CRIMINAL LAW

AND

ITS ADMINISTRATION

By

FRED E. INBAU
John Henry Wigmore Professor of Law
Northwestern University

JAMES R. THOMPSON
United States Attorney for the Northern District of Illinois;
Former Associate Professor of Law,
Northwestern University

JAMES B. ZAGEL
Chief, Criminal Justice Division, Office
of Attorney General of Illinois

SECOND EDITION

Mineola, N. Y.
THE FOUNDATION PRESS, INC.
1974

Library of Congress Catalog Card Number: 74–83850

Inbau et al.,–Crim.Law and Admin. 2nd Ed.
2nd Reprint—1976

PREFACE

This book is designed, as was its earlier (1970) edition, for college level instruction, in the criminal law and its administration, to police officers enrolled in college courses, and to other college students interested in careers in law enforcement. It utilizes the casebook method of instruction rather than a textual treatment. This is precisely the method law professors employ in the instruction of law students in all phases of the law.

The advantages of the casebook method are primarily two-fold: (a) the acquisition of information as to what the law is, and (b) it affords a means for obtaining an insight into why and how appellate courts arrive at their decisions. Such a book also affords an opportunity for the interchange of viewpoints between students and instructor as to the wisdom of the law as it now exists and the direction into which it may, or should be, headed.

In addition to carefully selected sets of appellate court opinions, including those of the Supreme Court of the United States, *Criminal Law and Its Administration* contains some introductory textual and note materials which impliment the objectives of the presentation of the main case reports. Also included is a reproduction of those portions of the Constitution of the United States and its Amendments which are relevant to the general problems regarding the law of crimes and the procedures by which that law is to be enforced.

Many of the court opinions in the cases which comprise this casebook have been condensed, and footnotes were either omitted completely or reduced in number. Otherwise this book would be of unmanageable size.

F. E. I.
J. R. T.
J. B. Z.

July, 1974

*

SUMMARY OF CONTENTS

*

TABLE OF CONTENTS

TABLE OF CASES

The principal cases are in italic type. Cases cited or discussed are in roman. References are to Pages.

†

CRIMINAL LAW
AND ITS
ADMINISTRATION

Chapter 1

OUTLINE OF CRIMINAL PROCEDURE

The procedure followed in a criminal case is not the same for all states, but the differences are rather slight as regards basic concepts and principles. In essential respects there is also very little difference between the procedure of the state courts and that which exists in the federal courts.

The following outline of criminal procedure is here presented for the purpose of familiarizing the beginning law student with the basic procedures that are involved or referred to in the case reports he will be encountering in subsequent chapters.

PROCEDURE BETWEEN ARREST AND TRIAL

In most states there is a statutory provision to the effect that an arrested person must be taken without unnecessary delay before the nearest judge or magistrate. What happens after presentation to the judge or magistrate will depend upon whether the arrested person is accused of a felony or a misdemeanor. If the charge is for a misdemeanor, the judge or magistrate will sometimes have the power and authority to hear the case himself, and he will usually proceed with the trial unless the accused demands trial by jury or a continuance is requested or ordered for some reason. If the offense charged is a felony, the judge or magistrate before whom the accused is brought will ordinarily lack the constitutional or legislative authority to conduct trials for crimes of that degree of seriousness, and in such instances he only conducts what is known as a "preliminary hearing."

The Right to an Attorney

The Sixth Amendment of the Constitution of the United States provides that "in all criminal prosecutions, the accused shall enjoy the right . . . to have the assistance of Counsel for his defense".

And the Supreme Court of the United States has held that where incarceration may be a consequence of the prosecution the defendant is entitled to appointed counsel in the event he cannot afford one. A "preliminary hearing", of course, is a part of the "criminal prosecution".

Preliminary Hearing

A preliminary hearing is a relatively informal proceeding by means of which a determination is made as to whether there are reasonable grounds for believing the accused committed the offense—as to whether it is fair, under the circumstances, to require the accused to stand a regular trial. If after such a hearing the judge or magistrate decides that the accusation is without probable cause, the accused will be discharged. This discharge, however, will not bar a grand jury indictment if subsequently developed evidence (or the same evidence presented on the preliminary hearing) satisfies the grand jury that the accusation is well founded.

If the preliminary hearing judge or magistrate decides that the accusation is a reasonable one, the accused will be "bound over" to the grand jury—that is, held in jail until the charge against him is presented for grand jury consideration, or, if the offense is a bailable one, the accused may be released after a bond of a certain amount is given to insure his presence until the grand jury has acted in the matter. (The nature and composition of a "grand jury" and the difference between it and a "petit" or "trial jury" is described later in this outline.)

The Habeas Corpus Writ

In the event an arrested person is not formally charged with an offense and is not taken before a judge or other magistrate "without unnecessary delay" he, or rather someone on his behalf, may petition a judge for a "writ of habeas corpus" and thereby attempt to secure his release or at least compel the police to file a specific charge against him, in which latter event he may seek his release on bond. If the court issues the writ, the police or other custodians of the arrested person are required, either immediately or at an early designated time, to bring him into court (that is, "you have the body," which is the literal meaning of the term "habeas corpus"), and to explain to the court the reason or justification for holding the accused person in custody.

Upon the police showing adequate cause, a court may continue the hearing in order to give the police a little more time to conduct a further investigation before making the formal charge against the arrestee. Many times, however, the police are required to file their charges immediately or release the prisoner.

Coroner's Inquest

At this point in a discussion of criminal procedure, mention should be made of a proceeding peculiar to homicide cases, which comes into operation soon after a killing or discovered death. This is the "coroner's inquest."

The coroner's inquest is a very old proceeding and its function was and still is to determine "the cause of death." The verdict of the coroner's jury, which is made up, in some states, of six laymen selected by the coroner or one of his deputies, is not binding on the prosecuting attorney, grand jury or court. In effect, it is merely an advisory finding which can be either accepted or completely ignored. For instance, even though a coroner's jury returns a verdict of "accidental death," a grand jury, either upon its own initiative or upon evidence presented by the prosecutor, may find that death resulted because of someone's criminal act and charge that person with the offense.

In some jurisdictions the office of coroner has been replaced by what is known as a medical examiner system. Whereas the coroner is usually an elected official (who may or may not be a physician), a medical examiner must be a physician appointed by a state or county officer or agency; moreover, in many jurisdictions he must be a forensic pathologist, specially trained for the position. He, in turn, has the power of appointing assistants who are physicians already trained for the purpose or at least in the process of receiving such training.

The Grand Jury

Misdemeanors are usually prosecuted upon an "information" filed by the prosecuting attorney after he has received and considered the sworn complaint of the victim or of some other person with knowledge of the facts. As regards felonies, however, many states require that the matter must first be submitted to a "grand jury." Then, after hearing the alleged facts related by the victim or other persons, the grand jury determines whether there are reasonable grounds for proceeding to an actual trial of the person charged.

A grand jury is usually composed of 23 citizen-voters, 16 of whom constitute a quorum. The votes of 12 members are necessary to the return of an "indictment." This indictment is also known as a "true bill."

The consideration of a felony charge by a grand jury is in no sense of the word a trial. Only the state's evidence is presented and considered; the suspected offender is usually not even heard nor is his lawyer present to offer evidence in his behalf.

The primary reason for requiring consideration of felony cases by a grand jury is to offer another safeguard to accused persons against arbitrary action by a prosecuting attorney, for without its indictment there can be no trial in felony cases. The indictment is required even in cases where the person charged has already had a preliminary hearing into the reasonableness of the charges against him.

The Arraignment and Plea

Following an indictment, the next step in felony cases is the appearance of the accused person before a judge who is empowered to try felony cases. The indictment is read to the defendant or the essence of its contents is made known to him; in other words, he is advised of the criminal charges made against him. If he pleads guilty, the judge can sentence him immediately or take the matter under advisement for a decision at an early date. If the accused pleads "not guilty," a date is then set for his actual trial.

In some states, and in the federal system, the defendant may enter a plea of "nolo contendere," a plea which has the same effect as a plea of guilty, except that the admission thereby made cannot be used as evidence in any other action.

Pre-trial Motions

After the formal charge has been made against the accused, he may, in advance of trial, seek to terminate the prosecution's case, or at least seek to better prepare his defense, by utilizing a procedure known as making or filing a "motion." A motion is merely a request for a court ruling or order that will afford the defendant the assistance or remedy he is thereby seeking. Some of the more frequently used motions are the following:

Motion to Quash the Indictment: With this motion the defendant may question the legal sufficiency of the indictment. If the court decides that the indictment adequately charges a criminal offense, and that it was obtained in accordance with the prescribed legal procedures, the motion will be overruled; otherwise the indictment will be considered invalid and "quashed." Even after an indictment has been thus rejected and set aside, the prosecutor may nevertheless proceed to obtain another and proper indictment. Moreover, the prosecution is entitled to appeal from a court order quashing an indictment, since at this stage of the proceedings the defendant has not been placed in jeopardy and consequently a subsequent indictment and trial would not constitute a violation of his constitutional privilege against "double jeopardy."

Motion for a Bill of Particulars: Although the indictment, if valid, will ordinarily contain all the allegations of fact necessary for the defendant to prepare his defense, he may, by a motion for a "bill of particulars," obtain further details respecting the accusation.

Motion for a Change of Venue: A defendant may attempt to avoid trial before a particular judge or in the city, county, or district where the crime occurred by seeking a "change of venue." In instances where this appears to be necessary in order that the defendant may receive a fair trial, the motion for a change of venue will be granted.

Motion to Suppress Evidence: A defendant has the privilege of filing with the court, normally in advance of trial, a "motion to suppress" evidence which he contends has been obtained from him in an unconstitutional manner. The evidence in question may be, on the one hand, a tangible item such as a gun, narcotics, or stolen property or, on the other hand, an intangible item such as a confession. If the court is satisfied that the evidence has been illegally obtained, it will order the evidence suppressed, which means that it cannot be used at the trial. If the court decides that the evidence was lawfully obtained, it is usable against the defendant at the trial.

THE TRIAL

In all states, and in the federal system, the accused is entitled to "a speedy trial." This right to an early trial is guaranteed by the various constitutions, and the constitutional provisions are generally supplemented by legislative enactments particularizing and specifically limiting the pre-trial detention period. In Illinois, for instance, once a person is jailed upon a criminal charge, he must be tried within 120 days, unless the delay has been occasioned by him, or is necessitated by a hearing to determine his mental competency to stand trial. If the accused is out on bail, he can demand trial within 160 days. In either instance, however, if the court determines that the prosecution has exercised, without success, due diligence to obtain evidence material to the case, and that there are reasonable grounds to believe that such evidence will be forthcoming, the time for trial may be extended for another 60 days. Such time limits vary from state to state, but the consistent rule is that unless the accused person is tried within the specified period of time he must be released and is thereafter immune from prosecution for that offense.

The Federal Rules of Criminal Procedure provide, in Rule 50(b), that the District Court of each federal district shall prepare a plan for the prompt disposition of criminal cases, which plan is to include rules relating to the time limits for pre-trial procedures, the trial itself, sentencing, and status reports.

Prior to the adoption of this Rule in 1972, the Second Circuit Court of Appeals had already adopted one which provided that top priority should be given to imprisoned and high-risk released defendants. It further provided that the Government must be ready for trial within 90 days if the accused is being detained, and within 6 months in all other cases. Furthermore, guidelines were provided for the granting of continuances and procedures were established for the reporting of the status of all cases to the chief judge of that Circuit.

Responding to the requirements of Rule 50(b), the district court judges of the Northern District of Illinois adopted the following time limits: the accused must be brought to the trial court, for "arraignment and plea" within 20 days if he is in custody, and 30 days if he is not in custody; and there must be a trial within 90 days following a "not guilty" plea if the accused is in custody, and within

180 days if not in custody. The plan does provide, however, that the time limits may be extended by the court in the interest of justice, and that the Government's failure to conform to the prescribed limits shall not bar a prosecution, but in such latter situation the defendant must be released from custody.

Jury Trial—Trial by Judge Alone

A person accused of a "serious crime", which is considered to be one for which there may be incarceration beyond six months, is entitled to trial by jury, as a matter of constitutional right. However, he may waive this right and elect to be tried by a judge alone. In some jurisdictions the defendant has an absolute right to this waiver (e. g., Illinois); in others (e. g., the federal system) it is conditioned upon the concurrence of the judge and the prosecution.

If the case is tried without a jury, the judge hears the evidence and decides for himself whether the defendant is guilty or not guilty. Where the trial is by a jury, the jury determines the facts and the judge serves more or less as an umpire or referee; it is his function to determine what testimony or evidence is legally "admissible," that is, to decide what should be heard or considered by the jury. But the ultimate decision as to whether the defedant is guilty is one to be made by the jury alone.

Jury Selection

In the selection of the jurors, usually twelve in number, who hear the defendant's case, his attorney as well as the prosecuting attorney are usually permitted to question a larger number who have been chosen for jury service from the list of registered voters. In the federal system, however, most trial judges will do practically all of the questioning, with very little opportunity for questioning accorded the prosecutor and defense counsel. Nevertheless, each lawyer has a certain number of "peremptory challenges" which means that he can arbitrarily refuse to accept as jurors a certain number of those who appear as prospective jurors. In some states, by statutory provision, the defendant in larceny cases has ten such challenges and the state has an equal number; in a murder case the defendant and the state each have twenty peremptory challenges; and in minor criminal cases, such as petit larceny, the challenges are five in number for each side. And in all cases, if any prospective juror's answers to the questions of either attorney reveal a prejudice or bias which prevents him from being a fair and impartial juror, the judge, either on his own initiative or at the suggestion of either counsel, will dismiss that person from jury service. Although the desired result is not always achieved, the avowed purpose of this practice of permitting lawyers to question prospective jurors is to obtain twelve jurors who will be fair to both sides of the case.

Opening Statements

After the jury is selected, both the prosecuting attorney and the defense lawyer are entitled to make "opening statements" in which each outlines what he intends to prove. The purpose of this is to acquaint the jurors with each side of the case, so that it will be easier for them to follow the evidence as it is presented.

The Prosecution's Evidence

After the opening statements the prosecuting attorney produces the prosecution's testimony and evidence. He has the burden of proving the state's case "beyond a reasonable doubt." If at the close of the prosecution's case the judge is of the opinion that reasonable jurors could not conclude that the charge against the defendant has been proved, he will "direct a verdict" of acquittal. That ends the matter and the defendant goes free—forever immune from further prosecution for the crime, just the same as if a jury had heard all the evidence and found him "not guilty."

The Defendant's Evidence

If the court does not direct the jury, at the close of the prosecution's case, to find the defendant not guilty, the defendant may, if he wishes, present evidence in refutation. He himself may or may not testify, and if he chooses not to appear as a witness, the prosecuting attorney is not permitted to comment upon that fact to the jury. The basis for this principle, whereby the defendant is not obligated to speak in his own behalf, is the constitutional privilege which protects a person from self-incrimination.

The prosecution is given an opportunity to rebut the defendant's evidence, if any, and the presentation of testimony usually ends at that point. Then, once more, defense counsel will try to persuade the court to "direct a verdict" in favor of the defendant. If the court decides to let the case go to the jury, the prosecuting attorney and defense counsel make their "closing arguments."

Closing Arguments

In their closing arguments the prosecutor and defense counsel review and analyze the evidence and attempt to persuade the jury to render a favorable verdict.

Instructions of the Court to the Jury

After the closing arguments are completed, the judge in most jurisdictions will read and give to the jury certain written instructions as to the legal principles which should be applied to the facts of the case as determined by the jury. The judge also gives the jury certain written forms of possible verdicts. The jury then retires to the jury room where they are given an adequate opportunity to deliberate upon the matter, away from everyone, including the judge himself.

The Verdict of the Jury

When the jury has reached a decision, they advise the bailiff that they have reached a verdict and then return to the court room. The foreman, usually selected by the jurors themselves to serve as their leader and spokesman, announces the verdict of the jury. Insofar as jury participation is concerned, the case is then at an end.

If the verdict is "not guilty" the defendant is free forever from any further prosecution by that particular state or jurisdiction for the crime for which he was tried. If found "guilty," then, in most types of cases and in most jurisdictions, it becomes the function of the trial judge to fix the sentence within the legislatively prescribed limitations.

In the event the jurors are unable to agree upon a verdict—and it must be unanimous in most states—the jury, commonly referred to as a "hung jury," is discharged and a new trial date may be set for a retrial of the case before another jury.

The Motion for a New Trial

After a verdict of "guilty" there are still certain opportunities provided the defendant to obtain his freedom. He may file a "motion for a new trial," in which he alleges certain "errors" committed in the course of his trial; and if the trial judge agrees, the conviction is set aside and the defendant may be tried again by a new jury and usually before a different judge. Where this motion for a new trial is "overruled" or "denied," the judge will then proceed to sentence the defendant.

The Sentence

In cases tried without a jury, the judge, of course, will determine the sentence to be imposed. In jury cases the practice varies among the states, with most of them following the practice of confining the jury function to a determination of guilt or innocence and permitting the judge to fix the penalty. For the crimes of murder and rape, however, most of the states place both responsibilities upon the jury.

In some states there are statutory provisions which prescribe that upon conviction of a felony the defendant must be sentenced for a specified minimum-maximum term in the penitentiary—for example, 1 year to 10 years for burglary—and the determination of the appropriate time of his release within that period is to be made by a "parole board," whose judgment in that respect is based upon the extent of the convict's rehabilitation, the security risk involved, and similar factors. In many states a judge is permitted to set a minimum-maximum period anywhere within the minimum-maximum term prescribed by the legislature. In other words, the sentence given for grand larceny may be one to ten years, the statutory range, or 1 to 2, 9 to 10, or any other combination between 1 to 10. This minimum-maximum term means that he cannot be released before serving the minimum period, less "time off for good behavior," nor can he be kept in the penitentiary longer than the maximum period, less "time off for good behavior." In between this minimum-maximum period the convict is eligible for "parole," a procedure to be subsequently described.

In instances where imprisonment is fixed at a specified number of years, rather than for an indeterminate period, the law usually provides that the convicted person must serve one-third of the sentence before becoming eligible for parole.

PROBATION

In certain types of cases, a judge is empowered, by statute, to grant "probation" to a convicted person. This means that instead of sending the defendant to the penitentiary the court permits him to remain at liberty but upon certain conditions prescribed by law and by the judge. His background must first be investigated by a probation officer for the purpose of determining whether he is the kind of person who may have "learned his lesson" by the mere fact of being caught and convicted, or whether he could be rehabilitated outside of prison better than behind prison walls. In other words, would any useful purpose be served for him or society by sending him to prison?

Among the conditions of a defendant's probation, the court may require him to make restitution of money stolen, or reparations to a person he physically injured. Some state statutes provide that for a period of up to six months in misdemeanor cases, and up to five years in felony cases, a defendant on probation will be subjected to the supervision of a probation officer and, in general, must remain on "good behavior" during the period fixed by the court. A failure to abide by the conditions prescribed by the court will subject the defendant to a sentence in the same manner and form as though he had been denied probation and sentenced immediately after his conviction for the offense.

PAROLE

A penitentiary sentence of a specified term or number of years does not necessarily mean that a convicted person will remain in the penitentiary for that particular period of time. Under certain conditions and circumstances he may be released earlier "on parole," which means a release under supervision until the expiration of his sentence or until the expiration of a period otherwise specified by law. For instance, a person sentenced "for life" is, in some states, eligible for release "on parole" at the end of twenty years, with a subsequent five year period of parole supervision. One sentenced for a fixed number of years, for example 14 years for murder, may be eligible for parole in some states after he has served one-third that period of time. And a person who has been given an indeterminate minimum-maximum sentence, such as to 5 to 10 years for grand larceny, may be eligible for a parole after he has served the 5 year minimum, less time off for good behavior.

The manner of computing time off for good behavior, or "good time," varies among the states. Illinois has a system based on yearly credits; under this arrangement, the amount of the credit granted increases as the amount of time served by the obedient prisoner increases. Accordingly, one month off is granted for good behavior in the first year, two months for the second year, and so on up to a maximum of six months off for good behavior in the sixth year and in each succeeding year. The inmate is allowed to accumulate these credits. Thus, under the Illinois system, a prisoner who received a minimum-maximum sentence of 3 to 5 years and who served "good time", would be eligible for parole after serving 2 years and 6 months of his sentence.

A violation of the conditions of the parole will subject the parolee to possible return to prison for the remainder of his unexpired sentence.

POST-CONVICTION REMEDIES

The Appeal:

After sentence has been pronounced, the defendant may appeal his conviction to a reviewing court. The reviewing court will examine all or part of the written record of what happened at the trial, and consider the written and oral arguments of both the defense attorney and the prosecutor. It will then render a written decision and opinion which will either reverse or affirm the trial court conviction and state the reasons for the decision. If the trial court's decision is "reversed and remanded", it means that the defendant's conviction is nullified, although he may be tried over again by another jury. A decision of "reversed" ordinarily means that in addition to an improper trial there appears to be insufficient competent evidence upon which to try the defendant again, and consequently the prosecuting attorney may not make a second attempt to win a conviction.

A decision of the state's highest court affirming a conviction is, in nearly all instances, a final disposition of the case, and there is nothing else the convicted person can do but submit to the judgment of the trial court. But if the appeal involved a *federal* constitutional question or issue the defendant is entitled to seek a review of the state appellate court decision by the Supreme Court of the United States. Such requests, known as petitions for a *writ of certiorari,* are rarely granted, however.

Collateral Attacks:

In addition to the appeal itself, nearly all states in recent years have provided additional post-conviction remedies by which a defendant may attack his conviction. Such "collateral" remedies are known, variously, as proceedings in habeas corpus, post-conviction petitions, or by other titles. A defendant may thereby seek a re-litigation, in a trial court, of an issue that had been considered and decided on the direct appeal; or he may attempt to raise an entirely new issue. Moreover, the decision with respect to a collateral attack may be the subject of an appeal to a reviewing court.

Even after a conviction is upheld against collateral attack in the state courts, if a federal constitutional question had been presented, the convicted person has yet another remedy available—the *federal* writ of habeas corpus. The Supreme Court of the United States has held that a state court judgment of conviction resulting from a trial which involved a substantial error of federal constitutional dimension is void, and a prisoner held pursuant to a void judgment is unlawfully confined and subject to release by a federal court upon a writ of habeas corpus. In considering the petition for the writ a federal district judge may also order another "evidentiary hearing". And he has the power to remand the case to the state court for a new trial or for the outright release of the defendant, depending upon the kind of error committed and the evidence still available to the state.

APPEALS BY THE PROSECUTION

Only the defendant has a right to appeal the result of a trial; to permit the prosecution to appeal from a verdict of acquittal or a trial judge's finding of not guilty has been held to violate the constitutional protection against double jeopardy.

In a growing number of jurisdictions, however, the prosecution is being accorded the right to appeal certain decisions of a pre-trial nature. The Illinois Criminal Code, for example, provides for prosecution appeals from a trial court order dismissing the charge against a defendant, or from an order suppressing a confession or other evidence alleged to have been illegally obtained.

Chapter 2

CONSTITUTIONAL LIMITATIONS ON THE LEGISLATIVE POWER TO CREATE AND DEFINE CRIMINAL OFFENSES

A. FREEDOM OF SPEECH

SECTION 1. FREEDOM OF EXPRESSION BY INDIVIDUAL PROTESTERS

SCHENCK v. UNITED STATES

Supreme Court of the United States, 1919.
249 U.S. 47, 39 S.Ct. 247.

MR. JUSTICE HOLMES delivered the opinion of the court.

This is an indictment in three counts. The first charges a conspiracy to violate the Espionage Act of June 15, 1917 . . . by causing and attempting to cause insubordination, &c., in the military and naval forces of the United States, and to obstruct the recruiting and enlistment service of the United States, when the United States was at war with the German Empire, to-wit, that the defendants wilfully conspired to have printed and circulated to men who had been called and accepted for military service under the Act of May 18, 1917, a document set forth and alleged to be calculated to cause such insubordination and obstruction. The count alleges overt acts in pursuance of the conspiracy, ending in the distribution of the document set forth. The second court alleges a conspiracy to commit an offence against the United States, to-wit, to use the mails for the transmission of matter declared to be non-mailable . . . to-wit, the above mentioned document, with an averment of the same overt acts. The third count charges an unlawful use of the mails for the transmission of the same matter and otherwise as above. The defendants were found guilty on all the counts. They set up the First Amendment to the Constitution forbidding Congress to make any law abridging the freedom of speech, or of the press . . . .

* * *

The document in question upon its first printed side recited the first section of the Thirteenth Amendment, said that the idea embodied in it was violated by the Conscription Act and that a conscript is little better than a convict. In impassioned language it intimated that conscription was despotism in its worst form and a monstrous wrong against humanity in the interest of Wall Street's chosen few. It said "Do not submit to intimidation," but in form at least confined itself to peaceful measures such as a petition for the repeal of the act. The other and later printed side of the sheet was headed "Assert Your Rights." It stated reasons for alleging that any one violated the Constitution when he refused to recognize "your right to assert your opposition to the draft," and went on "If you do not assert and support your rights, you are helping to deny or disparage rights which it is the solemn duty of all citizens and residents of the United States to retain." It described the arguments on the other side as coming from cunning politicians and a mercenary capitalist press, and even silent consent to the conscription law as helping to support an infamous conspiracy. It denied the power to send our citizens away to foreign shores to shoot up the people of other lands, and added that words could not express the condemnation such cold-blooded ruthlessness deserves, &c., &c., winding up "You must do your share to maintain, support and uphold the rights of the people of this country." Of course the document would not have been sent unless it had been intended to have some effect, and we do not see what effect it could be expected to have upon persons subject to the draft except to influence them to obstruct the carrying of it out. The defendants do not deny that the jury might find against them on this point.

But it is said, suppose that that was the tendency of this circular, it is protected by the First Amendment to the Constitution. Two of the strongest expressions are said to be quoted respectively from well-known public men. It well may be that the prohibition of laws abridging the freedom of speech is not confined to previous restraints, although to prevent them may have been the main purpose, as intimated in Patterson v. Colorado, 205 U.S. 454, 462, 27 S.Ct. 556. We admit that in many places and in ordinary times the defendants in saying all that was said in the circular would have been within their constitutional rights. But the character of every act depends upon the circumstances in which it is done. Aikens v. Wisconsin, 195 U.S. 194, 205, 206, 25 S.Ct. 3. The most stringent protection of free speech would not protect a man in falsely shouting fire in a theatre and causing a panic. It does not even protect a man from an injunction against uttering words that may have all the effect of force. Gompers v. Bucks Stove & Range Co., 221 U.S. 418, 439, 31 S.Ct. 492. The question in every case is whether the words used are used in such circumstances and are of such a nature as to create a clear and present danger that they will bring about the substantive evils that Congress has a right to prevent. It is a question of proximity and degree. When a nation is at war many things that might be said in time of peace are such a hindrance to its effort that their utterance will not be endured so long as men fight and that no Court could regard them as protected by any constitutional right. It seems to be admitted that if an actual obstruction of the recruiting service were proved, liability for words that produced that effect might be enforced. The statute of 1917 in § 4 punishes conspiracies to obstruct as well as actual obstruction. If the act, (speaking, or circulating a paper,) its tendency and the intent with which it is done are the same, we perceive no ground for saying that success alone warrants making the act a crime. . . .

Judgments affirmed.

COHEN v. CALIFORNIA

Supreme Court of the United States, 1971.
403 U.S. 15, 91 S.Ct. 1780.

MR. JUSTICE HARLAN delivered the opinion of the Court.

This case may seem at first blush too inconsequential to find its way into our books, but the issue it presents is of no small constitutional significance.

Appellant Paul Robert Cohen was convicted in the Los Angeles Municipal Court of violating that part of California Penal Code § 415 which prohibits "maliciously and willfully disturb[ing] the peace or quiet of any neighborhood or person * * * by * * * offensive conduct * * *." He was given 30 days' imprisonment. The facts upon which his conviction rests are detailed in the opinion of the Court of Appeal of California, Second Appellate District, as follows:

> "On April 26, 1968, the defendant was observed in the Los Angeles County Courthouse in the corridor outside of division 20 of the municipal court wearing a jacket bearing the words 'Fuck the Draft' which were plainly visible. There were women and children present in the corridor. The defendant was arrested. The defendant testified that he wore the jacket knowing that the words were on the jacket as a means of informing the public of the depth of his feelings against the Vietnam War and the draft.
>
> "The defendant did not engage in, nor threaten to engage in, nor did anyone as the result of his conduct in fact commit or threaten to commit any act of violence. The defendant did not make any loud or unusual noise, nor was there any evidence that he uttered any sound prior to his arrest." . . .

In affirming the conviction the Court of Appeal held that "offensive conduct" means "behavior which has a tendency to provoke *others* to acts of violence or to in turn disturb the peace," and that the State had proved this element because on the facts of this case, "[i]t was certainly reasonably foreseeable that such conduct might cause others to rise up to commit a violent act against the person of the defendant or attempt to forceably remove his jacket." . . . The California Supreme Court declined review by a divided vote. . . . We now reverse.

I

In order to lay hands on the precise issue which this case involves, it is useful first to canvass various matters which this record does *not* present.

The conviction quite clearly rests upon the asserted offensiveness of the *words* Cohen used to convey his message to the public. The only "conduct" which the State sought to punish is the fact of communication. Thus, we deal here with a conviction resting solely upon "speech," . . . not upon any separately identifiable conduct which allegedly was intended by Cohen to be perceived by others as expressive of particular views but which, on its face, does not necessarily convey any message and hence arguably could be regulated without effectively repressing Cohen's ability to express himself. . . . Further, the State certainly lacks power to punish Cohen for the underlying content of the message the inscription conveyed. At least so long as there is no showing of an intent to incite disobedience to or disruption of the draft, Cohen could not, consistently with the First and Fourteenth Amendments, be punished for asserting the evident position on the inutility or immorality of the draft his jacket reflected. . . .

Appellant's conviction, then, rests squarely upon his exercise of the "freedom of speech" protected from arbitrary governmental interference by the Constitution and can be justified, if at all, only as a valid regulation of the manner in which he exercised that freedom, not as a permissible prohibition on the substantive message it conveys. This does not end the inquiry, of course, for the First and Fourteenth Amendments have never been thought to give absolute protection to every individual to speak whenever or wherever he pleases or to use any form of address in any circumstances that he chooses. In this vein, too, however, we think it important to note that several issues typically associated with such problems are not presented here.

In the first place, Cohen was tried under a statute applicable throughout the entire State. Any attempt to support this conviction on the ground that the statute seeks to preserve an appropriately decorous atmosphere in the courthouse where Cohen was arrested must fail in the absence of any language in the statute that would have put appellant on notice that certain kinds of otherwise permissible speech or conduct would nevertheless, under California law, not be tolerated in certain places. . . . No fair reading of the phrase "offensive conduct" can be said sufficiently to inform the ordinary person that distinctions between certain locations are thereby created.

In the second place, as it comes to us, this case cannot be said to fall within those relatively few categories of instances where prior decisions have established the power of government to deal more comprehensively with certain forms of individual expression simply upon a showing that such a form was employed. This is not, for example, an obscenity case. Whatever else may be necessary to give rise to the States' broader power to prohibit obscene expression, such expression must be, in some significant way, erotic. [Roth v. United States, . . . infra this casebook, p. 253]. It cannot plausibly be maintained that this vulgar allusion to the Selective Service System would conjure up such psychic stimulation in anyone likely to be confronted with Cohen's crudely defaced jacket.

This Court has also held that the States are free to ban the simple use, without a demonstration of additional justifying circumstances, of so-called "fighting words," those personally abusive epithets which, when addressed to the ordinary citizen, are, as a matter of common knowledge, inherently likely to provoke violent reaction. Chaplinsky v. New Hampshire, 315 U.S. 568, 62 S.Ct. 766 (1942). While the four-letter word displayed by Cohen in relation to the draft is not uncommonly employed in a personally provocative fashion, in this instance it was clearly not "directed to the person of the hearer." . . . No individual actually or likely to be present could reasonably have regarded the words on appellant's jacket as a direct personal insult. Nor do we have here an instance of the exercise of the State's police power to prevent a speaker from intentionally provoking a given group to hostile reaction. Cf. Feiner v. New York, 340 U.S. 315, 71 S.Ct. 303 (1951); Terminiello v. Chicago, 337 U.S. 1, 69 S.Ct. 894 (1949). There is, as noted above, no showing that anyone who saw Cohen was in fact violently aroused or that appellant intended such a result.

Finally, in arguments before this Court much has been made of the claim that Cohen's distasteful mode of expression was thrust upon unwilling or unsuspecting viewers, and that the State might therefore legitimately act as it did in order to protect the sensitive from otherwise unavoidable exposure to appellant's crude form of protest. Of course, the mere presumed presence of unwitting listeners or viewers does not serve automatically to justify curtailing all speech capable of giving offense. . . . While this Court has recognized that government may properly act in many situations to prohibit intrusion into the privacy of the home of unwelcome views and ideas which cannot be totally banned from the public dialogue, . . . we have at the same time consistently stressed that "we are often 'captives' outside the sanctuary of the home and subject to objectionable speech." . . . The ability of government, consonant with the Constitution, to shut off discourse solely to protect others from hearing it is, in other words, dependent upon a showing that substantial privacy interests are being invaded in an essentially intolerable manner. Any broader view of this authority would effectively empower a majority to silence dissidents simply as a matter of personal predilections.

In this regard, persons confronted with Cohen's jacket were in a quite different posture than, say, those subjected to the raucous emissions of sound trucks blaring outside their residences. Those in the Los Angeles courthouse could effectively avoid further bombardment of their sensibilities simply by averting their eyes. And, while it may be that one has a more substantial claim to a recognizable privacy interest when walking through a courthouse corridor than, for example, strolling through Central Park, surely it is nothing like the interest in being free from unwanted expression in the confines of one's own home. Given the subtlety and complexity of the factors involved, if Cohen's "speech" was otherwise entitled to constitutional protection, we do not think the fact that some unwilling "listeners" in a public building may have been briefly exposed to it can serve to justify this breach of the peace conviction where, as here, there was no evidence that persons powerless to avoid appellant's conduct did in fact object to it, and where that portion of the statute upon which Cohen's conviction rests evinces no concern, either on its face or as construed by the California courts, with the special plight of the captive auditor, but, instead, indiscriminately sweeps within its prohibitions all "offensive conduct" that disturbs "any neighborhood or person." . . .

II

Against this background, the issue flushed by this case stands out in bold relief. It is whether California can excise, as "offensive conduct," one particular scurrilous epithet from the public discourse, either upon the theory of the court below that its use is inherently likely to cause violent reaction or upon a more general assertion that the States, acting as guardians of public morality, may properly remove this offensive word from the public vocabulary.

The rationale of the California court is plainly untenable. At most it reflects an "undifferentiated fear or apprehension of disturbance [which] is not enough to overcome the right to freedom of expression." Tinker v. Des Moines Indep. Community School Dist., 393 U.S. 503, 508, 89 S.Ct. 733, 737 (1969). We have been shown no evidence that substantial numbers of citizens are standing ready to strike out physically at whoever may assault their sensibilities with execrations like that uttered by Cohen. There may be some persons about with such lawless and violent proclivities, but that is an insufficient base upon which to erect, consistently with constitutional values, a governmental power to force persons who wish to ventilate their dissident views into avoiding particular forms of expression. The argument amounts to little more than the self-defeating proposition that to avoid physical censorship of one who has not sought to provoke such a response by a hypothetical coterie of the violent and lawless, the States may more appropriately effectuate that censorship themselves. . . .

Admittedly, it is not so obvious that the First and Fourteenth Amendments must be taken to disable the States from punishing public utterance of this unseemly expletive in order to maintain what they regard as a suitable level of discourse within the body politic. We think, however, that examination and reflection will reveal the shortcomings of a contrary viewpoint.

At the outset, we cannot overemphasize that, in our judgment, most situations where the State has a justifiable interest in regulating speech will fall within one or more of the various established exceptions, discussed above but not applicable here, to the usual rule that governmental bodies may not prescribe the form or content of individual expression. Equally important to our conclusion is the constitutional backdrop against which our decision must be made. The constitutional right of free expression is powerful medicine in a society as diverse and populous as ours. It is designed and intended to remove governmental restraints from the arena of public discussion, putting the decision as to what views shall be voiced largely into the hands of each of us, in the hope that use of such freedom will ultimately produce a more capable citizenry and more perfect polity and in the belief that no other approach would comport with the premise of individual dignity and choice upon which our political system rests. . . .

To many, the immediate consequence of this freedom may often appear to be only verbal tumult, discord, and even offensive utterance. These are, however, within established limits, in truth necessary side effects of the broader enduring values which the process of open debate permits us to achieve. That the air may at times seem filled with verbal cacophony is, in this sense not a sign of weakness but of strength. We cannot lose sight of the fact that, in what otherwise might seem a trifling and annoying instance of individual distasteful abuse of a privilege, these fundamental societal values are truly implicated. That is why "[w]holly neutral futilities * * * come under the protection of free speech as fully as do Keats' poems or Donne's sermons," . . . and why "so long as the means are peaceful, the communication need not meet standards of acceptability," . . .

Against this perception of the constitutional policies involved we discern certain more particularized considerations that peculiarly call for reversal of this conviction. First, the principle contended for by the State seems inherently boundless. How is one to distinguish this from any other offensive word? Surely the State has no right to cleanse public debate to the point where it is grammatically palatable to the most squeamish among us. Yet no readily ascertainable general principle exists for stopping short of that result were we to affirm the judgment below. For, while the particular four-letter word being litigated here is perhaps more distasteful than most others of its genre, it is nevertheless often true that one man's vulgarity is another's lyric. Indeed, we think it is largely because governmental officials cannot make principled distinctions in this area that the Constitution leaves matters of taste and style so largely to the individual.

Additionally, we cannot overlook the fact, because it is well illustrated by the episode involved here, that much linguistic expression serves a dual communicative function: it conveys not only ideas capable of relatively precise, detached explication, but otherwise inexpressible emotions as well. In fact, words are often chosen as much for their emotive as their cognitive force. We cannot sanction the view that the Constitution, while solicitous of the cognitive content of individual speech has little or no regard for that emotive function which practically speaking, may often be the more important element of the overall message sought to be communicated. Indeed, as Mr. Justice Frankfurter has said, "[o]ne of the prerogatives of American citizenship is the right to criticize public men and measures—and that means not only informed and responsible criticism but the freedom to speak, foolishly and without moderation." . . .

Finally, and in the same vein, we cannot indulge the facile assumption that one can forbid particular words without also running a substantial risk of suppressing ideas in the process. Indeed, governments might soon seize upon the censorship of particular words as a convenient guise for banning the expression of unpopular views. We have been able, as noted above, to discern little social benefit that might result from running the risk of opening the door to such grave results.

It is, in sum, our judgment that, absent a more particularized and compelling reason for its actions, the State may not, consistently with the First and Fourteenth Amendments, make the simple public display here involved of this single four-letter expletive a criminal offense. Because that is the only arguably sustainable rationale for the conviction here at issue, the judgment below must be reversed.

Reversed.

MR. JUSTICE BLACKMUN, with whom THE CHIEF JUSTICE and MR. JUSTICE BLACK join.

I dissent, . . .

Cohen's absurd and immature antic, in my view, was mainly conduct and little speech. . . . The California Court of Appeal appears so to have described it, . . . and I cannot characterize it otherwise. Further, the case appears to me to be well within the sphere of Chaplinsky v. New Hampshire, . . . where Mr. Justice Murphy, a known champion of First Amendment freedoms, wrote for a unanimous bench. As a consequence, this Court's agonizing over First Amendment values seem misplaced and unnecessary. * * *

NOTES

1. The *Chaplinsky* case, to which the court referred in *Cohen*, involved a situation where the defendant, on a public street, addressed another person as a "God damned racketeer" and a "damned Fascist", adding that the whole city government was composed of "Fascists or agents of Fascists". The defendant was charged with violating a statute providing that "No person shall address any offensive, derisive or annoying word to another person [in any public place] . . ." His conviction was upheld by the Supreme Court, on the ground that the statute was intended to do no more than prohibit "face-to-face words plainly likely to cause a breach of the peace"; and that the limited scope of the statute was not an impingement of the constitutional right to free expression.

Compare Gooding, Warden v. Wilson, 405 U.S. 518, 92 S.Ct. 1103 (1972), which held unconstitutional, on grounds of violation of free speech as well as vagueness, a Georgia statute which provided that "[a]ny person who shall, without provocation, use to or of another, and in his presence . . . opprobrious words or abusive language, tending to cause a breach of the peace . . . shall be guilty of a misdemeanor."

The vagueness issue will be discussed in the Due Process section, infra.

2. Consider the validity of the following provision (§ 25–30) of the Code of the City of Miami Beach, Florida:

Communism and Nazism—Wearing and display of symbols prohibited

"Criminal communism and criminal nazism are doctrines that existing constitutional government should be overthrown by force, violence or other unlawful means. The hammer and sickle and the swastika are the respective symbols of such doctrines. Experience has demonstrated that the wearing or display of such symbols under given conditions and circumstances constitute incitements to riot, and other serious disturbances and will inevitably disrupt the peace, quiet and good order of the community and of its citizens and residents. It is therefore unlawful for any person to wear or to display, in any manner, either the hammer and sickle or the swastika on any public street or way or in any building to which the public has access; provided, that the foregoing shall not be applicable to any bona fide theatrical production or drama; and provided further; that the provisions of this section pertaining to the hammer and sickle shall not be applicable to any person duly accredited by the United States of America as an official representative of the U.S.S.R. or to any ceremony or function held or conducted under the auspices or with the approval of the State Department of the United States of America."

In Tinker v. Des Moines Independent Community School Districts, 393 U.S. 503, 89 S.Ct. 733 (1969), the Supreme Court held with two Justices dissenting, that in the absence of facts reasonably indicative of substantial disruption or material interference with school activities, the school authorities could not prohibit the wearing of black armbands by students in protest of the Vietnam hostilities.

SECTION 2. DEMONSTRATIONS

CITY OF CHICAGO v. GREGORY

Supreme Court of Illinois, 1968.
39 Ill.2d 48, 233 N.E.2d 422.

MR. JUSTICE HOUSE delivered the opinion of the court.

These consolidated appeals involve the conviction of 40 civil rights marchers under two provisions of the disorderly conduct ordinance of the city of Chicago.[1] In cause number 39983 defendant Dick Gregory and four other defendants were found guilty in a jury trial before a magistrate in the circuit court of Cook County and each defendant was fined $200. In cause number 39984 the other 35 defendants were found guilty in a trial before a magistrate on a stipulation of facts adduced at the Gregory trial and each defendant was fined $25. The defendant Gregory was charged with disorderly conduct in that he "did make or aid in making an improper noise, disturbance, breach of peace, or diversion tending to a breach of the peace within the limits of the city." A constitutional question gives us jurisdiction.

The gist of the occurrence giving rise to the arrest and conviction of defendants was a march by 65 to 85 persons around the home of the mayor of Chicago. The marchers carried signs, sang songs and chanted slogans protesting the retention of Dr. Benjamin C. Willis as Superintendent of Schools of Chicago and his handling of school segregation problems in the city. In order to avert what the police believed would become a riot, the marchers were ordered to stop their demonstration and upon their refusal they were arrested.

The city in its brief has taken the position that residential picketing is *per se* a violation of the city ordinance. Extremely strong arguments have been advanced for the proposition that the constitutional rights of free speech, free assembly and freedom to petition for redress of grievances do not protect marches, demonstrations and picketing of a residence or residences—even of the privately owned

[1.] The disorderly conduct ordinance in effect at the time of the events described in this case (Section 193 of the Municipal Code of Chicago) read, in part, as follows:
"All persons who shall make, aid, countenance, or assist in making any improper noise, riot, disturbance, breach of the peace, or diversion tending to a breach of the peace, within the limits of the city; all persons who shall collect in bodies or crowds for unlawful purposes, or for any purpose, to the annoyance or disturbance of other persons; . . . shall be deemed guilty of disorderly conduct, and upon conviction thereof, shall be severally fined not less than one dollar nor more than two hundred dollars for each offense."

homes of public officials. (See Kamin, Residential Picketing and the First Amendment, 61 N.W.L.Rev. 177 (1966); . . . Furthermore, our legislature has now enacted a statute prohibiting residential picketing [infra note 3, p. 209] based on the following declaration of policy: "The Legislature finds and declares that men in a free society have the right to quiet enjoyment of their homes; that the stability of community and family life cannot be maintained unless the right to privacy and a sense of security and peace in the home are respected and encouraged; that residential picketing, however, just the cause inspiring it, disrupts home, family and communal life; that residential picketing is inappropriate in our society where the jealously guarded rights of free speech and assembly have always been associated with respect for the rights of others. For these reasons the Legislature finds this Article to be necessary." . . . nine other States (Colorado, Connecticut, Florida, Hawaii, Kansas, Michigan, Nebraska, Utah and Wisconsin) have enacted statutory prohibitions of residential picketing.

A review of the record shows, however, that the arrests were not made on the basis of residential picketing nor did the trial proceed on that theory. Under these circumstances, we will assume, for the purposes of this opinion, as did the police and the magistrates below, that the residential picketing was not in and of itself a violation of the city ordinance.

Lieutenant Hougeson testified that on August 2, 1965, he was in charge of the "task force" of the Chicago police department and that his assignment for that day was to protect a group of people who were going to march. He explained that the task force is a unit which provides extra police protection to a district to help handle crowds at a sporting or public event or to combat a high crime rate in a certain district. On this day he had 40 police officers and 4 sergeants. About 4:00 P.M. he went to Buckingham Fountain in Grant Park on Chicago's lake front just east of the Loop, where approximately 65 marchers had assembled. He observed Dick Gregory addressing the marchers and heard him say, "First we will go over to the snake pit [city hall]. When we leave there, we will go out to the snake's house [the mayor's home]. Then, we will continue to go out to Mayor Daley's home until he fires Ben Willis [Superintendent of Schools]."

About 4:30 P.M. the marchers, two abreast, walked out of the park and went to the city hall in the loop. The marchers then walked south on State Street to 35th Street and then proceeded west to Lowe Avenue, a distance of about 5 miles from the city hall. The mayor's home is at 3536 South Lowe Avenue. The demonstrators had increased in number to about 85 and they arrived at the mayor's home about 8:00 o'clock P.M. In addition to the police, the marchers were accompanied by their attorney and an assistant city counsel. At the suggestion of an assistant city counsel, Gregory had agreed that the group would quit singing at 8:30 P.M. Commander Pierson, district commander of the 9th police district which encompasses this area, met Lieutenant Hougeson at the corner of 35th and Lowe and assumed command of the police operations.

There were about 35 people on the corner and a group of about 6 or 8 youngsters carrying a sign "We love Mayor Daley" tried to join the marchers but the police stopped them. As the demonstrators started south into the 3500 block of Lowe Avenue, Gregory testified he went back through the line to tell everyone just to keep singing and to keep marching. "Don't stop and don't answer any one back. Don't worry about anything that is going to be said to you. Just keep marching. If anyone hits you or anything, try to remember what they look like, but above all means, do not hit them back. Keep the line straight and keep it tight." The demonstrators chanted "Ben Willis must go, Snake Daley, also;" "Ben Willis must go—When?—Now;" "We are going to the home of the snake, the snake pit is down the street;" "Hey, Hey, what do you know, Ben Willis must go" and "Hey, Hey, what do you know, Mayor Daley must go also." They carried signs which read: "Daley fire Willis;" "Defacto, Desmacto, it is still segregation;" "Ben Willis must go—now;" and "Mayor Daley, fire Ben Willis." They also sang the civil rights songs, "We Shall Overcome" and "We Shall Not Be Moved."

The police ordered the taverns closed during the march. Police from the task force, the 9th district and other districts surrounded the block in which the mayor's home is located. There were about 10 officers at each of the four intersections and about 10 officers spread along each of the four blocks. The rest of the 100 police officers assigned to the march accompanied the demonstrators as they marched around the block. The police tried to keep all spectators across the street from the marchers. They were equipped with walkie-talkie radios to relay reports of conditions to each other and they had a bullhorn with which they addressed the spectators and the demonstrators.

As the marchers started around the block the first time, the neighbors began coming out of their homes. On the second time around the block some of the residents had moved their lawn sprinklers onto the sidewalk and the demonstrators went into the street just long enough to get around the water. On the third trip around the block the water sprinklers had been removed, presumably by order of the police. Gregory himself testified to several instances when the police kept the crowd that was accumulating from interfering with the march. "One of the neighborhood people stood in front of the line, and we just stopped. This individual didn't move and we didn't move. After a few minutes, the officers standing on the corner asked him to move and he moved." He said that on their fourth trip around the block (about 8:30 P.M.) people were yelling out the windows and the police made spectators in door ways close the doors. About 8:30 P.M. the demonstrators quit their singing and chanting and marched quietly. Shortly before 9:00 P.M. 100 to 150 spectators formed a line of march ahead of the demonstrators. Gregory said "the lieutenant [Hougheson] asked me if I would hold up the line until they got those people out of the way. I said, I will hold up the line, but they have just as much right to march peacefully as we have." The spectators were ordered to move. In order to avoid the appearance that the marchers were following the 100 to 150 spectators who had been ordered to move, Gregory said his group marched straight south crossing 36th Street thus taking them one block south of the block which they had been marching. They had to stop when they crossed 36th Street while the police opened a pathway through about 300 spectators they had confined on the corner across the street.

Sergeant Golden testified that between 8:00 o'clock and 9:00 o'clock the crowd increased steadily to a few hundred, but that from 9:00 o'clock until about 9:20 o'clock the people just seemed to come from everywhere until it reached between 1,000 and 1,200. During this time the crowd became unruly. There was shouting and threats, "God damned nigger, get the hell out of here;" "Get out of here niggers—go back where you belong or we will get you out of here" and "Get the hell out of here or we will break your blankety-blank head open." Cars were stopped in the streets with their horns blowing. There were Ku Klux Klan signs and there was singing of the Alabama Trooper song. Children in the crowd were playing various musical instruments such as a cymbal, trumpet and drum.

Rocks and eggs were also being thrown at the marchers from the crowd. The police were dodging the rocks and eggs and attempted to catch the persons who threw them. Sergeant Golden explained the problem. "You could see these teen-agers behind the crowd. You could see a boil of activity and something would come over our heads and I or my partner would go down to try to apprehend who was doing it. You couldn't see who was doing it. They would vanish into the crowd." He further testified that about 9:25 P.M., "They were saying, 'Let's get them,' and with this they would step off the curb to try to cross 35th Street and we would push them back with force. Once in a while somebody would run out, and we would grab ahold of them and throw them back into the crowd."

About 9:30 P.M. Commander Pierson told Gregory the situation was dangerous and becoming riotous. He asked Gregory if he would co-operate and lead the marchers out of the area. The request to leave the area was made about five times. Pierson then ld the marchers that any of them who wished to leave the area would iven a police escort. Three of the marchers accepted the proposal ere escorted out of the area. The remaining demonstrators sted and taken away in two police vans.

e have gone into considerable detail in describing the to the arrest of defendants, only a complete reading give one a true picture of the dilemma confront- ing the entire march from 4:30 P.M. until 9:30 e accompanied by their attorney who advised them, and the police were accompanied by an assistant city attorney who advised them. In short the record shows a determined effort by the police to allow the marchers to peacefully demonstrate and at the same time maintain order.

The defendants place heavy reliance on a footnote statement in Brown v. Louisiana, . . . that "Participants in an orderly demonstration in a public place are not chargeable with the danger, unprovoked except by the fact of the constitutionally protected demonstration itself, that their critics might react wih disorder or violence;" a statement in Watson v. City of Memphis, . . . quoted in Cox v. Louisiana, . . ., that "The compelling answer to this contention is that constitutional rights may not be denied simply because of hostility to their assertion or exercise;" and a statement in Wright v. Georgia, . . . that " * * * the possibility of disorder by others cannot justify exclusion of persons from a place if they otherwise have a constitutional right * * * to be present." They contend that their conduct was peaceful and that they were charged and convicted solely on the reaction of the crowd.

The Supreme Court in recent years has had occasion to reverse a number of breach-of-the-peace convictions based on civil rights activities. In none of these cases has there been a public disorder or imminent threat of public disorder. Garner v. Louisiana, . . . involved sit-ins, by Negroes at lunch counters catering only to whites. The court pointed out, "Although the manager of Kress' Department Store testified the only conduct which he considered disruptive was the petitioners' mere presence at the counter, he did state that he called the police because he 'feared that some disturbance might occur.' However, his fear is completely unsubstantiated by the record." . . . Taylor v. Louisiana, . . . concerned a sit-in by Negroes in a waiting room at a bus depot, reserved "for whites only." The court noted, " * * * immediately upon petitioners' entry into the waiting room many of the people therein became restless and that some onlookers climbed onto seats to get a better view. Nevertheless, respondent admits these persons moved on when ordered to do so by the police. There was no evidence of violence." . . . Edwards v. South Carolina, . . . involved a peaceful march by Negroes around the State House. The court commented, "There was no violence or threat of violence on their [marchers] part, or on the part of any member of the crowd watching them. Police protection was 'ample'." . . . Wright v. Georgia, . . . concerned 6 Negro boys playing basketball in a public park. The court noted, "The only evidence to support this contention is testimony of one of the police officers that 'The purpose of asking them to leave was to keep down trouble, which looked like to me might start—there were five or six cars driving around the park at the time, white people.' But that officer also stated that this 'was [not] unusual traffic for that time of day.' And the park was 50 acres in area." . . . Cox v. Louisiana, . . . involved the conviction of the leader of some 2,000

Negroes who demonstrated in the vicinity of a courthouse and jail to protest the arrest of fellow demonstrators. The court explained, "There is no indication, however, that any member of the white group threatened violence. * * * As Inspector Trigg testified, they could have handled the crowd." . . . Finally Brown v. Louisiana, . . . concerned a sit-in by 5 Negroes in the reading room of a public library maintained on a racially segregated basis. The court mentioned, "There was * * * no disorder, no intent to provoke a breach of the peace and no circumstances indicating that a breach might be occasioned by petitioners' actions." . . . The court in two of these cases, *Cox* and *Edwards*, in commenting on the lack of violence or threat of violence remarked that the situations were "a far cry from the situation in Feiner v. New York, . . ."

In Feiner v. New York, . . . defendant was convicted of disorderly conduct when he refused a police order to stop haranguing about 80 "restless" listeners. The court pointed out: "The exercise of the police officers' proper discretionary power to prevent a breach of the peace was thus approved by the trial court and later by two courts on review. The courts below recognized petitioner's right to hold a street meeting at this locality, to make use of loud-speaking equipment in giving his speech, and to make derogatory remarks concerning public officials and the American Legion. They found that the officers in making the arrest were motivated solely by a proper concern for the preservation of order and protection of the general welfare, and that there was no evidence which could lend color to a claim that the acts of the police were a cover for suppression of petitioner's views and opinions." The court concluded, "The findings of the state courts as to the existing situation and the imminence of greater disorder coupled with petitioner's deliberate defiance of the police officers convince us that we should not reverse this conviction in the name of free speech." . . .

In his dissenting opinion Justice Black stated "The Court's opinion apparently rests on this reasoning: The policeman, under the circumstances detailed, could reasonably conclude that serious fighting or even riot was imminent; therefore he could stop petitioner's speech to prevent a breach of peace; accordingly, it was 'disorderly conduct' for petitioner to continue speaking in disobedience of the officer's request." . . . He then stated the record failed to show any imminent threat of riot or uncontrollable disorder. He next stated "The police of course have power to prevent breaches of the peace. But if, in the name of preserving order, they ever can interfere with a lawful public speaker, they first must make all reasonable efforts to protect him." . . . Finally he disagreed with the majority's "statement that petitioner's disregard of the policeman's unexplained request amounted to such 'deliberate defiance' as would justify an arrest or conviction for disorderly conduct. * * * For at least where time allows, courtesy and explanation of commands are basic elements of good official conduct in a democratic society. * * * Petitioner was entitled to know why he should cease doing a lawful act." . . .

Justice Frankfurter in a concurring opinion summarized the situation this way: "As was said in Hague v. C. I. O., . . . untrolled official suppression of the speaker 'cannot be made a substitute for the duty to maintain order.' . . . Where conduct is within the allowable limits of free speech, the police are peace officers for the speaker as well as for his hearers. But the power effectively to preserve order cannot be displaced by giving a speaker complete immunity. * * * *It is not a constitutional principle that, in acting to preserve order, the police must proceed against the crowd, whatever its size and temper, and not against the speaker.*" (Emphasis added.) . . .

Applying the facts of this case to the rationale of the foregoing opinions we believe defendants were not denied their right to free speech, free assembly and freedom to petition for redress of grievances. First, the record is clear that there was some violence (throwing rocks and eggs) and an imminent threat of extreme public disorder. This immediately distinguishes this case from *Garner, Taylor, Edwards, Cox, Wright* and *Brown* discussed above. In fact the violence and imminent threat of a riot appears to have been greater here than in *Feiner*.

This brings us to the vital issue in the case of whether Justice Frankfurter's appraisal of *Feiner* that "It is not a constitutional principle that, in acting to preserve order, the police must proceed against the crowd, whatever its size and temper, and not against the speaker" can be reconciled with the Statement in *Brown* that "Participants in an orderly demonstration in a public place are not chargeable with the danger, unprovoked except by the fact of the constitutionally protected demonstration itself, that their critics might react with disorder or violence." We think the statements are harmonious when read in light of Justice Black's observation in his dissenting opinion in *Feiner* that "The police of course have power to prevent breaches of the peace. But, if, in the name of preserving order, they ever can interfere with a lawful public speaker, they first must make all reasonable efforts to protect him."

The record before us shows that the police made all reasonable efforts to protect the marchers before asking them to stop the demonstration. While no parade permit had been sought by the group and there had been no direct contact between representatives of the group and the police, the police did know of the planned march and a task force of 44 policemen were assigned to maintain order during the march. The 44 policemen went to Buckingham Fountain in Grant Park at 4:00 P.M. and accompanied the demonstrators while they marched to the city hall for a short demonstration and then marched about 5 miles south to 35th and Lowe. The police kept hostile spectators from interfering with the march around the block bounded by 35th Street, Union Avenue, 36th Street and Lowe Avenue. The taverns in the area were closed, barricades were placed at strategic points, there was radio communication among the police assigned to the area, and spectators were kept across the street. Water sprinklers which were turned on during the demonstration and interfered with the march were removed, persons in doorways were told to get back and close the doors, counterdemonstrators who tried to join the marchers were ordered across the street, a group of 150 countermarchers were ordered out of the demonstrators' line of march, and a pathway was cleared through several hundred spectators when the marchers deviated from their course around the block in which the mayor lived, and spectators who broke police lines and tried "to get" the demonstrators were forcefully thrown back into the crowd. Before the demonstration was ended there were about 100 policemen trying to maintain order in this one block area.

It is evident that there was adequate and determined police protection for the demonstrators from 4 o'clock in the afternoon until 9:30 in the evening while the demonstrators marched from Grant Park to the city hall and then to the mayor's home on the south side of Chicago. The demonstration around the mayor's home lasted 1½ hours during which the police were able to control the hostile crowd. It was between 9:00 and 9:25 that the crowd grew quickly in size and anger to the point where the police felt they could no longer control the situation.

Furthermore, we do not have here an "unexplained request" by the police as was apparently the case in *Feiner*. Commander Pierson told Gregory that the situation was becoming dangerous, that he was having difficulty containing the crowd and that there might be a riot. He asked Gregory five times to lead the marchers out. Gregory then went along the line of marchers and said "We will not leave; we have not broken any law; we will not resist if we are arrested." Commander Pierson then told the demonstrators that any of them who wished to leave would be given a police escort out of the area. After three of the demonstrators left, the rest were arrested.

We hold that under the circumstances of this case defendants were not denied any right of free speech, free assembly or freedom to petition for redress of grievances.

Defendants also argue that the disorderly conduct ordinance of the city is unconstitutionally vague as applied to free expression and free assembly. We interpret the ordinance as authorizing the action taken by police under the circumstances disclosed by this record. (See City of Chicago v. Williams, 45 Ill.App.2d 327, 195 N.E.2d 425.) It does not authorize the police to stop a peaceful demonstration merely because a hostile crowd may not agree with the views of the demontrators. It is only where there is an imminent threat of violence, the police have made all reasonable efforts to protect the demonstrators, the police have requested that the demonstration be stopped and explained the request, if there be time, and there is a refusal of the police request, that an arrest for an otherwise lawful demonstration may be made. As so interpreted we believe the ordinance is not so overly broad in scope as to be unconstitutionally vague or that it delegates undue discretion to the police. This is the type of conduct with which we are here faced and which is prohibited by the ordinance. * * *

The judgments of the circuit court of Cook County are affirmed.

NOTES

1. The foregoing Illinois Supreme Court decision was reversed by the Supreme Court of the United States in Gregory v. City of Chicago, 394 U.S. 111, 89 S.Ct. 946 (1969), in a short opinion by Mr. Chief Justice Warren, in which he stated, in part:

"Petitioners' march, if peaceful and orderly, falls well within the sphere of conduct protected by the First Amendment. . . . There is no evidence in this record that petitioners' conduct was disorderly. Therefore, . . . convictions so totally devoid of evidentiary support violate due process.

"The opinion of the Supreme Court of Illinois suggests that petitioners were convicted not for the manner in which they conducted their march but rather for their refusal to disperse when requested to do so by Chicago police. . . . However reasonable the police request may have been and however laudable the police motives, petitioners were charged and convicted for holding a demonstration, not for a refusal to obey a police officer. ['The trial judge charged solely in terms of the Chicago ordinance. Neither the ordinance nor the charge defined disorderly conduct as the refusal to obey a police order.'] As we said in Garner v. Louisiana, . . .: '[I]t is as much a denial of due process to send an accused to prison following conviction for a charge that was never made as it is to convict him upon a charge for which there is no evidence to support that conviction.'

"Finally, since the trial judge's charge permitted the jury to convict for acts clearly entitled to First Amendment protection, Stromberg v. California, . . . independently requires reversal of these convictions."

Following are excerpts from the concurring opinion of Justice Black, in which he was joined by Justice Douglas:

"I agree with the Illinois Supreme Court that the 'record shows a determined effort by the police to allow the marchers to peacefully demonstrate and at the same time maintain order.' I also think the record shows that outside of the marching and propagandizing of their views and protests, Gregory and his group while marching did all in their power to maintain order. Indeed, in the face of jeers, insults, and assaults with rocks and eggs, Gregory and his group maintained a decorum that speaks well for their determination simply to tell their side of their grievances and complaints. Even the 'snake' and 'snake pit' invectives used by Gregory and his demonstrators, unlike some used by their hecklers, remained within the general give-and-take of heated political argument. Thus both police and demonstrators made their best efforts faithfully to discharge their responsibilities as officers and citizens, but they were nevertheless unable to restrain the hostile hecklers within decent and orderly bounds. These facts disclosed by the record point unerringly to one conclusion, namely, that when groups with diametrically opposed, deep-seated views are permitted to air their emotional grievances, side by side, on city streets, tranquility and order cannot be maintained even by the joint efforts of the finest and best officers and of those who desire to be the most law-abiding protestors of their grievances.

"It is because of this truth, and a desire both to promote order and to safeguard First Amendment freedoms, that this Court has repeatedly warned States and governmental units that they cannot regulate conduct connected with these freedoms through use of sweeping, dragnet statutes that may, because of vagueness, jeopardize these freedoms. In those cases, however, we have been careful to point out that the Constitution does not bar enactment of laws regulating conduct, even though connected with speech, press, assembly, and petition, if such laws specifically bar only the conduct deemed obnoxious and are carefully and narrowly aimed at that forbidden conduct. . . . The dilemma revealed by this record is a crying example of a need for some such narrowly drawn law. It is not our duty and indeed not within our power to set out and define with precision just what statutes can be lawfully enacted to deal with situations like the one confronted here by police and protestors, both of whom appear to us to have been conscientiously trying to do their duties as they understood them. Plainly, however, no mandate in our Constitution leaves States and governmental units powerless to pass laws to protect the public from the kind of boisterous and threatening conduct that disturbs the tranquility of spots selected by the people either for homes, wherein they can escape the hurly-burly of the outside business and political world, or for public and other buildings that require peace and quiet to carry out their functions, such as courts, libraries, schools, and hospitals.

"The disorderly conduct ordinance under which these petitioners were charged and convicted is not, however, a narrowly drawn law, particularly designed to regulate certain kinds of conduct such as marching or picketing or demonstrating along the streets or highways. Nor does it regulate the times or places or manner of carrying on such activities. To the contrary, it might better be described as a meat-ax ordinance, gathering in one comprehensive definition of an offense a number of words which have a multiplicity of meanings, some of which would cover activity specifically protected by the First Amendment. The average person charged with its violation is necessarily left uncertain as to what conduct and attitudes of mind would be enough to convict under it. Who, for example, could possibly foresee what kind of noise or protected speech would be held to be 'improper'? That, of course, would depend on sensibilities, nerves, tensions, and on countless other things. As pointed out in Cantwell v. Connecticut, . . . common-law breach of peace is at its best a confusing offense that may imperil First Amendment rights. But how infinitely more doubtful and uncertain are the boundaries of an offense including any 'diversion tending to a breach of the peace . . . '! Moreover, the ordinance goes on to state that it shall be a crime for persons to 'collect in bodies or crowds for unlawful purposes, or for any purpose, to the annoyance or disturbance of other persons . . ..' Such language could authorize conviction simply because the form of the protest displeased some of the onlookers, and of course a conviction on that ground would encroach on First Amendment rights. . . . And it must be remembered that only the tiniest bit of petitioners' conduct could possibly be thought illegal here—that is, what they did after the policeman's order to leave the area. The right 'peaceably to assemble, and to petition the Government for a redress of grievances' is specifically protected by the First Amendment. For the entire five-mile march, the walking by petitioners in a group, the language, and the chants and songs were all treated by the city's assistant attorney and its specially detailed policemen as lawful, not lawless, conduct.

"The so-called 'diversion tending to a breach of the peace' here was limited entirely and exclusively to the fact that when the policeman in charge of the special police detail concluded that the hecklers observing the march were dangerously close to rioting and that the demonstrators and others were likely to be engulfed in that riot, he ordered Gregory and his demonstrators to leave, and Gregory—standing on what he deemed to be his constitutional rights—refused to do so. The 'diversion' complained of on the part of Gregory and the other marchers was not any noise they made or annoyance or disturbance of 'other persons' they had inflicted. Their guilt of 'disorderly conduct' therefore turns out to be their refusal to obey instanter an individual policeman's command to leave the area of the Mayor's home. Since neither the city council nor the state legislature had enacted a narrowly drawn statute forbidding disruptive picketing or demonstrating in a residential neighborhood, the conduct involved here could become 'disorderly' only if the policeman's command was a law which the petitioners were bound to obey at their peril. But under our democratic system of government, lawmaking is not entrusted to the moment-to-moment judgment of the policeman on his beat. Laws, that is valid laws, are to be made by representatives chosen to make laws for the future, not by police officers whose duty is to enforce laws already enacted and to make arrests only for conduct already made criminal. One of our proudest boasts is that no man can be convicted of crime for conduct, innocent when engaged in, that is later made criminal. . . . To let a policeman's command become equivalent to a criminal statute comes dangerously near making our government one of men rather than of laws. . . . There are ample ways to protect the domestic tranquility without subjecting First Amendment freedoms to such a clumsy and unwieldy weapon.

"The City of Chicago, recognizing the serious First Amendment problems raised by the disorderly conduct ordinance as it is written, argues that these convictions should nevertheless be affirmed in light of the narrowing construction placed on the ordinance by the Illinois Supreme Court in this case. That court held that the ordinance

> 'does not authorize the police to stop a peaceful demonstration merely because a hostile crowd may not agree with the views of the demonstrators. It is only where there is an imminent threat of violence, the police have made all reasonable efforts to protect the demonstrators, the police have requested that the demonstration be stopped and explained the request, if there be time, and there is a refusal of the police request, that an arrest for an otherwise lawful demonstration may be made.'

This interpretation of the ordinance is, of course, binding on this Court, and the construction of the Illinois Supreme Court is as authoritative [illegible] this limitation were written into the ordinance itself. But this ca[illegible] the end of our problem. The infringement of First Amendment rights will not be cured if the narrowing construction is so unforeseeable that men of common intelligence could not have realized the law's limited scope at the only relevant time, when their acts were committed, . . . or if the law remains excessively sweeping even as narrowed, ... Petitioners particularly press the Court to dispose of the case on this latter ground. They raise troublesome questions concerning the extent to which, even under the narrowed construction, guilt still depends on the mere refusal to obey a policeman's order. And they suggest that the scope of the police obligation to attempt first to deal with the hostile audience is still not made sufficiently clear.

"It is not necessary for the Court to resolve such issues in the present case, however, because the Chicago ordinance, as applied here, infringed on First Amendment rights for an even more fundamental reason. Whatever the validity of the Illinois Supreme Court's construction, this was simply not the theory on which these petitioners were convicted. In explaining the elements of the offense to the jury, the trial judge merely read the language of the ordinance. The jury was not asked to find whether, as the Illinois Supreme Court's construction apparently requires, there was 'an imminent threat of violence,' or whether the police had 'made all reasonable efforts to protect the demonstrators.' Rather, it was sufficient for the jury to decide that petitioners had made an 'improper noise' or a 'diversion tending to a breach of the peace,' or had 'collect[ed] in bodies or crowds for unlawful purposes, or for any purpose, to the annoyance or disturbance of other persons.'

"In fact, far from taking account of the limiting factors stressed by the Illinois Supreme Court, the judge's charge was based on precisely the opposite theory. The jury was instructed, over petitioners' objection, that 'the fact that persons other than these Defendants may or may not have violated any laws or may or may not have been arrested should not be considered by you in determining the guilt or innocence of these Defendants.' The significance of this instruction in the context of the evidence at trial is of course apparent—the jury was simply told to ignore questions concerning the acts of violence committed by the crowd of onlookers and attempts made by the police to arrest those directly responsible for them. * * *

"At the time the petitioners were tried, the Illinois Supreme Court had not yet announced its narrowing construction of the Chicago disorderly conduct ordinance. The trial judge's instructions supplied the jury only with the unadorned language of the statute. Thus it is entirely possible that the jury convicted the petitioners on the ground that Gregory and the others who demonstrated with him had, in the language of the ordinance, 'collect[ed] in bodies or crowds . . . to the annoyance or disturbance of other persons,' simply because the form of their protest had displeased some of the onlookers. . . .

"In agreeing to the reversal of these convictions, however, I wish once more to say that I think our Federal Constitution does not render the States powerless to regulate the conduct of demonstrators and picketers, conduct which is more than 'speech,' more than 'press,' more than 'assembly,' and more than 'petition,' as those terms are used in the First Amendment. Narrowly drawn statutes regulating the conduct of demonstrators and picketers are not impossible to draft. And narrowly drawn statutes regulating these activities are not impossible to pass if the people who elect their legislators want them passed. Passage of such laws, however, like the passage of all other laws, constitutes in the final analysis a choice of policies by the elected representatives of the people.

"I, of course, do not mean to say or even to intimate that freedom of speech, press, assembly, or petition can be abridged so long as the First Amendment remains unchanged in our Constitution. But to say that the First Amendment grants those broad rights free from any exercise of governmental power to regulate conduct, as distinguished from speech, press, assembly, or petition, would subject all the people of the Nation to the uncontrollable whim and arrogance of speakers, and writers, and protesters, and grievance bearers. * * * Were the authority of government so trifling as to permit anyone with a complaint to have the vast power to do anything he pleased, wherever he pleased, and whenever he pleased, our customs and our habits of conduct, social, political, economic, ethical, and religious, would all be wiped out, and become no more than relics of a gone but not forgotten past. Churches would be compelled to welcome into their buildings invaders who came but to scoff and jeer; streets and highways and public buildings would cease to be available for the purposes for which they were constructed and dedicated whenever demonstrators and picketers wanted to use them for their own purposes. And perhaps worse than all other changes, homes, the sacred retreat to which families repair for their privacy and their daily way of living, would have to have their doors thrown open to all who desired to convert the occupants to new views, new morals, and a new way of life. Men and women who hold public office would be compelled, simply because they did hold public office, to lose the comforts and privacy of an unpicketed home. I believe that our Constitution, written for the ages, to endure except as changed in the manner it provides, did not create a government with such monumental weaknesses. Speech and press are, of course, to be free, so that public matters can be discussed with impunity. But picketing and demonstrating can be regulated like other conduct of men. I believe that the homes of men, sometimes the last citadel of the tired, the weary, and the sick, can be protected by government from noisy, marching, tramping, threatening picketers and demonstrators bent on filling the minds of men, women, and children with fears of the unknown."

2. The disorderly conduct ordinance on the books at the time of the Gregory incident was declared unconstitutional by a federal district judge for the Northern District of Illinois, and it has been replaced by the following provisions of Chapter 193–1 of the Municipal Code of Chicago. Does it measure up to the standards prescribed in the concurring opinion of Justices Black and Douglas?

A person commits disorderly conduct when he knowingly:

(a) Does any act in such unreasonable manner as to provoke, make or aid in making a breach of peace; or

(b) Does or makes any unreasonable or offensive act, utterance, gesture or display which, under the circumstances, creates a clear and present danger of a breach of peace or imminent threat of violence; or

(c) Refuses or fails to cease and desist any peaceful conduct or activity likely to produce a breach of peace where there is an imminent threat of violence, and where the police have made all reasonable efforts to protect the otherwise peaceful conduct and activity, and have requested that said conduct and activity be stopped and explained the request if there be time; or

(d) Fails to obey a lawful order of dispersal by a person known by him to be a peace officer under circumstances where three or more persons are committing acts of disorderly conduct in the immediate vicinity, which acts are likely to cause substantial harm or serious inconvenience, annoyance or alarm; or

(e) Assembles with three or more persons for the purpose of using force or violence to disturb the public peace; or * * *

Related to the subject matter of (c) above, but outside the context of "disorderly conduct" is another Chicago Municipal Code provision (Ch. 11, Sec. 11–33), which reads as follows:

(a) Any person who knowingly shall resist or obstruct the performance by one known to the person to be a peace officer of any authorized act within his official capacity or shall knowingly interfere or prevent a peace officer from discharging his duty as such officer and whoever shall in any manner knowingly assist any person in the custody of any member of the police department to escape or attempt to escape from such custody, shall be fined not less than $25.00 nor more than $500.00.

(b) For the purposes of this section "resist" shall mean passive as well as active resistance.

In the light of the foregoing, consider the case of City of Chicago v. Meyer, 44 Ill.2d 1, 253 N.E.2d 400 (1969). The defendant had been making anti-war speeches on several occasions from a table on a sidewalk and four or five of his associates distributed pamphlets to members of the audience and passers-by. Their activities did not obstruct the sidewalk. However, about 11 o'clock one night about 100 to 200 persons gathered around, and they became "loud and boisterous", and two of them tore down a sign which the defendant had on display, and several spectators set fire to some leaflets. The police dispersed the crowd and they instructed defendant to also leave. He refused to do so and was arrested. He was charged with violating both of the above quoted ordinances, and convicted. However, the Supreme Court of Illinois reversed the disorderly conviction under Chapter 193–1, upon the authority of *Gregory,* but it sustained the conviction under Chapter 11, Section 11–33.

3. In *Gregory* the Illinois Supreme Court declined to hold that "residential picketing" was, as a matter of law, disorderly conduct. In considering that fact, plus the language of the concurring opinions of Justices Black and Douglas of the Supreme Court of the United States, does the following provision of the Illinois Criminal Code violate the First Amendment guarantee of freedom of speech?

RESIDENTIAL PICKETING

21.1–2 Prohibition—Exceptions. It is unlawful to picket before or about the residence or dwelling of any person, except when the residence or dwelling is used as a place of business. However, this Article does not apply to a person peacefully picketing his own residence or dwelling and does not prohibit the peaceful picketing of a place of employment involved in a labor dispute or the place of holding a meeting or assembly on premises commonly used to discuss subjects of general public interest.

21.1–3. Penalty. Any person who violates Section 21.1–2 shall be fined not more than $500 or imprisoned not more than 6 months, or both.

4. Consider the "Uniform Public Assembly Act", approved and recommended for enactment in all states, at the August, 1972 annual meeting of the National Conference of Commissioners on Uniform State Laws:

SECTION 1. [*Purposes; Rules of Construction.*] This Act shall be liberally construed and applied to promote its underlying purposes and policies, which are to:

(1) facilitate the free and unrestrained exercise of the constitutional rights of free speech and peaceable assembly by all who wish to exercise these rights within this State;

(2) impose only those limitations on public assemblies required to prevent substantial harm to public health and safety or to prevent unreasonable impairment of normal use of a public place;

(3) establish fair procedures for scheduling the time and place, and for prescribing the manner for holding public assemblies to assure adequate protection of the public health and safety;

(4) promote cooperation among governmental units and agencies to assist individuals in the free exercise of their rights of free speech and peaceable assembly; and

(5) make uniform the law with respect to the subject of this Act among those states which enact it.

SECTION 2. [*Definitions.*] As used in this Act:

(1) "permit" means a written statement, issued by a permit officer, authorizing the holding of a public assembly under stated conditions as to time, place, and manner;

(2) "permit officer" means the officer designated by the governing body of the political subdivision to receive and act upon applications for permits to hold public assemblies under this Act;

(3) "permit reviewing authority" means the board of 3 or more officials designated by the governing body of a political subdivision to hear appeals from decisions of the permit officer under this Act;

(4) "person" means an individual, corporation, government, governmental subdivision or agency, business trust, estate, trust, partnership or association, or any other legal entity;

(5) "political subdivision" means a city, town, village, or other incorporated place if the public assembly is or will be held therein and means the [county], [parish] if the public assembly is or will be held outside an incorporated place;

(6) "public assembly" means a gathering in a public place of 50 or more individuals which the general public is permitted to attend, with or without an admission charge;

(7) "public place" means (i) a place with respect to which the federal or state government, a political subdivision, or governmental agency normally has authority to control or prohibit use by the general public or (ii) a place with respect to which a private person permits use by the general public.

SECTION 3. [*Permit; When to Obtain.*]

(a) If there is no reasonable likelihood that a public assembly will substantially harm the public health or safety or substantially impair normal use of a public place, a person who intends to hold this kind of public assembly need not secure a permit but may apply for a permit to receive the protection and assistance afforded by this Act.

(b) If there is a reasonable likelihood that a public assembly will substantially harm the public health or safety or substantially impair normal use of a public place, a person who intends to hold this kind of public assembly shall apply for a permit.

SECTION 4. [*To Whom Application Made.*] An application for a permit to hold a public assembly shall be filed with the permit officer of the political subdivision.

SECTION 5. [*Contents of Application.*]

(a) An application for a permit to hold a public assembly shall be in writing and signed by an individual authorized to act for the person sponsoring the public assembly.

(b) The application shall state:

(1) the date and hours the public assembly is to be held;

(2) the name, residence address, and telephone number of the applicant, the principal officers of the applicant, the individual making the application, and any other individual authorized to represent the applicant in applying for the permit;

(3) the designation and location of the public place where the public assembly is to be held;

(4) that the requested use by the applicant of the designated place has been granted by the person having authority to grant the use of the public place if it is not freely accessible to the general public without advance reservation;

(5) the estimated number of persons expected to participate in or attend the public assembly;

(6) the general nature of the public assembly and the arrangements made to protect the public health and safety during the conduct of the public assembly, including arrangements with respect to traffic direction, crowd control and sanitation facilities;

(7) the name of any other political subdivision to which application has been or will be made to hold the public assembly; and

(8) any additional information the applicant wishes to furnish.

SECTION 6. [*Time for Filing Application.*]

(a) An application for a permit to hold a public assembly shall be filed at least 9 days before the day on which the public assembly is to be held.

(b) However, if the public assembly is to be held within 9 days after a specific and unanticipated event or announcement of public importance and in response to it, the application shall be filed within 24 hours after the event or announcement and at least 36 hours before the public assembly is to be held.

(c) The permit officer may receive and act upon an application to hold a public assembly even though the application was not filed in time.

SECTION 7. [*Receipt of Application.*]

(a) Upon receipt of an application for a permit to hold a public assembly, the permit officer shall note the time of filing on the application and shall forthwith mail or otherwise deliver a copy of the application to the principal officers of the applicant named in the application.

(b) At the request of the permit officer, the individual authorized to represent the applicant and the law enforcement and health officers designated by the permit officer shall meet with the permit officer to negotiate mutually satisfactory conditions under which the public assembly may be held to avoid substantial harm to the public health or safety and to minimize the effect of or avoid substantial impairment of normal use of the public place.

(c) If the public assembly is to be held in more than one political subdivision, the permit officers of the political subdivisions concerned shall coordinate their consideration of the applications for permits pending before them. At the request of the applicant, the permit officers of the political subdivisions concerned shall meet jointly with the individual authorized to represent the applicant and the appropriate law enforcement and health officers to negotiate mutually satisfactory conditions under which the public assembly may be held to avoid substantial harm to the public health and safety and to minimize the effect of or avoid substantial impairment of the normal use of the public place.

SECTION 8. [*Action on Application.*]

(a) The permit officer shall (1) issue the permit as requested, (2) issue the permit subject to conditions (Sections 9 and 10), or (3) apply to the [district] court for an order enjoining the holding of the public assembly [Section 11]. If the permit officer fails to take timely action on the application, he is deemed to have granted the permit as requested [Section 8(c)].

(b) The permit officer shall give the applicant immediate notice in writing of his action on the application.

(c) A permit officer is deemed to have granted a permit on the terms requested, if:

(1) an application is filed under Section 6(a) and the officer does not issue a permit or proceed under Section 11 within 10

days after the application is filed or not less than 4 days before the public assembly is to be held, whichever is earlier, or

(2) an application is filed under Section 6(b) and the officer does not issue a permit or proceed under Section 11 within 24 hours after the application is filed or not less than 18 hours before the public assembly is to be held, whichever is earlier.

(d) By agreement in writing the applicant and the permit officer may modify the time requirements of subsection (c).

SECTION 9. [*Criteria for Imposing Conditions on Permit.*]

(a) If there is a reasonable likelihood that a public assembly will substantially harm the public health or safety or substantially impair normal use of a public place, the permit officer shall grant the permit upon conditions reasonably necessary to avoid substantial harm to the public health or safety and to minimize the effect of or avoid substantial impairment of normal use of a public place.

(b) In determining whether to grant a permit only upon compliance with conditions, the permit officer shall consider whether:

(1) a permit has been granted to others to hold a public assembly at the same time in the same or a nearby public place;

(2) public sanitation facilities are adequate;

(3) noise, litter, or pollution of water or air will be generated by the public assembly;

(4) traffic generated by the public assembly will affect normal traffic movement;

(5) the time and place are suitable in view of the number of persons expected to attend;

(6) food, water, and emergency medical services are accessible to the persons attending;

(7) there is substantial potential that the public assembly will precipitate criminal activity that will increase the task of controlling the crowd and managing the public assembly;

(8) there is sufficient time to permit law enforcement and health officers and other public authorities to make the necessary arrangements to avoid substantial harm to the public health and safety;

(9) the public assembly will substantially impair the provision of fire and police protection and medical and other essential public services;

(10) the public assembly will unreasonably interfere with the quiet enjoyment of a residential community;

(11) there is an alternate public place that will reasonably serve the objectives of the public assembly if there will likely be substantial harm to the public health or safety or substantial impairment of normal use of the proposed public place;

(12) there is substantial potential for material injury to property at or near the public place;

(13) there is a special relationship between the subject of the public assembly and the public place that makes it reasonable to impose extraordinary burdens on the public place affected and the individuals residing or present in nearby areas; and

(14) the imposition of conditions on the permit will materially interfere with the reasonable and lawful objectives of the public assembly.

SECTION 10. [*Permissible Conditions.*]

(a) In granting a permit the permit officer may impose reasonable conditions as to the time, place, and manner of holding the public assembly so as to avoid substantial harm to the public health or safety and to minimize the effect of or avoid substantial impairment of the normal use of a public place. These conditions may include designating a different time or place; restricting duration of the public assembly; requiring installation of temporary sanitation facilities; requiring provision of emergency medical services; requiring the applicant to establish crowd control procedures; requiring trained parade marshals; and requiring the applicant to designate representatives to maintain liaison with law enforcement officers during the public assembly to facilitate dealing with emergencies that may rise.

(b) If there is an admission charge, the permit officer may impose a condition requiring the person holding the public assembly to reimburse the political subdivision for the cost of additional law enforcement officers required and to furnish a bond in a reasonable amount to insure reimbursement.

SECTION 11. [*Injunction Against Public Assembly.*] If there is a reasonable likelihood that a public assembly will substantially harm the public health or safety and this cannot be avoided by imposition of conditions (Sections 9 and 10), the permit officers shall inform the applicant or the person requested to apply (Section 13) that he will not grant the permit and shall forthwith apply to the [district] court for an order enjoining the applicant and other interested persons from holding the public assembly.

SECTION 12. [*Modification of Terms of Permit.*]

(a) If there is a material change in the contemplated circumstances of the public assembly after a permit is granted, the applicant shall promptly inform the permit officer of the change.

(b) By agreement with the applicant, the permit officer at any time may amend the terms of the permit to impose additional or different conditions (Sections 9 and 10). Upon the basis of material change in the contemplated circumstances reported by the applicant or determined by the permit officer presenting a reasonable likelihood that the public assembly will substantially harm the public health or safety or substantially impair normal use of a public place not authorized by the permit, the permit officer may impose additional or different conditions (Sections 9 and 10). Unless there is agreement or the applicant informs the permit officer of a change in the contemplated circumstances, the permit officer may amend the terms of the permit only by action taken and communicated to the applicant in writing stating the reason therefor at least 3 days before the day on which the public assembly is to begin.

(c) If the permit officer is unable to give the notice required by subsection (b) of additional or different conditions or the change in contemplated circumstances reported to or determined by the permit officer is such that there is a reasonable likelihood that the public assembly will substantially harm the public health or safety and this cannot be avoided by imposition of additional or different conditions (Sections 9 and 10), the permit officer shall so inform the applicant and forthwith apply to the [district] court for an order enjoining the applicant and other interested persons from holding the public assembly or for other appropriate relief.

SECTION 13. [*Application Requested by Permit Officer.*] If the permit officer determines that a public assembly is to be held that presents a reasonable likelihood that it will substantially harm the public health or safety or substantially impair normal use of a public place and this can be avoided or minimized by imposition of conditions (Sections 9 and 10) upon holding the public assembly and that no application for a permit has been made, the permit officer at least 5 days before the date on which the public assembly is to be held may request any person whom he reasonably believes to be organizing the public assembly to apply for a permit to hold it. The person requested may apply for a permit within 10 days after the request or 5 days before the announced date for the public assembly, whichever is earlier; in any case he shall have 24 hours within which to file the application. If the person fails to apply within the time required, the permit officer may issue a permit for the public assembly upon conditions reasonably necessary to avoid substantial harm to the public health or safety and to minimize the effect of or avoid substantial impairment of normal use of a public place (Sections 9 and 10), in which case, at least 3 days before the public assembly is to be held, he shall deliver the permit to any person whom he reasonably believes to be organizing the public assembly and shall publicize the permit and its conditions.

SECTION 14. [*Judicial Order Relating to Public Assembly.*] When a permit officer applies to the [district] court for a restraining order injunctive relief, or other order (Sections 11, 12(c), and 13), the court shall expedite the proceedings to afford timely relief and cause appropriate notice to be given. Upon a hearing the court may grant the permit as requested, grant a permit upon specified conditions, or enjoin the holding of the public assembly if there is a reasonable likelihood that the public assembly will substantially harm public health or safety and this cannot be avoided by the imposition of conditions on the permit.

SECTION 15. [*Rights Under Permit.*] Conduct constituting free and unrestrained exercise of the constitutional rights of free speech and peaceable assembly and permitted by the terms of a permit as to the time, place, and manner of holding a public assembly is deemed not to violate any statute, ordinance, rule, or regulation.

SECTION 16. [*Management of Public Assembly.*]

(a) Consistent with terms of the permit, a person granted a permit to hold a public assembly is entitled to determine the order of events of the public assembly.

(b) The political subdivision shall take all necessary steps by the provision of necessary personnel, equipment, materials, and facilities to assure freedom to exercise rights of free speech and peaceable assembly and prevent persons from interfering with or disrupting the conduct of a public assembly for which a permit has been issued.

(c) If the highest ranking law enforcement officer in charge determines that a public assembly for which a permit has been granted is not proceeding as authorized and that there is a substantial impairment of normal use of a public place not authorized by the permit or that there is imminent or existing danger that substantial harm to the public health or safety will occur, he shall marshal available resources to obtain compliance with the permit. He shall take appropriate steps to control any interference with or disruption of the conduct of the public assembly. He shall communicate with representatives of the person holding the public assembly to obtain their assistance. If, after taking these measures, the highest ranking law enforcement officer in charge determines that the public assembly cannot continue as authorized because of an imminent or existing danger that substantial harm to the public health or safety will occur, he shall limit the public assembly or otherwise impose conditions upon its conduct to the extent reasonably necessary to remove the danger. If the emergency measures taken and those that may reasonably be taken do or would not remove the imminent or existing danger, the highest ranking law enforcement officer in charge may postpone or cancel the public assembly and, if necessary, disperse the participants and bystanders.

(d) If a public assembly is held for which no permit has been granted and which substantially harms public health or safety or substantially impairs normal use of a public place, law enforcement and health officers shall take only those steps reasonably necessary to remove the substantial harm or impairment. However, if necessary to remove an imminent or existing danger of substantial harm to the public health or safety, the highest ranking law enforcement officer in charge may cancel the public assembly and disperse the participants and bystanders.

SECTION 17. [*Petition for Administrative Review.*]

(a) Within 30 days after the permit officer mails or delivers to the applicant a copy of the permit with conditions, including amended conditions, imposed by the permit officer, the applicant may petition the permit reviewing authority for review of the decision of the permit officer. No other person, including a political subdivision may obtain under this Act administrative or judicial review of the decision of the permit officer. The petition shall be in writing, set forth the grounds for review, and have attached a copy of the petitioner's application for a permit. The applicant shall deliver or mail to the permit officer a copy of his petition for review.

(b) Unless the applicant requests a postponement, the permit reviewing authority shall forthwith set a time for hearing the petition for review to be within 10 days after the petition for review is filed but not less than 3 days before the proposed public assembly is to be held.

SECTION 18. [*Administrative Review.*]

(a) The permit reviewing authority shall conduct the hearing of a petition for review in an informal manner and afford the parties an opportunity for a full, fair, and impartial hearing. The parties shall be afforded an opportunity to present evidence and argument on all of the issues involved. A party may conduct the cross-examination required for a full and true disclosure of the facts. Irrelevant, immaterial, and unduly repetitious evidence may be excluded. Evidence commonly relied upon by reasonably prudent men in the conduct of their affairs may be admitted. If the applicant and the permit reviewing authority agree, the permit reviewing authority shall make a record of the proceedings.

(b) The permit reviewing authority shall make its decision upon the evidence presented to it and state in writing its decision and the findings and reasons therefor. The permit reviewing authority may exercise all authority granted by this Act to the permit officer. Within 3 days after the petition for review is heard, the permit reviewing authority shall deliver or mail to the parties its written decision and the findings and reasons therefor. If the permit reviewing authority fails to deliver or mail to the applicant its written decision within 3 days after the petition for review is heard but not less than 3 days before the proposed public assembly is to be held, the applicant may treat the petition for review as having been denied.

SECTION 19. [*Judicial Review.*]

(a) Within 30 days after the applicant's petition for review is denied he may petition the [district] court for review of the denial. The petition shall contain a copy of the application, any decision of the permit reviewing authority, and state the grounds for reversal of the decision.

(b) If the decision by the permit officer from which an appeal is taken is made 5 or less days before the day on which the public assembly is proposed to be held, the applicant may petition the [district] court directly for a review of the action of the permit officer without first seeking review by the permit reviewing authority. In that case the petition shall set forth a copy of the application, the decision of the permit officer, and the grounds for reversal of the permit officer's decision.

(c) The court shall hear the petition for review de novo without a jury and receive evidence, and make a record of the proceedings. Upon the evidence presented the court shall make findings and order that the permit be granted either upon the terms requested or conditions stated by the court, or enjoin the holding of the public assembly if there is a reasonable likelihood that it will substantially harm the public health or safety and this cannot be avoided by the imposition of conditions on the permit.

SECTION 20. [*Consolidation of Court Proceedings.*] If an action is brought in the [district] court concerning a public assembly, all subsequent actions brought concerning the public assembly, upon motion of any party, shall be joined with the first action and heard before the same court.

SECTION 21. [*Appeals.*] A party may obtain a review of a final judgment of the [district] court by appeal to the [supreme court]. The appeal shall be taken as in other civil cases. The taking of an appeal does not operate to stay the order of the [district] court, but the [supreme court] may stay the order pending determination of the appeal.

SECTION 22. [*Records.*] The permit officer shall keep for 5 years copies of all applications to hold a public assembly, his actions thereon, and permits. The file containing this material shall be open to reasonable inspection by any individual during regular office hours of the political subdivision.

SECTION 23. [*Penalties.*]

(a) A person who willfully (1) violates a provision of a permit to hold a public assembly with knowledge of the provision; (2) disobeys a reasonable and lawful order of an individual known by him to be a law enforcement officer to cease disrupting or interfering with the conduct of a public assembly; or (3) disobeys a reasonable and lawful order of a law enforcement officer issued pursuant to Section 16 is guilty of [an offense] [a misdemeanor] and upon conviction may be fined not more than $[ ] or imprisoned for not more than [ ] days or both.

(b) It is a defense to a prosecution under this Section that the prohibition under which the violation is charged was issued in violation of the Constitution of the United States or this State or of this Act.

SECTION 24. [*Inapplicability of Act.*] This Act does not affect the authority of an owner of private property to regulate the use of his property or of a person responsible for the use of public property to schedule the use thereof.

SECTION 25. [*Temporary Permit Officer and Permit Reviewing Authorities.*] Until the governing body of the political subdivision designates otherwise, the [city manager] [chief of police] shall serve as the permit officer and the [city council] [board of aldermen] shall serve as the permit reviewing authority of the [city] [town] [village] or other incorporated place and the [county manager] [county attorney] [sheriff] shall serve as the permit officer and the [county commissioners court] [board of supervisors] shall serve as the permit reviewing authority of the [county] [parish].

* * *

SECTION 3. SYMBOLISM

UNITED STATES v. O'BRIEN

Supreme Court of the United States, 1968.
391 U.S. 367, 88 S.Ct. 1673.

[The defendant (in March, 1966) burned his Selective Service registration certificate (draft card) on the steps of a courthouse in the presence of a sizeable crowd. He said he did it to publicly influence others to adopt his anti war beliefs. He was arrested and charged with violating a federal statute making it a criminal offense for anyone to knowingly destroy or mutilate such certificates. In essence he claimed he was exercising his constitutional right to "symbolic free speech". Following are excerpts from the opinion of the Supreme Court upholding the defendant's conviction. The federal statute involved in the case is Section 462(b) of the Universal Military Training and Service Act of 1948—Title 50 (App), United States Code, as amended in 1965.]

MR. CHIEF JUSTICE WARREN delivered the opinion of the Court.

* * *

We note at the outset that the 1965 Amendment plainly does not abridge free speech on its face, and we do not understand O'Brien to argue otherwise. . . . [It] deals with conduct having no connection with speech. It prohibits the knowing destruction of certificates issued by the Selective Service System, and there is nothing necessarily expressive about such conduct. The Amendment does not distinguish between public and private destruction, and it does not punish only destruction engaged in for the purpose of expressing views. . . . A law prohibiting destruction of Selective Service certificates no more abridges free speech on its face than a motor vehicle law prohibiting the destruction of drivers' licenses, or a tax law prohibiting the destruction of books and records.

O'Brien nonetheless argues that the 1965 Amendment is unconstitutional in its application to him, and is unconstitutional as enacted because what he calls the "purpose" of Congress was "to suppress freedom of speech." We consider these arguments separately.

O'Brien first argues that the 1965 Amendment is unconstitutional as applied to him because his act of burning his registration certificate was protected "symbolic speech" within the First Amendment. His argument is that the freedom of expression which the First Amendment guarantees includes all modes of "communication of ideas by conduct," and that his conduct is within this definition because he did it in "demonstration against the war and against the draft."

We cannot accept the view that an apparently limitless variety of conduct can be labeled "speech" whenever the person engaging in the conduct intends thereby to express an idea. However, even on the assumption that the alleged communicative element in O'Brien's conduct is sufficient to bring into play the First Amendment, it does not necessarily follow that the destruction of a registration certificate is constitutionally protected activity. This Court has held that when "speech" and "nonspeech" elements are combined in the same course of conduct, a sufficiently important governmental interest in regulating the nonspeech element can justify incidental limitations on First Amendment freedoms. To characterize the quality of the governmental interest which must appear, the Court has employed a variety of descriptive terms: compelling; substantial; subordinating; paramount; cogent; strong. Whatever imprecision inheres in these terms, we think it clear that a government regulation is sufficiently justified if it is within the constitutional power of the Government; if it furthers an important or substantial governmental interest; if the governmental interest is unrelated to the suppression of free expression; and if the incidental restriction on alleged First Amendment freedoms is no greater than is essential to the furtherance of that interest. We find that the 1965 Amendment . . . meets all of these requirements, and consequently that O'Brien can be constitutionally convicted for violating it.

The constitutional power of Congress to raise and support armies and to make all laws necessary and proper to that end is broad and sweeping. . . . The power of Congress to classify and conscript manpower for military service is "beyond question." . . . Pursuant to this power, Congress may establish a system of registration for individuals liable for training and service, and may require such individuals within reason to cooperate in the registration system. The issuance of certificates indicating the registration and eligibility classification of individuals is a legitimate and substantial administrative aid in the functioning of this system. And legislation to insure the continuing availability of issued certificates serves a legitimate and substantial purpose in the system's administration.

O'Brien's argument to the contrary is necessarily premised upon his unrealistic characterization of Selective Service certificates. He essentially adopts the position that such certificates are so many pieces of paper designed to notify registrants of their registration or classification, to be retained or tossed in the wastebasket according to the convenience or taste of the registrant. Once the registrant has received notification, according to this view, there is no reason for him to retain the certificates. O'Brien notes that most of the information on a registration certificate serves no notification purpose at all; the registrant hardly needs to be told his address and physical characteristics. We agree that the registration certificate contains much information of which the registrant needs no notification. This circumstance, however, does not lead to the conclusion that the certificate serves no purpose, but that, like the classification certificate, it serves purposes in addition to initial notification. Many of these purposes would be defeated by the certificates' destruction or mutilation. Among these are:

1. The registration certificate serves as proof that the individual described thereon has registered for the draft. The classification certificate shows the eligibility classification of a named but undescribed individual. Voluntarily displaying the two certificates is an easy and painless way for a young man to dispel a question as to whether he might be delinquent in his Selective Service obligations. Correspondingly, the availability of the certificates for such display relieves the Selective Service System of the administrative burden it would otherwise have in verifying the registration and classification of all suspected delinquents. Further, since both certificates are in the nature of "receipts" attesting that the registrant has done what the law requires, it is in the interest of the just and efficient administration of the system that they be continually available, in the event, for example, of a mix-up in the registrant's file. Additionally, in a time of national crisis, reasonable availability to each registrant of the two small cards assures a rapid and uncomplicated means for determining his fitness for immediate induction, no matter how distant in our mobile society he may be from his local board.

2. The information supplied on the certificates facilitates communication between registrants and local boards, simplifying the system and benefiting all concerned. To begin with, each certificate bears the address of the registrant's local board, an item unlikely to be committed to memory. Further, each card bears the registrant's Selective Service number, and a registrant who has his number readily available so that he can communicate it to his local board when he supplies or requests information can make simpler the board's task in locating his file. Finally, a registrant's inquiry, particularly through a local board other than his own, concerning his eligibility status is frequently answerable simply on the basis of his classification certificate; whereas, if the certificate were not reasonably available and the registrant were uncertain of his classification, the task of answering his questions would be considerably complicated.

3. Both certificates carry continual reminders that the registrant must notify his local board of any change of address, and other specified changes in his status. The smooth functioning of the system requires that local boards be continually aware of the status and whereabouts of registrants, and the destruction of certificates deprives the system of a potentially useful notice device.

4. The regulatory scheme involving Selective Service certificates includes clearly valid prohibitions against the alteration, forgery, or similar deceptive misuse of certificates. The destruction or

mutilation of certificates obviously increases the difficulty of detecting and tracing abuses such as these. Further, a mutilated certificate might itself be used for deceptive purposes.

The many functions performed by Selective Service certificates establish beyond doubt that Congress has a legitimate and substantial interest in preventing their wanton and unrestrained destruction and assuring their continuing availability by punishing people who knowingly and wilfully destroy or mutilate them. And we are unpersuaded that the pre-existence of the non-possession regulations in any way negates this interest. * * *

. . . Finally, the 1965 Amendment . . . is concerned with abuses involving *any* issued Selective Service certificates, not only with the registrant's own certificates. The knowing destruction or mutilation of someone else's certificates would therefore violate the statute . . .

* * *

. . . We perceive no alternative means that would more precisely and narrowly assure the continuing availability of issued Selective Service certificates than a law which prohibits their wilful mutilation or destruction. . . . The 1965 Amendment prohibits such conduct and does nothing more. In other words, both the governmental interest and the operation of the 1965 Amendment are limited to the noncommunicative aspect of O'Brien's conduct. The governmental interest and the scope of the 1965 Amendment are limited to preventing harm to the smooth and efficient functioning of the Selective Service System. When O'Brien deliberately rendered unavailable his registration certificate, he wilfully frustrated this governmental interest. For this noncommunicative impact of his conduct, and for nothing else, he was convicted. * * *

MR. JUSTICE HARLAN, concurring.

The crux of the Court's opinion, which I join, is of course its general statement . . . that:

> "a government regulation is sufficiently justified if it is within the constitutional power of the Government; if it furthers an important or substantial governmental interest; if the governmental interest is unrelated to the suppression of free expression; and if the incidental restriction on alleged First Amendment freedoms is no greater than is essential to the furtherance of that interest."

I wish to make explicit my understanding that this passage does not foreclose consideration of First Amendment claims in those rare instances when an "incidental" restriction upon expression, imposed by a regulation which furthers an "important or substantial" governmental interest and satisfies the Court's other criteria, in practice has the effect of entirely preventing a "speaker" from reaching a significant audience with whom he could not otherwise lawfully communicate. This is not such a case, since O'Brien manifestly could have conveyed his message in many ways other than by burning his draft card.

[JUSTICE DOUGLAS' dissent is omitted because it concerns itself only with the constitutionality of the draft and he wanted to have that issue decided by the Court.]

STREET v. NEW YORK

Supreme Court of the United States, 1969.
394 U.S. 576, 89 S.Ct. 1354.

MR. JUSTICE HARLAN delivered the opinion of the Court.

Appellant Street has been convicted in the New York courts of violating [a New York law], which makes it a misdemeanor "publicly [to] mutilate, deface, defile, or defy, trample upon, or cast contempt upon either by words or act [any flag of the United States]." He was given a suspended sentence. We must decide whether, in light of all the circumstances, that conviction denied to him rights of free expression protected by the First Amendment and assured against state infringement by the Fourteenth Amendment. . . .

According to evidence given at trial, the events which led to the conviction were these. Appellant testified that during the afternoon of June 6, 1966, he was listening to the radio in his Brooklyn apartment. He heard a news report that civil rights leader James Meredith had been shot by a sniper in Mississippi. Saying to himself, "They didn't protect him," appellant, himself a Negro, took from his drawer a neatly folded, 48-star American flag which he formerly had displayed on national holidays. Appellant left his apartment and carried the still-folded flag to the nearby intersection of St. James Place and Lafayette Avenue. Appellant stood on the northeast corner of the intersection, lit the flag with a match, and dropped the flag on the pavement when it began to burn.

Soon thereafter, a police officer halted his patrol car and found the burning flag. The officer testified that he then crossed to the northwest corner of the intersection, where he found appellant "talking out loud" to a small group of persons. The officer estimated that there were some 30 persons on the corner near the flag and five to 10 on the corner with appellant. The officer testified that as he approached within 10 or 15 feet of appellant, he heard appellant say, "We don't need no damn flag," and that when he asked appellant whether he had burned the flag appellant replied: "Yes; that is my flag; I burned it. If they let that happen to Meredith, we don't need an American flag." Appellant admitted making the latter response, but he denied that he said anything else and asserted that he always had remained on the corner with the flag.

Later the same day, appellant was charged, by an information sworn to before a judge of the New York City Criminal Court, with having committed "the crime of Malicious Mischief in that [he] did wilfully and unlawfully defile, cast contempt upon and burn an American Flag, in violation of . . . the Penal Law, under the following circumstances: * * * [he] did wilfully and unlawfully set fire to an American Flag and shout, 'If they did that to Meredith, We don't need an American Flag.' "

Appellant was tried before another Criminal Court judge, sitting without a jury, and was convicted of malicious mischief . . . He was subsequently given a suspended sentence. . . .

Street argues that his conviction was unconstitutional for three different reasons. *First,* he claims that [the statute] is overbroad both on its face and as applied, because [it] makes it a crime "publicly [to] defy * * * or cast contempt upon [an American flag] *by words* * * *." (Emphasis added.) *Second,* he contends that [it] is vague and imprecise because it does not clearly define the conduct which it forbids. *Third,* he asserts that New York may not constitutionally punish one who publicly destroys or damages an American flag as a means of protest, because such an act constitutes expression protected by the Fourteenth Amendment. We deem it unnecessary to consider the latter two arguments, for we hold that [the statute] was unconstitutionally applied in appellant's case because it permitted him to be punished merely for speaking defiant or contemptuous words about the American flag. In taking this course, we resist the pulls to decide the constitutional issues involved in this case on a broader basis than the record before us imperatively requires.

Though our conclusion is a narrow one, it requires pursuit of four lines of inquiry: (1) whether the constitutionality of the "words" part of the statute was passed upon by the New York Court of Appeals; (2) whether, if appellant's conviction may have rested in whole or in part on his utterances and if the statute as thus applied is unconstitutional, these factors in themselves require reversal; (3) whether Street's words may in fact have counted independently in his conviction; and (4) whether the "words" provision of the statute, as presented by this case, is unconstitutional.

I.

The New York Court of Appeals did not mention in its opinion the constitutionality of the "words" part . . . Hence, in order to vindicate our jurisdiction to deal with this particular issue, we must inquire whether that question was presented to the New York courts in such a manner that it was necessarily decided by the New York Court of Appeals when it affirmed appellant's conviction. . . .

. . . there appears to be no doubt that the issue of the constitutionality of the "words" part of the statute was raised in appellant's briefs in both the Appellate Division and the Court of Appeals, and the State does not suggest the contrary.

We therefore conclude that the question is properly before us.

II.

We next consider whether it is our duty to reverse if we find, as we do in Parts III and IV, infra, that Street's words could have been an independent cause of his conviction and that a conviction for uttering such words would violate the Constitution.

That such is our duty is made apparent by a number of decisions of this Court. [The leading one of which is Stromberg v. California].

It is true that in the present case the general verdict was rendered by a judge, not a jury. However, if the ground of the judge's decision cannot be ascertained from the record, then the danger of unconstitutional conviction is not significantly less than . . . Hence, we conclude that . . . appellant's conviction must be set aside if we find that it could have been based solely upon his words and that a conviction resting on such a basis would be unconstitutional—a matter to which we shall turn in a moment.

Moreover, even assuming that the record precludes the inference that appellant's conviction might have been based solely on his words, we are still bound to reverse if the conviction could have been based upon both his words and his act.

. . . appellant . . . was charged with two acts violative of the statute: burning a flag and publicly speaking defiant or contemptuous words about the flag; and evidence was introduced to show the commission of both acts. Here too the verdict was general and the sentence a single penalty. Hence, unless the record negates the possibility that the conviction was based on both alleged violations, [the judgment must be affirmed as to both or as to neither.]

. . . when a single-count indictment or information charges the commission of a crime by virtue of having done both a constitutionally protected act and one which may be unprotected, and a guilty verdict ensues without elucidation, there is an unacceptable danger that the trier of fact will have regarded the two acts as "intertwined" and have rested the conviction on both together. . . . There is no comparable hazard when the indictment or information is in several counts and the conviction is explicitly declared to rest on findings of guilt on certain of those counts, for in such instances there is positive evidence that the trier of fact considered each count on its own merits and separately from the others.

III.

We turn to considering whether appellant's words could have been the sole cause of his conviction, or whether the conviction could have been based on both his words and his burning of the flag. . . . The sworn information which charged appellant with the crime of malicious mischief . . . recited not only that appellant had burned an American flag but also that he "[did] shout, 'If they did that to Meredith, We don't need an American flag.'" . . . the statute which appellant was charged with violating made it a crime not only publicly to mutilate a flag but also "publicly [to] defy * * * or cast contempt upon [any American flag] by words."

The State argues that appellant's words were at most used to establish his unlawful intent in burning the flag. However, after a careful examination of the comparatively brief trial record, we find ourselves unable to say with certainty that appellant's words were not an independent cause of his conviction. While it is true that at trial greater emphasis was placed upon appellant's action in burning the flag than upon his words, a police officer did testify to the utterance of the words. The State never announced that it was relying exclusively upon the burning. The trial judge never indicated during the trial that he regarded appellant's words as relating solely to intent. The judge found appellant guilty immediately after the end of the trial, and he delivered no oral or written opinion.

In the face of an information explicitly setting forth appellant's words as an element of his alleged crime, and of appellant's subsequent conviction under a statute making it an offense to speak words of that sort, we find this record insufficient to eliminate the possibility either that appellant's words were the sole basis of his conviction or that appellant was convicted for both his words and his deed.

IV.

We come finally to the question whether, in the circumstances of this case, New York may constitutionally inflict criminal punishment upon one who ventures "publicly [to] defy * * * or cast contempt upon [any American flag] by words * * *."

The relevant evidence introduced at appellant's trial, considered in the light most favorable to the State, must be taken to establish the following. At the time of his arrest, appellant was standing on a street corner and speaking to a small crowd; on the opposite corner lay the burning flag. Appellant said to the crowd: "We don't need no damn flag"; and when questioned by a police officer appellant stated: "If they let that happen to Meredith, we don't need an American flag." According to the officer, the crowds which gathered around appellant and around the flag did not obstruct the street or sidewalk and were neither unruly nor threatening.

In these circumstances, we can think of four governmental interests which might conceivably have been furthered by punishing appellant for his words: (1) an interest in deterring appellant from vocally inciting others to commit unlawful acts; (2) an interest in preventing appellant from uttering words so inflammatory that they would provoke others to retaliate physically against him, thereby causing a breach of the peace; (3) an interest in protecting the sensibilities of passers-by who might be shocked by appellant's words about the American flag; and (4) an interest in assuring that appellant, regardless of the impact of his words upon others, showed proper respect for our national emblem.

In the circumstances of this case, we do not believe that any of these interests may constitutionally justify appellant's conviction . . . for speaking as he did. We begin with the interest in preventing incitement. Appellant's words, taken alone, did not urge anyone to do anything unlawful. They amounted only to somewhat excited public advocacy of the idea that the United States should abandon, at least temporarily, one of its national symbols. It is clear that the Fourteenth Amendment prohibits the States from imposing criminal punishment for public advocacy of peaceful change in our institutions. . . . Even assuming that appellant's words might be found incitive when considered together with his simultaneous burning of the flag, [the statute] does not purport to punish only those defiant or contemptuous words which amount to incitement, and there is no evidence that the state courts regarded the statute as so limited. Hence, a conviction for words could not be upheld on this basis. . . .

Nor could such a conviction be justified on the second ground mentioned above: the possible tendency of appellant's words to provoke violent retaliation. Though it is conceivable that some listeners might have been moved to retaliate upon hearing appellant's disrespectful words, we cannot say that appellant's remarks were so inherently inflammatory as to come within that small class of "fighting words" which are "likely to provoke the average person to retaliation, and thereby cause a breach of the peace." Chaplinsky v. New Hampshire . . . . And even if appellant's words might be found within that category, [the statute] is not narrowly drawn to punish only words of that character, and there is no indication that it was so interpreted by the state courts. . . .

Again, such a conviction could not be sustained on the ground that appellant's words were likely to shock passers-by. Except perhaps for appellant's incidental use of the word "damn," upon which no emphasis was placed at trial, any shock effect of appellant's speech must be attributed to the content of the ideas expressed. It is firmly settled that under our Constitution the public expression of ideas may not be prohibited merely because the ideas are themselves offensive to some of their hearers. . . . And even if such a conviction might be upheld on the ground of "shock," there is again no indication that the state courts regarded the statute as limited to that purpose.

Finally, such a conviction could not be supported on the theory that by making the above-quoted remarks about the flag appellant failed to show the respect for our national symbol which may properly be demanded of every citizen. In West Virginia State Board of Educ. v. Barnette, . . . this Court held that to require unwilling schoolchildren to salute the flag would violate rights of free expression assured by the Fourteenth Amendment. In his opinion for the Court, Mr. Justice Jackson wrote words which are especially apposite here:

> "The case is made difficult not because the principles of its decision are obscure but because the flag involved is our own. Nevertheless, we apply the limitations of the Constitution with no fear that freedom to be intellectually and spiritually diverse or even contrary will disintegrate the social organization. * * * [F]reedom to differ is not limited to things that do not matter much. That would be a mere shadow of freedom. The test of its substance is the right to differ as to things that touch the heart of the existing order.
>
> "If there is any fixed star in our constitutional constellation, it is that no official high or petty, can prescribe what shall be orthodox in politics, nationalism, religion, or other matters of opinion or force citizens to confess by word or act their faith therein. If there are any circumstances which permit an exception, they do not now occur to us." . . .

We have no doubt that the constitutionally guaranteed "freedom to be intellectually * * * diverse and even contrary," and the "right to differ as to things that touch the heart of the existing order," encompass the freedom to express publicly one's opinions about our flag, including those opinions which are defiant or contemptuous.

Since appellant could not constitutionally be punished . . . for his speech, and since we have found that he may have been so punished, his conviction cannot be permitted to stand. In so holding, we reiterate that we have no occasion to pass upon the validity of this conviction insofar as it was sustained by the state courts on the basis that Street could be punished for his burning of the flag, even though the burning was an act of protest. Nor do we perceive any basis for our BROTHER WHITE's fears that our decision today may be taken to require reversal whenever a defendant is convicted for burning a flag in protest, following a trial at which his words have been introduced to prove some element of that offense. Assuming that such a conviction would otherwise pass constitutional muster, a matter about which we express no view, nothing in this opinion would render the conviction impermissible merely because an element of the crime was proved by the defendant's words rather than in some other way. . . .

We add that disrespect for our flag is to be deplored no less in these vexed times than in calmer periods of our history. . . . Nevertheless, we are unable to sustain a conviction that may have rested on a form of expression, however distasteful, which the Constitution tolerates and protects.

Reversed and remanded.

MR. CHIEF JUSTICE WARREN, dissenting.

* * * In my opinion a reading of the short trial record leaves no doubt that appellant was convicted solely for burning the American flag.

* * *

I believe that the States and the Federal Government do have the power to protect the flag from acts of desecration and disgrace. But because the Court has not met the issue, it would serve no purpose to delineate my reasons for this view. However, it is difficult for me to imagine that, had the Court faced this issue, it would have concluded otherwise. Since I am satisfied that the constitutionality of appellant's conduct should be resolved in this case and am convinced that this conduct can be criminally punished, I dissent.

[Appendix omitted.]

MR. JUSTICE BLACK, dissenting.

I agree with the excellent opinion written by Chief Judge Fuld for a unanimous Court of Appeals, upholding the New York statute which this Court now holds unconstitutional as applied. The entire state court construed the statute as applied to this appellant as making it an offense publicly to burn an American flag in order to protest something that had occurred. In other words the offense which that court sustained was the burning of the flag and not the making of any statements about it. The Court seems to console itself for holding this New York flag-burning law unconstitutional as applied by saying that, as it reads the record, the conviction could have been based on the words spoken by the appellant as he was burning the flag. Those words indicated a desire on appellant's part to degrade and defame the flag. If I could agree with the Court's interpretation of the record as to the possibility of the conviction's resting on these spoken words, I would firmly and automatically agree that the law is unconstitutional. I would not feel constrained, as the Court seems to be, to search my imagination to see if I could think of interests the State may have in suppressing this freedom of speech.

I would not balance away the First Amendment right that speech not be abridged in any fashion whatsoever. But I accept the unanimous opinion of the New York Court of Appeals that the conviction does not and could not have rested merely on the spoken words but that it rested entirely on the fact that the defendants had publicly burned the American flag—against the law of the State of New York.

It passes my belief that anything in the Federal Constitution bars a State from making the deliberate burning of the American flag an offense. It is immaterial to me that words are spoken in connection with the *burning*. It is the *burning* of the flag that the State has set its face against. . . . The talking that was done took place "as an integral part of conduct in violation of a valid criminal statute" against burning the American flag in public. I would therefore affirm this conviction.

* * *

[The dissenting opinions of Justices White and Fortas are omitted.]

NOTES

1. In State v. Kasnett, 30 Ohio App.2d 77, 283 N.E.2d 636 (1972), the Ohio Court of Appeals upheld the flag defilement conviction of a youth who had sewed and worn a flag on the portion of his jeans which covered his anus. The court distinguished the use of the flag in this way from both the sewing of a flag patch on the shoulder of a uniform, and the use of the flag as a complete garment (e. g.; a shirt or a cape).

2. A most unique usage was made of the American flag in the case of People v. Radich, 26 N.Y.2d 114, 308 N.Y.S.2d 846, 257 N.E.2d 30 (1970). The defendant, a proprietor of an art gallery, publicly displayed and exposed for sale certain "constructions", comparable to sculptures, for which the flag was used in the form of the human penis, erect and protruding from the upright member of a cross. He was prosecuted under a New York statute prohibiting the mutilation, defilement, etc. of the American flag. His defense was that this was "protest art". The New York Court of Appeals upheld his conviction (5 to 2), which was affirmed by an evenly divided (4–4) decision of the Supreme Court of the United States, 401 U.S. 531 (1971).

SECTION 4. SURVEILLANCE OF PROTESTERS

ANDERSON v. SILLS

Supreme Court of New Jersey, 1970.
56 N.J. 210, 265 A.2d 678.

WEINTRAUB, C. J. This is a declaratory judgment suit brought as a class action against the Attorney General and local law enforcement officials, also as a class. The complaint alleges violation of plaintiffs' First Amendment rights of speech and association. The complaint revolves about a memorandum, entitled "Civil Disorders—The Role of Local, County and State Government" (herein Memorandum), prepared by the Attorney General of the State and sent to local law enforcement officials. * * *

I.

The Memorandum suggests guidelines based upon the intensity of the disorders and the ability of the municipality to cope with them. It describes the primary duty of each municipality, the basis for a call upon neighboring municipal and county resources, the basis for a call for limited State Police assistance, and finally the basis for State intervention. It recommends advance planning as to each of the stages just mentioned and in comprehensive fashion discusses the problems to be anticipated and the facilities and resources available.

Virtually at the end of the Memorandum appears the following statement which plaintiffs stress:

Potential Problems

Our State Police have been working closely with local police in various communities throughout the State in a continuing effort to keep abreast of potential civil disorder problems. In that respect, therefore, we are already familiar generally with basic problems in these communities. However, these problems change and we should never become over confident to the end that we lose sight of the cause, as well as the effect of civil disturbances. The State Police Central Security Unit has distributed Security Summary Reports Form 421 and Security Incident Reports Form 420 to each police department. It is necessary that these reports be used routinely to inform the State Police of the situation in your community. We urge you to see that this vital intelligence is communicated to this central bureau for evaluation and dissemination.

Plaintiffs say the Memorandum will result in police invasion of their First Amendment rights and build that complaint upon the content of forms 420 and 421 and the instructions for their preparation contained in the Memorandum.

Form 420 calls for a report of an "incident." As the instructions related to the form explain, the "incident" may be "anticipated" or "in progress" or "completed." The form calls for a statement of the "type" of incident and the instructions give as "*Examples:* Civil disturbance, riot, rally, protest, demonstration, march, confrontation, etc." The form calls for the names of the organizations of groups involved in the "incident," and the instructions suggest as "*Examples of types:* Left wing, Right wing, Civil Rights, Militant, Nationalistic, Pacifist, Religious, Black Power, Ku Klux Klan, Extremist, etc." and as "*Examples of How Involved:* Sponsor, co-sponsor, supporter, assembled group, etc."

Form 421 relates to an individual, as distinguished from an incident. Among the instructions appear: "*Spouses Full Name*—Type full name of spouse. If wife, include maiden name or names by any other marriages," and "*Associates*—Enter names and addresses of associates, include aliases and nicknames. List additional associates in Narrative." The "Narrative" portion of the forms reads: "citizenship/naturalization data—parental background/occupation—armed forces service/draft status—membership, affiliation and/or status with organizations or groups—education background—habits or traits—places frequented—parole/probation data on immediate family—financial/credit status—include other records of past activities, findings and/or observations."

On the basis of the several items we have just collated plaintiffs envision that a mere rally, protest, demonstration or march of a pacifist group will precipitate a police dossier of everyone who attends, including therein his butcher's and banker's opinion of his credit. Adverting then to the portion of the Memorandum quoted above which says it is "necessary that these reports be used routinely to inform the State Police of the situation in your community" and urges that the intelligence be communicated "to this central bureau for evaluation and dissemination," plaintiffs enlarge upon their hypothetical horribles and see each such citizen harried amid his family, friends, and business associates. There is not an iota of evidence that anything of the kind has occurred or will, or that any person has been deterred by that prospect.

The individual plaintiffs themselves do not claim to have been deterred. In their affidavits on the motion for judgment, one plaintiff says she is chairman of the Students for a Democratic Society at St. Peter's College, and as an example of her activity she tells of "a sit-in at the office of the President." She adds that during a student strike which followed, "pickets were photographed by two men in plain clothes in an unmarked car" but there is no evidence as to their identity. The husband of that affiant says he has participated in a number of marches, rallies, and protests in opposition to the Viet Nam war, in support of burners of draft cards, and in protest of some alleged "racist policies" of a large religious organization. He adds that he hopes to be a lawyer and fears the Memorandum "may hinder my chances at being accepted at the law school of my choice"; that although "I have thus far not been deterred from exercising my First Amendment rights by the existence of the aforesaid memorandum, its existence is a factor which I must weigh in deciding whether or not to speak or act on a particular occasion;" and that "as an organizer of rallies, marches, protests and demonstrations, I feel that I must warn potential participants that, pursuant to the Attorney General's Memorandum they are subject to being investigated and classified by the police despite the lawfulness of our activity." Another affiant says she is a member of an urban renewal association and has picketed in support of its aims and as well against some alleged "racist policies" of the religious organization already referred to but she says that she feels "the existence of the memorandum may deter me from exercising my First Amendment rights in the future." She says she is "particularly concerned lest a police investigation such as that directed by the memorandum lead my landlord to believe that I had done something illegal." Another affiant describes his activities, including picketing of police headquarters, a stand-in at a bank, a sit-in at a mayor's office, and the distribution of anti-war leaflets and peace marches. He says "I cannot say that I will be deterred in the future from exercising my First Amendment rights" but he believes that "police surveillance, investigation, and cataloguing, and * * * disseminating the garnered information" may jeopardize his right to associate with others "should my activities become subject to the Attorney General's memorandum." The final affiant, the president of the Jersey City Branch of the NAACP, says that "once our organization and its members are investigated and categorized as per the memorandum, other persons in the community who are potential supporters * * * will disassociate themselves from any NAACP activity and a valuable audience will be lost."

The foregoing is a résumé of the record upon which the trial court held that the portion of the Memorandum we quoted above, entitled "Potential Problems," and forms 420 and 421 violate the First Amendment, and granted sweeping injunctive relief we will discuss later in this opinion. There was no evidence that the Memorandum was intended or has been read by local police officials to call for any action which invades a constitutionally protected area. There was no evidence that the Attorney General intended to intimidate anyone. Nor does it appear that he even sought to publicize the use of these forms. Indeed, according to the affidavit of Lieutenant Goch of the State Police submitted on the motion for reconsideration, there is no form 420 or 421 as to any of the plaintiffs, and there is no index file on any of them except one, and as to him only because of an arrest record going back to 1963.

II.

Defendants contend that since plaintiffs have not been harmed they lack "standing" to sue. We do not require that injury shall be experienced as a condition for suit, . . . and there is good reason to permit the strong to speak for the weak or the timid in First Amendment matters. Nonetheless the prospect of wrongful conduct must be real and not fanciful, . . . for the chance of error is substantial if an issue is accepted in a setting that is merely hypothetical. . . . Especially is this so when the decision depends upon striking a balance between competing constitutional values.

In this connection it is important to note what is and is not before us. We are not dealing with a statute imposing criminal liability for its violation, . . .

Here, the Memorandum imposes no liability or obligation or restriction whatever upon the citizen. Nor does it order the policeman to take action against a citizen upon the pain of discipline if the policeman does not comply. It is no more than a communication to law enforcement agencies about their respective powers and duties. It is wholly informative and advisory. It does not command; it merely encourages cooperation among all agencies concerned with the problem of civil disorders.

This is not to say that only statutes, regulations, or binding directives may spawn a First Amendment problem. But it would be unreasonable to require that intragovernmental communications be drafted with a precision the Constitution demands of a legislative enactment. The writer of the Memorandum could well assume the reader would be aware of the limitations of his office and would understand that the writer was not advocating anything arbitrary, oppressive, or foolish. The police are much too occupied for idle investigations. We think it preposterous to suppose that the Memorandum was intended or was understood to recommend round-the-clock surveillance of every person who attends an anti-war meeting.

When the Memorandum and forms 420 and 421 are read without strain, the common sense of the situation readily emerges. There have been serious disorders involving heavy losses of life and property. The police function is pervasive. It is not limited to the detection of past criminal events. Of at least equal importance is the responsibility to prevent crime. . . . In the current scene, the preventive role requires an awareness of group tensions and preparations to head off disasters as well as to deal with them if they appear. To that end the police must know what forces exist, what groups or organizations could be enmeshed in public disorders. This is not to ask the police to decide which are "good" and which are "bad." In terms of civil disorders, their respective virtues are irrelevant, for a group is of equal concern to the police whether it is potentially the victim or the aggressor. The police interest is in the explosive possibilities and not in the merits of the colliding philosophies. And it must be evident that a riot or the threat of one may best be ended with the aid of private citizens who because of their connections with the discordant groups can persuade them from a course of violence. Hence a police force would fail in its obligation if it did not know who could be called upon to help put out the burning fuse or the fire.

In the summer of 1967 there were serious riots. Both the President of the United States and the Governor of this State appointed commissions to study the problem and to make recommendations. The Report of the National Advisory Commission on Civil Disorders (March 1, 1968) in its "Supplement on Control of Disorders" encouraged the preparations which the Memorandum here involved seeks to achieve. It reads (p. 269):

> *Intelligence*—The absence of accurate information both before and during a disorder has created special control problems for police. Police departments must develop means to obtain adequate intelligence for planning purposes, as well as on-the-scene information for use in police operations during a disorder.
>
> An intelligence unit staffed with full-time personnel should be established to gather, evaluate, analyze, and disseminate information on potential as well as actual civil disorders. It should provide police administrators and commanders with reliable information essential for assessment and decisionmaking. It should use undercover police personnel and informants but it should also draw on community leaders, agencies, and organizations in the ghetto.

In his affidavit accepted by the trial court, Lieutenant Goch of the State Police described the activities of its Central Security Unit. He stated in part:

> At the present time information concerning crime and criminals is gathered by the intelligence unit in the Organized Crime Task Force in the New Jersey State Police and information concerning extremist organizations and incidents concerning disturbances arising out of racial, social and economic tensions is gathered by the central security unit, the human relations unit and the civil disturbance unit.
>
> Specifically, some of the past and present reasons for the accumulation of information by the State Police are: (a) to aid in the evaluation and determination of the probability of unlawful disorders, large-scale violence, and potential riots; (b) to aid in the determination of supplemental police manpower needs; (c) to facilitate decisions and planning for coping with disorders anticipated or in

progress; (d) to aid in the assessment of tension within communities and possible causes of unrest; (e) to aid in familiarization with the past activities of professional agitators, their tactics and control over their followings; and (f) to furnish information for meetings of the Governor with officials of various State Departments including the Department of Community Affairs, Department of Education, Department of Institutions and Agencies, Division on Civil Rights, Office of Attorney General, and Division of State Police for their study of the causes of civil disorder, so that this information can be used by the Governor and appropriate governmental agencies to alleviate present tensions and prevent future and potential disorders.

He pointed out that forms 420 and 421 were prepared prior to the Memorandum and were not devised for it. He emphasized that the forms deal with public incidents only, and are simply suggestive of the kinds of information the State Police believe should be on hand; that like information had always been received through liaison with police agencies; that in fact most of the information called for in these forms can be obtained from newspaper clippings; that such information as appears with respect to these plaintiffs was received from news clippings or other agencies, rather than by way of these forms; that information from all sources is integrated, and is available to public agencies only on a "need-to-know basis," and is never available to private interests.

Other affidavits accepted on the motion for reconsideration spell out the measures taken to keep up with a fast-moving scene and to anticipate explosive situations. They repel the notion that the program was intended or has been used to harass anyone. * * *

The State Police have, for example, supplied information on occasion that a particular group would be holding a public meeting at a particular time and place and that a volatile situation could develop. Thereafter members of this agency and others contact these groups or mentioned leaders to avert the development of disorders. * * *

It of course is not our purpose here to resolve a factual issue. We refer to the affidavits simply because on their face they assert a purpose to discharge a plain duty of government and thus confirm the purpose avowed in the Memorandum.

It is a serious matter for the judiciary to interfere with the preventive measures devised by the executive branch of government in response to its constitutional obligation to protect all the citizens. Surely, such interference may not rest upon a hypothetical exposition of what could happen under a set of forms in the hands of an officer indifferent to the restraints upon his office. Rather the premise must be accepted, absent proof the other way, that the

Memorandum assumed a lawful exercise of the judgment and discretion vested in the local police. The Memorandum did not originate the duty of the local police unit to decide what situations harbor the potential of disaster and what data should be gathered for responsible performance in office. The forms do not enlarge upon that power and responsibility. Rather, being designed for many situations, the forms are necessarily comprehensive, leaving it to the local authorities to decide in their judgment what incidents are worthy of note and what information should be obtained as to the individuals concerned or involved.

Nor should an injunction issue on the assumption that there will be unwarranted police action because a judge cannot on the basis of his own experience understand the relevancy of the spouse's full name, or the employer's name, or of "armed forces service/draft status," or "data on immediate family" or "financial/credit status," to mention some items plaintiffs stress in their academic attack. Law enforcement is a speciality, and its needs may not be within the expertise of a court. That is why a hearing is essential for an informed decision in a case of this kind. It may well be that a hearing will establish that some of these items are wholly unrelated to the police obligation with respect to anyone involved in any type of incident, but we should not merely assume that this is so. We cannot know how little we know until we listen.

III.

For these reasons the issue as projected by plaintiffs on the motion for summary judgment was a mere abstraction. The trial court should have denied the motion on that account. For the same reasons we will not deal with the merits. Nonetheless some observations may be helpful upon the remand.

Here we are dealing with the critical power of government to gather intelligence to enable it to satisfy the very reason for its being—to protect the individual in his person and things. The question in the case is not merely whether there are some individuals who might be "chilled" in their speech or associations by reason of the police activity here involved. Rather the critical question is whether that activity is legal, and although the amount of "chill" might in a given case be relevant to the issue of legality, the fact of "chill" is not itself pivotal. Indeed, the very existence of this Court may "chill" some who would speak or act more freely if there were no accounting before us for trespasses against others. But government there must be, for without it no value could be worth very much. The First Amendment itself would be meaningless if there were no constituted authority to protect the individual from suppression by others who disapprove of him or the company he keeps. Hence the First Amendment rights must be weighed against the competing interests of the citizen. If there is no intent to control the content of speech, an overriding public need may be met even though the measure adopted to that end operates incidentally to limit the unfettered exercise of the First Amendment right. . . . If a properly drawn measure is within the power of government, it is no objection that the exercise of speech or association is thereby "chilled." . . .

The power to investigate is basic. So the cases recognize a vast power to investigate in the legislative branch so long as the inquiry is relevant to the legislative function. . . . An administrative agency may on its own initiative investigate to see that there is compliance with law within the ambit of its responsibility. . . . So, too, a grand jury may inquire as to whether a crime occurred and who was the culprit, and its power to compel testimony does not depend upon the existence of "probable cause" either as to the fact of a crime or the culpability of the suspect.

The investigatory obligation of the police is surely no less extensive than the grand jury's. Indeed, the preventive role of the police necessarily implies a duty to gather data along a still wider range. The "stop-and-frisk" rule rests upon that preventive duty, . . . There is the power of surveillance. It includes even the deceptive use of undercover agents to infiltrate situations in which criminal events have occurred or may be anticipated. . . .

No doubt there may be situations in which judicial intervention would be warranted. One court intervened when it found the police surveillance was conducted in a manner which was unnecessarily obtrusive and unnecessarily interfered with legitimate business activity, . . . and another enjoined surveillance of a private meeting of a labor union when the presence of the police was manifest and operated to prevent free discussion, . . . But the power of surveillance is so imperative that even though it was found in United States v. McLeod, 385 F.2d 734 (5 Cir. 1967), that the police illegally intended by sham arrests and baseless prosecutions to frustrate the right to vote of a racial minority and should be enjoined in those respects, nonetheless the court would not restrain police surveillance of public meetings, . . . * * *

The basic approach must be that the executive branch may gather whatever information it reasonably believes to be necessary to enable it to perform the police roles, detectional and preventive. A court should not interfere in the absence of proof of bad faith or arbitrariness. * * *

We are not unmindful of the unfortunate polarization within our society, and we can understand how in that light some may fear that officials will unlawfully take sides. Yet, to deny to government, on that account, the authority it must have to fulfill its mission would heighten that fear or even make it a reality. Lawlessness has a tyranny of its own, and it would be folly to deprive government of its power to deal with that tyranny merely because of a figment of a fear that government itself may run amuck. It should be remembered, too, that our form of government has a built-in safeguard against tyranny in office. The total power of government is divided among the three branches to prevent despotic behavior within any of them. The delicate balance would be upset if the judiciary interfered with another branch upon nothing more than a fear that its officers will be unfaithful to their oaths or unequal to their responsibility. A public official who intentionally turns his office to an arbitrary end is already accountable under the criminal law for such misconduct. It will be time enough for a court to act injunctively when the threat of misbehavior is real. * * *

NOTES

1. In Laird v. Tatum, 408 U.S. 1, 92 S.Ct. 2318 (1972), the Supreme Court held that respondents were not entitled to declarative and injunctive relief on a claim that the U.S. Army was invading their rights by "surveillance of lawful civilian political activity". The Court found that since respondents alleged that the "mere existence" of the Army's date gathering system produced a constitutionally impermissible chilling effect upon their First Amendment rights, without demonstrating "the precise connection between the existence of the challenged system and their own alleged chills", they therefore failed to present a justiciable controversy. The Court stated that "allegations of a subjective 'chill' are not an adequate substitute for a claim of specific present objective harm or a threat of specific future harm."

2. With regard to the constitutional right of "association" referred to in Anderson v. Sills, consider the following excerpts from the dissenting opinions of Justices White and Harlan in U. S. v. Robel, 389 U.S. 258, 88 S.Ct. 419 (1967): "The right of association is not mentioned in the Constitution. It is a judicial construct appended to the First Amendment rights to speak freely, to assemble, and to petition for redress of grievances. . . . If men may speak as individuals, they may speak in groups as well. If they may assemble and petition, they must have the right to associate to some extent. In this sense the right of association simply extends constitutional protection to First Amendment rights when exercised with others rather than by an individual alone. . . ."

B. FREEDOM OF THE PRESS—THE OBSCENITY ISSUE

ROTH v. UNITED STATES ; ALBERTS v. CALIFORNIA

Supreme Court of the United States, 1957.
354 U.S. 476, 77 S.Ct. 1304.

MR. JUSTICE BRENNAN delivered the opinion of the Court.

The constitutionality of a criminal obscenity statute is the question in each of these cases. In Roth, the primary constitutional question is whether the federal obscenity statute [1] violates the provision of the First Amendment that "Congress shall make no law * * * abridging the freedom of speech, or of the press * * *." In Alberts, the primary constitutional question is whether the obscenity provisions of the California Penal Code [2] invade the freedoms of speech and press as they may be incorporated in the liberty protected from state action by the Due Process Clause of the Fourteenth Amendment.

Other constitutional questions are: whether these statutes violate due process,[3] because too vague to support conviction for crime;

1. The federal obscenity statute provided, in pertinent part:

"Every obscene, lewd, lascivious, or filthy book, pamphlet, picture, paper, letter, writing, print or other publication of an indecent character; and—

* * * * * *

"Every written or printed card, letter, circular, book, pamphlet, advertisement, or notice of any kind giving information, directly or indirectly, where, or how, or from whom, or by what means any of such mentioned matters, articles, or things may be obtained or made, * * * whether sealed or unsealed * * *

* * * * * *

"Is declared to be nonmailable matter and shall not be conveyed in the mails or delivered from any post office or by any letter carrier.

"Whoever knowingly deposits for mailing or delivery, anything declared by this section to be nonmailable, or knowingly takes the same from the mails for the purpose of circulating or disposing thereof, or of aiding in the circulation or disposition thereof, shall be fined not more than $5,000 or imprisoned not more than five years or both." 18 U.S.C. § 1461, 18 U.S.C.A. § 1461.

The 1955 amendment of this statute, 69 Stat. 183, is not applicable to this case.

2. The California Penal Code provides, in pertinent part:

"Every person who wilfully and lewdly, either:

* * * * * *

"3. Writes, composes, stereotypes, prints, publishes, sells, distributes, keeps for sale, or exhibits any obscene or indecent writing, paper, or book; or designs, copies, draws engraves, paints, or otherwise prepares any obscene or indecent picture or print; or molds, cuts, casts, or otherwise makes any obscene or indecent figure; or,

"4. Writes, composes, or publishes any notice or advertisement of any such writing, paper, book, picture, print or figure; * * *

* * * * * *

"6. * * * is guilty of a misdemeanor * * *." West's Cal.Penal Code Ann., 1955, § 311.

3. In Roth, reliance is placed on the Due Process Clause of the Fifth Amendment, and in Alberts, reliance is placed upon the Due Process Clause of the Fourteenth Amendment.

whether power to punish speech and press offensive to decency and morality is in the States alone, so that the federal obscenity statute violates the Ninth and Tenth Amendments (raised in Roth); and whether Congress, by enacting the federal obscenity statute, under the power delegated by Art. I, § 8, cl. 7, to establish post offices and post roads, pre-empted the regulation of the subject matter (raised in Alberts).

Roth conducted a business in New York in the publication and sale of books, photographs and magazines. He used circulars and advertising matter to solicit sales. He was convicted by a jury in the District Court for the Southern District of New York upon 4 counts of a 26-count indictment charging him with mailing obscene circulars and advertising, and an obscene book, in violation of the federal obscenity statute. His conviction was affirmed by the Court of Appeals for the Second Circuit. We granted certiorari.

Alberts conducted a mail-order business from Los Angeles. He was convicted by the Judge of the Municipal Court of the Beverly Hills Judicial District (having waived a jury trial) under a misdemeanor complaint which charged him with lewdly keeping for sale obscene and indecent books, and with writing, composing and publishing an obscene advertisement of them, in violation of the California Penal Code. The conviction was affirmed by the Appellate Department of the Superior Court of the State of California in and for the County of Los Angeles. We noted probable jurisdiction.

The dispositive question is whether obscenity is utterance within the area of protected speech and press. Although this is the first time the question has been squarely presented to this Court, either under the First Amendment or under the Fourteenth Amendment, expressions found in numerous opinions indicate that this Court has always assumed that obscenity is not protected by the freedoms of speech and press. . . .

The guaranties of freedom of expression in effect in 10 of the 14 States which by 1792 had ratified the Constitution, gave no absolute protection for every utterance. Thirteen of the 14 States provided for the prosecution of libel, and all of those States made either blasphemy or profanity, or both, statutory crimes. As early as 1712, Massachusetts made it criminal to publish "any filthy, obscene, or profane song, pamphlet, libel or mock sermon" in imitation or mimicking of religious services. . . . Thus, profanity and obscenity were related offenses.

In light of this history, it is apparent that the unconditional phrasing of the First Amendment was not intended to protect every utterance. This phrasing did not prevent this Court from concluding that libelous utterances are not within the area of constitutionally protected speech. . . . At the time of the adoption of the First Amendment, obscenity law was not as fully developed as libel law, but there is sufficiently contemporaneous evidence to show that obscenity, too, was outside the protection intended for speech and press.

The protection given speech and press was fashioned to assure unfettered interchange of ideas for the bringing about of political and social changes desired by the people. . . .

All ideas having even the slightest redeeming social importance —unorthodox ideas, controversial ideas, even ideas hateful to the prevailing climate of opinion—have the full protection of the guaranties, unless excludable because they encroach upon the limited area of more important interests. But implicit in the history of the First Amendment is the rejection of obscenity as utterly without redeeming social importance. This rejection for that reason is mirrored in the universal judgment that obscenity should be restrained, reflected in the international agreement of over 50 nations, in the obscenity laws of all of the 48 States, and in the 20 obscenity laws enacted by the Congress from 1842 to 1956. We hold that obscenity is not within the area of constitutionally protected speech or press.

It is strenuously urged that these obscenity statutes offend the constitutional guaranties because they punish incitation to impure sexual *thoughts*, not shown to be related to any overt antisocial conduct which is or may be incited in the persons stimulated to such *thoughts*. In Roth, the trial judge instructed the jury: "The words 'obscene, lewd and lascivious' as used in the law, signify that form of immorality which has relation to sexual impurity and has a tendency to excite lustful *thoughts*." (Emphasis added.) In Alberts, the trial judge applied the test . . . whether the material has "a substantial tendency to deprave or corrupt its readers by inciting lascivious *thoughts* or arousing lustful desires." (Emphasis added.) It is insisted that the constitutional guaranties are violated because convictions may be had without proof either that obscene material will perceptibly create a clear and present danger of antisocial conduct, or will probably induce its recipients to such conduct. But, in light of our holding that obscenity is not protected speech, the complete answer to this argument is in the holding of this Court in Beauharnais v. People of State of Illinois . . . :

> "Libelous utterances not being within the area of constitutionally protected speech, it is unnecessary, either for us or for the State courts, to consider the issues behind the phrase 'clear and present danger.' Certainly no one would contend that obscene speech, for example, may be punished only upon a showing of such circumstances. Libel, as we have seen, is in the same class."

. . . sex and obscenity are not synonymous. Obscene material is material which deals with sex in a manner appealing to prurient interest.[4] The portrayal of sex, *e. g.*, in art, literature, and

4. . . . material having a tendency to excite lustful thoughts. Webster's New International Dictionary (Unabridged, 2d ed., 1949) defines *prurient*, in pertinent part, as follows:

"* * * Itching; longing; uneasy with desire or longing; of persons, having itching, morbid, or lascivious longings; of desire, curiosity, or propensity, lewd * * *."

Pruriency is defined, in pertinent part, as follows:

"* * * Quality of being prurient; lascivious desire or thought. * * *"

scientific works, is not itself sufficient reason to deny material the constitutional protection of freedom of speech and press. Sex, a great and mysterious motive force in human life, has indisputably been a subject of absorbing interest to mankind through the ages; it is one of the vital problems of human interest and public concern. As to all such problems, this Court said in Thornhill v. State of Alabama . . . :

> "The freedom of speech and of the press guaranteed by the Constitution embraces at the least the liberty to discuss publicly and truthfully *all matters of public concern* without previous restraint or fear of subsequent punishment. The exigencies of the colonial period and the efforts to secure freedom from oppressive administration developed a broadened conception of these liberties as adequate to supply the public need for *information and education with respect to the significant issues of the times.* * * * Freedom of discussion, if it would fulfill its historic function in this nation, must embrace *all issues about which information is needed or appropriate to enable the members of society to cope with the exigencies of their period.*" (Emphasis added.)

The fundamental freedoms of speech and press have contributed greatly to the development and well-being of our free society and are indispensable to its continued growth. Ceaseless vigilance is the watchword to prevent their erosion by Congress or by the States. The door barring federal and state intrusion into this area cannot be left ajar; it must be kept tightly closed and opened only the slightest crack necessary to prevent encroachment upon more important interests. It is therefore vital that the standards for judging obscenity safeguard the protection of freedom of speech and press for material which does not treat sex in a manner appealing to prurient interest.

The early leading standard of obscenity allowed material to be judged merely by the effect of an isolated excerpt upon particularly susceptible persons. Regina v. Hicklin, [1868] L.R. 3 Q.B. 360. Some American courts adopted this standard but later decisions have rejected it and substituted this test: whether to the average person, applying contemporary community standards, the dominant theme

See also Mutual Film Corp. v. Industrial Comm., 236 U.S. 230, 242, 35 S.Ct. 387, 390, 59 L.Ed. 552, where this Court said as to motion pictures: "* * * They take their attraction from the general interest, eager and wholesome it may be, in their subjects, but a *prurient interest may be excited and appealed to* * * *." (Emphasis added.)

We perceive no significant difference between the meaning of obscenity developed in the case law and the definition of the A.L.I., Model Penal Code, § 207.10(2) (Tent. Draft No. 6, 1957), viz.:

"* * * A thing is obscene if, considered as a whole, its predominant appeal is to prurient interest, i. e., a shameful or morbid interest in nudity, sex, or excretion, and if it goes substantially beyond customary limits of candor in description or representation of such matters. * * *" . . .

of the material taken as a whole appeals to prurient interest. The Hicklin test, judging obscenity by the effect of isolated passages upon the most susceptible persons, might well encompass material legitimately treating with sex, and so it must be rejected as unconstitutionally restrictive of the freedoms of speech and press. On the other hand, the substituted standard provides safeguards adequate to withstand the charge of constitutional infirmity.

Both trial courts below sufficiently followed the proper standard. Both courts used the proper definition of obscenity. In addition, in the Alberts case, in ruling on a motion to dismiss, the trial judge indicated that, as the trier of facts, he was judging each item as a whole as it would affect the normal person, and in Roth, the trial judge instructed the jury as follows:

> "* * * The test is not whether it would arouse sexual desires or sexual impure thoughts in those comprising a particular segment of the community, the young, the immature or the highly prudish or would leave another segment, the scientific or highly educated or the so-called worldly-wise and sophisticated indifferent and unmoved. * * *
>
> "The test in each case is the effect of the book, picture or publication considered as a whole, not upon any particular class, but upon all those whom it is likely to reach. In other words, you determine its impact upon the average person in the community. The books, pictures and circulars must be judged as a whole, in their entire context, and you are not to consider detached or separate portions in reaching a conclusion. You judge the circulars, pictures and publications which have been put in evidence by present-day standards of the community. You may ask yourselves does it offend the common conscience of the community by present-day standards.
>
> * * * * * * * * * *
>
> "In this case, ladies and gentlemen of the jury, you and you alone are the exclusive judges of what the common conscience of the community is, and in determining that conscience you are to consider the community as a whole, young and old, educated and uneducated, the religious and the irreligious—men, women and children."

It is argued that the statutes do not provide reasonably ascertainable standards of guilt and therefore violate the constitutional requirements of due process. . . . The federal obscenity statute makes punishable the mailing of material that is "obscene, lewd, lascivious, or filthy * * * or other publication of an indecent character." The California statute makes punishable, *inter alia*, the keeping for sale or advertising material that is "obscene or indecent." The thrust of the argument is that these words are not sufficiently precise because they do not mean the same thing to all people, all the time, everywhere.

Many decisions have recognized that these terms of obscenity statutes are not precise. This Court, however, has consistently held that lack of precision is not itself offensive to the requirements of due process. "* * * [T]he Constitution does not require impossible standards"; all that is required is that the language "conveys sufficiently definite warning as to the proscribed conduct when measured by common understanding and practices * * *." . . . These words, applied according to the proper standard for judging obscenity, already discussed, give adequate warning of the conduct proscribed and mark "* * * boundaries sufficiently distinct for judges and juries fairly to administer the law * * *. That there may be marginal cases in which it is difficult to determine the side of the line on which a particular fact situation falls is no sufficient reason to hold the language too ambiguous to define a criminal offense * * *." . . . [5]

In summary, then, we hold that these statutes, applied according to the proper standard for judging obscenity, do not offend constitutional safeguards against convictions based upon protected material, or fail to give men in acting adequate notice of what is prohibited.

Roth's argument that the federal obscenity statute unconstitutionally encroaches upon the powers reserved by the Ninth and Tenth Amendments to the States and to the people to punish speech and press where offensive to decency and morality is hinged upon his contention that obscenity is expression not excepted from the sweep of the provision of the First Amendment that "*Congress* shall make *no law* * * * abridging the freedom of speech, or of the press * * *." (Emphasis added.) That argument falls in light of our holding that obscenity is not expression protected by the First Amendment. We therefore hold that the federal obscenity statute punishing the use of the mails for obscene material is a proper exercise of the postal power delegated to Congress by Art. I, § 8, cl. 7. * * *

Alberts argues that because his was a mail-order business, the California statute is repugnant to Art. 1, § 8, cl. 7, under which the Congress allegedly pre-empted the regulatory field by enacting the federal obscenity statute punishing the mailing or advertising by mail of obscene material. The federal statute deals only with actual mailing; it does not eliminate the power of the state to punish "keeping for sale" or "advertising" obscene material. The state statute in no way imposes a burden or interferes with the federal postal functions. "* * * The decided cases which indicate the limits

5. It is argued that because juries may reach different conclusions as to the same material, the statutes must be held to be insufficiently precise to satisfy due process requirements. But, it is common experience that different juries may reach different results under any criminal statute. That is one of the consequences we accept under our jury system. . . .

of state regulatory power in relation to the federal mail service involve situations where state regulation involved a direct, physical interference with federal activities under the postal power or some direct, immediate burden on the performance of the postal functions * * *." . . .

The judgments are affirmed.

Affirmed.

MR. CHIEF JUSTICE WARREN, concurring in the result.

I agree with the result reached by the Court in these cases, but, because we are operating in a field of expression and because broad language used here may eventually be applied to the arts and sciences and freedom of communication generally, I would limit our decision to the facts before us and to the validity of the statutes in question as applied. * * *

That there is a social problem presented by obscenity is attested by the expression of the legislatures of the forty-eight States as well as the Congress. To recognize the existence of a problem, however, does not require that we sustain any and all measures adopted to meet that problem. The history of the application of laws designed to suppress the obscene demonstrates convincingly that the power of government can be invoked under them against great art or literature, scientific treatises, or works exciting social controversy. Mistakes of the past prove that there is a strong countervailing interest to be considered in the freedoms guaranteed by the First and Fourteenth Amendments.

The line dividing the salacious or pornographic from literature or science is not straight and unwavering. Present laws depend largely upon the effect that the materials may have upon those who receive them. It is manifest that the same object may have a different impact, varying according to the part of the community it reached. But there is more to these cases. It is not the book that is on trial; it is a person. The conduct of the defendant is the central issue, not the obscenity of a book or picture. The nature of the materials is, of course, relevant as an attribute of the defendant's conduct, but the materials are thus placed in context from which they draw color and character. A wholly different result might be reached in a different setting.

The personal element in these cases is seen most strongly in the requirement of *scienter*. Under the California law, the prohibited activity must be done "wilfully and lewdly." The federal statute limits the crime to acts done "knowingly." In his charge to the jury, the district judge stated that the matter must be "calculated" to corrupt or debauch. The defendants in both these cases were engaged in the business of purveying textual or graphic matter openly advertised to appeal to the erotic interest of their customers. They were plainly engaged in the commercial exploitation of the morbid and shameful craving for materials with prurient effect. I believe that the State and Federal Governments can constitutionally punish such conduct. That is all that these cases present to us, and that is all we need to decide.

I agree with the Court's decision in its rejection of the other contentions raised by these defendants.

MR. JUSTICE HARLAN, concurring in the result in [the Alberts case] and dissenting in [the Roth case].

I regret not to be able to join the Court's opinion. I cannot do so because I find lurking beneath its disarming generalizations a number of problems which not only leave me with serious misgivings as to the future effect of today's decisions, but which also, in my view, call for different results in these two cases.

I.

My basic difficulties with the Court's opinion are threefold. First, the opinion paints with such a broad brush that I fear it may result in a loosening of the tight reins which state and federal courts should hold upon the enforcement of obscenity statutes. Second, the Court fails to discriminate between the different factors which, in my opinion, are involved in the constitutional adjudication of state and federal obscenity cases. Third, relevant distinctions between the two obscenity statutes here involved, and the Court's own definition of "obscenity," are ignored.

In final analysis, the problem presented by these cases is how far, and on what terms, the state and federal governments have power to punish individuals for disseminating books considered to be undesirable because of their nature or supposed deleterious effect upon human conduct. Proceeding from the premise that "no issue is presented in either case, concerning the obscenity of the material involved," the Court finds the "dispositive question" to be "whether obscenity is utterance within the area of protected speech and press," and then holds that "obscenity" is not so protected because it is "utterly without redeeming social importance." This sweeping formula appears to me to beg the very question before us. The Court seems to assume that "obscenity" is a peculiar *genus* of "speech and press," which is as distinct, recognizable, and classifiable as poison ivy is among other plants. On this basis the *constitutional* question before us simply becomes, as the Court says, whether "obscenity," as an abstraction, is protected by the First and Fourteenth Amendments, and the question whether a *particular* book may be suppressed becomes a mere matter of classification, of "fact," to be entrusted to a factfinder and insulated from independent constitutional judgment. But surely the problem cannot be solved in such a generalized fashion. Every communication has an individuality and "value" of its own. The suppression of a particular writing or other tangible form of expression is, therefore, an *individual* matter, and in the nature of things every such suppression raises an individual constitutional problem, in which a reviewing court must determine for *itself* whether the attacked expression is suppressable within constitutional standards. Since those standards do not readily lend themselves to generalized definitions, the constitutional problem in the last analysis becomes one of particularized judgments which appellate courts must make for themselves.

I do not think that reviewing courts can escape this responsibility by saying that the trier of the facts, be it a jury or a judge, has labeled the questioned matter as "obscene," for, if "obscenity" is to be suppressed, the question whether a particular work is of that character involves not really an issue of fact but a question of constitutional *judgment* of the most sensitive and delicate kind. Many juries might find that Joyce's "Ulysses" or Bocaccio's "Decameron" was obscene, and yet the conviction of a defendant for selling either book would raise, for me, the gravest constitutional problems, for no such verdict could convince me, without more, that these books are "utterly without redeeming social importance." In short, I do not understand how the Court can resolve the constitutional problems now before it without making its own independent judgment upon the character of the material upon which these convictions were based. I am very much afraid that the broad manner in which the Court has decided these cases will tend to obscure the peculiar responsibilities resting on state and federal courts in this field and encourage them to rely on easy labeling and jury verdicts as a substitute for facing up to the tough individual problems of constitutional judgment involved in every obscenity case.

My second reason for dissatisfaction with the Court's opinion is that the broad strides with which the Court has proceeded has led it to brush aside with perfunctory ease the vital constitutional considerations which, in my opinion, differentiate these two cases. It does not seem to matter to the Court that in one case we balance the power of a State in this field against the restrictions of the Fourteenth Amendment, and in the other the power of the Federal Government against the limitations of the First Amendment. I deal with this subject more particularly later.

Thirdly, the Court has not been bothered by the fact that the two cases involve different statutes. In California the book must have a "tendency to deprave or corrupt its readers"; under the federal statute it must tend "to stir sexual impulses and lead to sexually impure thoughts." The two statutes do not seem to me to present the same problems. Yet the Court compounds confusion when it superimposes on these two statutory definitions a third, drawn from the American Law Institute's Model Penal Code, Tentative Draft No. 6: "A thing is obscene if, considered as a whole, its predominant appeal is to prurient interest." The bland assurance that this definition is the same as the ones with which we deal flies in the face of the authors' express rejection of the "deprave and corrupt" and "sexual thoughts" tests: . . .

. . . there is a significant distinction between the definitions used in the prosecutions before us, and the American Law Institute formula. If, therefore, the latter is the correct standard, as my Brother BRENNAN elsewhere intimates, then these convictions should surely be reversed. Instead, the Court merely assimilates the various tests into one indiscriminate potpourri.

I now pass to the consideration of the two cases before us.

II.

I concur in the judgment of the Court in No. 61, Alberts v. People of State of California. * * *

In judging the constitutionality of this conviction, we should remember that our function in reviewing state judgments under the Fourteenth Amendment is a narrow one. We do not decide whether the policy of the State is wise, or whether it is based on assumptions scientifically substantiated. We can inquire only whether the state action so subverts the fundamental liberties implicit in the Due Process Clause that it cannot be sustained as a rational exercise of power. . . .

What, then, is the purpose of this California statute? Clearly the state legislature has made the judgment that printed words *can* "deprave or corrupt" the reader—that words can incite to antisocial or immoral action. The assumption seems to be that the distribution of certain types of literature will induce criminal or immoral sexual conduct. It is well known, of course, that the validity of this assumption is a matter of dispute among critics, sociologists, psychiatrists, and penologists. There is a large school of thought, particularly in the scientific community, which denies any causal connection between the reading of pornography and immorality, crime, or delinquency. Others disagree. Clearly it is not our function to decide this question. That function belongs to the state legislature. Nothing in the Constitution requires California to accept as truth the most advanced and sophisticated psychiatric opinion. It seems to me clear that it is not irrational, in our present state of knowledge, to consider that pornography can induce a type of sexual conduct which a State may deem obnoxious to the moral fabric of society. In fact the very division of opinion on the subject counsels us to respect the choice made by the State.

Furthermore, even assuming that pornography cannot be deemed ever to cause, in an immediate sense, criminal sexual conduct, other interests within the proper cognizance of the States may be protected by the prohibition placed on such materials. The State can reasonably draw the inference that over a long period of time the indiscriminate dissemination of materials, the essential character of which is to degrade sex, will have an eroding effect on moral standards. And the State has a legitimate interest in protecting the privacy of the home against invasion of unsolicited obscenity.

Above all stands the realization that we deal here with an area where knowledge is small, data are insufficient, and experts are divided. Since the domain of sexual morality is pre-eminently a matter of state concern, this Court should be slow to interfere with state legislation calculated to protect that morality. It seems to me that nothing in the broad and flexible command of the Due Process Clause forbids California to prosecute one who sells books whose dominant tendency might be to "deprave or corrupt" a reader. I agree with the Court, of course, that the books must be judged as a whole and in relation to the normal adult reader.

What has been said, however, does not dispose of the case. It still remains for us to decide whether the state court's determination that this material should be suppressed is consistent with the Fourteenth Amendment; and that, of course, presents a federal question as to which we, and not the state court, have the ultimate responsibility. And so, in the final analysis, I concur in the judgment because, upon an independent perusal of the material involved, and in light of the considerations discussed above, I cannot say that its suppression would so interfere with the communication of "ideas" in any proper sense of that term that it would offend the Due Process Clause. I therefore agree with the Court that appellant's conviction must be affirmed.

III.

I dissent in . . . Roth v. United States.

We are faced here with the question whether the federal obscenity statute, as construed and applied in this case, violates the First Amendment to the Constitution. To me, this question is of quite a different order than one where we are dealing with state legislation under the Fourteenth Amendment. I do not think it follows that state and federal powers in this area are the same, and that just because the State may suppress a particular utterance, it is automatically permissible for the Federal Government to do the same.

. . .

The Constitution differentiates between those areas of human conduct subject to the regulation of the States and those subject to the powers of the Federal Government. The substantive powers of the two governments, in many instances, are distinct. And in every case where we are called upon to balance the interest in free expression against other interests, it seems to me important that we should keep in the forefront the question of whether those other interests are state or federal. Since under our constitutional scheme the two are not necessarily equivalent, the balancing process must needs often produce different results. Whether a particular limitation on speech or press is to be upheld because it subserves a paramount governmental interest must, to a large extent, I think, depend on whether that government has, under the Constitution, a direct substantive interest, that is, the power to act, in the particular area involved.

The Federal Government has, for example, power to restrict seditious speech directed against it, because that Government certainly has the substantive authority to protect itself against revolution. . . . But in dealing with obscenity we are faced with the converse situation, for the interests which obscenity statutes purportedly protect are primarily entrusted to the care, not of the Federal Government, but of the States. Congress has no substantive power over sexual morality. Such powers as the Federal Government has in this field are but incidental to its other powers, here the postal power, and are not of the same nature as those possessed by the States, which bear direct responsibility for the protection of the local moral fabric. * * *

Not only is the federal interest in protecting the Nation against pornography attenuated, but the dangers of federal censorship in this field are far greater than anything the States may do. It has often been said that one of the great strengths of our federal system is that we have, in the forty-eight States, forty-eight experimental social laboratories. "State statutory law reflects predominantly this capacity of a legislature to introduce novel techniques of social control. The federal system has the immense advantage of providing forty-eight separate centers for such experimentation." . . . Different States will have different attitudes toward the same work of literature. The same book which is freely read in one State might be classed as obscene in another. And it seems to me that no overwhelming danger to our freedom to experiment and to gratify our tastes in literature is likely to result from the suppression of a borderline book in one of the States, so long as there is no uniform nation-wide suppression of the book, and so long as other States are free to experiment with the same or bolder books.

Quite a different situation is presented, however, where the Federal Government imposes the ban. The danger is perhaps not great if the people of one State, through their legislature, decide that "Lady Chatterley's Lover" goes so far beyond the acceptable standards of candor that it will be deemed offensive and non-sellable, for the State next door is still free to make its own choice. At least we do not have one uniform standard. But the dangers to free thought and expression are truly great if the Federal Government imposes a blanket ban over the Nation on such a book. The prerogative of the States to differ on their ideas of morality will be destroyed, the ability of States to experiment will be stunted. The fact that the people of one State cannot read some of the works of D. H. Lawrence seems to me, if not wise or desirable, at least acceptable. But that no person in the United States should be allowed to do so seems to me to be intolerable, and violative of both the letter and spirit of the First Amendment. * * *

MR. JUSTICE DOUGLAS, with whom MR. JUSTICE BLACK concurs, dissenting.

When we sustain these convictions, we make the legality of a publication turn on the purity of thought which a book or tract instills in the mind of the reader. I do not think we can approve that standard and be faithful to the command of the First Amendment, which by its terms is a restraint on Congress and which by the Fourteenth is a restraint on the States. * * *

By these standards punishment is inflicted for thoughts provoked, not for overt acts nor antisocial conduct. This test cannot be squared with our decisions under the First Amendment. . . . This issue cannot be avoided by saying that obscenity is not protected by the First Amendment. The question remains, what is the constitutional test of obscenity?

The tests by which these convictions were obtained require only the arousing of sexual thoughts. Yet the arousing of sexual thoughts and desires happens every day in normal life in dozens of ways. . . .

The test of obscenity the Court endorses today gives the censor free range over a vast domain. To allow the State to step in and punish mere speech or publication that the judge or the jury thinks has an *undesirable* impact on thoughts but that is not shown to be a part of unlawful action is drastically to curtail the First Amendment. . . .

If we were certain that impurity of sexual thoughts impelled to action, we would be on less dangerous ground in punishing the distributors of this sex literature. But it is by no means clear that obscene literature, as so defined, is a significant factor in influencing substantial deviations from the community standards. * * *

The absence of dependable information on the effect of obscene literature on human conduct should make us wary. It should put us on the side of protecting society's interest in literature, except and unless it can be said that the particular publication has an impact on action that the government can control.

As noted, the trial judge in the Roth case charged the jury in the alternative that the federal obscenity statute outlaws literature dealing with sex which offends "the common conscience of the community." That standard is, in my view, more inimical still to freedom of expression.

The standard of what offends "the common conscience of the community" conflicts, in my judgment, with the command of the First Amendment that "Congress shall make no law * * * abridging the freedom of speech, or of the press." Certainly that standard would not be an acceptable one if religion, economics, politics or philosophy were involved. How does it become a constitutional standard when literature treating with sex is concerned?

Any test that turns on what is offensive to the community's standards is too loose, too capricious, too destructive of freedom of expression to be squared with the First Amendment. Under that test, juries can censor, suppress, and punish what they don't like, provided the matter relates to "sexual impurity" or has a tendency "to excite lustful thoughts." This is community censorship in one of its worst forms. It creates a regime where in the battle between the literati and the Philistines, the Philistines are certain to win. If experience in this field teaches anything, it is that "censorship of obscenity has almost always been both irrational and indiscriminate." . . . The test adopted here accentuates that trend.

I assume there is nothing in the Constitution which forbids Congress from using its power over the mails to proscribe *conduct* on the grounds of good morals. No one would suggest that the First Amendment permits nudity in public places, adultery, and other phases of sexual misconduct.

. . . Government should be concerned with anti-social conduct, not with utterances. Thus, if the First Amendment guarantee of freedom of speech and press is to mean anything in this field, it must allow protests even against the moral code that the standard of the day sets for the community. In other words, literature should not be suppressed merely because it offends the moral code of the censor.

The legality of a publication in this country should never be allowed to turn either on the purity of thought which it instills in the mind of the reader or on the degree to which it offends the community conscience. By either test the role of the censor is exalted, and society's values in literary freedom are sacrificed.

The Court today suggests a third standard. It defines obscene material as that "which deals with sex in a manner appealing to prurient interest." Like the standards applied by the trial judges below, that standard does not require any nexus between the literature which is prohibited and action which the legislature can regulate or prohibit. Under the First Amendment, that standard is no more valid than those which the courts below adopted.

I do not think that the problem can be resolved by the Court's statement that "obscenity is not expression protected by the First Amendment." . . . Unlike the law of libel, . . . there is no special historical evidence that literature dealing with sex was intended to be treated in a special manner by those who drafted the First Amendment. In fact, the first reported court decision in this country involving obscene literature was in 1821. . . . I reject too the implication that problems of freedom of speech and of the press are to be resolved by weighing against the values of free expression, the judgment of the Court that a particular form of that expression has "no redeeming social importance." The First Amendment, its prohibition in terms absolute, was designed to preclude courts as well as legislatures from weighing the values of speech against silence. The First Amendment puts free speech in the preferred position.

Freedom of expression can be suppressed if, and to the extent that, it is so closely brigaded with illegal action as to be an inseparable part of it. . . . As a people, we cannot afford to relax that standard. For the test that suppresses a cheap tract today can suppress a literary gem tomorrow. All it need do is to incite a lascivious thought or arouse a lustful desire. The list of books that judges or juries can place in that category is endless.

I would give the broad sweep of the First Amendment full support. I have the same confidence in the ability of our people to reject noxious literature as I have in their capacity to sort out the true from the false in theology, enonomics, politics, or any other field.

NOTE

A statute designed to prohibit the dissemination of "obscene" or "harmful" materials to minors, which materials may not be deemed to be so for adults, has been held constitutionally valid by a 6 to 3 decision of Supreme Court. The statutory expression "harmful to minors" was not considered so vague as to fail to put a legitimate disseminator on notice, and, consequently, a conviction under the statute was not in violation of due process. Ginsberg v. N. Y., 390 U.S. 629, 88 S.Ct. 1274 (1968).

STANLEY v. GEORGIA

Supreme Court of the United States, 1969.
394 U.S. 557, 89 S.Ct. 1243.

MR. JUSTICE MARSHALL delivered the opinion of the Court.

An investigation of appellant's alleged bookmaking activities led to the issuance of a search warrant for appellant's home. Under authority of this warrant, federal and state agents secured entrance. They found very little evidence of bookmaking activity, but while looking through a desk drawer in an upstairs bedroom, one of the federal agents, accompanied by a state officer, found three reels of eight-millimeter film. Using a projector and screen found in an upstairs living room, they viewed the films. The state officer concluded that they were obscene and seized them. Since a further examination of the bedroom indicated that appellant occupied it, he was charged with possession of obscene matter and placed under arrest. He was later indicted for "knowingly hav[ing] possession of obscene matter" in violation of Georgia law. Appellant was tried before a jury and convicted. The Supreme Court of Georgia affirmed. . . .

Appellant raises several challenges to the validity of his conviction. We find it necessary to consider only one. Appellant argues here, and argued below, that the Georgia obscenity statute, insofar as it punishes mere private possession of obscene matter, violates the First Amendment, as made applicable to the States by the Fourteenth Amendment. For reasons set forth below, we agree that the mere private possession of obscene matter cannot constitutionally be made a crime.

The court below saw no valid constitutional objection to the Georgia statute, even though it extends further than the typical statute forbidding commercial sales of obscene material. It held that "[i]t is not essential to an indictment charging one with possession of obscene matter that it be alleged that such possession was 'with intent to sell, expose or circulate the same.' " . . . The State and appellant both agree that the question here before us is whether "a statute imposing criminal sanctions upon the mere [knowing] possession of obscene matter" is constitutional. In this context, Georgia concedes that the present case appears to be one of "first impression * * * on this exact point," but contends that since "obscenity is not within the area of constitutionally protected speech or press," . . . the States are free, subject to the limits of other provisions of the Constitution, . . . to deal with it any way deemed necessary, just as they may deal with possession of other things thought to be detrimental to the welfare of their citizens. If the State can protect the body of a citizen, may it not, argues Georgia, protect his mind?

It is true that *Roth* does declare, seemingly without qualification, that obscenity is not protected by the First Amendment. . . . [However] none of the statements cited by the Court in *Roth* for the proposition that "this Court has always assumed that obscenity is not protected by the freedoms of speech and press" were made in the context of a statute punishing mere private possession of obscene material; the cases cited deal for the most part with use of the mails to distribute objectionable material or with some form of public distribution or dissemination. Moreover, none of this Court's decisions subsequent to *Roth* involved prosecution for private possession of obscene materials. . . .

In this context, we do not believe that this case can be decided simply by citing *Roth*. *Roth* and its progeny certainly do mean that the First and Fourteenth Amendments recognize a valid governmental interest in dealing with the problem of obscenity. But the assertion of that interest cannot, in every context, be insulated from all constitutional protections. . . . That holding cannot foreclose an examination of the constitutional implications of a statute forbidding mere private possession of such material.

It is now well established that the Constitution protects the right to receive information and ideas. "This freedom [of speech and press] * * * necessarily protects the right to receive * * *."

. . . This right to receive information and ideas, regardless of their social worth, . . . is fundamental to our free society. Moreover, in the context of this case—a prosecution for mere possession of printed or filmed matter in the privacy of a person's own home—that right takes on an added dimension. For also fundamental is the right to be free, except in very limited circumstances, from unwanted governmental intrusions into one's privacy.

These are the rights that appellant is asserting in the case before us. He is asserting the right to read or observe what he pleases—the right to satisfy his intellectual and emotional needs in the privacy of his own home. He is asserting the right to be free from state inquiry into the contents of his library. Georgia contends that appellant does not have these rights, that there are certain types of materials that the individual may not read or even possess. Georgia justifies this assertion by arguing that the films in the present case are obscene. But we think that mere categorization of these films as "obscene" is insufficient justification for such a drastic invasion of personal liberties guaranteed by the First and Fourteenth Amendments. Whatever may be the justifications for other statutes regulating obscenity, we do not think they reach into the privacy of one's own home. If the First Amendment means anything, it means that a State has no business telling a man, sitting alone in his own house, what books he may read or what films he may watch. Our whole constitutional heritage rebels at the thought of giving government the power to control men's minds.

And yet, in the face of these traditional notions of individual liberty, Georgia asserts the right to protect the individual's mind from the effects of obscenity. We are not certain that this argument amounts to anything more than the assertion that the State has the right to control the moral content of a person's thoughts. To some, this may be a noble purpose, but it is wholly inconsistent with the philosophy of the First Amendment. . . . Nor is it relevant that obscenity in general, or the particular films before the Court, are arguably devoid of any ideological content. The line between the transmission of ideas and mere entertainment is much too elusive for this Court to draw, if indeed such a line can be drawn at all. . . . Whatever the power of the state to control public dissemination of ideas inimical to the public morality, it cannot constitutionally premise legislation on the desirability of controlling a person's private thoughts.

Perhaps recognizing this, Georgia asserts that exposure to obscenity may lead to deviant sexual behavior or crimes of sexual violence. There appears to be little empirical basis for that assertion. But more importantly, if the State is only concerned about literature inducing antisocial conduct, we believe that in the context of private consumption of ideas and information we should adhere to the view that "[a]mong free men, the deterrents ordinarily to be applied to prevent crime are education and punishment for violations of the law * * *." . . . Given the present state of knowledge, the State may no more prohibit mere possession of obscenity on the ground that it may lead to antisocial conduct than it may prohibit possession of chemistry books on the ground that they may lead to the manufacture of homemade spirits.

It is true that in *Roth* this Court rejected the necessity of proving that exposure to obscene material would create a clear and present danger of antisocial conduct or would probably induce its recipients to such conduct. . . . But that case dealt with public distribution of obscene materials and such distribution is subject to different objections. For example, there is always the danger that obscene material might fall into the hands of children, or that it might intrude upon the sensibilities or privacy of the general public. . . . No such dangers are present in this case.

Finally, we are faced with the argument that prohibition of possession of obscenity is a necessary incident to statutory schemes prohibiting distribution. That argument is based on alleged difficulties of proving an intent to distribute or in producing evidence of actual distribution. We are not convinced that such difficulties exist, but even if they did we do not think that they would justify infringement of the individual's right to read or observe what he pleases. Because that right is so fundamental to our scheme of individual liberty, its restriction may not be justified by the need to ease the administration of otherwise valid criminal laws.

We hold that the First and Fourteenth Amendments prohibit making mere private possession of obscene material a crime. . . . *Roth* and the cases following that decision are not impaired by today's holding. As we have said, the States retain broad power to regulate obscenity; that power simply does not extend to mere possession by the individual in the privacy of his own home. Accordingly, the judgment of the court below is reversed and the case is remanded for proceedings not inconsistent with this opinion.

It is so ordered.

Judgment reversed and case remanded.

[The concurring opinion of Justice Black is omitted. We have also omitted the concurring opinion by Justices Stewart, Brennan, and White, who considered the extent of the search to be a violation of the Fourth Amendment's prohibition against unreasonable searches and seizures—a subject we are leaving for subsequent discussion.]

NOTES

1. In Memoirs v. Massachusetts, 383 U.S. 413, 418, 383 S.Ct. 975, 977 (1966), a three Justice plurality of the Supreme Court enunciated a new test of obscenity:

> ". . . Under [the *Roth*] definition as elaborated in subsequent cases, three elements must coalesce: it must be established that (a) the dominant theme of the material taken as a whole appeals to a pruri-

ent interest in sex; (b) the material is patently offensive because it affronts contemporary community standards relating to the description or representation of sexual matters; and (c) the material is utterly without redeeming social value.

". . . A book cannot be proscribed unless it is found to be *utterly* without redeeming social value. This is so even though the book is found to possess the requisite prurient appeal and to be patently offensive. Each of the three federal constitutional criteria is to be applied independently; the social value of the book can neither be weighed against nor canceled by its prurient appeal or patent offensiveness."

In a companion case, Ginzburg v. United States, 383 U.S. 463, 86 S.Ct. 942 (1966), the Court held that materials which might not be obscene when judged in the abstract could be found to be so when viewed "against a background of commercial exploitation of erotica solely for the sake of their prurient appeal", and that "in close cases evidence of pandering may be probative with respect to the nature of the material in question and thus satisfy the *Roth* test". (Pp. 466, 945; 477, 949.) And in Mishkin v. New York, 383 U.S. 502, 86 S.Ct. 958 (1966), the Court held that material which was designed to appeal to "a clearly defined deviant sexual group, rather than the public at large, the prurient-appeal requirement of the *Roth* test is satisfied if the dominant theme of the material taken as a whole appeals to the prurient interest in sex of the members of that group". (Pp. 508; 963.)

2. In Miller v. California, 413 U.S. 15, 93 S.Ct. 2607 (1973), the Supreme Court re-examined the obscenity issue and abandoned the plurality opinion expressed in *Memoirs*. The Court said that the *Memoirs* rule "produced a drastically altered test that called on the prosecution to prove a negative, *i. e.*, that the material was 'utterly without redeeming social value'—a burden virtually impossible to discharge under our criminal standards of proof". The Court then proceeded to formulate a new test:

"(a) whether 'the average person, applying contemporary community standards' would find that the work, taken as a whole, appeals to the prurient interest, (b) whether the work depicts or describes, in a patently offensive way, sexual conduct specifically defined by the applicable state law, and (c) whether the work, taken as a whole, lacks serious literary, artistic, political, or scientific value."

The Court then set forth a description of sexual conduct which the states could proscribe:

"(a) Patently offensive representations or descriptions of ultimate sexual acts, normal or perverted, actual or simulated.

"(b) Patently offensive representations or descriptions of masturbation, excretory functions, and lewd exhibition of the genitals."

Under this test, the Court assumed that "no one will be subject to prosecution for the sale or exposure of obscene materials unless these materials depict or describe patently offensive 'hard core' sexual conduct specifically defined by the regulating state law, as written or construed". Finally, the Court held it was proper to instruct a jury that "contemporary community standards" were those of the state and not an abstract "national" standard since "it is neither realistic nor constitutionally sound to read the First Amendment as requiring that the people of Maine or Mississippi accept public depiction of conduct found tolerable in Las Vegas, or New York City".

In Kaplan v. California, **413 U.S. 115,** 93 S.Ct. 2680 (1973), the Court held that written material, without pictures, could be obscene.

3. If the *Miller* test is intended to reach only depiction of "patently offensive 'hard core' sexual conduct", does it make any difference whether the test is (1) that the material be "utterly without redeeming social value", or (2) that the material "lacks serious literary, artistic, political or scientific values"? Could a lay jury distinguish between the two tests? Could a lay jury distinguish between *state* contemporary community standards and *national* contemporary standards, and particularly when the Court has held, in the companion case of Paris Adult Theatre v. Slaton, **413 U.S. 49,** 93 S.Ct. 2628 (1973), that expert testimony on this point is not constitutionally required?

4. In the *Paris* case the Court categorically rejected the theory that "obscene, pornographic films acquire constitutional immunity from state regulation simply because they are exhibited for consenting adults". In United States v. Orito, **413 U.S. 139,** 93 S.Ct. 2674 (1973), the Court held that the federal government may lawfully ban the interstate shipment of obscenity for personal use, and in United States v. 12 200-Ft. Reels of Super 8mm. Film, 413 U.S. 123, 93 S.Ct. 2665 (1973), the same conclusion was reached as to the importation of such materials. Can these cases be squared with the rationale in *Stanley*?

C. FREEDOM OF RELIGION

PEOPLE v. WOODY

Supreme Court of California, 1964.
61 Cal.2d 716, 40 Cal.Rptr. 69, 394 P.2d 813.

TOBRINER, JUSTICE. On April 28, 1962, a group of Navajos met in an Indian hogan in the desert near Needles, California, to perform a religious ceremony which included the use of peyote. Police officers, who had observed part of the ceremony, arrested defendants, who were among the Indians present. Defendants were later convicted of violating section 11500 of the Health and Safety Code, which prohibits the unauthorized possession of peyote. We have concluded that since the defendants used the peyote in a bona fide pursuit of a religious faith, and since the practice does not frustrate a compelling interest of the state, the application of the statute improperly defeated the immunity of the First Amendment of the Constitution of the United States.

When the police entered the hogan and charged the participants with the use of peyote, one of the Indians handed the officers a gold-colored portrait frame containing a photostatic copy of the articles of incorporation of the Native American Church of the State of California. The articles declared: "That we as a people place explicit faith and hope and belief in the Almighty God and declare full, competent, and everlasting faith in our Church things which and by which we worship God. That we further pledge ourselves to work for unity with the sacramental use of peyote and its religious use."

The state stipulated at trial that at the time of the arrest defendants and the other Indians were performing a religious ceremony which involved the use of peyote. Defendants pleaded not guilty to the crime of illegal possession of narcotics, contending that their possession of peyote was incident to the observance of their faith and that the state could not constitutionally invoke the statute against them without abridging their right to the free exercise of their religion. The trial proceeded without a jury; the court held defendants guilty and imposed suspended sentences.

Defendants' defense, if any, must lie in their constitutional objection. We do not doubt that even though technically peyote is an "hallucinogen" rather than a narcotic, the state, pursuant to the police power, may proscribe its use. . . . Only if the application of the proscription improperly infringes upon the immunity of the First Amendment can defendants prevail; their case rests upon that Amendment, which is operative upon the states by means of the Fourteenth Amendment . . .

Although the prohibition against infringement of religious belief is absolute, the immunity afforded religious practices by the

First Amendment is not so rigid. * * * But the state may abridge religious practices only upon a demonstration that some compelling state interest outweighs the defendants' interests in religious freedom. * * *

The first step requires an exploration into the particulars of this case to determine whether section 11500 of the Health and Safety Code imposes any burden upon the free exercise of defendants' religion. An examination of the record as to the nature of peyote and its role in the religion practiced by defendants as members of the Native American Church of California compels the conclusion that the statutory prohibition most seriously infringes upon the observance of the religion.

The plant Lophophora williamsii, a small, spineless cactus, found in the Rio Grande Valley of Texas and northern Mexico, produces peyote, which grows in small buttons on the top of the cactus. Peyote's principal constituent is mescaline. When taken internally by chewing the buttons or drinking a derivative tea, peyote produces several types of hallucinations, depending primarily upon the user. In most subjects it causes extraordinary vision marked by bright and kaleidoscopic colors, geometric patterns, or scenes involving humans or animals. In others it engenders hallucinatory symptoms similar to those produced in cases of schizophrenia, dementia praecox, or paranoia. Beyond its hallucinatory effect, peyote renders for most users a heightened sense of comprehension; it fosters a feeling of friendliness toward other persons.

Peyote, as we shall see, plays a central role in the ceremony and practice of the Native American Church, a religious organization of Indians. Although the church claims no official prerequisites to membership, no written membership rolls, and no recorded theology, estimates of its membership range from 30,000 to 250,000, the wide variance deriving from differing definitions of a "member." As the anthropologists have ascertained through conversations with members, the theology of the church combines certain Christian teachings with the belief that peyote embodies the Holy Spirit and that those who partake of peyote enter into direct contact with God.

Peyotism discloses a long history. A reference to the religious use of peyote in Mexico appears in Spanish historical sources as early as 1560. Peyotism spread from Mexico to the United States and Canada; American anthropologists describe it as well established in this country during the latter part of the nineteenth century. Today, Indians of many tribes practice Peyotism. Despite the absence of recorded dogma, the several tribes follow surprisingly similar ritual and theology; the practices of Navajo members in Arizona practically parallel those of adherents in California, Montana, Oklahoma, Wisconsin, and Saskatchewan.

The "meeting," a ceremony marked by the sacramental use of peyote, composes the cornerstone of the peyote religion. The meeting convenes in an enclosure and continues from sundown Saturday to sunrise Sunday. To give thanks for the past good fortune or find guidance for future conduct, a member will "sponsor" a meeting and supply to those who attend both the peyote and the next morning's breakfast. The "sponsor," usually but not always the "leader," takes charge of the meeting; he decides the order of events and the amount of peyote to be consumed. Although the individual leader exercises an absolute control of the meeting, anthropologists report a striking uniformity of its ritual.

A meeting connotes a solemn and special occasion. Whole families attend together, although children and young women participate only by their presence. Adherents don their finest clothing, usually suits for men and fancy dresses for the women, but sometimes ceremonial Indian costumes. At the meeting the members pray, sing, and make ritual use of drum, fan, eagle bone, whistle, rattle and prayer cigarette, the symbolic emblems of their faith. The central event, of course, consists of the use of peyote in quantities sufficient to produce an hallucinatory state.

At an early but fixed stage in the ritual the members pass around a ceremonial bag of peyote buttons. Each adult may take four, the customary number, or take none. The participants chew the buttons, usually with some difficulty because of extreme bitterness; later, at a set time in the ceremony any member may ask for more peyote; occasionally a member may take as many as four more buttons. At sunrise on Sunday the ritual ends; after a brief outdoor prayer, the host and his family serve breakfast. Then the members depart. By morning the effects of the peyote disappear; the users suffer no aftereffects.

Although peyote serves as a sacramental symbol similar to bread and wine in certain Christian churches, it is more than a sacrament. Peyote constitutes in itself an object of worship; prayers are directed to it much as prayers are devoted to the Holy Ghost. On the other hand, to use peyote for nonreligious purposes is sacrilegious. Members of the church regard peyote also as a "teacher" because it induces a feeling of brotherhood with other members; indeed, it enables the participant to experience the Deity. Finally, devotees treat peyote as a "protector." Much as a Catholic carries his medallion, an Indian G.I. often wears around his neck a beautifully beaded pouch containing one large peyote button. . . .

The record thus establishes that the application of the statutory prohibition of the use of peyote results in a virtual inhibition of the practice of defendants' religion. To forbid the use of peyote is to remove the theological heart of Peyotism. Having reached this conclusion, we must undertake the second step in the analysis of the constitutional issue: a determination of whether the state has demonstrated that "compelling state interest" which necessitates an abridgement of defendants' First Amendment right. . . .

The state asserts that the compelling reason for the prohibition of Peyotism lies in its deleterious effects upon the Indian community, and even more basically, in the infringement such practice would place upon the enforcement of the narcotic laws because of the difficulty of detecting fraudulent claims of an asserted religious use of peyote. The prosecution further claims that the cases support these positions. We set forth the reasons why we believe the contentions to be unfounded.

The People urge that "the use of peyote by Indians in place of medical care, the threat of indoctrination of small children," and the "possible correlation between the use of this drug and the possible propensity to use some other more harmful drug" justify the statutory prohibition. The record, however, does not support the state's chronicle of harmful consequences of the use of peyote.

The evidence indicates that the Indians do not in fact employ peyote in place of proper medical care; and, as the Attorney General with fair objectivity admits, "there was no evidence to suggest that Indians who use peyote are more liable to become addicted to other narcotics than non-peyote-using Indians." Nor does the record substantiate the state's fear of the "indoctrination of small children"; it shows that Indian children never, and Indian teenagers rarely, use peyote. Finally, as the Attorney General likewise admits, the opinion of scientists and other experts is "that peyote * * * works no permanent deleterious injury to the Indian. * * *" Indeed, as we have noted, these experts regard the moral standards of members of the Native American Church as higher than those of Indians outside the church.

The Attorney General also argues that since "peyote could be regarded as a symbol, one that obstructs enlightenment and shackles the Indian to primitive conditions" the responsibility rests with the state to eliminate its use. We know of no doctrine that the state, in its asserted omniscience, should undertake to deny to defendants the observance of their religion in order to free them from the suppositious "shackles" of their "unenlightened" and "primitive condition."

Turning to the state's second contention, that the threat of fraudulent assertions of religious immunity will render impossible the effective enforcement of the narcotic laws, we note that [in earlier cases before this Court, and in this one] the state produced no evidence that spurious claims of religious immunity would in fact preclude effective administration of the law or that other "forms of regulation" would not accomplish the state's objectives.

That other states have excepted from the narcotic laws the use of peyote, and have not considered such exemption an impairment to enforcement, weakens the prosecution's forebodings. New Mexico in 1959, and Montana in 1957, amended their narcotics laws to provide that the prohibition against narcotics "shall not apply to the possession, sale or gift of peyote for religious sacramental purposes by any bona fide religious organization incorporated under the laws of the state." Arizona has reached a similar result by judicial decree.

That the state's showing of "compelling interest" cannot lie in untested assertions that recognition of the religious immunity will interfere with the enforcement of the state statute, finds illustration in the Minnesota litigation culminating in In re Jenison (1963) 267

Minn. 136, 125 N.W.2d 588 [which involved a criminal contempt conviction of a woman who refused to serve on a jury because of religious objections]. The United States Supreme Court reversed *per curiam* and remanded the case to the Minnesota Supreme Court . . . Upon remand the state court reversed the conviction, stating that "there has been an inadequate showing that the state's interest in obtaining competent jurors requires us to override relator's right to the free exercise of her religion. Consequently we hold that until and unless further experience indicates that the indiscriminate invoking of the First Amendment poses a serious threat to the effective functioning of our jury system, any person whose religious convictions prohibit compulsory jury duty shall henceforth be exempt." . . .

We turn to the several cases cited by the Attorney General which uphold statutes restricting religious practices. The People principally rely upon Reynolds v. United States which ruled that Congress could constitutionally apply to Mormons a prohibition against polygamy. The Mormon doctrine of polygamy rested in alleged devine origin and imposed upon male members, circumstances permitting, the observance of the practice upon pain of eternal damnation.

The Supreme Court held that the history of the laws against polygamy showed that the condemnation of the practice was a matter of the gravest social importance. It found in polygamy the seed of destruction of a democratic society. Viewing the practice as highly injurious to its female adherents, the Court classed polygamy with such religious rites as sacrifice of human beings and funereal immolation of widows.

Reynolds v. United States must be distinguished from the instant case for two fundamental reasons. The test of constitutionality calls for an examination of the degree of abridgement of religious freedom involved in each case. Polygamy, although a basic tenet in the theology of Mormonism, is not essential to the practice of the religion; peyote, on the other hand, is the *sine qua non* of defendants' faith. It is the sole means by which defendants are able to experience their religion; without peyote defendants cannot practice their faith. Second, the degree of danger to state interests in Reynolds far exceeded that in the instant case. The Court in Reynolds considered polygamy as a serious threat to democratic institutions and injurious to the morals and well-being of its practitioners. As we have heretofore indicated, no such compelling state interest supports the prohibition of the use of peyote. * * *

Finally, we deal with the Attorney General's argument that our present conclusion requires an inquiry in each case into the bona fides of a particular defendant's beliefs, an inquiry which is both difficult and "repugnant to the spirit of our law. . . . ". Yet the trier of fact need inquire only into the question of whether the defendants' belief in Peyotism is honest and in good faith. . . . although judicial examination of the truth or validity of religious beliefs is foreclosed by the First Amendment, the courts of necessity must ask whether the claimant holds his belief honestly and in good faith or whether he seeks to wear the mantle of religious immunity merely as a cloak for illegal activities.

In so doing, we impose no undue burden upon the trier of fact. We do not doubt the capacity of judge and jury to distinguish between those who would feign faith in an esoteric religion and those who would honestly follow it. . . . Thus the court makes a factual examination of the bona fides of the belief and does not intrude into the religious issue at all; it does not determine the nature of the belief but the nature of defendants' adherence to it.

* * *

In the instant case, of course, we encounter no problem as to the bona fide nature of defendants' assertion of the free exercise clause. The state agrees, and the evidence amply demonstrates, that defendants' use of peyote was for a religious purpose.

We have weighed the competing values represented in this case on the symbolic scale of constitutionality. On the one side we have placed the weight of freedom of religion as protected by the First Amendment; on the other, the weight of the state's "compelling interest." Since the use of peyote incorporates the essence of the religious expression, the first weight is heavy. Yet the use of peyote presents only slight danger to the state and to the enforcement of its laws; the second weight is relatively light. The scale tips in favor of the constitutional protection. * * *

NOTES

1. In reaching a result contrary to the Woody case, the Supreme Court of North Carolina said, in State v. Bullard, 267 N.C. 599, 148 S.E. 2d 565 (1966): "Even if he [the defendant] were sincere, the first amendment could not protect him. It is true that this amendment permits a citizen complete freedom of religion. He may belong to any church or to no church and may believe whatever he will, however fantastic, illogical or unreasonable, but nowhere does it authorize him in the exercise of his religion to commit acts, which constitute threats to the public safety, morals, peace and order. * * * The defendant may believe what he will as to peyote and marijuana and he may conceive that one is necessary and the other is advisable in connection with his religion. But it is not a violation of his constitutional rights to forbid him, in the guise of his religion, to possess a drug which will produce hallucinatory symptoms similar to those produced in cases of schizophrenia, dementia praecox, or paranoia, and his position cannot be sustained here—in law nor in morals" The court's use of the phrases "guise of his religion" and "nor in morals" should probably be read in light of its earlier conclusion that "Some doubt may be cast upon the validity of the defendant's claim that he uses these drugs only in connection with his religion. The officers testified that in their discussion with him at the time the drugs were found in his apartment that the defendant made no mention of his religion nor the

need for the drugs in connection therewith. A jury might well have found that this claim was a defense invented by the defendant long after his arrest", although, at the time of appeal, he claimed to be "a Peyotist with Buddhist leanings and that he has recently joined the Neo-American Church".

2. May a state, in the exercise of the police power, forbid persons to handle poisonous snakes, though the practice is both a religious and a voluntary one? In State v. Massey, 229 N.C. 734, 51 S.E.2d 179 (1949), the court held that the public safety factor outweighed the freedom of religion one.

D. THE RIGHT OF PRIVACY

ROE v. WADE

Supreme Court of the United States, 1973.
410 U.S. 113, 93 S.Ct. 705.

[The majority and minority opinions in this case occupied 64 pages in the official U. S. reporter, so they obviously had to be condensed extensively for casebook usage. Although the following excerpts deal primarily with the right of privacy issue, we have retained certain tangentially related ones, for the reason that the subject of abortion is not treated elsewhere in the casebook. Students with a greater interest in the subject than is here presented will have access, of course, to the unabridged opinions themselves.]

MR. JUSTICE BLACKMUN delivered the opinion of the Court.

* * *

The Texas statutes that concern us here . . . make it a crime to "procure an abortion," as therein defined, or to attempt one, except with respect to "an abortion procured or attempted by medical advice for the purpose of saving the life of the mother." Similar statutes are in existence in a majority of the States. . . .

* * *

Jane Roe, a single woman who was residing in Dallas County, Texas, instituted this federal action in March 1970 against the District Attorney of the county. She sought a declaratory judgment that the Texas criminal abortion statutes were unconstitutional on their face, and an injunction restraining the defendant from enforcing the statutes. * * *

The principal thrust of appellant's attack on the Texas statutes is that they improperly invade a right, said to be possessed by the pregnant woman, to choose to terminate her pregnancy. Appellant would discover this right in the concept of personal "liberty" embodied in the Fourteenth Amendment's Due Process Clause; or in personal, marital, familial, and sexual privacy said to be protected by the Bill of Rights or its penumbras, . . . Before addressing this claim, we feel it desirable briefly to survey, in several aspects, the history of abortion, for such insight as that history may afford us, and then to examine the state purposes and interests behind the criminal abortion laws.

It perhaps is not generally appreciated that the restrictive criminal abortion laws in effect in a majority of States today are of relatively recent vintage. Those laws, generally proscribing abortion or its attempt at any time during pregnancy except when necessary to preserve the pregnant woman's life, are not of ancient or even of common law origin. Instead, they derive from statutory changes effected, for the most part, in the latter half of the 19th century.

1. *Ancient attitudes.* These are not capable of precise determination. We are told that at the time of the Persian Empire abortifacients were known and that criminal abortions were severely punished. We are also told, however, that abortion was practiced in Greek times as well as in the Roman Era, and that "it was resorted to without scruple." The Ephesian, Soranos, often described as the greatest of the ancient gynecologists, appears to have been generally opposed to Rome's prevailing free-abortion practices. He found it necessary to think first of the life of the mother, and he resorted to abortion when, upon this standard, he felt the procedure advisable. Greek and Roman law afforded little protection to the unborn. If abortion was prosecuted in some places, it seems to have been based on a concept of a violation of the father's right to his offspring. Ancient religion did not bar abortion.

2. *The Hippocratic Oath.* What then of the famous Oath that has stood so long as the ethical guide of the medical profession and that bears the name of the great Greek (460(?)–377(?) B.C.), who has been described as the Father of Medicine, the "wisest and the greatest practitioner of his art," and the "most important and most complete medical personality of antiquity," who dominated the medical schools of his time, and who typified the sum of the medical knowledge of the past? The Oath varies somewhat according to the particular translation, but in any translation the content is clear: "I will give no deadly medicine to anyone if asked, nor suggest any such counsel; and in like manner I will not give to a woman a pessary to produce abortion," or "I will neither give a deadly drug to anybody if asked for it, nor will I make a suggestion to this effect. Similarly, I will not give to a woman an abortive remedy."

Although the Oath is not mentioned in any of the principal briefs in this case, . . . it represents the apex of the development of strict ethical concepts in medicine, and its influence endures to this day. Why did not the authority of Hippocrates dissuade abortion practice in his time and that of Rome? The late Dr. Edelstein provides us with a theory: . . . . The Oath was not uncontested even in Hippocrates' day; only the Pythagorean school of philosophers frowned upon the related act of suicide. Most Greek thinkers, on the other hand, commended abortion, at least prior to viability. . . . For the Pythagoreans, however, it was a matter of dogma. For them the embryo was animate from the moment of conception, and abortion meant destruction of a living being. The abortion clause of the Oath, therefore, "echoes Pythagorean doctrines," and "[i]n no other stratum of Greek opinion were such views held or proposed in the same spirit of uncompromising austerity."

Edelstein then concludes that the Oath originated in a group representing only a small segment of Greek opinion and that it certainly was not accepted by all ancient physicians. He points out that medical writings down to Galen (130–200 A.D.) "give evidence of the violation of almost every one of its injunctions." But with the end of antiquity a decided change took place. Resistance against suicide and against abortion became common. The Oath came to be popular. The emerging teachings of Christianity were in agreement with the Pythagorean ethic. The Oath "became the nucleus of all medical ethics" and "was applauded as the embodiment of truth." Thus, suggests Dr. Edelstein, it is "a Pythagorean manifesto and not the expression of an absolute standard of medical conduct."

This, it seems to us, is a satisfactory and acceptable explanation of the Hippocratic Oath's apparent rigidity. It enables us to understand, in historical context, a long accepted and revered statement of medical ethics.

3. *The Common Law.* It is undisputed that at the common law, abortion performed *before* "quickening"—the first recognizable movement of the fetus *in utero*, appearing usually from the 16th to the 18th week of pregnancy—was not an indictable offense. The absence of a common law crime for pre-quickening abortion appears to have developed from a confluence of earlier philosophical, theological, and civil and canon law concepts of when life begins. These disciplines variously approached the question in terms of the point at which the embryo or fetus became "formed" or recognizably human, or in terms of when a "person" came into being, that is, infused with a "soul" or "animated." A loose consensus evolved in early English law that these events occurred at some point between conception and live birth. This was "mediate animation." Although Christian theology and the canon law came to fix the point of animation at 40 days for a male and 80 days for a female, a view that persisted until the 19th century, there was otherwise little agreement about the precise time of formation or animation. There was agreement, however, that prior to this point the fetus was to be regarded as part of the mother and its destruction, therefore, was not homicide. Due to continued uncertainty about the precise time when animation occurred, to the lack of any empirical basis for the 40–80 day view, and

perhaps to Acquinas' definition of movement as one of the two first principles of life, Bracton focused upon quickening as the critical point. The significance of quickening was echoed by later common law scholars and found its way into the received common law in this country.

Whether abortion of a *quick* fetus was a felony at common law, or even a lesser crime, is still disputed. Bracton, writing early in the 13th century, thought it homicide. But the later and predominant view, following the great common law scholars, has been that it was at most a lesser offense. In a frequently cited passage, Coke took the position that abortion of a woman "quick with childe" is "a great misprision and no murder." Blackstone followed, saying that while abortion after quickening had once been considered manslaughter (though not murder), "modern law" took a less severe view. A recent review of the common law precedents argues, however, that those precedents contradict Coke and that even post-quickening abortion was never established as a common law crime. This is of some importance because while most American courts ruled, in holding or dictum, that abortion of an unquickened fetus was not criminal under their received common law, others followed Coke in stating that abortion of a quick fetus was a "misprision," a term they translated to mean "misdemeanor." That their reliance on Coke on this aspect of the law was uncritical and, apparently in all the reported cases, dictum (due probably to the paucity of common law prosecutions for post-quickening abortion), makes it now appear doubtful that abortion was ever firmly established as a common law crime even with respect to the destruction of a quick fetus.

4. *The English statutory law.* England's first criminal abortion statute . . . came in 1803. It made abortion of a quick fetus, § 1, a capital crime, but in § 2 it provided lesser penalties for the felony of abortion before quickening, and thus preserved the quickening distinction. This contrast was continued in the general revision of 1828 . . . It disappeared, however, together with the death penalty, in 1837 . . . and did not reappear in the Offenses Against the Person Act of 1861 . . . that formed the core of English anti-abortion law until the liberalizing reforms of 1967. * * *

[The 1967 Abortion Act] permits a licensed physician to perform an abortion where two other licensed physicians agree (a) "that the continuance of the pregnancy would involve risk to the life of the pregnant woman, or of injury to the physical or mental health of the pregnant woman or any existing children of her family, greater than if the pregnancy were terminated," or (b) "that there is a substantial risk that if the child were born it would suffer from such physical or mental abnormalities as to be seriously handicapped." The Act also provides that, in making this determination, "account may be taken of the pregnant woman's actual or reasonably foreseeable environment." It also permits a physician, without the concurrence of others, to terminate a pregnancy where he is of the good faith opinion that the abortion "is immediately necessary to save the life or to prevent grave permanent injury to the physical or mental health of the pregnant woman."

5. *The American law.* In this country the law in effect in all but a few States until mid-19th century was the pre-existing English common law. Connecticut, the first State to enact abortion legislation, adopted in 1821 that part of [the early English act] that related to a woman "quick with child." The death penalty was not imposed. Abortion before quickening was made a crime in that State only in 1860. In 1828 New York enacted legislation that, in two respects, was to serve as a model for early anti-abortion statutes. First, while barring destruction of an unquickened fetus as well as a quick fetus, it made the former only a misdemeanor, but the latter second-degree manslaughter. Second, it incorporated a concept of therapeutic abortion by providing that an abortion was excused if it "shall have been necessary to preserve the life of such mother, or shall have been advised by two physicians to be necessary for such purpose." By 1840, when Texas had received the common law, only eight American States had statutes dealing with abortion. It was not until after the War Between the States that legislation began generally to replace the common law. Most of these initial statutes dealt severely with abortion after quickening but were lenient with it before quickening. Most punished attempts equally with completed abortions. While many statutes included the exception for an abortion thought by one or more physicians to be necessary to save the mother's life, that provision soon disappeared and the typical law required that the procedure actually be necessary for that purpose.

Gradually, in the middle and late 19th century the quickening distinction disappeared from the statutory law of most States and the degree of the offense and the penalties were increased. By the end of the 1950's a large majority of the States banned abortion, however and whenever performed, unless done to save or preserve the life of the mother. The exceptions, Alabama and the District of Columbia, permitted abortion to preserve the mother's health. Three other States permitted abortions that were not "unlawfully" performed or that were not "without lawful justification," leaving interpretation of those standards to the courts. In the past several years, however, a trend toward liberalization of abortion statutes has resulted in adoption, by about one-third of the States, of less stringent laws, most of them patterned after the ALI Model Penal Code, . . .

It is thus apparent that at common law, at the time of the adoption of our Constitution, and throughout the major portion of the 19th century, abortion was viewed with less disfavor than under most American statutes currently in effect. Phrasing it another way, a woman enjoyed a substantially broader right to terminate a pregnancy than she does in most States today. At least with respect to the early stage of pregnancy, and very possibly without such a limitation, the opportunity to make this choice was present in this country well into the 19th century. Even later, the law continued for some time to treat less punitively an abortion procured in early pregnancy.

6. *The position of the American Medical Association.* The anti-abortion mood prevalent in this country in the late 19th century was shared by the medical profession. Indeed, the attitude of the profession may have played a significant role in the enactment of stringent criminal abortion legislation during that period. * * *

. . . [In 1967 the AMA's] Committee on Human Reproduction urged the adoption of a stated policy of opposition to induced abortion except when there is "documented medical evidence" of a threat to the health or life of the mother, or that the child "may be born with incapacitating physical deformity or mental deficiency," or that a pregnancy "resulting from legally established statutory or forcible rape or incest may constitute a threat to the mental or physical health of the patient," and two other physicians "chosen because of their recognized professional competency have examined the patient and have concurred in writing," and the procedure "is performed in a hospital accredited by the Joint Commission on Accreditation of Hospitals." The providing of medical information by physicians to state legislatures in their consideration of legislation regarding therapeutic abortion was "to be considered consistent with the principles of ethics of the American Medical Association." This recommendation was adopted by the House of Delegates. . . .

In 1970, after the introduction of a variety of proposed resolutions, and of a report from its Board of Trustees, a reference committee noted "polarization of the medical profession on this controversial issue"; division among those who had testified; a difference of opinion among AMA councils and committees; "the remarkable shift in testimony" in six months, felt to be influenced "by the rapid changes in state laws and by the judicial decisions which tend to make abortion more freely available;" and a feeling "that this trend will continue." On June 25, 1970, the House of Delegates adopted preambles and most of the resolutions proposed by the reference committee. The preambles emphasized "the best interests of the patient," "sound clinical judgment," and "informed patient consent," in contrast to "mere acquiescence to the patient's demand." The resolutions asserted that abortion is a medical procedure that should be performed by a licensed physician in an accredited hospital only after consultation with two other physicians and in conformity with state law, and that no party to the procedure should be required to violate personally held moral principles. . . . The AMA Judicial Council rendered a complementary opinion. * * *

[Omitted here are the reported position of the American Public Health Association, and that of the American Bar Association. The latter organization's House of Delegates in 1972 approved the Uniform Abortion Act drafted by the Conference of Commissioners on Uniform State Laws. It appears in footnote 40 of the court's opinion.] * * *

Three reasons have been advanced to explain historically the enactment of criminal abortion laws in the 19th century and to justify their continued existence.

It has been argued occasionally that these laws were the product of a Victorian social concern to discourage illicit sexual conduct. Texas, however, does not advance this justification in the present case, and it appears that no court or commentator has taken the argument seriously. The appellants and *amici* contend, moreover, that this is not a proper state purpose at all and suggest that if it were, the Texas statutes are overbroad in protecting it since the law fails to distinguish between married and unwed mothers.

A second reason is concerned with abortion as a medical procedure. When most criminal abortion laws were first enacted, the procedure was a hazardous one for the woman. This was particularly true prior to the development of antisepsis. Antiseptic techniques, of course, were based on discoveries by Lister, Pasteur, and others first announced in 1867, but were not generally accepted and employed until about the turn of the century. Abortion mortality was high. Even after 1900, and perhaps until as late as the development of antibiotics in the 1940's, standard modern techniques such as dilation and curettage were not nearly so safe as they are today. Thus it has been argued that a State's real concern in enacting a criminal abortion law was to protect the pregnant woman, that is, to restrain her from submitting to a procedure that placed her life in serious jeopardy.

Modern medical techniques have altered this situation. Appellants and various *amici* refer to medical data indicating that abortion in early pregnancy, that is, prior to the end of first trimester, although not without its risk, is now relative safe. Mortality rates for women undergoing early abortions, where the procedure is legal, appear to be as low as or lower than the rates for normal childbirth. Consequently, any interest of the State in protecting the woman from an inherently hazardous procedure, except when it would be equally dangerous for her to forgo it, has largely disappeared. Of course, important state interests in the area of health and medical standards do remain. The State has a legitimate interest in seeing to it that abortion, like any other medical procedure, is performed under circumstances that insure maximum safety for the patient. This interest obviously extends at least to the performing physician and his staff, to the facilities involved, to the availability of aftercare, and to adequate provision for any complication or emergency that might arise. The prevalence of high mortality rates at illegal "abortion mills" strengthens, rather than weakens, the State's interest in regulating the conditions under which abortions are performed. Moreover, the risk to the woman increases as her pregnancy continues. Thus the State retains a definite interest in protecting the woman's own health and safety when an abortion is proposed at a late stage of pregnancy.

The third reason is the State's interest—some phrase it in terms of duty—in protecting prenatal life. Some of the argument for this justification rests on the theory that a new human life is present from the moment of conception. The State's interest and general obligation to protect life then extends, it is argued, to prenatal life. Only when the life of the pregnant mother herself is at stake, balanced against the life she carries within her, should the interest of the embryo or fetus not prevail. Logically, of course, a legitimate state interest in this area need not stand or fall on acceptance of the belief that life begins at conception or at some other point prior to live birth. In assessing the State's interest, recognition may be given to the less rigid claim that as long as at least *potential* life is involved, the State may assert interests beyond the protection of the pregnant woman alone.

Parties challenging state abortion laws have sharply disputed in some courts the contention that a purpose of these laws, when enacted, was to protect prenatal life. Pointing to the absence of legislative history to support the contention, they claim that most state laws were designed solely to protect the woman. Because medical advances have lessened this concern, at least with respect to abortion in early pregnancy, they argue that with respect to such abortions the laws can no longer be justified by any state interest. There is some scholarly support for this view of original purpose. The few state courts called upon to interpret their laws in the late 19th and early 20th centuries did focus on the State's interest in protecting the woman's health rather than in preserving the embryo and fetus. Proponents of this view point out that in many States, including Texas, by statute or judicial interpretation, the pregnant woman herself could not be prosecuted for self-abortion or for cooperating in an abortion performed upon her by another. They claim that adoption of the "quickening" distinction through received common law and state statutes tacitly recognizes the greater health hazards inherent in late abortion and impliedly repudiates the theory that life begins at conception.

It is with these interests, and the weight to be attached to them, that this case is concerned.

The Constitution does not explicitly mention any right of privacy. In a line of decisions, however, going back perhaps as far as

[1891] . . ., the Court has recognized that a right of personal privacy, or a guarantee of certain areas or zones of privacy, does exist under the Constitution. In varying contexts the Court or individual Justices have indeed found at least the roots of that right in the First Amendment, . . . ; in the Fourth and Fifth Amendments, . . . ; in the penumbras of the Bill of Rights, . . . ; in the Ninth Amendment, . . . ; or in the concept of liberty guaranteed by the first section of the Fourteenth Amendment, . . . These decisions make it clear that only personal rights that can be deemed "fundamental" or "implicit in the concept of ordered liberty," . . . are included in this guarantee of personal privacy. They also make it clear that the right has some extension to activities relating to marriage, . . . procreation, . . . contraception, . . . family relationships, . . . and child rearing and education, . . .

This right of privacy, whether it be founded in the Fourteenth Amendment's concept of personal liberty and restrictions upon state action, as we feel it is, or, as the District Court determined, in the Ninth Amendment's reservation of rights to the people, is broad enough to encompass a woman's decision whether or not to terminate her pregnancy. The detriment that the State would impose upon the pregnant woman by denying this choice altogether is apparent. Specific and direct harm medically diagnosable even in early pregnancy may be involved. Maternity, or additional offspring, may force upon the woman a distressful life and future. Psychological harm may be imminent. Mental and physical health may be taxed by child care. There is also the distress, for all concerned, associated with the unwanted child, and there is the problem of bringing a child into a family already unable, psychologically and otherwise, to care for it. In other cases, as in this one, the additional difficulties and continuing stigma of unwed motherhood may be involved. All these are factors the woman and her responsible physician necessarily will consider in consultation.

On the basis of elements such as these, appellants and some *amici* argue that the woman's right is absolute and that she is entitled to terminate her pregnancy at whatever time, in whatever way, and for whatever reason she alone chooses. With this we do not agree. Appellants' arguments that Texas either has no valid interest at all in regulating the abortion decision, or no interest strong enough to support any limitation upon the woman's sole determination, is unpersuasive. The Court's decisions recognizing a right of privacy also acknowledge that some state regulation in areas protected by that right is appropriate. As noted above, a state may properly assert important interests in safeguarding health, in maintaining medical standards, and in protecting potential life. At some point in pregnancy, these respective interests become sufficiently compelling to sustain regulation of the factors that govern the abortion decision. The privacy right involved, therefore, cannot be said to be absolute. In fact, it is not clear to us that the claim asserted by some *amici* that one has an unlimited right to do with one's body as one pleases bears a close relationship to the right of privacy previously articulated in the Court's decisions. The Court has refused to recognize an unlimited right of this kind in the past. Jacobson v. Massachusetts . . . (vaccination); Buck v. Bell, . . . (sterilization).

We therefore conclude that the right of personal privacy includes the abortion decision, but that this right is not unqualified and must be considered against important state interests in regulation. * * *

The appellee and certain *amici* argue that the fetus is a "person" within the language and meaning of the Fourteenth Amendment. In support of this they outline at length and in detail the well-known facts of fetal development. If this suggestion of personhood is established, the appellant's case, of course, collapses, for the fetus' right to life is then guaranteed specifically by the Amendment. The appellant conceded as much on reargument. On the other hand, the appellee conceded on reargument that no case could be cited that holds that a fetus is a person within the meaning of the Fourteenth Amendment.

The Constitution does not define "person" in so many words. Section 1 of the Fourteenth Amendment contains three references to "person." The first, in defining "citizens," speaks of "persons born or naturalized in the United States." The word also appears both in the Due Process Clause and in the Equal Protection Clause. "Person" is used in other places in the Constitution: in the listing of qualifications for representatives and senators [etc.], and in the Fifth, Twelfth, and Twenty-second Amendments as well as in §§ 2 and 3 of the Fourteenth Amendment. But in nearly all these instances, the use of the word is such that it has application only postnatally. None indicates, with any assurance, that it has any possible pre-natal application.

All this, together with our observation, supra, that throughout the major portion of the 19th century prevailing legal abortion practices were far freer than they are today, persuades us that the word "person," as used in the Fourteenth Amendment, does not include the unborn. . . .

This conclusion, however, does not of itself fully answer the contentions raised by Texas, and we pass on to other considerations.

The pregnant woman cannot be isolated in her privacy. She carries an embryo, and, later, a fetus, if one accepts the medical definitions of the developing young in the human uterus. The situation therefore is inherently different from marital intimacy, or bedroom possession of obscene material, or marriage, or procreation, or education, ... As we have intimated above, it is reasonable and appropriate for a State to decide that at some point in time another interest, that of health of the mother or that of potential human life, becomes significantly involved. The woman's privacy is no longer sole and any right of privacy she possesses must be measured accordingly.

Texas urges that, apart from the Fourteenth Amendment, life begins at conception and is present throughout pregnancy, and that, therefore, the State has a compelling interest in protecting that life from and after conception. We need not resolve the difficult question of when life begins. When those trained in the respective disciplines of medicine, philosophy, and theology are unable to arrive at any consensus, the judiciary, at this point in the development of man's knowledge, is not in a position to speculate as to the answer.

It should be sufficient to note briefly the wide divergence of thinking on this most sensitive and difficult question. There has always been strong support for the view that life does not begin until live birth. This was the belief of the Stoics. It appears to be the predominant, though not the unanimous, attitude of the Jewish faith. It may be taken to represent also the position of a large segment of the Protestant community, insofar as that can be ascertained; organized groups that have taken a formal position on the abortion issue have generally regarded abortion as a matter for the conscience of the individual and her family. As we have noted, the common law found greater significance in quickening. Physicians and their scientific colleagues have regarded that event with less interest and have tended to focus either upon conception or upon live birth or upon the interim point at which the fetus becomes "viable," that is, potentially able to live outside the mother's womb, albeit with artificial aid. Viability is usually placed at about seven months (28 weeks) but may occur earlier, even at 24 weeks. The Aristotelian theory of "mediate animation," that held sway throughout the Middle Ages and the Renaissance in Europe, continued to be official Roman Catholic dogma until the 19th century, despite opposition to this "ensoulment" theory from those in the Church who would recognize the existence of life from the moment of conception. The latter is now, of course, the official belief of the Catholic Church. As one of the briefs *amicus* discloses, this is a view strongly held by many non-Catholics as well, and by many physicians. Substantial problems for precise definition of this view are posed, however, by new embryological data that purport to indicate that conception is a "process" over time, rather than an event, and by new medical techniques such as menstrual extraction, the "morning-after" pill, implantation of embryos, artificial insemination, and even artifical wombs.

In areas other than criminal abortion the law has been reluctant to endorse any theory that life, as we recognize it, begins before live birth or to accord legal rights to the unborn except in narrowly defined situations and except when the rights are contingent upon live birth. For example, the traditional rule of tort law had denied recovery for prenatal injuries even though the child was born alive. That rule has been changed in almost every jurisdiction. In most States recovery is said to be permitted only if the fetus was viable, or at least quick, when the injuries were sustained, though few courts have squarely so held. In a recent development, generally opposed by the commentators, some States permit the parents of a stillborn child to maintain an action for wrongful death because of prenatal injuries. Such an action, however, would appear to be one to vindicate the parents' interest and is thus consistent with the view that the fetus, at most, represents only the potentiality of life. Similarly, unborn children have been recognized as acquiring rights or interests by way of inheritance or other devolution of property, and have been represented by guardians *ad litem*. Perfection of the interests involved, again, has generally been contingent upon live birth. In short, the unborn have never been recognized in the law as persons in the whole sense.

In view of all this, we do not agree that, by adopting one theory of life, Texas may override the rights of the pregnant woman that are at stake. We repeat, however, that the State does have an important and legitimate interest in preserving and protecting the health of the pregnant woman, whether she be a resident of the State or a nonresident who seeks medical consultation and treatment there, and that it has still *another* important and legitimate interest in protecting the potentiality of human life. These interests are separate and distinct. Each grows in substantiality as the woman approaches term and, at a point during pregnancy, each becomes "compelling."

With respect to the State's important and legitimate interest in the health of the mother, the "compelling" point, in the light of present medical knowledge, is at approximately the end of the first trimester. This is so because of the now established medical fact, referred to above that until the end of the first trimester mortality in abortion is less than mortality in normal childbirth. It follows that, from and after this point, a State may regulate the abortion procedure to the extent that the regulation reasonably relates to the preservation and protection of maternal health. Examples of permissible state regulation in this area are requirements as to the qualifications of the person who is to perform the abortion; as to the licensure of that person; as to the facility in which the procedure is to be performed, that is, whether it must be a hospital or may be a clinic or some other place of less-than-hospital status; as to the licensing of the facility; and the like.

This means, on the other hand, that, for the period of pregnancy prior to this "compelling" point, the attending physician, in consultation with his patient, is free to determine, without regulation by the State, that in his medical judgment the patient's pregnancy should be terminated. If that decision is reached, the judgment may be effectuated by an abortion free of interference by the State.

With respect to the State's important and legitimate interest in potential life, the "compelling" point is at viability. This is so because the fetus then presumably has the capability of meaningful life outside the mother's womb. State regulation protective of fetal life after viability thus has both logical and biological justifications. If the State is interested in protecting fetal life after viability, it may go so far as to proscribe abortion during that period except when it is necessary to preserve the life or health of the mother.

Measured against these standards, the Texas Penal Code, in restricting legal abortions to those "procured or attempted by medical advice for the purpose of saving the life of the mother," sweeps too broadly. The statute makes no distinction between abortions performed early in pregnancy and those performed later, and it limits to a single reason, "saving" the mother's life, the legal justification for the procedure. The statute, therefore, cannot survive the constitutional attack made upon it here. * * *

To summarize and to repeat:

1. A state criminal abortion statute of the current Texas type, that excepts from criminality only a *life saving* procedure on behalf of the mother, without regard to pregnancy stage and without recognition of the other interests involved, is violative of the Due Process Clause of the Fourteenth Amendment.

(a) For the stage prior to approximately the end of the first trimester, the abortion decision and its effectuation must be left to the medical judgment of the pregnant woman's attending physician.

(b) For the stage subsequent to approximately the end of the first trimester, the State, in promoting its interest in the health of the mother, may, if it chooses, regulate the abortion procedure in ways that are reasonably related to maternal health.

(c) For the stage subsequent to viability the State, in promoting its interest in the potentiality of human life, may, if it chooses, regulate, and even proscribe, abortion except where it is necessary, in appropriate medical judgment, for the preservation of the life or health of the mother.

2. The State may define the term "physician" . . . to mean only a physician currently licensed by the State, and may proscribe any abortion by a person who is not a physician as so defined. * * *

[The concurring opinions of Chief Justice Burger and of Justices Douglas and Stewart are omitted.]

MR. JUSTICE REHNQUIST, dissenting.

The Court's opinion brings to the decision of this troubling question both extensive historical fact and a wealth of legal scholarship. While its opinion thus commands my respect, I find myself nonetheless in fundamental disagreement with those parts of it which invalidate the Texas statute in question, and therefore dissent.

The Court's opinion decides that a State may impose virtually no restriction on the performance of abortions during the first trimester of pregnancy. Our previous decisions indicate that a necessary predicate for such an opinion is a plaintiff who was in her first trimester of pregnancy at some time during the pendency of her law suit. While a party may vindicate his own constitutional rights, he may not seek vindication for the rights of others. . . . The Court's statement of facts in this case makes clear, however, that the record in no way indicates the presence of such a plaintiff. We know only that plaintiff Roe at the time of filing her complaint was a pregnant woman; for aught that appears in this record, she may have been in her *last* trimester of pregnancy as of the date the complaint was filed.

Nothing in the Court's opinion indicates that Texas might not constitutionally apply its proscription of abortion as written to a woman in that stage of pregnancy. Nonetheless, the Court uses her complaint against the Texas statute as a fulcrum for deciding that States may impose virtually no restrictions on medical abortions performed during the *first* trimester of pregnancy. In deciding such a hypothetical lawsuit the Court departs from the longstanding admonition that it should never "formulate a rule of constitutional law broader than is required by the precise facts to which it is to be applied." . . .

Even if there were a plaintiff in this case capable of litigating the issue which the Court decides, I would reach a conclusion opposite to that reached by the Court. I have difficulty in concluding, as the Court does, that the right of "privacy" is involved in this case. Texas by the statute here challenged bars the performance of a medical abortion by a licensed physician on a plaintiff such as Roe. A transaction resulting in an operation such as this is not "private" in the ordinary usage of that word. Nor is the "privacy" which the Court finds here even a distant relative of the freedom from searches and seizures protected by the Fourth Amendment to the Constitution which the Court has referred to as embodying a right to privacy.

. . .

If the Court means by the term "privacy" no more than that the claim of a person to be free from unwanted state regulation of consensual transactions may be a form of "liberty" protected by the Fourteenth Amendment, there is no doubt that similar claims have been upheld in our earlier decisions on the basis of that liberty. I agree with the statement of MR. JUSTICE STEWART in his concurring opinion that the "liberty," against deprivation of which without due process the Fourteenth Amendment protects, embraces more than the rights found in the Bill of Rights. But that liberty is not guaranteed absolutely against deprivation, but only against deprivation without due process of law. The test traditionally applied in the area of social and economic legislation is whether or not a law such as that challenged has a rational relation to a valid state objective. . . . The Due Process Clause of the Fourteenth Amendment undoubtedly does place a limit on legislative power to enact laws such as this, albeit a broad one. If the Texas statute were to prohibit an abortion even where the mother's life is in jeopardy, I have little doubt that such a statute would lack a rational relation to a valid state objective. . . . But the Court's sweeping invalidation of any restrictions on abortion during the first trimester is impossible to justify under that standard, and the conscious weighing of competing factors which the Court's opinion apparently substitutes for the established test is far more appropriate to a legislative judgment than to a judicial one. * * *

The fact that a majority of the States, reflecting after all the majority sentiment in those States, have had restrictions on abortions for at least a century seems to me as strong an indication there is that the asserted right to an abortion is not "so rooted in the traditions and conscience of our people as to be ranked as fundamental," . . . Even today, when society's views on abortion are changing, the very existence of the debate is evidence that the "right" to an abortion is not so universally accepted as the appellants would have us believe.

To reach its result the Court necessarily has had to find within the Scope of the Fourteenth Amendment a right that was apparently completely unknown to the drafters of the Amendment. As early as 1821, the first state law dealing directly with abortion was enacted by the Connecticut legislature. . . . By the time of the adoption of the Fourteenth Amendment in 1868 there were at least 36 laws enacted by state or territorial legislatures limiting abortion. While many States have amended or updated their laws, 21 of the laws on the books in 1868 remain in effect today. Indeed, the Texas statute struck down today was, as the majority notes, first enacted in 1857 and "has remained substantially unchanged to the present time."

There apparently was no question concerning the validity of this provision or of any of the other state statutes when the Fourteenth Amendment was adopted. The only conclusion possible from this history is that the drafters did not intend to have the Fourteenth Amendment withdraw from the States the power to legislate with respect to this matter.

Even if one were to agree that the case which the Court decides were here, and that the enunciation of the substantive constitutional law in the Court's opinion were proper, the actual disposition of the case by the Court is still difficult to justify. The Texas statute is struck down *in toto*, even though the Court apparently concedes that at later periods of pregnancy Texas might impose these selfsame statutory limitations on abortion. My understanding of past practice is that a statute found to be invalid as applied to a particular plaintiff, but not unconstitutional as a whole, is not simply "struck down" but is instead declared unconstitutional as applied to the fact situation before the Court. . . .

MR. JUSTICE WHITE, with whom MR. JUSTICE REHNQUIST joins, dissenting.

At the heart of the controversy in these cases are those recurring pregnancies that pose no danger whatsoever to the life or health of the mother but are nevertheless unwanted for any one or more of a variety of reasons—convenience, family planning, economics, dislike of children, the embarrassment of illegitimacy, etc., The common claim before us is that for any one of such reasons, or for no reason at all, and without asserting or claiming any threat to life or health, any woman is entitled to an abortion at her request if she is able to find a medical advisor willing to undertake the procedure.

The Court for the most part sustains this position: During the period prior to the time the fetus becomes viable, the Constitution of the United States values the convenience, whim or caprice of the putative mother more than the life or potential life of the fetus; the Constitution, therefore, guarantees the right to an abortion as against any state law or policy seeking to protect the fetus from an abortion not prompted by more compelling reasons of the mother.

With all due respect, I dissent. I find nothing in the language or history of the Constitution to support the Court's judgment. The Court simply fashions and announces a new constitutional right for pregnant mothers and, with scarcely any reason or authority for its action, invests that right with sufficient substance to override most existing state abortion statutes. The upshot is that the people and the legislatures of the 50 States are constitutionally disentitled to weigh the relative importance of the continued existence and development of the fetus on the one hand against a spectrum of possible impacts on the mother on the other hand. As an exercise of raw judicial power, the Court perhaps has authority to do what it does today; but in my view its judgment is an improvident and extravagant exercise of the power of judicial review which the Constitution extends to this Court.

The Court apparently values the convenience of the pregnant mother more than the continued existence and development of the life or potential life which she carries. Whether or not I might agree with that marshalling of values, I can in no event join the Court's judgment because I find no constitutional warrant for imposing such an order of priorities on the people and legislatures of the States. In a sensitive area such as this, involving as it does issues over which reasonable men may easily and heatedly differ, I cannot accept the Court's exercise of its clear power of choice by interposing a constitutional barrier to state efforts to protect human life and by investing mothers and doctors with the constitutionally protected right to exterminate it. This issue, for the most part, should be left with the people and to the political processes the people have devised to govern their affairs.

It is my view, therefore, that the Texas statute is not constitutionally infirm because it denies abortions to those who seek to serve only their convenience rather than to protect their life or health. Nor is this plaintiff, who claims no threat to her mental or physical health, entitled to assert the possible rights of those women whose pregnancy assertedly implicates their health. . . .

NOTE

In the companion case of Doe v. Bolton, 410 U.S. 179, 93 S.Ct. 739, not only did a majority of the court re-affirm what had been decided in *Roe* but it also declared unconstitutional a 1968 Georgia "therapeutic abortion" statute because the Court found invalid certain conditions that were attached to the performance of the abortions authorized by the statute. The conditions prescribed in the statute were: (1) that the abortion be performed in a hospital accredited by a "Joint Commission on Accreditation of Hospitals"; (2) that the procedure be approved by the hospital staff abortion committee; (3) that the performing physician's judgment be confirmed by the independent examination of two other licensed physicians; and (4) that the woman be a resident of Georgia. The Court found (1) objectionable because Georgia placed no restriction on the performance of nonabortion surgery in hospitals without the commission's accreditation, and there was no showing that there was a particular need for it in abortion cases; (2) was "unduly restrictive of the patient's rights and needs"; (3) had no rational connection with a patient's needs and unduly infringed upon the physician's right to practice; and (4) was not based upon any policy of preserving state-supported facilities for Georgia's residents, since the restriction also applied to private hospitals and to privately retained physicians.

E. THE RIGHT TO BEAR ARMS

UNITED STATES v. MILLER

Supreme Court of the United States, 1939.
307 U.S. 174, 59 S.Ct. 816.

MR. JUSTICE MCREYNOLDS delivered the opinion of the Court.

An indictment in the District Court Western District Arkansas, charged that Jack Miller and Frank Layton "did unlawfully, knowingly, wilfully, and feloniously transport in interstate commerce from the town of Claremore in the State of Oklahoma to the town of Siloam Springs in the State of Arkansas a certain firearm, to-wit, a double barrel 12-gauge Stevens shotgun having a barrel less than 18 inches in length, bearing identification number 76230, said defendants, at the time of so transporting said firearm in interstate commerce as aforesaid, not having registered said firearm as required by Section 1132d of Title 26, United States Code . . . and not having in their possession a stamp-affixed written order for said firearm as provided by Section 1132c, Title 26, United States Code . . . and the regulations issued under authority of the said Act of Congress known as the 'National Firearms Act' approved June 26, 1934, contrary to the form of the statute in such case made and provided, and against the peace and dignity of the United States."

A duly interposed demurrer alleged: The National Firearms Act . . . offends the inhibition of the Second Amendment to the Constitution—"A well regulated Militia, being necessary to the security of a free State, the right of people to keep and bear Arms, shall not be infringed."

The District Court held that section eleven of the Act violates the Second Amendment. It accordingly sustained the demurrer and quashed the indictment.

The cause is here by direct appeal. * * *

In the absence of any evidence tending to show that possession or use of a "shotgun having a barrel of less than eighteen inches in length" at this time has some reasonable relationship to the preservation or efficiency of a well regulated militia, we cannot say that the Second Amendment guarantees the right to keep and bear such an instrument. Certainly it is not within judicial notice that this weapon is any part of the ordinary military equipment or that its use could contribute to the common defense. . . .

The Constitution as originally adopted granted to the Congress power—"To provide for calling forth the Militia to execute the Laws of the Union, suppress Insurrections and repel Invasions; To provide for organizing, arming, and disciplining, the Militia, and for governing such Part of them as may be employed in the Service of the United States, reserving to the States respectively, the Appointment of the Officers, and the Authority of training the Militia according to the discipline prescribed by Congress." With obvious purpose to assure the continuation and render possible the effectiveness of such forces the declaration and guarantee of the Second Amendment were made. It must be interpreted and applied with that end in view.

The Militia which the States were expected to maintain and train is set in contrast with Troops which they were forbidden to keep without the consent of Congress. The sentiment of the time strongly disfavored standing armies; the common view was that adequate defense of country and laws could be secured through the Militia—civilians primarily, soldiers on occasion.

The signification attributed to the term Militia appears from the debates in the Convention, the history and legislation of Colonies and States, and the writings of approved commentators. These show plainly enough that the Militia comprised all males physically capable of acting in concert for the common defense. "A body of citizens enrolled for military discipline." And further, that ordinarily when called for service these men were expected to appear bearing arms supplied by themselves and of the kind in common use at the time.

Blackstone's Commentaries, Vol. 2, Ch. 13, p. 409 points out "that king Alfred first settled a national militia in this kingdom," and traces the subsequent development and use of such forces.

Adam Smith's Wealth of Nations, Book V, Ch. 1, contains an extended account of the Militia. It is there said: "Men of republican principles have been jealous of a standing army as dangerous to liberty." "In a militia, the character of the labourer, artificer, or tradesman, predominates over that of the soldier: in a standing army, that of the soldier predominates over every other character; and in this distinction seems to consist the essential difference between those two different species of military force."

"The American Colonies In The 17th Century," Osgood, Vol. 1, ch. XIII, affirms in reference to the early system of defense in New England—

"In all the colonies, as in England, the militia system was based on the principle of the assize of arms. This implied the general obligation of all adult male inhabitants to possess arms, and, with certain exceptions, to cooperate in the work of defence." "The possession of arms also implied the possession of ammunition, and the authorities paid quite as much attention to the latter as to the former." "A year later [1632] it was ordered that any single man who had not furnished himself with arms might be put out to service, and this became a permanent part of the legislation of the colony [Massachusetts]."

Also "Clauses intended to insure the possession of arms and ammunition by all who were subject to military service appear in all the important enactments concerning military affairs. Fines were the penalty for delinquency, whether of towns or individuals. According to the usage of the times, the infantry of Massachusetts consisted of pikemen and musketeers. The law, as enacted in 1649 and thereafter, provided that each of the former should be armed with a pike, corselet, head-piece, sword, and knapsack. The musketeer should carry a 'good fixed musket,' not under bastard musket bore, not less than three feet, nine inches, nor more than four feet three inches in length, a priming wire, scourer, and mould, a sword, rest, bandoleers, one pound of powder, twenty bullets, and two fathoms of match. The law also required that two-thirds of each company should be musketeers." * * *

Most if not all of the States have adopted provisions touching the right to keep and bear arms. Differences in the language employed in these have naturally led to somewhat variant conclusions concerning the scope of the right guaranteed. But none of them seem to afford any material support for the challenged ruling of the court below. * * *

We are unable to accept the conclusion of the court below and the challenged judgment must be reversed. The cause will be remanded for further proceedings.

MR. JUSTICE DOUGLAS took no part in the consideration or decision of this cause.

NOTES

1. For an interesting article on this Second Amendment right, see Sprecher, The Lost Amendment, 51 A.B.A.J. 554, 665 (1965), in which the author suggests that the spirit of the 2nd Amendment should be preserved. He added: "We have come to rely so heavily on the law that often we are helpless in the face of those who operate outside the law . . . We should find the lost Second Amendment and determine that it affords the right to arm a state militia and also the right of the individual to keep and bear arms".

2. Legislation controlling the use of weapons has long been a source of litigation interpreting the scope and meaning of the Second Amendment. In 1840 the Arkansas Supreme Court, in State v. Buzzard, 4 Ark. 18, at 27, said of a concealed weapons statute:

> "The act in question does not . . . detract any thing from the power of the people to defend their free state and the established institutions of the country. It inhibits only the bearing of certain arms concealed. This is simply a regulation as to the manner of bearing such arms as are specified".

Jurisdictions with very strict legislation governing the possession and use of firearms and other weapons have successfully prosecuted individuals carrying concealed weapons—even on their own property. People ex rel. Darling v. Warden of City Prison, 154 App.Div. 413, 139 N.Y.S. 277 (1913). The broad application of concealed weapons statutes can be seen in the case of People v. Wilmot, 18 App.Div.2d 695, 236 N.Y.S.2d 11 (1962). In that case appellant sought the reversal of his conviction for carrying a concealed paintbrush. His efforts were successful, the court having considered that it was not surprising that a painter on his way home from work should be carrying a paintbrush.

3. Legislation has been upheld which outlaws the interstate sale of weapons by unlicensed persons, United States v. Kraase, 340 F.Supp. 147 (E.D.Wis.1972), and also a law prohibiting convicted felons from possessing firearms, United States v. Synnes, 438 F.2d 764 (8th Cir. 1971).

4. As regards the adding of handguns to the classes of weapons and destructive devices which are prohibited from general possession, consider Justice Douglas' words in his dissenting opinion in Adams v. Williams, 407 U.S. 143, 92 S.Ct. 1921 at 1925 (1972):

> "There is no reason why all pistols should not be barred to everyone except the police".

F. THE SELF-INCRIMINATION PRIVILEGE

SECTION 1. THE PHYSICAL EVIDENCE—COMMUNICATION DELINEATION

SCHMERBER v. CALIFORNIA

Supreme Court of the United States, 1966.
384 U.S. 757, 86 S.Ct. 1826.

MR. JUSTICE BRENNAN delivered the opinion of the Court.

Petitioner was convicted in Los Angeles Municipal Court of the criminal offense of driving an automobile while under the influence of intoxicating liquor. He had been arrested at a hospital while receiving treatment for injuries suffered in an accident involving the automobile that he had apparently been driving. At the direction of a police officer, a blood sample was then withdrawn from petitioner's body by a physician at the hospital. The chemical analysis of this sample revealed a percent by weight of alcohol in his blood at the time of the offense which indicated intoxication, and the report of this analysis was admitted in evidence at the trial. Petitioner objected to receipt of this evidence of the analysis on the ground that the blood had been withdrawn despite his refusal, on the advice of his counsel, to consent to the test. He contended that in that circumstance the withdrawal of the blood and the admission of the analysis in evidence denied him due process of law under the Fourteenth Amendment, as well as specific guarantees of the Bill of Rights secured against the States by that Amendment; his privilege against self-incrimination under the Fifth Amendment; his right to counsel under the Sixth Amendment; and his right not to be subjected to unreasonable searches and seizures in violation of the Fourth Amendment. The Appellate Department of the California Superior Court rejected these contentions and affirmed the conviction. In view of constitutional decisions since we last considered these issues we granted certiorari. We affirm.

[Only the self-incrimination portion of the case is included herein.]

[Breithaupt v. Abram, 352 U.S. 432, 77 S.Ct. 408 (1957)] summarily rejected an argument that the withdrawal of blood and the admission of the analysis report involved in that state case violated the Fifth Amendment privilege of any person not to "be compelled in any criminal case to be a witness against himself." Citing Twining v. State of New Jersey, 211 U.S. 78, 29 S.Ct. 14 (1964). But that case, holding that the protections of the Fourteenth Amendment do not embrace this Fifth Amendment privilege, has been succeeded by Malloy v. Hogan, 378 U.S. 1, 8, 84 S.Ct. 1489, 1493. We there held that "[t]he Fourteenth Amendment secures against state invasion the same privilege that the Fifth Amendment guarantees against federal infringement—the right of a person to remain silent unless he chooses to speak in the unfettered exercise of his own will, and to suffer no penalty . . . for such silence." We therefore must now decide whether the withdrawal of the blood and admission in evidence of the analysis involved in this case violated petitioner's privilege. We hold that the privilege protects an accused only from being compelled to testify against himself, or otherwise provide the State with evidence of a testimonial or communicative nature,[1] and that the withdrawal of blood and use of the analysis in question in this case did not involve compulsion to these ends.

It could not be denied that in requiring petitioner to submit to the withdrawal and chemical analysis of his blood the State compelled him to submit to an attempt to discover evidence that might be used to prosecute him for a criminal offense. He submitted only after the police officer rejected his objection and directed the physician to proceed. The officer's direction to the physician to administer the test over petitioner's objection constituted compulsion for the purposes

1. A dissent suggests that the report of the blood test was "testimonial" or "communicative," because the test was performed in order to obtain the testimony of others, communicating to the jury facts about petitioner's condition. Of course, all evidence received in court is "testimonial" or "communicative" if these words are thus used. But the Fifth Amendment relates only to acts on the part of the person to whom the the privilege applies, and we use these words subject to the same limitations. A nod or headshake is as much a "testimonial" or "communicative" act in this sense as are spoken words. But the terms as we use them do not apply to evidence of acts noncommunicative in nature as to the person asserting the privilege, even though, as here, such acts are compelled to obtain the testimony of others.

of the privilege. The critical question, then, is whether petitioner was thus compelled "to be a witness against himself." [2]

If the scope of the privilege coincided with the complex of values it helps to protect, we might be obliged to conclude that the privilege was violated. In Miranda v. Arizona . . . [1966], the Court said of the interests protected by the privilege: "All these policies point to one overriding thought: the constitutional foundation underlying the privilege is the respect a government—state or federal—must accord to the dignity and integrity of its citizens. To maintain a 'fair state-individual balance,' to require the government 'to shoulder the entire load,' . . . to respect the inviolability of the human personality, our accusatory system of criminal justice demands that the government seeking to punish an individual produce the evidence against him by its own independent labors, rather than by the cruel, simple expedient of compelling it from his own mouth." The withdrawal of blood necessarily involves puncturing the skin for extraction, and the percent by weight of alcohol in that blood, as established by chemical analysis, is evidence of criminal guilt. Compelled submission fails on one view to respect the "inviolability of the human personality." Moreover, since it enables the State to rely on evidence forced from the accused, the compulsion violates at least one meaning of the requirement that the State procure the evidence against an accused "by its own independent labors."

As the passage in *Miranda* implicitly recognizes, however, the privilege has never been given the full scope which the values it helps to protect suggest. History and a long line of authorities in lower courts have consistently limited its protection to situations in which the State seeks to submerge those values by obtaining the evidence against an accused through "the cruel, simple expedient of compelling it from his own mouth. . . . In sum, the privilege is fulfilled only when the person is guaranteed the right 'to remain silent unless he chooses to speak in the unfettered exercise of his own will.'" The leading case in this Court is Holt v. United States, 218 U.S. 245, 31 S.Ct. 2. There the question was whether evidence was admissible that the accused, prior to trial and over his protest, put on a blouse that fitted him. It was contended that compelling the accused to submit to the demand that he model the blouse violated the privilege. Mr. Justice Holmes, speaking for the Court, rejected the argument as "based upon an extravagant extension of the 5th Amendment," and went on to say: "[T]he prohibition of compelling a man in a criminal court to be witness against himself is a prohibition of the use of physi-

2. Many state constitutions, including those of most of the original Colonies, phrase the privilege in terms of compelling a person to give "evidence" against himself. But our decision cannot turn on the Fifth Amendment's use of the word "witness." "[A]s the manifest purpose of the constitutional provisions, both of the states and of the United States, is to prohibit the compelling of testimony of a self-incriminating kind from a party or a witness, the liberal construction which must be placed upon constitutional provisions for the protection of personal rights would seem to require that the constitutional guaranties, however differently worded, should have as far as possible the same interpretation . . . ." Counselman

cal or moral compulsion to extort communications from him, not an exclusion of his body as evidence when it may be material. The objection in principle would forbid a jury to look at a prisoner and compare his features with a photograph in proof." [3]

It is clear that the protection of the privilege reaches an accused's communications, whatever form they might take, and the compulsion of responses which are also communications, for example, compliance with a subpoena to produce one's papers. Boyd v. United States, 116 U.S. 616, 6 S.Ct. 524. On the other hand, both federal and state courts have usually held that it offers no protection against compulsion to submit to fingerprinting, photographing, or measurements, to write or speak for identification, to appear in court, to stand, to assume a stance, to walk, or to make a particular gesture. The distinction which has emerged, often expressed in different ways, is that the privilege is a bar against compelling "communications" or "testimony," but that compulsion which makes a suspect or accused the source of "real or physical evidence" does not violate it.

Although we agree that this distinction is a helpful framework for analysis, we are not to be understood to agree with past applications in all instances. There will be many cases in which such a distinction is not readily drawn. Some tests seemingly directed to obtain "physical evidence," for example, lie detector tests measuring changes in body function during interrogation, may actually be directed to eliciting responses which are essentially testimonial. To compel a person to submit to testing in which an effort will be made to determine his guilt or innocence on the basis of physiological responses, whether willed or not, is to evoke the spirit and history of the Fifth Amendment. Such situations call to mind the principle that the protection of the privilege "is as broad as the mischief against which it seeks to guard." Counselman v. Hitchcock, 142 U.S. 547, 562.

In the present case, however, no such problem of application is presented. Not even a shadow of testimonial compulsion upon or enforced communication by the accused was involved either in the extraction or in the chemical analysis. Petitioner's testimonial capacities were in no way implicated; indeed, his participation, except as a donor, was irrelevant to the results of the test, which depend on chemical analysis and on that alone.[4] Since the blood test evidence,

v. Hitchcock, 142 U.S. 547, 584–585, 12 S.Ct. 195, 206. 8 Wigmore, Evidence § 2252 (McNaughton rev. 1961).

3. Compare Wigmore's view, "that the privilege is limited to testimonial disclosures. It was directed at the employment of legal process to *extract from the person's own lips* an admission of guilt, which would thus take the place of other evidence." 8 Wigmore, Evidence § 2263 (McNaughton rev. 1961). California adopted the Wigmore formulation. Our holding today, however, is not to be understood as adopting the Wigmore formulation.

4. This conclusion would not necessarily govern had the State tried to show that the accused had incriminated himself when told that he would have to be tested. Such incriminating evidence may be an unavoidable byproduct of the compulsion to take the test, especially for an individual who fears the extraction or opposes it on religious grounds. If it wishes to compel persons to submit to such attempts to discover evidence, the State may have to forego the advan-

although an incriminating product of compulsion, was neither petitioner's testimony nor evidence relating to some communicative act or writing by the petitioner, it was not inadmissible on privilege grounds.

* * *

[The concurring opinion of Justices Harlan and Stewart is omitted.]

MR. JUSTICE BLACK with whom MR. JUSTICE DOUGLAS joins, dissenting.

I would reverse petitioner's conviction. I agree with the Court that the Fourteenth Amendment made applicable to the States the Fifth Amendment's provision that "No person . . . shall be compelled in any criminal case to be a witness against himself . . . ." But I disagree with the Court's holding that California did not violate petitioner's constitutional right against self-incrimination when it compelled him, against his will, to allow a doctor to puncture his blood vessels in order to extract a sample of blood and analyze it for alcoholic content, and then used that analysis as evidence to convict petitioner of a crime.

The Court admits that "the State compelled [petitioner] to submit to an attempt to discover evidence [in his blood] that might be [and was] used to prosecute him for a criminal offense." To reach the conclusion that compelling a person to give his blood to help the State convict him is not equivalent to compelling him to be a witness against himself strikes me as quite an extraordinary feat. The Court, however, overcomes what had seemed to me to be an insuperable obstacle to its conclusion by holding that

> ". . . the privilege protects an accused only from being compelled to testify against himself, or otherwise provide the State with evidence of a testimonial or communicative nature, and that the withdrawal of blood and use of the analysis in question in this case did not involve compulsion to these ends."

I cannot agree that this distinction and reasoning of the Court justify denying petitioner his Bill of Rights' guarantee that he must not be compelled to be a witness against himself.

In the first place it seems to me that the compulsory extraction of petitioner's blood for analysis so that the person who analyzed it could give evidence to convict him had both a "testimonial" and a

tage of any *testimonial* products of administering the test—products which would fall within the privilege. Indeed, there may be circumstances in which the pain, danger, or severity of an operation would almost inevitably cause a person to prefer confession to undergoing the "search," and nothing we say today should be taken as establishing the permissibility of compulsion in that case. But no such situation is presented in this case. . . .

"communicative nature." The sole purpose of this project which proved to be successful was to obtain "testimony" from some person to prove that petitioner had alcohol in his blood at the time he was arrested. And the purpose of the project was certainly "communicative" in that the analysis of the blood was to supply information to enable a witness to communicate to the court and jury that petitioner was more or less drunk.

I think it unfortunate that the Court rests so heavily for its very restrictive reading of the Fifth Amendment's privilege against self-incrimination on the words "testimonial" and "communicative." These words are not models of clarity and precision as the Court's rather labored explication shows. Nor can the Court, so far as I know, find precedent in the former opinions of this Court for using these particular words to limit the scope of the Fifth Amendment's protection. There is a scholarly precedent, however, in the late Professor Wigmore's learned treatise on evidence. He used "testimonial" which, according to the latest edition of his treatise . . . means "communicative" . . . as a key word in his vigorous and extensive campaign designed to keep the privilege against self-incrimination "within limits the strictest possible." 8 Wigmore, Evidence § 2251 (3d ed. 1940), p. 318. Though my admiration for Professor Wigmore's scholarship is great, I regret to see the word he used to narrow the Fifth Amendment's protection play such a major part in any of this Court's opinions.

I am happy that the Court itself refuses to follow Professor Wigmore's implication that the Fifth Amendment goes no further than to bar the use of forced self-incriminating statements coming from a "person's own lips." It concedes, as it must so long as Boyd v. United States, stands, that the Fifth Amendment bars a State from compelling a person to produce papers he has that might tend to incriminate him. It is a strange hierarchy of values that allows the State to extract a human being's blood to convict him of a crime because of the blood's content but proscribes compelled production of his lifeless papers. Certainly there could be few papers that would have any more "testimonial" value to convict a man of drunken driving than would an analysis of the alcoholic content of a human being's blood introduced in evidence at a trial for driving while under the influence of alcohol. In such a situation blood, of course, is not oral testimony given by an accused but it can certainly "communicate" to a court and jury the fact of guilt.

The Court itself expresses its own doubts, if not fears, of its own shadowy distinction between compelling "physical evidence" like blood which it holds does not amount to compelled self-incrimination, and "eliciting responses which are essentially testimonial." And in explanation of its fears the Court goes on to warn that

> "To compel a person to submit to testing [by lie detectors for example] in which an effort will be made to determine his guilt or innocence on the basis of physiological responses,

> whether willed or not, is to evoke the spirit and history of the Fifth Amendment. Such situations call to mind the principle that the protection of the privilege 'is as broad as the mischief against which it seeks to guard.' Counselman v. Hitchcock."

A basic error in the Court's holding and opinion is its failure to give the Fifth Amendment's protection against compulsory self-incrimination the broad and liberal construction that *Counselman* and other opinions of this Court have declared it ought to have.

The liberal construction given the Bill of Rights' guarantee in Boyd v. United States, supra, which Professor Wigmore criticized severely, . . . makes that one among the greatest constitutional decisions of this Court. In that case all the members of the Court decided that civil suits for penalties and forfeitures incurred for commission of offenses against the law,

> ". . . are within the reason of criminal proceedings for all the purposes of . . . that portion of the fifth amendment which declares that no person shall be compelled in any criminal case to be a witness against himself; . . . within the meaning of the fifth amendment to the constitution . . ."

Obviously the Court's interpretation was not completely supported by the literal language of the Fifth Amendment. Recognizing this, the Court announced a rule of constitutional interpretation that has been generally followed ever since, particularly in judicial construction of Bill of Rights guarantees:

> "A close and literal construction [of constitutional provisions for the security of persons and property] deprives them of half their efficacy, and leads to gradual depreciation of the right, as if it consisted more in sound than in substance. It is the duty of courts to be watchful for the constitutional rights of the citizen, and against any stealthy encroachments thereon."

The Court went on to say . . . that to require "an owner to produce his private books and papers, in order to prove his breach of the laws, and thus to establish the forfeiture of his property, is surely compelling him to furnish evidence against himself." The Court today departs from the teachings of *Boyd*. Petitioner Schmerber has undoubtedly been compelled to give his blood "to furnish evidence against himself," yet the Court holds that this is not forbidden by the Fifth Amendment. With all deference I must say that the Court here gives the Bill of Rights' safeguard against compulsory self-incrimination a construction that would generally be considered too narrow and technical even in the interpretation of an ordinary commercial contract.

The Court apparently, for a reason I cannot understand, finds some comfort for its narrow construction of the Fifth Amendment in this Court's decision in Miranda v. Arizona. I find nothing whatever in the majority opinion in that case which either directly or indirectly supports the holding in this case. In fact I think the interpretive constitutional philosophy used in *Miranda*, unlike that used in this case, gives the Fifth Amendment's prohibition against compelled self-incrimination a broad and liberal construction in line with the wholesome admonitions in the *Boyd* case. The closing sentence in the Fifth Amendment section of the Court's opinion in the present case is enough by itself, I think, to expose the unsoundness of what the Court here holds. That sentence reads:

> "Since the blood test evidence, although an incriminating product of compulsion, was neither petitioner's testimony nor evidence relating to some communicative act or writing by the petitioner, it was not inadmissible on privilege grounds."

How can it reasonably be doubted that the blood test evidence was not in all respects the actual equivalent of "testimony" taken from petitioner when the result of the test was offered as testimony, was considered by the jury as testimony, and the jury's verdict of guilt rests in part on that testimony? The refined, subtle reasoning and balancing process used here to narrow the scope of the Bill of Rights' safeguard against self-incrimination provides a handy instrument for further narrowing of that constitutional protection, as well as others, in the future. Believing with the Framers that these constitutional safeguards broadly construed by independent tribunals of justice provide our best hope for keeping our people free from governmental oppression, I deeply regret the Court's holding. . . .

[The separate dissenting opinion of Justice Douglas and the one by Justice Fortas are omitted.]

NOTES

1. Consider the following alternative to the procedure utilized by the police in *Schmerber*—a provision of the Uniform Vehicle Code, prepared by the National Commission on Uniform Traffic Laws and Ordinances, as revised in 1968, and by Supplement I, 1972:

§ 6–205.1—Revocation of license for refusal to submit to chemical tests [generally known as the "implied consent law"].

(a) Any person who operates a motor vehicle upon the highways of this State shall be deemed to have given consent, subject to the provisions of § 11–902.1, to a chemical test or tests of his blood, breath, or urine for the purpose of determining the alcoholic or drug content of his blood if arrested for any offense arising out of acts alleged to have been committed while the person was driving or in actual physical control of a motor vehicle while under the influence of alcohol or any drugs. The test or tests shall be administered at the direction of a law enforcement officer having reasonable grounds to believe the person to have been driving or in actual physical control of a motor vehicle upon the highways of this State while under the influence of alcohol or any drugs. The law enforcement agency by which such officer is employed shall designate which of the aforesaid tests shall be administered.

(b) Any person who is dead, unconscious or who is otherwise in a condition rendering him incapable of refusal, shall be deemed not to have withdrawn the consent provided by paragraph (a) of this section and the test or tests may be administered subject to the provisions of § 11-902.1.

(c) If a person under arrest refuses upon the request of a law enforcement officer to submit to a chemical test designated by the law enforcement agency as provided in paragraph (a) of this section, none shall be given, but the department, upon the receipt of a sworn report of the law enforcement officer that he had reasonable grounds to believe the arrested person had been driving or was in actual physical control of a motor vehicle upon the highways of this State while under the influence of alcohol or any drug and that the person had refused to submit to the test upon the request of the law enforcement officer, shall revoke his license subject to review as hereinafter provided.

(d) Upon revoking the license, as hereinbefore in this section directed, the department shall immediately notify the person in writing and upon his request shall afford him an opportunity for a hearing in the same manner and under the same conditions as is provided in § 6-206(c) for notification and hearings in the cases of discretionary suspension of licenses, except that the scope of such a hearing for the purposes of this section shall cover the issues of whether a law enforcement officer had reasonable grounds to believe the person had been driving or was in actual physical control of a motor vehicle upon the highways of this State while under the influence of alcohol or any drug, whether the person was placed under arrest, and whether he refused to submit to the test upon request of the officer. Whether the person was informed that his privilege to drive would be revoked if he refused to submit to the test shall not be an issue. The department shall order that the revocation either be rescinded or sustained.

(e) If the revocation is sustained after such a hearing, the person whose license has been revoked, under the provisions of this section, shall have the right to file a petition in the appropriate court to review the final order of revocation by the department.

2. Where a driver has refused to submit to a chemical test for intoxication, a number of jurisdictions, either by statute or by decision law, permit comment to be made upon that fact at the trial. See Campbell v. Superior Court, 106 Ariz. 542, 479 P.2d 685 (1971), and the cases from other states cited therein. The physical characteristic of the test distinguishes such a holding from that of the United States Supreme Court in Griffin v. California, 380 U.S. 609, 85 S.Ct. 1229 (1965), prohibiting prosecutorial comment on the defendant's failure to *testify*. For the viewpoint contrary to the above Arizona case, and for the law that prevails in the various jurisdictions, consult 87 A.L.R.2d 370.

3. For an excellent analysis of the cases involving "strip" searching, retrieving objects from body cavities, and obtaining body fluid or breath for analysis in drunk driving cases, consult McIntyre and Chabraja, The Intensive Search of a Suspect's Body and Clothing, 58 J.Crim.L., C. & P.S. 18 (1967).

SECTION 2. LIMITATIONS UPON COMPELLED COMMUNICATIONS

CALIFORNIA v. BYERS

Supreme Court of the United States, 1971.
402 U.S. 424, 91 S.Ct. 1535.

MR. CHIEF JUSTICE BURGER announced the judgment of the Court and an opinion in which MR. JUSTICE STEWART, MR. JUSTICE WHITE, and MR. JUSTICE BLACKMUN join.

This case presents the narrow but important question of whether the constitutional privilege against compulsory self-incrimination is infringed by California's so-called "hit and run" statute which requires the driver of a motor vehicle involved in an accident to stop at the scene and give his name and address. Similar "hit and run" or "stop and report" statutes are in effect in all 50 States and the District of Columbia.

* * *

Section 20002(a)(1) of the California Vehicle Code provides:

> "The driver of any vehicle involved in an accident resulting in damage to any property including vehicles shall immediately stop the vehicle at the scene of the accident and shall then and there * * * [l]ocate and notify the owner or person in charge of such property of the name and address of the driver and owner of the vehicle involved * * *."[1]

Byers demurred on the ground that it violated his privilege against compulsory self-incrimination. His demurrer was ultimately sustained by the California Supreme Court. That court held that the privilege protected a driver who "reasonably believes that compliance with the statute will result in self-incrimination." Here the court found that Byers' apprehensions were reasonable because compliance with § 20002(a)(1) confronted him with "substantial hazards of self-incrimination." Nevertheless the court upheld the validity of the statute by inserting a judicially-created use restriction on the disclosures which it required. [Editors' note: What the California court held and said was that the compelled disclosures and the fruits of such disclosures may not be used in a criminal prosecution

1. As an alternative § 20002(a)(2) requires that the driver shall "[l]eave in a conspicuous place on the vehicle or other property damaged a written notice giving the name and address of the driver and of the owner of the vehicle involved and a statement of the circumstances thereof and shall without unnecessary delay notify the police department * * *."

The California Supreme Court did not pass upon this part of the statute, and we express no opinion as to its validity. The violation of either part of the statute leaves the driver liable to imprisonment for up to six months or to a fine of up to $500.

The California Vehicle Code also requires drivers involved in accidents resulting in personal injury or death to file accident reports, but there is a statutory use restriction for these compelled disclosures. §§ 20012–20013.

relating to the accident.] The court concluded, however, that it would be "unfair" to punish Byers for his failure to comply with the statute because he could not reasonably have anticipated the judicial promulgation of the use restriction.[2] We granted certiorari, to assess the validity of the California Supreme Court's premise that without a use restriction § 20002(a)(1) would violate the privilege against compulsory self-incrimination. We conclude that there is no conflict between the statute and the privilege.

(1)

Whenever the Court is confronted with the question of a compelled disclosure that has an incriminating potential, the judicial scrutiny is invariably a close one. Tension between the State's demand for disclosures and the protection of the right against self-incrimination are likely to give rise to serious questions. Inevitably these must be resolved in terms of balancing the public need on the one hand, and the individual claim to constitutional protections on the other; neither interest can be treated lightly.

An organized society imposes many burdens on its constituents. It commands the filing of tax returns for income; it requires producers and distributors of consumer goods to file informational reports on the manufacturing process and the content of products, on the wages, hours, and working conditions of employees. Those who borrow money on the public market or issue securities for sale to the public must file various information reports; industries must report periodically the volume and content of pollutants discharged into our waters and atmosphere. Comparable examples are legion.

In each of these situations there is some possibility of prosecution—often a very real one—for criminal offenses disclosed by or deriving from the information which the law compels a person to supply. Information revealed by these reports could well be "a link in a chain" of evidence leading to prosecution and conviction. But under our holdings the mere possibility of incrimination is insufficient to defeat the strong policies in favor of a disclosure called for by statutes like the one challenged here.

United States v. Sullivan, 274 U.S. 259, 47 S.Ct. 607 (1927), shows that an application of the privilege to the California statute is not warranted. There a bootlegger was prosecuted for failure to file an income tax return. He claimed that the privilege against compulsory self-incrimination afforded him a complete defense because filing a return would have tended to incriminate him by revealing the unlawful source of his income. Speaking for the Court,

2. Presumably the California holding contemplated that persons who fail to comply with the statute in the future will be subject to prosecution and conviction since the use restriction removed the justification for a reasonable apprehension of self-incrimination. Our disposition removes the premise upon which the use restriction rested.

Mr. Justice Holmes rejected this claim on the ground that it amounted to "an extreme if not an extravagant application of the Fifth Amendment." at 607.[3] Sullivan's tax return, of course, increased his risk of prosecution and conviction for violation of the National Prohibition Act. But the Court had no difficulty in concluding that an extension of the privilege to cover that kind of mandatory report would have been unjustified. In order to invoke the privilege it is necessary to show that the compelled disclosures will themselves confront the claimant with "substantial hazards of self-incrimination."

The components of this requirement were articulated in Albertson v. SACB . . . (1965), and later in Marchetti v. United States (1968), Grosso v. United States . . . (1968), and Haynes v. United States . . . (1968). In *Albertson* the Court held that an order requiring registration by individual members of a Communist organization violated the privilege. There *Sullivan* was distinguished:

> "In *Sullivan* the questions in the income tax return were neutral on their face and directed at the public at large, but here they are directed at a *highly selective group inherently suspect of criminal activities.* Petitioners' claims are not asserted in an *essentially noncriminal* and *regulatory area* of inquiry, but against an inquiry in an area permeated with criminal statutes, where response to any of the * * * questions in context might involve the petitioners in the admission of a crucial element of a crime." (emphasis added).

Albertson was followed by *Marchetti* and *Grosso* where the Court held that the privilege afforded a complete defense to prosecutions for noncompliance with federal gambling tax and registration requirements. It was also followed in *Haynes* where petitioner had been prosecuted for failure to register a firearm as required by federal statute. In each of these cases the Court found that compliance with the statutory disclosure requirements would confront the petitioner with "substantial hazards of self-incrimination." . . .

In all of these cases the disclosures condemned were only those extracted from a "highly selective group inherently suspect of criminal activities" and the privilege was applied only in "an area permeated with criminal statutes"—not in "an essentially noncriminal and regulatory area of inquiry." . . .

Although the California Vehicle Code defines some criminal offenses, the statute is essentially regulatory, not criminal. The Cali-

3. "As the defendant's income was taxed, the statute of course required a return. * * * In the decision that this was contrary to the Constitution we are of opinion that the protection of the Fifth Amendment was pressed too far. If the form of return provided called for answers that the defendant was privileged from making he could have raised the objection in the return, *but could not on that account refuse to make any return at all.*" (emphasis added).

fornia Supreme Court noted that § 20002(a)(1) was not intended to facilitate criminal convictions but to promote the satisfaction of civil liabilities arising from automobile accidents. In *Marchetti* the Court rested on the reality that almost everything connected with gambling is illegal under "comprehensive" state and federal statutory schemes. The Court noted that in almost every conceivable situation compliance with the statutory gambling requirements would have been incriminating. Largely because of these pervasive criminal prohibitions, gamblers were considered by the Court to be "a highly selective group inherently suspect of criminal activities."

In contrast, § 20002(a)(1), like income tax laws, is directed at all persons—here all persons who drive automobiles in California. This group, numbering as it does in the millions, is so large as to render § 20002(a)(1) a statute "directed at the public at large." . . . It is difficult to consider this group as either "highly selective" or "inherently suspect of criminal activities." Driving an automobile, unlike gambling, is a lawful activity. Moreover, it is not a criminal offense under California law to be a driver "involved in an accident." An accident may be the fault of others; it may occur without any driver having been at fault. No empirical data is suggested in support of the conclusion that there is a relevant correlation between being a driver and criminal prosecution of drivers. So far as any available information instructs us, most accidents occur without creating criminal liability even if one or both of the drivers are guilty of negligence as a matter of tort law.

The disclosure of inherently illegal activity is inherently risky. Our decisions in *Albertson* and the cases following illustrate that truism. But disclosures with respect to automobile accidents simply do not entail the kind of substantial risk of self-incrimination involved in *Marchetti, Grosso,* and *Haynes.* Furthermore, the statutory purpose is noncriminal and self-reporting is indispensible to its fulfillment.

(2)

Even if we were to view the statutory reporting requirement as incriminating in the traditional sense, in our view it would be the "extravagant" extension of the privilege Justice Holmes warned against to hold that it is testimonial in the Fifth Amendment sense. Compliance with § 20002(a)(1) requires two things: first, a driver involved in an accident is required to stop at the scene; second, he is required to give his name and address. The act of stopping is no more testimonial—indeed less so in some respects—than requiring a person in custody to stand or walk in a police lineup, to speak prescribed words, to give samples of handwriting, fingerprints or blood. . . . Disclosure of name and address is an essentially neutral act. Whatever the collateral consequences of disclosing name and address, the statutory purpose is to implement the state police power to regulate use of motor vehicles.

* * *

Stopping in compliance with § 20002(a)(1) . . . does not provide the State with "evidence of a testimonial or communicative nature" within the meaning of the Constitution. It merely provides the State and private parties with the driver's identity for, among other valid state needs, the study of causes of vehicle accidents and related purposes, always subject to the driver's right to assert a Fifth Amendment privilege concerning specific inquiries.

Petitioner argues that since the statutory duty to stop is imposed only on the "driver of any vehicle involved in an accident," a driver's compliance is testimonial because his action gives rise to an inference that he believes that he was the "driver of a vehicle involved in an accident." From this, the petitioner tells us, it can be further inferred that he was indeed the operator of an "accident involved" vehicle. In [United States v. Wade (1967)], however, the Court rejected the notion that such inferences are communicative or testimonial. There the petitioner was placed in a lineup to be viewed by persons who had witnessed a bank robbery. At one point he was compelled to speak the words alleged to have been used by the perpetrator. Despite the inference that the petitioner uttered the words in his normal undisguised voice, the Court held that the utterances were not of a "testimonial" nature in the sense of the Fifth Amendment privilege even though the speaking might well have led to identifying him as the bank robber. Furthermore, the Court noted in *Wade* that no question was presented as to the admissibility in evidence at trial of anything said or done at the lineup. . . . Similarly no such problem is presented here. Of course, a suspect's normal voice characteristics, like his handwriting, blood, fingerprints, or body may prove to be the crucial link in a chain of evidentiary factors resulting in prosecution and conviction. Yet such evidence may be used against a defendant.

After having stopped, a driver involved in an accident is required by § 20002(a)(1) to notify the driver of the other vehicle of his name and address. A name, linked with a motor vehicle, is no more incriminating than the tax return, linked with the disclosure of income, . . . It identifies but does not by itself implicate anyone in criminal conduct.

Although identity, when made known, may lead to inquiry that in turn leads to arrest and charge, those developments depend on different factors and independent evidence. Here the compelled disclosure of identity could have led to a charge that might not have been made had the driver fled the scene; but this is true only in the same sense that a taxpayer can be charged on the basis of the contents of a tax return or failure to file an income tax form. There is no constitutional right to refuse to file an income tax return or to flee the scene of an accident in order to avoid the possibility of legal involvement.

The judgment of the California Supreme Court is vacated and the case is remanded for further proceedings not inconsistent with this opinion.

Vacated and remanded.

[Justice Harland wrote a very lengthy concurring opinion. Due to its length, and to the fact that what he had to say is discussed in the dissenting opinion, we are herewith reporting what we consider to be the core of his viewpoint.]

MR. JUSTICE HARLAN, concurring in the judgment.

* * *

. . . If the privilege is extended to the circumstances of this case, it must, I think, be potentially available in every instance where the government relies on self-reporting. And the considerable risks to efficient government of a self-executing claim of privilege will require acceptance of, at the very least, a use restriction of unspecified dimensions. Technological progress creates an ever-expanding need for governmental information about individuals. If the individual's ability in any particular case to perceive a genuine risk of self-incrimination is to be a sufficient condition for imposition of use restrictions on the government in all self-reporting contexts, then the privilege threatens the capacity of the government to respond to societal needs with a realistic mixture of criminal sanctions and other regulatory devices. To the extent that our *Marchetti-Grosso* line of cases appears to suggest that the presence of perceivable risks of incrimination in and of itself justifies imposition of a use restriction on the information gained by the Government through compelled self-reporting, I think that line of cases should be explicitly limited by this Court.

* * *

MR. JUSTICE BLACK, with whom MR. JUSTICE DOUGLAS and MR. JUSTICE BRENNAN join, dissenting.

Since the days of Chief Justice John Marshall this Court has been steadfastly committed to the principle that the Fifth Amendment's prohibition against compulsory self-incrimination forbids the Federal Government to compel a person to supply information which can be used as a "link in a chain of testimony" needed to prosecute him for a crime. . . . It is now established that the Fourteenth Amendment makes that provision of the Fifth Amendment applicable to the States. . . . The plurality opinion, if agreed to by a majority of the Court, would practically wipe out the Fifth Amendment's protection against compelled self-incrimination. This protective constitutional safeguard against arbitrary government was first most clearly declared by Chief Justice Marshall in the trial of Aaron Burr in 1807. In erasing this principle from the Constitution the plurality opinion retreats from a cherished guarantee of liberty fashioned by James Madison and the other founders of what they gladly proclaimed to be our free government. One need only read with care the past cases cited in today's opinions to understand the shrinking process to which the Court today subjects a vital safeguard of our Bill of Rights.

The plurality opinion labors unsuccessfully to distinguish this case from our previous holdings enforcing the Fifth Amendment guarantee against compelled self-incrimination. . . . The plurality opinion appears to suggest that those previous cases are not controlling because respondent Byers would not have subjected himself to a "substantial risk of self-incrimination" by stopping after the accident and providing his name and address as required by California law. This suggestion can hardly be taken seriously. A California driver involved in an accident causing property damage is in fact very likely to have violated one of the hundreds of state criminal statutes regulating automobiles which comprise most of two volumes of the California Code. More important, the particular facts of this case demonstrate that Byers would have subjected himself to a "substantial risk of self-incrimination" had he given his name and address at the scene of the accident. He has now been charged not only with failing to give his name but also with passing without maintaining a safe distance as prohibited by California Vehicle Code § 21750. It is stipulated that the allegedly improper passing caused the accident from which Byers left without stating his name and address. In a prosecution under § 21750, the State will be required to prove that Byers was the driver who passed without maintaining a safe distance. Thus if Byers had stopped and provided his name and address as the driver involved in the accident, the State could have used that information to establish an essential element of the crime under § 21750. It seems absolutely fanciful to suggest that he would not have faced a "substantial risk of self-incrimination" by complying with the disclosure statute.

The plurality opinion also seeks to distinguish this case from our previous decisions on the ground that § 20002(a)(1) requires disclosure in an area not "permeated with criminal statutes" and because it is not aimed at a "highly selective group inherently suspect of criminal activities." Of course these suggestions ignore the fact that *this particular respondent* would have run a serious risk of self-incrimination by complying with the disclosure statute. Furthermore, it is hardly accurate to suggest that the activity of driving an automobile in California is not "an area permeated with criminal statutes." And it is unhelpful to say the statute is not aimed at an "inherently suspect" group because it applies to "all persons who drive automobiles in California." The compelled disclosure is required of all persons who drive automobiles in California *who are involved in accidents causing property damage.* If this group is not "suspect" of illegal activities, it is difficult to find such a group.

The plurality opinion purports to rely on United States v. Sullivan to support its result. But *Sullivan* held only that a taxpayer could not defeat a prosecution for failure to file a tax return on the grounds that his income was illegally obtained. The Court there suggested that the defendant could lawfully have refused to answer particular questions on the return if they tended to incriminate him.[4] Here, unlike *Sullivan*, the only information that the State requires Byers to disclose greatly enhances the probability of conviction for crime. As I have pointed out, if Byers had stopped and identified himself as the driver of the car in the accident, he would have handed the State an admission to use against him at trial on a charge of failing to maintain a safe distance while passing. Thus Byers' failure to stop is analogous to a refusal to answer a particular incriminating question on a tax return, an act protected by the Fifth Amendment under this Court's decision in *Sullivan*.

I also find unacceptable the alternative holding that the California statute is valid because the disclosures it requires are not "testimonial" (whatever that term may mean). Even assuming that the Fifth Amendment prohibits the State only from compelling a man to produce "testimonial" evidence against himself, the California requirement here is still unconstitutional. What evidence can possibly be more "testimonial" than a man's own statement that he is a person who has just been involved in an automobile accident inflicting property damage? Neither United States v. Wade, . . . nor any other case of this Court has ever held that the State may convict a man by compelling him to admit that he is guilty of conduct constituting an element of a crime. Yet the plurality opinion apparently approves precisely that result.

My BROTHER HARLAN'S opinion makes it clear that today the Court "balances" the importance of a defendant's Fifth Amendment right not to be forced to help convict himself against the government's interest in forcing him to do so. As in previous decisions, this balancing inevitably results in the dilution of constitutional guarantees. . . . By my BROTHER HARLAN'S reasoning it appears that the scope of the Fifth Amendment's protection will now depend on what value a majority of nine Justices chooses to place on this explicit constitutional guarantee as opposed to the government's interest in convicting a man by compelling self-incriminating testimony. In my view, vesting such power in judges to water down constitutional rights does indeed "embark us" on BROTHER HARLAN'S "uncharted and treacherous seas."

I can only assume that the unarticulated premise of the decision is that there is so much crime abroad in this country at pres-

4. "If the form of return provided called for answers that the defendant was privileged from making he could have raised the objection in the return, but could not on that account refuse to make any return at all. We are not called on to decide what, if anything, he might have withheld. Most of the items warranted no complaint. It would be an extreme if not an extravagant application of the Fifth Amendment to say that it authorized a man to refuse to state the amount of his income because it had been made in crime." . . .

ent that Bill of Rights' safeguards against arbitrary government must not be completely enforced. I can agree that there is too much crime in the land for us to treat criminals with favor. But I can never agree that we should depart in the slightest way from the Bill of Rights' guarantees that give this country its high place among the free nations of the world. If we affirmed the State Supreme Court, California could still require persons involved in accidents to stop and give their names and addresses. The State would only be denied the power to violate the Fifth Amendment by using the fruits of such compelled testimony against them in criminal proceedings. Instead of criticizing the Supreme Court of California for its rigid protections of individual liberty, I would without more ado affirm its judgment.

MR. JUSTICE BRENNAN, with whom MR. JUSTICE DOUGLAS and MR. JUSTICE MARSHALL join, dissenting.

* * *

Much of the plurality's confusion appears to stem from its misunderstanding of the language, embodied in several of this Court's opinions, regarding questions "directed at a highly selective group inherently suspect of criminal activities." . . . The plurality seems to believe that membership in such a suspect group is somehow an indispensable foundation for any Fifth Amendment claim. Of course this is not so, unless the plurality is now prepared to assume that . . . [four of our prior decisions] were based respectively upon the unarticulated premises that bankrupts, businessmen, policemen, and lawyers are all "group[s] inherently suspect of criminal activities." Instead, in the words of the California Supreme Court, "in each case the crime-directed character of the registration requirement was * * * important only insofar as it supported the claims of the specific petitioners that they faced 'substantial hazards of self-incrimination' justifying invocation of the privilege." . . . That this is so is evident from our emphasis in *Marchetti* that "we do not hold that these wagering tax provisions are as such constitutionally impermissible * * *. If, in different circumstances, a taxpayer is not confronted by substantial hazards of self-incrimination * * * nothing we decide today would shield him from the various penalties prescribed by the wagering tax statutes." The point is that in both *Albertson* and *Marchetti*, petitioners arrived in this Court accompanied by a record showing only that they had failed to register, respectively, as Communists and as a gambler, and that in fact they were such. Since neither of these facts was necessarily criminal, we had to determine whether the petitioner faced "real and appreciable" or merely "imaginary and unsubstantial" hazards when they refused to register. That the petitioners belonged in each case to an inherently suspect group was relevant to that question, and that alone. By contrast, in the present case we are dealing with a record which demonstrates, as found by all three courts below, that respondent was charged by California both with illegal passing which resulted in an accident, and with failing to report himself as one of the drivers involved in that accident. It is hard to imagine a record demonstrating a more substantial hazard of self-incrimination than this. Yet the plurality somehow conclude that respondent did not face the "substantial risk of self-incrimination involved in *Marchetti*." . . .

* * *

Similarly, I do not believe that the force of my BROTHER BLACK'S reasoning may be avoided by my BROTHER HARLAN'S approach. He quite candidly admits that our prior cases compel the conclusion that respondent was entitled to rely on the privilege against self-incrimination as a defense to prosecution for failure to stop and report his involvement in an accident. He would simply limit those cases because he believes that technological progress has made the privilege against self-incrimination a "threat" to "realistic" government that we can no longer afford. To the extent that this argument calls for refutation, it is adequately disposed of in Mr. Justice Brandeis' dissenting opinion in Olmstead v. United States . . . Our society is not endangered by the Fifth Amendment. "The dangers of which we must really beware are * * * that we shall fall prey to the idea that in order to preserve our free society some of the liberties of the individual must be curtailed, at least temporarily. How wrong that kind of a program would be is surely evident from the mere statement of the proposition."

In any event my BROTHER HARLAN'S opinion is consistent neither with the present record nor its own premises. As to the first, my BROTHER HARLAN appears to believe that the imposition of use restrictions on the present statute would threaten the capacity of California "to respond to societal needs with a realistic mixture of criminal sanctions and other regulatory devices." . . . If so, this threat passed unperceived by the California Supreme Court: that court stated that its imposition of a use restriction "will neither frustrate any apparent significant legislative purpose nor unduly hamper criminal prosecutions of drivers involved in accidents resulting in damage to the property of others." . . . It seems to have passed unnoticed by the California Legislature as well. The present statute applies to drivers involved in accidents causing property damage. . . . [Another one] requires similar, albeit more detailed, reports from drivers involved in accidents resulting in either personal injury or death. Yet the California Legislature itself imposed use restrictions upon the use of such reports. It is one thing to respect a State's assertion that imposition of a particular requirement will unduly hamper a legitimate state interest. It is quite another to flout the conclusion of the State's Supreme Court—and, so far as appears, of the state legislature as well—that imposition of a particular requirement is not at all inconsistent with the asserted state interests.

* * *

[The subject of compelled testimony before an administrative agency or judicial tribunal will be subsequently discussed in Chapter 14.]

G. CRUEL AND UNUSUAL PUNISHMENT

ROBINSON v. CALIFORNIA

Supreme Court of the United States, 1962.
370 U.S. 660, 82 S.Ct. 1417.

MR. JUSTICE STEWART delivered the opinion of the Court.

A California statute makes it a criminal offense for a person to "be addicted to the use of narcotics." [1] This appeal draws into question the constitutionality of that provision of the state law, as construed by the California courts in the present case.

The appellant was convicted after a jury trial in the Municipal Court of Los Angeles. The evidence against him was given by two Los Angeles police officers. Officer Brown testified that he had had occasion to examine the appellant's arms one evening on a street in Los Angeles some four months before the trial. The officer testified that at that time he had observed "scar tissue and discoloration on the inside" of the appellant's right arm, and "what appeared to be numerous needle marks and a scab which was approximately three inches below the crook of the elbow" on the appellant's left arm. The officer also testified that the appellant under questioning had admitted to the occasional use of narcotics.

Officer Lindquist testified that he had examined the appellant the following morning in the Central Jail in Los Angeles. The officer stated that at that time he had observed discolorations and scabs on

1. The statute is § 11721 of the California Health and Safety Code. It provides:

"No person shall use, or be under the influence of, or be addicted to the use of narcotics, excepting when administered by or under the direction of a person licensed by the State to prescribe and administer narcotics. It shall be the burden of the defense to show that it comes within the exception. Any person convicted of violating any provision of this section is guilty of a misdemeanor and shall be sentenced to serve a term of not less than 90 days nor more than one year in the county jail. The court may place a person convicted hereunder on probation for a period not to exceed five years and shall in all cases in which probation is granted require as a condition thereof that such person be confined in the county jail for at least 90 days. In no event does the court have the power to absolve a person who violates this section from the obligation of spending at least 90 days in confinement in the county jail."

the appellant's arms, and he identified photographs which had been taken of the appellant's arms shortly after his arrest the night before. Based upon more than ten years of experience as a member of the Narcotic Division of the Los Angeles Police Department, the witness gave his opinion that "these marks and the discoloration were the result of the injection of hypodermic needles into the tissue into the vein that was not sterile." He stated that the scabs were several days old at the time of his examination, and that the appellant was neither under the influence of narcotics nor suffering withdrawal symptoms at the time he saw him. This witness also testified that the appellant had admitted using narcotics in the past.

The appellant testified in his own behalf, denying the alleged conversations with the police officers and denying that he had ever used narcotics or been addicted to their use. He explained the marks on his arms as resulting from an allergic condition contracted during his military service. His testimony was corroborated by two witnesses.

The trial judge instructed the jury that the statute made it a misdemeanor for a person "either to use narcotics, or to be addicted to the use of narcotics * * * That portion of the statute referring to the 'use' of narcotics is based upon the 'act' of using. That portion of the statute referring to 'addicted to the use' of narcotics is based upon a condition or status. They are not identical. * * * To be addicted to the use of narcotics is said to be a status or condition and not an act. It is a continuing offense and differs from most other offenses in the fact that [it] is chronic rather than acute; that it continues after it is complete and subjects the offender to arrest at any time before he reforms. The existence of such a chronic condition may be ascertained from a single examination, if the characteristic reactions of that condition be found present."

The judge further instructed the jury that the appellant could be convicted under a general verdict if the jury agreed *either* that he was of the "status" *or* had committed the "act" denounced by the statute. "All that the People must show is either that the defendant did use a narcotic in Los Angeles County, or that while in the City of Los Angeles he was addicted to the use of narcotics * * *."

Under these instructions the jury returned a verdict finding the appellant "guilty of the offense charged." An appeal was taken to the Appellate Department of the Los Angeles County Superior Court, "the highest court of a State in which a decision could be had" in this case. . . . Although expressing some doubt as to the constitutionality of "the crime of being a narcotic addict," the reviewing court in an unreported opinion affirmed the judgment of conviction, citing two of its own previous unreported decisions which had upheld the constitutionality of the statute. We noted probable jurisdiction of this appeal . . . because it squarely presents the issue whether the statute as construed by the California courts in this case is repugnant to the Fourteenth Amendment of the Constitution.

The broad power of a State to regulate the narcotic drugs traffic within its borders is not here in issue. More than forty years ago, in Whipple v. Martinson, 256 U.S. 41, 41 S.Ct. 425, 65 L.Ed. 819, this Court explicitly recognized the validity of that power: "There can be no question of the authority of the state in the exercise of its police power to regulate the administration, sale, prescription and use of dangerous and habit-forming drugs * * *. The right to exercise this power is so manifest in the interest of the public health and welfare, that it is unnecessary to enter upon a discussion of it beyond saying that it is too firmly established to be successfully called in question." . . .

Such regulation, it can be assumed, could take a variety of valid forms. A State might impose criminal sanctions, for example, against the unauthorized manufacture, prescription, sale, purchase, or possession of narcotics within its borders. In the interest of discouraging the violation of such laws, or in the interest of the general health or welfare of its inhabitants, a State might establish a program of compulsory treatment for those addicted to narcotics.[2] Such a program of treatment might require periods of involuntary confinement. And penal sanctions might be imposed for failure to comply with established compulsory treatment procedures. . . . Or a State might choose to attack the evils of narcotics traffic on broader fronts also—through public health education, for example, or by efforts to ameliorate the economic and social conditions under which those evils might be thought to flourish. In short, the range of valid choice which a State might make in this area is undoubtedly a wide one, and the wisdom of any particular choice within the allowable spectrum is not for us to decide. Upon that premise we turn to the California law in issue here.

It would be possible to construe the statute under which the appellant was convicted as one which is operative only upon proof of the actual use of narcotics within the State's jurisdiction. But the California courts have not so construed this law. Although there was evidence in the present case that the appellant had used narcotics in Los Angeles, the jury were instructed that they could convict him even if they disbelieved that evidence. The appellant could be convicted, they were told, if they found simply that the appellant's "status" or "chronic condition" was that of being "addicted to the use of narcotics." And it is impossible to know from the jury's verdict that the defendant was not convicted upon precisely such a finding.

The instructions of the trial court, implicitly approved on appeal, amounted to "a ruling on a question of state law that is as binding on us as though the precise words had been written" into the statute. Terminiello v. Chicago, 337 U.S. 1, 4, 69 S.Ct. 894, 895,

2. California appears to have established just such a program in §§ 5350–5361 of its Welfare and Institutions Code. The record contains no explanation of why the civil procedures authorized by this legislation were not utilized in the present case.

93 L.Ed. 1131. "We can only take the statute as the state courts read it." Id., at 6, 69 S.Ct. at 896. Indeed, in their brief in this Court counsel for the State have emphasized that it is "the proof of addiction by circumstantial evidence * * * by the tell-tale track of needle marks and scabs over the veins of his arms, that remains the gist of the section."

This statute, therefore, is not one which punishes a person for the use of narcotics, for their purchase, sale or possession, or for antisocial or disorderly behavior resulting from their administration. It is not a law which even purports to provide or require medical treatment. Rather, we deal with a statute which makes the "status" of narcotic addiction a criminal offense, for which the offender may be prosecuted "at any time before he reforms." California has said that a person can be continuously guilty of this offense, whether or not he has ever used or possessed any narcotics within the State, and whether or not he has been guilty of any antisocial behavior there.

It is unlikely that any State at this moment in history would attempt to make it a criminal offense for a person to be mentally ill, or a leper, or to be afflicted with a venereal disease. A State might determine that the general health and welfare require that the victims of these and other human afflictions be dealt with by compulsory treatment, involving quarantine, confinement, or sequestration. But, in the light of contemporary human knowledge, a law which made a criminal offense of such a disease would doubtless be universally thought to be an infliction of cruel and unusual punishment in violation of the Eighth and Fourteenth Amendments. . . .

We cannot but consider the statute before us as of the same category. In this Court counsel for the State recognized that narcotic addiction is an illness. Indeed, it is apparently an illness which may be contracted innocently or involuntarily.[3] We hold that a state law which imprisons a person thus afflicted as a criminal, even though he has never touched any narcotic drug within the State or been guilty of any irregular behavior there, inflicts a cruel and unusual punishment in violation of the Fourteenth Amendment. To be sure, imprisonment for ninety days is not, in the abstract, a punishment which is either cruel or unusual. But the question cannot be considered in the abstract. Even one day in prison would be a cruel and unusual punishment for the "crime" of having a common cold.

We are not unmindful that the vicious evils of the narcotics traffic have occasioned the grave concern of government. There are, as we have said, countless fronts on which those evils may be legitimately attacked. We deal in this case only with an individual pro-

3. Not only may addiction innocently result from the use of medically prescribed narcotics, but a person may even be a narcotics addict from the moment of his birth. [citation here to many supporting authorities.]

vision of a particularized local law as it has so far been interpreted by the California courts.

Reversed.

[MR. JUSTICE FRANKFURTER took no part in the case. MR. JUSTICE DOUGLAS' concurring opinion is omitted.]

MR. JUSTICE HARLAN, concurring. I am not prepared to hold that on the present state of medical knowledge it is completely irrational and hence unconstitutional for a State to conclude that narcotics addiction is something other than an illness nor that it amounts to cruel and unusual punishment for the State to subject narcotics addicts to its criminal law. Insofar as addiction may be identified with the use or possession of narcotics within the State (or, I would suppose, without the State), in violation of local statutes prohibiting such acts, it may surely be reached by the State's criminal law. But in this case the trial court's instructions permitted the jury to find the appellant guilty on no more proof than that he was present in California while he was addicted to narcotics. Since addiction alone cannot reasonably be thought to amount to more than a compelling propensity to use narcotics, the effect of this instruction was to authorize criminal punishment for a bare desire to commit a criminal act.

If the California statute reaches this type of conduct, and for present purposes we must accept the trial court's construction as binding, . . . it is an arbitrary imposition which exceeds the power that a State may exercise in enacting its criminal law. Accordingly, I agree that the application of the California statute was unconstitutional in this case and join the judgment of reversal.

MR. JUSTICE CLARK, dissenting. The Court finds § 11721 of California's Health and Safety Code, making it an offense to "be addicted to the use of narcotics," violative of due process as "a cruel and unusual punishment." I cannot agree.

The statute must first be placed in perspective. California has a comprehensive and enlightened program for the control of narcotism based on the overriding policy of prevention and cure. It is the product of an extensive investigation made in the mid-Fifties by a committee of distinguished scientists, doctors, law enforcement officers and laymen appointed by the then Attorney General, now Governor, of California. The committee filed a detailed study entitled "Report on Narcotic Addiction" which was given considerable attention. No recommendation was made therein for the repeal of § 11721, and the State Legislature in its discretion continued the policy of that section.

Apart from prohibiting specific acts such as the purchase, possession and sale of narcotics, California has taken certain legislative steps in regard to the status of being a narcotic addict—a condition commonly recognized as a threat to the State and to the individual. The Code deals with this problem in realistic stages. At its incipiency narcotic addiction is handled under § 11721 of the Health and

Safety Code which is at issue here. It provides that a person found to be addicted to the use of narcotics shall serve a term in the county jail of not less than 90 days nor more than one year, with the minimum 90-day confinement applying in all cases without exception. Provision is made for parole with periodic tests to detect readdiction.

The trial court defined "addicted to narcotics" as used in § 11721 in the following charge to the jury:

> "The word 'addicted' means, strongly disposed to some taste or practice or habituated, especially to drugs. In order to inquire as to whether a person is addicted to the use of narcotics is in effect an inquiry as to his habit in that regard. Does he use them habitually? To use them often or daily is, according to the ordinary acceptance of those words, to use them habitually."

There was no suggestion that the term "narcotic addict" as here used included a person who acted without volition or who had lost the power of self-control. Although the section is penal in appearance—perhaps a carry-over from a less sophisticated approach—its present provisions are quite similar to those for civil commitment and treatment of addicts who have lost the power of self-control, and its present purpose is reflected in a statement which closely follows § 11721: "The rehabilitation of narcotic addicts and the prevention of continued addiction to narcotics is a matter of statewide concern." California Health and Safety Code, § 11728.

Where narcotic addiction has progressed beyond the incipient, volitional stage, California provides for commitment of three months to two years in a state hospital. California Welfare and Institutions Code, § 5355. For the purposes of this provision, a narcotic addict is defined as

> "any person who habitually takes or otherwise uses *to the extent of having lost the power of self-control* any opium, morphine, cocaine, or other narcotic drug as defined in Article 1 of Chapter 1 of Division 10 of the Health and Safety Code." California Welfare and Institutions Code, § 5350. (Emphasis supplied.)

This proceeding is clearly civil in nature with a purpose of rehabilitation and cure. Significantly, if it is found that a person committed under § 5355 will not receive substantial benefit from further hospital treatment and is not dangerous to society, he may be discharged—but only after a minimum confinement of three months. § 5355.1.

Thus, the "criminal" provision applies to the incipient narcotic addict who retains self-control, requiring confinement of three months to one year and parole with frequent tests to detect renewed use of drugs. Its overriding purpose is to cure the less seriously addicted person by preventing further use. On the other hand, the "civil" commitment provision deals with addicts who have lost the power of self-control, requiring hospitalization up to two years. Each deals with a different type of addict but with a common purpose. This is most apparent when the sections overlap: if after civil commitment of an addict it is found that hospital treatment will not be helpful, the addict is confined for a minimum period of three months in the same manner as is the volitional addict under the "criminal" provision.

In the instant case the proceedings against the petitioner were brought under the volitional-addict section. There was testimony that he had been using drugs only four months with three to four relatively mild doses a week. At arrest and trial he appeared normal. His testimony was clear and concise, being simply that he had never used drugs. The scabs and pocks on his arms and body were caused, he said, by "overseas shots" administered during army service preparatory to foreign assignment. He was very articulate in his testimony but the jury did not believe him, apparently because he had told the clinical expert while being examined after arrest that he had been using drugs, as I have stated above. The officer who arrested him also testified to like statements and to scabs—some 10 or 15 days old—showing narcotic injections. There was no evidence in the record of withdrawal symptoms. Obviously he could not have been committed under § 5355 as one who had completely "lost the power of self-control." The jury was instructed that narcotic "addiction" as used in § 11721 meant strongly disposed to a taste or practice or habit of its use, indicated by the use of narcotics often or daily. A general verdict was returned against petitioner, and he was ordered confined for 90 days to be followed by a two-year parole during which he was required to take periodic Nalline tests.

The majority strikes down the conviction primarily on the grounds that petitioner was denied due process by the imposition of criminal penalties for nothing more than being in a status. This view point is premised upon the theme that § 11721 is a "criminal" provision authorizing a punishment, for the majority admits that "a State might establish a program of compulsory treatment for those addicted to narcotics" which "might require periods of involuntary confinement." I submit that California has done exactly that. The majority's error is in instructing the California Legislature that hospitalization is the *only treatment* for narcotics addiction—that anything less is a punishment denying due process. California has found otherwise after a study which I suggest was more extensive than that conducted by the Court. Even in California's program for hospital commitment of nonvolitional narcotic addicts—which the majority approves—it is recognized that some addicts will not respond to or do not need hospital treatment. As to these persons its provisions are identical to those of § 11721—confinement for a period of not less than 90 days. Section 11721 provides this confinement as treatment for the volitional addicts to whom its provisions apply, in addition to parole with frequent tests to detect and prevent further use of drugs. The fact that § 11721 might be labeled "criminal" seems irrelevant,[4] not only to the majority's own "treatment" test but to the "concept of ordered liberty" to which the States must attain under the Fourteenth Amendment. The test is the overall purpose and effect of a State's act, and I submit that California's program relative to narcotic addicts—including both the "criminal" and "civil" provisions—is inherently one of treatment and lies well within the power of a State.

However, the case in support of the judgment below need not rest solely on this reading of California law. For even if the overall statutory scheme is ignored and a purpose and effect of punishment is attached to § 11721, that provision still does not violate the Fourteenth Amendment. The majority acknowledges, as it must, that a State can punish persons who purchase, possess or use narcotics. Although none of these acts are harmful to society *in themselves,* the State constitutionally may attempt to deter and prevent them through punishment because of the grave threat of future harmful conduct which they pose. Narcotics addiction—including the incipient, volitional addiction to which this provision speaks—is no different. California courts have taken judicial notice that "the inordinate use of a narcotic drug tends to create an irresistible craving and forms a habit for its continued use until one becomes an addict, and he respects no convention or obligation and will lie, steal, or use any other base means to gratify his passion for the drug, being lost to all considerations of duty or social position." . . . Can this Court deny the legislative and judicial judgment of California that incipient, volitional narcotic addiction poses a threat of serious crime similar to the threat inherent in the purchase or possession of narcotics? And if such a threat is inherent in addiction, can this Court say that California is powerless to deter it by punishment?

It is no answer to suggest that we are dealing with an involuntary status and thus penal sanctions will be ineffective and unfair. The section at issue applies only to persons who use narcotics often or even daily but not to the point of losing self-control. When dealing with involuntary addicts California moves only through § 5355 of its Welfare Institutions Code which clearly is not penal. Even if it could be argued that § 11721 may not be limited to volitional addicts, the petitioner in the instant case undeniably retained the power of self-control and thus to him the statute would be constitutional. Moreover, "status" offenses have long been known and recognized in the criminal law. A ready example is drunkenness, which plainly is as involuntary after addiction to alcohol as is the taking of drugs.

Nor is the conjecture relevant that petitioner may have acquired his habit under lawful circumstances. There was no suggestion by him to this effect at trial, and surely the State need not rebut all possible lawful sources of addiction as part of its prima facie case.

4. Any reliance upon the "stigma" of a misdemeanor conviction in this context is misplaced, as it would hardly be different from the stigma of a civil commitment for narcotics addiction.

The argument that the statute constitutes a cruel and unusual punishment is governed by the discussion above. Properly construed, the statute provides a treatment rather than a punishment. But even if interpreted as penal, the sanction of incarceration for 3 to 12 months is not unreasonable when applied to a person who has voluntarily placed himself in a condition posing a serious threat to the State. Under either theory, its provisions for 3 to 12 months' confinement can hardly be deemed unreasonable when compared to the provisions for 3 to 24 months' confinement under § 5355 which the majority approves.

I would affirm the judgment.

MR. JUSTICE WHITE, dissenting. If appellant's conviction rested upon sheer status, condition or illness or if he was convicted for being an addict who had lost his power of self-control, I would have other thoughts about this case. But this record presents neither situation. And I believe the Court has departed from its wise rule of not deciding constitutional questions except where necessary and from its equally sound practice of construing state statutes, where possible, in a manner saving their constitutionality.

I am not at all ready to place the use of narcotics beyond the reach of the States' criminal laws. I do not consider appellant's conviction to be a punishment for having an illness or for simply being in some status or condition, but rather a conviction for the regular, repeated or habitual use of narcotics immediately prior to his arrest and in violation of the California law. As defined by the trial court, addiction *is* the regular use of narcotics and can be proved only by evidence of such use. To find addiction in this case the jury had to believe that appellant had frequently used narcotics in the recent past.[5] California is entitled to have its statute and the record so read, particularly where the State's only purpose in allowing prosecutions for addiction was to supersede its own venue requirements applicable to prosecutions for the use of narcotics and in effect to allow convictions for use where there is no precise evidence of the county where the use took place.

Nor do I find any indications in this record that California would apply § 11721 to the case of the helpless addict. I agree with my BROTHER CLARK that there was no evidence at all that appellant had lost the power to control his acts. There was no evidence of any use

5. This is not a case where a defendant is convicted "even though he has never touched any narcotic drug within the State or been guilty of any irregular behavior there." The evidence was that appellant lived and worked in Los Angeles. He admitted before trial that he had used narcotics for three or four months, three or four times a week, usually at his place with his friends. He stated to the police that he had last used narcotics at 54th and Central in the City of Los Angeles on January 27, 8 days before his arrest. According to the State's expert, no needle mark or scab found on appellant's arms was newer than 3 days old and the most recent mark might have been as old as 10 days, which was consistent with appellant's own pretrial admissions. The State's evidence was that appellant had used narcotics at least 7 times in the 15 days immediately preceding his arrest.

within 3 days prior to appellant's arrest. The most recent marks might have been 3 days old or they might have been 10 days old. The appellant admitted before trial that he had last used narcotics 8 days before his arrest. At the trial he denied having taken narcotics at all. The uncontroverted evidence was that appellant was not under the influence of narcotics at the time of his arrest nor did he have withdrawal symptoms. He was an incipient addict, a redeemable user, and the State chose to send him to jail for 90 days rather than to attempt to confine him by civil proceedings under another statute which requires a finding that the addict has lost the power of self-control. In my opinion, on this record, it was within the power of the State of California to confine him by criminal proceedings for the use of narcotics or for regular use amounting to habitual use.[6]

The Court clearly does not rest its decision upon the narrow ground that the jury was not expressly instructed not to convict if it believed appellant's use of narcotics was beyond his control. The Court recognizes no degrees of addiction. The Fourteenth Amendment is today held to bar any prosecution for addiction regardless of the degree or frequency of use, and the Court's opinion bristles with indications of further consequences. If it is "cruel and unusual punishment" to convict appellant for addiction, it is difficult to understand why it would be any less offensive to the Fourteenth Amendment to convict him for use on the same evidence of use which proved he was an addict. It is significant that in purporting to reaffirm the power of the States to deal with the narcotics traffic, the Court does not include among the obvious powers of the State the power to punish for the use of narcotics. I cannot think that the omission was inadvertent.

The Court has not merely tidied up California's law by removing some irritating vestige of an outmoded approach to the control of narcotics. At the very least, it has effectively removed California's power to deal effectively with the recurring case under the statute where there is ample evidence of use but no evidence of the precise location of use. Beyond this it has cast serious doubt upon the power of any State to forbid the use of narcotics under threat of criminal punishment. I cannot believe that the Court would forbid the application of the criminal laws to the use of narcotics under any circumstances. But the States, as well as the Federal Government, are now on notice. They will have to await a final answer in another case.

Finally, I deem this application of "cruel and unusual punishment" so novel that I suspect the Court was hard put to find a way to ascribe to the Framers of the Constitution the result reached today rather than to its own notions of ordered liberty. If this case involved economic regulation, the present Court's allergy to substantive due process would surely save the statute and prevent the Court from imposing its own philosophical predilections upon state legisla-

6. Health and Safety Code § 11391 expressly permits and contemplates the medical treatment of narcotics addicts confined to jail.

tures or Congress. I fail to see why the Court deems it more appropriate to write into the Constitution its own abstract notions of how best to handle the narcotics problem, for it obviously cannot match either the States or Congress in expert understanding.

I respectfully dissent.

NOTES

1. In 1965 the California legislature transferred the provisions for the commitment and treatment of addicts from the Penal Code to the Welfare and Institutions Code. See People v. Reynoso, 64 Cal.2d 432, 50 Cal. Rptr. 468, 412 P.2d 812 (1966).

2. As regards prosecutions for "being under the influence", or for the "use" of narcotics, consider the following:

In State v. Margo, 40 N.J. 188, 191 A.2d 43 (1963) the court distinguished a New Jersey statute making it a criminal offense "to use" or be "under the influence of narcotics" from the one in Robinson by saying that addiction was something distinct from being under the influence. (The case does not reveal that defendant was a confirmed addict, although there were needle scars on his arm.) The court said *"Our statute does not punish for an unsatisfied craving for drugs.* Rather it *denounces the state of being under the influence* . . . . the statute deals with being under the influence . . . to obviate an issue as to whether the drug was taken here or in another jurisdiction." And the court added that if a person could be prosecuted for use, because it is an anti-social act, he can be prosecuted for being under the influence, which offends society's interest in the same way.

In People v. Nettles, 34 Ill.2d 52, 213 N.E.2d 536 (1966), the Illinois Supreme Court held that an addict could be prosecuted for "possession".

In Watson v. U. S., 141 U.S.App.D.C. 335, 439 F.2d 442 (1970), the defendant, an addict, had been convicted of having purchased and of having facilitated the concealment sale of heroin. (Under the federal statute possession is "sufficient evidence to authorize conviction unless the defendant explains the possession to the satisfaction of the jury"). The D. C. Court of Appeals, en banc, affirmed the conviction but remanded the case for resentencing, with consideration to be given to the National Addict Rehabilitation Act. In a footnote (#15) the court referred a 5th circuit case which cautioned that in view of the rehabilitation procedures in that Act great caution should be exhibited in any "extension of *Robinson*". Nevertheless the D. C. Court of Appeals had this to say:

> " . . . if *Robinson's* deployment of the Eighth Amendment as a barrier to California's making addiction a crime means anything, it must also mean in all logic that (1) Congress either did not intend to expose the non-trafficking addict possessor to criminal punishment, or (2) its effort to do so is as unavailing constitutionally as that of the California legislature."

In his concurring opinion one of the judges (457–458) said that "today's opinion leads clearly to the conclusion that the federal narcotics law involved in this case do not apply to nontrafficking addicts in possession of narcotics for their own use".

3. If a nontrafficking addict cannot be prosecuted for use or possession, as *Watson,* supra, seems to hold, what about prosecutions for the crimes addicts commit in order to support their habits?

In Wheeler v. U. S., a decision of the District of Columbia Court of Appeals, 276 A.2d 722 (D.C.App.1971), the defendant was prosecuted for violating a provision of the District of Columbia's Criminal Code which prohibits the possession of narcotics paraphernalia. He argued that in view of *Robinson* he could not be convicted for conduct incidental to the conviction. In rejecting this contention the court pointed out that Congress, in the preamble to the rehabilitation act, stated that "The Congress intends that Federal Criminal laws shall be enforced against drug users . . . and [the act] shall not be used to substitute treatment for punishment in cases of crimes committed by drug users". The court said that it would be "a paradox if the eighth amendment must be read today as invalidating the measures enacted by Congress to deter narcotics users from persisting in habits ruinous to their health and character as well as to protect the public from dangerous crimes committed by them".

4. If narcotic addiction is not punishable criminally, may a chronic alcoholic be found guilty for violating a law prohibiting public intoxication?

In Powell v. Texas, 392 U.S. 651, 88 S.Ct. 2145 (1968), the Supreme Court, in a 5–4 decision, held that the conviction for public intoxication of a person who was to some degree compelled to drink did not amount to "cruel and unusual punishment" where it did not appear that he was unable to stay off the streets on the occasion in question.

The Minnesota Supreme Court, in State v. Fearon, 233 Minn. 90, 166 N.W.2d 720, (1969) held that since a chronic alcoholic does not drink by choice he cannot be punished for his subsequent drunkenness in a public place. For a general review of the case law, see 40 A.L.R.3d 321.

FURMAN v. GEORGIA

JACKSON v. GEORGIA

BRANCH v. TEXAS

Supreme Court of the United States, 1972.
408 U.S. 238, 92 S.Ct. 2726.

PER CURIAM [Petitioner Furman was convicted of murder and sentenced to death; Petitioners Jackson and Branch were convicted of rape and sentenced to death.] Certiorari was granted limited to the following question: "Does the imposition and carrying out of the death penalty in [these cases] constitute cruel and unusual punishment in violation of the Eighth and Fourteenth Amendments?" . . . The Court holds that the imposition and carrying out of the death penalty in these cases constitutes cruel and unusual punishment in violation of the Eighth and Fourteenth Amendments. The judgment in each case is therefore reversed insofar as it leaves undisturbed the death sentence imposed, and the cases are remanded for further proceedings. So ordered.

Judgment in each case reversed in part and cases remanded.

MR. JUSTICE DOUGLAS, MR. JUSTICE BRENNAN, MR. JUSTICE STEWART, MR. JUSTICE WHITE and MR. JUSTICE MARSHALL filed separate opinions in support of judgments.

MR. CHIEF JUSTICE BURGER, MR. JUSTICE BLACKMUN, MR. JUSTICE POWELL and MR. JUSTICE REHNQUIST filed separate dissenting opinions.

[The reproduction of all of the opinions required 118 pages in the Supreme Court Reporter; they obviously had to be considerably reduced for casebook purposes. This also necessitated the omission of all of the 360 footnotes.]

MR. JUSTICE DOUGLAS, concurring.

In these three cases the death penalty was imposed, one of them for murder, and two for rape. In each the determination of whether the penalty should be death or a lighter punishment was left by the State to the discretion of the judge or of the jury. In each of the three cases the trial was to a jury. They are here on petitions for certiorari which we granted limited to the question whether the imposition and execution of the death penalty constitutes "cruel and unusual punishments" within the meaning of the Eighth Amendment as applied to the States by the Fourteenth. I vote to vacate each judgment, believing that the exaction of the death penalty does violate the Eighth and Fourteenth Amendments.

That the requirements of due process ban cruel and unusual punishment is now settled. Louisiana ex rel. Francis v. Resweber . . . ; Robinson v. California, . . .

It has been assumed in our decisions that punishment by death is not cruel, unless the manner of execution can be said to be inhuman and barbarous. In re Kemmler, . . . It is also said in our opinions that the proscription of cruel and unusual punishments "is not fastened to the obsolete, but may acquire meaning as public opinion becomes enlightened by a humane justice." . . . A like statement was made in Trop v. Dulles, . . . that the Eighth Amendment "must draw its meaning from the evolving standards of decency that mark the progress of a maturing society."

The generalities of a law inflicting capital punishment is one thing. What may be said of the validity of a law on the books and what may be done with the law in its application do or may lead to quite different conclusions.

It would seem to be incontestable that the death penalty inflicted on one defendant is "unusual" if it discriminates against him by reason of his race, religion, wealth, social position, or class, or if it is imposed under a procedure that gives room for the play of such prejudices.

There is evidence that the provision of the English Bill of Rights of 1689 from which the language of the Eighth Amendment was taken was concerned primarily with selective or irregular application of harsh penalties and that its aim was to forbid arbitrary and discriminatory penalties of a severe nature.

* * *

The words "cruel and unusual" certainly include penalties that are barbaric. But the words, at least when read in light of the English proscription against selective and irregular use of penalties, suggest that it is "cruel and unusual" to apply the death penalty—or any other penalty—selectively to minorities whose numbers are few, who are outcasts of society, and who are unpopular, but whom society is willing to see suffer though it would not countenance general application of the same penalty across the boards . . .

The Court in McGautha v. California, . . . noted that in this country there was almost from the beginning a "rebellion against the common-law rule imposing a mandatory death sentence on all convicted murderers." The first attempted remedy was to restrict the death penalty to defined offenses such as "premeditated" murder. But juries took "the law into their own hands" and refused to convict on the capital offense.

> "In order to meet the problem of jury nullification, legislatures did not try, as before, to refine further the definition of capital homicides. Instead they adopted the method of forthrightly granting juries the discretion which they had been exercising in fact."

The Court concluded "In light of history, experience, and the present limitations of human knowledge, we find it quite impossible to say that committing to the untrammeled discretion of the jury the power to pronounce life or death in capital cases is offensive to any thing in the Constitution."

The Court refused to find constitutional dimensions in the argument that those who exercise their discretion to send a person to death should be given standards by which that discretion should be exercised.

A recent witness before the Committee of the Judiciary, United States House of Representatives, Ernest van den Haag, . . . stated:

> "Any penalty, a fine, imprisonment or the death penalty could be unfairly or unjustly applied. The vice in this case is not in the penalty but in the process by which it is inflicted. It is unfair to inflict unequal penalties on equally guilty parties, or on any innocent parties, *regardless of what the penalty is.*
>
> "I conclude that this vice must be corrected, if it exists, not by changing penalties but by changing the processes by which they are judicially inflicted."

But those who advance that argument overlook *McGautha.*

We are now imprisoned in the *McGautha* holding. Indeed the seeds of the present cases are in *McGautha.* Juries (or judges, as the case may be) have practically untrammeled discretion to let an accused live or insist that he die.

The high service rendered by the "cruel and unusual" punishment clause of the Eighth Amendment is to require legislatures to write penal laws that are evenhanded, nonselective, and nonarbitrary, and to require judges to see to it that general laws are not applied sparsely, selectively, and spottily to unpopular groups.

A law that stated that anyone making more than $50,000 would be exempt from the death penalty would plainly fall, as would a law that in terms said that Blacks, those who never went beyond the fifth grade in school, or those who made less than $3,000 a year, or those who were unpopular or unstable should be the only people executed. A law which in the overall view reaches that result in practice has no more sanctity than a law which in terms provides the same.

Thus, these discretionary statutes are unconstitutional in their operation. They are pregnant with discrimination and discrimination is an ingredient not compatible with the idea of equal protection of the laws that is implicit in the ban on "cruel and unusual" punishments.

Any law which is nondiscriminatory on its face may be applied in such a way as to violate the Equal Protection Clause of the Fourteenth Amendment. . . . Such conceivably might be the fate of a mandatory death penalty, where equal or lesser sentences were imposed on the elite, a harsher one on the minorities or members of the lower castes. Whether a mandatory death penalty would otherwise be constitutional is a question I do not reach.

I concur in the judgments of the Court.

MR. JUSTICE BRENNAN, concurring.

The question presented in these cases is whether death is today a punishment for crime that is "cruel and unusual" and consequently, by virtue of the Eighth and Fourteenth Amendments, beyond the power of the State to inflict.

Almost a century ago, this Court observed that "[d]ifficulty would attend the effort to define with exactness the extent of the constitutional provision which provides that cruel and unusual punishments shall not be inflicted." . . . Less than 15 years ago, it was again noted that "[t]he exact scope of the constitutional phrase 'cruel and unusual' has not been detailed by this Court." . . . Those statements remain true today. The Cruel and Unusual Punishments Clause, like the other great clauses of the Constitution, is not susceptible to precise definition. Yet we know that the values and ideals it embodies are basic to our scheme of government. And we know also that the Clause imposes upon this Court the duty, when the issue is properly presented, to determine the constitutional validity of a challenged punishment, whatever that punishment may be. In these cases, "[t]hat issue confronts us, and the task of resolving it is inescapably ours." . . . .

We have very little evidence of the Framers' intent in including the Cruel and Unusual Punishments Clause among those restraints upon the new Government enumerated in the Bill of Rights.

* * *

. . . we cannot now know exactly what the Framers thought "cruel and unusual punishments" were. Certainly they intended to ban torturous punishments, but the available evidence does not support the further conclusion that *only* torturous punishments were to be outlawed. . . .

* * *

Judicial enforcement of the Clause, then, cannot be evaded by invoking the obvious truth that legislatures have the power to prescribe punishments for crimes. That is precisely the reason the Clause appears in the Bill of Rights. The difficulty arises, rather, in formulating the "legal principles to be applied by the courts" when a legislatively prescribed punishment is challenged as "cruel and unusual." In formulating those constitutional principles, we must avoid the insertion of "judicial conception[s] of . . . wisdom or propriety," . . . yet we must not, in the guise of "judicial restraint," abdicate our fundamental responsibility to enforce the Bill of Rights. Were we to do so, the "constitution would indeed be as easy of application as it would be deficient in efficacy and power. Its general principles would have little value and be converted by precedent into impotent and lifeless formulas. Rights declared in words might be lost in reality." . . . The Cruel and Unusual Punishments Clause would become, in short, "little more than good advice." . . .

Ours would indeed be a simple task were we required merely to measure a challenged punishment against those that history has long condemned. That narrow and unwarranted view of the Clause, however, was left behind with the 19th century. Our task today is more complex. We know "that the words of the [Clause] are not precise, and that their scope is not static." We know, therefore, that the Clause "must draw its meaning from the evolving standards of decency that mark the progress of a maturing society." . . . That knowledge, of course, is but the beginning of the inquiry.

The primary principle is that a punishment must not be so severe as to be degrading to the dignity of human beings. Pain, certainly, may be a factor in the judgment. The infliction of an extremely severe punishment will often entail physical suffering. . . . Yet the Framers also knew "that there could be exercises of cruelty by laws other than those which inflicted bodily pain or mutilation." . . . Even though "[t]here may be involved no physical mistreatment, no primitive torture," . . . severe mental pain may be inherent in the infliction of a particular punishment. . . .

* * *

In determining whether a punishment comports with human dignity, we are aided also by a second principle inherent in the Clause—that the State must not arbitrarily inflict a severe punishment. This principle derives from the notion that the State does not respect human dignity when, without reason, it inflicts upon some people a severe punishment that it does not inflict upon others. Indeed, the very words "cruel and unusual punishments" imply condemnation of the arbitrary infliction of severe punishments. And, as we now know, the English history of the Clause reveals a particular concern with the establishment of a safeguard against arbitrary punishments. . . .

* * *

A third principle inherent in the Clause is that a severe punishment must not be unacceptable to contemporary society. Rejection by society, of course, is a strong indication that a severe punishment does not comport with human dignity. In applying this principle, however, we must make certain that the judicial determination is as objective as possible. Thus, for example, Weems v. United States, . . . and Trop v. Dulles . . . suggest that one factor that may be considered is the existence of the punishment in jurisdictions other than those before the Court . . . another factor to be considered is the historic usage of the punishment.

* * *

The question under this principle, then, is whether there are objective indicators from which a court can conclude that contemporary society considers a severe punishment unacceptable. Accordingly, the judicial task is to review the history of a challenged punishment and to examine society's present practices with respect to its use. Legislative authorization, of course, does not establish acceptance. The acceptability of a severe punishment is measured not by its availability, for it might become so offensive to society as never to be inflicted, but by its use.

The final principle inherent in the Clause is that a severe punishment must not be excessive. A punishment is excessive under this principle if it is unnecessary: The infliction of a severe punishment by the State cannot comport with human dignity when it is nothing more than the pointless infliction of suffering. If there is a significantly less severe punishment adequate to achieve the purposes for which the punishment is inflicted, . . . the punishment inflicted is unnecessary and therefore excessive.

* * *

The question, then, is whether the deliberate infliction of death is today consistent with the command of the Clause that the State may not inflict punishments that do not comport with human dignity. I will analyze the punishment of death in terms of the principles set out above and the cumulative test to which they lead: It is a denial of human dignity for the State arbitrarily to subject a person to an unusually severe punishment that society has indicated it does not regard as acceptable and that cannot be shown to serve any penal purpose more effectively than a significantly less drastic punishment. Under these principles and this test, death is today a "cruel and unusual" punishment.

Death is a unique punishment in the United States. In a society that so strongly affirms the sanctity of life, not surprisingly the common view is that death is the ultimate sanction. This natural human feeling appears all about us. There has been no national debate about punishment, in general or by imprisonment, comparable to the debate about the punishment of death. No other punishment has been so continuously restricted, . . . nor has any State yet abolished prisons, as some have abolished this punishment. And those States that still inflict death reserve it for the most heinous crimes. Juries, of course, have always treated death cases differently, as have governors exercising their commutation powers. . . . Some legislatures have required particular procedures, such as two-stage trials and automatic appeals, applicable only in death cases. "It is the universal experience in the administration of criminal justice that those charged with capital offenses are granted special considerations." . . . (all States require juries of 12 in death cases). This Court, too, almost always treats death cases as a class apart. And the unfortunate effect of this punishment upon the functioning of the judicial process is well known; no other punishment has a similar effect.

* * *

Death is truly an awesome punishment. The calculated killing of a human being by the State involves, by its very nature, a denial of the executed person's humanity. The contrast with the plight of a person punished by imprisonment is evident. An individual in prison does not lose "the right to have rights." A prisoner retains, for example, the constitutional rights to the free exercise of religion, to be free of cruel and unusual punishments, and to treatment as a "person" for purposes of due process of law and the equal protection of the laws. A prisoner remains a member of the human family. Moreover, he retains the right of access to the courts. His punishment is not irrevocable. Apart from the common charge, grounded upon the recognition of human fallibility, that the punishment of death must inevitably be inflicted upon innocent men, we know that death has been the lot of men whose convictions were unconstitutionally secured in view of later, retroactively applied, holdings of this Court. The punishment itself may have been unconstitutionally inflicted, . . . yet the finality of death precludes relief. An executed person has indeed "lost the right to have rights." As one 19th century proponent of punishing criminals by death declared, "When a man is hung, there is an end of our relations with him. His execution is a way of saying, 'You are not fit for this world. Take your chance elsewhere.'"

In comparison to all other punishments today, then, the deliberate extinguishment of human life by the State is uniquely degrading to human dignity. I would not hesitate to hold, on that ground alone, that death is today a "cruel and unusual" punishment, were it not that death is a punishment of long-standing usage and acceptance in this country. I therefore turn to the second principle—that the State may not arbitrarily inflict an unusually severe punishment.

* * *

When a country of over 200 million people inflicts an unusually severe punishment no more than 50 times a year, the inference is strong that the punishment is not being regularly and fairly applied. To dispel it would indeed require a clear showing of nonarbitrary infliction.

* * *

In sum, the punishment of death is inconsistent with all four principles: Death is an unusually severe and degrading punishment; there is a strong probability that it is inflicted arbitrarily; its rejection by contemporary society is virtually total; and there is no reason to believe that it serves any penal purpose more effectively than the less severe punishment of imprisonment. The function of these principles is to enable a court to determine whether a punishment comports with human dignity. Death, quite simply, does not.

MR. JUSTICE STEWART, concurring.

The penalty of death differs from all other forms of criminal punishment, not in degree but in kind. It is unique in its total irrevocability. It is unique in its rejection of rehabilitation of the convict as a basic purpose of criminal justice. And it is unique, finally, in its absolute renunciation of all that is embodied in our concept of humanity.

For these and other reasons, at least two of my Brothers have concluded that the infliction of the death penalty is constitutionally impermissible in all circumstances under the Eighth and Fourteenth Amendments. Their case is a strong one. But I find it unnecessary to reach the ultimate question they would decide. . . .

* * *

Legislatures—state and federal—have sometimes specified that the penalty of death shall be the mandatory punishment for every person convicted of engaging in certain designated criminal conduct. Congress, for example, has provided that anyone convicted of acting as a spy for the enemy in time of war shall be put to death. The

Rhode Island Legislature has ordained the death penalty for a life term prisoner who commits murder. Massachusetts has passed a law imposing the death penalty upon anyone convicted of murder in the commission of a forcible rape. An Ohio law imposes the mandatory penalty of death upon the assassin of the President of the United States or the Governor of a State.

If we were reviewing death sentences imposed under these or similar laws, we would be faced with the need to decide whether capital punishment is unconstitutional for all crimes and under all circumstances. We would need to decide whether a legislature—state or federal—could constitutionally determine that certain criminal conduct is so atrocious that societys' interest in deterrence and retribution wholly outweighs any considerations of reform or rehabilitation of the perpetrator, and that, despite the inconclusive empirical evidence, only the automatic penalty of death will provide maximum deterrence.

On that score I would say only that I cannot agree that retribution is a constitutionally impermissible ingredient in the imposition of punishment. The instinct for retribution is part of the nature of man, and channeling that instinct in the administration of criminal justice serves an important purpose in promoting the stability of a society governed by law. When people begin to believe that organized society is unwilling or unable to impose upon criminal offenders the punishment they "deserve," then there are sown the seeds of anarchy—of self-help, vigilante justice, and lynch law.

The constitutionality of capital punishment in the abstract is not, however, before us in these cases. For the Georgia and Texas legislatures have not provided that the death penalty shall be imposed upon all those who are found guilty of forcible rape. And the Georgia Legislature has not ordained that death shall be the automatic punishment for murder. In a word, neither State has made a legislative determination that forcible rape and murder can be deterred only by imposing the penalty of death upon all who perpetrate those offenses. As Mr. Justice White so tellingly puts it, the "legislative will is not frustrated if the penalty is never imposed."

Instead, the death sentences now before us are the product of a legal system that brings them, I believe, within the very core of the Eighth Amendment's guarantee against cruel and unusual punishments, a guarantee applicable against the States through the Fourteenth Amendment. . . . In the first place, it is clear that these sentences are "cruel" in the sense that they excessively go beyond, not in degree but in kind, the punishments that the state legislatures have determined to be necessary. . . . In the second place, it is equally clear that these sentences are "unusual" in the sense that the penalty of death is infrequently imposed for murder, and that its imposition for rape is extraordinarily rare. But I do not rest my conclusion upon these two propositions alone.

These death sentences are cruel and unusual in the same way that being struck by lightning is cruel and unusual. For, of all the people convicted of rapes and murders in 1967 and 1968, many just as reprehensible as these, the petitioners are among a capriciously selected random handful upon whom the sentence of death has in fact been imposed. My concurring Brothers have demonstrated that, if any basis can be discerned for the selection of these few to be sentenced to die, it is the constitutionally impermissible basis of race. . . . But racial discrimination has not been proved, and I put it to one side. I simply conclude that the Eighth and Fourteenth Amendments cannot tolerate the infliction of a sentence of death under legal systems that permit this unique penalty to be so wantonly and so freakishly imposed.

MR. JUSTICE WHITE, concurring.

The facial constitutionality of statutes requiring the imposition of the death penalty for first degree murder, for more narrowly defined categories of murder or for rape would present quite different issues under the Eighth Amendment than are posed by the cases before us. In joining the Court's judgment, therefore, I do not at all intimate that the death penalty is unconstitutional *per se* or that there is no system of capital punishment that would comport with the Eighth Amendment. That question, ably argued by several of my Brethren, is not presented by these cases and need not be decided.

The narrower question to which I address myself concerns the constitutionality of capital punishment statutes under which (1) the legislature authorizes the imposition of the death penalty for murder or rape; (2) the legislature does not itself mandate the penalty in any particular class or kind of case (that is, legislative will is not frustrated if the penalty is never imposed) but delegates to judges or juries the decisions as to those cases, if any, in which the penalty will be utilized; and (3) judges and juries have ordered the death penalty with such infrequency that the odds are now very much against imposition and execution of the penalty with respect to any convicted murderer or rapist. It is in this context that we must consider whether the execution of these petitioners violates the Eighth Amendment.

I begin with what I consider a near truism: that the death penalty could so seldom be imposed that it would cease to be a credible deterrent or measurably to contribute to any other end of punishment in the criminal justice system. It is perhaps true that no matter how infrequently those convicted of rape or murder are executed, the penalty so imposed is not disproportionate to the crime and those executed may deserve exactly what they received. It would also be clear that executed defendants are finally and completely incapacitated from again committing rape or murder or any other crime. But when imposition of the penalty reaches a certain degree of infrequency, it would be very doubtful that any existing general need for retribution would be measurably satisfied. Nor could it be said with confidence that society's need for specific deterrence justifies death for so few when for so many in like circumstances life imprisonment or shorter prison terms are judged sufficient, or that community values are measurably reenforced by authorizing a penalty so rarely invoked.

Most important, a major goal of the criminal law—to deter others by punishing the convicted criminal—would not be substantially served where the penalty is so seldom invoked that it ceases to be the credible threat essential to influence the conduct of others. For present purposes I accept the morality and utility of punishing one person to influence another. I accept also the effectiveness of punishment generally and need not reject the death penalty as a more effective deterrent than a lesser punishment. But common sense and experience tell us that seldom-enforced laws become ineffective measures for controlling human conduct and that the death penalty, unless imposed with sufficient frequency, will make little contribution to deterring those crimes for which it may be exacted.

The imposition and execution of the death penalty are obviously cruel in the dictionary sense. But the penalty has not been considered cruel and unusual punishment in the constitutional sense because it was thought justified by the social ends it was deemed to serve. At the moment that it ceases realistically to further these purposes, however, the emerging question is whether its imposition in such circumstances would violate the Eighth Amendment. It is my view that it would, for its imposition would then be the pointless and needless extinction of life with only marginal contributions to any discernible social or public purposes. A penalty with such negligible returns to the State would be patently excessive and cruel and unusual punishment violative of the Eighth Amendment.

It is also my judgment that this point has been reached with respect to capital punishment as it is presently administered under the statutes involved in these cases. Concededly, it is difficult to prove as a general proposition that capital punishment, however administered, more effectively serves the ends of the criminal law than does imprisonment. But however that may be, I cannot avoid the conclusion that as the statutes before us are now administered, the penalty is so infrequently imposed that the threat of execution is too attenuated to be of substantial service to criminal justice.

MR. JUSTICE MARSHALL, concurring.

* * *

Perhaps the most important principle in analyzing "cruel and unusual" punishment questions is one that is reiterated again and again in the prior opinions of the Court: i. e., the cruel and unusual language "must draw its meaning from the evolving standards of decency that mark the progress of a maturing society." Thus, a penalty which was permissible at one time in our Nation's history is not necessarily permissible today.

* * *

. . . It is not improper at this point to take judicial notice of the fact that for more than 200 years men have labored to demonstrate that capital punishment serves no purpose that life imprisonment could not serve equally as well. And they have done so with great success. Little if any evidence has been adduced to prove the contrary. The point has now been reached at which deference to the legislatures is tantamount to abdication of our judicial roles as factfinders, judges, and ultimate arbiters of the Constitution. We know that at some point the presumption of constitutionality accorded legislative acts gives way to a realistic assessment of those acts. This point comes when there is sufficient evidence available so that judges can determine not whether the legislature acted wisely, but whether it had any rational basis whatsoever for acting. We have this evidence before us now. There is no rational basis for concluding that capital punishment is not excessive. It therefore violates the Eighth Amendment.

* * *

Assuming knowledge of all the facts presently available regarding capital punishment, the average citizen would, in my opinion, find it shocking to his conscience and sense of justice. For this reason alone capital punishment cannot stand.

In striking down capital punishment, this Court does not malign our system of government. On the contrary, it pays homage to it. Only in a free society could right triumph in difficult times, and could civilization record its magnificent advancement. In recognizing the humanity of our fellow beings, we pay ourselves the highest tribute. We achieve "a major milestone in the long road up from barbarism" and join the approximately 70 other jurisdictions in the world which celebrate their regard for civilization and humanity by shunning capital punishment.

MR. CHIEF JUSTICE BURGER, with whom MR. JUSTICE BLACKMUN, MR. JUSTICE POWELL, and MR. JUSTICE REHNQUIST join, dissenting.

At the outset it is important to note that only two members of the Court, MR. JUSTICE BRENNAN and MR. JUSTICE MARSHALL, have concluded that the Eighth Amendment prohibits capital punishment for all crimes and under all circumstances. MR. JUSTICE DOUGLAS has also determined that the death penalty contravenes the Eighth Amendment, although I do not read his opinion as necessarily requiring final abolition of the penalty. . . . the constitutional prohibition against "cruel and unusual punishments" cannot be construed to bar the imposition of the punishment of death.

MR. JUSTICE STEWART and MR. JUSTICE WHITE have concluded that petitioners' death sentences must be set aside because prevailing sentencing practices do not comply with the Eighth Amendment. . . . I believe this approach fundamentally misconceives the nature of the Eighth Amendment guarantee and flies directly in the face of controlling authority of extremely recent vintage.

If we were possessed of legislative power, I would either join with MR. JUSTICE BRENNAN and MR. JUSTICE MARSHALL or, at the very least, restrict the use of capital punishment to a small category of the most heinous crimes. Our constitutional inquiry, however, must be divorced from personal feelings as to the morality and efficacy of the death penalty and be confined to the meaning and applicability of the uncertain language of the Eighth Amendment. There is no novelty in being called upon to interpret a constitutional provision that is less than self-defining, but of all our fundamental guarantees, the ban on "cruel and unusual punishments" is one of the most difficult to translate into judicially manageable terms. The widely divergent views of the Amendment expressed in today's opinions reveal the haze that surrounds this constitutional command. Yet it is essential to our role as a court that we not seize upon the enigmatic character of the guarantee as an invitation to enact our personal predilections into law.

Although the Eighth Amendment literally reads as prohibiting only those punishments that are both "cruel" and "unusual," history compels the conclusion that the Constitution prohibits all punishments of extreme and barbarous cruelty, regardless of how frequently or infrequently imposed.

The most persuasive analysis of Parliament's adoption of the English Bill of Rights of 1689—the unquestioned source of the Eighth Amendment wording—suggests that the prohibition against "cruel and unusual punishments" was included therein out of aversion to severe punishments not legally authorized and not within the jurisdiction of the courts to impose. To the extent that the term "unusual" had any importance in the English version, it was apparently intended as a reference to illegal punishments.

From every indication, the framers of the Eighth Amendment intended to give the phrase a meaning far different from that of its English precursor. The records of the debates in several of the State conventions called to ratify the 1789 draft Constitution submitted prior to the addition of the Bill of Rights show that the framers' exclusive concern was the absence of any ban on tortures. The later inclusion of the "cruel and unusual punishment" clause was in response to these objections. There was no discussion of the inter-relationship of the terms "cruel" and "unusual," and there is nothing in the debates supporting the inference that the Founding Fathers would have been receptive to torturous or excessively cruel punishments even if usual in character or authorized by law.

* * *

In the 181 years since the enactment of the Eighth Amendment, not a single decision of this Court has cast the slightest shadow of a doubt on the constitutionality of capital punishment.

* * *

By limiting its grants of certiorari, the Court has refused even to hear argument on the Eighth Amendment claim on two occasions in the last four years. . . . In these cases the Court confined its attention to the procedural aspects of capital trials, it being implicit that the punishment itself could be constitutionally imposed. Nonetheless, the Court has now been asked to hold that a punishment clearly permissible under the Constitution at the time of its adoption and accepted as such by every member of the Court until today, is suddenly so cruel as to be incompatible with the Eighth Amendment.

Before recognizing such an instant evolution in the law, it seems fair to ask what factors have changed that capital punishment should now be "cruel" in the constitutional sense as it has not been in the past. It is apparent that there has been no change of constitutional significance in the nature of the punishment itself. Twentieth century modes of execution surely involve no greater physical suffering than the means employed at the time of the Eighth Amendment's adoption. And although a man awaiting execution must inevitably experience extraordinary mental anguish, no one suggests that this anguish is materially different from that experienced by condemned men in 1791, even though protracted appellate review processes have greatly increased the waiting time on "death row." To be sure, the ordeal of the condemned man may be thought cruel in the sense that all suffering is thought cruel. But if the Constitution proscribed every punishment producing severe emotional stress, then capital punishment would clearly have been impermissible in 1791.

* * *

There are no obvious indications that capital punishment offends the conscience of society to such a degree that our traditional deference to the legislative judgment must be abandoned. It is not a punishment such as burning at the stake that everyone would ineffably find to be repugnant to all civilized standards. Nor is it a punishment so roundly condemned that only a few aberrant legislatures have retained it on the statute books. Capital punishment is authorized by statute in 40 States, the District of Columbia and in the federal courts for the commission of certain crimes. On four occasions in the last 11 years Congress has added to the list of federal crimes punishable by death. . . .

* * *

Today the Court has not ruled that capital punishment is *per se* violative of the Eighth Amendment; nor has it ruled that the punishment is barred for any particular class or classes of crimes. The substantially similar concurring opinions of MR. JUSTICE STEW-

ART and MR. JUSTICE WHITE, which are necessary to support the judgment setting aside petitioners' sentences, stop short of reaching the ultimate question. The actual scope of the Court's ruling, which I take to be embodied in these concurring opinions, is not entirely clear. This much, however, seems apparent: if the legislatures are to continue to authorize capital punishment for some crimes, juries and judges can no longer be permitted to make the sentencing determination in the same manner they have in the past. This approach—not urged in oral arguments or briefs—misconceives the nature of the constitutional command against "cruel and unusual punishments," disregards controlling case law, and demands a rigidity in capital cases which, if possible of achievement, cannot be regarded as a welcome change. Indeed the contrary seems to be the case.

As I have earlier stated, the Eighth Amendment forbids the imposition of punishments that are so cruel and inhumane as to violate society's standards of civilized conduct. The Amendment does not prohibit all punishments the States are unable to prove necessary to deter or control crime. The Amendment is not concerned with the process by which a State determines that a particular punishment is to be imposed in a particular case. And the Amendment most assuredly does not speak to the power of legislatures to confer sentencing discretion on juries, rather than to fix all sentences by statute.

The critical factor in the concurring opinions of both MR. JUSTICE STEWART and MR. JUSTICE WHITE is the infrequency with which the penalty is imposed. This factor is taken not as evidence of society's abhorrence of capital punishment—the inference that petitioners would have the Court draw—but as the earmark of a deteriorated system of sentencing. It is concluded that petitioners' sentences must be set aside, not because the punishment is impermissibly cruel, but because juries and judges have failed to exercise their sentencing discretion in acceptable fashion.

To be sure, there is a recitation cast in Eighth Amendment terms: petitioners' sentences are "cruel" because they exceed that which the legislatures have deemed necessary for all cases; petitioners' sentences are "unusual" because they exceed that which is imposed in most cases. This application of the words of the Eighth Amendment suggests that capital punishment can be made to satisfy Eighth Amendment values if its rate of imposition is somehow multiplied; it seemingly follows that the flexible sentencing system created by the legislatures, and carried out by juries and judges, has yielded more mercy than the Eighth Amendment can stand. The implications of this approach are mildly ironical. . . .

Since there is no majority of the Court on the ultimate issue presented in these cases, the future of capital punishment in this country has been left in an uncertain limbo. Rather than providing a final and unambiguous answer on the basic constitutional question, the collective impact of the majority's ruling is to demand an undetermined measure of change from the various state legislatures and the Congress. While I cannot endorse the process of decisionmaking that has yielded today's result and the restraints which that result imposes on legislative action, I am not altogether displeased that legislative bodies have been given the opportunity, and indeed unavoidable responsibility, to make a thorough re-evaluation of the entire subject of capital punishment. If today's opinions demonstrate nothing else, they starkly show that this is an area where legislatures can act far more effectively than courts.

The legislatures are free to eliminate capital punishment for specific crimes or to carve-out limited exceptions to a general abolition of the penalty, without adherence to the conceptual strictures of the Eighth Amendment. The legislatures can and should make an assessment of the deterrent influence of capital punishment, both generally and as affecting the commission of specific types of crimes. If legislatures come to doubt the efficacy of capital punishment, they can abolish it, either completely or on a selective basis. If new evidence persuades them that they have acted unwisely, they can reverse their field and reinstate the penalty to the extent it is thought warranted. An Eighth Amendment ruling by judges cannot be made with such flexibility or discriminating precision.

The world-wide trend toward limiting the use of capital punishment, a phenomenon we have been urged to give great weight, hardly points the way to a judicial solution in this country under a written Constitution. Rather, the change has generally come about through legislative action, often on a trial basis and with the retention of the penalty for certain limited classes of crimes. Virtually nowhere has change been wrought by so crude a tool as the Eighth Amendment. The complete and unconditional abolition of capital punishment in this country by judicial fiat would have undermined the careful progress of the legislative trend and foreclosed further inquiry on many as yet unanswered questions in this area.

Quite apart from the limitations of the Eighth Amendment itself, the preference for legislative action is justified by the inability of the courts to participate in the debate at the level where the controversy is focused. The case against capital punishment is not the product of legal dialectic, but rests primarily on factual claims, the truth of which cannot be tested by conventional judicial processes. The five opinions in support of the judgment differ in many respects, but they share a willingness to make sweeping factual assertions, unsupported by empirical data, concerning the manner of imposition and effectiveness of capital punishment in this country. Legislatures will have the opportunity to make a more penetrating study of these claims with the familiar and effective tools available to them as they are not to us.

The highest judicial duty is to recognize the limits on judicial power and to permit the democratic processes to deal with matters falling outside of those limits. The "hydraulic pressures" that Holmes spoke of as being generated by cases of great import have propelled the Court to go beyond the limits of judicial power, while fortunately leaving some room for legislative judgment.

MR. JUSTICE BLACKMUN, dissenting.

I join the respective opinions of THE CHIEF JUSTICE, MR. JUSTICE POWELL, and MR. JUSTICE REHNQUIST, and add only the following, somewhat personal, comments.

Cases such as these provide for me an excruciating agony of the spirit. I yield to no one in the depth of my distaste, antipathy, and, indeed, abhorrence, for the death penalty, with all its aspects of physical distress and fear and of moral judgment exercised by finite minds. That distaste is buttressed by a belief that capital punishment serves no useful purpose that can be demonstrated. For me, it violates childhood's training and life's experiences, and is not compatible with the philosophical convictions I have been able to develop. It is antagonistic to any sense of "reverence for life." Were I a legislator, I would vote against the death penalty for the policy reasons argued by counsel for the respective petitioners and expressed and adopted in the several opinions filed by the Justices who vote to reverse these convictions.

If the reservations expressed by my BROTHER STEWART (which, as I read his opinion, my BROTHER WHITE shares) were to command support, namely, that capital punishment may not be unconstitutional so long as it be mandatorily imposed, the result, I fear, will be that statutes stricken down today will be reenacted by state legislatures to prescribe the death penalty for specifed crimes without any alternative for the imposition of a lesser punishment in the discretion of the judge or jury, as the case may be. This approach, it seems to me, encourages legislation that is regressive and of an antique mold, for it eliminates the element of mercy in the imposition of punishment. I thought we had passed beyond that point in our criminology long ago.

* * *

MR. JUSTICE POWELL, with whom THE CHIEF JUSTICE, MR. JUSTICE BLACKMUN, and MR. JUSTICE REHNQUIST join, dissenting.

* * *

Whether one views the question as one of due process or of cruel and unusual punishment, as I do for convenience in this case, the issue is essentially the same. The fundamental premise upon which neither standard is based is that notions of what constitutes cruel and unusual punishment or due process do evolve. Neither the Congress nor any state legislature would today tolerate pillorying, branding, or cropping or nailing of the ears—punishments that were in existence during our colonial era. Should, however, any such punishment be prescribed, the courts would certainly enjoin its execution. . . . Likewise no court would approve any method of implementation of the death sentence found to involve unnecessary cruelty in light of presently available alternatives. Similarly, there may well be a process of evolving attitude with respect to the application of the death sentence for particular crimes. . . .

But we are not asked to consider the permissibility of any of the several methods employed in carrying out the death sentence. Nor are we asked, at least as part of the core submission in these cases, to determine whether the penalty might be a grossly excessive punishment for some specific criminal conduct. Either inquiry would call for a discriminating evaluation of particular means, or of the relationship between particular conduct and its punishment. Petitioners' principal argument goes far beyond the traditional process of case-by-case inclusion and exclusion. Instead the argument insists on an unprecedented constitutional rule of absolute prohibition of capital punishment for any crime, regardless of its depravity and impact on society. In calling for a precipitous and final judicial end to this form of penalty as offensive to evolving standards of decency, petitioners would have this Court abandon the traditional and more refined approach consistently followed in its prior Eighth Amendment precedents. What they are saying, in effect, is that the evolutionary process has come suddenly to an end; that the ultimate wisdom as to the appropriateness of capital punishment under all circumstances, and for all future generations, has somehow been revealed.

* * *

Any attempt to discern contemporary standards of decency through the review of objective factors must take into account several overriding considerations which petitioners choose to discount or ignore. In a democracy the first indicator of the public's attitude must always be found in the legislative judgments of the people's chosen representatives. MR. JUSTICE MARSHALL's opinion today catalogues the salient statistics. Forty States, the District of Columbia, and the Federal Government still authorize the death penalty for a wide variety of crimes. . . .

At the state level, New York, among other States, has recently undertaken reconsideration of its capital crimes. A law passed in 1967 restricted the use of capital punishment to the crimes of murder of a police officer and murder by a person serving a sentence of life imprisonment. . . .

I pause here to state that I am at a loss to understand how those urging this Court to pursue a course of *absolute* abolition as a matter of constitutional judgment can draw any support from the New York experience. As is also the case with respect to recent legislative activity in Canada and Great Britain, New York's decision to restrict the availability of the death penalty is a product of refined and discriminating legislative judgment, reflecting not the total rejection of capital punishment as inherently cruel, but indicating a desire to limit it to those circumstances in which legislative judgment deems retention to be in the public interest. No such legislative flexibility is permitted by the contrary course petitioners urge this Court to follow.

In addition to the New York experience, a number of other States have undertaken reconsideration of capital punishment in recent years. In four States the penalty has been put to a vote of the people through public referenda—a means likely to supply objective evidence of community standards. In Oregon a referendum seeking abolition of capital punishment failed in 1958 but was subsequently approved in 1964. Two years later the penalty was approved in Colorado by a wide margin. In Massachusetts, in 1968, in an advisory referendum, the voters there likewise recommended retention of the penalty. In 1970, approximately 64% of the voters in Illinois approved the penalty. In addition, the National Commission on Reform of Federal Criminal Laws reports that legislative committees in Massachusetts, Pennsylvania, and Maryland recommended abolition, while committees in New Jersey and Florida recommended retention. . . .

* * *

Members of this Court know, from the petitions and appeals that come before us regularly, that brutish and revolting murders continue to occur with disquieting frequency. Indeed, murders are so commonplace in our society that only the most sensational receive significant and sustained publicity. It could hardly be suggested that in any of these highly publicized murder cases—the several senseless assassinations or the too numerous shocking multiple murders that have stained this country's recent history—the public has exhibited any signs of "revulsion" at the thought of executing the convicted murderers. The public outcry, as we all know, has been quite to the contrary. Furthermore, there is little reason to suspect that the public's reaction would differ significantly in response to other less publicized murders. It is certainly arguable that many such murders, because of their senselessness or barbarousness, would evoke a public demand for the death penalty rather than a public rejection of that alternative. Nor is there any rational basis for arguing that the public reaction to any of these crimes would be muted if the murderer were "rich and powerful." The demand for the ultimate sanction might well be greater, as a wealthy killer is hardly a sympathetic figure. While there might be specific cases in which capital punishment would be regarded as excessive and shocking to the conscience of the community, it can hardly be argued that the public's dissatisfaction with the penalty in particular cases would translate into a demand for absolute abolition.

In pursuing the foregoing speculation, I do not suggest that it is relevant to the appropriate disposition of these cases. The purpose of the digression is to indicate that judicial decisions cannot be founded on such speculations and assumptions however appealing they may seem.

But the discrimination argument does not rest alone on a projection of the assumed effect on public opinion of more frequent executions. Much also is made of the undeniable fact that the death penalty has a greater impact on the lower economic strata of society, which include a relatively higher percentage of persons of minority racial and ethnic group backgrounds. The argument drawn from this fact is two-pronged. In part it is merely an extension of the speculation approach pursued by petitioners, *i. e.*, that public revulsion is suppressed in callous apathy because the penalty does not affect persons from the white middle class who comprise the majority in this country. This aspect, however, adds little to the infrequency rationalization for public apathy which I have found unpersuasive.

As MR. JUSTICE MARSHALL's opinion today demonstrates, the argument does have a more troubling aspect. It is his contention that if the average citizen were aware of the disproportionate burden of capital punishment borne by the "poor, the ignorant, and the underprivileged," he would find the penalty "shocking to his conscience and sense of justice" and would not stand for its further use. This argument, like the apathy rationale, calls for further speculation on the part of the Court. It also illuminates the quicksands upon which we are asked to base this decision. Indeed, the two contentions seem to require contradictory assumptions regarding the public's moral attitude toward capital punishment. The apathy argument is predicated on the assumption that the penalty is used against the less influential elements of society, that the public is fully aware of this, and that it tolerates use of capital punishment only because of a callous indifference to the offenders who are sentenced. MR. JUSTICE MARSHALL's argument, on the other hand, rests on the contrary assumption that the public does not know against whom the penalty is enforced and that if the public were educated to this fact it would find the punishment intolerable. Neither assumption can claim to be an entirely accurate portrayal of public attitude; for some acceptance of capital punishment might be a consequence of hardened apathy based on the knowledge of infrequent and uneven application, while for others acceptance may grow only out of ignorance. More significantly, however, neither supposition acknowledges what, for me, is a more basic flaw.

Certainly the claim is justified that this criminal sanction falls more heavily on the relatively impoverished and underprivileged elements of society. The "have-nots" in every society always have been subject to greater pressure to commit crimes and to fewer constraints than their more affluent fellow citizens. This is, indeed, a tragic byproduct of social and economic deprivation, but it is not an argument of constitutional proportions under the Eighth or Fourteenth Amendment. The same discriminatory impact argument could be made with equal force and logic with respect to those sentenced to prison terms. The Due Process Clause admits of no distinction between the deprivation of "life" and the deprivation of "liberty." If discriminatory impact renders capital punishment cruel and unusual, it likewise renders invalid most of the prescribed penalties for crimes of violence. The root causes of the higher incidence of criminal penalties on "minorities and the poor" will not be cured by abolishing the system of penalties. Nor, indeed, could any society have a viable system of criminal justice if sanctions were abolished or ameliorated because most of those who commit crimes happen to be underprivileged. The basic problem results not from the penalties imposed for criminal conduct but from social and economic factors that have plagued humanity since the beginning of recorded history, frustrating all efforts to create in any country at any time the perfect society in which there are no "poor," no "minorities" and no "underprivileged." The causes underlying this problem are unrelated to the constitutional issue before the Court.

With deference and respect for the views of the Justices who differ, it seems to me that all these studies—both in this country and elsewhere—suggest that as a matter of policy and precedent this is a classic case for the exercise of our oft-announced allegiance to judicial restraint. I know of no case in which greater gravity and delicacy have attached to the duty that this Court is called on to perform whenever legislation—state or federal—is challenged on constitutional grounds. It seems to me that the sweeping judicial action undertaken today reflects a basic lack of faith and confidence in the democratic process. Many may regret, as I do, the failure of some legislative bodies to address the capital punishment issue with greater frankness or effectiveness. Many might decry their failure either to abolish the penalty entirely or selectively, or to establish standards for its enforcement. But impatience with the slowness, and even the unresponsiveness, of legislatures is no justification for judicial intrusion upon their historic powers. Rarely has there been a more appropriate opportunity for this Court to heed the philosophy of Mr. Justice Oliver Wendell Holmes. As Mr. Justice Frankfurter reminded the Court in *Trop*:

> "the whole of [Mr. Justice Holmes'] work during his thirty years of service on this Court should be a constant reminder that the power to invalidate legislation must not be exercised as if, either in constitutional theory or in the act of government, it stood as the sole bulwark against unwisdom or excesses of the moment." . . .

MR. JUSTICE REHNQUIST, with whom THE CHIEF JUSTICE, MR. JUSTICE BLACKMUN, and MR. JUSTICE POWELL join, dissenting.

The Court's judgment today strikes down a penalty that our Nation's legislators have thought necessary since our country was founded. My BROTHERS DOUGLAS, BRENNAN, and MARSHALL would at one fell swoop invalidate laws enacted by Congress and 40 of the 50 state legislatures and would consign to the limbo of unconstitutionality under a single rubric penalties for offenses as varied and unique as murder, piracy, mutiny, highjacking, and desertion in the face of the enemy. My BROTHERS STEWART and WHITE, asserting reliance on a more limited rationale—the reluctance of judges and juries actually to impose the death penalty in the majority of capital cases—join in the judgment in these cases. Whatever its precise rationale, today's holding necessarily brings into sharp relief the fundamental question of the role of judicial review in a democratic society. . . .

* * *

The courts in cases properly before them have been entrusted under the Constitution with the last word, short of constitutional amendment, as to whether a law passed by the legislature conforms to the Constitution. But just because courts in general, and this Court in particular, do have the last word, the admonition of Mr. Justice Stone in United States v. Butler must be constantly borne in mind:

> "[W]hile unconstitutional exercise of power by the executive and legislative branches of the government is subject to judicial restraint, the only check upon our own exercise of power is our own sense of self-restraint."

* * *

NOTES

1. A number of state legislatures have changed their capital punishment statutory provisions in an effort to avoid the faults described in *Furman.* Consider the following attempts in California and Florida.

California

§ 190. Murder; punishment

Every person guilty of murder in the first degree shall suffer death if any one or more of the special circumstances enumerated in Section 190.2 have been charged and found to be true in the manner provided in Section 190.1. Every person otherwise guilty of murder in the first degree shall suffer confinement in the state prison for life. Every person guilty of murder in the second degree is punishable by imprisonment in the state prison from five years to life.

§ 190.1 Death penalty; determination of guilt; right to counsel; separate determination of special circumstances; trier of fact; retrial after dismissal of jury

In any case in which the death penalty is to be imposed as the penalty for an offense only upon the finding of the truth of the special circumstances enumerated in Section 190.2, the guilt or innocence of the person charged shall first be determined without a finding as to penalty. In any such case the person charged shall be represented by counsel. If such a person has been found guilty of such an offense, and has been found sane on any plea of not guilty by reason of insanity, and any one or more of the special circumstances enumerated in Section 190.2 have been charged, there shall be further proceedings on the issue of the special circumstances charged. In any such proceedings the person shall be represented by counsel. The determination of the truth of any or all of the special circumstances charged shall be made by the trier of fact on the evidence presented. In case of a reasonable doubt whether a special circumstance is true, the defendant is entitled to a finding that it is not true. The trier of fact shall make a special finding that each special circumstance charged is either true or not true. Wherever a special circumstance requires proof of the commission or attempted commission of a crime, such crime shall be charged and proved pursuant to the general law applying to the trial and conviction of a crime.

If the defendant was convicted by the court sitting without a jury, the trier of fact shall be a jury unless a jury is waived by the defendant with the consent of the defendant's counsel, in which case the trier of fact shall be the court. If the defendant was convicted by a plea of guilty the trier of fact shall be a jury unless a jury is waived by the defendant with the consent of his counsel. If the defendant was convicted by a jury, the trier of fact shall be the same jury unless, for good cause shown, the court discharges that jury, in which case a new jury shall be drawn to determine the issue of whether or not any of the special circumstances charged are true or not true.

If the trier of fact finds, as to any person convicted of any offense under Section 190 requiring further proceedings that any one or more of the special circumstances enumerated in Section 190.2 as charged is true, the defendant shall suffer the penalty of death, and neither the finding that any of the remaining special circumstances charged is not true, nor if the trier of fact is a jury, the inability of the jury to agree on the issue of the truth or untruth of any of the remaining special circumstances charged, shall prohibit the imposition of such penalty.

In any case in which the defendant has been found guilty by a jury, and the same or another jury is unable to reach a unanimous verdict that one or more of the special circumstances charged are true, and does not reach a unanimous verdict that all of such special circumstances charged are not true, the court shall dismiss the jury and shall order a new jury impaneled to try the issues, but the issue of guilt shall not be retried by such jury, nor shall such jury retry the issue of the truth of any of the special circumstances which were found by a unanimous verdict of the previous jury to be untrue. If such new jury is unable to reach a unanimous verdict that one or more of the special circumstances it is trying are true, the court shall dismiss the jury and impose the punishment of confinement in the state prison for life.

§ 190.2 Death penalty; special circumstances

The penalty for a person found guilty of first-degree murder shall be death in any case in which the trier of fact pursuant to the further proceedings provided for in Section 190.1 makes a special finding that:

(a) The murder was intentional and was carried out pursuant to an agreement with the defendant. "An agreement," as used in this subdivision, means an agreement by the person who committed the murder to accept valuable consideration for the act of murder from any person other than the victim.

(b) The defendant personally committed the act which caused the death of the victim and any of the following additional circumstances exist:

(1) The victim is a peace officer, [which includes correctional, parole and probation officers], who, while engaged in the performance of his duty, was intentionally killed, and the defendant knew or reasonably should have known that such victim was a peace officer engaged in the performance of his duties.

(2) The murder was willful, deliberate and premeditated and the victim was a witness to a crime who was intentionally killed for the purpose of preventing his testimony in any criminal proceeding.

(3) The murder was willful, deliberate and premeditated and was committed during the commission or attempted commission of any of the following crimes:

(i) Robbery, ...

(ii) Kidnapping, ... Brief movements of a victim which are merely incidental to the commission of another offense and which do not substantially increase the victim's risk of harm over that necessarily inherent in the other offense do not constitute kidnapping within the meaning of this paragraph.

(iii) Rape by force or violence, . . . ; or by threat of great and immediate bodily harm, ...

(iv) The performance of lewd or lascivious acts upon the person of a child under the age of 14, ...

(v) Burglary . . . of an inhabited dwelling housing entered by the defendant with an intent to commit grand or petit larceny or rape.

(4) The defendant has in this or in any prior proceeding been convicted of more than one offense of murder of the first or second degree. For the purpose of this paragraph an offense committed in another jurisdiction which if committed in California would be punishable as first or second degree murder shall be deemed to be murder of the first or second degree.

§ 190.3 Death penalty; exclusions; persons under 18; person not personally present at nor physically aiding in commission of act causing death

(a) Notwithstanding any other provision of law, the death penalty shall not be imposed upon any person who was under the age of 18 years at the time of the commission of the crime. The burden of proof as to the age of such person shall be upon the defendant.

(b) Except when the trier of facts finds that a murder was committed pursuant to an agreement as defined in subdivision (a) of Section 190.2, or when a person is convicted of [procuring, by willful perjury or subornation of perjury, the execution of an innocent person], the death penalty shall not be imposed upon any person who is a principal in the commission of a capital offense unless he was personally present during the commission of the act or acts causing death, and directly committed or physically aided in the commission of such act or acts.

Florida

921.141 Sentence of death or life imprisonment for capital felonies; further proceedings to determine sentence

(1) Upon conviction or adjudication of guilt of a defendant of a capital felony the court shall conduct a separate sentencing proceeding to determine whether the defendant should be sentenced to death or life imprisonment . . . . The proceeding shall be conducted by the trial judge before the trial jury as soon as practicable. If the trial jury has been waived or if the defendant pleaded guilty, the sentencing proceeding shall be conducted before a jury empaneled for that purpose unless waived by the defendant. In the proceeding, evidence may be presented as to any matter that the court deems relevant to sentence, and shall include matters relating to any of the aggravating or mitigating circumstances enumerated in subsections (6) and (7) of this section. Any such evidence which the court deems to have probative value may be received, regardless of its admissibility under the exclusionary rules of evidence, provided that the defendant is accorded a fair opportunity to rebut any hearsay statements; and further provided that this subsection shall not be construed to authorize the introduction of any evidence secured in violation of the Constitution of the United States or of the State of Florida. The state and the defendant or his counsel shall be permitted to present argument for or against sentence of death.

(2) After hearing all the evidence, the jury shall deliberate and render an advisory sentence to the court based upon the following matters:

(a) Whether sufficient aggravating circumstances exist as enumerated in subsection (6), and

(b) Whether sufficient mitigating circumstances exist as enumerated in subsection (7), which outweigh aggravating circumstances found to exist, and

(c) Based on these considerations whether the defendant should be sentenced to life or death.

(3) Notwithstanding the recommendation of a majority of the jury, the court after weighing the aggravating and mitigating circumstances shall enter a sentence of life imprisonment or death, but if the court imposes a sentence of death, it shall set forth in writing its findings upon which the sentence of death is based as to the facts:

(a) That sufficient aggravating circumstances exist as enumerated in subsection (6), and

(b) That there are insufficient mitigating circumstances, as enumerated in subsection (7), to outweigh the aggravating circumstances. In each case in which the court imposes the death sentence, the determination of the court shall be supported by specific written findings of fact based upon the circumstances in subsections (6) and (7) and based upon the records of the trial and the sentencing proceedings.

(4) If the court does not make the findings requiring the death sentence, the court shall impose sentence of life imprisonment . . . .

(5) The judgment of conviction and sentence of death shall be subject to automatic review by the Supreme Court of Florida within sixty (60) days after certification by the sentencing court of the entire record unless time is extended an additional period not to exceed thirty (30) days by the Supreme Court for good cause shown. Such review by the Su-

preme Court shall have priority over all other cases, and shall be heard in accordance with rules promulgated by the Supreme Court.

(6) Aggravating circumstances.—Aggravating circumstances shall be limited to the following:

(a) The capital felony was committed by a person under sentence of imprisonment;

(b) The defendant was previously convicted of another capital felony or of a felony involving the use or threat of violence to the person;

(c) The defendant knowingly created a great risk of death to many persons;

(d) The capital felony was committed while the defendant was engaged or was an accomplice in the commission of, or an attempt to commit, or flight after committing or attempting to commit any robbery, rape, arson, burglary, kidnaping, aircraft piracy, or the unlawful throwing, placing or discharging of a destructive device or bomb;

(e) The capital felony was committed for the purpose of avoiding or preventing a lawful arrest or effecting an escape from custody;

(f) The capital felony was committed for pecuniary gain;

(g) The capital felony was committed to disrupt or hinder the lawful exercise of any governmental function or the enforcement of laws.

(h) The capital felony was especially heinous, atrocious or cruel.

(7) Mitigating circumstances.—Mitigating circumstances shall be the following:

(a) The defendant has no significant history of prior criminal activity;

(b) The capital felony was committed while the defendant was under the influence of extreme mental or emotional disturbance;

(c) The victim was a participant in the defendant's conduct or consented to the act;

(d) The defendant was an accomplice in the capital felony committed by another person and his participation was relatively minor;

(e) The defendant acted under extreme duress or under the substantial domination of another person;

(f) The capacity of the defendant to appreciate the criminality of his conduct or to conform his conduct to the requirements of law was substantially impaired;

(g) The age of the defendant at the time of the crime.

H. DUE PROCESS OF LAW

SECTION 1. POLICE POWER AND STATUTORY VAGUENESS

PAPACHRISTOU ET AL. v. CITY OF JACKSONVILLE

Supreme Court of the United States, 1972.
405 U.S. 156, 92 S.Ct. 839.

MR. JUSTICE DOUGLAS delivered the opinion of the Court.

This case involves eight defendants who were convicted in a Florida municipal court of violating a Jacksonville, Florida, vagrancy ordinance.[1] Their convictions, entailing fines and jail sentences (some of which were suspended), were affirmed by the Florida Circuit Court in a consolidated appeal, and their petition for certiorari was denied by the District Court of Appeals, . . . The case is here on a petition for certiorari, which we granted. . . . For reasons which will appear, we reverse.[2]

1. Jacksonville Ordinance Code § 26–57 provided at the time of these arrests and convictions as follows:
"Rogues and vagabonds, or dissolute persons who go about begging, common gamblers, persons who use juggling or unlawful games or plays, common drunkards, common night walkers, thieves, pilferers or pickpockets, traders in stolen property, lewd, wanton and lascivious persons, keepers of gambling places, common railers and brawlers, persons wandering or strolling around from place to place without any lawful purpose or object, habitual loafers, disorderly persons, persons neglecting all lawful business and habitually spending their time by frequenting houses of ill fame, gaming houses, or places where alcoholic beverages are sold or served, persons able to work but habitually living upon the earnings of their wives or minor children shall be deemed vagrants and, upon conviction in the Municipal Court shall be punished [90 days imprisonment, $500 fine, or both.]
We are advised that at present the Jacksonville vagrancy ordinance is § 330.107 and identical with the earlier one except that "juggling" has been eliminated.

2. Florida also has a vagrancy statute . . . which reads quite closely on the Jacksonville ordinance. . . . [It] makes the commission of any Florida misdemeanor a Class D offense against the City of Jacksonville. In 1971 Florida made minor amendments to its statute.

[The statute] was declared unconstitutionally overbroad in Lazarus v. Faircloth, D.C., 301 F.Supp. 266. The Court said: "All loitering, loafing, or idling on the streets and highways of a city, even though habitual, is not necessarily detrimental to the public welfare nor is it under all circumstances an interference with travel upon them. It may be and often is entirely innocuous. The statute draws no distinction between conduct that is calculated to harm and that which is essentially innocent." See also Smith v. Florida, 404 U.S. —, 92 S. Ct. 848, 30 L.Ed.2d —.

The Florida disorderly conduct ordinance, covering "loitering about any hotel, block, barroom, dramshop, gambling house or disorderly house, or wandering about the streets either by night or by day without any known lawful means of support or without being able to give a satisfactory account of themselves" has also been held void for "excessive broadness and vagueness" by the Florida Supreme Court, Headley v. Selkowitz, 171 So.2d 368, 370.

At issue are five consolidated cases. Margaret Papachristou, Betty Calloway, Eugene Eddie Melton, and Leonard Johnson were all arrested early on a Sunday morning, and charged with vagrancy—"prowling by auto."

Jimmy Lee Smith and Milton Henry were charged with vagrancy—"vagabonds."

Henry Edward Heath and a co-defendant were arrested for vagrancy—"loitering" and "common thief."

Thomas Owen Campbell was charged with vagrancy—"common thief."

Hugh Brown was charged with vagrancy—"disorderly loitering on street" and "disorderly conduct—resisting arrest with violence."

The facts are stipulated. Papachristou and Calloway are white females. Melton and Johnson are black males. Papachristou was enrolled in a job-training program sponsored by the State Employment Service at Florida Junior College in Jacksonville. Calloway was a typing and shorthand teacher at a state mental institution located near Jacksonville. She was the owner of the automobile in which the four defendants were arrested. Melton was a Vietnam war veteran who had been released from the Navy after nine months in a veterans' hospital. On the date of his arrest he was a part-time computer helper while attending college as a full-time student in Jacksonville. Johnson was a tow-motor operator in a grocery chain warehouse and was a lifelong resident of Jacksonville.

At the time of their arrest the four of them were riding in Calloway's car on the main thoroughfare in Jacksonville. They had left a restaurant owned by Johnson's uncle where they had eaten and were on their way to a night club. The arresting officers denied that the racial mixture in the car played any part in the decision to make the arrest. The arrest, they said, was made because the defendants had stopped near a used-car lot which had been broken into several times. There was, however, no evidence of any breaking and entering on the night in question.

Of these four charged with "prowling by auto" none had been previously arrested except Papachristou who had once been convicted of a municipal offense.

Jimmy Lee Smith and Milton Henry (who is not a petitioner) were arrested between 9 and 10 a.m. on a weekday in downtown Jacksonville, while waiting for a friend who was to lend them a car so they could apply for a job at a produce company. Smith was a part-time produce worker and part-time organizer for a Negro political group. He had a common-law wife and three children supported by him and his wife. He had been arrested several times but convicted only once. Smith's companion, Henry, was an 18-year-old high school student with no previous record of arrest.

This morning it was cold, and Smith had no jacket, so they went briefly into a dry cleaning shop to wait, but left when requested to do so. They thereafter walked back and forth two or three times over a two-block stretch looking for their friend. The store owners, who apparently were wary of Smith and his companion, summoned two police officers who searched the men and found neither had a weapon. But they were arrested because the officers said they had no identification and because the officers did not believe their story.

Heath and a codefendant were arrested for "loitering" and for "common thief." Both were residents of Jacksonville, Heath having lived there all his life and being employed at an automobile and body shop. Heath had previously been arrested but his codefendant had no arrest record. Heath and his companion were arrested when they drove up to a residence shared by Heath's girlfriend and some other girls. Some police officers were already there in the process of arresting another man. When Heath and his companion started backing out of the driveway, the officers signaled to them to stop and asked them to get out of the car, which they did. Thereupon they and the automobile were searched. Although no contraband or incriminating evidence was found, they were both arrested, Heath being charged with being a "common thief" because he was reputed to be a thief. The codefendant was charged with "loitering" because he was standing in the driveway, an act which the officers admitted was done only at their command.

Campbell was arrested as he reached his home very early one morning and was charged with "common thief." He was stopped by officers because he was traveling at a high rate of speed, yet no speeding charge was placed against him.

Brown was arrested when he was observed leaving a downtown, Jacksonville, hotel by a police officer seated in a cruiser. The police testified he was reputed to be a thief, narcotics pusher, and generally opprobrious character. The officer called Brown over to the car, intending at that time to arrest him unless he had a good explanation for being on the street. Brown walked over to the police cruiser, as commanded, and the officer began to search him, apparently preparatory to placing him in the car. In the process of the search he came on two small packets which were later found to contain heroin. When the officer touched the pocket where the packets were, Brown began to resist. He was charged with "disorderly loitering on the street" and "disorderly conduct—resisting arrest with violence." While he was also charged with a narcotics violation, that charge was *nolled*.

Jacksonville's ordinance and Florida's statute were "derived from early English law," . . . and employ "archaic language" in their definitions of vagrants. The history is an often-told tale. The breakup of feudal estates in England led to labor shortages which in turn resulted in the Statutes of Laborers, designed to stabilize the labor force by prohibiting increases in wages and prohibiting the movement of workers from their home areas in search of improved conditions. Later vagrancy laws became criminal aspects of the poor laws. The series of laws passed in England on the subject became increasingly severe. But "the theory of the Elizabethan poor laws no longer fits the facts," . . . The conditions which spawned these laws may be gone, but the archaic classifications remain.

This ordinance is void-for-vagueness, both in the sense that it "fails to give a person of ordinary intelligence fair notice that his contemplated conduct is forbidden by the statute," . . . and because it encourages arbitrary and erratic arrests and convictions. . . .

Living under a rule of law entails various suppositions, one of which is that "All [persons] are entitled to be informed as to what the State commands or forbids." Lanzetta v. New Jersey, . . .

Lanzetta is one of a well-recognized group of cases insisting that the law give fair notice of the offending conduct. . . . In the field of regulatory statutes governing business activities, where the acts limited are in a narrow category, greater leeway is allowed. . . .

The poor among us, the minorities, the average householder are not in business and not alerted to the regulatory schemes of vagrancy laws; and we assume they would have no understanding of their meaning and impact if they read them. Nor are they protected from being caught in the vagrancy net by the necessity of having a specific intent to commit an unlawful act. . . .

The Jacksonville ordinance makes criminal activities which by modern standards are normally innocent. "Nightwalking" is one. Florida construes the ordinance not to make criminal one night's wandering, . . . only the "habitual" wanderer or as the ordinance describes it "common night walkers." We know, however, from experience that sleepless people often walk at night, perhaps hopeful that sleep-inducing relaxation will result.

Luis Munoz-Marin, former Governor of Puerto Rico, commented once that "loafing" was a national virtue in his Commonwealth and that it should be encouraged. It is, however, a crime in Jacksonville.

"Persons able to work but habitually living on the earnings of their wives or minor children"—like habitually living "without visible means of support"—might implicate unemployed pillars of the community who have married rich wives.

"Persons able to work but habitually living on the earnings of their wives or minor children" may also embrace unemployed people out of the labor market, by reason of a recession or disemployed by reason of technological or so-called structural displacements.

Persons "wandering or strolling" from place to place have been extolled by Walt Whitman and Vachel Lindsay. The qualification "without any lawful purpose or object" may be a trap for innocent acts. Persons "neglecting all lawful business and habitually spending their time by frequenting . . . places where alcoholic beverages are sold or served" would literally embrace many members of golf clubs and city clubs.

Walkers and strollers and wanderers may be going to or coming from a burglary. Loafers or loiterers may be "casing" a place for a holdup. Letting one's wife support him is an intra-family matter, and normally of no concern to the police. Yet it may, of course, be the setting for numerous crimes.

The difficulty is that these activities are historically part of the amenities of life as we have known it. They are not mentioned in the Constitution or in the Bill of Rights. These unwritten amenities have been in part responsible for giving our people the feeling of independence and self-confidence, the feeling of creativity. These amenities have dignified the right of dissent and have honored the right to be nonconformists and the right to defy submissiveness. They have encouraged lives of high spirits rather than hushed, suffocating silence.

They are embedded in Walt Whitman's writings especially in his Song of the Open Road. They are reflected too, in the spirit of Vachel Lindsay's I Want to go Wandering and by Henry D. Thoreau.

This aspect of the vagrancy ordinance before us is suggested by what this Court said in 1875 about a broad criminal statute enacted by Congress: "It would certainly be dangerous if the legislature could set a net large enough to catch all possible offenders, and leave it to the courts to step inside and say who could be rightfully detained, and who should be set at large." . . .

While that was a federal case, the due process implications are equally applicable to the States and to this vagrancy ordinance. Here the net cast is large, not to give the courts the power to pick and choose but to increase the arsenal of the police. . . .

* * *

Where the list of crimes is so all-inclusive and generalized as that one in this ordinance, those convicted may be punished for no more than vindicating affronts to police authority: . . .

Another aspect of the ordinance's vagueness appears when we focus, not on the lack of notice given a potential offender, but on the effect of the unfettered discretion it places in the hands of the Jacksonville police. Caleb Foote, an early student of this subject, has called the vagrancy-type law as offering "punishment by analogy." Such crimes, though long common in Russia, are not compatible with our constitutional system. We allow our police to make arrests only on "probable cause," a Fourth and Fourteenth Amendment standard applicable to the States as well as to the Federal Government. Arresting a person on suspicion, like arresting a person for investigation, is foreign to our system, even when the arrest is for past criminality. Future criminality, however, is the common justification for the presence of vagrancy statutes. . . . Florida has indeed construed her vagrancy statute "as necessary regulations," *inter alia,* "to deter vagabondage and prevent crimes." . . .

A direction by a legislature to the police to arrest all "suspicious" persons would not pass constitutional muster. A vagrancy prosecution may be merely the cloak for a conviction which could not be obtained on the real but undisclosed grounds for the arrest. . . .

Those generally implicated by the imprecise terms of the ordinance—poor people, nonconformists, dissenters, idlers—may be required to comport themselves according to the life-style deemed appropriate by the Jacksonville police and the courts. Where, as here, there are no standards governing the exercise of the discretion granted by the ordinance, the scheme permits and encourages an arbitrary and discriminatory enforcement of the law. It furnishes a convenient tool for "harsh and discriminatory enforcement by prosecuting officials, against particular groups deemed to merit their displeasure." . . . It results in a regime in which the poor and the unpopular are permitted to "stand on a public sidewalk . . . only at the whim of any police officer." . . .

A presumption that people who might walk or loaf or loiter or stroll or frequent houses where liquor is sold, or who are supported by their wives or who look suspicious to the police are to become future criminals is too precarious for a rule of law. The implicit presumption in these generalized vagrancy standards—that crime is being nipped in the bud—is too extravagant to deserve extended treatment. Or course, vagrancy statutes are useful to the police. Of course they are nets making easy the round-up of so-called undesirables. But the rule of law implies equality and justice in its application. Vagrancy laws of the Jacksonville type teach that the scales of justice are so tipped that even-handed administration of the law is not possible. The rule of law, evenly applied to minorities as well as majorities, to the poor as well as the rich, is the great mucilage that holds society together.

The Jacksonville ordinance cannot be squared with our constitutional standards and is plainly unconstitutional.

Reversed.

MR. JUSTICE POWELL and MR. JUSTICE REHNQUIST took no part in the consideration or decision of this case.

NOTES

1. Consider the validity of the following section (250.6) of the American Law Institute's Model Penal Code:

> Loitering or Prowling: A person commits a violation if he loiters or prowls in a place, at a time, or in a manner not usual for law-abiding individuals under circumstances that warrant alarm for the safety of persons and property in the vicinity. Among the circumstances which may be considered in determining whether

> such alarm is warranted is the fact that the actor takes flight upon appearance of a police officer, refuses to identify himself, or manifestly endeavors to conceal himself or any object. Unless flight by the actor or other circumstances makes it impracticable, a police officer shall prior to any arrest for an offense under the section afford the actor an opportunity to dispel any alarm which would otherwise be warranted, by requesting him to identify himself and explain his presence and conduct. No person shall be convicted of an offense under this section if the police officer did not comply with the preceding sentence, or if it appears at trial that the explanation given by the actor was true, and if believed by the police officer at the time, would have dispelled the alarm.

2. New York and Colorado have statutory provisions which read as follows (§ 240.36, Penal Code, and 40–8–24, respectively):

> A person is guilty of loitering when he loiters or remains in any place with one or more persons for the purpose of unlawfully using or possessing a dangerous drug (the definition of which appears elsewhere in the two codes).

The purpose of such a law is to take care of the law enforcement problem whereby upon the approach of law enforcement officers some members of a crowd will throw their drugs on the ground and thus render it impossible to determine which ones actually had possession. Is it sufficiently narrow and clear to withstand constitutional scrutiny?

Because of the large number of arrests made under this statute, the District Attorney of New York City issued a directive to the police of that city advising them that "dragnet" or "mass" arrests are not authorized by the statute, and that a gathering of known addicts is not of and by itself a violation of the law. They were further advised that "intention" may be inferred only from the presence of dangerous drugs or paraphernalia commonly associated with dangerous drugs, such as a bottle cap, eye dropper, empty glassine envelope, etc., and accompanying circumstances excluding every possibility except intent to use or possess a dangerous drug. The order said that "visual observation of dangerous drugs or paraphernalia is an essential requisite to an arrest", N. Y. Times, Nov. 3, 1970.

A predecessor to the foregoing N.Y. statute made it an offense to loiter in the common areas of a building for the purpose of using or possessing any narcotic drug. It was held to be "clear and unambiguous", prohibiting no more than "loitering or congregating for the purpose of committing a criminal act". "It certainly is", said the New York Court of Appeals in its unanimous opinion, "a reasonable legislative response to a criminal problem". The case itself was one involving the defendant and two other men. Defendant had dropped a bottle cap when he saw the police; one of the other men had a hypodermic needle and an eye-dropper; and the third one had empty glassine envelopes in his possession. People v. Pagnotta, 25 N.Y.2d 333, 253 N.E.2d 202, 48 ALR 1271 (1969).

PEOPLE v. JOHNSON

Court of Appeals of New York, 1959.
6 N.Y.2d 549, 190 N.Y.S.2d 694, 161 N.E.2d 9.

DYE, JUDGE. The defendant-appellant had been convicted, following a trial without a jury, of disorderly conduct in violation of section 722–b of the Penal Law. That section provides: "§ 722–b. Loitering in school buildings. Any person not the parent or legal guardian of a pupil in regular attendance at said school who loiters in or about any school building or grounds without written permission from the principal, custodian or other person in charge thereof, or in violation of posted rules or regulations governing the use thereof, shall be guilty of disorderly conduct."

The proof establishes, without any serious doubt, that this defendant and a male companion who, by the way, has not been charged with any violation although he was with the defendant at all times on or about March 21, 1958, entered the Baldwin Senior High School in Baldwin, N. Y., between 2:30 and 2:45 p. m., to meet two friends who were in the school. Concededly, neither of them were within the exception of the statute, that is, neither was the parent nor the guardian of a student in regular attendance at such school, and had no written permission to be there.

They hung about in the main lobby for about 10 minutes and then, at the suggestion of one of the students whom they had planned to meet and whom they saw as they passed through the lobby, went to the second floor and waited in the corridor outside their home room. Several minutes later when the class was dismissed the defendant and his companion and their two student friends walked down the stairs and out through the lobby and on the school grounds. When outside the defendant put an unlighted cigarette in his mouth. A teacher who was present asked him three different times to remove it and when he did not the teacher reached to take it out of his mouth. The defendant countered by knocking off the teacher's hat and punching him in the stomach, following which he left. There was also evidence that several weeks before, for good reason which had no bearing on the within charge, the defendant had been warned by a teacher to keep out of the school.

When the defendant took the stand in his own behalf, he did not contradict any of the People's proof as to the main issue. By his own statement, he admitted he knew he was not supposed to be in the school and grounds but contented himself in denying a series of collateral matters with prior alleged conduct in and about the school establishment which had no relation to the violation charged. In fact his challenge to the conviction is not directed mainly to the sufficiency of the People's proof, but to the validity of the statute as a constitutional enactment for lack of standards and appropriate definition.

In People v. Diaz, 4 N.Y.2d 469, 176 N.Y.S.2d 313, 151 N.E.2d 871, and People v. Bell, 306 N.Y. 110, 115 N.E.2d 821, we dealt with a loitering statute. In Diaz we set aside a conviction had under a city ordinance which provided that no person shall lounge or loiter about any street or street corner because the prohibiting language was too vague, indefinite and uncertain to define a crime, since the ordinance made no distinction between conduct calculated to harm and that which is essentially innocent in the use of a public street.

There is a vast difference between a statute or ordinance dealing with loitering on a public street or street corner as in Diaz (supra), and a statute which prohibits any person who does not come within the named exceptions to loiter in or about any school building or grounds without written permission of the principal, custodian or other person in charge thereof, or in violation of posted rules and regulations governing the use thereof. A school is in a sense public in that it is endowed and operated by the taxpayers' money, but it is not public in the sense that any member of the public may use it for his own personal purposes, and is justifiably the proper subject for proscribed acts such as loitering. A school building being of such a restricted public nature, the attack upon section 722–b on constitutional grounds is wholly without merit. Read in the light of the nature of a school building, the statute is sufficiently clear and unambiguous to inform the public of the proscribed act. On its face it simply states that any person who loiters (a term which has by long usage acquired a common and accepted meaning) without permission of the specified persons is guilty of disorderly conduct.

Nor is there any merit to defendant's contention that the statute was not intended to make criminal an otherwise innocent activity. Loitering in school buildings, or on school grounds, is not an innocent activity. It is common knowledge that law enforcement agencies and school authorities are continuously and increasingly harassed by the presence of unauthorized persons invading the precincts of our schools such, for instance, as dope peddlers, sex offenders, idlers and trouble makers in general, and other persons harboring some illegitimate purpose involving the innocence of immature school children and youth. Then, too, there is the ever present threat of fire and disaster from indiscriminate and careless use of cigarettes in and about the school corridors and buildings. The authorities, we know, are not only charged with the duty of providing children with a proper education, but while so doing must be watchful of their moral and physical safety and well-being. It was for these and other reasons that the enactment of section 722–b was sponsored by the law enforcement authorities and parent organizations, leading boards of education and other civic-minded groups. The nature of the activity carried on in a school building incident to the teaching and protection of children compels restriction against persons loitering in and about the building and grounds wherein these activities are carried on. This interpretation does not conflict with or limit our decision in People v. Bell (supra) which dealt with loitering in and about railway property by a person "who [was] unable to give a satisfactory explanation of his presence".

Here the statute makes definite and certain that one does not qualify as an implied invitee or licensee who needs written permission to frequent a school else he is a trespasser and may be punished for loitering. Here the defendant conceded that he did not come within the statutory exceptions nor did he have permission to enter the school premises and this in face of prior warning to keep out.

The judgment appealed from should be affirmed.

CONWAY, CHIEF JUDGE (concurring). I agree with JUDGE DYE.

I should like to add a word about the reasons stated in the dissenting opinion for the passage of the act in question. I was in Chicago at a Conference of the Chief Justices at the time, within the last two years, when the nearly one hundred children, who had been burned to death in a school fire there, were buried. Anyone who witnessed any part of the tragedy on that day of sorrow would feel that one of the reasons for the adoption of the act was to prevent just such occurrences. Stupid or thoughtless young people can do as much harm to the defenseless as wicked ones.

I have not seen in the record any concession by anyone that the defendant was in the school for any good purpose. He had been warned previously to stay out of the school, in which he did not belong. Nevertheless he returned. He was carrying a cigarette, and whether or not, at the moment, it was lighted or unlighted is not too important.

I do not think that the citations of cases involving railroad stations where people are accustomed to go to see their friends off on trains or to meet them is pertinent. Those places are public places—not school buildings crowded with children.

VAN VOORHIS, JUDGE (concurring). "Loiter" assumes different meanings according to the circumstances. As this word is construed in Judge DYE's opinion, I think that it signifies in section 722–b of the Penal Law that every person not the parent or legal guardian of a pupil in regular attendance at a school is forbidden to enter the school building or grounds without written permission from the principal, custodian or other person in charge—except for the purpose of obtaining such permission. Necessarily the teaching and maintenance staffs of the school are excepted. Posted rules or regulations governing the use of the school building or grounds may provide for the admission of other persons on other occasions, and the use of such buildings and grounds is, of course, subject also to the provisions of the Education Law, § 1 et seq. This is the gist of Judge DYE's opinion, as I read it, with which I agree. The rigor of section 722–b, thus construed, is a proper exercise of the police power in view of the problem of maintaining order in the schools, nor is the term "loitering" defective on account of vagueness in defining the offense if "loitering" is construed in this manner.

FULD, JUDGE (dissenting). The defendant, a youngster, 17 years old, went into a high school to meet two friends who were students there and wound up with a conviction for disorderly conduct on the ground that his waiting around for his friends constituted loitering in the building in violation of section 722–b of the Penal Law.

That section was designed to exclude from school areas degenerates, narcotics peddlers, vandals and the like. The statute was broadly worded—to punish one who "loiters" about a school building—but it certainly was never designed to render innocent conduct criminal. The word "loitering" is both broad and nebulous, but what it signifies—not only by dictionary definition, but in ordinary everyday speech—is staying about or around a place without any purpose at all, aimlessly and idly, or for some illegal or illicit purpose.

The defendant was in the school building for a legitimate reason and he did nothing wrong or improper while he was there. Placing a cigarette in his mouth on the steps of the building as he was going out, even if unwise, did not render him a criminal or constitute "loitering." We should give to the statute a reasonable and sensible construction by interpreting it in such a way that it will exclude from our schools only those who are disorderly or have no legitimate motive for being in or about a school building. We should not read it to exclude those who are there, at the end of the school day, to meet friends who attend the school—certainly a good and sufficient reason.

The Legislature, by enacting section 722–b, may have desired to facilitate the conviction of those in a school building for some illicit purpose, but surely it could not have been its design to render criminal and punishable the perfectly innocent conduct of the defendant. Had the Legislature intended, as is suggested by Judge Dye and Judge Van Voorhis, an all-inclusive statute, a statute designed to prohibit everyone, except a parent or guardian of a pupil, from *entering* a school building, it would have been a simple matter for the Legislature to have expressly so provided. The term "loiter" which is found in the statute indicates a quite different intent.

If, on the other hand, the section is to be construed as the People urge, and as this court is holding, then, it seems to me, it runs afoul of the requirements of constitutional due process. Indeed, as this court wrote of other legislation which also condemned "loitering" (People v. Diaz, supra), a statute "must be informative on its face * * * and so explicit that 'all men subject to its penalties may know what acts it is their duty to avoid' (United States v. Brewer, 139 U.S. 278, 288, 11 S.Ct. 538, 541, 35 L.Ed. 190 * * *). While the term 'loiter' or 'loitering' has by long usage acquired a common and accepted meaning * * * it does not follow that by itself, and without more, such term is enough to inform a citizen of its criminal implications and, by the same token, leave it open to arbitrary enforcement."

I would reverse the judgment and dismiss the information.

DESMOND, FROESSEL and BURKE, JJ., concur with DYE, J.

CONWAY, C. J., and VAN VOORHIS, J., concur with DYE, J., each in a separate memorandum.

FULD, J., dissents in an opinion.

Judgment affirmed.

COATES v. CITY OF CINCINNATI

Supreme Court of the United States, 1969.
402 U.S. 611, 91 S.Ct. 1686.

MR. JUSTICE STEWART delivered the opinion of the Court.

A Cincinnati, Ohio, ordinance makes it a criminal offense for "three or more persons to assemble . . . on any of the sidewalks . . . and there conduct themselves in a manner annoying to persons passing by . . . ." The issue before us is whether this ordinance is unconstitutional on its face.

The appellants were convicted of violating the ordinance, and the convictions were ultimately affirmed by a closely divided vote in the Supreme Court of Ohio, upholding the constitutional validity of the ordinance. . . . The record brought before the reviewing courts tells us no more than that the appellant Coates was a student involved in a demonstration and the other appellants were pickets involved in a labor dispute. For throughout this litigation it has been the appellants' position that the ordinance on its face violates the First and Fourteenth Amendments of the Constitution. . . .

In rejecting this claim and affirming the convictions the Ohio Supreme Court did not give the ordinance any construction at variance with the apparent plain import of its language. The court simply stated:

> "The ordinance prohibits, *inter alia*, 'conduct . . . annoying to persons passing by.' The word 'annoying' is a widely used and well understood word; it is not necessary to guess its meaning. 'Annoying' is the present participle of the transitive verb 'annoy' which means to trouble, to vex, to impede, to incommode, to provoke, to harass or to irritate.
>
> "We conclude, as did the Supreme Court of the United States in Cameron v. Johnson, . . . in which the issue of the vagueness of a statute was presented, that the ordinance 'clearly and precisely delineates its reach in words of common understanding. It is a "precise and narrowly drawn regulatory statute [ordinance] evincing a legislative judgment that certain specific conduct be . . . proscribed."' " . . .

Beyond this, the only construction put upon the ordinance by the state court was its unexplained conclusion that "the standard of conduct which it specifies is not dependent upon each complainant's sensitivity." But the court did not indicate upon whose sensitivity a violation does depend—the sensitivity of the judge or jury, the sensitivity of the arresting officer, or the sensitivity of a hypothetical reasonable man.

We are thus relegated, at best, to the words of the ordinance itself. If three or more people meet together on a sidewalk or street corner, they must conduct themselves so as not to annoy any police officer or other person who should happen to pass by. In our opinion this ordinance is unconstitutionally vague because it subjects the exercise of the right of assembly to an unascertainable standard, and unconstitutionally broad because it authorizes the punishment of constitutionally protected conduct.

Conduct that annoys some people does not annoy others. Thus, the ordinance is vague, not in the sense that it requires a person to conform his conduct to an imprecise but comprehensible normative standard, but rather in the sense that no standard of conduct is specified at all. As a result, "men of common intelligence must necessarily guess at its meaning." . . . .

It is said that the ordinance is broad enough to encompass many types of conduct clearly within the city's constitutional power to prohibit. And so, indeed, it is. The city is free to prevent people from blocking sidewalks, obstructing traffic, littering streets, committing assaults, or engaging in countless other forms of antisocial conduct. It can do so through the enactment and enforcement of ordinances directed with reasonable specificity toward the conduct to be prohibited. . . . It cannot constitutionally do so through the enactment and enforcement of an ordinance whose violation may entirely depend upon whether or not a policeman is annoyed.

But the vice of the ordinance lies not alone in its violation of the due process standard of vagueness. The ordinance also violates the constitutional right of free assembly and association. Our decisions establish that mere public intolerance or animosity cannot be the basis for abridgment of these constitutional freedoms. . . . The First and Fourteenth Amendments do not permit a State to make criminal the exercise of the right of assembly simply because its exercise may be "annoying" to some people. If this were not the rule, the right of the people to gather in public places for social or political purposes would be continually subject to summary suspension through the good-faith enforcement of a prohibition against annoying conduct. And such a prohibition, in addition, contains an obvious invitation to discriminatory enforcement against those whose association together is "annoying" because their ideas, their lifestyle, or their physical appearance is resented by the majority of their fellow citizens.

The ordinance before us makes a crime out of what under the Constitution cannot be a crime. It is aimed directly at activity protected by the Constitution. We need not lament that we do not have before us the details of the conduct found to be annoying. It is the ordinance on its face that sets the standard of conduct and warns against transgression. The details of the offense could no more serve to validate this ordinance than could the details of an offense charged under an ordinance suspending unconditionally the right of assembly and free speech.

The judgment is reversed.

MR. JUSTICE BLACK.

* * *

This Court has long held that laws so vague that a person of common understanding cannot know what is forbidden are unconstitutional on their face. . . . Likewise, laws which broadly forbid conduct or activities which are protected by the Federal Constitution, such as, for instance, the discussion of political matters, are void on their face. . . . On the other hand, laws which plainly forbid conduct which is constitutionally within the power of the State to forbid but also restrict constitutionally protected conduct may be void either on their face or merely as applied in certain instances. As my Brother WHITE states in his opinion (with which I substantially agree), this is one of those numerous cases where the law could be held unconstitutional because it prohibits both conduct which the Constitution safeguards and conduct which the State may constitutionally punish. Thus, the First Amendment which forbids the State to abridge freedom of speech, would invalidate this city ordinance if it were used to punish the making of a political speech, even if that speech were to annoy other persons. In contrast, however, the ordinance could properly be applied to prohibit the gathering of persons in the mouths of alleys to annoy passersby by throwing rocks or by some other conduct not at all connected with speech. It is a matter of no little difficulty to determine when a law can be held void on its face and when such summary action is inappropriate. This difficulty has been aggravated in this case, because the record fails to show in what conduct these defendants had engaged to annoy other people. In my view, a record showing the facts surrounding the conviction is essential to adjudicate the important constitutional issues in this case. I would therefore vacate the judgment and remand the case with instructions that the trial court give both parties an opportunity to supplement the record so that we may determine whether the conduct actually punished is the kind of conduct which it is within the power of the State to punish.

MR. JUSTICE WHITE, with whom THE CHIEF JUSTICE and MR. JUSTICE BLACKMUN join, dissenting.

The claim in this case, in part, is that the Cincinnati ordinance is so vague that it may not constitutionally be applied to any conduct. But the ordinance prohibits persons from assembling with others and "conduct[ing] themselves in a manner annoying to persons passing by . . . ." Cincinnati Code of Ordinances § 901–L6. Any man of average comprehension should know that some kinds of conduct, such as assault or blocking passage on the street, will annoy others and are clearly covered by the "annoying conduct" standard of the ordinance. It would be frivolous to say that these and many other kinds of conduct are not within the foreseeable reach of the law.

It is possible that a whole range of other acts, defined with unconstitutional imprecision, is forbidden by the ordinance. But as a general rule, when a criminal charge is based on conduct constitutionally subject to proscription and clearly forbidden by a statute, it is no defense that the law would be unconstitutionally vague if applied to other behavior. Such a statute is not vague on its face. It may be vague as applied in some circumstances, but ruling on such a challenge obviously requires knowledge of the conduct with which a defendant is charged.

In Williams v. United States, 341 U.S. 97 (1951), a police officer was charged under federal statutes with extracting confessions by force and thus, under color of law, depriving the prisoner there involved of rights, privileges, and immunities secured or protected by the Constitution and laws of the United States, contrary to 18 U.S.C. § 242. The defendant there urged that the standard—rights, privileges, and immunities secured by the Constitution—was impermissibly vague and, more particularly, that the Court was often so closely divided on illegal-confession issues that no defendant could be expected to know when he was violating the law. The Court's response was that, while application of the statute to less obvious methods of coercion might raise doubts about the adequacy of the standard of guilt, in the case before it, it was "plain as a pikestaff that the present confessions would not be allowed in evidence whatever the school of thought concerning the scope and meaning of the Due Process Clause." The claim of facial vagueness was thus rejected.

So too in United States v. National Dairy Corp., where we considered a statute forbidding sales of goods at "unreasonably" low prices to injure or eliminate a competitor, 15 U.S.C. § 13a, we thought the statute gave a seller adequate notice that sales below cost were illegal. The statute was therefore not facially vague, although it might be difficult to tell whether certain other kinds of conduct fell within this language. We said: "In determining the sufficiency of the notice a statute must of necessity be examined in the light of the conduct with which a defendant is charged." . . . This approach is consistent with the host of cases holding that "one to whom application of a statute is constitutional will not be heard to attack the statute on the ground that impliedly it might also be taken as applying to other persons or other situations in which its application might be unconstitutional." . . .

Our cases, however, including *National Dairy*, recognize a different approach where the statute at issue purports to regulate or proscribe rights of speech or press protected by the First Amendment. . . . Although a statute may be neither vague, overbroad, nor otherwise invalid as applied to the conduct charged against a particular defendant, he is permitted to raise its vagueness or unconstitutional overbreadth as applied to others. And if the law is found deficient in one of these respects, it may not be applied to him either, until and unless a satisfactory limiting construction is placed on the statute. . . . The statute, in effect, is stricken down on its face. This result is deemed justified since the otherwise continued existence of the statute in unnarrowed form would tend to suppress constitutionally protected rights. . . .

Even accepting the overbreadth doctrine with respect to statutes clearly reaching speech, the Cincinnati ordinance does not purport to bar or regulate speech as such. It prohibits persons from assembling and "conduct[ing]" themselves in a manner annoying to other persons. Even if the assembled defendants in this case were demonstrating and picketing, we have long recognized that picketing is not solely a communicative endeavor and has aspects which the State is entitled to regulate even though there is incidental impact on speech. In Cox v. Louisiana (1965), the Court held valid on its face a statute forbidding picketing and parading near a courthouse. This was deemed a valid regulation of conduct rather than pure speech. The conduct reached by the statute was "subject to regulation even though [it was] intertwined with expression and association." The Court then went on to consider the statute as applied to the facts of record.

In the case before us, I would deal with the Cincinnati ordinance as we would with the ordinary criminal statute. The ordinance clearly reaches certain conduct but may be illegally vague with respect to other conduct. The statute is not infirm on its face and since we have no information from this record as to what conduct was charged against these defendants, we are in no position to judge the statute as applied. That the ordinance may confer wide discretion in a wide range of circumstances is irrelevant when he may be dealing with conduct at its core.

I would therefore affirm the judgment of the Ohio Supreme Court.

NOTES

1. A Kentucky statute provided that "a person is guilty of disorderly conduct if, with intent to cause public inconvenience, annoyance or alarm, or recklessly creating a risk thereof, he . . . congregates with other persons in a public place and refuses to comply with a lawful order of the police to disperse . . .". In Colten v. Kentucky, 407 U.S. 104, 92 S.Ct. 1953 (1972), a police officer requested the defendant several times to leave a congested roadside where a friend of his in another car was being ticketed for a traffic offense. Defendant refused, was arrested for disorderly conduct, and convicted. The majority of the Court held that the statute was not impermissibly vague or broad. It laid down these basic principles:

> "The root of the vagueness doctrine is a rough idea of fairness. It is not a principle designed to convert into a constitutional dilemma the practical difficulties in drawing criminal statutes

both general enough to take into account a variety of human conduct and sufficiently specific to provide fair warning that certain kinds of conduct are prohibited. We agree with the Kentucky court when it said: 'We believe that citizens who desire to obey the statute will have no difficulty in understanding it . . . .'

* * *

"As the Kentucky statute was construed by the state court, a crime is committed only where there is no bona fide intention to exercise a constitutional right—in which event, by definition, the statute infringes no protected speech or conduct—or where the interest so clearly outweighs the collective interest sought to be asserted that the latter must be deemed insubstantial."

2. Consider the issue of vagueness as it may arise under the following provision of the U.S.Code (Ch. 102) dealing with riots:

Section 2101.

(a) (1) Whoever travels in interstate or foreign commerce or uses any facility of interstate or foreign commerce, including, but not limited to, the mail, telegraph, telephone, radio, or television, with intent—

(A) to incite a riot; or

(B) to organize, promote, encourage, participate in, or carry on a riot; or

(C) to commit any act of violence in furtherance of a riot; or

(D) to aid or abet any person in inciting or participating in or carrying on a riot or committing any act of violence in furtherance of a riot;

and who either during the course of any such travel or use or thereafter performs or attempts to perform any other overt act for any purpose specified in subparagraph (A), (B), (C), or (D) of this paragraph—

Shall be fined not more than $10,000, or imprisoned not more than five years, or both.

(b) In any prosecution under this section, proof that a defendant engaged or attempted to engage in one or more of the overt acts described in subparagraph (A), (B), (C), or (D) of paragraph (1) of subsection (a) and (1) has traveled in interstate or foreign commerce, or (2) has use of or used any facility of interstate or foreign commerce, including but not limited to, mail, telegraph, telephone, radio, or television, to communicate with or broadcast to any person or group of persons prior to such overt acts, such travel or use shall be admissible proof to establish that such defendant traveled in or used such facility of interstate or foreign commerce.

* * *

Section 2102

(a) As used in this chapter, the term "riot" means a public disturbance involving (1) an act or acts of violence by one or more persons part of an assemblage of three or more persons, which act or acts shall constitute a clear and present danger of, or shall result in, damage or injury to the property of any other person or to the person of any other individual or (2) a threat or threats of the commission of an act or acts of violence by one or more persons part of an assemblage of three or more persons having, individually or collectively, the ability of immediate execution of such threat or threats, where the performance of the threatened act or acts of violence would constitute a clear and present danger of, or would result in, damage or injury to the property of any other person or to the person of any other individual.

(b) As used in this chapter, the term "to incite a riot", or "to organize, promote, encourage, participate in, or carry on a riot", includes, but is not limited to, urging or instigating other persons to riot, but shall not be deemed to mean the mere oral or written (1) advocacy of ideas or (2) expression of belief, not involving advocacy of any act or acts of violence or assertion of the rightness of, or the right to commit, any such act or acts.

In National Mobilization Com. to End the War in Vietnam, 411 F.2d 934 (7th Cir. 1969), the court upheld the statute's validity, saying that statutes are not unconstitutional "because there are marginal cases in which it is difficult to draw the line".

GOODING, WARDEN v. WILSON

Supreme Court of the United States, 1972.
405 U.S. 518, 92 S.Ct. 1103.

MR. JUSTICE BRENNAN delivered the opinion of the Court.

Appellee was convicted in Superior Court, Fulton County, Georgia, on two counts of using opprobrious words and abusive language in violation of Georgia Code § 26–6303, which provides: "Any person who shall, without provocation, use to or of another, and in his presence . . . opprobrious words or abusive language, tending to cause a breach of the peace . . . shall be guilty of a misdemeanor."

* * *

Section 26–6303 punishes only spoken words. It can therefore withstand appellee's attack upon its facial constitutionality only if, as authoritatively construed by the Georgia courts, it is not susceptible of application to speech, although vulgar or offensive, that is protected by the First and Fourteenth Amendments, . . . Only the Georgia courts can supply the requisite construction, since of course "we lack jurisdiction authoritatively to construe state legislation." . . . It matters not that the words appellee used might have been constitutionally prohibited under a narrowly and precisely drawn statute. At least when statutes regulate or proscribe speech and when "no readily apparent construction suggests itself as a vehicle for rehabilitating the statutes in a single prosecution," . . . the transcendent value to all society of constitutionally protected expression is deemed to justify allowing "attacks on overly broad statutes with no requirement that the person making the attack demonstrate that his own conduct could not be regulated by a statute drawn with the requisite narrow specificity," . . . This is deemed necessary because persons whose expression is constitutionally protected may well refrain from exercising their rights for fear of criminal sanctions provided by a statute susceptible of application to protected expression.

* * *

The constitutional guarantees of freedom of speech forbid the States from punishing the use of words or language not within "narrowly limited classes of speech." Chaplinsky v. New Hampshire, . . . Even as to such a class, however, because "the line between speech unconditionally guaranteed and speech which may legitimately be regulated, suppressed, or punished is finely drawn," . . . "[i]n every case the power to regulate must be so exercised as not, in attaining a permissible end, unduly to infringe the protected freedom," . . . . In other words, the statute must be carefully drawn or be authoritatively construed to punish only unprotected speech and not be susceptible of application to protected expression. "Because First Amendment freedoms need breathing space to survive, government may regulate in the area only with narrow specificity." . . .

Appellant does not challenge these principles but contends that the Georgia statute is narrowly drawn to apply only to a constitutionally unprotected class of words—"fighting" words—"those which by their very utterance inflict injury or tend to incite an immediate breach of the peace." . . . In *Chaplinsky*, we sustained a conviction under Chapter 378, § 2, of the Public Laws of New Hampshire, which provided: "No person shall address any offensive, derisive or annoying word to any other person who is lawfully in any street or other public place, nor call him by any offensive or derisive name . . . ." Chaplinsky was convicted for addressing to another on a public sidewalk the words, "You are a God damned racketeer," and "a damned Fascist and the whole government of Rochester are Fascists or agents of Fascists." Chaplinsky challenged the constitutionality of the statute as inhibiting freedom of expression because it was vague and indefinite. The Supreme Court of New Hampshire, however, "long before the words for which Chaplinsky was convicted," sharply limited the statutory language "offensive, derisive or annoying word" to "fighting" words . . .

* * *

Appellant argues that the Georgia appellate courts have by construction limited the proscription of § 26–6303 to "fighting" words, as the New Hampshire Supreme Court limited the New Hampshire statute. . . . We have, however, made our own examination of the Georgia cases, both those cited and others discovered in research. That examination brings us to the conclusion, in agreement with the courts below, that the Georgia appellate decisions have not construed § 26–6303 to be limited in application, as in *Chaplinsky*, to words that "have a direct tendency to cause acts of violence by the person to whom, individually, the remark is addressed."

The dictionary definitions of "opprobrious" and "abusive" give them greater reach than "fighting" words. . . .

* * *

MR. JUSTICE POWELL and MR. JUSTICE REHNQUIST, took no part in the consideration or decision of this case.

MR. CHIEF JUSTICE BURGER, dissenting.

I fully join in MR. JUSTICE BLACKMUN's dissent against the bizarre result reached by the Court. It is not merely odd, it is nothing less than remarkable that a court can find a state statute void on its face, not because of its language—which is the traditional test—but because of the way courts of that State have applied the statute in a few isolated cases, decided as long ago as 1905 and generally long before this Court's decision in Chaplinsky v. New Hampshire, ... Even if all of those cases had been decided yesterday, they do nothing to demonstrate that the narrow language of the Georgia statute has any significant potential for sweeping application to suppress or deter important protected speech.

In part the Court's decision appears to stem from its assumption that a statute should be regarded in the same light as its most vague clause, without regard to any of its other language. . . . The statute at bar, however, does not prohibit language "tending to cause a breach of the peace." Nor does it prohibit the use of "opprobrious words or abusive language" without more. Rather, it prohibits use "to or of another, and in his presence, opprobrious words or abusive language, tending to cause a breach of the peace." If words are to bear their common meaning, and are to be considered in context, rather than dissected with surgical precision using a semantical scalpel, this statute has little potential for application outside the realm of "fighting words" which this Court held beyond the protection of the First Amendment in *Chaplinsky.* Indeed, the language used by the *Chaplinsky* Court to describe words properly subject to regulation bears a striking resemblance to that of the Georgia statute, which was enacted many, many years before *Chaplinsky* was decided. And, if the early Georgia cases cited by the majority establish any proposition, it is that the statute, as its language so clearly indicates, is aimed at preventing precisely that type of personal, face-to-face abusive and insulting language likely to provoke a violent retaliation—self help, as we euphemistically call it—which the *Chaplinsky* case recognized could be validly prohibited. The facts of the case now before the Court demonstrate that the Georgia statute is serving that valid and entirely proper purpose. There is no persuasive reason to wipe the statute from the books, unless we want to encourage victims of such verbal assaults to seek their own private redress.

* * *

MR. JUSTICE BLACKMUN, with whom THE CHIEF JUSTICE joins, dissenting.

It seems strange indeed that in this day a man may say to a police officer, who is attempting to restore access to a public building, "White son of a bitch, I'll kill you" and "You son of a bitch, I'll choke you to death," and say to an accompanying officer, "You son of a bitch, if you ever put your hands on me again, I'll cut you all to pieces," and yet constitutionally cannot be prosecuted and convicted under a state statute which makes it a misdemeanor to "use to or of another, and in his presence, opprobrious words or abusive language, tending to cause a breach of the peace. . . . " This, however, is precisely what the Court pronounces as the law today.

The Supreme Court of Georgia, when the conviction was appealed, unanimously held the other way. . . . Surely any adult who can read—and I do not exclude this appellee-defendant from that category—should reasonably expect no other conclusion. The words of Georgia Code § 26–6303 are clear. They are also concise. They are not, in my view, overbroad or incapable of being understood. Except perhaps for the "big" word "opprobrious"—and no point is made of its bigness—any Georgia schoolboy would expect that this defendant's fighting and provocative words to the officers were covered by § 26–6303. Common sense permits no other conclusion. This is demonstrated by the fact that the appellee, and this Court, attacks the statute not as it applies to the appellee, but as it conceivably might apply to others who might utter other words.

The Court reaches its result by saying that the Georgia statute has been interpreted by the State's courts so as to be applicable in practice to otherwise constitutionally protected speech. It follows, says the Court, that the statute is overbroad and therefore is facially unconstitutional and to be struck down in its entirety. Thus Georgia apparently is to be left with no valid statute on its books to meet Wilson's bullying tactic. This result, achieved by what is indeed a very strict construction, will be totally incomprehensible to the State of Georgia, to its courts, and to its citizens.

The Court would justify its conclusion by unearthing a 66-year-old decision, . . ., of the Supreme Court of Georgia, and two intermediate appellate court cases over 55 years old, . . . broadly applying the statute in those less permissive days, and by additional reference to (a) a 1956 Georgia intermediate appellate court decision, . . . which, were it the first and only Georgia case, would surely not support today's decision, and (b) another intermediate appellate court decision . . . (1961), relating not to § 26–6303, but to another statute.

This Court appears to have developed its overbreadth rationale in the years since these early Georgia cases. The State's statute, therefore, is condemned because the State's courts have not had an opportunity to adjust to this Court's modern theories of overbreadth.

I wonder, now that § 26–6303 is voided, just what Georgia can do if it seeks to proscribe what the Court says it still may constitutionally proscribe. The natural thing would be to enact a new statute reading just as § 26–6303 reads. But it, too, presumably would be overbroad unless the legislature would add words to the effect that it means only what this Court says it may mean and no more.

* * *

For me, Chaplinsky v. New Hampshire . . . was good law when it was decided and deserves to remain as good law now. A unanimous Court, including among its members Chief Justice Stone and Justices Black, Reed, Douglas and Murphy, obviously thought it was good law. But I feel that by decisions such as this one . . ., despite its protestations to the contrary, is merely paying lip service to *Chaplinsky*. As the appellee states in a footnote to his brief, p. 14, "Although there is no doubt that the state can punish 'fighting words' this appears to be about all that is left of the decision in *Chaplinsky*." If this is what the overbreadth doctrine means, and if this is what it produces, it urgently needs reexamination. The Court has painted itself into a corner from which it, and the States, can extricate themselves only with difficulty.

I. EQUAL PROTECTION OF THE LAW

McLAUGHLIN v. FLORIDA

Supreme Court of the United States, 1964.
379 U.S. 184, 85 S.Ct. 283.

MR. JUSTICE WHITE delivered the opinion of the Court.

At issue in this case is the validity of a conviction under § 798.05 of the Florida statutes, providing that:

> "Any negro man and white woman, or any white man and negro woman, who are not married to each other, who shall habitually live in and occupy in the nighttime the same room shall each be punished by imprisonment not exceeding twelve months, or by fine not exceeding five hundred dollars."

Because the section applies only to a white person and a Negro who commit the specified acts and because no couple other than one made up of a white and a Negro is subject to conviction upon proof of the elements comprising the offense it proscribes, we hold § 798.05 invalid as a denial of the equal protection of the laws guaranteed by the Fourteenth Amendment. * * *

The elements of the offense as described by the trial judge are the (1) habitual occupation of a room at night, (2) by a Negro and a white person (3) who are not married. The State presented evidence going to each factor, appellants' constitutional contentions were overruled and the jury returned a verdict of guilty. Solely on the authority of Pace v. Alabama, . . . the Florida Supreme Court affirmed and sustained the validity of § 798.05 as against appellants' claims that the section denied them equal protection of the laws guaranteed by the Fourteenth Amendment. . . .

It is readily apparent that § 798.05 treats the interracial couple made up of a white person and a Negro differently than it does any other couple. No couple other than a Negro and a white person can be convicted under § 798.05 and no other section proscribes the precise conduct banned by § 798.05. Florida makes no claim to the contrary in this Court. However, all whites and Negroes who engage in the forbidden conduct are covered by the section and each member of the interracial couple is subject to the same penalty.

In this situation, Pace v. Alabama is relied upon as controlling authority. In our view, however, *Pace* represents a limited view of the Equal Protection Clause which has not withstood analysis in the subsequent decisions of this Court. In that case, the Court let stand a conviction under an Alabama statute forbidding adultery or fornication between a white person and a Negro and imposing a greater penalty than allowed under another Alabama statute of general application and proscribing the same conduct whatever the race of the participants. The opinion acknowledged that the purpose of the Equal Protection Clause "was to prevent hostile and discriminating State legislation against any person or class of persons" and that equality of protection under the laws implies that any person, "whatever his race . . . shall not be subjected, for the same offence, to any greater or different punishment." But taking quite literally its own words, "for the same *offence*" (emphasis supplied), the Court pointed out that Alabama had designated as a separate offense the commission by a white person and a Negro of the identical acts forbidden by the general provisions. There was, therefore, no impermissible discrimination because the difference in punishment was "directed against the offence designated" and because in the case of each offense all who committed it, white and Negro were treated alike. Under *Pace* the Alabama law regulating the conduct of both Negroes and whites satisfied the Equal Protection Clause since it applied equally to and among the members of the class which it reached without regard to the fact that the statute did not reach other types of couples performing the identical conduct and without any necessity to justify the difference in penalty established for the two offenses. Because each of the Alabama laws applied equally to those to whom it was applicable, the different treatment accorded interracial and intraracial couples was irrelevant.[1]

1. Had the Court been presented with a statute that, for example, prohibited any Negro male from having carnal knowledge of a white female and penalized only the Negro, such a statute would unquestionably have been held to deny equal protection even though it applied equally to all to whom it applied. See Strauder v. West Virginia, 100 U.S. 303, 306–308; Ho Ah Kow v. Nunan, 12 Fed.Cas. 252 (No. 6546) (C.C.D.Cal.1879) (Field,

This narrow view of the Equal Protection Clause was soon swept away. While acknowledging the currency of the view that "if the law deals alike with all of a certain class" it is not obnoxious to the Equal Protection Clause and that "as a general proposition, this is undeniably true," the Court in Gulf, C. & S. F. R. Co. v. Ellis, . . . said that it was "equally true that such classification cannot be made arbitrarily. . . . " Classification "must always rest upon some difference which bears a reasonable and just relation to the act in respect to which the classification is proposed, and can never be made arbitrarily and without any such basis." "[A]rbitrary selection can never be justified by calling it classification." . . .

Judicial inquiry under the Equal Protection Clause, therefore, does not end with a showing of equal application among the members of the class defined by the legislation. The courts must reach and determine the question whether the classifications drawn in a statute are reasonable in light of its purpose—in this case, whether there is an arbitrary or invidious discrimination between those classes covered by Florida's cohabitation law and those excluded. That question is what *Pace* ignored and what must be faced here.

Normally, the widest discretion is allowed the legislative judgment in determining whether to attack some, rather than all, of the manifestations of the evil aimed at; and normally that judgment is given the benefit of every conceivable circumstance which might suffice to characterize the classification as reasonable rather than arbitrary and invidious. . . . But we deal here with a classification based upon the race of the participants, which must be viewed in light of the historical fact that the central purpose of the Fourteenth Amendment was to eliminate racial discrimination emanating from official sources in the States. This strong policy renders racial classifications "constitutionally suspect" . . .; and subject to the "most rigid scrutiny" . . .; and "in most circumstances irrelevant" to any constitutionally acceptable legislative purpose. . . . Thus it is that racial classifications have been held invalid in a variety of contexts. See, e. g., Virginia Board of Elections v. Hamm . . . (designation of race in voting and property records); Anderson v. Martin . . . (designation of race on nomination papers and ballots); Watson v. City of Memphis . . . (segregation in public parks and playgrounds); Brown v. Board of Education . . . (segregation in public schools).

We deal here with a racial classification embodied in a criminal statute. In this context, where the power of the State weighs most

J.) ("Chinese Pigtail" case). Because of the manifest inadequacy of any approach requiring only equal application to the class defined in the statute, one may conclude that in *Pace* the Court actually ruled *sub silentio* that the different treatment meted out to interracial and intraracial couples was based on a reasonable legislative purpose. If the Court did reach that conclusion it failed to articulate it or to give its reasons, and for the reasons stated infra we reject the contention presented here that the criminal statute presently under review is grounded in a reasonable legislative policy.

heavily upon the individual or the group, we must be especially sensitive to the policies of the Equal Protection Clause which, as reflected in congressional enactments dating from 1870, were intended to secure "the full and equal benefit of all laws and proceedings for the security of persons and property" and to subject all persons "to like punishment, pains, penalties, taxes, licenses, and exactions of every kind, and to no other."

Our inquiry, therefore, is whether there clearly appears in the relevant materials some overriding statutory purpose requiring the proscription of the specified conduct when engaged in by a white person and a Negro, but not otherwise. Without such justification the racial classification contained in § 798.05 is reduced to an invidious discrimination forbidden by the Equal Protection Clause.

The Florida Supreme Court, relying upon Pace v. Alabama, found no legal discrimination at all and gave no consideration to statutory purpose. The State in its brief in this Court, however, says that the legislative purpose of § 798.05, like the other sections of chapter 798, was to prevent breaches of the basic concepts of sexual decency; and we see no reason to quarrel with the State's characterization of this statute, dealing as it does with illicit extramarital and premarital promiscuity.

We find nothing in this suggested legislative purpose, however, which makes it essential to punish promiscuity of one racial group and not that of another. There is no suggestion that a white person and a Negro are any more likely habitually to occupy the same room together than the white or the Negro couple or to engage in illicit intercourse if they do. Sections 798.01–798.05 indicate no legislative conviction that promiscuity by the interracial couple presents any particular problems requiring separate or different treatment if the suggested over-all policy of the chapter is to be adequately served. Sections 798.01–798.03 deal with adultery, lewd cohabitation and fornication, in that order. All are of general application. Section 798.04 prohibits a white and a Negro from living in a state of adultery or fornication and imposes a lesser period of imprisonment than does either § 798.01 or § 798.02, each of which is applicable to all persons. Simple fornication by the interracial couple is covered only by the general provision of § 798.03. This is not, therefore, a case where the class defined in the law is that from which "the evil mainly is to be feared," Patsone v. Pennsylvania . . . ; or where the "[e]vils in the same field may be of different dimensions and proportions, requiring different remedies" . . . ; or even one where the State has done as much as it can as fast as it can . . . . That a general evil will be partially corrected may at times, and without more, serve to justify the limited application of a criminal law; but legislative discretion to employ the piecemeal approach stops short of permitting a State to narrow statutory coverage to focus on a racial group. Such classifications bear a far heavier burden of justification. . . .

Florida's remaining argument is related to its law against interracial marriage . . . which, in the light of certain legislative history of the Fourteenth Amendment, is said to be immune from attack under the Equal Protection Clause. Its interracial cohabitation law, § 798.05, is likewise valid, it is argued, because it is ancillary to and serves the same purpose as the miscegenation law itself.

We reject this argument, without reaching the question of the validity of the State's prohibition against interracial marriage or the soundness of the arguments rooted in the history of the Amendment. For even if we posit the constitutionality of the ban against the marriage of a Negro and a white, it does not follow that the cohabitation law is not to be subjected to independent examination under the Fourteenth Amendment. "[A]ssuming, for purposes of argument only, that the basic prohibition is constitutional," in this case the law against interracial marriage, "it does not follow that there is no constitutional limit to the means which may be used to enforce it." . . . Section 798.05 must therefore itself pass muster under the Fourteenth Amendment; and for reasons quite similar to those already given, we think it fails the test.

There is involved here an exercise of the state police power which trenches upon the constitutionally protected freedom from invidious official discrimination based on race. Such a law, even though enacted pursuant to a valid state interest, bears a heavy burden of justification, as we have said, and will be upheld only if it is necessary, and not merely rationally related, to the accomplishment of a permissible state policy. . . . Those provisions of chapter 798 which are neutral as to race express a general and strong state policy against promiscuous conduct, whether engaged in by those who are married, those who may marry or those who may not. These provisions, if enforced, would reach illicit relations of any kind and in this way protect the integrity of the marriage laws of the State, including what is claimed to be a valid ban on interracial marriage. These same provisions, moreover, punish premarital sexual relations as severely or more severely in some instances than do those provisions which focus on the interracial couple. Florida has offered no argument that the State's policy against interracial marriage cannot be as adequately served by the general, neutral, and existing ban on illicit behavior as by a provision such as § 798.05 which singles out the promiscuous interracial couple for special statutory treatment. In short, it has not been shown that § 798.05 is a necessary adjunct to the State's ban on interracial marriage. We accordingly invalidate § 798.05 without expressing any views about the State's prohibition of interracial marriage, and reverse these convictions.

Reversed.

MR. JUSTICE STEWART, with whom MR. JUSTICE DOUGLAS joins, concurring.

I concur in the judgment and agree with most of what is said in the Court's opinion. But the Court implies that a criminal law of the kind here involved might be constitutionally valid if a State could show "some overriding statutory purpose." This is an implication in which I cannot join, because I cannot conceive of a valid legislative purpose under our Constitution for a state law which makes the color of a person's skin the test of whether his conduct is a criminal offense. These appellants were convicted, fined, and imprisoned under a statute which made their conduct criminal only because they were of different races. So far as this statute goes, their conduct would not have been illegal had they both been white, or both Negroes. There might be limited room under the Equal Protection Clause for a civil law requiring the keeping of racially segregated public records for statistical or other valid public purposes. . . . But we deal here with a criminal law which imposes criminal punishment. And I think it is simply not possible for a state law to be valid under our Constitution which makes the criminality of an act depend upon the race of the actor. Discrimination of that kind is invidious *per se*.

NOTES

1. In Loving v. Virginia, 388 U.S. 1, 87 S.Ct. 1817 (1967), the Court, on the authority of the McLaughlin case, voided prohibitions against interracial marriage.

2. The limitations imposed upon state action in the creation and definition of crime are not always concerned with unequal application based on race. For example, in State ex rel. Flores v. Tahash, 272 Minn. 451, 138 N.W.2d 626 (1966), the petitioner, convicted of the unlawful possession of 85 bottles of empirin compound with codeine phosphate, and sentenced to 10 to 40 years in the penitentiary, attacked the statute defining the offense on the ground that the legislature had not outlawed the possession of other exempt narcotics containing a higher percentage of codeine. Consider the following excerpt from the court's opinion affirming the conviction:

"* * * A pharmaceutical expert called by counsel for defendant testified in the following manner:

> 'Q. Now Doctor, can you make some comparison for us as to the amount of codeine which would be consumed, say, in a teaspoonful of syrup, cough syrup, as compared with one tablet of empirin compound with codeine phosphate, assuming that this was a $\frac{1}{8}$ grain tablet of codeine?
>
> 'A. The maximum amount of codeine that an exempt codeine-containing cough syrup may contain, as you stated, is one grain of codeine phosphate per fluid ounce. The usual dose of such a preparation would be one teaspoonful. This would be approximately $\frac{1}{6}$ of an ounce. So that the amount of codeine contained in a teaspoonful of such a cough syrup would be about $\frac{1}{6}$ grain.
>
> 'Q. $\frac{1}{6}$ grain?
>
> 'A. A teaspoonful of such an exempt codeine containing cough syrup would therefore contain more codeine phosphate than would be contained in one—$\frac{1}{8}$ grain codeine phosphate empirin compound with codeine phosphate.'

"While the defendant concedes that possession of tablets containing codeine in the amounts found on his person is a violation of the statute, he asserts that under the evidence the statute denies him the equal protection of the laws guaranteed by the State and Federal Constitutions. It is essentially defendant's position that to prohibit the sale of a tablet with 1/8 of a grain of codeine and at the same time exempt the sale of cough syrup containing as much as 1/6 of a grain of codeine per teaspoon results in an arbitrary and unreasonable classification. The state, on the other hand, argues that the classification is proper because (1) liquid cough syrup is more difficult to conceal than tablets; (2) its cost would be prohibitive if available only by prescription; and (3) the benefit and convenience to the public in securing cough syrup over the counter outweigh the potential dangers inherent in permitting its purchase without a prescription.

"With respect to the test to be applied in considering the propriety of a legislative classification, we have recently held . . . 'In deciding whether classification in a given situation offends constitutional principles, the rules of construction generally governing legislation are relevant. In this area there is a growing judicial tendency to permit the exercise of broad discretion. The fact that measures taken are not directed at all of the evils to be corrected does not invalidate the application of the statute if the problem is dealt with according to practical exigencies and experience in a manner which is germane to its solution.' For the reasons advanced by the state, we are of the opinion the classification is reasonable and the statute therefore valid. * * *"

3. Sometimes the contention of a denial of equal protection of the laws is raised against a statutory scheme which, because it strives for flexibility in sentencing, may make different defendants liable for varying penalties for committing the same act. In Black v. Gladden, 237 Or. 631, 393 P.2d 190 (1964), the defendant was convicted of shoplifting goods valued at $2.30 and sentenced to a term not to exceed six years. In seeking post-conviction release he contended that he was denied equal protection of the laws since there was "no rational distinction between the acts proscribed in . . . the larceny statute [a misdemeanor], and the acts proscribed in . . . the shoplifting statute [a felony], and that, therefore, if two persons do identical acts of taking, one may be charged by the grand jury or magistrate with a felony and the other with a misdemeanor without any guiding standard to guide them in making the distinction". This, said the petitioner, violates the rule which says "that if there is no rational basis for distinguishing the acts committed by one person from the acts committed by another, the acts of one cannot be treated solely as a felony and the acts of the other solely as a misdemeanor."

In rejecting the argument, the court held that since there "is a reasonable basis for regarding theft committed in a store or other mercantile establishment as a *separate social evil,* distinct from theft committed under other circumstances", it was "clearly a matter for legislative discretion" which did not "give rise to a constitutional objection". (Emphasis added.)

In People v. Harper, 1 Mich.App. 480, 136 N.W.2d 768 (1965), the court held constitutional a statutory scheme of regulation which punished the unlawful sale of narcotics by unlicensed persons with greater severity than it punished unlawful sale by licensed persons. Portions of the court's opinion are set forth below:

"QUINN, JUDGE.

"* * * The gist of appellant's argument to establish unconstitutionality is that because a licensed person who sells narcotics unlawfully is subject to a maximum penalty of 10 years . . . and an unlicensed person who does the same thing is subject to a minimum sentence of 20 years and a maximum of life . . . the latter is denied equal protection of the law as guaranteed by U.S.Const. art. 14 and Const.1908, art. 2, § 1. Appellant is not licensed. The precise question for decision is whether the classification 'licensed' and 'unlicensed' is reasonable. . . .

"The standards of classification are:

> " '1. The equal-protection clause of the 14th Amendment does not take from the state the power to classify in the adoption of police laws, but admits of the exercise of a wide scope of discretion in that regard, and avoids what is done only when it is without any reasonable basis, and therefore is purely arbitrary. 2. A classification having some reasonable basis does not offend against that clause merely because it is not made with mathematical nicety, or because in practice it results in some inequality. 3. When the classification in such a law is called in question, if any state of facts reasonably can be conceived that would sustain it, the existence of that state of facts at the time the law was enacted must be assumed. 4. One who assails the classification in such a law must carry the burden of showing that it does not rest upon any reasonable basis, but is essentially arbitrary.' "

The statutes here involved were enacted to control manufacture, possession, and distribution of narcotic drugs. In order to facilitate and regulate the legitimate trade in these products, certain people are licensed. . . . By licensing this group, the legislature places severe controls over their contact with narcotics. . . . Every transaction that they make is governed by law and the records that they keep are subject to close scrutiny by the appropriate authorities. . . . The licensing act is aimed primarily at safeguarding and regulating legitimate trade of narcotics. The act under which respondent was convicted and sentenced is directed solely at suppressing illegal traffic in narcotics. The purpose of the two acts is entirely different, and it is a reasonable basis for the classifications 'licensed' and 'unlicensed'.

"The statutes involved are not unconstitutional. Writ denied."

4. The conviction of a woman for being "a common scold" was voided in State v. Palendrano, 120 N.J.Super. 336, 293 A.2d 747 (1972). Among the grounds for the decision was the element of unequal protection, since only a woman, and not a man, could be subject to prosecution, whereas a man might be just as "troublesome and angry" by "wrangling" among his neighbors.

5. A Massachusetts statute made it a criminal offense for "whoever . . . gives away . . . any drug, medicine, instrument or article whatever for the prevention of conception", except that a registered physician could administer to or prescribe the same for any *married* person. It also authorized the sale by a pharmacist to any *married* person presenting a physician's prescription. The defendant, who was neither a physician nor a pharmacist, exhibited contraceptive articles in the course of delivering a lecture to a group of college students, and at the end of his lecture he gave a young *unmarried woman* a contraceptive vaginal foam. His Massachusetts conviction was reversed by the Supreme Court of the United States—Eisenstadt v. Baird, 405 U.S. 438, 92 S.Ct. 1029 (1972)—upon the privacy principle and also because of its violation of the rights of single persons under the Equal Protection Clause of the Fourteenth Amendment.

Chapter 3

FEDERAL CRIMINAL JURISDICTION

A. DIRECT FEDERAL INTEREST OFFENSES

There is no federal common law jurisdiction in criminal cases. United States v. Hudson, 11 U.S. (14 Cranch) 32 (1812). Thus, every congressional enactment in the criminal area must be based upon a constitutional provision which specifically authorizes Congress to legislate in a given field. The Tenth Amendment to the Constitution reserves to the states all powers not expressly delegated to the federal government by the Constitution.

Those areas in which the federal government has a direct interest pose no problem. The most obvious direct federal interest offenses are violations of the Internal Revenue Laws. The judiciary has taken the position that, given the broad grant of constitutional power vested in Congress to collect taxes, it will not restrain an exercise of the taxing power because of the onerous and burdensome results to taxpayers. McCray v. United States, 195 U.S. 27, 24 S.Ct. 769 (1904). Congress, not the courts, has the right to select the objects of taxation and the measures for implementing the collection process. Thus, without inquiring into the reasons underlying Congress' decision to select a particular subject for taxation the courts will not limit any tax unless there are provisions in the tax statute extraneous to a constitutionally authorized taxing need. United States v. Kahriger, 345 U.S. 22, 73 S.Ct. 510 (1954).

In this manner, the courts have recognized Congress' power to collect taxes whether the business involved is lawful or unlawful, Wainer v. United States, 299 U.S. 92, 57 S.Ct. 79 (1936), although the method of reporting the income subject to taxation may generate fifth amendment self-incrimination problems. See Marchetti v. United States, 390 U.S. 39, 88 S.Ct. 697 (1968). Consequently, the taxing power has been upheld in a wide variety of situations. E. g., United States v. Singer, 82 U.S. (15 Wall.) 111 (1872) (distilled spirits); United States v. Gullett, 322 F.Supp. 272 (D.Colo.1972) (transfer of firearms); United States v. Gross, 313 F.Supp. 1330 (D.Ind.1970), aff'd, 451 F.2d 1355 (7th Cir. 1971) (firearms dealers). But compare Harper v. Virginia Bd. of Elections, 383 U.S. 663, 86 S.Ct. 1079 (1966) (state poll tax unconstitutional).

The same federal interest, of course, exists with respect to the United States mails. Consequently, there is little question that Congress had the right to punish the use of the mails in execution of a scheme to defraud. 18 U.S.C.A. § 1341. However, the precise definition of the type of "scheme" that may be prosecuted under the statute has been a source of considerable consternation.

UNITED STATES v. STATES

United States Court of Appeals, 8th Cir., 1973.
488 F.2d 761.

MATTHES, SENIOR CIRCUIT JUDGE. * * *

Before trial appellants moved to dismiss [their] indictment [under the mail fraud statute] asserting that it failed to allege that anyone had been defrauded of any money or property, and consequently failed to state an offense against the United States. . . . [After their motion was denied] appellants waived a jury and a bench trial resulted in their convictions. Their appeals challenge the court's action in entertaining the charge.

* * *

The indictment charges that the defendants devised a scheme to defraud the voters and residents of the third and nineteenth wards of the City of St. Louis and the Board of Election Commissoners of the City of St. Louis by the use of fraudulent voter registrations and applications for absentee ballots. It is alleged that the purpose of the scheme to defraud was to influence the outcome of the election of the Republican Committeeman for the nineteenth ward and the Democratic Committeeman for the third ward "for the purpose of securing and controlling said political offices and the political influence and financial benefits of said offices * * *." It is further alleged that as part of the scheme to defraud, the defendants submitted false and fraudulent voter registration affidavits bearing the names of false and fictitious persons with false addresses and caused the St. Louis Board of Election Commissioners to place absentee ballots for the fictitious persons in an authorized depository for mail matter.

* * *

At the outset of their claim for reversal the appellants submit that the very language of 18 U.S.C.A. § 1341 mandates a holding that there is an offense under the statute only if money or property is involved in the scheme to defraud. Appellants argue that the first phrase of § 1341, dealing with "any scheme or artifice to defraud," must be read in conjunction with the second phrase, concerning "obtaining money or property by means of false or fraudulent pretenses, representations, or promises," which was added to the statute by a subsequent amendment.* Appellants suggest that

* **§ 1341. Frauds and swindles**

Whoever, having devised or intending to devise any scheme or artifice to defraud, or for obtaining money or property by means of false or fraudulent pretenses, representations, or promises, or to sell, dispose of, loan, exchange, alter, give away, distribute,

the second phrase was added to the predecessor of § 1341 because Congress believed that the "scheme to defraud" language included only frauds perpetrated without misrepresentations. They argue that the explicit "money or property" limitation in the added passage reveals that Congress believed that the first phrase in the original legislation dealt only with schemes to defraud of money or property.

But no case or legislative history is cited by the appellants supporting such an interpretation of legislative intent, nor does there appear to be any authority justifying such a construction of the statute. Moreover, not only does the appellants' conjunctive construction of the two phrases place a very strained and limited meaning on the broad wording of the first phrase, but a reading of the statute as a whole reveals that the two phrases in question are part of an uninterrupted listing of a series of obviously diverse schemes which result in criminal sanctions if the mails are used. The more natural construction of the wording in the statute is to view the two phrases independently, rather than complementary of one another. Indeed, numerous courts have construed the "scheme or artifice to defraud" language of § 1341 without reference to the "obtaining money or property" phrase.

* * *

Consequently, we hold that the language of the statute on its face does not preclude a finding that a "scheme or artifice to defraud" need not concern money or property. Since the statutory wording itself does not conclusively resolve the issue presented by the appellants, and since the legislative history does not deal with the scope and meaning of the provision of the statute in issue, we examine judicial opinions construing § 1341 for assistance in definitely determining whether the statute should apply to the facts of this case.

Initially, it should be noted that the concept of fraud in § 1341 is to be construed very broadly. . . . In Blachly v. United States [380 F.2d 665 (5th Cir. 1967)], the court observed:

> "The crime of mail fraud is broad in scope. * * * The fraudulent aspect of the scheme to "defraud" is measured by a nontechnical standard. * * * Law puts its imprimatur on the accepted moral standards and condemns

supply, or furnish or procure for unlawful use any counterfeit or spurious coin, obligation, security, or other article, or anything represented to be or intimated or held out to be such counterfeit or spurious article, for the purpose of executing such scheme or artifice or attempting so to do, places in any post office or authorized depository for mail matter, any matter or thing whatever to be sent or delivered by the Postal Service, or takes or receives therefrom, any such matter or thing, or knowingly causes to be delivered by mail according to the direction thereon, or at the place at which it is directed to be delivered by the person to whom it is addressed, any such matter or thing, shall be fined not more than $1,000 or imprisoned not more than five years, or both.

conduct which fails to match the "reflection of moral uprightness, of fundamental honesty, fair play and right dealing in the general and business life of the members of society." This is indeed broad. For as Judge Holmes once observed, "[t]he law does not define fraud; it needs no definition. It is as old as falsehood and as versable as human ingenuity."

Likewise, the definition of fraud in § 1341 is to be broadly and liberally construed to further the purpose of the statute; namely, to prohibit the misuse of the mails to further fraudulent enterprises. Accordingly, many courts have construed the term "scheme or artifice to defraud" to include within its ambit widely diverse schemes. [For instance, a divorce mill granting decrees of questionable validity; bribery of public officials; bribery of an oil company employee to gain the company's geophysical maps; mailing an extortion note; and ballot tampering by election officials.] * * *

There are also cases concerning bribery schemes which support the view that money or tangible property need not be involved in the scheme to defraud in order for the mail fraud statute to be invoked. Beginning with Shushan v. United States, the term "scheme or artifice to defraud" [included] an operation to bribe and corrupt public officials in order to gain advantages and special treatment. In *Shushan* there is the implication that a scheme to gain personal favors from public officials is a scheme to defraud the public, although the interest lost by the public can be described no more concretely than as an intangible right to the proper and honest administration of government. "[T]here must be a purpose to do wrong which is inconsistent with moral uprightness." This concept, that a scheme to defraud of certain intangible rights is grounds for prosecution under § 1341 if the mails are used, is more explicitly stated in United States v. Faser . . . (1969). In *Faser*, the defendants were indicted under the mail fraud statute after they accepted bribes to deposit public funds in a certain bank. There, as here, the defendants contended the indictment failed to state an offense because it did not allege that someone was actually defrauded out of something tangible that can be measured in terms of money or property. In rejecting that argument the court specifically discussed whether a fraudulent scheme must entail money or property in order for there to be an offense under § 1341. As an alternative ground for overruling the motion to dismiss, the court stated:

> "[I]t is further the opinion of this Court that the thing out of which it is charged that the State was defrauded need not necessarily be that which can be measured in terms of money or property. It is the opinion of this Court that it is a violation of the statute in question if a person defrauds the State out of the 'loyal and faithful services of an employee.' * * *

"Thus it seems quite clear that even if the thing out of which the State was allegedly defrauded was not susceptible of measurement in terms of money or physical property, a valid indictment may still result therefrom."

. . . In [a number of cases the courts have] upheld the mail fraud indictment on the ground that the mails had been used in a scheme to defraud a corporation of the "honest and faithful services" of one or more employees. . . . These cases serve as persuasive authority for the proposition that in a prosecution for use of the mails to further and execute a vote fraud scheme the indictment states an offense even though it does not contain allegations that anyone was defrauded of any property or money. Nevertheless, the appellants argue that the application of the mail fraud statute to the facts of this case will result in a "policing" of state election procedure, and that Congress has never explicitly authorized such widespread intervention into state affairs. The appellants' argument misinterprets the purpose of the mail fraud legislation. The focus of the statute is upon the misuse of the Postal Service, not the regulation of state affairs, and Congress clearly has the authority to regulate such misuse of the mails. [In Badders v. United States (1916), the court said:] "The overt act of putting a letter into the postoffice of the United States is a matter that Congress may regulate. * * * Whatever the limits to its power, it may forbid any such acts done in furtherance of a scheme it regards as contrary to public policy, whether it can forbid the scheme or not." The purpose of 18 U.S.C. § 1341 is to prevent the Postal Service from being used to carry out fraudulent schemes, regardless of what is the exact nature of the scheme and regardless of whether it happens to be forbidden by state law. . . . "Congress definitely intends that the misuse of the mails shall be controlled even though it be its policy to leave the control of elections to the several States."

The appellants' argument presents no justification for refusing to apply the mail fraud statutes to the facts of this case. The prosecution of appellants in federal court for mail fraud does not interfere with the state's enforcement of its election laws. There are no grounds for dismissing the indictment under the principles of comity or the abstention doctrine or under any other principle of federalism.

* * *

Affirmed.

ROSS, CIRCUIT JUDGE (concurring).

I reluctantly concur. The law, as capably expressed by Judge Matthes, leaves us no other alternative.

However, I cannot believe that it was the original intent of Congress that the Federal Government should take over the prosecution of every state crime involving fraud just because the mails have been used in furtherance of that crime. The facts in this case show that this election fraud was purely a state matter. It should have been prosecuted in state court. [The federal government's decision to prosecute this case] relieved the state of its duty to police the violation of its local election laws and helped create a precedent which will encourage the same sort of unwarranted federal preemption in the future.

NOTES

1. The federal instrumentality involved under § 1341 is, of course, the use of the mails. Each mailing is a separate offense under the statute; and the offender can receive independent, consecutive sentences for every item mailed. However, to be convicted, the accused must not only participate in a scheme, but also cause the use of the mails in furtherance of that scheme. The use of the mails in furtherance of the scheme is the essential requisite of federal jurisdiction.

By a 5–4 vote, the Supreme Court of the United States, resolving an issue upon which the federal appellate courts had split, held that mailings of invoices for collection were not in furtherance of a fraudulent credit card scheme. Mr. Justice Rehnquist's opinion for the narrow majority in United States v. Maze, —— U.S. ——, 94 S.Ct. 645 (1974), considered both the "furtherance" and "causation" requirements:

"In February 1971 respondent Thomas E. Maze moved to Louisville, Kentucky, and there shared an apartment with Charles L. Meredith. In the spring of that year respondent's fancy lightly turned to thoughts of the sunny Southland, and he thereupon took Meredith's BankAmericard and his 1968 automobile and headed for Southern California. By presenting the BankAmericard and signing Meredith's name, respondent obtained food and lodging at motels located in California, Florida, and Louisiana. Each of these establishments transmitted to the Citizens Fidelity Bank and Trust Company in Louisville, which had issued the BankAmericard to Meredith, the invoices representing goods and services furnished to respondent. Meredith, meanwhile, on the day after respondent's departure from Louisville, notified the Louisville bank that his credit card had been stolen.

"Upon respondent's return to Louisville he was indicted on four counts of violation of the federal mail fraud statute . . .

* * *

"The indictment charged that respondent had obtained goods and services at four specified motels by presenting Meredith's BankAmericard for payment and representing himself to be Meredith, and that respondent knew that each merchant would cause the sales slips of the purchases to be delivered by mail to the Louisville bank which would in turn mail them to Meredith for payment. The indictment also charged that the delay in this mailing would enable the respondent to continue purchasing goods and services for an appreciable period of time.

"Respondent was tried by a jury in the United States District Court for the Western District of Kentucky. At trial, representatives of the four motels identified the sales invoices from the transactions on Meredith's BankAmericard which were forwarded to the Louisville bank by their motels. An official of the Louisville bank testified that all of the sales invoices for those transactions were received by the bank in due course through the mail, and that this was the customary method by which invoices representing BankAmericard purchases were transmitted to the Louisville bank. The jury found respondent guilty as charged on all counts, and he appealed the judgment of conviction to the Court of Appeals for the Sixth Circuit. That court reversed the judgment as to the mail fraud statute . . . . 468 F.2d 529 (CA6 1972). Because of an apparent conflict among the courts of appeals as to the circumstances under which the fraudulent use of a credit card may violate the mail fraud statute, we granted the Government's petition for certiorari.

* * *

"In Pereira v. United States, 347 U.S. 1, 9, 74 S.Ct. 358, 363 (1954), the Court held that one 'causes' the mails to be used where he 'does an act with knowledge that the use of mails will follow in the ordinary course of business, or where such use can reasonably be foreseen, even though not actually intended . . . .' We assume, . . . that the evidence would support a finding by the jury that Maze 'caused' the mailings of the invoices he signed from the out-of-state motels to the Louisville bank. But the more difficult question is whether these mailings were sufficiently closely related to respondent's scheme so as to bring his conduct within the statute.

"Under the statute, the mailing must be 'for the purpose of executing the scheme, as the statute requires,' Kann v. United States, 323 U.S. 88, 94, 65 S.Ct. 148, 151 (1944), but 'it is not necessary that the scheme contemplate the use of the mails as an essential element,'

* * *

"The defendant in *Pereira*, supra, was charged with having defrauded a wealthy widow of her property after having married her. The Court describes the conduct of defendant in these words:

> 'Pereira asked his then wife if she would join him in the hotel venture and advance $35,000 towards the purchase price of $78,000. She agreed. It was then agreed, between her and Pereira, that she would sell some securities that she possessed in Los Angeles, and bank the money in a bank of his choosing in El Paso. On June 15, she received a check for $35,000 on the Citizens National Bank of Los Angeles from her brokers in Los Angeles, and gave it to Pereira, who endorsed it for collection to the State National Bank in El Paso. The check cleared, and on June 18, a cashier's check for $35,000 was drawn in favor of Pereira.'

"Thus the mailings in *Pereira* played a significant part in enabling the defendant in that case to acquire dominion over the $35,000 with which he ultimately absconded. Unlike the mailings in *Pereira* the mailings here were directed to the end of adjusting accounts between the motel proprietor, the Louisville bank, and Meredith, all of whom had to a greater or lesser degree been the victims of respondent's scheme. Respondent's scheme reached fruition when he checked out of the motel, and there is no indication that the success of his scheme depended in any way on which of his victims ultimately bore the loss. Indeed, from his point of view, he probably would have preferred to have the invoices misplaced by the various motel personnel and never mailed at all.

* * *

"Congress could have drafted the mail fraud statute so as to require only that the mails be in fact used as a result of the fraudulent scheme. But it did not do this; instead, it required that the use of the mails be 'for the purpose of executing such a scheme or artifice. . . .' Since the mailings in this case were not for that purpose, the judgment of the Court of Appeals is affirmed."

2. Based upon the judicial recognition of "reasonable foreseeability" of the use of the mails, causation is not ordinarily difficult to prove. In United States v. Strauss, 452 F.2d 375 (7th Cir. 1971), certiorari denied, 405 U.S. 989, 92 S.Ct. 1252 (1972), a defendant who was not alleged to possess any special knowledge of banking procedures was convicted of perpetrating a "check kiting" scheme. The mailing which supported the § 1341 violation consisted of "advice letters" transmitted by victim banks. Affirming the conviction, the court held:

> Although, it was not the normal practice of these banks to utilize the mails in the bank collection process, the evidence shows the practice of sending advice letters through the mails was not an isolated one and could reasonably have been anticipated under the circumstances.

Situations similar to that in *Strauss* are abundant: the deposit of a check drawn on an out-of-state bank; the mailing from an attorney for adjusters to an attorney for claimants caused by a doctor in the execution of an inflated bills scheme; the mailing of a newspaper caused by one who solicited victims through advertisements; etc.

3. "Furtherance" is far more difficult to prove. "[T]he important question is whether the use of the mails was significantly related to those operative facts making the fraud possible or constituting the fraud." Adams v. United States, 312 F.2d 137, 140 (5th Cir. 1963). In United States v. Chason, 451 F.2d 301, 303 (2d Cir. 1971), the court said: "[t]he real test is the extent of the contribution which the mails make to the success of the entire scheme". Thus, the mailing must bear a direct relationship to the scheme charged. Compare Richardson v. United States, 150 F.2d 58 (6th Cir. 1945) (mailed assurance that cotton bore quality rating cards did not further a scheme which involved the submission of fraudulent samples of cotton rating examiners and the subsequent obtaining of loans secured by the misrated cotton); McLendon v. United States, 2 F.2d 660 (6th Cir. 1924) (mailing referring to hunting capabilities of dog did not further scheme to misrepresent pedigrees).

A great deal of litigation has involved the question of whether a mailing was in furtherance of a scheme. How could a fraud statute eliminating this requirement be drawn? Would it be constitutional? Would it be advisable?

B. THE NECESSARY AND PROPER CLAUSE

In conjunction with the specific authority to create laws in a number of enumerated areas, the Necessary and Proper clause of the Constitution, U.S.Const. Art. I, § 8, cl. 18, provides Congress with the power to legislate in areas that will facilitate the execution of the powers vested in the federal government. In Logan v. United States, 144 U.S. 283, 12 S.Ct. 617 (1892), the Supreme Court recognized the applicability of this clause. There, taking cognizance of the propriety of the civil rights conspiracy statute, the Court upheld the right of federal authorities to protect prisoners in their custody:

> Among the powers which the Constitution expressly confers upon Congress is the power to make all laws necessary and proper for carrying into execution the powers specifically granted to it, and all other powers vested by the Constitution in the government of the United States, or in any department or officer thereof. In the exercise of this general power of legislation, Congress may use any means, appearing to it most eligible and appropriate, which are adapted to the end to be accomplished, and are consistent with the letter and the spirit of the Constitution.
>
> Although the Constitution contains no grant, general or specific, to Congress of the power to provide for the punishment of crimes, except piracies and felonies on the high seas, offences against the law of nations, treason, and counterfeiting the securities and current coin of the United States, no one doubts the power of Congress to provide for the punishment of all crimes and offences against the United States, whether committed within one of the States of the Union, or within territory over which Congress has plenary and exclusive jurisdiction.
>
> To accomplish this end, Congress has the right to enact laws for the arrest and commitment of those accused of any such crime or offence, and for holding them in safe custody until indictment and trial; and persons arrested and held pursuant to such laws are in the exclusive custody of the United States, and are not subject to the judicial process or executive warrant of any State. The United States, having the absolute right to hold such prisoners, have an equal duty to protect them, while so held, against assault or injury from any quarter. The existence of that duty on the part of the government necessarily implies a corresponding right of the prisoners to be so protected; and this right of the

prisoners is a right secured to them by the Constitution and laws of the United States.

Therefore, notwithstanding the fact that the Constitution may not specifically grant Congress the power to regulate conduct in certain areas, where a given piece of legislation may be characterized as an incident of sovereignty which inheres in the government, it will be upheld under the Necessary and Proper Clause. Congress, thus, has the power to create, define and punish offenses whenever it is necessary and proper, by law, to do so to effectuate the objects of government.

The cases upholding this rationale are manifold. See, e. g., United States v. O'Brien, 391 U.S. 367, 88 S.Ct. 1673 (1968) (draft card laws); Dennis v. United States, 341 U.S. 494, 71 S.Ct. 857 (1951) (right of government to protect itself against violent overthrow); Baender v. Barnett, 255 U.S. 224, 41 S.Ct. 271 (1921) (counterfeiting laws in aid of power to coin money); Selective Draft Law Cases, 245 U.S. 366, 38 S.Ct. 159 (1918) (conscription laws in aid of power to raise armed forces); Ex Parte Jackson, 96 U.S. 727, 24 S.Ct. 877 (1877) (mail fraud statute in aid of power to establish post offices); Joyce v. United States, 147 U.S.App. D.C. 128, 454 F.2d 971 (1971) (flag desecration statute); United States v. Pizzarusso, 388 F.2d 8 (2d Cir. 1968) (false visa application laws in aid of power to regulate foreign affairs); Dropps v. United States, 34 F.2d 15 (8th Cir. 1929) (statute prohibiting bribery of federal officials).

The direct federal interest offenses and those covered by the umbrella of the Necessary and Proper Clause have not posed substantial difficulty in recent years. Rather, contemporary litigation has revolved around Congress' power to proscribe traditional state offenses under the Commerce Clause.

C. THE COMMERCE CLAUSE

PEREZ v. UNITED STATES

Supreme Court of the United States, 1971.
402 U.S. 146, 91 S.Ct. 1357.

MR. JUSTICE DOUGLAS delivered the opinion of the Court.

The question in this case is whether Title II of the Consumer Credit Protection Act, 18 U.S.C. § 891 et seq., as construed and applied to petitioner, is a permissible exercise by Congress of its powers under the Commerce Clause of the Constitution. Petitioner's conviction after trial by jury and his sentence were affirmed by the Court of Appeals, one judge dissenting. 426 F.2d 1073. We granted the petition for a writ of certiorari because of the importance of the question presented. We affirm that judgment.

Petitioner is one of the species commonly known as "loan sharks" which Congress found are in large part under the control of "organized crime." [1] "Extortionate credit transactions" are defined as those characterized by the use or threat of the use of "violence or other criminal means" in enforcement.[2] There was ample evidence showing petitioner was a "loan shark" who used the threat of violence as a method of collection. He loaned money to one Miranda, owner of a new butcher shop, making a $1,000 advance to be repaid in installments of $105 per week for 14 weeks. After paying at this rate for six or eight weeks, petitioner increased the weekly payment to $130. In two months Miranda asked for an additional loan of $2,000 which was made, the agreement being that Miranda was to pay $205 a week. In a few weeks petitioner increased the weekly payment to $330. When Miranda objected, petitioner told him about a customer who refused to pay and ended up in a hospital. So Miranda paid. In a few months petitioner increased his demands to $500 weekly which Miranda paid, only to be advised that at the end of the week petitioner would need $1,000. Miranda made that payment by not paying his suppliers; but faced with a $1,000 payment the next week, he sold his butcher shop. Petitioner pursued Miranda, first making threats to Miranda's wife and then telling Miranda he

1. Section 201(a) of Title II contains the following findings by Congress:

"(1) Organized crime is interstate and international in character. Its activities involve many billions of dollars each year. It is directly responsible for murders, willful injuries to person and property, corruption of officials, and terrorization of countless citizens. A substantial part of the income of organized crime is generated by extortionate credit transactions.

"(2) Extortionate credit transactions are characterized by the use, or the express or implicit threat of the use, of violence or other criminal means to cause harm to person, reputation, or property as a means of enforcing repayment. Among the factors which have rendered past efforts at prosecution almost wholly ineffective has been the existence of exclusionary rules of evidence stricter than necessary for the protection of constitutional rights.

"(3) Extortionate credit transactions are carried on to a substantial extent in interstate and foreign commerce and through the means and instrumentalities of such commerce. Even where extortionate credit transactions are purely intrastate in character, they nevertheless directly affect interstate and foreign commerce."

2. Section 891 of 18 U.S.C. (1964 ed., Supp. V) provides in part:

"(6) An extortionate extension of credit is any extension of credit with respect to which it is the understanding of the creditor and the debtor at the time it is made that delay in making repayment or failure to make repayment could result in the use of violence or other criminal means to cause harm to the person, reputation, or property of any person.

"(7) An extortionate means is any means which involves the use, or an express or implicit threat of use, of violence or other criminal means to cause harm to the person, reputation, or property of any person."

could have him castrated. When Miranda did not make more payments, petitioner said he was turning over his collections to people who would not be nice but who would put him in the hospital if he did not pay. Negotiations went on, Miranda finally saying he could only pay $25 a week. Petitioner said that was not enough, that Miranda should steal or sell drugs if necessary to get the money to pay the loan, and that if he went to jail it would be better than going to a hospital with a broken back or legs. He added, "I could have sent you to the hospital, you and your family, any moment I want with my people."

Petitioner's arrest followed. Miranda, his wife, and an employee gave the evidence against petitioner who did not testify or call any witnesses. Petitioner's attack was on the constitutionality of the Act, starting with a motion to dismiss the indictment.

The constitutional question is a substantial one.

* * *

The Commerce Clause reaches, in the main, three categories of problems. First, the use of channels of interstate or foreign commerce which Congress deems are being misused, as, for example, the shipment of stolen goods (18 U.S.C. §§ 2312–2315) or of persons who have been kidnaped (18 U.S.C. § 1201). Second, protection of the instrumentalities of interstate commerce, as, for example, the destruction of an aircraft (18 U.S.C. § 32), or persons or things in commerce, as, for example, thefts from interstate shipments (18 U.S.C. § 659). Third, those activities affecting commerce. It is with this last category that we are here concerned.

Chief Justice Marshall in Gibbons v. Ogden, 9 Wheat. 1, 195, said:

> "The genius and character of the whole government seem to be, that its action is to be applied to all the external concerns of the nation, and to those internal concerns which affect the States generally; but not to those which are completely within a particular State, which do not affect other States, and with which it is not necessary to interfere, for the purpose of executing some of the general powers of the government. The completely internal commerce of a State, then, may be considered as reserve for the State itself."

* * *

In United States v. Darby, 312 U.S. 100, the decision sustaining an Act of Congress which prohibited the employment of workers in the production of goods "for interstate commerce" at other than prescribed wages and hours, *a class of activities* was held properly regulated by Congress without proof that the particular intrastate activity against which a sanction was laid had an effect on commerce. A unanimous Court said:

> "Congress has sometimes left it to the courts to determine whether the intrastate activities have the prohibited effect on the commerce, as in the Sherman Act. It has sometimes left it to an administrative board or agency to determine whether the activities sought to be regulated or prohibited have such effect, as in the case of the Interstate Commerce Act, and the National Labor Relations Act, or whether they come within the statutory definition of the prohibited Act, as in the Federal Trade Commission Act. And sometimes Congress itself has said that a particular activity affects the commerce, as it did in the present Act, the Safety Appliance Act and the Railway Labor Act. In passing on the validity of legislation of the *class* last mentioned the only function of courts is to determine whether the particular activity regulated or prohibited is within the reach of the federal power."

That case is particularly relevant here because it involved a criminal prosecution, a unanimous Court holding that the Act was "sufficiently definite to meet constitutional demands." Petitioner is clearly *a member of the class* which engages in "extortionate credit transactions" as defined by Congress and the description of that class has the required definiteness.

It was the "class of activities" test which we employed in Atlanta Motel v. United States, 379 U.S. 241, to sustain an Act of Congress requiring hotel or motel accommodations for Negro guests. The Act declared that " 'any inn, hotel, motel, or other establishment which provides lodging to transient guests' affects commerce *per se*." That exercise of power under the Commerce Clause was sustained.

> "[O]ur people have become increasingly mobile with millions of people of all races traveling from State to State; . . . Negroes in particular have been the subject of discrimination in transient accommodations, having to travel great distances to secure the same; . . . often they have been unable to obtain accommodations and have had to call upon friends to put them up overnight . . . and . . . these conditions had become so acute as to require the listing of available lodging for Negroes in a special guidebook. . . ."

* * *

Where the *class of activities* is regulated and that *class* is within the reach of federal power, the courts have no power "to excise, as trivial, individual instances" of the class. Maryland v. Wirtz, 392 U.S. 183, 193.

Extortionate credit transactions, though purely intrastate, may in the judgment of Congress affect interstate commerce. In an analogous situation, Mr. Justice Holmes, speaking for a unanimous Court, said: "[W]hen it is necessary in order to prevent an evil to make the law embrace more than the precise thing to be prevented it may do so." Westfall v. United States, 274 U.S. 256, 259. In that case an officer of a state bank which was a member of the Federal Reserve System issued a fraudulent certificate of deposit and paid it from the funds of the state bank. It was argued that there was no loss to the Reserve Bank. Mr. Justice Holmes replied, "But every fraud like the one before us weakens the member bank and therefore weakens the System." In the setting of the present case there is a tie-in between local loan sharks and intrastate crime.

The findings by Congress are quite adequate on that ground. The McDade Amendment in the House, as already noted, was the one ultimately adopted. As stated by Congressman McDade it grew out of a "profound study of organized crime, its ramifications and its implications" undertaken by some 22 Congressmen in 1966–1967. 114 Cong.Rec. 14391. The results of that study were included in a report, The Urban Poor and Organized Crime, submitted to the House on August 29, 1967, which revealed that "organized crime takes over $350 million a year from America's poor through loan-sharking alone." See 113 Cong.Rec. 24460–24464. Congressman McDade also relied on The Challenge of Crime in a Free Society, A Report by the President's Commission on Law Enforcement and Administration of Justice (February 1967) which stated that loan sharking was "the second largest source of revenue for organized crime," and is one way by which the underworld obtains control of legitimate businesses.

The Congress also knew about New York's Report, An Investigation of the Loan Shark Racket (1965). See 114 Cong.Rec. 1428–1431. That report shows the loan shark racket is controlled by organized criminal syndicates, either directly or in partnership with independent operators; that in most instances the racket is organized into three echelons, with the top underworld "bosses" providing the money to their principal "lieutenants," who in turn distribute the money to the "operators" who make the actual individual loans; that loan sharks serve as a source of funds to bookmakers, narcotics dealers, and other racketeers; that victims of the racket include all classes, rich and poor, businessmen and laborers; that the victims are often coerced into the commission of criminal acts in order to repay their loans; that through loan sharking the organized underworld has obtained control of legitimate businesses, including securities brokerages and banks which are then exploited; and that "[e]ven where extortionate credit transactions are purely intrastate in character, they nevertheless directly affect interstate and foreign commerce."

 * * *

The essence of all these reports and hearings was summarized and embodied in formal congressional findings. They supplied Congress with the knowledge that the loan shark racket provides organized crime with its second most lucrative source of revenue, exacts millions from the pockets of people, coerces its victims into the commission of crimes against property, and causes the takeover by racketeers of legitimate businesses. See generally 114 Cong.Rec. 14391, 14392, 14395, 14396.

We have mentioned in detail the economic, financial, and social setting of the problem as revealed to Congress. We do so not to infer that Congress need make particularized findings in order to legislate. We relate the history of the Act in detail to answer the impassioned plea of petitioner that all that is involved in loan sharking is a traditionally local activity. It appears, instead, that loan sharking in its national setting is one way organized interstate crime holds its guns to the heads of the poor and the rich alike and syphons funds from numerous localities to finance its national operations.

Affirmed.

MR. JUSTICE STEWART, dissenting.

Congress surely has power under the Commerce Clause to enact criminal laws to protect the instrumentalities of interstate commerce, to prohibit the misuse of the channels or facilities of interstate commerce, and to prohibit or regulate those intrastate activities that have a demonstrably substantial effect on interstate commerce. But under the statute before us a man can be convicted without any proof of interstate movement, of the use of the facilities of interstate commerce, or of facts showing that his conduct affected interstate commerce. I think the Framers of the Constitution never intended that the National Government might define as a crime and prosecute such wholly local activity through the enactment of federal criminal laws.

In order to sustain this law we would, in my view, have to be able at the least to say that Congress could rationally have concluded that loan sharking is an activity with interstate attributes that distinguish it in some substantial respect from other local crime. But it is not enough to say that loan sharking is a national problem, for all crime is a national problem. It is not enough to say that some loan sharking has interstate characteristics, for any crime may have an interstate setting. And the circumstance that loan sharking has an adverse impact on interstate business is not a distinguishing attribute, for interstate business suffers from almost all criminal activity, be it shoplifting or violence in the streets.

Because I am unable to discern any rational distinction between loan sharking and other local crime, I cannot escape the conclusion that this statute was beyond the power of Congress to enact. The definition and prosecution of local, intrastate crime are reserved to the States under the Ninth and Tenth Amendments.

NOTE

Perez centered upon a congressional finding that commerce was affected by the interstate aspect of organized crime's control over loansharking activities. Did Congress intend to limit the statutes considered in *Perez* to cases in which the government could prove that a particular defendant was a member of organized crime? How could such proof be submitted to a jury without prejudicing a defendant?

In United States v. Keresty, 334 F.Supp. 461 (W.D.Pa.1971), affirmed 465 F.2d 36 (3d Cir. 1972), certiorari denied 409 U.S. 991 (1973), defendants, charged with the collection of a local gambling debt upon which no interest was added, argued that 18 U.S.C.A. § 894, a part of the statutory scheme considered in *Perez*, was expressly limited to proven loansharking activities and, if not, the statute was unconstitutional, absent a showing that particular local extortionate activities affected interstate commerce. Noting that *Perez* disposed of the second prong of defendants' claim, the court rejected the "loansharking" contention thusly:

> "The language which structures the Act, however, is clear and precise. If it is broad, it is broad for the purpose of assuring that its application is not limited to traditional conceptions. It proscribes specific rather than generic activities. And it is the specific activities with which [defendants] were charged which were within its proscriptions however unconventional."

Expanding upon the trial judge's decision on the constitutional question, the Third Circuit, tracing the legislative history of the Act, effectively rejected the contention:

> "It is sufficient that Congress has defined a limited class of credit transactions, i. e., those involving extortionate means of extension and collection, as having a substantial effect on interstate commerce. That this particular transaction cannot be directly tied to organized crime, does not affect the validity of the congressional approach employed here. So long as the goal is within the power of Congress, we will not substitute our judgment for the judgment of Congress as to the wisdom of this particular statutory scheme."

REWIS v. UNITED STATES

United States Supreme Court, 1971.
401 U.S. 808, 91 S.Ct. 1056.

MR. JUSTICE MARSHALL delivered the opinion of the Court.

In this case, petitioners challenge their convictions under the Travel Act, 18 U.S.C. § 1952, which prohibits interstate travel in furtherance of certain criminal activity.[1] Although the United States Court of Appeals for the Fifth Circuit narrowed an expansive interpretation of the Act, the Court of Appeals affirmed petitioners' convictions. For the reasons stated below, we reverse.

Petitioners, James Rewis and Mary Lee Williams, were convicted along with two other defendants in the United States District Court for the Middle District of Florida. Their convictions arose from a lottery, or numbers operation, which petitioners admittedly ran in Yulee, Florida, a small community located a few miles south of the Georgia-Florida state line. Petitioners are Florida residents, and there is no evidence that they at any time crossed state lines in connection with the operation of their lottery. The other two convicted defendants are Georgia residents who traveled from their Georgia homes to place bets at petitioners' establishment in Yulee.

The District Court instructed the jury that mere bettors in a lottery violated Florida law, and that if the bettors traveled interstate for the purpose of gambling, they also violated the Travel Act. Presumably referring to petitioners, the District Court further charged that a defendant could be found guilty under the aiding and abetting statute, without proof that he personally performed every act constituting the charged offense. On appeal, the Fifth Circuit held that § 1952 did not make it a federal crime merely to cross a state line for the purpose of placing a bet and reversed the convictions of the two Georgia residents because the evidence presented at trial was insufficient to show that they were anything other than customers of the gambling operation. However, the Court of Appeals

1. 18 U.S.C. § 1952 provides in pertinent part:

"(a) Whoever travels in interstate or foreign commerce or uses any facility in interstate or foreign commerce, including the mail, with intent to—

"(1) distribute the proceeds of any unlawful activity; or

"(2) commit any crime of violence to further any unlawful activity; or

"(3) otherwise promote, manage, establish, carry on, or facilitate the promotion, management, establishment, or carrying on, of any unlawful activity, and thereafter performs or attempts to perform any of the acts specified in subparagraphs (1), (2), and (3), shall be fined not more than $10,000 or imprisoned for not more than five years, or both.

"(b) As used in this section 'unlawful activity' means (1) any business enterprise involving gambling, liquor on which the Federal excise tax has not been paid, narcotics, or prostitution offenses in violation of the laws of the State in which they are committed or of the United States, or (2) extortion, bribery, or arson in violation of the laws of the State in which committed or of the United States."

upheld petitioners' convictions on the grounds that operators of gambling establishments are responsible for the interstate travel of their customers.

We agree with the Court of Appeals that it cannot be said, with certainty sufficient to justify a criminal conviction, that Congress intended that interstate travel by mere customers of a gambling establishment should violate the Travel Act.[2] But we are also unable to conclude that conducting a gambling operation frequented by out-of-state bettors, by itself, violates the Act. Section 1952, prohibits interstate travel with the intent to "promote, manage, establish, carry on or facilitate" certain kinds of illegal activity; and the ordinary meaning of this language suggests that the traveler's purpose must involve more than the desire to patronize the illegal activity. Legislative history of the Act is limited, but does reveal that § 1952 was aimed primarily at organized crime and, more specifically at persons who reside in one State while operating or managing illegal activities located in another. In addition, we are struck by what Congress did not say. Given the ease with which citizens of our Nation are able to travel and the existence of many multi-state metropolitan areas, substantial amounts of criminal activity, traditionally subject to state regulation, are patronized by out-of-state customers. In such a context, Congress would certainly recognize that an expansive Travel Act would alter sensitive federal-state relationships, could overextend limited federal police resources, and might well produce situations in which the geographic origin of customers, a matter of happenstance, would transform relatively minor state offenses into federal felonies. It is not for us to weigh the merits of these factors, but the fact that they are not even discussed in the legislative history of § 1952 strongly suggests that Congress did not intend that the Travel Act should apply to criminal activity solely because that activity is at times patronized by persons from another State. In short, neither statutory language nor legislative history supports such a broad ranging interpretation of § 1952. And even if this lack of support were less apparent, ambiguity concerning the ambit of criminal statutes should be resolved in favor of lenity. . . .

The Government concedes as much, but offers an alternative construction of the Travel Act—that the Act is violated whenever the operator of an illegal establishment can reasonably foresee that customers will cross state lines for the purpose of patronizing the illegal operation or whenever the operator actively seeks to attract business from another State. The first half of this proposed interpretation—reasonable foreseeability of interstate patronage—does not merit acceptance. Whenever individuals actually cross state

2. Both parties correctly concede that the questions in this case are solely statutory. No issue of constitutional dimension is presented.

lines for the purpose of patronizing a criminal establishment, it will almost always be reasonable to say that the operators of the establishment could have foreseen that some of their customers would come from out-of-state. So, for practical purposes, this alternative construction is almost as expansive as interpretations that we have already rejected. In addition, there is little, if any, evidence that Congress intended that foreseeability should govern criminal liability under § 1952.

There may, however, be greater support for the second half of the Government's proposed interpretation—that active encouragement of interstate patronage violates the Act. Of course, the conduct deemed to constitute active encouragement must be more than merely conducting the illegal operation; otherwise, this interpretation would only restate other constructions which we have rejected. Still, there are cases in which federal courts have correctly applied § 1952 to those individuals whose agents or employees cross state lines in furtherance of illegal activity . . . and the Government argues that the principles of those decisions should be extended to cover persons who actively seek interstate patronage. Although we are cited to no cases which have gone so far and although much of what we have said casts substantial doubt on the Government's broad argument, there may be occasional situations in which the conduct encouraging interstate patronage so closely approximates the conduct of a principal in a criminal agency relationship that the Travel Act is violated. But we need not rule on this part of the Government's theory because it is not the interpretation of § 1952 under which petitioners were convicted. The jury was not charged that they must find that petitioners actively sought interstate patronage. And we are not informed of any action by petitioners, other than actually conducting their lottery, that was designed to attract out-of-state customers. As a result, the Government's proposed interpretation of the Travel Act cannot be employed to uphold these convictions.

Reversed.

MR. JUSTICE WHITE took no part in the decision in this case.

NOTE

Based upon a reading of the legislative history of the Travel Act, the courts have come to the conclusion that Congress did not intend to use all of its broad powers under the Commerce Clause, and have narrowly construed the statute. Thus, although there is no requirement that the travel or use of a facility be in furtherance of the unlawful activity, as there is in the mail fraud statute, on the face of the statute, the decisions have read a "furtherance" requirement into the Act.

A review of the legislative history and the cases considering § 1952 is found in Judge Friendly's opinion in United States v. Archer, 486 F.2d 670 (2d Cir. 1973), where the court found the Travel Act inapplicable to interstate and foreign telephone calls caused by federal agents. Refusing to hold that "manufactured jurisdiction" amounted to entrapment, the court simply found the phone calls too incidental to support federal intervention into a local offense. To support its decision, the court reviewed a wealth of case law presenting varied factual situations:

"Of our own decisions under the Travel Act, the most illuminating for present purposes is United States v. Corallo (1969). Although that case, like this one, involved corruption of a local official, the evidence there disclosed numerous telephone calls from New York to Connecticut for the very purpose of arranging the bribe and distributing the proceeds among the conspirators. On that basis Judge Medina concluded, that 'the extensive references in the record to interstate telephone calls that were actually made justify the inference that the use of interstate telephone calls was not a casual and incidental occurrence but the fulfillment of an integral part of the conspiratorial consensus.' In United States v. DeSapio (1970), the interstate acts were much less numerous, but one of them, the meeting at Fried's horsefarm which was reached by interstate travel at his suggestion, was the occasion when, on the Government's proof, the entire conspiracy was hatched. In United States v. Cassino (1972), several of the conspirators engaged in weekly travel from New York to New Jersey for meetings in furtherance of the conspiracy. Finally, in our most recent encounter with the Travel Act, United States v. Kahn (1973), where there was extensive interstate travel and use of the mails, Judge Smith distinguished *Rewis* and the Seventh Circuit decisions cited below on the ground that in them 'the defendants themselves engaged in no interstate activities, and that the total interstate travel aspect of the enterprises was either marginal or unforeseen.'

"Of the other circuits the Seventh has had most to say concerning how purposeful and important to the enterprise the use of interstate facilities must be. United States v. Altobello (1971) held it was not enough that a Philadelphian who was the victim of extortion in Chicago gave as part payment the proceeds of a check he cashed on a Philadelphia bank, which cleared through the mails. In United States v. McCormick (1971), an Indiana lottery operator advertised in a local newspaper for salesmen, and some copies of the newspaper were mailed out of the state. The court again refused to permit application of the Travel Act, finding that 'the activities engaged in by defendant were essentially local' and that the role played by the interstate mailings was 'a matter of happenstance' and 'minimal and incidental' to the operation of the illegal lottery. The decision in United States v. Lee (1971), cited by the Government, indicates no contrary view; in that case employees of an Indiana gambling establishment regularly crossed state lines, and the court distinguished both *Altobello* and *Rewis* by pointing to the 'continual interstate travel by employees of the illegal venture.' Two cases from other circuits holding the interstate aspect insufficient are United States v. Hawthorne, 356 F.2d 740 (4 Cir.), cert. denied, 384 U.S. 908, 86 S.Ct. 1344 (1966) [moving self and family from Indiana to West Virginia where illegal gambling enterprise was to be undertaken]; and United States v. Judkins, 428 F.2d 333 (6 Cir. 1970) [calls from Arkansas to appellant's house of prostitution in Tennessee not shown to have a business purpose].

"It is with this background that we consider the three telephone calls which the Government claims to have brought this case within 18 U.S.C. § 1952(a)(3)."

Upon the basis of these decisions, the court concluded that the various telephone calls were "insufficient to transform this sordid, federally provoked incident of local corruption into a crime against the United States."

Does *Rewis* compel the result reached in *Archer* and the cases it relies upon? How should the Travel Act be amended to alter these results? Is such an amendment advisable?

UNITED STATES v. DeMET

United States Court of Appeals, 7th Cir., 1973.
486 F.2d 816.

FAIRCHILD, CIRCUIT JUDGE. Defendant was convicted by a jury of obstructing, delaying and affecting commerce and the movement of articles in commerce by extortion in violation of 18 U.S.C. § 1951, commonly called the Hobbs Act.[1] On this appeal defendant asserts error in . . . . insufficiency of the evidence as to extortion and effect on interstate commerce . . . . We have considered these contentions, find none meritorious and affirm the conviction.

Viewing the evidence in a light most favorable to support the verdict, the following facts appear:

Louis King owned a Chicago cocktail lounge called "The Scene" during the period covered by the indictment, November, 1969 to February, 1970. King purchased some of the beer for his business from the Chicago branch of Anheuser-Busch. It was brewed outside Illinois. Some of the liquor he purchased came from distilleries in other states or countries.

During the period of the indictment, defendant was a Chicago police officer and vice coordinator assigned to the district where the Scene was located.

In late November or early December, 1969, defendant and several other police officers visited the Scene. They sat at the bar

1. In pertinent part, § 1951 provides:

"(a) Whoever in any way or degree obstructs, delays, or affects commerce or the movement of any article or commodity in commerce, by robbery or extortion or attempts or conspires so to do, or commits or threatens physical violence to any person or property in furtherance of a plan or purpose to do anything in violation of this section shall be fined not more than $10,000 or imprisoned not more than twenty years, or both.

(b) As used in this section—

(1) . . . .

(2) The term "extortion" means the obtaining of property from another, with his consent, induced by wrongful use of actual or threatened force, violence, or fear, or under color of official right.

(3) The term "commerce" means commerce within the District of Columbia, or any Territory or Possession of the United States; all commerce between any point in a State, Territory, Possession, or the District of Columbia and any point outside thereof; all commerce between points within the same State through any place outside such State; and all other commerce over which the United States has jurisdiction."

and defendant asked King how it was going and whether King had any problems. King described how a police sergeant would come into the lounge on weekend nights and require payment of $10 or $20 in exchange for not enforcing a late night parking ordinance which went into effect one hour before closing. King also told defendant that police officers would come on week nights and unjustifiably accuse him of staying open after hours.

This conversation occurred at about 2:00 A.M. when the lounge was busy. Defendant asked if there was a more quiet place where they could talk. King led defendant to a back room. Once in the room, defendant said, "In order to avoid all this bullshit why don't you pay so much a month." King asked, "Now, what's the mutuels?" To which defendant replied, "Well you tell us." King offered $50.00 a month, a sum which defendant found acceptable. King and his wife made the payment to defendant.

King testified that he paid the money to defendant because he feared that if he did not pay it might jeopardize his liquor license and lead to more "harassment."

Just before Christmas, 1969, defendant and three other officers all in plain clothes entered the Scene Lounge. During conversation with King one of the officers mentioned that a gift had been given or would be given to the "Commander." One of the officers asked what King was going to give. King displayed a bottle of Grand Metaxa. Then one of the officers asked, "Well what about us?" King replied, "O.K. Stop around Christmas and I will have something for you."

King testified that he inferred from this conversation that if he didn't cooperate he might be charged with liquor violations or risk loss of his license.

Later during the Christmas week, defendant stopped at the Scene between 7:00 and 8:00 P.M. before it had opened for business. He had previously called to make sure someone would be there. King had two cases of liquor and two extra bottles waiting for him when he arrived, and assisted in loading the cases into defendant's car. King estimated the value to be over $300.00.

Sometime between Christmas, 1969 and New Year's Day, King had another conversation with defendant at the police station. King complained to defendant that even though he was paying $50.00 a month, he had been forced to pay $300.00 to a sergeant and a patrolman the previous evening. Defendant professed ignorance of the incident and suggested that they go see the "boss." Defendant and King then went to the district commander's office. Defendant went in to see the commander and, after a few minutes, King was invited into his office.

In the presence of defendant, King related to the commander the incident of the previous night. King then asked, "Why am I paying $50.00 a month when I am brought into the station for after hours and forced to pay $300.00 a month?" The commander replied, "I will take care of this. Don't worry about it."

In January, 1970, defendant again visited King at the Scene in the company of other police officers. Defendant asked to see King for a few minutes. The two then went to a back room. King called his wife; Mrs. King came in and gave defendant $50.00.

Following the payments, the Scene had no further parking problems.

* * *

Alleged Failure to Prove Extortion.

Under § 1951 extortion is defined as "the obtaining of property from another, with his consent, induced by wrongful use of actual or threatened fear, or under color of official right." The government's proof was directed to showing that King feared economic loss should he not comply with defendant's demands.

Defendant contends that the government's proof was an insufficient basis upon which to convict for extortion. Because King admitted his encounters with the defendant were friendly and defendant never said nor intimated he would cause "trouble," defendant contends that King's conduct was not motivated by fear as required by § 1951. Rather, defendant argues, King willingly gave money to defendant because it brought certain advantages (such as non-enforcement of parking restrictions) to which he was not lawfully entitled. Thus, in essence, defendant argues that he was merely receiver of bribes and could therefore not be guilty of extortion.

Fear, as used in § 1951, includes not only fear of physical violence but fear of economic harm, as well. . . . It is not necessary that this fear be a consequence of a direct threat, it is enough that the circumstances surrounding the alleged extortion render the victim's fear reasonable. . . .

Indeed, fear may be present even if confrontations between the victim and the alleged extorter appear friendly:

> "The fact that relations between the victims and the extorters were often cordial is not inconsistent with extortion. Knowing that they were at the mercy of the Attorney General's office, it is a fair inference that the victims felt that to save their businesses they had to keep the extorters satisfied." United States v. Hyde (1971).

Finally, it is important to note that the economic loss which the victim fears may be a consequence of action which the alleged extorter has a duty to take:

> "It is the wrongful use of an otherwise valid power that converts dutiful action into extortion. If the purpose and effect are to intimidate others, forcing them to pay, the action

constitutes extortion. Put another way, it is the right to impartial determination of the issue on the merits (i. e. whether to enforce the law or whether to picket or strike) that the victim is deprived of when these actions are taken for the purpose of coercing him into paying. The distinction from bribery is therefore the initiative and purpose on the part of the official and the fear and lack of voluntariness on the part of the victim." United States v. Hyde, supra.

While portions of King's testimony taken with other evidence may be consistent with defendant's view that King freely gave money and liquor to obtain advantages, the jury could reasonably infer from all the circumstances, including defendant's official position, that King was in fear of harm to his business, his fear was reasonable, and defendant exploited it to extort money and liquor.

If early morning customers of the Scene had their cars ticketed, they might take their business elsewhere or at least leave earlier. An arrest for staying open after hours could lead to loss of the liquor license. Defendant, the vice coordinator of the district, promised to eliminate these concerns in exchange for a monthly payment. There was support for a finding that King believed that implicit in defendant's offer was the threat of continued "parking problems" and other harassment if the money (and later liquor) was not forthcoming.

In arguing for acquittal, defendant's counsel presented his view of the facts, i. e. that King was a willing participant and that any fear which King felt was unreasonable. The jury was instructed that in order for defendant's conduct to be considered extortion defendant must obtain the money through a wrongful use of fear, including fear of economic harm, and that the fear must be reasonable. Thus the issue of whether King gave money to defendant voluntarily in order to obtain certain advantages or out of fear that if the money was not forthcoming he would be subject to police harassment was squarely presented to the jury.

The jury apparently thought King's conduct was induced by fear and that defendant's conduct constituted extortion. We cannot say the verdict was not supported by substantial evidence.

Alleged Failure to Affect Interstate Commerce.

Extortion is an offense against the United States when the extorter "in any way or degree obstructs, delays or affects commerce or the movement of any article or commodity in commerce, . . ." 18 U.S.C. § 1951(a). In order to satisfy the interstate commerce element, the government offered proof that some of the beer and liquor purchased for the Scene had out of state origins, that in one instance a national corporation shipped its product across state lines to a Chicago warehouse from which it was delivered to the Scene and that in another instance a local company purchased liquor from out of state producers and then resold it to the Scene and others.

Relying primarily on cases applying the Fair Labor Standards Act, defendant argues that by the time the Scene acquired these beverages they were no longer in interstate commerce and that any extortion therefore could have no effect on interstate commerce. Because of differences in the statutes, such decisions are not controlling as to the requisite manner or degree of interference with commerce that may justify conviction under the Hobbs Act. . . .

Although King's business was primarily local, depletion of King's assets by the goods and money extorted, or the cessation of his business if he did not yield and his fears were realized, would tend to reduce the demand for and amount of beer and liquor moving into Illinois. The effect on interstate commerce would exist, though small by most standards, and only indirectly caused by defendant's acts. There are obvious questions as to the most desirable division between the states and the federal government of the function of enforcing good order, but given the existence of an impact of defendant's conduct on interstate commerce, the question is whether the Hobbs Act must be construed as stopping some margin short of full application of the commerce power.

"The commerce clause endows Congress with full and plenary power to do anything and everything necessary to protect interstate commerce—The specific question is whether in the statute involved the Congress has seen fit to exercise all of its power." Walling v. Goldblatt Bros. (1942).

When a law purports to regulate activities "in commerce" something less than the full commerce power is exercised. On the other hand, a law which regulates matters "affecting" interstate commerce is within, though a more nearly full application of, the commerce power.

Section 1951 clearly contemplates a full application of the commerce power. It proscribes extortion which "in any way or degree obstructs, delays, or affects commerce or the movement of any article or commodity in commerce . . . ." In United States v. Stirone, 361 U.S. 212, 215, 4 L.Ed.2d 252, 255 (1960), the Supreme Court said of the Hobbs Act:

> "'That Act speaks in broad language, manifesting a purpose to use all the constitutional power Congress has to punish interference with interstate commerce by extortion, robbery or physical violence.' The Act outlaws such interference 'in any way or degree.'"[2]

2. We have considered the Supreme Court's 1971 interpretation of the Travel Act as a less than full application of the commerce power, and the policy factors the Court suggests Congress may have considered, Rewis v. United States, 401 U.S. 808, 812 (1971). The two statutes are differently structured. We do not conclude that we are authorized, in a Hobbs Act case, to create a formula under which an impact on interstate commerce is to be dismissed as *de minimis*.

Because Congress has seen fit to exercise its full power under the commerce clause, extortionate conduct having an arguably *de minimis* effect on commerce may nevertheless be punished. Battaglia v. United States (1967) (extortion resulted in a pool table from an out-of-state source being kept from use); United States v. Augello (1971) (assets of drive-in restaurant which purchased mostly from an out-of-state concern depleted by $100; proprietor, in addition, gave $200 from his personal funds.). . . .

Where the victim of extortion, as here, customarily obtains inventory which has come from outside the state, obstruction and delay of, and effect upon commerce may, for the purpose of the Hobbs Act, be found in curtailment of the victim's potential as a buyer of such goods. This may be traced either through the depletion of his assets by his fulfillment of the extortionate demands or the harm which would follow if the threats were carried out.

* * *

The judgment is affirmed.

SWYGERT, CHIEF JUDGE, concurring.

Several years ago I took issue by dissent with a holding of this court that a depletion of corporate reserves comprised an "interference with interstate commerce" within the meaning of the Hobbs Act where a corporation was engaged in interstate commerce. My concern was centered on the unlimited reach of the doctrine espoused by the majority:

> "If a depletion of reserves is all that is necessary to show the requisite affect on commerce, then a threat of any kind to extract money made to a person who happens to operate a business engaged to any extent in interstate commerce comes within the statute's proscription. Under this rationale, a retail store owner, for example, would be afforded federal protection from extortion, regardless of the nature or the likely affect of the threat, simply because his stock of merchandise had in some measure moved in interstate commerce."

Exactly what I apprehended in 1968 has today come to pass. My misgivings, however, did not persuade my brethren in *Amabile,* and I stand by the decision reached in this case as the law of the circuit.

I would also narrow what some might read to be the holding of the majority on the question of extortion under the Hobbs Act. DeMet was prosecuted below for a violation of that portion of the Hobbs Act which makes illegal "the obtaining of property from another, with his consent, induced by wrongful use of actual or threatened fear." As my colleagues recognize, the proof of the Government was directed to demonstrating a fear of economic loss on the part of King. Proof of fear may not have been necessary had the Government chosen to rely on another provision to the Hobbs Act, namely, that prohibiting "the obtaining of property from another, with his consent, . . . *under color of official right.*" (emphasis supplied). It is, of course, hardly appropriate to render a decision on that issue in this case, and I express no views on it.*

NOTE

The Hobbs Act "speaks in broad language, manifesting a purpose to use all the constitutional power Congress has to punish interference with interstate commerce by extortion. . . ." Stirone v. United States, 361 U.S. 212, 215 (1960). Thus, *DeMet* correctly held that "extortionate conduct having an arguably *de minimus* effect on commerce may nevertheless be punished". In this manner, the courts recognized that "the Hobbs Act not only forbids extortion which interferes with interstate commerce but also extortion which affects interstate commerce". United States v. Gill, 490 F.2d 233 (7th Cir., 1973). See also United States v. Malinsky, 19 F.R.D. 426, 428 (S.D.N.Y.1956) ("The substantiality of the effect is not left to judicial determination. The only question is whether the prohibited activity is within the reach of Congress").

Commerce may be affected either as a direct result of the extortionate transaction or by a depletion of the resources of a business operating in interstate commerce. The latter theory is predicated on the notion that the business would have been in a position to purchase more or better quality merchandise from out of state if the extortionate payment had not been made. For example, in United States v. Tropiano, 418 F.2d 1069 (2d Cir. 1969), certiorari denied, 397 U.S. 1021 (1970), defendants, engaged in the rubbish removal business, were charged with threatening to harm certain individuals engaged in the same business for soliciting accounts in the city in which defendants operated. At trial, the government's sole evidence in support of the interstate commerce aspect of the offense was the fact that the victim purchased refuse removal trucks from an out of state corporation. In response to defendants' claim that this proof was insufficient, the court said:

> "[The victim's] surrender of his right to solicit additional customers in [the city] automatically limited his future orders for receptacles for new customers and the trucks required to serve such customers."

Tropiano not only recognized the depletion of resources theory, but it also indicated that a potential affect on commerce is sufficient to confer

* It is worthy of note, however, that an argument has been made in the literature that this provision renders criminal any reception of money (not rightfully due) "under color of official right" by a police officer or other public official, without reference to whether the facts which surround the receipt characterize the action as bribery or extortion. See Stern, Prosecutions of Local Political Corruption Under the Hobbs Act: The Unnecessary Distinction Between Bribery and Extortion. 3 Seton Hall L.Rev. 1 (1971).

federal jurisdiction. Because "Congress has the power to deal with extortion or attempted extortion actually or *potentially* affecting interstate commerce," Hulahan v. United States, 214 F.2d 441, 445 (8th Cir.), certiorari denied, 348 U.S. 856 (1954), "it is enough that the extortion 'in any way or degree' . . . affects commerce, though its affect be merely potential or subtle". United States v. Augello, 451 F.2d 1167, 1169–70 (2d Cir. 1971), certiorari denied, 405 U.S. 1070 (1972). Thus, in United States v. Pranno, 385 F.2d 387 (7th Cir. 1967), certiorari denied, 390 U.S. 944 (1968), the court affirmed the Hobbs Act conviction of two defendants who extorted a large sum from the owner and contractor of a proposed manufacturing plant by threatening to withhold a building permit. Because the extortionate demands were met, the permit was granted and the construction of the plant was not delayed. The movement of construction materials in interstate commerce was not, therefore, actually affected. The court, nevertheless, held that "it was only necessary to prove that delay *would have been caused* had the owner and contactor refused payment. . . ." (emphasis added).

Pranno is consistent with the cases which have considered similar situations. For example, in United States v. Hyde, 448 F.2d 815 (5th Cir. 1971), cert. denied, 404 U.S. 1058 (1972), defendant claimed that the extorted companies had not commenced interstate operations until several months after payment was made. This claim was rejected on the ground that the interstate commerce element can be established by expectation at the time of the extortionate transaction:

> "The companies were formed, and registration for a stock sale was sought, with a stated purpose of going into the activities that support a finding of interstate commerce. Neither the statute nor the Constitution requires that the company be engaged in an interstate transaction at the moment of the extortion to support federal jurisdiction."

Does the extraordinarily broad reading of the Hobbs Act trench upon state's rights? See Note, The Scope of Federal Criminal Jurisdiction Under the Commerce Clause, 1972 U.Ill.L.F. 805, 822:

"[I]t should be noted that the use of the commerce clause as an expansive basis for federal intervention in the area of crime control has not been opposed by the states, though similar federal intervention in economic affairs faced heavy resistance. State acquiescence, if not encouragement, can be attributed to several factors: the federal government has not preempted state powers; federal intervention has helped states deal with problems serious enough to override the usual states' rights fears; and the federal government has entered this area gradually, reluctantly, and primarily with programs aimed at organized crime, a problem generally felt to be incapable of solution by the states acting alone."

Chapter 4

HOMICIDE

A. MURDER

COMMONWEALTH v. WEBSTER

Supreme Judicial Court of Massachusetts, 1850.
59 Mass. 295, 386.

The defendant, professor of chemistry, in the medical college, in Boston, attached to the university at Cambridge, was indicted in the municipal court at the January term, 1850, for the murder of Dr. George Parkman, at Boston, on the 23d of November, 1849. . . .

The government introduced evidence, that George Parkman, quite peculiar in person and manners, and very well known to most persons in the city of Boston, left his home in Walnut Street in Boston in the forenoon of the 23d of November, 1849, in good health and spirits; and that he was traced through various streets of the city until about a quarter before two o'clock of that day, when he was seen going towards and about to enter the medical college: That he did not return to his home: That on the next day a very active, particular, and extended search was commenced in Boston and the neighboring towns and cities, and continued until the 30th of November; and that large rewards were offered for information about Dr. Parkman: That on the 30th of November certain parts of a human body were discovered, in and about the defendant's laboratory in the medical college; and a great number of fragments of human bones and certain blocks of mineral teeth, imbedded in slag and cinders, together with small quantities of gold, which had been melted, were found in an assay furnace of the laboratory: That in consequence of some of these discoveries the defendant was arrested on the evening of the 30th of November: That the parts of a human body so found resembled in every respect the corresponding portions of the body of Dr. Parkman, and that among them all there were no duplicate parts; and that they were not the remains of a body which had been dissected: That the artificial teeth found in the furnace were made for Dr. Parkman by a dentist in Boston in 1846, and refitted in his mouth by the same dentist a fortnight before his disappearance: That the defendant was indebted to Dr. Parkman on certain notes, and was pressed by him for payment; that the defendant has said that on the 23d of November, about nine o'clock in the morning, he left word at Dr. Parkman's house, that if he would come to the medical college at half past one o'clock on that day, he would pay him; and that, as he said, he accordingly had an interview with Dr. Parkman at half past one o'clock on that day, at his laboratory in the medical college: That the defendant then had no means of paying, and that the notes were afterwards found in his possession. . . .

[The defendant was tried before the Chief Justice, and Justices Wilde, Dewey and Metcalf. The opinion of the court on the law of the case was given in the charge to the jury as follows:]

SHAW, C. J. Homicide, of which murder is the highest and most criminal species, is of various degrees, according to circumstances. The term, in its largest sense, is generic, embracing every mode by which the life of one man is taken by the act of another. Homicide may be lawful or unlawful; it is lawful when done in lawful war upon an enemy in battle, it is lawful when done by an officer in the execution of justice upon a criminal, pursuant to a proper warrant. It may also be justifiable, and of course lawful, in necessary self-defence. But it is not necessary to dwell on these distinctions; it will be sufficient to ask attention to the two species of criminal homicide, familiarly known as murder and manslaughter.

In seeking for the sources of our law upon this subject, it is proper to say, that whilst the statute law of the commonwealth declares that "Every person who shall commit the crime of murder shall suffer the punishment of death for the same;" yet it nowhere defines the crimes of murder or manslaughter, with all their minute and carefully-considered distinctions and qualifications. For these, we resort to that great repository of rules, principles, and forms, the common law. This we commonly designate as the common law of England; but it might now be properly called the common law of Massachusetts. It was adopted when our ancestors first settled here, by general consent. It was adopted and confirmed by an early act of the provincial government, and was formally confirmed by the provision of the constitution declaring that all the laws which had theretofore been adopted, used, and approved, in the province or state of Massachusetts bay, and usually practiced on in the courts of law, should still remain and be in full force until altered or repealed by the legislature. So far, therefore, as the rules and principles of the common law are applicable to the administration of criminal law, and have not been altered and modified by acts of the colonial or provincial government or by the state legislature, they have the same force and effect as laws formally enacted.

By the existing law, as adopted and practiced on, unlawful homicide is distinguished into murder and manslaughter.

Murder, in the sense in which it is now understood, is the killing of any person in the peace of the commonwealth, with *malice aforethought*, either express or implied by law. Malice, in this definition, is used in a technical sense, including not only anger, hatred, and revenge, but every other unlawful and unjustifiable motive. It is not confined to ill-will towards one or more individual persons, but is intended to denote an action flowing from any wicked and corrupt motive, a thing done *malo animo*, where the fact has been attended with such circumstances as carry in them the plain indications of a heart regardless of social duty, and fatally bent on mischief. And therefore malice is implied from any deliberate or cruel act against another, however sudden.

Manslaughter is the unlawful killing of another without malice; and may be either voluntary, as when the act is committed with a real design and purpose to kill, but through the violence of sudden passion, occasioned by some great provocation, which in tenderness for the frailty of human nature the law considers sufficient to palliate the criminality of the offence; or involuntary, as when the death of another is caused by some unlawful act not accompanied by any intention to take life.

From these two definitions, it will be at once perceived, that the characteristic distinction between murder and manslaughter is malice, express or implied. It therefore becomes necessary, in every case of homicide proved, and in order to an intelligent inquiry into the legal character of the act, to ascertain with some precision the nature of legal malice, and what evidence is requisite to establish its existence.

Upon this subject, the rule as deduced from the authorities is, that the implication of malice arises in every case of intentional homicide; and, the fact of killing being first proved, all the circumstances of accident, necessity, or infirmity, are to be satisfactorily established by the party charged, unless they arise out of the evidence produced against him to prove the homicide, and the circumstances attending it. If there are, in fact, circumstances of justification, excuse, or palliation, such proof will naturally indicate them. But where the fact of killing is proved by satisfactory evidence, and there are no circumstances disclosed, tending to show justification or excuse, there is nothing to rebut the natural presumption of malice. This rule is founded on the plain and obvious principle, that a person must be presumed to intend to do that which he voluntarily and wilfully does in fact do, and that he must intend all the natural, probable, and usual consequences of his own acts. Therefore, when one person assails another violently with a dangerous weapon, likely to kill and which does in fact destroy the life of the party assailed, the natural presumption is, that he intended death or other great bodily harm; and, as there can be no presumption of any proper motive or legal excuse for such a cruel act, the consequence follows, that, in the absence of all proof to the contrary, there is nothing to rebut the presumption of malice. On the other hand, if death, though wilfully intended, was inflicted immediately after provocation given by the deceased, supposing that such provocation consisted of a blow or an assault, or other provocation on his part, which the law deems adequate to excite sudden and angry passion and create heat of blood, this fact rebuts the presumption of malice; but still, the homicide being unlawful, because a man is bound to curb his passions, is criminal, and is manslaughter.

In considering what is regarded as such adequate provocation, it is a settled rule of law, that no provocation by words only, however opprobrious, will mitigate an intentional homicide, so as to reduce it to manslaughter. Therefore, if, upon provoking language given, the party immediately revenges himself by the use of a dangerous and deadly weapon likely to cause death, such as a pistol discharged at the person, a heavy bludgeon, an axe, or a knife; if death ensues, it is a homicide not mitigated to manslaughter by the circumstances, and so is homicide by malice aforethought, within the true definition of murder. It is not the less malice aforethought, within the meaning of the law, because the act is done suddenly after the intention to commit the homicide is formed; it is sufficient that the malicious intention precedes and accompanies the act of homicide. It is manifest, therefore, that the words "malice aforethought," in the description of murder, do not imply deliberation, or the lapse of considerable time between the malicious intent to take life and the actual execution of that intent, but rather denote purpose and design, in contradistinction to accident and mischance.

In speaking of the use of a dangerous weapon, and the mode of using it upon the person of another, I have spoken of it as indicating an intention to kill him, or do him great bodily harm. The reason is this. Where a man, without justification or excuse, causes the death of another by the intentional use of a dangerous weapon likely to destroy life, he is responsible for the consequences, upon the principle already stated, that he is liable for the natural and probable consequences of his act. Suppose, therefore, for the purpose of revenge, one fires a pistol at another, regardless of consequences, intending to kill, maim, or grievously wound him, as the case may be, without any definite intention to take his life; yet, if that is the result, the law attributes the same consequences to homicide so committed, as if done under an actual and declared purpose to take the life of the party assailed. . . .

The true nature of manslaughter is, that it is homicide mitigated out of tenderness to the frailty of human nature. Every man, when assailed with violence or great rudeness, is inspired with a sudden impulse of anger, which puts him upon resistance before time for cool reflection; and if, during that period, he attacks his assailant with a weapon likely to endanger life, and death ensues, it is regarded as done through heat of blood or violence of anger, and not through malice, or that cold-blooded desire of revenge which more properly constitutes the feeling, emotion, or passion of malice.

The same rule applies to homicide in mutual combat, which is attributed to sudden and violent anger occasioned by the combat, and not to malice. When two meet, not intending to quarrel, and angry words suddenly arise, and a conflict springs up in which blows are given on both sides, without much regard to who is the assailant, it is mutual combat. And if no unfair advantage is taken in the outset, and the occasion is not sought for the purpose of gratifying malice, and one seizes a weapon and strikes a deadly blow, it is regarded as homicide in heat of blood; and though not excusable, because a man is bound to control his angry passions, yet it is not the higher offence of murder.

We have stated these distinctions, not because there is much evidence in the present case which calls for their application, but that the jury may have a clear and distinct view of the leading principles in the law of homicide. There seems to have been little evidence in the present case that the parties had a contest. There is some evidence tending to show the previous existence of angry feelings; but unless these feelings resulted in angry words, and words were followed by blows, there would be no proof of heat of blood in mutual combat, or under provocation of an assault, on the one side or the other; and the proof of the defendant's declarations, as to the circumstances under which the parties met and parted, as far as they go, repel the supposition of such a contest.

With these views of the law of homicide, we will proceed to the further consideration of the present case. The prisoner at the bar is charged with the wilful murder of Dr. George Parkman. This charge divides itself into two principal questions, to be resolved by the proof: first, whether the party alleged to have been murdered came to his death by an act of violence inflicted by any person; and if so, secondly, whether the act was committed by the accused. . . .

This case is to be proved, if proved at all, by circumstantial evidence; because it is not suggested that any direct evidence can be given, or that any witness can be called to give direct testimony, upon the main fact of the killing. It becomes important, therefore, to state what circumstantial evidence is; to point out the distinction between that and positive or direct evidence.

The distinction, then, between direct and circumstantial evidence, is this. Direct or positive evidence is when a witness can be called to testify to the precise fact which is the subject of the issue on trial; that is, in a case of homicide, that the party accused did cause the death of the deceased. Whatever may be the kind of force of the evidence, that is the fact to be proved. But suppose no person was present on the occasion of the death, and of course that no one can be called to testify to it; is it wholly unsusceptible of legal proof? Experience has shown that circumstantial evidence may be offered in such a case; that is, that a body of facts may be proved of so conclusive a character, as to warrant a firm belief of the fact, quite as strong and certain as that on which discreet men are accustomed to act, in relation to their most important concerns. It would be injurious to the best interests of society, if such proof could not avail in judicial proceedings. If it was necessary always to have positive evidence, how many criminal acts committed in the community, destructive of its peace and subversive of its order and security, would go wholly undetected and unpunished?

The necessity, therefore, of resorting to circumstantial evidence, if it is a safe and reliable proceeding, is obvious and absolute. Crimes are secret. Most men, conscious of criminal purposes, and about the execution of criminal acts, seek the security of secrecy and darkness. It is therefore necessary to use all modes of evidence besides that of direct testimony, provided such proofs may be relied on as leading to safe and satisfactory conclusions; and, thanks to a beneficent providence, the laws of nature and the relations of things to each other are so linked and combined together, that a medium of proof is often thereby furnished, leading to inferences and conclusions as strong as those arising from direct testimony. . . . The evidence must establish the *corpus delicti*, as it is termed, or the offence committed as charged; and, in case of homicide, must not only prove a death by violence, but must, to a reasonable extent, exclude the hypothesis of suicide, and a death by the act of any other person. This is to be proved beyond reasonable doubt.

Then, what is reasonable doubt? It is a term often used, probably pretty well understood, but not easily defined. It is not mere possible doubt; because every thing relating to human affairs, and depending on moral evidence, is open to some possible or imaginary doubt. It is that state of the case, which, after the entire comparison and consideration of all the evidence, leaves the minds of the jurors in that condition and they cannot say they feel an abiding conviction, to a moral certainty, of the truth of the charge. The burden of proof is upon the prosecutor. All the presumptions of law independent of evidence are in favor of innocence; and every person is presumed to be innocent until he is proved guilty. If upon such proof there is reasonable doubt remaining, the accused is entitled to the benefit of it by an acquittal. For it is not sufficient to establish a probability, though a strong one arising from the doctrine of chances, that the fact charged is more likely to be true than the contrary; but the evidence must establish the truth of the fact to a reasonable and moral certainty; a certainty that convinces and directs the understanding, and satisfies the reason and judgment of those who are bound to act conscientiously upon it. This we take to be proof beyond reasonable doubt; because if the law, which mostly depends upon considerations of a moral nature, should go further than this, and require absolute certainty, it would exclude circumstantial evidence altogether. . . .

[The jury returned a verdict of guilty, and the defendant's sentence of death by hanging was sustained by the Supreme Judicial Court of Massachusetts. Subsequently, Dr. Webster confessed:

"On Tuesday the 20th of November, I sent the note to Dr. Parkman. . . . It was to ask Dr. Parkman to call at my rooms on Friday the 23d, after my lecture. . . . My purpose was, if he should accede to the proposed interview, to state to him my embarrassments and utter inability to pay him at present, to apologize for those things in my conduct which had offended him, to throw myself upon his mercy, to beg for further time and indulgence for the sake of my family, if not for my own, and to make as good promises to him as I could have any hope of keeping. . . .

"Dr. Parkman agreed to call on me, as I proposed.

"He came, accordingly, between half-past one and two. . . . He immediately addressed me with great energy: 'Are you ready for me, sir? Have you got the money?' I replied, 'No, Dr. Parkman'; and was then beginning to state my condition and make my appeal to him. He would not listen to me, but interrupted me with much vehemence. He called me 'scoundrel' and 'liar', and went on heaping upon me the most bitter taunts and opprobrious epithets. . . . I cannot tell how long the torrent of threats and invectives continued, and I can now recall to memory but a small portion of what he said. At first I kept interposing, trying to pacify him, so that I might obtain the object for which I had sought the interview. But I could not stop him, and soon my own temper was up. I forgot everything. I felt nothing but the sting of his words. I was excited to the highest degree of passion; and while he was speaking and gesticulating in the most violent and menacing manner, thrusting the letter and his fist into my face, in my fury I seized whatever was the handiest,—it was a stick of wood,—and dealt him an instantaneous blow with all the force that passion could give it. I did not know, nor think, nor care where I should hit him, nor how hard, nor what the effect would be. It was on the side of his head, and there was nothing to break the force of the blow. He fell instantly upon the pavement. . . . Perhaps I spent ten minutes in attempts to resuscitate him; but I found that he was absolutely dead. . . .

"My next move was to get the body into the sink which stands in the small private room. By setting the body partially erect against the corner, and getting up into the sink myself, I succeeded in drawing it up. There it was entirely dismembered. . . .

"There was a fire burning in the furnace of the lower laboratory. . . . The head and viscera were put in to that furnace that day. . . .

"When the body had been thus all disposed of, I cleared away all traces of what had been done. I took up the stick with which the fatal blow had been struck. It proved to be the stump of a large grape vine, say two inches in diameter, and two feet long. . . . I had carried it in from Cambridge . . . for the purpose of showing the effect of certain chemical fluids in coloring wood. . . . I put it into the fire. . . ."

The full confession appears in Bemis, Report of the Case of John W. Webster, pp. 564–71 (1850).

Had the above story been told at the trial, and believed, should the jury, in light of the judge's charge, have convicted Dr. Webster of murder or manslaughter?] *

* For an interesting account of the trial of Dr. Webster, see the article by Justice Robert Sullivan, "The Murder Trial of Dr. Webster, Boston, 1850", in 51 Mass.L.Q. 367 (1966) and 52 ibid., 67 (1967).

NOTES

Malice aforethought

1. As Chief Justice Shaw noted in his charge to the jury in the Webster case, supra, "[T]he characteristic distinction between murder and manslaughter is malice, express or implied."

With respect to the meaning and significance of the term "malice," consider the following:

"The meaning of 'malice aforethought', which is the distinguishing criterion of murder, is certainly not beyond the range of controversy. The first thing that must be said about it is that neither of the two words is used in its ordinary sense. . . . 'It is now only an arbitrary symbol. For the "malice" may have in it nothing really malicious; and need never be really "aforethought", except in the sense that every desire must necessarily come before—though perhaps only an instant before—the act which is desired. The word "aforethought", in the definition, has thus become either false or else superfluous. The word "malice" is neither; but it is apt to be misleading, for it is not employed in its original (and its popular) meaning.' 'Malice aforethought' is simply a comprehensive name for a number of different mental attitudes which have been variously defined at different stages in the development of the law, the presence of any one which in the accused has been held by the courts to render a homicide particularly heinous and therefore to make it murder. . . . As Stephen put it '. . . when a particular state of mind came under their notice the Judges called it malice or not according to their view of the propriety of hanging particular people. . . .'." Report of the Royal Commission on Capital Punishment, 26–28 (1953).

Also consider the following, from Gov. of the Virgin Islands v. Lake, 362 F.2d 770 (3d Cir. 1966):

" 'The proof of homicide, as necessarily involving malice,' the Supreme Court said in Stevenson v. United States, 1896, . . . 'must show the facts under which the killing was effected, and from the whole facts and circumstances surrounding the killing the jury infers malice or its absence. Malice in connection with the crime of killing is but another name for a certain condition of a man's heart or mind; and as no one can look into the heart or mind of another, the only way to decide upon its condition at the time of a killing is to infer it from the surrounding facts, and that inference is one of fact, for a jury. The presence or absence of this malice or mental condition marks the boundary which separates the two crimes of murder and manslaughter.' " . . .

2. Under the common law, even in the absence of intent to kill or inflict great bodily harm, a wilful or unjustified act or omission, the natural tendency of which was to cause death or great physical harm, afforded sufficient basis for a finding of implied malice. Such a result was based on the principle that a man is to be presumed to have intended the natural and probable consequences of his acts. In Wellar v. People, 30 Mich. 16 (1874), which involved a death allegedly due to the defendant's kicking of the victim, the court explained the doctrine in these terms:

"It is not necessary in all cases that one held for murder must have intended to take the life of the person he slays by his wrongful act. It is not always necessary that he must have intended a personal injury to such person. But it is necessary that the intent with which he acted shall be equivalent in legal character to a criminal purpose aimed against life. . . . The willful use of a deadly weapon, without excuse or provocation, in such a manner as to imperil life, is almost universally recognized as showing a felonious intent. . . . But where the weapon or implement used is not one likely to kill or maim, the killing is held to be manslaughter, unless there is an actual intent which shows a felonious purpose. . . . If respondent willfully and violently kicked the deceased in such a way as he must have known would endanger her life, and her life was destroyed in that way, an actual intention of killing would not be necessary, as in such case the death would have been a result he might fairly be held to regard as likely."

Courts have stated that malice may be inferred from the use of a deadly weapon, or the use of any other weapon in a deadly manner. E. g., Pannill v. Commonwealth, 185 Va. 244, 38 S.E.2d 457 (1946).

3. It should also be noted that malice, express or implied, need not be exhibited toward the specific person killed. Thus in Banks v. State, 85 Tex.Cr.R. 165, 211 S.W. 217 (1919), which involved the firing of shots into a moving train and resulted in the death of one of the crew, the court said:

"One who deliberately used a deadly weapon in such reckless manner as to evince a heart regardless of social duty and fatally bent on mischief, as is shown by firing into a moving train upon which human beings necessarily are, cannot shield himself from the consequences of his acts by disclaiming malice. Malice may be toward a group of persons as well as toward an individual. It may exist without former grudges or antecedent menaces. The intentional doing of any wrongful act in such manner and under such circumstances as that the death of a human being may result therefrom is malice."

Similarly, where a defendant fired a pistol into a crowd of persons engaged in some altercation at a dance, as a result of which a man was killed, the court held that the conduct would be murder if the defendant fired intentionally, even though he had no intent to kill anyone or shoot at a particular individual. Smith v. State, 124 Ga. 213, 52 S.E. 329 (1905).

Mercy Killings

1. Malice may be present even though the motive for a killing is of the highest order. Thus, a "mercy killing" is usually murder, inasmuch as it constitutes an intentional taking of life, without provocation or other mitigation, and without legal justification or excuse. The present state of the law concerning euthanasia is well summarized in the following excerpt from Williams, The Sanctity of Life and the Criminal Law, 318–26 (1957):

"Under the present law, voluntary euthanasia would, except in certain narrow circumstances, be regarded as suicide in the patient who consents and murder in the doctor who administers; even on a lenient view, most lawyers would say that it could not be less than manslaughter in the doctor, the punishment for which, according to the jurisdiction and the degree of manslaughter, can be anything up to imprisonment for life.

"More specifically, the following principles may be stated:

"(a) If the doctor gives the patient a fatal injection with the intention of killing him, and the patient dies in consequence, the doctor is a common murderer because it is his hand that caused the death. Neither the consent of the patient, nor the extremity of his suffering, nor the imminence of death by natural causes, nor all of these factors taken together, is a defence. . . .

"(b) If the doctor furnishes poison (for example, an overdose of sleeping tablets) for the purpose of enabling the patient to commit suicide, and the patient takes it accordingly and dies, this is suicide and a kind of self-murder in the patient, and the doctor, as an abettor, again becomes guilty of murder. So, at any rate, is it in strict legal theory. . . .

"(c) A case that may be thought to be distinguishable from both of those already considered is that of the administration of a fatal dose of a drug where this dose is in fact the minimum necessary to deaden pain. Where a patient is suffering from an incurable and agonizing disease, and ordinary quantities of a drug fail to render the pain tolerable, many doctors will give the minimum dose necessary to kill the pain, knowing that this minimum is at the same time an amount that is likely to kill the patient. In other words, with the choice of either doing nothing, or killing both the pain and the patient, the doctor chooses the latter course. . . . Thus a point is reached at which, proceeding upon the same principles as he has followed heretofore, and which have so far been lawful, the doctor is led to give what he knows is likely to be an immediately fatal dose. It would be extremely artificial to say that this last dose, which is administered upon the same principle as all the previous ones, is alone unlawful. . . . [The physician's] legal excuse . . . rests upon the doctrine of necessity, there being at this junction no way of relieving pain without ending life. In this limited form the excuse of necessity would be likely to be accepted by a judge, and to this extent it may be held that euthanasia is permitted under the existing law. . . .

"(d) We come, finally, to the problem of killing by inaction. 'Mercy-killing' by omission to use medical means to prolong life is probably lawful. Although a physician is normally under a duty to use reasonable care to conserve his patient's life, he is probably exempted from that duty if life has become a burden to the patient."

In 1972, a Milwaukee judge held that a terminally ill person had a legal right to refuse medical or surgical treatment which could prolong life. The hospital administrator had asked that a guardian be appointed for the patient for the purpose of authorizing the amputation of a gangrenous left leg, caused by hardening of the arteries, which was likely to kill the patient before the week's end. Since Wisconsin law requires that an adult person be mentally incompetent before a guardian can be appointed, the Catholic judge visited the patient at the hospital and was reported stating: "In no way was this lady mentally ill. She knew what the consequences of her decision would be and I was not about to declare her incompetent. I say let Mrs. Raasch depart in God's own peace." Chicago Today, Jan. 26, 1972, p. 7.

2. Administration of the law in this area reflects a contemporary conflict between the thought that euthanasia is less reprehensible than other forms of murder, and the idea that, morally, such homicide can-

not be condoned. Consider the following histories of two cases of euthanasia:

(a) Louis Repouille filed a petition for naturalization on September 22, 1944, and the federal district court entered an order granting the petition. The federal district attorney appealed on the ground that the petitioner had not established the fact of "good moral character" for the five-year period preceding his petition in that it was alleged and proved at the district court hearing that the petitioner had, during that period, deliberately put to death his thirteen-year-old son. The Court of Appeals for the Second Circuit reversed the order of the district court and dismissed Repouille's petition, but without prejudice to the filing of a second petition. 165 F.2d 152 (1947). In rendering the court's decision, Judge Learned Hand stated:

"His reason for this tragic deed was that the child had 'suffered from birth from a brain injury which destined him to be an idiot and a physical monstrosity malformed in all four limbs. The child was blind, mute, and deformed. He had to be fed; the movements of his bladder and bowels were involuntary, and his entire life was spent in a small crib'. Repouille had four other children at the time, towards whom he has always been a dutiful and responsible parent; it may be assumed that his act was to help him in their nurture, which was being compromised by the burden imposed upon him in the care of the fifth. The family was altogether dependent upon his industry for its support. He was indicted for manslaughter in the first degree; but the jury brought in a verdict of manslaughter in the second degree with a recommendation of the 'utmost clemency'; and the judge sentenced him to not less than five years or more than ten, execution to be stayed, and the defendant to be placed on probation, from which he was discharged in December, 1945. Concededly, except for this act he conducted himself as a person of 'good moral character' during the five years before he filed his petition. Indeed, if he had waited before filing his petition from September 22, to October 14, 1944, he would have had a clear record for the necessary period, and would have been admitted without question. . . .

"It is reasonably clear that the jury which tried Repouille did not feel any moral repulsion at his crime. Although it was inescapably murder in the first degree, not only did they bring in a verdict that was flatly in the face of the facts and utterly absurd—for manslaughter in the second degree presupposes that the killing has not been deliberate—but they coupled even that with a recommendation which showed that in substance they wished to exculpate the offender. Moreover, it is also plain, from the sentence which he imposed, that the judge could not have seriously disagreed with their recommendation.

"One might be tempted to seize upon all this as a reliable measure of current morals; and no doubt it should have its place in the scale; but we should hesitate to accept it as decisive, when, for example, we compare it with the fate of a similar offender in Massachusetts, who, although he was not executed, was imprisoned for life. Left at large as we are, without means of verifying our conclusion, and without authority to substitute our individual beliefs, the outcome must needs be tentative; and not much is gained by discussion. We can say no more than that, quite independently of what may be the current moral feeling as to legally administered euthanasia, we feel reasonably secure in holding that only a minority of virtuous persons would deem the practice morally justifiable, while it remains in private hands, even when the provocation is as overwhelming as it was in this instance."

(b) The Massachusetts case referred to by the Court in the preceding paragraph was Com. v. Noxon, 319 Mass. 495, 66 N.E.2d 814 (1946). The history of the Noxon case, particularly that portion of it occurring after the above decision on the Repouille petition, sheds light on the many factors which affect the ultimate outcome of such cases. The following brief history is taken from the January 17, 1949, issue of Newsweek Magazine:

"When John F. Noxon was charged in 1943 with electrocuting his incurably Mongoloid 6-month-old son Larry, the newspapers labeled the case a 'mercy killing'. Noxon pleaded innocent. He insisted that the death had been accidental—that it was only by chance the boy had come in contact with a metal tray that touched a short-circuited radio wire.

"The wealthy Pittsfield, Mass., lawyer's trial became much more than a simple attempt to arrive at facts. In a heavily Catholic state, the idea of mercy killing was anathema. Noxon's social position and his personality —dour and uncommunicative—lost him much sympathy among those who might have supported him. After a sensational trial, he was found guilty and sentenced to the electric chair.

"But Noxon's lawyer, ex-Gov. Joseph B. Ely, did not give up. When the State Supreme Court rejected his appeal, Ely turned to Gov. Maurice J. Tobin. His argument: Noxon, half-crippled by infantile paralysis, would be punished enough if his sentence was commuted to life imprisonment. Although a Catholic, Tobin agreed and won the approval of his nine-man Executive Council. Noxon was moved from the condemned row in the state prison at Charleston to the Norfolk prison colony where thenceforth he served as prison librarian.

"Last month Gov. Robert F. Bradford, Ely's onetime law partner, who was defeated for reelection in November, asked the Pardon and Parole Committee of his council to consider a further reduction of Noxon's sentence—from life to six-years-to-life, making parole possible at once. This time, Tobin, now Secretary of Labor, advised against further leniency. More sensationally, District Attorney William J. Foley openly charged that Bradford was deliberately turning loose murderers in the last days of his administration and hinted at corruption.

"In the midst of the hullabaloo, Bradford's committee, headed by Lt. Gov. Arthur Coolidge, approved the governor's recommendation. Then the full council, by a 6-to-3 vote, granted the reduction in sentence. Last week the State Parole Board closed the books on the controversial case by releasing Noxon. On Friday, Jan. 7, 1949, he walked out of the Norfolk prison colony."

Another unusual case history is discussed in Note, 34 Notre Dame Law. 460 (1959).

3. Present attitudes regarding legislative change in the law concerning euthanasia include (1) the view that the status quo has sufficient flexibility, through such factors as the jury system and the pardoning power, to afford just treatment in each case according to its merits; (2) the position that the penalty for a killing motivated by mercy should be reduced; and (3) the view that euthanasia should be legalized within cer-

tain narrow bounds and placed under state supervision and control. These positions are ably discussed and evaluated in Silving, Euthanasia: A Study in Comparative Criminal Law, 103 U.Pa.L.Rev. 350 (1954). See also, Kamisar, Some Non-Religious Views Against Proposed "Mercy-Killing" Legislation, 42 Minn.L.Rev. 969 (1958), and Williams, "Mercy-Killing" Legislation—A Rejoinder, 43 Minn.L.Rev. 1 (1958). Also see Levinsohn, Voluntary Mercy Deaths, 8 J.For.Med. 57 (1961), and Sanders, Euthanasia: None Dare Call It Murder, 60 J.Crim.L., C. & P.S. 351 (1969).

4. Suicide is the intentional killing of oneself. At common law it was a felony, punishable by forfeiture of goods and ignominous burial; attempted suicide was a misdemeanor. Since forfeiture of goods as a punishment for crime has largely been abandoned, and ignominous burial is no longer practiced, it might be said that the successful suicide has not committed any offense, since he cannot be punished. Some states still punish the unsuccessful (attempted) suicide by statute. Note, 40 N.C.L.Rev. 323 (1962).

The Unborn Child

1. Since the common law of homicide refers to the killing of a "human being," the courts in this country have generally not considered the aborting of an unknown child to be a homicide. The child must be shown to have achieved an independent circulation. E. g., Clarke v. State, 117 Ala. 1, 23 So. 671 (1898); Keeler v. Superior Court of Amador County, 2 Cal.3d 619, 87 Cal.Rptr. 481, 470 P.2d 617 (1970); State v. Dickinson, 23 Ohio App.2d 259, 263 N.E.2d 253, reversed 275 N.E.2d 599 (1971). Once the fetus has emerged totally and the breathing process started, it is not needed that the umbilical cord be severed; it achieves the status of a "human being". Jackson v. Commonwealth, 265 Ky. 295, 96 S.W.2d 1014 (1936). But see, Morgan v. State, 148 Tenn. 417, 256 S.W. 433 (1923), suggesting that an independent circulation cannot be established until after the umbilical cord is severed.

The infliction of injuries upon an unborn child who dies after having been born alive may be considered homicide. In Abrams v. Foshee, 3 Iowa 274 (1856), the court held that if a child is born alive and subsequently dies as a result of potions or bruises while still in the womb, the person administering the potions or bruises with intent to produce a miscarriage could be convicted of murder.

2. Because it is sometimes very difficult to establish that the issue was born alive, which proof is needed to support a prosecution for murder or manslaughter, some states have specially provided that concealment of an infant death is a misdemeanor. For example, the Illinois Criminal Code (§ 9–4) provides as follows:

> (a) A person commits the offense of concealing the death of a bastard when that person conceals the death of any issue of a human body which if born alive would be a bastard.
>
> (b) Nothing herein contained shall be so construed as to prevent any person from being indicted for the murder or manslaughter of such bastard child.

R. v. ONUFREJCZYK

Court of Criminal Appeals.
[1955] 1 All Eng.R. 247.

[The evidence was that the defendant and one Sykut had a farm which was a financial failure. The defendant was trying, unsuccessfully, to borrow money to buy out Sykut's interest, in order to avoid a sale of the farm by auction. On or about December 14th, Sykut disappeared. On December 18th, defendant told a sheriff's officer that Sykut had gone to another city to see a doctor. Later, however, he said that three men had forced Sykut into a car at gun point and driven him away from the farm. He also wrote letters suggesting that Sykut had returned to Poland. Sykut's wife, who lived in Poland, had not heard from him, however, well after the time it would have taken him to reach Poland. The defendant was still trying to borrow money, and he tried to persuade a friend to go to a solicitor with him and impersonate Sykut. He was also arranging for a woman to draft some supposed agreements and forge Sykut's signature to them. In addition, he tried to get a blacksmith to say that Sykut had fetched a horse at the blacksmith's on December 17th, when Sykut had actually called for the horse on the 14th.]

LORD GODDARD, C. J., delivered the judgment of the court: The appellant, who is a Pole and who has been in this country since 1947, was convicted of the murder of another Pole, Sykut, his partner.

The principal question that has been argued, is whether there was proof of what the law calls a corpus delicti. In this case the remarkable fact, which has remained remarkable and unexplained, is that the body of this man, who was last seen so far as anybody knows on Dec. 14, 1953, has completely disappeared and there is no trace whatever either of him, or of his clothes, or of his ashes. It has been submitted to us that the law is that, unless the body can be found or an account can be given of the death, there is no proof of a corpus delicti. Corpus delicti means, first, that a crime has been committed, that is to say that the man is dead, and that his death has been caused by a crime.

There is, apparently, no reported case in English law where a man has been convicted of murder and there has been no trace of the body at all. But it is, we think, clear that the fact of death can be proved, like any other fact can be proved, by circumstantial evidence, that is to say, by evidence of facts which lead to one conclusion, provided the jury are satisfied and are warned that the evidence must lead to one conclusion only. . . .

. . . The case for the prosecution was:—This man has disappeared. He has completely gone from the ken of mankind. It is impossible to believe that he is alive now. I suppose it would have been possible for him to have got out of the country and become immured behind what is sometimes called the Iron Curtain; but here you have facts which point irresistably towards the appellant being the person who knows and who disposed of that man in one form or another. It may be that it would be desirable to emphasise to the jury that the first thing to which they must apply their mind is: Was a murder committed? Speaking for myself, I think that the way the learned judge put it in the two passages which I have read did sufficiently direct the attention of the jury to the fact that they had to be satisfied of that, and, if they were satisfied of the death, and the violent death, of this man, they need not go any further. It is, no doubt, true that the prosecution relied considerably on certain minute spots of blood which were found in the kitchen when it was scientifically examined, spots so small that they might easily have escaped the attention of somebody who was trying to wash or wipe up blood. The appellant did not deny that the blood that was found, although it was a minute quantity, on the wall of the kitchen, and, I think, on the ceiling of the kitchen, was the blood of his partner. He said that its presence there was due to the fact that his partner had cut his hand in the field with, I think, one of the tractors, and on coming in must have shaken his hand and shaken off some blood. That, of course, was a possibility and it was put to the jury. It was also a possibility that Sykut was disposed of in the kitchen, but there is no evidence that he was and, a matter which has been very properly stressed by counsel for the appellant, there is no evidence here how Sykut met his death. This court is of the opinion, however, that there was evidence on which the jury could infer that he met his death, that he was dead; and, if he was dead, the circumstances of the case point to the fact that his death was not a natural death. Then, if that establishes, as it would, a corpus delicti, the evidence was such that the jury were entitled to find that the appellant murdered his partner. . . .

We have come to the conclusion that there was evidence on which the jury were entitled to find that the appellant's partner was murdered and that the appellant was the murderer. Accordingly, this appeal is dismissed.

NOTES

1. For other murder cases in which the corpus delicti was established by circumstantial evidence alone, consider the following:

(a) In People v. Scott, 176 Cal.App.2d 458, 1 Cal.Rptr. 600 (1959), the defendant's wife, a woman in excellent health, disappeared. Although her glasses and dentures were found in a trash pile, no traces of her body were ever found. Before his arrest the defendant had told his friends a number of conflicting stories and lies by way of trying to explain his wife's disappearance. He also forged her name on checks and had obtained large sums of her money. The affirmance of his murder conviction was disapproved in 34 Tul.L.Rev. 820 (1960).

(b) In Commonwealth v. Burns, 409 Pa. 619, 187 A.2d 552 (1963), the Supreme Court of Pennsylvania held that circumstantial evidence, which included proof of complete, sudden termination of a long-established, consistent pattern of living of the alleged victim, a healthy, 49-year old woman, who was last seen lying on the floor in defendant's presence in an apparently helpless condition with blood on her head, was sufficient to prove the corpus delicti.

(c) In King v. Horry, [1952] N.Z.L.R. 111, the defendant, George Horry, in 1942, while using an alias, married one Eileen Turner, in New Zealand. He had told her and her parents a number of fine things about himself; however, he concealed the fact that he was an ex-convict. After marriage Eileen converted all of her assets, about 1,000 pounds, into cash to take on their honeymoon. The day after the marriage, and while at a sea resort, she and George talked to her attorney about her finances. They also visited some friends to whom they told of plans to leave New Zealand the next day. George told them that a secret military mission precluded his giving them any further details about their trip. This was the last time Eileen was seen. The next day George, alone, was back in the town where he and Eileen had been married. (It was later established that he had never left New Zealand.) He opened a bank account in an amount of 767 pounds. Five months later he married another woman.

Shortly after Eileen's disappearance her parents received a letter, postmarked "Australia" and signed "George and Eileen," in which it was stated that they were leaving Australia for England. George said Eileen was busy visiting someone else. (It was later established that George, while still in New Zealand, had arranged for another person in Australia to mail the letter from there.) Thereafter George called on Eileen's parents and told them that he and Eileen had left Australia for England on the "Empress of India", and that the ship had been torpedoed and that he last saw Eileen in a life boat. He said he had been picked up by a British warship. In fact, no "Empress of India" ever existed.

Nine years after Eileen's disappearance George was prosecuted for murder and his conviction was sustained on appeal. See comment on the case in Morris, Corpus Delicti and Circumstantial Evidence, 68 L.Q.R. 391 (1952).

(d) For other interesting cases and readings upon the subject, consult R. v. Workman and Huculak (Alberta App.Div., Dec. 19, 1962), 5 Cr.L.Q. 403; Comm. v. Lettrich, 346 Pa. 497, 31 A.2d 155 (1943); and People v. Kirby, 223 Mich. 440, 194 N.W. 142 (1923). And for a very interesting discussion of a case somewhat similar to the Onufrejczyk case, see Hilling, The Case of Decasto Earl Mayer and Marry Ellen Smith, 22 Wash.L. Rev. 79 (1947). Also, for an account of case convictions for murders where no killings had ever occurred, see Borchand, Convicting the Innocent (1932). For a very recent case involving the corpus delicti issue, see Comm. v. Burns, 409 Pa. 619, 187 A.2d 552 (1963).

2. In the United States, there is disagreement among the courts as to what constitutes the corpus delicti. Some courts require only that the particular loss or injury involved in the case be proved. Other courts—probably a majority—also require proof that the loss or injury was caused by a criminal act. Some courts go even further and require a third element—proof that the accused himself committed the crime involved.

Wigmore favored the first of these views, commenting about the view of the courts in the second category that it "makes the rule much more difficult for the jury to apply amid a complex mass of evidence, and tends to reduce the rule to a juggling formula." 7 Wigmore Evidence, § 2072 (3d ed. 1940). A different opinion is expressed in Note, The Corpus Delicti—Confession Problem, 43 J.Crim.L., C. & P.S. 214, 215 (1952), where it is stated that the second view "demands the proof of a crime and no more or less. The first view, however, can be criticized for requiring proof of less than an actual crime and thereby failing to provide adequate protection from unwarranted prosecution." As for the view held by the courts in the third category, Wigmore asserted it is "too absurd to be argued with."

The courts are also in disagreement as to what degree of proof is required to establish the elements which comprise the corpus delicti. A majority of the court held that the corpus delicti need not be proved beyond a reasonable doubt. See, e. g., State v. Kindle, 71 Mont. 58, 227 P. 65 (1924). For a contrary holding, see Roberts v. State, 210 Miss. 777, 50 So. 2d 356 (1951). Compare also People v. Rife, 382 Ill. 588, 48 N.E.2d 367 (1943) and People v. Franklin, 415 Ill. 514, 114 N.E.2d 661 (1953). However, when the evidence of the corpus delicti is only circumstantial, there is a tendency to require a higher degree of proof.

"If any principle can be deduced from the numerous cases, it is that the strictness of the evidence requirement varies with the particular facts of each case." Comment, 43 J.Crim.L., C. & P.S. 214 (1952).

New York, North Dakota and Texas have statutes requiring direct evidence of the corpus delicti in all homicide cases.

3. A majority of courts hold that the corpus delicti cannot be established solely by an extra-judicial confession of the accused. Some independent corroboration is required. Hogan v. State, 235 Ind. 271, 132 N.E. 2d 908 (1956); People v. Nachowicz, 340 Ill. 480, 172 N.E. 812 (1930). For a discussion of the wisdom of this rule, see Note, The Corpus Delicti—Confession Problem, supra.

4. Contrary to a prevailing misconception, proof of corpus delicti is a requirement of all criminal cases and not merely in homicide cases. In Commonwealth v. Leslie, 424 Pa. 331, 227 A.2d 900 (1967), the defendant confessed that he had started the fire which destroyed a summer cottage. While the police had suspected as much, they could not uncover any evidence that the fire had been started deliberately. In reversing the conviction, the Supreme Court of Pennsylvania, while recognizing that the corpus delicti could be proved by circumstantial evidence, found that the state had relied on the confession alone to prove the corpus delicti and held that this was insufficient. Proof of corpus delicti is one of the most difficult tasks facing the prosecution in arson cases. See Comment, 45 J. Crim.L., C. & P.S. 185 (1954). For corpus delicti issues in other crimes, see: Jefferson v. Sweat, 76 So.2d 494 (Fla.1954); People v. Jefferson, 1 Ill.App.3d 484, 275 N.E.2d 176 (1971).

PEOPLE v. CARUSO

Court of Appeals of New York, 1927.
246 N.Y. 437, 159 N.E. 390.

[The defendant was convicted of murder in the first degree under a New York statute which, so far as is here relevant, defines first degree murder as "The killing of a human being, unless it is excusable or justifiable, . . . from a deliberate and premeditated design to effect the death of the person killed. . . ."]

ANDREWS, J. This judgment must be reversed. . . . Francesco Caruso, an illiterate Italian, 35 years old, came to this country about 1911. He worked as a laborer, and in the early part of 1927 was living with his wife and six small children in an apartment in Brooklyn. On Friday, February 11th, one of these children, a boy of six, was ill with a sore throat. That day and the next he treated the boy with remedies bought at a drug store. The child grew worse, and at 10 o'clock of the night of the 12th he sent for a Dr. Pendola, who had been recommended to him, but with whom he was not acquainted.

What followed depends upon a statement made by Caruso and upon his testimony on the stand. Any proper inferences may be drawn therefrom. The belief that what he said was false, however, or any reasoning based upon his failure to call friendly witnesses, will not supply the want of affirmative testimony of the facts necessary to constitute the crime. Those facts, if they exist, must be inferred from his own admissions.

Some time between 10:30 and 11 in the evening Dr. Pendola arrived. The child had diphtheria. Caruso was sent out to buy some antitoxin, and, when he returned the doctor administered it. He then gave Caruso another prescription with instructions as to its use, and left promising to return in the morning.

Caruso watched the child all night, giving remedies every half hour. "About 4 o'clock in the morning," he testified, "my child was standing up to the bed, and asked me to, he says, 'Papa' he said, 'I am dying.' I say that time, I said, 'You don't die.' I said, 'I will help you every time.' The same time that child he will be crazy—look like crazy, that time—don't want to stay any more inside. All I can do, I keep my child in my arms, and I held him in my arms from 4 o'clock until 8 o'clock in the morning. After 8 o'clock in the morning the poor child getting worse—the poor child in the morning he was"—(slight interruption in the testimony while the defendant apparently stops to overcome his emotion). "The poor child that time, and he was asking me, 'Papa,' he said, 'I want to go and sleep.' So I said, 'All right, Giovie, I will put you in the sleep.' I take my Giovie, and I put him in the bed, and he started to sleep, to wait until the doctor came, and the doctor he never came. I waited from 10 o'clock, the doctor he never came."

Then, after trying in vain to get in touch with the doctor, he sent for an ambulance from a drug store.

"When I go home I seen my child is got up to the bed that time, and he says to me, 'Papa, I want to come with you.' I take my child again up in my arms, and I make him look to the backyard to the window. He looked around the yard about a couple of minutes, and after, when he looked around, he says to me, 'Papa, I want to go to sleep again.' I said, "All right, Giovie, I will put you in the sleep.' I put my child on the bed. About a few seconds my child is on the bed, my child says to me, he says, 'Papa, I want to go to the toilet.' I said, 'All right, Giovie, I will take you to the toilet.' So I was trying to pick up the child, and make him go to the toilet, when I held that child I felt that leg—that child started to shake up in my arms. My wife know about better than me—I cannot see good myself in the face, so she tell what kind of shakes he do, and she has told me, she says, 'Listen, Frank, why the child has died already.' I said, 'All right, you don't cry. No harm, because you make the child scared.' That time I go right away and put the child on the bed. When I put the child, before I put my hand to the pillow, my child said to me, 'Goodbye, Papa, I am going already.' So that time I put my hands to my head—I said, 'That child is dead. I don't know what I am going to do myself now.' That time I never said nothing, because I said 'Jesus, my child is dead now. Nobody will get their hands on my child.' "

About 12 o'clock Dr. Pendola arrived. The child had been dead for some time. He was told, and then Caruso says the doctor laughed, and he "lost his head." This seems incredible. Yet Caruso apparently believed it, for his testimony on the stand is a repetition of the same charge made in his statement that same night, before it is likely that a man of Caruso's mentality would be preparing a false defense. The probability is there was, from one cause or another, some twitching of the facial muscles that might be mistaken for a smile.

Besides the delay of the doctor and the smile was another circumstance, which, if true, would exasperate Caruso. He says, and again this appears in the statement as well as in his testimony on the trial, that, when he was buying the antitoxin, the druggist told him that the dose was too large for a child of the age of his son. This he told the doctor. The latter was indignant, and paid no heed to the warning. The druggist denied any such conversation, and apparently the dose was proper. But it seems probable that something occurred that left on Caruso's mind the impression that the death of his child was caused by malpractice. At least, immediately after the death, he told an ambulance surgeon that Dr. Pendola had killed his child by an injection, and also complained of his delay in not coming that morning. And within a short time he made the same charge to others.

Then followed some talk. Caruso accused the doctor of killing his child. The doctor denied it. Caruso attacked him in anger, choked him until he fell to the floor, then went to a closet ten or twelve feet away, took a knife, and stabbed him twice in the throat, so killing him. Caruso then took his family to the janitor's apartment downstairs, and himself went to his brother's house on Staten Island, where he was arrested that night. He made no attempt whatever to conceal the facts of the homicide, and his departure cannot fairly be viewed as a flight, indicating consciousness of guilt. . . .

. . . Conviction here of murder in the first degree is not justified by the weight of the evidence. The jury might find that the intent to kill existed. While in his testimony on the stand Caruso denies such an intent, and says that in his rage he did not know what he was doing, yet in his statement he expressly admits his intent to kill, and the inference that the intent existed might also be drawn from the two wounds in the neck inflicted with a large knife.

But was there premeditation and deliberation? This seems to have been the question which troubled the jury. They considered their verdict for six hours—twice returning for definitions of homicide and of deliberation and premeditation. Time to deliberate and premeditate there clearly was. Caruso might have done so. In fact, however, did he?

Until the Saturday evening Caruso had never met Dr. Pendola. Nothing occurred at that interview that furnished any motive for murder. Then came nervous strain and anxiety culminating in grief, deep and genuine, for the death of his child. Brooding over his loss, blaming the doctor for his delay in making the promised visit, believing he had killed the boy by his treatment, the doctor finally enters. And, when told of the child's death he appears to laugh. This, added to his supposed injuries, would fully account for the gust of anger that Caruso says he felt. Then came the struggle and the homicide.

As has been said, Caruso had the time to deliberate, to make a choice whether to kill or not to kill—to overcome hesitation and doubt—to form a definite purpose. And, where sufficient time exists, very often the circumstances surrounding the homicide justify—indeed require—the necessary inference. Not here, however. No plan to kill is shown, no intention of violence when the doctor arrived—only grief and resentment. Not until the supposed laugh did the assault begin. "If the defendant inflicted the wound in a sudden transport of passion, excited by what the deceased then said and by the preceding events which, for the time, disturbed her reasoning faculties and deprived her of the capacity to reflect, or while under the influence of some sudden and uncontrollable emotion excited by the final culmination of her misfortunes, as indicated by the train of events which have been related, the act did not constitute murder in the first degree. Deliberation and premeditation imply the capacity at the time to think and reflect, sufficient volition to make a choice and by the use of these powers to refrain from doing a wrongful act." (People v. Barberi.) When the supposed laugh came, there was apparent cause for excitement and anger. There was enough to indicate hot blood and unreflecting action. There was immediate provocation. People v. Ferraro, 161 N.Y. 365, 375, 55 N.E. 931. The attack seems to have been the instant effect of impulse. Nor does the fact that the stabbing followed the beginning of the attack by some time affect this conclusion. It was all one transaction under the peculiar facts of this case. If the assault was not deliberated or premeditated, then neither was the infliction of the fatal wound.

With due consideration of all the facts presented there is insufficient evidence to justify a conviction of murder in the first degree. Doubtless, on this record the defendant might be convicted of some crime, either murder in the second degree, or, if his testimony on the stand is accepted, manslaughter in the first degree. Either verdict might be sustained on the facts. Not the one actually rendered.

The judgment of conviction should be reversed, and a new trial ordered.

Judgment reversed, etc.

NOTES

1. Statutory Degrees of Murder

At the common law, there were no degrees of murder. Any homicide, committed with malice aforethought, express or implied, constituted murder. Death, of course, was the penalty for murder under the common law.

In order to lessen the penalty attaching to certain forms of murder not thought to warrant the punishment of death, many states statutorily divided the crime of murder into degrees, with a sliding scale of penalties appropriate to the various degrees.

2. The Definition of Murder in Recent Criminal Codes

In one of the most recent criminal codes the drafters have avoided the usage of such language as "malice aforethought" and "deliberate and premeditated".

The Illinois Criminal Code provides (in § 9–1):

> (a) A person who kills an individual without lawful justification commits murder if, in performing the acts which cause the death:
>
> (1) He either intends to kill or do great bodily harm to that individual or another, or knows that such acts will cause death to that individual or another; or
>
> (2) He knows that such acts create a strong probability of death or great bodily harm to that individual or another; or
>
> (3) He is attempting or committing a forcible felony other than voluntary manslaughter.

PEOPLE v. WALSH

Court of Appeals of New York, 1933.
262 N.Y. 140, 186 N.E. 422.

CROUCH, JUDGE. The four defendants were jointly indicted in the common-law form for murder in the first degree. The fatal shot was fired by the defendant Walsh. The case was tried and submitted to the jury solely as a felony murder. The felony charged was robbery in a restaurant speakeasy. The victim was Joseph P. Burke, a police officer. All the defendants were found guilty and were sentenced to death.

The trial judge, after telling the jury that the point for them to decide was whether or not a felony had been committed, and, if so, whether Officer Burke was killed while it was in progress, charged as follows: "I am going to charge you as a matter of law in this case that if you believe the testimony of the People's witnesses, if you believe the events, if you are satisfied beyond a reasonable doubt that the events transpired as detailed by the People's witnesses, if that testimony is accepted by you, then Officer Burke was killed while these defendants were participating in a felony, and if that is the case, then your only verdict can be one of murder in the first degree. If you find that is not the case, if you are not satisfied by the testimony of the People's witnesses, of course, your verdict must be not guilty."

And also as follows: "If you find in this case that the defendants were acting in concert, if you find that they were engaged in the commission of a felony—the felony of robbery, if you find and you are satisfied beyond a reasonable doubt that the killing occurred as detailed by the People's witnesses, then you should find them guilty. If you are not so satisfied, you should acquit them."

If upon any hypothesis, warranted by the testimony of the people's witnesses, the jury could have found that the commission of the robbery had come to an end before the killing took place, the instructions above quoted constitute prejudicial error. Their purport was something more than a mere statement that the people's testimony sufficed to make out a case of felony murder, if the jurors believed it. There was a clear direction to the jury, not that they could find, but that they must find the defendants guilty, if they believed the facts were as the people's witnesses testified. The jury was precluded from finding the facts in accordance with the people's testimony, and at the same time finding Walsh was not engaged in the commission of a felony when he killed Officer Burke.

The testimony of the people's witnesses disclosed the following facts: In the city of New York, on the northwest corner of Seventh avenue and West 136th street, ground floor, was located a restaurant speakeasy having a front entrance on Seventh avenue and a side entrance on West 136th street, opening through a small vestibule into a rear room taken up with tables. The front room, separated from the rear by a screen or partition, contained a bar and a lunch counter. There were two doors between the bar room and the rear room. Immediately north of this establishment fronting on Seventh avenue was a stationery and cigar store. Back of both was a room, referred to as the "entry," with a toilet used in common. Doors led into the entry both from the rear room of the restaurant and from the rear of the stationery store. There was thus, by passing through the stationery store into the entry, a third means of access to the restaurant. The vestibule of the side entrance above referred to was a small compartment about three by four feet. The inner door contained a peek hole window, had a snap lock, and was always kept closed by means of an automatic check. The outer door was always unlocked. Shortly before 8 a. m., on Sunday morning, June 12, 1932, in an automobile driven by defendant Kelly, the four defendants came to this place for the purpose of robbing it. The automobile was parked nearby with the motor running. Kelly remained outside across 136th street. A. Celentano then entered the restaurant by the front door and bought a glass of beer and a package of cigarettes. The only occupants of the restaurant were the barkeeper and the porter. A few minutes later J. Celentano and Walsh came in together through the front door. Both had guns. The two occupants were told to put up their hands, and did so. Four dollars were taken from the porter's pocket, and sixteen or seventeen dollars from the cash register at the back of the bar. The two occupants were taken to the entry at the rear; the porter remained there, but the barkeeper came back and went behind the bar. Walsh remained in or near the entry to guard the porter, while the two Celentanos rifled the safe and the drawers back of the bar. While so engaged, a colored man and woman knocked at the side door which was opened by Walsh, who ordered them into the entry where the porter was. Walsh remained at or near the doorway of the entry. About this time three police officers, Regan, Rhodes, and Burke, on their way to go on post, were informed at the corner of Seventh avenue and 136th street that something was wrong in the restaurant. Thereupon Officer Burke stationed himself at the side door on 136th street, and Officers Regan and Rhodes went to the front door. They could not get in. Officer Rhodes, evidently familiar with the premises, left Officer Regan and entered the stationery store to get in the restaurant through the back entry. Officer Regan kicked at the front door which was thereupon opened by one of the Celentanos. He entered, revolver in hand, told the Celentanos to throw up their hands, and proceeded to search them. Officer Rhodes, coming through the stationery store by way of the back entry, joined Officer Regan within a minute or two. He did not see Walsh. Walsh from where he had been standing had a view of the front door. It is a fair inference that he saw what happened when Officer Regan entered, and immediately started to make his escape through the side door into 136th street. The porter, who was in the entry, testified he saw Officer Regan come in the front door, and that at that moment Walsh walked away from him. The barkeeper testifies that after Officer

Regan entered and rounded up the Celentanos, he heard the side door close, and that, right after the door closed, Officer Rhodes walked in from the entry. After Rhodes rejoined Regan they made the two Celentanos lie face down on the floor, and completed the searching. Walsh, in the vestibule, opened the outside door, saw Officer Burke standing at the left near the outside wall, drew back, closed the door, then partly opened it again, reached out and fired the fatal shot. Thereupon he fled in the direction of Eighth avenue and was subsequently captured. Kelly, the lookout, heard the shot and saw a fellow running down the street. After a short time he went to the car, drove away, abandoned the car, and was subsequently arrested.

It is possible to have a factual situation in a case of felonious homicide where only one conclusion can be drawn as to whether or not the homicide took place during the commission of the felony. There have been such cases in this court. . . . The instances where a trial judge may charge the point as matter of law are, however, exceptional. . . .

Whether the robbery here was still in progress when the shot was fired depends largely upon inferences to be drawn from the conduct of Walsh. The prosecution admits that the two Celentanos were under arrest, and hence no act by either of them thereafter prolonged its commission. Kelly was across the street as a lookout and aid in the "getaway." In a legal sense he was aiding in the commission of the robbery. . . . In a practical sense, his mere presence could hardly be said to prolong the commission of a robbery if it had otherwise ended. It may be assumed that Walsh stood within the four walls of the building when he fired the shot. That is an important but not a conclusive circumstance. . . . The jury could have found that the inner door of the vestibule had closed and locked behind him. If that was so, he was in effect definitely outside the restaurant proper. But neither is that alone conclusive. He might have been entirely outside the building when he shot and still have been engaged in the robbery, if he was getting away with the loot or was doing anything to aid his confederates in getting away with it. . . But there is no evidence to show that he had any of the loot. The inference is to the contrary. The jury could have found that his entire conduct from the moment Officer Regan entered the restaurant constituted flight, and hence "desistance or abandonment" of the robbery. . . .

In short, even upon the testimony of the prosecution alone, the question of whether or not the homicide occurred during the commission of the felony was one of fact. It should have been left to the jury under instructions pointing out generally that the killing to be felony murder must occur while the actor or one or more of his confederates is engaged in securing the plunder or in doing something immediately connected with the underlying crime . . . ; that escape may, under certain unities of time, manner, and place, be a matter so immediately connected with the crime as to be part of its commission . . . ; but that, where there is no reasonable doubt of a complete intervening desistance from the crime, as by the abandonment of the loot and running away, the subsequent homicide is not murder in the first degree without proof of deliberation and intent. . . .

CRANE, J. (dissenting). These men were committing robbery. When caught at it, Walsh tried to shoot his way out. He killed while he and his associates were committing a felony. Therefore, I am for affirmance, even though there were slight errors in the charge.

Judgments of conviction reversed, etc.

NOTES

1. Compare the principal case with Comm. v. Doris, 287 Pa. 547, 135 A. 313 (1926). Doris and three companions robbed the occupants of a bank car transporting funds. In the course of the robbery, Doris was captured; however, his companions fled from the scene. In the chase that followed, one of the pursuing policemen was shot and killed by the felons, who were captured a short time thereafter. Doris was separately tried, convicted of first degree murder committed "in the perpetration of . . . robbery", and sentenced to death. The Pennsylvania Supreme Court affirmed. "The proof of the common purpose to take, by force, the money of the bank, carry it away, and make a safe escape, may be inferred from the attending circumstances. Whether such a criminal intent existed was a question for the jury, and the evidence warranted their conclusion. . . . It is urged that the escape and flight are not to be considered as part of the perpetration of the robbery, which, it is claimed, had been completed . . . and thereafter no responsibility attached to any individual for the act of the other. . . . Whether the act of departing is a continuous part of the attempted or accomplished crime is for the jury."

2. The felony-murder doctrine was applied in Comm. v. De Moss, 401 Pa. 395, 165 A.2d 14 (1960) to convict for murder a robbery conspirator who was in another state at the time of the robbery-murder.

3. Consider the above decisions in light of the following analysis appearing in 24 J.Crim.L. & C. 598 (1933):

"The decisions . . . may be generalized into two formulas: either the common design to rob did include the common design to kill if necessary to escape, in which case the accessory should suffer the same penalty as the one killing; or that it did not, and then the design to kill in order to escape was a totally new one which must be proved, i. e., it must be proved that the accessory was accomplice to the *new design* before he may be held for murder. . . . Those courts that adhere to the first view make the vital assumption, that *when armed criminals commit robbery they are prepared to kill* in order to effect their escape. Those that follow the second view contend that persons may be prepared to rob, and yet not prepared to 'resist to the death' but may prefer to surrender if caught. . . . The situations arising under the second formula are usually tried as conspiracy cases, and it must be shown that the conspiracy extended not only to the robbery but also to the killing. . . ."

4. One aspect of the felony-murder doctrine that has been a troublesome one for the courts has arisen in cases where, in the course of a dangerous felony, (a) a police officer is killed during an exchange of shots between

felons and police and no proof is offered at trial that the fatal shot came from the gun of a felon, or else the prosecution attempts to secure a murder conviction even when there is evidence the fatal shot accidently came from another officer's gun; (b) the victim of a felony kills one of two or more felons, and a surviving felon is prosecuted for the murder of his co-felon; and (c) one felon is accidentally killed by a co-felon, who is then prosecuted for murder of the slain individual.

In a series of Pennsylvania cases the Supreme Court of Pennsylvania first held that in a shoot-out between felons and police, during which a police officer is killed, the felons are guilty of first degree murder, regardless of who fired the fatal shot. Commonwealth v. Almeida, 362 Pa. 596, 68 A.2d 595 (1949).

Subsequent to the *Almeida* case the Pennsylvania Supreme Court was required to rule on the following fact situation, in Commonwealth v. Thomas, 382 Pa. 639, 117 A.2d 204 (1955): Thomas and a confederate committed a robbery. While fleeing from the scene, the confederate was shot and killed by the store owner. Thomas was indicted for murder of his co-felon. However, the trial court sustained Thomas' demurrer to the commonwealth's evidence and the decision was appealed. The Supreme Court, with three justices dissenting, reversed the judgment of the lower court. In so doing, the court stated:

"The sole question is whether defendant can be convicted of murder under this state of facts. That is, can a co-felon be found guilty of murder where the victim of an armed robbery justifiably kills the other felon as they flee from the scene of the crime? . . . If the defendant sets in motion the physical power of another, he is liable for its result. . . . Commonwealth v. Almeida. . . . As has been said many times, such a rule is equally consistent with reason and sound public policy, and is essential to the protection of human life. The felon's robbery set in motion a chain of events which were or should have been within his contemplation when the motion was initiated. He therefore should be held responsible for *any death* which by direct and almost inevitable sequence results from the initial criminal act. . . . We can see no sound reason for distinction merely because the one killed was a co-felon."

Following the above action of the Supreme Court in the *Thomas* case, the District Attorney of Philadelphia moved the trial court for entry of a *nolle prosequi* on the murder indictment, and the court approved the motion. At the same time, Thomas pleaded guilty to an indictment charging him with armed robbery and was sentenced to the penitentiary. The Pennsylvania penalty for armed robbery is a fine not exceeding ten thousand dollars, or imprisonment in solitary confinement at labor for not exceeding twenty years, or both.

A few years later, the Pennsylvania Supreme Court again found it necessary to struggle with the felony-murder concept. The occasion was the case of Commonwealth v. Redline, 391 Pa. 486, 137 A.2d 472 (1958), where the defendant and his accomplice perpetrated a robbery and, while fleeing from the scene, engaged in a gun battle with the police. The accomplice was killed by a policeman, and defendant was indicted for and convicted of the murder of the accomplice. Here, the Supreme Court changed its mind and overruled *Thomas*, holding that felony-murder applies only if the killing is done by one of the felons, and not if the killing is done by a police officer or a bystander. The court did not overrule

Almeida, although it expressed its dissatisfaction with that case, because the two cases could be distinguished on the basis that in *Almeida* the victim of the killing was a police officer, while in *Redline,* the victim was one of the felons.

On the same day that the Supreme Court of Pennsylvania decided the *Redline* case, it handed down a decision in Com. v. Bolish, 391 Pa. 550, 138 A.2d 447 (1958). Bolish and one Flynn planned an arson, and in carrying out the plan Flynn was fatally injured by an explosion which occurred when he placed a jar of gasoline on an electric hot plate. Bolish was convicted of first degree murder and sentenced to life imprisonment. The judgment was affirmed on appeal, the court rejecting the defendant's contention that the felony-murder doctrine does not apply to the death of an accomplice resulting from the accomplice's own act. The court stated that the defendant "was actively participating in the felony which resulted in death. The element of malice, present in the design of defendant, necessarily must be imputed to the resulting killing, and made him responsible for the death. . . . The fact that the victim was an accomplice does not alter the situation, since his own act which caused his death was in furtherance of the felony." Two justices dissented.

Is the *Bolish* case distinguishable from *Redline?*

The conviction and death sentence in the *Almeida* case were eventually set aside by a federal district court, upon a habeas corpus hearing, because of the fact that the prosecution had suppressed evidence establishing that the fatal bullet was actually fired by a police officer and not by one of the felons. 104 F.Supp. 321 (E.D.Pa.1951), affirmed 195 F.2d 815 (3d Cir. 1952). Almeida was retried. He pled guilty and received a life sentence.

The Pennsylvania Supreme Court finally settled the whole matter to its satisfaction in Commonwealth ex rel. Smith v. Myers, 438 Pa. 218, 261 A.2d 550 (1970). It overruled the original *Almeida* case in the following colorful conclusion: "We thus give *Almeida* burial, taking it out of its limbo, and plunging it downward into the bowels of the earth". Similarly colorful language was used in the dissenting opinion of Chief Justice Bell, in which he started off by saying:

> This is the age of Crime and Criminals, and the peace-loving citizen is the forgotten man. Murder, robbery and rape are rampant, and this tidal wave of ruthless crime, violence and widespread lawlessness which too often goes unpunished is due in considerable part to recent pro-criminal decisions of the highest Courts in our State and Country. No matter how guilty a convicted criminal undoubtedly is, no matter how terrible his crime was, or how many crimes he has previously committed, the highest Courts of our Country (1) have in recent years extended and continue to *expand* the so-called rights of criminals, and (2) are completely oblivious of the rights, the security, the safety and the welfare of the law-abiding public. * * *

5. Compare the course of the history of the felony-murder doctrine in Pennsylvania with the following two California cases:

(a) In People v. Washington, 62 Cal.2d 777, 44 Cal.Rptr. 442, 402 P.2d 130 (1965), the defendant was convicted of murder for participating in a robbery in which his accomplice was killed by the victim of the robbery. Upon his appeal he urged the court to confine a felon's homicide responsibility to situations where the victim was an *innocent* person. Here, of course, the person killed was one of the felons. Although ultimately reversing the defendant's conviction the majority of the California Supreme Court (per Chief Justice Traynor) expressed the view that a distinction based upon a consideration of the person killed would make the defendant's criminal liability turn upon the marksmanship of the police and the victims of the felony during which the killing occurred. The court preferred to face up to the basic issue as to whether a felon can be convicted of murder for the killing of *any* person by another who is resisting the robbery; and it held that there could be no conviction in such instances. It interpreted the language of the California felony-murder statute to mean that for a killing to occur in the "perpetration", or in an "attempt to perpetrate" a felony, it had to be done by one of the felons; in other words, in furtherance of the felony. The court rejected the causation theory upon which the opposite result would have been reached. Also, as regards the prosecution's contention that responsibility for any death would serve to prevent dangerous felonies, the court said:

"Neither the common-law rationale of the rule nor the Penal Code supports this contention. In every robbery there is a possibility that the victim will resist and kill. The robber has little control over such a killing once the robbery is undertaken as this case demonstrates. To impose an additional penalty for the killing would discriminate between robbers, not on the basis of any difference in their own conduct, but solely on the basis of the response by others that the robber's conduct happened to induce. An additional penalty for a homi^cide committed by the victim would deter robbery haphazardly at best."

Two justices dissented; they expressed the view that the rule adopted by the court contained the following implicit advice to would-be felons:

"Henceforth in committing certain crimes, including robbery, rape and burglary, you are free to arm yourselves with a gun and brandish it in the faces of your victims without fear of a murder conviction unless you or your accomplice pulls the trigger. If the menacing effect of your gun causes a victim or policeman to fire and kill an innocent person or a cofelon, you are absolved of responsibility for such killing unless you shoot first."

They added:

"Obviously this advance judicial absolution removes one of the most meaningful deterrents to the commission of armed felonies."

On the other hand, in Taylor v. Superior Court, 3 Cal.3d 578, 477 P.2d 131 (1970), a sharply divided California Supreme Court upheld the conviction of murder of the driver of a getaway car where one of his accomplices, who were engaged in a robbery and assault with a deadly weapon, was shot and killed by the robbery victim. The court cited with approval the following language from its earlier case of People v. Gilbert:

> When the defendant or his accomplice, with a conscious disregard for life, intentionally commits an act that is likely to cause death, and his victim or a police officer kills in reasonable response to such act, the defendant is guilty of murder. In such a case, the killing is attributable, not merely to the commission of a felony, but to the intentional act of the defendant or his accomplice committed with conscious disregard for life.

6. All of the foregoing problems become rather inconsequential, of course, in the absence of capital punishment (either by state choice or by court mandate). Wisconsin, which abolished capital punishment long before the *Furman* decision of the Supreme Court of the United States, resolved the felony-murder doctrine in this fashion:

> *Third-Degree Murder.* Whoever in the course of committing or attempting to commit a felony causes the death of another human being as a natural and probable consequence of the commission of or attempt to commit the felony, may be imprisoned not more than 15 years in excess of the maximum provided by law for the felony.

COMMONWEALTH v. CHEEKS

Supreme Court of Pennsylvania, 1966.
423 Pa. 67, 223 A.2d 291.

EAGEN, JUSTICE. On May 22, 1964, after a nine-day trial, the appellant, Bernard Cheeks, was convicted by a jury of murder in the first degree and punishment was fixed at life imprisonment . . .

The crime involved the robbery and stabbing on October 11, 1963, of Joe Henry Howell by four young males on a public street in Philadelphia . . . * * *

The Commonwealth's medical trial testimony may be summarized as follows: Upon Howell's admission to the hospital at 2:10 a. m. o'clock in the early morning following the occurrence, an examination disclosed an obvious penetrating wound of the abdomen in the area of the umbilicus. Since the extent of the wound was not ascertainable from an exterior examination, an operation was deemed necessary and was performed. It disclosed a puncture of the abdominal cavity, measuring about one inch in length, and it also disclosed that the only interior damage therefrom was to the mesentery, a leaf of tissue attached to the intestines through which the blood vessels course and supply nourishment to these organs. However, during the operation the whole gastro-intestinal tract was manually handled and checked for wounds.

In order to prevent a common post-operative complication,[1] a "Levin" tube was inserted in the patient through the nostril to the stomach to suction off damaging secretions and air that might accumulate in that organ. Following the operation and after coming out of the anesthesia, the patient, Howell, was uncooperative, disorientated, resisted treatment, demonstrated delirium tremens, hallucinations, wouldn't stay in bed and wandered into the hospital halls and the rooms of other patients. Out of precaution, he was then tied to

1. Following such an operation, the intestines and bowels frequently do not function normally causing secretions and air to remain unduly in the stomach, resulting in abnormal distention and possible serious consequences.

the bed. However, he managed to pull out the tube three times and developed hiccups.[2]

On October 15th, the abdomen became markedly distended. This followed a period during which the patient had continued to be uncooperative and had again extracted the tube. However, the abdominal distention was described as "secondary to the operation, and not secondary to pulling out the tube." It was also stated that the operation itself "produced a temporary paralysis in the intestine which caused accumulation of the gas and fluids and it was necessary to remove the fluids to keep the man alive."

As a result of the above described complication, another longer "Cantor" tube was inserted. This had a bag of mercury at the end for weight purposes and had to be positioned under a fluoroscope or x-ray machine. Howell pulled out this tube on at least two occasions, the second of these instances occurred on October 18th, in the x-ray room, just as the process of inserting the tube was about completed. As a result a gag reaction immediately followed, causing a large amount of gastric material in the stomach to be sucked into the lungs. A tracheotomy was hurriedly performed without material result. Howell expired about 1:30 p. m. o'clock on the same day from suffocation, resulting in heart stoppage due to lack of oxygen in the lungs.

Under this proof, it is our studied conclusion that the question of causal connection was for the jury to resolve. The fact that the stabbing was not the immediate cause of death is not controlling. [As pointed out in the *Peters* case, Pa.1964], one charged with homicide cannot escape liability merely because the blow he inflicted is not mortal, or the immediate cause of death. If his blow is the legal cause, i. e., if it started a chain of causation which led to the death, he is guilty of homicide. . . .

In this case, the stabbing necessitated the operation; the operation was the direct cause of the stomach complication and abdominal distention; the insertion of the tubes was required to alleviate this condition and to save the victim's life. The fact that the victim, while in a weakened physical condition and disorientated mental state, pulled out the tubes and created the immediate situation, which resulted in his death, is not such an intervening and independent act sufficient to break the chain of causation or events between the stabbing and the death. * * *

COHEN, JUSTICE (dissenting). In Commonwealth v. Root [an earlier decision of the Supreme Court of Pennsylvania], we held that "the tort liability concept of proximate cause has no proper place in prosecutions for criminal homicide and more direct causal connection

2. One medical expert stated that this condition and behavior was in no way attributable to the operation or medication. However, another such expert testified, that the abnormal retention of fluids and gases in the stomach produced a chemical reaction and the mental confusion, which in turn caused the confused behavior of the patient and resulted in his pulling out the tubes.

is required for conviction". A reading of the majority opinion discloses that in concluding that defendant's act was the proximate cause of death and that defendant is criminally responsible therefor, a weighty reliance has been placed upon precedent grounded upon the application of the tort liability concept of proximate cause. This reliance blatantly violates the principles of Root. I, accordingly, dissent.

B. MANSLAUGHTER

SECTION 1. VOLUNTARY MANSLAUGHTER

STATE v. FLORY

Supreme Court of Wyoming, 1929.
40 Wyo. 184, 276 P. 458.

BLUME, C. J. The defendant was convicted of murder in the second degree for killing E. T. Ostrum on January 16, 1928, and he appeals.

The deceased, aged between 65 to 70 years, was the father of Daisy Flory, the wife of defendant, who is about 21 years of age, and who married defendant in 1923. The mother and father of Daisy were, it seems, divorced, for a number of years prior to the homicide in question in this case. The father apparently was not well acquainted with his daughter and paid little attention to her, although he sent her some small presents when her two children, age 3 years and 1 year, respectively, were born. At the time of the homicide and for some time prior thereto, the deceased lived on a farm in Campbell county, Wyo., the defendant on a farm in Montana; the distance, by road, between the two places being about 50 miles. The deceased was engaged in farming and in performing common labor. The defendant was a "dry farmer" in the summer and a trapper in the winter. Deceased wrote to his daughter in the summer of 1927, wanting to visit her, and she and her husband invited him to come. He arrived on the day after Thanksgiving, during the absence of the defendant, who came home on November 30th. The visit between the deceased and defendant was pleasant, and it was agreed, in fact, upon suggestion of the deceased, that the latter might somewhat later, move over to defendant's place, build himself a house, and in the meantime occupy the "bunkhouse" on defendant's place. He was invited to continue his visit at that time until after Christmas, which he agreed to do. Defendant left home, to go trapping, about the middle of December, and returned, as was expected, on the afternoon of December 23d. He claims that during this time the deceased made indecent proposals to

Daisy Flory, defendant's wife, and raped her and committed incest upon her on the morning of December 23d. According to the testimony, defendant was not told thereof until later, although she immediately indicated to him that she did not want her father to stay longer and did not want him to move as had been planned. Deceased left on December 26th, first to visit at another place and then to go home. On January 3, 1928, defendant had occasion to go to Ostrum's place to get some poison for coyotes and to tell him not to move. During this time the deceased mentioned to defendant that he had discussed with Daisy the subject of not having any more children, and he gave defendant a package containing a silk sponge and three rubbers, used for prevention of conception, stating that while at Sheridan, a few days previously he had bought nine of them. Defendant had never discussed the subject with his wife, and when he arrived home and showed her the package, she was perturbed, exclaimed, "O, God!" and from that time to the morning of January 15th she gradually told him of the details of the indecent advances and rape above mentioned, telling the final scenes on the morning of the date last mentioned, and that deceased had said: "Don't be foolish and say anything about this." The defendant thereupon took his gun, as he was accustomed to do when going on trips, with the intention, as he testified, of going to deceased's home and getting an explanation of the latter's conduct. He stopped overnight at the house of Mr. Hudsonpillar, and the next morning went to the house of deceased, arriving there about 11 o'clock in the forenoon, finding the deceased at home. The house is nearly 24 feet square, entered by a door in the south into a large room occupying the whole of the south 13 feet. The north side of the house is divided between a kitchen, about 9 x 10 feet in area, in the northwest corner, and a storeroom in the northeast corner, each being connected with the large room by a door. No one else was there, and the only living witness to the tragedy is the defendant himself. He testified at length, and his testimony, condensed, is about as follows:

"I took the gun along in because I knew he was stouter than I and I knew he could handle me. I had no intentions when I went in of killing the man at all. He says 'Hello' to me, and I walked towards him, and I said 'What made you rape Daisy.' And he came right straight towards me. I looked at both hands, but he didn't have anything in them, and he says to me 'Let's talk it over,' and I says to him, 'Don't come any closer,' and he turned around and walked back, and I walked after him—to see what he was going to do, and when he got to the stove (in the northwest corner of the kitchen) he says 'Let's talk it over.' He was facing me in a stooped-over position and I says to him 'Charley, do you know you just about ruined my home?' And he says 'I will keep the girl,' and when he said that, I says 'You are a pretty son of a bitch to keep your daughter.' I was thinking of some of the things he had done, was pretty nervous, and that man he just sprang after me, and when he did I jerked the rifle back, and just then I heard the report of the gun, and I saw him fall, and I turned around and went out. At no time did he deny he didn't rape his daughter. When I jerked the rifle back, I have no recollection of pulling the trigger with my finger. I didn't intend to shoot him when I jerked the rifle back, and it surprised me, and I turned around and went out. I had fear when he came at me. He had the meanest look in his face of any man I ever saw, and I knew he could handle me, if he got hold of me. I was giddy when I went out."

On cross-examination he testified, among other things:

"I was mad on my way over there and when I got there, but not any madder than any one else under the circumstances. I didn't tell Hudsonpillar I was going to Ostrum's. I didn't want to talk to him about it. I can't say that I was mad when I got to Hudsonpillar's. The gun was cocked when I took it out of the scabbard; I didn't examine it, but usually carry it with the safety on. I didn't rap when I went in. As I was opening the door, on the south, he showed up in the kitchen. I went right in; had the gun in the right hand. I walked towards the deceased; deceased was in the kitchen; I walked close to the kitchen door, keeping my eyes on deceased; I pointed the gun at him, when he came toward me the first time, and shouted at him 'Don't come any closer,' and he went back into the kitchen. I went next to the door. He had nothing in his hands, but when he sprang for me, I don't think so. I saw nothing in them. When he said 'I can keep the girl' it made me mad. I didn't take my eyes off Ostrum. I must have taken the safety off the gun when he rushed at me the first time. It looked like to me he was rushing for the rifle, and when he rushed towards me, I jerked the rifle, and that was when the shot was fired. I didn't intend to shoot him. The gun went off accidentally. I didn't intend to shoot him, and it got me so I couldn't stay there and look at him, I was intending to get away from him as he came toward me. I jerked the gun back and went backwards, and the gun went off. I was standing right in the door (leading to the kitchen). I knew he was dead the way he fell. I later gave myself up at Sheridan."

On re-examination he testified that he wept twice while going to Ostrum's. . . .

The defendant contends that the information given him by his wife as to the rape and incest committed upon her by the decedent so aroused his passions and deprived him of such self-control that his act cannot be held to be murder. The incest and rape, if true, could not justify the killing of the deceased. . . . But the evidence may be admissible for the purpose of mitigation and to reduce the crime to manslaughter. . . . The state contends that the testimony was not admissible in this case, because ample time—at least a day and probably longer—had elapsed after the defendant had been informed of the acts of decedent; further, that defendant's own testimony shows that when he was at Hudsonpillar's during the evening and night of January 15, 1928, his blood had cooled and he was no longer perturbed. Counsel for the defendant say that when he, on the morning of January 16th, met the deceased, and the latter did not deny the rape and said that he would keep his daughter, this was heaping insult upon injury and vividly recalled to defendant's mind what had been told him on the previous days. There is other testimony which shows to some extent at least that defendant's mind was perturbed on his way to Ostrum's. We are inclined to agree with defendant's contention. The crime of deceased, if true, was most heinous and was calculated to create a most violent passion in the mind of the defendant, and it is hardly to be expected that it would, as a matter of law, subside within so short a time, especially when, as testified, a situation arose by which past facts were clearly recalled. Courts are not altogether agreed as to whether the question of cooling time is one of law or one for the jury. Some hold it to be a question of law and that 24 hours is sufficient for the mind to cool. . . . We think, however, that the weight of authority is that, in cases like that at bar, the question of cooling time depends on the circumstances and is ordinarily one for the jury. . . .

In [State v. Thomas, 169 Iowa 591, 151 N.W. 842] it is said: "Where the want of provocation is so clear as to admit of no reasonable doubt that the alleged provocation could not have had any tendency to produce such state of mind in ordinary men, the evidence thereof should be excluded; but if there be a reasonable doubt as to whether the alleged provocation had such tendency, it is the safer rule to let the issue go to the jury under proper instructions. Of course, the reasonableness or adequacy of the provocation must depend on the facts of each particular case. In some cases, the courts declare that only actual personal knowledge of the wife's infidelity will extenuate the crime of killing by the husband to manslaughter. . . . But others with better reason hold that information of the recent liaison of the wife with a paramour, reaching the husband for the first time, may be shown as likely to have thrown him into ungovernable passion. . . . The circumstances of each case necessarily must determine the admissibility of the evidence as well as its bearing on the different issues presented. Again, it is to be remarked that there is no definite time within which the passions when aroused by such a wrong may be said to have so far subsided and reason to have resumed its sway to such an extent as that thereafter the killing may be denounced as in vengeance alone. The question is one of reasonable time and dependent on all the facts of the case. While the time may be so long as to exclude all doubt on the subject and exact the exclusion of the evidence in so far as offered in extenuation, more frequently it should be submitted to the jury under proper instructions. . . ."

The court, in fact, permitted the defendant to show that the wife of the defendant told him of the commission of the rape and incest, but excluded all details, and collateral facts tending to show the state of the defendant's mind. In this we think there was error. While no cases discuss the point directly . . ., courts seem to have admitted the details told a defendant as a matter of course, and the reasons for that are plain. In the first place, a bare statement of the ultimate fact might give the jury the impression that it is fabricated, while a detailed statement might add credibility to the witness. Again, the pertinent inquiry is as to what was the condition of the defendant's mind as the result of what has been told him. In order to determine that, the jury must, mentally, be placed as near as possible in the position of the defendant, in order to be able to judge properly. Details of an atrocious character would be more apt to affect the mind of the defendant, just as details are more apt to affect the mind of any one else. . . . It is true, of course, as argued, that the details might prejudice and inflame the minds of the jury; if so, the same details would be apt to inflame the mind of the defendant, and that is the very point that was to be determined by the jury. . . .

We have a case here, accordingly, in which we find that there is no error in the case, except as to the refusal to admit evidence which, if admitted, might have induced the jury to find the degree of the crime to be no greater than that of manslaughter. . . . [T]he state may elect by writing, filed in this case within 30 days, to take a new trial, in which event the judgment will be reversed and the cause remanded for a new trial. Unless that is done, the judgment will stand reversed as to murder in the second degree and affirmed for manslaughter, and the case will be remanded to the district court with direction to cause the prisoner to be brought before it to be resentenced for that crime, taking into consideration the time already served by the defendant, and to make all other necessary orders not inconsistent herewith.

Remanded, with directions.

BEDDER v. DIRECTOR OF PUBLIC PROSECUTIONS

House of Lords, 1954.
2 All Eng.R. 801.

LORD SIMONDS, L. C.: My Lords, this appeal raises once more a question of importance in the criminal law. Your Lordships, I think, agree with me that, on examination, the question appears to be amply covered by the highest authority, but the answer can usefully be restated.

The appellant, a youth of eighteen years, was convicted on May 27, 1954, at Leicester Assizes of the murder of Doreen Mary Redding, a prostitute. He appealed to the Court of Criminal Appeal on the substantial ground of misdirection, claiming that the learned judge who tried the case had wrongly directed the jury on the test of provocation and that, had they been rightly directed, they might have found him guilty not of murder but of manslaughter only. The Court of Criminal Appeal dismissed his appeal, holding that the jury had been rightly directed.

The relevant facts, so far as they bear on the question of provocation, can be shortly stated. The appellant has the misfortune to be sexually impotent, a fact which he naturally well knew and, according to his own evidence had allowed to prey on his mind. On the night of the crime he saw the prostitute with another man, and when they had parted, went and spoke to her and was led by her to a quiet court off a street in Leicester. There he attempted in vain to have intercourse with her whereupon—and I summarise the evidence in the way most favourable to him—she jeered at him and attempted to get away. He tried still to hold her and then she slapped him in the face and punched him in the stomach: he grabbed her shoulders and pushed her back from him whereat (I use his words),

"She kicked me in the privates. Whether it was her knee or foot, I do not know. After that I do not know what happened till she fell".

She fell, because he had taken a knife from his pocket and stabbed her with it twice, the second blow inflicting a mortal injury. It was in these circumstances that the appellant pleaded that there had been such provocation by the deceased as to reduce the crime from murder to manslaughter, and the question is whether the learned judge rightly directed the jury on this issue. In my opinion, the summing-up of the learned judge was impeccable. Adapting the language used in this House in the cases of Mancini v. Public Prosecutions Director, [1941] 3 All E.R. 272; and Holmes v. Public Prosecutions Director, [1946] 2 All E.R. 124 . . ., he thus directed the jury:

"Provocation would arise if the conduct of the deceased woman, Mrs. Redding, to the prisoner was such as would cause a reasonable person, and actually caused the person to lose his self-control suddenly and to drive him into such a passion and lack of self-control that he might use violence of the degree and nature which the prisoner used here. The provocation must be such as would reasonably justify the violence used, the use of a knife", . . . and a little later he addressed them thus:

"The reasonable person, the ordinary person, is the person you must consider when you are considering the effect which any acts, any conduct, any words, might have to justify the steps which were taken in response thereto, so that an unusually excitable or pugnacious individual, or a drunken one or a man who is sexually impotent is not entitled to rely on provocation which would not have led an ordinary person to have acted in the way which was in fact carried out. There may be, members of the jury, infirmity of mind and instability of character, but if it does not amount to insanity, it is no defence. Likewise infirmity of body or affliction of the mind of the assailant is not material in testing whether there has been provocation by the deceased to justify the violence used so as to reduce the act of killing to manslaughter. They must be tested throughout this by the reactions of a reasonable man to the acts, or series of acts, done by the deceased woman". . . .

My Lords, . . . I am at a loss to know what other direction than that which he gave could properly have been given by the learned judge to the jury in this case. The argument, as I understood it, for the appellant was that the jury, in considering the reaction of the hypothetical reasonable man to the acts of provocation, must not only place him in the circumstances in which the accused was placed, but must also invest him with the personal physical peculiarities of the accused. Learned counsel, who argued the case for the appellant with great ability, did not, I think, venture to say that he should be invested with mental or temperamental qualities which distinguished him from the reasonable man: for this would have been directly in conflict with . . . the recent decision of the House in Mancini's case which I have cited. But he urged that the reasonable man should be invested with the peculiar physical qualities of the accused, as in the present case with the characteristic of impotence, and the question should be asked: what would be the reaction of the impotent reasonable man in the circumstances? For that proposition I know of no authority: nor can I see any reason in it. It would be plainly illogical not to recognise an unusually excitable or pugnacious temperament in the accused as a matter to be taken into account but yet to recognise for that purpose some unusual physical characteristic, be it impotence or another. Moreover, the proposed distinction appears to me to ignore the fundamental fact that the temper of a man which leads him to react in such and such a way to provocation is, or may be, itself conditioned by some physical defect. It is too subtle a refinement for my mind or, I think, for that of a jury to grasp that the temper may be ignored but the physical defect taken into account.

It was urged on your Lordships that the hypothetical reasonable man must be confronted with all the same circumstances as the accused, and that this could not be fairly done unless he was also invested with the peculiar characteristics of the accused. But this makes nonsense of the test. Its purpose is to invite the jury to consider the act of the accused by reference to a certain standard or norm of conduct and with this object the "reasonable" or the "average" or the "normal" man is invoked. If the reasonable man is then deprived in whole or in part of his reason, or the normal man endowed with abnormal characteristics, the test ceases to have any value. This is precisely the consideration which led this House in Mancini's case to say that an unusually excitable or pugnacious person is not entitled to rely on provocation which would not have led an ordinary person to act as he did. In my opinion, then, the Court of Criminal Appeal was right in approving the direction given to the jury by the learned judge and this appeal must fail.

NOTES

1. The Test of the Reasonable Man

(a) Compare the approach of the Lords in the above case with the comments regarding provocation contained in the 1953 Report of the Royal Commission on Capital Punishment, pp. 51–53:

"[The proposal has been put before us that], in considering whether there is provocation sufficient to reduce the crime to manslaughter, the sole test should be whether the accused was in fact deprived of self-control and that the jury should not be required to consider also whether a 'reasonable man' would have been so deprived. . . .

"[The suggestion is] prompted by the feeling that objective tests of provocation are unsatisfactory and inequitable, and that the question whether a crime is murder or manslaughter ought to depend only on whether the accused did in fact commit it in ungovernable passion caused by sudden provocation, of whatever kind. . . .

"[The argument suggesting] that this test of the 'reasonable man' should be abolished . . . was simple and direct. This test, it is said, is inequitable. . . . As Mr. Nield put it, 'the jury should be permitted to determine the effect of the provocation on this particular man whom they have seen and may have heard and whose circumstances have probably been described to them.'

"This proposal was strongly opposed by the Judges who gave evidence before us. . . . Lord Cooper observed that if the existing rule was changed, 'there might be circumstances in which a bad-tempered man would be acquitted and a good-tempered man would be hanged, which, of course, is neither law nor sense.'

"We recognize the force of the Judge's objections. . . . We think that this argument is in principle sound, at least so far as minor abnormalities of character are concerned. . . .

"Nevertheless we feel sympathy with the view which prompted the proposal that provocation should be judged by the standard of the accused. The objections of the Judges take no account of that fundamental difference between the law of murder and the law applicable to all other crimes. . . . In the case of the other crimes the court can and does take account of extenuating circumstances in assessing the sentence; in the case of murder alone the sentence is fixed and automatic. Provocation is in essence only an extenuating circumstance. . . . The rule of law that provocation may, within narrow bounds, reduce murder to manslaughter, represents an attempt by the courts to reconcile the preservation of the fixed penalty for murder with a limited concession to natural human weakness, but it suffers from the common defects of a compromise. . . .

"We have indeed no doubt that if the criterion of the 'reasonable man' was strictly applied by the courts and the sentence of death was carried out in cases where it was so applied, it would be too harsh in its operation. In practice, however, the courts not infrequently give weight to factors personal to the prisoner in considering a plea of provocation, and where there is a conviction of murder such factors are taken into account by the Home Secretary and may often lead to commutation of the sentence. The application of the test does not therefore lead to any eventual miscarriage of justice. At the same time, as we have seen, there are serious objections of principle to its abrogation. In these circumstances we do not feel justified in recommending any change in the existing law."

2. Provocation

In situations where a homicide is committed in the heat of passion brought on by provoking circumstances, several types of provocation have traditionally been recognized as legally sufficient to reduce the grade of the homicide from murder to voluntary manslaughter.

(a) *Assault and battery.* The law takes account of the possibility that an assault and battery may so provoke a "reasonable man" that he may lose his powers of reason and judgment and kill as a consequence. The states are not uniform, however, in their treatment of this type of provocation.

Some jurisdictions follow a flexible rule and regard assault alone as legally adequate provocation where the particular circumstances appear sufficient to excite the passions of a reasonable man. Other jurisdictions require an actual battery, as a matter of law, before sufficient provocation is deemed to exist.

(b) *Adultery.* Adultery amounts to sufficient provocation where a husband discovers his wife in the act of intercourse and kills either her or her paramour. Sheppard v. State, 243 Ala. 497, 10 So.2d 822 (1942). It has also been held that adequate provocation may exist where a mistake of fact leads to the homicide, the husband finding his wife in suspicious circumstances and having a reasonable belief that she has committed adultery. State v. Yanz, 74 Conn. 177, 50 A. 37 (1901).

In marked contrast to the common law, under which paramour killings are manslaughter at least, several states have statutes providing that such killings are justifiable. The following provision appears in the Texas Penal Code (Vernon's Ann.P.C. art. 1220):

> Homicide is justifiable when committed by the husband upon one taken in the act of adultery with the wife, provided the killing takes place before the parties to the act have separated. Such circumstances cannot justify a homicide when it appears that there has been on the part of the husband, any connivance in or assent to the adulterous connection.

As interpreted in Price v. State, 18 Tex.App. 474 (1885), the above statement "taken in the act of adultery" does not mean that the husband must be an actual eyewitness to the physical act. "It is sufficient if he sees them in bed together, or leaving that position, or in such a position as indicates with reasonable certainty to a rational mind that they have just then committed the adulterous act, or were then about to commit it."

Although a husband in Texas is justified in killing his wife's paramour, there is no privilege to use a razor merely to maim and torture. Sensobaugh v. State, 92 Tex.Cr.R. 417, 244 S.W. 379 (1922).

Similar statutes are also in effect in New Mexico and Utah. See New Mexico Statutes, 1953 Comp. §§ 41–2411–41–2416, and the Utah Code Annotated 1953, 76–30–10(4). A like result has also been achieved in Georgia by judicial decision. See Gibson v. State, 44 Ga.App. 264, 161 S.E. 158 (1931), and cases cited therein. In Delaware, the punishment for manslaughter of a paramour found in the act of adultery with the defendant's wife is a fine of between $100 and $1,000 and imprisonment for not more than one year. 11 Del.Code § 575(b). Where the wife is the victim the punishment is a fine of up to $10,000, or imprisonment up to thirty years, or both. Ibid., § 575(a).

For a discussion of the so-called "unwritten law" by which jury acquittals are often achieved in paramour killing cases under color of self-defense, see Inbau, Scientific Reasoning and Jury Verdicts, 16 Postgraduate Medicine, No. 4 (1954). The frequently successful use of the defense of insanity in such cases is described in 19 Neb.Law Bull. 146 (1940).

(c) *Trespass.* By one view, trespass constitutes legally sufficient provocation for a homicide committed in the heat of passion. Under another view, however, trespass is regarded as too minor an incident to qualify as legal incitement.

(d) *Acts against third persons.* It is generally held that certain acts such as murder, rape, etc. committed by one against a close relative of the slayer constitute sufficient provocation.

(e) *Words and gestures.* Strongly entrenched in the United States is the almost uniform rule that words or gestures, alone, are never sufficient provocation for an intentional homicide.

Informational language, as opposed to words which in themselves constitute the incitement, may qualify as adequate provocation where the fact communicated would be sufficient, and where the slayer has not previously known of the matter revealed.

Contemporary appraisal of the law concerning words as provocation indicates dissatisfaction with the inflexibility of a rule which fails to grant legal recognition to the inciting character of language which may be regarded as highly provoking by the general community.

3. Cooling of Blood

(a) Consider the following comments of the court in In re Fraley, 3 Okl.Cr. 719, 109 P. 295 (1910), and compare them with the statements of the court on this subject in the preceeding main case of State v. Flory.

"[I]t was stated by counsel for the petitioner . . . that the deceased, some nine or ten months previously, had shot and killed the son of the petitioner . . . and it is urged here that when the petitioner saw the deceased . . . the recollection of that event must have engendered in him a passion which overcame him; that the killing was committed in the heat of such passion, was without premeditation, and therefore was not murder. To this we cannot assent. . . . In Ragland v. State . . ., four hours intervening between the provocation and the killing was held as a matter of law to be sufficient cooling time to preclude the reduction of a homicide to manslaughter. Perry v. State . . . and Rockmore v. State . . . each hold three days as a matter of law sufficient cooling time. Commonwealth v. Aiello . . . holds from one to two hours sufficient, and State v. Williams . . . holds fifteen minutes sufficient. And the authorities are all agreed that the question is not alone whether the defendant's passion in fact cooled, but also was there sufficient time in which the passion of a reasonable man would cool. If in fact the defendant's passion did cool, which may be shown by circumstances, such as the transaction of other business in the meantime, rational conversations upon other subjects, evidence of preparation for the killing, etc., then the length of time intervening is immaterial. But if in fact it did not cool, yet if such time intervened between the provocation and the killing that the passion of the average man would have cooled and his reason have resumed its sway, then still there is not reduction of the homicide to manslaughter. . . . If the fatal wound be inflicted immediately following a sufficient provocation given, then the question as to whether the defendant's passion thereby aroused had in fact cooled, or as to whether or not such time had elapsed that the passion of a reasonable man would have cooled, is a question of fact to be determined upon a consideration of all the facts and circumstances in evidence; but when an unreasonable period of time has elapsed between the provocation and the killing, then the court is authorized to say as a matter of law that the cooling time was sufficient."

(b) With regard to the application of the "reasonable man" test in this area, compare the following statement of the court in State v. Hazlett, 16 N.D. 426, 113 N.W. 374 (1907):

"Where the evidence shows that a homicide was committed, in the heat of passion and with provocation, we think the jury, in determining whether there was sufficient cooling time for the passion to subside and reason to resume its sway, should be governed, not by the standard of an ideal, reasonable man, but they should determine such question from the standpoint of the defendant in the light of all the facts and circumstances disclosed by the evidence. . . . We are aware that some courts have held to the contrary, but we are convinced that the rule as above announced is the more reasonable and just one."

Justifiable Use of Force

1. Self Defense

The use of force to defend one's self is an undisputed right. It is only with respect to the manner in which he does it, or the circumstances under which it occurs, that there are differences and uncertainties in the law. For instance, when a person who is free from fault is faced with a threat of great bodily danger, may he stand his ground and kill his assailant, or is he under an obligation to retreat?

The American Law Institute, in its Model Penal Code provides (in § 3.04 of its Tentative Draft No. 8) that:

> The use of deadly force is not justifiable . . . if the actor knows . . . that he can avoid the necessity of using such force with complete safety by retreating or by surrendering possession of a thing to a person asserting a claim of right thereto or by complying with a demand that he abstain from any action which he has no duty to take, except that:
>
> (1) the actor is not obliged to retreat from his dwelling or place of work, unless he was the initial aggressor . . .

In adopting the "retreat to the wall" doctrine the drafters of the code, in their commentary, offer the following justification (ibid p. 23):

"There is a sense in which a duty to retreat may be regarded as a logical derivative of the underlying justifying principle of self-defense, belief in the necessity of the protective action; the actor who knows he can retreat with safety also knows that the necessity can be avoided in that way. The logic of this position never has been accepted when moderate force is used in self-defense; here all agree that the actor may stand his ground and estimate necessity upon that basis. When the resort is to deadly force, however, Beale argued that the common law was otherwise, that the law of homicide demanded that the estimation of necessity take account of the possibility of safe retreat. . . . Perkins has challenged this conclusion in the case of actors free from fault in bringing on the struggle, urging that it was only true with respect to aggressors or cases of mutual combat. . . . American jurisdictions have divided on the question, no less in crime than tort, with the preponderant position favoring the right to stand one's ground. . . . In a famous opinion Justice Holmes advanced what seems to be a median position: 'Rationally the failure to retreat is a circumstance to be considered with all the others in order to determine whether the defendant went farther than he was justified in doing; not a categorical proof of guilt.' . . . This would apparently remit the issue to the jury, without a legal mandate on the point. . . .

"The Institute has deemed considerations of this kind decisive with respect to torts and it is clear that they apply with equal force to penal law."

The majority of states, however, permit one to stand his own ground and meet force with force, as long as the defender is not the original aggressor. (LaFave & Scott, Criminal Law, 1972, at 395.)

2. Defense of Others

The law recognizes the right of a person to kill in defense of not only his own life but also that of another. Two doctrines bear upon this privilege to defend others: (1) the rule that one may defend a close relative, and (2) the rule that one may take life if necessary to prevent a dangerous or forcible felony. In application to specific situations, these principles are frequently cumulative. Thus, if one kills the assailant of a near relative, he may invoke his specific right to defend a member of his family, as well as his general privilege to interfere to prevent a felonious assault.

Cases involving defense of a party who, at the time of the killing, was engaged in an affray brought on by his own misconduct have resulted in disagreement among the courts as to whether the "assistant" must "stand in the shoes" of the wrongdoer, or instead be judged according to the reasonableness of his own conduct in interfering to protect one whose life seemed to be unlawfully endangered.

It is a matter of speculation as to which view is the more socially tolerable. In other words, will a person who sees a close relative in great and immediate danger pause to determine whether the relative was himself free from fault?

3. Prevention of a Felony

The right to take life to prevent the commission of a felony is confined to the prevention of a *dangerous* felony. A corollary of this principle is the rule that homicide is not justifiable when committed for the protection of mere property rights or interests, although the punishment for such killings is usually of the manslaughter grade rather than murder.

4. Defense of Habitation

Defense of the habitation against a dangerous intruder is a right which stems from the law's early view that a man's home is his "fortress" or "castle." This privilege permits one to take the life of an intending trespasser, if the dweller reasonably believes that the threatened entry is for the purpose of committing a felony or inflicting great bodily harm upon an occupant of the house. The rule is even broader in some jurisdictions, allowing the occupant to prevent an intrusion the apparent purpose of which is an assault or other violence non-felonious in nature. The right to defend the habitation permits one to use non-deadly force to prevent a mere civil trespass, although it does not countenance the use of deadly force for that purpose. Where deadly force is inflicted upon a trespasser, however, aggravating circumstances of the trespass may constitute such provocation as to make the killing manslaughter, rather than murder.

The rule allows defense of the habitation by guests or servants of the household, where the occupant himself would be justified in making a defense. It has also been held to encompass the protection of one's place of business, in addition to his dwelling.

One is not bound to retreat from his own house, even if he may do so with safety, in order to avoid taking the life of an assailant. He may stand his ground and kill the aggressor if it becomes necessary.

The use of spring guns or traps for the protection of property or dwellings, resulting in the death of an intruder, may expose the owner of the property to liability for homicide, although some cases have suggested that where the landowner would have been entitled to use similar force if he had been present, the use of the device was lawful.

5. Defense of Property Other Than Dwelling

Ordinarily, deadly force cannot be used to protect property or to preserve a lawful right of possession. Use of such force, to be justified, must be sanctioned under a different principle, such as that of self defense, defense of dwelling, or preventing a felony.

[Case citations in support of the foregoing report on the "Justifiable Use of Force" may be found in Cases and Comments on Criminal Law, by Inbau, Thompson, and Moenssens (1973), 489–494.]

SECTION 2. INVOLUNTARY MANSLAUGHTER

COMMONWEALTH v. FEINBERG

Superior Court of Pennsylvania, 1967.
211 Pa.Super. 100, 234 A.2d 913.
Aff'd 433 Pa. 558, 253 A.2d 636.

MONTGOMERY, JUDGE. These appeals are from judgments of sentence imposed following appellant's conviction on five charges of involuntary manslaughter. They arose by reason of the deaths of five individuals from methyl alcohol (methanol) poisoning due to their consumption of Sterno, a jelly-like substance prepared and intended for heating purposes. It is solidified alcohol popularly called "canned heat" but has additives specified by the United States government to render it unfit for drinking purposes.

Appellant Max Feinberg was the owner of a cigar store handling tobacco, candy, etc., in the skid-row section of Philadelphia and sold to residents of that area Sterno in two types of containers, one for home use and one for institutional use. Such sales were made under circumstances from which it could be reasonably concluded that appellant knew the purchasers were intending to use it for drinking purposes by diluting it with water or other beverages, and not for its intended use. Prior to December, 1963, there had been no known fatal consequences resulting from this practice, presumably for the reason that the product then sold by appellant contained only four per cent methyl alcohol (methanol). However, on December 21, 1963 appellant bought from the Richter Paper Company ten additional cases of institutional Sterno containing seventy-two cans each, unaware that it contained fifty-four per cent methanol, although the lid of each container was marked "Institutional Sterno. Danger. Poison; Not for home use. For commercial and industrial use only", and had a skull and crossbones imprinted thereon. Nevertheless appellant ignored this warning and sold part of this supply in the same manner he had previously dispensed his other supply of the product. The containers of the regular Sterno and the institutional type previously sold contained no such warning and were merely marked "Caution. Flammable. For use only as a fuel." The only difference in the containers previously sold was that the institutional type was so marked but had no wrap-around label as was affixed to the container intended for regular use. Both containers were the same size, as were the containers sold after December 21st which did not contain wrap-around labels. Between December 23 and December 30, 1963, thirty-one persons died in this area as a result of methyl alcohol poisoning. After hearing of their deaths, appellant, on December 28, 1963 returned to the Richter Paper Company four cases and forty-two cans which remained unsold from the ten cases he had purchased on December 21, 1963, at which time he remarked about the change in markings on the cans. Appellant was the only purchaser in the Philadelphia area of this new institutional product from the Richter Company. The methanol content of institutional Sterno had been increased by the manufacturer from four per cent to fifty-four per cent in September, 1963 but the new product was not marketed until December, 1963. Richter received the first shipment of it on December 11, and another on December 17, 1963. The chemical contents of the new institutional product were not stated on the container; nor was the appellant informed otherwise of any change in the contents of that product except by the notice of its dangerous contents for home use, as previously recited.

It is the contention of the appellant that his convictions on the charges of involuntary manslaughter cannot be sustained . . . as a result of any criminal negligence on his part. * * *

There remains the question of whether the Commonwealth has established that the deaths under consideration were due to the criminal negligence of the appellant. Involuntary manslaughter consists of the killing of another person without malice and unintentionally, but in doing some unlawful act not amounting to a felony, or in doing some lawful act in an unlawful way. Where the act in itself is not unlawful, to make it criminal the negligence must be of such a departure from prudent conduct as to evidence a disregard of human life or an indifference to consequences. . . .

We are satisfied that the record clearly establishes that appellant, in the operation of his small store with part-time help, knew that he was selling Sterno in substantial quantities to a clientele that was misusing it; that in order to profit more from such sales he induced Richter Paper Company to procure for him a supply of the institutional product because the cost of same was less than the regular type with labels; that he was aware of the "poison" notice and warning of harmful effects of the new shipment received on December 21, 1963 but nevertheless placed it in stock for general sale by himself and his employees; and thereafter sold several hundred cans of it; and that he dispensed it without warning his purchasers of the harmful effect it would have if misused for drinking purposes, and without directing their attention to the warning on the containers.

If the deaths of these five persons were the result of appellant's actions, it justifies his conviction for involuntary manslaughter. Although a more culpable degree of negligence is required to establish a criminal homicide than is required in a civil action for damages, we find the appellant's actions as fully meeting the definition and requirement of proof set forth in Commonwealth v. Aurick, 342 Pa. 282, 19 A.2d 920 (1941). In the light of the recognized weaknesses of the purchasers of the product, and appellant's greater concern for profit than with the results of his actions, he was grossly negligent and demonstrated a wanton and reckless disregard for the welfare of those whom he might reasonably have expected to use the product for drinking purposes. * * *

We find no merit in appellant's argument that there is no evidence to prove he ever sold a can of the new institutional Sterno. The evidence clearly shows that he was in full charge of the operation of the store when the bulk of the new product was sold. Harold was only a part-time employe coming in after school and on Saturdays, and during this period appellant's wife and family were in Florida, which left appellant as the one who made the bulk of the sales.

Nor do we find any merit in his argument that he was unaware of the warning on the cans. He must have handled many of them during the course of events when almost four hundred cans were sold. The circumstances established by the evidence sufficiently supports a finding that he did know of the change in markings but disregarded it. As far as instructing anyone else to sell the product, the fact that it was available for sale in an opened carton under the counter is sufficient to indicate an implied authorization.

The facts in this case do not indicate the prosecution of a person for acts done by another without his knowledge or consent. Appellant was the active participant with full knowledge. He, personally, and through his part-time employe, acting under his orders, committed the crimes. . . .

The judgments of sentence, therefore, are affirmed in the cases of Lynwood Scott; John Streich; James Newsome; and Juanita Williams; and the judgment is reversed and appellant discharged in the case of Edward Harrell.

HOFFMAN, J., files a dissenting opinion.

* * *

PEOPLE v. MARSHALL

Supreme Court of Michigan, 1961.
362 Mich. 170, 106 N.W.2d 842.

SMITH, JUSTICE. At approximately 3:00 a. m. on the morning of February 4, 1958, a car driven by Neal McClary, traveling in the wrong direction on the Edsel Ford Expressway, crashed head-on into another vehicle driven by James Coldiron. The drivers of both cars were killed. Defendant William Marshall has been found guilty of involuntary manslaughter of Coldiron. At the time that the fatal accident took place, he, the defendant William Marshall, was in bed at his place of residence. His connection with it was that he owned the car driven by McClary, and as the evidence tended to prove, he voluntarily gave his keys to the car to McClary, with knowledge that McClary was drunk.

The principal issue in the case is whether, upon these facts, the defendant may be found guilty of involuntary manslaughter. It is axiomatic that "criminal guilt under our law is personal fault." . . . As Sayre . . . puts the doctrine "it is of the very essence of our deep-rooted notions of criminal liability that guilt be personal and individual." This was not always true in our law, nor is it universally true in all countries even today, but for us it is settled doctrine.

The State relies on a case, Story v. United States, . . . in which the owner, driving with a drunk, permitted him to take the wheel, and was held liable for aiding and abetting him "in his criminal negligence." The owner, said the court, sat by his side and permitted him "without protest so recklessly and negligently to operate the car as to cause the death of another." . . . If defendant Marshall had been by McClary's side an entirely different case would be presented, but on the facts before us Marshall, as we noted, was at home in bed. The State also points out that although it is only a misdemeanor to drive while drunk, yet convictions for manslaughter arising out of drunk driving have often been sustained. It argues from these cases that although it was only a misdemeanor for an owner to turn his keys over to a drunk driver, nevertheless a conviction for manslaughter may be sustained if such driver kills another. This does not follow from such cases as Story, supra. In the case before us death resulted from the misconduct of driver. The accountability of the owner must rest as a matter of general principle, upon his complicity in such misconduct. In turning his keys over, he was guilty of a specific offense, for which he incurred a specific penalty. Upon these facts he cannot be held a principal with respect to the fatal accident: the killing of Coldiron was not counselled by him, accomplished by another acting jointly with him, nor did it occur in the attempted achievement of some common enterprise.

This is not to say that defendant is guilty of nothing. He was properly found guilty of violation of paragraph (b) of section 625 of the Michigan vehicle code which makes it punishable for the owner of an automobile knowingly to permit it to be driven by a person "who is under the influence of intoxicating liquor." The State urges that this is not enough, that its manslaughter theory, above outlined, "was born of necessity," and that the urgency of the drunk-driver problem "has made it incumbent upon responsible and concerned law enforcement officials to seek new approaches to a new problem within the limits of our law." What the State actually seeks from us is an interpretation that the manslaughter statute imposes an open-end criminal liability. That is to say, whether the owner may ultimately go to prison for manslaughter or some lesser offense will depend upon whatever unlawful act the driver commits while in the car. Such a theory may be defensible as a matter of civil liability but [in his American Rights, 85, 86] Gellhorn's language in another criminal context is equally applicable here: "It is a basic proposition in a constitutional society that crimes should be defined in advance, and not after action has been taken." We are not unaware of the magnitude of the problem presented, but the new approaches demanded for its solution rest with the legislature, not the courts.

The view we have taken of the case renders it unnecessary to pass upon other allegations of error. The verdict and sentence on that count of the information dealing with involuntary manslaughter are set aside and the case remanded to the circuit court for sentencing on the verdict of the jury respecting the violation, as charged, of section 625(b) of the Michigan Vehicle Code, discussed hereinabove.

NOTES

1. Many states have enacted "Negligent Homicide" or "Reckless Homicide" statutes. An Oregon statute, though repealed in 1971, provided that death caused by the driving of a motor vehicle in a "negligent manner" constitutes "negligent homicide", and "negligent" is defined as "a want of such attention to the natural or probable consequences of the act or omission referred to as a prudent man ordinarily bestows in acting in his own concerns." In State v. Wohahn, 204 Or. 84, 282 P.2d 675 (1955), the Supreme Court of Oregon upheld the constitutionality of this statute against the contention that it was vague, indefinite and a violation of due process. In discussing the purpose of this type of legislation, the court said: "Negligent homicide statutes were adopted after the manslaughter acts had proved ineffective as a means of repressing the negligence in motor vehicle operation which was causing deaths upon the public thoroughfares. Possibly the success of the new legislation, if it in truth achieved any, resulted from the fact that in common understanding manslaughter acts deal with brutal killings by a debased type of individual, whereas the motorist is generally a reputable citizen, and the wrong committed by him which brought someone to his death finds its counterpart in the driving of many others."

2. Suppose two motorists are involved in a "drag race", during which one of them is killed. Is the competitor guilty of involuntary manslaughter? What about a participant in a game of "Russian Roulette"?

In Commonwealth v. Atencio, 345 Mass. 627, 189 N.E.2d 223 (1963), a "Russian Roulette" survivor's conviction of involuntary manslaughter was sustained. The court distinguished that conduct from a "drag race" situation on the ground that there was "skill" involved in the latter, whereas "Russian Roulette" involves only a matter of chance, with a high likelihood of someone being killed.

Perhaps the simplest solution to the "drag race" problem is the effective enforcement of legislation outlawing it and providing much higher penalties than ordinary speeding or reckless driving.

Chapter 5

SEX OFFENSES AND RELATED PROBLEMS

A. RAPE

COMMONWEALTH v. BURKE

Supreme Judicial Court of Massachusetts, 1870.
105 Mass. 376.

GRAY, J. The defendant has been indicted and convicted for aiding and assisting Dennis Green in committing a rape upon Joanna Caton. The single exception taken at the trial was to the refusal of the presiding judge to rule that the evidence introduced was not sufficient to warrant a verdict of guilty. The instructions given were not objected to, and are not reported in the bill of exceptions. The only question before us therefore is, whether, under any instructions applicable to the case, the evidence would support a conviction.

That evidence, which it is unnecessary to state in detail, was sufficient to authorize the jury to find that Green, with the aid and assistance of this defendant, had carnal intercourse with Mrs. Caton, without her previous assent, and while she was, as Green and the defendant both knew, so drunk as to be utterly senseless and incapable of consenting, and with such force as was necessary to effect the purpose.

All the statutes of England and of Massachusetts, and all the text books of authority, which have undertaken to define the crime of rape, have defined it as the having carnal knowledge of a woman by force and against her will. The crime consists in the enforcement of a woman without her consent. The simple question, expressed in the briefest form, is, Was the woman willing or unwilling? The earlier and more weighty authorities show that the words "against her will," in the standard definitions, mean exactly the same thing as "without her consent;" and that the distinction between these phrases, as applied to this crime, which has been suggested in some modern books, is unfounded.

The most ancient statute upon the subject is that of Westm. I. c. 13, making rape (which had been a felony at common law) a misdemeanor, and declaring that no man should "ravish a maiden within age, neither by her own consent, nor without her consent, nor a wife or maiden of full age, nor other woman against her will," on penalty of fine and imprisonment, either at the suit of a party or of the king. The St. of Westm. II, c. 34, ten years later, made rape felony again, and provided that if a man should "ravish a woman, married, maiden, or other woman, where she did not consent, neither before nor after," he should be punished with death, at the appeal of the party; "and likewise, where a man ravisheth a woman, married lady, maiden, or other woman, with force, although she consent afterwards," he should have a similar sentence upon prosecution in behalf of the king.

It is manifest upon the face of the Statutes of Westminster, and is recognized in the oldest commentaries and cases, that the words "without her consent" and "against her will" were used synonymously; and that the second of those statutes was intended to change the punishment only, and not the definition of the crime, upon any indictment for rape—leaving the words "against her will," as used in the first statute, an accurate part of the description. . . .

Coke treats the two phrases as equivalent; for he says: "Rape is felony by the common law declared by parliament, for the unlawful and carnal knowledge and abuse of any woman above the age of ten years against her will, or of a woman child under the age of ten years with her will or against her will;" although in the latter case the words of the St. of Westm. I. (as we have already seen) were "neither by her own consent, nor without her consent." 3 Inst. 60. Coke elsewhere repeatedly defines rape as "the carnal knowledge of a woman by force and against her will." Co.Lit. 123 b. 2 Inst. 180. A similar definition is given by Hale, Hawkins, Comyn, Blackstone, East and Starkie, who wrote while the Statutes of Westminster were in force; as well as by the text writers of most reputation since the St. of 9 Geo. IV, c. 31, repealed the earlier statutes, and assuming the definition of the crime to be well established, provided simply that "every person convicted of the crime of rape shall suffer death as a felon." . . . There is authority for holding that it is not even necessary that an indictment, which alleges that the defendant "feloniously did ravish and carnally know" a woman, should add the words "against her will." . . . However, that may be, the office of those words, if inserted, is simply to negative the woman's previous consent. Stark.Crim.Pl. 431 note.

In the leading modern English case of The Queen v. Camplin, the great majority of the English judges held that a man who gave intoxicating liquor to a girl of thirteen, for the purpose, as the jury found, "of exciting her, not with the intention of rendering her insensible, and then having sexual connection with her," and made her quite drunk, and, while she was in a state of insensibility, took advantage of it, and ravished her, was guilty of rape. It appears indeed by the judgment delivered by Patteson, J., in passing sentence, as reported in 1 Cox Crim.Cas. 220, and 1 C. & K. 746, as well by the contemporaneous notes of Parke, B., printed in a note to 1 Denison, 92, and of Alderson, B., as read by him in The Queen v. Page, 2 Cox Crim.Cas.

133, that the decision was influenced by its having been proved at the trial that, before the girl became insensible the man had attempted to procure her consent, and had failed. But it further appears by those notes that Lord Denman, C. J., Parke, B., and Patteson, J., thought that the violation of any woman without her consent, while she was in a state of insensibility and had no power over her will, by a man knowing at the time that she was in that state, was a rape, whether such state was caused by him or not; for example, as Alderson, B., adds, "in the case of a woman insensibly drunk in the streets, not made so by the prisoner." And in the course of the argument this able judge himself said that it might be considered against the general presumable will of a woman that a man should have unlawful connection with her. The later decisions have established the rule in England that unlawful and forcible connection with a woman in a state of unconsciousness at the time, whether that state has been produced by the act of the prisoner or not, is presumed to be without her consent, and is rape. . . .

The earliest statute of Massachusetts upon the subject was passed in 1642, and, like the English Statutes of Westminster, used "without consent" as synonymous with "against her will," as is apparent upon reading its provisions, which were as follows: 1st. "If any man shall unlawfully have carnal copulation with any woman child under ten years old, he shall be put to death, whether it were with or without the girl's consent." 2d. "If any man shall forcibly and without consent ravish any maid or woman that is lawfully married or contracted, he shall be put to death." 3d. "If any man shall ravish any maid or single woman, committing carnal copulation with her by force, against her will, that is above the age of ten years, he shall be either punished with death, or with some other grievous punishment, according to circumstances, at the discretion of the judges." 2 Mass.Col.Rec. 21. Without dwelling upon the language of the first of these provisions, which related to the abuse of female children, it is manifest that in the second and third, both of which related to the crime of rape, strictly so called, and differed only in the degree of punishment, depending upon the question whether the woman was or was not married or engaged to be married, the legislature used the words "without consent," in the second provision, as precisely equivalent to "against her will," in the third. The later revisions of the statute have abolished the difference in punishment, and therefore omitted the second provision, and thus made the definition of rape in all cases the ravishing and carnally knowing a woman "by force and against her will." . . . But they cannot, upon any proper rule of construction of a series of statutes in pari materia, be taken to have changed the description of the offence.

We are therefore unanimously of opinion that the crime, which the evidence in this case tended to prove, of a man's having carnal intercourse with a woman, without her consent, while she was, as he knew, wholly insensible so as to be incapable of consenting, and with such force as was necessary to accomplish the purpose, was rape. If it were otherwise, any woman in a state of utter stupefaction, whether caused by drunkenness, sudden disease, the blow of a third person, or drugs which she had been persuaded to take even by the defendant himself, would be unprotected from personal dishonor. The law is not open to such a reproach.

NOTES

1. The present day statutory law adopts the view of the present case. See McKinney's N.Y.Penal Law, §§ 130.20–130.35, and also the Illinois Criminal Code (S.H.A. ch. 38) § 11–1, which reads as follows:

> (a) A male person of the age of 14 years and upwards who has sexual intercourse with a female, not his wife, by force and against her will, commits rape. Intercourse by force and against her will includes, but is not limited to, any intercourse which occurs in the following situations:
>
> (1) Where the female is unconscious; or
>
> (2) Where the female is so mentally deranged or deficient that she cannot give effective consent to intercourse.
>
> (b) Sexual intercourse in rape occurs when there is any penetration of the female sex organ by the male sex organ.
>
> (c) Penalty. A person convicted of rape shall be imprisoned in the penitentiary for an indeterminate term with a minimum of not less than one year.

The codes of these two states also remove another early ambiguity by providing, as does New York (McKinney's Penal Code § 130.00) that "any sexual penetration, however slight, is sufficient to complete the crime."

It is, however, not necessary that emission occur, though some states have indicated that lack of emission may be a strong circumstance indicating lack of penetration. Coles v. Peyton, 389 F.2d 224 (4th Cir. 1968), decided under Virginia law.

2. Some states, by statute, have attempted (as does Wisconsin, in W.S.A. 944.01 of its Criminal Code) to define "force and against her will" to mean "either that her utmost resistance is overcome and prevented by physical violence or that her will to resist is overcome by threats of imminent physical violence likely to cause great bodily harm."

Consent is deemed vitiated, then, by fraud or imposition. See 70 ALR2d 824. So will the intercourse with a mentally deficient woman be deemed to be without her consent. 31 ALR3d 1227.

3. While non-chastity of the victim is not a defense—even a prostitute can be raped—evidence of the character of the woman as to unchastity is generally admissible on the issue of whether she consented or not. Where the defense is consent, it has been held that the prosecution may introduce evidence that the victim was a virgin prior to the alleged rape, as a circumstance to be considered on the improbability of consent. State v. Aveen, 284 Minn. 194, 169 N.W.2d 749 (1969).

In order to be guilty of rape, the offender must be at least 14 years of age. This early common law concept, still retained in most jurisdictions, is not based on considerations of physical capacity, but rather on a belief that sexual intercourse by one below that age should not be punished as rape. Accordingly, in Foster v. Commonwealth, 96 Va. 306, 31 S.E. 503 (1898), it was held that a boy under 14 years of age is conclusively presumed to be incapable of committing the crime of rape, or of attempting to commit it, whatever may be the real facts. Therefore, evidence to rebut the presumption is inadmissible. (However, the court added that where the boy assists another in an attempted rape, he may be convicted as a principal in the second degree, and punished the same as the principal in the first degree.)

4. The principal case deals with "forcible rape", as distinguished from "statutory rape"—an offense based solely upon the age of the female and without reference to force, consent or chastity. The usual age below which the act is rape is 16.

STATE v. WHEELER

Supreme Judicial Court of Maine, 1954.
150 Me. 332, 110 A.2d 578.

TAPLEY, JUSTICE. . . . The respondent was indicted for the crime of rape. The case was tried at the October Term, 1953, of the Superior Court for the County of Sagadahoc and State of Maine before a jury. Jury found respondent guilty. Respondent excepted to rulings as to the admissibility of evidence and to the refusal of the presiding Justice to direct a verdict of not guilty at the conclusion of the testimony.

The indictment charged the respondent with rape of a female of the age of sixteen years. The act was alleged to have occurred on September 28, 1953 at Bowdoinham, Maine. The prosecutrix resided in the Town of South Freeport, Maine and on the twenty-seventh day of September, 1953, she went to the Town of Richmond where she was accustomed to spending considerable time. There is much testimony in the record relating to her activities with three boys with whom she was acquainted. It appears that during the evening of September 27th she went to ride with these boys for a distance of one or two miles from Richmond and that during this ride she was submitted to physical violence by being slapped on the face and having her arm twisted in an attempt to remove a portion of her clothing; that she was forcibly ejected from the car and later made her way back to Richmond; that following her return to Richmond she was again approached by the same boys, caused to re-enter the car and then taken to a point outside of Richmond where the car was stopped and an attempt made by one of them to rape her. During this attempt, a car passing the parked car of the boys was stopped by one of them. This car was operated by the respondent. The prosecutrix was transferred from the boys' car to that of the respondent. He drove some distance, stopped his automobile on a side road and there committed the act complained of, for which he was indicted, tried and found guilty.

The State must prove beyond a reasonable doubt that the respondent carnally knew the prosecutrix by force, without her consent or against her will. . . . The element of force and the act against her will are inconsistent with consent. It is obvious, of course, if the prosecutrix willingly consented to the act, there would be no rape.

During the course of the trial the State presented a witness in the person of one Donald Shields, a boy of sixteen years of age, who testified in direct examination that he was a passenger in the back seat of the respondent's car and was present at the time of the alleged rape. The substance of his testimony was that no act of intercourse occurred between the respondent and the prosecutrix. After completion of his direct testimony there was no cross-examination by the defense. Later he was called to the stand by the State and at that time testified that his testimony in direct was false and that he so testified because he was requested and urged to do so by the respondent.

The State's case was predicated on the testimony of the prosecutrix with very little, if any, corroboration. There is no statute in Maine requiring corroboration on the part of the prosecutrix in cases of this nature and it is well settled that a verdict based on the uncorroborated testimony of a complainant will not be disturbed on the mere fact of lack of corroboration. State v. Newcomb, 146 Me. 173, at page 181, 78 A.2d 787. Corroboration, if there is corroboration, must come from sources other than the prosecutrix. Although corroboration is not necessary, it is well for the purpose of this case to analyze the record to determine what corroboration, if any, there is present. The cases hold that where corroboration to any reasonable degree is lacking, it becomes necessary to scrutinize and analyze the testimony of the prosecutrix with great care. Her testimony as to the acts complained of must be such they would be within the realms of probability and credibility.

75 C.J.S. Rape, § 78, page 560:

> "At common law, and in the absence of a statute requiring corroboration, it is generally held that the unsupported testimony of the prosecutrix, if not contradictory *or incredible, or inherently improbable,* if believed by the jury, is sufficient to sustain a conviction of rape . . . ." (Italics ours.)

The prosecutrix testified that soon after the alleged act occurred she complained to her mother. The mother did not appear as a witness in corroboration of the complainant. There was medical testimony resulting from the examination of the girl but this did not disclose in any way that she had been raped by the defendant.

There is evidence that the complainant suffered some injury to her jaw and she complained of a soreness in the vicinity of her ribs. This condition, according to her own testimony, resulted from the violent physical treatment that she received from the three boys.

This fact is further established by the testimony of the boys. The prosecutrix furnishes the only testimony of the actual act of rape.

The testimony of the prosecutrix is of such sordid nature that a detailed account will serve no good purpose. It is suffice to say that the prosecutrix' narration of the rape is inherently improbable and incredible and does not meet the test of common sense. . . .

Reversed.

NOTES

1. For another application of the "implausibility" rule enunciated in the principal case, see Penn v. State, 237 Ind. 374, 146 N.E.2d 240 (1957), in which the defendant was prosecuted for the statutory rape of a "baby sitter," aged 16, who testified that she became pregnant as a result of intercourse with the defendant, Penn. She testified that "when Mr. and Mrs. Penn would return from the evening out, [Penn] would usually go to bed, but that prosecutrix and Mrs. Penn would usually stay up late—popping corn, talking and watching television. They were friends. That, on prior occasions, prosecutrix slept on the davenport in the living room, but that beginning in October she slept in [Penn's] bed with Penn and his wife. Prosecutrix testified that on these occasions the accused would there have intercourse first with one and then the other, with knowledge of both. . . . Both Penn and his wife flatly denied the entire story of any sexual relations between prosecutrix and appellant." In reversing the defendant's conviction, the Supreme Court of Indiana said:

"Ordinarily reasonable men know that a wife will not knowingly and willingly share the sex life of her husband. Experience teaches that where another woman enters the sex life of her husband a wife does not remain on good terms with the other woman. She does not thereafter invite the other woman to her home to visit, pop corn, and watch television. Especially, she will not share her husband and aid and abet the act by inviting the other woman to her home and accompanying her to the bed of her husband. . . . We conclude therefore that in this case the uncorroborated testimony of the prosecutrix was so improbable and incredible that no reasonable man could say that the appellant's guilt had been proved beyond a reasonable doubt." [1]

1. As another example of a member of an appellate court drawing on human experience in order to deal with cases in this area, consider the majority opinion of Pearson, C. J., in State v. Neely, 74 N.C. 425 (1876), where the defendant was convicted of assault with intent to commit rape:

"A majority of the Court are of the opinion that there was evidence to be left to the jury as to the intent charged. For my own part, I think the evidence plenary, and had I been on the jury would not have hesitated one moment.

"I see a chicken-cock drop his wings and take after a hen; my experience and observation assure me that his purpose is sexual intercourse; no other evidence is needed.

"Whether the cock supposes that the hen is running by female instinct to increase the estimate of her favor and excite passion, or whether the cock intends to carry his purpose by force and against her will, is a question about which there may be some doubt: as for instance, if she is a setting hen and 'makes flight', not merely amorous resistance. There may be evidence from experience and observation of the nature of the animals and of male and female instincts fit to be left to the jury, upon all of the circumstances and surroundings of the case, was the pursuit made with the expectation that he would be gratified voluntarily, or was it made with the intent to have his will against her will and by force? Upon

In People v. Taylor, 48 Ill.2d 91, 268 N.E.2d 865 (1971), a conviction was reversed where the record showed that the complaining witness had testified that as she was getting out of the defendant's car, where the alleged forcible rape occurred, she kissed him goodbye.

2. British and American courts have frequently quoted with approval in sex offense cases the ancient admonition of Sir Matthew Hale that ". . . it is an accusation easily made and hard to be proved, and harder to be depended by the party accused, though ever so innocent; . . ." It is necessary, Hale continued, to "be the more cautious upon trials of offenses of this nature wherein the court and jury may with so much ease be imposed upon without great care and vigilance; the heinousness of the offense many times transporting the judge and jury with so much indignation that they are over hastily carried to the conviction of the person accused thereof by the confident testimony, sometimes of malicious and false witnesses". 1 Hale, Pleas of the Crown, 635, 636. Undoubtedly, concern over convicting the innocent, on the one hand, and indignation produced by this species of crime, on the other, have strongly influenced both the substantive doctrines and the evidentiary rules in this area.

3. As illustrated by the Wheeler case, supra, the courts in many states have held that, in the absence of statute, the testimony of the prosecutrix need not be supported by other corroborative evidence. In Fogg v. Commonwealth, 208 Va. 541, 159 S.E.2d 616 (1968), the court said that the prosecutrix's testimony alone is sufficient, if it is credible and the jury believes the accused to be guilty beyond a reasonable doubt? Some courts, however, have indicated that the judge may be under a duty to caution the jury in placing reliance on such uncorroborated testimony, and other modifications and qualifications have been introduced. Consider, for instance, the requirement that although the prosecuting witness' testimony need not be corroborated, it must nevertheless be "clear and convincing". People v. Polak, 360 Ill. 440, 196 N.E. 513 (1935).

In State v. Klein, 200 N.W.2d 288 (N.D.1972), the court stated that corroboration of actual penetration was not required and affirmed a conviction even though a doctor who examined the complaining witness within four hours after the alleged rape found no evidence of penetration.

Statutes have been enacted in a number of States requiring corroboration of the prosecutrix's testimony in prosecutions for rape and other sexual offenses. Problems of the kind and quantum of corroborative evidence have frequently arisen. See 60 A.L.R. 1124 (1929); 30 J.Crim.L. & C. 788 (1940); 30 Mich.L.Rev. 1291 (1932). See also 7 Wigmore, Evidence (3d ed.1940) §§ 2061–62.

4. (a) Consider, as regards protection against false accusations in sex cases, the following analysis and recommendation contained in 3 Wigmore on Evidence, § 924a (3d ed.1940):

"There is . . . at least one situation in which chastity may have a direct connection with veracity, viz. when a *woman or young girl testifies*

the case of the cock and the hen, can any one seriously insist that a jury has no right to call to their assistance their own experience and observation of the nature of animals and of male and female instincts. . . .

"The prisoner had some intent when he pursued the woman. There is no evidence tending to show that his intent was to kill her or to rob her; so that intent must have been to have sexual intercourse. . . ."

as complainant against a man charged with a sexual crime,—*rape, rape under age, seduction, assault.* Modern psychiatrists have amply studied the behavior of errant young girls and women coming before the courts in all sorts of cases. Their psychic complexes are multifarious, distorted partly by inherent defects, partly by diseased derangements or abnormal instincts, partly by bad social environment, partly by temporary physiological or emotional conditions. One form taken by these complexes is that of contriving false charges of sexual offences by men. The unchaste (let us call it) mentality finds incidental but direct expression in the narration of imaginary sex-incidents of which the narrator is the heroine or the victim. On the surface the narration is straightforward and convincing. The real victim, however, too often in such cases is the innocent man; for the respect and sympathy naturally felt by any tribunal for a wronged female helps to give easy credit to such a plausible tale.

"No doubt any judge of a criminal Court and any prosecuting attorney can corroborate this with instances from his own observation. But the lamentable thing is that the orthodox rules of Evidence in most instances prevent adequate probing of the testimonial mentality of a woman-witness, so as to reveal the possible falsity of such charges. Judging merely from the reports of cases in the appellate courts, one must infer that many innocent men have gone to prison because of tales whose falsity could not be exposed. And the situation of injustice has become the more extreme, because in some States the so-called age of consent has been raised to 16 or 18 years (thus making consent immaterial below that age) and in a few States even life imprisonment may be imposed; so that a plausible tale by an attractive, innocent-looking girl may lead to a life-sentence for the accused, because the rules of Evidence (and the judge's unacquaintance with modern psychiatry) permit no adequate probing of the witness' veracity.

"The modern realist movement having insisted on removing the veil of romance which enveloped all womanhood since the days of chivalry, it is now allowable for judges to look at the facts. The facts are that there exist occasionally female types of excessive or perverted sexuality, just as there are such male types; and that these are often accompanied by a testimonial plausibility which should not be taken at its face value. Only an inquiry into the social and mental history will reveal the degree of credibility. This inquiry the law of Evidence ought to permit to the fullest extent, rejecting the hindrance of rules that were framed without an understanding of these facts.

"No judge should ever let a sex-offence charge go to the jury unless the female complainant's social history and mental makeup have been examined and testified to by a qualified physician.

"It is time that the Courts awakened to the sinister possibilities of injustice that lurk in believing such a witness without careful psychiatric scrutiny."

(b) Compare Weihofen, Testimonial Competence and Credibility, 34 Geo.Wash.L.Rev. 53 (1965):

" . . . to meet the danger [of false testimony in sex cases], mental examination of the complainant has been urged for every sex case—or at least for every case lacking corroboration. But until psychiatry can tell us more about the mental conditions that can have a bearing on testimony in these cases, and can devise techniques that meet the test of general scientific acceptance for determining the actual effect of the mental condition on credibility in the particular case, it is probably premature to call for such universal examination of all complainants in sex cases. We need fuller studies of the psychopathology of accusation, not only of rape but of crime generally, and also of the phenomenon of false confessions.

Professor Weihofen's article not only deals with witness competence and credibility in sex cases, but also with the problem generally.

Also see Conrad, Psychiatric Lie Detection, 21 Fed.Rules Dec. 199 (1958).

(c) Following are some of the cases involving the issue of psychiatric examinations of complaining witnesses in sex cases:

Burton v. State, 232 Ind. 246, 111 N.E.2d 892 (1953). This was a sodomy case involving a prosecutrix who was ten years old. The court said: "This record is wholly silent that the state took any steps whatever to determine the prosecutrix was not a fantast, or was not under the compelling domination of her mother. . . . With such a record before us we fail to find any evidence that would convince us beyond a reasonable doubt of the appellant's guilt. . . . By this decision we do not hold that in every case where a sexual offense is charged there should be a psychiatric examination of the prosecutrix. There are many cases where the facts and circumstances leave no doubt of the guilt of the accused, but the record here does not present such a case."

In a dissenting opinion, Draper, J., commented as follows: " . . . No objection was made to the testimony of this child because she had not been cleared by a psychiatrist. None such could be made. Our legislature has not seen fit to require such as a condition precedent to the right to testify in court, and I do not believe this court has any right to impose it. I do not hold lightly the language found in Wigmore's Treatise on Evidence (3rd Ed.), Vol. 3, § 924a. . . . I think it merits the careful consideration of the General Assembly. But if the suggestions therein made are to become the law in Indiana, it should be made law by the legislature. Procedural methods and safeguards should be established and clearly pointed out. To say that a woman may not testify against a man in a sex case unless she first submits to a psychiatric examination covering, perhaps, a period of many months, in the absence of legislation requiring it, seems to me to be an unwarranted arrogation of authority which this court does not have. . . ."

In a later case, however, the Indiana Supreme Court adopted the dissenting view of Judge Draper in the foregoing case. Wedmore v. State, 237 Ind. 212, 143 N.E.2d 649 (1957).

(d) The Supreme Court of California has expressed the following viewpoint, in Ballard v. Superior Court, San Diego County, 64 Cal.2d 159, 49 Cal. Rptr. 302, 410 P.2d 838 (1966):

" . . . a general rule requiring a psychiatric examination of complaining witnesses in every sex case or, as an alternative, in any such case that rests upon the uncorroborated testimony of the complaining witness would, in many instances, not be necessary or appropriate. Moreover, victims of sex crimes might be deterred by such an absolute requirement from disclosing such offenses.

"Rather than formulate a fixed rule in this matter we believe that discretion should repose in the trial judge to order a psychiatric examination of the complaining witness in a case involving a sex violation if the defendant presents a compelling reason for such an examination. . . . * * *

"We therefore believe that the trial judge should be authorized to order the prosecutrix to submit to a psychiatric examination if the circumstances indicate a necessity for an examination. Such necessity would generally arise only if little or no corroboration supported the charge and if the defense raised the issue of the effect of the complaining witness' mental or emotional condition upon her veracity. Thus, in rejecting the polar extremes of an absolute prohibition and an absolute requirement that the prosecutrix submit to a psychiatric examination, we have accepted a middle ground, placing the matter in the discretion of the trial judge.

"The complaining witness should not, and realistically cannot, be forced to submit to a psychiatric examination or to cooperate with a psychiatrist. In the event that the witness thus refuses to cooperate, however, a comment on that refusal should be permitted."

5. Consider Mosley v. Commonwealth, 420 S.W.2d 679 (Ky.1967):

"Appellant was convicted of the crime of rape and sentenced to ten years' servitude in the state penitentiary. The sole ground for reversal of the conviction is that the trial court erred in excluding the testimony of James Gay, a psychologist, concerning the mental condition of the prosecuting witness at the time of the alleged rape.

"The record reflects that for several months prior to May 11, 1966, the date of the alleged offense, Geraldine Eden, the prosecuting witness, had been staying in the home of Elihu Asher where she was employed as a full-time baby-sitter. Geraldine, who is 27 years of age, testified that during the evening of May 11, 1966, the Ashers had left their residence to go bowling. Appellant, an acquaintance of Geraldine and a relative of Asher entered the Asher home for the purpose of staying overnight. Geraldine stated that after the Asher children went to bed, appellant tried to make love to her and when she resisted his amorous advances he forcibly tied her hands behind her back, pushed her down on a couch, removed her underclothing and raped her.

"Appellant, age 54, testified that upon his arrival at the Asher residence Geraldine informed him that she wanted to talk with him before he retired. He had waited only a short time when Geraldine came over and sat beside him on a couch where they immediately began making love and Geraldine voluntarily submitted to sexual intercourse with him as she had on several previous occasions. He stated that following the intercourse they went to the kitchen and Geraldine prepared a snack for them. When they were later questioned that night as to their conduct, appellant stated that much to his surprise Geraldine claimed he had raped her.

"Appellant urges that the court erred in refusing to permit the jury to consider, for the purpose of impeaching Geraldine's credibility, the testimony of Doctor Gay concerning Geraldine's mental condition. Doctor Gay has obtained a Ph. D. degree in psychology and has been licensed by the state of Kentucky as a clinical psychologist. (KRS 319.010 defines the practice of clinical psychology to include the administration of tests for the purpose of psychological diagnosis, classification and evaluation and recognizes services involving the reeducation, guidance or readjustment of the patient.) He is a member of the American and Kentucky Psychological

Associations and is presently the psychologist in charge of the Fayette County Program, a special program at Eastern State Hospital for out-patient treatment.

"Doctor Gay, who is in charge of the treatment of Geraldine's mental disorder, testified, by way of avowal out of the presence of the jury, that Geraldine had entered a state hospital for mental treatment during October 1961. At that time she was complaining that her father and brothers had molested her sexually during her adolescence. She was discharged from the hospital in January 1962 and readmitted for treatment on a voluntary basis during 1964. She has been treated by Doctor Gay since September 1965.

"While Doctor Gay beleved that Geraldine was in a state of remission at the time of the alleged rape, it was his opinion that she is schizophrenic and is an immature individual. She could not tolerate frustration, was easily disturbed and had a guilt complex. Doctor Gay stated that schizophrenia is a complex phenomenon, that it is a disturbance of behavorial effect and thinking which has not been found to be caused or related to any physical or organic condition, but it has a psychiatric origin, i. e. an emotional basis. He further stated that one of the manifestations of schizophrenic reaction is fantasies and when asked whether Geraldine's fantasies extend to the area of sex, he answered, "In this particular case I think it does."

"Since the Commonwealth relied upon the uncorroborated testimony of Geraldine to establish its case against appellant, the principal question at issue had reference to the credit to be given to the testimony of Geraldine. Therefore, Doctor Gay's testimony may have had an important impact on the jury as it tended to impeach Geraldine's credibility.

"It is our opinion that the proffered testimony of Doctor Gay was relevant and competent and should have been received, not in extenuation of rape, but for its bearing upon the question of the weight to be accorded Geraldine's testimony. For this reason the court should admonish the jury that the expert testimony should be considered by it only for the purpose of affecting the credibility of this witness, if it does so." * * *

6. The Polygraph ("Lie-Detector") Technique has been of great value in sex offense investigations, and particularly as a safeguard against false accusations. See Reid & Inbau, Truth and Deception: The Polygraph ("Lie-Detector") Technique (1966).

B. THE ISSUE OF HOMOSEXUALITY—AND OTHER DEVIATE SEXUAL CONDUCT

With regard to the extent to which the law should attempt to control deviate sexual conduct, consider the following excerpts from Kinsey, Pomeroy and Martin, Sexual Behavior in the Human Male (1948):

> A. "*Mouth-genital contact.* Mouth-genital contacts of some sort, with the subject as either the active or the passive member in the relationship, occur at some time in the histories of nearly 60 per cent of all males. . . . " (Page 371)

B. "*Animal Contacts.* In the total population, only one male in twelve or fourteen (estimated at about 8%) ever has sexual experience with animals. . . . Frequencies of animal contact are similarly low taken as a whole. For most individuals, they do not occur more than once or twice, or a few times in a lifetime." (Page 670)

C. "*Homosexuality.* 37 per cent of the total male population has at least some overt homosexual experience to the point of orgasm between adolescence and old age. This accounts for nearly 2 males out of every 5 that one may meet.

"50 per cent of the males who remain single until age 35 have had overt homosexual experience to the point of orgasm, since the onset of adolescence." (Page 650)

(For the incidence of sexual deviancy in females, see Kinsey, Pomeroy, Martin and Gebhard, Sexual Behavior in the Human Female (1953).)

Examine and evaluate the following provisions of the Model Penal Code (Tent.Dr. #4, 1955), as well as the comments of the draftsmen with respect to these provisions:

Section 207.5. *Sodomy and Related Offenses.*

(1) *Deviate Sexual Intercourse by Force or Its Equivalent.* A person who causes another to carry out or submit to an act of deviate sexual intercourse commits a felony of the second degree [1] if:

(a) The victim is compelled to participate by force or violence, or out of fear that death or serious physical injury

1. The punishment provision of the Model Penal Code are as follows:

Section 6.03. *Fines.* A person who has been convicted of an offense may be sentenced to pay a fine not exceeding:

(1) $10,000, when the conviction is of a felony of the first or second degree;

(2) $5,000, when the conviction is of a felony of the third degree;

(3) $1,000, when the conviction is of a misdemeanor;

(4) $500, when the conviction is of a petty misdemeanor or a violation;

(5) Any higher amount equal to double the pecuniary gain derived from the offense by the offender;

(6) Any higher amount specifically authorized by statute.

Section 6.06. *Sentence of Imprisonment for Felony; Ordinary Terms.* A person who has been convicted of a felony may be sentenced to imprisonment, as follows:

(1) In the case of a felony of the first degree, [other than a capital crime] for a term the minimum of which shall be fixed by the Court at not less than one year nor more than ten years, and the maximum of which shall be life imprisonment;

(2) In the case of a felony of the second degree, for a term the minimum of which shall be fixed by the Court at not less than one year nor more than three years, and the maximum of which shall be ten years;

(3) In the case of a felony of the third degree, for a term the minimum of which shall be fixed by the Court at not less than one year nor more than two years, and the maximum of which shall be five years.

Section 6.08. *Sentence of Imprisonment for Misdemeanors and Petty Misde-*

or extreme pain is about to be inflicted on him or a member of his family, or by threat to commit any felony of the first degree; or

(b) For the purpose of preventing the victim from resisting, the actor administers or employs, without the victim's knowledge or consent, drugs, intoxicants, or other substance or force resulting in a major deficiency of ordinary power to make judgments or control behavior; or

(c) The victim is unconscious or physically powerless to resist; or

(d) The victim is less than 10 years old (whether or not the actor is aware of that).

(2) *Gross Imposition.* A person who causes another to carry out or submit to an act of deviate sexual intercourse in situations not covered by subsection (1) commits a felony of the third degree if:

(a) The victim is compelled to participate by any intimidation [which would prevent resistance by a person of ordinary resolution] [reasonably calculated to prevent resistance]; or

(b) The actor knows that the victim's submission is due to substantially complete incapacity to appraise or control his own behavior, but this paragraph shall not apply where a victim over 18 years of age loses that capacity as a result of voluntary use of drugs [or intoxicants] in the company of the actor; or

(c) The victim submits because he is unaware that a sexual act is being committed upon him; or

(d) The victim is less than 18 years old, and the actor is at least 5 years older than the victim, but it shall be a defense under this paragraph if the actor proves that the victim had previously engaged promiscuously in deviate sexual intercourse.

(3) *Minor Wards and Persons in Custody.* A person who causes another to carry out or submit to an act of deviate sexual intercourse in situations not covered by subsections (1) and (2) commits a misdemeanor if:

(a) The victim is less than 21 years old and the actor is charged with his care, treatment, protection, or education; or

meanors; Ordinary Terms. A person who has been convicted of a misdemeanor or a petty misdemeanor may be sentenced to imprisonment for a definite term which shall be fixed by the Court and shall not exceed one year in the case of a misdemeanor or three months in the case of a petty misdemeanor.

The Code also provides for the imposition of heavier penalties, or "extended terms," in certain specified situations. See §§ 7.03, 7.04, 6.07 and 6.09.

(b) The victim is in custody of law or detained in a hospital, school or other institution and the actor is associated in any capacity with his custody or control or with the institution or authority having such custody or control.

(4) *Consensual Sodomy; Public Solicitation.* A person who engages in an act of deviate sexual intercourse [2] or who in any public place solicits another with whom he had no previous acquaintance to engage in deviate sexual intercourse commits a misdemeanor.

. . .

(6) *Definition. Deviate Sexual Intercourse* means penetration by the male sex organ into any opening of the body of a human being [other than natural intercourse] or animal . . . and any

2. The Reporters of the Model Penal Code proposed that consensual relations between adults be excluded from criminal punishment. They supported their proposal in the following terms:

"Our proposal to exclude from the criminal law all sexual practices not involving force, adult corruption of minors, or public offense is based on the following grounds. No harm to the secular interests of the community is involved in atypical sex practice in private between consenting adult partners. This area of private morals is the distinctive concern of spiritual authorities. It has been so recognized in a recent report by a group of Anglican clergy, with medical and legal advisers, calling upon the British Government to reexamine its harsh sodomy law. The distinction between civil and religious responsibilities in this area is reflected in the penal codes of such predominantly Catholic countries as France, Italy, Mexico and Uruguay, none of which attempt to punish private misbehavior of this sort. The Penal Codes of Denmark, Sweden and Switzerland also stay out of this area. On the other hand, the German Code of 1871, still in force, contains broad and severe provisions directed particularly against male homosexuality.

"As in the case of illicit heterosexual relations, existing law is substantially unenforced, and there is no prospect of real enforcement except against cases of violence, corruption of minors and public solicitation. Statutes that go beyond that permit capricious selection of a very few cases for prosecution and serve primarily the interest of blackmailers. Existence of the criminal threat probably deters some people from seeking psychiatric or other assistance for their emotional problems; certainly conviction and imprisonment are not conducive to cures. Further, there is the fundamental question of the protection to which every individual is entitled against state interference in his personal affairs when he is not hurting others. Lastly, the practicalities of police administration must be considered. Funds and personnel for police work are limited, and it would appear to be poor policy to use them to any extent in this area when large numbers of atrocious crimes remain unsolved. Even the necessary utilization of police in cases involving minors or public solicitation raises special problems of police morale, because of the entrapment practices that enforcement seems to require, and the temptation to bribery and extortion." (Tentative Draft No. 4 (1955), pp. 277–79).

Although the Advisory Committee unanimously approved the proposal, the Council of the Institute, at its March 1955 meeting, voted in favor of criminal punishment. Some members felt that, although the Reporters' position was a rational one, it would be totally unacceptable to American legislatures and hence would prejudice acceptance of the Code generally. Other members of the Council opposed the position on the ground that sodomy is a cause or symptom of moral decay and therefore should be repressed by law. Accordingly, subsection (4) of Section 207.5 was revised to reflect the Council's position.

sexual penetration of the vulva or anus of a female by another female or by an animal.

COMMENTS OF DRAFTSMEN

Deviate Sexual Intercourse

The statutes of nearly all states punish fellatio (oral stimulus of the male sex organ), cunnilingus (oral stimulus of the female sex organ), anal intercourse (sodomy originally meant anal intercourse between men, but by extension the term has been applied to all anal and oral intercourse as well as buggery and *necrophilia*), and bestiality (copulation between human and animal). The term buggery is used to refer collectively to bestiality plus anal intercourse. In a few states and in England, fellatio and cunnilingus are not included so that the offense is limited to bestiality and anal intercourse by males. One result is to make male homosexuality a grave offense while leaving Lesbianism unpunished in these jurisdictions. Where mouth-genital contact is held not to be covered by the sodomy law, it may be punishable under statutes dealing with lewd and lascivious behavior. The distinction thus drawn between two closely related types of sexual deviation results in a preposterous difference in maximum sentence: e. g. twenty years for anal sodomy, three years for oral. . . . And the law reaches into the very privacy of the marriage chamber to punish husband and wife who depart from its standards. Punishment provided under present law, aside from the indeterminate sentences of the "sex psychopath" laws, is extremely severe. Maximum imprisonment ranges from three years to life, with ten years most common (seventeen states) and twenty years the next most frequent (nine states). Twenty-nine states fix minimum sentences from one to seven years. Six jurisdictions provide for aggravated penalties if sodomy is committed on a child: (fourteen years—California; fifteen years—Washington; sixteen years—District of Columbia, Georgia, New Jersey; eighteen years—New York).

Deviate sexual intercourse as defined in subsection (6) of Section 207.5 is somewhat broader than existing laws dealing with unnatural intercourse insofar as it includes digital penetration of a female by another female and penetration by inanimate objects. These activities seem to fall within the basic concept of the unnatural intercourse offense, namely, violation of bodily integrity in a manner that simulates normal intercourse. . . .

Age Disparity

Commentators agree that disparity of age is an important consideration. Overt homosexual practice typically begins in youth, and while a certain amount of it will undoubtedly continue to arise spontaneously among the youthful, it seems advisable to attempt to deter seduction of the young by older perverts, while avoiding criminality for occasional or experimental adolescent experience with contemporaries. Paragraph (d) of subsection (2) seeks to accomplish this by making 18 the "age of consent" and requiring a five year age disparity. The reasons for using 18 rather than 16 . . . are (1) belief that emotional instability of adolescence probably is more prolonged among males; (2) it seems desirable to afford protection against seduction during the normal years of secondary education; and (3) the hypothesis that homosexual seduction is more likely to precipitate a fixed pattern of undesirable behavior and maladjustment.

NOTE

Following the same general views of the drafters of the Model Penal Code, the new Illinois Criminal Code (art. 11, ch. 38, S.H.A.) has eliminated deviate sexual conduct as a crime except where force is involved, or where it occurs in a public place, or where there is a specified age disparity between the parties.

C. FORNICATION AND ADULTERY

With regard to adultery and fornication, compare and appraise the following statutory provisions. Also give consideration to the fact that in some jurisdictions (e. g., Louisiana) such conduct is not criminally proscribed.

Wisconsin Criminal Code

§ 944.15 *Fornication.* Whoever has sexual intercourse with a person not his spouse may be fined not more than $200 or imprisoned not more than 6 months or both.

§ 944.16 *Adultery.* Either of the following may be fined not more than $1,000 or imprisoned not more than 3 years or both:

(1) A married person who has sexual intercourse with a a person not his spouse; or

(2) A person who has sexual intercourse with a person who is married to another.

Texas Penal Code

Arts. 499–504. "Adultery" is the living together and carnal intercourse with each other, or habitual carnal intercourse with each other without living together, of a man and woman when either is lawfully married to some other person. . . .

When adultery has been committed, both parties are guilty, though only one may be married.

Every one guilty of adultery shall be fined not less than one hundred nor more than one thousand dollars.

"Fornication" is the living together and carnal intercourse with each other, or habitual carnal intercourse with each other without living together, of a man and woman, both being unmarried.

Every one guilty of fornication shall be fined not less than fifty nor more than five hundred dollars.

Illinois Criminal Code

§ 11–7.

(a) Any person who cohabits or has sexual intercourse with another not his spouse commits adultery, if the behavior is open and notorious,[1] and

(1) The person is married and the other person involved in such intercourse is not his spouse; or

(2) The person is not married and knows that the other person involved in such intercourse is married.

[Adultery is a Class A misdemeanor, punishable for any term up to one year.]

§ 11–8.

(a) Any person who cohabits or has sexual intercourse with another not his spouse commits fornication if the behavior is open and notorious.

[Fornication is a Class B misdemeanor, punishable up to 6 months.]

Consider the following comments of the draftsmen of the Model Penal Code (tentative draft #4, 1955), at 204–10:

"Sexual intercourse outside the bounds of lawful matrimony is widely, but not universally, criminal in the United States. . . .

"At the present time 11 of the 48 states have no fornication statute, and only 18 punish a single act of intercourse between unmarried persons (four of these by fine alone). The rest of the states

1. As to the meaning of "open and notorious" consider the drafters' commentary:

"Since it is the scandalousness, the affront to public decency and the marital institution that is of pivotal concern in this crime, notoriety must extend not only to the sexual intercourse of cohabitation, but must also extend to the fact of the absence of the marital relationship between parties engaging in such behavior."

This concept prevailed under the earlier case law interpreting the same phrase used in the earlier Illinois statutory provision. People v. Potter, 319 Ill. App. 409, 49 N.E.2d 307 (1943).

require either a continuous or an "open and notorious" relationship, or both. Fornication is not criminal in England or, generally speaking, in the rest of the world. If a married person is involved, the number of American states punishing a single act of illicit intercourse rises to 30 (four of these by fine alone). Abroad, we find adultery excluded from the category of crime in England, Japan, the U.S.S.R. and Uruguay, among others. In France, Italy and Argentina criminal penalties apply to an adulterous wife and her paramour, but a husband's adultery is criminal only if he keeps a mistress, i. e., a continuous relationship, or for infractions carried out within his marital abode. The German and Swiss Penal Codes punish adultery only "if because of it, the marriage is dissolved." Generally in foreign law, and in a few American States, prosecution is authorized only on complaint of the spouse.

"American penal laws against illicit intercourse are generally unenforced. This is particularly remarkable in view of the fact that thousands of cases of adultery are made a matter of judicial record in divorce proceedings, . . . There is some indication that these laws, like other dead letter statutes, may lend themselves to discriminatory enforcement, e. g., where the parties involved are of different races, or where a political figure is involved. . . . Considerations of the foregoing character account for the omission of fornication and adultery from the Louisiana Penal Code of 1942. . . . The reporters for the . . . Code . . . prepared an article on adultery which was rejected by the Council of the Louisiana State Law Institute. Its advisory committee was 'virtually unanimous' against it, on the grounds that

'to make such conduct a crime will do more harm than good, in that it will not prevent illicit and promiscuous relations by faithless husbands or wives, and the prosecutions will rarely occur except in blackmail or semi-blackmail situations.'

"Another ground of opposition was that impossibility of enforcement would tend to bring the law into disrepute. Prosecutors report that criminal complaints are generally filed as a lever to secure favorable divorce settlements, and that the complaints are almost always withdrawn or abandoned before the case can come to trial. Even if the case is successfully prosecuted, a sentence of imprisonment is imposed only in exceptional circumstances, as in a recent Massachusetts case where the male paramour was sentenced to 3 years imprisonment for adultery after the adulterous wife killed her husband in a family quarrel.

"The reluctance to prosecute finds some justification in evidence that a large proportion of the population is guilty at one time or another of this breach of sexual mores. Kinsey reports that one-half of the married males and one-fourth of the married females commit at least one adulterous act during married life, and one of every six of the females who had never had such relations wanted or would consider having them. The pattern of adulterous relations is extremely sporadic. There are typically many acts within a short time period and then none for long periods. One-third of the females reported less than a total of ten acts; two-fifths had only one partner. The male seldom had extra-marital intercourse with the same partner for more than a brief period (a summer, a vacation). Adulterous relationships are often idealized in a literary representations, and are revealed in the intimate biographies of prominent and respected figures.

"Pre-marital intercourse is also very common and widely tolerated, so that prosecution for this offense is rare. Criminal complaints are frequently filed solely as a means of compelling the putative father to provide support for the mother and child. A substantial number of convictions of fornication occur in the course of rape prosecutions, where the possibility of conviction of the lesser offense offers an opportunity for prosecution and defense to bargain for a plea of guilty, or for a jury to reach a compromise verdict when there is reason to believe that the woman may have consented.

" . . . We deem it inappropriate for the government to attempt to control behavior that has no substantial significance except as to the morality of the actor. Such matters are best left to religious, educational and other social influences. . . . [I]t must be recognized, as a practical matter, that in a heterogeneous community such as ours, different individuals and groups have widely divergent views of the seriousness of various moral derelictions. . . .

Contrast the above expressed views with those of Professor Frank E. Horack, Jr. in 44 Ill.L.Rev. 149 (1949):

" . . . [F]rom the assumption of the necessity of the family in the social system we create the institution of monogamous marriage and build custom, mores and laws to support it. A host of legislative and judicial rules support and promote the relationship: tort actions against those who invade the relation; tax exemption; statutory actions for wives against gamblers and tavern owners; the sex laws; homestead exemptions; participation of the wife in the conveyancing of realty; the reduction in penalties for crimes of violence resulting from invasion of the marriage relation, *et cetera, et cetera*. . . .

"These and many other sanctions in themselves have little meaning, except as they in a cumulative fashion tend to encourage the creation of the marriage relation and protect it from external interference. Most of the sex laws have similar objectives. It is significant to note that of the six forms of sexual outlet that Kinsey analyzes only those which most directly challenge the sexual integrity of the marriage relationship have been made criminal, even though the remaining may be subject to social or religious condemnation. Thus, there is little doubt as to the social objectives of the system of sex regulation.

"Once a rule has been established, however, the rule will operate and must operate with some degree of uniformity and thus, in particular cases, result in what may be believed to be an unfair, unwise, or unscientific consequence. This cannot be totally avoided for law is force and law is power, and the very nature of society requires that when its goals are not achieved by the suasion of custom, morality and religion, then the law must operate. Even within the legal framework, however, through the device of the jury, the special handling of juvenile offenders, mental cases, and all persons under the probation system, the unrelenting vigor of the rule may be adjusted to the needs of particular individuals. The failure of the legal rule in particular cases does not require a condemnation of the major postulates upon which it is founded unless the adjustment of legal rule is so impossible or the consequences are so grossly unrealistic as to condemn the whole system. In a sense this is the crux of the lawyer's problem in the Kinsey Report. Does it on the one hand disclose that the institution of the family is an inappropriate postulate for our social organization, or on the other disclose that the secondary sanctions for the support of the family are so unrealistic as to serve no useful purpose in the maintenance and protection of that relationship?

"In substance the data discloses that although there is only one legally approved channel for sexual outlet—sexual intercourse within the bonds of monogamous marriage—practically all human males on one or more occasions in their lives whether married or unmarried, find sexual outlet in other ways. Accepting this as a fact the legal question then is, does this almost universal practice establish the impracticability of any sex laws, the need for the adjustment in those we now have, or change in their administration?

"The data on violations, however, is probably no more startling than similar data would be if procured from studies of the same intensity relating to other illegal conduct. Any person who will honestly relate his boyhood activities and any person engaged in 'boys' work' or experienced in law enforcement activity knows that the concept of property is not well fixed in the consciousness of young boys regardless of social or economic strata. What we are pleased to dismiss as boyish enthusiasm, pranks, and minor indiscretions fit our concept of both petty and grand larceny, the malicious destruction of property and a host of other crimes. Auto theft is a serious crime, yet many young boys, particularly those who do not have access to automobiles, 'borrow' cars for the thrill of the ride with little concern for the rights of the owner and yet probably with little or no 'intent to steal' in the traditional sense.

" . . . In other words, though the rule of law must be rigid, it requires a full measure of understanding, compassion and flexibility in its administration. Dr. Kinsey apparently does not understand this dichotomy of the law, for he suggests that '85% of the younger male population could be convicted as sex offenders if law enforcement officials were as efficient as most people expect them to be.' And we might add 85% similarly could be convicted as common thieves. The real point is that 'most people' don't expect the law to be enforced under these circumstances.

"It is an easy step from this premise to the next—that sex offenders are badly treated after apprehension. Probably so. . . . Unfortunately, it is not reserved for sex offenders alone. Likewise, the disparity between the judgment of policemen in apprehension and the attitude of the judge in sentencing is probably as common in the area of non-sex offenses. In sum, in the course of the survey Dr. Kinsey has had opportunity to study the operation of law as it affects sex offenders, but his observations and his shock need not be reserved for sex offenders.

"Further testing of these hypotheses make clear the necessity for caution. Many of the crimes which, if considered as independent prohibitions might seem artificial and unreal, take significance and seem valid when viewed as secondary sanctions necessary for the promotion of the primary postulate—the protection of the family relationship. Thus, the conclusions concerning the validity of statutes prohibiting extra-marital intercourse even if biologically unsound make perfectly good sense in terms of protecting the interest which most husbands and wives have in the maintenance of the marriage relation. And while in rejoinder it may be pointed out that the sanction of the marriage relation as measured by the divorce rate perhaps is not as firmly held as it was by earlier generations, adultery as a cause of divorce still speaks of the interest of one spouse in maintaining the relation on an exclusively monogamous basis.

". . . Society intends to protect individuals against the violent sex crimes and no substantial portion of the population is prepared to abandon the family relation as the basis of social organization even admitting of substantial violation of its tenets. Legislative change of either the primary and secondary sanctions is not to be expected.

"It is, of course, possible to argue that some of these indirect sanctions are unnecessary to the protection of the family relation and it is equally possible to assert that extra-marital intercourse 'properly understood' is neither an invasion of the relation or dangerous to it. The difficulty with maintaining this proposition is that in our democratic society we have carefully preserved the right of the people through their elected representatives to make laws that they believe to be desirable. This concept of our governmental organization reserves to all the people the right to establish their own standards. This right encompasses the power to be wrong, quite as much as the power to be correct. It means that our society may establish standards of morals and enact them into law even though they attempt to exact conduct from society which is higher than a majority can attain. Indeed there are many who assert that it is only in this fashion that 'progress' is made. . . ."

NOTE

As previously noted, in Illinois deviate sexual conduct among consenting adults in private is not a criminal offense. Consequently, homosexuals who openly live together and publicly profess their status are not subject to punishment, whereas the Criminal Code of Illinois punishes open and notorious adultery (§ 11–7, ch. 38, S.H.A.) and also fornication (§ 11–8, ch. 38, S.H.A.). May this not be an unconstitutional distinction favoring homosexual conduct over heterosexual behavior?

The state courts, in states which profess to punish both deviate sexual conduct and adultery and fornication, have generally upheld the validity of the statutes when constitutional issues were raised. See 41 ALR3d 1338.

D. MISCELLANEOUS SEX OFFENSES

Among other commonly encountered sex offenses are those designed to protect children ("contributing," "indecent liberties," or however they may be titled), incest, prostitution, public indecency, etc. In connection with the latter, the California Supreme Court said, in In Re Smith, 7 Cal.3d 362, 497 P.2d 807 (1972), that nude sunbathing on an isolated beach without any other sexual act being performed, does not satisfy the requirements of the crime prohibiting the willful or lewd exposure of the private parts of the body. The Tenth Circuit Court of Appeals, in United States v. Hymans, 463 F.2d 615 (10th Cir. 1972) did not similarly view male and female defendants who had engaged in "skinny dipping" and were arrested while they were sunning themselves on the bank, eating watermelons. The court said it was not "persuaded by such nostalgic authorities as James Whitcomb Riley's 'The Old Swimming Hole', or Mark Twain's 'Adventures of Huckleberry Finn'," and affirmed a conviction for indecent exposure in a national forest.

See also the cases and notes collected in the earlier chapter dealing with First Amendment rights, particularly the section on Obscenity.

E. "SEXUALLY DANGEROUS" PERSONS LEGISLATION

Over a period of many years, approximately thirty states, and the District of Columbia, have enacted legislation designed to institutionalize potentially dangerous sex offenders "for treatment and cure". The objective has been to institutionalize such persons to prevent their commission of rapes and other serious sexual or sex related offenses.

In some jurisdictions, there can only be a "sexually dangerous persons" proceeding against someone who is already "charged with a criminal offense". Others do not so confine the proceeding. For example, the District of Columbia in its 1970 Code (§§ 22–3503 to 22–3511) allows for a "sexual psychopath" proceeding against any person whenever it shall appear to the United States Attorney or any of his assistants that by a course of repeated misconduct in sexual matters a person has evidenced such a lack of power to control his sexual impulses as to be dangerous to others "because he is likely to attack or otherwise inflict injury, loss, pain, or other evil on the objects of his desire".

As a general rule, statutes of this type have been rarely used. Ordinarily the individual only comes to the attention of a prosecutor after he has committed a crime for which he can be sent away on a criminal charge, and perhaps on one that will result in a penitentiary sentence from which he is far less likely to be released on parole than upon release from a mental institution as "cured". There are also a number of constitutional obstacles—e. g., the self-incrimination privilege as regards a compulsory psychiatric examination.

Some scholars feel that the only constructive preventive measures are community level and school programs aimed at seeking out and treating deviational characteristics among *children*.

[For further information and references upon the subject, consult Cases and Comments on Criminal Law, by Inbau, Thompson, and Moenssens (1973), 551–559.]

Chapter 6

MISAPPROPRIATION AND RELATED PROPERTY OFFENSES

A. LARCENY

Larceny, generally speaking, is the crime of stealing. Technically, it consists of several specific elements, namely

a. a taking and

b. a carrying away

c. of the personal property

d. of another

e. with intent to steal.

An act which lacks any one of these elements cannot be larceny.

To understand why the law of larceny is so technical as to require the fulfillment of all of these elements, reference must be made to the history of the offense.

First, larceny was the only form of theft criminally punished under the early common law. The offense was narrowly construed, inasmuch as many forms of deception were not commonly regarded as criminal. The social and economic community lacked the complexity of modern times, and it was thought that with the exercise of ordinary prudence one could protect himself from most sorts of deception. For example, it was held in 1761 that it was not a crime to "make a fool of another" by deliberately delivering fewer goods than were ordered. The civil law was relied upon to correct such a deception; the criminal law would intervene only if the fraud was one which common care could not prevent, such as the use of false weights and measures. As commerce increased, the criminal law expanded to punish new forms of theft; however, the law of larceny had become so fixed that gaps were filled by the addition of new crimes, such as embezzlement and false pretenses, rather than by redefining larceny.

Second, the technicalities surrounding the law of larceny derive to some extent from the fact that grand larceny (larceny of goods having a certain minimum value) was a capital offense. Gradually, as attitudes towards the death penalty changed, judges became reluctant to impose the death penalty upon thieves, especially since the amount which divided grand and petit larceny was very low. Thus, judges would frequently rely upon technicalities to acquit in larceny cases.

The complex nature of the law of theft has little justification today. Some efforts have been made to simplify the law in this area. Notably, several states have abolished the separate offenses of larceny, embezzlement, etc., and combined them in a new crime called "theft." Until such time, however, as reform in this area is general, it is necessary to understand some of the complexities of the law of larceny, as well as the offenses that have been developed to supplement larceny in the field of theft.

THE ELEMENTS OF LARCENY

1. *The Taking*

It should be stressed at the outset that the "taking" refers to a taking of *possession* of the personal goods of another. Thus, one can take possession of goods over which he has mere *custody,* and such a taking amounts to larceny if the other requirements are present. However, if actual possession is never acquired by the thief, or by one acting at his direction or instigation, larceny has not been committed. Moreover, there is no taking unless the object is first in someone else's possession, either actual or constructive.

The taking can be effected by the hands of the thief, by a mechanical device, or even by an animal trained for that purpose, or by an innocent human being acting under the thief's direction. A "lifting up" of an object by any one of these means is a "taking."

2. *The Carrying Away*

A good illustration of the meaning of the requirement of "carrying away" is the case of a person who took some beaded bags from a show case and put them in the pocket of an overcoat he was carrying on his arm. When a salesman's suspicion was aroused the defendant departed from the store but left his overcoat behind, with the merchandise in it, on a counter about six feet away from the one from which he had taken the objects. This was held to be a "carrying away" within the meaning of the larceny provision of the Illinois Criminal Code then in effect.

Carrying away, without achieving actual possession, however, is insufficient. In a case where the defendant lifted an overcoat from a store dummy and started to walk away with it, but it was secured to the dummy by a chain, which the defendant was unable to break, it was held that the defendant was not guilty of larceny, inasmuch as he never had actual possession of the coat.

3. *Personal Property*

Under common law, only personal property, and not something that might be considered part of the realty, could be the subject of larceny. An illustration of this is a case where a tombstone was taken from a grave in a cemetery. It was held that there could be no larceny of "anything adhering to the soil".

Certain animals were not considered personalty at common law. The theft of a dog, cat, monkey, or fox was not deemed a larceny. However, those animals of a domestic nature that were useful for the sustenance of life came under the umbrella of personalty and could therefore be the subject of a larceny. They included cows, horses, hogs, and chickens.

4. *Another's Property*

According to the common law, one co-owner cannot be guilty of larceny from another co-owner. Thus, a partner who steals partnership property is not guilty of larceny. Likewise, at common law, a spouse does not commit larceny by taking property from the other spouse.

5. *Intent to Steal*

This required element of larceny is not only an historical one, but one of the highest importance today, either under the common law or modern statutory concepts. No one can be guilty of larceny, or of theft as defined under recently enacted statutes or codes, unless he had the intent to permanently deprive the owner of the property that was taken and carried away.

Because of the requirement of an intent to steal, it is often difficult to obtain larceny convictions in cases involving so-called "joyriding". Where an automobile is taken with the intent to use it for a few hours and then return it to the place where taken, or to leave it in a place where the owner will be likely to recover it, all of the elements of larceny are usually present except for the intent to steal. As a consequence, most states have enacted special legislation concerning this offense. Section 206.6 of the Model Penal Code, for example, provides: "A person who takes the vehicle of another without his consent, under circumstances not amounting to theft, commits a petty misdemeanor."

In shoplifting situations, many merchants are under the impression that the offense is not completed until the goods are taken out of the store, for until then the "intent to steal" cannot be established. But the intent to steal is provable by other factors, such as the carrying of goods from one floor to another. In other words, conduct on the part of the accused that is clearly inconsistent with the ordinary behavior of customers can be used as evidence of intent to steal. According to this test, therefore, a person should not be arrested while he is carrying an unconcealed piece of merchandise in the direction of clerks whom he could conceivably be approaching for an inquiry about the merchandise or where it conceivably appears that he is taking it to a better lighted place for closer inspection. In such instances the accused could reasonably offer such explanations as evidence of no intent to steal. On the other hand, the taking of an object from a counter, placing it in a bag or purse, and walking away from the counter without paying for it, is conduct unbecoming a customer and may reasonably be taken as evidence of intent to steal.

COWAN v. STATE

Supreme Court of Arkansas, 1926.
171 Ark. 1018, 287 S.W. 201.

WOOD, J. Bert Cowan was indicted in the Crawford circuit court for the crime of grand larceny. The indictment, in apt language, charged him with the crime of grand larceny in the stealing of two automobile license plates of the total value of $16, the personal property of Paul W. Sheridan.

One of the witnesses introduced by the state testified that he worked for the Paul Sheridan Motor Company in Van Buren, Crawford county, Ark., and that he saw Cowan on or about the 31st day of May, 1926, in Crawford county, Ark., trying to get a license tag off of a Ford car which belonged to Paul Sheridan. Witness went for the sheriff.

The sheriff testified that he saw the defendant take a license tag off of a Ford touring car and stick it under the bib of his overalls, and witness arrested him. The law fixes as the regular price of license for a Ford touring car the sum of $16 from the 1st of January to the 21st of June.

The defendant offered to prove by the sheriff and other witnesses that the replacement cost of the license tags is $1. The court refused to allow the witness to so testify, to which ruling the defendant duly excepted.

The defendant was convicted and sentenced by judgment of the court to imprisonment in the state penitentiary for a period of one year, from which judgment he duly prosecutes this appeal.

The law requires every person who owns and desires to operate an automobile in this state to pay a fee for the registration and licensing of such automobile a minimum of $15 per annum. . . . It is made the duty of the commissioner of state lands, highways, and improvements, when the automobile has been duly registered and the license fee duly paid, to issue to the applicant a registration card and a set of registration plates bearing the number that has been assigned to such motor vehicle. . . . The possession of these registration cards and license plates is evidence of the fact that the owner and operator of the car has complied with the law requiring registration and payment of the license fee. It is unlawful for the owner of any automobile to display any registration plate or plates that are not furnished by the state highway commissioner, and the owner of any motor vehicle subject to the payment of a license fee who fails to pay the same when due, in addition to the license fee, is subject to a penalty for the operation of the car without paying a license. . . .

Under the above and other provisions . . . and the testimony in this case, it is obvious that the stealing of automobile license plates evidencing the right to own and operate an automobile from January 1st to June 21st constituted grand larceny. The only method by which the appellant could lawfully obtain a license plate to operate his car in this state was by complying with the [above] provisions . . . , and in order to obtain such license plates it would be necessary for him to pay not less than the sum of $15. Registration cards and license plates, under the law, are not the subject of barter and sale. They evidence the right of the owner of the particular car that has been registered and for which license plates have been issued to operate that car. These original license plates cannot be obtained by any one lawfully without the payment of the license fee. Intrinsically, to be sure, the metal license plates were worth but little or nothing, merely the cost of the metal and the manufacture thereof into plates, but as an evidence of the right to own and operate a car they were worth the sum of $16. The effect of the provisions of the Harrelson Law is to fix the value of license plates at not less than $15. The value of the license plates which appellant stole was $16, as shown by the undisputed evidence in this case. It is not a question of what the owner of the automobile would have to pay in order to replace them; the question is, what was the value of the plates to the owner when he obtained them—that is, what he had to pay for same in order to obtain them as an evidence of the right to operate his car in this state. The value of these particular plates should be measured by what these particular plates cost, and not by what replacement plates would cost, for appellant was not charged and was not convicted of stealing license plates which had been replaced. He was charged and convicted of stealing automobile license plates of the value of $16. To obtain these license plates, the owner had to pay $16, and if appellant, as before stated, had lawfully obtained the same, he would have had to pay the sum of $16 therefor. When motor vehicle license plates are stolen, the thief intends not only to deprive the owner of the car of the evidence of his right to operate such car on the highways of this state, but he also intends to deprive the state of the license fee which he would have to pay as an evidence of his right to operate a motor vehicle. He therefore intends to steal the property of another and to convert the same permanently to his own use of more than the value of $10. In such case the lucri causa is complete, and under the law the offender is guilty of grand larceny. See sections 2484 and 2488, C. & M. Digest.

The trial court ruled correctly in holding that the offered testimony was inadmissible, and its judgment is therefore affirmed.

McCulloch, C. J. (dissenting). The offense of larceny consists of stealing, taking, and carrying away the property of another, and the degree of the offense is fixed according to the value of the property stolen. Crawford & Moses' Digest, §§ 2483, 2486. The extent of the value is unimportant further than it fixes the degree of the offense, but the property stolen must be of some value. It is not contended in the present case that the two automobile license tags which were stolen were entirely without value, however trifling it may have been, but the contention is that it is limited to the intrinsic value of the tags themselves, and not the value of the privilege, of which the tags constitute mere evidence. I think that counsel for appellant is right in this contention and that the offense made out is only that of petit larceny.

At common law, things without intrinsic value, such as choses in action, were not subjects of larceny, . . . but our statutes place such property on the same basis as the money value which choses in action represent, and provide in express terms that such character of property may be the subject of larceny. . . . The stealing of a license tag does not, however, come within the provision of that section, for it is not a "banknote, bond, bill, note, receipt, or any instrument of writing whatever."

It is contended that the case comes within the terms of the following section of the statute:

"Section 2484. Larceny shall embrace every theft which unlawfully deprives another of his money or other personal property, or those means and muniments by which the right and title to property, real or personal, may be ascertained." . . .

I do not think this is true, for the theft of the tags does not deprive the owner of personal property of the value of the license evidenced by the tags, nor of "those means and muniments by which the right and title to property, real or personal, may be ascertained." The license to use the car on the public highway is a personal privilege, and its use is limited to the particular car named in the license. This privilege does not constitute property within the meaning of the statute; therefore the license tags do not constitute "means and muniments by which the right and title to property, real or personal, may be ascertained." But, even if so regarded, the value amounts to the sum of $1, which would be required to replace the tags, as that is the extent of the owner's loss. In other words, the value could not in any event exceed the replacement cost.

My conclusion is that the judgment should be reversed, with directions to the court to sentence appellant for petit larceny.

NOTES

1. Determining the value of stolen property is usually a function of the jury. Where the evidence is in conflict, the jury's determination will not be disturbed. In a larceny prosecution for the theft of dogs alleged to be worth $100 each, the defendant introduced evidence that they had no commercial value whatever. The court said that the verdict of guilty of grand larceny settled this conflict against the defendant. Blankenship v. Commonwealth, 133 Va. 638, 112 S.E. 622 (1922).

2. In People v. Fognini, 374 Ill. 161, 28 N.E.2d 95 (1940), the defendants were charged with the larceny of two suits of clothes. The jury returned a verdict of guilty and found the value of the property stolen to be

the sum of $30. In reversing the decision and remanding the cause for a new trial, the Supreme Court of Illinois stated:

"It is argued, as one of the reasons for reversal, that the proof failed to show the fair, cash market value of these suits on the date of the larceny.

"Three witnesses testified as to this matter and the evidence offered by them is substantially alike. It appears from the testimony that the two suits in question were old stock and had been on the shelves of the company three and one-half years. . . . One of the witnesses said he thought the suits had cost $18.50 and that they were worth $20 apiece.

"Over repeated objections and motions to strike, the witnesses were all questioned by the assistant State's attorney as to the 'fair, cash value' of the merchandise omitting the word 'market' from the question. . . . It is clear from the evidence that these suits had proved unmarketable over a period of three and one-half years by any usual retail methods. . . . Whether or not there was a market through some cut rate or special sale means, was not proved or touched upon by the evidence. The verdict of the jury that the suits were worth $15 each is not supported by any evidence.

"In those types of larceny where the value of the property is material, that value must be alleged and proved, and the proof must show the fair, cash market value at the time and place of the theft. . . ."

To the same effect see Fugate v. State, 80 Okl.Cr.R. 200, 158 P.2d 177 (1945) ("the expression 'market value' relates to buying and selling, so that another equivalent expression might be said to be 'reasonable selling price.' "). See also People v. Herring, 396 Ill. 364, 71 N.E.2d 682 (1947).

3. Defendant, a turnstile maintainer in the New York subway system, was tried for the theft of fares deposited by subway passengers in the station turnstiles. The first larceny involved approximately $1,500, alleged to have been taken over a period of 11 months, while the second charge involved the theft of more than $370 over a period of 10 months. The defendant was convicted of grand larceny, although he had contended at the trial that since the takings occurred over a period of time and in no one instance exceeded $100 (the jurisdiction's statutory dividing line between grand and petty larceny), he was guilty only of a number of petty larcenies. In affirming the defendant's conviction, the New York Court of Appeals, in People v. Cox, 286 N.Y. 137, 36 N.E.2d 84 (1941), said:

"There is evidence sufficient in the case at bar to sustain the verdict of the jury that the entire taking was governed by a single intent and a general illegal design. This total sum stolen by defendant . . . under the two counts of the indictment was stolen pursuant to this general fraudulent design which was created before the misappropriations began and continued throughout the entire period. If the jury did not find such to be the fact, they were instructed to acquit the defendant. It is submitted that the record supports the above finding of the jury rather than that there were a number of isolated transactions or distinct larcenies coincident solely in method, place or time. . . . Here there was a continuing larceny by a thief operating under a single purpose to carry out a general fraudulent plan. We have first the formulation of a plan for systemized thievery, then the adoption of the plan by persons able to make it effective, and lastly its subsequent realization, together with the taking of the necessary steps to preserve a continuing operation unmolested. . . . Logic and reason join . . . in holding that the People may prosecute for a single crime a defendant who, pursuant to a single intent and one general fraudulent plan, steals in the aggregate as a felon and not as a petty thief. If this were not so, a crime of grand larceny would go unpunished and a felon escape because the law classified him only as a petty thief."

Compare Camp v. State, 7 Okl.Cr.R. 531, 124 P. 331 (1912). In that case, the defendant was tried and convicted of grand larceny based on the theft of various items of clothing from a dry goods store over a period of several months. In reversing the defendant's conviction, the Criminal Court of Appeals of Oklahoma stated:

"We have examined the record carefully, and fail to find any testimony that the value of the property taken at any one time exceeded $20 [the statutory dividing line between grand and petit larceny]. Counsel for appellant made this point in their brief, and insisted that, under the evidence, appellant should not have been convicted for more than petit larceny. It was therefore the duty of the attorney for the state, if there was any evidence in the record showing that goods had been taken at any one time worth exceeding $20, to call our attention to it. As he has not done so, and as we have been unable to find such testimony, we feel that we should sustain the contention of counsel for appellant, and hold that the testimony in this case does not support a verdict for grand larceny."

B. EMBEZZLEMENT

WARREN v. STATE

Supreme Court of Indiana 1945.
223 Ind. 552, 62 N.E.2d 624.

RICHMAN, CHIEF JUSTICE. Waiving a jury appellant was tried and convicted of larceny of four cans of Prestone. The only question presented is whether the finding is contrary to law. The evidence leaves no doubt that for more than six months he continued to take property of his employer and convert it to his own use, but he contends that his employment was such as to make his crime embezzlement rather than larceny.

He was employed as a member of a maintenance crew under a foreman in Plant No. 2 of the Allison Division of General Motors Corporation. The plant contained tanks for reception and storage of gasoline, oil and Prestone. To a storage building housing Prestone both the foreman and appellant had keys. "The Chief Engineer . . . had exclusive control in Plant No. 2 of this Prestone." Appellant was not authorized to remove Prestone from the building except on requisition from some other person in authority. One of appellant's duties was to receive gasoline. A confederate (who pleaded guilty to the same affidavit upon which appellant was tried) was employed by a trucking company to deliver gasoline to the plant and thus obtained ingress. His truck was used to take away Prestone abstracted by appellant from the storage building. The Prestone was sold and the proceeds divided by appellant and the truck driver. A statement signed by appellant, and admitted in evidence, related numerous such transactions from June through August, 1943. In November they "took out some 30 to 35 drums of Prestone," each containing 55 gallons and sold them for $83 per drum. Appellant's employer became suspicious and early in January, 1944, investigators observed appellant surreptitiously placing four cans in the truck. It was followed away from the plant and the cans, containing Prestone, were recovered. No contention is made by appellant that he had a requisition when he took this Prestone. There was other testimony more favorable to appellant's theory, but upon appeal we look only to the evidence tending to support the finding.

The facts related bring the case within the rule of Colip v. State [1899] . . . and cases from other jurisdictions cited in a note in 125 A.L.R. at p. 368, holding that an employe who has "mere custody of personal property, as distinguished from legal possession" and with animo furandi converts same to his own use is guilty of larceny. Here there was no "relation of special trust in regard to the article appropriated" which this court in Colip v. State, supra, said was necessary to an embezzlement. Appellant had access to the storage building but the Prestone therein was in the possession of the employer. We see no essential difference between this case and the hypothetical case of the watchman referred to in the following quotation from Vinnedge v. State [1906]:

"Where there is at most but a naked possession or control—that is, a bare charge—or where the access consists of a mere physical propinquity as an incident of the employment, the felonious appropriation should be regarded as larceny. The reference in the embezzlement statute to officers, agents, attorneys, clerks, servants, and employés is plainly indicative of the intent to limit the denouncement of the statute to cases in which such persons have, as an element of their employment, a special trust concerning the money, article, or thing of value that involves an actual possession thereof or a special right of access to or control over the same. This requirement would not be satisfied, as we may indicate by way of illustration, by the mere control or possession, or physical opportunity of access, which a watchman in charge of a store might have. As before indicated, the relationship contemplated by the statute is one of special trust and confidence; a relationship in which there inheres, either for the particular transaction or for all purposes, a special right of access to, or control or possession of, the money, article, or thing of value which is appropriated."

Usually a watchman carries a key. Appellant's key made access easier but did not give him possession. We regard as immaterial the fact that he was bonded against embezzlement. It perhaps was a circumstance which the court might have taken into consideration in determining the relationship of the parties, but it was in no sense controlling. Appellant's contention that animus furandi was not proved is controverted by the evidence showing that the crime was preceded by similar consummated thefts over a period of many months. Similar transactions may be shown to prove felonious intent, knowledge and other similar states of mind. . . .

The cases relied upon by appellant belong to another category. Davis v. State [1925] recognizes the principle quoted from Colip v. State, supra, but holds that the facts establish the crime of embezzlement. The appellant therein received money as treasurer of an association and later converted it to his own use. He had exclusive possession and control of the fund under a trust to account to his employer. In Jones v. State [1877] a merchant gave his employe some money in an unsealed envelope, directing him to deliver it to other merchants as the purchase price of a load of flour. On the day he succumbed to temptation and fled with the money to another state. State v. Wingo [1883] had similar facts. Each employe was given exclusive possession of the property under a special trust and later formed the felonious intent. . . .

Judgment affirmed.

NOTES

1. There is little or no justification today for the distinction between larceny and embezzlement. Both the offenses of larceny and embezzlement, as well as many related ones, can be adequately covered under a general statutory offense of "Theft". See, for example, Article 16 (S.H.A. ch. 38) of the Illinois Criminal Code.

2. In view of the fact that in many instances thefts by employees from their employers are never reported to the law enforcement authorities because of restitution being made by the employee, or someone on his behalf, attorneys should be mindful of the offense known as "compounding a felony" or as "misprision of felony". Consider, for instance, the following provision in the Illinois Criminal Code (S.H.A. ch. 38, § 32–1):

> A person compounds a crime when he receives or offers to another any consideration for a promise not to prosecute or aid in the prosecution of an offender.

The United States Code (18 U.S.C.A.) contains the following provision:

> § 4. Misprision of felony
>
> Whoever, having knowledge of the actual commission of a felony cognizable by a court of the United States, conceals and does not as soon as possible make known the same to some judge or other person in civil or military authority under the United States, shall be fined not more than $500 or imprisoned not more than three years, or both.

In a 1948 English case, R. v. Aberg, 32 Crim.App.Reps. 144, Lord Chief Justice Goddard said that "misprision of felony is an offense which is described in the books, but which has been generally regarded nowadays as obsolete or fallen into desuetude". But thirteen years later the House of Lords declared that the offense of misprision of felony still existed in all its vigor. Sykes v. Director of Public Prosecution, [1961] 3 All Eng.L.R.

33, held that if one knows that a felony has been committed and fails to report it, he is guilty of misprision of felony. Concealment, it was held, need not involve a positive act; mere omission is sufficient. Exempted, apparently, are persons within a privileged relationship with the felon (e. g., lawyers, clergyman), for the court in the Sykes case referred to "a claim of right made in good faith". For full text of the Sykes case, see infra p. 425.

A similar "misprision of felony" concept prevails in Australia. See R. v. Crimmins, [1959] V.R. 270.

C. FALSE PRETENSES

CHAPLIN v. UNITED STATES

United States Court of Appeals, D.C.1946.
157 F.2d 697.

CLARK, ASSOCIATE JUSTICE. This is an appeal from a conviction under the first count of an indictment charging appellant and his wife with obtaining money by false pretenses.

Of the several points raised by appellant we think one to be of controlling significance. He urges that the indictment failed to charge a crime because the one statement which he is alleged to have made relating to a subsisting fact was not traversed and no evidence was introduced to prove that the one statement was false.

To examine this contention we turn to the indictment. It is there charged that appellant and his wife, co-defendant below, ". . . with intent to defraud, feloniously did pretend and represent to one Violette McMullen, then and there being, that they, the said Sydney A. Chaplin and the said Dorothy Chaplin, were engaged in the wine and liquor business in Alexandria, Virginia, and that if she, the said Violette McMullen, would advance certain money, they, . . . *would* purchase certain liquor stamps with said money and . . . *would* return . . . any money so advanced . . ." (Italics added.) In the traversing clause, it is charged that the defendants ". . . would not purchase such liquor stamps and would not return . . . the money advanced . . . as they . . . well knew."

It appears from the indictment that the prosecution's case was necessarily founded on the defendants' *intention*, at the time of acquiring the money, not to do two things promised: (1) buy stamps, and (2) repay the money. Both of these promises relate to things the defendants were to do in the future. The prosecution did not prove that the defendants misrepresented their business connection. On the contrary, it appears from the record that the appellant and his wife were in the liquor business, that they did own a large quantity of wine for which state stamps were required and that they did buy some small amount of tax stamps. The question for our decision comes down to whether the "present intention" of the defendants not to return the money and not to buy the stamps as they said they would relates to a "present or past existing fact" such as will support a conviction for the crime of false pretenses. The rule stated in Wharton's Criminal Law, 12th Ed., § 1439, is that: "A false pretense, under the statute, must relate to a past event or existing fact. Any representation with regard to a future transaction is excluded. Thus, for instance, a false statement, that a draft which the defendant exhibits to the prosecutor has been received from a house of good credit abroad, and is for a valuable consideration, on the faith of which he obtains the prosecutor's goods, is within the law; a promise to deposit with him such a draft at some future time, though wilfully and intentionally false, and the means of prosecutor's parting possession with his property, is not. So a pretense that the party would do an act that he did not mean to do (as a pretense that he would pay for goods on delivery) was ruled by all the judges not to be a false pretense under the Statute of Geo. II., and the same rule is distinctly recognized in this country, it being held that the statement of an intention is not a statement of an existing fact." We think the great weight of authority sustains this statement of the rule and compels us to answer the question in the negative.

In its brief, the government was most candid on this point, stating that Commonwealth v. Althause, 207 Mass. 32, 93 N.E. 202, . . . from which a quotation of dictum was taken did not represent the weight of authority. The same may be said for the other two cases cited to support the prosecution's position on the point. . . . It appears from a study of these cases that the courts concerned found no difficulty in applying the rule on "intention" which has long been used in actions at law for fraud and deceit. We think it unnecessary to discuss the advisability of transplanting this concept to criminal actions. There is a vast difference between subjecting a defendant to criminal penalties and providing for the redress of wrongs through civil actions.

A majority of the courts having this problem placed before them have not subscribed to the theory that "intention", as manifest by false and misleading promises, standing alone, is a *fact* in the sense required for a conviction on the charge of false pretenses. . . .

Not only is the rule deeply rooted in our law, but moreover, we think the reasons upon which it is founded are no less cogent today than they were when the early cases were decided under the English statute cited by *Wharton*, supra. It is of course true that then, as now, the intention to commit certain crimes was ascertained by looking backward from the act and finding that the accused intended to do what he did do. However, where as here, the act complained of—namely, failure to repay money or use it as specified at the time of borrowing—is as consonant with ordinary commercial default as with criminal conduct, the danger of applying this technique to prove the crime is quite apparent. Business affairs would be materially incumbered by the ever present threat that a debtor might be subjected to criminal penalties if the prosecutor and jury were of the view that at the time of borrowing he was mentally a cheat. The risk of prosecuting one who is guilty of nothing more than a failure or inability to pay his debts is a very real consideration. It is not enough to say that if innocent the accused would be found not guilty. The social stigma attaching to one accused of a crime as well as the burdens incident to the defense would, irrespective of the outcome, place a devastating weapon in the hands of a disgruntled or disappointed creditor.

The business policy, as well as the difficulties and dangers inherent in a contrary rule are illustrated by the earlier English cases. In Rex v. Goodhall, 1821, . . . the accused was found to have obtained a quantity of meat, promising to pay for it but not so intending. In reversing the jury's verdict of guilty the court said: "It was merely a promise for future conduct, and common prudence and caution would have prevented any injury arising from the breach of it." Again, in Reg. v. Oates, 1855, Dears C.C. 459, 6 Cox C.C. 540, where the accused was charged with making a fraudulent overcharge for work performed the court discharged the prisoner saying: "Is a shopkeeper who knowingly charges for an article more than it is worth, liable to an indictment under this statute? . . . to hold the statute applicable to such a case would shake many transactions which, though certainly not fair in themselves are still not indictable."

In Reg. v. Woodman, 1879, . . . the prosecution advanced precisely the same argument that is urged here, contending that the defendant's intention was the existing fact about which the misrepresentation had been made. To this the court responded: "How can you define a man's mind? It is a mere promissory false pretence."

If we were to accept the government's position the way would be open for every victim of a bad bargain to resort to criminal proceedings to even the score with a judgment proof adversary. No doubt in the development of our criminal law the zeal with which the innocent are protected has provided a measure of shelter for the guilty. However, we do not think it wise to increase the possibility of conviction by broadening the accepted theory of the weight to be attached to the mental attitude of the accused.

In view of the foregoing we do not think it necessary to review the other points raised by appellant.

Reversed.

EDGERTON, ASSOCIATE JUSTICE (dissenting). The court holds that "the great weight of authority . . . compels us". This is a new rule and an important one. I think it is erroneous.

Usually there are good reasons for a doctrine which is widely accepted, and uniformity itself has some value even in criminal law. Accordingly we should consider the weight of authority elsewhere for what it may be worth. But we should not determine our action by a count of foreign cases regardless of logic, consistency, and social need.

"The social value of a rule has become a test of growing power and importance". We should decide the question before us "in accordance with present-day standards of wisdom and justice rather than in accordance with some outworn and antiquated rule of the past" which was never adopted here. To let judges who lived and died in other times and places make our decisions would be to abdicate as judges and serve as tellers. . . .

Considered without regard to the foreign cases on which the court relies, the indictment is plainly valid. No doubt a promise is commonly an undertaking, but it is always an assertion of a present intention to perform. "I will" means among other things "I intend to." It is so understood and it is meant to be so understood. Intention is a fact and present intention is a present fact. A promise made without an intention to perform is therefore a false statement about a present fact. This factual and declarative aspect of a promise is not a new discovery. It has come to be widely recognized in civil actions for deceit.

In criminal cases most courts and text writers have clung to an old illusion that the same words cannot embody both a promise and a statement of fact. But this tradition that in a criminal case "the statement of an intention is not a statement of an existing fact" has begun to break down. It is an obvious fiction. The meaning of words is the same whether their author is prosecuted civilly or criminally or not at all. The fiction that a promise made without intent to perform does not embody a misrepresentation conflicts with the facts, with the deceit cases, and with the interest of society in protecting itself against fraud. An Act of Congress makes it a crime in the District of Columbia to obtain money "by any false pretense, with intent to defraud." Congress did not exempt, and the court should not exempt, a pretense conveyed by words which also convey a promise. As a matter of plain English there could be no clearer case of false and fraudulent pretense than a borrower's pretense that he intends to repay money which he actually does not intend to repay.

The old illusion that a promise states no facts is not the only source of the old tolerance of falsehoods regarding intention. That a fool and his money are soon parted was once accepted as a sort of natural law. In 1821 the fact that "common prudence and caution would have prevented any injury" seemed to an English court a good reason for refusing to penalize an injury which had been intentionally inflicted by a false promise. The fact that common agility in dodging an intentional blow would have prevented any injury would not have seemed a reason for refusing to penalize a battery. Fools were fair game though cripples were not. But in modern times, no one not talking law would be likely to deny that society should protect mental as well as physical helplessness against intentional injuries.

Though the court decides the case on the basis of authority, the opinion concludes with a defense of the prevailing rule. But to justify this rule it would be necessary to show that false pretenses regarding intention are a harmless way of obtaining money, or else that intention cannot be proved in prosecutions for false pretenses as it is constantly proved in other criminal prosecutions and in civil actions for deceit.

Difficulties of proof are seldom greater in criminal cases than in civil, except that the prosecution must prove its case beyond a reasonable doubt. No peculiar difficulty of proof distinguishes this crime from others. Intentions of one sort or another must be proved in most criminal cases. They are usually proved by conduct. It is inherently no more difficult to prove an intent not to perform a promise than, for example, an intent to monopolize, to commit a felony, or to receive goods knowing them to be stolen. Appellant's conduct showed his intent. After getting $375 from a nurse by promising to buy liquor stamps and repay the money, he made the same promise a few days later and got $700 more. He said he needed the money to get the stamps. Yet he bought less than $40 worth of stamps, if any, during the next six weeks, and there is no evidence that he bought any stamps at any later time. Meanwhile he continued to borrow money from the woman. He made no repayments at any time. The jury might well conclude, as it did, that the difference between his promises and his performance was not accidental but was part of his original plan. The court does not suggest that the proof of his original intention was insufficient. If it were thought to be insufficient, the conviction should be reversed on that ground. The rule which the court adopts will make prosecutions impossible even when admissions or other evidence make guilt obvious.

No peculiar danger to innocent men distinguishes this crime from others. No honest borrower who fails to repay a loan, or changes his mind about the use which he intended to make of the money, is likely to be charged with obtaining it by false pretenses. Prosecutions are not undertaken without evidence and convictions do not withstand attack unless they are supported by sufficient evidence. The danger of a counter suit for malicious prosecution is always present to discourage unfounded charges. The court's picture of a flood of indictments against honest business men is unconvincing. No such flood has been observed in the few jurisdictions which have adopted the modern rule. . . .

There is, as the court says, a vast difference between criminal penalties and civil redress. It is the more unfortunate to hold, as the court does, that a common sort of fraud is not a crime. Since civil redress is not punitive but compensatory, the decision means that the law of the District of Columbia offers no deterrent to this sort of fraud. If a swindler has property which can be taken in execution on a civil judgment, he may not always win by practicing this fraud. But he cannot lose. If he perseveres he will win in the long run, for he will not always be sued to judgment. And one who has no property on which execution can be levied is bound to win as often as he can find a victim.

NOTES

1. The viewpoint expressed by the dissent in the above case is the one adopted in the A.L.I. Model Penal Code, which provides, in 206.2 as follows:

Theft by Deception

(1) *General.* A person commits theft if he obtains property of another by means of deception. A person deceives if he purposely:

(a) creates or reinforces an impression which is false and which he does not believe to be true; or

(b) prevents another from acquiring information which the actor knows would influence the other party in the transaction; or

(c) fails to disclose a lien, adverse claim, or other legal impediment to the enjoyment of property being sold or otherwise transferred or encumbered, regardless of the legal validity of the impediment and regardless of any official record disclosing its existence;

(d) fails to correct a false impression previously created or reinforced by him; or

(e) fails to correct a false impression which he knows to be influencing another to whom he stands in a relationship of special trust and confidence.

(2) *Value, Law, Opinion, Intention; False Promises.* Deception may relate to value, law, opinion, intention or other state of mind. A promise which creates the impression that the promisor intends that the promise shall be performed is deception if he does not have that intention at the time of the promise; but the non-existence of that intention shall not be inferred from the fact alone that the promise was not performed.

(3) *Puffing Excepted.* Exaggerated commendation of wares in communications addressed to the public or to a class or group shall not be deemed deceptive if:

(a) it would be unlikely to mislead the ordinary person of the class or group addressed; and

(b) there is no deception other than as to the actor's belief in the commendation; and

(c) the actor was not in a position of special trust and confidence in relation to the misled party.

"Commendation of wares" includes representation that the price asked is low.

(4) *Non-pecuniary Deception Excepted.* A person does not commit theft by deception where, in a business transaction, the only deception is as to matters having no pecuniary significance.

2. The Illinois Criminal Code (S.H.A. ch. 38) provides, in § 16–1(b), that a person commits theft when he knowingly "obtains by deception control over property of the owner", and, in § 15–4(e), that "deception" means to knowingly "promise performance which the offender does not intend to perform or knows will not be performed". "Failure to perform", however, "standing alone is not evidence that the offender did not intend to perform" (§ 15–4(e)).

3. With regard to overdrawn checks or checks on defunct or non-existing bank accounts, consider the following from the Illinois Criminal Code (S.H.A. ch. 38, § 17–1):

A person commits a deceptive practice when:

* * *

(d) With intent to obtain control over property or to pay for property, labor or services of another, he issues or delivers a check or other order upon a real or fictitious depository for the payment of money, knowing that it will not be paid by the depository. Failure to have sufficient funds or credit with the depository when the check or other order is issued or delivered is prima facie evidence that the offender knows that it will not be paid by the depository; . . .

4. The problem of credit card frauds has become an increasingly troublesome and complex one. Rather than attempt an analysis or statutory treatment here, and particularly in view of the statutory variances, we suggest that the classroom discussion concern itself with the statute of the particular jurisdiction in which the class is conducted.

Comprehensive Theft Statutes

Several states, following the pioneering proposals of the American Law Institute (Art. 206, A.L.I. Penal Code, Tent.Draft # 2), have enacted general theft statutes which have abolished the separate offenses of larceny, embezzlement, and false pretenses. See Wisconsin Criminal Code, W.S.A. 943.-20, and Illinois Criminal Code (S.H.A. ch. 38), Art. 16.

D. RECEIVING STOLEN PROPERTY

PEOPLE v. RIFE

Supreme Court of Illinois, 1943.
382 Ill. 588, 48 N.Ed.2d 367.

THOMPSON, JUSTICE. Plaintiff in error, Noah D. Rife, and his wife, Mabel, operators of a junk yard in the city of Danville, were jointly indicted at the January term, 1941, of the circuit court of Vermilion county, charged in three counts with receiving, buying and aiding in concealing 132 pounds of engine brass and 167 pounds of journal brass, and in a fourth count with receiving, buying and aiding in concealing 299 pounds of brass, all of the property of and stolen from Benjamin Wham, trustee of the Chicago and Eastern Illinois Railway Company, a corporation. Each of the counts charged that defendant knew that said brass had been stolen. Defendants pleaded not guilty and were tried by a jury. Plaintiff in error was found guilty and the value of the property received was found to be $9.35. His wife, the other defendant, was found not guilty. Motion for a new trial was denied and plaintiff in error was sentenced to the Illinois State Penal Farm at Vandalia for one year and fined $1,000. . . .

The roundhouse foreman in the Chicago and Eastern Illinois railway yards at Chicago, in October, 1940, supervised the replacing of brass on engines 3643 and 1908. The old brass taken off these engines was loaded in two freight cars, sealed and shipped to the railroad shops or roundhouse at Danville. One of these cars arrived on October 22, 1940, and was unloaded and put in the bins at the Danville shops on October 22 and 23. The other car came in November 2, 1940, and from that time until it was unloaded on November 8, stood upon the company's track at the storeroom in the Danville yards of the C. & E. I. On November 5, 1940, plaintiff in error bought 187 pounds of railroad brass from [a boy named Henry Brandon]. On the day previous he had also bought brass from Brandon. On November 5, 1940, W. B. Sloan, the chief of police of the railway company, Theodore Alberts, general foreman of the company, and Robert Meade, a deputy sheriff, went to the junk yard of plaintiff in error, where they recovered 132 pounds of railway-engine brass and 167 pounds of journal brass. This brass was positively identified by Mr. Alberts from the engine numbers, 3643 and 1908, and the patent number A-D 830 stamped on the various pieces.

The contention is made that the evidence is not sufficient to prove beyond a reasonable doubt that the brass described in the indictment was ever stolen, and also that the evidence is not sufficient to prove beyond a reasonable doubt that plaintiff in error knew the brass had been stolen at the time he purchased it from Henry Brandon. Before there can be a conviction for receiving stolen property the evidence must show beyond a reasonable doubt, first, that the property has, in fact, been stolen by a person other than the one charged with receiving the property; second, that the one charged with receiving it has actually received it or aided in concealing it; third, that the person so receiving the stolen property knew that it was stolen at the time of receiving it; and, fourth, that he received the property for his own gain or to prevent the owner from again possessing it. . . . But while it is true that these four propositions must all be proved beyond a reasonable doubt, it is also true that neither is required to be established by direct evidence. Circumstantial evidence may be resorted to for the purpose of proving the corpus delicti as well as for the purpose of connecting the accused with the crime. . . . There is no invariable rule as to the quantum of proof necessary to establish the corpus delicti. Each case must depend, in a measure, upon its own particular circumstances. . . . Circumstantial evidence is legal evidence and there is no legal distinction between direct and circumstantial evidence so far as weight and effect are concerned. . . . It is not necessary that someone testify, in so many words, to the theft of this brass and that plaintiff in error had knowledge of such theft at the time he purchased the brass from Henry Brandon, but such facts may be shown by circumstantial evidence. The brass found in the Rife junk yard was positively identified as brass which had been removed from the Chicago and Eastern Illinois engines in Chicago and shipped to Danville, within twenty days at the most, previous to that time. It was conclusively proved by the evidence that this brass was shipped from Chicago to Danville for use in the railroad shops there, and received at the C. & E. I. shops at Danville, where it was in the exclusive possession of the railway company on its own private premises. It then disappeared. It must have been taken by somebody. The only conclusion that can follow, under all the circumstances, is that a larceny had been committed. There was no contention by the plaintiff in error on the trial that the brass was not stolen. Indeed, his wife testified that he had told her that Henry Brandon had stolen it. In the case of People v. Feeley . . . where department-store merchandise, including shirts, ties, socks, and other wearing apparel, was discovered in an automobile, this court held that the fact that none of the articles had been wrapped in packages by the stores, but had been stuffed in large quantities in cardboard boxes, and the finding of the shoplifters' boxes in the automobile, were circumstances sufficiently proving the theft of such merchandise. In the Feeley case, supra, there was no evidence that the merchandise had been missed or was known to be stolen before found in the automobile. It is not necessary in the instant case, to warrant the jury in finding that a larceny of the brass had been committed, for the evidence to show that it had been missed by the employees of the Chicago and Eastern Illinois Railway Company or that they knew that it had been stolen. . . .

Plaintiff in error testified that when Brandon sold him the brass, he told him that the brass was not stolen, that he had found it, that it was all right for plaintiff in error to buy it, and that if any one inquired he could say that he had bought it from Brandon. He also testified that the possession of a large amount of heavy brass by [a boy] who claimed to have found it did not arouse his suspicions. . . .

There was no direct evidence that plaintiff in error purchased the brass in question knowing it to have been stolen. The People relied upon circumstantial evidence for such proof, but this does not militate against the prosecution. . . . Knowledge that property was stolen is seldom susceptible of direct proof, but may be inferred from all the surrounding facts and circumstances. . . . Circumstances which will induce a belief in the mind of a reasonable person that property has been stolen are sufficient proof of such guilty knowledge. . . . The knowledge need not be that actual or positive knowledge which one acquires from personal observation of the fact, but it is sufficient if the circumstances accompanying the transaction be such as to make the accused believe the goods had been stolen. This knowledge of the accused is an essential element of the offense and must be found by the jury as a fact. In determining whether the fact existed, the jury will be justified in presuming that the accused acted rationally and that whatever would convey knowledge or induce belief in the mind of a reasonable person, would, in the absence of countervailing evidence, be sufficient to apprise him of the like fact, or induce in his mind the like impression and belief. . . .

In the instant case plaintiff in error, after recent and repeated warnings to be on the alert for stolen railroad brass and to notify the sheriff's office of any suspicious circumstances, failed to report the circumstance to the officers when [a boy] offered him a large amount of such brass with no explanation other than that he had found it and had not stolen it. Plaintiff in error made no inquiry into the details of the [boy's] improbable story of his acquisition of such a large amount of brass. The story of plaintiff in error, of his purchase of this brass in good faith and innocence, is not supported either by any direct or circumstantial evidence. On the contrary, all the evidence points conclusively to, and is sufficient to warrant the jury in believing, beyond a reasonable doubt, that plaintiff in error knew when he purchased this brass that he was handling stolen property. . . . All of the evidence, and facts and circumstances in evidence, in the instant case, when considered together, cannot consistently be reconciled with any theory other than that of the guilt of the accused. Upon a review of the record in a criminal case, it is the duty of this court to consider the evidence, and if it does not establish guilt beyond a reasonable doubt, the conviction must be reversed. We have carefully considered all of the evidence, both that of the People and that of plaintiff in error, and we cannot say that it is not amply sufficient to justify the jury in believing beyond a reasonable doubt that the plaintiff in error is guilty of the crime with which he is charged. . . .

The judgment will therefore be affirmed.

Judgment affirmed.

COMMONWEALTH v. OWENS

Supreme Court of Pennsylvania, 1970.
441 Pa. 318, 271 A.2d 230.

ROBERTS, JUSTICE. It has been the law in the criminal courts of Pennsylvania that a defendant's unexplained possession of recently stolen goods is sufficient proof of his guilt of the crime of receiving stolen goods. Although the statute defining that crime provides as an express element that the defendant knew or had reason to know that the goods in question had been stolen, it has been reasoned that such scienter may be presumed from evidence of mere possession. . . .

This case raises a serious question as to the continuing validity of this presumption in light of the United States Supreme Court's recent decisions in Leary v. United States (1969), and Turner v. United States (1970). . . .

At approximately 11:10 P.M. on the evening of January 31, 1967, Dr. Dick Kazin parked and left his automobile on Craft Avenue in the Oakland section of Pittsburgh. Upon returning to the car some twenty minutes later, he discovered one of the car's front windows broken and three handguns and two snow tires missing from within.

On February 19, 1967, Lieutenant O'Connell of the Pittsburgh police force went to the grocery store of one Earl Harris armed with a search warrant seeking contraband moonshine whiskey. Not only did the search for the moonshine prove fruitful, but O'Connell also found one of the pistols that had been stolen from Kazin less than three weeks earlier. At appellant's trial Harris testified that he had purchased the pistol from appellant for a total price of $30, paying $20 in cash with a balance of $10. In partial corroboration of this story Harris' wife Velma testified that appellant had come into the grocery store seeking payment of the $10 balance and attempting to sell a second pistol which he showed to her at that time. Velma Harris admitted, however, that appellant had offered no clue as to how he had come into possession of either of the weapons.

The foregoing is the sum of the prosecution's case.

Appellant testified in his own behalf and admitted having met Harris in prison many years earlier and having seen him on the street several times in the subsequent years. However, he denied any connection with the stolen gun or its sale or attempted sale to Harris. He further denied all of Velma Harris' testimony concerning his supposed demand for a $10 balance and attempt to sell a second gun.

The trier of fact was of course free to credit the testimony of Earl and Velma Harris and to disbelieve that of appellant, but the former established at most only that appellant possessed a stolen pistol at some time less than three weeks after its theft. Thus the presumption of guilty knowledge is the sole basis upon which appellant's conviction can rest, and it is to an assessment of this presumption that we must turn.

The general teaching of *Leary* and *Turner* is that a criminal presumption is unconstitutional "unless it can at least be said with substantial assurance that the presumed fact is more likely than not to flow from the proved fact on which it is made to depend." . . .

Leary reversed a conviction for the possession of marihuana knowing the same to have been illegally imported, by invalidating the statutory presumption that such knowledge may be presumed from evidence of mere possession. The Court admitted that information concerning the factual accuracy of the presumption was " 'not within specialized judicial competence or completely commonplace,' " and that significant weight should be accorded to Congress's presumed investigation as to the soundness of the presumption. Nevertheless, in the absence of an actual legislative record documenting the accuracy of the presumption, the Court felt free to and did survey other available data on the subject. From such a survey the Court was willing to assume that the majority of marihuana consumed in the United States was illegally imported but deemed this an insufficient basis for concluding that "a majority of marihuana possessors either are cognizant of the apparently high rate of importation or otherwise have become aware that *their* marihuana was grown abroad." . . .

Turner dealt with an almost identical knowledge presumption concerning possession of cocaine and heroin. The Court struck down the presumption as applied to cocaine on the basis of its finding that large amounts of coca leaves, the raw material from which cocaine is derived, are legally imported for medicinal purposes. Respecting heroin, however, the Court sustained the presumption in light of evidence that virtually all domestically consumed heroin is illegally imported and that this fact concerning the source of heroin is not only widely and popularly known but especially known to those who traffic in the drug, "unless they practice a studied ignorance to which they are not entitled." . . .

The "more likely than not" test coupled with the examples provided by *Leary* and *Turner* as to how that test should be applied in a given case leave us with little doubt that the knowledge presumption concerning receipt of stolen goods is constitutionally infirm, at least as applied to the circumstances of this case, and we so hold. We reiterate that there is nothing whatever in the record touching upon how appellant originally came into possession of the stolen pistol, and the possibilities of innocent acquisition seem myriad: a gift, payment for services rendered, payment of a debt, purchase from a seemingly reputable dealer in used guns. The only empirical data furnished to us by either party casts considerable doubt upon the probable factual strength of the knowledge presumption. A staff report submitted to the National Commission on the Causes and Prevention of Violence: Firearms and Violence in American Life, ch. 3, at 13–15, estimates that there were 24,000,000 handguns in the United States in 1968, that 54% of all handguns acquired in 1968 were sold used, and that among low income groups 71% of all used firearms were obtained from a friend or a private party. While these figures do not enable us to construct with any degree of accuracy the relative percentages of transfers of stolen and nonstolen guns, they nevertheless do indicate the probability that substantial numbers of used guns are transferred in seemingly innocent circumstances. . . .

* * *

In response, the Commonwealth urges that the wisdom of common experience suffices to demonstrate that a possessor of a recently stolen pistol more likely than not knew or had reason to know that the weapon had been stolen. We fear, however, that the Commonwealth attributes to us and demands of us not merely a sensitivity to the dictates of common experience but a degree of clairvoyance which we do not and shall never possess. . . .

* * *

The order of the Superior Court is reversed and the motion in arrest of judgment is granted and the judgment of sentence is vacated.

EAGEN, J., concurs in the result.

BELL, C. J., filed a dissenting opinion in which COHEN, J., joined.

POMEROY, J., dissents.

BELL, CHIEF JUSTICE (dissenting).

Defendant was tried on June 12, 1967, without a jury, and was found guilty of receiving stolen goods and sentenced to three years' imprisonment. Defendant's motion for arrest of judgment and a discharge, or in the alternative a new trial, was denied by the lower Court. The Superior Court affirmed, per curiam, and we granted allocatur. . . .

* * *

It has been the long and well established law of Pennsylvania that possession of recently stolen property raises a presumption of knowledge that the property had been stolen. . . .

* * *

Many Superior Court cases reiterate (although at times in slightly different language) this well and widely established presumption of guilt from mere possession of recently stolen property. . . .

In a vain attempt to avoid the above-mentioned well established principles of law, the majority base their Opinion upon Leary v. United States and Turner v. United States. *Leary* and *Turner* are clearly distinguishable on their facts. In *Leary*, the United States Supreme Court held unconstitutional a statutory provision which raised a presumption of knowledge of *illegal importation of marijuana* from the mere possession of marijuana. In *Turner*, the United States Supreme Court held that a statutory presumption of knowledge of *illegal importation of cocaine* from mere possession of cocaine was invalid because much more cocaine is lawfully produced in this country than is smuggled into this country. Furthermore, in *Turner*, a statutory presumption of knowledge of the *illegal importation of heroin* from the mere possession of heroin was upheld because the overwhelming evidence is that the heroin consumed in the United States is *illegally imported*. It is important to note that these two decisions are limited to the particular statutory presumptions in light of the particular circumstances of each case and do not decry or invalidate the Constitutionality of presumptions generally.

The prior decisions of this Court were not written on the sand to be washed away by each wave of new Justices. When crime is running rampant in our cities (and indeed throughout Pennsylvania and our entire Country) and terrifying our law-abiding citizens, this is no time to overrule well settled principles of law to aid criminals and those accused of crime and further jeopardize the safety and security of Society.

For the above reasons, I vigorously dissent.

COHEN, J., joins in this dissenting Opinion.

UNITED STATES v. BROCATO

United States Court of Appeals, 8th Circuit 1971.
437 F.2d 1157, cert. denied 402 U.S. 1010, 91 S.Ct. 2196.

PER CURIAM. In this case, John and Albert Brocato appeal their convictions for knowingly possessing property stolen from an interstate shipment in violation of 18 U.S.C. § 659. They claim that the evidence was insufficient to show possession and that the trial court erred in giving an instruction which permitted the jury to infer defendants' guilty knowledge from their possession of recently stolen property. We find these claims lacking in merit.

The evidence showed that 280 Singer nine-inch portable television sets being transported in interstate commerce disappeared from a truck during the morning of November 6, 1969, at Kansas City, Missouri. Two days later, approximately 100 of the sets were seen in the storage area of a Bertsch and Vegder store located at 9401 Blue Ridge Boulevard, Kansas City, Missouri. This firm did not sell Singer television sets.

The evidence further shows that appellant Albert Brocato leased a Ford Econoline rental truck on November 8, 1969, and that appellant John Brocato drove the truck to the Bertsch and Vegder store that afternoon, where he talked with Anthony LaTore, the store manager. FBI agents placed the store under surveillance that day. The next day, Sunday, November 9, Anthony LaTore opened the store and he and the two appellants proceeded to load some of the television sets into the leased truck. FBI agents then arrested the three men and found 55 television sets present: 15 in the truck, 5 on the loading dock and 35 in the storage area of the store.

Subsequently, the three arrested persons were indicted for unlawfully possessing chattels of a value in excess of $100.00, that is, 55 Singer nine-inch television sets, which had been stolen from an interstate shipment. The LaTore prosecution was severed from that against these appellants.

The evidence in this case clearly shows that appellants exercised dominion and thus possessed the property in question within the meaning of the statute. . . .

Moreover, we have repeatedly upheld instructions which permit an inference of guilty knowledge from possession of recently stolen property. . . . See Judge Lay's opinion in United States v.

Jones, 418 F.2d 818 (8th Cir. 1969), for a detailed discussion of the historical antecedents of these instructions.

The trial court in this case phrased the instruction as follows:

> You are instructed that possession of property recently stolen, if not satisfactorily explained, is a circumstance from which you, the jury, may reasonably draw the inference and find, in the light of the surrounding circumstances shown by the evidence in the case, if you so find, that the person in possession knew the property had been stolen.
>
> * * * * * * * * * *
>
> Possession may be satisfactorily explained by facts and circumstances in evidence independent of any testimony or other evidence from any accused.

Pursuant to this instruction, the appellants might have explained the circumstances of their possession of the stolen property in question. John Brocato, however, contends that his prior felony conviction stood in the way of his taking the stand in his own defense. Thus, he argues, the giving of the instruction infringed upon his right against self-incrimination.

Such contention is without merit in this case. Appellants could have presented evidence other than their own testimony to explain the circumstances; yet neither appellant produced any affirmative evidence. Albert Brocato, whose conduct was entwined with that of John Brocato, declined to take the stand, although he apparently possessed no prior criminal record. Thus, appellant John Brocato demonstrates no infringement of his Fifth Amendment right against self-incrimination.

Accordingly, we affirm.

E. ROBBERY *

LEAR v. STATE

Supreme Court of Arizona, 1931.
39 Ariz. 313, 6 P.2d 426.

ROSS, J. The appellant was convicted of robbery. He appeals and assigns as error the insufficiency of the evidence to sustain the conviction and the giving of erroneous instructions.

The prosecuting witness, George Gross, testified that around 7 o'clock on the morning of August 12, 1931, he opened the Campbell Quality Shop, located in Buckeye, Maricopa county; that just about

* Robbery is traditionally classified as a crime against the person; however, since the ultimate purpose of the crime is the misappropriation of property, it is included in this section.

that time appellant entered the store and inquired about purchasing some shirts and shoes; that in the meantime he had taken a box of currency and a bag of silver out of the store safe; had placed the currency in the cash register and the bag of silver on the counter; that, while he was in the act of untying or unrolling the bag of silver, and while it was on the counter, appellant grabbed it from his hands and ran out of the back door; that appellant said no word at the time, exhibited no arms, and used no force other than to grab the bag as stated above. Appellant admitted taking the bag of silver and that it contained $33.

It was the contention of appellant at the trial, and is his contention here, that the facts do not show that he committed the crime of robbery. This crime is defined by our statute, section 4602, Revised Code of 1928, as follows: "Robbery is the felonious taking of personal property in the possession of another, from his person or immediate presence and against his will, accomplished by means of force or fear. The fear may be either of an unlawful injury to the person or property of the person robbed, or of a relative or member of his family; or of an immediate and unlawful injury to the person or property of any one in the company of the person robbed at the time of the robbery."

The crimes of robbery and larceny are not the same. The former is classified as a crime against the person and the latter as a crime against property. In robbery there is, in addition to a felonious taking, a violent invasion of the person. If the person is not made to surrender the possession of the personal property by means of force or fear, the dominant element of robbery is not present. The mere taking of property in possession of another, from his person or immediate presence and against his will, is not robbery. Such taking must be accomplished by force or fear to constitute robbery.

The element of fear is not in the case. Appellant made no threat or demonstration. He simply grabbed the bag of silver from the hands of the prosecuting witness and ran away with it. There was no pulling or scrambling for possession of the bag. Was the force employed by appellant the kind of force necessary to constitute robbery? We think not. As we read the cases and textwriters, "the force used must be either before, or at the time of the taking, and must be of such a nature as to show that it was intended to overpower the party robbed, and prevent his resisting, and not merely to get possession of the property stolen." . . . * * *

F. BURGLARY *

1. The Common Law

At common law the offense of burglary consisted of a *breaking* and *entering* of the *dwelling house* of another, in the *nighttime*, with *intent* to commit a felony. The problems which have arisen over the years with respect to each of these elements are perhaps as complex as those concerning the elements of larceny. Fortunately, many of the early troublesome issues have been obviated by statute. Familiarity with some of the major common law rules is nevertheless helpful to an understanding of the legislation in this area.

a. *Breaking.* The requirement of a "breaking" or "breach" means that the burglar must make a trespassory entry involving the creation of an opening into the dwelling. In State v. Boon, 35 N.C. 227, 229 (1852), the court stated: "Passing an imaginary line is a 'breaking of the close,' and will sustain an action of trespass *quare clausum fregit.* In burglary more is required—there must be a breaking, moving or putting aside of something material, which constitutes a part of the dwelling-house, and is relied on as a security against intrusion."

The breaking may be into any part of a building and need not be a breaking in from the outside. Opening the door of an inner room is therefore sufficient. Davidson v. State, 86 Tex.Cr.R. 243, 216 S.W. 624 (1919).

Constructive breaking occurs under certain circumstances where no force is used to make a way for the entry. The use of a trick or an artifice to gain entry is one type of constructive breaking. In Nichols v. State, 68 Wis. 416, 32 N.W. 543 (1887), for example, the burglar gained entry by concealing himself in a box. In Le Mott's Case, 84 Eng.Rep. 1073 (1650), the burglars merely told a maid that they wanted to speak to the master, and when she opened the door for them they entered and robbed him. Another type of constructive breaking occurs when one who has access to the dwelling, such as a servant, conspires to let another into the house. See Regina v. Johnson, Car. & M. 218, 174 Eng.Rep. 479 (1841).

Entering a dwelling which one has a right to enter at the time entry is made does not constitute a breaking because there is no trespass. Thus, using a key to enter a building which one has an unrestricted right to enter is not a breaking. People v. Kelley, 253 App. Div. 430, 3 N.Y.S.2d 46 (1938); Davis v. Commonwealth, 132 Va. 521, 110 S.E. 356 (1922). However, if the entry by use of a key is

* The common law crimes of burglary and arson, which are treated in this section, are crimes against the habitation; under modern legislation, however, they have, as here, been grouped with the property offenses.

made at an unauthorized time, a trespass exists and a breaking occurs. State v. Corcoran, 82 Wash. 44, 143 P. 453 (1914).

b. *Entering.* An entry is made if any part of the body is inside the dwelling, even if only a hand or finger intrudes for the purpose of the breaking. State v. Whitaker, 275 S.W.2d 316 (Mo.1955); Regina v. O'Brien, 4 Cox C.C. 400 (1850); Franco v. State, 42 Tex. 276 (1875). An entry may also be made by inserting an object into the dwelling; however, the object must be inserted for the purpose of carrying out the felonious design, and it is insufficient if the instrument is used only to effect the breach. Walker v. State, 63 Ala. 49 (1879); Rex v. Rust, 1 Mood.C.C. 183 (1828). The entry must be "consequent upon the breaking," so that if one enters a dwelling through an open door and then opens an inner door but does not go through it, the requirement of entry is lacking. Regina v. Davis, 6 Cox C.C. 369 (1854).

c. *The dwelling house of another.* (1) A dwelling house, under the rules of common law burglary, is a building habitually used as a place to sleep. Rex v. Stock, Russ. & R. 185, 2 Leach C.C. 1015, 7 Taunt. 339 (1810). It may be a store or other place of business, if someone regularly sleeps there, State v. Outlaw, 72 N.C. 551 (1875); but the fact that someone may sleep there from time to time is insufficient, State v. Jenkins, 50 N.C. 430 (1858). If a building is regularly used as a residence during a certain time of the year, for example a summer home, it qualifies as a dwelling house even during the period when it is not occupied. State v. Bair, 112 W.Va. 655, 166 S.E. 369 (1932). The test is whether the occupant intends to return. State v. Meerchouse, 34 Mo. 344 (1864). A building that no one has yet moved into is not considered a dwelling house for purposes of burglary. Woods v. State, 186 Miss. 463, 191 So. 283 (1939).

Rooms in an inn, hotel, or apartment building are the dwellings of the occupants, unless the occupants are merely transients. People v. Carr, 255 Ill. 203, 99 N.E. 357 (1912). Where the rooms are occupied by transients, however, the rooms are considered the dwelling house of the landlord, whether or not the landlord lives in the building. See Rodgers v. People, 86 N.Y. 360 (1881).

The dwelling house is considered to include not only the dwelling itself but also buildings which are "within the curtilage." The purpose of including buildings used in connection with the dwelling is to protect against the dangers resulting from the likelihood that a dweller who hears a prowler in the nighttime will go forth to protect his family and property. Thus a garage is considered part of the dwelling house where it is in reasonable proximity to the house. Harris v. State, 41 Okl.Cr. 121, 271 P. 957 (1928). A cellar is also within the "curtilage" even though it has no entrance from the dwelling itself and must be entered from the outside. Mitchell v. Commonwealth, 88 Ky. 349, 11 S.W. 209 (1889).

The dwelling house must be that "of another," in the sense that it must be occupied by another. It need not be owned by victim, inasmuch as burglary at common law is a crime against the habitation and not against property. One may therefore burglarize a building leased to, and occupied by, someone else. Smith v. People, 115 Ill. 17, 3 N.E. 733 (1885). The dweller, however, cannot burglarize his own dwelling, even though it has other occupants. Clarke v. Commonwealth, 66 Va. 908 (1874).

d. *Nighttime.* As an element of burglary, nighttime is the period of time between sunset and sunrise, and it is not considered night if there is enough natural daylight so that one can discern the countenance of another man's face. People v. Griffin, 19 Cal. 578 (1862). Both the breaking and entering must occur during the nighttime, but they need not occur on the same night. Rex v. Smith, Russ. & Ry. 417, 168 Eng.Rep. 874 (1820).

e. *With intent to commit a felony.* Although burglary is commonly thought of as an offense committed with intent to steal, the required intent actually includes the intent to commit any felony. It is not necessary that the felony in fact be committed, Wilson v. State, 24 Conn. 56 (1855); however, both the breaking and entering must be made with the necessary intent. Colbert v. State, 91 Ga. 705, 17 S.E. 840 (1893).

At common law both grand and petit larceny were felonies, but petit larceny is now frequently made a misdemeanor by statute; however, it is also commonly provided that burglarious intent exists where there is an intent to commit a felony "or to steal."

2. Legislation

Modern legislation on burglary has made a number of changes in the common law, generally broadening the scope of the offense. Following are the various changes as revealed in an excellent analysis of the modern law of burglary in Note, A Rationale of the Law of Burglary, 57 Colum.L.Rev. 1009 (1951):

(1) All jurisdictions now include virtually all buildings in the scope of the crime, although most jurisdictions attach a more severe penalty to the offense where a dwelling is involved.

(2) A few jurisdictions dispense with the requirement of "entry."

(3) A few jurisdictions dispense with the requirement of "breaking," but some of these require a trespass instead. Others provide a higher penalty where a "breaking" occurs. Where breaking is retained, some jurisdictions provide that absent a "breaking in," a "breaking out" will suffice.

(4) All jurisdictions recognize daytime burglaries, although some provide a more severe penalty for burglaries committed at night.

(5) The jurisdictions define burglarious intent in four principal ways: (a) intent to commit a felony; (b) intent to commit a felony or larceny; (c) intent to commit any crime (with respect to one or more degrees or forms of burglary); and (d) intent to commit certain specified crimes. A few jurisdictions dispense entirely with the requirement of an intent to commit another crime for the lowest degree or form of burglary.

(6) Many jurisdictions have added new elements to the common law crime of burglary. For example, some make special provisions for armed burglary and burglary involving the use of (or attempt or intent to use) explosives, and some require for the offense of first degree burglary that someone be in the building at the time of the offense.

For a modern code provision covering the offense of burglary, consider the following from the 1961 Illinois Criminal Code (S.H.A. ch. 38):

> **§ 19—1. Burglary**
>
> (a) A person commits burglary when without authority he knowingly enters or without authority remains within a building, housetrailer, watercraft, aircraft, motor vehicle (as defined in the Illinois Motor Vehicle Law) railroad car, or any part thereof, with intent to commit therein a felony or theft. . . .

The problem of establishing the requisite "intent" in this or any other similar burglary statute is illustrated in the next principal case.

Modern statutes of "housebreaking," the day-time burglary of a dwelling offense, still require interpretation on what constitutes a dwelling. In Holtman v. State, 278 A.2d 82 (Md.Spec.App.1971) a conviction for daytime housebreaking was reversed upon a showing that the defendant had broken into a church. Though it may be the "mansion house of God", the court did not consider it a dwelling within the meaning of the burglary law. On the other hand, an Illinois court construed a "car wash" to be a building falling within the modern Illinois burglary statute above. People v. Blair, 1 Ill.App.3d 6, 272 N.E.2d 404 (1971).

PEOPLE v. SCHNELLER

Illinois Appellate Court, 1966.
69 Ill.App.2d 50, 216 N.E.2d 510.

PRESIDING JUSTICE DRUCKER. The defendant, George W. Schneller, was found guilty of burglary after a bench trial and was sentenced to the penitentiary for a term of not less than one nor more than four years. In this appeal defendant contends that he was not proven guilty beyond a reasonable doubt of the crime of burglary as charged in the indictment.

Officer Robert Hanson testified that on March 13, 1964, at approximately 7:30 P.M. he proceeded to the Chicago Historical Society pursuant to a radio assignment notifying him that the ADT electric alarm system was sounding, and that other officers arrived shortly thereafter; that upon investigation he found the doors secured but he noticed a door at the north end of the building open and close; that men from the ADT system arrived and opened the door; and that they entered with police dogs and found the defendant near a snow plow and a mimeograph machine. The officer further testified that a showcase had been pried open and a small white shirt type button was on the floor; that two buttons were missing from defendant's shirt; that they found a screwdriver, some long-nosed pliers, sunglasses and a handkerchief; and that near the door they found an automatic pistol and flashlight; and that the aforesaid tools were found in a room which contained machinery or large equipment, not small tools.

Paul Angle, director of the museum, testified as to the condition of the showcase and also identified some guns which were found in a bag and on the floor as those which were formerly in the showcase.

Edward Stashinski, an employee of the museum, testified as to his encounter with the defendant on March 11 (two days before the occurrence in question) at about 4:35 P.M. (which was after the second bell had rung as notice to visitors to leave the building) in the basement work area of the museum which the public is not allowed to enter. He stated that some people stray from the public portion of the museum to that portion which is not public but only during working hours, whereas his encounter with defendant was after working hours; that in his three and one-half years of employment at the museum no one, to his knowledge, has ever wandered into this particular area; and that:

> [I]t is a work area where there are prized possessions where we do not allow people, and have posted the doorways and stairwells to this specifically, so in this case it is not just a question of slipping off out of the exhibit area as through an open door to see what is beyond the door, it is a case of coming down into the bowels of the building and so to see what is there, so this is not what they usually do, to come down the stairwell to do this.

Defendant testified in his own behalf and denied that he entered with the aforementioned tools. He stated that he visited the museum on March 13 at about 3:45 P.M.; that as he entered the main corridor he noticed a man and woman arguing; that he went to the woman's defense and was struck by the man; and that he could remember nothing thereafter until placed in police custody (at about 7:30 P.M.).

Under prior law (Ill.Rev.Stat., 1959, ch. 38, § 84) the crime of burglary was complete when one entered "willfully and maliciously" with intent to commit a felony. In People v. Kelley, 274 Ill. 556, 113 N.E. 926, the defendant was convicted of burglary under that statute after he entered a store when it was open to the public and allegedly took money from a customer. In reversing the conviction the Supreme Court stated at page 558 that:

> The intent is an essential element of the crime of burglary and must be proved beyond a reasonable doubt. There is no evidence as to the intent with which the defendant entered the store, unless it is found in his conduct after entering. . . . He may have taken advantage of the opportunity to commit larceny, but his presence in the store is as consistent with his innocence as with his guilt of the criminal intent at the time of his entry.

It can be inferred that if the prosecution in that case had shown the requisite intent at the time of defendant's entry into the store it would have been considered a burglary. It was of no consequence under that statute whether the entry was with or without authority.

However, under [the Illinois Code, supra p. 325 of this casebook] the crime of burglary is complete when a person knowingly enters into or remains within a building "without authority" with the intent to commit a felony or theft. The State, electing to indict the defendant for "knowingly entering without authority" instead of "remaining without authority," contends that whoever enters a building with the intent to commit a felony ipso facto enters without authority. . . .

The authority which clothes an invitee who enters a public museum is not unlimited because the invitation itself is not unlimited. The opening of a museum's doors to the public is an invitation to enter for the lawful purpose of viewing the exhibits on display. The authority of one who accepts such invitation is necessarily coincident with the terms of the offer, and it would be contrary to reason and ordinary human understanding to deduce that the welcome extended under those circumstances includes authority to enter for any different purpose, especially one which is unlawful or criminal. We therefore hold that the entry into an establishment which is open to the public, with the intent to commit a felony or theft, is without authority.

In a bench trial it is the function of the trial court to determine the credibility of the witnesses and the weight to be afforded their testimony. . . . A reviewing court will not substitute its opinion for that of the trier of fact unless the proof is so unsatisfactory as to justify a reasonable doubt of the defendant's guilt. . . . In the instant case, the presence of a screwdriver, pliers, a flashlight and an automatic pistol, the circumstances surrounding the defendant's arrest and his conduct only two days prior to his arrest constitute sufficient evidence to justify the finding of the trial court that defendant entered the museum with the intent to commit a theft. Therefore the decision of the trial court is affirmed.

G. THE TERMINOLOGY OF THEFT: PROBLEMS OF CONSTRUCTION

UNITED STATES v. TURLEY

Supreme Court of the United States, 1957.
352 U.S. 407, 77 S.Ct. 397.

MR. JUSTICE BURTON delivered the opinion of the Court.

This case concerns the meaning of the word "stolen" in the following provision of the National Motor Vehicle Theft Act, commonly known as the Dyer Act:

> "Whoever transports in interstate or foreign commerce a motor vehicle or aircraft, knowing the same to have been stolen, shall be fined not more than $5,000 or imprisoned not more than five years, or both."

The issue before us is whether the meaning of the word "stolen," as used in this provision, is limited to a taking which amounts to common-law larceny, or whether it includes an embezzlement or other felonious taking with intent to deprive the owner of the rights and benefits of ownership. For the reasons hereafter stated, we accept the broader interpretation.

In 1956, an information based on this section was filed against James Vernon Turley in the United States District Court for the District of Maryland. It charged that Turley, in South Carolina, lawfully obtained possession of an automobile from its owner for the purpose of driving certain of their friends to the homes of the latter in South Carolina, but that, without permission of the owner and with intent to steal the automobile, Turley converted it to his own use and unlawfully transported it in interstate commerce to Baltimore, Maryland, where he sold it without permission of the owner. The information thus charged Turley with transporting the automobile in interstate commerce knowing it to have been obtained by embezzlement rather than by common-law larceny.

Counsel appointed for Turley moved to dismiss the information on the ground that it did not state facts sufficient to constitute an offense against the United States. He contended that the word "stolen" as used in the Act referred only to takings which constitute common-law larceny and that the acts charged did not. The District Court agreed and dismissed the information. . . . The United States concedes that the facts alleged in the information do not constitute common-law larceny, but disputes the holding that a motor vehicle obtained by embezzlement is not "stolen" within the meaning of the Act. . . .

Decisions involving the meaning of "stolen" as used in the National Motor Vehicle Theft Act did not arise frequently until comparatively recently. Two of the earlier cases interpreted "stolen" as meaning statutory larceny as defined by the State in which the taking occurred. The later decisions rejected that interpretation but divided on whether to give "stolen" a uniformly narrow meaning restricted to common-law larceny, or a uniformly broader meaning inclusive of embezzlement and other felonious takings with intent to deprive the owner of the rights and benefits of ownership. The Fifth, Eighth and Tenth Circuits favored the narrow definition while the Fourth, Sixth and Ninth Circuits favored the broader one. We agree that in the absence of a plain indication of an intent to incorporate diverse state laws into a federal criminal statute, the meaning of the federal statute should not be dependent on state law. . . .

We recognize that where a federal criminal statute uses a common-law term of established meaning without otherwise defining it, the general practice is to give that term its common-law meaning. But "stolen" (or "stealing") has no accepted common-law meaning. On this point the Court of Appeals for the Fourth Circuit recently said:

> "But while 'stolen' is constantly identified with larceny, the term was never at common law equated or exclusively dedicated to larceny. 'Steal' (originally 'stale') at first denoted in general usage a taking through secrecy, as implied in 'stealth,' or through stratagem, according to the Oxford English Dictionary. Expanded through the years, it became the generic designation for dishonest acquisition, but it never lost its initial connotation. Nor in law is 'steal' or 'stolen' a word of art. Blackstone does not mention 'steal' in defining larceny—"the felonious taking and carrying away of the personal goods of another'—or in expounding its several elements. . . ."

Webster's New International Dictionary (2d ed., 1953) likewise defines "stolen" as "Obtained or accomplished by theft, stealth, or craft . . . ." Black's Law Dictionary (4th ed., 1951) states that "steal" "may denote the criminal taking of personal property either by larceny, embezzlement, or false pretenses." Furthermore, "stolen" and "steal" have been used in federal criminal statutes, and the courts interpreting those words have declared that they do not have a necessary common-law meaning coterminous with larceny and exclusive of other theft crimes. Freed from a common-law meaning, we should give "stolen" the meaning consistent with the context in which it appears.

> "That criminal statutes are to be construed strictly is a proposition which calls for the citation of no authority. But this does not mean that every criminal statute must be given the narrowest possible meaning in complete disregard of the purpose of the legislature." . . .

It is, therefore, appropriate to consider the purpose of the Act and to gain what light we can from its legislative history.

By 1919, the law of most States against local theft had developed so as to include not only common-law larceny but embezzlement, false pretenses, larceny by trick, and other types of wrongful taking. The advent of the automobile, however, created a new problem with which the States found it difficult to deal. The automobile was uniquely suited to felonious taking whether by larceny, embezzlement or false pretenses. It was a valuable, salable article which itself supplied the means for speedy escape. "The automobile [became] the perfect chattel for modern large-scale theft." This challenge could be best met through use of the Federal Government's jurisdiction over interstate commerce. The need for federal action increased with the number, distribution and speed of the motor vehicles until, by 1919, it became a necessity. The result was the National Motor Vehicle Theft Act.

This background was reflected in the Committee Report on the bill presented by its author and sponsor, Representative Dyer. . . This report, entitled "Theft of Automobiles," pointed to the increasing number of automobile thefts, the resulting financial losses, and the increasing cost of automobile theft insurance. It asserted that state laws were inadequate to cope with the problem because the offenders evaded state officers by transporting the automobiles across state lines where associates received and sold them. Throughout the legislative history Congress used the word "stolen" as synonymous with "theft," a term generally considered to be broader than "common-law larceny." To be sure, the discussion referred to "larceny" but nothing was said about excluding other forms of "theft." The report stated the object of the Act in broad terms, primarily emphasizing the need for the exercise of federal powers. No mention is made of a purpose to distinguish between different forms of theft, as would be expected if the distinction had been intended.

"Larceny" is also mentioned in Brooks v. United States, 1925, . . . This reference, however, carries no necessary implication excluding the taking of automobiles by embezzlement or false pretenses. Public and private rights are violated to a comparable degree whatever label is attached to the felonious taking. A typical example of common-law larceny is the taking of an unattended automobile. But an automobile is no less "stolen" because it is rented, transported interstate, and sold without the permission of the owner (embezzlement). The same is true where an automobile is purchased with a worthless check, transported interstate, and sold (false pretenses). Professional thieves resort to innumerable forms of theft and Congress presumably sought to meet the need for federal action effectively rather than to leave loopholes for wholesale evasion.

We conclude that the Act requires an interpretation of "stolen" which does not limit it to situations which at common law would be considered larceny. The refinements of that crime are not related to the primary congressional purpose of eliminating the interstate traffic in unlawfully obtained motor vehicles. The Government's interpretation is neither unclear nor vague. "Stolen" as used in 18 U.S.C. § 2312, . . . includes all felonious takings of motor vehicles with intent to deprive the owner of the rights and benefits of ownership, regardless of whether or not the theft constitutes common-law larceny.

Reversed and remanded.

MR. JUSTICE FRANKFURTER, whom MR. JUSTICE BLACK and MR. JUSTICE DOUGLAS join, dissenting.

If Congress desires to make cheating, in all its myriad varieties, a federal offense when employed to obtain an automobile that is then taken across a state line, it should express itself with less ambiguity than by language that leads three Courts of Appeals to decide that it has not said so and three that it has. If "stealing" (describing a thing as "stolen") be not a term of art, it must be deemed a colloquial, everyday term. As such, it would hardly be used, even loosely, by the man in the street to cover "cheating." Legislative drafting is dependent on treacherous words to convey, as often as not, complicated ideas, and courts should not be pedantically exacting in construing legislation. But to sweep into the jurisdiction of the federal courts the transportation of cars obtained not only by theft but also by trickery does not present a problem so complicated that the Court should search for hints to find a command. When Congress has wanted to deal with many different ways of despoiling another of his property and not merely with larceny, it has found it easy enough to do so, as a number of federal enactments attest. . . . No doubt, penal legislation should not be artificially restricted so as to allow escape for those for whom it was with fair intendment designed. But the principle of lenity which should guide construction of criminal statutes, . . . precludes extending the term "stolen" to include every form of dishonest acquisition. This conclusion is encouraged not only by the general consideration governing the construction of penal laws; it also has regard for not bringing to the federal courts a mass of minor offenses that are local in origin until Congress expresses, if not an explicit, at least an unequivocal, desire to do so.

I would affirm the judgment.

H. RELATED PROPERTY OFFENSES

SECTION 1. ARSON

1. The Common Law

Arson at common law is the malicious (or, as sometimes stated, wilful and malicious) burning of the dwelling house of another. Like burglary, arson at common law is an offense against habitation, and what has been stated above with respect to "the dwelling house of another" in connection with burglary likewise applies to arson.

a. *Malicious.* The burning must be malicious to constitute arson; consequently, an accidental or negligent burning is not sufficient. Morris v. State, 124 Ala. 44, 27 So. 336 (1900). It is not necessary, however, that destruction of the dwelling be intended, or that the motive be one of ill will. For example, a prisoner in a jail is guilty of arson where he burns a hole in the building solely for the purpose of making an escape. Smith v. State, 23 Tex.App. 357, 5 S.W. 219 (1887); Lockett v. State, 63 Ala. 5 (1879). Contra, State v. Mitchell, 27 N.C. 350 (1845); People v. Cotteral, 18 Johns. 115 (N.Y.1820). An intent to commit an unlawful act the probable consequence of which is a burning is sufficient, where the act is performed without regard to the consequences. State v. Laughlin, 53 N.C. 321 (1861). See also, Regina v. Faulkner, 13 Cox C.C. 550 (1877).

b. *Burning.* Arson is not committed unless some part of the structure of the dwelling house is actually damaged by fire. Blackening or discoloration is insufficient; the fiber of some part of the structural material of the building must be at least slightly damaged. People v. Oliff, 361 Ill. 237, 197 N.E. 777 (1935); State v. Spiegel, 11 Iowa 701, 83 N.W. 722 (1900).

2. The Statutes

As in the case of burglary, the crime of arson has been considerably broadened by modern legislation. The great majority of jurisdictions in the United States have adopted the Model Arson Law. Five principal changes are effected by this law:

(1) The property burned (except in the case of personal property) does not have to be that of another person.

(2) Where a dwelling house is involved, there is no requirement that it be occupied, even occasionally. It may be vacant.

(3) All types of buildings and structures are made the subject of arson.

(4) The intentional burning of the personal property of another, where the property has a value of twenty-five dollars or more, is made arson.

(5) The intentional burning of any property insured against fire damage, where the burning is for the purpose of defrauding the insurer, is made a felony, although it is not called arson.

An example of a modern statutory version of arson is the following from the Illinois Criminal Code, § 20–1:

> A person commits arson when, by means of fire or explosive, he knowingly:
>
> (a) Damages any real property, or any personal property having a value of $150 or more, of another without his consent; or
>
> (b) With intent to defraud an insurer, damages any property or any personal property having a value of $150 or more.
>
> Property "of another" means a building or other property, whether real or personal, in which a person other than the offender has an interest which the offender has no authority to defeat or impair, even though the offender may also have an interest in the building or property.
>
> Penalty.
>
> A person convicted of arson shall be imprisoned in the penitentiary for any indeterminate term with a minimum of not less than one year.

SECTION 2. MALICIOUS MISCHIEF

The malicious destruction of, or damage to, the property of another is a common law misdemeanor. State v. Watts, 48 Ark. 56, 2 S.W. 342 (1886). In both the United States and England, however, a number of statutes have been enacted to cover most forms of malicious mischief, making some forms felonies and others misdemeanors. Where a particular offense of this character is not covered by statute, it is punishable as a common law offense in those states which retain common law crimes; moreover, the statutes frequently employ a comprehensive section to cover the malicious injury of any real or personal property of another not specifically made criminal by a separate provision.

Consider the following, from the Illinois Criminal Code, § 21–1:

> **Criminal Damage to Property**
>
> Whoever commits any of the following acts shall be fined not to exceed $500.00 or imprisoned in a penal institution other than the penitentiary not to exceed one year, or both or for the commission of any act enumerated in subsection (a) or (f) when the damage to property exceeds $150

may be imprisoned in the penitentiary for not more than five years or both fined and imprisoned:

(a) Knowingly damages any property of another without his consent; or

(b) Recklessly by means of fire or explosive damages property of another; or

(c) Knowingly starts a fire on the land of another without his consent; or

(d) Knowingly injures a domestic animal of another without his consent; or

(e) Knowingly deposits on the land or in the building of another, without his consent, any stink bomb or any offensive smelling compound and thereby intends to interfere with the use by another of the land or building.

(f) Damages any property, other than property described in Subsection 20–1(3), with intent to defraud an insurer.

SECTION 3. FORGERY

SMITH v. STATE

Court of Special Appeals of Maryland, 1969.
7 Md.App. 457, 256 A.2d 357.

MURPHY, CHIEF JUDGE. Maryland Code, Article 27, Section 44, provides in part that if any person "shall falsely make, forge or counterfeit * * * any * * * bill of exchange * * * with intention to defraud any person whomsoever, [he] shall be deemed a felon * * *."

Appellant was indicted under this statute, the indictment charging that on May 11, 1968 he did, with intent feloniously to defraud, "falsely make, forge, and counterfeit a certain bill of exchange, to wit, * * * a certain *blank* check of Arundel Engineering Construction Co., Inc., * * * drawn on the Maryland National Bank, Baltimore, Maryland." (Emphasis supplied.)

The evidence at the trial showed that on May 11, 1968, the police, acting under a valid search and seizure warrant, searched appellant's living premises and seized various printing machines and implements utilized in their operation, including a mechanical checkwriter and a printer's typeset containing composed type. At the request of the police, appellant ran off an imprint from the composed type, revealing a blank check purportedly that of the Arundel Engineering Construction Co., drawn on the Maryland National Bank of Baltimore, Maryland. The blank check form contained the usual bank check numbers and purported on its face to be drawn against

Arundel's payroll account in the Bank. The space on the check for the payee's name, the amount of money for which drawn, and the authorized signature of the payor were all blank. The evidence showed that appellant did not have permission to print checks for Arundel, and that Arundel had no account with the Maryland National Bank.

Appellant, an accomplished printer, admitted composing the type for the blank Arundel checks. He testified that he was preparing to publish a book on the detection of check forgeries and had no intention of attempting to negotiate any of these checks. The evidence showed that no checks of Arundel made from the plates seized from appellant were ever passed or negotiated.

Appellant was also separately charged under Section 44 with having falsely made, forged and counterfeited on various dates five checks of Spring Grove Hospital, payable to designated individuals in specified amounts, as set forth in the indictments, all checks being drawn on the American National Bank and signed by L. B. Smyth. The evidence showed that these checks had been forged and were completely bogus, that they were dishonored because Spring Grove Hospital maintained no account with the American National Bank, and the payor L. B. Smyth was unknown to the Hospital authorities and hence not an authorized signature.

Through the testimony of an F.B.I. expert, the State showed that the composed typeface seized by police from appellant's residence on May 11, 1968, when compared with the print of the Spring Grove checks, revealed certain similar defects in the letter faces, indicating that the Arundel and Spring Grove checks were made from the same plates.

Appellant denied any responsibility for or knowledge of printing, forging or uttering the Spring Grove checks and no evidence was adduced to show any connection between L. B. Smyth and the appellant.

At the conclusion of the trial the court, sitting without a jury, concluded that appellant made all the checks in question with the printing equipment seized from him on May 11, 1968. The court convicted appellant under all six indictments with having falsely made, forged and counterfeited each of the six checks, as charged in the respective indictments. Appellant was sentenced under each indictment to concurrent terms of four years under the jurisdiction of the Department of Correction.

On this appeal, appellant contends that the evidence was insufficient to convict him of any of the offenses. We agree.

Forgery has been defined as a false making or material alteration, with intent to defraud, of any writing which, if genuine, might apparently be of legal efficacy or the foundation of a legal liability. . . . More succinctly, forgery is the fraudulent making of a false writing having apparent legal significance. . . . It is thus clear that one of the essential elements of forgery is a writing in such form as to be apparently of some legal efficacy and hence capable of defrauding or deceiving. . . . In Arnold v. Cost, . . . it was held in effect that a person cannot be convicted of the forgery of a paper absolutely invalid upon its face and which could not operate to the prejudice of another. If then the instrument is entirely valueless on its face and of no binding force or effect for any purpose of harm, liability or injury to anyone, all authorities agree that it cannot be the subject of forgery. . . .

By common definition forgery is false making, . . . and as used in Section 44, we think the terms "falsely make" and "forge" are synonymous, both describing a spurious or fictitious making relating to the genuineness of execution of an instrument. . . . Similarly, the term "counterfeit" in common parlance signifies the fabrication of a false image or representation; counterfeiting an instrument means falsely making it; and in its broadest sense it means the making of a copy without authority or right and with a view to deceive or defraud by passing the copy as original or genuine. . . . under the National Stolen Property Act which penalizes the transportation of "falsely made, forged, altered, or counterfeited securities" the quoted words were ejusdem generis and usually employed to denounce the crime of forgery. In light of these principles, and bearing in mind that as originally enacted in 1799, Section 44 was entitled "An Act for the more effectual preventing of forgery," we think the terms "falsely make, forge or counterfeit," as used in the Section, are virtually synonymous and were collectively intended to proscribe the crime of forgery.

While a check drawn on a bank may constitute a bill of exchange within the meaning of Section 44, . . . the Arundel check (Indictment #3767) was entirely blank in all its operative parts. It contained no payee's name, no payor's signature, no date, and specified no amount. In this condition, it obviously was an instrument without legal efficacy as a bill of exchange. Consequently, it was not a writing capable of defrauding and hence was not a forgery under Section 44. . . .

And for the same reasons that the blank Arundel check was not a forgery, neither was it a counterfeit within the meaning of the statute, the terms "forge" and "counterfeit," as heretofore indicated, being synonymously employed.

We make the additional observation that it was at the direction of the police that appellant ran off an imprint of the blank Arundel check. In no event could appellant be convicted of having falsely made, forged or counterfeited a document which he reproduced under these circumstances.

While there was evidence to show inferentially that the blank check forms used in connection with the five Spring Grove checks were printed by the appellant, and that these checks subsequently were the subject of forgeries, there was no evidence to show that appellant was responsible for, or had any connection with, the authorizing signature "L. B. Smyth," nor was there any showing that he endorsed, negotiated, or attempted to endorse or negotiate the checks. At most, the evidence showed that appellant composed the type from which the blank Spring Grove checks were subsequently imprinted. Under these circumstances, the judgment of the trial judge was clearly erroneous in having convicted appellant of having forged these checks. . . .

Chapter 7

CRIMINAL RESPONSIBILITY AND THE DEFENSE OF MENTAL IMPAIRMENT

A. THE MENTAL ELEMENT IN CRIME: IGNORANCE OF LAW AND MISTAKE OF LAW AND FACT

MORISSETTE v. UNITED STATES

Supreme Court of the United States, 1952.
342 U.S. 246, 72 S.Ct. 240.

MR. JUSTICE JACKSON delivered the opinion of the Court. . . .

On a large tract of uninhabited and untilled land in a wooded and sparsely populated area of Michigan, the Government established a practice bombing range over which the Air Force dropped simulated bombs at ground targets. These bombs consisted of a metal cylinder about forty inches long and eight inches across, filled with sand and enough black powder to cause a smoke puff by which the strike could be located. At various places about the range signs read "Danger—Keep Out—Bombing Range." Nevertheless, the range was known as good deer country and was extensively hunted.

Spent bomb casings were cleared from the targets and thrown into piles "so that they will be out of the way." They were not stacked or piled in any order but were dumped in heaps, some of which had been accumulating for four years or upwards, were exposed to the weather and rusting away.

Morissette, in December of 1948, went hunting in this area but did not get a deer. He thought to meet expenses of the trip by salvaging some of these casings. He loaded three tons of them on his truck and took them to a nearby farm, where they were flattened by driving a tractor over them. After expending this labor and trucking them to market in Flint, he realized $84.

Morissette, by occupation, is a fruit stand operator in summer and a trucker and scrap iron collector in winter. An honorably discharged veteran of World War II, he enjoys a good name among his neighbors and has had no blemish on his record more disreputable than a conviction for reckless driving.

The loading, crushing and transporting of these casings were all in broad daylight, in full view of passers-by, without the slightest effort at concealment. When an investigation was started, Morissette voluntarily, promptly and candidly told the whole story to the authorities, saying that he had no intention of stealing but thought the property was abandoned, unwanted and considered of no value to the Government. He was indicted, however, on the charge that he "did unlawfully, wilfully and knowingly steal and convert" property of the United States of the value of $84, in violation of 18 U.S.C. § 641, 18 U.S.C.A. § 641, which provides that "whoever embezzles, steals, purloins, or knowingly converts" government property is punishable by fine and imprisonment. Morissette was convicted and sentenced to imprisonment for two months or to pay a fine of $200. The Court of Appeals affirmed, one judge dissenting.

On his trial, Morissette, as he had at all times told investigating officers, testified that from appearances he believed the casings were cast-off and abandoned, that he did not intend to steal the property, and took it with no wrongful or criminal intent. The trial court, however, was unimpressed, and ruled: "[H]e took it because he thought it was abandoned and he knew he was on government property. . . . That is no defense. . . . I don't think anybody can have the defense they thought the property was abandoned on another man's piece of property." The court stated: "I will not permit you to show this man thought it was abandoned. . . . I hold in this case that there is no question of abandoned property." The court refused to submit or to allow counsel to argue to the jury whether Morissette acted with innocent intention. It charged: "And I instruct you that if you believe the testimony of the government in this case, he intended to take it. . . . He had no right to take this property. . . . [A]nd it is no defense to claim that it was abandoned, because it was on private property. . . . And I instruct you to this effect: That if this young man took this property (and he says he did), without any permission (he says he did), that was on the property of the United States Government (he says it was), that it was of the value of one cent or more (and evidently it was), that he is guilty of the offense charged here. If you believe the government, he is guilty. . . . The question on intent is whether or not he intended to take the property. He says he did. Therefore, if you believe either side, he is guilty." Petitioner's counsel contended, "But the taking must have been with a felonious intent." The court ruled, however: "That is presumed by his own act."

The Court of Appeals suggested that "greater restraint in expression should have been exercised", but affirmed the conviction because "As we have interpreted the statute, appellant was guilty of its violation beyond a shadow of doubt, as evidenced even by his own admissions." Its construction of the statute is that it creates several separate and distinct offenses, one being knowing conversion of government property. The court ruled that this particular offense requires no element of criminal intent. This conclusion was thought to be required by the failure of Congress to express such a requisite and this Court's decisions in United States v. Behrman, and United States v. Balint.

In those cases this Court did construe mere omission from a criminal enactment of any mention of criminal intent as dispensing with it. If they be deemed precedents for principles of construction generally applicable to federal penal statutes, they authorize this conviction. . . .

The contention that an injury can amount to a crime only when inflicted by intention is no provincial or transient notion. It is as universal and persistent in mature systems of law as belief in freedom of the human will and a consequent ability and duty of the normal individual to choose between good and evil. A relation between some mental element and punishment for a harmful act is almost as instinctive as the child's familiar exculpatory "But I didn't mean to," and has afforded the rational basis for a tardy and unfinished substitution of deterrence and reformation in place of retaliation and vengeance as the motivation for public prosecution. Unqualified acceptance of this doctrine by English common law in the Eighteenth Century was indicated by Blackstone's sweeping statement that to constitute any crime there must first be a "vicious will." Common-law commentators of the Nineteenth Century early pronounced the same principle. . . .

Crime as a compound concept, generally constituted only from concurrence of an evil-meaning mind with an evil-doing hand, was congenial to an intense individualism and took deep and early root in American soil. As the states codified the common law of crimes, even if their enactments were silent on the subject, their courts assumed that the omission did not signify disapproval of the principle but merely recognized that intent was so inherent in the idea of the offense that it required no statutory affirmation. Courts, with little hestitation or division, found an implication of the requirement as to offenses that were taken over from the common law. The unanimity with which they have adhered to the central thought that wrongdoing must be conscious to be criminal is emphasized by the variety, disparity and confusion of their definitions of the requisite but elusive mental element. However, courts of various jurisdictions, and for the purposes of different offenses, have devised working formulae, if not scientific ones, for the instruction of juries around such terms as "felonious intent," "criminal intent," "malice aforethought," "guilty knowledge," "fraudulent intent," "wilfulness," "*scienter*," to denote guilty knowledge, or "*mens rea*," to signify an evil purpose or mental culpability. By use or combination of these various tokens, they have sought to protect those who were not blameworthy in mind from conviction of infamous common-law crimes.

However, the Balint and Behrman offenses belong to a category of another character, with very different antecedents and origins. The crimes there involved depend on no mental element but consist only of forbidden acts or omissions. This, while not expressed by the Court, is made clear from examination of a century-old but accelerating tendency, discernible both here and in England, to call into existence new duties and crimes which disregard any ingredient of intent. The industrial revolution multiplied the number of workmen exposed to injury from increasingly powerful and complex mechanisms, driven by freshly discovered sources of energy, requiring higher precautions by employers. Traffic of velocities, volumes and varieties unheard of came to subject the wayfarer to intolerable casualty risks if owners and drivers were not to observe new cares and uniformities of conduct. Congestion of cities and crowding of quarters called for health and welfare regulations undreamed of in simpler times. Wide distribution of goods became an instrument of wide distribution of harm when those who dispersed food, drink, drugs, and even securities, did not comply with reasonable standards of quality, integrity, disclosure and care. Such dangers have engendered increasingly numerous and detailed regulations which heighten the duties of those in control of particular industries, trades, properties or activities that affect public health, safety or welfare.

While many of these duties are sanctioned by a more strict civil liability, lawmakers, whether wisely or not, have sought to make such regulations more effective by invoking criminal sanctions to be applied by the familiar technique of criminal prosecutions and convictions. This has confronted the courts with a multitude of prosecutions, based on statutes or administrative regulations, for what have been aptly called "public welfare offenses." These cases do not fit neatly into any of such accepted classifications of common-law offenses, such as those against the state, the person, property, or public morals. Many of these offenses are not in the nature of positive aggressions or invasions, with which the common law so often dealt, but are in the nature of neglect where the law requires care, or inaction where it imposes a duty. Many violations of such regulations result in no direct or immediate injury to person or property but merely create the danger or probability of it which the law seeks to minimize. While such offenses do not threaten the security of the state in the manner of treason, they may be regarded as offenses against its authority, for their occurrence impairs the efficiency of controls deemed essential to the social order as presently constituted. In this respect, whatever the intent of the violator, the injury is the same, and the consequences are injurious or not according to fortuity. Hence, legislation applicable to such offenses, as a matter of policy, does not specify intent as a necessary element. The accused, if he does not will the violation, usually is in a position to prevent it with no more care than society might reasonably expect and no more exertion than it might reasonably exact from one who assumed his responsibilities. Also, penalties commonly are relatively small, and conviction does no grave damage to an offender's reputation. Under such considerations, courts have turned to construing statutes and regulations which make no mention of intent as dispensing with it and holding that the guilty act alone makes out the crime. This has not, however, been without expressions of misgiving.

The pilot of the movement in this country appears to be a holding that a tavernkeeper could be convicted for selling liquor to an habitual drunkard even if he did not know the buyer to be such. . . . Later came Massachusetts holdings that convictions for selling adulterated milk in violation of statutes forbidding such sales require no allegation or proof that defendant knew of the adulteration. . . . Departures from the common-law tradition, mainly of these general classes, were reviewed and their rationale appraised by Chief Justice Cooley, as follows: "I agree that as a rule there can be no crime without a criminal intent, but this is not by any means a universal rule. . . . Many statutes which are in the nature of police regulations, as this is, impose criminal penalties irrespective of any intent to violate them, the purpose being to require a degree of diligence for the protection of the public which shall render violation impossible." . . .

Neither this Court nor, so far as we are aware, any other has undertaken to delineate a precise line or set forth comprehensive criteria for distinguishing between crimes that require a mental element and crimes that do not. We attempt no closed definition, for the law on the subject is neither settled nor static. The conclusion reached in the Balint and Behrman cases has our approval and adherence for the circumstances to which it was there applied. A quite different question here is whether we will expand the doctrine of crimes without intent to include those charged here.

Stealing, larceny, and its variants and equivalents, were among the earliest offenses known to the law that existed before legislation; they are invasions of rights of property which stir a sense of insecurity in the whole community and arouse public demand for retribution, the penalty is high and, when a sufficient amount is involved, the infamy is that of a felony, which, says Maitland, is " . . . as bad a word as you can give to man or thing." State courts of last resort, on whom fall the heaviest burden of interpreting criminal law in this country, have consistently retained the requirement of intent in larceny-type offenses. If any state has deviated, the exception has neither been called to our attention nor disclosed by our research.

Congress, therefore, omitted any express prescription of criminal intent from the enactment before us in the light of an unbroken course of judicial decision in all constituent states of the Union holding intent inherent in this class of offense, even when not expressed in a statute. Congressional silence as to mental elements in an Act merely adopting into federal statutory law a concept of crime already so well defined in common law and statutory interpretation by the states may warrant quite contrary inferences than the same silence in creating an offense new to general law, for whose definition the courts have no guidance except the Act. Because the offenses before this Court in the Balint and Behrman cases were of this latter class, we cannot accept them as authority for eliminating intent from offenses incorporated from the common law. Nor do exhaustive studies of state court cases disclose any well-considered decisions applying the doctrine of crime without intent to such enacted common-law offenses. . . .[1]

1. Sayre, Public Welfare Offenses, 33 Col.L.Rev. 55, 73, 84, cites and classifies a large number of cases and concludes that they fall roughly into sub-

The Government asks us by a feat of construction radically to change the weights and balances in the scales of justice. The purpose and obvious effect of doing away with the requirement of a guilty intent is to ease the prosecution's path to conviction, to strip the defendant of such benefit as he derived at common law from innocence of evil purpose, and to circumscribe the freedom heretofore allowed juries. Such a manifest impairment of the immunities of the individual should not be extended to common-law crimes on judicial initiative. . . .

We hold that mere omission from § 641 of any mention of intent will not be construed as eliminating that element from the crimes denounced.

It is suggested, however, that the history and purposes of § 641 imply something more affirmative as to elimination of intent from at least one of the offenses charged under it in this case. The argument does not contest that criminal intent is retained in the offenses of embezzlement, stealing and purloining, as incorporated into this section. But it is urged that Congress joined with those, as a new, separate and distinct offense, knowingly to convert government property, under circumstances which imply that it is an offense in which the mental element of intent is not necessary.

Congress has been alert to what often is a decisive function of some mental element in crime. It has seen fit to prescribe that an evil state of mind, described variously in one or more such terms as "intentional," "wilful," "knowing," "fraudulent" or "malicious," will make criminal an otherwise indifferent act, or increase the degree of the offense or its punishment. Also, it has at times required a specific intent or purpose which will require some specialized knowledge or design for some evil beyond the common-law intent to do injury. The law under some circumstances recognizes good faith or blameless intent as a defense, partial defense, or as an element to be considered in mitigation of punishment. . . . In view of the care that has been bestowed upon the subject, it is significant that we have not found, nor has our attention been directed to, any instance in which Congress has expressly eliminated the mental element from a crime taken over from the common law.

Congress, by the language of this section, has been at pains to incriminate only "knowing" conversions. But, at common law there are unwitting acts which constitute conversions. In the civil tort, except for recovery of exemplary damages, the defendant's knowledge, intent, motive, mistake, and good faith are generally irrelevant. If

divisions of (1) illegal sales of intoxicating liquor, (2) sales of impure or adulterated food or drugs, (3) sales of misbranded articles, (4) violations of antinarcotic Acts, (5) criminal nuisances, (6) violations of traffic regulations, (7) violations of motor-vehicle laws, and (8) violations of general police regulations, passed for the safety, health or well-being of the community.

one takes property which turns out to belong to another, his innocent intent will not shield him from making restitution or indemnity, for his well-meaning may not be allowed to deprive another of his own.

Had the statute applied to conversions without qualification, it would have made crimes of all unwitting, inadvertent and unintended conversions. Knowledge, of course, is not identical with intent and may not have been the most apt words of limitation. But knowing conversion requires more than knowledge that defendant was taking the property into his possession. He must have had knowledge of the facts, though not necessarily the law, that made the taking a conversion. In the case before us, whether the mental element that Congress required be spoken of as knowledge or as intent, would not seem to alter its bearing on guilt. For it is not apparent how Morissette could have knowingly or intentionally converted property that he did not know could be converted, as would be the case if it was in fact abandoned or if he truly believed it to be abandoned and unwanted property.

It is said, and at first blush the claim has plausibility, that, if we construe the statute to require a mental element as part of criminal conversion, it becomes a meaningless duplication of the offense of stealing, and that conversion can be given meaning only by interpreting it to disregard intention. But here again a broader view of the evolution of these crimes throws a different light on the legislation.

It is not surprising if there is considerable overlapping in the embezzlement, stealing, purloining and knowing conversion grouped in this statute. What has concerned codifiers of the larceny-type offense is that gaps or crevices have separated particular crimes of this general class and guilty men have escaped through the breaches. The books contain a surfeit of cases drawing fine distinctions between slightly different circumstances under which one may obtain wrongful advantages from another's property. The codifiers wanted to reach all such instances. . . . Knowing conversion adds significantly to the range of protection of government property without interpreting it to punish unwitting conversions. . . .

We find no grounds for inferring any affirmative instruction from Congress to eliminate intent from any offense with which this defendant was charged.

As we read the record, this case was tried on the theory that even if criminal intent were essential its presence (a) should be decided by the court (b) as a presumption of law, apparently conclusive, (c) predicated upon the isolated act of taking rather than upon all of the circumstances. In each of these respects we believe the trial court was in error. . . .

We think presumptive intent has no place in this case. A conclusive presumption which testimony could not overthrow would effectively eliminate intent as an ingredient of the offense. A presumption which would permit but not require the jury to assume intent from an isolated fact would prejudge a conclusion which the jury should reach of its own volition. A presumption which would permit the jury to make an assumption which all the evidence considered together does not logically establish would give to a proven fact an artificial and fictional effect. In either case, this presumption would conflict with the overriding presumption of innocence with which the law endows the accused and which extends to every element of the crime. Such incriminating presumptions are not to be improvised by the judiciary. Even congressional power to facilitate convictions by substituting presumptions for proof is not without limit. Tot v. United States, 319 U.S. 463, 63 S.Ct. 1241, 87 L.Ed. 1519.

Moreover, the conclusion supplied by presumption in this instance was one of intent to steal the casings, and it was based on the mere fact that defendant took them. The court thought the only question was, "Did he intend to take the property?" That the removal of them was a conscious and intentional act was admitted. But that isolated fact is not an adequate basis on which the jury should find the criminal intent to steal or knowingly convert, that is, *wrongfully* to deprive another of possession of property. Whether that intent existed, the jury must determine, not only from the act of taking, but from that together with defendant's testimony and all of the surrounding circumstances.

Of course, the jury, considering Morissette's awareness that these casings were on government property, his failure to seek any permission for their removal and his self-interest as a witness, might have disbelieved his profession of innocent intent and concluded that his assertion of a belief that the casings were abandoned was an afterthought. Had the jury convicted on proper instructions it would be the end of the matter. But juries are not bound by what seems inescapable logic to judges. They might have concluded that the heaps of spent casings left in the hinterland to rust away presented an appearance of unwanted and abandoned junk, and that lack of any conscious deprivation of property or intentional injury was indicated by Morissette's good character, the openness of the taking, crushing and transporting of the casings, and the candor with which it was all admitted. They might have refused to brand Morissette as a thief. Had they done so, that too would have been the end of the matter.

Reversed.

NOTES

1. Professor Jerome Hall in his book, General Principles of Criminal Law (2d ed. 1960), devotes a chapter to the problems of strict liability. In connection with proposed substitutes for strict liability, he suggests the following (at pp. 351–353):

"Any current estimate of strict liability must take account of the vastly improved procedural and administrative facilities that now abound. Summary judicial hearings have been greatly improved; various techniques for arriving at judgments by conference, requiring mere recordation in court, are available; administration and administrative law have been greatly improved and expanded in the past quarter of a century. In short, the sole *raison d'être* of strict liability no longer exists—the problem posed by statistics can now be met by available legal institutions. . . . The continued recital of the rationalizations of a century ago loses any modicum of persuasiveness when the insistent claims of principle can be satisfied.

"The elimination of punitive strict liability would not restrict the inducements made by prosecutors to obtain pleas of guilty to the relevant criminal charges. The general features of contemporary criminal procedure, characterized by the disposal of the greatest part of the business by prosecutors and judges sitting without juries, would obtain here too. The bulk of the problem of protecting public welfare would be transferred to licensing and administrative agencies, . . . leaving the willful violations to be disposed of by specialized criminal courts or by special procedure. Against these unscrupulous individuals, the criminal law, sharpened to allow adequate dealing with crimes that are very serious in modern conditions, would be used much more frequently than in the past. On the other hand, the trial of reputable persons in a criminal court would be discontinued. Instead, sound legislation, . . . inspection, licensing, information, . . . investigation by boards, informal conferences, and publicity would provide much more likely means of influencing legitimate business.

"For the incompetents who simply cannot conform to decent standards, even after warning, information and counsel by regulatory boards, there is no alternative save to bar them from the pursuit of activities which are harmful to the public—whether that is driving an automobile, supplying milk or operating a public bar. It is undoubtedly true that the penal law functions much less onerously than would revocation of a license to do business. But this does not support the continuance of an anomalous strict 'penal' liability. The community is entitled to protection from inefficient persons who engage in potentially dangerous vocations or activities. They are certainly not restrained or improved by the perfunctory imposition of petty fines, nor for that matter by much severer penalties. The only proper recourse in some cases (very few, presumably, by comparison with those who improve their course of business after notice and assistance are received) must be the termination of the business or other activity. To make that depend on criminal behavior is to confuse immorality with inefficiency. To confine revocation of a license to the former is to ignore a major cause of injury to important social interests."

2. Assume a person marries another in the reasonable but mistaken belief, that his previous marriage was legally dissolved. Is he guilty of the offense of bigamy? Suppose a male has sexual intercourse with a female whom he reasonably believes to be above the "age of consent" (e. g., the statutory age being 16 within that jurisdiction; she is 15, but looks to be about 18). Is he guilty of "statutory rape"?

The offense of "statutory rape" has been dealt with in the same manner as the offense of bigamy, insofar as the mistaken belief of an offender that the girl was above the age of consent is concerned. Most jurisdictions treat the offense as a strict liability crime. However, a minority of jurisdictions allow the reasonable mistake as to age defense, either by judicial fiat, or by statute. The Illinois Criminal Code, for instance, provides that "It shall be an affirmative defense to indecent liberties with a child [the Illinois equivalent of statutory rape] that: (1) The accused reasonably believed the child was of the age of 16 or upwards at the time of the act giving rise to the charge: . . ." (§ 11-4—a felony.)

PEOPLE v. YOUNG

Court of Appeals of New York, 1962.
11 N.Y.2d 274, 183 N.E.2d 319.

PER CURIAM. Whether one, who in good faith aggressively intervenes in a struggle between another person and a police officer in civilian dress attempting to effect the lawful arrest of the third person, may be properly convicted of assault in the third degree is a question of law of first impression here.

The opinions in the court below [the Appellate Division of the Supreme Court] in the absence of precedents in this State carefully expound the opposing views found in other jurisdictions. The majority in the Appellate Division have adopted the minority rule in the other States that one who intervenes in a struggle between strangers under the mistaken but reasonable belief that he is protecting another who he assumes is being unlawfully beaten is thereby exonerated from criminal liability . . . The weight of authority holds with the dissenters below that one who goes to the aid of a third person does so at his own peril . . . .

While the doctrine espoused by the majority of the court below may have support in some States, we feel that such a policy would not be conducive to an orderly society. We agree with the settled policy of law in most jurisdictions that the right of a person to defend another ordinarily should not be greater than such person's right to defend himself. Subdivision 3 of section 246 of the Penal Law, Consol.Laws, c. 40, does not apply as no offense was being committed on the person of the one resisting the lawful arrest. Whatever may be the public policy where the felony charged requires proof of a specific intent and the issue is justifiable homicide . . ., it is not relevant in a prosecution for assault in the third degree where it is only necessary to show that the defendant knowingly struck a blow.

In this case there can be no doubt that the defendant intended to assault the police officer in civilian dress. The resulting assault was forceful. Hence motive or mistake of fact is of no significance as the defendant was not charged with a crime requiring such intent or knowledge. To be guilty of third degree assault "It is sufficient that the defendant voluntarily intended to commit the unlawful act of touching" . . . . Since in these circumstances the aggression was inexcusable the defendant was properly convicted.

Accordingly, the order of the Appellate Division should be reversed and the information reinstated.

FROESSEL, JUDGE (dissenting). [Concurrence by VAN VOORHIS, J.] The law is clear that one may kill in defense of another when there is reasonable, though mistaken, ground for believing that the person slain is about to commit a felony or to do some great personal injury to the apparent victim . . .; yet the majority now hold, for the first time, that in the event of a simple assault under similar circumstances, the mistaken belief, no matter how reasonable, is no defense.

Briefly, the relevant facts are these: On a Friday afternoon at about 3:40, Detectives Driscoll and Murphy, not in uniform, observed an argument taking place between a motorist and one McGriff in the street in front of premises 64 West 54th Street, in midtown Manhattan. Driscoll attempted to chase McGriff out of the roadway in order to allow traffic to pass, but McGriff refused to move back; his actions caused a crowd to collect. After identifying himself to McGriff, Driscoll placed him under arrest. As McGriff resisted, defendant "came out of the crowd" from Driscoll's rear and struck Murphy about the head with his fist. In the ensuing struggle Driscoll's right kneecap was injured when defendant fell on top of him. At the station house, defendant said he had not known or thought Driscoll and Murphy were police officers.

Defendant testified that while he was proceeding on 54th Street he observed two white men, who appeared to be 45 or 50 years old, pulling on a "colored boy" (McGriff), who appeared to be a lad about 18, whom he did not know. The men had nearly pulled McGriff's pants off, and he was crying. Defendant admitted he knew nothing of what had transpired between the officers and McGriff, and made no inquiry of anyone; he just came there and pulled the officer away from McGriff.

Defendant was convicted of assault third degree. In reversing upon the law and dismissing the information, the Appellate Division held that one is not "criminally liable for assault in the third degree if he goes to the aid of another who he mistakenly, but *reasonably*, believes is being unlawfully beaten, and thereby injures one of the apparent assaulters" (emphasis supplied). While in my opinion the majority below correctly stated the law, I would reverse here and remit so that the Appellate Division may pass on the question of whether or not defendant's conduct was reasonable in light of the circumstances presented at the trial . . .

As the majority below pointed out, assault is a crime derived from the common law (People v. Katz, 290 N.Y. 361, 365, 49 N.E.2d 482, 484). Basic to the imposition of criminal liability both at common law and under our statutory law is the existence in the one who committed the prohibited act of what has been variously termed a guilty mind, a *mens rea* or a criminal intent . . .

Criminal intent requires an awareness of wrongdoing. When conduct is based upon mistake of fact reasonably entertained, there can be no such awareness and, therefore, no criminal culpability. In People ex rel. Hegeman v. Corrigan, 195 N.Y. 1, 12, 87 N.E. 792, 796, we stated: "it is very apparent that the innocence or criminality of the intent in a particular act generally depends on the knowledge or belief of the actor at the time. An honest and *reasonable* belief in the existence of circumstances which, if true, would make the act for which the defendant is prosecuted innocent, would be a good defense." (Emphasis supplied.)

It is undisputed that defendant did not know that Driscoll and Murphy were detectives in plain clothes engaged in lawfully apprehending an alleged disorderly person. If, therefore, defendant *reasonably* believed he was lawfully assisting another, he would not have been guilty of a crime. Subdivision 3 of section 246 of the Penal Law provides that it is not unlawful to use force "When committed either by the party about to be injured or *by another person in his aid or defense, in preventing or attempting to prevent an offense against his person,* * * * if the force or violence used is not more than sufficient to prevent such offense" (emphasis supplied). The law is thus clear that if defendant entertained an "honest and reasonable belief" . . ., that the facts were as he perceived them to be, he would be exonerated from criminal liability.

By ignoring one of the most basic principles of criminal law—that crimes *mala in se* require proof of at least general criminal intent—the majority now hold that the defense of mistake of fact is "of no significance". We are not here dealing with one of "a narrow class of exceptions" . . . where the Legislature has created crimes which do not depend on *criminal* intent but which are complete on the mere intentional doing of an act *malum prohibitum* . . .

There is no need, in my opinion, to consider the law of other States, for New York policy clearly supports the view that one may act on appearances reasonably ascertained, as does New Jersey . . . Our Penal Law (§ 1055), to which I have already alluded, is a statement of that policy. The same policy was expressed by this court in People v. Maine, . . . There, the defendant observed his brother fighting in the street with two other men; he stepped in and stabbed to death one of the latter. The defense was justifiable homicide under the predecessor of section 1055. The court held it reversible error to admit into evidence the declarations of the defendant's brother, made before defendant happened upon the scene, which tended to show that the brother was the aggressor. We said: "Of course, the acts and conduct of the defendant must be judged solely with reference to the situation as it was when he first and afterwards saw it." Mistake of relevant fact, reasonably entertained, is thus a defense to homicide under section 1055 . . . and one who kills in defense of another and proffers this defense of justification is to be judged according to the circumstances as they appeared to him (People v. Maine, . . .).

The mistaken belief, however, must be one which is reasonably entertained and the question of reasonableness is for the trier of the facts . . . "The question is not, merely, what did the accused believe? but also, what did he have the right to believe?" . . .

Although the majority of our courts are now purporting to fashion a policy "conducive to an orderly society", by their decision they have defeated their avowed purpose. What public interest is promoted by a principle which would deter one from coming to the aid of a fellow citizen who he has reasonable ground to apprehend is in imminent danger of personal injury at the hands of assailants? Is it reasonable to denominate, as justifiable homicide, a slaying committed under a mistaken but reasonably held belief, and deny this same defense of justification to one using less force? Logic, as well as historical background and related precedent, dictates that the rule and policy expressed by our Legislature in the case of homicide, which is an assault resulting in death, should likewise be applicable to a much less serious assault not resulting in death.

I would reverse the order appealed from and remit the case to the Appellate Division pursuant to section 543–b of the Code of Criminal Procedure "for determination upon the questions of fact raised in that court".

NOTE

In United States v. Freed, 401 U.S. 601, 91 S.Ct. 1112 (1971), the accused had been charged with possessing unregistered hand grenades, in violation of a federal statute. There was no allegation that he knew the hand grenades were unregistered or that it was against the law to possess them. Speaking for the Supreme Court, Justice Douglas stated:

> The Act requires no specific intent or knowledge that the hand grenades were unregistered. It makes it unlawful for any person "to receive or possess a firearm which is not registered to him." By the lower court decisions at the time that requirement was written into the Act the only knowledge required to be proved was knowledge that the instrument possessed was a firearm.
>
> The presence of a "vicious will" or *mens rea* was long a requirement of criminal responsibility. But the list of exceptions grew, especially in the expanding regulatory area involving activities affecting public health, safety, and welfare. * * *
>
> At the other extreme is Lambert v. California, 355 U.S. 225, in which a municipal code made it a crime to remain in Los Angeles for more than five days without registering if a person had been convicted of a felony. Being in Los Angeles is not *per se* blameworthy. The mere failure to register we held, was quite "unlike the commission of acts, or the failure to act under circumstances that should alert the doer to the consequences of his deed." The fact that the ordinance was a convenient law enforcement technique did not save it.
>
> In United States v. Dotterweich, 320 U.S. 277, 284, a case dealing with the imposition of a penalty on a corporate officer whose firm shipped adulterated and misbranded drugs in violation of the Food and Drug Act, we approved the penalty "though consciousness of wrongdoing be totally wanting."
>
> The present case is in the category neither of *Lambert* nor *Morissette*, but is closer to *Dotterweich*. This is a regulatory measure in the interest of the public safety, which may well be premised on the theory that one would hardly be surprised to learn that possession of hand grenades is not an innocent act. They are highly dangerous offensive weapons, no less dangerous than the narcotics involved in United States v. Balint, 258 U.S. 250, 254, where a de-

fendant was convicted of sale of narcotics against his claim that he did not know the drugs were covered by a federal act.

In his concurring opinion Justice Brennan stated, in part:

* * *

The Court's discussion of the intent the Government must prove to convict appellees of violation of 26 U.S.C. § 5861(d) (1964 ed., Supp. V) does not dispel the confusion surrounding a difficult, but vitally important, area of the law. This case does not raise questions of "consciousness of wrongdoing" or "blameworthiness." If the ancient maxim that "ignorance of the law is no excuse" has any residual validity, it indicates that the ordinary intent requirement—*mens rea*—of the criminal law does not require knowledge that an act is illegal, wrong, or blameworthy. Nor is it possible to decide this case by a simple process of classifying the statute involved as a "regulatory" or a "public welfare" measure. To convict appellees of possession of unregistered hand grenades, the Government must prove three material elements: (1) that appellees possessed certain items; (2) that the items possessed were hand grenades; and (3) that the hand grenades were not registered. The Government and the Court agree that the prosecutor must prove knowing possession of the items and also knowledge that the items possessed were hand grenades. Thus, while the Court does hold that no intent at all need be proved in regard to one element of the offense—the unregistered status of the grenades—knowledge must still be proved as to the other two elements. Consequently, the National Firearms Act does not create a crime of strict liability as to all its elements. It is no help in deciding what level of intent must be proved as to the third element to declare that the offense falls within the "regulatory" category.

. . . I think we must recognize, first, that "[t]he existence of a *mens rea* is the rule of, rather than the exception to, the principles of Anglo-American criminal jurisprudence;" second, that *mens rea* is not a unitary concept, but may vary as to each element of a crime; and third, that Anglo-American law has developed several identifiable and analytically distinct levels of intent, *e. g.*, negligence, recklessness, knowledge, and purpose. To determine the mental element required for conviction, each material element of the offense must be examined and the determination made what level of intent Congress intended the Government to prove, taking into account constitutional considerations, as well as the common-law background, if any, of the crime involved.

. . . we may therefore properly infer that Congress meant that the Government must prove knowledge with regard to the first two elements of the offense under the amended statute.

The third element—the unregistered status of the grenades—presents more difficulty. Proof of intent with regard to this element would require the Government to show that the appellees knew that the grenades were unregistered or negligently or recklessly failed to ascertain whether the weapons were registered. It is true that such a requirement would involve knowledge of law, but it does *not* involve "consciousness of wrongdoing" in the sense of knowledge that one's actions were prohibited or illegal. Rather, the definition of the crime, as written by Congress, requires proof of circumstances that involve a legal element, namely whether the grenades were registered in accordance with federal law. The knowledge involved is solely knowledge of the circumstances that the law has defined as material to the offense. . . .

Therefore, as with the first two elements, the question is solely one of congressional intent. And while the question is not an easy one, two factors persuade me that proof of *mens rea* as to the unregistered status of the grenades is not required. First, as the Court notes, the case law under the provisions replaced by the current law dispensed with proof of intent in connection with this element. Second, the firearms covered by the Act are major weapons such as machineguns and sawed-off shotguns; deceptive weapons such as flashlight guns and fountain pen guns; and major destructive devices such as bombs, grenades, mines, rockets, and large caliber weapons including mortars, antitank guns, and bazookas. Without exception, the likelihood of governmental regulation of the distribution of such weapons is so great that anyone must be presumed to be aware of it. In the context of a taxing and registration scheme, I therefore think it reasonable to conclude that Congress dispensed with the requirement of intent in regard to the unregistered status of the weapon, as necessary to effective administration of the statute.

B. INFANCY

STATE v. MONAHAN

Supreme Court of New Jersey, 1954.
15 N.J. 34, 104 A.2d 21.

JACOBS, J. Prompted by mid-Twentieth Century sociological precepts, our Legislature has directed that children under 16 who commit any offenses which would be criminal if committed by adults, shall not be triable in criminal proceedings but shall be dealt with exclusively by our specialized juvenile courts. The legal issue presented to us is whether this clear statutory mandate may be judicially disregarded to enable a first degree murder trial in the County Court of a 15-year-old boy who participated in a robbery with his father during which his father killed two persons.

In April, 1953 Eugene Monahan and his 15-year-old son Michael were indicted for the murder of William Diskin and Sebastian Weilandics. Eugene Monahan has been tried, convicted and sentenced to death and his appeal is pending before this court. The State concedes that the victims were killed by the father and not the son but asserts that since the homicides occurred during a robbery in which the son participated, the son was equally triable for murder in the first degree, punishable by death unless there is a recommendation of life imprisonment. . . . A motion was made for transfer of the proceeding against the son to the Juvenile and Domestic Relations Court on the ground that under N.J.S. 2A:85-4, N.J.S.A., and N.J.S. 2A:4-14, N.J.S.A., it was cognizable exclusively in that court. The motion was denied and an appeal was taken. . . .

The principle of removing or mitigating the criminal responsibility of children has ancient origins. In the early case of State v. Aaron. . . ., Chief Justice Kirkpatrick restated the settled common law doctrine, adapted from earlier Roman law, that since a child under seven "cannot have discretion to discern between good and evil" he is incapable of committing crime; between the ages of seven and 14 he is subject to a rebuttable presumption of incapacity; and after 14 he is presumptively capable. . . . Although the common law rule precluded criminal convictions of many young offenders, there are instances in which it failed to do so, with shocking consequences. Blackstone cites cases in which children of very tender age were drastically condemned as adult criminals; he refers to the hanging of an eight-year-old for maliciously burning some barns; to the hanging of a ten-year-old who had killed one of his companions; and to the burning of a girl of 13 who had killed her mistress. . . . Similar illustrations in our own State are not lacking. In 1818 a boy of 11 was tried for murder . . ., and in 1828 a boy of 13 was hanged for an offense which he committed when he was 12. . . . . During most of the Nineteenth Century, child and adult offenders were treated alike although intermittent steps were taken towards their separate confinement. It was not until the turn of the century that modern concepts really began to take form; they embodied the upward movement in the child's age of criminal responsibility, the extended recognition of society's obligation as *parens patriae* to care for delinquent children, and the creation of independent juvenile courts. . . .

The first juvenile court in this country was established in Cook County, Illinois, by an 1899 act which provided that the child offender was to be considered a ward of the state under control of the juvenile court; proceedings were there to be conducted informally with rehabilitative supervision rather than retributive punishment in mind, and without public indictment, trial by jury and other incidents of criminal causes. Thereafter the other states adopted legislation which was comparable though specific provisions varied. Attacks on the legislation based on the absence of indictment, trial by jury and the other constitutional guarantees applicable to criminal proceedings were quickly rejected. . . . In the Fisher case [213 Pa. 48, 62 A. 200] the Supreme Court of Pennsylvania pointed out that the juvenile court proceeding is not "the trial of a child charged with a crime, but is mercifully to save it from such an ordeal, with the prison or penitentiary in its wake, if the child's own good and the best interests of the state justify such salvation." In the Lindsay case [257 Ill. 328, 100 N.E. 894] the Supreme Court of Illinois noted that the "prerogative of the state, arising out of its power and duty, as *parens patriae*, to protect the interest of infants, has always been exercised by courts of chancery" and has not been questioned for generations. In the Lewis case [260 N.Y. 171, 183 N.E. 354] the New York Court of Appeals stated that there is no doubt about the power of the legislature "to say that an act done by a child shall not be a crime." And in the recent Morin case [95 N.H. 518, 68 A.2d 670] the Supreme Court of New Hampshire, in rejecting an attack on its statute relating to delinquent children, said:

> "We think it sufficiently plain that the act in question is designed to permit the exercise of the powers of the state as 'parens patriae,' for the purpose of rehabilitating minor children, and not of punishing them for the commission of a crime. 'It is generally held that the purpose of such statutes is not penal, but protective. It is not that the child shall be punished for breach of a law or regulation, but that he shall have a better chance to become a worthy citizen.' . . . Similar statutes have been universally upheld over objections based upon constitutional grounds. . . .

In In re Paniecki [N.J.1935] . . ., Vice-Chancellor Backes had occasion to deal with the issue of whether a 15-year-old boy, charged with murder, was triable in the same manner as an adult in the Court of Oyer and Terminer. The vice chancellor held that he was, expressing the sweeping view that the Legislature had no power "to vest jurisdiction in the juvenile court to try the crime of murder (or any other indictable offense) without a jury." He did not consider any of the many cases to the contrary throughout the states and if his view had ultimately prevailed it would have struck a mortal blow to the juvenile court movement in our State. . . .

Immediately after Vice-Chancellor Backes had rendered his decision in the Daniecki case, holding that the 15-year-old boy before him was triable for murder in the same manner as an adult, the Legislature took affirmative steps to obviate its effects. It provided in L. 1935, c. 285, that a person under the age of 16 shall be deemed incapable of committing a crime under the common law or statute law of this State; and in L.1935, c. 284, in defining delinquency cognizable exclusively in the juvenile court, it included conduct which, if committed by any one 16 or over, would constitute a felony, high misdemeanor, misdemeanor or other offense. The statutory language was unmistakable in design. . . .

In In re Mei . . . [N.J.1937], the question was again raised as to whether a 15-year-old was triable for murder in the same manner as an adult; the court held that he was notwithstanding the express terms of L.1935, cc. 284, 285. It did not suggest that the Legislature intended to exclude murder from its comprehensive enactments; nor did it adopt the sweeping view of unconstitutionality expressed in the Daniecki case and later rejected in the Goldberg case. Instead, it rested on the unprecedented ground that since the charge of murder is "so horrible in fact and in the contemplation of society" it must remain "a crime within the purview of the Constitution, whatever name and whatever treatment may be appended to it by the Legislature." . . . Viewed strictly as a legal ground it has no supporting basis whatever since the Constitution makes no pertinent mention of murder and the guarantees, when applicable, govern murder and other indictable common law offenses with like force. Viewed strictly as an emotional ground it concededly may not be given any controlling effect.

In approximately half the states the jurisdiction of the juvenile court over children under 16 is exclusive, even where the offense would constitute murder if committed by an adult. . . . The Standard Juvenile Court Act as revised in 1949 likewise vests exclusive jurisdiction in the juvenile court over all children under 16. It also provides for jurisdiction over children from 16 to 18 but states that if the child is 16 or over and is charged "with an offense which would be a felony if committed by an adult" the juvenile court may, in its discretion, certify the child for criminal proceedings. To remove any doubts, it expressly directs that "no child under sixteen years of age shall be so certified." Judicial opinions sustaining such legislation are now legion and the Mei decision stands alone in its notion that a child of seven or over, charged with murder, must be tried in the same manner as an adult regardless of what the Legislature says on the subject. Although the decision is devoid of supporting reason and authority, the suggestion is advanced that since it was rendered many years ago it should be permitted to stand until altered by the Legislature. This approach might have some merit if the Mei decision turned on a matter of statutory construction but the fact is that the court there asserted an absence of constitutional power which no amount of legislation could supply. . . . In any event, the pertinent legislative enactments after the Mei case clearly reaffirm the plain statutory purpose to vest in the juvenile court, exclusive jurisdiction over children under 16 regardless of the severity of their offenses. . . . In 1946 the Legislature, in dealing with juvenile court jurisdiction over persons between the ages of 16 and 18, expressly stated that the juvenile court may refer the matter to the prosecutor for criminal trial where the offense was of a "heinous nature." L.1946, c. 77; N.J.S. 2A:4–15, N.J.S.A. . . . No comparable provision was ever adopted with respect to children under 16, thus evidencing the legislative purpose of preserving the exclusive jurisdiction of the juvenile court in such instances. . . . When our statutes relating to civil and criminal justice were recently revised, the Legislature re-enacted its comprehensive declarations that a person under the age of 16 shall be deemed incapable of committing a crime, . . . and that juvenile delinquency shall include any act which, if committed by an adult, would constitute a felony, high misdemeanor, misdemeanor or other offense. . . .

A majority of the court is satisfied that our present legislation lawfully vests exclusive jurisdiction in the juvenile court over misconduct by children under 16, including misconduct which would constitute murder or other heinous crime if committed by an adult. Accordingly, the order entered below is set aside and the matter is remanded to the Juvenile and Domestic Relations Court of Union County for further proceedings in accordance with the governing statutes and rules of court.

HEHER, J., concurring in result. [The concurring opinion of HEHER, J., is omitted.] For reversal: JUSTICES HEHER, BURLING, JACOBS and BRENNAN—4. For affirmance: CHIEF JUSTICE VANDERBILT, and JUSTICES OLIPHANT and WACHENFELD—3.

OLIPHANT, J. (dissenting). I find myself compelled to dissent in this case because I differ basically with the approach and reasoning of the majority opinion. . . .

The majority . . . have in effect overruled the holding in the Mei case and assert that under the *parens patriae* doctrine, both on psychological and sociological grounds, the State and the Legislature have the power to treat such a crime when committed by an infant on a psychological or sociological basis and bring it within the definition of juvenile delinquency as set forth in the statute. . . .

. . . [T]he nub of the problem here presented revolves around the statutory provision, N.J.S. 2A:85-4, N.J.S.A., which provides:

> "A person under the age of 16 years is deemed incapable of committing a crime."

This provision seemingly ignores the fundamental fact of the law of nature as applied to man and facts of everyday existence which are of common knowledge and public notice.

I cannot comprehend the reasoning that suggests that marauding gangs of little hoodlums armed with guns, knives, switch knives or other lethal weapons are to be considered as a matter of law incapable of committing the crime of murder. Infants under the age of 21 years, according to statistics, perpetrate a high percentage of the heinous crimes committed throughout the country, and the situation has reached such serious proportions that it is a threat to the public welfare and safety of the law-abiding citizen. . . .

At the common law and in this State, insofar as a crime is concerned, the inability to form a criminal intent is a matter of defense. As to children under the age of seven years there is a conclusive presumption that the child was *doli incapax,* or incapable of entertaining a criminal intent, and no evidence can or should be received to show capacity in fact. Between the ages of seven and 14 the presumption is rebuttable, but the State or prosecution has the burden of showing that the infant has sufficient intelligence to distinguish between right and wrong and to understand the nature and illegality of the particular act. Over the age of 14 children were and are presumed to be *doli capax* and therefore responsible. The presumption is rebuttable but the burden of proof is upon the defendant to establish that he did not have sufficient intelligence to understand the nature and consequences of his act. These rules are consistent with the nature of man and the natural use of his faculties of intellect and will, and his freedom to acquire the necessary knowledge to make the distinction between right and wrong. They are rules to determine the ultimate fact of the ability of an individual to distinguish between right and wrong. The point in life when a person is capable of making this distinction may vary, but once it is reached that person, whether it be an adult or a child, is capable of criminal intent. . .

The views expressed here were of sufficient moment to induce the Legislatures in many states to remove the charge of murder from the field of juvenile delinquency. It is indeed a curious anomaly that in this country, where civilization in some respects has reached its highest peak insofar as the welfare and comfort of an individual is concerned and where the educational opportunities are practically unlimited for a child, we are brought face to face with a statute that in effect denied that the normal child is a rational human being insofar as the highest crime against nature is concerned. I doubt that even in the primitive state of civilization there is any society that subscribes to such a proposition. Bluntly, the statute practically says that a child, within defined age limits, is not a rational being but merely an animal without the will or mind to control its baser animal instincts. . . .

I am unable to subscribe to nor can I find support for the legal theory by which the Legislature can declare that those young in years but old in crime and depravity are incapable of committing the crime of murder. Many such are experienced criminals. A prominent jurist recently said: "The whole problem of juvenile and adolescent delinquency has become worse and is now a scandal." . . .

I would affirm the order of the court below in denying the motion for the transfer of the indictments to the Juvenile and Domestic Relations Court.

WACHENFELD, J. (dissenting).

Over the many years our present procedure in reference to these matters has worked out quite satisfactorily. No hue or cry of great injustice has been heard, nor is there a single case the disposition of which has offended the public's sense of essential fairness.

The method of disposing of these cases has now been changed, not by legislative enactment, where the power admittedly resides, but by a new judicial interpretation. In re Mei . . ., which has stood for 17 years, is overruled and is no longer the law.

Up until now, all who committed murder, whether old or young, were held strictly accountable to the law. If the offender appreciated the difference between right and wrong, he was answerable in a court of law for the highest crime known, the taking of another's life.

Today's youth is more precocious than yesterday's. His aggressiveness has not been diminished, and the record unfortunately shows his propensity for going out of bounds has not decreased. The child who flounts authority is becoming too prevalent, and the seriousness of these infractions is becoming increasingly grim. Juvenile delinquency is still one of our foremost problems, and its solution is being vainly sought by educator, legislator and many public agencies.

How, then, will this change in the law affect the dilemma confronting us? Will it help or hinder? Those of tender age who are likely to commit the crime involved will certainly not be additionally deterred by the knowledge that the punishment for it has practically been abolished and the worst that can befall them for committing a felony murder under the new rule is confinement in a reformatory or correctional institution for the term fixed by the trustees, not to exceed in any case a few years.

Erring youth indeed offers a fertile field for remedial effort, but I doubt if in this instance we are making much of a contribution.

The police now cannot keep track of those they have apprehended and referred to the Juvenile Court. The disposition there is confidential and secret and makes better law enforcement by those responsible for it more difficult. To the classification of the offenses so processed we now add the crime of murder. I have grave fears of its consequences.

I cannot embrace many of the expressions in Justice Oliphant's dissent, but I feel obligated to state briefly the reasons why I would adhere to the decision in In re Mei, supra, and therefore affirm the judgment below.

NOTES

1. Many jurisdictions specify the minimum age for criminal responsibility by statute. The Model Penal Code, too, in § 4.10 (Tentative Draft No. 7), suggests an abandonment of the common law approach to the defense of infancy, and provides that a person may not be tried for or convicted of an offense which he committed when he was under sixteen, or one committed when he was sixteen or seventeen unless the juvenile court lacks jurisdiction over the person because of his age or waives jurisdiction.

In New York, the age of capacity is 16 (McKinney's N.Y. Penal Law § 30.00); in Illinois, 13 (Ill.Cr.Code, § 6–1, ch. 38, S.H.A.). In a number of states, the common law rules of infancy still pertain (e. g. Clay v. State, 143 Fla. 204, 196 So. 462 [1940]), or have been embodied in a statute. In California, for instance, Penal Code § 26 provides that children under the age of 14 are incapable of committing crimes, "in the absence of clear proof that at the time of committing the act charged against them, they knew its wrongfulness." (West's Ann.Calif.Codes.)

A number of states give concurrent jurisdiction to juvenile courts and criminal courts over acts committed by children over the minimum age of capacity but below the age of 17 or 18. In Illinois, a recent amendment to the Illinois Juvenile Court Act (Ill.Rev.Stats. ch. 37, § 702–7, effective Jan. 1, 1973), sets up the following procedure:

§ 702–7. Criminal Prosecutions Limited

(1) Except as provided in this Section, no minor who was under 17 years of age at the time of the alleged offense may be prosecuted under the criminal laws of this State or for violation of an ordinance of any political subdivision thereof.

(2) Subject to paragraph (1) of Section 2–8, any minor alleged to have committed a traffic, boating or fish and game law violation or an offense punishable by fine only may be prosecuted therefor and if found guilty punished under any statute or ordinance relating thereto, without reference to the procedures set out in this Act.

(3) If a petition alleges commission by a minor 13 years of age or over of an act which constitutes a crime under the laws of this State, and, on motion of the State's Attorney, a Juvenile Judge, designated by the Chief Judge of the Circuit to hear and determine such motions, after investigation and hearing but before commencement of the adjudicatory hearing, finds that it is not in the best interests of the minor or of the public to proceed under this Act, the court may enter an order permitting prosecution under the criminal laws.

(a) In making its determination on a motion to permit prosecution under the criminal laws, the court shall consider among other matters: (1) whether there is sufficient evidence upon which a grand jury may be expected to return an indictment; (2) whether there is evidence that the alleged offense was committed in an aggressive and premeditated manner; (3) the age of the minor; (4) the previous history of the minor; (5) whether there are facilities particularly available to the Juvenile Court for the treatment and rehabilitation of the minor; and (6) whether the best interest of the minor and the security of the public may require that the minor continue in custody or under supervision for a period extending beyond his minority. The burden and standard of proof shall be the same as under Section 5–1 of this Act. (b) If criminal proceedings are instituted, the petition shall be dismissed insofar as the act or acts involved in the criminal proceedings are concerned. Taking of evidence in an adjudicatory hearing in any such case is a bar to criminal proceedings based upon the conduct alleged in the petition.

(4) Nothing in this Act prohibits or limits the prosecution of any minor for an offense committed on or after his 17th birthday even though he or she is at the time of the offense a ward of the court.

(5) If a petition alleges commission by a minor 13 years of age or over of an act which constitutes a crime under the laws of this State, the minor, with the consent of his counsel, may, at any time before commencement of the adjudicatory hearing, file with the court a motion that criminal prosecution be ordered and that the petition be dismissed insofar as the act or acts involved in the criminal proceedings are concerned. If such a motion is filed as herein provided, the court shall enter its order accordingly.

C. INTOXICATION

PEOPLE v. GUILLETT

Supreme Court of Michigan, 1955.
342 Mich. 1, 69 N.W.2d 140.

BUTZEL, JUSTICE. Lawrence Guillett was informed against for assault with intent to commit rape. He pleaded not guilty and was tried in circuit court where a jury found him guilty of the crime charged. Appellant *in propria persona* has appealed from his conviction on various grounds. The complainant had agreed to spend an evening with him. He, with two other friends, called for her and they visited a tavern where each of them consumed three glasses of beer. She and appellant then went to the home of the latter's parents, and later purchased a bottle of wine out of which she took one glass which she only partially consumed while he apparently finished the bottle. They sat together on a davenport and he made indecent advances which she repulsed. After she arose he then struck her, knocked her down and continued his attempt to commit rape. During a struggle she grabbed a telephone receiver and struck him so many blows on the head that he required hospitalization. She then escaped, ran across the road and the police and an ambulance were summoned. Appellant's mother testified that he had been drinking for several days and that he had come home drunk earlier that day, but she left him to go to work shortly after 3 p. m. His father said that he appeared "dozy."

In view of the testimony the trial judge in his charge to the jury stated:

> "Now, there has been injected here to a great extent, the question of intoxication. I will give you an instruction on that.
>
> "It is a well settled law in this state that voluntary drunkenness is not a defense to crime. A man who puts himself in a position to have no control over his actions must be held to intend the consequences. The safety of the community requires this rule. Intoxication is so easily counterfeited, and, when real, is so often resorted to as a means of nerving a person up to the commission of some deliberate act, and withal is so inexcusable in itself, that the law has never recognized it as an excuse for crime.
>
> "In the case of an offense such as the one charged, committed during a period of intoxication, the law presumes the defendant to have intended the obscuration and perversion of his faculties which followed his voluntary intoxication. He must be held to have purposely blinded his moral

> perception and set his will free from the control of reason—to have suppressed the guards and invited the mutiny; and should therefore be held responsible as well for the vicious excesses of the will thus set free as for the acts done by its prompting."

Defendant has assigned error on the ground that the charge as given was incomplete and therefore misleading because it failed to state that intoxication may serve to negative the existence of the intent required for conviction of the crime charged.

We must conclude that the charge was erroneous. In Roberts v. People, 19 Mich. 401, 418, 420, the defendant was convicted of assault with intent to commit murder. On appeal, after considering the necessity for finding intent in fact, or specific intent, Justice Christiancy discussed the issue of whether drunkenness might negative the existence of that intent. He concluded:

> "In determining the question whether the assault was committed with the intent charged, it was therefore material to inquire whether the defendant's mental faculties were so far overcome by the effect of intoxication, as to render him incapable of entertaining the intent. And for this purpose, it was the right and the duty of the jury—as upon the question of intent of which this forms a part—to take into consideration the nature and the circumstances of the assault, the actions, conduct and demeanor of the defendant, and his declaration before, at the time, and after the assault; and especially to consider the nature of the intent, and what degree of mental capacity was necessary to enable him to entertain the simple intent to kill, under the circumstances of this case—or, which is the same thing, how far the mental faculties must be obscured by intoxication to render him incapable of entertaining that particular intent. . . .
>
> "But the Circuit Court held, in effect that no extent of intoxication could have the effect to disprove the intent; treating the intent as an inference of law for the Court, rather than a question of fact for the jury. In this we think there was error."

. . . A consideration of later Michigan authority reveals that Roberts v. People, supra, remains as the most eloquent and correct statement of law on the subject. Thus in People v. Walker, 38 Mich. 156, Judge Cooley wrote an opinion reversing a conviction of larceny stating:

> "While it is true that drunkenness cannot excuse crime, it is equally true that when a certain intent is a necessary element in a crime, the crime cannot have been committed when the intent did not exist. In larceny the crime does not consist in the wrongful taking of the property, for that might be a mere trespass; but it consists in the wrongful

taking with felonious intent; and if the defendant, for any reason whatever, indulged no such intent, the crime cannot have been committed. This was fully explained by Mr. Justice Christiancy in Roberts v. People, 19 Mich. 401, and is familiar law."

. . . It is to be noted that we are here concerned with intoxication insofar as it might negative the requisite intent, as distinguished from insanity or delirium tremens brought on by intoxication, the latter, if present, being a complete excuse rather than a partial one as here. . . .

It is important in this decision to emphasize that intoxication may only negative the existence of *specific intent.* Examination of the cases reveals that where the rule was applied it was done so in cases where the crime charged also involved a specific intent. Apparently the trial judge in the instant case did not realize this. For the most part his charge was in the exact words of Justice Cooley in People v. Garbutt, 17 Mich. 9. However, it should have been noted that the crime involved in that case was murder, not a specific intent crime, or as was said in Roberts v. People, supra, 19 Mich. at page 417:

"The correctness of the principle laid down by this Court in People v. Garbutt (17 Mich. 9–19), is not denied; that 'a man who voluntarily puts himself into a condition to have no control of his actions, must be held to intend the consequences.' But this, it is insisted, includes only the consequences which do actually ensue—the crime actually committed; and not in this case the intent charged, if the defendant was at the time incapable of entertaining it, and did not in fact entertain it."

"We think this reasoning is entirely sound, and it is well supported by authority."

The crime of assault with intent to rape involves a specific intent. . . . The charge was therefore erroneous. . . .

The error here is one of omission. The charge is one of half-truth and misleading. The effect of the instruction given in this case was to instruct the jury that any and all evidence of intoxication had absolutely no bearing on appellant's guilt of the crime charged. It has been said that a charge stating some elements of a crime but omitting others "would have a natural tendency to cause a jury to believe that those stated were exclusive." . . . It was therefore prejudicial to the appellant. It was reversible error. . . .

D. THE INSANITY DEFENSE AND INCOMPETENCY TO STAND TRIAL

SECTION 1. THE M'NAGHTEN (RIGHT-WRONG) TEST

DANIEL M'NAGHTEN'S CASE

House of Lords, 1843.
10 Cl. & F. 200, 8 Eng.Reprint 718.

The prisoner had been indicted for [the murder of Edward Drummond, private secretary to Sir Robert Peel.] . . . The prisoner pleaded Not guilty.

Evidence having been given of the fact of the shooting of Mr. Drummond, and of his death in consequence thereof, witnesses were called on the part of the prisoner, to prove that he was not, at the time of committing the act, in a sound state of mind. . . .

LORD CHIEF JUSTICE TINDAL (in his charge):—The question to be determined is, whether at the time the act in question was committed, the prisoner had or had not the use of his understanding, so as to know that he was doing a wrong or wicked act. If the jurors should be of opinion that the prisoner was not sensible, at the time he committed it, that he was violating the laws both of God and man, then he would be entitled to a verdict in his favour: but if, on the contrary, they were of opinion that when he committed the act he was in a sound state of mind, then their verdict must be against him.

Verdict, Not guilty, on the ground of insanity.

This verdict, and the question of the nature and extent of the unsoundness of mind which would excuse the commission of a felony of this sort, having been made the subject of debate in the House of Lords, it was determined to take the opinion of the Judges on the law governing such cases. . . .

LORD CHIEF JUSTICE TINDAL . . . The first question proposed by your Lordships is this: "What is the law respecting alleged crimes committed by persons afflicted with insane delusion in respect of one or more particular subjects or persons: as, for instance, where at the time of the commission of the alleged crime the accused knew he was acting contrary to law, but did the act complained of with a view, under the influence of insane delusion, of redressing or revenging some supposed grievance or injury, or of producing some supposed public benefit?"

In answer to which question, assuming that your Lordships inquiries are confined to those persons who labour under such partial delusions only, and are not in other respects insane, we are of opinion that, notwithstanding the party accused did the act complained of with a view, under the influence of insane delusion, of redressing or revenging some supposed grievance or injury, or of producing some public benefit, he is nevertheless punishable according to the nature of the crime committed, if he knew at the time of committing such crime that he was acting contrary to law; by which expression we understand your Lordships to mean the law of the land.

Your Lordships are pleased to inquire of us, secondly, "What are the proper questions to be submitted to the jury, where a person alleged to be afflicted with insane delusion respecting one or more particular subjects or persons, is charged with the commission of a crime (murder, for example), and insanity is set up as a defence?" And, thirdly, "In what terms ought the question to be left to the jury as to the prisoner's state of mind at the time when the act was committed?" And as these two questions appear to us to be more conveniently answered together, we have to submit our opinion to be, that the jurors ought to be told in all cases that every man is to be presumed to be sane, and to possess a sufficient degree of reason to be responsible for his crimes, until the contrary be proved to their satisfaction; and that to establish a defence on the ground of insanity, it must be clearly proved that, at the time of the committing of the act, the party accused was labouring under such a defect of reason, from disease of the mind, as not to know the nature and quality of the act he was doing; or, if he did know it, that he did not know he was doing what was wrong. The mode of putting the latter part of the question to the jury on these occasions has generally been, whether the accused at the time of doing the act knew the difference between right and wrong: which mode, though rarely, if ever, leading to any mistake with the jury, is not, as we conceive, so accurate when put generally and in the abstract, as when put with reference to the party's knowledge of right and wrong in respect to the very act with which he is charged. If the question were to be put as to the knowledge of the accused solely and exclusively with reference to the law of the land, it might tend to confound the jury, by inducing them to believe that an actual knowledge of the law of the land was essential in order to lead to a conviction; whereas the law is administered upon the principle that every one must be taken conclusively to know it, without proof that he does know it. If the accused was conscious that the act was one which he ought not to do, and if that act was at the same time contrary to the law of the land, he is punishable; and the usual course therefore has been to leave the question to the jury, whether the party accused had a sufficient degree of reason to know that he was doing an act that was wrong; and this course we think is correct, accompanied with such observations and explanations as the circumstances of each particular case may require.

The fourth question which your Lordships have proposed to us is this:—"If a person under an insane delusion as to existing facts, commits an offence in consequence thereof, is he thereby excused?" To which question the answer must of course depend on the nature of the delusion: but, making the same assumption as we did before, namely, that he labours under such partial delusion only, and is not in other respects insane, we think he must be considered in the same situation as to responsibility as if the facts with respect to which the delusion exists were real. For example, if under the influence of his delusion he supposes another man to be in the act of attempting to take away his life, and he kills that man, as he supposes, in self-defence, he would be exempt from punishment. If his delusion was that the deceased had inflicted a serious injury to his character and fortune, and he killed him in revenge for such supposed injury, he would be liable to punishment. . . .

NOTES

1. There were several rules which antedated the *M'Naghten* test. See the Calendar of Close Rolls, Edward I, 7 Edward I p. 518 (1278) ("Whilst suffering from madness"); Fitz Herbert, New Natura Brevium, 233 B (1794) ("He . . . who cannot account or number twenty pence nor can tell who was his father or mother, nor how old he is"); I Hale, Pleas of the Crown, 30 (1847) ("such a person as labouring under melancholy distempers hath yet ordinarily as great understanding, as ordinarily a child of fourteen years hath, is such a person as may be guilty of . . . felony").

Consider finally the very old rule commonly called the "Wild Beast Test":

TRIAL OF EDWARD ARNOLD

Kingston Assizes 1724 16 How.St.T.R. 695, 764.

JUSTICE TRACY, charging the jury: . . . If a man be deprived of his reason, and consequently of his intention, he cannot be guilty; . . . punishment is intended for example, and to deter other persons from wicked designs; but the punishment of a madman, a person that hath no design, can have no example. This is on one side. On the other side, we must be very cautious; it is not every frantic and idle humour of a man, that will exempt him from justice, and the punishment of the law. When a man is guilty of a great offence, it must be very plain and clear, before a man is allowed such an exemption; therefore it is not every kind of frantic humour or something unaccountable in a man's actions, that points him out to be such a madman as is to be exempted from punishment: it must be a man that is totally deprived of his understanding and memory, and doth not know what he is doing, no more than an infant, than a brute, or a wild beast, such a one is never the object of punishment . . .

2. As regards the history of the M'Naghten Rules themselves, consider the following from the opinion of Chief Judge Biggs of the Third Cir-

cuit Court of Appeals in U. S. v. Currens, 290 F.2d 751 (1961), at pp. 448–449:

". . . The M'Naghten Rules . . . were engendered by the excitement and fear which grew out of the acquittal of Daniel M'Naghten who had attempted to assassinate Sir Robert Peel, Prime Minister of England, but who instead shot Peel's private secretary, Drummond, because M'Naghten had mistaken Drummond for Peel. The offense against Drummond followed a series of attempted assassinations of members of the English Royal House, including Queen Victoria herself, and attacks on the Queen's ministers. Some of these were considered to have grown out of Anti-Corn-Law League plots. When M'Naghten was acquitted at his trial . . . public indignation, led by the Queen, ran so high that the Judges of England were called before the House of Lords to explain their conduct. A series of questions were propounded to them. Their answers, really an advisory opinion which were delivered by Lord Chief Justice Tindal for all fifteen Judges, save Mr. Justice Maule, constitute what are now known as the M'Naghten Rules. . . ."

KNIGHTS v. STATE

Supreme Court of Nebraska, 1899.
58 Neb. 225, 78 N.W. 508.

SULLIVAN, J. In the district court of Washington county, George Knights was convicted of the crime of arson, and sentenced to imprisonment in the penitentiary for a term of 12 years. . . .

In relation to the defense of insanity, upon which the prisoner relied, the court said to the jury, in the twelfth instruction: "You are instructed that the law presumes that every person is sane, and it is not necessary for the state to introduce evidence of sanity in the first instance. When, however, any evidence has been introduced tending to prove insanity of an accused, the burden is then upon the state to establish the fact of the accused's sanity, the same as any other material fact to be established by the state to warrant a conviction. If the testimony introduced in this case tending to prove that the defendant was insane at the time of the alleged burning described in the information raises in your mind a reasonable doubt of his sanity at the time of the alleged burning, then your verdict should be acquittal." It is contended that this instruction gave the jury to understand that the burden of establishing his insanity rested upon the defendant up to a certain point in the trial, and was then shifted from him to the state. . . . [T]here can be no room to doubt that the court, in the instruction now under consideration, stated the correct doctrine in unmistakable terms. In this case the jury were informed that the law presumes sanity, but that, when the defendant produced evidence tending to prove insanity, the state was charged with a burden which did not previously rest upon it. The court did not say nor imply that the burden of proving insanity was ever on the accused, or that there was a shifting of the burden from him to the state. The substance of what the court did say was that, when the legal presumption of sanity encountered opposing evidence, the law then, for the first time, imposed on the state the onus of showing the prisoner's sanity by the proper measure of proof. . . .

PEOPLE v. WOOD

Court of Appeals of New York, 1962.
12 N.Y.2d 69, 187 N.E.2d 116.

FROESSEL, JUDGE. On July 4, 1960 the bodies of John Rescigno and Frederick Sess, aged 62 and about 77 respectively, were discovered in the "little house" they shared in Astoria, Queens County. In addition to other wounds, Sess had sustained multiple skull fractures. On Rescigno's body were about 16 wounds; his jugular vein had been severed. Defendant, Frederick Charles Wood, aged 50, was convicted of murder first degree (two counts) and sentenced to death.

Wood was taken into custody on July 5th. During the automobile trip to the station house, he told a detective that he had received the cut on his right thumb during a barroom altercation, but when asked the same question later at the police station, he replied that he had been cut by glass fragments while striking Rescigno with a bottle. He thereupon admitted having killed Sess and Rescigno on June 30, 1960, and gave a particularized account of how and why he did so. This statement, recorded in shorthand, transcribed, and signed by defendant, was admitted in evidence at trial without objection.

Defendant made no attempt to controvert the evidence which overwhelmingly established that he killed Rescigno and Sess. His sole defense was insanity. Ordinarily, under these circumstances, we would say little more about the evidence relating to the commission of the crimes. Here, however, since it is indicative of Wood's state of mind on June 30th, we set forth in some detail his statement made to an Assistant District Attorney on July 5th.

Almost at the outset of the interrogation, Wood was asked if he had done something "wrong" in Astoria on the night of June 30th. He replied that he had, that he "knocked off those two guys", "did them in", "killed two men". Defendant then related that at about 3:00 p. m. on June 30th, while he was panhandling on Broadway, New York City, he saw John Rescigno, whom he had never met before, leaving a tavern. Wood had panhandled two dollars, but "was looking for more". He "figured" Rescigno was a "lush" and "might be good for a score". Rescigno purchased a bottle of wine. Defendant obtained an invitation from Rescigno to stay at the latter's house that night. He "figured" he "could make a score" because Rescigno "had been drinking like hell", and defendant "knew what the score was and he didn't".

During the subway ride to Astoria, Rescigno said he was a "pensioner", showed Wood his social security card, and "intimate[d] he has quite a bit of money", at which point defendant "developed an idea I would try to take [rob] him during the evening sometime". When they arrived at the house between 7:00 and 8:00 p. m., the "apartment" was dark, and Rescigno did not turn on the lights. At the time, defendant saw Sess in bed in a bedroom.

They drank some beer; Rescigno took a drink of muscatel "and he gets silly drunk", "mumbles unintelligibly", but Wood finally understood that he suggested they "go to bed together". Continuing: "* * * I don't like degenerates. I always had a distaste for them. * * * I knew right then he sealed his fate. I know I'm going to knock him off that night. Not only for his money but for the satisfaction of knocking off a degenerate." But he could not "knock him off right away because [he had] to figure out the angles". Therefore Wood went "along with the gag", gave Rescigno "a mushy kiss", suggested they take it easy, have some more drinks, and told him he was going to stay all night.

Defendant went to the kitchen to find a weapon. Because it was dark and he did not want to turn on the lights, the only weapon he could find was an empty beer bottle. He took the bottle and a package of cigarettes to Rescigno's bedroom, offered Rescigno a cigarette because "just as soon as he reached for the cigarette I had the intention of knocking his brains out, which I did". After rendering the victim unconscious, Wood severed his jugular vein with a piece of jagged glass from the broken bottle. Blood was spurting out, but Wood stood to one side in order to keep from soiling his clothes.

After taking two or three dollars from Rescigno's clothes, Wood remembered a man sleeping in the other room, whom he "figured" he "might as well finish * * * off just on the grounds he might be a degenerate also". Defendant returned to the kitchen "figuring out the best weapon to use on this guy". He found a heavy coal shovel, lifted it "to see if it had the right amount of heft", beat Sess on the head with the shovel, then "flailed him unmercifully" with a chair. Wood, in his own language, "was satisfied in my mind he couldn't recover".

Thereupon defendant went to the kitchen, where he washed, and combed his hair—"I could pass for a Sunday school teacher any place on the face of the earth". He then returned to the bedroom, searched Sess' pockets looking for money but "unfortunately" found none. Defendant did not wish to remain long because he felt that Sess' "loud [dying] noise" and the barking of a dog "would tip off the neighbors that something was *wrong*" (emphasis supplied).

Before departing, however, Wood wrote two notes which were found under a cigarette holder on a table in the kitchen. One reads: "And God bless the Parole Board. They're real intelligent people"; the other states: "Now, aren't these two murders a dirty shame.

I'm so-o sorry." Wood engaged in this "little caper" to "dress the two knock offs up a bit", and because he has "a flair for the dramatics at times".

The first witness for the *defense* was the Assistant District Attorney, who had testified for the People regarding Wood's statement. He now related what Wood told him during the time the statement was being transcribed. Defendant spoke, among other things, about three murders he had committed in the past. He subsequently described them orally and in writing to the psychiatrists who examined him at Bellevue Hospital prior to trial, and who testified with reference thereto. In 1925 when he was about 15 years old, and because "he couldn't have her", Wood injected arsenic into some cream puffs which he sent to a girl, Cynthia Longo, who died as a result thereof. Thereafter, when he was about 21 years old, he bludgeoned 140 times and stabbed to death a woman he encountered one night. Having contracted syphilis and gonorrhea from another woman, thus becoming angry at women generally, he picked this stranger to kill.

In 1942 defendant murdered John Loman because the latter made a disparaging remark about Wood's girl friend. Wood caused Loman to become very drunk, attempted to asphyxiate him with gas, and when this failed to achieve the desired result, he bashed in Loman's head. With the help of his girl friend, Wood hid the body, planning to dismember it later and dispose of the parts. When arrested, he denied his guilt, and the authorities had a " 'hell of a time' " attempting to prove premeditation. Though convicted of murder second degree, defendant said he was " 'actually guilty of Murder in the First Degree' ". He was sentenced to from 20 years to life, only to be paroled less than a month before the present homicides.

Defendant further told the Assistant District Attorney that after the jury's verdict in the Loman case, but prior to sentence, he slashed his wrists in a suicide "attempt", because he did not want to spend a lot of time in prison, and felt he could obtain better treatment in a hospital. He was sent to Dannemora State Hospital, where he enjoyed himself and was allowed to play cards, but when certain privileges were withdrawn, he became dissatisfied and felt it was time to tell the psychiatrist he was not insane. Defendant boasted that "Anytime I wanted to, I knew I could get out of there because I wasn't insane"; he "could fool anybody", he was "fooling the psychiatrist all along" and "could do it anytime". He succeeded.

After the hospital released him, Wood was transferred to prison, where he determined to and did become a model prisoner as he sorely wanted to gain freedom. Paroled and assigned to Albany district, Wood obtained employment in a laundry. He was not happy there, however, knew that eventually he would begin drinking again, in which event he would lose his job and be returned to prison, and, therefore, decided to lose himself in New York City.

Although the four defense psychiatrists testified in answer to hypothetical questions that on June 30th defendant was laboring under such defect of reason as to know neither the nature nor the quality of his acts nor that they were wrong, their conclusions were largely weakened by lengthy and vigorous cross-examinations. By contrast, the People's two psychiatric experts, who testified that Wood was legally sane, were together asked but six questions on cross-examination, to two of which objections were sustained.

When the defense psychiatrists had testified, defendant, against the advice of his attorneys, took the stand, after having been duly cautioned, and stated that, although he was "very sick" while at Bellevue for examination, "at the time I committed the crime, the two murders, I knew the nature and I knew the quality of my act. I was sane then, perfectly sane, and I am perfectly sane now". He made this statement, he testified, because he had "been living on borrowed time" since 1926, and furthermore he did not "relish the prospect of going back to prison for the rest of my life or to any insane asylum". He was not cross-examined.

Defendant now merely urges that the People failed to establish beyond a reasonable doubt that he knew the acts were wrong. We now consider this contention. In substance, the expert testimony for the defense was that Wood had schizophrenic reaction, an illness from which he had suffered since about 1926, though "not probably an organic illness". In this connection, the defense psychiatrists stated that although defendant's memory was good, his sensorium clear, he was unaware of the full significance and consequences of his acts, though he knew their physical nature and quality, and that his judgment was impaired, his reasoning defective. Further, defendant told the psychiatrists at Bellevue that he considered himself to be "God's emissary" to take and to save life, and that he was presently charged with the duty of seeking out and killing those whom he believed were degenerates. Their cross-examination established beyond peradventure that Wood knew it was against the law to kill a human being.

One of the People's psychiatrists, Dr. Winkler, who first examined Wood in July, 1960 at Kings County Hospital and interviewed him in April, 1961, testified that defendant had a "highly pathological personality * * * a severe personality disorder", which manifested itself early in his life, but had not "deteriorated" since. Dr. Winkler noted that though defendant had been subjected to extensive hospital observation during the course of his lifetime, the diagnosis of schizophrenic reaction was made *for the first time* at Bellevue in the Fall of 1960. The witness further stated that Wood cannot be called "mentally ill or psychotic", and that his moral judgment was not distorted by illness or disease, but had "never developed". Another "peculiarity", Dr. Winkler testified, was defendant's "inability to control his impulses", a pathological sign but not "legal insanity". During three weeks' observation at the hospital in July, 1960, Wood had not shown any evidence of a psychotic condition.

Regarding the "God's emissary" delusion, Dr. Winkler entertained "definite doubts" that this was "a firm, fixed belief" and gave his reasons therefor. It is of some significance that Wood made this assertion for the *first* time in a psychiatric examination during the latter part of January or in February, 1961, seven months after the homicides with which he was charged, and following the administration of sodium amytal, a drug which, according to Dr. Winkler, might induce delusions. The Kings County Hospital report of July, 1960 does not contain a reference to this delusion. Most significant is the fact that Wood did not mention the delusion in his July 5th statement, but admitted he did something "wrong" on June 30th, namely, killed two men. Indeed, he stated then that *he* "always had a distaste" for degenerates, and had killed Rescigno partly "for the satisfaction of" killing a degenerate, and partly to steal money. It may also be noted that the "God's emissary" delusion and degeneracy had nothing to do with his previous three murders.

Moreover, he did not just kill Rescigno when he ascertained the latter was a degenerate, but first had to "figure out the angles", made sure his intended victim was drunk, and then distracted him by offering a cigarette. After the killings, defendant did not tarry long, being apprehensive that Sess' dying noises and the barking of a dog would alert neighbors to the fact "that something was *wrong*" (emphasis supplied). The People's psychiatrist, Dr. D'Angelo, supported Dr. Winkler in his view that defendant knew the nature and quality of his acts and that they were wrong.

In People v. Schmidt, . . . Judge Cardozo, discussing the meaning of the word "wrong" as used in section 1120, Consol.Laws, c. 40 of the Penal Law, held that there are certain circumstances in which the word "ought not to be limited to legal wrong." Continuing: "Knowledge that an act is forbidden by law will in most cases permit the inference of knowledge that, according to the accepted standards of mankind, it is also condemned as an offense against good morals. Obedience to the law is itself a moral duty. If, however, there is an insane delusion that God has appeared to the defendant and ordained the commission of a crime, we think it cannot be said of the offender that he knows the act to be wrong. It is not enough, to relieve from criminal liability, that the prisoner is morally depraved [citation]. It is not enough that he has views of right and wrong at variance with those that find expression in the law. The variance must have its origin in some disease of the mind. . . . * * * Cases will doubtless arise where criminals will take shelter behind a professed belief that their crime was ordained by God * * *. We can safely leave such fabrications to the common sense of juries." . . .

As defendant concedes in his brief, the Trial Judge correctly charged the jury on the meaning of the word "wrong" when he stated: "When it speaks of the defendant's ignorance of his act as wrong, the law does not mean to permit the individual to be his own judge of what is right or wrong. It says that the individual has sufficient knowledge that an act was wrong if its perpetrator knows that his act is against the law and against the commonly accepted standards of morality and conduct which prevail in the community of mankind. He must know that his act was contrary to the laws of God and man." The Trial Judge then stated an example which is so strikingly parallel to defendant's claim that the jury could not have failed to see the point.

Of course the question as to whether Wood knew it was wrong to kill when he killed Sess and Rescigno was a question of fact for the jury, and, as we stated in People v. Horton, . . . "if the record in its entirety presents a fair conflict in the evidence, or if conflicting inferences can properly be drawn from it, '* * * the determination of the jury will not be interfered with, unless it is clearly against the weight of evidence, or appears to have been influenced by passion, prejudice, mistake or corruption.' . . . We see nothing in the record to take the instant case out of this general rule. Of course the fact that a defendant was suffering from some type of mental disorder . . . , or that he had a psychopathic personality . . . , or that his "moral perceptions were of low order" . . . , or that he had an irresistible impulse to commit the crime . . . , does not immunize him from criminal responsibility. . . .

There was abundant evidence here upon which the jury reasonably could have rejected entirely the defense that Wood considered himself to be "God's emissary". Moreover, the jury, having been properly instructed, could reasonably have found that defendant was operating under a standard of morality he had set up for himself and which applied only to him. The law does not excuse for such moral depravity or "views of right and wrong at variance with those that find expression in the law" . . . While the very nature and circumstances of the present homicides, as well as the expert testimony on both sides, make clear that Wood was not well balanced mentally, the weight of evidence clearly supports the determination, implicit in the verdict, that he knew not only the nature and quality of his acts, but also that they were wrong, as that term was correctly defined and exemplified by the trial court. Under these circumstances we have no right to interfere with the verdict. . . .

Defendant also contends that he was denied a fair trial on the issue of insanity by reason of various rulings of the court and certain conduct and comment of the prosecutor. One of these contentions relates to the remarks of the prosecutor in his summation concerning two of the defense psychiatrists. Specifically he referred to them as "the two happiness boys", as "those two idiots—I am sorry, those two psychiatrists"; he "charged" them with being "ignorant, stupid, incompetent", and scoffed at their titles of "Diplomate". These remarks were clearly improper, and cannot be justified or excused by anything that transpired earlier in the trial. Although we have been disturbed by this aspect of the case, we have concluded that these remarks, now complained of, did not deprive defendant of a fair trial. Only the first of these comments was objected to at the trial, and it was stricken. Counsel did not object to the summation upon the ground that it or any part thereof was inflammatory, nor make a motion for a mistrial. While objection need not be voiced in a capital case to preserve a question for our review, we are of the opinion, on the present record, that the prosecutor's remarks had no influence upon the jury.

We have examined the other contentions of the defendant and find no merit to them.

The judgment appealed from should be affirmed.

FULD, JUDGE (dissenting). I agree with the court that, upon the record before us, the People have established that the defendant was legally sane under the law of this State as it now stands . . . , but I cannot refrain from observing that the result demonstrates the unreality, if not the invalidity, of our present standards for determining criminal responsibility. This case serves to confirm the view, frequently expressed over the years, that section 1120 of the Penal Law should be amended and the "right-wrong" test which now controls our decisions changed.

However, since the issue of the defendant's insanity under section 1120 seems to me so extremely close, I do not believe that we may disregard the prosecutor's concededly inexcusable and improper remarks, relating to the defense psychiatrists, as technical error under section 542 of the Code of Criminal Procedure.

DESMOND, C. J., and VAN VOORHIS, J., dissent and vote to reverse and to dismiss the indictment upon the ground that by the clear weight of evidence this defendant is insane under the rule of section 1120 of the Penal Law in which connection we express our strong disapproval of the prosecutor's inexcusable ridicule of the court-appointed psychiatrists.

NOTE

In 1965 the New York legislature changed the test of insanity. See infra p. 378.

SECTION 2. THE IRRESISTIBLE IMPULSE TEST

As a supplement to the M'Naghten test, a number of jurisdictions have adopted the so-called "irresistible impulse" test. Under that test, the jury is instructed that it must acquit the defendant if it finds that the diseased mind of the accused rendered him incapable of exercising the normal governing power of the will so as to control his actions under the compulsion of an insane impulse to act. The rule is not a recent one, since an instruction based on the same concept was given as early as 1844 in a Massachusetts case. Chief Justice Shaw's jury instruction in Commonwealth v. Rogers read, in part:

> If then it is proved, to the satisfaction of the jury, that the mind of the accused was in a diseased and unsound state, the question will be, whether the disease existed to so high a degree, that for the time being it overwhelmed the reason, conscience, and judgment, and whether the prisoner, in committing the homicide acted from an irresistible and uncontrollable impulse, if so, then the act was not the act of a voluntary agent, but the involuntary act of the body, without the concurrence of a mind directing it.

Consider the following paragraph from Moenssens, Moses & Inbau, Scientific Evidence in Criminal Cases, 1973 (Chapter 3 on "Forensic Psychiatry", § 3.03(2)):

> The motivation for formulating the irresistible impulse rule arose from the psychiatrist's difficulty in perceiving the various forms of compulsive behavior within the M'Naghten definition of legal insanity. Compulsive behavior such as kleptomania, pyromania, and dipsomania occurs when the actor does know right from wrong and does contemplate the consequences of his normative violation, knowing it is wrong, but nevertheless persists in the act because of an inner force which he is powerless to resist. Psychiatrists might not categorize this individual as insane in the right-wrong sense; consequently, if such behavior is to be exempted from responsibility, the irresistible impulse is a necessary adjunct to *M'Naghten.*

SECTION 3. THE DURHAM TEST

In Durham v. United States, 94 U.S.App.D.C. 228, 214 F.2d 862 (1954) defendant Durham, an individual with a long history of mental illness, appealed from his conviction for housebreaking on the grounds that the existing tests in the District of Columbia for determining criminal responsibility (the right-wrong test supplemented by the irresistible impulse test) were not satisfactory criteria for determining criminal responsibility.

The Court of Appeals for the District of Columbia accepted the argument of a large number of medico-legal writers that the right-wrong test is based upon an entirely obsolete and misleading conception of the nature of insanity. It accepted the view of psychiatry that man is an integrated personality of which reason is only one element, not the sole determinant of his conduct. Therefore the right-wrong test, because it considers knowledge or reason alone, is an inadequate guide to mental responsibility for criminal behavior. The fundamental objection to the right-wrong test is that it is made to rest upon any particular symptom. In attempting to define insanity in terms of a symptom, courts have assumed an impossible role.

Turning to the "irresistible impulse test", the court found that test inadequate because based upon the misleading implication that 'diseased mental condition(s)' produce only sudden, momentary or spontaneous inclinations to commit unlawful acts. Such a test gives no recognition to mental illness characterized by brooding and reflection.

Finally, the court concluded that a broader test should be adopted and formulated the rule that an accused is not criminally responsible if his unlawful act was the "product of mental disease or mental defect". It went on to say, "We use 'disease' in the sense of a condition which is considered capable of either improving or deteriorating. We use 'defect' in the sense of a condition which is not considered capable of either improving or deteriorating and which may be either congenital, or the result of injury, or the residual effect of a physical or mental disease".

In essence this test permits a jury to find a defendant not guilty by reason of insanity if it believes beyond a reasonable doubt that the accused suffered from a mental disease or defect and that there was sufficient causal connection between the mental abnormality and the accused's unlawful act to excuse the defendant from criminal responsibility for it.

SECTION 4. THE AMERICAN LAW INSTITUTE (A.L.I.) TEST, AND THE BRAWNER SUPPLEMENTATION

The response of other jurisdictions to *Durham* was less than enthusiastic. Perhaps this was due in part to the increasing popularity of the A.L.I. test. The American Law Institute, in Tentative Draft No. 4 of its Model Penal Code, proposed the following insanity test:

> (1) A person is not responsible for criminal conduct if at the time of such conduct as a result of mental disease or defect he lacks substantial capacity either to appreciate the criminality of his conduct or to conform his conduct to the requirements of law.
>
> (2) The terms "mental disease or defect" do not include an abnormality manifested only by repeated criminal or otherwise anti-social conduct.

As the A.L.I. test became adopted in more jurisdictions, the *Durham* rule lost what little stature it had achieved. Then on June 23, 1972, the Court of Appeals for the District of Columbia, in United States v. Brawner, 471 F.2d 969 (D.C.Cir. 1972), abandoned *Durham* and accepted the A.L.I. test. The court continued to adhere, however, to the definition of "mental disease or defect" it had earlier articulated in McDonald v. United States, 114 U.S.App. D.C. 120, 312 F.2d 847 (1962): "mental disease or defect includes any abnormal condition of the mind which substantially affects mental or emotional processes and substantially impairs behavior controls." The principal reason for the *Brawner* departure from *Durham* was the undue dominance gained by experts giving testimony on insanity. This dominance occurred because of the broad area of relevance encompassed by the *Durham*'s "product" concept which "did not signify a reasonably identifiable common ground that was also shared by the nonlegal experts, and the laymen serving on the jury as the representatives of the community. Accordingly, the court decided:

> The experts have meaningful information to impart, not only to the existence of mental illness or not, but also on its relationship to the incident charged as an offense. In the interest of justice this valued information should be available, and should not be lost or blocked by requirements that unnaturally restrict communication between the experts and the jury. The more we have pondered the problem the more convinced we have become that the sound solution lies not in further shaping of the *Durham* "product" approach in more refined molds, but in adopting the ALI's formulation as the linchpin of our jurisprudence.

The ALI's formulation retains the core requirement of a meaningful relationship between the mental illness and the incident charged. The language in the ALI rule is sufficiently in the common ken that its use in the courtroom, or in preparation for trial, permits a reasonable three-way communication—between (a) the law-trained, judges and lawyers; (b) the experts and (c) the jurymen—without insisting on a vocabulary that is either stilted or stultified, or conducive to a testimonial mystique permitting expert dominance and encroachment on the jury's function. There is no indication in the available literature that any such untoward development has attended the reasonably widespread adoption of the ALI rule in the Federal courts and a substantial number of state courts.

With respect to the caveat paragraph in subsection (2) of the Model Penal Code test, which excludes from the concept of mental disease or defect abnormalities that are manifested only by repeated criminal or otherwise anti-social conduct, the *Brawner* court took notice of the fact that there was a split among the jurisdiction which had adopted the ALI test concerning this provision. Some courts had concluded to adopt the caveat, which excluded the defense of insanity for the so-called psychopathic personalities or sociopaths, while other jurisdictions had specifically decided to omit it from the test. The *Brawner* case pragmatically adopted the caveat paragraph as a rule for application by the judge, to avoid miscarriage of justice, but not for inclusion in instructions to the jury.

NOTES

1. The court's opinion in the 1972 case of United States v. Brawner was written by Circuit Judge Leventhal. Chief Judge Bazelon, who had written the Durham v. United States opinion in 1954 wrote a separate opinion in *Brawner*, concurring in part and dissenting in part. He stated, in part: "We are unanimous in our decision today to abandon the formulation of criminal responsibility adopted eighteen years ago in Durham. . . . But the adoption of this new test [ALI] is largely an anticlimax, for even though *Durham*'s language survived until today's decision, the significant differences between our approach and the approach of the ALI test vanished many years ago". Chief Judge Bazelon then proceeds to dispel the notion that the court's action achieved "uniformity" in the federal courts and also expresses the pessimistic view that the ALI test will not produce significantly better results than those obtained under *Durham*. The two opinions, read together (and some 70 pages long) provide an excellent analysis of the insanity defense problem.

2. The A.L.I. test sometimes with slight revisions, has been adopted in the following federal cases: United States v. Freeman, 357 F.2d 606 (2d Cir. 1966); United States v. Currens, 290 F.2d 751 (3d Cir. 1961); United States v. Chandler, 393 F.2d 920 (4th Cir. 1968); Blake v. United States, 407 F.2d 908 (5th Cir. 1969); United States v. Smith, 404 F.2d 720 (6th Cir. 1968); United States v. Shapiro, 383 F.2d 680 (7th Cir. 1967); Pope v. United States, 372 F.2d 710 (8th Cir. 1967); Wade v. United States,

426 F.2d 64 (9th Cir. 1972); Wion v. United States, 325 F.2d 420 (10th Cir. 1963); United States v. Brawner, supra, (D.C.Cir. 1972).

Many states, too, have adopted the A.L.I. formulation, whether by statute (e. g., Illinois, Maryland, Montana, Vermont), or by judicial decision, as in State v. White, 93 Idaho 153, 456 P.2d 797 (1969), Hill v. State, 252 Ind. 601, 251 N.E.2d 429 (1969), Terry v. Commonwealth, 371 S.W.2d 862 (Ky.1963); and Commonwealth v. McHoul, 352 Mass. 544, 226 N.E.2d 556 (1967). Some courts, on the other hand, have rejected the A.L.I. test and retained M'Naghten, (e. g., State v. White, 60 Wash.2d 551, 374 P.2d 942 (1962)). Compare: State v. Griffin, 99 Ariz. 43, 406 P.2d 397 (1965); State v. Lucas, 30 N.J. 37, 152 A.2d 50 (1959); State v. Harkness, 160 N.W.2d 324 (Iowa, 1968); Kuk v. State, 80 Nev. 291, 392 P.2d 630 (1964).

3. A few states have enacted statutory or code provisions adopting slightly modified versions of the A.L.I. text.

The Illinois Criminal Code (S.H.A. ch. 38, § 6–2) provides as follows:

(a) A person is not criminally responsible for conduct if at the time of such conduct, as a result of mental disease or mental defect, he lacks substantial capacity either to appreciate the criminality of his conduct or to conform his conduct to the requirements of law.

(b) The terms "mental disease or mental defect" do not include an abnormality manifested only by repeated criminal or otherwise antisocial conduct.

The McKinney's N.Y. Penal Law (§ 30.05) reads as follows:

1. A person is not criminally responsible for conduct if at the time of such conduct, as a result of mental disease or defect, he lacks substantial capacity to know or appreciate either:

(a) The nature and consequence of such conduct; or

(b) That such conduct was wrong.

HOLLOWAY v. UNITED STATES

United States Court of Appeals, D.C.Cir., 1945.
80 U.S.App.D.C. 3, 148 F.2d 665.

[Defendant was convicted of rape. He appealed on the sole ground that the record disclosed such substantial doubt of his sanity that the verdict should be set aside. The record disclosed that in 1940 the defendant was held in Gallinger Hospital for mental observation. Later he was confined in a federal hospital as a mental patient. And, in 1943, he was again committed to Gallinger Hospital as a mental patient. He was later released, not as recovered, in the custody of his mother, with further directions for the treatment of his mental disorders. Some months after this release he raped two women on the same day. Following is the Court of Appeals' opinion affirming the defendant's conviction.]

ARNOLD, J. The application of [the tests for insanity], however they are phrased, to a borderline case can be nothing more than a moral judgment that it is just or unjust to blame the defendant for what he did. Legal tests of criminal insanity are not and cannot be the result of scientific analysis or objective judgment. There is no objective standard by which such a judgment of an admittedly abnormal offender can be measured. They must be based on the instinctive sense of justice of ordinary men. . . .

[W]hen psychiatrists attempt on the witness stand to reconcile the therapeutic standards of their own art with the moral judgment of the criminal law they become confused. Thus it is common to find groups of distinguished scientists of the mind testifying on both sides and in all directions with positiveness and conviction. This is not because they are unreliable or because those who testify on one side are more skillful or learned than those who testify on the other. It is rather because to the psychiatrist mental cases are a series of imperceptible gradations from the mild psychopath to the extreme psychotic, whereas criminal law allows for no gradations. It requires a final decisive moral judgment of the culpability of the accused. For purposes of conviction there is no twilight zone between abnormality and insanity. An offender is wholly sane or wholly insane.

A complete reconciliation between the medical tests of insanity and the moral tests of criminal responsibility is impossible. The purposes are different; the assumptions behind the two standards are different. For that reason the principal function of a psychiatrist who testifies on the mental state of an abnormal offender is to inform the jury of the character of his mental disease. The psychiatrist's moral judgment reached on the basis of his observations is relevant. But it cannot bind the jury except within broad limits. To command respect criminal law must not offend against the common belief that men who talk rationally are in most cases morally responsible for what they do.

The institution which applies our inherited ideas of moral responsibility to individuals prosecuted for crime is a jury of ordinary men. These men must be told that in order to convict they should have no reasonable doubt of the defendant's sanity. After they have declared by their verdict that they have no such doubt their judgment should not be disturbed on the ground it is contrary to expert psychiatric opinion. Psychiatry offers us no standard for measuring the validity of the jury's moral judgment as to culpability. To justify a reversal circumstances must be such that the verdict shocks the conscience of the court.

NOTE

XYY Chromosomal Defect as Evidence of Insanity

The XYY chromosomal defect found in some members of the human population has recently been urgd as a defense to criminal responsibility. The XYY theory is that certain individuals, due to their body chemistry, are unable to control their cognitive and/or volitional functions and, hence, should not be held responsible for their unlawful acts.

Biologically speaking, the normal human cell is made up of 46 chromosomes, comprised of 22 pairs of autosomal chromosomes (22 Xs and 22 Ys), plus the 45th and 46th chromosomes which are either X or Y sex chromosomes. XX is female and XY is male. The X chromosome is thought by some scientists to be responsible for the passive attitude in the personality makeup, while the Y chromosome is believed to control the aggressive potential, although other scientists dismiss this theory as a chauvinistic gratuity unfounded in medical science. When a male has an extra Y chromosome constituting an XYY chromosomal makeup, it is theorized that he may become intensely aggressive, display anti-social behavior, and also have a relatively low intelligence. It is also theorized he may be unable to control his behavior.

People v. Tanner, 13 Cal.App.3d 596, 91 Cal.Rptr. 656 (1970) is an example of one of the first judicial responses in this country to the problem presented by the XYY individual to traditional theories of criminal responsibility. *Tanner* held that a trial judge did not abuse his discretion in finding the evidence insufficient to establish the legal insanity of an XYY individual charged with assault with intent to murder in a state where the M'Naghten "right-wrong" test had to be met in order to establish legal insanity.

The defendant's witnesses included two geneticists who presented lengthy and complex testimony and documentary evidence concerning XYY syndrome. This evidence indicated that XYY individuals exhibit aggressive behavior as a result of their chromosomal abnormality. The court found such evidence deficient in three principal respects: First, that studies of XYY individuals were few, rudimentary in scope, and inconclusive because they indicated only that aggressive behavior may be one manifestation of XYY syndrome, but not that all XYY individuals were by nature involuntarily aggressive; *Second,* that the experts could not demonstrate a causal relationship between the assault in question and the defendant's chromosomal abnormality; and *Third,* that the experts did not testify that the possession of an extra Y chromosome results in legal insanity under the state's version of the M'Naghten rule. See also Millard v. State, 814 Md.App. 419, 261 A.2d 227 (1970).

Query: Would XYY syndrome fare better under the A.L.I. insanity test?

SECTION 5. INCOMPETENCY

1. *Incompetency to Stand Trial.* A person cannot be brought to trial if his mental condition at that time is such that he is "unable to understand the nature and purpose of the proceedings against him, or to assist in his defense". Whenever that condition is found to exist (by a judge or jury), he will be committed to a mental institution and can only be tried thereafter if and when he improves sufficiently to satisfy the above stated requirements.

2. *Incompetency at Time of Scheduled Execution.* In death penalty cases there can be no execution if prior to the time of the scheduled event the sentenced person develops a mental condition

that will not permit him "to understand the nature and purpose" of the sentence of death.

(With regard to the various and complex issues that may arise as to the competency of an accused person to stand trial, consult Inbau, Thompson, and Moenssens, Cases and Comments on Criminal Law (1973), 729–745.)

Chapter 8

ENTRAPMENT

SHERMAN v. UNITED STATES

Supreme Court of the United States, 1958.
356 U.S. 369, 78 S.Ct. 819.

MR. CHIEF JUSTICE WARREN delivered the opinion of the Court.

The issue before us is whether petitioner's conviction should be set aside on the ground that as a matter of law the defense of entrapment was established. Petitioner was convicted under an indictment charging three sales of narcotics in violation of 21 U.S.C. § 174, 21 U.S.C.A. § 174. A previous conviction had been reversed on account of improper instructions as to the issue of entrapment. In the second trial, as in the first, petitioner's defense was a claim of entrapment: an agent of the Federal Government induced him to take part in illegal transactions when otherwise he would not have done so.

In late August 1951, Kalchinian, a government informer, first met petitioner at a doctor's office where apparently both were being treated to be cured of narcotics addiction. Several accidental meetings followed, either at the doctor's office or at the pharmacy where both filled their prescriptions from the doctor. From mere greetings, conversation progressed to a discussion of mutual experiences and problems, including their attempts to overcome addiction to narcotics. Finally Kalchinian asked petitioner if he knew of a good source of narcotics. He asked petitioner to supply him with a source because he was not responding to treatment. From the first, petitioner tried to avoid the issue. Not until after a number of repetitions of the request, predicated on Kalchinian's presumed suffering, did petitioner finally acquiesce. Several times thereafter he obtained a quantity of narcotics which he shared with Kalchinian. Each time petitioner told Kalchinian that the total cost of narcotics he obtained was twenty-five dollars and that Kalchinian owed him fifteen dollars. The informer thus bore the cost of his share of the narcotics plus the taxi and other expenses necessary to obtain the drug. After several such sales Kalchinian informed agents of the Bureau of Narcotics that he had another seller for them. On three occasions during November 1951, government agents observed petitioner give narcotics to Kalchinian in return for money supplied by the Government.

At the trial the factual issue was whether the informer had convinced an otherwise unwilling person to commit a criminal act or whether petitioner was already predisposed to commit the act and exhibited only the natural hesitancy of one acquainted with the narcotic trade. The issue of entrapment went to the jury, and a conviction resulted. Petitioner was sentenced to imprisonment for ten years.

The Court of Appeals for the Second Circuit affirmed. We granted certiorari.

In Sorrells v. United States, 287 U.S. 435, 53 S.Ct. 210, this Court firmly recognized the defense of entrapment in the federal courts. The intervening years have in no way detracted from the principles underlying that decision. The function of law enforcement is the prevention of crime and the apprehension of criminals. Manifestly, that function does not include the manufacturing of crime. Criminal activity is such that stealth and strategy are necessary weapons in the arsenal of the police officer. However, "A different question is presented when the criminal design originates with the officials of the Government, and they implant in the mind of an innocent person the disposition to commit the alleged offense and induce its commission in order that they may prosecute." Then stealth and strategy become as objectionable police methods as the coerced confession and the unlawful search. Congress could not have intended that its statutes were to be enforced by tempting innocent persons into violations.

However, the fact that government agents "merely afford opportunities or facilities for the commission of the offense does not" constitute entrapment. Entrapment occurs only when the criminal conduct was "the product of the *creative* activity" of law-enforcement officials. (Emphasis supplied.) To determine whether entrapment has been established, a line must be drawn between the trap for the unwary innocent and the trap for the unwary criminal. The principles by which the courts are to make this determination were outlined in *Sorrells*. On the one hand, at trial the accused may examine the conduct of the government agent; and on the other hand, the accused will be subjected to an "appropriate and searching inquiry into his own conduct and predisposition" as bearing on his claim of innocence.

We conclude from the evidence that entrapment was established as a matter of law. In so holding, we are not choosing between conflicting witnesses, nor judging credibility. Aside from recalling Kalchinian, who was the Government's witness, the defense called no witnesses. We reach our conclusion from the undisputed testimony of the prosecution's witnesses.

It is patently clear that petitioner was induced by Kalchinian. The informer himself testified that, believing petitioner to be undergoing a cure for narcotics addiction, he nonetheless sought to persuade petitioner to obtain for him a source of narcotics. In Kalchinian's own words we are told of the accidental, yet recurring, meetings, the ensuing conversations concerning mutual experiences in regard to narcotics addiction, and then of Kalchinian's resort to sympathy. One request was not enough, for Kalchinian tells us that additional ones were necessary to overcome, first, petitioner's refusal, then his evasiveness, and then his hesitancy in order to achieve capitulation. Kalchinian not only procured a source of narcotics but apparently also induced petitioner to return to the habit. Finally, assured of a catch, Kalchinian informed the authorities so that they could close the net. The Government cannot disown Kalchinian and insist it is not responsible for his actions. Although he was not being paid, Kalchinian was an active government informer who had but recently been the instigator of at least two other prosecutions. Undoubtedly the impetus for such achievements was the fact that in 1951 Kalchinian was himself under criminal charges for illegally selling narcotics and had not yet been sentenced. It makes no difference that the sales for which petitioner was convicted occurred after a series of sales. They were not independent acts subsequent to the inducement but part of a course of conduct which was the product of the inducement. In his testimony the federal agent in charge of the case admitted that he never bothered to question Kalchinian about the way he had made contact with petitioner. The Government cannot make such use of an informer and then claim disassociation through ignorance.

The Government sought to overcome the defense of entrapment by claiming that petitioner evinced a "ready complaisance" to accede to Kalchinian's request. Aside from a record of past convictions, which we discuss in the following paragraph, the Government's case is unsupported. There is no evidence that petitioner himself was in the trade. When his apartment was searched after arrest, no narcotics were found. There is no significant evidence that petitioner even made a profit on any sale to Kalchinian. The Government's characterization of petitioner's hesitancy to Kalchinian's request as the natural wariness of the criminal cannot fill the evidentiary void.

The Government's additional evidence in the second trial to show that petitioner was ready and willing to sell narcotics should the opportunity present itself was petitioner's record of two past narcotics convictions. In 1942 petitioner was convicted of illegally selling narcotics; in 1946 he was convicted of illegally possessing them. However, a nine-year-old sales conviction and a five-year-old possession conviction are insufficient to prove petitioner had a readiness to sell narcotics at the time Kalchinian approached him, particularly when we must assume from the record he was trying to overcome the narcotics habit at the time.

The case at bar illustrates an evil which the defense of entrapment is designed to overcome. The government informer entices someone attempting to avoid narcotics not only into carrying out an illegal sale but also into returning to the habit of use. Selecting the proper time, the informer then tells the government agent. The set-up is accepted by the agent without even a question as to the manner in which the informer encountered the seller. Thus the Government plays on the weaknesses of an innocent party and beguiles him into committing crimes which he otherwise would not have attempted. Law enforcement does not require methods such as this.

It has been suggested that in overturning this conviction we should reassess the doctrine of entrapment according to principles announced in the separate opinion of Mr. Justice Roberts in Sorrells v. United States, 287 U.S. 435, 453, 53 S.Ct. 210, 217. To do so would be to decide the case on grounds rejected by the majority in *Sorrells* and, so far as the record shows, not raised here or below by the parties before us. We do not ordinarily decide issues not presented by the parties and there is good reason not to vary that practice in this case.

At least two important issues of law enforcement and trial procedure would have to be decided without the benefit of argument by the parties, one party being the Government. Mr. Justice Roberts asserted that although the defendant could claim that the Government had induced him to commit the crime, the Government could not reply by showing that the defendant's criminal conduct was due to his own readiness and not to the persuasion of government agents. The handicap thus placed on the prosecution is obvious. Furthermore, it was the position of Mr. Justice Roberts that the factual issue of entrapment—now limited to the question of what the government agents did—should be decided by the judge, not the jury. Not only was this rejected by the Court in *Sorrells,* but where the issue has been presented to them, the Courts of Appeals have since *Sorrells* unanimously concluded that unless it can be decided as a matter of law, the issue of whether a defendant has been entrapped is for the jury as part of its function of determining the guilt or innocence of the accused.

To dispose of this case on the ground suggested would entail both overruling a leading decision of this Court and brushing aside the possibility that we would be creating more problems than we would supposedly be solving.

The judgment of the Court of Appeals is reversed and the case is remanded to the District Court with instructions to dismiss the indictment.

Reversed and remanded.

MR. JUSTICE FRANKFURTER, whom MR. JUSTICE DOUGLAS, MR. JUSTICE HARLAN, and MR. JUSTICE BRENNAN join, concurring in the result.

Although agreeing with the Court that the undisputed facts show entrapment as a matter of law, I reach this result by a route different from the Court's.

Today's [ruling] fails to give the doctrine of entrapment the solid foundation that the decisions of the lower courts and criticism of learned writers have clearly shown is needed. Instead it accepts without re-examination the theory espoused in Sorrells v. United States, 287 U.S. 435, 53 S.Ct. 210, over strong protest by Mr. Justice Roberts, speaking for Brandeis and Stone, JJ., as well as himself. The fact that since the *Sorrells* case the lower courts have either ignored its theory and continued to rest decision on the narrow facts of each case, or have failed after penetrating effort to define a satisfactory generalization is proof that the prevailing theory of the *Sorrells* case ought not to be deemed the last word. In a matter of this kind the Court should not rest on the first attempt at an explanation for what sound instinct counsels. It should not forego re-examination to achieve clarity of thought, because confused and inadequate analysis is too apt gradually to lead to a course of decisions that diverges from the true ends to be pursued.

It is surely sheer fiction to suggest that a conviction cannot be had when a defendant has been entrapped by government officers or informers because "Congress could not have intended that its statutes were to be enforced by tempting innocent persons into violations." In these cases raising claims of entrapment, the only legislative intention that can with any show of reason be extracted from the statute is the intention to make criminal precisely the conduct in which the defendant has engaged. That conduct includes all the elements necessary to constitute criminality. Without compulsion and "knowingly," where that is requisite, the defendant has violated the statutory command. If he is to be relieved from the usual punitive consequences, it is on no account because he is innocent of the offense described. In these circumstances, conduct is not less criminal because the result of temptation, whether the tempter is a private person or a government agent or informer.

The courts refuse to convict an entrapped defendant, not because his conduct falls outside the proscription of the statute, but because, even if his guilt be admitted, the methods employed on behalf of the Government to bring about conviction cannot be countenanced. As Mr. Justice Holmes said in Olmstead v. United States, 277 U.S. 438, 470, 48 S.Ct. 564, 575 (dissenting), in another connection, "It is desirable that criminals should be detected, and to that end that all available evidence should be used. It also is desirable that the Government should not itself foster and pay for other crimes, when they are the means by which the evidence is to be obtained. . . . [F]or my part I think it a less evil that some criminals should escape than that the Government should play an ignoble part." Insofar as they are used as instrumentalities in the administration of criminal justice, the federal courts have an obligation to set their face against enforcement of the law by lawless means or means that violate rationally vindicated standards of justice, and to refuse to sustain such methods by effectuating them. They do this in the exercise of a recognized jurisdiction to formulate and apply "proper standards for the enforcement of the federal criminal law in the federal courts," an obligation that goes beyond the conviction of the particular defendant before the court. Public confidence in the fair and honorable administration of justice, upon which ultimately depends the rule of law, is the transcending value at stake.

The formulation of these standards does not in any way conflict with the statute the defendant has violated, or involve the initiation of a judicial policy disregarding or qualifying that framed by Congress. A false choice is put when it is said that either the defendant's conduct does not fall within the statute or he must be convicted. The statute is wholly directed to defining and prohibiting the substantive offense concerned and expresses no purpose, either permissive or prohibitory, regarding the police conduct that will be tolerated in the detection of crime. A statute prohibiting the sale of narcotics is as silent on the question of entrapment as it is on the admissibility of illegally obtained evidence. It is enacted, however, on the basis of certain presuppositions concerning the established legal order and the role of the courts within that system in formulating standards for the administration of criminal justice when Congress itself has not specifically legislated to that end. Specific statutes are to be fitted into an antecedent legal system.

It might be thought that it is largely an academic question whether the court's finding a bar to conviction derives from the statute or from a supervisory jurisdiction over the administration of criminal justice; under either theory substantially the same considerations will determine whether the defense of entrapment is sustained. But to look to a statute for guidance in the application of a policy not remotely within the contemplation of Congress at the time of its enactment is to distort analysis. It is to run the risk, furthermore, that the court will shirk the responsibility that is necessarily in its keeping, if Congress is truly silent, to accommodate the dangers of overzealous law enforcement and civilized methods adequate to counter the ingenuity of modern criminals. The reasons that actually underlie the defense of entrapment can too easily be lost sight of in the pursuit of a wholly fictitious congressional intent.

The crucial question, not easy to answer, to which the court must direct itself is whether the police conduct revealed in the particular case falls below standards, to which common feelings respond, for the proper use of governmental power. For answer it is wholly irrelevant to ask if the "intention" to commit the crime originated with the defendant or government officers, or if the criminal conduct was the product of "the creative activity" of law-enforcement officials. Yet in the present case the Court repeats and purports to apply these unrevealing tests. Of course in every case of this kind the intention that the particular crime be committed originates with the police, and without their inducement the crime would not have occurred. But . . . where the police in effect simply furnished the opportunity for the commission of the crime, . . . this is not enough to enable the defendant to escape conviction.

The intention referred to, therefore, must be a general intention or predisposition to commit, whenever the opportunity should arise, crimes of the kind solicited, and in proof of such a predisposition evidence has often been admitted to show the defendant's reputation, criminal activities, and prior disposition. The danger of prejudice in such a situation, particularly if the issue of entrapment must be submitted to the jury and disposed of by a general verdict of guilty or innocent, is evident. The defendant must either forego the claim of entrapment or run the substantial risk that, in spite of instructions, the jury will allow a criminal record or bad reputation to weigh in its determination of guilt of the specific offense of which he stands charged. Furthermore, a test that looks to the character and predisposition of the defendant rather than the conduct of the police loses sight of the underlying reason for the defense of entrapment. No matter what the defendant's past record and present inclinations to criminality, or the depths to which he has sunk in the estimation of society, certain police conduct to ensnare him into further crime is not to be tolerated by an advanced society. And in the present case it is clear that the Court in fact reverses the conviction because of the conduct of the informer Kalchinian, and not because the Government has failed to draw a convincing picture of petitioner's past criminal conduct. Permissible police activity does not vary according to the particular defendant concerned; surely if two suspects have been solicited at the same time in the same manner, one should not go to jail simply because he has been convicted before and is said to have a criminal disposition. No more does it vary according to the suspicions, reasonable or unreasonable, of the police concerning the defendant's activities. Appeals to sympathy, friendship, the possibility of exorbitant gain, and so forth, can no more be tolerated when directed against a past offender than against an ordinary law-abiding citizen. A contrary view runs afoul of fundamental principles of equality under law, and would espouse the notion that when dealing with the criminal classes anything goes. The possibility that no matter what his past crimes and general disposition the defendant might not have committed the particular crime unless confronted with inordinate inducements, must not be ignored. Past crimes do not forever outlaw the criminal and open him to police practices, aimed at securing his repeated conviction, from which the ordinary citizen is protected. The whole ameliorative hopes of modern penology and prison administration strongly counsel against such a view.

This does not mean that the police may not act so as to detect those engaged in criminal conduct and ready and willing to commit further crimes should the occasion arise. Such indeed is their obligation. It does mean that in holding out inducements they should act in such a manner as is likely to induce to the commission of crime only these persons and not others who would normally avoid crime and through self-struggle resist ordinary temptations. This test shifts attention from the record and predisposition of the particular defendant to the conduct of the police and the likelihood, objectively considered, that it would entrap only those ready and willing to commit crime. It is as objective a test as the subject matter permits, and will give guidance in regulating police conduct that is lacking when the reasonableness of police suspicions must be judged or the criminal disposition of the defendant retrospectively appraised. It draws directly on the fundamental intuition that led in the first instance to the outlawing of "entrapment" as a prosecutorial instrument. The power of government is abused and directed to an end for which it was not constituted when employed to promote rather than detect crime and to bring about the downfall of those who, left to themselves, might well have obeyed the law. Human nature is weak enough and sufficiently beset by temptations without government adding to them and generating crime.

What police conduct is to be condemned, because likely to induce those not otherwise ready and willing to commit crime, must be picked out from case to case as new situations arise involving different crimes and new methods of detection. The *Sorrells* case involved persistent solicitation in the face of obvious reluctance, and appeals to sentiments aroused by reminiscences of experiences as companions in arms in the World War. Particularly reprehensible in the present case was the use of repeated requests to overcome petitioner's hesitancy, coupled with appeals to sympathy based on mutual experiences with narcotics addiction. Evidence of the setting in which the inducement took place is of course highly relevant in judging its likely effect, and the court should also consider the nature of the crime involved, its secrecy and difficulty of detection, and the manner in which the particular criminal business is usually carried on.

As Mr. Justice Roberts convincingly urged in the *Sorrells* case, such a judgment, aimed at blocking off areas of impermissible police conduct, is appropriate for the court and not the jury. "The protection of its own functions and the preservation of the purity of its own temple belongs only to the court. It is the province of the court and of the court alone to protect itself and the government from such prostitution of the criminal law. The violation of the principles of justice by the entrapment of the unwary into crime should be dealt with by the court no matter by whom or at what stage of the proceedings the facts are brought to its attention." 287 U.S., at 457, 53 S.Ct., at 218 (separate opinion). Equally important is the consideration that a jury verdict, although it may settle the issue of entrapment in the particular case, cannot give significant guidance for official conduct for the future. Only the court, through the gradual evolution of explicit standards in accumulated precedents, can do this with the degree of certainty that the wise administration of criminal justice demands.

KADIS v. UNITED STATES

United States Court of Appeals, 1st Cir. 1967.
373 F.2d 370.

ALDRICH, CHIEF JUDGE. Defendants, the Walnut Drug Corp. and two individual pharmacists, were convicted of violating 21 U.S.C. § 331(k) by refilling prescriptions for two drugs, librium and dexedrine, without obtaining authorization from the prescriber. They appeal on the ground that the two pharmacists were entrapped by agents of the Food and Drug Administration.

The facts are largely undisputed. In September 1964 the FDA office in Boston received a telephone call from a person who identified himself as Wilfred Chagnon, the treasurer of the Massachusetts Pharmacy Association. The caller said that the Walnut Drug Corp. was refilling librium and other drugs without authorization. Two agents were assigned to investigate. One obtained a medical prescription for librium, the other for dexedrine. Neither prescription referred to refills. Each agent went in plain clothes to the Walnut Pharmacy and had his prescription filled. Thereafter, over a period of about three months, the agents returned to the pharmacy a number of times and successfully asked for refills. The transactions are typically reflected by the following testimony of one of the agents.

> "[Kadis] came to the cash register in front of me, placed a prescription envelope on the counter in front of me. He said, 'Does the doctor want you to keep on taking these?' I said, 'I don't know.' He said, 'Of course you have been in to see him, and he probably said to continue.' I looked at him and said, 'I have not been back to see him since I got the prescription.' At that time I handed him a ten dollar bill.
>
> "He said, 'You will be going back to see him pretty soon, won't you?'
>
> "I said, 'I suppose I should' I replied, 'It is one of those things,' and he said 'We are supposed to keep track of how many tablets you take. It is just a technicality.'
>
> "I nodded my head. He handed me my change."

The defendants' principal claim is that they were entrapped as a matter of law because the government agents had inadequate grounds to seek them out.

The doctrine of entrapment as developed by the courts is far from simple, and has led to a number of misunderstandings. Thirty-five years ago, in Sorrells v. United States, the Court said, "[T]he question whether it [entrapment] precludes prosecution or affords a ground of defense, and, if so, upon what theory, has given rise to conflicting opinions." Unhappily, this statement is no less true today. We believe that one reason for the confusion is that there may not be general agreement about "the true ends to be pursued." In *Sorrells*, the Court said, [Entrapment occurs] when the criminal design originates with the officials of the government, and they implant in the mind of an innocent person the disposition to commit the alleged offense and induce its commission in order that they may prosecute." See also Sherman v. United States. It can be argued that this definition suggests two different objectives: to prevent prosecution of persons who were innocent until corrupted by government agents, and to preclude certain police conduct whether the particular defendant was innocent or not.[1]

In the original *Sherman* appeal, Judge Learned Hand divided the issue of entrapment into two subsidiary questions: whether the police had induced the crime, and whether the defendant was predisposed, that is, whether the inducement had been directed towards an innocent man, or one already corrupt. The court placed the

1. In both *Sorrells* and *Sherman* concurring minorities contended that the sole proper purpose of the doctrine of entrapment was to prevent certain police activities. In both cases the Court rejected this view.

burden as to the first issue on the defendant, and the burden as to the second on the government. This separation has given rise to an increasing number of problems. We believe the time has come to review not only the problems, but the rationale underlying the division itself.

Although Judge Hand placed the burden of showing inducement upon the defendant, he did not define the quantum of burden. Subsequently, in United States v. Pugliese, the court reversed a conviction as plain error because the district court had failed to make clear to the jury that this burden was only to prove inducement by a fair preponderance, and not beyond a reasonable doubt. [We, too, have] held that the defendant's evidence must merely preponderate. Later, however, since it was clear that the government must show the predisposition of the defendant beyond a reasonable doubt, and since we were troubled by the potential confusion introduced by requiring the jury to be instructed on two different burdens, we held that there is no burden of proof on the defendant even as to inducement. All that we [then] required was that there be some evidence indicating that the defendant was induced.

Consideration of inducement as a separate issue has encouraged the previously mentioned thought, that one of the "ends" to be achieved by the doctrine of entrapment is to police the police, to prevent certain antisocial police conduct—no matter how corrupt the defendant may, in fact, have been. There are really two claims. The first, which is advanced in the case at bar in its most extreme form, is that no inducement of any kind is justified unless the police had prior grounds warranting the initiation of their activity. We rejected this contention in Whiting v. United States, 321 F.2d 72 (1963). So have a number of other circuits. We adhere to that view.

At the other end of the spectrum, it is argued that extreme forms of inducement are socially offensive, and should defeat any prosecution based thereon. We see no purpose in debating the wisdom of such a principle, for there is a more ready answer. Extreme police tactics, for example, of badgering, or making massive appeals to the sympathy of an obviously reluctant person, will mean that as a matter of law the government cannot be found to have sustained its burden of proving that it did not corrupt an innocent or unwilling man. No situation suggests itself in which such police behavior, if conceded or found, would not necessarily create a reasonable doubt that the defendant was ready and willing to commit the crime when he was approached. Since an acquittal would thereby be required, we see no reason for making ethical appraisals of the police behavior.

We find, in sum, that consideration of inducement as a separate issue serves no useful purpose, and we believe it to be a mistake. We will no longer bifurcate entrapment into sub-issues of inducement and predisposition, . . . Henceforth we will look, singly, at the ultimate question of entrapment. If the defendant shows, through government witnesses or otherwise, some indication that a government agent corrupted him, the burden of disproving entrapment will be on the government; but such a showing is not made simply by evidence of a solicitation. There must be some evidence tending to show unreadiness.

While this conclusion modifies our prior decisions, we do not feel it to be at variance with the position thus far taken by the Supreme Court, which has never distinguished between the issues of inducement and predisposition, nor condemned the act of inducement apart from its effect on an innocent man. In Sherman v. United States, 1958, 356 U.S. 369, 78 S.Ct. 819, very forceful, what might well be described as offensive, inducement resulted in a directed acquittal not by virtue of singling out the acts of inducement for criticism, but because the Court held that in the face of such massive inducement the government could not sustain the burden of proving that the defendant had not been corrupted. More recently, in Osborn v. United States, 1966, 385 U.S. 323, 87 S.Ct. 429, in a situation in which inducement, as such, could have raised interesting questions, the Court made no mention of it. There a government agent who managed to gain employment with an attorney defending a criminal case remarked that one of the prospective jurors was his cousin. The attorney "jumped up" and said, "Let's go outside and talk about it," and immediately suggested the possibility of offering a bribe. It is difficult to say that the agent's remark did not induce the offense in the broad sense of the word. The Court's sole observation, however, was, "At [most, the] statement afforded the petitioner 'opportunities or facilities' for the commission of a criminal offense, and that is a far cry from entrapment."

One question remains: when has the defendant shown "some evidence" of entrapment, viz., when is the burden placed upon the government to show that the defendant was not in fact corrupted by the government agent. The amount need not be so substantial as to require, if uncontroverted, a directed verdict of acquittal, but it must be more than a mere scintilla. It cannot be enough, for example, where the defendant readily agreed to engage in a criminal act, to show that he enjoys a good reputation. However, any evidence, whether introduced by the defense or by the prosecution, that the government agents went beyond a simple request and pleaded or argued with the defendant, should be enough. Evidence that the defendant resisted the criminal suggestion raises the question whether his hesitation exhibited the conscience of the upright, or merely the circumspection of the criminal. Evidence that on other occasions the defendant refused to engage in acts similar to those with which he is charged tends to prove that he was not ready and willing, and equally creates a jury issue. On the other hand, evidence, as in the case at bar, of unwillingness to commit much more serious or otherwise noncomparable crimes, would seem insufficient.

Whether in the present case there was enough evidence, we need not determine. The court in fact submitted the question to the jury with clear and accurate instructions, and fully explained the burden that was upon the government. Defendants have shown no prejudicial error.

Affirmed.

UNITED STATES v. RUSSELL

Supreme Court of the United States, 1973.
411 U.S. 423, 93 S.Ct. 1637.

MR. JUSTICE REHNQUIST delivered the opinion of the Court.

Respondent Richard Russell was charged in three counts of a five count indictment returned against him and codefendants John and Patrick Connolly.[1] After a jury trial in the District Court, in which his sole defense was entrapment, respondent was convicted on all three counts of having unlawfully manufactured and processed methamphetamine ("speed") and of having unlawfully sold and delivered that drug in violation of 21 U.S.C. §§ 331(q)(1), (2), 360a (a), (b) (Supp. V, 1964). He was sentenced to concurrent terms of two years in prison for each offense, the terms to be suspended on the condition that he spend six months in prison and be placed on probation for the following three years. On appeal the United States Court of Appeals for the Ninth Circuit, one judge dissenting, reversed the conviction solely for the reason that an undercover agent supplied an essential chemical for manufacturing the methamphetamine which formed the basis of respondent's conviction. The court concluded that as a matter of law "a defense to a criminal charge may be founded upon an intolerable degree of governmental participation in the criminal enterprise." [We reverse.]

There is little dispute concerning the essential facts in this case. On December 7, 1969, Joe Shapiro, an undercover agent for the Federal Bureau of Narcotics and Dangerous Drugs, went to respondent's home on Whidbey Island in the State of Washington where he met with respondent and his two codefendants, John and Patrick Connolly. Shapiro's assignment was to locate a laboratory where it was believed that methamphetamine was being manufactured illicitly. He told the respondent and the Connollys that he represented an organization in the Pacific Northwest that was interested in controlling the manufacture and distribution of methamphetamine. He then made an offer to supply the defendants with the chemical phenyl-2-propanone, an essential ingredient in the manufacture of methamphetamine, in return for one-half of the drug produced. This offer was made on the condition that Agent Shapiro be shown a sample of the drug which they were making and the laboratory where it was being produced.

1. John Connolly did not appear for trial. Patrick Connolly was tried with the respondent and found guilty of all five counts against him. The validity of his conviction is not before us in this proceeding.

During the conversation Patrick Connolly revealed that he had been making the drug since May 1969 and since then had produced three pounds of it.[2] John Connolly gave the agent a bag containing a quantity of methamphetamine that he represented as being from "the last batch that we made." Shortly thereafter, Shapiro and Patrick Connolly left respondent's house to view the laboratory which was located in the Connolly house on Whidbey Island. At the house Shapiro observed an empty bottle bearing the chemical label phenyl-2-propanone.

By prearrangement Shapiro returned to the Connolly house on December 9, 1969, to supply 100 grams of propanone and observe the chemical reaction. When he arrived he observed Patrick Connolly and the respondent cutting up pieces of aluminum foil and placing them in a large flask. There was testimony that some of the foil pieces accidentally fell on the floor and were picked up by the respondent and Shapiro and put into the flask.[3] Thereafter Patrick Connolly added all of the necessary chemicals, including the propanone brought by Shapiro, to make two batches of methamphetamine. The manufacturing process having been completed the following morning, Shapiro was given one-half of the drug and respondent kept the remainder. Shapiro offered to buy, and the respondent agreed to sell, part of the remainder for $60.

About a month later Shapiro returned to the Connolly house and met with Patrick Connolly to ask if he was still interested in their "business arrangement." Connolly replied that he was interested but that he had recently obtained two additional bottles of phenyl-2-propanone and would not be finished with them for a couple of days. He provided some additional methamphetamine to Shapiro at that time. Three days later Shapiro returned to the Connolly house with a search warrant and, among other items, seized an empty 500-gram bottle of propanone and a 100-gram bottle, not the one he had provided, that was partially filled with the chemical.

There was testimony at the trial of respondent and Patrick Connolly that phenyl-2-propanone was generally difficult to obtain. At the request of the Bureau of Narcotics and Dangerous Drugs, some chemical supply firms had voluntarily ceased selling the chemical.

At the close of the evidence, and after receiving the District Judge's standard entrapment instruction,[4] the jury found the re-

2. At trial Patrick Connolly admitted making this statement to Agent Shapiro but asserted that the statement was not true.

3. Agent Shapiro did not otherwise participate in the manufacture of the drug or direct any of the work.

4. The District Judge stated the governing law on entrapment as follows: "Where a person has the willingness and the readiness to break the law, the mere fact that the government agent provides what appears to be a favorable opportunity is not entrapment." He then instructed the jury to acquit respondent if it had a "reasonable doubt whether the defendant

spondent guilty on all counts charged. On appeal the respondent conceded that the jury could have found him predisposed to commit the offenses, but argued that on the facts presented there was entrapment as a matter of law. The Court of Appeals agreed, although it did not find the District Court had misconstrued or misapplied the traditional standards governing the entrapment defense. Rather, the court in effect expanded the traditional notion of entrapment, which focuses on the predisposition of the defendant, to mandate dismissal of a criminal prosecution whenever the court determines that there has been "an intolerable degree of governmental participation in the criminal enterprise." In this case the court decided that the conduct of the agent in supplying a scarce ingredient essential for the manufacture of a controlled substance established that defense.

This new defense was held to rest on either of two alternative theories. One theory is based on two lower court decisions which have found entrapment, regardless of predisposition, whenever the government supplies contraband to the defendants. The second theory, a nonentrapment rationale, is based on a recent Ninth Circuit decision that reversed a conviction because a government investigator was so enmeshed in the criminal activity that the prosecution of the defendants was held to be repugnant to the American criminal justice system. The court below held that these two rationales constitute the same defense, and that only the label distinguishes them. In any event, it held that "[b]oth theories are premised on fundamental concepts of due process and evince the reluctance of the judiciary to countenance 'overzealous law enforcement.'"

* * *

In the instant case respondent asks us to reconsider the theory of the entrapment defense as it is set forth in the majority opinions in *Sorrells* and *Sherman* [discussed in the preceding main cases]. His principal contention is that the defense should rest on constitutional grounds. He argues that the level of Shapiro's involvement in the manufacture of the methamphetamine was so high that a criminal prosecution for the drug's manufacture violates the fundamental principles of due process. The respondent contends that the same factors that led this Court to apply the exclusionary rule to illegal searches and seizures and confessions should be considered here. But he would have the Court go further in deterring undesirable official conduct by requiring that any prosecution be barred absolutely because of the police involvement in criminal activity. The analogy is imperfect in any event, for the principal reason behind the adoption of the exclusionary rule was the government's "failure to observe its own laws." Unlike the situations giving rise

had the previous intent or purpose to commit the offense . . . and did so only because he was induced or persuaded by some officer or agent of the government." No exception was taken by respondent to this instruction.

to the holdings in *Mapp* and *Miranda*, the government's conduct here violated no independent constitutional right of the respondent. Nor did Shapiro violate any federal statute or rule or commit any crime in infiltrating the respondent's drug enterprise.

Respondent would overcome this basic weakness in his analogy to the exclusionary rule cases by having the Court adopt a rigid constitutional rule that would preclude any prosecution when it is shown that the criminal conduct would not have been possible had not an undercover agent "supplied an indispensable means to the commission of the crime that could not have been obtained otherwise, through legal or illegal channels." Even if we were to surmount the difficulties attending the notion that due process of law can be embodied in fixed rules, and those attending respondent's particular formulation, the rule he proposes would not appear to be of significant benefit to him. For on the record presented it appears that he cannot fit within the terms of the very rule he proposes.

The record discloses that although the propanone was difficult to obtain it was by no means impossible. The defendants admitted making the drug both before and after those batches made with the propanone supplied by Shapiro. Shapiro testified that he saw an empty bottle labeled phenyl-2-propanone on his first visit to the laboratory on December 7, 1969. And when the laboratory was searched pursuant to a search warrant on January 10, 1970, two additional bottles labeled phenyl-2-propanone were seized. Thus, the facts in the record amply demonstrate that the propanone used in the illicit manufacture of methamphetamine not only *could* have been obtained without the intervention of Shapiro but was in fact obtained by these defendants.

While we may some day be presented with a situation in which the conduct of law enforcement agents is so outrageous that due process principles would absolutely bar the government from invoking judicial processes to obtain a conviction, the instant case is distinctly not of that breed. Shapiro's contribution of propanone to the criminal enterprise already in process was scarcely objectionable. The chemical is by itself a harmless substance and its possession is legal. While the government may have been seeking to make it more difficult for drug rings, such as that of which respondent was a member, to obtain the chemical, the evidence described above shows that it nonetheless was obtainable. The law enforcement conduct here stops far short of violating that "fundamental fairness, shocking to the universal sense of justice," mandated by the Due Process Clause of the Fifth Amendment.

The illicit manufacture of drugs is not a sporadic, isolated criminal incident, but a continuing, though illegal, business enterprise. In order to obtain convictions for illegally manufacturing drugs, the gathering of evidence of past unlawful conduct frequently proves to be an all but impossible task. Thus in drug-related offenses law enforcement personnel have turned to one of the only practicable means of detection: the infiltration of drug rings and a limited participation in their unlawful present practices. Such infiltration is a recognized and permissible means of apprehension; if that be so, then the supply of some item of value that the drug ring requires must, as a general rule, also be permissible. For an agent will not be taken into the confidence of the illegal entrepreneurs unless he has something of value to offer them. Law enforcement tactics such as this can hardly be said to violate "fundamental fairness" or "shocking to the universal sense of justice."

Respondent also urges, as an alternative to his constitutional argument, that we broaden the nonconstitutional defense of entrapment in order to sustain the judgment of the Court of Appeals. This Court's opinions in Sorrells v. United States, supra, and Sherman v. United States, supra, held that the principal element in the defense of entrapment was the defendant's predisposition to commit the crime. Respondent conceded in the Court of Appeals, as well he might, "that he may have harbored a predisposition to commit the charged offenses." Yet he argues that the jury's refusal to find entrapment under the charge submitted to it by the trial court should be overturned and the views of Justices Roberts and Frankfurter, concurring in *Sorrells* and *Sherman*, respectively, which make the essential element of the defense turn on the type and degree of governmental conduct, be adopted as the law.

We decline to overrule these cases. *Sorrells* is a precedent of long standing that has already been once reexamined in *Sherman* and implicitly there reaffirmed. Since the defense is not of a constitutional dimension, Congress may address itself to the question and adopt any substantive definition of the defense that it may find desirable.[5]

* * *

. . . [It does not] seem particularly desirable for the law to grant complete immunity from prosecution to one who himself planned to commit a crime, and then committed it, simply because government undercover agents subjected him to inducements which might have seduced a hypothetical individual who was not so predisposed. . . .

Several decisions of the United States district courts and courts of appeals have undoubtedly gone beyond this Court's opinions in *Sorrells* and *Sherman* in order to bar prosecutions because of what they thought to be for want of a better term "overzealous law enforcement." But the defense of entrapment enunciated in those opinions was not intended to give the federal judiciary a "chancel-

5. A bill currently before the Congress contemplates an express statutory formulation of the entrapment defense. S. 1, 93d Cong., 1st Sess., § 1–3B2 (1973).

lor's foot" veto over law enforcement practices of which it did not approve. . . .

Respondent's concession in the Court of Appeals that the jury finding as to predisposition was supported by the evidence is, therefore, fatal to his claim of entrapment. He was an active participant in an illegal drug manufacturing enterprise which began before the government agent appeared on the scene, and continued after the government agent had left the scene. He was, in the words of *Sherman*, supra, not an "unwary innocent" but an "unwary criminal." The Court of Appeals was wrong, we believe, when it sought to broaden the principle laid down in *Sorrels* and *Sherman*. Its judgment is therefore

Reversed.

MR. JUSTICE DOUGLAS, with whom MR. JUSTICE BRENNAN concurs, dissenting.

* * *

In my view, the fact that the chemical ingredient supplied by the federal agent might have been obtained from other sources is quite irrelevant. Supplying the chemical ingredient used in the manufacture of this batch of "speed" made the United States an active participant in the unlawful activity. . . .

* * *

Federal agents play a debased role when they become the instigators of the crime, or partners in its commission, or the creative brain behind the illegal scheme. That is what the federal agent did here when he furnished the accused with one of the chemical ingredients needed to manufacture the unlawful drug.

MR. JUSTICE STEWART, with whom MR. JUSTICE BRENNAN and MR. JUSTICE MARSHALL join, dissenting.

* * *

The purpose of the entrapment defense, then, cannot be to protect persons who are "otherwise innocent." Rather, it must be to prohibit unlawful governmental activity in instigating crime.

* * *

. . . In my view, a person's alleged "predisposition" to crime should not open him to government participation in the criminal transaction that would be otherwise unlawful. . . .

* * *

It is the Government's duty to prevent crime, not to promote it. Here, the Government's agent asked that the illegal drug be produced for him, solved his quarry's practical problems with the assurance that he could provide the one essential ingredient that was difficult to obtain, furnished that element as he had promised, and bought the finished product from the respondent—all so that the respondent could be prosecuted for producing and selling the very drug for which the agent had asked and for which he had provided the necessary component. Under the objective approach that I would follow, this respondent was entrapped, regardless of his predisposition or "innocence."

NOTE

In People v. Strong, 21 Ill.2d 320, 172 N.E.2d 765 (1961), the Illinois Supreme Court made the following ruling:

> While we are sympathetic to the problems of enforcement agencies in controlling the narcotics traffic, and their use of informers to that end, we cannot condone the action of one acting for the government in supplying the very narcotics that gave rise to the alleged offense. . . . This is more than mere inducement. In reality the government is supplying the *sine qua non* of the offense.

Chapter 9

UNCOMPLETED CRIMINAL CONDUCT AND CRIMINAL COMBINATIONS

A. UNCOMPLETED CRIMINAL CONDUCT

SECTION 1. ATTEMPT

PEOPLE v. PALUCH

Appellate Court of Illinois, Second District, 1966.
78 Ill.App.2d 356, 222 N.E.2d 508.

DAVIS, JUSTICE. The defendant, Michael Paluch, was charged, in the Circuit Court of the 18th Judicial Circuit, DuPage County, with attempting to practice barbering without a certificate of registration as a barber in violation of Ill.Rev.Stat.1965, ch. 16¾, par. 14.92(b) (1). The case was tried before the court without a jury and the defendant was found guilty as charged and a fine in the sum of $25 was imposed. The defendant contends that the evidence was not sufficient to sustain the judgment.

On November 5, 1965, Ernie Pinkston, an agent of the barber's union, went to a barber shop located in Glen Ellyn. It was 9:00 A.M. and the shop was not yet open. He then saw the defendant unlock the rear door and enter the shop. Shortly thereafter, he went to the front door and asked the defendant if the shop was open. The defendant unlocked the door, admitted Pinkston, walked over to the barber chair, put on his smock and offered the chair to Pinkston. The defendant had his own barber tools—clipping shears, razors and combs.

Pinkston then showed the defendant his business card and asked to see his license. The defendant twice motioned to a particular license which, in fact, was not his. No one else was in the shop at the time. When later asked if he worked at the shop, the defendant answered "yes" and admitted that he had no license.

Both the defendant and the State refer to the Criminal Code of 1961, . . . with reference to the elements necessary to establish the offense of an "attempt," which provides:

> "A person commits an attempt when, with intent to commit a specific offense, he does any act which constitutes a substantial step toward the commission of that offense."

Two elements must be present to constitute an attempt: (1) an intent to commit a specific offense, and (2) an act which is a substantial step towards its commission. The defendant contends that all that can be shown by the record in this case is a mere preparation to do something, but that no act constituting a substantial step toward barbering was committed. . . .

As pointed out in the Committee Comments to par. 8–4 of the Criminal Code . . . the determination of when the preparation to commit an offense ceases and the perpetration of the offense begins, is a troublesome problem. The distinction between the preparation and the attempt is largely a matter of degree, and whether certain given conduct constitutes an actual attempt is a question unique to each particular case.

In order to constitute an attempt, it is not requisite that the act of the defendant is necessarily the last deed immediately preceding that which would render the substantive crime complete. . . . In Commonwealth v. Peaslee . . . [1901], Mr. Justice Holmes, as Chief Justice of the Supreme Judicial Court of Massachusetts, discussed the considerations necessary in determining whether there were sufficient acts to constitute an attempt to commit an offense under circumstances where further acts were required to perpetrate the offense. He there noted that the acts may then be nothing more than preparation to commit an offense which is not punishable, but also stated that given preparations may constitute an attempt, the determining factor being a matter of degree. As illustrative of this comment, his opinion states:

> "If the preparation comes very near to the accomplishment of the act, the intent to complete it renders the crime so probable that the act will be a misdemeanor, although there is still a locus poenitentiae, in the need of a further exertion of the will to complete the crime. As was observed in a recent case, the degree of proximity held sufficient may vary with circumstances, including, among other things, the apprehension which the particular crime is calculated to excite."

The crux of the determination of whether the acts are sufficient to constitute an attempt really is whether, when given the specific intent to commit an offense, the acts taken in furtherance thereof are such that there is a dangerous proximity to success in carrying out the intent. In Hyde v. United States . . . (1911), Mr. Justice Holmes, in his dissenting opinion, . . . adequately delineates the distinction between the mere preparation to commit an offense and an attempt to perpetrate the offense, in these words:

> "But combination, intention, and overt act may all be present without amounting to a criminal attempt,—as if all that were done should be an agreement to murder a man 50 miles away, and the purchase of a pistol for the purpose. There must be dangerous proximity to success. But when that exists the overt act is the essence of the offense."

The language of par. 8–4 of the Criminal Code, stating that there must be a substantial step toward the commission of the offense indicates that it is not necessary for an "attempt" that the last proximate act to the completion of the offense be done. In addition, the Illinois Supreme Court has likewise considered this problem. In People v. Woods, . . . it stated:

> "Mere preparation to commit a crime, of course, does not constitute an attempt to commit it. We feel however that an attempt does exist where a person, with intent to commit a specific offense, performs acts which constitute substantial steps toward the commission of that offense."

The defendant, who conceded that he worked at the barber shop, was the only person there. He had a key and unlocked the shop. He had barber tools. He had a fraudulent license which was posted near the barber chair. He admitted Pinkston to the shop, put on his smock—as it was referred to by the witness—and motioned him to the chair. At this point the defendant was precluded from barbering without a certification of registration, only by the fact that the witness showed the defendant his business card and did not get into the chair. These facts are sufficient to establish the defendant's attempt to violate the statute, as charged.

The defendant argues that barber tools need not be used exclusively for barbering, and that there is nothing to establish that he had a specific intent to practice barbering. In view of the foregoing facts, we find it unbelievable that the defendant had any intent other than to barber and to use the barbering tools, chair and shop for that purpose.

The acts of the defendant were not of such serious character and consequence that he could be expected to feel genuinely apprehensive about what he was doing. The degree of proximity to the actual commission of a crime necessary for there to be an attempt is, in part, determined by the apprehension which the particular crime is calculated to excite. The greater the apprehension, the greater the likelihood that a would-be offender will not follow through with his intended plans. Inasmuch as the offense involved was only a misdemeanor and the penalty inconsequential, there was no cause for serious apprehension on the part of the defendant in connection with the commission of this particular offense, and it was inconceivable that at this late moment he would repent and alter his course of conduct out of fear or concern. He had then taken substantial steps toward the commission of the act of barbering without a certificate of registration. His intention and overt acts resulted in conduct in the very close proximity to the commission of the offense and constituted an attempt. . . .

Judgment affirmed.

MORAN, PRESIDING JUSTICE (dissenting).

I agree with the majority opinion up to the point where it holds that the defendant was guilty of certain acts which constituted a substantial step toward the commission of the offense charged. It is this facet of the case alone with which I disagree.

While it is true that the distinction between the preparation and the substantial step toward the commission of an act, is one of degree, and must be determined by the circumstances of each case; nevertheless, I believe the facts in the case at bar are insufficient to establish the act which constitutes a substantial step toward the commission of the offense.

The majority opinion relies upon, among others, People v. Woods . . . (1962); however, in that case the defendant commenced toward performance of the act by giving the complaining witness a sedative, although not taken by her, nevertheless it was directed toward her. There was, in addition, the fact that the defendant had received a fee for services to be rendered; the fact that instruments needed to perform the operation were in a pan on the stove; and the fact that the complaining witness stated she was ready and began to remove her clothing.

In the case at bar, while there is no doubt that the necessary intent was present, still there is no evidence that the defendant took a "first step" toward commission of the intended crime against Pinkston, the complaining witness. Pinkston, the only one present other than the defendant at the time of the alleged "act", testified that the defendant unlocked the barbershop door, walked back to the barber chair and put on his smock. He further testified that he, Pinkston, walked over and set his briefcase down and the defendant "offered me to get into the chair; at that, I handed him my business card." Thereafter, Pinkston looked around to see where his license was but did not see it. In addition, the defendant had his own barber tools present.

This is the only evidence offered to establish the act which together with the intent is a necessary element to constitute the offense of an "attempt." I would concede that if Pinkston had sat in the barber chair, as offered, and an over-garment placed upon him, then it could be said that a substantial step toward the commission of the offense charged had taken place—even though not one hair was clipped from his head. However, this is not the evidence. The best that can be said of the evidence adduced in this case toward the charge of attempting to practice barbering without a certificate of registration as a barber, is that the defendant started preparing himself but never got to the point of preparing the person against whom the attempt was to have been made. Therefore, I must, and do, dissent from my learned colleagues.

NOTES

1. In Martin v. Commonwealth, 195 Va. 1107, 81 S.E.2d 574 (1954), defendant was charged with attempt to commit pandering by feloniously placing a female in his dwelling house for the purpose of causing her "to cohabit" with male persons. It appeared that after taking the girl to his apartment, the defendant solicited three young men to have sexual intercourse with the girl upon payment of money to him. He took the boys to his room, where the girl was lying in bed nude. One of the boys said he would go get the necessary money, but when he returned shortly thereafter the defendant had already been arrested by the police. The question arose whether the attempt to commit pandering had occurred when the girl had not yet commenced any preparation to have sexual relations with the boys nor had the defendant received the money. In that regard, the court stated:

> It is well settled in this jurisdiction that in criminal law an attempt is an unfinished crime, and is compounded of two elements, the intent to commit the crime and the doing of some direct act towards its consummation, but falling short of the execution of the ultimate design; that it need not be the last proximate act towards the consummation of the crime in contemplation, but is sufficient if it be an act apparently adopted to produce the result intended; mere preparation is not sufficient. . . .
>
> The defendant contends that the acts charged amounted to nothing more than a mere preparation to commit a crime, and that the allegations do not show any overt act towards its accomplishment. . . .
>
> The undisputed evidence shows that the defendant did everything but receive money in the pursuance of his plans. He placed the female in his room, exhibited her lying in bed nude to three male persons, and solicited money from those persons for the purpose of causing her to have sexual intercourse with them. One of the males went to get the money to be paid to Martin, but the intervention of the police prevented payment and the final consummation of the intended crime. This was not due to any fault or change of plans on Martin's part. He performed direct ineffectual acts towards the commission of the offense of pandering, and when he did this, the attempt to commit the offense was complete. . . .

2. In People v. Rizzo, 246 N.Y. 334, 158 N.E. 888 (1927), the defendant and others planned to hold up a man carrying money for a payroll from the bank to a company. Armed with firearms, they started out in an automobile looking for the carrier of the money, whom Rizzo claimed to be able to identify. They drove from the bank to the company and back in an attempt to spot the carrier, but failed to find him. Meanwhile they were watched and followed by police officers who moved in and arrested the defendant and his cohorts. In reversing the conviction of attempt to commit robbery the court held that the acts of the defendant and his friends had not progressed to the point of nearness to commission of the act as is required for a conviction for attempt. They were looking for the man who was transporting the money, but they had not seen nor

discovered him at the time they were arrested. The court said: "In a word, these defendants had planned to commit a crime, and were looking around the city for an opportunity to commit it, but the opportunity fortunately never came. Men would not be guilty of an attempt at burglary if they had planned to break into a building and were arrested while they were hunting about the streets for the building not knowing where it was. Neither would a man be guilty of an attempt to commit murder if he armed himself and started out to find the person whom he had planned to kill but could not find him."

MERRITT v. COMMONWEALTH

Supreme Court of Appeals of Virginia, 1935.
164 Va. 653, 180 S.E. 395.

HUDGINS, JUSTICE. This writ of error brings under review proceedings of a trial in which the accused was convicted of attempted murder, and sentenced to eight years in the penitentiary. The first error assigned is to the action of the court in overruling the demurrer to the indictment. The indictment, with some parts deleted, reads thus:

"The Grand Jurors . . . present that, Lewis Merritt did, on the 25th day of March, 1934, . . . feloniously attempt to commit the crime of murder *by then and there* with a pistol, . . . charged and loaded . . . which . . . he, . . . then and there feloniously, wilfully and of his malice aforethought, did point at and towards one P. H. Trull, he, the said Lewis Merritt, at this time being close enough to the said P. H. Trull, to be within carrying distance of said pistol, and so the jurors of the Commonwealth of Virginia, upon their oaths do say that Lewis Merritt, then and there, *in the manner and form above set forth, did attempt to kill and murder* the said P. *T.* Trull, against the peace and dignity of the Commonwealth of Virginia." (Italics supplied.) . . .

The indictment should charge both the intent and the overt act. Under [our] statute, we have held that where the intent appeared as a part of the act alleged, it need not be expressly stated. In Cunningham's Case, . . . and Broaddus v. Commonwealth, . . . the charge was that the accused, with force and arms, violently and feloniously made an assault upon the prosecutrix, and did attempt "to ravish and carnally know" her "against her will and by force."

In each of these, and other, cases, it was held that the specific intent to commit the crime charged was sufficiently alleged and might be inferred, either from the nature of the act alleged or from the use of the word "attempt" in the indictment, as "attempt" embraces the full meaning of "intent"; the only distinction between an "intent" and an "attempt" as used was that the former implies purpose only, while the latter implies both purpose and the effort to carry that purpose into effect.

In the case at bar, the indictment alleged that the accused did "attempt to commit murder." This part of the indictment does not state against whom the attempt was directed. The indictment proceeds to tell how the commonwealth claims the attempt to commit murder was accomplished, i. e., "by then and there" feloniously and maliciously pointing a loaded pistol at Trull, who was in gunshot range. Even if the jury had believed that the accused pointed a loaded gun at Trull, they would not have been justified in finding him guilty of an attempted murder, unless they believed that at the time he pointed the pistol he had formed the purpose, the intent, to murder, and the act was done in furtherance of that specific intent.

The indictment concludes by stating that the accused "then and there, in the manner and form above stated," i. e., by pointing a loaded pistol, "did attempt to kill and murder." The conclusion is unescapable that the only crime charged in the indictment is an assault, with no specific intent to kill and murder alleged. . . .

If the commonwealth desired to prosecute the accused for a higher degree of crime than an assault with a deadly weapon, the indictment should have clearly alleged the necessary elements which constituted the particular crime; that is, if the commonwealth intended to prove that the act was done in furtherance of a specific purpose, the design to murder Trull, this intent should have been alleged in the indictment.

"An act may be evil in itself, or evil by reason of the intent prompting it, or being in itself evil may be rendered more so by the intent. In an attempt, the act may be either evil or indifferent in itself; but whether it is the one or the other, its special reprehensible quality, as an element in this form of indictable wrong is derived from the particular intent whence it proceeds." Bishop On Criminal Law (9th Ed.) vol. 1, p. 521.

In Fields v. Commonwealth . . . [Va.], the indictment was similar in many respects to the one here in question. There it was alleged that the accused "did discharge and shoot off at and towards one David Tabb" a pistol, "she [the accused] . . . being close enough to the said David Tabb to be within carrying distance of said pistol." One of the objections raised to the indictment was that it "does not allege that the intent existed to kill him." The court in discussing the question thus raised, said:

"It is the settled law of this state that an indictment for murder need not expressly allege the intent to kill, and that an indictment for murder at common law (which does not expressly charge the intent to kill) is valid and sufficient to support a verdict of murder in the first degree, if the evidence introduced on the trial is sufficient to establish that the murder was of that degree. . . . On the same principle we are of opinion that an indictment for an attempt to commit murder at common law is valid and sufficient to support a verdict, such as that rendered in the instant case, convicting the accused of an attempt to commit murder in the first degree, if the evidence was sufficient to prove the commission of that crime."

The fallacy in this statement is that while a person may be guilty of murder though there was no actual intent to kill, he cannot be guilty of an attempt to commit murder unless he has a specific intent to kill. . . . A common example illustrating this principle is: "If one from a house-top recklessly throw a billet of wood upon the sidewalk where persons are constantly passing, and it fall upon a person passing by and kill him, this would be by the common law murder. But if, instead of killing, it inflicts only a slight injury, the party could not be convicted of an assault with intent to commit murder." . . .

"Where the substantive crime intended requires a specific intent, though this intent does not in the same sense as in the other case aggravate what is done, still it adds a culpability which mere general malevolence could not give. So that the indictable attempt exists only when the act, short of the substantive crime, proceeds from the specific intent to do the entire evil thing, thus imparting to so much as is done a special culpability. When we say that a man attempted to do a given wrong, we mean that he intended to do it specifically; and proceeded a certain way in the doing. The intent in the mind covers the thing in full; the act covers it only in part. . . .

The statute, section 4767, does not undertake to state what shall constitute an attempt to commit a crime. It provides that every person who makes an attempt, and in such attempt does any act towards its commission, shall be punished. The common-law definition of attempt is not changed.

"The two elements—of an evil intent and a simultaneous resulting act constitute, in combination only, an indictable attempt—the same as in any other crime. This is not the only way to state the proposition. The authorities are in substantial agreement as to the essentials of the crime though they differ in their form of expression. It has therefore been stated that the following elements are involved in the crime: 1. the intent; 2. the performance of some act toward carrying it out; 3. failure to consummate. An actual crime must be in contemplation." Bishop on Criminal Law (9th Ed.) vol. 1, p. 519. . . .

The intent is the purpose formed in a man's mind, and is usually proved by his conduct, sometimes by his statements; the necessary intent constituting one element in an attempt is the intent in fact, as distinguished from an intent in law. From the act alleged, the law infers a general evil intent, on the principal that a man intends the probable and necessary consequences of his act. The act charged here is an assault. In order to raise this assault to a more substantive crime, it must be done with a specific intent to take life. This intent cannot be inferred from the act alleged. . . .

The indictment in question did not allege that the assault was committed upon Trull with the specific intent to kill and murder him. We cannot infer the specific intent to kill and murder from the allegation that the accused maliciously pointed the loaded pistol at Trull. From this allegation, a general evil purpose may be inferred, but not the specific design to kill.

For the reasons stated, the judgment of the trial court is reversed, the verdict of the jury set aside, and the case remanded for such further proceedings as the commonwealth may be advised.

Reversed and remanded.

NOTE

What is the status of one who intends to commit a crime and takes certain steps toward its perpetration but who voluntarily abandons the project prior to its completion? It seems clear that if the requisite elements of an attempt are present, abandonment due to some extrinsic cause, such as the unexpected arrival of police officers or the intended victim, will be of no effect. See, e. g., People v. Carter, 73 Cal.App. 495, 238 P. 1059 (1925). However, as stated in People v. Von Hecht, 133 Cal.App.2d 25, 283 P.2d 764 (1955), "Abandonment is a defense if the attempt to commit a crime is freely and voluntarily abandoned before the act is put in process of final execution and where there is no outside cause prompting such abandonment."

If the plans of a would-be offender are abandoned before the "act is put in process of final execution", is this really a defense of abandonment, or should we rather say that the offense of attempt had not yet been committed because the defendant's act, though preparation for an offense, had not yet reached the stage of a "substantial step" needed to constitute the offense of attempt?

PEOPLE v. ROLLINO

Supreme Court, Queens County, N.Y., 1962.
37 Misc.2d 14, 233 N.Y.S.2d 580.

J. IRWIN SHAPIRO, JUSTICE. At the conclusion of his trial without a jury . . . under an indictment charging him with Grand Larceny, Second Degree, defendant has moved for its dismissal and thereby revived the question whether a would-be thief can be guilty of either a consummated or an attempted larceny when the coveted property is turned over to him with the knowledge and consent of the owner, by one of its agents, by pre-arrangement with the police, in order to supply a basis for the miscreant's criminal prosecution.

The development of attempts to commit crimes apparently stems from the decision of the Kings Bench in Rex. v. Schofield, Cald. 397 (1784). There, the defendant was tried for arson. He had placed a lighted candle among combustibles in a certain house, with intent to burn it. There was, however, no proof of burning adduced. The court held that the *completion* of the criminal act was not required to constitute criminality if the attempt was committed with the necessary intent. It logically inquired:

> "* * * Is it no offence to set fire to a train of gunpowder with intent to burn a house, because by accident, or the interposition of another, the mischief is prevented?" (p. 400)

That attempts were indictable as such was restated and definitively determined in Rex v. Higgins, 2 East 5 (1801). Fifty-six years later, the question of "impossibility" was raised for the first time in Regina v. McPherson, Dears. & B. 197, 201 (1857), when Baron Bramwell said:

> "* * * The argument that a man putting his hand into an empty pocket might be convicted of an attempt to steal, appeared to me at first plausible; but suppose a man, believing a block of wood to be a man who was his deadly enemy, struck it a blow intending to murder, could he be convicted of attempting to murder the man he took it to be?"

Subsequently, in Regina v. Collins, 9 Cox C.C. 497, 169 Eng.Rep. 1477 (1864) the Court expressly held that attempted larceny was not made out by proof that the defendant pickpocket actually inserted his hand into the victim's empty pocket with intent to steal, Chief Justice Cockburn declaring, at page 499:

> "We think that an attempt to commit a felony can only be made out when, if no interruption had taken place, the attempt could have been carried out successfully, and the felony completed of the attempt to commit which the party is charged."

This very broad language, encompassing as it did all forms of "impossibility", was subsequently rejected by the English courts and it was held that the inability of the pickpocket to steal from an empty pocket did not preclude his conviction of an attempted larceny. Regina v. Ring, 17 Cox C.C. 491, 66 L.T.(N.S.) 300 (1892). The determination in that case, generally speaking, represents the existing state of the law in the United States (Sayre, Criminal Attempts, 41 Harvard Law Review 821, 855).

In this country it is generally held that a defendant may be charged with an attempt where the crime was not completed because of "physical or factual impossibility" whereas a "legal impossibility" in the completion of the crime precludes prosecution for an attempt (Smith, "Two Problems in Criminal Attempts" 70 Harvard Law Review 422).

What is a "legal impossibility" as distinguished from a "physical or factual impossibility" has over a long period of time perplexed our courts and has resulted in many irreconcilable decisions and much philosophical discussion by legal scholars in numerous articles and papers in law school publications and by text writers. [The court's long list of references is omitted.]

The reason for the "impossibility" of completing the substantive crime ordinarily falls into one of two categories: (1) where the act if completed would not be criminal, a situation which is usually described as a "legal impossibility" and (2) where the basic or substantive crime is impossible of completion, simply because of some physical or factual condition unknown to the defendant, a situation which is usually described as a "factual impossibility".

The authorities in the various States and the text-writers are in general agreement that where there is a "legal impossibility" of completing the substantive crime, the accused cannot be successfully charged with an attempt, whereas in those cases in which the "factual impossibility" situation is involved, the accused may be convicted of an attempt. Detailed discussion of the subject is unnecessary to make it clear that it is frequently most difficult to compartmentalize a particular set of facts as coming within one of the categories rather than the other. Examples of the so-called "legal impossibility" situations are:

(a) A person accepting goods which he believes to have been stolen, but which were not in fact stolen goods, is not guilty of an attempt to receive stolen goods. . . .

(b) It is not an attempt to commit subornation of perjury where the false testimony solicited, if given, would have been immaterial to the case at hand and hence not perjurious. . . .

(c) An accused who offers a bribe to a person believed to be a juror, but who is not a juror, is not guilty of an attempt to bribe a juror. . . .

(d) An official who contracts a debt which is unauthorized and a nullity, but which he believes to be valid, is not guilty of an attempt to illegally contract a valid debt. . . .

(e) A hunter who shoots a stuffed deer believing it to be alive is not guilty of an attempt to shoot a deer out of season. . . .

Examples of cases in which *attempt* convictions have been sustained on the theory that all that prevented the consummation of the completed crime was a "factual impossibility" are:

(a) The picketing of an empty pocket . . .

(b) An attempt to steal from an empty receptacle . . . or an empty house . . .

(c) Where defendant shoots into the intended victim's bed, believing he is there, when in fact he is elsewhere . . .

(d) Where the defendant erroneously believing that the gun is loaded points it at his wife's head and pulls the trigger . . .

(e) Where the woman upon whom the abortion operation is performed is not in fact pregnant . . .

The foregoing lines of demarcation laid down in the cases and by text writers as to when an attempt may and may not be successfully charged has been roundly criticized. Thus in Hall, General Principles of Criminal Law, 2d ed., p. 589 (1960) the writer says:

> "* * * There are no degrees of impossibility and no sound basis for distinguishing among the conditions necessary for commission of the intended harm."

And in 40 Yale Law Journal, supra, at page 71 we find Judge Thurman W. Arnold saying, with regard to the artificiality of the distinctions attempted to be made, the following:

> "The distinctions * * * are ingenious, but * * * they lead us either to absurd results or else to no results."

In an exhaustive and extremely well considered opinion on this subject in United States v. Thomas and McClellan, (13 U.S.C.M.A. 278, 32 C.M.R. 278) decided on September 7, 1962 we find the United States Court of Military Appeals dealing with this subject and saying:

> "The lack of logic between some of the holdings, supra; the inherent difficulty in assigning a given set of facts to a proper classification; the criticism of existing positions in this area; and, most importantly, the denial of true and substantial justice by these artificial holdings have led, quite naturally, to proposals for reform in the civilian legal concepts of criminal attempts."

In that case the accused, among other things, were charged with an attempt to commit the crime of rape. It appeared, however, that the female with whom they had been drinking had died of a heart attack. They thought she was merely unconscious and decided to have sexual intercourse with her. The trial officer charged that "there was no requirement that the victim be alive before the accused could be convicted of attempted rape." The Board of Review disagreed holding that there could not be an attempt to commit the crime of rape because as a "legal impossibility" there could not be a consummated rape with a corpse, a live female being a necessary party to the accomplishment of that crime. The Board of Review concluded thusly because, it said, "an attempt to commit a crime must be directed to an object on which it is possible to commit the crime". The United States Military Court of Appeals agreed that if the case before it were in a Civil Court the Board of Review's determination would be correct, but it held that "to follow civilian authorities into the intricacies and artificial distinctions they draw in the field of criminal attempts * * * would lead military jurisprudence into the morass of confusion as to criminal attempts in which civilian jurisprudence finds itself immobilized, and from which heroic efforts are being made to extricate it."

Some Courts have by "heroic efforts" taken what I consider to be a progressive and more modern view on the subject than is permitted by the decisional law in this State. Thus, California has now abandoned the . . . rationale that a person accepting goods which he believes to have been stolen, but which was not in fact stolen goods, is not guilty of an attempt to receive stolen goods and imposes a liability for the attempt . . .

Returning now from the discussion of "attempts" to the facts in this case which I find to be as follows:

Prior to and at the time of the occurrences resulting in this prosecution, one Edwin Martinez was an employee of Long Island Drug Company, a division of the Ketcham Company, Inc., with a stock of drugs and drug products in its wholesale business establishment on New York Boulevard in Queens County. A short time before the date charged in the indictment defendant Rollino proposed that Martinez should steal from his employer certain of the products that it stocked, as opportunity permitted, and for which the defendant would pay Martinez. Although the latter pretended to agree to the proposal he promptly reported the matter to an official of Long Island Drug Company and he in turn called in a private detective agency. At the suggestion of one of the agency's operators a responsible official of the Long Island Drug Company gave Martinez a package containing drug products having a wholesale value of $187.00, with instructions to bring it to the defendant in ostensible pursuance of the latter's criminal plan. When informed of the availability of the merchandise, Rollino directed Martinez to meet him at a specified time in a designated parking lot in Queens County.

Martinez went to the parking lot in his Nash automobile. There he was joined by the defendant, who entered the car and received the package, for which Martinez asked $25.00. Rollino offered—and his pseudo-accomplice accepted—$15.00 in payment therefor with defendant promising that he would do better the next time. Fearful that they were being watched, defendant told Martinez to leave the package in the Nash, lock it, hand over the keys and leave the lot. When Martinez complied, Rollino also left the parking lot but returned in his own car about a half-hour later and stopped directly behind the Nash. He then got out, walked over to the Nash, reached in and picked up the package but, after a period of indecision in which he looked about the parking lot with evident apprehension, he put the package down again, closed the door and started to walk away. At that point the police, who had been called in by the detective agency, moved in and apprehended the defendant. Of course, he had been under their surveillance the whole time. When questioned, Rollino said that he had been sent to pick up the package by a man whom he knew only as James Dunne. When asked why, if that was the case, he didn't take it, his only explanation was that he was scared and changed his mind about picking it up. His explanation of his status in the matter, as Dunne's messenger, was, of course, untrue.

The evidence convinces me, beyond reasonable doubt, that defendant intended and endeavored to steal drugs or drug products from Long Island Drug Company by counseling and, as he thought, inducing and procuring its employee to do so . . . and that, on the date of the crime for which he was tried before me, he acted directly and overtly to realize, as he hoped, the gain contemplated by his previous incitement. The discretion that he gave his pretended accomplice as to what would be stolen, and when, would not, of course, create any uncertainty of Rollino's criminal liability had Martinez really acted corruptly, in advancement of defendant's plan. . . . But the employee had remained faithful to his employer and what defendant assumed to be the fruit of his crime had, in fact, been brought to him with the owner's knowledge and consent.

Although it has been said that "(i)t is * * * no longer necessary, to constitute larceny, that the property should have been taken from the possession of the owner by a trespass . . . the idea remains basic to the concept of what has come to be known as "common law larceny", that "(i)f an individual owner voluntarily delivers his property to one who wishes to steal it, there is no trespass" . . . and consequently "no crime committed by the defendant * * * because it was with the full consent" . . . . . A taking without consent is the *sine qua non* of that form of larceny . . . and the charge is unsupportable if the owner or his authorized agent voluntarily consents to the taking, even if it is done only for the purpose of catching the thief and even though neither of them otherwise encouraged the evil-doer to adopt and execute the criminal plan. . . .

As the Court put it in one sentence in Stanton Motor Corp. v. Rosetti [N.Y.]:

> "An essential element of common law larceny is the taking of the property of another without his consent and against his will."

Having determined that the defendant in this case may not be found guilty of the completed act of larceny because the drugs were not in fact taken from the owner without its consent, the next question is whether, under such circumstances, he may be found guilty of an attempt to commit larceny. . . .

The answer would seem to be "no" for the very fact that prevents a conviction for the completed crime of larceny also precludes a conviction of an attempted larceny. "(I)n the present case, the act, which it was doubtless the intent of the defendant to commit would not have been a crime if it had been consummated" (People v. Jaffe . . . [N.Y.]), and "an unsuccessful attempt to do that which is not a crime, when effectuated, cannot be held to be an attempt to commit the crime specified" (People v. Teal . . . [N.Y.]). When the owner's agent offered the drugs to Rollino, to entrap him, defendant "succeeded in what he attempted, but what he did was not criminal" (People v. Jelke . . . [N.Y.]). Since the completed act did not and could not as a *matter of law* constitute a larceny it is *legally impossible* for defendant to be guilty of an attempted larceny.

The Mills, Jaffe and Teal cases have been the subject of analytic discussion and much criticism and while the comment on Jaffe and Teal in the Jelke case, supra . . . is a summary and therefore not necessarily an approval of the rule of law laid down in those cases, that rule of law has never been modified or overruled in this state and it must, accordingly, be accepted and enforced by this Court.

The defendant's moral guilt is unquestionable. He intended to commit the crime of grand larceny and did everything that he could to implement and effectuate his criminal purpose and intent. That he cannot be adjudged legally guilty is due entirely to the existing state of the decisional and statutory law on the subject. Clearly a modification of the law in this regard, to make it less favorable to criminal elements, is called for but this Court may only adjudicate; it may not legislate.

In this connection, attention is called to the proposal of The American Law Institute for the adoption of a "Model Penal Code" which in Article 5.01 defines "Criminal Attempts" in the following manner:

> "(1) *Definition of attempt.* A person is guilty of an attempt to commit a crime if, acting with the kind of culpability otherwise required for commission of the crime, he:
>
> "(a) purposely engages in conduct which would constitute the crime if the attendant circumstances were as he believes them to be; or
>
> "(b) when causing a particular result is an element of the crime, does or omits to do anything with the purpose of causing or with the belief that it will cause such result, without further conduct on his part; or
>
> "(c) purposely does or omits to do anything which, under the circumstances as he believes them to be, is a substantial step in a course of conduct planned to culminate in his commission of the crime."

Tentative Draft No. 10 of the Model Penal Code (p. 25) makes obvious the reason and necessity for the adoption of the proposed Article 5.01 when it says:

> "* * * It should suffice, therefore, to indicate at this stage what we deem to be the major results of the draft. They are:
>
> "(a) to extend the criminality of attempts by sweeping aside the defense of impossibility (including the distinction between so-called factual and legal impossibility) and by drawing the line between attempt and non-criminal preparation further away from the final act; the crime becomes essentially one of criminal purpose implemented by an overt act strongly corroborative of such purpose; * * *."

The motion to dismiss the indictment is granted since an element essential to defendant's legal guilt of either a larceny or an attempted larceny of the kind here charged is entirely lacking. . . .

NOTES

1. In 1967, New York, by legislation, changed the rule in the foregoing case. See Sections 110 and 110.10 of the McKinney's Penal Law, which read as follows:

> § 110. A person is guilty of an attempt to commit a crime when, with intent to commit a crime, he engages in conduct which tends to effect the commission of such crime.

> § 110.10 If the conduct in which a person engages otherwise constitutes an attempt to commit a crime pursuant to section 110, it is no defense to a prosecution for such attempt that the crime charged to have been attempted was, under the attendant circumstances, factually or legally impossible of commission, if such crime could have been committed had the attendant circumstances been as such person believed them to be.

2. Compare the Illinois Criminal Code (S.H.A. ch. 38), which provides as follows:

> § 8–4(a) *Elements of the Offense.* A person commits an attempt when, with intent to commit a specific offense, he does any act which constitutes a substantial step toward the commission of that offense.

> § 8–4(b) *Impossibility.* It shall not be a defense to a charge of attempt that because of a misapprehension of the circumstances it would have been impossible for the accused to commit the offense attempted.

3. California, by decision law, follows a rule in accordance with the above statutory provisions. People v. Meyers, 213 Cal.App.2d 518, 28 Cal. Rptr. 753 (1963).

Consider Waters v. State, 2 Md.App. 216, 234 A.2d 147 (1967), in which an 80 year old man was convicted of assault with intent to commit rape. He contended that physical inability to engage in "sexual activity" precluded a conviction of an offense based upon "intent to rape". In affirming defendant's conviction the court said: "While there can be no attempt in a case involving legal impossibility, as attempting to do what is not a crime is not attempting to commit a crime, factual impossibility of success does not prevent the attempt from being made. Physical incapacity to commit a crime does not affect the capacity of one to be guilty of an attempt. Thus a man who is physically impotent may be guilty of an attempt to commit rape."

In State v. Ray, 63 Wash.2d 224, 386 P.2d 423 (1963), it was held that in a prosecution for attempted rape, the fact that the defendant's "zipper stuck" was no defense.

Since at common law an accused under the age of fourteen is conclusively presumed to be incapable of committing the crime of rape, whatever the real facts may be, "it logically follows, as a plain legal deduction, that he was also incapable in law of an attempt to commit it. . . . " Foster v. Commonwealth, 96 Va. 306, 31 S.E. 503 (1898). But in Preddy v. Commonwealth, 184 Va. 765, 36 S.E.2d 549 (1946), the court held that a 67-year old man was properly convicted of attempting to rape a ten-year old girl, even though the defendant might have been impotent. See, in this connection, the excellent note on impossibility of consummation of substantive crime as a defense to conspiracy or attempt prosecutions at 37 ALR3d 375 (1971).

SECTION 2. SOLICITATION

STATE v. BLECHMAN

Supreme Court of New Jersey, 1946.
135 N.J.L. 99, 50 A.2d 152.

HEHER, JUSTICE. Plaintiff-in-error challenges what is said to be a judgment of conviction upon an indictment charging that on October 11, 1944, he did "counsel" one George Polos to set fire to a certain dwelling house in the City of Hackensack, with intent to prejudice and defraud the insurers thereof against loss or damage by fire, in contravention of R.S. 2:109–4, N.J.S.A., which provides that one who shall, with that intent, "willfully or maliciously set fire to, or burn, or aid, counsel, procure or consent to the setting fire to or burning, of any" such insured building or chattels shall be guilty of a high misdemeanor. . . .

At common law, it is a misdemeanor for one to counsel, incite or solicit another to commit either a felony or a misdemeanor, certainly so if the misdemeanor is of an aggravated character, even though the solicitation is of no effect, and the crime counseled is not in fact committed. The gist of the offense is the solicitation. It is not requisite that some act should be laid to have been done in pursuance of the incitement. While the bare intention to commit evil is not indictable, without an act done, the solicitation, itself, is an act done toward the execution of the evil intent and therefore indictable. An act done with a criminal intent is punishable by indictment. It was said by an eminent common-law judge (Lawrence, J., in Rex v. Higgins, 2 East 5) that under the common law all offenses of a public nature, i. e. "all such acts or attempts as tend to the prejudice of the community," are indictable; and it goes without saying that an attempt to incite another to commit arson or a kindred offense is prejudicial to the community and public in its nature. [citing numerous cases]
. . .

The solicitation constitutes a substantive crime in itself, and not an abortive attempt to perpetrate the crime solicited. It falls short of an attempt, in the legal sense, to commit the offense solicited. An attempt to commit a crime consists of a direct ineffectual overt act toward the consummation of the crime, done with an intent to commit the crime. Neither intention alone nor acts in mere preparation will suffice. There must be an overt act directly moving toward the commission of the designed offense—such as will apparently result, in the usual and natural course of events, if not hindered by extraneous causes, in the commission of the crime itself. . . .

Of course, at common law one who counsels, incites or solicits another to commit a felony, is indictable as a principal or an accessory before the fact, if the designed felony is accomplished, depending upon his presence and participation or absence at the time of its commission. . . .

Let the judgment be affirmed.

NOTES

1. Illustrative of solicitation statutes are the following:

West's Ann. California Pen.Code, § 653f. Every person who solicits another to offer or accept or join in the offer or acceptance of a bribe, or to commit or join in the commission of murder, robbery, burglary, grand theft, receiving stolen property, extortion, rape by force and violence, perjury, subornation of perjury, forgery, or kidnaping, is punishable by imprisonment in the county jail not longer than one year or in the state prison not longer than five years, or by fine of not more than five thousand dollars. Such offense must be proved by the testimony of two witnesses, or of one witness and corroborating circumstances.

§ 8–1, Illinois Criminal Code (S.H.A. ch. 38): A person commits solicitation when, with intent that an offense be committed, he commands, encourages or requests another to commit that offense.

B. CRIMINAL COMBINATIONS—CONSPIRACIES

The various elements that comprise the offense of "conspiracy" and the evidentiary problems encountered in its prosecution are of considerably less concern to police officers than to criminal law practitioners and the courts. Nevertheless, it is an offense with which the police must be familiar and there are a few of its aspects that are of practical concern to them. The following proposed statutory provisions, and the note material thereafter, should suffice.

THE PROPOSED OFFICIAL DRAFT OF THE MODEL PENAL CODE OF THE AMERICAN LAW INSTITUTE, 1962:

Section 5.03. Criminal Conspiracy

(1) *Definition of Conspiracy.* A person is guilty of conspiracy with another person or persons to commit a crime if with the purpose of promoting or facilitating its commission he:

(a) agrees with such other person or persons that they or one or more of them will engage in conduct which constitutes such crime or an attempt or solicitation to commit such crime; or

(b) agrees to aid such other person or persons in the planning or commission of such crime or of an attempt or solicitation to commit such crime.

(2) *Scope of Conspiratorial Relationship.* If a person guilty of conspiracy, as defined by Subsection (1) of this Section, knows that a person with whom he conspires to commit a crime has conspired with another person or persons to commit the same crime, he is guilty of conspiring with such other person or persons, whether or not he knows their identity, to commit such crime.

(3) *Conspiracy With Multiple Criminal Objectives.* If a person conspires to commit a number of crimes, he is guilty of only one conspiracy so long as such multiple crimes are the object of the same agreement or continuous conspiratorial relationship.

* * *

(5) *Overt Act.* No person may be convicted of conspiracy to commit a crime, other than a felony of the first or second degree, unless an overt act in pursuance of such conspiracy is alleged and proved to have been done by him or by a person with whom he conspired.

(6) *Renunciation of Criminal Purpose.* It is an affirmative defense that the actor, after conspiring to commit a crime, thwarted the success of the conspiracy, under circumstances manifesting a complete and voluntary renunciation of his criminal purpose.

(7) *Duration of Conspiracy.* [: . . .]

(a) conspiracy is a continuing course of conduct which terminates when the crime or crimes which are its object are committed or the agreement that they be committed is abandoned by the defendant and by those with whom he conspired; and

(b) such abandonment is presumed if neither the defendant nor anyone with whom he conspired does any overt act in pursuance of the conspiracy during the applicable period of limitation; and

(c) if an individual abandons the agreement, the conspiracy is terminated as to him only if and when he advises those with whom he conspired of his abandonment or he informs the law enforcement authorities of the existence of the conspiracy and of his participation therein.

Section 5.04. Incapacity, Irresponsibility or Immunity of Party to Solicitation or Conspiracy

(1) Except as provided in Subsection (2) of this Section, it is immaterial to the liability of a person who solicits or conspires with another to commit a crime that:

(a) he or the person whom he solicits or with whom he conspires does not occupy a particular position or have a particular characteristic which is an element of such crime, if he believes that one of them does; or

(b) the person whom he solicits or with whom he conspires is irresponsible or has an immunity to prosecution or conviction for the commission of the crime.

(2) It is a defense to a charge of solicitation or conspiracy to commit a crime that if the criminal object were achieved, the actor would not be guilty of a crime under the law defining the offense . . . .

THE FINAL REPORT OF THE NATIONAL COMMISSION ON REFORM OF FEDERAL CRIMINAL LAWS (1971):

§ 1004. Criminal Conspiracy.

(1) Offense. A person is guilty of conspiracy if he agrees with one or more persons to engage in or cause the performance of conduct which, in fact, constitutes a crime or crimes, and any one or more of such persons does an act to effect an objective of the conspiracy. The agreement need not be explicit but may be implicit in the fact of collaboration or existence of other circumstances.

(2) Parties to Conspiracy. If a person knows or could expect that one with whom he agrees has agreed or will agree with another to effect the same objective, he shall be deemed to have agreed with the other, whether or not he knows the other's identity.

(3) Duration of Conspiracy. A conspiracy shall be deemed to continue until its objectives are accomplished, frustrated or abandoned. "Objectives" includes escape from the scene of the crime, distribution of booty, and measures, other than silence, for concealing the crime or obstructing justice in relation to it. A conspiracy shall be deemed to have been abandoned if no overt act to effect its objectives has been committed by any conspirator during the applicable period of limitations.

(4) Defense Precluded. It is no defense to a prosecution under this section that the person with whom such person is alleged to have conspired has been acquitted, has not

been prosecuted or convicted, has been convicted of a different offense, is immune from prosecution, or is otherwise not subject to justice.

* * *

NOTES

1. As regards the underlying concept of the conspiracy offense, as well as the common law definition and requirements, consider the following from State v. Carbone, 10 N.J. 329, 91 A.2d 571 (1952):

"At common law, a conspiracy consists not merely in the intention but in the agreement of two or more persons (not being husband and wife) to do an unlawful act, or to do a lawful act by unlawful means. So long as such a design rests in intention only, it is not indictable. When two agree to carry it into effect, the very plot is an act in itself, and the act of each of the parties, promise against promise, *actus contra actum*, capable of being enforced if lawful, punishable if for a criminal object or for the use of criminal means. The agreement is an advancement of the intention which each has conceived in his mind; the mind proceeds from a secret intention to the overt act of mutual consultation and agreement. . . . It is not requisite, in order to constitute a conspiracy at common law, that the acts agreed to be done be such as would be criminal if done; it is enough if the acts agreed to be done, although not criminal, be wrongful, *i. e.*, amount to a civil wrong. The gist of the offense of conspiracy lies, not in doing the act, nor effecting the purpose for which the conspiracy is formed, nor in attempting to do them, nor in inciting others to do them, but in the forming of the scheme or agreement between the parties. . . . The offense depends on the unlawful agreement and not on the act which follows it; the latter is not evidence of the former. . . . The combination itself is vicious and gives the public an interest to interfere by indictment. . . . The external or overt act of the crime is concert by which initial consent to a common purpose is exchanged. . . . In order to render one criminally liable for conspiracy at common law, it must be shown that he entered into an agreement as thus defined with one or more persons, whether charged with him in the indictment or not, and whether known or unknown. . . .

"But it is not essential that there be direct contact between the parties, or that all enter into the conspiratorial agreement at one and the same time. 'It may be that the alleged conspirators have never seen each other, and have never corresponded. One may have never heard the name of the other, and yet by the law they may be parties to the same common criminal agreement.' . . . 'What has to be ascertained is always the same matter: is it true to say, * * * that the acts of the accused were done in pursuance of a criminal purpose held in common between them?' One who joins a conspiracy after its formation is equally guilty with the original conspirators. . . .

". . . an agreement or combination between two or more persons to commit a crime constitutes a conspiracy punishable as a misdemeanor, if with certain exceptions there be an overt act in furtherance of the object of the agreement by one or more of the parties. . . . The union is invested with a potentiality for evil that renders the plan criminal in itself, and punishable as such if an act be done to effect its object. . . .

". . . Overt acts proved against one or more of the prisoners may be looked to as against all of them to show the nature and object of the conspiracy. . . .

"Where two or more persons have entered into a conspiracy to perpetrate a crime, the acts and declarations of one of the conspirators in furtherance of the common object are deemed in law the facts and declarations of all. This on the theory of a joint or mutual agency *ad hoc* for the prosecution of the common plan. . . ."

2. The "overt act" requirement specified in the preceding note, as well as in the American Law Institute's proposed statute, was defined by Justice Holmes in Hyde v. United States, 225 U.S. 347, 388, 32 S.Ct. 793, 810 (1912), in the following manner: "The overt act is simply evidence that the conspiracy has passed beyond words and is on foot when the act is done."

In a commentary to the proposal of the National Commission on Reform of Federal Criminal Laws, the following statement appears with respect to the word "act" used therein: ". . . as in existing law any act to effect an objective of the conspiracy suffices for criminal liability; the act need not constitute a 'substantial step' as is required in the case of attempt. An alternative to the text would be to adopt the substantial step requirement on the theory that otherwise the act may be innocent in itself and not particularly corroborative of the existence of a conspiracy."

3. One of the most advantageous features of a conspiracy case, insofar as the prosecution is concerned, and one of which the police should be mindful, is the fact that whatever any one conspirator says or does in *furtherance of the conspiracy* is usable as evidence against all of the other conspirators. In other words, each one acts as an agent of the others in effectuating their objective.

Concealment efforts may or may not be considered "in furtherance" of the conspiracy, depending upon the circumstances of the particular case. The following language from the Supreme Court decision in Grunewald v. United States, 353 U.S. 391, at 405, 77 S.Ct. 963, at 974 (1956), should be helpful in making the delineation:

". . . a vital distinction must be made between acts of concealment done in furtherance of the *main* criminal objectives of the conspiracy, and acts of concealment done after these central objectives have been attained, for the purpose only of covering up after the crime. Thus the Government argues in its brief that 'in the crime of kidnapping, the acts of conspirators in hiding while waiting for ransom would clearly be planned acts of concealment which would be in aid of the conspiracy to kidnap. So here, there can be no doubt that . . . all acts of concealment, whether to hide the identity of the conspirators or the action theretofore taken, were unquestionably in furtherance of the initial conspiracy . . . .' We do not think the analogy is valid. Kidnapers in hiding, waiting for ransom, commit acts of concealment in furtherance of the objectives of the conspiracy itself, just as repainting a stolen car would be in furtherance of a conspiracy to steal; in both cases the successful accomplishment of the crime necessitates concealment. More closely analogous to our case would be conspiring kidnapers who cover their traces after the main conspiracy is finally ended—i. e., after they have abandoned the kidnaped person and then take care to escape detection. In the latter case, as here, the acts of covering up can by themselves indicate nothing more than that the conspirators do not wish to be apprehended—a concomitant, certainly, of every crime since Cain attempted to conceal the murder of Abel from the Lord.

C. PARTIES TO THE CRIME—ACCESSORIES BEFORE AND AFTER THE FACT

Normally, criminal liability is predicated upon the doing of an act, usually by the defendant. Early in the development of the common law, however, the courts recognized that criminal liability could be predicated upon conduct done by a party other than the defendant, for whose conduct the defendant would be held responsible. Consider, in this connection, the following excerpt from Usselton v. The People, 149 Ill. 612, 36 N.E. 952 (1894):

"By the ancient common law, existing prior to the reign of Henry IV,—the latter part of the fourteenth and beginning of the fifteenth centuries,—those persons only were considered principals who committed the overt act, while those who were present, aiding and abetting, were deemed accessories at the fact, and those who, not being present had advised or encouraged the perpetration of the crime, were deemed accessories before the fact. During that reign it seems to have been settled as the law that he who was present, aiding and abetting in the perpetration of the crime, was to be considered as a principal, the courts holding that all who were actually or constructively present, but not actively participating in the crime, were principals of the second degree. (1 Russell on Crimes, (Greenl. ed.) 26; 1 Bishop on Crim.Law, 648.) And this continued to be the common law as it was adopted in this State.

"An accessory before the fact, at common law, is defined by Sir Mathew Hale to be 'one who, being absent at the time of the commission of the offense, doth yet procure, counsel or command another to commit it.' And absence, it is said, is indispensably necessary to constitute one an accessory, for if he be actually or constructively present when the felony is committed, he is an aider and abettor, and not an accessory before the fact, (1 Hale's P.C. 615; 4 Blackstone's Com. 36, 37; 1 Archbold on Crim.Pl. and Pr. 14;) or, as defined by Bishop, (1 Crim.Law, 673): 'An accessory before the fact is one whose will contributes to another's felonious act, committed while too far himself from the act to be a principal.' No distinction was made in the punishment of a principal and of an accessory before the fact by the common law, the principle that what one does by the agency of another he does by himself, applying equally in criminal and civil cases. Broom's Legal Maxims, (2d ed.) 643.

At common law, an accessory before the fact, without his consent, could only be tried after the conviction of the principal. While the principal remained amenable to indictment and conviction, the accessory had the right to insist upon the conviction of the principal offender before he was put upon trial, for, as said by Blackstone, (book 4, 323), "*non constitit* whether any felony was committed or no, till the principal was attainted, and it might so happen that the accessory be convicted one day and the principal acquitted the next, which would be absurd.' And this absurdity might happen wherever the trial of the principal might occur subsequently to that of the accessory. This was subject to the exception, that where the accessory was indicted with the principal he might waive the right, and thereupon they might be put upon trial jointly.

"It seems that the distinction between accessories before the fact and principals, up to a late date, at least, has been retained in England. By Statute 7, Geo. IV, chap. 64, sec. 9, it is provided that persons who shall counsel, procure or command any other person to commit a felony shall be deemed guilty of a felony, and may be indicted and convicted, either as accessory before the fact to the principal felony, together with the principal felon, or after his conviction, or may be indicted and convicted of a substantive felony, whether the principal felon shall have been convicted or not, etc. (See 11 and 12 Vic. 46, sec. 1.) And such seems to be the rule in some of the States which have adopted, in substance, Statute 7, Geo. IV. In this State, however, the distinction between accessories before the fact and principals has been abolished. By section 2, division 2, of the Criminal Code, (par. 331, Starr & Curtis,) it is provided: 'An accessory is he who stands by and aids, abets or assists, or who, not being present aiding, abetting or assisting, hath advised, encouraged, aided or abetted the perpetration of the crime. He who thus aids, abets, assists, advises or encourages shall be considered as principal, and punished accordingly.' It is to be observed that in the definition of accessories are included those who were principals in the second degree at common law,—that is, those standing by, aiding and abetting,—as well as those who, not being present, had advised and encouraged the perpetration of the crime, and it is expressly provided that all persons who are thus defined to be accessories shall be deemed principals, and punished accordingly. It necessarily follows, that none of the rights of the defendant incident to the prosecution of the defendant as an accessory,—such as, that he may insist upon the conviction of the principal before his arraignment and trial,—can inhere, for the reason that he is himself to be considered and regarded as a principal in the crime charged. All stand before the law as principals in the perpetration of the crime. By the express provision of the succeeding section of the Code, every person falling within the definition of an accessory thus given may be put upon trial with the principal actor in the perpetration of the crime, or before or after the latter's conviction, or whether he is amenable to justice or not, and 'punished as principal.'

"It is observable, that the advising or encouraging of another to commit a felony is not created into a substantive felony, of itself, but is made to so connect the offender with the principal felony that he becomes a principal in its commission. There is, in the nature of things, no difference in the degree of moral turpitude between the man whose will has procured the commission of a crime, and the one who willfully carries out his malignant purpose. . . ."

In defining the relationships and responsibilities of the parties to criminal offenses, modern statutory treatment has, in general, obliterated the common law distinctions between "principals" and "accessories before the fact". The Illinois Criminal Code, for instance, contains the following provisions:

ARTICLE 5. PARTIES TO CRIME

§ 5–1. **Accountability for Conduct of Another.]** A person is responsible for conduct which is an element of an offense if the conduct is either that of the person himself, or that of another and he is legally accountable for such conduct as provided in Section 5–2, or both.

§ 5–2. **When Accountability Exists.]** A person is legally accountable for the conduct of another when:

(a) Having a mental state described by the statute defining the offense, he causes another to perform the conduct, and the other person in fact or by reason of legal incapacity lacks such a mental state; or

(b) The statute defining the offense makes him so accountable; or

(c) Either before or during the commission of an offense, and with the intent to promote or facilitate such commission, he solicits, aids, abets, agrees or attempts to aid, such other person in the planning or commission of the offense. However, a person is not so accountable, unless the statute defining the offense provides otherwise, if:

(1) He is a victim of the offense committed; or

(2) The offense is so defined that his conduct was inevitably incident to its commission; or

(3) Before the commission of the offense, he terminates his effort to promote or facilitate such commission, and does one of the following: wholly deprives his prior efforts of effectiveness in such commission, or gives timely warning to the proper law enforcement authorities, or otherwise makes proper effort to prevent the commission of the offense.

§ 5–3. **Separate Conviction of Person Accountable.]** A person who is legally accountable for the conduct of another which is an element of an offense may be convicted upon proof that the offense was committed and that he was so accountable, although the other person claimed to have committed the offense has not been prosecuted or convicted, or has been convicted of a different offense or degree of offense, or is not amenable to justice, or has been acquitted.

SYKES v. DIRECTOR OF PUBLIC PROSECUTIONS

House of Lords, 1961.
3 W.L.R. 371.

LORD DENNING. My Lords, this case raises the question whether there is today such an offense as misprision of felony. Mr. Edward Clarke says that there has never been such an offense known to our law; or if there has, he says, it has ceased to be an offense by becoming obsolete. The Solicitor-General says that there always has been such an offense and the present case is a good example of its continuing usefulness. The facts giving rise to the question were as follows:

About March 18, 1960, thieves got into the weapon armoury at a United States Air Force station in Norfolk. They stole 100 pistols, 4 submachine-guns and about 1,960 rounds of ammunition. They hired a taxi and took the stolen goods to Manchester. They took them into the house of a man named Kenny. A day or two later a man named Whittle brought a van to Kenny's house and took the "stuff" to the house of a man named Black.

On March 23, 1960, Sykes comes into the story. We do not know how he came to know about the guns and ammunition but we know that he went up to an Irishman named Kerwin who was a waiter in a Manchester club and asked him: "Have you any contacts with the I.R.A.?" Kerwin said: "I don't want to talk about it in the club." They talked about it later: and they went to a hotel where they met two men. One of them was Kenny (the man who first received the guns in Manchester) and the other was a man named Tucker (who has not appeared in the story before). Kenny said they had 100 revolvers, some submachine-guns and ammunition for sale. Kerwin led them to think that he had contacts with the I.R.A. and would have to go to London to see them. But instead of going to London, he went to the police and acted under their instructions.

On March 27, 1960, Kerwin (prompted thereto by the police) told Sykes that he had arranged to dispose of the guns but he needed a sample to convince the organisation that the guns were there. Kerwin that night asked Sykes what he expected to gain financially and he said: "Half of what Tucker gets for his share."

On March 28, 1960, Kenny took a sample of one of the pistols and gave it to Kerwin (who gave it to the police). Later the police disguised themselves as would-be purchasers of the guns. They were taken to Black's house and shown the goods. Whereupon the police officers disclosed their identity, and arrested Kenny, Whittle and Black. They took possession of the stolen property. Afterwards they arrested Tucker and Sykes.

In the early morning of March 29, 1960, at the police station, the superintendent said to Sykes: "I have reason to believe that you were the man who first got into touch with an Irishman and asked him to contact the I.R.A. so that they could buy the guns and that you have been actively helping Kenny and Tucker in arranging for the sale of these guns during the past week." Sykes said: "Look, Inspector, that can't be possible. I don't know this man Kenny and I haven't seen Tucker for four months."

All five men were taken before the magistrates. Kenny, Tucker, Whittle and Black were charged with receiving the goods, knowing them to have been stolen. Sykes was charged as being accessory after the fact. After the evidence was taken, counsel for Sykes urged strongly that he ought not to be committed for trial on the charge of being accessory: there was no evidence that he had taken any active steps to conceal the felony or had done any act for *the purpose* of assisting the others to escape conviction. . . . But the magistrates committed all five men for trial.

When counsel was instructed to draft the indictment, he was so impressed by the argument which had been urged before the magistrates that he did not put in a count charging Sykes with being an accessory after the fact but charged him with misprision of felony.
* * *

There remains the . . . point whether active concealment is an essential ingredient of [misprision of felony]. Now the ingredients of the offense can best be seen by comparing it with offenses of like degree which have other ingredients.

First: *Accessory after the fact.* The classic definition of an accessory after the fact is when a person, knowing a felony to have been committed, receives, relieves, comforts, or assists the felon, see 1 Hale P.C. 618, 4 Black. 37. These are all *active* acts of assistance from which it can be inferred that he assented to the felon going free, in contrast to misprision which consists of concealment only, from which no inference of assent need be drawn. It might be thought that the acts of assistance given by Sykes in the present case would be such as to make him an accessory after the fact. But it has been said that, to make a man an accessory, the assistance must be given to the felon *personally,* in order to prevent or hinder him from being apprehended or tried or suffering punishment . . so that if the assistance was not given the felon personally, but only indirectly by persuading witnesses not to give evidence against him

. . . or if the acts of assistance were done, not to hinder the arrest of the felon, but with another motive, such as to avoid arrest himself . . . or to make money for himself without regard to what happened to the felon (as in the present case), he would not be guilty as an accessory after the fact. It was these limitations on the offense of being an accessory that led to Sykes being charged with misprision of felony. * * *

This review of the authorities shows that the essential ingredients of misprision of felony are:

1. *Knowledge.* The accused man must know that a felony has been committed by someone else. His knowledge must be proved in the way in which the prosecution have been accustomed in other crimes when knowledge is an ingredient, such as receiving, accessory after the fact, compounding a felony, and so forth. That is to say, there must be evidence that a reasonable man in his place, with such facts and information before him as the accused had, would have known that a felony had been committed. From such evidence the jury may infer that the accused man himself had knowledge of it. He need not know the difference between felony and misdemeanour—many a lawyer has to look in the books for the purpose—but he must at least know that a serious offense has been committed: or, as the commissioners of 1840 put it, an offense of an "aggravated complexion": for after all, that is still, broadly speaking, the difference between a felony and misdemeanour. Felonies are the serious offenses. Misdemeanours are the less serious. If he knows that a serious offense has been committed—and a lawyer on turning up the books sees it is a felony—that will suffice. This requirement that it must be a serious offense disposes of many of the supposed absurdities, such as boys stealing apples, which many laymen would rank as a misdemeanour and no one would think he was bound to report to the police. It means that misprision comprehends an offense which is of so serious a character that an ordinary law-abiding citizen would realise he ought to report it to the police.

2. *Concealment.* The accused man must have "concealed or kept secret" his knowledge. He need not have done anything active: but it is his duty by law to disclose to proper authority all material facts known to him relative to the offence. It is not sufficient to tell the police that a felony has been committed. He must tell the name of the man who did it, if he knows it; the place, and so forth. All material facts known to him . . . . If he fails or refuses to perform this duty when there is a reasonable opportunity available to him to do so, then he is guilty of misprision. He can perform this duty by reporting to the police or a magistrate or anyone else in lawful authority. Failure to do so is a misprision of felony.

Misprision of felony is itself a misdemeanour and is punishable by fine and imprisonment. Whatever limitations may have existed in olden days on the period of imprisonment that might be imposed, the only limitation now is that it must not be an inordinately heavy sentence.

My Lords, it was said that this offence is out of date. I do not think so. The arm of the law would be too short if it was powerless to reach those who are "contact" men for thieves or assist them to gather in the fruits of their crime; or those who indulge in gang warfare and refuse to help in its suppression. There is no other offence of which such persons are guilty save that of misprision of felony.

I am not dismayed by the suggestion that the offence of misprision is impossibly wide: for I think it is subject to just limitations. Non-disclosure may be due to a claim of right made in good faith. For instance, if a lawyer is told by his client that he has committed a felony, it would be no misprision in the lawyer not to report it to the police, for he might in good faith claim that he was under a duty to keep it confidential. Likewise with doctor and patient, and clergyman and parishioner. There are other relationships which may give rise to a claim in good faith that it is in the public interest not to disclose it. For instance, if an employer discovers that his servant has been stealing from the till, he might well be justified in giving him another chance rather than reporting him to the police. Likewise with the master of a college and a student. But close family or personal ties will not suffice where the offence is of so serious a character that it ought to be reported. In 1315 it was held that it was the duty of a brother to raise hue and cry against his own brother and he was fined for not doing so . . . and in 1938 a mistress was found guilty of misprision for shielding her lover . . . . The judges have not been called upon further to define the just limitations to misprision, but I do not doubt their ability to do so, if called upon.

My Lords, there was some discussion before us whether a man was bound to disclose a contemplated felony which comes to his knowledge, such as a planned raid on a bank. There is a striking passage in Lambard's Eirenarcha (1614), p. 289, which says that failure to do so is misprision of felony . . . and the commissioners who reported on the Criminal Law in 1843 were clearly in favour of it. They said: "The necessity for making such disclosures extends, perhaps, with greater force, to the knowledge of a meditated crime, the perpetration of which may, by means of such a disclosure, be prevented, than it does to the knowledge of one already committed." This is good sense and may well be good law. I would therefore reserve this point which does not arise in the present case. * * *

LORD GODDARD * * *

Though in my opinion the offence should be sparingly prosecuted, I am by no means prepared to say that it has no use in our criminal law at the present day; it may well be used when there is technical difficulty in framing a charge of being an accessory after the fact to a felony, and counsel who had acted for the prosecution told us that was the reason for using it in the instant case.

Moreover, it is almost a common-place in these days to find the police appealing for persons whom they think must be able to throw light on some serious crime to come forward and give their assistance. And there have been instances quite recently in wounding cases arising out of gang warfare of refusing to assist the police as to the identity of the attackers, whether from fear of reprisals or from a mistaken sense of loyalty. It is very easy to poke ridicule at the offence and say that it obliges people to inform against a boy stealing an apple. The law is nowadays administered with dignity and common sense. And if it is said it obliges a father to inform against his son, or vice versa, I would answer that in the case of a really heinous crime be it so.

In my opinion, therefore, misprision of felony is today an indictable misdemeanour at common law, and a person is guilty of the crime if knowing that a felony has been committed he conceals his knowledge from those responsible for the preservation of the peace, be they constables or justices, within a reasonable time and having a reasonable opportunity for so doing. What is a reasonable time and opportunity is a question of fact for a jury, and also whether the knowledge that he has is so definite that it ought to be disclosed. A man is neither bound nor would he be wise to disclose rumours or mere gossip, but if facts are within his knowledge that would materially assist in the detection and arrest of a felon he must disclose them as it is a duty he owes to the State. The gist of the offence is concealment which may be passive, that is mere non-disclosure, or active in destroying or hiding evidence, though in the latter case it would probably often amount to being an accessory after the fact, and I would add that where it is thought possible and proper to charge a person as an accessory it is preferable to do so rather than have recourse to the offence of misprision. * * *

Appeal Dismissed.

NOTES

In the United States there is generally lacking any obligation upon the part of anyone to report a criminal offense or reveal the identity of its perpetrator. The closest we have come in this country are the offenses of "compounding a felony" or "misprision of felony" (previously discussed, p. 305), or those prohibitions upon the concealment of fugitives.

Chapter 10

THE LAW OF ARREST

A. HISTORICAL BACKGROUND *

Origin of the Police Department

The conditions in England during the centuries in which the law of arrest was being cast into its present shape, the seventeenth and eighteenth, were very different from those prevailing today in either England or the United States. Police departments were unknown, for it was not until 1829 that Sir Robert Peel persuaded the English Parliament to pass an act creating a police force for the city of London. In his honor the policemen were called "Bobbies", a nickname which London policemen still bear. Of course, Peel's idea was not entirely new; if it had been, Parliament would probably not have enacted it. For some years previously, various experiments had been tried and different sections of London had attempted to maintain groups of watchmen, but these men were usually ill-trained and always too few in number to provide satisfactory police protection. Outside of London, there were virtually no police officers, though in some places small groups of men undertook without compensation to keep the peace. There was thus nothing at all comparable to police departments, as we know them, before 1829. . . .

Up to the time of Sir Robert Peel, the methods of policing England differed little from those used in the days of the Norman kings. The Crown appointed sheriffs and constables among whose manifold duties was that of arresting wrongdoers, but the principal burden of keeping the peace lay on the community as a whole. Hence arose the institutions of the posse comitatus and the hue and cry. When a serious crime was committed and the offender could be tracked, the hue and cry was raised. It was then the duty of all the neighbors to seize their weapons and aid in the pursuit, which continued from county to county until the offender was captured or had escaped. Furthermore, sheriffs and constables often called upon ordinary citizens to form a posse comitatus and assist in making arrests. . . . This practice is still common in the more sparsely settled parts of this country

* From an article by the late Professor Sam Bass Warner, which was published in 26 A.B.A.J. 151 (1940) and in 31 J.Crim.L. & C. 111 (1940). The historical information it reveals should receive consideration when an analysis is made of present day cases involving arrest and detention procedures.

where police officers are few and hundreds of citizens somtimes take part in man-hunts, the modern equivalent of the hue and cry.

Right of Private Persons to Make Arrests

For the most part, however, victims of crimes were supposed, with the aid of their relatives and neighbors, to do their own detective work and themselves to arrest and prosecute offenders. . . . In fact, the right of private persons to make arrests was in nearly all respects equal to that of sheriffs and constables. So adequate did it seem, that when the "Bobbies" were created they were given no additional powers. They differed from private persons only in being employed to do that which the latter could do if so inclined. . . .

When a suspect was apprehended, he found himself in a sorry plight. Persons charged with serious offenses were rarely granted their freedom on bail. For example, even as late as 1800, the highly respectable Mrs. Leigh Perrot, aunt of Jane Austen, was unable to persuade the judges to admit her to bail, though she was accused merely of shoplifting. She had to spend the winter in jail in spite of her wealth, the absurdity of the charge, and the special trip her husband took to London in an effort to persuade the Court of King's Bench to release her on bail. . . .

In 1823, Sir Robert Peel also started the great reform which transformed prisons from business enterprises operated for the benefit of the keepers into liabilities of the taxpayers. Everywhere prior to that date and in some places until recently, jailers had been able to make a profit out of their unfortunate charges. Dickens' account of Mr. Pickwick's experiences in prison indicates some of the more legitimate ways in which this was done. Every incident of prison life, from admission to discharge, was made the occasion for levying fees. Fees were charged for the privilege of detention in this or that part of the prison, for a separate room, for a bed, for a mattress, for the use of bedclothes, etc., etc. When a prisoner was acquitted, he was not released until he paid all the fees due, including a fee for discharge. . . . What happened to prisoners unable to pay their fees depended upon the century and the humanitarian instincts of the jailer. In Massachusetts at the end of the seventeenth century such unfortunates might be sold for life or a period of years into the service of anybody willing to pay their fees. . . .

Sufferings of Persons in Jail Awaiting Trial

Since jailers were held responsible for escapes and many jails were constructed for some other purpose and hence easy to break out of, prisoners were often kept in irons. Those without means to buy better accommodations were frequently huddled together in dark, filthy rooms, in close proximity to depravity and disease. Under such conditions imprisonment until the next term of court was often equivalent to a death sentence, especially during the frequent periods when the prisons were swept by a malignant form of typhus known as "gaol fever". In 1759 an English authority estimated that each year a fourth of the people in prison died there. . . .

These misfortunes awaited persons thrown into prison pending trial, but an even worse fate, if that were possible, might result from arrest. During the centuries when the law of arrest was developing, kidnaping was much more prevalent than at present. As arrests were commonly made by private persons, the victim must often have been in doubt whether he was being arrested for crime, seized for ransom, or perhaps shanghaied for service as an English seaman or even as a slave on a foreign galley.

Arrests With and Without a Warrant

Such a state of affairs naturally developed a law strictly circumscribing the right to arrest and prescribing the disposition of the prisoner after arrest, with little distinction between the right of private citizens and public officials to make arrests. It was expected that most arrests would be made after the issuance of a warrant, whereas today the vast majority of arrests are made without a warrant. Hence, the right to arrest for a misdemeanor was with a few exceptions limited to misdemeanors amounting to a breach of the peace and then only when committed in the presence of the person making the arrest. This is still the law in many states, but in the majority police officers, and sometimes even private citizens, have been given the right to arrest for any misdemeanor committed in their presence. . . .

Either an officer or a private person could, and still can, arrest for a felony actually committed either when it was committed in his presence or he has reasonable cause to believe that the person to be arrested committed it. There also developed at the beginning of the nineteenth century the rule prevailing in many American states, that an officer may arrest whenever he has reasonable cause to believe that the person to be arrested has committed a felony, even though no felony has in fact been committed. . . .[1]

1. Also with regard to the historical background of the law of arrest, see the interesting article entitled The First Urban Policeman, by Martin A. Kelly, 1 J. Police Sci. & Adm. 56 (1973).

B. DEFINITION AND LEGISLATIVE PROVISIONS

SECTION 1. DEFINITION OF ARREST

"An arrest is the taking of another into custody for the actual or purported purpose of bringing the other before a court, body or official, or of otherwise securing the administration of the law. . .

"Mere words will not constitute an arrest, while on the other hand no actual physical touching is essential. . . . an assertion of authority and purpose to arrest followed by submission of the arrestee constitutes an arrest. There can be no arrest without either touching or submission." Perkins, Elements of Police Science 223, 227 (1942).

"Arrest is the taking of a person into custody in order that he may be forthcoming to answer for the commission of an offense." Sec. 18, Code of Criminal Procedure, American Law Institute.

" 'Arrest' means the taking of a person into custody." Sec. 102–5 of the 1963 Illinois Code of Criminal Procedure. "An arrest is made by an actual restraint of the person or by his submission to custody." Sec. 107–5, *ibid.*

SECTION 2. ILLUSTRATIVE LEGISLATIVE PROVISIONS REGARDING ARRESTS BY THE POLICE AS WELL AS BY PRIVATE CITIZENS

At the present time, the arrest rights of police officers and of private citizens are usually prescribed by legislative enactments, and they vary to a considerable extent, from jurisdiction to jurisdiction, as will be observed from the following selections:

Statutes and Code Provisions

California

Penal Code (Part 2 of Criminal Procedure):

§ 836. A peace officer may make an arrest in obedience to a warrant, or may . . . without a warrant, arrest a person:

1. Whenever he has reasonable cause to believe that the person to be arrested has committed a public offense in his presence.

2. When a person arrested has committed a felony, although not in his presence.

3. Whenever he has reasonable cause to believe that the person to be arrested has committed a felony, whether or not a felony has in fact been committed.

§ 837. A private person may arrest another:

1. For a public offense committed or attempted in his presence.

2. When the person arrested has committed a felony, although not in his presence.

3. When a felony has been in fact committed, and he has reasonable cause for believing the person arrested to have committed it.

(According to § 16, "crimes and public offenses" include "felonies", "misdemeanors", and "infractions". § 17 provides: "A felony is a crime which is punishable with death or by imprisonment in the state prison. Every other crime or public offense is a misdemeanor except offenses that are classified as infractions.")

Illinois

Code of Criminal Procedure:

§ 107–2. **Arrest by Peace Officer.** A peace officer may arrest a person when:

(a) He has a warrant commanding that such person be arrested; or

(b) He has reasonable grounds to believe that a warrant for the person's arrest has been issued in this State or in another jurisdiction; or

(c) He has reasonable grounds to believe that the person is committing or has committed an offense [defined in § 102–15 as "a violation of any penal statute of this State"].

§ 107–3. **Arrest by Private Person.** Any person may arrest another when he has reasonable grounds to believe that an offense other than an ordinance violation is being committed.

§ 107–4. **Arrest by Peace Officer from Other Jurisdiction.** (a) As used in this Section:

(1) "State" means any State of the United States and the District of Columbia.

(2) "Peace Officer" means any peace officer or member of any duly organized State, County, or Municipal peace unit or police force of another State.

(3) "Fresh pursuit" means the immediate pursuit of a person who is endeavoring to avoid arrest.

(b) Any peace officer of another State who enters this State in fresh pursuit and continues within this State in fresh pursuit of a person in order to arrest him on the ground that he has committed an offense in the other State has the same authority to arrest and hold the person in custody as peace officers of this State have to arrest and hold a person in custody on the ground that he has committed an offense in this State.

(c) If an arrest is made in this State by a peace officer of another State in accordance with the provisions of this Section he shall without unnecessary delay take the person arrested before the circuit court of the county in which the arrest was made. Such court shall conduct a hearing for the purpose of determining the lawfulness of the arrest. If the court determines that the arrest was lawful it shall commit the person arrested, to await for a reasonable time the issuance of an extradition warrant by the Governor of this State, or admit him to bail for such purpose. If the court determines that the arrest was unlawful it shall discharge the person arrested.

[In addition to the citizen arrest power in § 107–3, the Code, in § 107–8, also imposes an obligation upon male persons over the age of 18 to aid a police officer in making an arrest if such aid is requested.]

Michigan

Code of Criminal Procedure (Title 28):

§ 28.874(15). Any peace officer may, without a warrant, arrest a person—

(a) For the commission of any felony or misdemeanor committed in his presence;

(b) When such person has committed a felony although not in the presence of the officer;

(c) When a felony in fact has been committed and he has reasonable cause to believe that such person has committed it;

(d) When he has reasonable cause to believe that a felony has been committed and reasonable cause to believe that such person has committed it;

(e) When he has received positive information by written, telegraphic, teletypic, telephonic, radio or other authoritative source that another officer holds a warrant for such arrest;

(f) When he has received such positive information broadcast from any recognized police or other governmental radio station, or teletype, as may afford him reasonable cause to believe that a felony has been committed and reasonable cause to believe that such person has committed it;

(g) When he has reasonable cause to believe that such person is an escaped convict, or has violated a condition of parole from any prison, or has violated a condition of probation imposed by any court, or has violated any condition of a pardon granted by the executive.

§ 28.875(16). A private person may make an arrest—

(a) For a felony committed in his presence;

(b) When the person to be arrested has committed a felony although not in his presence;

(c) When summoned by any peace officer to assist said officer in making an arrest.

New York

Criminal Procedure Law:

§ 140.10.

1. Subject to the provisions of subdivision two, a police officer may arrest a person for:

> (a) Any offense when he has reasonable cause to believe that such person has committed such offense in his presence; and
>
> (b) A crime when he has reasonable cause to believe that such person has committed such crime, whether in his presence or otherwise.

2. A police officer may arrest a person for a petty offense, pursuant to subdivision one, only when:

> (a) Such offense was committed or believed by him to have been committed within the geographical area of such police officer's employment; and
>
> (b) Such arrest is made in the county in which such offense was committed or believed to have been committed or in an adjoining county; except that the police officer may follow such person in continuous close pursuit, commencing either in the county in which the offense was or is believed to have been committed or in an adjoining county, in and through any county of the state, and may arrest him in any county in which he apprehends him.

3. A police officer may arrest a person for a crime, pursuant to subdivision one, whether or not such crime was committed within the geographical area of such police officer's employment, and he may make such arrest within the state, regardless of the situs of the commission of the crime. In addition, he may, if necessary, pursue such person outside the state and may arrest him in any state the laws of which contain provisions equivalent [to New York law].

§ 140.30.

1. Subject to the provisions of subdivision two, any person may arrest another person (a) for a felony when the latter has in fact committed such felony, and (b) for any offense when the latter has in fact committed such offense in his presence.

2. Such an arrest, if for a felony, may be made anywhere in the state. If the arrest is for an offense other than a felony, it may be made only in the county in which such offense was committed.

[When an arrest is made in accordance with this provision, according to § 140.35, the arrester "must inform the person whom he is arresting of the reason for such arrest unless he encounters physical resistance, flight or other factors rendering such procedure impractical".]

According to § 10.00 of the Penal Code, the words "offense" and "crime" are differentiated as follows:

> "Offense" means conduct for which a sentence to a term of imprisonment or to a fine is provided by any law of this state or by any law, local law or ordinance of a political subdivision of this state, or by any order, rule or regulation of any governmental instrumentality authorized by law to adopt the same.
>
> "Crime" means a misdemeanor or a felony.

And in New York (also in § 10.00), the distinction between "misdemeanor" and "felony" is set out in the following terms:

> "Misdemeanor" means an offense, other than a "traffic infraction," for which a sentence to a term of imprisonment in excess of fifteen days may be imposed, but for which a sentence to a term of imprisonment in excess of one year cannot be imposed.
>
> "Felony" means an offense for which a sentence to a term of imprisonment in excess of one year may be imposed.

Texas

Code of Criminal Procedure:

Art. 14.01 Offense within view

(a) A peace officer or any other person, may, without a warrant, arrest an offender when the offense is committed in his presence or within his view, if the offense is one classed as a felony or as an offense against the public peace.

(b) A peace officer may arrest an offender without a warrant for any offense committed in his presence or within his view.

Art. 14.03 Authority of peace officers

Any peace officer may arrest, without warrant, persons found in suspicious places and under circumstances which reasonably show that such persons have been guilty of some felony or breach of the peace, or threaten, or are about to commit some offense against the laws.

Federal

There is no single act regarding the arrest powers of federal officers generally. The matter is dealt with by separate statutes pertaining to particular groups of officers. For instance, there is a separate provision for FBI agents, and it authorizes an arrest, without warrant, for "any offense against the United States committed in their presence, or for any felony cognizable under the laws of the United States if they have reasonable grounds to believe that the person to be arrested has committed or is committing such felony." (18 U.S.C.A. § 3052.) Another statute confers a similar power upon marshals and their deputies. (18 U.S.C.A. § 3053.)

Separate statutes provide similar arrest powers for offenses that are the province of the Secret Service (18 USC § 3056), the Bureau of Narcotics and Dangerous Drugs (26 USC § 7607), the Postal Inspectors (18 USC § 3061), and the I.R.S. enforcement agents (26 USC § 7608). Bureau of Prisons enforcement personnel may make warrantless arrests for specified offenses only if they have "reasonable grounds to believe that the arrested person is guilty of such offense, and if there is likelihood of his escaping before a warrant can be obtained for his arrest." (18 USC § 3050).

The District of Columbia, however, has its own provisions with regard to arrest powers. They are as follows in the District of Columbia Code:

§ 23–581. Arrests without warrant by law enforcement officers

(a) (1) A law enforcement officer may arrest, without a warrant having previously been issued therefor—

(A) a person whom he has probable cause to believe has committed or is committing a felony;

(B) a person whom he has probable cause to believe has committed or is committing an offense in his presence;

(C) a person whom he has probable cause to believe has committed or is about to commit any offense listed in paragraph (2) and, unless immediately arrested, may not be apprehended, may cause injury to others, or may tamper with, dispose of, or destroy evidence.

(2) The offenses referred to in subparagraph (C) of paragraph (1) are the following:

(A) The following offenses specified in the Act entitled "An Act to establish a code of law for the District of Columbia", approved March 3, 1901, and listed in the following table:

Offense:	**Specified in—**
Assault	section 806 (D.C.Code, sec. 22–504).
Petit larceny	section 827 (D.C.Code, sec. 22–2202).
Receiving stolen goods	section 829 (D.C.Code, sec. 22–2205).
Unlawful entry	section 824 (D.C.Code, sec. 22–3102).

(B) Attempts to commit the following offenses specified in such Act and listed in the following table:

Offense:	**Specified in—**
Burglary	section 823 (D.C.Code, sec. 22–1801).
Grand larceny	section 826 (D.C.Code, sec. 22–2201).
Unauthorized use of vehicles	section 826b (D.C.Code, sec. 22–2204).

(b) A law enforcement officer may, even if his jurisdiction does not extend beyond the District of Columbia, continue beyond the District, if necessary, a pursuit commenced within the District of a person who has committed an offense or whom he has probable cause to believe has committed or is committing a felony, and may arrest that person in any State the laws of which contain provisions equivalent to those of section 23–901 [which permits the arrest in D. C. by officers from other jurisdictions in fresh pursuit of the intended arrestee].

§ 23–582. Arrests without warrant by other persons

(a) A special policeman shall have the same powers as a law enforcement officer to arrest without warrant for offenses committed within premises to which his jurisdiction extends, and may arrest outside the premises on fresh pursuit for offenses committed on the premises.

(b) A private person may arrest another—

(1) whom he has probable cause to believe is committing in his presence—

(A) a felony, or

(B) an offense enumerated in section 23–581(a)(2); or

(2) in aid of a law enforcement officer or special policeman, or other person authorized by law to make an arrest.

(c) Any person making an arrest pursuant to this section shall deliver the person arrested to a law enforcement officer without unreasonable delay.

Ordinances

In addition to the arrest rights covered by state statutes, there are, in some jurisdictions, city and county ordinances dealing with the subject. Although such ordinances seldom differ from or exceed the arrest rights set forth in the statutes themselves, there are instances where they are broader. For example, note the following with respect to the State of Illinois and the City of Chicago:

Although the Criminal Code, as previously noted, provides that a peace officer may arrest a person when he has reasonable grounds to believe that the person is committing or has committed an offense (meaning a violation of any penal statute of the state), Section 11–25 of the Municipal Code of Chicago grants to members of its police department the power

> "(1) to arrest or cause to be arrested, with or without process, all persons who break the peace, or are found violating any municipal ordinance or any criminal law of the State; (2) to commit arrested persons for examination; (3) if necessary, to detain arrested persons in custody overnight or Sunday in any safe place, or until they can be brought before the proper court; and (4) to exercise all other powers as conservators of the peace as are provided in this code."

This ordinance was enacted pursuant to authorization conferred by the Illinois legislature upon Illinois municipalities to prescribe the duties and powers of police officers. Ch. 24, §§ 11–1–1, 11–1–2, Ill. Rev.Stats.

Missouri presents another example, with respect to the arrest powers of the Kansas City police department, which is accorded considerably more power than is provided for the police of Missouri generally. In Kansas City, police officers may make an arrest when they "have reason to believe that any person has committed or is about to commit within the city . . . any breach of the peace or violation of law and order." Vernon's Annot. Mo. Stats. § 84.440.

NOTE

Warrants for Arrest. Fairly typical of the legislative conditions for the issuance of court orders—warrants—for arrest is the following provision of the Illinois Criminal Code (Art. 107–9):

(a) When a complaint is presented to a court charging that an offense has been committed it shall examine upon oath or affirmation the complainant or any witnesses.

(b) The complaint shall be in writing and shall:

(1) State the name of the accused if known, and if not known the accused may be designated by any name or description by which he can be identified with reasonable certainty;

(2) State the offense with which the accused is charged;

(3) State the time and place of the offense as definitely as can be done by the complainant; and

(4) Be subscribed and sworn to by the complainant.

(c) A warrant shall be issued by the court for the arrest of the person complained against if it appears from the contents of the complaint and the examination of the complainant or other witnesses, if any, that the person against whom the complaint was made has committed an offense.

(d) The warrant of arrest shall:

(1) Be in writing;

(2) Specify the name of the person to be arrested or if his name is unknown, shall designate such person by any name or description by which he can be identified with reasonable certainty;

(3) Set forth the nature of the offense;

(4) State the date when issued and the municipality or county where issued;

(5) Be signed by the judge of the court with the title of his office;

(6) Command that the person against whom the complaint was made be arrested and brought before the court issuing the warrant or if he is absent or unable to act before the nearest or most accessible court in the same county; and

(7) Specify the amount of bail.

(e) The warrant shall be directed to all peace officers in the State. It shall be executed by the peace officer, or by a private person specially named therein, and may be executed in any county in the State.

SECTION 3. ARREST IMMUNITY

Certain individuals may be exempt from arrest on a temporary or permanent basis, depending upon the nature of the arrest, and the person's occupation and activities. The exemption in some cases is common law, but generally it is pursuant to statute. The exemption from civil arrest is far more common than one for criminal detention.

The broadest arrest immunity is conferred upon diplomats of a foreign nation, their families and staffs. These individuals are not subject to the criminal laws of the host country.

Statutory immunity from civil arrest has been conferred upon public officials in the performance of their official duties, military personnel, and officers of the court while attending or traveling to and from court. This latter privilege arose from the common law.

Article 1, § 6 of the United States Constitution provides that Senators and Representatives "shall in all cases, except Treason, Felony and Breach of the Peace, be privileged from arrest during their attendance at the session of their respective Houses, and in going to and returning from the same". This phrase removes criminal offenses from the Congressional arrest immunity.

SECTION 4. DETENTION SHORT OF ARREST

In addition to the power of arrest, law enforcement officers, and also private persons, have the right, under certain conditions, to detain persons short of an actual arrest. The police, for instance, have the right to stop a motorist who has violated a traffic law and issue to him a notice or citation to appear in court at a designated time on the charge filed by the officer who observed the violation. This is not an arrest because, according to the definitions previously discussed, there is no intention on the part of the officer to take the motorist into "custody" to answer the charge. Such a detention has been sanctioned on the theory that the use of the highways by motorists is a privilege and not an absolute right, and the privilege may be subjected to various conditions, including the stopping to check upon driver licenses and car registrations.

Also, as will be discussed in detail later on in this casebook, there is the right of the police to "stop-and-frisk", under reasonable circumstances, persons whom they reasonably suspect of criminality.

A property owner, merchant, or an agent of either one, may, under certain circumstances detain a person on the premises whom they reasonably believe to be in wrongful possession of property belonging to the property owner or merchant. Such a detention, however, is permissible only when done in a reasonable manner and only for the time reasonably necessary to investigate the facts. Although this right has a common law foundation, there are many state statutes which specifically recognize it and delineate its extent and limitations.

C. POST–ARREST REQUIREMENTS AND INITIAL JUDICIAL INQUIRY

Illlustrative of the obligations imposed upon a person who has effected an arrest are the following:

Sec. 109–1(a), Illinois Code of Criminal Procedure:

A person arrested without a warrant shall be taken without unnecessary delay before the nearest and most accessible judge in that county, and a charge shall be filed. A person arrested on a warrant shall be taken without unnecessary delay before the judge who issued the warrant or if he is absent or unable to act before the nearest or most accessible judge in the same county.

Sec. 28.873, Michigan Code of Criminal Procedure:

A private person who has made an arrest must without unnecessary delay, take the person arrested before the most convenient magistrate in the county in which the offense was committed or deliver him to a peace officer, who must without unnecessary delay take him before such magistrate. The peace officer or private person so taking the person arrested before such magistrate must lay before the magistrate a complaint stating the offense for which the person was arrested.

Rule 5(a) of the Federal Rules of Criminal Procedure:

An officer making an arrest under a warrant issued upon a complaint or any person making an arrest without a warrant shall take the arrested person without unnecessary delay before the nearest available commissioner or before any other nearby officer empowered to commit persons charged with offenses against the laws of the United States. When a person arrested without a warrant is brought before a commissioner or other officer, a complaint shall be filed forthwith.

Arrest statutes generally make no provision for the release of an arrestee by the police themselves, even after it becomes apparent that the person arrested is innocent of the offense for which he has been arrested. Accordingly, such a person is held in custody until he can be brought before a magistrate, as required by a literal interpretation of arrest statute provisions. Some courts hold that a police release is unlawful and may be the basis for a civil action on the part of the arrestee. When an arrestee of this type is taken before a magistrate he is, in some localities, charged with "disorderly conduct," found guilty, and sentence suspended. All this is done with court cooperation, and it is supposed to "protect" the police from false arrest suits. As a practical matter it does have that effect; legally, speaking, however, it does not.

Some police departments have developed a practice, without actual legal authorization, however, of permitting a commanding officer to release innocent arrestees. Seldom, of course, does a person who is released in this manner resort to legal action on the theory that his police release was not legally authorized.

Section 134(f) of the Restatement of Torts provides that whenever a police officer ascertains beyond a reasonable doubt that he was mistaken in making the arrest without a warrant he is no longer privileged to keep the person in custody and must release him, unless the person desires to be taken before a court to have the stigma officially removed. The section also provides for release in cases of mistaken identity.

The 1963 Illinois Code of Criminal Procedure (§ 107–6) contains the following provision:

> A peace officer who arrests a person without a warrant is authorized to release the person without requiring him to appear before a court when the officer is satisfied that there are no grounds for criminal complaint against the person arrested.

New York has a similar provision (§ 140.40 of its Criminal Procedure Law):

> . . . a police officer is not required to take an arrested person into custody or to take any other action prescribed in this section on behalf of the arresting person if he has rea-

sonable cause to believe that the arrested person did not commit the alleged offense or that the arrest was otherwise unauthorized.

The reasons for the insistence in a democratic society that the police take arrested persons before a judicial officer are obvious; to follow any other practice would deprive the arrestee of an impartial evaluation of the reasonableness for holding him for further proceedings. This evaluation is known as a "preliminary hearing".

Preliminary Hearing

A preliminary hearing is a relatively informal proceeding by means of which a determination is made as to whether there are reasonable grounds for believing the accused committed the offense—as to whether it is fair, under the circumstances, to require the accused to stand a regular trial. If after such a hearing the judge or magistrate decides that the accusation is without probable cause, the accused will be discharged. This discharge, however, will not bar a grand jury indictment if subsequently developed evidence (or the same evidence presented on the preliminary hearing) satisfies the grand jury that the accusation is well founded.

In the event an arrested person is not formally charged with an offense and is not taken before a judge or other magistrate "without unnecessary delay" he, or rather someone on his behalf, may petition a judge for a "writ of habeas corpus" and thereby attempt to secure his release or at least compel the police to file a specific charge against him, in which latter event he may seek his release on bond. If the court issues the writ, the police or other custodians of the arrested person are required, either immediately or at an early designated time, to bring him into court (that is, "you have the body," which is the literal meaning of the term "habeas corpus"), and to explain to the court the reason or justification for holding the accused person in custody.

Upon the police showing adequate cause, a court may continue the hearing in order to give the police a little more time to conduct a further investigation before making the formal charge against the arrestee. Many times, however, the police are required to file their charges immediately or release the prisoner.

D. LEGAL CONSEQUENCES OF AN ILLEGAL ARREST AND OF A FAILURE TO COMPLY WITH THE LAW RESPECTING THE PRESCRIBED DISPOSITION OF AN ARRESTEE

A person who makes an illegal arrest or who violates the rights and privileges of the arrestee subjects himself to the possibility of a civil suit by the arrestee. Under certain circumstances he may even subject himself to a criminal prosecution. Moreover, if the illegal arrest is made by a law enforcement officer, the evidence he seizes from the arrestee is subject to suppression by reason of the "exclusionary rule". The details of that rule will be subsequently revealed.

With respect to the court rule or statutory requirement as to the disposition of the arrestee, some courts hold, in effect, that "unnecessary delay" means a delay for any reason other than the unavailability of a committing magistrate or circumstances such as distance, lack of ready transportation, etc., which may prevent a quick presentation of the arrestee to a magistrate. Other courts, however, take the view that "unnecessary delay" means only "unreasonable delay" and consequently the police are permitted to hold an arrestee for a "reasonable" length of time, with reasonableness being determined by all the surrounding circumstances and factors in the particular case.[2]

NOTE

In 1943, and again in 1957, the Supreme Court of the United States held, in McNabb v. United States, 318 U.S. 332, 63 S.Ct. 608 (1943), and Mallory v. United States, 354 U.S. 449, 77 S.Ct. 1356 (1957), that where *federal officers* interrogated an arrested person instead of taking him "without unnecessary delay" before a United States commissioner or a federal judge, as required by law, any confession obtained during the period of delay was inadmissible in evidence, regardless of its voluntariness or trustworthiness. This the Court did in the exercise of its "supervisory power" over lower federal courts.

Since the *McNabb-Mallory* rule was not based upon constitutional "due process" considerations, or upon any other provision of the Bill of Rights, the rule was not binding upon the states. Of all the states, only Michigan was inclined to adopt a similar rule. See People v. Hamilton, 359 Mich. 410, 102 N.W.2d 738 (1960) and People v. McCager, 367 Mich. 116, 116 N.W. 2d 205 (1962), in which the Michigan Supreme Court said that Michigan was "the first state to adopt the exclusionary rule principle announced in McNabb v. United States". (In *McCager* the confession was made four days after the defendant's arrest.) But within a short time Michigan qualified the application of the rule to such an extent as to effectively discard it. In People v. Farmer, 380 Mich. 198, 156 N.W.2d 504 (1968), the court held that the rule was applicable only where the delay in taking an arrestee before a

2. For example: Mooradian v. Davis, 302 Mich. 484, 5 N.W.2d 435 (1942); People v. Jackson, 23 Ill.2d 274, 178 N.E.2d 299 (1961).

magistrate was "for the purpose of coercing a confession". In *Farmer* the court found that there were "no circumstances to support a claim of involuntariness" such as appeared in the *Hamilton* case or in the subsequent one of People v. Ubbes, 374 Mich. 571, 132 N.W.2d 669 (1965). (A similar experiment in Delaware and Wisconsin is discussed in Inbau & Reid, Criminal Interrogation and Confessions (2d ed. 1967, at 167–168.)

In June, 1968 Congress abolished the *McNabb-Mallory* rule in the Omnibus Crime Control and Safe Streets Act. The act provides that although a federal officer's delay in taking an arrestee before a federal judicial officer is a factor that may be considered by the judge and jury, the delay alone is not controlling as regards the admissibility of a confession.

Since the *McNabb-Mallory* rule was not of constitutional dimension, this provision of the Act should be held constitutionally valid.

Although the Omnibus Act provision is directed at federal cases, it, along with Michigan's experimentation with the *McNabb-Mallory* rule, will probably dissuade many state courts from adopting such a rule.

E. EXTRADITION OF ACCUSED PERSONS LOCATED IN OTHER JURISDICTIONS

There are instances where a person charged with a crime is located in another jurisdiction or country. To effect his return from another country there must exist a treaty providing for mutual extradition of fugitives; in the absence of a treaty there is no legal right to the return of a fugitive. With regard to interstate situations there is a provision in the Constitution (Art. IV, Sec. 2) which reads as follows:

> A Person charged in any State with Treason, Felony, or other Crime, who shall flee from Justice, and be found in another State, shall on Demand of the executive Authority of the State from which he fled, be delivered up, to be removed to the State having Jurisdiction of the Crime.

In implementation of this constitutional authorization, practically all of the states have adopted the Uniform Extradition Act. It sets forth the procedures which must be followed, and it even covers case situations where the wanted person has not actually fled from, nor was he physically present in the demanding state at the time of the offense; all that is required is a charge that the wanted person committed an act within the host state or in a third state "intentionally resulting in a crime in the state whose executive authority is making the demand".[3]

3. For information regarding extradition as well as other aspects of the interstate crime control problem see: The Handbook on Interstate Crime Control (prepared by the Council of State Governments, 1313 E. 60th St., Chicago, Ill. 60637).

NOTE

The fact that a fugitive may have been illegally arrested, or even kidnapped, for return to the state where the crime was committed does not affect the court's jurisdiction to try the case. Frisbie v. Collins, 342 U.S. 519, 72 S.Ct. 509 (1952); United States v. Sobel, 142 F.Supp. 515 (D.C.N.Y. 1956); People v. Griffith, 130 Colo. 475, 276 P.2d 559 (1954).

In the case of Adolph Eichmann, the chief executioner of millions of Jews during the Nazi regime in Germany, the Supreme Court of Israel relied heavily upon American case law to justify its right to try Eichmann, who had been kidnapped in Argentina and flown to Israel for trial. See Pearlman, The Capture and Trial of Adolph Eichmann (1963) 112.

Chapter 11

SEARCHES AND SEIZURES

A. PROBABLE CAUSE FOR ARREST

DRAPER v. UNITED STATES

Supreme Court of the United States, 1959.
358 U.S. 307, 79 S.Ct. 329.

MR. JUSTICE WHITTAKER delivered the opinion of the Court.

. . .

The evidence offered at the hearing on the motion to suppress was not substantially disputed. It established that one Marsh, a federal narcotic agent with 29 years' experience, was stationed at Denver; that one Hereford had been engaged as a "special employee" of the Bureau of Narcotics at Denver for about six months, and from time to time gave information to Marsh regarding violations of the narcotic laws, for which Hereford was paid small sums of money, and that Marsh had always found the information given by Hereford to be accurate and reliable. On September 3, 1956, Hereford told Marsh that James Draper (petitioner) recently had taken up abode at a stated address in Denver and "was peddling narcotics to several addicts" in that city. Four days later, on September 7, Hereford told Marsh "that Draper had gone to Chicago the day before [September 6] by train [and] that he was going to bring back three ounces of heroin [and] that he would return to Denver either on the morning of the 8th of September or the morning of the 9th of September also by train." Hereford also gave Marsh a detailed physical description of Draper and of the clothing he was wearing, and said that he would be carrying "a tan zipper bag," and habitually "walked real fast."

On the morning of September 8, Marsh and a Denver police officer went to the Denver Union Station and kept watch over all incoming trains from Chicago, but they did not see anyone fitting the description that Hereford had given. Repeating the process on the morning of September 9, they saw a person, having the exact physical attributes and wearing the precise clothing described by Hereford, alight from an incoming Chicago train and start walking "fast" toward the exit. He was carrying a tan zipper bag in his right hand and the left was thrust in his raincoat pocket. Marsh, accompanied by the police officer, overtook, stopped and arrested him. They then searched him and found the two "envelopes containing heroin" clutched in his left hand in his raincoat pocket, and found the syringe in the tan zipper bag. Marsh then took him (petitioner) into custody. Hereford died four days after the arrest and therefore did not testify at the hearing on the motion.

26 U.S.C. (Supp. V) § 7607, added by § 104(a) of the Narcotic Control Act of 1956, 70 Stat. 570, 26 U.S.C.A. § 7607, provides, in pertinent part:

"The Commissioner . . . and agents, of the Bureau of Narcotics . . . may—

. . .

"(2) Make arrests without warrant for violations of any law of the United States relating to narcotic drugs . . . where the violation is committed in the presence of the person making the arrest or where such person has reasonable grounds to believe that the person to be arrested has committed or is committing such violation."

The crucial question for us then is whether knowledge of the related facts and circumstances gave Marsh "probable cause" within the meaning of the Fourth Amendment, and "reasonable grounds" within the meaning of § 104(a), supra, to believe that petitioner had committed or was committing a violation of the narcotic laws. If it did, the arrest, though without a warrant, was lawful. . . .

Petitioner . . . contends (1) that the information given by Hereford to Marsh was "hearsay" and, because hearsay is not legally competent evidence in a criminal trial, could not legally have been considered, but should have been put out of mind, by Marsh in assessing whether he had "probable cause" and "reasonable grounds" to arrest petitioner without a warrant, and (2) that, even if hearsay could lawfully have been considered, Marsh's information should be held insufficent to show "probable cause" and "reasonable grounds" to believe that petitioner had violated or was violating the narcotic laws and to justify his arrest without a warrant.

Considering the first contention, we find petitioner entirely in error. Brinegar v. United States, 338 U.S. 160, 172–173, 69 S.Ct. 1302, 1309, has settled the question the other way. There, in a similar situation, the convict contended "that the factors relating to inadmissibility of the evidence [for] *purposes of proving guilt at the trial,* deprive[d] the evidence as a whole of sufficiency to show probable cause for the search . . . ." (Emphasis added.) But this Court, rejecting that contention, said: "[T]he so-called distinction places a wholly unwarranted emphasis upon the criterion of admissibility in evidence, to prove the accused's guilt, of facts relied upon to show probable cause. The emphasis, we think, goes much too far in confusing and disregarding the difference between what is required to prove guilt in a criminal case and what is required to show probable cause for arrest or search. It approaches requiring (if it does not in practical effect require) proof sufficient to establish guilt in order to substantiate the existence of probable cause. There is a large difference between the two things to be proved [guilt and probable cause], as well as between the tribunals which determine them, and therefore a like difference in the *quanta* and modes of proof required to establish them." . . . .

Nor can we agree with petitioner's second contention that Marsh's information was insufficient to show probable cause and reasonable grounds to believe that petitioner had violated or was violating the narcotic laws and to justify his arrest without a warrant. The information given to narcotic agent Marsh by "special employee" Hereford may have been hearsay to Marsh, but coming from one employed for that purpose and whose information had always been found accurate and reliable, it is clear that Marsh would have been derelict in his duties had he not pursued it. And when, in pursuing that information, he saw a man, having the exact physical attributes and wearing the precise clothing and carrying the tan zipper bag that Hereford had described, alight from one of the very trains from the very place stated by Hereford and start to walk at a "fast" pace toward the station exit, Marsh had personally verified every facet of the information given him by Hereford except whether petitioner had accomplished his mission and had the three ounces of heroin on his person or in his bag. And surely, with every other bit of Hereford's information being thus personally verified, Marsh had "reasonable grounds" to believe that the remaining unverified bit of Hereford's information—that Draper would have the heroin with him—was likewise true.

"In dealing with probable cause . . . as the very name implies, we deal with probabilities. These are not technical; they are the factual and practical considerations of everyday life on which reasonable and prudent men, not legal technicians, act." Brinegar v. United States. Probable cause exists where "the facts and circumstances within their [the arresting officer's] knowledge and of which they had reasonably trustworthy information [are] sufficient in themselves to warrant a man of reasonable caution in the belief that" an offense has been or is being committed. Carroll v. United States, 267 U.S. 132, 162, 45 S.Ct. 280, 288. . . .

We believe that, under the facts and circumstances here, Marsh had probable cause and reasonable grounds to believe that petitioner was committing a violation of the laws of the United States relating to narcotic drugs at the time he arrested him. The arrest was therefore lawful, and the subsequent search and seizure, having been made incident to that lawful arrest, were likewise valid. It follows that petitioner's motion to suppress was properly denied and that the seized heroin was competent evidence lawfully received at the trial.

Affirmed.

THE CHIEF JUSTICE and MR. JUSTICE FRANKFURTER took no part in the consideration or decision of this case.

MR. JUSTICE DOUGLAS, dissenting.

Of course, the education we receive from mystery stories and television shows teaches that what happened in this case is efficient police work. The police are tipped off that a man carrying narcotics will step off the morning train. A man meeting the precise description does alight from the train. No warrant for his arrest has been—or as I see it, could then be—obtained. Yet he is arrested; and narcotics are found in his pocket and a syringe in the bag he carried. This is the familiar pattern of crime detection which has been dinned into public consciousness as the correct and efficient one. It is however, a distorted reflection of the constitutional system under which we are supposed to live.

With all due deference, the arrest made here on the mere word of an informer violated the spirit of the Fourth Amendment and the requirement of the law, . . . governing arrests in narcotics cases. If an arrest is made without a warrant, the offense must be committed in the presence of the officer or the officer must have "reasonable grounds to believe that the person to be arrested has committed or is committing" a violation of the narcotics law. The arresting officers did not have a bit of evidence, known to them and as to which they could take an oath had they gone to a magistrate for a warrant, that petitioner had committed any crime. The arresting officers did not know the grounds on which the informer based his conclusion; nor did they seek to find out what they were. They acted solely on the informer's word. In my view that was not enough.

The rule which permits arrest for felonies, as distinguished from misdemeanors, if there are reasonable grounds for believing a crime has been or is being committed . . . grew out of the need to protect the public safety by making prompt arrests. Yet, apart from those cases where the crime is committed in the presence of the officer, arrests without warrants, like searches without warrants, are the exception, not the rule in our society. Lord Chief Justice Pratt in Wilkes v. Wood, condemned not only the odious general warrant, in which the name of the citizen to be arrested was left blank, but the whole scheme of seizures and searches under "a discretionary power" of law officers to act "wherever their suspicions may chance to fall"—a practice which he denounced as "totally subversive of the liberty of the subject." See III May, Constitutional History of England, c. XI. Wilkes had written in 1762, "To take any man into custody, and deprive him of his liberty, without having some seeming foundation at least, on which to justify such a step, is inconsistent with wisdom and sound policy." The Life and Political Writings of John Wilkes, p. 372.

George III in 1777 pressed for a bill which would allow arrests on suspicion of treason committed in America. The words were "suspected of" treason and it was to these words that Wilkes addressed himself in Parliament. "There is not a syllable in the Bill of the degree of probability attending the suspicion. . . . Is it possible,

Sir, to give more despotic powers to a bashaw of the Turkish empire? What security is left for the devoted objects of this Bill against the malice of a prejudiced individual, a wicked magistrate . . . ?" The Speeches of Mr. Wilkes, p. 102.

These words and the complaints against which they were directed were well known on this side of the water. Hamilton wrote about "the practice of arbitrary imprisonments" which he denounced as "the favorite and most formidable instruments of tyranny." Federalist No. 84. The writs of assistance, against which James Otis proclaimed, were vicious in the same way as the general warrants, since they required no showing of "probable cause" before a magistrate, and since they allowed the police to search on suspicion and without "reasonable grounds" for believing that a crime had been or was being committed. Otis' protest was eloquent; but he lost the case. His speech, however, rallied public opinion. "Then and there," wrote John Adams, "the child Independence was born." 10 Life and Works of John Adams (1856), p. 248. . . .

The Court is quite correct in saying that proof of "reasonable grounds" for believing a crime was being committed need not be proof admissible at the trial. It could be inferences from suspicious acts, e. g., consort with known peddlers, the surreptitious passing of a package, an intercepted message suggesting criminal activities, or any number of such events coming to the knowledge of the officer. . . . But, if he takes the law into his own hands and does not seek the protection of a warrant, he must act on some evidence known to him. This important requirement should be strictly enforced, lest the whole process of arrest revert once more to whispered accusations by people. When we lower the guards as we do today, we risk making the role of the informer—odious in our history—once more supreme. . . .

Here the officers had no evidence—apart from the mere word of an informer—that petitioner was committing a crime. The fact that petitioner walked fast and carried a tan zipper bag was not evidence of any crime. The officers knew nothing except what they had been told by the informer. If they went to a magistrate to get a warrant of arrest and relied solely on the report of the informer, it is not conceivable to me that one would be granted. For they could not present to the magistrate any of the facts which the informer may have had. They could swear only to the fact that the informer had made the accusation. They could swear to no evidence that lay in their own knowledge. They could present, on information and belief, no facts which the informer disclosed. No magistrate could issue a warrant on the mere word of an officer, without more. We are not justified in lowering the standard when an arrest is made without a warrant and allowing the officers more leeway than we grant the magistrate.

With all deference I think we break with tradition when we sustain this arrest. . . .

BECK v. OHIO

Supreme Court of the United States, 1964.
379 U.S. 89, 85 S.Ct. 223.

MR. JUSTICE STEWART delivered the opinion of the Court.

On the afternoon of November 10, 1961, the petitioner, William Beck, was driving his automobile in the vicinity of East 115th Street and Beulah Avenue in Cleveland, Ohio. Cleveland police officers accosted him, identified themselves, and ordered him to pull over to the curb. The officers possessed neither an arrest warrant nor a search warrant. Placing him under arrest, they searched his car but found nothing of interest. They then took him to a nearby police station where they searched his person and found an envelope containing a number of clearing house slips "beneath the sock of his leg." The petitioner was subsequently charged in the Cleveland Municipal Court with possession of clearing house slips in violation of a state criminal statute. He filed a motion to suppress as evidence the clearing house slips in question, upon the ground that the police had obtained them by means of an unreasonable search and seizure in violation of the Fourth and Fourteenth Amendments. After a hearing the motion was overruled, the clearing house slips were admitted in evidence, and the petitioner was convicted. His conviction was affirmed by an Ohio Court of Appeals, and ultimately by the Supreme Court of Ohio, with two judges dissenting. We granted certiorari to consider the petitioner's claim that, under the rule of Mapp v. Ohio, the clearing house slips were wrongly admitted in evidence against him because they had been seized by the Cleveland police in violation of the Fourth and Fourteenth Amendments.

Although the police officers did not obtain a warrant before arresting the petitioner and searching his automobile and his person, the Supreme Court of Ohio found the search nonetheless constitutionally valid as a search incident to a lawful arrest. And it is upon that basis that the Ohio decision has been supported by the respondent here. See Draper v. United States; Ker v. California, 374 U.S. 23, 83 S.Ct. 1623.

There are limits to the permissible scope of a warrantless search incident to a lawful arrest, but we proceed on the premise that, if the arrest itself was lawful, those limits were not exceeded here. The constitutional validity of the search in this case, then, must depend upon the constitutional validity of the petitioner's arrest. Whether that arrest was constitutionally valid depends in turn upon whether, at the moment the arrest was made, the officers had probable cause to make it—whether at that moment the facts and circumstances within their knowledge and of which they had reasonably trustworthy information were sufficient to warrant a prudent man in believing that the petitioner had committed or was committing an offense. Brinegar v. United States, 338 U.S. 160, 175–176, 69 S.Ct. 1302, 1310–1311; Henry v. United States, 361 U.S. 98, 102, 80 S.Ct. 168, 171. "The rule of probable cause is a practical, nontechnical conception affording the best compromise that has been found for accommodating . . . often opposing interests. Requiring more would unduly hamper law enforcement. To allow less would be to leave law-abiding citizens at the mercy of the officers' whim or caprice." Brinegar v. United States, supra. . . .

The trial court made no findings of fact in this case. The trial judge simply made a conclusory statement: "A lawful arrest has been made, and this was a search incidental to that lawful arrest." The Court of Appeals merely found "no error prejudicial to the appellant." In the Supreme Court of Ohio, Judge Zimmerman's opinion contained a narrative recital which is accurately excerpted in the dissenting opinions filed today. But, putting aside the question of whether this opinion can fairly be called the opinion of the court, such a recital in an appellate opinion is hardly the equivalent of findings made by the trier of the facts. In any event, after giving full scope to the flexibility demanded by "a recognition that conditions and circumstances vary just as do investigative and enforcement techniques," we hold that the arrest of the petitioner cannot on the record before us be squared with the demands of the Fourth and Fourteenth Amendments.

The record is meager, consisting only of the testimony of one of the arresting officers, given at the hearing on the motion to suppress. As to the officer's own knowledge of the petitioner before the arrest, the record shows no more than that the officer "had a police picture of him and knew what he looked like," and that the officer knew that the petitioner had "a record in connection with clearing house and scheme of chance." Beyond that, the officer testified only that he had "information" that he had "heard reports," that "someone specifically did relate that information," and that he "knew who that person was." There is nowhere in the record any indication of what "information" or "reports" the officer had received, or, beyond what has been set out above, from what source the "information" and "reports" had come. The officer testified that when he left the station house, "I had in mind looking for [the petitioner] in the area of East 115th Street and Beulah, stopping him if I did see him make a stop in that area." But the officer testified to nothing that would indicate that any informer had said that the petitioner could be found at that time and place. Cf. Draper v. United States. And the record does not show that the officers saw the petitioner "stop" before they arrested him, or that they saw, heard, smelled, or otherwise perceived anything else to give them ground for belief that the petitioner had acted or was then acting unlawfully.

No decision of this Court has upheld the constitutional validity of a warrantless arrest with support so scant as this record presents. The respondent relies upon Draper v. United States. But in that case the record showed that a named special employee of narcotics agents who had on numerous occasions given reliable information had told the arresting officer that the defendant, whom he described minutely, had taken up residence at a stated address and was selling narcotics to addicts in Denver. The informer further had told the officer that the defendant was going to Chicago to obtain narcotics and would be returning to Denver on one of two trains from Chicago, which event in fact took place. In complete contrast, the record in this case does not contain a single objective fact to support a belief by the officers that the petitioner was engaged in criminal activity at the time they arrested him.

An arrest without a warrant bypasses the safeguards provided by an objective predetermination of probable cause, and substitutes instead the far less reliable procedure of an after-the-event justification for the arrest or search, too likely to be subtly influenced by the familiar shortcomings of hindsight judgment. "Whether or not the requirements of reliability and particularity of the information on which an officer may act are more stringent where an arrest warrant is absent, they surely cannot be less stringent than where an arrest warrant is obtained. Otherwise, a principal incentive now existing for the procurement of arrest warrants would be destroyed." Wong Sun v. United States, 371 U.S. 471, 479–480, 83 S.Ct. 407, 413. Yet even in cases where warrants were obtained, the Court has held that the Constitution demands a greater showing of probable cause than can be found in the present record.

When the constitutional validity of an arrest is challenged, it is the function of a court to determine whether the facts available to the officers at the moment of the arrest would "warrant a man of reasonable caution in the belief" that an offense has been committed. Carroll v. United States, 267 U.S. 132, 162, 45 S.Ct. 280, 288. If the court is not informed of the facts upon which the arresting officers acted, it cannot properly discharge that function. All that the trial court was told in this case was that the officers knew what the petitioner looked like and knew that he had a previous record of arrests or convictions for violations of the clearing house law. Beyond that, the arresting officer who testified said no more than that someone (he did not say who) had told him something (he did not say what) about the petitioner. We do not hold that the officer's knowledge of the petitioner's physical appearance and previous record was either inadmissible or entirely irrelevant upon the issue of probable cause. See Brinegar v. United States, 338 U.S. 160, 172–174, 69 S.Ct. 1302, 1309–1310. But to hold that knowledge of either or both of these facts constituted probable cause would be to hold that anyone with a previous criminal record could be arrested at will.

It is possible that an informer did in fact relate information to the police officer in this case which constituted probable cause for the petitioner's arrest. But when the constitutional validity of that arrest was challenged, it was incumbent upon the prosecution to show with considerably more specificity than was shown in this case what the informer actually said, and why the officer thought the information was credible. We may assume that the officers acted in good faith in arresting the petitioner. But "good faith on the part of the arresting officers is not enough." Henry v. United States. If subjective good faith alone were the test, the protections of the Fourth Amendment would evaporate, and the people would be "secure in their persons, houses, papers, and effects," only in the discretion of the police.

Reversed. . . .

[The dissenting opinions of Justices Black, Clark and Harlan have been omitted. They were of the view that the facts found by the Ohio Supreme Court, and the inferences drawn from the testimony of the prosecution's witnesses satisfied the probable cause element.]

HILL v. CALIFORNIA

Supreme Court of the United States, 1971.
401 U.S. 797, 91 S.Ct. 1106.

MR. JUSTICE WHITE delivered the opinion of the Court.

On June 4, 1966, four armed men robbed a residence in Studio City, California. On June 5, Alfred Baum and Richard Bader were arrested for possession of narcotics; at the time of their arrest, they were driving petitioner Hill's car, and a search of the car produced property stolen in the Studio City robbery the day before. Bader and Baum both admitted taking part in the June 4 robbery, and both implicated Hill. Bader told the police that he was sharing an apartment with Hill at 9311 Sepulveda Boulevard. He also stated that the guns used in the robbery and other stolen property were in the apartment. On June 6, Baum and Bader again told the police that Hill had been involved in the June 4 robbery.

One of the investigating officers then checked official records on Hill, verifying his prior association with Bader, his age and physical description, his address, and the make of his car. The information the officer uncovered corresponded with the general descriptions by the robbery victims and the statements made by Baum and Bader.

Hill concedes that this information gave the police probable cause to arrest him, and the police undertook to do so on June 6. Four officers went to the Sepulveda Boulevard apartment, verified the address, and knocked. One of the officers testified: "The door was opened and a person who fit the description exactly of Archie Hill, as I had received it from both the cards and from Baum and Bader, answered the door. . . . We placed him under arrest for robbery."

The police had neither an arrest nor a search warrant. After arresting the man who answered the door, they asked him whether he was Hill and where the guns and stolen goods were. The arrestee replied that he was not Hill, that his name was Miller, that it was Hill's apartment and that he was waiting for Hill. He also claimed that he knew nothing about any stolen property or guns, although the police testified that an automatic pistol and a clip of ammunition were lying in plain view on a coffee table in the living room where the arrest took place. The arrestee then produced identification indicating that he was in fact Miller, but the police were unimpressed and proceeded to search the apartment—living room, bedroom, kitchen area, and bath—for a period which one officer described as "a couple of hours."

During the course of the search, the police seized several items: rent receipts and personal correspondence bearing Hill's name from a dresser drawer in the bedroom; a starter pistol, two switchblade knives, a camera and case stolen in the Studio City robbery, and two hoodmasks made from white T-shirts, all from the bedroom; a .22-caliber revolver from under the living room sofa; and two pages of petitioner Hill's diary from a bedroom dresser drawer.

On October 20, 1966, Hill was found guilty of robbery on the basis of evidence produced at the preliminary hearing and the trial. Eyewitnesses to the robbery were unable to identify Hill; the only substantial evidence of his guilt consisted of the items seized in the search of his apartment. In sustaining the admissibility of the evidence, the trial judge ruled that the arresting officers had acted in the good-faith belief that Miller was in fact Hill. * * *

Based on our own examination of the record, we find no reason to disturb either the findings of the California courts that the police had probable cause to arrest Hill and that the arresting officers had a reasonable, good-faith belief that the arrestee Miller was in fact Hill, or the conclusion that "[w]hen the police have probable cause to arrest one party, and when they reasonably mistake a second party for the first party, then the arrest of the second party is a valid arrest." The police unquestionably had probable cause to arrest Hill; they also had his address and a verified description. The mailbox at the indicated address listed Hill as the occupant of the apartment. Upon gaining entry to the apartment, they were confronted with one who fit the description of Hill received from various sources. That person claimed he was Miller, not Hill. But aliases and false identifications are not uncommon. Moreover, there was a lock on the door and Miller's explanation for his mode of entry was not convincing.[1] He also denied knowledge of firearms in the apartment although a pistol

1. Petitioner points out that the officers had no idea how Miller gained access to the Hill apartment, and asserts that it was improper for them to assume that he was lawfully there. It is undisputed that Miller was the only occupant of the apartment. One of the officers testified that there was a lock on the door and that he had asked Miller how he had gotten into the apartment; Miller made no specific reply, except to reiterate that he had come in and was waiting for Hill, the tenant.

and loaded ammunition clip were in plain view in the room.[2] The upshot was that the officers in good faith believed Miller was Hill and arrested him. They were quite wrong as it turned out, and subjective good-faith belief would not in itself justify either the arrest or the subsequent search. But sufficient probability, not certainty, is the touchstone of reasonableness under the Fourth Amendment and on the record before us the officers' mistake was understandable and the arrest a reasonable response to the situation facing them at the time.

Nor can we agree with petitioner that however valid the arrest of Miller, the subsequent search violated the Fourth Amendment. It is true that Miller was not Hill; nor did Miller have authority or control over the premises, although at the very least he was Hill's guest. But the question is not what evidence would have been admissible against Hill (or against Miller for that matter) if the police, with probable cause to arrest Miller, had arrested him in Hill's apartment and then carried out the search at issue. Here there was probable cause to arrest Hill and the police arrested Miller in Hill's apartment, reasonably believing him to be Hill. In these circumstances the police were entitled to do what the law would have allowed them to do if Miller had in fact been Hill, that is, to search incident to arrest and to seize evidence of the crime the police had probable cause to believe Hill had committed. When judged in accordance with "the factual and practical considerations of everyday life on which reasonable and prudent men, not legal technicians, act," the arrest and subsequent search were reasonable and valid under the Fourth Amendment. * * *

1. *Draper*, *Beck* and *Hill* all refer to the general standards by which the existence of probable cause is judged. Consider in connection with those cases the following additional observations in Browne v. State, 24 Wis. 2d 491, 129 N.W.2d 175, 180 (1964):

> "Probable cause to arrest refers to the quantum of evidence which would lead a reasonable man to believe that the defendant probably committed a crime. While the standard is objective . . it is not necessary that the evidence be sufficient to prove ultimate guilt beyond a reasonable doubt or even that it be sufficient to

2. Petitioner also claims that it was unreasonable for the officers to disregard Miller's proffered identification. However, Miller's answer to the question about firearms could reasonably be regarded as evasive, and his subsequent production of identification as therefore entitled to little weight. Petitioner stresses that Miller was subsequently booked in his own name when taken to the station house, arguing that this demonstrates that the officers' belief that Miller was Hill was unreasonable. However, the trial judge found that the arresting officer was not responsible for the booking procedures under which Miller would be booked under whatever name he gave at the station house. This conclusion is buttressed by the fact that Miller was not released from custody for a day and a half, after a thorough check of his identification revealed that he had in fact told the truth about his identity, despite his evasiveness in dealing with the officers at the apartment.

> prove that guilt is more probable than not. It is only necessary that the information lead a reasonable officer to believe that guilt is more than a possibility."

Also consider this judicial language:

> "Probable cause . . . is to be viewed from the vantage point of a prudent, reasonable cautious police officer on the scene at the time of the arrest, guided by his experience and training. . . It is 'a plastic concept whose existence depends on the facts and circumstances of the particular case' . . . Because of the kaleidoscopic myriad that goes into the probable cause mix 'seldom does a decision in one case handily dispose of the next' . . . It is however, the totality of these facts and circumstances which is the relevant consideration. . . . Viewed singly these factors may not be dispositive, yet when viewed in unison the puzzle may fit." United States v. Davis, 458 F.2d 819, 821 (D.C.Cir. 1972).

See Davis v. United States, 409 F.2d 458, 460 (D.C.Cir. 1969) ("conduct innocent in the eyes of the untrained may carry entirely different 'messages' to the experienced or trained observer").

> "Probable cause to arrest refers to that quantum of evidence which would lead a reasonable man to believe that the defendant probably committed a crime. While the standard is objective . . . it is not necessary that the evidence be sufficient to prove ultimate guilt beyond a reasonable doubt or even that it be sufficient to prove that guilt is more probable than not. It is only necessary that the information lead a reasonable officer to believe that guilt is more than a possibility." Browne v. State, 24 Wis.2d 491, 129 N.W.2d 175, 180 (1964).

In Houser v. Geary, 465 F.2d 193, 196 (9th Cir. 1972), with respect to mistaken inferences as the basis for police action, the court held that "These inferences might be wrong in fact, but they are . . . more reasonable than not, and that is enough for probable cause".

2. Assuming that it is permissible for the police to *ask* questions of citizens, United States v. Brown, 436 F.2d 702 (9th Cir. 1970), it is clear that the citizen does not have to *answer* them. Lloyd v. Douglas, 313 F. Supp. 1364 (S.D.Iowa 1970). A citizen's refusal to answer does not give rise to probable cause to arrest, but if he does answer and his answers are evasive, contradictory or patently false they may be considered as elements contributing to the existence of probable cause. In *Hill,* the Court thought the suspect's evasive answers helped the police to establish probable cause to arrest. Consider the following situation in People v. Rosemond, 26 N.Y.2d 101, 257 N.E.2d 23 (1970):

> On January 4, 1966, while on a motor patrol, a policeman observed defendant and another man enter, empty-handed, an apartment building at 102 Patchen Avenue, Brooklyn. This was at 12:10 p. m. The patrol continued around the block and came back to the Patchen Avenue address a short time later.
>
> At this time the officer saw defendant and his companion coming out of the building, one carrying a plaid zippered suitcase, the other a plaid plastic shopping bag. The officer followed them

until they started to enter a hallway around the corner from the place where they were first seen.

The officer testified: "At that time * * * I approached them. I asked the defendant, Rosemond, what did he have in the package. He said he didn't know."

. . .

The police can and should find out about unusual situations they see, as well as suspicious ones. It is unwise, and perhaps futile, to codify them or to prescribe them precisely in advance as a rule of law. To a very large extent what is unusual enough to call for inquiry must rest in the professional experience of the police.

But reasonable ground to suspect a felony goes forward should not be the sole criterion on which inquiry may be activitated. Nor is inquiry interdicted even though most of what it elicits may be quite innocent.

For example, men carrying a cash register out of a grocery store may very well be taking it out for repair; but they may not; and under conditions of manner and attitude difficult to lay down categorically, police would be quite warranted in finding out by asking questions.

. . .

In the background of what the police had observed immediately before the answers given would have made it perfectly manifest to anyone that a criminal enterprise was afoot.

. . .

From the moment the defendant Rosemond made the highly suggestive sort of answer that he did not know what he had in the bag he had just carried out of the house, there was reasonable ground to arrest him and his companion at least for larceny, since then the situation became clear and a larceny was probable.

See also Commonwealth v. DeFlemingue, 463 Pa. 450, 299 A.2d 246 (1973).

3. If a suspect may refuse to answer questions and his refusal to respond cannot be used to establish probable cause for arrest, what can be said of the situation of a suspect who flees when he sees the police? Consider and compare the following cases:

(a) In re Harvey, 222 Pa. Super. 222, 295 A.2d 93, 94–95 (1972):

"On January 3, 1972, Officers Roberts and Stevenson were patrolling the area of Woodstock and Norris Streets in an unmarked police vehicle. According to Officer Roberts' testimony, the officers were assigned to that area ". . . specifically to try to curb the number of gang shootings which had taken place in the area, and also the shooting of residents and bystanders to these gang activities." At approximately 8:55 p. m. the officers were proceeding west on Norris Street, approaching Woodstock Street, when they observed three young males, including appellant, going north on Woodstock from Norris. Officer Roberts testified that the police vehicle was brought to a stop and both officers approached the three males on foot "for investigation." The officer then stated that "the defendant appeared to move away from the other two boys." The officer then called to appellant, and when appellant approached the officer, appellant was pulled by his coat and belt. The officer stated that he felt an object inside appellant's left coat pocket. Officer Roberts then "frisked" appellant and seized a revolver.

. . .

"In the instant case the police officers, when seizing appellant, had no information that he was committing any illegal acts, or that he was armed and dangerous. The officers had no information that either appellant or his companions were members of a gang or were involved in a gang incident. At the time appellant was seized, there was nothing in appellant's conduct from which the officer could reasonably infer that criminal activity was afoot and that appellant was armed. Appellant's failure to immediately heed the officer's command to stop was not sufficient to justify the officer's touching and holding of appellant."

(b) People v. Siegenthaler, 7 Cal.3d 465, 499 P.2d 499, 500–02 (1972):

"The record . . . discloses that at 2:45 a. m. officers in a marked police vehicle stopped at an intersection in Los Angeles. One of the officers observed three men on foot who after looking in the direction of the vehicle, immediately ran off in the opposite direction. The officers were in a commercial area where there had been many burglaries of business establishments although they were not aware that any particular burglary had recently taken place. They nevertheless pursued the men and saw some discard objects which on examination proved to be a business-type checkbook and a checkwriter. The officers continued the pursuit and apprehended the three men, one of whom was defendant.

"The abandoned checkbook bore the name of the Ideal Brush Company at a nearby address. An investigation at that address was conducted by other officers who reported that the premises appeared to have been recently burglarized.

"Defendant was observed late at night in a commercial area where there had been a high incidence of burglaries. His only inducement to flee, insofar as appears, was the appearance of a marked police vehicle and police officers who took notice of defendant and his companions. In no way could defendant claim that the officers infringed any right which induced defendant's actions. . . . Nevertheless he fled and in doing so discarded evidence which, together with the flight and other circumstances, would necessarily lead a prudent man to conscientiously entertain a strong suspicion that defendant and his companions had committed a burglary. . . . the officers were thus armed with probable cause for his arrest. . . ."

(c) Consider the situation in which an individual indicates shock or fear upon seeing a police officer, as in McWilliams v. United States, 298 A.2d 38 (D.C.Ct.App.1972):

"Officer Daniels of the Metropolitan Police testified at the hearing on appellant's motion to suppress that on the morning of November 11, 1971, he entered Bonanza Cleaners, a dry cleaning establishment at 4309 Deane Avenue, N.E. for the purpose of using the rest room. Upon entering the men's room, located at the rear of the premises, he observed appellant, whom he had seen on other occasions and recognized as an employee, standing in front of the sink. Appellant looked at the officer in a startled manner, stepped back from the sink, and "froze". The officer then noticed a small black coin purse on the left side of the sink. He stepped toward the sink and again appellant stepped back. Officer Daniels picked up the purse and opened it. Upon observing several small packets containing a white powdery substance, he asked appellant: "What you got here?" Appellant replied: "You know." The officer then identified himself and formally placed appellant under arrest. A subsequent search of appellant's person disclosed a needle, syringe and cooker wrapped in foil in his left pants pocket.

"The officer testified that he looked into the purse only because he was "curious". He also testified that the Metropolitan Police Department has a narcotics display with a sample purse of that type and that on about ten other occasions he himself had seen similar purses used by addicts to carry their paraphernalia. * * *

"The factors cited by the Government as constituting probable cause are (1) appellant's quick looks at the officer, (2) his freezing against the wall, (3) his startled expression, and (4) the sight of a coin purse similar to those in which the officer had found narcotics in the past. While it is true that "[c]onduct innocent in the eyes of the untrained may carry entirely different 'messages' to the experienced or trained observer", we think that, under all the circumstances, probable cause was lacking. The sight of an employee standing beside a sink in his employer's rest room, who appears startled upon seeing a policeman, is not adequate justification for an arrest or a search. Additionally, Officer Daniels, by his own admission, did not have reason to believe a crime was being committed when he looked into appellant's purse and opened it only out of curiosity. We therefore conclude there was no probable cause to arrest prior to the search and, as a consequence, the search constituted a violation of appellant's rights under the Fourth Amendment."

Reversed.

4. In *Draper*, the officers relied upon the word of a proven informer. Suppose an officer is approached by an ordinary citizen who claims to have witnessed or suffered the commission of a crime. Since the officer has no prior experience with the alleged victim or witness, may he give credence to their statements? Consider the following:

(a) United States ex rel. Cardaio v. Casscles, 446 F.2d 632, 635–37 (2nd Cir. 1971):

"On June 1, 1964, the Manhattan police received information that narcotics could be found in an apartment at 31 Bedford Street, Manhattan. Lieutenant Mulligan and other officers went to that address. While they were waiting at the door of the apartment, Tod Konrad appeared. In answer to the officer's inquiry, Konrad said that he had marijuana in his apartment. He further remarked that he was "a nervous wreck" because the night before he had been "stuck up" and robbed of approximately eight pounds of marijuana. He said that one of his assailants was armed with a gun. He characterized this man as a "beatnik type of kid," with long hair, about twenty years old, whose name was Nick. He gave the officers Nick's telephone number. It was a Queens number. . . .

"Detective King ascertained that the telephone number was that of Nicholas Cardaio of 43–10 Auburndale Lane, Queens. Petitioner lived at that address, a two-family house. The other apartment in the house was occupied by petitioner's father, also named Nicholas Cardaio. It is not entirely clear whether the telephone number was that of the father or the son.

"[The police then effected a warrantless arrest of petitioner] . . . Konrad's information was first hand. It was based on his personal knowledge. He said that the marijuana had been taken from him by a robber at gunpoint. He gave the police a description of his assailant as a young man, about twenty, "a beatnik type" with long hair. He furnished his name, "Nick," and his telephone number. Investigation confirmed that the telephone was listed under the name of a "Nick", i. e., Nicholas Cardaio. When the officers arrived at the Auburndale Lane house, they inquired if "Nick" was there and were told that he was. Upon entering, they observed petitioner, who presumably conformed to Konrad's description. The fact that there was another Nicholas Cardaio, petitioner's father, at that address, is immaterial. The description obviously could not apply to the father. There is no doubt that Konrad's information led the police directly to petitioner. It was sufficient to induce a reasonable belief on their part that petitioner was the man who had committed the crime.

. . .

". . . We have found no case in which evidence of previous reliability of the informant has been thought necessary where the information comes from the person who is himself the victim of the crime about which he complains. To require such proof would create a standard impossible of attainment, as a practical matter, for, as has been pointed out:

> 'Most victims of crime are total strangers to arresting officers as are most of the persons they arrest.'

"In United States ex rel. Walls v. Mancusi, 406 F.2d 505 (2d Cir. 1969), this court found probable cause where the victim of a holdup, previously unknown to the police, told a nearby policeman of the attack and gave a description of the assailants. To be sure, the culprits were still in sight and were observed running away, thereby tending to corroborate the victim's accusation. We do not regard that fact, however, as such a vital distinction as to require a different result in the present case. In *Pendergrast,* the victim picked out the defendant from a crowd of onlookers, and defendant stoutly denied the accusation prior to his arrest. In Brown v. United States, 125 U.S.App.D.C. 43, 365 F.2d 976 (1966), information broadcast over a police radio which came from an unknown victim, reporting a robbery and giving a somewhat inaccurate description of the defendant and his automobile, was held sufficient. The court pointed out that "the victim's report has the virtue of being based on personal observation," and "is less likely to be colored by self-interest than is that of an informant."

"We hold that the police were entitled to rely upon Konrad's information and that it afforded them probable cause to arrest petitioner."

(b) A different rationale exists for establishing the reliability of named "citizen-informers" as opposed to the traditional idea of unnamed police contacts or informers who usually themselves are criminals. Information supplied to officers by the traditional police informer is not given in the spirit of a concerned citizen, but often is given in exchange for some concession, payment, or simply out of revenge against the subject. The nature of these persons and the information which they supply convey a certain impression of unreliability, and it is proper to demand that some evidence of their credibility and reliability be shown. One practical way of making such a showing is to point to accurate information which they have supplied in the past.

However, an ordinary citizen who reports a crime which has been committed in his presence, or that a crime is being or will be committed, stands on much different ground than a police informer. He is a witness to criminal activity who acts with an intent to aid the police in law enforcement because of his concern for society or for his own safety. He does not expect any gain or concession in exchange for his information. An informer of this type usually would not have more than one opportunity to supply information to the police, thereby precluding proof of his reliability by pointing to previous accurate information which he has supplied.

It would be unreasonable to demand the same showing of prior reliability in the case of such an informer as in the case of a "traditional police informer." Rather, the reliability of such a person should be evaluated from the nature of his report, his opportunity to hear and see the matters reported, and the extent to which it can be verified by independent police investigation. State v. Paszek, 50 Wis.2d 619, 184 N.W.2d 837 (1971). See also United States v. Hakler, 442 F.2d 1172, 1174–75 (9th Cir. 1971) (crime victim is presumed reliable); Brooks v. United States, 416 F.2d 1044, 1049 (5th Cir. 1969) (local law enforcement officers are reliable informants).

Consult Thompson and Starkman, The Citizen Informant Rule, 64 J. Crim.L. & C. 163 (1973).

(c) The same rule of presumed reliability applies to accomplices. See United States v. Long, 449 F.2d 288, 292–93 (8th Cir. 1971). The reason for the rule is somewhat different in accomplice cases. The courts rely on personal knowledge of the accomplice and upon the fact that he is not anonymous. The courts also consider the fact that he is making an admission against his own interest by declaring his own involvement in illegal conduct. Such an admission has been thought to be likely to be true. See United States v. Harris, 403 U.S. 573 (1971).

5. The source of information given to officers is not limited to identified citizens and anonymous police informers. In recent years the use of computer information and credit card checks have become significant. With respect to computer reports, it has been held that the police may rely upon computer reports to make arrests but that the ultimate validity of the arrest will be determined by the sufficiency of the information on which the computer report was based, i. e. whether the officer originating the report had enough information to justify an arrest. United States v. Williams, 459 F.2d 44 (9th Cir. 1972).

The credit card check problem was the subject of United States v. Wilson, 465 F.2d 1290 (7th Cir. 1972). Judge Duffy, speaking for the majority of the panel (p. 1294), said:

> "The total information available to the officers at the time of their apprehension of the defendant was the radio communique from headquarters based on a phone call from Mr. Mayhaus who asserted that he had cause to believe that a person of defendant's description possibly possessed a stolen credit card. The basis of the information possessed by Mayhaus had been supplied by the unidentified person in the American Express Division of Texaco Oil Company. With this information as the basis for their actions, the three state troopers felt justified, upon viewing a car of the description recited in the phone call and subsequent radio bulletin, in stopping the car and conducting a full search of defendant.
>
> . . . .

"We are of the opinion it is still a requirement that an informant's report be "made from direct observations and personal knowledge". United States v. Squella Avendano, 447 F.2d 575, 581 (5th Cir. 1971).

"It is obvious that Mr. Mayhaus had no personal knowledge that the credit card was stolen. His report was based on a telephone call to an unidentified person who himself could have had no personal knowledge that the card was stolen.

. . .

"We hold that the arresting officer did not have probable cause to arrest the defendant herein because the radio bulletin relied on was inadequate and the arresting officer had no independent information to corroborate the alleged facts stated in the bulletin."

"PELL, CIRCUIT JUDGE (dissenting):

". . . A known individual, the assistant manager of a truck stop where Wilson had purchased gasoline, had called the American Express Company and was informed that the card was stolen. Although the identity of the person to whom he talked at American Express is not indicated, it would do violence to reason to assume that upon the assistant manager's calling the telephone number that he had for this very purpose, some interloper would come on the line and purport to speak on behalf of the credit card issuer.

"It is at this point, it seems to me, that we must take cognizance of conditions in the present-day marketplace. We would be closing our eyes to the realities of modern commercial practices relating to the widespread use of credit cards—realities which should properly be judicially cognizable—if we were to ignore the extent of thievery and consequent abuse of credit cards. We are all familiar with the store clerk who checks a credit card number against a list prepared by a nameless clerk or an equally anonymous computer showing credit cards that are not to be honored.

"For many years we have recognized the reliability of records made in the regular course of business and have accepted such records into evidence for their truth. 28 U.S.C. § 1732. I find this no far-fetched analogy to the present situation. The assistant manager was using the established procedures for the detection of nonviable credit cards, and, as a result of the use of those procedures in the regular course of his business, he learned that the particular card had been stolen. This information was communicated through police channels with specificity regarding the possessor. Reasonable cause existed for the arrest which occurred, and the incidental search was made in part for the very purpose of locating the stolen credit card.

"Any more cumbersome procedure when coupled with the mobility of individuals misusing credit cards would mean that, for all practical purposes, the chances of apprehending the misuser would be so minimal as to be virtually nonexistent. An insistence that the "unidentified person" at the American Express Company or any other issuing company have personal knowledge of the theft would impose a condition impossible to meet."

On a re-hearing, en banc, the Court of Appeals adopted the views of Judge Pell and overruled the panel decision. 479 F.2d 936.

6. It is fairly common for several officers to participate in an investigation in such a manner that no single officer knows enough about the case to establish probable cause although the collective knowledge of the officers establishes probable cause. In this connection consider the following from State v. Stark, 288 Minn. 286, 179 N.W.2d 597, 600 (1971):

"The arresting officer was a patrolman who did not personally know all these facts but, as a matter of police routine, he had been told that defendant was wanted for robbery and he had been given the defendant's photograph. When he was given the order to arrest the defendant, it appeared that the defendant was about to flee. Defendant argues that because the arresting officer did not have sufficient knowledge or information to establish probable cause, the arrest was illegal. This is not the correct test. The test is whether the law-enforcement agency as a corporate body possessed sufficient information to establish probable cause. Smith v. United States, 123 App.D.C. 202, 358 F.2d 833; Farrow v. State, 233 Md. 526, 197 A.2d 434. In this case probable cause was established by all information possessed by police as a unit and therefore the arrest was lawful." See also United States v. Stratton, 453 F.2d 36, 37 (8th Cir. 1972); Stassi v. United States, 410 F.2d 946, 952 (5th Cir. 1969) ("The officers were working in close concert with each other and the knowledge of one of them was the knowledge of all").

7. Must the police know exactly the crime for which they arrest? Consider the following from People v. Georgev, 38 Ill.2d 165, 230 N.E.2d 851 (1967):

"We deem that the circumstances here reasonably indicated to the lone officer who stopped the defendant's car that he had probable cause to believe he was confronted with a crime other than the simple automobile regulatory violations. The auto the accused occupied was "running with fictitious plates," as the officer testified. The defendant and Cantu each claimed to have been the driver of the auto. The defendant did not have any driver's license and Cantu did not have a valid one. The officer observed rolls of coins on the floor of the auto and an adding machine on the rear seat of the car, partially covered by a coat. It was 2:00 A.M. Considering all of the circumstances surrounding the officer's encounter with the defendant and Cantu, the officer as a reasonably prudent person was justified in the belief that a crime, such as auto theft, burglary or knowing possession of stolen property, had been committed and that evidence confirming such belief could be found in the auto occupied by the defendant and Cantu. The search's validity was not impaired by the fact that the officer did not know of the specific offense that the search might disclose."

B. PROBABLE CAUSE FOR A WARRANT

SPINELLI v. UNITED STATES

Supreme Court of the United States, 1969.
393 U.S. 410, 89 S.Ct. 584.

MR. JUSTICE HARLAN delivered the opinion of the Court.

William Spinelli was convicted under 18 U.S.C. § 1952 of traveling to St. Louis, Missouri, from a nearby Illinois suburb with the intention of conducting gambling activities proscribed by Missouri law. * * * At every appropriate stage in the proceedings in the lower courts, the petitioner challenged the constitutionality of the warrant which authorized the FBI search that uncovered the evidence necessary for his conviction. * * *

Believing it desirable that the principles of [Aguilar v. Texas, 378 U.S. 108, 84 S.Ct. 1509 (1964)] should be further explicated, we granted certiorari, our writ being later limited to the question of the constitutional validity of the search and seizure. For reasons that follow we reverse.

In *Aguilar*, a search warrant had issued upon an affidavit of police officers who swore only that they had "received reliable information from a credible person and do believe" that narcotics were being illegally stored on the described premises. While recognizing that the constitutional requirement of probable cause can be satisfied by hearsay information, this Court held the affidavit inadequate for two reasons. First, the application failed to set forth any of the "underlying circumstances" necessary to enable the magistrate independently to judge of the validity of the informant's conclusion that the narcotics were where he said they were. Second, the affiant-officers did not attempt to support their claim that their informant was " 'credible' or his information 'reliable.' " The Government is, however, quite right in saying that the FBI affidavit in the present case is more ample than that in *Aguilar*. Not only does it contain a report from an anonymous informant, but it also contains a report of an independent FBI investigation which is said to corroborate the informant's tip. We are, then, required to delineate the manner in which *Aguilar*'s two-pronged test should be applied in these circumstances.

In essence, the affidavit, reproduced in full in the Appendix to this opinion, contained the following allegations:

1. The FBI had kept track of Spinelli's movements on five days during the month of August 1965. On four of these occasions, Spinelli was seen crossing one of two bridges leading from Illinois into St. Louis, Missouri, between 11 a. m. and 12:15 p. m. On four of the five days, Spinelli was also seen parking his car in a lot used by residents of an apartment house at 1108 Indian Circle Drive in

St. Louis, between 3:30 p. m. and 4:45 p. m. On one day, Spinelli was followed further and seen to enter a particular apartment in the building.

2. An FBI check with the telephone company revealed that this apartment contained two telephones listed under the name of Grace P. Hagen, and carrying the numbers WYdown 4–0029 and WYdown 4–0136.

3. The application stated that "William Spinelli is known to this affiant and to federal law enforcement agents and local law enforcement agents as a bookmaker, an associate of bookmakers, a gambler, and an associate of gamblers."

4. Finally it was stated that the FBI "has been informed by a confidential reliable informant that William Spinelli is operating a handbook and accepting wagers and disseminating wagering information by means of the telephones which have been assigned the numbers WYdown 4–0029 and WYdown 4–0136."

There can be no question that the last item mentioned, detailing the informant's tip, has a fundamental place in this warrant application. Without it, probable cause could not be established. The first two items reflect only innocent-seeming activity and data. Spinelli's travels to and from the apartment building and his entry into a particular apartment on one occasion could hardly be taken as bespeaking gambling activity; and there is surely nothing unusual about an apartment containing two separate telephones. Many a householder indulges himself in this petty luxury. Finally, the allegation that Spinelli was "known" to the affiant and to other federal and local law enforcement officers as a gambler and an associate of gamblers is but a bald and unilluminating assertion of suspicion that is entitled to no weight in appraising the magistrate's decision. Nathanson v. United States, 290 U.S. 41, 46, 54 S.Ct. 11, 12 (1933).

So much indeed the Government does not deny. Rather, following the reasoning of the Court of Appeals, the Government claims that the informant's tip gives a suspicious color to the FBI's reports detailing Spinelli's innocent-seeming conduct and that, conversely, the FBI's surveillance corroborates the informant's tip, thereby entitling it to more weight. It is true, of course, that the magistrate is obligated to render a judgment based upon a commonsense reading of the entire affidavit. United States v. Ventresca, 380 U.S. 102, 108, 85 S.Ct. 741, 745 (1964). We believe, however, that the "totality of circumstances" approach taken by the Court of Appeals paints with too broad a brush. Where, as here, the informer's tip is a necessary element in a finding of probable cause its proper weight must be determined by a more precise analysis.

The informer's report must first be measured against *Aguilar*'s standards so that its probative value can be assessed. If the tip is found inadequate under *Aguilar*, the other allegations which corroborate the information contained in the hearsay report should then be considered. At this stage as well, however, the standards enunciated in *Aguilar* must inform the magistrate's decision. He must ask: Can it fairly be said that the tip, even when certain parts of it have been corroborated by independent sources, is as trustworthy as a tip which would pass *Aguilar's* tests without independent corroboration? *Aguilar* is relevant at this stage of the inquiry as well because the tests it establishes were designed to implement the long-standing principle that probable cause must be determined by a "neutral and detached magistrate," and not by "the officer engaged in the often competitive enterprise of ferreting out crime." A magistrate cannot be said to have properly discharged his constitutional duty if he relies on an informer's tip which—even when partially corroborated—is not as reliable as one which passes *Aguilar's* requirements when standing alone.

Applying these principles to the present case, we first consider the weight to be given the informer's tip when it is considered apart from the rest of the affidavit. It is clear that a Commissioner could not credit it without abdicating his constitutional function. Though the affiant swore that his confidant was "reliable," he offered the magistrate no reason in support of this conclusion. Perhaps even more important is the fact that *Aguilar's* other test has not been satisfied. The tip does not contain a sufficient statement of the underlying circumstances from which the informer concluded that Spinelli was running a bookmaking operation. We are not told how the FBI's source received his information—it is not alleged that the informant personally observed Spinelli at work or that he had ever placed a bet with him. Moreover, if the informant came by the information indirectly, he did not explain why his sources were reliable. Compare Jaben v. United States, 381 U.S. 214, 85 S.Ct. 1365 (1965). In the absence of a statement detailing the manner in which the information was gathered, it is especially important that the tip describe the accused's criminal activity in sufficient detail so that the magistrate may know that he is relying on something more substantial than a casual rumor circulating in the underworld or an accusation based merely on an individual's general reputation.

The detail provided by the informant in Draper v. United States, 358 U.S. 307, 79 S.Ct. 329 (1959), provides a suitable benchmark. While Hereford, the FBI's informer in that case did not state the way in which he had obtained his information he reported that Draper had gone to Chicago the day before by train and that he would return to Denver by train with three ounces of heroin on one of two specified mornings. Moreover Hereford went on to describe with minute particularity the clothes that Draper would be wearing upon his arrival at the Denver station. A magistrate, when confronted with such detail, could reasonably infer that the informant had gained his information in a reliable way. Such an inference cannot be made in the present case. Here, the only facts supplied were that Spinelli was using two specified telephones and that these phones were being used in gambling operations. This meager report could easily have been obtained from an offhand remark heard at a neighborhood bar.

Nor do we believe that the patent doubts *Aguilar* raises as to the report's reliability are adequately resolved by a consideration of the allegations detailing the FBI's independent investigative efforts. At most, these allegations indicated that Spinelli could have used the telephones specified by the informant for some purpose. This cannot by itself be said to support both the inference that the informer was generally trustworthy and that he had made his charge against Spinelli on the basis of information obtained in a reliable way. Once again, *Draper* provides a relevant comparison. Independent police work in that case corroborated much more than one small detail that had been provided by the informant. There, the police, upon greeting the inbound Denver train on the second morning specified by informer Hereford, saw a man whose dress corresponded precisely to Hereford's detailed description. It was then apparent that the informant had not been fabricating his report out of whole cloth; since the report was of the sort which in common experience may be recognized as having been obtained in a reliable way, it was perfectly clear that probable cause had been established.

We conclude, then, that in the present case the informant's tip —even when corroborated to the extent indicated—was not sufficient to provide the basis for a finding of probable cause. This is not to say that the tip was so insubstantial that it could not properly have counted in the magistrate's determination. Rather, it needed some further support. When we look to the other parts of the application, however, we find nothing alleged which would permit the suspicions engendered by the informant's report to ripen into a judgment that a crime was probably being committed. As we have already seen, the allegations detailing the FBI's surveillance of Spinelli and its investigation of the telephone company records contain no suggestion of criminal conduct when taken by themselves—and they are not endowed with an aura of suspicion by virtue of the informer's tip. Nor do we find that the FBI's reports take on a sinister color when read in light of common knowledge that bookmaking is often carried on over the telephone and from premises ostensibly used by others for perfectly normal purposes. Such an argument would carry weight in a situation in which the premises contain an unusual number of telephones or abnormal activity is observed, cf. McCray v. Illinois, 386 U.S. 300, 302, 87 S.Ct. 1056, 1057 (1967), but it does not fit this case where neither of these factors is present. All that remains to be considered is the flat statement that Spinelli was "known" to the FBI and others as a gambler. But just as a simple assertion of police suspicion is not itself a sufficient basis for a magistrate's finding of probable cause, we do not believe it may be used to give additional weight to allegations that would otherwise be insufficient.

The affidavit, then, falls short of the standards set forth in *Aguilar, Draper*, and our other decisions that give content to the notion of probable cause. In holding as we have done, we do not retreat from the established propositions that only the probability, and not a prima facie showing, of criminal activity is the standard of probable cause, Beck v. Ohio, 379 U.S. 89, 96, 85 S.Ct. 223, 228 (1964); that affidavits of probable cause are tested by much less rigorous standards than those governing the admissibility of evidence at trial. McCray v. Illinois, 386 U.S. 300, 311, 87 S.Ct. 1056, 1062 (1967); that in judging probable cause issuing magistrates are not to be confined by niggardly limitations or by restrictions on the use of their common sense. United States v. Ventresca, 380 U.S. 102, 108, 85 S.Ct. 741, 745 (1964); and that their determination of probable cause should be paid great deference by reviewing courts, Jones v. United States, 362 U.S. 257, 270–271, 80 S.Ct. 725, 735–736 (1960). But we cannot sustain this warrant without diluting important safeguards that assure that the judgment of a disinterested judicial officer will interpose itself between the police and the citizenry.

The judgment of the Court of Appeals is reversed and the case is remanded to that court for further proceedings consistent with this opinion.

It is so ordered.

Reversed and remanded.

MR. JUSTICE MARSHALL took no part in the consideration or decision of this case.

APPENDIX

AFFIDAVIT IN SUPPORT OF SEARCH WARRANT.

I, Robert L. Bender, being duly sworn, depose and say that I am a Special Agent of the Federal Bureau of Investigation, and as such am authorized to make searches and seizures.

That on August 6, 1965, at approximately 11:44 a. m., William Spinelli was observed by an Agent of the Federal Bureau of Investigation driving a 1964 Ford convertible, Missouri license HC3–649, onto the Eastern approach of the Veterans Bridge leading from East St. Louis, Illinois, to St. Louis, Missouri.

That on August 11, 1965, at approximately 11:16 a. m., William Spinelli was observed by an Agent of the Federal Bureau of Investigation driving a 1964 Ford convertible, Missouri license HC3–649, onto the Eastern approach of the Eads Bridge leading from East St. Louis, Illinois, to St. Louis, Missouri.

Further, at approximately 11:18 a. m. on August 11, 1965, I observed William Spinelli driving the aforesaid Ford convertible from the Western approach of the Eads Bridge into St. Louis, Missouri.

Further, at approximately 4:40 p. m. on August 11, 1965, I observed the aforesaid Ford convertible, bearing Missouri license HC3–649, parked in a parking lot used by residents of The Chieftain Manor Apartments, approximately one block east of 1108 Indian Circle Drive.

On August 12, 1965, at approximately 12:07 p. m. William Spinelli was observed by an Agent of the Federal Bureau of Investigation driving the aforesaid 1964 Ford convertible onto the Eastern approach of the Veterans Bridge from East St. Louis, Illinois, in the direction of St. Louis, Missouri.

Further, on August 12, 1965, at approximately 3:46 p. m., I observed William Spinelli driving the aforesaid 1964 Ford convertible onto the parking lot used by the residents of The Chieftain Manor Apartments approximately one block east of 1108 Indian Circle Drive.

Further, on August 12, 1965, at approximately 3:49 p. m., William Spinelli was observed by an Agent of the Federal Bureau of Investigation entering the front entrance of the two-story apartment building located at 1108 Indian Circle Drive, this building being one of The Chieftain Manor Apartments.

On August 13, 1965, at approximately 11:08 a. m., William Spinelli was observed by an Agent of the Federal Bureau of Investigation driving the aforesaid Ford convertible onto the Eastern approach of the Eads Bridge from East St. Louis, Illinois, heading towards St. Louis, Missouri.

Further, on August 13, 1965, at approximately 11:11 a. m., I observed William Spinelli driving the aforesaid Ford convertible from the Western approach of the Eads Bridge into St. Louis, Missouri.

Further, on August 13, 1965, at approximately 3:45 p. m., I observed William Spinelli driving the aforesaid 1964 Ford convertible onto the parking area used by residents of The Chieftain Manor Apartments, said parking area being approximately one block from 1108 Indian Circle Drive.

Further, on August 13, 1965, at approximately 3:55 p. m., William Spinelli was observed by an Agent of the Federal Bureau of Investigation entering the corner apartment located on the second floor in the southwest corner, known as Apartment F, of the two-story apartment building known and numbered as 1108 Indian Circle Drive.

An August 16, 1965, at approximately 3:22 p. m., I observed William Spinelli driving the aforesaid Ford convertible onto the parking lot used by the residents of The Chieftain Manor Apartments approximately one block east of 1108 Indian Circle Drive.

Further, an Agent of the F. B. I. observed William Spinelli alight from the aforesaid Ford convertible and walk toward the apartment building located at 1108 Indian Circle Drive.

The records of the Southwestern Bell Telephone Company reflect that there are two telephones located in the southwest corner apartment on the second floor of the apartment building located at 1108 Indian Circle Drive under the name of Grace P. Hagen. The numbers listed in the Southwestern Bell Telephone Company records for the aforesaid telephones are WYdown 4–0029 and WYdown 4–0136.

William Spinelli is known to this affiant and to federal law enforcement agents and local law enforcement agents as a bookmaker, an associate of bookmakers, a gambler, and an associate of gamblers.

The Federal Bureau of Investigation has been informed by a confidential reliable informant that William Spinelli is operating a handbook and accepting wagers and disseminating wagering information by means of the telephones which have been assigned the numbers WYdown 4–0029 and WYdown 4–0136.

/s/ Robert L. Bender,
Robert L. Bender,

Special Agent Federal Bureau of Investigation.

Subscribed and sworn to before me this 18th day of August, 1965, at St. Louis, Missouri.

/s/ William R. O'Toole.

MR. JUSTICE WHITE, concurring.

An investigator's affidavit that he has seen gambling equipment being moved into a house at a specified address will support the issuance of a search warrant. The oath affirms the honesty of the statement and negatives the lie or imagination. Personal observation attests to the facts asserted—that there is gambling equipment on the premises at the named address.

But if the officer simply avers, without more, that there is gambling paraphernalia on certain premises, the warrant should not issue, even though the belief of the officer is an honest one, as evidenced by his oath, and even though the magistrate knows him to be an experienced, intelligent officer who has been reliable in the past. This much was settled in Nathanson v. United States, 290 U.S. 41, 54 S.Ct. 11 (1933), where the Court held insufficient an officer's affidavit swearing he had cause to believe that there was illegal liquor on the premises for which the warrant was sought. The unsupported assertion or belief of the officer does not satisfy the requirement of probable cause.

What is missing in *Nathanson* and like cases is a statement of the basis for the affiant's believing the facts contained in the affidavit—the good "cause" which the officer in *Nathanson* said he had. If an officer swears that there is gambling equipment at a certain address, the possibilities are (1) that he has seen the equipment; (2) that he has observed or perceived facts from which the presence of the equipment may reasonably be inferred; and (3) that he has obtained the information from someone else. If (1) is true, the affidavit is good. But in (2), the affidavit is insufficient unless the perceived facts are given, for it is the magistrate, not the officer, who is to judge the existence of probable cause. With respect to (3), where the officer's information is hearsay, no warrant should issue absent good cause for crediting that hearsay. Because an affidavit asserting, without more, the location of gambling equipment at a particular address does not claim personal observation of any of the facts by the officer, and because of the likelihood that the information came from an unidentified third party, affidavits of this type are unacceptable.

Neither should the warrant issue if the officer states that there is gambling equipment in a particular apartment and that his information comes from an informant, named or unnamed, since the honesty of the informant and the basis for his report are unknown. Nor would the missing elements be completely supplied by the officer's oath that the informant has often furnished reliable information in the past. This attests to the honesty of the informant, but Aguilar v. Texas, supra, requires something more—did the information come from observation, or did the informant in turn receive it from another? Absent additional facts for believing the informant's report, his assertion stands no better than the oath of the officer to the same effect. Indeed, if the affidavit of an officer, known by the magistrate to be honest and experienced, stating that gambling equipment is located in a certain building is unacceptable, it would be quixotic if a similar statement from an honest informant were found to furnish probable cause. A strong argument can be made that both should be acceptable under the Fourth Amendment, but under our cases neither is. The past reliability of the informant can no more furnish probable cause for believing his current report than can previous experience with the officer himself.

If the affidavit rests on hearsay—an informant's report—what is necessary under *Aguilar* is one of two things: the informant must declare either (1) that he has himself seen or perceived the fact or facts asserted; or (2) that his information is hearsay, but there is good reason for believing it—perhaps one of the usual grounds for crediting hearsay information. The first presents few problems: since the report, although hearsay, purports to be first-hand observation, remaining doubt centers on the honesty of the informant, and that worry is dissipated by the officer's previous experience with the informant. The other basis for accepting the informant's report is more complicated. But if, for example, the informer's hearsay comes from one of the actors in the crime in the nature of admission against interest, the affidavit giving this information should be held sufficient.

I am inclined to agree with the majority that there are limited special circumstances in which an "honest" informant's report, if sufficiently detailed, will in effect verify itself—that is, the magistrate when confronted with such detail could reasonably infer that the informant had gained his information in a reliable way. Detailed information may sometimes imply that the informant himself has observed the facts. Suppose an informant with whom an officer has had satisfactory experience states that there is gambling equipment in the living room of a specified apartment and describes in detail not only the equipment itself but the appointments and furnishments in the apartment. Detail like this, if true at all must rest on personal observation of either the informant or of someone else. If the latter, we know nothing of the third person's honesty or sources; he may be fabricating a wholly false report. But it is arguable that on these facts it was the informant himself who has perceived the facts, for the information reported is not usually the subject of casual day-to-day conversation. Because the informant is honest and it is probable that he has viewed the facts, there is probable cause for the issuance of a warrant.

So too in the special circumstances of Draper v. United States, 358 U.S. 307, 79 S.Ct. 329 (1959), the kind of information related by the informant is not generally sent ahead of a person's arrival in a city except to those who are intimately connected with making careful arrangements for meeting him. The informant, posited as honest, somehow had the reported facts, very likely from one of the actors in the plan, or as one of them himself. The majority's suggestion is that a warrant could have been obtained based only on the informer's report. I am inclined to agree, although it seems quite plain that if it may be so easily inferred from the affidavit that the informant has himself observed the facts or has them from an actor in the event, no possible harm could come from requiring a statement to that effect, thereby removing the difficult and recurring questions which arise in such situations.

Of course, *Draper* itself did not proceed on this basis. Instead the Court pointed out that when the officer saw a person getting off the train at the specified time, dressed and conducting himself precisely as the informant had predicted, all but the critical fact with respect to possessing narcotics had then been verified and for that reason the officer had "reasonable grounds" to believe also that Draper was carrying narcotics. Unquestionably, verification of arrival time, dress and gait reenforced the honesty of the informant—he had not reported a made up story. But if what *Draper* stands for is that the existence of the tenth and critical fact is made sufficiently probable to justify the issuance of a warrant by verifying nine other facts coming from the same source, I have my doubts about that case.

In the first place, the proposition is not that the tenth fact may be logically inferred from the other nine or that the tenth fact is usually found in conjunction with the other nine. No one would suggest that just anyone getting off the 10:30 train dressed as Draper was, with a brisk walk and carrying a zipper bag, should be arrested for carrying narcotics. The thrust of *Draper* is not that the verified facts have independent significance with respect to proof of the tenth. The argument instead relates to the reliability of the source: because an informant is right about some things, he is more probably right about other facts, usually the critical, unverified facts.

But the Court's cases have already rejected for Fourth Amendment purposes the notion that the past reliability of an officer is sufficient reason for believing his current assertions. Nor would it suffice, I suppose, if a reliable informant states there is gambling equipment in Apartment 607 and then proceeds to describe in detail Apartment 201, a description which is verified before applying for the warrant. He was right about 201, but that hardly makes him more believable about the equipment in 607. But what if he states that there are narcotics locked in a safe in Apartment 300, which is described in detail, and the apartment manager verifies everything but the contents of the safe? I doubt that the report about the narcotics is made appreciably more believable by the verification. The informant could still have gotten his information concerning the safe from others about whom nothing is known or could have inferred the presence of narcotics from circumstances which a magistrate would find unacceptable.

The tension between *Draper* and the *Nathanson-Aguilar* line of cases is evident from the course followed by the majority opinion. First, it is held that the report from a reliable informant that Spinelli is using two telephones with specified numbers to conduct a gambling business plus Spinelli's reputation in police circles as a gambler does not add up to probable cause. This is wholly consistent with *Aguilar* and *Nathanson*: the informant did not reveal whether he had personally observed the facts or heard them from another, and if the latter, no basis for crediting the hearsay was presented. Nor were the facts, as MR. JUSTICE HARLAN says, of such a nature that they normally would be obtainable only by the personal observation of the informant himself. The police, however, did not stop with the informant's report. Independently, they established the existence of two phones having the given numbers and located them in an apartment house which Spinelli was regularly frequenting away from his home. There remained little question but that Spinelli was using the phones, and it was a fair inference that the use was not for domestic but for business purposes. The informant had claimed the business involved gambling. Since his specific information about Spinelli using two phones with particular numbers had been verified, did not his allegation about gambling thereby become sufficiently more believable if the *Draper* principle is to be given any scope at all? I would think so, particularly since information from the informant which was verified was not neutral, irrelevant information but was material to proving the gambling allegation: two phones with different numbers in an apartment used away from home indicates a business use in an operation, like bookmaking, where multiple phones are needed. The *Draper* approach would reasonably justify the issuance of a warrant in this case, particularly since the police had some awareness of Spinelli's past activities. The majority, however, while seemingly embracing *Draper,* confines that case to its own facts. Pending full scale reconsideration of that case, on the one hand, or of the *Nathanson-Aguilar* cases on the other, I join the opinion of the Court and the judgment of reversal, especially since a vote to affirm would produce an equally divided Court.

MR. JUSTICE BLACK, dissenting.

In my view, this Court's decision in Aguilar v. Texas, 378 U.S. 108, 84 S.Ct. 1509 (1964) was bad enough. That decision went very far toward elevating the magistrate's hearing for issuance of a search warrant to a full-fledged trial, where witnesses must be brought forward to attest personally to all the facts alleged. But not content with this, the Court today expands *Aguilar* to almost unbelievable proportions. Of course, it would strengthen the probable cause presentation if eyewitnesses could testify that they saw the defendant commit the crime. It would be stronger still if these witnesses could explain in detail the nature of the sensual perceptions on which they based their "conclusion" that the person they had seen was the defendant and that he was responsible for the events they observed. Nothing in our Constitution, however, requires that the facts be established with that degree of certainty and with such elaborate specificity before a policeman can be authorized by a disinterested magistrate to conduct a carefully limited search.

The Fourth Amendment provides that "no warrants shall issue but upon probable cause, supported by oath or affirmation, and particularly describing the place to be searched, and the persons or things to be seized." In this case a search warrant was issued supported by an oath and particularly describing the place to be searched and the things to be seized. The supporting oath was three printed pages and the full text of it is included in an Appendix to the Court's opinion. The magistrate, I think properly, held the information set forth sufficient facts to show "probable cause" that the defendant was violating the law. Six members of the Court of Appeals also agreed that the affidavit was sufficient to show probable cause. A majority of this Court today holds, however, that the magistrate and all of these judges were wrong In doing so, they substitute their own opinion for that of the local magistrate and the circuit judges, and reject the *en banc* factual conclusion of the Eighth Circuit and reverse the judgment based upon that factual conclusion. I cannot join in any such disposition of an issue so vital to the administration of justice, and dissent as vigorously as I can.

I repeat my belief that the affidavit given the magistrate was more than ample to show probable cause of the defendant's guilt. The affidavit meticulously set out facts sufficient to show the following:

1. The defendant had been shown going to and coming from a room in an apartment which contained two telephones listed under

the name of another person. Nothing in the record indicates that the apartment was of that large and luxurious type which could only be occupied by a person to whom it would be a "petty luxury" to have two separate telephones, with different numbers, both listed under the name of a person who did not live there.

2. The defendant's car had been observed parked in the apartment's parking lot. This fact was, of course, highly relevant in showing that the defendant was extremely interested in some enterprise which was located in the apartment.

3. The FBI had been informed by a reliable informant that the defendant was accepting wagering information by telephones—the particular telephones located in the apartment the defendant had been repeatedly visiting. Unless the Court, going beyond the requirements of the Fourth Amendment, wishes to require magistrates to hold trials before issuing warrants, it is not necessary—as the Court holds—to have the affiant explain "the underlying circumstances from which the informer concluded that Spinelli was running a bookmaking operation."

4. The defendant was known by federal and local law enforcement agents as a bookmaker and an associate of gamblers. I cannot agree with the Court that this knowledge was only a "bald and unilluminating assertion of suspicion that is entitled to no weight in appraising the magistrate's decision." Although the statement is hearsay that might not be admissible in a regular trial, everyone knows, unless he shuts his eyes to the realities of life, that this is a relevant fact which, together with other circumstances, might indicate a factual probability that gambling is taking place.

The foregoing facts should be enough to constitute probable cause for anyone who does not believe that the only way to obtain a search warrant is to prove beyond a reasonable doubt that a defendant is guilty. Even *Aguilar*, on which the Court relies, cannot support the contrary result, at least as that decision was written before today's massive escalation of it. * * *

[The dissenting opinions of MR. JUSTICE FORTAS and MR. JUSTICE STEWART are omitted.]

NOTES

1. In United States v. Harris, 403 U.S. 573, 91 S.Ct. 2075 (1971), the Court sustained a search warrant based upon the following affidavit:

"Roosevelt Harris has had a reputation with me for over 4 years as being a trafficker of nontaxpaid distilled spirits, and over this period I have received numerous information [*sic*] from all types of persons as to his activities. Constable Howard Johnson located a sizeable stash of illicit whiskey in an abandoned house under Harris' control during this period of time. This date, I have received information from a person who fears for their [sic] life and property should their name be revealed. I have interviewed this person, found this person to be a prudent person, and have, under a sworn verbal statement, gained the following information: This person has personal knowledge of and has purchased illicit whiskey from within the residence described, for a period of more than 2 years, and most recently within the past two weeks, has knowledge of a person who purchased illicit whiskey within the past two days from the house, has personal knowledge that the illicit whiskey is consumed by purchasers in the out-building known as and utilized as the 'dance hall,' and has seen Roosevelt Harris go to the other outbuilding located about 50 yards from the residence, on numerous occasions, to obtain the whiskey for this person and other persons."

The Court was not in agreement why the warrant was valid. Four members of the Court (Burger, Black, Stewart and Blackmun) held that the personal and recent observations of the informant distinguished the case from Spinelli and the allegation that the informer was "prudent" presents adequate probable cause.

Four members of the Court (Burger, Black, White and Blackmun) ruled that there was a special basis for crediting the informer's tip since the informer made an admission against his own interest i. e., he admitted personal participation in the crime. "People do not lightly admit a crime and place critical evidence in the hands of the police in the form of their own admissions. Admissions of crime . . . carry their own indicia of credibility—sufficient at least to support a finding of probable cause to search".

Three members of the Court (Burger, Black and Blackmun) ruled that it was not necessary for a warrant to allege that the informant had previously given correct information and that Spinelli was wrong when it held that a magistrate could not rely upon a suspect's prior reputation for involvement in criminal activities.

Four members of the Court (Harlan, Douglas, Brennan and Marshall) dissented. The dissenters conceded that the information given by the informer was, if credible, sufficient to establish probable cause. The dissenters thought that there was insufficient grounds to establish the informer's credibility. First, the vague allegation the informer was "prudent" is not enough to establish credibility. Second the mere fact that personal knowledge is claimed is not sufficient and, although information given to the police may be so thoroughly detailed as to support a finding of reliability, the information in this case is not so detailed. [Ed. Note An example of reliance on extensive detail to establish credibility is found in State v. Perry, 59 N.J. 383, 283 A.2d 330 (1971).] Third, the informer who makes a declaration against interest should not be deemed reliable for that reason alone. Fourth, the dissenters reiterated the Spinelli rule against considering a suspect's reputation. The dissenters suggested that it would be better practice for the government to bring the informer to the magistrate who could assess his credibility for himself while still maintaining the secrecy of his identity. Alternatively, the dissenters suggested that the agent should tell the magistrate of the informer's general background, employment, personal attributes that enable him to observe and relate accurately, position in the community, reputation with others, personal connection with the suspect, or any other circumstances which suggest the probable absence of any motivation to falsify, the apparent motivation for supplying the information, the presence or absence of a criminal record or association with known criminals, and the like.

2. In State v. Appleton, 297 A.2d 363 (Me.1972) the court found the "declaration against interest" theory especially persuasive where the informer not only admitted the purchase of illegal drugs but actually turned the drugs over to the police since his "action in and of itself involved him

in the commission of a crime . . . an informant is not likely to turn over to the police such criminal evidence unless he is certain in his own mind that his story implicating the persons occupying the premises where the sale took place will withstand police scrutiny."

DAWSON v. STATE

Court of Special Appeals of Maryland, 1971.
11 Md.App. 694, 276 A.2d 680.

MOYLAN, JUDGE. The appellants, Donald Lee Dawson and Frances M. Dawson, husband and wife were convicted . . . of unlawfully maintaining a premises for the purpose of selling lottery tickets. . . .

On this appeal, they [contend] that the search warrant for their home was issued and executed without adequate probable cause having been shown to justify its issuance. . . .

The Dual Analysis of Probable Cause

The existence of probable cause to justify the issuance of either a search and seizure warrant or an arrest warrant may be predicated upon either or both of two broad categories of information—1) the direct observation of the affiant applying for the warrant (or of the affiants on supporting affidavits . . . or 2) hearsay information furnished to the affiant by someone else and then recited by the affiant in his affidavit. It is axiomatic that probable cause may be based upon the direct observation of the affiant himself. * * * It is equally well-established that probable cause may be based upon hearsay information alone and need not reflect the direct personal observation of the affiant. * * * It follows that probable cause may also be based upon a combination of direct observation and hearsay information.

Confusion somehow manages to creep into the cases, however, where the affidavit offered to support probable cause is based upon the mixed predicate of both direct observation and hearsay information. That confusion is engendered by the failure to grasp the unifying principle—to appreciate that both of the broad categories of information are evaluated by the same general standards of measurement. The apparent difference in the standards is simply one of surface application and not of theoretical significance.

Whether the information being evaluated is the direct observation of the affiant or is hearsay information, the issuing magistrate is required to perform the same intellectual surgery. In determining the existence *vel non* of probable cause, the magistrate must make two distinct determinations. The number and the nature of these determinations do not vary, whether the specimen being analyzed is direct observation or hearsay information. He must:

(1) Evaluate the truthfulness of the source of the information; and

(2) Evaluate the adequacy of the factual premises furnished by that source to support the validity of the source's conclusion.

In the first instance, he is judging the integrity of a person. In the second instance, he is judging the logic of a proposition. * * *

In evaluating the truthfulness of the source of the information, the magistrate is presented with no problem in dealing with the affiant-observer. "The oath affirms the honesty of the statement and negatives the lie or imagination." *Spinelli,* 393 U.S. at 423, 89 S.Ct. at 592 (concurring opinion by White, J.). The oath, as a trustworthiness device, establishes, *per se,* the credibility of the affiant-source and, thereby, the reliability of his directly observed information. Where the source of the information, however, is an absent, non-swearing declarant (an informant), the pathway to the establishment of that source's credibility is more circuitous. The issuing magistrate must have, as a substitute for the oath, some other reason to be persuaded of the credibility of the source of the information.

In deciding whether he is so persuaded, the magistrate must perform the same analysis whether the non-swearing source is named or unnamed.

His evaluation, in theory, will be the same in either case. The practical distinction is that in dealing with a named source, the very naming of the source and the relationship of the source to the observed information may go a long way (or even be sufficient unto itself), under the facts of a particular case, to establish the credibility of that source or the reliability of his information. * * *

Where the source of the information is unnamed, however, the method of persuading the magistrate is more involved. He must be furnished sufficient background information for him to judge for himself the credibility of the unnamed source and/or the reliability of that source's information. * * * The credibility of the person and the reliability of the information are but alternative aspects of the same trustworthiness phenomenon. To conclude that trustworthiness is probably present, the magistrate must be convinced either 1) that the source himself, as a person, is inherently honest and credible, or 2) in the absence of such proof of character of the man, that the information is furnished by that source under circumstances redolent with insurances of trustworthiness. Credibility and reliability may operate alternatively or in combination to establish probable trustworthiness.

In evaluating the credibility of different types of sources, the practical applications may vary, but the common denominator of all such decisions is that the issuing magistrate must have before him enough circumstances to be able to judge for himself the honesty of the source of the information, whether that source be an affiant, a named non-swearing informant or an unnamed non-swearing informant. The magistrate may no more accept an affiant's assertion that his source (named or unnamed) is credible in lieu of a recitation of facts from which the magistrate may draw that conclusion for himself than he may accept an affiant's assertion that the affiant himself is credible as a substitute for the affiant's taking of the oath. The concluding, in either case, is only for the magistrate.

Once the magistrate has decided that the information is trustworthy, he has still only half completed his ultimate determination. He must still decide what the information is worth. He has decided that the source is not lying; but he has not yet decided whether the source is mistaken. The magistrate's second function is now to evaluate the information which he is accepting as true and to see what probabilities emerge from that available data. Again, he may not accept the conclusion of either the affiant-observer or the non-swearing informant. He must take from either of those sources his facts and then arrive at his own conclusion as to the significance of those facts. * * *

In the case of the affiant-observer, the magistrate cannot accept the affiant's mere conclusion that "A probably committed a crime" or that "B probably contains contraband." The magistrate needs to know what the observations were so that he can conclude for himself whether that observed data persuades him that "A probably committed a crime" or that "B probably contains contraband." * * * By the same logic, the magistrate may not accept the non-sworn hearsay conclusion of even a credible informant any more than he may accept the sworn conclusion of a credible affiant-observer. * * * Again, he needs to know just what the informant saw and just what the informant heard to warrant the informant's conclusion.[1] At issue here is not the informant's credibility but the informant's thinking process—not his integrity but his ratiocination.

In applying then these tools of analysis to an application based upon a mixed predicate of direct observation and hearsay information, the issuing magistrate may, after evaluating both the trustworthiness of the source of the information and the weight and worth of the information itself, reach one of four conclusions:

(1) That the direct observation is adequate unto itself to establish probable cause; . . .

(2) That the hearsay information is adequate unto itself to establish probable cause; . . .

1. If the informant himself is offering not direct observation but hearsay twice compounded, the entire evaluation process must begin again at a second level of remoteness. The primary informant must then pass along sufficient data in sufficient detail so that the magistrate may again judge for himself 1) the credibility of the secondary informant and 2) the worth of that secondary informant's information. If, in some extreme hypothetical situation, the secondary informant should be a mere conduit for hearsay thrice compounded from a tertiary informant, the evaluation process is escalated to yet another level of remoteness and so on ad infinitum. Ultimately, the magistrate must have the benefit of someone's firsthand observation in order to evaluate the worth of the information and must have also satisfactory proof of the credibility of every person involved in the chain of transmission of the information from the initial observer to the magistrate himself.

(3) That neither the direct observation nor the hearsay information, standing alone, is adequate to establish probable cause but that the two combined do add up to the establishment of such probable cause; . . .

(4) That even the sum total of the direct observation plus the hearsay information does not establish probable cause.

The most logical procedure to follow in evaluating a warrant application is to look first at the hearsay information. If the affiant has furnished the issuing magistrate enough of the underlying circumstances to persuade the magistrate 1) that the informant is credible or his information otherwise reliable and 2) that the informant's conclusion was validly arrived at, probable cause is established. What *Spinelli* refers to as "*Aguilar*'s two-pronged test" has been met. If, on the other hand, the information furnished about the informant and the information furnished from the informant fail to pass muster by either or both of *Aguilar*'s prongs, the informant's information is still not rendered valueless. "Rather, it need[s] some further support."

In search of that "further support," the magistrate may then look to the direct observation recounted by the affiant. That direct observation may serve a dual function. As substance in its own right, it bears directly on the question of probable cause. It may also serve the ancillary and concomitant function of corroborating or verifying the hearsay information. Initially, the trustworthiness of an informant's information may not have been adequately established intrinsically because either 1) the magistrate was not persuaded that the informant was, by proven past performance or testimonials as to character, or otherwise, inherently credible or 2) the magistrate was not persuaded that the information was otherwise reliable by virtue of having been furnished under circumstances reasonably insuring trustworthiness.

The necessary trustworthiness may then be established extrinsically by the independent verification of the affiant's direct observation. If some of the significant details of the informant's story are shown to be, in fact, true, that encourages the magistrate to believe that all of the story is probably true. The Supreme Court outlined this procedure in *Spinelli:*

> "The informer's report must first be measured against *Aguilar*'s standards so that its probative value can be assessed. If the tip is found inadequate under *Aguilar*, the other allegations which corroborate the information contained in the hearsay report should then be considered. At this stage as well, however, the standards enunciated in *Aguilar* must inform the magistrate's decision. He must ask: Can it fairly be said that the tip, even when certain parts of it have been corroborated by independent sources, is as trustworthy as a tip which would pass *Aguilar*'s tests without independent corroboration?"

The Warrant in This Case

The substance of the affidavit of Detective Fyfe in support of the application for the search and seizure warrant consists of nine paragraphs. The first paragraph lists the investigative experience of Detective Fyfe and ends with his conclusion that gambling activities are being conducted at the suspected premises. Paragraphs three through nine contain the direct observations of Detective Fyfe himself. Only the second paragraph deals with the hearsay information. That paragraph contains not simply Detective Fyfe's description of the confidential informant but also the information furnished to Detective Fyfe by the confidential informant. The paragraph recites:

> "That on Thursday April 17, 1969 your affiant interviewed a confidential source of information who has given reliable information in the past relating to illegal gambling activities which has resulted in the arrest and conviction of persons arrested for illegal gambling activities and that the source is personally known to your affiant. That this source related that there was illegal gambling activities taking place at 8103 Legation Road, Hyattsville Prince George's County, Maryland by a one Donald Lee Dawson. That the source further related that the source would call telephone # 577–5197 and place horse and number bets with Donald Lee Dawson."

A moment's analysis reveals that the first sentence relates to the "credibility/reliability" prong of the *Aguilar* test and that the second and third sentences relate to the "conclusionary validity" prong of the *Aguilar* test.

In looking at the "conclusionary validity" prong first, *Aguilar* is satisfied by the recitation in this case. It is clear that the confidential informant is not passing on mere hearsay or idle rumor that he has picked up from some secondary source. He has related that he has personally called telephone number 577–5197 and has personally placed horse and number bets with the appellant. His knowledge is first hand. His facts support his conclusion. With respect to meeting this prong of the *Aguilar* test, the hearsay recitation in the case at bar is diametrically contrary to that found to be inadequate in *Spinelli*.

The information furnished by the affiant about his confidential source is more borderline, however, in meeting the "credibility/reliability" prong of the *Aguilar* test. In that the recitation includes the assertion that the informant's information in the past has resulted in the "conviction of persons arrested for illegal gambling activities," the circumstances go further to establish credibility than they did in *Spinelli*, wherein the confidential source was simply described as "a confidential reliable informant," with no further recitation cataloging any results flowing from that source's information, even in vague, general terms. * * * It may well be that the facts here recited are enough to establish the credibility of the informant. In view of the strong independent verification hereinafter to be discussed, however, it is unnecessary for the State to rely exclusively on such recitation.

Even were we to assume, arguendo, that the trustworthiness of the confidential information has not been directly established because 1) the circumstances furnished to support the informant's credibility have been not quite adequate and 2) no circumstances have been furnished to show that the information is otherwise reliable, we must now explore the third avenue to trustworthiness. We must look to the direct observations of the affiant and see whether enough verification of parts of the informant's story exists to foster the conclusion that the whole story is probably true. Our analysis of the direct observations leads us to conclude that ample verification does exist; that the confidential information is sufficiently corroborated to be as trustworthy as that information would need to be to "pass *Aguilar*'s tests without independent corroboration." In looking at "the other parts of the application," we find ample allegations "which would permit the suspicions engendered by the informant's report to ripen into a judgment that a crime was probably being committed."

A discreet surveillance was conducted on the appellant's movements for six consecutive working days—Friday, April 18, 1969, through Thursday, April 24, 1969, excluding only the intervening Sunday. The pattern of conduct that emerged strongly suggested that the appellant was a middle-echelon executive in the gambling business—a business that can conveniently accommodate both bets on the horses and bets on the day's winning number, since both wagering activities are geared to the same hourly schedule and both look to the same sporting events for the winning and losing results.

The appellant urges strongly that not one of his observed activities could not easily have been engaged in by an innocent man. That is true. It is also beside the point. What the appellant ignores is that probable cause emerges not from any single constituent activity but, rather, from the overall pattern of activities. Each fragment of conduct may communicate nothing of significance, but the broad mosaic portrays a great deal. The whole may, indeed, be greater than the sum of its parts.

In the gambling business particularly, with its sophisticated pyramidal structure, only the lower-level operatives—the street writers—are vulnerable to surveillance that may yield directly-observed illicit transactions. The management level of the gambling syndicate is generally isolated from compromising contact with the better. Even at the management level, however, each echelon of command has its own telltale pattern of activity. The patterns are distinct. One does not expect the backer, the layoff man or the office manager —except when he is careless—to carry brown paper bags or to engage in overheard conversation about a three digit number, anymore than one expects the president of a bank to stand at a teller's cage. The office manager does not behave as does the pick-up man; the backer does not behave as does the writer. If the law, in its wisdom, were not to realize this—that different levels of the pyramid display different behavioral characteristics—it would be condemning law enforcement to the frustrating and never-ending futility of merely annoying the syndicate by reeling in occasionally its little fish—the low-level attrition that is little more than a license to do business to multi-million-dollar-a-year underworld cartels.

The affiant ascertained that the appellant, less than three years before the current observations, had been arrested and convicted of gambling violations. In interpreting otherwise ambiguous conduct, a man's history of criminal activity may well be of probative force. Although, as we observed in Silbert v. State, 10 Md.App. 56, 65, 267 A.2d 770, a convicted gambler does not forever after walk through life "enveloped in probable cause," he, nevertheless, is burdened by a history that does at least lend interpretative color to otherwise ambiguous activity.

The appellant seeks to equate the sworn fact of his criminal conviction for gambling in the present affidavit with the assertion condemned in *Spinelli*, that Spinelli was "known" to the affiant there as a "bookmaker." The appellant misreads *Spinelli*. The fact that a man is "known" as a gambler could be highly relevant where a proper factual foundation is laid for either the affiant's or the informant's conclusion. What was there condemned was not the probative force and relevance of a suspect being a known gambler, but simply the bald conclusory assertion of that fact with no factual basis furnished to the magistrate in support of the assertion. The court there said:

> "All that remains to be considered is the flat statement that Spinelli was 'known' to the FBI and others as a gambler. But just as a simple assertion of police suspicion is not itself a sufficient basis for a magistrate's finding of probable cause, we do not believe it may be used to give additional weight to allegations that would otherwise be insufficient."

The unsubstantiated assertion in *Spinelli* is, therefore, in no way analogous to the sworn recitation of the appellant's criminal record in the case at bar.

The appellant—an able-bodied adult male—was observed over portions of two work weeks to be engaged in no apparent legitimate employment. There are, of course, possible innocent hypotheses to explain this. There is also the hypothesis that there was no time for other employment because the gambling business is a full-time job that permits of little or no moonlighting in the legitimate sector. The appellant's history is a relevant factor in weighing the conflicting hypotheses which might account for this, otherwise unexplained, occupational inactivity in mid-April.

The affiant ascertained that the appellant had two telephones in his residence—not two instruments but two separate lines. This is not at all unusual. Neither, however, is it the norm. The affiant also ascertained that both of those telephone lines had silent listings. This is not highly unusual; it is, nevertheless, unusual. There are again, of course, possible innocent hypotheses. In weighing the hypotheses, however, the circumstances surrounding the telephones are not to be viewed in a vacuum. When the normal telephonic capacity of a house is doubled, when steps are taken both to cloak the phones at least partially in secrecy and to keep unwanted callers off the lines, and when a man who has been convicted of gambling in the past and is currently manifesting no means of legitimate livelihood is at home in close proximity to those phones during the busy hours of a bookmaking operation—an operation carried on in large measure by telephone—a pattern begins to emerge.

Another factor was added to the equation when the affiant observed that one of the appellant's silent listings—577–5197—was picked up in the course of a September, 1966, raid on a lottery operation in College Park. It is axiomatic that different outposts of a gambling operation need to know how to establish communication with each other.

On each day of observation, the appellant was observed to purchase an Armstrong Scratch Sheet, which gives information about horses running at various tracks that day. The purchase of an Armstrong Scratch Sheet is not, of itself, illegal. It, nevertheless, reveals to the prudent and reasonable mind that the purchaser has some interest in horseraces. That interest, of course, might be simply that of a bettor. It might, on the other hand, be that of a receiver or transmitter of bets. In weighing the relative probabilities, the reasonable mind cannot ignore the number and the privacy of the appellant's telephones, the time when the appellant is near those telephones, the appellant's criminal history and the appellant's apparent lack of legitimate employment.

On each morning of observation, the appellant was observed to leave his house between 9:02 and 10:20—to wit, at 9:02, 10:00, 10:20, 9:30, 10:00 and 9:30, respectively. On each day of observation, the appellant was observed to return to his house between 11:20 a. m. and 12:06 p. m.—to wit, at 11:50, 11:20, 11:53, 12:06, 11:55 and 11:48, respectively. On each day of observation, the appellant was observed, once he had returned to his house, to remain steadfastly in that house until after 6 p. m. The affiant, whose experience and expertise in gambling investigations was amply set out in the first paragraph of the affidavit, averred that the hours between noon and 6 p. m. are those when horse and number bets can be placed and when the results of the betting become available.

On each day of observation, the appellant was observed, during his morning rounds, to stop at a number of places, including liquor stores and restaurants, for periods of no more than several minutes in duration. Except for the Armstrong Scratch Sheets, he was never observed to purchase anything from any of the stores he visited. He was never observed to eat or drink anything at any of the restaurants he visited. The conduct of the appellant on these regular morning rounds is not viewed by the prudent and reasonable mind in a vacuum, but, rather, in meaningful conjunction with all of the other known data about him recounted in the application. The brevity and the frequency of the stops and the methodical regularity of the daily regimen are classic characteristics of the pick-up man phase of a gambling operation. He picks up the "action" (money and/or lists of bets) from the previous day or evening from prearranged locations—"drops." At the same time, he delivers cash to the appropriate locations for the pay-off of yesterday's successful players.

On one of the days of observation, the appellant was observed in close association during all of the day's activities—both upon the morning rounds and in the appellant's house throughout the afternoon—with a William Abdo, who was known by the affiant to have been arrested in 1966 along with the appellant for alleged gambling violations. It is not to permit "guilt by association" to reason that one's association may, at least, lend interpretive color to otherwise ambiguous activity.

In reviewing the observations, the ultimate question for the magistrate must be What is revealed by the whole pattern of activity? In the case at bar, the various strands of observation, insubstantial unto themselves, together weave a strong web of probable guilt.

The appellant seeks to equate the independent verification in this case to that in *Spinelli.* The two situations could not be in greater contrast. On five days, Spinelli was observed to drive across a Mississippi bridge from Illinois to St. Louis, Missouri, at between 11 a. m. and 12:15 p. m. On four occasions, Spinelli was observed to arrive at a parking lot near a suspected premises at between 3:30 p. m. and 4:45 p. m. No account at all was given of his activities in the St. Louis area during the approximate four-hour interval between crossing the bridge and arriving at the parking lot. On one occasion, Spinelli was observed to enter the apartment listed to a Grace Hagen. As in the instant case, two telephones were in the Hagen apartment. Unlike the instant case, the telephones were not unlisted. In *Spinelli,* there were no observations placing Spinelli in close proximity to the telephones throughout the rush-hour period of a bookmaking operation.

In *Spinelli,* unlike the case at bar, there were no observations of the "pick-up man"—type of activity, whatsoever. In *Spinelli,* unlike the case at bar, there was no observed association with a previously arrested gambler. In *Spinelli,* unlike the case at bar, there was no daily purchase of an Armstrong Scratch Sheet to evidence some daily interest in horseraces. In *Spinelli,* unlike the case at bar, neither Spinelli's telephone number nor Grace Hagen's telephone number had been picked up in a raided gambling headquarters. In

Spinelli, unlike the case at bar, Spinelli was not a convicted gambler. The affiant's conclusion there that he was a "known" gambler failed to merit consideration because of the absence of any factual basis for that conclusion.

Finally, the confidential hearsay information in *Spinelli* was so inadequate, under *Aquilar*, as to lend no interpretative color to the direct observations. In contrast, the confidential hearsay information was very substantial and would lend significant interpretative color to the direct observations here, if any further interpretative color, indeed, were needed. The hearsay information may, of course, reinforce the direct observation just as the direct observation may reinforce the hearsay information. There is no one-way street from direct observation to hearsay information. Rather, each may simultaneously cross-fertilize and enrich the other.

The direct observation in the case at bar may well be adequate unto itself to establish probable cause for the issuance of the search warrant. It is unnecessary to decide that question, however, since the direct observation amply verified the already significant confidential hearsay information and boosted it above *Aguilar's* threshold. The trustworthiness of the informant's assertion that he placed racing bets with the appellant over one of the unlisted telephone numbers —577–5197—was clearly extrinsically established. That the combination then of 1) the verified hearsay information and 2) the direct observation, as substance in its own right, served to establish probable cause is patent. * * *

Affirmed.

NOTES

1. For cases concerning the presumed reliability of citizen informers and others, refer to the material at Note 4 in Section A (Probable Cause for Arrest) of this Chapter.

2. The *Dawson* opinion approved the technique of establishing reliability by alleging that previous information led to arrests and convictions of other persons. *Spinelli* indicated that the mere assertion that there was a "reliable informant" was insufficient. What would the result be if it were alleged that the informant "has proved reliable in the past"? See State v. Ebron, 61 N.J. 207, 294 A.2d 1 (1972) (holding that such an allegation is sufficient).

3. Frequently, police officers may have probable cause to believe that A committed a burglary, that several valuable pieces of jewelry were taken and that A resides at a certain address. Do they have probable cause to believe that the stolen articles are hidden or kept in A's *home*? Most courts adopt the principle that a suspect's own home may be searched, and also accept the principle that "evidence of [a suspect's] continued presence or, at least, of frequent visits [will mark] the premises as a logical target for a search warrant, despite . . . lack of a possessory interest in the premises" Commonwealth v. DeMasi, — Mass. —, 283 N.E.2d 845 (1972). Some courts reject this principle. See United States v. Flanigan, 423 F.2d 745

(5th Cir. 1970). The issue is not fully settled. In United States v. Barley, 458 F.2d 408 (9th Cir. 1972) the court was faced with this problem: In writing for the majority, Judge Hufstedler held:

"The affidavit in support of the search of the house is no better than the affidavit for the automobile warrant. The affidavit simply discloses that Bailey had been seen at the house and that Cochran was arrested there. No facts are recited from which it could be inferred that Bailey and Cochran were other than casual social guests at the residence. At the trial, there was no evidence that Bailey and Cochran had leased the house, but that fact was not before the issuing magistrate.

> '[A]ll data necessary to show probable cause for the issuance of a search warrant must be contained within the four corners of a written affidavit given under oath.'

"In short, there is nothing but conjecture to sustain the conclusion that the house contained the objects of the search. As we observed in United States v. Lucarz (9th Cir. 1970) 430 F.2d 1051, 1055:

> '[S]imply from the existence of probable cause to believe a suspect guilty, [it does not follow in all cases] that there is also probable cause to search his residence. If that were so, there would be no reason to distinguish search warrants from arrest warrants, and cases like Chimel v. California, . . . would make little sense.' "

In dissent, Judge Kilkenny wrote:

"The affidavit supporting the issuance of the warrant for the search of the home reveals that appellant's female co-conspirator in the bank robbery, the lady who used the large brown manila envelope to carry the money obtained in the robbery, was arrested at 2256 E. Prince Road, Tucson, Arizona. The affidavit reveals that the home had been under surveillance for some time and that appellant was observed in the premises on April 23, 1971, and at other subsequent times prior to the arrest. The affidavit clearly sets forth the joint activities of appellant and the female co-conspirator immediately prior to and at the time of the robbery. From the facts stated in the affidavit, the Magistrate could reasonably infer: (1) that appellant or his co-conspirator, or both, were occupying the premises; (2) that as occupants, they might well have concealed on the premises a portion of the fruits of the robbery or the clothing which they wore at the time; and (3) probable cause existed for the issuance of the warrant. The logic employed by our court in *Lucarz,* supra, is here of particular significance. I quote from the opinion:

" 'The affidavit demonstrated the theft of the sort of materials that one would expect to be hidden at appellant's place of residence, both because of their value and bulk.'

"The affidavit should be interpreted in a common sense and realistic manner, United States v. Ventresca, and the warrant should issue when a man of reasonable caution would be of the belief that the items to be seized were in a particular location."

4. If the police have probable cause to believe that narcotics will be at a certain premises on a certain day in the future, may the police secure a warrant prior to the time the contraband arrives and thereafter execute the warrant on the day the narcotics arrive? The Court of Appeals of New

York approved such a practice after a thorough review of the applicable decisions of other courts. The Court sustained the "anticipatory" warrant despite the existence of a state statute which required that warrants be executed as soon as possible after issuance. The Court held that another statute which provided that unexecuted warrants would become void ten days after issuance was the controlling statute and it allowed a ten-day leeway to the police for the execution of warrants. See People v. Glen, 30 N.Y.2d 252, 282 N.E.2d 614 (1972).

5. Except in cases where anticipatory warrants may be sought, probable cause for a search refers to the probability that a crime has been committed *and* the probability that the specified items related to the crime are presently at the place to be searched. Thus the failure to specify in the affidavit when the relevant observations were made may invalidate a warrant. See Dean v. State, 46 Ala.App. 365, 242 So.2d 411 (1970). The passage of time between the observations and the application for a warrant may dissipate probable cause. See People v. Wright, 367 Mich. 611, 116 N.W.2d 756 (1963) (six days before warrant issued). When the information concerns an ongoing concern rather than an isolated transaction, ordinarily there is more reason to believe that evidence will remain despite a passage in time. See United States v. Harruff, 352 F.Supp. 224 (E.D.Mich.1972) (eleven days since last observations, warrant valid because operation had been in operation for six weeks before date of last observations).

Because probable cause for arrest refers to the probability that a particular individual has committed a crime, probable cause for arrest does not grow stale. However, a due process claim may be made by a defendant who asserts that the delay in the arrest prevented him from presenting an adequate defense. See United States v. Marion, 404 U.S. 307, 92 S.Ct. 455 (1972). Actual prejudice must be established. Compare Powell v. United States, 352 F.2d 705 (D.C.Cir.1965), with Ross v. United States, 349 F.2d 210 (D.C. Cir. 1965) and Woody v. United States, 125 U.S.App.D.C. 192, 370 F.2d 214 (1966).

With further regard to the effect of delay prior to arrest, consider Powell v. United States, 122 U.S.App.D.C. 229, 352 F.2d 705 (1965):

"BASTIAN, SENIOR CIRCUIT JUDGE: Appellant is one of 102 narcotics offenders against whom one Metropolitan Police Department undercover agent, Officer Rufus Moore, filed complaints in March 1963. During a period of about seven months beginning in August 1962. Officer Moore operated undercover for the Narcotics Squad and on October 10, and 11, 1962, he observed the transactions which led to the charges against appellant. On December 18, 1962, appellant was arrested on an unrelated charge of narcotic vagrancy (of which he was later acquitted) and, on January 18, 1963, he was committed to the District of Columbia Jail upon execution of a warrant charging him with violation of his parole from incarceration for a 1958 narcotics conviction. Thus, appellant was in jail serving the remainder of his 1958 sentence when the warrant based on Officer Moore's complaint was served upon him.

"At the outset, appellant complains that even though the police case against him was complete in October 1962 he was not arrested on those charges until March 1963, and he alleges that this five-month delay was purposeful, deliberate, vexatious, arbitrary and oppressive, and that he was prejudiced thereby. The alleged prejudice, says appellant, lies in his inability to recall the events of October 10 and 11, 1962, and to obtain witnesses who could lucidly support his sole affirmative defense of alibi. * * *

"Since the period with which we are concerned, that between commission of an offense and the arrest therefor, is to some extent covered by a statute of limitations, one might think that Congress had legislatively determined the question now raised. However, the issue here is not about the outer limits of a time period in which a prosecution may be initiated but about the problem of to what extent and under what circumstances the police may delay making an arrest once they have sufficient knowledge of a crime to support the arrest of a given individual for that crime.

"We think that an accused must show two things in order to invoke an exercise of our supervisory power because of alleged basic "unfairness," resulting from claimed delay in his arrest: that there was no legitimate reason for the delay, and that he was prejudiced by the delay. Appellant bears the burden of establishing his claim, and he has not met this burden in this case. The Government says that its undercover agents would be "blown," to use the vernacular, if they came to the surface to sign complaints as soon as an offender is detected and that the Government is entitled to maintain their usefulness by delaying arrests which would reveal them as agents. We believe this position to be both sound and substantial, for the Government, as the representative of the public, has a vested interest in operating at maximum efficiency in its enforcement of the law. Public interest in the proper administration of justice permits, if indeed it does not require the rights and interests of the public to be kept as well protected and free from prejudice as is possible, so long as that protection and freedom is consistent with the rights of an accused. Use of undercover agents is a necessary and accepted police practice, and the interest of the Government in keeping an agent's identity secret for a reasonable period is a legitimate basis for delaying the arrest of an individual wrongdoer while the agent is continuing his covert investigations. . . . Our view of the instant case is that it presents neither a due process question nor a case for exercise of our supervisory powers.

"Further, since it cannot be seriously argued that the police work wholly independently of the United States Attorney's office in these matters, it would seem that the acknowledged existence of governmental discretion in deciding whether or not to prosecute a given case tends to rebut appellant's claim of right to immediate arrest. We hold that the pre-arrest delay in this case was supported by a commendably legitimate reason. The efficacy of the undercover investigation which revealed appellant as a narcotics trafficker is demonstrated by the fact that 102 arrest warrants were issued for narcotics violations from this one investigation alone. To judicially disapprove of the police practice here involved would virtually end effective enforcement of narcotics laws, for surely it is within the realm of common knowledge and common sense that uniformed or otherwise known policemen are unable to penetrate the *sub rosa* world of the narcotics peddler. Extensive, time-consuming investigations by undercover operatives, who daily risk their lives, are required to get to the retail and wholesale sources of illicit narcotics.

"Since appellant has impeached neither the necessity for nor the investigative activities of Officer Moore, he has, in our opinion, fallen short of establishing his due process claim. As we said, both the absence of a valid reason for pre-arrest delay and the fact of prejudice are necessary to raise the due process claim. Appellant's claim that when he was arrested his memory of his whereabouts on or the events of October 10 and 11, 1962, was not clear might have found some support had he so testified, but on the record here we cannot say that this human failing, standing alone, has been shown to be of constitutional dimensions.

"In [Ross v. United States, 349 F.2d 210 (1965)] the respective positions taken by the members of the sitting division were extensively canvassed. The majority view there turns finally on the lack of adequate corroboration of the testimony of the undercover police officer. See note 4 of *Ross* and (3) of the last paragraph of the majority opinion in that case. Even so, *Ross* left open yet other cases, each to turn on its own facts. A seven-month delay there was too long, the court said, but a four-month delay might not be. . . .

"Though we do not consider it necessary to our decision, it should be noted that the narcotics sales for which appellant stands convicted were made, in the presence of Officer Moore, to one Atria Harris, a special employee of the Narcotics Squad. Harris, called as a *defense* witness, corroborated Officer Moore's testimony that the sales were made by appellant on the dates in question. Further, although appellant did not testify, his alibi defense was the testimony of his sister to the effect that appellant was in New York visiting her for an approximate two-month period which encompassed the dates of the sales. Obviously, the jury chose to disbelieve appellant's sister. . . .

"Affirmed.

"J. SKELLY WRIGHT, CIRCUIT JUDGE (dissenting):

"The panel opinion in this case looks 180 degrees in the opposite direction from the panel opinion in Ross v. United States, 349 F.2d 210 (1965), decided just two months ago. Moreover, it sanctions a system of law enforcement which, in my judgment, is fraught with the danger of convicting, and branding as criminal, defenseless and innocent people. As the panel opinion shows, appellant is one of 102 alleged narcotics offenders against whom a new policeman filed complaints all at one time. The majority opinion would approve convictions predicated on the uncorroborated testimony of the undercover policeman in spite of the fact that prosecution was purposefully delayed for a period of several months during which the accused-to-be, innocent or guilty, would have no way of knowing the Government was holding a charge against him.

"The policeman in this case, Officer Moore, followed the traditional pattern of narcotics investigations made by the Metropolitan Police Force. Under this pattern, a new policeman, working undercover, goes into the street, usually with a drug addict informant, and makes cases against other drug addicts by buying capsules of heroin. Customarily, the purchases of narcotics are made from persons the police officer has never seen before in his life and may never see again during the undercover investigation. The incident, however, is entered in the undercover policeman's diary as to time, date and place of each purchase, but no description of the seller, other than possibly a nickname, is recorded. There are no pictures in the policeman's diary. The only picture of the seller is in the mind of the undercover officer.

"At the appointed time, months after the purchases of narcotics, using his diary as his prop, the undercover policeman files charges against all of the persons from whom he has made buys, in this instance 102. He then goes out on the street with other officers to find the people accused. In his search the undercover officer's primary prop is his own mental picture of the sellers. I suggest that it defies human experience for any man, particularly a new policeman, to remember and to identify with absolute conviction the particular 102 faces, as distinguished from hundreds of others, that passed through his mind, many on just one occasion, during the kaleidoscope of his months-long undercover investigation. Indulging the unlikely assumption that he can remember the 102 particular faces, to suggest that he can allocate each face to the appropriate time and place shown in his diary offends credulity.

"Viewed from the standpoint of the people the policeman identifies, the situation is even more disconcerting. There is just no way in which an accused can protect himself against the stale charge in the policeman's diary plus the policeman's mental image of him as the offender. The accused has no way of knowing, to say nothing of proving, where he was at the time and on the day the policeman says his diary shows he made a sale of narcotics to the policeman. At the close of the undercover investigation, when arrest time came, Officer Moore in this case could have walked into the Negro slum area of Washington and picked up the first 102 people he found, charged them with the 102-odd sales shown in his diary, identified them on trial, and the persons so identified would doubtless be convicted in large numbers. They would be helpless to defend themselves. The people in this subculture simply do not have desk pads and social calendars to assist them in determining where they were at a particular time many months before. They live from day to day and one day is very much like another.

"I am not suggesting, of course, that Officer Moore would accuse the first 102 people he met. I am suggesting that in this kind of grab bag operation he could make mistakes in identification, and his mistakes would very likely wind up in the Lorton Reformatory serving five-, ten- or fifteen-year sentences. This spectre apparently does not disturb the majority of this panel. I find it frightening.

"The practice of this court in narcotics delay cases has been to remand to the District Court for hearing on the reasonableness of the delay and the prejudice to the defendant. Now that the guidelines for determining reasonableness and prejudice in this type of case have been set out in *Ross*, it is particularly appropriate that the District Court be permitted to apply these guidelines to this case after a proper evidentiary record on this issue is developed. I would, therefore, remand this case to the District Court for this purpose.

"I respectfully dissent."

6. Judicial decisions on the subject of warrants have focused almost exclusively on search warrants. This situation results from the absence of any rule which requires the use of a warrant to validate an arrest. Unlike the rules governing searches, there is no requirement that arrests be made with a warrant if it is possible or practical to secure one. United States v. Miles, 468 F.2d 482 (3rd Cir. 1972). Some courts are beginning to adopt a doctrine that requires arrest warrants, absent exigent circumstances, when an officer must enter a home to make an arrest. See Dorman v. United

States, 435 F.2d 385 (D.C.Cir. 1970); Vance v. North Carolina, 432 F.2d 985 (4th Cir. 1971). See also United States v. Wixom, 460 F.2d 206 (8th Cir. 1972). One other exception to the rule that arrest warrants are unnecessary arises in those states which adhere to a common law rule that an arrest for a misdemeanor committed outside the arresting officer's presence is illegal without a warrant. By definition this rule will rarely affect cases involving serious crimes unless during a search incident to an unlawful misdemeanor arrest an officer discovers evidence of a more significant crime. When arrest warrants are issued, they must meet the same basic probable cause standards applicable to search warrants. Whitely v. Warden, 401 U.S. 560, 91 S.Ct. 1031 (1971). In a case involving issuance of an arrest warrant for a person indicted by a grand jury, one court has refused to require a showing of probable cause beyond establishing that the person has been indicted. See People v. Morreno, 491 P.2d 575 (Colo.1971).

DIGEST OF TECHNICAL WARRANT REQUIREMENTS

1. Issuance of the Warrant

Warrants may be issued only by neutral, detached judicial officers. Neither prosecutors nor police officers may issue warrants. Coolidge v. New Hampshire, 403 U.S. 443, 91 S.Ct. 2022 (1971). Under some circumstances, a court clerk may issue an arrest warrant. Shadwick v. City of Tampa, 407 U.S. 345, 92 S.Ct. 2119 (1972). It should be noted that generally speaking, only law enforcement officers may execute a warrant.

The warrant is usually applied for on a pre-printed form containing blanks for names, addresses, items to be seized, etc., and a space for setting out the facts establishing probable cause. The warrant and the affidavit (or complaint or petition) for the warrant are usually prepared on separate pieces of paper. The process of preparing papers and presenting them to a magistrate is time-consuming. In rural areas or at odd hours of the night, there may be substantial delay before a warrant can be secured. But is the warrant inextricably linked to the traditional issuance procedures?

Consider the following statutes:

Calif.Penal Code, § 1526

(a) The magistrate may, before issuing the warrant, examine on oath the person seeking the warrant and any witnesses he may produce, and must take his affidavit or their affidavits in writing, and cause same to be subscribed by the party or parties making same.

(b) In lieu of the written affidavit required in subdivision (a), the magistrate may take an oral statement under oath which shall be recorded and transcribed. The transcribed statement shall be deemed to be an affidavit for the purposes of this chapter. In such cases, the recording of the sworn oral statement and the transcribed statement shall be certified by the magistrate receiving it and shall be filed with the clerk of the court.

§ 1528

* * * (b) The magistrate may orally authorize a peace officer to sign the magistrate's name on a duplicate original warrant. A duplicate original warrant shall be deemed to be a search warrant

for the purposes of this chapter, and it shall be returned to the magistrate as provided for in Section 1537. In such cases, the magistrate shall enter on the face of the original warrant the exact time of the issuance of the warrant and shall sign and file the original warrant and the duplicate original warrant with the clerk of the court as provided for in Section 1541.

Arizona Rev.Stat., § 13–1444

A. The magistrate may, before issuing the warrant, examine on oath the person or persons, seeking the warrant, and any witnesses produced, and must take his affidavit, or their affidavits, in writing, and cause the same to be subscribed by the party or parties making the affidavit. The magistrate may also, before issuing the warrant, examine any other sworn affidavit submitted to him which sets forth facts tending to establish probable cause for the issuance of the warrant.

B. The affidavit or affidavits must set forth the facts tending to establish the grounds of the application, or probable cause for believing they exist.

C. In lieu of, or in addition to, a written affidavit, or affidavits, as provided in subsection A, the magistrate may take an oral statement under oath which shall be recorded on tape, wire, or other comparable method. This statement may be given in person to the magistrate, or by telephone, radio, or other means of electronic communication. This statement shall be deemed to be an affidavit for the purposes of issuance of a search warrant. In such cases if a recording of the sworn statement has been made, the magistrate shall direct that the statement be transcribed and certified by the magistrate and filed with the court.

§ 13–1445(c)

* * *

C. The magistrate may orally authorize a peace officer to sign the magistrate's name on a search warrant if the peace officer applying for the warrant is not in the actual physical presence of the magistrate. This warrant shall be called a duplicate original search warrant and shall be deemed a search warrant for the purposes of this chapter. In such cases, the magistrate shall cause to be made an original warrant and shall enter the exact time of issuance of the duplicate original warrant on the face of the original warrant. Upon the return of the duplicate original warrant, the magistrate shall cause the original warrant and the duplicate original warrant to be filed as provided for in § 13–1453.

The California statute has been construed to authorize the applying for, and approving of, a warrant by telephone. See People v. Aguirre, 103 Cal. Rptr. 153 (Cal.Super.Ct.App.Dept.1972). If there is an adequate technique for preserving a permanent record of the oath, the affiant's statements and the court's authorization by tape recording or court reporter, it is difficult to see any constitutional objection to telephonic search warrants. Under the Arizona and California statutes, policemen or police vehicles would simply keep a supply of blank search warrant forms. If the warrant were needed quickly, the officers would fill in the necessary information, i. e. descriptions of premises to be searched and items to be seized, call the court, state under oath the facts constituting probable cause and, if the magistrate finds sufficient facts, the officer would sign the warrant with the magistrate's name in accordance with the magistrate's directions. Would the availability of such a warrant practice alleviate the practical problems of preserving the status quo at a home or other premises while a search warrant is sought?

2. Specifying the Place to be Searched

The place to be searched must be described with particularity. In the case of a single family residence this is usually done by giving the street address. In rural areas a rural route address may be given. In some cases a map may be incorporated into the warrant or a legal description (which is the surveyor's official description) of the property may be given. See United States v. Ortiz, 311 F.Supp. 880 (D.Colo.1970). Problems arise in cases involving multiple dwellings at a specific address. See People v. Avery, 173 Colo. 315, 478 P.2d 310 (1970). Often apartments do not have numbers and they should be described by location. Even this technique presents problems, for the police may not be able to secure an accurate description of the manner in which apartments are distributed. See United States v. Higgins, 428 F.2d 232 (7th Cir. 1970) (warrant for basement apartment in a building with three basement apartments). It may be advisable for officers to identify apartments by the name of the occupant if it is known, as well as apartment number or location.

Occasionally deficiencies occur in warrant descriptions. When the affidavit or complaint for the warrant contains a complete description the courts will construe the warrant and the affidavit together as one document and sustain the warrant. Moore v. United States, 461 F.2d 1236 (D.C.Cir. 1972) (warrant for entire second floor with several apartments is saved by the affidavit which mentioned a specific apartment). But see Giles v. State, 10 Md.App. 593, 271 A.2d 766 (1970). Some law enforcement officers will draft a warrant adding the specific statement that the material contained in the affidavit is incorporated in the warrant and made a part of the warrant.

Minor errors in street address are not always fatal, if the court can conclude that only one particular place is obviously referred to in the warrant and that the officers (who may well have conducted a surveillance of the place) could not have possibly been confused about the place to be searched. State v. Brasaccia, 58 N.J. 586, 279 A.2d 675 (1971); People v. Burrell, 8 Ill.App.3d 14, 288 N.E.2d 889 (1972); United States v. Sklaroff, 323 F.Supp. 296 (S.D.Fla.1971).

3. Specifying the Items to be Seized

A warrant must specifically describe the items to be seized. A general warrant is constitutionally prohibited and a warrant which simply authorizes a search of a certain premises without specifying what is to be seized is invalid.

There is no restriction on the number and kind of items that can be seized. Contraband, fruits, instrumentalities and evidence of a crime are all subject to seizure pursuant to warrant. Warden v. Hayden, 387 U.S.

294, 87 S.Ct. 1647 (1967). There are some state statutes which preclude the seizure of "mere evidence" but this restrictive rule is declining since the Supreme Court held it was not constitutionally required and would not be applied to federal officers. Warden v. Hayden, supra.

It is clear that if, during the course of lawfully executing a warrant, the police discover seizable items not named in the warrant they may seize the items. Warden v. Hayden, 387 U.S. 294, 87 S.Ct. 1647 (1967). This sort of police practice is usually justified under the "plain view" doctrine.

In determining what kind of description is sufficient, a rule of reason applies. "Gaming apparatus" may be sufficient, People v. Reid, 315 Ill. 597, 146 N.E. 504 (Ill.1925), while "stolen tires" may be insufficient, People v. Prall, 314 Ill. 515, 145 N.E. 610 (1924), because the tires clearly can be described by reference to a brand name or perhaps even serial number. "Narcotics paraphernalia" is generally good enough. People v. Henry, 173 Colo. 523, 482 P.2d 357 (1971), but see State v. Stewart, 129 Vt. 175, 274 A.2d 500 (1971) (inadequate to authorize seizure of "contraband, to wit: regulated drugs"). Contraband generally need not be described in great detail. Steele v. United States, 267 U.S. 498 (1925); U. S. v. Sultan, 463 F.2d 1066 (2nd Cir. 1972) (warrant description of "various merchandise and assets of Sultan, Inc." is adequate).

4. Specifying When the Warrant is to be Executed

The warrant itself will usually not contain specific requirements that a warrant be executed at any particular time. There are time limits applicable to warrants but these limits are usually prescribed by statute or court rule and vary from jurisdiction to jurisdiction. See Rule 41(d), Fed. Rules of Crim.Prac. (10 days); Ill.Rev.St., 1971, Ch. 38, Section 108–6 (96 hours). A delay in executing a warrant even when the statutory time limit is met may render the search unreasonable. This occurs when the delay in execution makes it likely that the evidence may no longer be at the place to be searched. See House v. United States, 411 F.2d 725 (D.C.Cir. 1969); United States v. Hepstead, 424 F.2d 269 (9th Cir. 1970). A delay in execution of a warrant may be required where the police secure a warrant before the items to be seized have arrived at the place to be searched, i. e., the "anticipatory" warrant. People v. Glen, 30 N.Y.2d 252, 282 N.E.2d 614 (N.Y. 1972).

Some jurisdictions require that warrants be executed only in daylight hours unless special procedures are followed and the warrant specifies that nighttime execution is permissible. Among the special procedures are requirements of securing the signatures of two magistrates, of showing a need for prompt execution of the warrant, or of producing "positive" affidavits. The restrictive nighttime search rule is purely a matter of local or statutory law. See United States v. Gooding, 477 F.2d 428 (D.C.Cir.1973), affd., 94 S.Ct. 1780 (1974). It has no constitutional basis.

5. Specifying the Person to be Searched or Arrested

The warrant must describe the person as well as the premises, if a person is to be searched or arrested. Ordinarily the person is identified by his name. If a person's name is not known, his physical appearance, nickname, and place of residence or place he frequents may be used to satisfy the specificity requirement. United States v. Ferrone, 438 F.2d 381 (3rd Cir. 1971) (John Doe warrant held valid where it names a white male, stocky build, black wavy hair, at a specific address in a specific apartment.)

C. POLICE ENTRY TO EXECUTE WARRANTS OR EFFECT ARRESTS

KER v. CALIFORNIA

Supreme Court of the United States, 1963.
374 U.S. 23, 83 S.Ct. 1623.

. . . It is contended that the lawfulness of the petitioners' arrests, even if they were based upon probable cause, was vitated by the method of entry. This Court, in cases under the Fourth Amendment, has long recognized that the lawfulness of arrests for federal offenses is to be determined by reference to state law insofar as it is not violative of the Federal Constitution. Miller v. United States, 357 U.S. 301, 78 S.Ct. 1190 (1958); United States v. Di Re, 332 U.S. 581, 68 S.Ct. 222 (1948); Johnson v. United States, 333 U.S. 10, 15, n. 5, 68 S.Ct. 367, 370 (1948). *A fortiori,* the lawfulness of these arrests by state officers for state offenses is to be determined by California law. California Penal Code, § 844, permits peace officers to break into a dwelling place for the purpose of arrest after demanding admittance and explaining their purpose. Admittedly the officers did not comply with the terms of this statute since they entered quietly and without announcement, in order to prevent the destruction of contraband. The California District Court of Appeal, however, held that the circumstances here came within a judicial exception which had been engrafted upon the statute by a series of decisions, and that the noncompliance was therefore lawful.

Since the petitioners' federal constitutional protection from unreasonable searches and seizures by police officers is here to be determined by whether the search was incident to a lawful arrest, we are warranted in examining that arrest to determine whether, notwithstanding its legality under state law, the method of entering the home may offend federal constitutional standards of reasonableness and therefore vitiate the legality of an accompanying search. We find no such offensiveness on the facts here. Assuming that the officers' entry by use of a key obtained from the manager is the legal equivalent of a "breaking," see Keiningham v. United States, 109 U.S.App.D.C. 272, 276, 287 F.2d 126, 130 (1960), it has been recognized from the early common law that such breaking is permissible in executing an arrest under certain circumstances. See Wilgus, Arrest Without a Warrant, 22 Mich.L.Rev. 541, 798, 800–806 (1924). Indeed, 18 U.S.C. § 3109, dealing with the execution of search warrants by federal officers, authorizes breaking of doors in words very similar to those of the California statute, both statutes including a requirement of notice of authority and purpose. In Miller v. United States, supra, this Court held unlawful an arrest, and therefore its accompanying search, on the ground that the District of Columbia officers before entering a dwelling did not fully satisfy the requirement of disclosing their identity and purpose. The Court stated that "the lawfulness of the arrest without warrant is to be determined by reference to state law. . . . By like reasoning the validity of the arrest of petitioner is to be determined by reference to the law of the District of Columbia." The parties there conceded and the Court accepted that the criteria for testing the arrest under District of Columbia law were "substantially identical" to the requirements of § 3109. Here, however, the criteria under California law clearly include an exception to the notice requirement where exigent circumstances are present. Moreover, insofar as violation of a federal statute required the exclusion of evidence in Miller, the case is inapposite for state prosecutions, where admissibility is governed by constitutional standards. Finally, the basis of the judicial exception to the California statute, as expressed by Justice Traynor in People v. Maddox, 294 P.2d, at 9, effectively answers the petitioners' contention:

> "It must be borne in mind that the primary purpose of the constitutional guarantees is to prevent unreasonable invasions of the security of the people in their persons, houses, papers, and effects, and when an officer has reasonable cause to enter a dwelling to make an arrest and as an incident to that arrest is authorized to make a reasonable search, his entry and his search are not unreasonable. Suspects have no constitutional right to destroy or dispose of evidence, and no basic constitutional guarantees are violated because an officer succeeds in getting to a place where he is entitled to be more quickly than he would, had he complied with section 844. Moreover, since the demand and explanation requirements of section 844 are a codification of the common law, they may reasonably be interpreted as limited by the common law rules that compliance is not required if the officer's peril would have been increased or the arrest frustrated had he demanded entrance and stated his purpose. Read v. Case, 4 Conn. 166, 170 [10 Am.Dec. 110]; see Restatement, Torts, § 206, comment d. Without the benefit of hindsight and ordinarily on the spur of the moment, the officer must decide these questions in the first instance."

No such exigent circumstances as would authorize noncompliance with the California statute were argued in Miller, and the Court expressly refrained from discussing the question, citing the Maddox case without disapproval.[1] Here justification for the officers' failure

1. Nor has the Court rejected the proposition that noncompliance may be reasonable in exigent circumstances subsequent to Miller. In Wong Sun v. United States, 371 U.S. 471, 83 S.Ct. 407 (1963), the Court held that federal officers had not complied with § 3109 in executing an arrest. There the Court noted that in Miller it had reserved the question of an exception in exigent circumstances and stated that "[h]ere, as in Miller, the Government claims no extraordinary circumstances—such as the imminent de-

to give notice is uniquely present. In addition to the officers' belief that Ker was in possession of narcotics, which could be quickly and easily destroyed, Ker's furtive conduct in eluding them shortly before the arrest was ground for the belief that he might well have been expecting the police.[2] We therefore hold that in the particular circumstances of this case the officers' method of entry, sanctioned by the law of California, was not unreasonable under the standards of the Fourth Amendment as applied to the States through the Fourteenth Amendment. . . .

MR. JUSTICE BRENNAN, with whom THE CHIEF JUSTICE, MR. JUSTICE DOUGLAS and MR. JUSTICE GOLDBERG join [dissenting].

. . .

Even if probable cause exists for the arrest of a person within, the Fourth Amendment is violated by an unannounced police intrusion into a private home, with or without an arrest warrant, except (1) where the persons within already know of the officers' authority and purpose, or (2) where the officers are justified in the belief that persons within are in imminent peril of bodily harm, or (3) where those within, made aware of the presence of someone outside (because, for example, there has been a knock at the door), are then engaged in activity which justifies the officers in the belief that an escape or the destruction of evidence is being attempted.

I.

It was firmly established long before the adoption of the Bill of Rights that the fundamental liberty of the individual includes protection against unannounced police entries. "[T]he Fourth Amendment did but embody a principle of English liberty, a principle old, yet newly won, that finds another expression in the maxim 'every man's home is his castle.'" Fraenkel, Concerning Searches and Seizures, 34 Harv.L.Rev. 361, 365 (1921); Frank v. Maryland, 359 U.S. 360, 376–382, 79 S.Ct. 804, 813–817 (dissenting opinion). As early as Semayne's Case, 5 Co.Rep. 91a, 91b, 77 Eng.Rep. 194, 195 (1603), it was declared that "[i]n all cases when the King is party, the sheriff (if the doors be not open) may break the party's house, either to arrest him, or to do other execution of the K[ing]'s process, if otherwise he cannot enter. *But before he breaks it, he ought to*

struction of vital evidence, or the need to rescue a victim in peril— . . . which excused the officer's failure truthfully to state his mission before he broke in."

2. A search of the record with the aid of hindsight may lend some support to the conclusion that, contra the reasonable belief of the officers, petitioners may not have been prepared for an imminent visit from the police. It goes without saying that in determining the lawfulness of entry and the existence of probable cause we may concern ourselves only with what the officers had reason to believe *at the time of their entry.* Johnson v. United States, 333 U.S. 10, 17, 68 S.Ct. 367, 370–371 (1948). As the Court said in United States v. Di Re, 332 U.S. 581, 595, 68 S.Ct. 222 (1948), "a search is not to be made legal by what it turns up. In law it is good *or bad* when it starts and does not change character from" what is dug up subsequently. (Emphasis added.)

signify the cause of his coming, and to make request to open doors . . . .." (Emphasis supplied.) Over a century later the leading commentators upon the English criminal law affirmed the continuing vitality of that principle. 1 Hale, Pleas of the Crown (1736), 583; see also 2 Hawkins, Pleas of the Crown (6th ed. 1787), c. 14, § 1; Foster, Crown Law (1762), 320–321. Perhaps its most emphatic confirmation was supplied only 35 years before the ratification of the Bill of Rights. In Curtis' Case, Fost. 135, 168 Eng.Rep. 67, decided in 1756, the defendant, on trial for the murder of a Crown officer who was attempting an entry to serve an arrest warrant, pleaded that because the officer had failed adequately to announce himself and his mission before breaking the doors, forceful resistance to his entry was justified and the killing was therefore justifiable homicide. In recognizing the defense the court repeated the principle that "peace-officers, having a legal warrant to arrest for a breach of the peace, may break open doors, *after having demanded admittance and given due notice of their warrant*"; the court continued that "no precise form of words is required in a case of this kind" because "[i]t is sufficient that the party hath notice, that the officer cometh not as a mere trespasser, but claiming to act under a proper authority . . . .." Fost., at 136–137, 168 Eng.Rep., at 68. (Emphasis supplied.) The principle was again confirmed not long after the Fourth Amendment became part of our Constitution. Abbott, C. J., said in Launock v. Brown, 2 B. & Ald. 592, 593–594, 106 Eng.Rep. 482, 483 (1819):

> ". . . I am clearly of opinion that, in the case of a misdemeanour, such previous demand is requisite . . . It is reasonable that the law should be so; for if no previous demand is made, how is it possible for a party to know what the object of the person breaking open the door may be? He has a right to consider it as an aggression on his private property, which he will be justified in resisting to the utmost."

The protections of individual freedom carried into the Fourth Amendment, undoubtedly included this firmly established requirement of an announcement by police officers of purpose and authority before breaking into an individual's home. The requirement is no mere procedural nicety or formality attendent upon the service of a warrant. Decisions in both the federal and state courts have recognized, as did the English courts, that the requirement is of the essence of the substantive protections which safeguard individual liberty. The Court of Appeals for the District of Columbia Circuit has said:

> ". . . there is no division of opinion among the learned authors . . . that even where an officer may have power to break open a door without a warrant, he cannot lawfully do so unless he first notifies the occupants as to the purpose of his demand for entry." Accarino v. United States, 179 F.2d 456, 462.

Similarly, the Supreme Judicial Court of Massachusetts declared in 1852:

> "The maxim of law that every man's house is his castle . . . has not the effect to restrain an officer of the law from breaking and entering a dwelling-house for the purpose of serving a criminal process upon the occupant. In such case the house of the party is no sanctuary for him, and the same may be forcibly entered by such officer after a proper notification of the purpose of the entry, and a demand upon the inmates to open the house, and a refusal by them to do so." Barnard v. Bartlett, 10 Cush. (Mass.) 501, 502–503; cf. State v. Smith, 1 N.H. 346.

Courts of the frontier States also enforced the requirement. For example, Tennessee's high court recognized that a police officer might break into a home to serve an arrest warrant only "after, demand for admittance and notice of his purpose," McCaslin v. McCord, 116 Tenn. 690, 708, 94 S.W. 79, 83; cf. Hawkins v. Commonwealth, 14 B.Mon. (53 Ky.) 395. Indeed, a majority of the States have enacted the requirement in statutes substantially similar to California Penal Code § 844 and the federal statute, 18 U.S.C. § 3109.

Moreover, in addition to carrying forward the protections already afforded by English law, the Framers also meant by the Fourth Amendment to eliminate once and for all the odious practice of searches under general warrants and writs of assistance against which English law had generally left them helpless. The colonial experience under the writs was unmistakably "fresh in the memories of those who achieved our independence and established our form of government." The problem of entry under a general warrant was not, of course, exactly that of unannounced intrusion to arrest with a warrant or upon probable cause, but the two practices clearly invited common abuses. One of the grounds of James Otis' eloquent indictment of the writs bears repetition here:

> "Now one of the most essential branches of English liberty is the freedom of one's house. A man's house is his castle; and whilst he is quiet he is as well guarded as a prince in his castle. This writ, if it should be declared legal, would totally annihilate this privilege. Custom-house officers may enter our houses when they please; we are commanded to permit their entry. Their menial servants may enter, may break locks, bars, and everything in their way: and whether they break through malice or revenge, no man, no court, can inquire. Bare suspicion without oath is sufficient." Tudor, Life of James Otis (1823), 66–67.

Similar, if not the same, dangers to individual liberty are involved in unannounced intrusions of the police into the homes of citizens. Indeed in two respects such intrusions are even more offensive to the sanctity and privacy of the home. In the first place service of the general warrants and writs of assistance was usually preceded at least by some form of notice or demand for admission. In the second place the writs of assistance by their very terms might be served only during daylight hours. By significant contrast, the unannounced entry of the Ker apartment occurred after dark, and such timing appears to be common police practice, at least in California.

It is much too late in the day to deny that a lawful entry is as essential to vindication of the protections of the Fourth Amendment as, for example, probable cause to arrest or a search warrant for a search not incidental to an arrest. This Court settled in Gouled v. United States, 255 U.S. 298, 305–306, 41 S.Ct. 261, 263, that a lawful entry is the indispensable predicate of a reasonable search. We held there that a search would violate the Fourth Amendment if the entry were illegal whether accomplished "by force or by an illegal threat or show of force" or "obtained by stealth instead of by force or coercion." Similarly, rigid restrictions upon unannounced entries are essential if the Fourth Amendment's prohibition against invasion of the security and privacy of the home is to have any meaning.

It is true, of course, that the only decision of this Court which forbids federal officers to arrest and search after an unannounced entry, Miller v. United States, did not rest upon constitutional doctrine but rather upon an exercise of this Court's supervisory powers. But that disposition in no way implied that the same result was not compelled by the Fourth Amendment. Miller is simply an instance of the usual practice of the Court not to decide constitutional questions when a nonconstitutional basis for decision is available. The result there drew upon analogy to a federal statute, similar in its terms to § 844, with which the federal officers concededly had not complied in entering to make an arrest. Nothing we said in Miller so much as intimated that, without such a basis for decision, the Fourth Amendment would not have required the same result. The implication, indeed, is quite to the contrary. For the history adduced in Miller in support of the nonconstitutional ground persuasively demonstrates that the Fourth Amendment's protections include the security of the householder against unannounced invasions by the police.

II.

The command of the Fourth Amendment reflects the lesson of history that "the breaking an outer door is, in general, so violent, obnoxious and dangerous a proceeding, that it should be adopted only in extreme cases, where an immediate arrest is requisite." 1 Burn, Justice of the Peace (28th ed. 1837), 275–276.

I have found no English decision which clearly recognizes any exception to the requirement that the police first give notice of their authority and purpose before forcibly entering a home. Exceptions were early sanctioned in American cases, e. g., Read v. Case, 4 Conn. 166, but these were rigidly and narrowly confined to situations not within the reason and spirit of the general requirement. Specifically, exceptional circumstances have been thought to exist only when, as one element, the facts surrounding the particular entry support a finding that those within actually knew or must have known of the officer's presence and purpose to seek admission. For example, the earliest exception seems to have been that "[i]n the case of an *escape* after arrest, the officer, on fresh pursuit of the offender to a house in which he takes refuge, may break the doors to recapture him, in the case of felony, without a warrant, and without notice or demand for admission to the house of the offender." Wilgus, Arrest Without a Warrant, 22 Mich.L.Rev. 541, 798, 804 (1924). The rationale of such an exception is clear, and serves to underscore the consistency and the purpose of the general requirement of notice: Where such circumstances as an escape and hot pursuit by the arresting officer leave no doubt that the fleeing felon is aware of the officer's presence and purpose, pausing at the threshold to make the ordinarily requisite announcement and demand would be a superfluous act which the law does not require. But no exceptions have heretofore permitted unannounced entries in the absence of such awareness on the part of the occupants—unless possibly where the officers are justified in the belief that someone within is in immediate danger of bodily harm.

Two reasons rooted in the Constitution clearly compel the courts to refuse to recognize exceptions in other situations when there is no showing that those within were or had been made aware of the officers' presence. The first is that any exception not requiring a showing of such awareness necessarily implies a rejection of the inviolable presumption of innocence. The excuse for failing to knock or announce the officer's mission where the occupants are oblivious to his presence can only be an almost automatic assumption that the suspect within will resist the officer's attempt to enter peacefully, or will frustrate the arrest by an attempt to escape, or will attempt to destroy whatever possibly incriminating evidence he may have. Such assumptions do obvious violence to the presumption of innocence. Indeed, the violence is compounded by another assumption, also necessarily involved, that a suspect to whom the officer first makes known his presence will further violate the law. It need hardly be said that not every suspect is in fact guilty of the offense of which he is suspected, and that not everyone who is in fact guilty will forcibly resist arrest or attempt to escape or destroy evidence.

The second reason is that in the absence of a showing of awareness by the occupants of the officers' presence and purpose, "loud noises" or "running" within would amount, ordinarily, at least, only to ambiguous conduct. Our decisions in related contexts have held that ambiguous conduct cannot form the basis for a belief of the officers that an escape or the destruction of evidence is being attempted. Wong Sun v. United States, 371 U.S. 471, 483–484, 83 S.Ct. 407, 415–416; Miller v. United States, supra.

Beyond these constitutional considerations, practical hazards of law enforcement militate strongly against any relaxation of the requirement of awareness. First, cases of mistaken identity are surely not novel in the investigation of crime. The possibility is very real that the police may be misinformed as to the name or address of a suspect, or as to other material information. That possibility is itself a good reason for holding a tight rein against judicial approval of unannounced police entries into private homes. Innocent citizens should not suffer the shock, fright or embarrassment attendant upon an unannounced police intrusion. Second, the requirement of awareness also serves to minimize the hazards of the officers' dangerous calling. We expressly recognized in Miller v. United States, supra, that compliance with the federal notice statute "is also a safeguard for the police themselves who might be mistaken for prowlers and be shot down by a fearful householder." Indeed, one of the principal objectives of the English requirement of announcement of authority and purpose was to protect the arresting officers from being shot as trespassers, ". . . for if no previous demand is made, how is it possible for a party to know what the object of the person breaking open the door may be? He has a right to consider it as an aggression on his private property, which he will be justified in resisting to the utmost." Launock v. Brown, 2 B. & Ald. 592, 594, 106 Eng.Rep. 482, 483 (1819).

These compelling considerations underlie the constitutional barrier against recognition of exceptions not predicated on knowledge or awareness of the officers' presence. State and federal officers have the common obligation to respect this basic constitutional limitation upon their police activities. I reject the contention that the courts, in enforcing such respect on the part of all officers, state or federal, create serious obstacles to effective law enforcement. Federal officers have operated for five years under the Miller rule with no discernible impairment of their ability to make effective arrests and obtain important narcotics convictions. Even if it were true that state and city police are generally less experienced or less resourceful than their federal counterparts (and the experience of the very police force involved in this case, under California's general exclusionary rule adopted judicially in 1955, goes very far toward refuting any such suggestion), the Fourth Amendment's protections against unlawful search and seizure do not contract or expand depending upon the relative experience and resourcefulness of different groups of law-enforcement officers. When we declared in Mapp that, because the rights of the Fourth Amendment were of no lesser dignity than those of the other liberties of the Bill of Rights absorbed in the Fourteenth, " . . . we can no longer permit [them] to be revocable at the whim of any police officer who, in the name of law enforcement itself, chooses to suspend [their] enjoyment"—I thought by these words we had laid to rest the very problems of constitutional dissonance which I fear the present case so soon revives.

III.

I turn now to my reasons for believing that the arrests of these petitioners were illegal. My BROTHER CLARK apparently recognizes that the element of the Kers' prior awareness of the officers' presence was essential, or at least highly relevant, to the validity of the officers' unannounced entry into the Ker apartment, for he says "Ker's furtive conduct in eluding them shortly before the arrest was ground for the belief that he *might well have been* expecting the police." (Emphasis supplied.) But the test under the "fresh pursuit" exception which my BROTHER CLARK apparently seeks to invoke depends not, of course, upon mere conjecture whether those within "might well have been" expecting the police, but upon whether there is evidence which shows that the occupants were in fact aware that the police were about to visit them. That the Kers were wholly oblivious to the officers' presence is the only possible inference on the uncontradicted facts; the "fresh pursuit" exception is therefore clearly unavailable. When the officers let themselves in with the passkey, "proceeding quietly," as my BROTHER CLARK says, George Ker was sitting in his living room reading a newspaper, and his wife was busy in the kitchen. The marijuana, moreover, was in full view on the top of the kitchen sink. More convincing evidence of the complete unawareness of an imminent police visit can hardly be imagined. Indeed, even the conjecture that the Kers "might well have been expecting the police" has no support in the record. That conjecture is made to rest entirely upon the unexplained U-turn made by Ker's car when the officers lost him after the rendezvous at the oil fields. But surely the U-turn must be disregarded as wholly ambiguous conduct; there is absolutely no proof that the driver of the Ker car knew that the officers were following it.

My BROTHER CLARK invokes chiefly, however, the exception allowing an unannounced entry when officers have reason to believe that someone within is attempting to destroy evidence. But the minimal conditions for the application of that exception are not present in this case. On the uncontradicted record, not only were the Kers completely unaware of the officers' presence, but, again on the uncontradicted record, there was absolutely no activity within the apartment to justify the officers in the belief that anyone within was attempting to destroy evidence. Plainly enough, the Kers left the marijuana in full view on top of the sink because they were wholly oblivious that the police were on their trail. My BROTHER CLARK recognizes that there is no evidence whatever of activity in the apartment, and is thus forced to find the requisite support for this element of the exception in the officers' testimony that, in their experience in the investigation of narcotics violations, *other* narcotics suspects had responded to police announcements by attempting to destroy evidence. Clearly such a basis for the exception fails to meet the requirements of the Fourth Amendment; if police experience in pursuing other narcotics suspects justified an unannounced police intrusion into a home, the Fourth Amendment would afford no protection at all.

The recognition of exceptions to great principles always creates, of course, the hazard that the exceptions will devour the rule. If mere police experience that some offenders have attempted to destroy contraband justifies unannounced entry in *any* case, and cures the total absence of evidence not only of awareness of the officers' presence but even of such an attempt in the *particular* case, I perceive no logical basis for distinguishing unannounced police entries into homes to make arrests for *any* crime involving evidence of a kind which police experience indicates might be quickly destroyed or jettisoned. Moreover, if such experience, without more, completely excuses the failure of arresting officers before entry, at any hour of the day or night, either to announce their purpose at the threshold or to ascertain that the occupant already knows of their presence, then there is likewise no logical ground for distinguishing between the stealthy manner in which the entry in this case was effected, and the more violent manner usually associated with totalitarian police of breaking down the door or smashing the lock.

My BROTHER CLARK correctly states that only when state law "is not violative of the Federal Constitution" may we defer to state law in gauging the validity of an arrest under the Fourth Amendment. Since the California law of arrest here called in question patently violates the Fourth Amendment, that law cannot constitutionally provide the basis for affirming these convictions. This is not a case of conflicting testimony pro and con the existence of the elements requisite for finding a basis for the application of the exception. I agree that we should ordinarily be constrained to accept the state fact-finder's resolution of such factual conflicts. Here, however, the facts are uncontradicted: the Kers were completely oblivious of the presence of the officers and were engaged in no activity of any kind indicating that they were attempting to destroy narcotics. Our duty then is only to decide whether the officers' testimony—that in their general experience narcotics suspects destroy evidence when forewarned of the officers' presence—satisfies the constitutional test for application of the exception. Manifestly we should hold that such testimony does not satisfy the constitutional test. The subjective judgment of the police officers cannot constitutionally be a substitute for what has always been considered a necessarily objective inquiry, namely, whether circumstances exist in the *particular* case which allow an unannounced police entry.

We have no occasion here to decide how many of the situations in which, by the exercise of our supervisory power over the conduct of federal officers, we would exclude evidence, are also situations which would require the exclusion of evidence from state criminal proceedings under the constitutional principles extended to the States by Mapp. But where the conduct effecting an arrest so clearly transgresses those rights guaranteed by the Fourth Amendment as does the conduct which brought about the arrest of these petitioners, we would surely reverse the judgment if this were a federal prosecution involving federal officers. Since our decision in Mapp has made the guarantees of the Fourteenth Amendment coextensive with those of the Fourth we should pronounce precisely the same judgment upon the conduct of these state officers.

[JUSTICE HARLAN concurred in the result of affirmance reached by JUSTICES CLARK, BLACK, STEWART, and WHITE, but he voiced a strong dissent from the view of all the Justices who were of the opinion that the federal standards of admissibility were binding on the states.]

STATE v. MITCHELL

Court of Appeals of Oregon, 1971.
6 Or.App. 378, 487 P.2d 1156.

SCHWAB, CHIEF JUDGE.

The defendants in this consolidated proceeding appeal from convictions of illegal possession of narcotics . . . * * *

The defendants were all arrested, indicted and convicted on the basis of evidence seized from a house in Portland. On April 30, 1970, four policemen arrived at the house armed with a valid search warrant.

The parties have stipulated that the police then

> "* * * knocked and opened the door all in one movement. They did not knock and wait for any period of time between the time when they knocked and opened * * * the officers identified themselves * * * after the door was opened."

The police then seized the narcotics and narcotics paraphernalia, but only after attempts were made by various defendants to hide this contraband after police entry. * * *

. . . where the existence of probable cause to search or arrest subjects privacy to invasion, the requirement furnishes a civility, particularly in an urban society, to lessen the likelihood of injury or conflict between the police and the citizen. As a civility, it is flexible in its application to the varying fact situations. It has even been suggested that, it is not of a degree of importance which requires the application of the exclusionary rule, see Kaplan, Search and Seizure: A No-Man's Land in the Criminal Law, 49 Cal.L.Rev. 475, 502 (1961), although the cases appear to be contra. . . .

The notice and refusal precondition for forcible entry has been adapted by the courts to the exigencies of this age of plentiful firearms and indoor plumbing. Landynski, Search and Seizure and the Supreme Court 166 (Johns Hopkins Press, Baltimore 1966). Traditionally, forcible entry has been allowed where "exigent circumstances" exist to justify the exception. Particularly in narcotics and gambling cases, recent cases have allowed exception to the rule as a practical necessity. Therefore, where notice would imperil the officer, facilitate escape or allow the destruction of evidence, the requirement is dispensed with. * * *

The officers' on-the-spot decision is of necessity a hasty judgment based upon the facts—or reasonably founded suspicion—of the moment. Severe judicial second-guessing is therefore inappropriate. The officer must be given a degree of latitude for good faith judgment as to his own possible peril, or as to the possibility for destruction of the evidence, fruits or instrumentalities of crime for which he is obliged to search. If the decision is reasonable under the "exigent circumstances," the entry is valid.

The exigencies of narcotics and gambling prosecutions have led to two types of treatment. In New York, it has been held by the Court of Appeals that, under their procedure, the issuing magistrate may actually "take judicial notice that [gambling paraphernalia] is easily secreted or destroyed if persons unlawfully in the possession thereof are notified in advance that the premises are to be searched." Thus, officers may be magisterially authorized to forcibly enter without announcement in any gambling case. People v. De Lago, 16 N.Y.2d 289, 266 N.Y.S.2d 353, 356, 213 N.E.2d 659, 661 (1965), cert. denied 383 U.S. 963, 86 S.Ct. 1235, 16 L.Ed.2d 305 (1966).

On the other hand, California has declined to allow a blanket exception to the requirement in all narcotics cases. See People v. Gastelo, 67 Cal.2d 586, 63 Cal.Rptr. 10, 432 P.2d 706 (1967). In the latter case, for no reason of record, officers entered surreptitiously and arrested defendant while she was asleep in her bed. The court held that: " * * * Just as the police must have sufficiently particular reason to enter at all, so must they have some particular reason to enter in the manner chosen * * *." * * *

What constitutes "exigent circumstances" is discussed in more detail, and we think well stated, in State v. Clarke et al., 242 So.2d 791 (DCA, Fla.App., filed July 1970). These, stated in substance, are:

(1) Where the person within already knows of the officer's authority and purpose; (2) where the officer is justified in the belief that the persons within are in imminent peril of bodily harm; (3) where the officer's peril would have been increased had he demanded entrance and stated the purpose; (4) where those within, made aware of the presence of someone outside, are engaged in activities which justify the officer in the belief that an escape or destruction of evidence is being attempted; or (5) where evidence would be destroyed if the officer announced his presence.

The remaining question with regard to the search is whether or not "exigent circumstances" existed in the cases at hand which justified the officers' entry without first giving notice of their authority and purpose. We hold that there was such an "exigent circumstance." Each case must necessarily be decided on its merits. Here the officers, having observed the crime of illegal possession of an easily-disposable quantity of marihuana, had good cause to believe that unannounced entry was necessary to prevent the destruction of the

evidence. Narcotics, particularly in the small amount the officers believed they could see through the window, are easily disposable by swallowing or through use of plumbing. Announcement and disclosure of purpose might well only have assisted the defendants in disposing of the goods seized. There is no constitutional right to time in which to dispose of evidence. Subsequent evidence proved that the officers' fears were well warranted—the defendants attempted to dispose of the evidence even after the officers had made their entry.
* * *

NOTE

The Colorado Supreme Court adopted a position similar to that espoused in Mitchell, holding that notice of entry is not required where "such notice is likely to result in the evidence subject to seizure being easily or quickly destroyed or disposed of," which is true in every case involving a search for narcotics. People v. Lujan, 484 P.2d 1238 (Colo.1971). Notice of entry has not been excused in gambling cases even when easily destructible "flash paper" is used in a bookmaking operation. See United States v. Likas, 448 F.2d 607 (7th Cir. 1971).

Consider Title 23, District of Columbia Code, Section 23–591:

(a) Any officer authorized by law to make arrests, or to execute search warrants, or any person aiding such an officer, may break and enter any premises, any outer or inner door or window of a dwelling house or other building, or any part thereof, any vehicle, or anything within such dwelling house, building or vehicle, or otherwise enter to execute search or arrest warrants, to make an arrest where authorized by law without a warrant, or where authorized by law without a warrant, or where necessary to liberate himself or a person aiding him in the execution of such warrant or in making such arrest.

(b) Breaking and entry shall not be made until after such officer or person makes an announcement of his identity and purpose and the officer reasonably believes that admittance to the dwelling house or other building or vehicle is being denied or unreasonably delayed.

(c) An announcement of identity and purpose shall not be required prior to such breaking and entry—

(1) if the warrant expressly authorizes breaking and entry without such a prior announcement, or

(2) if circumstances known to such officer or person at the time of breaking and entry, but, in the case of the execution of a warrant, unknown to the applicant when applying for such warrant, give him probable cause to believe that—

(A) such notice is likely to result in the evidence subject to seizure being easily and quickly destroyed or disposed of,

(B) such notice is likely to endanger the life or safety of the officer or another person,

(C) such notice is likely to enable the party to be arrested to escape, or

(D) such notice would be a useless gesture.

(d) Whoever, after notice is given under subsection (b) or after entry where such notice is unnecessary under subsection (c), destroys, conceals, disposes of, or attempts to destroy, conceal, or dispose of, or otherwise prevents or attempts to prevent the seizure of, evidence subject to seizure shall be fined not more than $5,000 or imprisoned for not more than 5 years, or both.

(e) As used in this section and in subchapter II and IV, the terms "break and enter" and "breaking and entering" include any use of physical force or violence or other unauthorized entry but do not include entry obtained by trick or strategem.

D. WARRANTLESS SEARCHES

In Coolidge v. New Hampshire, 403 U.S. 443, 91 S.Ct. 2022 (1971), the Supreme Court restated a basic tenet of recent search and seizure law respecting warrantless searches:

> "[T]he most basic constitutional rule in this area is that 'searches conducted outside the judicial process, without prior approval by judge or magistrate, are *per se* unreasonable under the Fourth Amendment—subject only to a few specifically established and well-delineated exceptions.' The exceptions are 'jealously and carefully drawn,' and there must be 'a showing by those who seek exemption . . . that the exigencies of the situation made that course imperative.' '[T]he burden is on those seeking the exemption to show the need for it.' "

As Coolidge v. New Hampshire makes clear, a warrant for search is constitutionally required except in certain well established circumstances. These exceptions to the rule will be discussed in turn. But it is clear, that apart from the classical doctrines of search incident to arrest, etc., there is a generalized rule which allows warrantless searches where there is a risk that evidence will disappear. The necessity of quick action may justify warrantless search or seizure. Thus if evidence is likely to disappear, no warrant need be secured. State v. Tarantola, 461 S.W.2d 848 (Mo.1971) (evidence burning); State v. Murphy, 2 Ore.App. 25, 465 P.2d 900 (1970) (fingernail scrapings); United States v. Johnson, 467 F.2d 630 (2nd Cir. 1972) (evidence contained in suitcases left out in public where anyone might take them); United States v. Brown, 457 F.2d 731 (1st Cir. 1972) (accomplices were at large and had access to the evidence to be seized). Consider also cases in which officers are in "hot pursuit" of a dangerous felon. In one case armed robbers engaged in a gun battle. One policeman was killed and one robber fled into an apartment building containing several dwelling units. The court held "it was not unreasonable [for the police] to have conducted a search of each unit for suspects and weapons". The robbery was committed by three or four gunmen. People v. Bradford, 28 Cal.App.3d 695, 104 Cal.Rptr. 852 (1972).

SECTION 1. SEARCH INCIDENT TO ARREST

CHIMEL v. CALIFORNIA

Supreme Court of the United States, 1969.
395 U.S. 752, 89 S.Ct. 2034.

MR. JUSTICE STEWART delivered the opinion of the Court.

This case raises basic questions concerning the permissible scope under the Fourth Amendment of a search incident to a lawful arrest.

The relevant facts are essentially undisputed. Late in the afternoon of September 13, 1965, three police officers arrived at the Santa Ana, California, home of the petitioner with a warrant authorizing his arrest for the burglary of a coin shop. The officers knocked on the door, identified themselves to the petitioner's wife and asked if they might come inside. She ushered them into the house, where they waited 10 or 15 minutes until the petitioner returned home from work. When the petitioner entered the house, one of the officers handed him the arrest warrant and asked for permission to "look around." The petitioner objected, but was advised that "on the basis of the lawful arrest," the officers would nonetheless conduct a search. No search warrant had been issued.

Accompanied by the petitioner's wife, the officers then looked through the entire three-bedroom house, including the attic, the garage, and a small workshop. In some rooms the search was relatively cursory. In the master bedroom and sewing room, however, the officers directed the petitioner's wife to open drawers and "to physically move contents of the drawers from side to side so that [they] might view any items that would have come from [the] burglary." After completing the search, they seized numerous items—primarily coins, but also several medals, tokens, and a few other objects. The entire search took between 45 minutes and an hour.

At the petitioner's subsequent state trial on two charges of burglary, the items taken from his house were admitted into evidence against him, over his objection that they had been unconstitutionally seized. He was convicted, and the judgments of conviction were affirmed by both the California District Court of Appeal and the California Supreme Court. Both courts accepted the petitioner's contention that the arrest warrant was invalid because the supporting affidavit was set out in conclusory terms, but held that since the arresting officers had procured the warrant "in good faith," and since in any event they had had sufficient information to constitute probable cause for the petitioner's arrest, that arrest had been lawful. From this conclusion the appellate courts went on to hold that the search of the petitioner's home had been justified, despite the absence of a search warrant, on the ground that it had been incident to a valid arrest. We granted certiorari in order to consider the petitioner's substantial constitutional claims.

Without deciding the question, we proceed on the hypothesis that the California courts were correct in holding that the arrest of the petitioner was valid under the Constitution. This brings us directly to the question whether the warrantless search of the petitioner's entire house can be constitutionally justified as incident to that arrest. The decisions of this Court bearing upon that question have been far from consistent, as even the most cursory review makes evident.

Approval of a warrantless search incident to a lawful arrest seems first to have been articulated by the Court in 1914 as dictum in Weeks v. United States, 232 U.S. 383, 34 S.Ct. 341, in which the Court stated:

> "What then is the present case? Before answering that inquiry specifically, it may be well by a process of exclusion to state what it is not. It is not an assertion of the right on the part of the Government, always recognized under English and American law, to search the person of the accused when legally arrested to discover and seize the fruits or evidences of crime."

That statement made no reference to any right to search the *place* where an arrest occurs, but was limited to a right to search the "person." Eleven years later the case of Carroll v. United States, 267 U.S. 132, 45 S.Ct. 280, brought the following embellishment of the *Weeks* statement:

> "When a man is legally arrested for an offense, whatever is found upon his person *or in his control* which it is unlawful for him to have and which may be used to prove the offense may be seized and held as evidence in the prosecution." (Emphasis added.)

Still, that assertion too was far from a claim that the "place" where one is arrested may be searched so long as the arrest is valid. Without explanation, however, the principle emerged in expanded form a few months later in Agnello v. United States, 269 U.S. 20, 46 S.Ct. 4 —although still by way of dictum:

> "The right without a search warrant contemporaneously to search persons lawfully arrested while committing crime and to search the place where the arrest is made in order to find and seize things connected with the crime as its fruits or as the

> means by which it was committed, as well as weapons and other things to effect an escape from custody, is not to be doubted. See Carroll v. United States, 267 U.S. 132, 158, 45 S.Ct. 280; Weeks v. United States, 232 U.S. 383, 392, 34 S.Ct. 341."

And in Marron v. United States, 275 U.S. 192, 48 S.Ct. 74, two years later, the dictum of *Agnello* appeared to be the foundation of the Court's decision. In that case federal agents had secured a search warrant authorizing the seizure of liquor and certain articles used in its manufacture. When they arrived at the premises to be searched, they saw "that the place was used for retailing and drinking intoxicating liquors." They proceeded to arrest the person in charge and to execute the warrant. In searching a closet for the items listed in the warrant they came across an incriminating ledger, concededly not covered by the warrant, which they also seized. The Court upheld the seizure of the ledger by holding that since the agents had made a lawful arrest, "[t]hey had a right without a warrant contemporaneously to search the place in order to find and seize the things used to carry on the criminal enterprise."

That the *Marron* opinion did not mean all that it seemed to say became evident, however, a few years later in Go-Bart Importing Co. v. United States, 282 U.S. 344, 51 S.Ct. 153, and United States v. Lefkowitz, 285 U.S. 452, 52 S.Ct. 420. In each of those cases the opinion of the Court was written by Mr. Justice Butler, who had authored the opinion in *Marron*. In *Go-Bart*, agents had searched the office of persons whom they had lawfully arrested, and had taken several papers from a desk, a safe, and other parts of the office. The Court noted that no crime had been committed in the agents' presence, and that although the agent in charge "had an abundance of information and time to swear out a valid [search] warrant, he failed to do so." In holding the search and seizure unlawful, the Court stated:

> "Plainly the case before us is essentially different from Marron v. United States, 275 U.S. 192, 48 S.Ct. 74. There, officers executing a valid search warrant for intoxicating liquors found and arrested one Birdsall who in pursuance of a conspiracy was actually engaged in running a saloon. As an incident to the arrest they seized a ledger in a closet where the liquor or some of it was kept and some bills beside the cash register. These things were visible and accessible and in the offender's immediate custody. There was no threat of force or general search or rummaging of the place."

This limited characterization of *Marron* was reiterated in *Lefkowitz*, a case in which the Court held unlawful a search of desk drawers and a cabinet despite the fact that the search had accompanied a lawful arrest.

The limiting views expressed in *Go-Bart* and *Lefkowitz* were thrown to the winds, however, in Harris v. United States, 331 U.S. 145, 67 S.Ct. 1098, decided in 1947. In that case, officers had obtained a warrant for Harris' arrest on the basis of his alleged involvement with the cashing and interstate transportation of a forged check. He was arrested in the living room of his four-room apartment, and in an attempt to recover two canceled checks thought to have been used in effecting the forgery, the officers undertook a thorough search of the entire apartment. Inside a desk drawer they found a sealed envelope marked "George Harris, personal papers." The envelope, which was then torn open, was found to contain altered selective service documents, and those documents were used to secure Harris' conviction for violating the Selective Training and Service Act of 1940. The Court rejected Harris' Fourth Amendment claim, sustaining the search as "incident to arrest."

Only a year after *Harris,* however, the pendulum swung again. In Trupiano v. United States, 334 U.S. 699, 68 S.Ct. 1229, agents raided the site of an illicit distillery, saw one of several conspirators operating the still, and arrested him, contemporaneously "seiz[ing] the illicit distillery." The Court held that the arrest and others made subsequently had been valid, but that the unexplained failure of the agents to procure a search warrant—in spite of the fact that they had had more than enough time before the raid to do so—rendered the search unlawful. The opinion stated:

> "It is a cardinal rule that, in seizing goods and articles, law enforcement agents must secure and use search warrants wherever reasonably practicable. . . . This rule rests upon the desirability of having magistrates rather than police officers determine when searches and seizures are permissible and what limitations should be placed upon such activities. . . . To provide the necessary security against unreasonable intrusions upon the private lives of individuals, the framers of the Fourth Amendment required adherence to judicial processes wherever possible. And subsequent history has confirmed the wisdom of that requirement.
>
> . . . .
>
> "A search or seizure without a warrant as an incident to a lawful arrest has always been considered to be a strictly limited right. It grows out of the inherent necessities of the situation at the time of the arrest. But there must be something more in the way of necessity than merely a lawful arrest."

In 1950, two years after *Trupiano,* came United States v. Rabinowitz, 339 U.S. 56, 70 S.Ct. 430, the decision upon which California primarily relies in the case now before us. In *Rabinowitz,* federal authorities had been informed that the defendant was dealing in stamps bearing forged overprints. On the basis of that information they secured a warrant for his arrest, which they executed at his one-room business office. At the time of the arrest, the officers "searched the desk, safe, and file cabinets in the office for about an hour and a half," and seized 573 stamps with forged overprints. The stamps were admitted into evidence at the defendant's trial and this

Court affirmed his conviction, rejecting the contention that the warrantless search had been unlawful. The Court held that the search in its entirety fell within the principle giving law enforcement authorities "[t]he right 'to search the place where the arrest is made in order to find and seize things connected with the crime . . . .'" *Harris* was regarded as "ample authority" for that conclusion. The opinion rejected the rule of *Trupiano* that "in seizing goods and articles, law enforcement agents must secure and use search warrants wherever reasonably practicable." The test, said the Court, "is not whether it is reasonable to procure a search warrant, but whether the search was reasonable."

Rabinowitz has come to stand for the proposition, *inter alia,* that a warrantless search "incident to a lawful arrest" may generally extend to the area that is considered to be in the "possession" or under the "control" of the person arrested. And it was on the basis of that proposition that the California courts upheld the search of the petitioner's entire house in this case. That doctrine, however, at least in the broad sense in which it was applied by the California courts in this case, can withstand neither historical nor rational analysis.

Even limited to its own facts, the *Rabinowitz* decision was, as we have seen, hardly founded on an unimpeachable line of authority. As Mr. Justice Frankfurter commented in dissent in that case, the "hint" contained in *Weeks* was, without persuasive justification, "loosely turned into dictum and finally elevated to a decision." And the approach taken in cases such as *Go-Bart, Lefkowitz,* and *Trupiano* was essentially disregarded by the *Rabinowitz* Court.

Nor is the rationale by which the State seeks here to sustain the search of the petitioner's house supported by a reasoned view of the background and purpose of the Fourth Amendment. Mr. Justice Frankfurter wisely pointed out in his *Rabinowitz* dissent that the Amendment's proscription of "unreasonable searches and seizures" must be read in light of "the history that gave rise to the words"—a history of "abuses so deeply felt by the Colonies as to be one of the potent causes of the Revolution . . . ." The Amendment was in large part a reaction to the general warrants and warrantless searches that had so alienated the colonists and had helped speed the movement for independence. In the scheme of the Amendment, therefore, the requirement that "no Warrants shall issue, but upon probable cause," plays a crucial part. As the Court put it in McDonald v. United States, 335 U.S. 451, 69 S.Ct. 191:

> "We are not dealing with formalities. The presence of a search warrant serves a high function. Absent some grave emergency, the Fourth Amendment has interposed a magistrate between the citizen and the police. This was done not to shield criminals nor to make the home a safe haven for illegal activities. It was done so that an objective mind might weigh

> the need to invade that privacy in order to enforce the law. The right of privacy was deemed too precious to entrust to the discretion of those whose job is the detection of crime and the arrest of criminals. . . . And so the Constitution requires a magistrate to pass on the desires of the police before they violate the privacy of the home. We cannot be true to that constitutional requirement and excuse the absence of a search warrant without a showing by those who seek exemption from the constitutional mandate that the exigencies of the situation made that course imperative."

Even in the *Agnello* case the Court relied upon the rule that "[b]elief, however well founded, that an article sought is concealed in a dwelling house furnishes no justification for a search of that place without a warrant. And such searches are held unlawful notwithstanding facts unquestionably showing probable cause." Clearly, the general requirement that a search warrant be obtained is not lightly to be dispensed with, and "the burden is on those seeking [an] exemption [from the requirement] to show the need for it . . . ." United States v. Jeffers, 342 U.S. 48, 51, 72 S.Ct. 93, 95.

Only last Term in Terry v. Ohio, 392 U.S. 1, 88 S.Ct. 1868, we emphasized that "the police must, whenever practicable, obtain advance judicial approval of searches and seizures through the warrant procedure," and that "[t]he scope of [a] search must be 'strictly tied to and justified by' the circumstances which rendered its initiation permissible." The search undertaken by the officer in that "stop and frisk" case was sustained under that test, because it was no more than a "protective . . . search for weapons." But in a companion case, Sibron v. New York, 392 U.S. 40, 88 S.Ct. 1889, we applied the same standard to another set of facts and reached a contrary result, holding that a policeman's action in thrusting his hand into a suspect's pocket had been neither motivated by nor limited to the objective of protection. Rather, the search had been made in order to find narcotics, which were in fact found.

A similar analysis underlies the "search incident to arrest" principle, and marks its proper extent. When an arrest is made, it is reasonable for the arresting officer to search the person arrested in order to remove any weapons that the latter might seek to use in order to resist arrest or effect his escape. Otherwise, the officer's safety might well be endangered, and the arrest itself frustrated. In addition, it is entirely reasonable for the arresting officer to search for and seize any evidence on the arrestee's person in order to prevent its concealment or destruction. And the area into which an arrestee might reach in order to grab a weapon or evidentiary items must, of course, be governed by a like rule. A gun on a table or in a drawer in front of one who is arrested can be as dangerous to the arresting officer as one concealed in the clothing of the person arrested. There is ample justification, therefore, for a search of the arrestee's person and the area "within his immediate control"—construing that phrase to mean the area from within which he might gain possession of a weapon or destructible evidence.

There is no comparable justification, however, for routinely searching rooms other than that in which an arrest occurs—or, for that matter, for searching through all the desk drawers or other closed or concealed areas in that room itself. Such searches, in the absence of well-recognized exceptions, may be made only under the authority of a search warrant. The "adherence to judicial processes" mandated by the Fourth Amendment requires no less.

This is the principle that underlay our decision in Preston v. United States, 376 U.S. 364, 84 S.Ct. 881. In that case three men had been arrested in a parked car, which had later been towed to a garage and searched by police. We held the search to have been unlawful under the Fourth Amendment, despite the contention that it had been incidental to a valid arrest. Our reasoning was straightforward:

> "The rule allowing contemporaneous searches is justified, for example, by the need to seize weapons and other things which might be used to assault an officer or effect an escape, as well as by the need to prevent the destruction of evidence of the crime—things which might easily happen where the weapon or evidence is on the accused's person or under his immediate control. But these justifications are absent where a search is remote in time or place from the arrest." [1]

The same basic principle was reflected in our opinion last Term in *Sibron.* That opinion dealt with *Peters* v. *New York,* No. 74, as well as with Sibron's case, and *Peters* involved a search that we upheld as incident to a proper arrest. We sustained the search, however, only because its scope had been "reasonably limited" by the "need to seize weapons" and "to prevent the destruction of evidence," to which *Preston* had referred. We emphasized that the arresting officer "did not engage in an unrestrained and thoroughgoing examination of Peters and his personal effects. He seized him to cut short his flight, and he searched him primarily for weapons."

It is argued in the present case that it is "reasonable" to search a man's house when he is arrested in it. But that argument is founded on little more than a subjective view regarding the acceptability of certain sorts of police conduct, and not on considerations relevant to Fourth Amendment interests. Under such an unconfined

1. Our holding today is of course entirely consistent with the recognized principle that, assuming the existence of probable cause, automobiles and other vehicles may be searched without warrants "where it is not practicable to secure a warrant because the vehicle can be quickly moved out of the locality or jurisdiction in which the warrant must be sought."—Carroll v. United States, 267 U.S. 132, 153; see Brinegar v. United States, 338 U.S. 160.

analysis, Fourth Amendment protection in this area would approach the evaporation point. It is not easy to explain why, for instance, it is less subjectively "reasonable" to search a man's house when he is arrested on his front lawn—or just down the street—than it is when he happens to be in the house at the time of arrest.[2] As Mr. Justice Frankfurter put it:

> "To say that the search must be reasonable is to require some criterion of reason. It is no guide at all either for a jury or for district judges or the police to say that an 'unreasonable search' is forbidden—that the search must be reasonable. What is the test of reason which makes a search reasonable? The test is the reason underlying and expressed by the Fourth Amendment: the history and the experience which it embodies and the safeguards afforded by it against the evils to which it was a response." United States v. Rabinowitz, 339 U.S., at 83, 70 S.Ct., at 443 (dissenting opinion).

Thus, although "[t]he recurring questions of the reasonableness of searches" depend upon "the facts and circumstances—the total atmosphere of the case," (opinion of the Court), those facts and circumstances must be viewed in the light of established Fourth Amendment principles.

It would be possible, of course, to draw a line between *Rabinowitz* and *Harris* on the one hand, and this case on the other. For *Rabinowitz* involved a single room, and *Harris* a four-room apartment, while in the case before us an entire house was searched. But such a distinction would be highly artificial. The rationale that allowed the searches and seizures in *Rabinowitz* and *Harris* would allow the searches and seizures in this case. No consideration relevant to the Fourth Amendment suggests any point of rational limitation, once the search is allowed to go beyond the area from which the person arrested might obtain weapons or evidentiary items.[3] The only reasoned distinction is one between a search of the person arrested and the area within his reach on the one hand, and more extensive searches on the other.[4]

2. Some courts have carried the *Rabinowitz* approach to just such lengths. See, *e. g.*, Clifton v. United States, 224 F.2d 329 (C.A.4th Cir.), certiorari denied 350 U.S. 894, 76 S. Ct. 152 (purchaser of illicit whiskey arrested in back yard of seller; search of one room of house sustained); United States v. Jackson, 149 F. Supp. 937 (D.C.D.C.), reversed on other grounds 102 U.S.App.D.C. 109, 250 F.2d 772) (suspect arrested half a block from his rented room; search of room upheld). But see James v. Louisiana, 382 U.S. 36, 86 S.Ct. 151 (*per curiam*).

3. Cf. Mr. Justice Jackson's dissenting comment in *Harris:*

"The difficulty with this problem for me is that once the search is allowed to go beyond the person arrested and the objects upon him or in his immediate physical control, I see no practical limit short of that set in the opinion of the Court—and that means to me no limit at all."

4. It is argued in dissent that so long as there is probable cause to search the place where an arrest occurs, a search of that place should be permitted even though no search warrant

The petitioner correctly points out that one result of decisions such as *Rabinowitz* and *Harris* is to give law enforcement officials the opportunity to engage in searches not justified by probable cause, by the simple expedient of arranging to arrest suspects at home rather than elsewhere. We do not suggest that the petitioner is necessarily correct in his assertion that such a strategy was utilized here,[5] but the fact remains that had he been arrested earlier in the day, at his place of employment rather than at home, no search of his house could have been made without a search warrant. In any event, even apart from the possibility of such police tactics, the general point so forcefully made by Judge Learned Hand in United States v. Kirschenblatt, 2d Cir., 16 F.2d 202, remains:

> "After arresting a man in his house, to rummage at will among his papers in search of whatever will convict him, appears to us to be indistinguishable from what might be done under a general warrant; indeed, the warrant would give more protection, for presumably it must be issued by a magistrate. True, by hypothesis the power would not exist, if the supposed offender were not found on the premises; but it is small consolation to know that one's papers are safe only so long as one is not at home."

Rabinowitz and *Harris* have been the subject of critical commentary for many years, and have been relied upon less and less in our own decisions. It is time, for the reasons we have stated, to hold that on their own facts, and insofar as the principles they stand for are inconsistent with those that we have endorsed today, they are no longer to be followed.

has been obtained. This position seems to be based principally on two premises: first, that once an arrest has been made, the additional invasion of privacy stemming from the accompanying search is "relatively minor"; and second, that the victim of the search may "shortly thereafter" obtain a judicial determination of whether the search was justified by probable cause. With respect to the second premise, one may initially question whether all of the States in fact provide the speedy suppression procedures the dissent assumes. More fundamentally, however, we cannot accept the view that Fourth Amendment interests are vindicated so long as "the rights of the criminal" are "protect[ed] . . . against introduction of evidence seized without probable cause." The Amendment is designed to prevent, not simply to redress, unlawful police action. In any event, we cannot join in characterizing the invasion of privacy that results from a top-to-bottom search of a man's house as "minor." And we can see no reason why, simply because some interference with an individual's privacy and freedom of movement has lawfully taken place, further intrusions should automatically be allowed despite the absence of a warrant that the Fourth Amendment would otherwise require.

5. Although the warrant was issued at 10:39 a. m. and the arrest was not made until late in the afternoon the State suggests that the delay is accounted for by normal police procedures and by the heavy workload of the officer in charge. In addition, that officer testified that he and his colleagues went to the petitioner's house "to keep from approaching him at his place of business to cause him any problem there."

Application of sound Fourth Amendment principles to the facts of this case produces a clear result. The search here went far beyond the petitioner's person and the area from within which he might have obtained either a weapon or something that could have been used as evidence against him. There was no constitutional justification, in the absence of a search warrant, for extending the search beyond that area. The scope of the search was, therefore, "unreasonable" under the Fourth and Fourteenth Amendments, and the petitioner's conviction cannot stand.

Reversed.

MR. JUSTICE WHITE, with whom MR. JUSTICE BLACK joins, dissenting.

Few areas of the law have been as subject to shifting constitutional standards over the last 50 years as that of the search "incident to an arrest." There has been a remarkable instability in this whole area, which has seen at least four major shifts in emphasis. Today's opinion makes an untimely fifth. In my view, the Court should not now abandon the old rule.

I.

The modern odyssey of doctrine in this field is detailed in the majority opinion. It began with Weeks v. United States, 232 U.S. 383, 34 S.Ct. 341 (1914), where the Court paused to note what the case before it was not. "It is not an assertion of the right on the part of the Government, always recognized under English and American law, to search the person of the accused when legally arrested to discover and seize the fruits or evidences of crime. This right has been uniformly maintained in many cases. . . . Nor is it the case of burglar's tools or other proofs of guilt found upon his arrest *within the control of the accused.*" *Id.*, at 392, 34 S.Ct., at 344. (Emphasis added.) This scope of search incident to arrest, extending to all items under the suspect's "control," was reaffirmed in a dictum in Carroll v. United States, 267 U.S. 132, 158, 45 S.Ct. 280, 287 (1925). Accord, Agnello v. United States, 269 U.S. 20, 30–31, 46 S.Ct. 4, 5–6 (1925) (holding that "the place where the arrest is made" may be searched "is not to be doubted"). The rule was reaffirmed in Marron v. United States, 275 U.S. 192, 199, 48 S.Ct. 74, 77 (1927) where the Court asserted that authority to search incident to an arrest "extended to all parts of the premises used for the unlawful purpose."

Within four years, this rule was qualified by two Prohibition Act cases, Go-Bart Importing Co. v. United States, 282 U.S. 344, 356–358, 51 S.Ct. 153, 157–158(1931), and United States v. Lefkowitz, 285 U.S. 452, 463–467, 52 S.Ct. 420, 422–424 (1932).

If *Go-Bart* and *Lefkowitz* represented a retreat from the rule of *Weeks, Carroll, Agnello,* and *Marron,* the vigor of the earlier rule was reaffirmed in Harris v. United States, 331 U.S. 145, 67 S.Ct. 1098

(1947) which has, but for one brief interlude, clearly been the law until today. The very next Term after *Harris*, in Trupiano v. United States, 334 U.S. 699, 68 S.Ct. 1229 (1948), the Court held unjustifiable the seizure of a still incident to the arrest of a man at the still site, even though the still was contraband, had been visible through an open door before entering the premises to be "searched," and although a crime was being committed in the officers' presence. Accord, that year, McDonald v. United States, 335 U.S. 451, 69 S.Ct. 191 (1948) (gambling game seen through transom before entry). Two years later, however, the Court returned to the *Harris* rule in United States v. Rabinowitz, 339 U.S. 56, 70 S.Ct. 430 (1950), where the Court held that the reasonableness of a search does not depend upon the practicability of obtaining a search warrant, and that the fact of a valid arrest is relevant to reasonableness. *Trupiano* was *pro tanto* overruled.

Such rapid reversals had occurred before, but they are rare. Here there had been two about-faces, one following hard upon the other. Justice Frankfurter objected in this language: "Especially ought the Court not reenforce needlessly the instabilities of our day by giving fair ground for the belief that Law is the expression of chance—for instance, of unexpected changes in the Court's composition and the contingencies in the choice of successors." 339 U.S., at 86, 70 S.Ct., at 444. Since that time, the rule of *Weeks, Marron, Harris,* and *Rabinowitz* has clearly been the law. *E.g.*, Abel v. United States, 362 U.S. 217, 80 S.Ct. 683 (1960) (Frankfurter, J., writing for the Court); Ker v. California, 374 U.S. 23, 83 S.Ct. 1623 (1963).

II.

The rule which has prevailed, but for very brief or doubtful periods of aberration, is that a search incident to an arrest may extend to those areas under the control of the defendant and where items subject to constitutional seizure may be found. The justification for this rule must, under the language of the Fourth Amendment, lie in the reasonableness of the rule. Terry v. Ohio, 392 U.S. 1, 9, 88 S.Ct. 1868, 1873 (1968); Sibron v. New York, 392 U.S. 40, 88 S.Ct. 1889 (1968); Elkins v. United States, 364 U.S. 206, 222, 80 S.Ct. 1437, 1446 (1960). The Amendment provides:

> "The right of the people to be secure in their persons, houses, papers, and effects, against unreasonable searches and seizures, shall not be violated, and no Warrants shall issue, but upon probable cause, supported by Oath or affirmation, and particularly describing the place to be searched, and the persons or things to be seized."

In terms, then, the Court must decide whether a given search is reasonable. The Amendment does not proscribe "warrantless searches" but instead it proscribes "unreasonable searches" and this Court has never held nor does the majority today assert that warrantless searches are necessarily unreasonable.

Applying this reasonableness test to the area of searches incident to arrests, one thing is clear at the outset. Search of an arrested man and of the items within his immediate reach must in almost every case be reasonable. There is always a danger that the suspect will try to escape, seizing concealed weapons with which to overpower and injure the arresting officers, and there is a danger that he may destroy evidence vital to the prosecution. Circumstances in which these justifications would not apply are sufficiently rare that inquiry is not made into searches of this scope, which have been considered reasonable throughout.

The justifications which make such a search reasonable obviously do not apply to the search of areas to which the accused does not have ready physical access. This is not enough, however, to prove such searches unconstitutional. The Court has always held, and does not today deny, that when there is probable cause to search and it is "impracticable" for one reason or another to get a search warrant, then a warrantless search may be reasonable. *E.g.,* even Trupiano v. United States, 334 U.S. 699, 68 S.Ct. 1229 (1948). This is the case whether an arrest was made at the time of the search or not.

This is not to say that a search can be reasonable without regard to the probable cause to believe that seizable items are on the premises. But when there are exigent circumstances, and probable cause, then the search may be made without a warrant, reasonably. An arrest itself may often create an emergency situation making it impracticable to obtain a warrant before embarking on a related search. Again assuming that there is probable cause to search premises at the spot where a suspect is arrested, it seems to me unreasonable to require the police to leave the scene in order to obtain a search warrant when they are already legally there to make a valid arrest, and when there must almost always be a strong possibility that confederates of the arrested man will in the meanwhile remove the items for which the police have probable cause to search. This must so often be the case that it seems to me as unreasonable to require a warrant for a search of the premises as to require a warrant for search of the person and his very immediate surroundings.

This case provides a good illustration of my point that it is unreasonable to require police to leave the scene of an arrest in order to obtain a search warrant when they already have probable cause to search and there is a clear danger that the items for which they may reasonably search will be removed before they return with a warrant. Petitioner was arrested in his home after an arrest whose validity will be explored below, but which I will now assume was valid. There was doubtless probable cause not only to arrest petitioner, but to search his house. He had obliquely admitted both to a neighbor, and to the owner of the burglarized store, that he had committed the burglary.[1] In light of this, and the fact that the neighbor had seen other admittedly stolen property in petitioner's house, there was surely probable cause on which a warrant could have issued to search the house for the stolen coins. Moreover, had the police simply arrested petitioner, taken him off to the station house, and later returned with a warrant,[2] it seems very likely that petitioner's wife, who in view of petitioner's generally garrulous nature must have known of the robbery, would have removed the coins. For the police to search the house while the evidence they had probable cause to search out and seize was still there cannot be considered unreasonable.

III.

This line of analysis, supported by the precedents of this Court, hinges on two assumptions. One is that the arrest of petitioner without a valid warrant was constitutional as the majority assumes; the other is that the police were not required to obtain a search warrant in advance, even though they knew that the effect of the arrest might well be to alert petitioner's wife that the coins had better be removed soon. Thus it is necessary to examine the constitutionality of the arrest since if it was illegal, the exigent circumstances which it created may not, as the consequences of a lawless act, be used to justify the contemporaneous warrantless search. But for the arrest, the warrantless search may not be justified. And if circumstances can justify the warrantless arrest, it would be strange to say that the Fourth Amendment bars the warrantless search, regardless

1. Before the burglary of the coin store, petitioner had told its owner that he was planning a big robbery, had inquired about the alarm system in the store, the state of the owner's insurance, and the location of the owner's most valuable coins. Petitioner wandered about the store the day before the burglary. After the burglary, petitioner called the store's owner and accused him of robbing the store himself for the insurance proceeds on a policy which, as petitioner knew, had just been reduced from $50,000 to $10,000 coverage. On being told that the robbery had been sloppy, petitioner excitedly claimed that it had been "real professional" but then denied the robbery. On the night of the robbery itself petitioner declined an invitation to a bicycle ride, saying he was "going to knock over a place" and that a coin shop was "all set." After the robbery, he told the same neighbor that he had started to break into the coin shop, but had stopped, and then denied the whole incident. The neighbor had earlier seen stacks of typewriters in petitioner's house. Asked whether they were "hot" petitioner replied, "Hotter than a $3 bill." On reading a newspaper description of the coin store burglary, the neighbor called the police.

2. There were three officers at the scene of the arrest, one from the city where the coin burglary had occurred, and two from the city where the arrest was made. Assuming that one policeman from each city would be needed to bring the petitioner in and obtain a search warrant, one policeman could have been left to guard the house. However, if he not only could have remained in the house against petitioner's wife's will, but followed her about to assure that no evidence was being tampered with, the invasion of her privacy would be almost as great as that accompanying an actual search. Moreover, had the wife summoned an accomplice, one officer could not have watched them both.

of the circumstances, since the invasion and disruption of a man's life and privacy which stem from his arrest are ordinarily far greater than the relatively minor intrusions attending a search of his premises.

Congress has expressly authorized a wide range of officials to make arrests without any warrant in criminal cases. United States Marshals have long had this power, which is also vested in the agents of the Federal Bureau of Investigation, and in the Secret Service and the narcotics law enforcement agency. That warrantless arrest power may apply even when there is time to get a warrant without fear that the suspect may escape is made perfectly clear by the legislative history of the statute granting arrest power to the FBI.

In United States v. Coplon, 185 F.2d 629, 633–636 (C.A.2d Cir. 1950), the court held that an arrest and search were invalid because there was an insufficient showing of danger of escape, and therefore there was time to obtain a warrant. The opinion, written by Judge Learned Hand and joined by Judges Swan and Frank, reviewed the common-law power of arrest, which permitted arrests for felonies committed in the past "if [the officer] had reasonable ground to suppose that the person arrested had committed the felony." However, the court concluded that this power of warrantless arrest had been limited by the congressional requirement that there must be a "likelihood of the person escaping before a warrant can be obtained for his arrest."

The next month the Congress was moved by this very decision to amend the law, consciously deleting the language upon which Judge Hand had relied so as to make it clear that warrantless arrests were authorized even if there was time to procure a warrant. Thereupon, the Court of Appeals for the District of Columbia, passing on the very same arrest which had induced the congressional action, held that this "unmistakable" revision made it clear that there was in the FBI a power to arrest without warrant even when there was time to procure one. For this reason, the court upheld the arrest and contemporaneous search. Coplon v. United States, 191 F.2d 749 (C.A.D.C. Cir. 1951). Certiorari was denied in both *Coplon* cases. 342 U.S. 920, 926, 72 S.Ct. 362, 363 (1962). Moreover, the statute under which the FBI exercises that power was later said by this Court to state the constitutional standard, Henry v. United States, 361 U.S. 98, 100, 80 S.Ct. 168 (1959), since it requires "reasonable grounds to believe that the person to be arrested has committed or is committing" a felony, 18 U.S.C. § 3052, before a warrantless arrest may be made. And the Court today has declined to review a warrantless arrest under the narcotics agent statute. Jamison v. United States, 395 U.S. 986, 89 S.Ct. 2135 (1969). See also my dissent in Shipley v. California, 395 U.S. 818, 89 S.Ct. 2053 (1969).

The judgment of Congress is that federal law enforcement officers may reasonably make warrantless arrests upon probable cause, and no judicial experience suggests that this judgment is infirm. Indeed, past cases suggest precisely the contrary conclusion. The validity of federal arrests was long governed by state law, United States v. Di Re, 332 U.S. 581, 589–592, 68 S.Ct. 222, 226–227 (1948), and no requirement that warrants be sought whenever there is time to do so was imposed either by common-law history or by decisions of this Court. This Court has upheld an executive arrest warrant for deportation, permitting the arrest to occur without prior judicial scrutiny, Abel v. United States, 362 U.S. 217, 80 S.Ct. 683 (1960). And this Court has regularly affirmed the validity of warrantless arrests without any indication whatever that there was no time to get a warrant, and indeed where all the circumstances pointed to the opposite conclusion. The lower federal courts have certainly been of the view that warrants are unnecessary even where there is time to obtain them.

In light of the uniformity of judgment of the Congress, past judicial decisions, and common practice rejecting the proposition that arrest warrants are essential wherever it is practicable to get them, the conclusion is inevitable that such arrests and accompanying searches are reasonable, at least until experience teaches the contrary. It must very often be the case that by the time probable cause to arrest a man is accumulated, the man is aware of police interest in him or for other good reasons is on the verge of flight. Moreover, it will likely be very difficult to determine the probability of his flight. Given this situation, it may be best in all cases simply to allow the arrest if there is probable cause, especially since that issue can be determined very shortly after the arrest.

Nor are the stated assumptions at all fanciful. It was precisely these facts which moved the Congress to grant to the FBI the power to arrest without a warrant without any showing of probability of flight. Both the Senate and House committees quoted the letter of the Acting Deputy Attorney General, Peter Campbell Brown, who in asking for the new legislation asserted: "Although it is recognized that in any felony case the person to be arrested may attempt to flee, it is also recognized that in any such case in which the defendant is arrested without a warrant in an emergency situation, such defendant may be able to present a rather convincing argument that he did not intend to flee." Some weight should be accorded this factual judgment by law enforcement officials, adopted by the Congress.

IV.

If circumstances so often require the warrantless arrest that the law generally permits it, the typical situation will find the arresting officers lawfully on the premises without arrest or search warrant. Like the majority, I would permit the police to search the person of a suspect and the area under his immediate control either to assure the safety of the officers or to prevent the destruction of evidence. And like the majority, I see nothing in the arrest alone furnishing probable cause for a search of any broader scope. However, where as here the existence of probable cause is independently established and would justify a warrant for a broader search for evidence, I would follow past cases and permit such a search to be carried out without a warrant, since the fact of arrest supplies an exigent circumstance justifying police action before the evidence can be removed, and also alerts the suspect to the fact of the search so that he can immediately seek judicial determination of probable cause in an adversary proceeding, and appropriate redress.

This view, consistent with past cases, would not authorize the general search against which the Fourth Amendment was meant to guard, nor would it broaden or render uncertain in any way whatsoever the scope of searches permitted under the Fourth Amendment. The issue in this case is not the breadth of the search, since there was clearly probable cause for the search which was carried out. No broader search than if the officers had a warrant would be permitted. The only issue is whether a search warrant was required as a precondition to that search. It is agreed that such a warrant would be required absent exigent circumstances.[3] I would hold that the fact of arrest supplies such an exigent circumstance, since the police had lawfully gained entry to the premises to effect the arrest and since delaying the search to secure a warrant would have involved the risk of not recovering the fruits of the crime.

The majority today proscribes searches for which there is probable cause and which may prove fruitless unless carried out immediately. This rule will have no added effect whatsoever in protecting the rights of the criminal accused at trial against introduction of evidence seized without probable cause. Such evidence could not be introduced under the old rule. Nor does the majority today give any added protection to the right of privacy of those whose houses there is probable cause to search. A warrant would still be sworn out for those houses, and the privacy of their owners invaded. The only possible justification for the majority's rule is that in some instances arresting officers may search when they have no

3. A search without a warrant "can survive constitutional inhibition only upon a showing that the surrounding facts brought it within one of the exceptions to the rule that a search must rest upon a search warrant. Jones v. United States, 357 U.S. 493, 499, 78 S.Ct. 1253, 1257; United States v. Jeffers, 342 U.S. 48, 51, 72 S.Ct. 93, 95." Rios v. United States, 364 U.S. 253, 261, 80 S.Ct. 1431, 1436 (1960); Stoner v. California, 376 U.S. 483, 486, 84 S.Ct. 889, 891 (1964). And "a search can be incident to arrest only if it is substantially contemporaneous with the arrest and is confined to the immediate vicinity of the arrest. Agnello v. United States, 269 U.S. 20, 46 S.Ct. 4." Stoner v. California, *supra*, at 486, 84 S.Ct. at 891; James v. Louisiana, 382 U.S. 36, 37, 86 S.Ct. 151 (1965). There is thus no question that a warrant to search petitioner's house would have been required had he not been arrested there. In such cases, the officers are not already lawfully on the premises, and there is not so often the same risk of the destruction of evidence nor the necessity to make an immediate search without the delay involved in securing a warrant.

probable cause to do so and that such unlawful searches might be prevented if the officers first sought a warrant from a magistrate. Against the possible protection of privacy in that class of cases, in which the privacy of the house has already been invaded by entry to make the arrest—an entry for which the majority does not assert that any warrant is necessary—must be weighed the risk of destruction of evidence for which there is probable cause to search, as a result of delays in obtaining a search warrant. Without more basis for radical change than the Court's opinion reveals, I would not upset the balance of these interests which has been struck by the former decisions of this Court.

In considering searches incident to arrest, it must be remembered that there will be immediate opportunity to challenge the probable cause for the search in an adversary proceeding. The suspect has been apprised of the search by his very presence at the scene, and having been arrested, he will soon be brought into contact with people who can explain his rights. As MR. JUSTICE BRENNAN noted in a dissenting opinion, joined by JUSTICES BLACK and DOUGLAS, and THE CHIEF JUSTICE, in Abel v. United States, 362 U.S. 217, 249–250, 80 S.Ct. 683, 702 (1959), a search contemporaneous with a warrantless arrest is specially safeguarded since "[s]uch an arrest may constitutionally be made only upon probable cause, the existence of which is subject to judicial examination, see Henry v. United States, 361 U.S. 98, 100, 80 S.Ct. 168, 169; and such an arrest demands the prompt bringing of the person arrested before a judicial officer, where the existence of probable cause is to be inquired into. Fed.Rules Crim.Proc. 5(a) and (c). . . . Mallory v. United States, 354 U.S. 449, 77 S.Ct. 1356; McNabb v. United States, 318 U.S. 332, 63 S.Ct. 608." And since that time the Court has imposed on state and federal officers alike the duty to warn suspects taken into custody, before questioning them, of their right to a lawyer. Miranda v. Arizona, 384 U.S. 436, 86 S.Ct. 1602 (1966); Orozco v. Texas, 394 U.S. 324, 89 S.Ct. 1095 (1969).

An arrested man, by definition conscious of the police interest in him, and provided almost immediately with a lawyer and a judge, is in an excellent position to dispute the reasonableness of his arrest and contemporaneous search in a full adversary proceeding. I would uphold the constitutionality of this search contemporaneous with an arrest since there was probable cause both for the search and for the arrest, exigent circumstances involving the removal or destruction of evidence, and a satisfactory opportunity to dispute the issues of probable cause shortly thereafter. In this case, the search was reasonable.

[The concurring opinion of Mr. Justice Harlan is omitted.]

NOTES

1. *Chimel* holds that a warrantless search may be made of the area in the immediate control of the arrested person. How far does this area extend? Does the right to search evaporate if the suspect is handcuffed or restrained from moving? Compare the following cases:

(a) United States v. Patterson, 447 F.2d 424 (10th Cir. 1971):

"The basic facts upon which there appears to be no substantial disagreement are that a certificate of deposit issued to a Steven N. Mudrick was removed from his safe deposit box at the Roeland Park State Bank and cashed at the bank. The value of the certificate was $3,000, together with accrued interest. Mr. Mudrick, who had been a patient at a hospital at the time, had not cashed the certificate nor authorized anyone else to do so. While a patient at the hospital, his apartment had been burglarized. Items taken included, among other things, blank checks, a .22-caliber revolver, and the key to his safe deposit box at the Roeland Park State Bank. Mr. Mudrick testified that he knew a Marty Boyer, that she had been in his apartment shortly before his going to the hospital, and that she knew of his plans to go into the hospital.

"An arrest warrant had been issued for Martha H. Carlson, also known as Mary Boyer, also known as Martha H. Patterson, the appellant's wife, in connection with a forged instrument she had uttered under Mudrick's name. Five officers served the warrant at the apartment of Mr. and Mrs. Patterson. Both Mr. and Mrs. Patterson were in the living room when the officers entered. The appellant was frisked and searched for weapons, but none was found. No search was made of Mrs. Patterson.

"In the process of making the arrest, one of the police detectives went into the kitchen where he saw a partially hidden folder or envelope sitting on a shelf in a cabinet. The cabinet was four to six feet away from where Mrs. Patterson was standing at the time. The folder was in partial view of the detective because the cabinet door was about half-way open. The detective removed the folder from the cabinet against Mrs. Patterson's protests and found, among other things, a check and checkbook bearing Steven Mudrick's name and a safe deposit box key. The detective testified he was searching for a pistol since he knew Mrs. Patterson was a suspect in the burglary of Mudrick's apartment and this was one of the items taken.

"Appellant's position here is that Mrs. Patterson's arrest occurring in the living room would thereby limit the search to only that room. The record discloses that Mrs. Patterson, of her own volition, had moved to the doorway between the kitchen-dining room area and the living room. Access to the kitchen-dining room area was available to her by merely turning around. This justified the detective's precautionary measure of entering the kitchen. Appellant also argues the search should have been limited to the living room by the fact that Mrs. Patterson, though standing in the doorway, was facing toward the living room. Surely he would not argue before this court that a weapon concealed on a table or in a drawer just beyond the doorway is any less dangerous than a weapon in the room being occupied.

"Patterson cites us to our recent decision in United States v. Baca, 417 F.2d 103 (10th Cir. 1969), as support for his argument that search warrant procedures should be strictly adhered to and not lightly dispensed with.

Our statement there was "the area within the immediate control of the defendant may be searched and evidence or weapons seized without a warrant when made incidental to a lawful arrest." We there held, inter alia, that such areas as the inside of bureau drawers, nightstand, under the bed, or any similar area within the same room were beyond Baca's immediate control and the search of these areas was a violation of his Fourth Amendment protections. That decision was based on the fact that Baca was handcuffed with his hands behind his back. He was thereby effectively prevented from gaining access to such potential hiding places. The record here clearly discloses Mrs. Patterson had access to the kitchen-dining room area. She was handcuffed only after the detective had entered the kitchen and discovered the envelope containing the evidence, whereupon she became agitated and had to be restrained. Until that time, that area continued within the area of her "immediate control".

"Appellant would have us extend our decision in *Baca* concerning loss of immediate control by bringing the court's attention to such factors present at the arrest as the presence of five officers, the arrest itself (thereby implying restraint and loss of control of the surrounding area), and the physical presence of the police detective between Mrs. Patterson and the cabinet. While these are restraints of sorts, we are not willing to hold these restraints to be as effective as the handcuffing in *Baca* to render the immediately surrounding area beyond the arrestee's immediate control.

"The detective's entry into the kitchen was reasonable in assuring the safety of the arresting officers. This area was within the immediate control of appellant's wife. Therefore, it was a reasonable search incident to a lawful arrest. The evidence obtained would be admissible since "objects falling in the plain view of an officer who has a right to be in the position to have that view are subject to seizure and may be introduced in evidence." Harris v. United States, 390 U.S. 234, 236, 88 S.Ct. 992, 993 (1968).

(b) United States v. Mehciz, 437 F.2d 145 (9th Cir. 1971):

"On September 29, 1969, Arthur Fluhr, Special Agent of the Bureau of Narcotics and Dangerous Drugs, received information from a reliable informant that a large shipment of LSD was being carried from southern California to Phoenix the next day. Fluhr's informant supplied the first name (Vance) of the person who would be carrying the drugs as well as the airline, flight number and arrival time, and described him as a white male about six feet tall, wearing long dark hair and missing a front tooth.

"Fluhr and other federal officers met the flight on its arrival. They stood near the gate and watched the deplaning passengers until they spotted the appellant Mehciz who fit the description they had been given. The officers allowed Mehciz to pass through the gate and past them when Fluhr called, 'Hey, Vance!' at which Mehciz turned around and looked at Fluhr.

"Mehciz was immediately placed under arrest. When arrested, he was carrying a small gray overnight suitcase. The officers took the suitcase and handcuffed Mehciz so that there was no danger that he would get to the suitcase, obtain a weapon or destroy any evidence that might be found inside.

"Fluhr opened the suitcase at the airport and found the LSD tablets inside.

"Appellant's argument here is that the suitcase was searched after it had been taken from his possession and after he had been handcuffed by the federal agents. Therefore, the suitcase was not 'within his immediate control' as that phrase is defined in *Chimel*. Rather than conduct the search at this time, appellant argues that the federal agents should have maintained their control over the suitcase and then secured a warrant authorizing them to open and search it. Appellant does *not* suggest that the officers could not have procured a warrant under these facts nor would such an argument have merit.

"We are not unimpressed by the logical conclusion which appellant draws from his interpretation of the *Chimel* rule, but we are convinced that a contrary result is required. In Chambers v. Maroney, the Court was faced with a warrantless search of the automobile which the defendants had been driving when lawfully arrested. The suggestion made here was also proposed to the Court there, that the automobile should have been impounded without a search until a search warrant could be obtained.

"The Court in *Chambers* expressly rejected the suggestion saying that '[f]or constitutional purposes, we see no difference between on the one hand seizing and holding a car before presenting the probable cause issue to a magistrate and on the other hand carrying out an immediate search without a warrant. Given probable cause to search, either course is reasonable under the Fourth Amendment.' We believe that the factors underlying the decision in *Chambers*, i. e., mobility and the lack of undue intrusion, apply with at least equal force to the suitcase involved here.

"There is little doubt but that the rule of *Chimel* is apparently not applicable to automobile searches per the decision in *Chambers*. The Supreme Court has expressly held that 'for the purposes of the Fourth Amendment there is a constitutional difference between houses and cars.' While we are not necessarily of the view that *Chimel* is limited to house searches, we think it only reasonable to conclude that there is a corresponding 'constitutional difference' between a house and a suitcase.

"Finally, we think our conclusion here is further fortified by Draper v. United States. In *Draper*, the federal narcotics agents learned from a reliable informant that a man would be arriving in Denver by train from Chicago and would be delivering a shipment of heroin. He was described in detail but not named. When Draper left the train, the agents saw that he conformed to the description they had been given. He was stopped, arrested and searched. The heroin was found in his hand and a needle (also introduced into evidence at his trial) was found during the course of an on-the-spot search of a small handbag which he was carrying and which was taken from him when he was arrested.

"The Court noted that the agents had verified everything told them by the informant 'except whether [Draper] had accomplished his mission and had the three ounces of heroin on his person or *in his bag*'. As here, "the arrest was therefore lawful, and the subsequent search and seizure, having been made incident to that lawful arrest, were likewise valid.

"We think that *Draper* is factually indistinguishable from the situation involved here. Our result is thus dictated by *Draper*, as well as by the logic of *Chambers*, and we find nothing in *Chimel* or any other post-*Draper* decisions of the Supreme Court that leave any doubt as to the continuing vitality of *Draper* as constitutional precedent. . . . "

2. Normally a search incident to an arrest occurs after the arrest is made. Is it necessary that the arrest be made *before* the search? As was said in Holt v. Simpson, 340 F.2d 853, 856 (7th Cir. 1966):

"When probable cause for an arrest exists independently of what the search produces, the fact that the search precedes the formal arrest is immaterial when the search and arrest are nearly simultaneous and constitute for all practical purposes but one transaction. To hold differently would be to allow a technical formality of time to control when there had been no real interference with the substantive rights of a defendant."

See Cupp v. Murphy, infra note 5.

It has been consistently held that the fact a seizure may have preceded the actual arrest by a few minutes is immaterial where it was part of one continuous transaction and the existence of probable cause preceded the seizure. Buick v. United States, 396 F.2d 912, 915 (9th Cir. 1968); Henderson v. United States, 405 F.2d 874 (5th Cir. 1968); United States v. Lucas, 360 F.2d 937 (6th Cir. 1966); Willson v. Superior Court, 46 Cal.2d 291, 294 P.2d 36, 38 (1956). The reason for the rule is based on common sense and upon the practical difficulty of determining in many cases, the exact moment of arrest. United States v. Skinner, 412 F.2d 98, 102–04 (8th Cir. 1969). A few courts have held that despite pre-existing probable cause, if an officer searches a person or the area in his control with the intention of arresting only if he find evidence during the search, the search cannot be justified as being incidental to an arrest. State v. Baker, 112 N.J.Super. 351, 271 A.2d 435 (1970).

3. Under *Chimel* the right to search the person who is arrested is clear. See Ricehill v. Brewer, 459 F.2d 537 (8th Cir. 1972). How extensive may this search be? The following cases all approved extensive searches. State v. Wood, 262 La. 259, 263 So.2d 28 (1972) (suspect's mouth); Gaddis v. State, 497 P.2d 1087 (Okl.Crim.1972) (pubic hairs taken from clothes of arrestee); People v. Pinette, 42 Mich.App. 250, 201 N.W.2d 692 (1972) (shoes of arrestee). See generally State v. Swartsfager, — Or.App. —, 501 P.2d 1321 (1972).

In United States v. Simpson, 453 F.2d 1028 (10th Cir. 1972), the defendant was properly arrested by state officers for unlawful possession of explosives. Simpson's person was searched and the contents of his wallet examined. These contents included the selective service cards of another person and Simpson was prosecuted for illegal possession of those cards in federal court. He challenged the legality of the search. The Court held:

The general rule is that incident to a lawful arrest, a search without a warrant may be made of portable personal effects in the immediate possession of the person arrested. The discovery during a search of a totally unrelated object which provides grounds for prosecution of a crime different than that which the accused was arrested for does not render the search invalid. Thus when Simpson's wallet was searched it was done incident to a lawful arrest and even though incriminating objects unrelated to the offense for which he was arrested were discovered, the search was valid. The incriminating Selective Service Certificate and Classification Card were admissible in evidence in the instant prosecution. We observe that although the general rule approved here does not require specific justification on a case-to-case basis, we take notice that knives and other small weapons can be secreted in wallets and that cards and addresses may disclose names of those who may have conspired with the person searched in the commission of the crime charged.

An excellent analysis of cases involving thorough searches of the person is found in McIntyre and Chabraja, The Intensive Search of a Suspect's Body and Clothing, 58 J.Crim.L., C., & P.S. 18 (1967).

4. In Cupp v. Murphy, 412 U.S. 292, 93 S.Ct. 2000 (1973) the Court dealt with problems of scope and timing of the search incident to arrest:

* * *

"The [courts below] all agreed that the police had probable cause to arrest the respondent at the time they detained him and scraped his fingernails. As the Oregon Court of Appeals said,

"At the time the detectives took these scrapings they knew:

"The bedroom in which the wife was found dead showed no signs of disturbance, which fact tended to indicate a killer known to the victim rather than to a burglar or other stranger.

"The decedent's son, the only other person in the house that night, did not have fingernails which could have made the lacerations observed on the victim's throat.

"The defendant and his deceased wife had had a stormy marriage and did not get along well.

"The defendant had, in fact, been at his home on the night of the murder. He left and drove back to central Oregon claiming that he did not enter the house or see his wife. He volunteered a great deal of information without being asked, yet expressed no concern or curiosity about his wife's fate . . .

"It is also undisputed that the police did not obtain an arrest warrant nor formally 'arrest' the respondent . . . The respondent was detained only long enough to take the fingernail scrapings, and was not formally 'arrested' until approximately one month later. Nevertheless, the detention of the respondent against his will constituted a seizure of his person, and the Fourth Amendment guarantee of freedom from 'unreasonable searches and seizures' is clearly implicated. * * *

"We believe this search was constitutionally permissible under the principles of Chimel v. California, 395 U.S. 752, 89 S.Ct. 2034. *Chimel* stands in a long line of cases recognizing an exception to the warrant requirement when a search is incident to a valid arrest. The basis for this exception is that when an arrest is made, it is reasonable for a police officer to expect the arrestee to use any weapons he may have and to attempt to destroy any incriminating evidence then in his possession. The Court recognized in *Chimel* that the scope of a warrantless search must be commensurate with the rationale that excepts the search from the warrant requirement. Thus a warrantless search incident to arrest, the Court held in *Chimel,* must be limited to the area 'into which an arrestee might reach.'

"Where there is no formal arrest, as in the case before us, a person might well be less hostile to the police and less likely to take conspicuous, immediate steps to destroy incriminating evidence on his person. Since he knows he is going to be released, he might be likely instead to be concerned with diverting attention away from himself. Accordingly, we do not hold that a full *Chimel* search would have been justified in this case without a formal arrest and without a warrant. But the respondent was not subjected to such a search.

"At the time Murphy was being detained at the station house, he was obviously aware of the detectives' suspicions. Though he did not have the full warning of official suspicion that a formal arrest provides, Murphy was sufficiently apprised of his suspected role in the crime to motivate him to attempt to destroy what evidence he could without attracting further attention. Testimony at trial indicated that after he refused to consent to the taking of fingernail samples, he put his hands behind his back and appeared to rub them together. He then put his hands in his pockets, and a 'metallic sound, such as keys or change rattling' was heard. The rationale of *Chimel*, in these circumstances, justified the police in subjecting him to the very limited search necessary to preserve the highly evanescent evidence they found under his fingernails, . . .

"On the facts of this case, considering the existence of probable cause, the very limited intrusion undertaken incident to the station house detention, and the ready destructibility of the evidence, we cannot say that this search violated the Fourth and Fourteenth Amendments."

5. The right to search a person lawfully arrested is related to the recognized right of the police to inventory the property of a person about to be incarcerated. Charles v. United States, 278 F.2d 386 (9th Cir. 1960); Westover v. United States, 394 F.2d 164 (9th Cir. 1968); People v. Glaubman, 175 Colo. 141, 485 P.2d 711 (1971); State v. Hohensee, 473 S.W.2d 379 (Mo.1971). Some cases suggest that if the arrestee may be released on bail or recognizance before any period of incarceration, inventory search cannot be justified. People v. Millard, 15 Cal.App.3d 759, 93 Cal.Rptr. 402 (1971); People v. Overlee, 174 Colo. 1202, 483 P.2d 222 (1971). Inventory searches may have limitations. For example, may the contents of a suitcase be inventoried? Compare United States v. Boyd, 436 F.2d 1203 (5th Cir. 1970), and United States v. Robbins, 424 F.2d 57 (6th Cir. 1970) (inventory of suitcase permitted), with the more restrictive opinion in Faubion v. United States, 424 F.2d 437 (10th Cir. 1970). The rationale for the inventory search is offered by Mr. Justice Thompson, concurring in Arabia v. State, 82 Nev. 453, 421 P.2d 952 (1966).

"One's right of personal privacy is dramatically diminished when he has been lawfully placed in jail. He must then submit to reasonable measures designed to promote jail security and the orderly handling of inmates. The segregation of prisoners and the inventorying of their personal belongings is a matter of internal police administration, and does not offend the purposes of the Fourth Amendment." Would materials found in a jail inventory be admissible if the defendant's custody was the product of an arrest without probable cause?

Once the property of the suspect has been inventoried and stored, the police may lose the right to make any further inspection of the property unless they secure a warrant. See Brett v. United States, 412 F.2d 401 (5th Cir. 1969). Would the police have any difficulty in securing a lawful warrant in this kind of situation?

6. Consider the following excerpts from United States v. Edwards, — U.S. —, 94 S.Ct. 1234 (1974):

"MR. JUSTICE WHITE delivered the opinion of the Court.

"The question here is whether the Fourth Amendment should be extended to exclude from evidence certain clothing taken from respondent Edwards while he was in custody at the city jail approximately 10 hours after his arrest.

"Shortly after 11 p. m. on May 31, 1970, respondent Edwards was lawfully arrested on the streets of Lebanon, Ohio and charged with attempting to break into that city's Post Office. He was taken to the local jail and placed in a cell. Contemporaneously or shortly thereafter, investigation at the scene revealed that the attempted entry had been made through a wooden window which apparently had been pried up with a pry bar, leaving paint chips on the window sill and wire mesh screen. The next morning, trousers and a T-shirt were purchased for Edwards to substitute for the clothing which he had been wearing at the time of and since his arrest. His clothing was then taken from him and held as evidence. Examination of the clothing revealed paint chips matching the samples that had been taken from the window. This evidence and his clothing were received at trial over Edwards' objection that neither the clothing nor the results of its examination were admissible because the warrantless seizure of his clothing was invalid under the Fourth Amendment.

"The Court of Appeals reversed. Expressly disagreeing with two other courts of appeals, it held that although the arrest was lawful and probable cause existed to believe that paint chips would be discovered on petitioner's clothing, the warrantless seizure of the clothing carried out 'after the administrative process and mechanics of arrest have come to a halt' was nevertheless unconstitutional under the Fourth Amendment. . . .

"The prevailing rule under the Fourth Amendment that searches and seizures may not be made without a warrant is subject to various exceptions. One of them permits warrantless searches incident to custodial arrests, and has traditionally been justified by the reasonableness of searching for weapons, instruments of escape and evidence of crime when a person is taken into official custody and lawfully detained.

"It is also plain that searches and seizures that could be made on the spot at the time of arrest may legally be conducted later when the accused arrives at the place of detention. . . . The Courts of Appeals have followed this same rule, holding that both the person and the property in his immediate possession may be searched at the station house after the arrest has occurred at another place and if evidence of crime is discovered, it may be seized and admitted in evidence. Nor is there any doubt that clothing or other belongings may be seized upon arrival of the accused at the place of detention and later subjected to laboratory analysis or that the test results are admissible at trial.

"Conceding all this, the Court of Appeals in this case nevertheless held that a warrant is required where the search occurs after the administrative mechanics of arrest have been completed and the prisoner is incarcerated. But even on these terms, it seems to us that the normal processes incident to arrest and custody had not been completed when Edwards was placed in his cell on the night of May 31. With or without probable cause, the authorities were entitled at that point in time not only to search Edwards' clothing but also to take it from him and keep it in official custody. There was testimony that this was the standard practice in this city. The police were also entitled to take from Edwards any evidence of the crime in his immediate possession, including his clothing. And the Court of Appeals acknowledged that contemporaneously with or shortly after the time Edwards went to his cell, the police had probable cause to believe that the articles of clothing he wore were themselves material evidence of the crime for which he had been arrested. But it was late at night; no substitute clothing was then available for Edwards to wear, and it would certainly have been unreasonable for the police to have stripped petitioner of his clothing and left him exposed in his cell throughout the night. When the substitutes were purchased the next morning, the clothing he had been wearing at the time of arrest was taken from him and subjected to laboratory analysis. This was no more than taking from petitioner the effects in his immediate possession that constituted evidence of crime. This was and is a normal incident of a custodial arrest, and reasonable delay in effectuating it does not change the fact that Edwards was no more imposed upon than he could have been at the time and place of the arrest or immediately upon arrival at the place of detention. The police did no more on June 1 than they were entitled to do incident to the usual custodial arrest and incarceration.

"Other closely related considerations sustain the examination of the clothing in this case. It must be remembered that on both May 31 and June 1 the police had lawful custody of Edwards and necessarily of the clothing he wore. When it became apparent that the articles of clothing were evidence of the crime for which Edwards was being held, the police were entitled to take, examine, and preserve them for use as evidence, just as they are normally permitted to seize evidence of crime when it is lawfully encountered. Chimel v. California. Surely, the clothes could have been brushed down and vacuumed while Edwards had them on in the cell, and it was similarly reasonable to take and examine them as the police did, particularly in view of the existence of probable cause linking the clothes to the crime. Indeed, it is difficult to perceive what is unreasonable about the police examining and holding as evidence these personal effects of the accused that they already have in their lawful custody as the result of a lawful arrest. * * *

". . . [Most cases in the courts of appeals] have long since concluded that once the defendant is lawfully arrested and is in custody, the effects in his possession at the place of detention that were subject to search at the time and place of his arrest may lawfully be searched and seized without a warrant even though a substantial period of time has elapsed between the arrest and subsequent administrative processing on the one hand and the taking of the property for use as evidence on the other. This is true where the clothing or effects are immediately seized upon arrival at the jail, held under the defendant's name in the 'property room' of the jail and at a later time searched and taken for use at the subsequent criminal trial. The result is the same where the property is not physically taken from the defendant until sometime after his incarceration.

"In upholding this search and seizure, we do not conclude that the warrant clause of the Fourth Amendment is never applicable to postarrest seizures of the effects of an arrestee.[1] But we do think that the Court of

1. Holding the Warrant Clause inapplicable in the circumstances present here does not leave law enforcement officials subject to no restraints. This type of police conduct "must [still] be tested by the Fourth Amend-

Appeals for the First Circuit captured the essence of situations like these when it said in United States v. DeLeo, supra, 422 F.2d, at 493:

'While the legal arrest of a person should not destroy the privacy of his premises, it does—for at least a reasonable time and to a reasonable extent—take his own privacy out of the realm of protection from police interest in weapons, means of escape and evidence.'

The judgment of the Court of Appeals is reversed.

"MR. JUSTICE STEWART, with whom MR. JUSTICE DOUGLAS, MR. JUSTICE BRENNAN, and MR. JUSTICE MARSHALL join, dissenting. * * *

. . . Since it is conceded here that the seizure of Edwards' clothing was not made pursuant to a warrant, the question becomes whether the Government has met its burden of showing that the circumstances of this seizure brought it within one of the 'jealously and carefully drawn' exceptions to the warrant requirement.

"The Court finds a warrant unnecessary in this case because of the custodial arrest of the respondent. But the mere fact of an arrest does not allow the police to engage in warrantless searches of unlimited geographic or temporal scope. Rather, the search must be spatially limited to the person of the arrestee and the area within his reach and must, as to time, be 'substantially contemporaneous with the arrest.'

"Under the facts of this case, I am unable to agree with the Court's holding that the search was 'incident' to Edwards' custodial arrest. The search here occurred fully 10 hours after he was arrested, at a time when the administrative processing and mechanics of arrest had long since come to an end. His clothes were not seized as part of an 'inventory' of a prisoner's effects, nor were they taken pursuant to a routine exchange of civilian clothes for jail garb. And the considerations that typically justify a warrantless search incident to a lawful arrest were wholly absent here.[2] * * *

". . . I see no justification for dispensing with the warrant requirement here. The police had ample time to seek a warrant, and no exigent circumstances were present to excuse their failure to do so. Unless the exceptions to the warrant requirement are to be 'enthroned into the rule,' this is precisely the sort of situation where the Fourth Amendment requires a magistrate's prior approval for a search.

"The Court says that the relevant question is 'not whether it was reasonable to procure a search warrant, but whether the search itself was reasonable.' Ante, at 7–8. Precisely such a view, however, was explicitly rejected in Chimel v. California, where the Court characterized the argument as 'founded on little more than a subjective view regarding the ac-

ment's general proscription against unreasonable searches and seizures." Terry v. Ohio. But the Court of Appeals here conceded that probable cause existed for the search and seizure of petitioner's clothing, and petitioner complains only that a warrant should have been secured. We thus have no occasion to express a view concerning those circumstances surrounding custodial searches incident to incarceration which might "violate the dictates of reason either because of their number or their manner of perpetration."

2. No claim is made that the police feared that Edwards either possessed a weapon or was planning to destroy the paint chips on his clothing. Indeed, the Government has not even suggested that he was aware of the presence of the paint chips on his clothing.

ceptability of certain sorts of police conduct, and not on considerations relevant to Fourth Amendment interests.' * * *

"The intrusion here was hardly a shocking one, and it cannot be said that the police acted in bad faith. The Fourth Amendment, however, was not designed to apply only to situations where the intrusion is massive and the violation of privacy shockingly flagrant. . . .

"Because I believe that the Court today unjustifiably departs from well-settled constitutional principles, I respectfully dissent."

7. In *Chimel*, the Court thought that the police should get a warrant before searching the home of an arrestee and implied that the police could watch the home in the interim. Would the use of the telephone search warrant solve the police problem of maintaining security over the premises while a warrant is secured? What are the limits of police security measures? Consider the following excerpts from People v. Block, 6 Cal.3d 239, 499 P.2d 961 (1971):

> "In the instant case, it seems evident that Officer Galloway had reasonable cause to believe, based upon facts available to him at the time he acted, that additional persons might be on the premises. The presence of six or seven persons downstairs, four of whom bore signs of recent marijuana use, together with the immediate direction of burning marijuana smoke and the discovery of a smoking marijuana roach and two pipes lying in plain sight on a coffee table reasonably indicated that a 'pot party' was in progress, involving an undetermined number of participants. The lights which illuminated the stairway and upstairs hall justified the further suspicion that other persons might be upstairs who were involved in the offenses charged, or who might pose a security risk for the arresting officers. Under these circumstances, it was entirely reasonable for Officer Galloway to act as he did."
>
> (Dissent):
>
> "The sole basis suggested by the majority for the asserted reasonable belief that suspects might be upstairs was that the officers had found a 'pot party' in progress downstairs. The superior court judge's rhetorical question succinctly answers the majority's point: 'How could you possibly say that an officer has a right to wander around a house, looking for people, just because there are two people, or four people, smoking a roach?' The absence of any specific facts indicating the presence of additional suspects reduces Officer Galloway's suspicion to a mere hunch, insufficient to warrant a search under the foregoing authorities. To infer that because six people were found in the house others might be present is just as illogical as to infer that because only one person was found in the living room others should be around the house somewhere.
>
> "I conclude that the mere fact that the officers found a 'pot party' downstairs does not, without additional facts, furnish probable cause to believe that further participants were upstairs. The reasoning of the majority in reaching a contrary result means that *a search for additional 'possible suspects' could be undertaken in every case where more than one suspect who may be engaged in criminal conduct is arrested.* The rule announced today allows the

> police to search throughout a house for other suspects pursuant to an arrest of two or more in a variety of situations involving a myriad of crimes where an officer could surmise that there may be more than one person involved in the crime. To permit such searches would totally emasculate *Chimel* and allow the police to search any areas except places like desk drawers which are so small that even a midget could not hide in one."

In United States v. Gamble, 473 F.2d 1274 (7th Cir. 1973), the court refused to sustain an inspection of the premises:

". . . On the night of February 7, 1970, Everett Davis appeared at the Harvey police station and complained that Gamble and two others, James Williams and Jerome Crowder, had abducted him at gun point and taken him to Gamble's home where they committed an aggravated battery and armed robbery. Williams and Crowder were immediately taken into custody. At the time Crowder was arrested, the police found and seized a weapon of the type which the complaining witness alleged had been used in the robbery.

"Gamble was the next object of police attention. At about 12:30 in the morning of February 8, approximately seven officers proceeded to Gamble's residence for the purpose of securing his arrest. They knocked on his door and received a response from a female voice inside, inquiring as to the identity of the knocker. After announcing their office and their intent to arrest Gamble, and upon hearing no reply but a 'rustling' noise from behind the door, the officers broke down the door and entered with guns drawn.

"Their initial entry carried them into the kitchen of Gamble's residence. To the officers' left was a doorway leading to a bedroom, to their right a blank kitchen wall. As they entered, Gamble and a woman were emerging from the bedroom; another woman was observed sitting at a table in the kitchen. Gamble was advised of his arrest, ordered to raise his hands, and was frisked after being placed against the kitchen wall opposite the bedroom entrance.

"One of the arresting officers then walked to the bedroom door and looked inside. Observing a figure on a bed to his left, the officer turned on the room light and determined than an infant child was lying on the bed. The officer entered the room and walked to the bed to 'see that the baby was all right.' He was closely followed by a second officer, who, looking about the room, observed and seized the weapon upon which this prosecution was based. While this was going on, other officers of the arrest team were conducting a thorough search of the rest of the residence, despite the fact that they possessed only a warrant for Gamble's arrest, not a warrant to search his premises. * * *

"This is not a case like United States v. Harris, 140 U.S.App.D.C. 270, 435 F.2d 74 (1970), where all three members of a robbery gang were at large, and police, finding two of the gang in an apartment, had reason to believe that the third was hiding elsewhere on the premises. At the time of Gamble's arrest, both Williams and Crowder were safely in police custody. People v. Block, 6 Cal.3d 239, 103 Cal.Rptr. 281, 499 P.2d 961 (1971), and United States v. Broomfield, 336 F.Supp. 179 (E.D.Mich.1972), relied upon by the Government, are similarly distinguishable; in each case it was found that arresting officers had reason to believe that suspected drug violators other than those arrested were located in rooms beyond the site of arrest.

"Indeed, the Government's reliance on these cases is misplaced, since it does not contend that the feared presence of dangerous criminal suspects other than Gamble justified the search. Instead, we are presented with a list of other facts said to constitute exigent circumstances:

1. The police upon numerous occasions had responded to calls of 'shots-fired' at defendant's address.

2. The outside of defendant's house resembled an embattled fortress; (a) the front door was boarded up due to a recent explosion, and (b) there were numerous bullet holes in the outside walls.

3. There had been a large gathering of 20–30 persons at defendant's house earlier in the day.

4. The defendant was accused of a violent crime involving a dangerous weapon.

5. The defendant was known to possess firearms, admitted to owning a handgun, and expressed a particular interest in automatic weapons.

6. The police heard 'rustling' noises from inside defendant's house after announcing their office and purpose.

"Only with difficulty might the first three of these circumstances be characterized 'exigent' as we understand that term. They could readily have been presented to a magistrate by the Harvey police before the arrest of Gamble was undertaken. The same cannot be said of the last item on the list. Nonetheless, police officers will almost always be confronted with 'rustling' noises when they knock on the door of an occupied home late at night; the party inside must awake, prepare himself to answer, and walk to the door. We think that arresting police must show considerably more than this to justify a search beyond *Chimel* limits even of the room directly behind the door, much less of rooms leading therefrom. The remaining reasons suggested by the Government relate only to Gamble and his violent propensities. Justifications like these were fully considered by the Court in *Chimel*, and warrant no search beyond the area within the immediate reach of the arrestee."

8. May an officer conduct a search of the companion of someone he arrests, at least to the extent of determining whether or not the companion is armed? Consider the following from United States v. Berryhill, 445 F. 2d 1189 (9th Cir. 1971):

"The postal inspectors had obtained a warrant for the arrest of defendant for the Kawa check theft and were looking for him. The arresting officers had knowledge of defendant's prior arrest history, including information that he usually had weapons close to him. Defendant and his wife, the former driving, the latter a front-seat passenger, were located in an automobile and were stopped to effectuate the arrest at a busy intersection. The arrest was made with drawn pistols covering both occupants of the car, defendant was required to disembark and spread-eagle against the car where he was searched for weapons, handcuffed and taken to the officer's car by Inspector Loffler. Inspector Michaelson observed that Mrs. Berryhill was clutching a handbag with a paper sack protruding from the top. The paper sack was too small for its contents and in the top of the sack, the officer saw what appeared to be several envelopes. Michaelson, covering Mrs. Berryhill with his firearm, searched the handbag for weapons and found the mail matter which is the subject of Counts VI and XIII. On interrogation, defendant said, 'Look here, officer, the mail in her purse is mine. I told her to put it in there and she does what I say because she is my wife.'

"We are here concerned with the right to search another occupant of the vehicle, Mrs. Clarice Berryhill, who was clutching the handbag in which the stolen mail matter described in Counts VI and XIII was found. The fact that envelopes were observed protruding from the top of the paper sack might arguably have supported the reasonableness of the search, but the arresting officer described it as purely a search for weapons. And the lawful arrest of Berryhill cannot legalize a personal search of a companion for evidence against her simply because she was there. United States v. Di Re, 332 U.S. 581, 68 S.Ct. 222 (1948). The Supreme Court, however, has clarified the right of peace officers to protect themselves from the reasonably anticipated possibility of assault. In Terry v. Ohio, 393 U.S. 1, 88 S.Ct. 1868 (1967), the Court affirmed the right of a limited search "to assure * * * that the person with whom he is dealing is not armed with a weapon that could unexpectedly and fatally be used against him" despite the absence of probable cause for an arrest. We think that *Terry* recognizes and common sense dictates that the legality of such a limited intrusion into a citizen's personal privacy extends to a criminal's companions at the time of arrest. It is inconceivable that a peace officer effecting a lawful arrest of an occupant of a vehicle must expose himself to a shot in the back from defendant's associate because he cannot, on the spot, make the nice distinction between whether the other is a companion in crime or a social acquaintance. All companions of the arrestee within the immediate vicinity, capable of accomplishing a harmful assault on the officer, are constitutionally subjected to the cursory 'pat-down' reasonably necessary to give assurance that they are unarmed."

UNITED STATES v. ROBINSON

Supreme Court of the United States, 1973.
414 U.S. 218, 94 S.Ct. 467.

MR. JUSTICE REHNQUIST delivered the opinion of the Court.

Respondent Robinson was convicted in United States District Court for the District of Columbia of the possession and facilitation of concealment of heroin . . . On his appeal . . . the Court of Appeals *en banc* reversed the judgment of conviction, holding that the heroin introduced in evidence against respondent had been obtained as a result of a search which violated the Fourth Amendment to the United States Constitution . . .

On April 23, 1968, at approximately 11 o'clock p. m., Officer Richard Jenks, a 15-year veteran of the District of Columbia Metropolitan Police Department, observed the respondent driving a 1965 Cadillac near the intersection of 8th and C Streets, Southeast, in the District of Columbia. Jenks, as a result of previous investigation following a check of respondent's operator's permit four days earlier, determined there was reason to believe that respondent was operating a motor vehicle after the revocation of his operator's permit. This is an offense defined by statute in the District of Columbia which carries a mandatory minimum jail term, a mandatory minimum fine, or both.

Jenks signaled respondent to stop the automobile, which respondent did, and all three of the occupants emerged from the car. At that point Jenks informed respondent that he was under arrest for "operating after revocation and obtaining a permit by misrepresentation." It was assumed by the majority of the Court of Appeals, and is conceded by the respondent here, that Jenks had probable cause to arrest respondent, and that he effected a full custody arrest.

In accordance with procedures prescribed in Police Department instructions.[1] Jenks then began to search respondent. He explained

1. The government introduced testimony at the evidentiary hearing upon the original remand by the Court of Appeals as to certain standard operating procedures of the Metropolitan Police Department. Sergeant Dennis C. Donaldson, a Metropolitan Police Department Training Division Instructor, testified that when a police officer makes "a full custody arrest" which he defined as where an officer "would arrest a subject and subsequently transport him to a police facility for booking," the officer is trained to make a full "field type search":

"Q. Would you describe the physical acts the officer is instructed to perform with respect to this field search in a full custody arrest situation?

"A. (Sgt. Donaldson). Basically, it is a thorough search of the individual. We would expect in a field search that the officer completely search the individual and inspect areas such as behind the collar, underneath the collar, the waistband of the trousers, the cuffs, the socks and shoes. Those are the areas we would ask a complete thorough search of.

"Q. What are the instructions in a field type search situation when an officer feels something on the outside of the garment?

"A. If it is a full custody arrest and he is conducting a field search, we expect him to remove anything and examine it to determine exactly what it is.

"THE COURT: That is a fully custody arrest. What is the last part of it?

"THE WITNESS: In conducting a field search, which is done any time there is a full custody arrest, we expect the officer to examine anything he might find on the subject.

"THE COURT: Would he do the same thing in a pat-down search?

"THE WITNESS: If he could determine in his pat-down or frisk by squeezing that it was not, in fact, a weapon that could be used against him, then we don't instruct him to go further.

"THE COURT: But in a field search, even though he may feel something that he believes is not a weapon, is he instructed to take it out?

"THE WITNESS: Yes, sir."

Sergeant Donaldson testified that officers are instructed to examine the "contents of all of the pockets" of the arrestee in the course of the field search. It was stated that these standard operating procedures were initiated by the police department "primarily, for [the officer's] own safety and secondly, for the safety of the individual he has placed under arrest and, thirdly, to search for evidence of the crime." While the officer is instructed to make a full field search of the person of the individual he arrests, he is instructed, and police department regulations provide, that in the case of a full custody arrest for driving after revocation, "areas beyond [the arrestee's] immediate control should not be searched because there is no probable cause to believe that the vehicle contains fruits, instrumentalities, contraband or eviat a subsequent hearing that he was "face to face" with the respondent, and "placed [his] hands on [the respondent], my right hand to his left breast like this (demonstrating) and proceeded to pat him down thus (with the right hand)." During this patdown, Jenks felt an object in the left breast pocket of the heavy coat respondent was wearing, but testified that he "couldn't tell what it was" and also that he "couldn't actually tell the size of it." Jenks then reached into the pocket and pulled out the object, which turned out to be a "crumpled up cigarette package." Jenks testified that at this point he still did not know what was in the package:

> "As I felt the package I could feel objects in the package but I couldn't tell what they were . . . . . I knew they weren't cigarettes."

The officer then opened the cigarette pack and found 14 gelatin capsules of white powder which he thought to be, and which later analysis proved to be, heroin. Jenks then continued his search of respondent to completion, feeling around his waist and trouser legs, and examining the remaining pockets. The heroin seized from the respondent was admitted into evidence at the trial which resulted in his conviction in the District Court. * * *

I

It is well settled that a search incident to a lawful arrest is a traditional exception to the warrant requirement of the Fourth Amendment. This general exception has historically been formulated into two distinct propositions. The first is that a search may be made of the *person* of the arrestee by virtue of the lawful arrest. The second is that a search may be made of the area within the control of the arrestee.

Examination of this Court's decisions in the area show that these two propositions have been treated quite differently. The validity of the search of a person incident to a lawful arrest has been regarded as settled from its first enunciation, and has remained virtually unchallenged until the present case. The validity of the second proposition, while likewise conceded in principle, has been subject to differing interpretations as to the extent of the area which may be searched.

Because the rule requiring exclusion of evidence obtained in violation of the Fourth Amendment was first enunciated in Weeks v. United States, 232 U.S. 383 (1914)., it is understandable that virtually all of this Court's search and seizure law has been developed since

dence of the offense of driving after revocation." Those regulations also provide that in the case of some traffic offenses, including the crime of operating a motor vehicle after revocation of an operator's permit, the officer shall make a summary arrest of the violator and take the violator, in custody, to the stationhouse for booking. D. C. Metropolitan Police Department General Order No. 3, series 1959 (April 24, 1959).

Such operating procedures are not, of course, determinative of the constitutional issues presented by this case.

that time. In *Weeks,* the Court made clear its recognition of the validity of a search incident to a lawful arrest:

> "What then is the present case? Before answering that inquiry specifically, it may be well by a process of exclusion to state what it is not. It is not an assertion of the right of the government, always recognized under English and American law, to search the person of the accused when legally arrested to discover and seize the fruits or evidences of crime. This right has been uniformly maintained in many cases."

Agnello v. United States, 269 U.S. 20 (1925), decided 11 years after *Weeks*, repeats the categorical recognition of the validity of a search incident to lawful arrest:

> "The right without a search warrant contemporaneously to search persons lawfully arrested while committing crime and to search the place where the arrest is made in order to find and seize things connected with the crime as well as weapons and other things to effect an escape from custody, is not to be doubted." Id., at 30.

Throughout the series of cases in which the Court has addressed the second proposition relating to a search incident to a lawful arrest—the permissible area beyond the person of the arrestee which such a search may cover—no doubt has been expressed as to the unqualified authority of the arresting authority to search the person of the arrestee. E. g., Carroll v. United States, 267 U.S. 132 (1925); Chimel v. California, 395 U.S. 752 (1969). In *Chimel,* where the Court overruled *Rabinowitz* and *Harris* as to the area of permissible search incident to a lawful arrest, full recognition was again given to the authority to search the person of the arrestee:

> "When an arrest is made, it is reasonable for the arresting officer to search the person arrested in order to remove any weapons that the latter might seek to use in order to resist arrest or effect his escape. Otherwise, the officer's safety might well be endangered, and the arrest itself frustrated. In addition, it is entirely reasonable for the arresting officer to search for and seize any evidence on the arrestee's person in order to prevent its concealment or destruction."

Three years after the decision in *Chimel* we upheld the validity of a search in which heroin had been taken from the person of the defendant after his arrest on a weapons charge, in Adams v. Williams, 407 U.S. 143 (1972), saying:

> "Under the circumstances surrounding Williams' possession of the gun seized by Sergeant Connolly, the arrest on the weapons charge was supported by probable cause, and the

search of his person and of the car incident to that arrest was lawful." *Id.*, at 149.

Thus the broadly stated rule, and the reasons for it, have been repeatedly affirmed in the decisions of this Court since Weeks v. United States nearly 60 years ago. Since the statements in the cases speak not simply in terms of an exception to the warrant requirement, but in terms of an affirmative authority to search, they clearly imply that such searches also meet the Fourth Amendment's requirement of reasonableness.

II

In its decision of this case, the majority of the Court of Appeals decided that even after a police officer lawfully places a suspect under arrest for the purpose of taking him into custody, he may not ordinarily proceed to fully search the prisoner. He must instead conduct a limited frisk of the outer clothing and remove such weapons that he may, as a result of that limited frisk, reasonably believe the suspect has in his possession. While recognizing that Terry v. Ohio, 392 U.S. 1 (1968), dealt with a permissible "frisk" incident to an investigative stop based on less than probable cause to arrest, the Court of Appeals felt that the principles of that case should be carried over to this probable cause arrest for driving while one's license is revoked. Since there would be no further evidence of such a crime to be obtained in a search of the arrestee, the Court held that only a search for weapons could be justified.

Terry v. Ohio did not involve an arrest for probable cause, and it made quite clear that the "protective frisk" for weapons which it approved might be conducted without probable cause. The Court's opinion explicitly recognized that there is a "distinction in purpose, character, and extent between a search incident to an arrest and a limited search for weapons":

> "The former, although justified in part by the acknowledged necessity to protect the arresting officer from assault with a concealed weapon is also justified on other grounds, and can therefore involve a relatively extensive exploration of the person. A search for weapons in the absence of probable cause to arrest, however, must, like any other search, be strictly circumscribed by the exigencies which justify its initiation. Thus it must be limited to that which is necessary for the discovery of weapons which might be used to harm the officer or others nearby, and may realistically be characterized as something less than a 'full' search even though it remains a serious intrusion.
>
> " . . . An arrest is a wholly different type of intrusion upon the individual freedom from a limited search for weapons, and the interests each is designed to serve are likewise quite different. An arrest is the initial stage

> of a criminal prosecution. It is intended to vindicate society's interest in having its laws obeyed, and it is inevitably accompanied by future interference with the individual's freedom of movement, whether or not trial or conviction ultimately follows. The protective search for weapons, on the other hand, constitutes a brief though far from inconsiderable, intrusion upon the sanctity of the person."

Terry, therefore, affords no basis to carry over to a probable cause arrest the limitations this Court placed on a stop-and-frisk search permissible without probable cause.

The Court of Appeals also relied on language in Peters v. New York, 392 U.S., at 66, a companion case to *Terry.* There the Court held that the police officer had authority to search Peters because he had probable cause to arrest him, and went on to say:

> " . . . the incident search was obviously justified 'by the need to seize weapons and other things which might be used to assault an officer or effect an escape, as well as by the need to prevent the destruction of evidence of the crime.' Moreover, it was reasonably limited in scope by these purposes. Officer Laskey did not engage in an unrestrained and thoroughgoing examination of Peters and his personal effects."

It is of course possible to read the second sentence from this quotation as imposing a novel limitation on the established doctrine set forth in the first sentence. It is also possible to read it as did Mr. Justice Harlan in his concurring opinion:

> "The second possible source of confusion is the Court's statement that Officer Laskey did not engage in an unrestrained and thorough-going examination of Peters and his personal effects. Ante, at 67. Since the Court found probable cause to arrest Peters, and since an officer arresting on probable cause is entitled to make a very full incident search, I assume that this is merely a factual observation. As a factual matter, I agree with it."

We do not believe that the Court in *Peters* intended in one unexplained and unelaborated sentence to impose a novel and far reaching limitation on the authority to search the person of an arrestee incident to his lawful arrest. While the language from *Peters* was quoted with approval in Chimel v. California, it is preceded by a full exposition of the traditional and unqualified authority of the arresting officer to search the arrestee's person. We do not believe that either *Terry* or *Peters,* when considered in the light of the previously discussed statements of this Court, justified the sort of limitation upon that authority which the Court of Appeals fashioned in his case.

III

Virtually all of the statements of this Court affirming the existence of an unqualified authority to search incident to a lawful arrest are dicta. We would not therefore be foreclosed by principles of *stare decisis* from further examination into history and practice in order to see whether the sort of qualifications imposed by the Court of Appeals in this case were in fact intended by the Framers of the Fourth Amendment or recognized in cases decided prior to *Weeks*. Unfortunately such authorities as exist are sparse. * * *

Spalding v. Preston, 21 Vt. 9 (1848), represents an early holding in this country that evidence may be seized from one who is lawfully arrested. In Closson v. Morrison, 47 N.H. 484 (1867), the Court made the following statement:

> "We think that an officer would also be justified in taking from a person whom he has arrested for crime, any deadly weapon he might find upon him, such as a revolver, a dirk, a knife, a sword cane, a slung shot, or a club, though it had not been used or intended to be used in the commission of the offense for which the prisoner had been arrested, and even though no threats of violence towards the officer had been made. A due regard for his own safety on the part of the officer, and also for the public safety, would justify a sufficient search to ascertain if such weapons were carried on the person of the prisoner, or were in his possession, and if found, to seize and hold them until the prisoner should be discharged, or until they can otherwise be properly disposed of.
>
> "So we think it might be with money or other articles of value, found upon the prisoner, by means of which, if left in his possession, he might procure his escape, or obtain tools, or implements, or weapons with which to effect his escape. We think the officer arresting a man for crime, not only may, but frequently should, make such searches and seizures; then in many cases they might be reasonable and proper, and courts would hold him harmless for so doing, when he acts in good faith, and from a regard to his own or the public safety, or the security of his prisoner."

. . .

Then Chief Judge Cardozo of the New York Court of Appeals summarized his understanding of the historical basis for the authority to search incident to arrest in these words:

> "The basic principle is this: search of the person is unlawful when the seizure of the body is a trespass, and the purpose of the search is to discover grounds as yet unknown for arrest or accusation. Search of the person becomes lawful when grounds for arrest and accusation have been dis-

> covered, and the law is in the act of subjecting the body of the accused to its physical dominion.
>
> "The distinction may seem subtle, but in truth it is founded in shrewd appreciation of the necessities of government. We are not to strain an immunity to the point at which human nature rebels against honoring it in conduct. The peace officer empowered to arrest must be empowered to disarm. If he may disarm, he may search, lest a weapon be concealed. The search being lawful, he retains what he finds if connected with the crime."

While these earlier authorities are sketchy, they tend to support the broad statement of the authority to search incident to arrest found in the successive decisions of this Court, rather than the restrictive one which was applied by the Court of Appeals in this case. The scarcity of case law before *Weeks* is doubtless due in part to the fact that the exclusionary rule there enunciated had been first adopted only 11 years earlier in Iowa; but it would seem to be also due in part to the fact that the issue was regarded as well-settled.

The Court of Appeals in effect determined that the *only* reason supporting the authority for a *full* search incident to lawful arrest was the possibility of discovery of evidence or fruits. Concluding that there could be no evidence or fruits in the case of an offense such as that with which respondent was charged, it held that any protective search would have to be limited by the conditions laid down in *Terry* for a search upon less than probable cause to arrest. Quite apart from the fact that *Terry* clearly recognized the distinction between the two types of searches, and that a different rule governed one than governed the other, we find additional reason to disagree with the Court of Appeals.

The justification or reason for the authority to search incident to a lawful arrest rests quite as much on the need to disarm the suspect in order to take him into custody as it does on the need to preserve evidence on his person for later use at trial. The standards traditionally governing a search incident to lawful arrest are not, therefore, commuted to the stricter *Terry* standards by the absence of probable fruits or further evidence of the particular crime for which the arrest is made.

Nor are we inclined, on the basis of what seems to us to be a rather speculative judgment, to qualify the breadth of the general authority to search incident to a lawful custodial arrest on an assumption that persons arrested for the offense of driving while their license has been revoked are less likely to be possessed of dangerous weapons than are those arrested for other crimes.[2] It is scarcely

2. Such an assumption appears at least questionable in light of the available statistical data concerning assaults on police officers who are in the course of making arrests. The danger to the police officer flows from the fact of the arrest, and its attendant proximity, stress and uncertainty, and not

open to doubt that the danger to an officer is far greater in the case of the extended exposure which follows the taking of a suspect into custody and transporting him to the police station than in the case of the relatively fleeting contact resulting from the typical *Terry*-type stop. This is an adequate basis for treating all custodial arrests alike for purposes of search justification.

But quite apart from these distinctions, our more fundamental disagreement with the Court of Appeals arises from its suggestion that there must be litigated in each case the issue of whether or not there was present one of the reasons supporting the authority for a search of the person incident to a lawful arrest. We do not think the long line of authorities of this Court dating back to *Weeks*, nor what we can glean from the history of practice in this country and in England, requires such a case by case adjudication. A police officer's determination as to how and where to search the person of a suspect whom he has arrested is necessarily a quick *ad hoc* judgment which the Fourth Amendment does not require to be broken down in each instance into an analysis of each step in the search. The authority to search the person incident to a lawful custodial arrest while based upon the need to disarm and to discover evidence, does not depend on what a court may later decide was the probability in a particular arrest situation that weapons or evidence would in fact be found upon the person of the suspect. A custodial arrest of a suspect based on probable cause is a reasonable intrusion under the Fourth Amendment; that intrusion being lawful, a search incident to the arrest requires no additional justification. It is the fact of the lawful arrest which establishes the authority to search, and we hold that in the case of a lawful custodial arrest a full search of the person is not only an exception to the warrant requirement of the Fourth Amendment, but is also a "reasonable" search under that Amendment.

IV

The search of respondent's person conducted by Officer Jenks in this case and the seizure from him of the heroin, were permissible under established Fourth Amendment law. While thorough, the search partook of none of the extreme or patently abusive characteristics which were held to violate the Due Process Clause of the Fourteenth Amendment in Rochin v. California, 342 U.S. 165 (1952). Since it is the fact of custodial arrest which gives rise to the authority

from the grounds for arrest. One study concludes that approximately 30% of the shootings of police officers occur when the officer approaches a person seated in a car. Bristow Police Officer Shootings—A Factual Evaluation, 54 J.Crim.L.C. & P.S. 93 (1963), cited in Adams v. Williams, 407 U.S. 143, 148 (1972). The Government in its brief notes that the Uniform Crime Reports, prepared by the Federal Bureau of Investigation, indicate that a significant percentage of police officer murders occur when the officers are making traffic stops. Brief for the United States, at 23. Those reports indicate that during January-March, 1973, 35 police officers were murdered; 11 of those officers were killed while engaged in traffic stops.

to search,[3] it is of no moment that Jenks did not indicate any subjective fear of the respondent or that he did not himself suspect that respondent was armed. Having in the course of a lawful search come upon the crumpled package of cigarettes he was entitled to inspect it; and when his inspection revealed the heroin capsules, he was entitled to seize them as "fruits, instrumentalities, or contraband" probative of criminal conduct. Warden v. Hayden, 387 U.S. 294, 299, 307 (1967). The judgment of the Court of Appeals holding otherwise is Reversed.

[MR. JUSTICE POWELL'S concurring opinion is omitted.]

MR. JUSTICE MARSHALL, with whom MR. JUSTICE DOUGLAS and MR. JUSTICE BRENNAN join, dissenting.

Certain fundamental principles have characterized this Court's Fourth Amendment jurisprudence over the years. Perhaps the most basic of these was expressed by Mr. Justice Butler, speaking for a unanimous Court in Go-Bart Co. v. United States, 282 U.S. 344 (1931): "There is no formula for the determination of reasonableness. Each case is to be decided on its own facts and circumstances." As we recently held, "The constitutional validity of a warrantless search is preeminently the sort of question which can only be decided in the concrete factual context of the individual case." Sibron v. New York, 392 U.S. 40, 59 (1968). And the intensive, at times painstaking, case by case analysis characteristic of our Fourth Amendment decisions bespeaks our "jealous regard for maintaining the integrity of individual rights." Mapp v. Ohio, 367 U.S. 643, 647 (1961).

In the present case, however, the majority turns its back on these principles, holding that "the fact of the lawful arrest" always establishes the authority to conduct a full search of the arrestee's person, regardless of whether in a particular case "there was present one of the reasons supporting the authority for a search of the person incident to a lawful arrest." The majority's approach represents a clear and marked departure from our long tradition of case-by-case adjudication of the reasonableness of searches and seizures under the Fourth Amendment. I continue to believe that "[t]he scheme of the Fourth Amendment becomes meaningful only when it is assured that at some point the conduct of those charged with enforcing the laws can be subjected to the more detached, neutral scrutiny of a judge who must evaluate the reasonableness of a particular search or seizure in light of the particular circumstances." Terry v. Ohio. Because I find the majority's reasoning to be at odds with these fundamental principles, I must respectfully dissent.

3. The majority opinion of the Court of Appeals also discussed its understanding of the law where the police officer makes what the court characterized as "a routine traffic stop," i. e., where the officer would simply issue a notice of violation and allow the offender to proceed. Since in this case the officer did make a full custody arrest of the violator, we do not reach the question discussed by the Court of Appeals.

I

On April 19, 1968, Officer Richard Jenks stopped a 1965 Cadillac driven by respondent at the intersection of Ninth and U Streets, N. W., in the District of Columbia, for what was called a "routine spot check." At that time, Officer Jenks examined respondent's temporary operator's permit, automobile registration card, and selective service classification card. Although he permitted respondent to go on his way, Officer Jenks pursued a discrepancy he had noted between the "1938" date of birth given on the operator's permit and the "1927" date of birth given on the selective service card. A check of police traffic records showed that an operator's permit issued to one Willie Robinson, Jr., born in 1927, had been revoked, and that a temporary operator's permit had subsequently been issued to one Willie Robinson born in 1938. The pictures on the revoked permit and on the application for the temporary permit were of the same man—the person stopped by Jenks for the routine check on April 19th. Having investigated the matter himself in this fashion, it is clear that Officer Jenks had probable cause to believe that respondent had violated a provision of the District of Columbia Motor Vehicle Code making it unlawful for any person to operate a motor vehicle in the District during the period for which his operator's permit is revoked.

Four days later, on April 23, 1968, while on duty in their patrol car, Officer Jenks and his partner saw respondent driving the same vehicle. They pulled up behind respondent's car and signalled it to stop. From all indications in the record, respondent immediately complied and brought his car to a stop alongside the curb, the officers parking their patrol car immediately behind his.

Respondent got out of his car and walked back towards the patrol car. Both Officer Jenks and his partner got out of the patrol car and started toward respondent's car. Officer Jenks asked respondent for his permit and registration card and, when shown the same permit respondent had given him four days earlier, informed respondent that he was under arrest for operating a motor vehicle after revocation of his operator's permit.

Jenks then began to search respondent. His normal procedure in conducting a search of an arrestee would be to "have him spread-eagle against a wall or something of that nature." But in Jenks' own words, "I think almost every search is different. It depends on the man's size and the nature of the crime." Since he had a substantial height and weight advantage over respondent, and because the arrest was only for a traffic offense, Jenks chose instead to conduct the search face-to-face, in contrast to his normal practice.

The first step in the search was for Jenks to place both his hands on respondent's chest and begin to pat him down. During this pat-down, Jenks felt something in the left breast pocket of respondent's heavy overcoat. Jenks later testified that he could not immediately tell what was in the pocket. The record does indicate, however, that the object did not feel like a gun and that Jenks had no particular indication it was a weapon of any kind. Nonetheless, he reached into the pocket and took the object out. It turned out to be a crumpled up cigarette package.

With the package now in his hands, Jenks could feel objects inside but could not tell what they were. It does not appear that Jenks had any reason to believe, or did in fact believe, that the objects were weapons of any sort. He nevertheless opened up the package and looked inside, thereby finding the gelatin capsules of heroin which were introduced against respondent at his trial for the possession and facilitation of concealment of heroin.

II

* * *

One need not go back to Blackstone's Commentaries, Holmes' Common Law, or Pollock and Maitland in search of precedent for the approach adopted by the Court of Appeals. Indeed, given that mass production of the automobile did not begin until the early decades of the present century, I find it somewhat puzzling that the majority even looks to these sources for guidance on the only question presented in this case: the permissible scope of a search of the person incident to a lawful arrest for violation of a motor vehicle regulation. The fact is that this question has been considered by several state and federal courts, the vast majority of which have held that absent special circumstances a police officer has no right to conduct a full search of the person incident to a lawful arrest for violation of a motor vehicle regulation.

In Barnes v. State, 25 Wis.2d 116, 130 N.W.2d 264 (1964), for example, police officers stopped a car for a brake light violation. Rather than simply issue a citation, the officers placed the driver under arrest. A full search of the driver's person was then conducted, including shining a flashlight into his overcoat pocket, disclosing a small quantity of marihuana and a package of cigarette papers. The Supreme Court of Wisconsin held the search of the driver's pocket unreasonable. While expressly holding that where a traffic offender is actually arrested, as distinguished from being given a summons, it is reasonable for the arresting officer to search his person for weapons, nevertheless the court held it unreasonable to look inside the driver's overcoat pocket with a flashlight. "We cannot conceive," the court said, "that this aspect of the search was a legitimate search for weapons. . . . We reject the state's contention that any search of the person of one lawfully arrested is a valid search."

In State v. Curtis, 290 Minn. 429, 190 N.W.2d 631 (1971), police officers stopped a car which had defective taillights and which had made an illegal right turn. The officers decided to take the driver down to the station house and searched him for weapons before putting him in the squad car. One of the officers felt the outside of the driver's pockets. As in Robinson's case, the officer "detected some object but couldn't tell what it was. It did not feel like a gun or knife." "Neither officer expressed any concern for his personal safety. There was no testimony that they suspected defendant of any other criminal activity or were aware of any dangerous propensities on his part." Nevertheless the officer reached into the pocket, resulting in the discovery of a package of marihuana. The Minnesota Supreme Court held the search unlawful. While recognizing "the concern for the injuries and loss of life experienced by police officers in face-to-face confrontations with traffic offenders," the court held that "the validity of a search for weapons following a traffic arrest depends on whether the officer had reasonable grounds to believe such a search was necessary for his own safety or to prevent an escape."

Of like import is the decision of the Oregon Supreme Court in State v. O'Neal, 251 Or. 163, 444 P.2d 951 (1968) (*en banc*). Here defendant's automobile was stopped because it had no rear license plate. When asked to produce an operator's license, the defendant produced a temporary operator's license issued to another person which had expired several years earlier. The officers then arrested defendant and placed him in the back seat of the police car. "One of the officers got in the police car and asked the defendant to remove his money from his wallet and give his wallet to the officer. The defendant did so and the officer took papers from the wallet and examined them. When the officer unfolded one piece of paper a half-smoked marihuana cigarette fell out." The court held the search unlawful. Again, while recognizing the officer's right to conduct a search incident to arrest in order to protect the officer and deprive the prisoner of potential means of escape, the court held:

> "The search of the wallet obviously had nothing to do with the officer's safety. The defendant testified that the officers 'patted him down' before placing him in the police car. The officers did not remember whether they had or not. In any event, it is difficult to see how defendant's wallet could have reasonably been believed to have contained a weapon." 251 Or., at 166, 444 P.2d, at 953.

See also People v. Marsh [and other cases cited]. The Tenth Circuit has likewise stated that it is "in complete agreement with the prevailing federal and state authority which condemns the search of persons and automobiles following routine traffic violations."

Accordingly, I think it disingenuous for the Court to now pronounce that what precedents exist on the question "tend to support the broad statement of the authority to search incident to arrest found in the successive decisions of this Court, rather than the restrictive one which was applied by the Court of Appeals in this case." It is disquieting, to say the least, to see the Court at once admit that "[v]irtually all of the statements of this Court affirming the existence of an unqualified authority to search incident to a lawful arrest are dicta" and concede that we are presented with an open question on which "further examination into history and practice" would be helpful, yet then conduct an examination into prior practice which is not only wholly superficial, but totally inaccurate and misleading.

The majority's attempt to avoid case-by-case adjudication of Fourth Amendment issues is not only misguided as a matter of principle, but is also doomed to fail as a matter of practical application. As the majority itself is well aware, the powers granted the police in this case are strong ones, subject to potential abuse. Although, in this particular case, Officer Jenks was required by Police Department regulation to make an in-custody arrest rather than to issue a citation, in most jurisdictions and for most traffic offenses the determination of whether to issue a citation or effect a full arrest is discretionary with the officer. There is always the possibility that a police officer, lacking probable cause to obtain a search warrant, will use a traffic arrest as a pretext to conduct a search. See, e. g., Almador-Gonzalez v. United States, 391 F.2d 308 (CA5 1968). I suggest this possibility not to impugn the integrity of our police, but merely to point out that case-by-case adjudication will always be necessary to determine whether a full arrest was effected for purely legitimate reasons or, rather, as a pretext for searching the arrestee. . . .

III

The majority states that "A police officer's determination as to how and where to search the person of a suspect whom he has arrested is necessarily a quick ad hoc judgment which the Fourth Amendment does not require to be broken down in each instance into an analysis of each step in the search." No precedent is cited for this broad assertion—not surprisingly, since there is none. Indeed, we only recently rejected such "a rigid all-or-nothing model of justification and regulation under the Amendment, [for] it obscures the utility of limitations upon the scope, as well as the initiation, of police action as a means of constitutional regulation. This Court has held in the past that a search which is reasonable at its inception may violate the Fourth Amendment by virtue of its intolerable intensity and scope." Terry v. Ohio. As we there concluded, "in determining whether the seizure and search were 'unreasonable' our inquiry is a dual one—whether the officer's action was justified at its inception, and whether it was reasonably related in scope to the circumstances which justified the interference in the first place."

As I view the matter, the search in this case divides into three distinct phases: the patdown of respondent's coat pocket; the removal of the unknown object from the pocket; and the opening of the crumpled up cigarette package.

A

No question is raised here concerning the lawfulness of the pat-down of respondent's coat pocket. The Court of Appeals unanimously affirmed the right of a police officer to conduct a limited frisk for weapons when making an in-custody arrest, regardless of the nature of the crime for which the arrest was made. * * *

B

With respect to the removal of the unknown object from the coat pocket, the first issue presented is whether that aspect of the search can be sustained as part of the limited frisk for weapons. The weapons search approved by the Court of Appeals was modeled upon the narrowly drawn protective search for weapons authorized in *Terry,* which consists "of a limited patting of the outer clothing of the suspect for concealed objects which might be used as instruments of assault."

It appears to have been conceded by the Government below that the removal of the object from respondent's coat pocket exceeded the scope of a *Terry* frisk for weapons, since under *Terry,* an officer may not remove an object from the suspect's pockets unless he has reason to believe it to be a dangerous weapon.

In the present case, however, Officer Jenks had no reason to believe and did not in fact believe that the object in respondent's coat pocket was a weapon. He admitted later that the object did not feel like a gun. See n. 1, supra. In fact, he did not really have any thoughts one way or another about what was in the pocket. As Jenks himself testified, "I just searched him. I didn't think about what I was looking for. I just searched him." Since the removal of the object from the pocket cannot be justified as part of a limited *Terry* weapons frisk, the question arises whether it is reasonable for a police officer, when effecting an in-custody arrest of a traffic offender, to make a fuller search of the person than is permitted pursuant to *Terry.*

The underlying rationale of a search incident to arrest of a traffic offender initially suggests as reasonable a search whose scope is similar to the protective weapons frisk permitted in *Terry.* A search incident to arrest, as the majority indicates, has two basic functions: the removal of weapons the arrestee might use to resist arrest or effect an escape, and the seizure of evidence or fruits of the crime for which the arrest is made, so as to prevent its concealment or destruction.

The Government does not now contend that the search of respondent's pocket can be justified by any need to find and seize evidence in order to prevent its concealment or destruction, for as the Court of Appeals found, there are no evidence or fruits of the offense with which respondent was charged. The only rationale for a search in this case, then, is the removal of weapons which the arrestee might use to harm the officer and attempt an escape. This rationale, of course, is identical to the rationale of the search permitted in *Terry*. As we said there, "The sole justification of the search in the present situation is the protection of the police officers and others nearby, and it must therefore be confined in scope to an intrusion reasonably designed to discover guns, knives, clubs, or other hidden instruments for the assault of the police officer." Terry v. Ohio, supra, 392 U.S., at 29. Since the underlying rationale of a *Terry* search and the search of a traffic violator are identical, the Court of Appeals held that the scope of the searches must be the same. And in view of its conclusion that the removal of the object from respondent's coat pocket exceeded the scope of a lawful *Terry* frisk, a conclusion not disputed by the Government nor challenged by the majority here, the plurality of the Court of Appeals held that the removal of the package exceeded the scope of a lawful search incident to arrest of a traffic violator.

The problem with this approach, however, is that it ignores several significant differences between the context in which a search incident to arrest for a traffic violation is made, and the situation presented in *Terry*. Some of these differences would appear to suggest permitting a more thorough search in this case than was permitted in *Terry*; other differences suggest a narrower, more limited right to search than was there recognized.

The most obvious difference between the two contexts relates to whether the officer has cause to believe that the individual he is dealing with possesses weapons which might be used against him. *Terry* did not permit an officer to conduct a weapons frisk of anyone he lawfully stopped on the street, but rather, only where "he has reason to believe that he is dealing with an armed and dangerous individual . . . ." While the policeman who arrests a suspected rapist or robber may well have reason to believe he is dealing with an armed and dangerous person, certainly this does not hold true with equal force with respect to persons arrested for motor vehicle violations of the sort involved in this case.

Nor was there any particular reason in this case to believe that respondent was dangerous. He had not attempted to evade arrest, but had quickly complied with the police both in bring his car to a stop after being signalled to do so and in producing the documents Officer Jenks requested. In fact, Jenks admitted that he searched respondent face-to-face rather than in spread-eagle fashion because he had no reason to believe respondent would be violent.

While this difference between the situation presented in *Terry* and the context presented in this case would tend to suggest a lesser authority to search here than was permitted in *Terry*, other distinctions between the two contexts suggest just the opposite. As the Court of Appeals noted, a crucial feature distinguishing the in-custody arrest from the *Terry* context "is not the greater likelihood that a person taken into custody is armed, but rather the increased likelihood of danger to the officer *if* in fact the person is armed." A *Terry* stop involves a momentary encounter between officer and suspect, while an in-custody arrest places the two in close proximity for a much longer period of time. If the individual happens to have a weapon on his person, he will certainly have much more opportunity to use it against the officer in the in-custody situation. The prolonged proximity also makes it more likely that the individual will be able to extricate any small hidden weapon which might go undetected in a weapons frisk, such as a safety pin or razor blade. In addition, a suspect taken into custody may feel more threatened by the serious restraint on his liberty than a person who is simply stopped by an officer for questioning, and may therefore be more likely to resort to force.

Thus, in some senses there is less need for a weapons search in the in-custody traffic arrest situation than in a *Terry* context; while in other ways, there is a greater need. Balancing these competing considerations in order to determine what is a reasonable warrantless search in the traffic arrest context is a difficult process, one for which there may be no easy analytical guideposts. We are dealing in factors not easily quantified and, therefore, not easily weighed one against the other. And the competing interests we are protecting—the individual's interest in remaining free from unnecessarily intrusive invasions of privacy and society's interest that police officers not take unnecessary risks in the performance of their duties—are each deserving of our most serious attention and do not themselves tip the balance in any particular direction.

As will be explained more fully below, I do not think it necessary to solve this balancing equation in this particular case. It is important to note, however, in view of the reasoning adopted by the majority, that available empirical evidence supports the result reached by the plurality of the Court of Appeals, rather than the result reached by the Court today.

The majority relies on statistics indicating that a significant percentage of police officer murders occur when the officers are making traffic stops. But these statistics only confirm what we recognized in *Terry*—that "American criminals have a long tradition of armed violence, and every year in this country many law enforcement officers are killed in the line of duty, and thousands more are wounded." Terry v. Ohio. As the very next sentence in *Terry* recognized, however, "Virtually all of these deaths and a substantial portion of the injuries are inflicted with guns and knives." The statistics relied on by the Government in this case support this observation. Virtually all of the killings are caused by guns and knives, the very type of weapons which will not go undetected in a properly conducted weapons frisk. It requires more than citation to these statistics, then, to support the proposition that it is reasonable for police officers to conduct more than a *Terry*-type frisk for weapons when seeking to disarm a traffic offender who is taken into custody.

C

The majority opinion fails to recognize that the search conducted by Officer Jenks did not merely involve a search of respondent's person. It also included a separate search of effects found on his person. And even were we to assume, *arguendo*, that it was reasonable for Jenks to remove the object he felt in respondent's pocket, clearly there was no justification consistent with the Fourth Amendment which would authorize his opening the package and looking inside.

To begin with, after Jenks had the cigarette package in his hands, there is no indication that he had reason to believe or did in fact believe that the package contained a weapon. More importantly, even if the crumpled up cigarette package had in fact contained some sort of small weapon, it would have been impossible for respondent to have used it once the package was in the officer's hands. Opening the package therefore did not further the protective purpose of the search. Even the dissenting judges on the Court of Appeals were forced to concede that "since the package was now in the officer's possession any risk of the prisoner's use of a weapon in the package had been eliminated."

It is suggested, however, that since the custodial arrest itself represents a significant intrusion into the privacy of the person, any additional intrusion by way of opening or examining effects found on the person is not worthy of constitutional protection. But such an approach was expressly rejected by the Court in *Chimel.* There it was suggested that since the police had lawfully entered petitioner's house to effect an arrest, the additional invasion of privacy stemming from an accompanying search of the entire house was inconsequential. The Court answered: "[W]e see no reason why, simply because some interference with an individual's privacy and freedom of movement has lawfully taken place, further intrusions should automatically be allowed despite the absence of a warrant that the Fourth Amendment would otherwise require."

The Fourth Amendment preserves the right of "the people to be secure in their persons, houses, papers, and effects, against unreasonable searches and seizures . . . ." *Chimel* established the principle that the lawful right of the police to interfere with the security of the person did not, standing alone, automatically confer the right to interfere with the security and privacy of his house. Hence, the mere fact of an arrest should be no justification, in and of itself, for invading the privacy of the individual's personal effects.

The Government argues that it is difficult to see what constitutionally protected "expectation of privacy" a prisoner has in the interior of a cigarette pack. One wonders if the result in this case would have been the same were respondent a businessman who was lawfully taken into custody for driving without a license and whose wallet was taken from him by the police. Would it be reasonable for the police officer, because of the possibility that a razor blade was hidden somewhere in the wallet, to open it, remove all the contents, and examine each item carefully? Or suppose a lawyer lawfully arrested for a traffic offense is found to have a sealed envelope on his person. Would it be permissible for the arresting officer to tear open the envelope in order to make sure that it did not contain a clandestine weapon—perhaps a pin or a razor blade? Would it not be more consonant with the purpose of the Fourth Amendment and the legitimate needs of the police to require the officer, if he has any question whatsoever about what the wallet or letter contains, to hold onto it until the arrestee is brought to the precinct station? [4]

4. Nor would it necessarily have been reasonable for the police to have opened the cigarette package at the police station. The Government argued below, as an alternative theory to justify the search in this case, that when a suspect is booked and is about to be placed in station house detention, it is reasonable to search his person to prevent the introduction of weapons or contraband into the jail facility and to inventory the personal effects found on the suspect. Since respondent's cigarette package would have been removed and opened at the station house anyway, the argument goes, the search might just as well take place in the field at the time of the arrest. This argument fails for two reasons. First, as the Court of Appeals had indicated in its opinion in United States v. Mills, the justification for station house searches is not the booking process itself, but rather the fact that the suspect will be placed in jail. In the District of Columbia, petty offenses of the sort involved in the present case are bailable, and, as the Government stipulated in *Mills*, the normal procedure is for offenders to be advised of the opportunity to post collateral at the station house and to avoid an inventory search unless they are unable or refuse to do so. One cannot justify a full search in the field on a subsequent event that quite possibly may never take place.

Second, even had it become necessary to place respondent in confinement, it is still doubtful whether one could justify opening up the cigarette package and examining its contents. The purposes of preventing the introduction of weapons or contraband into the jail facility are fully served simply by removing the package from the prisoner. It is argued that the police must inventory effects found on the prisoner in order to avoid a later claim by the prisoner that jail personnel stole his property. But as the Court of Appeals noted in *Mills*, the police can protect themselves against such claims by means involving a less extreme intrusion on privacy than would be entailed in opening up and examining the contents of all effects found on the person. As an example, the Court of Appeals suggested that the prisoner be given "an opportunity, like that accorded someone given a bathhouse locker for temporary use, to 'check' his belongings in a sealed envelope, perhaps upon executing a waiver releasing the officer of any responsibility."

The Government also suggested in oral argument before this Court that it would be administratively inconvenient to require a police officer, after removing an object from an arrestee, to hold onto the object rather than to look inside and determine what it contains. Mere administrative inconvenience, however, cannot justify invasion of Fourth Amendment rights. See *Chimel*, supra, 392 U.S., at 768 n. 16. One can no doubt imagine cases where the inconvenience might be so substantial as to interefere with the task of transporting the suspect into custody. While these situations might necessitate a different rule, certainly in this case there would have been no inconvenience whatsoever. Officer Jenks could easily have placed the cigarette package in his own pocket or handed it to his partner to hold onto until they reached the precinct station.

I, for one, cannot characterize any of these intrusions into the privacy of an individual's papers and effects as being negligible incidents to the more serious intrusion into the individual's privacy stemming from the arrest itself. Nor can any principled distinction be drawn between the hypothetical searches I have posed and the search of the cigarette package in this case. The only reasoned distinction is between warrantless searches which serve legitimate protective and evidentiary functions and those that do not.

The search conducted by Officer Jenks in this case went far beyond what was reasonably necessary to protect him from harm or to ensure that respondent would not effect an escape from custody. In my view, it therefore fell outside the scope of a properly drawn "search incident to arrest" exception to the Fourth Amendment's warrant requirement. I would affirm the judgment of the Court of Appeals holding that the fruits of the search should have been suppressed at respondent's trial.

GUSTAFSON v. FLORIDA

Supreme Court of the United States, 1973.
414 U.S. 260, 94 S.Ct. 488.

MR. JUSTICE REHNQUIST delivered the opinion of the Court.

Petitioner James Gustafson was convicted in a Florida trial court for unlawful possession of marihuana. At his trial the State introduced into evidence marihuana which had been seized from him during a search incident to his arrest on a charge of driving without an operator's license. * * *

At approximately 2 a. m., on January 12, 1969, Lieutenant Paul R. Smith, a uniformed municipal police officer of Eau Gallie, Florida, was on a routine patrol in an unmarked squad car when he observed a 1953 white Cadillac, bearing New York license plates, driving south through the town. Smith observed the automobile weave across the center line and back to the right side of the road "three or four" times. Smith testified that he observed the two occupants of the Cadillac look back; after they apparently saw the squad car, the car drove across the highway and behind a grocery store, and then headed south on another city street.

At that point Smith turned on his flashing light and pulled the Cadillac over to the side of the road. After stopping the vehicle, Smith asked petitioner, the driver, to produce his operator's license. Petitioner informed Smith that he was a student and that he had left his operator's license in his dormitory room in the neighboring city of Melbourne, Florida. Petitioner was then placed under arrest for failure to have his vehicle operator's license in his possession. It was conceded by the parties below and in this Court that the officer had probable cause to arrest upon learning that petitioner did not have his license in his possession, and that he took petitioner into custody in order to transport him to the stationhouse for further inquiry.

Smith then proceeded to search the petitioner's person. Smith testified that he patted down the clothing of the petitioner, "outside and inside, I checked the belt, the shirt pockets and all around the belt, completely around the inside." Upon completing his patdown, he testified, he placed his hand into the left front coat pocket of the coat petitioner was wearing. From that pocket he extracted a "long chain" and a Benson and Hedges cigarette box. Smith testified that he then "opened [the cigarette box] and it appeared there were marijuana cigarettes in the box. I had been shown this in training at the police department and these appeared to be marijuana to me."

I

Petitioner urges that there could be no evidentiary purpose for the search conducted by Smith, and therefore the authority to search for weapons incident to a lawful arrest is controlled by the standards laid down in Terry v. Ohio. Petitioner contends that this case is different from United States v. Robinson, ante, in that petitioner had experienced no previous encounters with the officer in this case, and the offense for which he was arrested was "benign or trivial in nature," carrying with it no mandatory minimum sentence as did the offense for which Robinson was arrested. Petitioner points out that here, unlike *Robinson*, there were no police regulations which required the officer to take petitioner into custody, nor were there police department policies requiring full scale body searches upon arrest in the field. Petitioner also points to the fact that here, as in *Robinson*, the officer expressed no fear for his own well-being or for that of others in dealing with the petitioner.

We have held today in United States v. Robinson that "it is the fact of the lawful arrest which establishes the authority to search, and . . . in the case of a lawful custodial arrest a full search of the person is not only an exception to the warrant requirement of the Fourth Amendment, but is also a 'reasonable' search under that Amendment." Our decision in *Robinson* indicates that the limitations placed by Terry v. Ohio, supra, on protective searches conducted in an investigatory stop situation based on less than probable cause are not to be carried over to searches made incident to lawful custodial arrests. We stated in *Robinson:*

> "The justification or reason for the authority to search incident to a lawful arrest rests quite as much on the need to disarm the suspect in order to take him into custody as it does on the need to preserve evidence on his person for later use at trial. Agnello v. United States, supra; Abel v. United States, 362 U.S. 217 (1960). The standards traditionally governing the search incident to lawful arrest are not, therefore, commuted to stricter *Terry* standards by the absence of

probable fruits or further evidence of the particular crime for which the arrest is made."

Neither Chimel v. California, 395 U.S. 752 (1969), nor Peters v. New York, 392 U.S. 40 (1968), relied upon by petitioner, purported to limit the traditional authority of the arresting officer to conduct a full search of the person of an arrestee incident to a lawful custodial arrest. United States v. Robinson. Indeed, as our decision in *Robinson* indicates, not only has this been established Fourth Amendment law since the decision in Weeks v. United States, 232 U.S. 383 (1914), but it was also the rule both at common law and in the early development of American law. United States v. Robinson. Though the officer here was not required to take the petitioner into custody by police regulations as he was in *Robinson,* and there did not exist a departmental policy establishing the conditions under which a full scale body search should be conducted, we do not find these differences determinative of the constitutional issue.[1] It is sufficient that the officer had probable cause to arrest the petitioner and that he lawfully effectuated the arrest and placed the petitioner in custody. In addition, as our decision in *Robinson* makes clear, the arguable absence of "evidentiary" purpose for a search incident to a lawful arrest is not controlling.[2] "The authority to search a person incident to a lawful custodial arrest, while based upon the need to disarm and to discover evidence, does not depend on what a court may later decide was the probability in a particular arrest situation that weapons or evidence would in fact be found upon the person of the suspect."

II

We hold therefore that upon arresting petitioner for the offense of driving his automobile without a valid operator's license, and taking him into custody, Smith was entitled to make a full search of petitioner's person incident to that lawful arrest. Since it is the fact

1. Smith testified that he wrote about eight to 10 traffic citations per week, and that about three or four out of every 10 persons he arrested for the offense of driving without a license were taken into custody to the police station. Smith indicated that an offender is more likely to be taken into custody if he does not reside in the city of Eau Gaille. Finally, Smith testified that after making a custodial arrest, he always searches the arrestee before placing him into the patrol car.

2. The State of Florida argues in this Court that there was an evidentiary purpose for the search of petitioner. It is contended that Smith's observation of the erratic motions of the car that petitioner was driving created a reasonable suspicion that the petitioner may have been under the influence of some intoxicant. Upon confronting petitioner after stopping the car, Smith indicated that he noticed that the petitioner's eyes were "bleary." The State argues that the officer had probable cause to arrest the petitioner for driving while intoxicated, and that Smith thought Gustafson was intoxicated when he confronted him. Since Smith did not detect an odor of alcohol during that confrontation, the State argues it was reasonable for the officer to search the petitioner's person for drugs that may have been the cause of the suspected intoxication. Florida makes it a criminal offense to drive while intoxicated not only by alcohol, but also by unlawful drugs.

of custodial arrest which gives rise to the authority to search, it is of no moment that Smith did not indicate any subjective fear of the petitioner or that he did not himself suspect that the petitioner was armed. Having in the course of his lawful search come upon the box of cigarettes, Smith was entitled to inspect it; and when his inspection revealed the homemade cigarettes which he believed to contain an unlawful substance, he was entitled to seize them as "fruits, instrumentalities or contraband" probative of criminal conduct. Harris v. United States, 331 U.S. 145, 154–155 (1947); Adams v. Williams, 407 U.S. 143, 149 (1972). The judgment of the Supreme Court of Florida is therefore

Affirmed.

MR. JUSTICE STEWART, concurring.

It seems to me that a persuasive claim might have been made in this case that the custodial arrest of the petitioner for a minor traffic offense violated his rights under the Fourth and Fourteenth Amendments. But no such claim has been made. Instead, the petitioner has fully conceded the constitutional validity of his custodial arrest. That being so, it follows that the incidental search of his person was also constitutionally valid. To hold otherwise would, as the Court makes clear in this case and in United States v. Robinson, mark an abrupt departure from settled constitutional precedent.

MR. JUSTICE MARSHALL, with whom MR. JUSTICE DOUGLAS and MR. JUSTICE BRENNAN join, dissenting.

I respectfully dissent for the reasons stated in my opinion in United States v. Robinson. The facts show that after arresting petitioner Gustafson for driving without possession of an operator's license, Officer Smith conducted a search of petitioner's person in which he removed a Benson and Hedges cigarette box. The officer put petitioner in the back seat of the squad car and then opened the cigarette box, disclosing marihuana cigarettes. As my Brother Stewart indicates, [in his opinion], no challenge was made either here or below with respect to the lawfulness of Officer Smith's decision to effect a full custodial arrest for this minor traffic offense. Whether or not it was lawful for the officer to have searched petitioner's person and removed the cigarette package before placing petitioner in the squad car, there was no justification for his opening the package and looking inside.

There was no reason to believe, and Officer Smith did not in fact believe, that petitioner was a dangerous person or that the package contained a weapon. The package's weight alone no doubt would have indicated that it did not contain a gun or knife. In any event, even were it possible that the package contained some sort of weapon—say a razor blade—there was no chance the petitioner could use it once it was in the officer's hands. The opening of the package had no connection whatsoever with the protective purpose of the search.

The State argues, and the Florida Supreme Court found, see 258 So.2d 1, 2 (Fla.1972), that Officer Smith had a reasonable suspicion petitioner was intoxicated, justifying searching for intoxicating drugs such as marihuana. Leaving aside the question whether the officer could search for intoxicants absent probable cause that petitioner had committed an offense involving intoxication, I do not find sufficient evidence in this record to support the conclusion that Officer Smith even had a reasonable suspicion petitioner was intoxicated. To begin with, Officer Smith neither arrested petitioner for driving while intoxicated nor did he give petitioner a sobriety test. See Fla.Stats. Ann. §§ 322.261 and 322.262 (1973 Supp.). Smith testified that petitioner did not have any trouble getting out of his car, did not have difficulty standing up, and did not slur his speech when answering the officer's questions. Nor did the fact that petitioner's car weaved across a lane justify such a suspicion. As Officer Smith testified, he did not arrest petitioner on a careless driving by weaving charge because there was simply not enough evidence. If there was not enough evidence to justify a charge for the weaving itself, I find it hard to understand how there could be enough evidence to suspect that petitioner was intoxicated. Officer Smith testified that petitioner's eyes looked bleary, but that was hardly surprising, since the arrest took place at 2 a. m.

The only need for a search in this case was to disarm petitioner to protect Officer Smith from harm while the two were together in the patrol car. The search conducted by Officer Smith went far beyond what was reasonably necessary to achieve that end. It therefore fell outside the scope of a properly drawn "search incident to arrest" exception to the Fourth Amendment's warrant requirement. I would reverse the judgment of the Florida Supreme Court holding that the fruits of the search could be admitted at respondent's trial.

PEOPLE v. SUPERIOR COURT (AND SIMON)

Supreme Court of California, 1972.
7 Cal.3d 186, 101 Cal.Rptr. 837, 496 P.2d 1205.

. . . Police Officer Erickson, the sole witness for the People, testified he was on routine vehicular patrol with his partner Officer Amic at 7:30 p. m. on March 9, 1970, when he saw a car "driving without headlights or taillights." He stopped the vehicle and defendant, its driver and sole occupant, "got out of the car voluntarily" and "started to play around under the dash." The officer asked defendant for his identification, and "He stated he had no identification, no registration for the car. I placed him under arrest for his traffic violation under authority of [section] 40302(a) of the Vehicle Code." The officer then searched defendant's person and found in his right front pants pocket a soft plastic bag containing 7.6 grams of marijuana.

On cross-examination counsel asked Officer Erickson, "Did you at any time fear for your life, thinking that [defendant] had a weapon on him?" The officer replied he did not, and further acknowledged that in his pat-down search of defendant he found no evidence of any weapon whatever.

Defendant took the stand and testified that his car was a 1957 MG convertible. On the evening in question defendant was driving on the street when the ignition caught fire, the car's lights went out, and smoke began issuing from under the dashboard. He promptly stopped the vehicle to deal with the problem. The police arrived on the scene a few moments later, but defendant was already standing outside his car with the driver's door open, waving his hands under the dashboard in an effort to clear the smoke. In short, according to defendant, he stopped his car because of the emergency and not because of any order of the police officers.

Defendant testified that before he was asked for identification the officers ordered him to stand spreadeagled against the police car for the purpose of a pat search. In the course of the search Officer Erickson felt a soft lump in defendant's pants pocket and asked what it was; when defendant failed to answer, the officer told him to remove it. Defendant did so, and handed the marijuana to the police.

The trial court found that the officers did stop defendant's vehicle and had "just cause" to do so inasmuch as "the officers told the truth when they asked the defendant for his identification and registration and that he stated that he had no registration or identification, and that it was a lawful arrest under 40302(a) of the Vehicle Code."

* * *

I

It is first contended that Officer Erickson had probable cause to arrest defendant on a charge of automobile theft, and hence that the search of defendant's person was justified as an incident to such an arrest. The facts which the People assert gave Officer Erickson probable cause to believe the car was stolen are, as found by the trial court, (1) that defendant was unable to produce a vehicle registration card or other proof of ownership, and (2) that defendant was unable to produce a driver's license or other personal identification. * * *

It would not be unreasonable for a thief to remove or destroy the registration card of an automobile he has taken; his purpose in so doing might be to prevent the true owner from being traced, to eliminate the discrepancy between the owner's name and his own, or to facilitate substitution of a forged card. It is also true that being a stranger to the vehicle he might not be able to present the card to an officer simply because he did not know where to find it.

On the other hand, a motorist's failure to have or produce the registration card for his vehicle could equally well be entirely innocent. A common instance is . . . when a registration card is necessarily removed from the vehicle for the purpose of application for renewal or transfer of registration. Renewal, of course, is an annual event and in contemporary American society automobiles are bought and sold—and titles thereto transferred—with considerable frequency. Moreover, it is not only a thief who may not immediately be able to find the registration card for presentation to an officer; the same difficulty could be experienced by a friend or relative to whom the car had been lent, or even a teenage child or spouse of the owner. * * *

A series of Court of Appeal decisions has found such probable cause, however, when the absence of a registration was coupled with certain other "suspicious circumstances." First, the opinions emphasize the circumstance—also relied on here by the People—that defendant was unable to produce a driver's license upon the officer's demand . . .

On its face, of course, the presence or absence of a driver's license has no bearing whatever on the matter of title to the vehicle. The only explanation thus far offered in the California cases of the relevance [is that] "To a certain extent, the fact that the driver of a car not registered in his name was also unlicensed might be additional evidence that he did not own the car in question, since few automobile owners are not licensed as operators." But this reasoning assumes that the driver is actually unlicensed rather than simply not in physical possession of his license. The latter alternative however, appears to be the fact in almost all the cited cases. Nor is this surprising, for unless the driver confesses outright that he is unlicensed the most the officer knows from personal observation is that he does not have a license "in his immediate possession." Admittedly, even a thief who does own a driver's license might pretend not to have it with him or deliberately fail to carry it, in order to conceal his identity and age in the event he is stopped by the police.

Nevertheless, it is equally likely that the true explanation for a motorist's failure to have his license with him is the most obvious, i. e., that he inadvertently left it in a different suit of clothing—or, in the case of a lady driver, in a different handbag. Such occasional forgetfulness is a fact of human nature, no doubt reinforced by the pressures and demands of modern life. Indeed, we daresay that at one time or another virtually every motorist has suffered the minor embarrassment of leaving his license at home. . . .

We conclude that the mere failure of a motorist to have his driver's license in his immediate possession is a circumstance of such generally innocent connotation that it cannot reasonably transform the coincident lack of a registration card into grounds to believe the motorist guilty of grand theft. "The mere absence of registration did not give the officer probable cause to think that the car was stolen. . . . The absence of license and identification makes it no more probable that the car was stolen." (United States v. Day (E.D.Pa.1971) 331 F.Supp. 254, 256.)

This does not mean, however, that police officers are wholly barred from making warrantless arrests for automobile theft on the basis of personal observation; it means only that something more is needed to justify such an arrest than the motorist's inability to produce a registration card or driver's license. The cited decisions of the Courts of Appeal demonstrate there usually have been additional suspicious circumstances which, taken with the considerations just discussed, combine to furnish the necessary probable cause.

To begin with, in several of the cases the officer observed that one or both of the vehicle's license plates were missing or improperly attached. Such conditions are not only violations of the code and hence grounds for stopping the vehicle and issuing a citation to the driver, they are also relevant to the probable cause question before us.

The lack of a license plate does not alone constitute probable cause to believe the car stolen: the plate may have fallen off, been damaged in an accident or removed by a third party; and in the case of a vehicle recently purchased, the temporary "paper plate" may have become obscured or dislodged. But this circumstance is also highly suspicious: "It is a matter of common knowledge that automobile thieves often switch license plates from one car to another in order to conceal the identity of the stolen vehicle". A thief's first step towards that concealment is to remove both original plates from the vehicle; if he possesses a stolen plate, he will then ordinarily attach it in the rear position; but if he has no such substitute, he may well prefer to drive without any plates rather than risk quick identification from a police "hot sheet." We conclude that when an officer stops a vehicle with missing or improperly attached license plates and in addition learns the motorist is unable to produce the registration card, he may reasonably entertain the belief that the vehicle is stolen.

Other observable circumstances relied on in the cases to invest the lack of a registration card with guilty significance are, for example, the motorist's evasive driving and failure to stop promptly when the officer signals him to do so, and reports of criminal activity in progress in the neighborhood; but as we admonished, the police must remain alert to the danger of abusing these justifications by invoking them on the basis of inadequate facts . . .

Secondly, even though the lack of a registration card does not alone furnish the necessary probable cause, it does give the officer reasonable grounds to inquire further into the matter, i. e., to ask the motorist for an explanation of its absence; and a number of the cases have emphasized the significance of answers by the motorist which are inconsistent, conflicting, or palpably false. Thus in [one case] the motorist first said he had bought the vehicle from a used car lot, then that he had bought it from a friend; in [a second case] the motorist said he had borrowed the vehicle from a used car dealer, but a windshield sticker showed the dealer had previously sold it to a third person unknown to the occupants; and in [another case] the motorist named the alleged owner of the vehicle, but the officer learned by radio that the last registered owner bore a different name. Such answers have no discernible innocent meaning, and may reasonably be taken to indicate consciousness of guilt. They constitute, accordingly, a further suspicious circumstance sufficient to support a belief that the vehicle is stolen.

In the case at bar there is no showing whatever that the license plates on defendant's car were missing or irregular, or that defendant gave inconsistent or false explanations as to its ownership. As noted, the only circumstances upon which the People rely in this regard are defendant's inability to produce his registration card and his driver's license. For the reasons stated above, those circumstances did not furnish Officer Erickson with probable cause to believe defendant was guilty of grand theft of the automobile; accordingly, the search of defendant could not be justified as an incident to such an arrest.

Indeed, there is no showing that the officer in fact believed defendant was guilty of automobile theft: he did not inform defendant that such was the ground for the arrest, and at the preliminary examination he testified only that he arrested defendant for the equipment violations and took him into custody because of his lack of identification. The purpose of the exclusionary rule—to deter unreasonable searches and seizures by law enforcement officers—would clearly be frustrated if the courts were required to uphold a search conducted on unreasonable grounds simply because the prosecuting authorities belatedly managed to devise an alternative theory on which the arresting officer *could* have acted reasonably if he had known of it. Compliance with the fundamental guarantees of the Fourth Amendment is not a game to be won by inventive counsel, but a practical, day-today responsibility of law enforcement personnel. Accordingly, just as a warrantless arrest or search cannot be justified by facts of which the officer was wholly unaware at the time so also it cannot be justified on theories thereafter invented for the consumption of reviewing courts.

II

The People's second contention is that the search was justified as an incident to Officer Erickson's arrest of defendant for traffic violations "under authority of [section] 40302(a) of the Vehicle Code." * * *

* * *

Proceeding to the merits, we inquire into the constitutionally permissible scope of a search of the person as an incident to an ordinary traffic arrest. * * *

* * * In the case of an ordinary traffic offense there are neither "instrumentalities" used to commit the crime nor "fruits" or "evidence" thereof, so that a search for such items as an incident to the driver's arrest is unreasonable per se, whether conducted in his vehicle (id. at p. 813, 91 Cal.Rptr. 729, 478 P.2d 449) or on his person.[1]

With respect to contraband, we said "in the typical traffic violation case . . . the 'circumstances justifying the arrest'—e. g., speeding, failing to stop, illegal turn, or defective lights— do *not* also furnish probable cause to search the interior of the car." If the arresting officer "cannot reasonably expect to discover either instrumentalities or fruits or seizable evidence of the offense; still less does the arrest give him reasonable grounds to believe, without more, that the vehicle contains contraband. . . . To justify that search, there must be independent probable cause to believe the vehicle does in fact contain contraband." This reasoning applies with equal force to a search of the driver, and to justify such a search there must likewise be independent probable cause to believe that contraband is in fact secreted on his person.

The scope of a search for weapons after a routine traffic arrest however, is a more complex problem which has evoked differing responses from the courts. * * *

* * * [In] People v. Graves (1968) 263 Cal.App.2d 719, 70 Cal.Rptr. 509. * * * a robbery suspect, was arrested on outstanding traffic warrants; a thorough search of his person was conducted, turning up a packet of marijuana cigarettes. In reviewing the legality of that search and seizure, the Court of Appeal declared as follows (at pp. 733–734, 70 Cal.Rptr. at p. 519): "A valid arrest for a traffic offense permits a search by the arresting officer of the arrestee's person for weapons, but does not justify a complete search of his person for evidence of other unrelated crimes unless the officer has probable cause for believing that the traffic offender is guilty of a crime other than the traffic offense for which he is being arrested."

To justify its rule allowing a routine weapons search in every traffic arrest situation, the Court of Appeal reasoned (at p. 734, 70 Cal.Rptr. at p. 519): "The rationale * * * that traffic offenders are usually noncriminals and therefore should not be subjected to the indignity of even a search for weapons must yield to the principle * * * that a police officer may make a reasonable self-protective search for weapons if he has a constitutionally adequate reasonable

1. [We have] recognized an exception to this rule when the motorist is arrested for driving under the influence of alcohol or other drug: "The presence of the latter substances in the vehicle is admissible as corroborating evidence of these crimes, and a reasonable search therefore may be conducted in the interior of the vehicle in which such an offender is apprehended, as an incident to that arrest." Their presence on his person, of course, is equally admissible, and he may be searched for such substances as a further incident to the arrest. That search, however, must remain reasonable in scope.

ground for doing so, * * * In the case of a valid arrest the constitutional adequacy is supplied by the arrest itself. . . ."

* * * It is true, as the *Graves* court emphasized (*ibid.*), that "the danger to the officer and the possibility of an escape are present if the arrestee possesses a weapon regardless of whether the weapon is in any way related to the crime for which he has been arrested." This is self-evident. Conversely, however, those dangers are also present when the officer has detained and is interrogating an armed suspect in circumstances which may still fall short of probable cause to effectuate the arrest. The participants are often unsure of the precise moment at which such a detention becomes an "arrest" in the legal sense (see Part II A, ante), and the suspect does not have significantly less incentive or temptation to use his weapon before than after that elusive moment. In short, the physical risk to the officer is created by the circumstances of the confrontation taken as a whole, not by the technical niceties of the law of arrest. The critical question remains, is this the kind of confrontation in which the officer can reasonably believe in the possibility that a weapon may be used against him?

The actual holding of *Graves* illustrates the point: in addition to the outstanding traffic warrants, the officer in that case had independent probable cause to arrest the defendant for five recent armed robberies, the last committed only three hours before he stopped the defendant for irregular driving. Fully aware of these facts, he approached the car with a drawn gun and immediately placed the defendant in handcuffs. Manifestly in such circumstances it was reasonable for the officer to believe that the arrestee was armed and dangerous, and to take appropriate precautionary measures. Nor is it necessary, to support such a belief, that the crime for which the suspect is arrested ordinarily be committed by means of offensive weapons. * * *

Our analysis here, however, deals with an arrest not for robbery or burglary or possession of narcotics, but for a simple traffic violation. In extending the authority for a weapons search to that class of arrests, the *Graves* court was apparently motivated by its judicial "knowledge" that "police officers have been killed or assaulted while making arrests for traffic offenses" and such arrests "frequently disclose that the arrestee is wanted by the authorities for the alleged commission of another crime or crimes or that he is a fugitive from justice." This concern for the safety of traffic officers is commendable, and we fully shared it. * * *

The question, nevertheless, is whether these risks eventuate "frequently," as the *Graves* court believed, or "occasionally," as we asserted * * * While statistical certainty is impossible, we adhere to [a] * * * commonsense appraisal of the situation: "Millions of such vehicles [involved in routine traffic violations] are stopped every year, and all but a small proportion are doubtless proceeding at the time on lawful business or innocent pleasure." * * * that "Just as the arresting officer in an ordinary traffic violation case cannot reasonably expect to find contraband in the offender's vehicle, so also he cannot expect to find weapons. To allow the police to routinely search for weapons in all such instances would likewise constitute an 'intolerable and unreasonable' intrusion into the privacy of the vast majority of peaceable citizens who travel by automobile. It follows that a warrantless search for weapons, like a search for contraband, must be predicated in traffic violation cases on specific facts or circumstances giving the officer reasonable grounds to believe that such weapons are present in the vehicle he has stopped."

This reasoning is equally applicable to a search of the driver. * * * We therefore conclude that when a police officer observes a traffic violation and stops the motorist for the purpose of issuing a citation, a pat-down search for weapons as an incident to that arrest must be predicated on specific facts or circumstances giving the officer reasonable grounds to believe that a weapon is secreted on the motorist's person. * * *

* * *

Turning to the facts before us, we observe that defendant was initially stopped for driving during darkness without lighted headlamps or taillamps. These are simple infractions, punishable upon a first conviction by a fine not exceeding $50. As noted earlier the same is true of defendant's inability to present his driver's license and registration card; and if he had produced any other "satisfactory evidence of his identity," he would have been entitled as a matter of right to be released immediately upon signing a promise to appear. Beyond these traffic violations, however, there were no other facts or circumstances from which Officer Erickson, as a reasonably prudent man, could have inferred that defendant was carrying a concealed weapon. Indeed, we have already pointed out that when asked on cross-examination, "Did you at any time fear for your life, thinking that [defendant] had a weapon on him?" Officer Erickson replied in the negative. The pat-down search of defendant cannot be justified as an incident to Officer Erickson's decision to cite him for the foregoing traffic offenses.

* * *

Pressing the analysis further, the People emphasize that Officer Erickson not only had probable cause to issue the traffic citations to defendant but was required by Vehicle Code section 40302 to take him into custody for transportation before a magistrate in order to make bail; this fact, it is urged, justified the search of defendant. * * *

When a suspect has been lawfully arrested on a criminal charge and undergoes the process of "booking" at a police station prior to being held in jail (Pen.Code, § 7, subd. (21)), it is ordinarily reasonable to conduct a search of his person for the purpose of preventing the introduction of weapons or contraband into the jail facility. From this premise the argument has been drawn that for the sake of safety a search of this kind need not be postponed until the actual booking but may reasonably be conducted "in the field," i. e., at the time of the arrest, whenever the suspect will be charged with a "jailable" offense.

Whatever the merits of this argument in generality, it is inapplicable to the case at hand. * * * Section 40302 requires that a person coming within its terms be taken "without unnecessary delay" before the "nearest or most accessible" magistrate having jurisdiction, and sections 40306 and 40307 prescribe the next step in the procedure: if a magistrate is available, section 40306 provides (a) the arresting officer shall file a complaint, (b) the arrestee shall be given at least five days' continuance to prepare his case and (c) "shall thereupon be released from custody" on his own recognizance or on bail; if on the other hand a magistrate is not available, section 40307 provides that the officer shall take the arrestee before (a) the clerk of the magistrate "who shall admit him to bail" or (b) the officer in charge of the most accessible jail "who shall admit him to bail" or release him upon a simple written promise to appear.

The clear and unmistakable import of these provisions, when read together, is that a person taken into custody pursuant to section 40302 must be transported *directly* to a magistrate or to one of the officials listed in section 40307, and must *immediately* be released on bail or written promise to appear. Accordingly, he cannot lawfully be subjected to the routine booking process used in the case of a nontraffic misdemeanant; nor can he be searched as an incident of that process, either in the field or at a police station. We conclude that the search of defendant in the case at bar cannot be justified as an incident to Officer Erickson's decision to take him into custody for transportation before a magistrate pursuant to section 40302.

WRIGHT, CHIEF JUSTICE (concurring). [Omitted]

* * *

BURKE, JUSTICE (concurring and dissenting).

* * *

I disagree, however, with certain statements constituting dictum of the majority, which are not mentioned by the Chief Justice. The statements suggest that * * * the legality of an arrest is tested solely on the basis of the legal theory employed by the officer in making the arrest. * * *

Under views expressed by United States Supreme Court justices the legality of an arrest is not tested—as the majority here indicate—solely on the basis of the legal theory employed by the officer in making the arrest. In Wainwright v. City of New Orleans, 392 U.S. 598, 88 S.Ct. 2243, wherein the court dismissed a writ of certiorari as improvidently granted, a concurring opinion by Justice Fortas (joined in by Justice Marshall) states that he is "not prepared to say that, regardless of the presence or absence of adequate cause for police action, the arrest [made on a charge of vagrancy while loitering] or the attempt by the officers to search [at the police station following the arrest] is unlawful" and that he "should want to know whether, in fact, there was constitutionally adequate cause for the police to suspect that the [petitioner] was the man sought for murder." A dissenting opinion by Chief Justice Warren expresses disagreement with Justice Fortas and states that it is irrelevant that the record does not permit a determination whether the petitioner could have been lawfully arrested for murder since he was not arrested or booked for murder. According to the dissent, "when a controversy arises over the legality of the arrest, the police should be held to the booked offense." The booked offense, of course, may differ from the offense the officer had in mind as the basis for the arrest. Thus both the foregoing views are contrary to the majority opinion in the instant case.

Both federal and state courts have upheld arrests on grounds other than that relied upon by the officer in making the arrest. (E. g., Klingler v. United States (8th Cir.) 409 F.2d 299, 304 [defendant arrested for vagrancy; held that there was not probable cause to arrest him for that crime but that the arrest was lawful since there was probable cause to arrest him for robbery]; People v. Superior Court (Johnson), 15 Cal.App.3d 146, 92 Cal.Rptr. 916 [defendant arrested for "investigation of burglary"; held that stated ground was inadequate but arrest was lawful since there was probable cause to believe him guilty of disorderly conduct and burglary and attempted burglary]; People v. Kelley, 3 Cal.App.3d 146, 83 Cal.Rptr. 287 [defendant arrested for drunk driving; held unnecessary to determine if probable cause to arrest him for that offense since there was probable cause to arrest him for being found in a public place under the influence of intoxicating liquor and possession in car upon highway of alcoholic beverage in open container]; People v. Walker, 273 Cal.App. 2d 720, 725, 78 Cal.Rptr. 439 [defendant arrested for robbery; held unnecessary to determine if probable cause to arrest him for that offense since there was probable cause to arrest him for possession of concealed weapons]; Commonwealth v. Lawton, 348 Mass. 129, 202 N.E.2d 824, 826 [defendant arrested for being abroad in the nighttime; held unnecessary to decide constitutionality of statute proscribing that offense since there was probable cause to arrest for breaking and entering, and arrest was therefore lawful]; see generally American Law Institute, A Model Code of Pre-arraignment Procedure (Propose Official Draft No. 1, April 10, 1972) at pp. 15–17 & 136.)

Penal Code section 841 requires that an officer inform the person to be arrested of, among other things, "the cause of the arrest." However, a failure to announce the cause of the arrest does not invalidate the arrest or search incident thereto, nor does the officer's announcement of the wrong offense have that effect.

SECTION 2. PLAIN VIEW SEIZURES

UNITED STATES v. WRIGHT

United States Court of Appeals, District of Columbia, 1971.
146 U.S.App.D.C. 126, 449 F.2d 1355.

PER CURIAM.

Appellant was convicted of grand larceny of a Chevrolet Corvette transmission, found by police in appellant's garage immediately before and at the time of his arrest. * * *

I. *Facts Relevant to the Issue Presented*

All the events took place on 18 May 1968, beginning at 5:00 a. m. when the police were notified that a 1967 Chevrolet Corvette had been stolen. By 4:20 p. m. Police Officers Huffstutler and Howard had located the Corvette, stripped of its transmission, engine, radiator, hood and steering wheel. From various pieces of evidence in and around the car Officer Huffstutler concluded that the Corvette had been stripped elsewhere, and by an examination of the terrain deduced the probable locale of the stripping within a three-block area. In a systematic survey of all streets and alleys they observed tell-tale sweepings of nuts and bolts in front of a three-car garage, and in addition several red rags of the type previously noted on the stripped Corvette. A comparison of the rags found at the two locations showed they were identical. The officers returned to the garage.

The three sliding doors of the garage were not completely closed because of their construction and age, leaving an opening of approximately eight or nine inches. Inside it was "relatively dark," so the officer employed his flashlight to look in through the gap. Lying ten feet away he noticed a transmission shaft. On his knees for a better view, he identified it as a Chevrolet product, and observed that the speedometer cable had been clipped. After returning to the stripped Corvette, a check of its speedometer cable showed it, too, had been clipped.

On notifying the Auto Squad of his discoveries, Officer Huffstutler was advised to go to the garage and recover the stolen transmission. Instead, he returned to his precinct and began to type an application for a search warrant. On reflection, he decided it was better then to return to the garage, interview its owner, and set in motion the procedure to take fingerprints from the Corvette.

On arrival at the garage Officer Huffstutler and his partner noted an automobile with its trunk open, parked so the trunk could be loaded from a little alleyway which led to the side door of the garage. Inside the open trunk were a steering wheel, clutch plate, and pressure plate, all 1967 Corvette equipment, and each of which corresponded to items stripped from the stolen car. With guns drawn the officers moved toward the open side door of the garage, and as they did appellant Wright and two others emerged. The three were arrested for possession of stolen property. Leaving them in custody, Officer Huffstutler entered the open door of the garage and located the Corvette transmission which had been moved to another place inside. * * *

II. *Legality of the Officer's First Look*

Appellant contends strenuously that his rights under the Fourth Amendment were violated not once but twice by illegal search of the garage. He argues that the officer's action in peering through the eight or nine-inch crack was a search, particularly since it was aided by artificial light; that such search was illegal; that this illegal search tainted the seizure thereafter of the auto transmission at the time of the arrest. As in Dorsey v. United States [125 U.S.App.D.C. 355, 372 F.2d 928 (1967)], "the Government argues there can be no question of an illegal search since there was no search at all."

There was no search here. There are at least two doctrines or perhaps two different characterizations of the same doctrine, which we have enunciated in previous decisions on which the officer's conduct was legally justified. For convenience they might be termed the "challenging situation" and "plain view" doctrines.

A. *A closer look at a challenging situation.*

In *Dorsey,* supra, two officers approached a parked car occupied by two recognized, known narcotics violators. Although it was 11:00 p. m. the officers could see the driver and the passenger were turned facing each other as though examining something on the seat. The officer on the driver's side directed his flashlight into the car and illuminated in Dorsey's hand a cellophane bag filled with white-powdered, gelatin capsules. When Dorsey placed the bag on the ledge of the glove compartment, the other officer reached through the open window, seized the bag, and placed Dorsey under arrest. As the driver complained of the officer flashing his light inside the car, the officer noticed that the driver was dropping heroin capsules on the floor. He, too, was arrested and nine heroin capsules were picked up off the floor.

Without either characterizing the officer's action as a search or attempting to justify it as a search, we held that

> "The essential inquiry, as is customarily the case in Fourth Amendment claims, is the reasonableness of the police conduct under the circumstances. * * * Reasonableness involves consideration of the nature of the police conduct as well as the occasion of its exercise. We think the evidence supported a view of that conduct as not transgressing the constitutional standard.
>
> "* * * When the officers suddenly saw [the appellants] situated as they were at the time and place in question, the

former were entitled to extend their preventive patrolling mission to the extent of approaching the car and observing what was going on inside. * * * We do not think the need to employ a visual aid at night in the form of a flashlight converts this form lawful into unlawful conduct. A car parked at 14th and U Streets at eleven o'clock at night, occupied by known narcotics offenders, bears little resemblance to a home or dwelling. If policemen are to serve any purpose of detecting and preventing crime by being out on the streets at all, *they must be able to take a closer look at challenging situations as they encounter them.* All we hold here is that this was one of those situations, and that the police response to it was a justifiable one which did not project their law enforcement responsibilities beyond permissible constitutional limits."

We think the facts and holding in *Dorsey*, supra, are comparable and decisive of appellant's contentions in regard to his first alleged illegal search.

B. *Plain view.*

James v. United States [135 U.S.App.D.C. 314, 418 F.2d 1150 (1969)] is equally dispositive of appellant's first claim and is closer on the operative facts. In *James* a police officer observed a partially stripped-down new Pontiac, and three days later observed that the stripping job had been completed. When he saw the new Pontiac the second time, completely stripped, the police officer entered the premises to investigate further, and in so doing secured the license number from the rear tag, the front license plate being missing.

On a pre-trial motion to suppress the District Court did exclude the rear license plate and the owner's manual found through the officer's entry on the unoccupied garage premises, but appellant also contended that all the stolen property discovered pursuant to a later issued search warrant should be suppressed, because this was the fruit of illegal observations by the officer from outside the garage which preceded his entry on the premises, and those observations violated his Fourth Amendment rights. The garage door was ajar and the officer was able to look under and observe parts and tools thrown about. In *James* we held that

"The police are free to observe circumstances in evidence that are in 'plain view' to the public * * * the plain view doctrine was reaffirmed in Harris v. United States, 390 U.S. 234, 88 S.Ct. 992, 19 L.Ed.2d 1067 (1968). That the policeman may have to crane his neck, or bend over, or squat, does not render the doctrine inapplicable, so long as what he saw would have been visible to any curious passerby. * *"

Whether it be considered that the transmission was in "plain view" to start with, or whether the officer took "a closer look at a challenging situation," we conclude that no rights of appellant protected by the Fourth Amendment were violated by Officer Huffstutler peering through the gap between the garage doors.

III. *Legality of the Seizure of the Transmission in the Garage*

Appellant contends with equal vigor that the seizure of the auto transmission was illegal as being the product of an illegal search either if the entry of Officer Huffstutler into the garage is considered independently, or if his entry is considered as the product of his previously illegal search by peering through the gap in the garage doors. * * *

A. *Plain view.*

All the authorities cited above in our discussion of the doctrine of "plain view" are equally applicable to Officer Huffstutler's seizure of the auto transmission. Obviously the doctrine of "plain view" would be a rather sterile doctrine if it extended only so far as police officers' looking. In all of the "plain view" cases, the viewing has been followed by a seizure of evidence.

We do not ignore that Officer Huffstutler had spotted the stolen auto transmission within ten feet of him, had noted the cut speedometer cable, had gone the few blocks to the stripped Corvette to see if its speedometer cable was cut (it was), then returned to the garage for a final look before going to his precinct. After a short time there he returned to the garage, made the arrests, and seized the auto transmission. All of the events from the time the two officers first came upon the stripped Corvette, searched the neighborhood, made their observations in the garage, went back to the stripped Corvette, went back to the garage, went to the precinct, returned to the garage for the third time—all took place in exactly two hours. The time interval from when Officer Huffstutler first spotted the stolen transmission is not certain, but it probably was more than an hour and not more than an hour and a half.

What appellant is contending for here is to write into the doctrine of "plain view" a continuous observation requirement. Is the officer required to keep his eye glued to the knothole while he motions for help with a free hand? If the officer had known the additional fact of the Corvette's speedometer cable being cut at the time he first saw the transmission, and had left his point of observation to return to his car to radio his headquarters, and then returned to the gap in the garage doors only to find the transmission had been moved out of his vision, would he then have been barred from moving inside the garage to seize what he was certain was stolen property? If an interruption of the officer's plain view of stolen property is allowed, how long an interruption is permitted?

In Creighton [v. United States, 132 U.S.App.D.C. 115, 406 F.2d 651 (1968)], the police had observed various items of property openly displayed in appellant's car, after he had been arrested for a traffic violation. Learning of a burglary later while appellant was still at the station house, police went to appellant's car and seized the stolen property. We held that the goods were in plain view, and that there was no search, hence no warrant was required. In *Creighton,* as in the case at bar, the original "plain view" of the stolen property by the officers occurred at a time when the officers did not *know* the items were stolen. In *Creighton* there was an interval after the sighting, during which a phone call turned up a report of a burglary; in *Wright* here there was an interval after the officer's first look, during which he checked the cut speedometer cable. In each case, after the clinching piece of information had been secured, the officer returned to the stolen property and seized it. No search was involved in either case.

In the circumstances of this case we believe that on the doctrine of "plain view" Officer Huffstutler was authorized to carry that doctrine to its logical conclusion, seize the stolen property he had observed, and that the one-hour to hour-and-a-half interval in which the other events connected with his investigation transpired did not preclude him from doing this. On his return to the garage at the time the arrests were made it was the officer's duty to follow up, see if the transmission was still there, and recover the stolen property if he could. Whether he could see the transmission through the open door is in our judgment immaterial. He had seen it in the garage no more than an hour and a half before; it was not an unreasonable seizure under the Fourth Amendment for him to step inside, identify it again, and have it moved out along with the other stolen automobile parts that were already in the process of being spirited away.

Our holding on this point finds support in the American Law Institute Tentative Draft No. 3 of A Model Code of Pre-Arraignment Procedure (1970), Part II, Search and Seizure. Section 6.06, Seizure Independent of Search, provides:

> An officer who, in the course of otherwise lawful activity, observes or otherwise becomes aware of the nature and location of things which he reasonably believes to be subject to seizure under Section SS 1.03, and which therefore can be seized without a search, may seize such things.

Section SS 1.03(b) lists as subject to search and seizure "contraband, the fruits of crime, or things otherwise criminally possessed."

It was not necessary for Officer Huffstutler to make a search to discover the auto transmission when he seized it at the time of the arrest. He had already observed the transmission and become aware that it was located inside the garage. He had carefully checked it to be the fruit of the crime he was investigating and, in the language of the American Law Institute draft, it was "subject to seizure (as fruits of crime) * * * and * * * therefore can be seized without a search."

The Commentary on this draft Section is illuminating:

"The authorization with respect to the seizure of things plainly observable in private premises does raise some questions under Johnson v. United States, 333 U.S. 10 [68 S.Ct. 367, 92 L.Ed. 436] (1948). There the opium was not visible but it was plainly observable by odor perceptible off the premises. Nevertheless entrance and seizure without a warrant was held unlawful. * * * However, although the *presence* of opium was observable, its location was not evident, and a search was in fact necessary; the authorization in the draft does not cover a search, but *only an entry for things already perceived and ready to hand.*" (Last emphasis supplied.) * * *

B. *Seizure to prevent removal of evidence.*

The police officer had seen the auto transmission shortly before, the other missing parts from the Corvette he was at the moment viewing in the trunk of another car, obviously in preparation to be hauled away. He was obligated to recover the stolen transmission without giving the miscreants a chance to spirit this away, too. The officers had no idea how many persons other than those visible were involved, hence

> "On the basis of such a plain view discovery of the fruits of a crime which were identified both by description and label, it was not only reasonable for the officers to seize them notwithstanding the absence of a search warrant, but it would have been a dereliction of their duty for them not to do so. To say that the police must leave evidence which they find (without engaging in an improper search) in order to go after a search warrant, on the assumption that the items will remain in the same place until they return with the warrant, is to ignore reality." [citing from United States v. Thweatt, 140 U.S.App.D.C. 120, 433 F.2d 1226, 1231 (1970)]

The officers were confronted with a situation which called for immediate action. The action which they took, the seizure of the stolen transmission, was the reasonable action to satisfy the exigent circumstances present.

* * *

[The dissenting opinion of JUDGE WRIGHT is omitted.]

COOLIDGE v. NEW HAMPSHIRE

Supreme Court of the United States, 1971.
403 U.S. 443, 91 Sup.Ct. 2022.

[The facts of this case and other parts of the opinion are in the subsequent "Automobile Searches" section of this Chapter. What appears here concerns only the applicability of the plain view doctrine to the seizure and search of Coolidge's car].

MR. JUSTICE STEWART delivered the opinion of the Court.

It is well established that under certain circumstances the police may seize evidence in plain view without a warrant. But it is important to keep in mind that, in the vast majority of cases, *any* evidence seized by the police will be in plain view, at least at the moment of seizure. The problem with the "plain view" doctrine has been to identify the circumstances in which plain view has legal significance rather than being simply the normal concomitant of any search, legal or illegal.

An example of the applicability of the "plain view" doctrine is the situation in which the police have a warrant to search a given area for specified objects, and in the course of the search come across some other article of incriminating character. Where the initial intrusion which brings the police within plain view of such an article is supported not by a warrant, but by one of the recognized exceptions to the warrant requirement, the seizure is also legitimate. Thus the police may inadvertently come across evidence while in "hot pursuit" of a fleeing suspect. And an object which comes into view during a search incident to arrest that is appropriately limited in scope under existing law may be seized without a warrant. Chimel v. California, 395 U.S. 752, 762–763. Finally, the "plain view" doctrine has been applied where a police officer is not searching for evidence against the accused, but nonetheless inadvertently comes across an incriminating object. Harris v. United States, 390 U.S. 234; Frazier v. Cupp, 394 U.S. 731; Ker v. California, 374 U.S. 23, 43. Cf. Lewis v. United States, 385 U.S. 206.

What the "plain view" cases have in common is that the police officer in each of them had a prior justification for an intrusion in the course of which he came inadvertently across a piece of evidence incriminating the accused. The doctrine serves to supplement the prior justification—whether it be a warrant for another object, hot pursuit, search incident to lawful arrest, or some other legitimate reason for being present unconnected with a search directed against the accused—and permits the warrantless seizure. Of course, the extension of the original justification is legitimate only where it is immediately apparent to the police that they have evidence before them; the "plain view" doctrine may not be used to extend a general exploratory search from one object to another until something incriminating at last emerges.

The rationale for the "plain view" exception is evident if we keep in mind the two distinct constitutional protections served by the warrant requirement. First, the magistrate's scrutiny is intended to eliminate altogether searches not based on probable cause. The premise here is that *any* intrusion in the way of search or seizure is an evil, so that no intrusion at all is justified without a careful prior determination of necessity. The second, distinct objective is that those searches deemed necessary should be as limited as possible. Here, the specific evil is the "general warrant" abhorred by the colonists, and the problem is not that of intrusion *per se*, but of a general, exploratory rummaging in a person's belongings. The warrant accomplishes this second objective by requiring a "particular description" of the things to be seized.

The "plain view" doctrine is not in conflict with the first objective because plain view does not occur until a search is in progress. In each case, this initial intrusion is justified by a warrant or by an exception such as "hot pursuit" or search incident to a lawful arrest, or by an extraneous valid reason for the officer's presence. And given the initial intrusion, the seizure of an object in plain view is consistent with the second objective, since it does not convert the search into a general or exploratory one. As against the minor peril to Fourth Amendment protections, there is a major gain in effective law enforcement. Where, once an otherwise lawful search is in progress, the police inadvertently come upon a piece of evidence, it would often be a needless inconvenience, and sometimes dangerous—to the evidence or to the police themselves—to require them to ignore it until they have obtained a warrant particularly describing it.

The limits on the doctrine are implicit in the statement of its rationale. The first of these is that plain view *alone* is never enough to justify the warrantless seizure of evidence. This is simply a corollary of the familiar principle discussed above, that no amount of probable cause can justify a warrantless search or seizure absent "exigent circumstances." Incontrovertible testimony of the senses that an incriminating object is on premises belonging to a criminal suspect may establish the fullest possible measure of probable cause. But even where the object is contraband, this Court has repeatedly stated and enforced the basic rule that the police may not enter and make a warrantless seizure.

The second limitation is that the discovery of evidence in plain view must be inadvertent. The rationale of the exception to the warrant requirement, as just stated, is that a plain view seizure will not turn an initially valid (and therefore limited) search into a "general" one, while the inconvenience of procuring a warrant to cover an inadvertent discovery is great. But where the discovery is anticipated, where the police know in advance the location of the evidence and intend to seize it, the situation is altogether different. The requirement of a warrant to seize imposes no inconvenience whatever, or at least none which is constitutionally cognizable in a legal system that regards warrantless searches as "per se unreasonable" in the absence of "exigent circumstances."

If the initial intrusion is bottomed upon a warrant which fails to mention a particular object, though the police know its location and intend to seize it, then there is a violation of the express constitutional requirement of "warrants . . . particularly describing . . . [the] things to be seized." The initial intrusion may, of course, be legitimated not by a warrant but by one of the exceptions to the warrant requirement, such as hot pursuit or search incident to lawful arrest. But to extend the scope of such an intrusion to the seizure of objects—not contraband nor stolen nor dangerous in themselves—which the police know in advance they will find in plain view and intend to seize, would fly in the face of the basic rule that no amount of probable cause can justify a warrantless seizure.

In the light of what has been said, it is apparent that the "plain view" exception cannot justify the police seizure of the Pontiac car in this case. The police had ample opportunity to obtain a valid warrant; they knew the automobile's exact description and location well in advance; they intended to seize it when they came upon Coolidge's property. And this is not a case involving contraband or stolen goods or objects dangerous in themselves.

The seizure was therefore unconstitutional, and so was the subsequent search at the station house. Since evidence obtained in the course of the search was admitted at Coolidge's trial, the judgment must be reversed and the case remanded to the New Hampshire Supreme Court. * * *

MR. JUSTICE BLACK, dissenting [regarding the "plain view" seizure issue].

I believe the seizure of petitioner's automobile was valid under the well-established right of the police to seize evidence in plain view at the time and place of arrest. The majority concedes that the police were rightfully at petitioner's residence to make a valid arrest at the time of the seizure. To use the majority's words, the "initial intrusion" which brought the police within plain view of the automobile was legitimate. The majority also concedes that the automobile was "plainly visible both from the street and from inside the house where Coolidge was actually arrested," and that the automobile itself was evidence which the police had probable cause to seize. Indeed, the majority appears to concede that the seizure of petitioner's automobile was valid under the doctrine upholding seizures of evidence in plain view at the scene of arrest, at least as it stood before today.

However, even after conceding that petitioner's automobile itself was evidence of the crime, that the police had probable cause to seize it as such, and that the automobile was in plain view at the time and place of arrest, the majority holds the seizure to be a violation of the Fourth Amendment because the discovery of the automobile was not "inadvertent." The majority confidently states: "What the 'plain view' cases have in common is that the police officer in each of them had a prior justification for an intrusion in the course of which he came inadvertently across a piece of evidence incriminating the accused." But the prior holdings of this Court not only fail to support the majority's statement, they flatly contradict it.

* * *

The majority confuses the historically justified right of the police to seize visible evidence of the crime in open view at the scene of arrest with the "plain view" exception to the requirement of particular description in search warrants. The majority apparently reasons that unless the seizure made pursuant to authority conferred by a warrant is limited to the particularly described object of seizure, the warrant will become a general writ of assistance. Evidently, as a check on the requirement of particular description in search warrants, the majority announces a new rule that items not named in a warrant cannot be seized unless their discovery was unanticipated or "inadvertent." The majority's concern is with the scope of the intrusion authorized by a warrant. But the right to seize items properly subject to seizure because in open view at the time of arrest is quite independent of any power to search for such items pursuant to a warrant. The entry in the present case did not depend for its authority on a search warrant but was concededly authorized by probable cause to effect a valid arrest. The intrusion did not exceed that authority. The intrusion was limited in scope to the circumstances which justified the entry in the first place—the arrest of petitioner. There was no general search; indeed, there was no search at all. The automobile itself was evidence properly subject to seizure and was in open view at the time and place of arrest.

Only rarely can it be said that evidence seized incident to an arrest is truly unexpected or inadvertent. Indeed, if the police officer had no expectation of discovering weapons, contraband, or other evidence, he would make no search.

* * *

[CHIEF JUSTICE BURGER and JUSTICE BLACKMUN joined JUSTICE BLACK's opinion on this issue.]

MR. JUSTICE WHITE, with whom THE CHIEF JUSTICE joins, concurring and dissenting.

. . . In my view, Coolidge's Pontiac was lawfully seized as evidence of the crime in plain sight and thereafter was lawfully searched.

* * *

. . . It is clear that effects may not be seized without probable cause but the law as to when a warrant is required to validate their seizure is confused and confusing. Part of the difficulty derives from the fact that effects enjoy derivative protection when located in a house or other area within reach of the Fourth Amendment. Under existing doctrine, effects seized in warrantless, illegal searches of houses are fruits of a constitutional violation and may not be received in evidence. But is a warrant required to seize contraband or criminal evidence when it is found by officers at a place where they are legally entitled to be at the time? Before a person is deprived of his possession or right to possession of his effects, must a magistrate confirm that what the officer has legally seen (and would be permitted to testify about, if relevant and material) is actually contraband or criminal evidence?

The issue arises in different contexts. First, the effects may be found on public property. Suppose police are informed that important evidence has been secreted in a public park. A search is made and the evidence found. Although the evidence was hidden rather than abandoned, I had not thought a search warrant was required for officers to make a seizzure, see United States v. Lee, 274 U.S. 559 (1927) (boat seized on public waters); Hester v. United States, 265 U.S. 57 (1924) (liquor seized in open field); any more than a warrant is needed to seize an automobile which is itself evidence of crime and which is found on a public street or in a parking lot.

Second, the items may be found on the premises of a third party who gives consent for an official search but who has no authority to consent to seizure of another person's effects. Frazier v. Cupp, 394 U.S. 731 (1969), would seem to settle the validity of the seizure without a warrant as long as the search itself involves no Fourth Amendment violation.

Third, the police may arrest a suspect in his home and in the course of a properly limited search discover evidence of crime. . . .

And, while Chimel v. California, supra, narrowed the permissible scope of incident searches to the person and the immediate area within reach of the defendant, it did not purport to re-establish the *Trupiano* rule that searches accompanying arrests are invalid if there is opportunity to get a warrant. . . .

Finally, officers may be on a suspect's premises executing a search warrant and in the course of the authorized search discover evidence of crime not covered by the warrant. . . .

In all of these situations, it is apparent that seizure of evidence without a warrant is not itself an invasion either of personal privacy or of property rights beyond that already authorized by law. Only the possessory interest of a defendant in his effects is implicated. And in these various circumstances, at least where the discovery of evidence is "inadvertent," the Court would permit the seizure because, it is said, "the minor peril to Fourth Amendment protections" is overridden by the "major gain in effective law enforcement" inherent in avoiding the "needless inconvenience" of procuring a warrant. Ante, at 467, 468. I take this to mean that both the possessory interest of the defendant and the importance of having a magistrate confirm that what the officer saw with his own eyes is in fact contraband or evidence of crime are not substantial constitutional considerations. Officers in these circumstances need neither guard nor ignore the evidence while a warrant is sought. Immediate seizure is justified and reasonable under the Fourth Amendment. . . .

The Court would interpose in some or all of these situations, however, a condition that the discovery of the disputed evidence be "inadvertent." If it is "anticipated," that is if "the police know in advance the location of the evidence and intend to seize it," the seizure is invalid. Id., at 2040.

I have great difficulty with this approach. Let us suppose officers secure a warrant to search a house for a rifle. While staying well within the range of a rifle search, they discover two photographs of the murder victim, both in plain sight in the bedroom. Assume also that the discovery of the one photograph was inadvertent but finding the other was anticipated. The Court would permit the seizure of only one of the photographs. But in terms of the "minor" peril to Fourth Amendment values there is surely no difference between these two photographs: the interference with possession is the same in each case and the officers' appraisal of the photograph they expected to see is no less reliable than their judgment about the other. And in both situations the actual inconvenience and danger to evidence remain identical if the officers must depart and secure a warrant. The Court, however, states that the State will suffer no constitutionally cognizable inconvenience from invalidating anticipated seizures since it had probable cause to search for the items seized and could have included them in a warrant.

This seems a punitive and extravagant application of the exclusionary rule. If the police have probable cause to search for a photograph as well as a rifle and they proceed to seek a warrant, they could have no possible motive for deliberately including the rifle but omitting the photograph. Quite the contrary is true. Only oversight or careless mistake would explain the omission in the warrant application if the police were convinced they had probable cause to search for the photograph. Of course, they may misjudge the facts and not realize they have probable cause for the picture, or the magistrate may find against them and not issue a warrant for it. In either event the officers may validly seize the photograph for which they had no probable cause to search but the other photograph is excluded from evidence when the Court subsequently determines that the officers, after all, had probable cause to search for it.

More important, the inadvertence rule is unnecessary to further any Fourth Amendment ends and will accomplish nothing. Police with a warrant for a rifle may search only places where rifles might be and must terminate the search once the rifle is found; the inadvertence rule will in no way reduce the number of places into which they may lawfully look. So, too, the areas of permissible search incident to arrest are strictly circumscribed by *Chimel*. Excluding evidence seen from within those areas can hardly be effective to operate to prevent wider, unauthorized searches. If the police stray outside the scope of an authorized *Chimel* search they are already in violation of the Fourth Amendment, and evidence so seized will be excluded; adding a second reason for excluding evidence hardly seems worth the candle. Perhaps the Court is concerned that officers, having the right to intrude upon private property to make arrests, will use that right as a pretext to obtain entry to search for objects in plain sight, cf. Chimel v. California, supra, at 767, but, if so, such a concern is unfounded. The reason is that under *Chimel* the police can enter only into those portions of the property into which entry is necessary to effect the arrest. Given the restrictions of *Chimel*, the police face a substantial risk that in effecting an arrest and a search incident thereto they will never enter into those portions of the property from which they can plainly see the objects for which they are searching and that, if they do not, those objects will be destroyed before they can return and conduct a search of the entire premises pursuant to a warrant. If the police in fact possess probable cause to believe that weapons, contraband, or evidence of crime is in plain view on the premises, it will be far safer to obtain a search warrant than to take a chance that in making an arrest they will come into plain view of the object they are seeking. It is only when they lack probable cause for a search—when, that is, discovery of objects in plain view from a lawful vantage point is inadvertent—that entry to make an arrest might, as a practical matter, assist the police in discovering an object for which they could not have obtained a warrant. But the majority in that circumstance would uphold their authority to seize what they see. I thus doubt that the Court's new rule will have any measurable effect on police conduct. It will merely attach undue consequences to what will most often be an unintended mistake or a misapprehension of some of this Court's probable-cause decisions, a failing which, I am afraid, we all have.

It is careful to note that Coolidge's car is not contraband, stolen, or in itself dangerous. Apparently, contraband, stolen, or dangerous materials may be seized when discovered in the course of an otherwise authorized search even if the discovery is fully anticipated and a warrant could have been obtained. The distinction the Court draws between contraband and mere evidence of crime is reminiscent of the confusing and unworkable approach that I thought Warden v. Hayden, supra, had firmly put aside.

Neither does the Court in so many words limit *Chimel;* on the contrary, it indicates that warrantless *Chimel*-type searches will not be disturbed, even if the police "anticipate that they will find specific evidence during the course of such a search." Ante, at 482. The Court also concedes that, when an arresting officer "comes within plain view of a piece of evidence, not concealed, although outside of the area under the immediate control of the arrestee, the officer may seize it, so long as the plain view was obtained in the course of an appropriately limited search of the arrestee." Id., at 466 n. 24. Yet today's decision is a limitation on *Chimel,* for in the latter example, the Court would permit seizure only if the plain view was inadvertently obtained. If the police, that is, fully anticipate that, when they arrest a suspect as he is entering the front door of his home, they will find a credit card in his pocket and a picture in plain sight on the wall opposite the door, both of which will implicate him in a crime, they may under today's decision seize the credit card but not the picture. This is a distinction that I find to be without basis and that the Court makes no attempt to explain. I can therefore conclude only that *Chimel* and today's holding are squarely inconsistent and that the Court, unable to perceive any reasoned distinction, has abandoned any attempt to find one.

The Court also fails to mention searches carried out with third-party consent. Assume for the moment that authorities are reliably informed that a suspect, subject to arrest, but not yet apprehended, has concealed specified evidence of his crime in the house of a friend. The friend freely consents to a search of his house and accompanies the officers in the process. The evidence is found precisely where the officers were told they would find it, and the officers proceed to seize it, aware, however, that the friend lacks authority from the suspect to confer possession on them. The suspect's interest in not having his possession forcibly interfered with in the absence of a warrant from a magistrate is identical to the interest of Coolidge, and one would accordingly expect the Court to deal with the question. Frazier v. Cupp, supra, indicates that a seizure in these circumstances would be lawful, and the Court today neither overrules nor distinguishes *Frazier* * * *.

Neither does the Court indicate whether it would apply the inadvertence requirement to searches made in public places, although one might infer from its approval of United States v. Lee, supra, which held admissible a chemical analysis of bootleg liquor observed by revenue officers in plain sight, that it would not.

Aware of these inconsistencies, the Court admits that "it would be nonsense to pretend that our decision today reduces Fourth Amendment law to complete order and harmony." Ante, at 483. But it concludes that logical consistency cannot be attained in constitutional law and ultimately comes to rest upon its belief "that the result reached in this case is correct. . . . " Id., at 484. It may be that constitutional law cannot be fully coherent and that constitutional principles ought not always be spun out to their logical limits, but this does not mean that we should cease to strive for clarity and consistency of analysis. Here the Court has a ready opportunity, one way or another, to bring clarity and certainty to a body of law that lower courts and law enforcement officials often find confusing. Instead, without apparent reason, it only increases their confusion by clinging to distinctions that are both unexplained and inexplicable.

II

In the case before us, the officers had probable cause both to arrest Coolidge and to seize his car. In order to effect his arrest, they went to his home—perhaps the most obvious place in which to look for him. They also may have hoped to find his car at home and, in fact, when they arrived on the property to make the arrest, they did find the 1951 Pontiac there. Thus, even assuming that the Fourth Amendment protects against warrantless seizures outside the house, but see Hester v. United States, supra, at 59, the fact remains that the officers had legally entered Coolidge's property to effect an arrest and that they seized the car only after they observed it in plain view before them. The Court, however, would invalidate this seizure on the premise that officers should not be permitted to seize effects in plain sight when they have anticipated they will see them.

Even accepting this premise of the Court, seizure of the car was not invalid. The majority makes an assumption that, when the police went to Coolidge's house to arrest him, they anticipated that they would also find the 1951 Pontiac there. In my own reading of the record, however, I have found no evidence to support this assumption. For all the record shows, the police, although they may have hoped to find the Pontiac at Coolidge's home, did not know its exact location when they went to make the arrest, and their observation of it in Coolidge's driveway was truly inadvertent. Of course, they did have probable cause to seize the car, and, if they had had a valid warrant as well, they would have been justified in looking for it in Coolidge's driveway—a likely place for it to be. But if the fact of probable cause bars this seizure, it would also bar seizures not only of cars found at a house, but also of cars parked in a parking lot, hidden in some secluded spot, or delivered to the police by a third party at the police station. This would simply be a rule that the existence of probable cause bars all warrantless seizures.

It is evident on the facts of this case that Coolidge's Pontiac was subject to seizure if proper procedures were employed. It is also apparent that the Pontiac was in plain view of the officers who had legally entered Coolidge's property to effect his arrest. I am satisfied that it was properly seized whether or not the officers expected that it would be found where it was. And, since the Pontiac was legally seized as evidence of the crime for which Coolidge was arrested, Cooper v. California, supra, authorizes its warrantless search while in lawful custody of the police. "It would be unreasonable to hold that the police, having to retain the car in their custody for such a length of time, had no right, even for their own protection, to search it. It is no answer to say that the police could have obtained a search warrant, for '[t]he relevant test is not whether it is reasonable to procure a search warrant, but whether the search was reasonable.' . . . Under the circumstances of this case, we cannot hold unreasonable under the Fourth Amendment the examination or search of a car validly held by officers for use as evidence . . . ."

NORTH v. SUPERIOR COURT

Supreme Court of California, 1972.
8 Cal.3d 301, 104 Cal.Rptr. 833, 502 P.2d 1305.

BURKE, JUSTICE.

According to evidence presented at the preliminary hearing, the victim a school girl, told Detective Neesan, the arresting officer, that on October 4, 1971, as she was walking home from school, she was pulled into a car at knifepoint by the driver. According to Neesan, the victim described the car as "a light blue two-door car. She thought it was a Ford fastback. . . ." The victim indicated that the car was "higher" than ordinary, had two front bucket seats separated by a center console containing a gear shift and glove box, and was equipped with what appeared to be custom carpeting of a "shag type, with long pile, possibly multicolored yellow and brown."

Following the alleged incident, the officers showed the victim a series of 13 photographs, from which she selected two persons as possible suspects; petitioner was one of the suspects she chose. Detective Neesan had known petitioner and was aware that he had been arrested on two prior occasions involving female victims "picked up in a vehicle while they were on the street." Neesan obtained and drove to petitioner's address where he observed a vehicle (a light blue two-door 1964 Ford) matching the description given by the victim. Neesan then determined that the vehicle was registered to a "female subject" but that a transfer notice was on file dated July 29, 1971. Neesan next asked the victim to review a police "mug book" containing photographs of automobiles and to try and pick out the suspect vehicle. She picked out a 1964 Ford as the car within which she had been abducted.

On October 5, at 8:30 p. m., Neesan drove back to petitioner's residence and arrested petitioner inside his apartment. Petitioner's wife was also present in the apartment. Petitioner asked Neesan if he could give his car keys to her, but Neesan refused since the car was to be towed to the police station. Later that night, the car was examined for fingerprints and various tests made and measurements taken. Although the fingerprints taken at this time were "negative," subsequent tests made on October 7, disclosed "positive" prints of the victim. The October 5 tests did indicate that the left rear tire was similar in design to the impression left at the crime scene, and that the car's "wheel span" matched measurements taken at the scene. Apparently, examination of the vehicle turned up additional evidence linking petitioner with the crime. No search warrant was obtained by the officers who seized and examined petitioner's car.

* * *

1. *The Seizure and Subsequent Examination of Petitioner's Car*

* * *

We [have previously set] forth the following principle "distilled" from the foregoing cases: "When officers, incidental to a lawful arrest, seize an automobile or other object in the reasonable belief that such object *is itself evidence* of the commission of the crime for which such arrest is made, any subsequent examination of said object undertaken for the purpose of determining its evidentiary value does not constitute a 'search' within the meaning of the Fourth Amendment.

* * *

Here, petitioner's car was seized contemporaneous with petitioner's arrest, as evidence of the alleged kidnapping; the car was believed to be the very instrumentality used to commit the kidnapping. Of course, since petitioner was arrested in his apartment, a *search* of the car could not have been made as "incident to arrest"; such searches must be limited to the area within the suspect's immediate control. (E. g., Chimel v. California, 395 U.S. 752, 89 S.Ct. 2034, 23 L.Ed.2d 685.) We are concerned, however, with a *seizure* of evidence in plain sight of arresting officers rather than a search for such evidence. . . . [T]his court has recognized an important exception to the rule announced in the *Chimel* case, supra, namely, that " 'objects falling in the plain view of an officer who has a right to be in a position to have that view are subject to seizure and may be introduced in evidence.' " Thus, in [an earlier case], we upheld the seizure of contraband found in plain view of officers conducting a post-arrest house search for additional suspects. Although the instant case involves the seizure of evidence of an offense rather than contraband itself, the cases no longer recognize a distinction between contraband and "mere evidence" for purposes of applying the Fourth Amendment. Petitioner's car was parked on a public street, in plain view of the arresting officers. Under [the] authorities cited above, the officers properly seized the car as evidence of the alleged kidnapping.

Petitioner contends, however, that our [rule] must be reexamined and modified in the light of the subsequent decision of the United States Supreme Court in Coolidge v. New Hampshire. *Coolidge,* properly understood, leaves [our holding] undisturbed.

In *Coolidge,* the police arrested a murder suspect in his house and thereupon seized his automobile and searched it later at the police station, finding physical evidence that the victim had been inside the vehicle. The record disclosed that the police had known for some time of the probable role of the car in the crime, and there were no "exigent circumstances" to justify a warrantless search. Accordingly, the plurality opinion of Justice Stewart concluded that the seizure could not be justified on the theory that the vehicle was itself the "instrumentality" of the crime and was discovered "in plain view" of the officers. Justice Stewart was of the opinion that the "plain view" doctrine is applicable only to the *inadvertent* discovery of incriminating evidence.

If the plurality opinion in *Coolidge* were entitled to binding effect as precedent, we would have difficulty distinguishing its holding from the instant case, for the discovery of petitioner's car was no more "inadvertent" than in *Coolidge*. However, that portion of Justice Stewart's plurality opinion which proposed the adoption of new restrictions to the "plain view" rule was signed by only four members of the court (Stewart, J., Douglas, J., Brennan, J., and Marshall, J.). Although concurring in the judgment, Justice Harlan declined to join in that portion of the opinion and the four remaining justices expressly disagreed with Justice Stewart on this point. . . .

It follows that the "plain view" issue raised by the plurality opinion was in fact considered by an equally divided court, and hence was not actually decided in *Coolidge*. As stated in [one of our earlier cases] involving a different aspect of the *Coolidge* plurality opinion, "under settled doctrine, the judgment of an equally divided United States Supreme Court 'is without force as precedent.' Thus we are bound to apply the [vehicle search] rule according to our present understanding of its scope."

We conclude that our decision in *Teale* correctly sets forth the present law regarding warrantless seizures of evidentiary items in plain view of arresting officers, and that the superior court in the instant case properly denied petitioner's motion to suppress evidence derived from the subsequent police examination of petitioner's vehicle.

[The remainder of the opinion concerning admissibility of defendant's conversations with his wife is omitted.]

[The concurring and dissenting opinion of CHIEF JUSTICE WRIGHT joined by JUSTICE MCCOMB is omitted.]

TOBRINER, JUSTICE, dissenting.

* * *

On the issue of the evidence acquired through examination of the automobile, I agree with the conclusion and reasoning of Justice Sullivan. In my opinion, the suppression of this evidence is required by the decision of the United States Supreme Court in Coolidge v. New Hampshire (1971) 403 U.S. 443, 91 S.Ct. 2022, 29 L.Ed.2d 564. Despite the divergent views expressed by the justices in that case, and the absence of a single majority opinion, the fact remains that the United States Supreme Court ordered suppression of the evidence obtained by examination of Coolidge's car. Unless we can find and articulate some reasonable distinction between the facts of *Coolidge* and of the present case, we must conclude that the Supreme Court would also exclude the evidence at issue in the present case.

In both *Coolidge* and the instant case the crime was committed inside the defendant's automobile. In both cases the defendant was arrested inside his home; his car was parked outside the residence and in plain sight from the public streets. In *Coolidge* the police had an invalid search warrant; here they had no warrant at all. In both cases the police impounded the cars, examined them meticulously, and through this examination discovered evidence introduced against defendant. In both cases the defendant objected to the introduction of the evidence, and in both the state sought to uphold the evidence on the ground that the automobile was evidence of the crime in plain sight from public vantage.

Justice Burke contends, in effect, that because *Coolidge* did not yield a clear majority opinion, that the decision of the Supreme Court in that case may be disregarded by this court. I would maintain to the contrary, that when a case comes before us which is in all material facts identical to *Coolidge*, we must treat *the result* reached in *Coolidge* as controlling, and exclude the evidence in question. I have stated briefly the material facts of his case and of *Coolidge* and can find no reasonable basis to distinguish the two cases.

PETERS, J., concurs.

SULLIVAN, JUSTICE (dissenting).

* * *

. . . the simple fact is that there is no support in *Coolidge* or other decisions of the high court for the seizure of the car on the mere basis that it is in plain view. * * *

As is well stated by Mr. Justice Stewart in Coolidge v. New Hampshire, "plain view *alone* is never enough to justify the warrantless seizure of evidence." The "plain view" doctrine merely allows an officer with a *prior justification* for a search to seize evidence which he inadvertently discovers. After all, "in the vast majority of cases, *any* evidence seized by the police will be in plain view, at least at the moment of seizure." Probable cause alone is not enough. If this exception to the requirement of a warrant were not so limited it would erode entirely the guarantee of the Fourth Amendment.

Detective Neesan discovered the automobile in plain view and had probable cause to believe it was connected with the crime under investigation; what he lacked, however, was either a warrant or exigent circumstances.[2] Since he had seen the car the day before he seized it, it cannot be argued that he found it inadvertently when he went to arrest defendant. The seizure is not lawful simply because the automobile was in plain view on the street.

Of course I recognize that there is some dispute whether the "plain view" section II–C of the *Coolidge* opinion is binding upon us, because it reflects the consensus of only a plurality of the Supreme Court. However, Mr. Justice Harlan, whose concurrence produced the fifth vote for the majority decision, specifically concurred with section II–D of Justice Stewart's opinion. That section is addressed primarily to Mr. Justice White's dissenting opinion, which "marshals the arguments that can be made against our interpretation of the 'automobile' and 'plain view' exceptions to the warrant requirement." (Coolidge v. New Hampshire, supra, 403 U.S. 443, 473, 91 S.Ct. 2022, 2042, 29 L.Ed.2d 564.) Such reference and several others to part II–

C (id. at p. 482, 91 S.Ct. 2022) of the plurality opinion suggest that Justice Harlan's limited concurrence sweeps more broadly than the majority would allow.

But apart from these considerations, the ineluctable fact remains that seizure of evidence of the crime on the mere basis that it is in plain view has no support in our decisional law. * * *

NOTE

The plain view doctrine operates on the premise that there is no "search". There is, however, a seizure and there must be probable cause to seize.

Assume police officers are executing a valid search warrant which authorizes the seizure of marijuana. In the course of the search one officer discovers several United States savings bonds bearing names and addresses different from that of the suspect. The officer took the bonds to a different room of the residence and gave them to another officer. That officer telephoned one of the persons whose names were on the bonds. That person told the police that the bonds were stolen. Until the call was made the officers had no knowledge that the bonds were stolen. Was the police conduct proper? Consider the views of the court deciding the case. Commonwealth v. Hawkins, 280 N.E.2d 665 (Mass.1972):

Tauro, C. J. . . .

Articles not named in a search warrant, except weapons or contraband, may be seized only if the police have probable cause to believe that they were stolen. . . .

In the instant case the police admitted they had no actual knowledge that the bonds had been stolen until after investigating their ownership. The mere fact that the names on the bonds were different from that of the defendant was insufficient to provide probable cause for their seizure. . . .

In the circumstances of this case it might appear to some that the defendant is being given unwarranted protection. However, if the situation in the instant case were transposed to a different setting, for example, to the home of a person of wealth, it would appear irrational to argue that United States government bonds could be taken from his possession, even momentarily, in order to establish their ownership. It is fundamental in our concept of justice that the denial of constitutional protection to the worst of men effectively serves to deny the same protection to the best of men.

Braucher, J. (dissenting)

I agree that the police did not have probable cause to believe that the bonds had been stolen. They acquired such probable cause only after they made a telephone call to an owner named on one of the bonds.

I also agree that the police had a right to look into the brown envelope in their search for drugs. But they were under a duty to keep the defendant's belongings in order and were therefore justified in noting that the articles were United States savings bonds with names and addresses different from that of the defendant. Such bonds are not transferable. 31 U.S.C. § 757c(a) (1970). 31 C.F.R. (1971) § 315.15. McDonald v. Hanahan, 328 Mass. 539, 540, 105 N.E.2d 240. Their presence in a small apartment being searched for narcotics warranted a further threshold inquiry. . . .

If a threshold inquiry is unreasonably extended, there is danger to the security guaranteed by the Fourth Amendment. . . . But in the present case the police made a telephone call which could have taken only a few minutes. There is no indication that it prolonged the concurrent search for narcotics. The telephone call was likely to produce a less serious invasion of an innocent defendant's privacy than the alternative of sending an officer out to investigate and to bring back a new warrant.

The record indicates that the police took the bonds from one room to another before they had probable cause. It does not indicate a definitive "seizure" until afterwards.

I do not believe that it is proper for either the police or this court to base a judgment on the assumed wealth or poverty of the defendant. If police, acting lawfully in searching a millionaire's mansion, found in a bureau drawer in his bedroom United States savings bonds bearing the names of several other people, they would have solid reason for making further inquiry. Millionaires have no more right to steal than anyone else.

SECTION 3. CONSENT SEARCHES

JUDD v. UNITED STATES

United States Court of Appeals, D.C.Cir. 1951.
190 F.2d 649.

WASHINGTON, CIRCUIT JUDGE.

This case presents the question whether the trial court was correct in denying a motion to suppress certain evidence on the ground that it was procured through a search and seizure which violated the Fourth Amendment.

Appellant Robert Judd was charged with the crimes of housebreaking and grand larceny, D.C.Code (1940 ed.) §§ 22–1801, 22–2201. He pleaded not guilty and after trial by jury was convicted on both counts. It is from the judgment of conviction that he appeals.

On the night of March 23–24, 1950, the office of the Standard Transfer & Storage Company, in Washington, D. C., was broken into and some $2,600 stolen in money and travellers' checks. The next day the police received information from someone identified only as "Harvey" that he had recently overheard his neighbor, Ernest White, discussing various housebreaking jobs, with several people, including appellant Judd. From this they concluded that the Standard Transfer larceny might be involved. Accordingly, police officers proceeded to the house where Ernest White lived and secreted themselves in a room adjoining White's. They heard White enter with another unidentified person and discuss leaving town for Philadelphia. After the person with White, still unidentified, had left, the police entered White's room, placed him under arrest, and commenced a search, locating some of the stolen checks. Appellant Judd was not in the room at that time and there was no evidence that he had been present earlier in the evening, or that he was the person who had come in with White. Shortly after the arrest of White, Judd entered the apartment and was immediately arrested. He denied any knowledge of the crime.

At the trial the sole affirmative evidence linking Judd with the crime was the testimony of a laboratory technician, that the print of a shoe taken from Judd's apartment matched a shoeprint found on a carton inside the Standard Transfer & Storage Company building, under or near a window which apparently had been entered for purposes of the theft. The shoe and a photographic copy of the impression on the box carton were introduced in evidence. It is Judd's contention that the shoe was captured by an unconstitutional search and seizure and should not have been admitted in evidence. If he is correct in that contention, the conviction, of course, cannot stand.

From the testimony on the motion to suppress, the following picture may be drawn: The appellant was arrested without a warrant at 11 o'clock at night, when he entered the premises of White. He was taken to jail and "booked on an open charge." He was not then formally committed. While held in custody for purposes of investigation, he was interrogated for several hours by police officers concerning general criminal activity, possible possession of burglar's tools at his home, and whether he had committed the Standard Transfer burglary. He was also asked whether he had certain items of clothing at home, including shoes. At approximately 2:00 A.M., in the custody of four police officers and while handcuffed, he was taken to his own home, which was in a different part of town. The apartment was then searched and the shoes found. Appellant testified that all this was against his will and without any consent. A police officer testified that while he and another officer were interrogating Judd at the jail concerning burglar's tools and his clothing and shoes, they asked him whether "he minded us going over to his room and taking a look, and he said no. . . . We asked him if he would go over and he said yes. . . . He didn't give us actual consent to search it. He gave us consent to go in there. I told him I was looking for a pair of shoes and he said it was all right to go over there . . . ." The other officer testified: "We questioned him as to whether he had any tools that could be used in ripping safes. . . . So, he said we would go out to his place and see, if we believed he had any of these things there. . . . I told him where we were going, and he was well aware of the fact that we were going to his home. He said he had nothing to conceal or hide out there, and it was perfectly all right for us to go out there."

This is the basis of the Government's case. The Government, admitting that no warrant had been obtained, contends that the appellant voluntarily consented to the search and seizure, thus making the issuance of a warrant unnecessary. There is no claim that consent was given when the officers reached the apartment, reliance being placed solely on the statements made by Judd while in jail. The Government argues that the validity of the arrest, never having been formally challenged, is not before us and, in any event, is irrelevant to the issue of consent.

Searches and seizures made without a proper warrant are generally to be regarded as unreasonable and violative of the Fourth Amendment. True, the obtaining of the warrant may on occasion be waived by the individual; he may give his consent to the search and seizure. But such a waiver or consent must be proved by clear and positive testimony, and it must be established that there was no duress or coercion, actual or implied. Amos v. United States, 255 U.S. 313, 41 S.Ct. 266; United States v. Kelih, D.C.S.D.Ill.1921, 272 F. 484. The Government must show a consent that is "unequivocal and specific" (Karwicki v. United States, 4 Cir., 55 F.2d 225, 226), "freely and intelligently given." Kovach v. United States, 6 Cir., 53 F.2d 639. Thus "invitations" to enter one's house, extended to armed officers of the law who demand entrance, are usually to be considered as invitations secured by force. United States v. Marquette, D.C.N.D.Cal. 1920, 271 F. 120. A like view has been taken where an officer displays his badge and declares that he has come to make a search (United States v. Slusser, D.C.S.D.Ohio 1921, 270 F. 818), even where the householder replies "All right." United States v. Marra, D.C.W.D. N.Y.1930, 40 F.2d 271. A finding of consent in such circumstances has been held to be "unfounded in reason". Herter v. United States, 9 Cir., 27 F.2d 521. Intimidation and duress are almost necessarily implicit in such situations; if the Government alleges their absence, it has the burden of convincing the court that they are in fact absent.

This burden on the Government is particularly heavy in cases where the individual is under arrest. Non-resistance to the orders or suggestions of the police is not infrequent in such a situation; true consent, free of fear or pressure, is not so readily to be found. United States v. Novero, D.C., 58 F.Supp. 275; United States v. McCunn, D.C.S.D.N.Y.1930, 40 F.2d 295. In fact, the circumstances of the defendant's plight may be such as to make any claim of actual consent "not in accordance with human experience", and explainable only on the basis of "physical or moral compulsion". Ray v. United States, 5 Cir., 84 F.2d 654, 656.

In the case at bar, do the circumstances justify the finding of consent? As we have noted, the appellant was arrested late at night without a warrant, booked on an open charge for "investigation,"[1] questioned for several hours by various police officers, then taken to his home some distance away, while handcuffed, and in custody of four officers. His statements while in jail, which are relied on as con-

1. While not controlling in this decision, we may note that Judd was not charged with housebreaking or any other offense until several hours after his arrest (and after the search); nor does it appear with certainty from the record before us that he was promptly taken before a committing magistrate, as required by Rule 5(a) of the Federal Rules of Criminal Procedure.

sent, may be summarized as: I have nothing to hide, you can go there and see for yourself. Conceivably, that is the calm statement of an innocent man; conceivably, again, it is but the false bravado of the small-time criminal. But, however it be characterized, it hardly establishes willing agreement that the officers search the household without first procuring a warrant.[2] Comparable statements have been held insufficient where the victim of the search was safely in his home,[3] his place of business,[4] or in his automobile.[5] Surely they acquire no more force when procured under the circumstances here present.[6] Further, the testimony of one officer was that Judd "didn't give us actual consent to search it. He gave us consent to go in there." Before a court holds that a defendant has waived his protection under the Fourth Amendment, "there must be convincing evidence to that effect." Nueslein v. District of Columbia, 73 App.D.C. 85, 89, 115 F.2d 690, 694. Here, the officers themselves do not appear completely convinced.

The relative credibility of the witnesses is not the central issue in this case.[7] The real issue is whether the evidence offered by the Government, taken at full value, meets the required standard. We hold that it does not; that there has not been a sufficient showing of true consent, free of duress and coercion. Standards of this sort must be maintained and enforced by the trial and appellate courts. If they are not, the guarantees of the Bill of Rights can quickly disappear through tacit nullification. We must hold that there was no consent and that the search and seizure were not permissible. Ac-

2. For example, Officer Friel testified: "We asked him [Judd] if he would go over [to his home] and he said yes." It seems obvious that there was not much else Judd could say under the circumstances. Similarly, where Officer Friel testified: "I asked him if he minded us going over to his room and taking a look, and he said no."

3. Herter v. United States, supra; Farris v. United States, 9 Cir., 24 F.2d 639; United States v. Marra, supra; Helfer v. State, 84 Okl.Cr. 304, 181 P.2d 862; Byrd v. State, 161 Tenn. 306, 30 S.W.2d 273.

4. United States v. McCunn, supra.

5. Graham v. State, Okl.Cr.App., 184 P.2d 984; Edwards v. State, 83 Okl. Cr. 340, 177 P.2d 143.

6. Gibson v. United States, 80 U.S.App. D.C. 81, 149 F.2d 381, certiorari denied sub nom. O'Kelley v. United States, 326 U.S. 724, 66 S.Ct. 29, on which the Government relies, is not in point. The court there merely held that evidence which is volunteered by a person while under illegal arrest, where he admits that he acted on a completely voluntary basis, is not inadmissible.

7. In this connection, the judge who heard the motion to suppress concluded his remarks by saying:

"The two police officers impressed the Court as gentlemen of probity. The defendant is unworthy of belief, because of his past conflicts with the law.

"He was placed on probation once for a serious offense; was arrested at a subsequent time for violation of probation. He was before this Court on a robbery charge on which he was acquitted for insufficiency of evidence, but he certainly has not been a good law-abiding citizen.

"He certainly is not entitled to ask the Court to accept his word as against officers of the law.

* * * * * *

"The motion to suppress is denied."

cordingly, the evidence was inadmissible and the motion to suppress should have been granted. The conviction cannot stand. . . .

Reversed and remanded.

CLARK, CIRCUIT JUDGE, dissents.

NOTES

1. What factors will indicate that a consent to search has been voluntarily given? Several were set forth by the court in United States v. Smith, 308 F.2d 657 (2d Cir. 1962). " . . . if the defendant permits a warrantless search of his home or establishment in the mistaken belief that he has nothing there which will incriminate him, it has been held that the search has been voluntarily consented to . . . if the defendant admits his guilt to the officer, instead of denying it to him, and then allows a search without a warrant, this strongly implies voluntary consent on his part . . . the degree of affirmative assistance given to the police by the suspect is often relevant in determining whether consent exists."

Where the police indicate they have a warrant but no warrant is produced at trial or the warrant turns out to be invalid, consent is vitiated. Bumper v. North Carolina, 391 U.S. 543, 88 S.Ct. 1788 (1968). The mere threat to get a warrant, however, has been held insufficient to negate voluntariness of consent. Barlow v. State, 280 A.2d 703 (Del.1971); State v. Douglas, 488 P.2d 1366 (Or.1971). Deception may vitiate consent. Commonwealth v. Brown, 437 Pa. 1, 261 A.2d 879 (1970) (officer told defendant he would sell gun and instead had a ballistics test run); Graves v. Beto, 424 F.2d 524 (5th Cir. 1970) (defendant told blood sample was for alcohol test but it was used to type his blood for comparison with blood stains in rape case); United States v. J. B. Kramer Grocery, 418 F.2d 987 (9th Cir. 1969) (false assertion of right to search without a warrant). In cases where an officer gains entry into premises, there is some issue as to whether consent to enter is necessarily vitiated. Thus an officer may not pose as a gas man to gain entry, but perhaps using a false name he gains entry into a room by making an appointment with a prostitute over the telephone is permissible. People v. St. Ives, 110 Ill.App.2d 37, 249 N.E.2d 97 (1969). Threats of force will make consent involuntary. Weed v. United States, 340 F.2d 827 (10th Cir. 1965) (officers with drawn guns said they could get warrant); Waldron v. United States, 219 F.2d 37 (D.C.Cir. 1955) (police told pregnant girl they could not be responsible for the conditions of the house if they had to get a warrant). Consider, State v. Redford, 27 Utah 2d 379, 496 P.2d 884 (1972) (police officer bought an automobile solely to acquire the right to search it).

2. A person who consents to a search may limit the scope of the search and those limitations must be respected. United States v. Dichiarinte, 445 F.2d 126 (7th Cir. 1971) (consent to search for narcotics does not confer authority to search for papers).

3. A consent may be invalid if the party giving the consent is mentally incompetent. See United States v. Elrod, 441 F.2d 353 (5th Cir. 1971).

STONER v. CALIFORNIA

Supreme Court of the United States, 1964.
376 U.S. 483, 84 S.Ct. 889.

MR. JUSTICE STEWART delivered the opinion of the Court.

The petitioner was convicted of armed robbery after a jury trial in the Superior Court of Los Angeles County, California. At the trial several articles which had been found by police officers in a search of the petitioner's hotel room during his absence were admitted into evidence over his objection. A District Court of Appeal of California affirmed the conviction, and the Supreme Court of California denied further review. We granted certiorari, limiting review "to the question of whether evidence was admitted which had been obtained by an unlawful search and seizure." For the reasons which follow, we conclude that the petitioner's conviction must be set aside.

The essential facts are not in dispute. On the night of October 25, 1960, the Budget Town Food Market in Monrovia, California, was robbed by two men, one of whom was described by eyewitnesses as carrying a gun and wearing horn-rimmed glasses and a grey jacket. Soon after the robbery a checkbook belonging to the petitioner was found in an adjacent parking lot and turned over to the police. Two of the stubs in the checkbook indicated that checks had been drawn to the order of the Mayfair Hotel in Pomona, California. Pursuing this lead, the officers learned from the Police Department of Pomona that the petitioner had a previous criminal record, and they obtained from the Pomona police a photograph of the petitioner. They showed the photograph to the two eyewitnesses to the robbery, who both stated that the picture looked like the man who had carried the gun. On the basis of this information the officers went to the Mayfair Hotel in Pomona at about 10 o'clock on the night of October 27. They had neither search nor arrest warrants. There then transpired the following events, as later recounted by one of the officers:

> "We approached the desk, the night clerk, and asked him if there was a party by the name of Joey L. Stoner living at the hotel. He checked his records and stated 'Yes, there is.' And we asked him what room he was in. He stated he was in Room 404 but he was out at this time.
>
> "We asked him how he knew that he was out. He stated that the hotel regulations required that the key to the room would be placed in the mail box each time they left the hotel. The key was in the mail box, that he therefore knew he was out of the room.
>
> "We asked him if he would give us permission to enter the room, explaining our reasons for this.
>
> "Q. What reasons did you explain to the clerk?
>
> "A. We explained that we were there to make an arrest of a man who had possibly committed a robbery in the

City of Monrovia, and that we were concerned about the fact that he had a weapon. He stated 'In this case, I will be more than happy to give you permission and I will take you directly to the room.'

"Q. Is that what the clerk told you?

"A. Yes, sir.

"Q. What else happened?

"A. We left one detective in the lobby, and Detective Oliver, Officer Collins, and myself, along with the night clerk, got on the elevator and proceeded to the fourth floor, and went to Room 404. The night clerk placed a key in the lock, unlocked the door, and says, 'Be my guest.' "

The officers entered and made a thorough search of the room and its contents. They found a pair of horn-rimmed glasses and a grey jacket in the room, and a .45-caliber automatic pistol with a clip and several cartridges in the bottom of a bureau drawer. The petitioner was arrested two days later in Las Vegas, Nevada. He waived extradition and was returned to California for trial on the charge of armed robbery. The gun, the cartridges and clip, the horn-rimmed glasses, and the grey jacket were all used as evidence against him at his trial.

The search of the petitioner's room by the police officers was conducted without a warrant of any kind, and it therefore "can survive constitutional inhibition only upon a showing that the surrounding facts brought it within one of the exceptions to the rule that a search must rest upon a search warrant." The District Court of Appeal thought the search was justified as an incident to a lawful arrest.[1] But a search can be incident to an arrest only if it is substantially contemporaneous with the arrest and is confined to the immediate vicinity of the arrest. Whatever room for leeway there may be in these concepts, it is clear that the search of the petitioner's hotel room in Pomona, California, on October 27 was not incident to his arrest in Las Vegas, Nevada, on October 29. The search was completely unrelated to the arrest, both as to time and as to place. See Preston v. United States, decided this day.

In this Court the respondent has recognized that the reasoning of the California District Court of Appeal cannot be reconciled with our decision in Agnello, nor, indeed, with the most recent California decisions. Accordingly, the respondent has made no argument that the search can be justified as an incident to the petitioner's arrest.

1. The court reasoned that the officers had probable cause to arrest the petitioner prior to their entry into the hotel room; that they were not obliged to accept as true the night clerk's statement that the petitioner was not in his room; that "it may be reasonably inferred that they entered his room for the purpose of making an arrest," that their observation of the glasses in plain sight reasonably led them to a further search; and that in the circumstances the arrest and the search and seizure were "part of the same transaction."

Instead, the argument is made that the search of the hotel room, although conducted without the petitioner's consent, was lawful because it was conducted with the consent of the hotel clerk. We find this argument unpersuasive.

Even if it be assumed that a state law which gave a hotel proprietor blanket authority to authorize the police to search the rooms of the hotel's guests could survive constitutional challenge, there is no intimation in the California cases cited by the respondent that California has any such law. Nor is there any substance to the claim that the search was reasonable because the police, relying upon the night clerk's expressions of consent, had a reasonable basis for the belief that the clerk had authority to consent to the search. Our decisions make clear that the rights protected by the Fourth Amendment are not to be eroded by strained applications of the law of agency or by unrealistic doctrines of "apparent authority." As this Court has said,

> "it is unnecessary and ill-advised to import into the law surrounding the constitutional right to be free from unreasonable searches and seizures subtle distinctions, developed and refined by the common law in evolving the body of private property law which, more than almost any other branch of law, has been shaped by distinctions whose validity is largely historical. . . . [W]e ought not to bow to them in the fair administration of the criminal law. To do so would not comport with our justly proud claim of the procedural protections accorded to those charged with crime." Jones v. United States, 362 U.S. 257, 266–267, 80 S.Ct. 725, 733–734.

It is important to bear in mind that it was the petitioner's constitutional right which was at stake here, and not the night clerk's nor the hotel's. It was a right, therefore, which only the petitioner could waive by word or deed, either directly or through an agent. It is true that the night clerk clearly and unambiguously consented to the search. But there is nothing in the record to indicate that the police had any basis whatsoever to believe that the night clerk had been authorized by the petitioner to permit the police to search the petitioner's room.

At least twice this Court has explicitly refused to permit an otherwise unlawful police search of a hotel room to rest upon consent of the hotel proprietor. Lustig v. United States, 338 U.S. 74, 69 S. Ct. 1372; United States v. Jeffers, 342 U.S. 48, 72 S.Ct. 93. In Lustig the manager of a hotel allowed police to enter and search a room without a warrant in the occupant's absence, and the search was held unconstitutional. In Jeffers the assistant manager allowed a similar search, and that search was likewise held unconstitutional.

It is true, as was said in Jeffers, that when a person engages a hotel room he undoubtedly gives "implied or express permission" to "such persons as maids, janitors or repairmen" to enter his room "in the performance of their duties." 342 U.S., at 51, 72 S.Ct. at 95. But the conduct of the night clerk and the police in the present case was of an entirely different order. In a closely analogous situation the Court has held that a search by police officers of a house occupied by a tenant invaded the tenant's constitutional right, even though the search was authorized by the owner of the house, who presumably had not only apparent but actual authority to enter the house for some purposes, such as to "view waste." Chapman v. United States, 365 U.S. 610, 81 S.Ct. 776. The Court pointed out that the officers' purpose in entering was not to view waste but to search for distilling equipment, and concluded that to uphold such a search without a warrant would leave tenants' homes secure only in the discretion of their landlords.

No less than a tenant of a house, or the occupant of a room in a boarding house, McDonald v. United States, 335 U.S. 451, 69 S.Ct. 191, a guest in a hotel room is entitled to constitutional protection against unreasonable searches and seizures. That protection would disappear if it were left to depend upon the unfettered discretion of an employee of the hotel. It follows that this search without a warrant was unlawful. Since evidence obtained through the search was admitted at the trial, the judgment must be reversed.

It is so ordered.

Judgment reversed.

NOTES

1. If the record did show that the police reasonably believed "that the night clerk had been authorized by the petitioner to permit the police to search the petitioner's room", would that have made a difference?

2. Suppose that a landlord rents a garage to a tenant who uses it to store stolen property. When suspicion falls upon the landlord, may he "exculpate" himself with the authorities by opening the garage and letting them search with his consent? This problem was presented in United States v. Botsch, 364 F.2d 542 (2d Cir. 1966), and the court sustained such a search. The court said:

"In the case before us, Stein [the landlord] not only possessed a key to the shack with Botsch's knowledge and approval, but Botsch expressly authorized him to use it for the purpose of accepting the deliveries which flowed from the fraudulent scheme. Thus, Stein and Botsch did not occupy a mere landlord-tenant relationship; Stein, having been made an unwitting accomplice by Botsch, had a vital interest in cooperating with the Inspectors so that he could remove any taint of suspicion cast upon him. Indeed, any individual under similar circumstances would have a right to promptly and voluntarily exculpate himself by establishing that his role in the alleged scheme was entirely innocent and passive. This right to exculpate oneself . . . distinguishes the . . . search from . . . Stoner v. California . . . ."

Is the *Botsch* case really distinguishable from *Stoner*? See the dissenting opinion of Judge Smith in the *Botsch* case. And see Chapman v. United States, 365 U.S. 610, 81 S.Ct. 776 (1961).

3. Must the person who consents to search be given a warning of his right to refuse?

In Schneckloth v. Bustamonte, 412 U.S. 218, 93 S.Ct. 2041 (1973), the Court said:

"We hold only that when the subject of a search is not in custody and the State attempts to justify a search on the basis of his consent, the Fourth and Fourteenth Amendments require that it demonstrate that the consent was in fact voluntarily given, and not the result of duress or coercion, express or implied. Voluntariness is a question of fact to be determined from all the circumstances, and while the subject's knowledge of a right to refuse is a factor to be taken into account, the prosecution is not required to demonstrate such knowledge as a prerequisite to establishing a voluntary consent."

With respect to one in custody being asked to consent to a search, some courts have required warnings. See e. g., United States v. Blalock, 255 F.Supp. 268 (E.D.Pa.1966); Perkins v. Henderson, 418 F.2d 441 (5th Cir. 1969). For a discussion of whether Miranda warnings are adequate see United States v. Noa, 443 F.2d 144 (9th Cir. 1971); State v. Custer, 251 So.2d 287 (Fla.App.1971). Other courts have said that warnings are unnecessary. United States ex rel. Coombs v. LaValle, 417 F.2d 523 (2d Cir. 1969); United States v. Malloy, 460 F.2d 243 (10th Cir. 1972). Many of the cases which hold that warnings are not required indicate that knowledge of the right to refuse (which warnings could supply) is a factor to be considered in determining the voluntariness of the consent. Some courts have made it a very significant factor. Rosenthall v. Henderson, 389 F.2d 514 (6th Cir. 1968). On the nature of warning required, see Schorr v. State, 499 P.2d 450 (Okl.Cr.1972) (warnings of rights are required) and Thomas v. States, 501 P.2d 1405 (Okl.Cr.1972) (unnecessary to advise the suspect of the purpose of the search).

4. The question of who may consent to a search other than the suspect himself has arisen in a large variety of situations. A summary of the general categories considered by the courts are given here.

(a) A landlord cannot consent to search of tenant's apartment. Chapman v. United States, 365 U.S. 610, 81 S.Ct. 776 (1961). The landlord may consent if it appears that the tenant has vacated the premises. See United States v. Kress, 446 F.2d 358 (7th Cir. 1971); Eisentrager v. Hocker, 450 F.2d 490 (9th Cir. 1971). A landlord may consent to search of common areas. Gillars v. United States, 182 F.2d 962 (D.C.Cir. 1950).

(b) Generally a university official cannot consent to a search of a student's dormitory room. United States v. Kress, 446 F.2d 358 (9th Cir. 1971); Commonwealth v. McCloskey, 217 Pa.Super. 432, 272 A.2d 271 (1970).

(c) Co-tenants can consent to search of property they share with each other. Frazier v. Cupp, 394 U.S. 731, 89 S.Ct. 1420 (1969); United States v. Cataldo, 433 F.2d 38 (2d Cir. 1970).

(d) A spouse who is a co-tenant can consent to search of jointly occupied premises, Commonwealth v. Martin, 358 Mass. 282, 264 N.E.2d 336 (1970), even if parties are antagonistic, State v. McCarthy, 23 Ohio 2d 87, 269 N.E.2d 424 (1971); People v. Koshiol, 45 Ill.2d 573, 262 N.E.2d 446 (1970). A mistress may also consent to the search if she has jointly occupied the premises for a period of time. White v. United States, 444 F.2d 724 (10th Cir. 1971); United States v. Wilson, 447 F.2d 1 (9th Cir. 1971).

However, some jurisdictions recognize some limits upon the authority for a particular seizure. Hawaii v. Evans, 45 Hawaii 622, 372 P.2d 365 (1962) (wife cannot consent to search of husband's possessions); United States ex rel. Casey v. Mazurkiewicz, 431 F.2d 839 (3rd Cir. 1970) (wife cannot consent to search of garage where husband is sole lessee and has only key). Other jurisdictions reject even these limitations. Dinkins v. State, 244 So.2d 148 (Fla.App.1971).

(e) Consent by parents or children pose knotty problems. Some courts hold that a parent can consent to the search of a child's room. State v. Schorr, 289 Minn. 175, 182 N.W.2d 878 (1971) (twenty-two-year-old son); Jones v. State, 13 Md.App. 309, 283 A.2d 184 (1971); People v. Daniels, 16 Cal.App.3d 36, 93 Cal.Rptr. 628 (1971) (adult son present in next room). However, where the son or daughter has exclusive use of a particular room, other courts have invalidated parental consent. Reeves v. Warden, 346 F.2d 915 (4th Cir. 1965). See People v. Daniels, supra (mother cannot consent to search of son's suitcase). Other relatives may have a right to consent under some circumstances. Consent by adult, married sister to search of home owned by the parents of her and her defendant brother has been held proper in Garr v. Commonwealth, 463 S.W.2d 109 (Ky.1971). See also State v. Boyle, 207 Kan. 833, 486 P.2d 849 (1971) (consent by defendant's older brother in parent's absence). However, the "exclusive use" doctrine may limit the scope of the search in these cases also. Thus in Shorry v. Warden, 401 F.2d 474 (4th Cir. 1968), a sister who owned a home was said not to be authorized to consent to the search of her brother's bedroom in her home. In People v. Overall, 7 Mich.App. 153, 151 N.W.2d 225 (1967), a grandmother was held not authorized to consent to the search of a room occupied by her grandson.

(f) A host may permit the search of the guest's room but not the search of closed recesses and the seizure of the guest's personal property. People v. Laursen, 22 Cal.App.3d 1033, 99 Cal.Rptr. 841 (1972). The exclusive use limitation may also be applied in these cases. Burger v. United States, 333 F.2d 210 (9th Cir. 1964). The right to clean a room of a paying or a non-paying guest may not authorize a host to consent to a search or a seizure. Purvis v. Wiseman, 298 F.2d 761 (D.Ore.1969).

(g) The area of employer-employee authority to consent is not well settled. See United States v. Blok, 188 F.2d 1019 (D.C.Cir. 1959) (employer's consent to search of employee's desk invalid); Braddock v. State, 127 Ga. 313, 194 S.E.2d 317 (1972) (truck owner may consent to search of his truck even though evidence discovered is used against employee-driver); People v. Smith, 204 N.W.2d 308 (Mich.App.1972) (employee cannot consent to police inspection of calculator owned by employer).

(h) Consent by bailee with whom a man leaves his property depends upon particular facts of bailment and extent to which bailor has relinquished control. See Pielaw v. United States, 8 F.2d 492 (9th Cir. 1925); Van Eichelberger v. United States, 252 F.2d 184 (9th Cir. 1958).

5. A situation analogous to third party consent occurs when, instead of consenting to a search, the third party seizes the evidence and brings it to the police. No question of the legality of the seizure will be raised in the criminal trial because no motion to suppress lies where the search was conducted by a private citizen acting on his own. Barnes v. United States, 373 F.2d 517 (5th Cir. 1967) (motel owner); People v. Hively, 173 Colo. 1458, 480 P.2d 558 (1971) (airline official); Cash v. Williams, 455 F.2d 1227 (6th Cir. 1972) (owner of private garage where police towed vehicle); People v.

Martin, 23 Cal.App.3d 172, 98 Cal.Rptr. 261 (1971) (hospital employee). Whenever the private citizen acts in concert with the police, state action will be found. Stapleton v. Superior Court, 70 Cal.2d 81, 447 P.2d 967 (1968).

UNITED STATES v. BLALOCK

United States District Court, E.D.Pa.1966.
255 F.Supp. 268.

JOSEPH S. LORD, III, DISTRICT JUDGE. This is a motion to suppress twenty-one twenty dollar bills seized by the F.B.I. in a search of defendant's hotel room in Miami, Florida. At defendant's trial, I denied the motion, but later found it necessary to grant a new trial and a new hearing on the motion prior thereto. From the testimony at that hearing I find these to have been the relevant circumstances:

Defendant was suspected of robbing the Parke Towne Branch of the Broad Street Trust Company. The bank had kept in its cash drawers "bait money", the serial numbers of which had previously been recorded. On the night of July 24, 1965, three agents of the F.B.I. encountered defendant as he entered his hotel lobby. They had no search warrant. After identifying themselves and after some preliminary questioning, defendant, accompanied by an agent, went to the men's room where he was frisked. The defendant and the agents then proceeded to his room. Defendant opened the door of the room and the party entered. One of the agents questioned defendant about the Philadelphia robbery, but defendant denied any knowledge of the crime. One of the agents then asked defendant whether, since he was not involved in the robbery, he would mind if they searched his room. Defendant replied that he had no objection. It was during the search which then ensued that the money was found.

Generally speaking, a warrantless search and seizure is regarded as unreasonable and violative of the Fourth Amendment. Judd v. United States, 190 F.2d 649 (1951). In order to overcome the prima facie unconstitutionality of the search here involved, the Government relies solely on the asserted consent of the defendant to the search, in other words, a waiver by defendant of his Fourth Amendment right. However, rights given by the Constitution are too fundamental and too precious for waiver lightly to be found. Commonwealth of Pennsylvania ex rel. Whiting v. Cavell, 244 F.Supp. 560, 567 (M.D.Pa., 1965), aff'd per curiam, 358 F.2d 132 (C.A.3, 1966). It is only where there is "an intentional relinquishment or abandonment of a known right or privilege." Johnson v. Zerbst, 304 U.S. 458, 464, 58 S.Ct. 1019, 1023 (1938) that an effective waiver can be found. "A search and seizure may be made without a search warrant if the individual freely and intelligently gives his unequivocal and specific consent to the search, uncontaminated by any duress or coercion, actual or implied. The Government has the burden of proving by clear and positive evidence that such consent was given. . . ." Channel v. United States, 285 F.2d 217, 219–220 (C.A.9, 1960). It is apparent that where consent is relied upon to validate a warrantless search, the Government must prove that the consent was (a) intelligent and (b) voluntary. In Wren v. United States, 352 F.2d 617, at page 618 (C.A. 10, 1965), the Court said:

> "It is fundamental in our judicial process, as guaranteed by the Fourth Amendment, that we are secure in our persons, houses, papers and effects against unreasonable searches and seizures. This constitutional right, like all others, may be waived by voluntary consent. In order to constitute a voluntary consent it must clearly appear that the search was voluntarily permitted or expressly invited and agreed to by the person whose right is involved. In addition, such person must be cognizant of his rights in the premises, the consent must not be contaminated by any duress or coercion and the government has the burden of proof. . . ."

First, the consent must have been "intelligent." Obviously, the requirement of an "intelligent" consent implies that the subject of the search must have been aware of his rights, for an intelligent consent can only embrace the waiver of a "known right." Johnson v. Zerbst, 304 U.S. 458, 58 S.Ct. 1019 (1938); United States ex rel. Mancini v. Rundle, 337 F.2d 268 (C.A.3, 1964). Certainly one cannot *intelligently* surrender that which he does not know he has. Cf. United States ex rel. Mancini v. Rundle, supra; Walker v. Pepersack, 316 F.2d 119 (C.A.4, 1963). The agents here properly warned defendant of his right to counsel and his right to remain silent, but they did not warn him of his right to refuse a warrantless search. The Fourth Amendment requires no less knowing a waiver than do the Fifth and Sixth. The requirement of knowledge in each serves the same purpose, i. e., to prevent the possibility that the ignorant may surrender their rights more readily than the shrewd. Conceivably, the assent of the defendant may have been "the false bravado of the small-time criminal," Judd, supra, 190 F.2d at 651; or it may have been an untutored submission to authority. Which it was could have been resolved by the officers at the scene. To require law enforcement agents to advise the subjects of investigation of their right to insist on a search warrant would impose no great burden, nor would it unduly or unnecessarily impede criminal investigation. Here, the evidence shows no such warning, nor is there any other evidence that Blalock was aware of his Fourth Amendment right. It cannot be said, then, that the Government has sustained its burden of showing that there was an intelligent waiver of a known right. Commonwealth of Pennsylvania ex rel. Whiting v. Cavell, 244 F.Supp. 560, 567 (M.D.Pa., 1965), aff'd per curiam, 358 F.2d 132 (C.A.3, 1966). This being so, we need not consider whether the consent was voluntary.

Defendant's motion to suppress will be granted. It is so ordered.

NOTE

A contrary result was reached in Gorman v. United States, 380 F. 2d 158 (1st Cir.1967), where the court refused to require that Fourth and

Sixth Amendment warnings precede a consent search when the defendant had been given the standard *Miranda* warnings. The court said "Although the analogy with *Miranda* . . . has a surface plausibility, we do not think that the *Miranda* prescription . . . must or ought to be mechanistically duplicated when circumstances indicate the advisability of requesting a search." The court held that the defendant ought to be aware that he was in the presence of persons not acting in his interest. Moreover, the court held, the *Miranda* warnings were designed to prevent the acquisition of unreliable, or self-incriminatory evidence, and to assure the right to counsel. "We therefore see no reason", said the court, "in policy or precedent automatically to borrow a procedure adapted to one set of constitutional rights at one stage of a criminal proceeding and apply it to a quite different right, serving quite different purposes, at another stage".

Even assuming that the court is correct—in holding that a person may infer that evidence found in a consent search will be used against him from the warning that he may remain silent in the face of interrogation—does it necessarily follow that the defendant would realize that he had a right to prevent the search without his consent? And, if not, could the resulting consent be a knowing and intelligent one?

SECTION 4. ABANDONED PROPERTY

ABEL v. UNITED STATES

Supreme Court of the United States, 1960.
362 U.S. 217, 80 Sup.Ct. 683.

MR. JUSTICE FRANKFURTER delivered the opinion of the Court.

The question in this case is whether [certain] items were properly admitted into evidence at the petitioner's trial for conspiracy to commit espionage. All . . . items were seized by officers of the Government without a search warrant. The seizures did not occur in connection with the exertion of the criminal process against petitioner. They arose out of his administrative arrest by the United States Immigration and Naturalization Service as a preliminary to his deportation. A motion to suppress these items as evidence, duly made in the District Court, was denied after a full hearing. 155 F.Supp. 8. Petitioner was tried, convicted and sentenced to thirty years' imprisonment and to the payment of a fine of $3,000. * * *

The . . . items, all in petitioner's possession at the time of his administrative arrest, the admissibility of which is in question were the following:

* * *

[A] a hollowed-out pencil containing 18 microfilms; and

[B] a block of wood, wrapped in sandpaper, and containing within it a small booklet with a series of numbers on each page, a so-called "cipher pad."

* * *

Petitioner was arrested by officers of the Immigration and Naturalization Service (hereafter abbreviated as I.N.S.) on June 21, 1957, in a single room in the Hotel Latham in New York City, his then abode.

* * *

After placing petitioner under arrest, the four I.N.S. agents undertook a search of his person and of all of his belongings in the room, and the adjoining bathroom, which lasted for from fifteen to twenty minutes. Petitioner did not give consent to this search; his consent was not sought. The F.B.I. agents observed this search but took no part in it. It was Schoenenberger's testimony to the District Court that the purpose of this search was to discover weapons and documentary evidence of petitioner's "alienage"—that is, documents to substantiate the information regarding petitioner's status as an alien which the I.N.S. had received from the F.B.I. During this search one of the challenged items of evidence, the one we have designated (2), a birth certificate for "Martin Collins," was seized. Weapons were not found, nor was any other evidence regarding petitioner's "alienage."

When the search was completed, petitioner was told to dress himself, to assemble his things and to choose what he wished to take with him. With the help of the I.N.S. agents almost everything in the room was packed into petitioner's baggage. A few things petitioner deliberately left on a window sill, indicating that he did not want to take them, and several other things which he chose not to pack up into his luggage he put into the room's wastepaper basket.

* * *

When petitioner's belongings had been completely packed, petitioner agreed to check out of the hotel. One of the F.B.I. agents obtained his bill from the hotel and petitioner paid it. Petitioner was then handcuffed and taken, along with his baggage, to a waiting automobile and thence to the headquarters of the I.N.S. in New York.

As soon as petitioner had been taken from the hotel an F.B.I. agent, Kehoe, who had been in the room adjoining petitioner's during the arrest and search and who, like the I.N.S. agents, had no search warrant, received permission from the hotel management to search the room just vacated by petitioner. Although the bill which petitioner had paid entitled him to occupy the room until 3 p. m. of that day, the hotel's practice was to consider a room vacated whenever a guest removed his baggage and turned in his key. Kehoe conducted a search of petitioner's room which lasted for about three hours. Among other things, he seized the contents of the wastepaper basket into which petitioner had put some things while packing his belongings. Two of the items thus seized were the challenged items of evidence we have designated [A] and [B]: a hollow pencil containing microfilm and a block of wood containing a "cipher pad."

* * *

We have left to the last the admissibility of the hollowed-out pencil and the block of wood containing a "cipher pad," because their admissibility is founded upon an entirely different set of considerations. These two items were found by an agent of the F.B.I. in the course of a search he undertook of petitioner's hotel room, immediately after petitioner had paid his bill and vacated the room. They were found in the room's wastepaper basket, where petitioner had put them while packing his belongings and preparing to leave. No pretense is made that this search by the F.B.I. was for any purpose other than to gather evidence of crime, that is, evidence of petitioner's espionage. As such, however, it was entirely lawful, although undertaken without a warrant. This is so for the reason that at the time of the search petitioner had vacated the room. The hotel then had the exclusive right to its possession, and the hotel management freely gave its consent that the search be made. Nor was it unlawful to seize the entire contents of the wastepaper basket, even though some of its contents had no connection with crime. So far as the record shows, petitioner had abandoned these articles. He had thrown them away. So far as he was concerned, they were *bona vacantia.* There can be nothing unlawful in the Government's appropriation of such abandoned property. The two items which were eventually introduced in evidence were assertedly means for the commission of espionage and were themselves seizable as such. These two items having been lawfully seized by the Government in connection with an investigation of crime, we encounter no basis for discussing further their admissibility as evidence.

Affirmed.

[The dissenting opinions of JUSTICE DOUGLAS and JUSTICE BRENNAN are omitted.]

NOTES

1. In United States v. Robinson, 430 F.2d 1141 (6th Cir. 1970), the prosecution introduced a hat seized from the defendant's room and used it as evidence to corroborate the testimony of two witnesses. The court resolved the question of the legality of the seizure in this way:

"The hat had been seized by FBI agents during a search of the appellant's apartment on January 8, 1968, some 34 days after his arrest for the Warren bank robbery. The evidence further showed that although appellant was continuously incarcerated during this intervening period, giving the agents an adequate opportunity to secure a search warrant, no warrant for the search was obtained. Instead, the agents merely sought and received the permission of the building manager to conduct the search of the apartment.

"Upon disclosure of the circumstances of the seizure of the hat, appellant moved for a mistrial on the grounds that the hat was the product of an illegal search of his apartment. The District Court denied the motion, holding that the apartment had been abandoned by appellant at the time of the search.

"The principal issue here is thus whether appellant had abandoned the apartment at the time of the search, it being undisputed that the building manager's consent to the search would be ineffective as a waiver of appellant's Fourth Amendment rights without an abandonment on his part. Whether premises have been abandoned so as to sanction the warrantless search raises a significant issue of the intent of the occupier of the premises, since his mere absence from the premises without an intent to abandon could not legitimize such a search. Friedman v. United States, 347 F.2d 697, 704 (8th Cir. 1965); United States v. Minker, 312 F.2d 632, 634–635 (3rd Cir. 1963). While the intent of one in possession of property often cannot be directly shown but must be inferred from his actions, abandonment will not be presumed. It must be clearly shown by the party asserting it. Coleman v. Maxwell, 387 F.2d 134, 135 (6th Cir. 1967). Moreover, where, as here, the party's absence from the premises is involuntary because of his arrest and incarceration, the government should bear an especially heavy burden of showing that he intended to abandon them. This the government has not done.

"In denying the appellant's motion for a mistrial, the District Court relied on the testimony of two witnesses to conclude that appellant had abandoned the apartment at the time of the search. The first witness was the building manager who permitted the FBI agents to search the apartment. Viewed most favorably to the government, his testimony was that he considered the apartment abandoned at the time of the search because the appellant had been absent therefrom without having paid any rent for over a month. However, as indicated the building manager's belief that appellant had abandoned the apartment was premised solely on the fact of appellant's absence and thus sheds no light on appellant's intention to return to the apartment. It was therefore totally irrelevant to the issue.

"The second witness was a Miss Shirley Case, a friend of appellant's wife, who testified that she and appellant's wife went to appellant's apartment (appellant and his wife were not living together at the time) and removed some of his belongings in December 1967. However, her entire testimony on this point was contained in her response to one leading question, and cannot be considered as evidence of an intent to abandon the premises on appellant's part. We must therefore conclude that the government failed to show that the premises had been abandoned by appellant at the time of the search, that the warrantless search of the premises was therefore unlawful, and that receipt of the hat into evidence constituted error."

3. The doctrine of abandoned property is sometimes applied when a suspect arrested by the police drops or throws some contraband to the ground. When a person discards incriminating evidence before an arrest occurs, then the property is generally seizable as abandoned property. See People v. Harris, 15 Cal.App.3d 498, 93 Cal.Rptr. 285 (1971).

If the abandonment occurs after the arrest, is the evidence admissible even if the arrest was illegal? Consider the following excerpt from State v. Smithers, 269 N.E.2d 874 (Ind.1971):

"DE BRULER, J.

"The State appeals on a reserved question of law alleging that the trial court erred in suppressing the evidence.

"Sergeant Mastin testified that he was called by Officers McKinney and Connors to the scene of a stopped car at around 12:45 a. m. on October 17th. Upon arrival at the scene Mastin was given the following information by the two officers: The officers thought there were juveniles in the car out after

11:00 p. m. curfew and they stopped the car to check the occupants to see if they were juveniles. When the car was stopped Connors observed the defendant, riding in the right front seat, put his arm out the car door and drop a brown manila envelope. Connors picked it up and asked defendant about it but he denied having possession of it. Mastin testified that after his arrival at the scene he looked in the envelope and found a substance that could have been marijuana. Mastin talked to the defendant who denied ever having the envelope. Mastin then permitted the car with defendant in it to proceed on its way.

"Appellant contends that the police legally obtained the envelope containing marijuana because the defendant had abandoned it. It is true that the police may legally seize abandoned property. Hardin v. State, 257 N.E. 2d 671 (Ind.1970). However, where police action triggers the abandonment, that action must be lawful or the evidence will be considered obtained in an illegal search and seizure within the meaning of the Fourth Amendment. Rios v. United States, 364 U.S. 253, 80 S.Ct. 1431 (1960). For purposes of the Fourth Amendment, there is no real abandonment if there is no lawful arrest or detention in the first instance because the "primary illegality would taint the abandonment and, as such, the abandonment could not justify the admission of the evidence." People v. Baldwin, 25 N.Y.2d 66, 250 N.E.2d 62 (1969). Therefore, the crucial issue is whether the police action in stopping the car, which precipitated the abandonment of the envelope, was lawful. If the police were justified in stopping the car then there was a "true abandonment" of the envelope by defendant, the evidence contained in the envelope was admissible in evidence and the trial court erred in suppressing it.

[The Court then held that under Indiana law, the arrests were illegal and the evidence was properly suppressed].

"ARTERBURN, C. J. (dissenting)

"I disagree with the majority opinion for the reason that no search is involved in this case, and there is nothing in the Constitution which prevents an officer or anyone else from picking up something from the street that has been abandoned or thrown away by a defendant or any third party. I go further and state that this includes articles thrown away in the act of excitement or fear, whatever the cause may be. In Von Hauger v. State 266 N.E.2d 197 (Ind.1971), the defendant dropped a package containing hypodermic needles and other apparatus used in drug injections and walked away when he saw the law enforcement officers. We held that the evidence so obtained was admissible.

"The defendant in this case was not searched nor seized. He was merely asked for his identification and driver's license. I think a police officer, and particularly a traffic officer, has not only the right, but at times the duty, to ask for the driver's license. In particular, I am thinking about road blocks that are necessary to be set up for the apprehension of fleeing criminals. Anything abandoned by fleeing persons is entirely open to seizure by anyone including police officers. The majority opinion is an unnecessary restriction upon law enforcement activities where a guilty conscience causes the party to flee or abandon articles which are incriminating. Again, I say there is no constitutional prohibition against the entry of the evidence which the appellant threw away or discarded in his case. It is an uncalled for stretching of the prohibition against unreasonable searches."

4. Compare the views expressed in two recent cases concerning the police search of trash:

(a) People v. Krivda, 5 Cal.3d 357, 486 P.2d 1262 (1971):

"BURKE, J.

"The question presented by this appeal is whether a householder who places contraband in trash barrels and subsequently places the barrels adjacent to the street for pickup by the rubbish collector may be deemed to have abandoned the trash at that location and to have forsaken any reasonable expectation of privacy with respect thereto.

"The People urge that the placement of the barrels near the sidewalk for collection constituted an abandonment of their contents. Indeed, had defendants simply cast their trash onto the sidewalk for anyone to pick over and cart away, we would have no difficulty finding that defendants had thereby foresaken any reasonable expectation of privacy with respect thereto.

"The placement of one's trash barrels onto the sidewalk for collection is not, however, necessarily an abandonment of one's trash to the police or general public. To the contrary, many municipalities have enacted ordinances which restrict the right to collect and haul away trash to licensed collectors, whose activities are carefully regulated. (See, e. g., Los Angeles County Ord. No. 5860, ch. IX, §§ 1611–1622, 1681–1691.) Moreover, these ordinances commonly prohibit unauthorized persons from tampering with trash containers. The provisions of these ordinances would appear to refute the view that the contents of one's trash barrels become public property when placed on the sidewalk for collection.

"Aside from municipal ordinances, there may exist an additional element of expected privacy whenever one consigns his property to the trash can, to be dumped, destroyed and forgotten. As stated in *Edwards*, 'The marijuana itself was not visible without "rummaging" in the receptacle. So far as appears defendants alone resided at the house. In the light of the combined facts and circumstances it appears that defendants exhibited an expectation of privacy, and we believe that expectation was reasonable under the circumstances of the case. We can readily ascribe many reasons why residents would not want their castaway clothing, letters, medicine bottles or other telltale refuse and trash to be examined by neighbors or others, *at least not until the trash had lost its identity and meaning by becoming part of a large conglomeration of trash elsewhere.* Half truths leading to rumor and gossip may readily flow from an attempt to "read" the contents of another's trash.' (People v. Edwards, 71 Cal.2d 1096, 1104, 458 P.2d 713, 718.)

"Similarly, in the instant case the contraband was concealed in paper sacks within the barrels, and was not visible without emptying or searching through the barrels' contents. The fact that the officers did not examine the contents until the trash had been placed into the well of the refuse truck does not distinguish *Edwards*, for at no time did defendants' trash lose its 'identity' by being mixed and combined with the 'conglomeration' of trash previously placed in the truck. Under such circumstances, we hold that defendants had a reasonable expectation that their trash would not be rummaged through and picked over by police officers acting without a search warrant. . . .

"We should hesitate to encourage a practice whereby our citizens' trash cans could be made the subject of police inspection without the protection of applying for and securing a search warrant.

"WRIGHT, C. J. (dissenting):

"I do not agree that the area protected by the Fourth Amendment proscription of unreasonable searches and seizures encompasses parkways immediately adjacent to public thoroughfares or pedestrian walkways or that the police action enlisting the assistance of the authorized trash collectors in separately picking up trash placed at the curb for pickup transmuted the collection into an unreasonable seizure. Moreover, in my view, a householder has neither a reasonable expectation of privacy as to his curbside trash, nor a right to expect that his trash will be commingled with that of others before it is subject to examination, governmental or otherwise. Whatever his hope may be as to the ultimate disposition of his trash, it does not, in my view, rise to a 'reasonable expectation of privacy.'

"The majority purport to find support for their conclusion that the police invaded defendants' reasonable expectation of privacy as to their trash container in Katz v. United States, where the court held that electronic eavesdropping on a telephonic conversation violated the defendant's privacy on which he justifiably relied. Since *Katz,* however, the court has further refined the constitutionally justifiable expectations which are protected by the Fourth Amendment. In United States v. White, 401 U.S. 745, 91 S.Ct. 1122 (1971), the Court emphasized the continued viability of Hoffa v. United States, 385 U.S. 293, 87 S.Ct. 408 (1966), and prior cases approving various means by which governmental agents or informers, using electronic equipment, record or transmit their conversations with wrongdoers who believe the conversation will remain private. If *White* and *Katz* have any applicability in areas other than electronic eavesdropping, it is in their holdings that an actual expectation of privacy based on a belief that a confederate or one believed to be a confederate will not reveal a defendant's secrets, is not a constitutionally justified expectation of privacy protected by the Fourth Amendment. In *White* the court explained: 'Inescapably, one contemplating illegal activities must realize and risk that his companions may be reporting to the police. If he sufficiently doubts their truthworthiness, the association will very probably end or never materialize. But if he has no doubts, or allays them, or risks what doubts he has, the risk is his.' Surely the defendant who discards his trash and places it at the curb to be picked up must also assume the risk that the collector of the rubbish may be an agent of the police or may permit the police to examine the unconglomerated trash once it is picked up. A 'constitutionally justifiable expectation of privacy' need not extend to the well of a trash truck."

(b) United States v. Dzialak, 441 F.2d 212 (2d Cir. 1971):

"Appellant's first claim is that the search by Harold Poling of the trash located in front of appellant's house was in violation of his right under the Fourth Amendment to be free from unreasonable searches and seizures. The District Court decided this question on a motion to suppress the items seized by Poling and held that the items taken had been abandoned by Dzialak and therefore that there was nothing unlawful about their seizure.

"Appellant argues that this was incorrect and places reliance upon an ordinance of the Town of Cheektowaga, which was in effect at the time of the seizures, and which prohibits anyone, except authorized employees of the Town of Cheektowaga, to rummage into, pick up, collect, move or otherwise interfere with articles or materials placed on the right of way of any public street for collection. It is argued that Dzialak may very well have relied on this ordinance when placing his trash out in the street and that this goes to negative any intent to abandon the articles in question.

"We are not persuaded. We think it abundantly clear that Dzialak abandoned the property. The town ordinance simply cannot change the fact that he 'threw [these articles] away' and thus there 'can be nothing unlawful in the Government's appropriation of such abandoned property.'"

SECTION 5. AUTOMOBILE SEARCHES

CHAMBERS v. MARONEY

Supreme Court of the United States, 1970
399 U.S. 42, 90 S.Ct. 1975.

MR. JUSTICE WHITE delivered the opinion of the Court.

The principal question in this case concerns the admissibility of evidence seized from an automobile, in which petitioner was riding at the time of his arrest, after the automobile was taken to a police station and was there thoroughly searched without a warrant. The Court of Appeals for the Third Circuit found no violation of petitioner's Fourth Amendment rights. We affirm.

I

During the night of May 20, 1963, a Gulf service station in North Braddock, Pennsylvania, was robbed by two men each of whom carried and displayed a gun. The robbers took the currency from the cash register; the service station attendant, one Stephen Kovacich, was directed to place the coins in his right hand glove, which was then taken by the robbers. Two teen-agers, who had earlier noticed a blue compact station wagon circling the block in the vicinity of the Gulf station, then saw the station wagon speed away from a parking lot close to the Gulf station; about the same time, they learned that the Gulf station had been robbed. They reported to police, who arrived immediately, that four men were in the station wagon and one was wearing a green sweater. Kovacich told the police that one of the men who robbed him was wearing a green sweater and the other was wearing a trench coat. A description of the car and the two robbers was broadcast over the police radio. Within an hour, a light blue compact station wagon answering the description and carrying four men was stopped by the police about two miles from the Gulf station. Petitioner was one of the men in the station wagon. He was wearing a green sweater and there was a trench coat in the car. The occupants were arrested and the car was driven to the police station. In the course of a thorough search of the car at the station, the police found concealed in a compartment under the dashboard two .38 caliber revolvers (one loaded with dumdum bullets), a right hand glove containing small change, and certain cards bearing the name of Raymond Havicon, the attendant at a Boron service station in McKeesport, Pennsylvania, who had been robbed at gun point on May 13, 1963. In the course of a warrant-authorized search of petitioner's home the day after petitioner's arrest, police found and seized certain .38 caliber ammunition, including some dumdum bullets similar to those found in one of the guns taken from the station wagon.

Petitioner was indicted for both robberies. His first trial ended in a mistrial but he was convicted of both robberies at the second trial. Both Kovacich and Havicon identified petitioner as one of the robbers. The materials taken from the station wagon were introduced into evidence, Kovacich identifying his glove and Havicon the cards taken in the May 13 robbery. The bullets seized at petitioner's house were also introduced over objections of petitioner's counsel. Petitioner was sentenced to a term of four to eight years' imprisonment for the May 13 robbery and to a term of two to seven years' imprisonment for the May 20 robbery, the sentences to run consecutively. Petitioner did not take a direct appeal from these convictions. In 1965, petitioner sought a writ of habeas corpus in the state court, which denied the writ after a brief evidentiary hearing; the denial of the writ was affirmed on appeal in the Pennsylvania appellate courts. Habeas corpus proceedings were then commenced in the United States District Court for the Western District of Pennsylvania. An order to show cause was issued. Based on the State's response and the state court record, the petition for habeas corpus was denied without a hearing. The Court of Appeals for the Third Circuit affirmed, . . . and we granted certiorari.

II

We pass quickly the claim that the search of the automobile was the fruit of an unlawful arrest. Both the courts below thought the arresting officers had probable cause to make the arrest. We agree. Having talked to the teen-age observers and to the victim Kovacich, the police had ample cause to stop a light blue compact station wagon carrying four men and to arrest the occupants, one of whom was wearing a green sweater and one of whom had a trench coat with him in the car.[1]

Even so, the search which produced the incriminating evidence was made at the police station some time after the arrest and cannot be justified as a search incident to an arrest: "Once an accused is under

1. In any event, as we point out below, the validity of an arrest is not necessarily determinative of the right to search a car if there is probable cause to make the search. Here, as will be true in many cases, the circumstances justifying the arrest are also those furnishing probable cause for the search.

arrest and in custody, then a search made at another place, without a warrant, is simply not incident to the arrest." Preston v. United States, 376 U.S. 364, 367, 84 S.Ct. 881, 883 (1964). Dyke v. Taylor Implement Mfg. Co., 391 U.S. 216, 88 S.Ct. 1472 (1968), is to the same effect; the reasons which have been thought sufficient to justify warrantless searches carried out in connection with an arrest no longer obtain when the accused is safely in custody at the station house.

There are, however, alternative grounds arguably justifying the search of the car in this case. In *Preston,* supra, the arrest was for vagrancy; it was apparent that the officers had no cause to believe that evidence of crime was concealed in the auto. In *Dyke,* supra, the Court expressly rejected the suggestion that there was probable cause to search the car. Here the situation is different, for the police had probable cause to believe that the robbers, carrying guns and the fruits of the crime, had fled the scene in a light blue compact station wagon which would be carrying four men, one wearing a green sweater and another wearing a trench coat. As the state courts correctly held, there was probable cause to arrest the occupants of the station wagon that the officers stopped; just as obviously was there probable cause to search the car for guns and stolen money.

In terms of the circumstances justifying a warrantless search, the Court has long distinguished between an automobile and a home or office. In Carroll v. United States, 267 U.S. 132, 45 S.Ct. 280 (1925), the issue was the admissibility in evidence of contraband liquor seized in a warrantless search of a car on the highway. After surveying the law from the time of the adoption of the Fourth Amendment onward, the Court held that automobiles and other conveyances may be searched without a warrant in circumstances which would not justify the search without a warrant of a house or an office, provided that there is probable cause to believe that the car contains articles that the officers are entitled to seize. The Court expressed its holding as follows:

"We have made a somewhat extended reference to these statutes to show that the guaranty of freedom from unreasonable searches and seizures by the Fourth Amendment has been construed, practically since the beginning of the government, as recognizing a necessary difference between a search of a store, dwelling house, or other structure in respect of which a proper official warrant readily may be obtained and a search of a ship, motor boat, wagon, or automobile for contraband goods, where it is not practicable to secure a warrant, because the vehicle can be quickly moved out of the locality or jurisdiction in which the warrant must be sought.

"Having thus established that contraband goods concealed and illegally transported in an automobile or other vehicle may be searched for without a warrant, we come now to consider under what circumstances such search may be made. . . . [T]hose lawfully within the country, entitled to use the public highways, have a right to free passage without interruption or search unless there is known to a competent official, authorized to search, probable cause for believing that their vehicles are carrying contraband or illegal merchandise.

. . .

"The measure of legality of such a seizure is, therefore, that the seizing officer shall have reasonable or probable cause for believing that the automobile which he stops and seizes has contraband liquor therein which is being illegally transported." 267 U.S., at 153–154, 155–156, 45 S.Ct. at 285–286.

The Court also noted that the search of an auto on probable cause proceeds on a theory wholly different from that justifying the search incident to an arrest:

"The right to search and the validity of the seizure are not dependent on the right to arrest. They are dependent on the reasonable cause the seizing officer has for belief that the contents of the automobile offend against the law." 267 U.S., at 158–159, 45 S.Ct. at 287.

Finding that there was probable cause for the search and seizure at issue before it, the Court affirmed the convictions.

Carroll was followed and applied in Husty v. United States, 282 U.S. 694, 51 S.Ct. 240 (1931), and Scher v. United States, 305 U.S. 251, 59 S.Ct. 174 (1938). It was reaffirmed and followed in Brinegar v. United States, 338 U.S. 160, 69 S.Ct. 1302 (1949). In 1964, the opinion in *Preston,* supra, cited both *Brinegar* and *Carroll* with approval. In Cooper v. California, 386 U.S. 58, 87 S.Ct. 788 (1967),[2] the Court read *Preston* as dealing primarily with a search incident to arrest and cited that case for the proposition that the mobility of a car may make the search of a car without a warrant reasonable "although the result might be the opposite in a search of a home, a store, or other fixed piece of property." The Court's opinion in *Dyke,* recognized that "[a]utomobiles, because of their mobility, may be searched without a warrant upon facts not justifying a warrantless search of a residence or office," citing *Brinegar* and *Carroll,* supra. However, because there was insufficient reason to search the car involved in the *Dyke* case, the Court did not reach the question of whether those cases "extend to a warrantless search, based upon probable cause, of an automobile which, having been stopped originally on a highway, is parked outside a courthouse." 391 U.S., at 222, 88 S.Ct. at 1476.[3]

2. *Cooper* involved the warrantless search of a car held for forfeiture under state law. Evidence seized from the car in that search was held admissible. In the case before us no claim is made that state law authorized that the station wagon be held as evidence or as an instrumentality of the crime; nor was the station wagon an abandoned or stolen vehicle. The question here is whether probable cause justifies a warrantless search in the circumstances presented.

3. Nothing said last term in Chimel v. California, 395 U.S. 752, 89 S.Ct. 2034 (1969), purported to modify or affect the rationale of *Carroll.* As the Court noted:

"Our holding today is of course entirely consistent with the recognized principle that, assuming the existence of probable cause, automobiles and other vehicles may be searched without warrants 'where it is not practicable to secure a warrant, because the vehicle can be quickly moved out of the locali-

Neither *Carroll*, supra, nor other cases in this Court require or suggest that in every conceivable circumstance the search of an auto even with probable cause may be made without the extra protection for privacy which a warrant affords. But the circumstances which furnish probable cause to search a particular auto for particular articles are most often unforeseeable; moreover, the opportunity to search is fleeting since a car is readily movable. Where this is true, as in *Carroll* and the case before us now, if an effective search is to be made at any time, either the search must be made immediately without a warrant or the car itself must be seized and held without a warrant for whatever period is necessary to obtain a warrant for the search.[4]

In enforcing the Fourth Amendment's prohibition against unreasonable searches and seizures, the Court has insisted upon probable cause as a minimum requirement for a reasonable search permitted by the Constitution. As a general rule, it has also required the judgment of a magistrate on the probable cause issue and the issuance of a warrant before a search is made. Only in exigent circumstances will the judgment of the police as to probable cause serve as a sufficient authorization for a search. *Carroll*, supra, holds a search warrant unnecessary where there is probable cause to search an automobile stopped on the highway; the car is movable, the occupants are alerted, and the car's contents may never be found again if a warrant must be obtained. Hence, an immediate search is constitutionally permissible.

Arguably, because of the preference for a magistrate's judgment, only the immobilization of the car should be permitted until a search warrant is obtained; arguably, only the "lesser" intrusion is permissible until the magistrate authorizes the "greater." But which is the "greater" and which the "lesser" intrusion is itself a debatable question and the answer may depend on a variety of circumstances. For constitutional purposes, we see no difference between on the one hand seizing and holding a car before presenting the probable cause issue to a magistrate and on the other hand carrying out an immediate search without a warrant. Given probable cause to search, either course is reasonable under the Fourth Amendment.

On the facts before us, the blue station wagon could have been searched on the spot when it was stopped since there was probable cause to search and it was a fleeting target for a search. The probable cause factor still obtained at the station house and so did the mobility of the car unless the Fourth Amendment permits a warrantless seizure

ty or jurisdiction in which the warrant must be sought.' Carroll v. United States, 267 U.S. 132, 153, 45 S.Ct. 280, 285, 69 L.Ed. 543; see Brinegar v. United States, 338 U.S. 160, 69 S.Ct. 1302, 93 L.Ed. 1879." 395 U.S., at 764 n. 9, 89 S.Ct. at 2040.

4. Following the car until a warrant can be obtained seems an impractical alternative since, among other things, the car may be taken out of the jurisdiction. Tracing the car and searching it hours or days later would of course permit instruments or fruits of crime to be removed from the car before the search.

of the car and the denial of its use to anyone until a warrant is secured. In that event there is little to choose in terms of practical consequences between an immediate search without a warrant and the car's immobilization until a warrant is obtained.[5] The same consequences may not follow where there is unforeseeable cause to search a house. But as *Carroll,* supra, held, for the purposes of the Fourth Amendment there is a constitutional difference between houses and cars. . . .

Affirmed.

MR. JUSTICE BLACKMUN took no part in the consideration or decision of this case.

(The concurring opinion of MR. JUSTICE STEWART is omitted.)

MR. JUSTICE HARLAN, concurring in part and dissenting in part.

I find myself in disagreement with the Court's disposition of this case in two respects. . . .

II

In sustaining the search of the automobile I believe the Court ignores the framework of our past decisions circumscribing the scope of permissible search without a warrant. The Court has long read the Fourth Amendment's proscription of "unreasonable" searches as imposing a general principle that a search without a warrant is not justified by the mere knowledge by the searching officers of facts showing probable cause. The "general requirement that a warrant be obtained" is basic to the Amendment's protection of privacy, and "the burden is on those seeking [an] exemption . . . to show the need for it." . . .

Fidelity to this established principle requires that, where exceptions are made to accommodate the exigencies of particular situations, those exceptions be no broader than necessitated by the circumstances presented. For example, the Court has recognized that an arrest creates an emergency situation justifying a warrantless search of the arrestee's person and of "the area from within which he might gain possession of a weapon or destructible evidence"; however, because the exigency giving rise to this exception extends only that far, the search may go no further. . . . Similarly we held in Terry v. Ohio, 392 U.S. 1, 88 S.Ct. 1868 (1968), that a warrantless search in a "stop and frisk" situation must "be strictly circumscribed by the exigencies which justify its initiation." Any intrusion beyond what is necessary for the personal safety of the officer or others nearby is forbidden.

5. It was not unreasonable in this case to take the car to the station house. All occupants in the car were arrested in a dark parking lot in the middle of the night. A careful search at that point was impractical and perhaps not safe for the officers, and it would serve the owner's convenience and the safety of his car to have the vehicle and the keys together at the station house.

Where officers have probable cause to search a vehicle on a public way, a further limited exception to the warrant requirement is reasonable because "the vehicle can be quickly moved out of the locality or jurisdiction in which the warrant must be sought." Carroll v. United States, 267 U.S. 132, 153, 45 S.Ct. 280, 285 (1923). Because the officers might be deprived of valuable evidence if required to obtain a warrant before effecting any search or seizure, I agree with the Court that they should be permitted to take the steps necessary to preserve evidence and to make a search possible.[1] Cf. ALI, Model Code of Pre-Arraignment Procedure § 6.03 (Tent. Dr. No. 3, 1970). The Court holds that those steps include making a warrantless search of the entire vehicle on the highway—a conclusion reached by the Court in *Carroll* without discussion—and indeed appears to go further and to condone the removal of the car to the police station for a warrantless search there at the convenience of the police.[2] I cannot agree that this result is consistent with our insistence in other areas that departures from the warrant requirement strictly conform to the exigency presented.

The Court concedes that the police could prevent removal of the evidence by temporarily seizing the car for the time necessary to obtain a warrant. It does not dispute that such a course would fully protect the interests of effective law enforcement; rather it states that whether temporary seizure is a "lesser" intrusion than warrantless search "is itself a debatable question and the answer may depend on a variety of circumstances."[3] I believe it clear that a warrantless search involves the greater sacrifice of Fourth Amendment values.

The Fourth Amendment proscribes, to be sure, unreasonable "seizures" as well as "searches." However, in the circumstances in which this problem is likely to occur the lesser intrusion will almost always be

1. Where a suspect is lawfully arrested in the automobile, the officers may, of course, perform a search within the limits prescribed by *Chimel* as an incident to the lawful arrest. However, as the Court recognizes, the search here exceeded those limits. Nor was the search here within the limits imposed by pre-*Chimel* law for searches incident to arrest; therefore, the retroactivity of *Chimel* is not drawn in question in this case. See Preston v. United States, 376 U.S. 364, 84 S.Ct. 881 (1964).

2. The Court disregards the fact that *Carroll* and each of this Court's decisions upholding a warrantless vehicle search on its authority, involved a search for contraband. . . . Although subsequent dicta have omitted this limitation, . . . the *Carroll* decision has not until today been held to authorize a general search of a vehicle for evidence of crime, without a warrant, in every case where probable cause exists.

3. The Court, unable to decide whether search or temporary seizure is the "lesser" intrusion, in this case authorizes both. The Court concludes that it was reasonable for the police to take the car to the station, where they searched it once to no avail. The searching officers then entered the station, interrogated petitioner and the car's owner, and returned later for another search of the car—this one successful. At all times the car and its contents were secure against removal or destruction. Nevertheless the Court approves the searches without even an inquiry into the officers' ability promptly to take their case before a magistrate.

the simple seizure of the car for the period—perhaps a day—necessary to enable the officers to obtain a search warrant. In the first place, as this case shows, the very facts establishing probable cause to search will often also justify arrest of the occupants of the vehicle. Since the occupants themselves are to be taken into custody, they will suffer minimal further inconvenience from the temporary immobilization of their vehicle. Even where no arrests are made, persons who wish to avoid a search—either to protect their privacy or to conceal incriminating evidence—will almost certainly prefer a brief loss of the use of the vehicle in exchange for the opportunity to have a magistrate pass upon the justification for the search. To be sure, one can conceive of instances in which the occupant, having nothing to hide and lacking concern for the privacy of the automobile, would be more deeply offended by a temporary immobilization of his vehicle than by a prompt search of it. However, such a person always remains free to consent to an immediate search, thus avoiding any delay. Where consent is not forthcoming, the occupants of the car have an interest in privacy that is protected by the Fourth Amendment even where the circumstances justify a temporary seizure. Terry v. Ohio, supra. The Court's endorsement of a warrantless invasion of that privacy where another course would suffice is simply inconsistent with our repeated stress on the Fourth Amendment's mandate of "adherence to judicial processes." E. g., Katz v. United States, 389 U.S., at 357, 88 S.Ct., at 514.[4]

Indeed, I believe this conclusion is implicit in the opinion of the unanimous Court in Preston v. United States, 376 U.S. 364, 84 S.Ct. 881 (1964). The Court there purported to decide whether a factual situation virtually identical to the one now before us was "such as to fall within *any* of the exceptions to the constitutional rule that a search warrant must be had before a search may be made." The Court concluded that no exception was available, stating that "since the men were under arrest at the police station and the car was in police custody at a garage, [there was no] danger that the car would be moved out of the locality or jurisdiction." The Court's reliance on the police custody of the car as its reason for holding "that the search of the car without a warrant failed to meet the test of reasonableness under the Fourth Amendment," ibid., can only have been based on the premise that the more reasonable course was for the police to retain custody of the car for the short time necessary to obtain a warrant. The Court expressly did not rely, as suggested today, on the fact that an arrest for vagrancy provided "no cause to believe that evidence of crime was concealed in the auto." . . . The Court now discards the approach

4. Circumstances might arise in which it would be impracticable to immobilize the car for the time required to obtain a warrant—for example, where a single police officer must take arrested suspects to the station, and has no way of protecting the suspects' car during his absence. In such situations it might be wholly reasonable to perform an on-the-spot search based on probable cause. However, where nothing in the situation makes impracticable the obtaining of a warrant, I cannot join the Court in shunting aside that vital Fourth Amendment safeguard.

taken in *Preston*, and creates a special rule for automobile searches that is seriously at odds with generally applied Fourth Amendment principles. * * *

STATE v. BOYKINS

Supreme Court of New Jersey, 1967.
50 N.J. 73, 232 A.2d 141.

WEINTRAUB, C. J. Defendant, indicted for possession of a narcotic drug, obtained a pretrial order suppressing evidence obtained by a search of an automobile in which he was a passenger. The Appellate Division granted leave to appeal and affirmed the order. We granted the State's petition for certification.

At 8:45 P.M. on September 14, 1965, two detectives in plain clothes, riding in an unmarked car, saw an automobile with four men, of whom defendant was one, proceeding along Bergen Street in the City of Newark at a high speed and in a reckless manner. Because of a red light defendant's car stopped 50 to 75 feet short of the intersection of Bergen Street with 18th Avenue. The detectives drew up on the left, identified themselves as police officers, and directed the driver to pull to the curb. The driver said he would, but when the light changed "he took off with his wheels screeching," swerving toward the police car in an effort to hit it, and then made a right turn into 18th Avenue. The police car had to be pulled sharply to the left to avoid the collision. The officers took up the chase at speeds in excess of 60 miles per hour. The police siren was turned on and shots were fired in the air and then at the car to disable it. Defendant's car narrowly missed two pedestrians, who had to climb a parked automobile "like a squirrel climbing a tree." The car turned into Jelliff Avenue "on two wheels . . . . managed to right itself and then came to a sudden stop" on the wrong side of the street, at the Waverly Freight Yards. Defendant, who was in a rear seat, and two others fled from the car, and stopped only after warning shots were fired. Other police cars, summoned during the chase, converged on the scene within a minute. Defendant became violent; it took four officers to confine him to a police car.

The fourth occupant of defendant's car, a passenger in the front, was dead at the scene. We gather that it was later determined that he had been hit by a bullet fired by the pursuing officers. The officers did not suggest they thought they were dealing with a homicide, and hence we will not consider that circumstance in deciding the issue before us. At the same time, it is irrelevant whether the shooting was warranted, and of course that matter was not tried.

Defendant and the others were searched on the spot. The search of defendant revealed nothing, and we gather that the search of the other men also produced no evidence of criminal involvement. But a search of the car, made at the scene while defendant and his companions were still there, revealed an open knife under the front seat on the driver's side and a brown manila envelope on the floor on the passenger's side. The envelope contained marijuana.

In granting the motion to suppress, the trial court discounted the claim that the driver of the fleeing car tried to commit an assault and battery in swerving toward the officers' car. The trial court then found that although the testimony warranted an arrest for speeding; reckless driving; or careless driving, an arrest for such traffic violations would not justify the search of the automobile. . . .

Noting that a search could be made as an incident to an arrest if reasonably necessary to protect the arresting officer from attack, to prevent escape, or to prevent destruction of evidence (84 N.J.Super. at pp. 434–435, 202 A.2d 448), the trial court found no basis for the search in the present case because the occupants were no longer in the car and in fact were securely handcuffed by the time the vehicle was searched, even though the time interval was no more than minutes. And while apparently recognizing that the behavior of the defendant and his companions was strongly suggestive of involvement in crime, the trial court emphasized that the State was not able to point to any specific criminal event, known to the officers at the time of arrest. . . .

The Appellate Division affirmed on the basis of the trial court's opinion.

Surely not every traffic violation will justify a search of every part of the vehicle. See, generally, annotation, 10 A.L.R.3d 314 (1966). A traffic violation as such will justify a search for things related to it. So, for example, if the operator is unable to produce proof of registration, the officer may search the car for evidence of ownership. People v. Prochnau, 59 Cal.Rptr. 265 (Ct.App.1967); Draper v. State of Maryland, 265 F.Supp. 718 (D.Md.1967); or if the officer has reason to believe the driver is under the influence of liquor or drugs, he may search the car for alcohol or narcotics, State v. Parker, 81 Idaho 51, 336 P.2d 318 (Sup.Ct.1959); People v. Jackson, 241 Cal.App.2d 189, 50 Cal.Rptr. 437 (Dist.Ct.App.1966). The State argues before us that the search here made could be justified on the latter ground. It could, if the officer had testified that the driver's behavior or condition had suggested he was under such influence but the record is silent in that regard.

If an officer decides to take a traffic violator into custody rather than to issue a summons, he may search the occupants and the car for weapons if he reasonably believes it necessary for his own protection or to prevent an escape. As noted above, the trial court rejected that basis for a search, saying that once the driver and his companions were securely handcuffed outside the car, there was no danger of injury to the officers or of escape. We assume the trial court found as well that the officers had already made a final decision not to transport the prisoners in defendant's car and that hence there was no need to search the automobile for weapons in connection with such use of it.

We need not pass upon the issue that limited context would raise, because the search was valid upon another basis. The facts recited above plainly suggest the driver and his passengers or one or more of them were involved in some substantial criminal affair. Ordinary men do not run the risks they ran to avoid a traffic ticket. There is no reason to suppose the driver doubted the detectives were in fact officers of the law. He acknowledged the order to pull to the curb and said he would. He was not in a desolate locale. On the contrary the scene was a populated area of a large city. Such behavior strongly suggests a probability that the occupants had on their persons or in the car contraband or instruments or the fruit of crime. It seems to us that in such circumstances the public interest requires that the men and the vehicle be searched even though at that stage the officers know of no specific offense, other than a traffic violation, upon which an arrest could be made.

The Fourth Amendment forbids only such searches as are unreasonable. The familiar doctrine that a search may be made as an incident to an arrest does not exhaust the subject of reasonable searches without a warrant. Rather it represents merely a category of reasonable searches. See People v. Webb, 56 Cal.Rptr. 902, 424 P.2d 342 (Sup.Ct.1967). This is made plain in Cooper v. State of California, 386 U.S. 58, 87 S.Ct. 788 (1967). There a search was made a week after the vehicle had been seized in connection with a narcotics violation. It was argued on the basis of Preston v. United States, 376 U.S. 364, 84 S.Ct. 881 (1964), that the search could not be deemed an incident of the arrest because it was not made at the time of the arrest. The Supreme Court said that *Preston* did not hold that a search without a warrant can be reasonable only if it is made as an incident to an arrest. It pointed out that in *Preston* the search was sought to be sustained solely upon that basis, and that that effort failed because (1) the offense for which the defendant was there arrested was vagrancy and since there could not be an instrument, fruit, or evidence of that offense in the vehicle, there could not be a search upon that premise, and (2) insofar as the protection of the arresting officers and prevention of an escape are concerned, there was no need for a search long after the defendant was jailed. Stressing that *Preston* held no more and did not say that to be reasonable a search without a warrant must be connected with an arrest, the Court proceeded to consider whether the basis asserted for the search in the case before it repelled a charge of unreasonableness. The Court could see nothing unreasonable in searching a car which the police held in custody as evidence in connection with a forfeiture proceeding, saying "It would be unreasonable to hold that the police, having to retain the car in their garage for such a length of time, had no right, even for their own protection, to search it" * * *

In Henry v. United States, 361 U.S. 98, 80 S.Ct. 168 (1959), the officers investigating a theft of liquor from an interstate shipment searched a truck and seized stolen radios. There was no probable cause for an arrest As to the search, the majority found no cause to believe the truck held stolen goods, saying (361 U.S. at pp. 103–104, 80 S.Ct. at p. 172):

> ". . . Riding in the car, stopping in an alley, picking up packages, driving away—these were all acts that were outwardly innocent. Their movements in the car had no mark of fleeing men or men acting furtively. The case might be different if the packages had been taken from a terminal or from an interstate trucking platform. But they were not. As we have said, the alley where the packages were picked up was in a residential section."

Thus it was recognized that suspicious behavior of the occupants of a vehicle may give good cause to search it.

In the case before us, the extraordinary behavior of the driver and his passengers generated an irresistible suspicion that there was something illicit upon them or in the car. There was accordingly ample basis for the search unless the Constitution requires that the officers know of some specific criminal event to which the search can be related. In considering whether knowledge of a specific criminal act is indispensable, it should be kept in mind that if such knowledge and a purpose to seize something specific related to such an event are required, the deficiency will bar as well a search under a warrant since the Fourth Amendment requires as to a warrant that the "things to be seized" shall be particularly described. The question then is not whether the obvious public interest in such a setting shall be protected by search under a warrant but whether the public interest can be protected at all.

We must recur to the basic proposition that the Fourth Amendment bars only searches that are unreasonable. "Since the Fourth Amendment speaks, not in terms that are absolute, but rather of unreasonableness, it necessarily calls for a continuing reconciliation of competing values. Preeminent in the galaxy of values is the right of the individual to live free from criminal attack in his home, his work, and the streets." State v. Davis, 50 N.J. 16, 231 A.2d 793 (1967). That primary individual right demands that government be equal to the reason for its being—the protection of the individual citizen, and in deciding whether a search is unreasonable if the officer does not know precisely what it will uncover, we must keep in mind that the police have a preventive role as well as the duty to deal with crimes already committed. And finally it is worth repeating that the immediate question is whether evidence of unimpeachable probative worth shall be suppressed with the obvious hurt to other individuals and to public values involved, not because the Fourth Amendment says that evidence illegally obtained shall not be used, but rather because the judiciary, believing it was unable to fashion a remedy for its breach, settled upon the sanction of suppression to compel obedience to its command.

Here we are not dealing with the privacy of a home, or of a place of business. We are not dealing with something which is immobile and is thereby limited in its usefulness to the criminal element. Rather the subject is a motor vehicle, which, for all its blessings, is high among the agencies of crime. The automobile is perfectly suited for that use. It provides cover for weapons, contraband, and the fruits of crime. It supplies a capacity to strike without warning and to leave without trace. No discussion of crime can ignore the automobile, or the fact that the incidence of crime is hinged directly to the amount of privacy we accord it.

The States remain free, and obliged, to devise "workable rules" of search and seizure to meet "the practical demands of effective criminal investigation and law enforcement." Ker v. State of California, 374 U.S. 23, 34, 83 S.Ct. 1623, 1630 (1963). In Brinegar v. United States, 338 U.S. 160, 176, 69 S.Ct. 1302, 1311 (1949), which involved a search of an automobile, the Court stressed that probable cause is "a practical, nontechnical conception" and that,

> ". . . Requiring more would unduly hamper law enforcement. To allow less would be to leave law-abiding citizens at the mercy of the officers' whim or caprice."

With these values in view, we have no difficulty in sustaining the search upon the basis of the conduct we have described. We see no trace of the general warrant. The place to be searched is specific and small—an automobile; and although the officers may have no precise reason to expect to find the product of a specific crime, it is reasonable to suspect at least the presence of a weapon. The weapon is so routinely an instrument of crimes of force or violence with which the automobile is closely identified that conduct which affords a well-grounded suspicion of some criminal involvement on the part of the occupant of a car supports also a well-grounded suspicion that a search of the vehicle will yield a weapon. To require more would, in the words of *Brinegar*, supra, "unduly hamper law enforcement," and surely it cannot be said that a search of a vehicle upon such a showing would "leave law-abiding citizens at the mercy of the officers' whim or caprice." We see nothing unreasonable about a search of an automobile in such circumstances. We see no threat to the privacy of the law-abiding citizen. Rather we see a much needed assurance for the primary right of the individual to be protected from criminal attack.

. . .

The judgment of the Appellate Division is reversed and the order of suppression in the trial court is set aside.

COOLIDGE v. NEW HAMPSHIRE

Supreme Court of the United States, 1971.
403 U.S. 443, 91 S.Ct. 2022, rehearing denied 404 U.S. 874, 92 S.Ct. 26.

[The defendant Coolidge was convicted of the murder of a fourteen year old girl. Upon the discovery of the victim's body a massive investigation was conducted and Coolidge became a possible suspect. he was fully cooperative with the police and took a Polygraph (lie-detector) test, after which he was released. During a short period of time when Coolidge was in custody on an unrelated charge (a theft from his employer to which he had confessed during a Polygraph examination), the police went to his home where his wife gave them four guns belonging to Coolidge and the clothes she thought Coolidge was wearing on the night the victim disappeared. At his trial the state offered firearms identification evidence that one of these guns was the murder weapon and that vacuum sweepings from the clothes indicated a high probability that the clothes had been in contact with the victim's body.

[After the guns and clothes were obtained, the investigation continued for two and a half weeks. During this period, Coolidge was not in custody. Additional evidence implicating Coolidge was then discovered. In light of the available evidence, the police chief applied for a warrant to search Coolidge's Pontiac car. The warrants were issued by the state attorney general, acting as a justice of the peace pursuant to state statute.

[The warrant was executed and the car was seized from the Coolidge driveway where it was parked and where it was plainly visible from the street. The car was towed to the police station where it was searched and vacuumed two days after its seizure. It was seized again eleven months later. Vacuum sweepings from the car were microscopically analyzed and introduced into evidence against Coolidge at his trial.

[The Court held that the warrant was invalid because a warrant could not be issued by a prosecutor or a police officer even if, under state law, they were designated as justices of the peace and therefore eligible to issue warrants. Such persons were not considered to be the neutral and detached magistrates required by the Constitution for the valid issuance of warrants. JUSTICE BLACK, joined by CHIEF JUSTICE BURGER and JUSTICE BLACKMUN dissented from this viewpoint, saying that "there is no language in the Fourth Amendment which provides any basis for disqualification of the state attorney general to act as a magistrate . . . [and, therefore, the attorney general's participation in the case at the time he issued the search warrant was] harmless error if it was error at all [because] a refusal to issue a warrant on the showing of probable cause made in this case would have been an abuse of discretion."

[After deciding that the warrant was invalid, the Court next considered arguments which sought to establish that the searches were valid without warrants.]

MR. JUSTICE STEWART delivered the opinion of the Court.*

A

The State's first theory is that the seizure on February 19 and subsequent search of Coolidge's Pontiac were "incident" to a valid arrest. We assume that the arrest of Coolidge inside his house was valid, so that the first condition of a warrantless "search incident" is met. And since the events in issue took place in 1964, we assess the State's argument in terms of the law as it existed before Chimel v. California, which substantially restricted the "search incident" exception to the warrant requirement, but did so only prospectively. But even under pre-*Chimel* law, the State's position is untenable.

The leading case in the area before *Chimel* was United States v. Rabinowitz, 339 U.S. 56, 70 S.Ct. 430, 94 L.Ed. 653, which was taken to stand "for the proposition, *inter alia,* that a warrantless search 'incident to a lawful arrest' may generally extend to the area that is considered to be in the 'possession' or under the 'control' of the person arrested." In this case, Coolidge was arrested inside his house; his car was outside in the driveway. The car was not touched until Coolidge had been removed from the scene. It was then seized and taken to the station, but it was not actually searched until two days later.

First, it is doubtful whether the police could have carried out a contemporaneous search of the car under *Rabinowitz* standards. For this Court has repeatedly held that, even under *Rabinowitz,* "[a] search may be incident to an arrest ' "only if it is substantially contemporaneous with the arrest and is confined to the *immediate* vicinity of the arrest. * * *" ' " These cases make it clear beyond any question that a lawful pre-*Chimel* arrest of a suspect outside his house could never by itself justify a warrantless search inside the house. There is nothing in search-incident doctrine (as opposed to the special rules for automobiles and evidence in "plain view," to be considered below) that suggests a different result where the arrest is made inside the house and the search outside and at some distance away.

Even assuming, *arguendo,* that the police might have searched the Pontiac in the driveway when they arrested Coolidge in the house, Preston v. United States, 376 U.S. 364, 84 S.Ct. 881, makes plain that they could not legally seize the car, remove it, and search it at their leisure without a warrant. In circumstances virtually identical to those here, Mr. Justice Black's opinion for a unanimous Court held

* The portion of the opinion excerpted here was joined by Justices DOUGLAS, BRENNAN and MARSHALL. Justice HARLAN agreed with the result but not with the reasons given for it.

that "[o]nce an accused is under arrest and in custody, then a search [of his car] made at another place, without a warrant, is simply not incident to the arrest." Search-incident doctrine, in short, has no applicability to this case.

B

The second theory put forward by the State to justify a warrantless seizure and search of the Pontiac car is that under Carroll v. United States, 267 U.S. 132, 45 S.Ct. 280, the police may make a warrantless search of an automobile whenever they have probable cause to do so, and, under our decision last Term in Chambers v. Maroney, whenever the police may make a legal contemporaneous search under *Carroll*, they may also seize the car, take it to the police station, and search it there. But even granting that the police had probable cause to search the car, the application of the *Carroll* case to these facts would extend it far beyond its original rationale.

Carroll did indeed hold that "contraband goods concealed and illegally transported in an automobile or other vehicle may be searched for without a warrant," provided that "the seizing officer shall have reasonable or probable cause for believing that the automobile which he stops and seizes has contraband liquor therein which is being illegally transported." Such searches had been explicitly authorized by Congress, and, as we have pointed out elsewhere, in the conditions of the time "[a]n automobile * * * was an almost indispensable instrumentality in large-scale violation of the National Prohibition Act, and the car itself therefore was treated somewhat as an offender and became contraband." In two later cases, each involving an occupied automobile stopped on the open highway and searched for contraband liquor, the Court followed and reaffirmed *Carroll*. And last Term in *Chambers*, supra, we did so again.

The underlying rationale of *Carroll* and of all the cases that have followed it is that there is

> "a necessary difference between a search of a store, dwelling house, or other structure in respect of which a proper official warrant readily may be obtained and a search of a ship, motor boat, wagon, or automobile for contraband goods, where *it is not practicable to secure a warrant*, because the vehicle can be quickly moved out of the locality or jurisdiction in which the warrant must be sought."

As we said in *Chambers*, "exigent circumstances" justify the warrantless search of "an automobile *stopped on the highway*," where there is probable cause, because the car is "movable, the occupants are alerted, and the car's contents may never be found again if a warrant must be obtained." "[T]he opportunity to search is fleeting * * *."

In this case, the police had known for some time of the probable role of the Pontiac car in the crime. Coolidge was aware that he was a suspect in the Mason murder, but he had been extremely cooperative throughout the investigation, and there was no indication that he meant to flee. He had already had ample opportunity to destroy any evidence he thought incriminating. There is no suggestion that, on the night in question, the car was being used for any illegal purpose, and it was regularly parked in the driveway of his house. The opportunity for search was thus hardly "fleeting." The objects that the police are assumed to have had probable cause to search for in the car were neither stolen nor contraband nor dangerous.

When the police arrived at the Coolidge house to arrest him, two officers were sent to guard the back door while the main party approached from the front. Coolidge was arrested inside the house, without resistance of any kind on his part, after he had voluntarily admitted the officers at both front and back doors. There was no way in which he could conceivably have gained access to the automobile after the police arrived on his property. When Coolidge had been taken away, the police informed Mrs. Coolidge, the only other adult occupant of the house, that she and her baby had to spend the night elsewhere and that she could not use either of the Coolidge cars. Two police officers then drove her in a police car to the house of a relative in another town, and they stayed with her there until around midnight, long after the police had had the Pontiac towed to the station house. The Coolidge premises were guarded throughout the night by two policemen.[1]

The word "automobile" is not a talisman in whose presence the Fourth Amendment fades away and disappears. And surely there is nothing in this case to invoke the meaning and purpose of the

1. It is frequently said that occupied automobiles stopped on the open highway may be searched without a warrant because they are "mobile," or "movable." No other basis appears for Mr. Justice WHITE's suggestion in his dissenting opinion that we should "treat searches of automobiles as we do the arrest of a person." In this case, it is, of course, true that even though Coolidge was in jail, his wife was miles away in the company of two plainclothesmen, and the Coolidge property was under the guard of two other officers, the automobile was in a literal sense "mobile." A person who had the keys and could slip by the guard could drive it away. We attach no constitutional significance to this sort of mobility.

First, a good number of the containers that the police might discover on a person's property and want to search are equally movable, e. g., trunks, suitcases, boxes, briefcases, and bags. How are such objects to be distinguished from an unoccupied automobile—not then being used for any illegal purpose—sitting on the owner's property? It is true that the automobile has wheels and its own locomotive power. But given the virtually universal availability of automobiles in our society there is little difference between driving the container itself away and driving it away in a vehicle brought to the scene for that purpose. Of course, if there is a criminal suspect close enough to the automobile so that he might get a weapon from it or destroy evidence within it, the police may make a search of appropriately limited scope. Chimel v. California. But if Carroll v. United States permits a warrantless search of an unoccupied vehicle, on private property and beyond the scope of a valid search incident to an arrest, then it would permit as well a warrantless search of a suitcase or a box. We have found no case that suggests such an extension of *Carroll*.

rule of Carroll v. United States—no alerted criminal bent on flight, no fleeting opportunity on an open highway after a hazardous chase, no contraband or stolen goods or weapons, no confederates waiting to move the evidence, not even the inconvenience of a special police detail to guard the immobilized automobile. In short, by no possible stretch of the legal imagination can this be made into a case where "it is not practicable to secure a warrant," and the "automobile exception," despite its label, is simply irrelevant.

Since *Carroll* would not have justified a warrantless search of the Pontiac at the time Coolidge was arrested, the later search at the station house was plainly illegal, at least so far as the automobile exception is concerned. *Chambers, supra,* is of no help to the State, since that case held only that, where the police may stop and search an automobile under *Carroll,* they may also seize it and search it later at the police station. Rather, this case is controlled by Dyke v. Taylor Implement Mfg. Co. There the police lacked probable cause to seize or search the defendant's automobile at the time of his arrest, and this was enough by itself to condemn the subsequent search at the station house. Here there was probable cause, but no exigent circumstances justified the police in proceeding without a warrant. As in *Dyke,* the later search at the station house was therefore illegal.

[The concurring opinion of MR. JUSTICE HARLAN is omitted, as is the separate opinion of CHIEF JUSTICE BURGER dissenting from the Court's ruling concerning the automobile search.]

MR. JUSTICE BLACK, dissenting as to the ruling on the automobile search.

* * *

It is important to point out that the automobile itself was evidence and was seized as such. Prior to the seizure the police had been informed by two witnesses that on the night of the murder they had seen an automobile parked near the point where the little girl's dead body was later discovered. Their description of the parked automobile matched petitioner's car. At the time of the seizure the identification of petitioner's automobile by the witnesses as the car they had seen on the night of the murder was yet to be made. The police had good reason to believe that the identification would be an important element of the case against the petitioner. Preservation of the automobile itself as evidence was a reasonable motivation for its seizure. Considered in light of the information in the hands of the New Hampshire police at the time of the seizure, I conclude that the seizure and search were constitutional, even had there been no search warrant, for the following and other reasons.

A

First, the seizure of petitioner's automobile was valid as incident to a lawful arrest. The majority concedes that there was probable cause for petitioner's arrest. Upon arriving at petitioner's residence to make that arrest, the police saw petitioner's automobile which they knew fitted the description of the car observed by two witnesses at the place where the murdered girl's body had been found. The police arrested the petitioner and seized the automobile. The majority holds that because the police had to go into petitioner's residence in order to place petitioner under arrest, the contemporaneous seizure of the automobile outside the house was not incident to that arrest. I cannot accept this elevation of form over reason.

After stating that Chimel v. California is inapplicable to this case, the majority goes on to formulate and apply a *per se* rule reaching far beyond *Chimel.* To do so, the majority employs a classic *non sequitur.* Because this Court has held that police arresting a defendant on the street in front of his house cannot go into that house and make a general search, it follows, says the majority, that the police having entered a house to make an arrest cannot step outside the house to seize clearly visible evidence. Even though the police, upon entering a doorway to make a valid arrest, would be authorized under the pre-*Chimel* law the majority purports to apply, to make a five-hour search of a four-room apartment, the majority holds that the police could not step outside the doorway to seize evidence they passed on their way in. The majority reasons that as the doorway locks the policeman out, once entered, it must lock him in.

The test of reasonableness cannot be governed by such arbitrary rules. Each case must be judged on its own particular facts. Here, there was no general exploration, only a direct seizure of important evidence in plain view from both inside as well as outside the house. On the facts of this case, it is my opinion that the seizure of petitioner's automobile was incident to his arrest and was reasonable under the terms of the Fourth Amendment.

B

Moreover, under our decision last Term in Chambers v. Maroney, the police were entitled not only to seize petitioner's car but also to search the car after it had been taken to the police station. The police had probable cause to believe that the car had been used in the commission of the murder and that it contained evidence of the crime. Under Carroll v. United States, and Chambers v. Maroney, such belief was sufficient justification for the seizure and the search of petitioner's automobile.

The majority reasons that the *Chambers* and *Carroll* rationale, based on the mobility of automobiles, is inapplicable here because the petitioner's car could have been placed under guard and, thereby, rendered immobile. But this Court explicitly rejected such reasoning in *Chambers:* "For constitutional purposes, we see no difference between on the one hand seizing and holding a car before presenting the probable cause issue to a magistrate and on the other hand carrying out an immediate search without a warrant. * * * The probable-cause factor still obtained at the station house and so did the mobility of the car * * *." This Court held there that the delayed search at the station house, as well as an immediate search at the time of seizure, was reasonable under the Fourth Amendment.

As a second argument for holding that the *Chambers* decision does not apply to this case, the majority reasons that the evidence could not have been altered or the car moved because petitioner was in custody and his wife was accompanied by police, at least until the police towed the car to the station. But the majority's reasoning depends on two assumptions: first, that the police should, or even could, continue to keep petitioner's wife effectively under house arrest; and, second, that no one else had any motivation to alter or remove the car. I cannot accept the first assumption, nor do I believe that the police acted unreasonably in refusing to accept the second.[2]

(CHIEF JUSTICE BURGER and JUSTICE BLACKMUN joined in this part of JUSTICE BLACK's opinion.)

MR. JUSTICE WHITE, dissenting as to the Court's ruling concerning the search of the car.

[In the major part of his opinion MR. JUSTICE WHITE advances the position that the search was lawful under the plain view doctrine. This doctrine was discussed earlier in this chapter. The remainder of his opinion is concerned with the application of specific automobile search doctrines discussed by the previous opinions.]

* * *

. . . it may be helpful to explain my reasons for relying on the plain-sight rule rather than on Chambers v. Maroney to validate this search.

Chambers upheld the seizure and subsequent search of automobiles at the station house rather than requiring the police to search

2. The majority attempts to rely on Preston v. United States, 376 U.S. 364, 84 S.Ct. 881, 11 L.Ed.2d 777 (1964), to support its holding that the police could not search petitioner's automobile at the station house. But this case is not *Preston*, nor is it controlled by *Preston*. The police arrested Preston for vagrancy. No claim was made that the police had any authority to hold his car in connection with that charge. The fact that the police had custody of Preston's car was totally unrelated to the vagrancy charge for which they arrested him; so was their subsequent search of the car. Here the officers arrested petitioner for murder. They seized petitioner's car as evidence of the crime for which he was arrested. Their subsequent search of the car was directly related to the reason petitioner was arrested and the reason his car had been seized and. therefore, was valid under this Court's decision in Cooper v. California (1967).

My Brother WHITE points out that the police in the present case not only searched the car immediately upon taking it to the station house, but also searched it 11 months and 14 months after seizure. We held in *Cooper*, where the search occurred one week after seizure, that the Fourth Amendment is not violated by the examination or search of a car validly held by officers for use as evidence in a pending trial. In my view the police are entitled to search a car whether detained for a week or for a year where that car is being properly held as relevant evidence of the crime charged.

cars immediately at the places where they are found. But *Chambers* did not authorize the indefinite detention of automobiles so seized; it contemplated some expedition in completing the searches so that automobiles could be released and returned to their owners. In the present case, however, Coolidge's Pontiac was not released quickly but was retained in police custody for more than a year and was searched not only immediately after seizure but also on two other occasions: one of them 11 months and the other 14 months after seizure. Since fruits of the later searches as well as the earlier one were apparently introduced in evidence, I cannot look to *Chambers* and would invalidate the later searches but for the fact that the police had a right to seize and detain the car not because it was a car, but because it was itself evidence of crime. It is only because of the long detention of the car that I find *Chambers* inapplicable, however, and I disagree strongly with the majority's reasoning for refusing to apply it.

As recounted earlier, arrest and search of the person on probable cause but without a warrant is the prevailing constitutional and legislative rule, without regard to whether on the particular facts there was opportunity to secure a warrant. Apparently, exigent circumstances are so often present in arrest situations that it has been deemed improvident to litigate the issue in every case.

In similar fashion, "practically since the beginning of the Government," Congress and the Court have recognized "a necessary difference between a search of a store, dwelling house or other structure in respect of which a proper official warrant readily may be obtained, and a search of a ship, motor boat, wagon or automobile, for contraband goods, where it is not practicable to secure a warrant because the vehicle can be quickly moved out of the locality or jurisdiction in which the warrant must be sought." As in the case of an arrest and accompanying search of a person, searches of vehicles on probable cause but without a warrant have been deemed reasonable within the meaning of the Fourth Amendment without requiring proof of exigent circumstances beyond the fact that a movable vehicle is involved. The rule has been consistently recognized, and was reaffirmed less than a year ago in Chambers v. Maroney, where a vehicle was stopped on the highway but was searched at the police station, there being probable cause but no warrant.

The majority now approves warrantless searches of vehicles in motion when seized. On the other hand, warrantless, probable-cause searches of parked but movable vehicles in some situations would be valid only upon proof of exigent circumstances justifying the search. Although I am not sure, it would seem that, when police discover a parked car that they have probable cause to search, they may not immediately search but must seek a warrant. But if before the warrant arrives, the car is put in motion by its owner or others, it may be stopped and searched on the spot or elsewhere. In the case before us, Coolidge's car, parked at his house, could not be searched without a valid warrant, although if Coolidge had been arrested as he drove away from his home, immediate seizure and subsequent search of the car would have been reasonable under the Fourth Amendment.

I find nothing in the language or the underlying rationale of the line of cases from *Carroll* to *Chambers* limiting vehicle searches as the Court now limits them in situations such as the one before us. Although each of those cases may, as the Court argues, have involved vehicles or vessels in motion prior to their being stopped and searched, each of them approved the search of a vehicle that was no longer moving and, with the occupants in custody, no more likely to move than the unattended but movable vehicle parked on the street or in the driveway of a person's house. In both situations the probability of movement at the instance of family or friends is equally real, and hence the result should be the same whether the car is at rest or in motion when it is discovered.

In Husty v. United States [282 U.S. 694], the police had learned from a reliable informant that Husty had two loads of liquor in automobiles of particular make and description parked at described locations. The officers found one of the cars parked and unattended at the indicated spot. Later, as officers watched, Husty and others entered and started to drive away. The car was stopped after having moved no more than a foot or two; immediate search of the car produced contraband. Husty was then arrested. The Court, in a unanimous opinion, sustained denial of a motion to suppress the fruits of the search, saying that "[t]he Fourth Amendment does not prohibit the search, without warrant, of an automobile, for liquor illegally transported or possessed, if the search is upon probable cause * * *." Further, "[t]he search was not unreasonable because, as petitioners argue, sufficient time elapsed between the receipt by the officer of the information and the search of the car to have enabled him to procure a search warrant. He could not know when Husty would come to the car or how soon it would be removed. In such circumstances we do not think the officers should be required to speculate upon the chances of successfully carrying out the search, after the delay and withdrawal from the scene of one or more officers which would have been necessary to procure a warrant. The search was, therefore, on probable cause, and not unreasonable * * *."

The Court apparently cites *Husty* with approval as involving a car in motion on the highway. But it was obviously irrelevant to the Court that the officers could have obtained a warrant before Husty attempted to drive the car away. Equally immaterial was the fact that the car had moved one or two feet at the time it was stopped. The search would have been approved even if it had occurred before Husty's arrival or after his arrival but before he had put the car in motion. The Court's attempt to distinguish *Husty* on the basis of the car's negligible movement prior to its being stopped is without force.

The Court states flatly, however, that this case is not ruled by the *Carroll-Chambers* line of cases but by Dyke v. Taylor Implement Mfg. Co. There the car was properly stopped and the occupants arrested for reckless driving, but the subsequent search at the station house could not be justified as incident to the arrest. Nor could the car itself be seized and later searched, as it was, absent probable cause to believe it contained evidence of crime. In *Dyke,* it was pointed out that probable cause did not exist at the time of the search, and we expressly rested our holding on this fact, noting that, "[s]ince the search was not shown to have been based upon sufficient cause," it was not necessary to reach other grounds urged for invalidating it. Given probable cause, however, we would have upheld the search in *Dyke.*

For Fourth Amendment purposes, the difference between a moving and movable vehicle is tenuous at best. It is a metaphysical distinction without roots in the commonsense standard of reasonableness governing search and seizure cases. Distinguishing the case before us from the *Carroll-Chambers* line of cases further enmeshes Fourth Amendment law in litigation breeding refinements having little relation to reality. I suggest that in the interest of coherence and credibility we either overrule our prior cases and treat automobiles precisely as we do houses or apply those cases to readily movable as well as moving vehicles and thus treat searches of automobiles as we do the arrest of a person. By either course we might bring some modicum of certainty to Fourth Amendment law and give the law enforcement officers some slight guidance in how they are to conduct themselves.

NOTES

What would be "exigent circumstances" to permit search of an unoccupied parked car where probable cause exists but no warrant has been secured? Consider the following:

> "An officer has probable cause to believe that a large quantity of stolen shoes were stored in a trailer parked in a private lot. A reliable informer said that the shoes were going to be moved to another location. The court approved the search of the trailer and seizure of the shoes without a warrant."

Upon such facts the court in United States v. Bozada, 473 F.2d 389 (8th Cir. 1973) said:

"In the matter at hand, exigent circumstances did exist. . . . The trailer was being used for an unlawful purpose—to transport stolen shoes, reliable information indicated that it was about to be moved, the tractor-trailer unit was hooked up ready for movement, the owner of the vehicle was not in custody, and there were others who appeared to be involved who were at large. * * * The opportunity to search was fleeting. Movement of the trailer appeared imminent. We are not impressed with the notion that a stake-out or limited seizure of the trailer should have been made while a search warrant was being procured. That could well pose more problems than it would solve. * * * Chambers v. Maroney."

The dissenting judges thought that the circumstances did not justify the police action:

"The truck was, of course, mobile but this fact alone is insufficient to justify a warrantless search. * * *

"Nor would the fact that the police had probable cause to believe that the truck contained stolen goods justify the warrantless search. Most vehicles which the police have probable cause to search contain evidence of a crime. Thus, to allow warrantless searches on this basis would swallow the warrant requirement in its exception—a result clearly not contemplated by the Coolidge Court.

"Of course, if the vehicle were being used at the time of the search for an illegal purpose, no warrant would be required. Coolidge v. New Hampshire. But, the term 'being used' requires that someone be in or at the vehicle at the time that the search is carried out. If this were not the case, then the court would have upheld the search in Coolidge because the police carrying out that search had good reason to believe that the vehicle contained evidence of a crime.

. . .

"We also reject the suggestion that the warrantless search can be justified because the police had reason to believe that the truck was to be moved. Sound police practice requires that the police assume that a vehicle containing stolen goods or evidence of a crime will be moved. Unless they act promptly on this assumption, they may lose the opportunity to apprehend those who have committed crimes. But the question remains what form of action is appropriate and constitutional.

"It was proper for the police to place the truck under surveillance, and they did just that. For nearly two hours, they watched and waited for someone to come for the unoccupied truck and no one did. During this two hours, they had adequate opportunity to secure a search warrant without incurring the risk that the car would be moved. There were three officers at the scene, their car was radio-equipped, and the courts were nearby. Thus, one of the policemen at the scene, or someone at headquarters, could have secured the warrant while the others remained at the parking lot.

"It would also have been proper for the police to have seized the vehicle if someone came for it before the warrant arrived.

"The majority relies on Chambers v. Maroney for the proposition that if there is probable cause to search, it is just as reasonable to carry out an immediate search as it is to temporarily seize the car and await a warrant. The Court in *Coolidge* made it clear, however, that *Chambers* cannot be viewed as supporting such reasoning. * * *

"We also reject the view that the police were excused from seeking a warrant because the hour was late and they would have difficulty in finding a judge to issue the warrant. The vital protections of the Fourth Amendment cannot be hinged upon the convenience of the police, prosecutors and judges. * * *

"If the processes of our government are such that police officers are unable to secure search warrants outside of ordinary business hours, then the cure for that problem is not to sacrifice the Fourth Amendment rights of our citizens, but to streamline the warrant procuring procedure."

See also United States v. Castalde, 453 F.2d 506 (7th Cir. 1971) (search of car on the street was permitted at 5:30 a. m. where the radiator was warm and the key was in the ignition); United States v. Ellis, 461 F.2d 962 (2d Cir. 1972) (two known culprits involved in the offense were still at large and because of this a warrantless search was justified).

2. There are other doctrines which are applied to justify the search of an automobile.

a. Some courts allow a search of an automobile when it has been abandoned. See United States v. Gibson, 421 F.2d 622 (5th Cir. 1970); United States v. Moore, 459 F.2d 1360 (D.C.Cir.1972) (car used for getaway is abandoned when driver loses control and flees from the car).

b. Where an automobile is subject to forfeiture under a statute which forfeits to the state any automobile involved in the commission of a crime, some courts have indicated that the police have the right to search the car. See Cooper v. California, 386 U.S. 58, 87 S.Ct. 788 (1967).

c. Another theory is one which allows the search of a vehicle which is lawfully seized as an instrumentality of the crime. See State v. Thompson, 285 Minn. 529, 173 N.W.2d 459 (1970). The Court in *Coolidge* mentioned this doctrine but did not rule upon its validity.

d. The most commonly used alternative justification for automobile searches is the inventory theory. As we noted in section 5 of this Chapter, the police may inventory the property of a person who has been arrested. When the property is carried on the arrestee's person the inventory serves to preserve the security of the jail where the arrestee is to be incarcerated, to protect the arrestee's property and to protect the officers against false claims of theft. In the auto inventory, the justifications are solely protection of the arrestee's property and the safeguarding against false claims of theft. Several courts accept the validity of automobile inventory searches. See State v. Hock, 54 N.J. 526, 257 A.2d 699 (1969); United States v. Boyd, 436 F.2d 1203 (5th Cir. 1971). In order that this inventory rule apply, it is essential that the police have lawfully obtained the vehicle in the first place. Some courts have regarded an inventory search of automobiles as potentially abusive and have held that contraband found during an evidence search cannot be used as evidence in a criminal prosecution. Mozzetti v. Superior Court, 4 Cal.3d 699, 484 P.2d 84 (1971). The case law is discussed at length in United States v. Lawson, 487 F.2d 468 (8th Cir. 1973).

e. In Cady v. Dombrowski, 413 U.S. 433, 93 S.Ct. 2523 (1973) the Court dealt with a case involving the seizure of bloodstained articles, used to link the accused with the commission of murder, from the trunk of his automobile. The accused was involved in a one-car accident in Wisconsin. The Court's opinion stated:

"At the scene, the police observed the 1967 Thunderbird and took various measurements relevant to the accident. Respondent was, in the opinion of the officers, drunk. He had informed them that he was a Chicago police officer. The Wisconsin policemen believed that Chicago police officers were required by regulation to carry their service revolvers at all times. After calling a towtruck to remove the disabled Thunderbird, and not finding the revolver on respondent's person, one of the officers looked into the front seat and glove compartment of that car for respondent's service revolver. No revolver was found. The wrecker arrived and the Thunderbird was towed to a privately owned service station in Kewaskum, approximately seven miles from the West Bend police station. It was left outside by the wrecker, and no police guard was posted. At 11:33 p. m. on the 11th respondent was taken directly to the West Bend police station from the accident scene, and, after being interviewed by an assistant district attorney, to whom respondent again stated that he was a Chicago policeman, respondent was formally arrested for drunken driving. Respondent was 'in a drunken condition' and 'incoherent at times.' Because of his injuries sustained in the accident, the same two officers took respondent to a local hospital. He lapsed into an unexplained coma, and a doctor, fearing the possibility of complications, had respondent hospitalized overnight for observation. One of the policemen remained at the hospital as a guard, and the other, Officer Weiss, drove at some time after 2 a. m. on the 12th to the garage to which the 1967 Thunderbird had been towed after the accident.

"The purpose for going to the Thunderbird, as developed on the motion to suppress, was to look for respondent's service revolver. Weiss testified that respondent did not have a revolver when he was arrested, and that the West Bend authorities were under the impression that Chicago police officers were required to carry their service revolvers at all times. He stated that the effort to find the revolver was 'standard procedure in our department.'

"Weiss opened the door of the Thunderbird and found, on the floor of the car, a book of Chicago police regulations and, between the two front seats, a flashlight which appeared to have 'a few spots of blood on it.' He then opened the trunk of the car, which had been locked, and saw various items covered with what was later determined to be type O blood. These included a pair of police uniform trousers, a pair of gray trousers, a nightstick with name 'Dombrowski' stamped on it, a raincoat, a portion of a car floor mat, and a towel. The blood on the car mat was moist. The officer removed these items to the police station.

. . .

" . . . state and local police officers, unlike federal officers, have much more contact with vehicles for reasons related to the operation of vehicles themselves. All States require vehicles to be registered and operators to be licensed. State and localities have enacted extensive and detailed codes regulating the condition and manner in which motor vehicles may be operated on public streets and highways.

"Because of the extensive regulation of motor vehicles and traffic, and also because of the frequency with which a vehicle can become disabled or involved in an accident on public highways, the extent of police-citizen contact in a home or office. Some such contacts will occur because the officer may believe the operator has violated a criminal statute, but many more will not be of that nature. Local police officers, unlike federal officers, frequently investigate vehicle accidents in which there is no claim of criminal liability and engage in what, for want of a better term, may be described as community caretaking functions, totally divorced from the detection, investigation, or acquisition of evidence relating to the violation of a criminal statute.

. . .

"Here we must decide whether a 'search' of the trunk of the 1967 Ford was unreasonable solely because the local officer had not previously obtained a warrant. And, if that be answered in the negative, we must then determine whether the warrantless search was unreasonable within the meaning of the Fourth and Fourteenth Amendments. In answering these questions, two factual considerations deserve emphasis. First the police had exercised a form of custody or control over the 1967 Thunderbird. Respondent's vehicle was disabled as a result of the accident, and constituted a nuisance along the highway. Respondent, being intoxicated (and later comatose), could not make arrangements to have the vehicle towed and stored. At the direction of the police, and for elemental reasons of safety, the automobile was towed to a private garage. Second, both the state courts and the district courts found as a fact that the search of the trunk to retrieve the revolver was 'standard procedure in [that police] department,' to protect the public from the possibility that a revolver would fall into untrained or perhaps malicious hands. Although the trunk was locked, the car was left outside, in a lot seven miles from the police station to which respondent had been taken, and no guard was posted over it.

. . .

" . . . the intrusion into the trunk of the 1967 Thunderbird at the garage was not unreasonable within the meaning of the Fourth and Fourteenth Amendments solely because a warrant had not been obtained by Officer Weiss after he left the hospital. The police did not have actual, physical custody of the vehicle, but the vehicle had been towed there at the officers' directions. These officers in a rural area were simply reacting to the effects of an accident—one of the recurring practical situations that results from the operation of motor vehicles and with which local police officers must deal every day. The Thunderbird was not parked adjacent to the dwelling place of the owner as in *Coolidge*, supra, nor simply momentarily unoccupied on a street. Rather, like an obviously abandoned vehicle, it represented a nuisance, and there is no suggestion in the record that the officers' action in exercising control over it by having it towed away was unwarranted either in terms of state law or sound police procedure.

"In *Harris* [390 U.S. 234, 88 S.Ct. 492] the justification for the initial intrusion into the vehicle was to safeguard the owner's property, and in *Cooper* [380 U.S. 58, 87 S.Ct. 788] it was to guarantee the safety of the custodians. Here the justification, while different, was as immediate and constitutionally reasonable as those in *Harris* and *Cooper*: concern for the safety of the general public who might be endangered if an intruder removed a revolver from the trunk of the vehicle. The record contains uncontradicted testimony to support the findings of the state courts and District Court. Furthermore, although there is no record basis for discrediting such testimony, it was corroborated by the circumstantial fact that at the time the search was conducted Officer Weiss was ignorant of the fact that a murder, or any other crime, had been committed. While perhaps in a metropolitan area the responsibility to the general public might have been discharged by the posting of a police guard during the night, what might be normal police procedure in such an area may be neither normal nor possible in Keyaskum, Wisconsin. The fact that the protection of the public might, in the abstract, have been accomplished by 'less intrusive' means does not, by itself, render the search unreasonable.

"The Court's previous recognition of the distinction between motor vehicles and dwelling places leads us to conclude that the type of caretaking 'search' conducted here of a vehicle that was neither in the custody nor on the premises of its owner, and that had been placed where it was by virtue of lawful police action, was not unreasonable solely because a warrant had not been obtained."

Does Cady v. Dombrowski approve the inventory search theory?

SECTION 6. THE "SECOND SEARCH"

BRETT v. UNITED STATES

United States Court of Appeals, Fifth Circuit, 1969.
412 F.2d 401.

GODBOLD, CIRCUIT JUDGE.

Appellant was arrested on the afternoon of February 18. He was searched at that time, though not thoroughly, and taken before the United States Commissioner and then to jail. There was testimony that customarily prisoners being booked into this jail are thoroughly searched. Appellant was given prison garb, and his clothing and effects were put in a bag in the prisoners' property room. There was no evidence that this was for any purpose other than routine safekeeping of the effects of an accused required to don prison garb when jailed. Three days later, for reasons not stated, Agent Corbit came to the jail and requested the deputy-custodian to inspect the contents of appellant's property bag, which still was in the property room. The deputy found in the watch pocket of appellant's trousers cellophane papers which he turned over to Corbit. On examination these were found to have in them traces of heroin. . . .

The search was invalid and the fruits not admissible for any purpose. The burden is upon the government to show that the search fell within one of the exceptions to the Fourth Amendment requirement of a warrant. No such showing was made.

This search was not incident to an arrest, because it was not even close to contemporaneous. The items introduced into evidence were not items seized at the time of arrest for subsequent use as evidence, . . . nor were they the result of a subsequent search or inspection of items so seized. This search was not a later look at items which had remained in police custody after having been discovered in an earlier and valid search. Nor was it like [a search] in which marihuana was validly found in a car at the time of arrest and the car, after being impounded, was searched more thoroughly the following day.

The "plain view" exception is inapplicable to the belated search of appellant's clothing.[1] The search was unrelated to the duties

1. In Evalt v. United States, 382 F.2d 424 (9th Cir. 1967) a post-arrest search of defendant's packsack by an FBI agent was held valid, but the search was to compare the serial numbers on money contained in the packsack and already observed by the sheriff with the serial numbers of money that had

of the police as guardians of the prisoner's property, to inventory or to protect property in their hands for safekeeping. The clothing was not in danger of being removed elsewhere, as in the case of automobiles, or of being destroyed, and it was not available to appellant as the source of escape weapons.

We note that there was ample opportunity to apply for a search warrant, to submit to a magistrate the evidence which the officer deemed sufficient to justify the late search of appellant's stored clothing. . . .

The fact that the police have custody of a prisoner's property for the purpose of protecting it while he is incarcerated does not alone constitute a basis for an exception to the requirement of a search warrant.

The government urges that the search be held valid by analogy to laboratory testing without a warrant of the clothing of a jailed person. We decline to accept the invitation. Examination of the laboratory test cases discloses that with few exceptions they are concerned with testing of clothing seized incident to arrest. * * *

Reversed and remanded.

ALDRICH, CIRCUIT JUDGE (dissenting in part).

With respect to the search of the defendant's clothing it seems to me that there is a material difference between breaking into the trunk of a car that has merely been taken into protective custody and reaching into the pocket of trousers removed from a prisoner. It is doubtless true that the fact that premises, whether real estate, or an automobile, could be searched at the time of the arrest does not mean that the police are free to return later. In such case what is involved is a new entry into property not truly possessed. The question in the case at bar should be the type of dominion which the authorities exercised over the clothes, whether mere custody, or full possession. *Cf.* Cooper v. California, 1967, 386 U.S. 58, 87 S.Ct. 788, 17 L.Ed.2d 730.

This may be tested by asking the question whether, had the defendant demanded the return of his clothes prior to trial, the demand would have been enforceable. I would say not. This must be the assumption in Miller v. Eklund, 9 Cir., 1966, 364 F.2d 976. My brethren would distinguish *Miller*, but I find it hard to think that if clothes can be introduced into evidence one cannot look into the pocket. I also find it hard to differentiate in principle between a

been stolen. Westover v. United States, 394 F.2d 164 (9th Cir. 1968) is similar to *Evalt* and to *Baskerville*, supra. It held that the police validly could look at the serial numbers on currency which had been taken from the prisoner at the time of arrest and put in the prisoners' property room. The numbers could have been listed when the money was taken into police custody because plainly visible, so the police could look at the bills again later. *Westover* rests squarely on Harris v. United States, 390 U.S. 234, 88 S.Ct. 992, 19 L.Ed.2d 1067 (1968), a "plain view" case.

search of the clothes three days after the arrest, and six hours after. Regardless of the court's jocosity, the arrest in *Caruso* was long over. The case there, and here, seems distinguishable from *Preston* not in terms of the number of hours after the arrest, but in terms of the nature of the possession.

The court would also distinguish the government's laboratory examination cases on the ground that in the case at bar the clothing was not "seized" at the time of the arrest. It is merely this court's legal conclusion that the clothing was not "seized" here—concededly it was taken.

* * *

By a process of distinguishing all other cases this court has become the first to hold, so far as appears, that a defendant's right of privacy is not infringed if his trousers are removed and searched today, but is invaded if the police return tomorrow to the clothes locker. I dislike being a disagreer, but this seems to me a pointless nicety.

STATE v. PIRES

Supreme Court of Wisconsin, 1972.
55 Wis.2d 597, 201 N.W.2d 153.

CONNOR T. HANSEN, JUSTICE.

The issue presented on this appeal is whether the inculpatory statements of the defendant were seized in violation of the fourth amendment of the United States Constitution and art. I, sec. 11, of the Wisconsin Constitution. The trial court found that the statements came into the possession of the police as a result of an unconstitutional search. The resolution of the issue requires a review of the facts upon which the trial court based its findings and determinations.

November 10, 1970, Robert Pires, husband of the defendant, came home from work about 5 o'clock p. m. and in the bedroom found the defendant lying across the bed. Also on the bed was his infant child who was cold and appeared dead. He testified he thought his child had died from a fall and that his wife was having a nervous breakdown. His wife had been under psychiatric care, and he first called her psychiatrist, then his brother, and finally he called for a police ambulance. He told the police his baby was dead and his wife was having a nervous breakdown. The police ambulance arrived shortly before 5:30 p. m. and took Pires, his wife, and the infant to the hospital. The officers with the ambulance took no items from the house. Pires gave no one else permission to enter the dwelling or remove anything from it. When the ambulance left, no one remained in the home.

Lieutenant Halaska testified he was in the Safety Building in Milwaukee at about 5:20 p. m. when he received a police radio dispatch to go to the defendant's address because of a report that there was supposedly the body of a child and a semi-conscious woman in the dwelling. When he arrived at the home, he observed no activity. Very shortly a police squad with two uniformed police officers arrived. They all went to the front door, rang the doorbell, received no response and found it locked. Halaska then stationed one of the officers at the front door and he and the other officer proceeded to the back door. They knocked on the door, received no response, and upon finding the door unlocked, entered the premises. They immediately began a search of the house for victims or someone responsible for the victims. They first went to the kitchen and then to the bedroom. Their search produced no one and they did not observe the inculpatory statements of the defendant that were lying on a stand near the bed.

Sometime very shortly after this search of the premises, it appears, Halaska somehow learned that the defendant and the child were at the hospital. About 5:40 p. m. Detective Schreiber arrived at the residence. Schreiber testified that Halaska and the two uniformed officers admitted him through the front door of the premises. He was told by these officers that the apparently-dead child and the defendant, both apparent victims of an overdose of drugs, had been conveyed to the hospital from the bedroom. After this conversation, the officers all went into the bedroom and while in the bedroom they observed a clipboard on a night stand next to the bed with a pad of paper. Examination revealed that the top four pages were the inculpatory statements of the defendant which are the subject of this appeal. The officers took possession of these writings.

Halaska's testimony is somewhat ambivalent. In response to an inquiry by the court, he testified he knew nobody was in the bedroom after the first search and that there was no further reason for him to make a further search of the room. Later, however, he testified that the first search was done rather quickly and, therefore, a second search was necessary. Halaska further testified that he had no knowledge that the police ambulance had arrived and departed until after the search. He does not identify what he means by the use of the words "the search." If he is referring to the first search of the premises, his testimony can be reconciled with that of Schreiber. If Halaska is referring to the completion of the second search, his testimony is in conflict with that of Schreiber.

The trial court determined that the officers, without a search warrant, had a legitimate reason to enter and search the premises for victims. As to the second search, the trial court, in effect, found that once the officers had determined no victims were in the bedroom they had no constitutional right to conduct a second warrantless search. The trial court determined the note was not in plain view and in order for the officers to see it they had to be searching for evidence and not victims. The trial court, therefore, found the second search to be unconstitutional and entered an order suppressing the evidence obtained on the second search of the premises.

* * *

The "emergency doctrine" or "exigent-circumstance rule" is founded upon the actions of police which are considered reasonable. The element of reasonableness is supplied by the compelling need to assist the victim or apprehend those responsible, not the need to secure evidence.

The trial court found that the initial intrusion into Pires' dwelling was justified under this doctrine. We agree. The fact that, in reality, no one was in the dwelling, does not alter the justification for the initial entry.

In State v. Davidson (1969), 44 Wis.2d 177, 170 N.W.2d 755, the police officers observed blood on the outside door and large quantities of blood and broken glass inside the house. This court held the police officers' warrantless intrusion reasonable. However, a warrantless entry into the dwelling three days later for a further search was held to be unconstitutional.

* * *

The difficulty in applying the exigent-circumstance rule to the instant case comes into focus as a result of the second intrusion into the bedroom. Halaska testified he did not see or observe the writings on the first examination of the bedroom. It appears he knew the baby and its mother were at the hospital before the officers made the second visit to the bedroom. Most important, however, is the fact that he testified that after his first entry into the Pires' bedroom, he knew nobody was in the bedroom and there was no reason to make further inquiry into the bedroom.

Therefore, if the seizure of the inculpatory writings is to escape the taint of unconstitutionality, the rationale of the exigent-circumstances rule, applicable to the first warrantless entry of the bedroom, must somehow be extended to the second entry of the bedroom. Under the facts of this case, we cannot justify the second entry under this rule.

A search, lawful at its inception, may become unlawful by broadening its intensity and scope unless further steps are taken that can independently satisfy constitutional requirements.

* * *

The sole justification for the warrantless search in the present case is the need to aid victims or to apprehend those who may be responsible. A search resting upon this rationale must be confined in scope to an intrusion reasonably designed to discover the victims or those who may be responsible. The second intrusion into the Pires' bedroom was not directed to either of these objectives.

Reasonableness of the search is, in the first instance, a substantive determination to be made by the trial court from the facts and circumstances of the case. The trial court, after hearing all the testimony and observing the demeanor of the witnesses, stated that he did not believe that the police officers went back into the bedroom the second time to look for a body but believe they were searching for evidence. The record supports such a determination.

After the officers had determined no one was present, victim or otherwise, the application of the "emergency rationale" terminated. Any further search beyond this point, unless further steps are taken to independently satisfy constitutional mandates, is unconstitutional. In the event authorities concluded further search was necessary, a search warrant should have been obtained. The dwelling was vacant; it could have been sealed off; and there was no evidence of any articles which were contraband or stolen or dangerous in themselves. We find no compelling reason as to why the authorities should not have secured a search warrant before conducting the second search.

* * *

In addition, we are of the opinion that the documents were not in "plain view" as the rule is generally understood and applied. The officers did not even see the documents on the first search of the bedroom. It was only after the officers were satisfied no one was in the room and were making the second search that they first observed the documents. Even then, only after Halaska picked the documents up and read them did he realize their contents. It was then that the inculpatory statements were seized.

The order of the trial court sustaining the motion to suppress the evidence is affirmed.

Order affirmed.

ROBERT W. HANSEN, JUSTICE (dissenting).

* * *

The majority opinion finds the police taking of the notes that were in plain view on the nightstand to be improper. Apparently, the majority views the husband's telephone call as solely a request for an ambulance, unaccompanied by a report of a situation calling for and requiring police investigation of the circumstances. If no more had been involved than his reporting he had found his wife unconscious on the bed, this interpretation of the telephone call might hold up. But the husband also informed police that alongside the unconscious body of his wife lay the cold and apparently lifeless body of his child. The unconscious wife and dead child, side by side on the bed, made accident (such as the wife's taking too many sleeping pills by mistake or the child's happening upon a bottle of iodine in a medicine chest) an unlikely explanation of what had happened. The husband's report to police was a report that a crime had likely been committed. Such report required and authorized police investigation.

The majority opinion rests the police entry in the bedroom, not upon consent or invitation, but upon "exigent circumstance rule," meaning required by the circumstances then and there present. The majority agrees with the trial court that the ". . . initial intrusion into Pires' dwelling was justified under this doctrine." However, the majority holds the "second intrusion into the Pires' bedroom" was not justified by the circumstances then exigent. This makes two police visits to the bedroom, separated by minutes, into two separate searches. This we would not do. If the police had a right to check or search the bedroom at all, as we see it, they had a right to recheck it. It is true that in one case this court upheld a contemporaneous search, but found tainted a second search, three days later. But that was three days later. Here, if the officers had the right to check the bedroom, we would hold they had the right, some minutes later, to recheck it.

Finding consent and invitation as the basis for the police being in the bedroom, first time or second, we do not reach or need the exigent circumstances rule. If we did, we would not limit it, as does the majority opinion, to ". . . the compelling need to assist the victim or apprehend those responsible, not the need to secure evidence." If the crime were rape, the circumstances exigent would not merely justify looking for another rape victim in the bedroom or to see if the rapist was hiding under the bed or in a closet. Criminals may return to the scene of their crimes on occasion, but they usually leave promptly after the crime has been completed. The police would have the right and duty to seek telltale clues which are in plain view and have been left behind by the perpetrator of the crime. Apprehension of a criminal is more often accomplished by discovering what he has left behind than by discovering that he has stayed behind.

Of course, as the majority opinion points out, search, lawful in its inception, may become unlawful if its scope or intensity are broadened. We see neither scope nor intensity broadened by stepping back into a bedroom to check or recheck it. Nor would we attach to the departure of the ambulance the importance given it in the majority opinion. If the husband, as we would hold, reported the probable commission of a crime in his home, the coming or going of the ambulance does not affect the consent given to the police to investigate circumstances surrounding the situation reported.

We would not consider important, or even relevant, the conclusion that the police, before entering the bedroom again, ". . . knew the baby and its mother were at the hospital." If this fact is at all controlling, the suggestion is that police officers complete their investigation before the ambulance leaves. Minutes are precious when it comes to saving lives. Police officers are entitled, and, as we see it, required to give priority to getting those in need of medical attention to the hospital. Having accomplished that task, they may resume their search.

It may well be, in light of the majority holding, that, upon receipt of a telephoned request from a homeowner for the dispatch of an ambulance to his home, reporting a situation that makes it reasonable to believe that a crime has been committed, the police are now required to ask, "Are you requesting that we investigate what has happened?" Given the predictable affirmative response, the invitation to enter and investigate the circumstances surrounding the incident would be express, not implied. We see no reason for requesting an express authorization where, as in the case before us, consent to investigate can be reasonably implied from the husband's report to the police. We would reverse the trial court's order which held inadmissible the notes observed and taken from the bedstand by the police, and we would find the police procedure followed in this case absolutely appropriate and completely correct.

I am authorized to state that MR. JUSTICE BRUCE F. BEILFUSS and MR. JUSTICE LEO B. HANLEY join in this dissent.

SECTION E. WIRETAPPING AND EAVESDROPPING

BERGER v. NEW YORK

Supreme Court of the United States, 1967.
388 U.S. 41, 87 S.Ct. 1873.

MR. JUSTICE CLARK delivered the opinion of the Court.

This writ tests the validity of New York's permissive eavesdrop statute [1] under the Fourth, Fifth, Ninth, and Fourteenth Amend-

1. "§ 813–a. Ex parte order for eavesdropping.
"An ex parte order for eavesdropping as defined in subdivisions one and two of section seven hundred thirty-eight of the penal law may be issued by any justice of the supreme court or judge of a county court or of the court of general sessions of the county of New York upon oath or affirmation of a district attorney, or of the attorney-general or of an officer above the rank of sergeant of any police department of the state or of any political subdivision thereof, that there is reasonable ground to believe that evidence of crime may be thus obtained, and particularly describing the person or persons whose communications, conversations or discussions are to be overheard or recorded and the purpose thereof, and, in the case of a telegraphic or telephonic communication, identifying the particular telephone number or telegraph line involved. In connection with the issuance of such an order the justice or judge may examine on oath the applicant and any other witness he may produce and shall satisfy himself of the existence of reasonable grounds for the granting of such application. Any such order shall be effective for the time specified therein but not for a period of more than two months unless extended or renewed by the justice or judge who signed and issued the original order upon satisfying himself that such extension or renewal is in the public interest. Any such order together with the papers upon which the application was based, shall be delivered to and retained by the applicant as authority for the eavesdropping authorized therein. A true copy of such order shall at all

ments. The claim is that the statute sets up a system of surveillance which involves trespassory intrusions into private, constitutionally protected premises, and is an invasion of the privilege against self-incrimination. . . .

Berger, the petitioner, was convicted on two counts of conspiracy to bribe the Chairman of the New York State Liquor Authority. The case arose out of the complaint of one Ralph Pansini to the District Attorney's office that agents of the State Liquor Authority had entered his bar and grill and without cause seized his books and records. Pansini asserted that the raid was in reprisal for his failure to pay a bribe for a liquor license. Numerous complaints had been filed with the District Attorney's office charging the payment of bribes by applicants for liquor licenses. On the direction of that office, Pansini, while equipped with a minifon recording device, interviewed an employee of the Authority. The employee advised Pansini that the price for a license was $10,000 and suggested that he contact attorney Harry Neyer. Neyer subsequently told Pansini that he worked with the Authority employee before and that the latter was aware of the going rate on liquor licenses downtown.

On the basis of this evidence an eavesdrop order was obtained from a Justice of the State Supreme Court, as provided by § 813–a. The order permitted the installation, for a period of 60 days, of a recording device in Neyer's office. On the basis of leads obtained from this eavesdrop a second order permitting the installation, for a like period, of a recording device in the office of one Harry Steinman was obtained. After some two weeks of eavesdropping a conspiracy was uncovered involving the issuance of liquor licenses for the Playboy and Tenement Clubs, both of New York City. Petitioner was indicted as "a go-between" for the principal conspirators, who though not named in the indictment were disclosed in a bill of particulars. Relevant portions of the recordings were received in evidence at the trial and were played to the jury, all over the objection of the petitioner. The parties have stipulated that the District Attorney "had no information upon which to proceed to present a case to the Grand Jury, or on the basis of which to prosecute" the petitioner except by the use of the eavesdrop evidence.

Eavesdropping is an ancient practice which at common law was condemned as a nuisance. IV Blackstone, Commentaries § 168.

The telephone brought on a new and more modern eavesdropper known as the "wiretapper."

Sophisticated electronic devices have now been developed (commonly known as "bugging") which are capable of eavesdropping on

times be retained in his possession by the judge or justice issuing the same, and, in the event of the denial of an application for such an order, a true copy of the papers upon which the application was based shall in like manner be retained by the judge or justice denying the same. As amended. L.1958, c. 676, eff. July 1, 1958."

anyone in most any given situation. They are to be distinguished from "wiretapping" which is confined to the interception of telegraphic and telephonic communications. Miniature in size—no larger than a postage stamp (3/8" x 3/8" x 1/8")—these gadgets pick up whispers within a room and broadcast them half a block away to a receiver. It is said that certain types of electronic rays beamed at walls or glass windows are capable of catching voice vibrations as they are bounced off the latter. Since 1940 eavesdropping has become a big business. Manufacturing concerns offer complete detection systems which automatically record voices under most any conditions by remote control. A microphone concealed in a book, a lamp, or other unsuspecting place in a room, or made into a fountain pen, tie clasp, lapel button, or cuff link increases the range of these powerful wireless transmitters to a half mile. Receivers pick up the transmission with interference-free reception on a special waive frequency. And, of late, a combination mirror transmitter has been developed which permits not only sight but voice transmission up to 300 feet. Likewise, parabolic microphones, which can overhear conversations without being placed within the premises monitored, have been developed. See Westin, Science, Privacy and Freedom, 66 Col.L.Rev. 1003, 1005–1010.

As science developed these detection techniques, law makers, sensing the resulting invasion of individual privacy, have provided some statutory protection for the public. Seven states, California, Illinois, Maryland, Massachusetts, Nevada, New York, and Oregon, prohibit surreptitious eavesdropping by mechanical or electronic device. However, all, save Illinois, permit official court-ordered eavesdropping. Some 36 states prohibit wiretapping. But of these, 27 permit "authorized" interception of some type. Federal law prohibits interception and divulging or publishing of the content of wiretaps without exception. In sum, it is fair to say that wiretapping on the whole is outlawed, except for permissive use by law enforcement officials in some states; while electronic eavesdropping is—save for seven states—permitted both officially and privately. And, in six of the seven states, electronic eavesdropping ("bugging") is permissible on court order. * * *

The Court was faced with its first wiretap case in 1928, Olmstead v. United States, 277 U.S. 438, 48 S.Ct. 564. There the interception of Olmstead's telephone line was accomplished without entry upon his premises and was, therefore, found not to be proscribed by the Fourth Amendment. The basis of the decision was that the Constitution did not forbid the obtaining of evidence by wiretapping unless it involved actual unlawful entry into the house. Statements in the opinion that "a conversation passing over a telephone wire" cannot be said to come within the Fourth Amendment's enumeration of "persons, houses, papers, and effects" have been negated by our subsequent cases as hereinafter noted. They found "conversation" was within the Fourth Amendment's protections, and that the use of electronic devices to capture it was a "search" within the meaning of the Amendment, and we so hold. In any event, Congress soon thereafter, and some say in answer to *Olmstead*, specifically prohibited the interception without authorization and the divulging or publishing of the contents of telephonic communications. And the *Nardone* cases (Nardone v. United States), 302 U.S. 379, 58 S.Ct. 275 (1937) and 308 U.S. 338, 60 S.Ct. 266 (1939), extended the exclusionary rule to wiretap evidence offered in federal prosecutions.

The first "bugging" case reached the Court in 1942 in Goldman v. United States, 316 U.S. 129, 62 S.Ct. 993. There the Court found that the use of a detectaphone placed against an office wall in order to hear private conversations in the office next door did not violate the Fourth Amendment because there was no physical trespass in connection with the relevant interception. And in On Lee v. United States, 343 U.S. 747, 72 S.Ct. 967 (1952), we found that since "no trespass was committed" a conversation between Lee and a federal agent, occurring in the former's laundry and electronically recorded, was not condemned by the Fourth Amendment. Thereafter in Silverman v. United States, 365 U.S. 505, 81 S.Ct. 679 (1961), the Court found "that the eavesdropping was accomplished by means of an unauthorized physical penetration into the premises occupied by the petitioners." A spike a foot long with a microphone attached to it was inserted under a baseboard into a party wall until it made contact with the heating duct that ran through the entire house occupied by Silverman, making a perfect sounding board through which the conversations in question were overheard. Significantly, the Court held that its decision did "not turn upon the technicality of a trespass upon a party wall as a matter of local law. It is based upon the reality of an actual intrusion into a constitutionally protected area." * * * The Fourth Amendment commands that a warrant issue not only upon probable cause supported by oath or affirmation, but also "particularly describing the place to be searched, and the persons or things to be seized." New York's statute lacks this particularization. It merely says that a warrant may issue on reasonable ground to believe that evidence of crime may be obtained by the eavesdrop. It lays down no requirement for particularity in the warrant as to what specific crime has been or is being committed, nor "the place to be searched," or "the persons or things to be seized" as specifically required by the Fourth Amendment. The need for particularity and evidence of reliability in the showing required when judicial authorization of a search is sought is especially great in the case of eavesdropping. By its very nature eavesdropping involves an intrusion on privacy that is broad in scope. As was said in Osborn v. United States, 385 U.S. 323, 87 S.Ct. 429 (1966), the "indiscriminate use of such devices in law enforcement raises grave constitutional questions under the Fourth and Fifth Amendments," and imposes "a heavier responsibility on this Court in its supervision of the fairness of procedures . . . ." There, two judges acting jointly authorized the installation of a device on the person of a prospective witness to record conversations between him and an attorney for a defendant then on trial in the United States District Court. The judicial authorization was based on an affidavit of the witness setting out in detail previous conversations between the witness and the attorney concerning the bribery of jurors in the case. The recording device was, as the Court said, authorized "under the most precise and discriminate circumstances, circumstances which fully met the 'requirement of particularity' " of the Fourth Amendment. The Court was asked to exclude the evidence of the recording of the conversations. The Court refused to do so, finding that the recording, although an invasion of the privacy protected by the Fourth Amendment, was admissible because of the authorization of the judges, based upon "a detailed factual affidavit alleging the commission of a specific criminal offense directly and immediately affecting the administration of justice . . . for the narrow and particularized purpose of ascertaining the truth of the affidavit's allegations." The invasion was lawful because there was sufficient proof to obtain a search warrant to make the search for the limited purpose outlined in the order of the judges. Through these "precise and discriminate" procedures the order authorizing the use of the electronic device afforded similar protections to those that are present in the use of conventional warrants authorizing the seizure of tangible evidence. Among other safeguards, the order described the type of conversation sought with particularity, thus indicating the specific objective of the Government in entering the constitutionally protected area and the limitations placed upon the officer executing the warrant. Under it the officer could not search unauthorized areas; likewise, once the property sought, and for which the order was issued, was found the officer could not use the order as a passkey to further search. In addition, the order authorized one limited intrusion rather than a series or a continuous surveillance. And, we note that a new order was issued when the officer sought to resume the search and probable cause was shown for the succeeding one. Moreover, the order was executed by the officer with dispatch, not over a prolonged and extended period. In this manner no greater invasion of privacy was permitted than was necessary under the circumstances. Finally the officer was required to and did make a return on the order showing how it was executed and what was seized. Through these strict precautions the danger of an unlawful search and seizure was minimized.

On the contrary, New York's statute lays down no such "precise and discriminate" requirements. * * * New York's broadside authorization rather than being "carefully circumscribed" so as to prevent unauthorized invasions of privacy actually permits general searches by electronic devices . . . . The Fourth Amendment's requirement that a warrant "particularly describ[e] the place to be searched, and the persons or things to be seized," repudiated these general warrants and "makes general searches . . . impossible and prevents the seizure of one thing under a warrant describing another. As to what is to be taken, nothing is left to the discretion of the officer executing the warrant."

We believe the statute here is equally offensive. First, as we have mentioned, eavesdropping is authorized without requiring belief that any particular offense has been or is being committed; nor that the property sought, the conversations, be particularly described. The purpose of the probable cause requirement of the Fourth Amendment to keep the state out of constitutionally protected areas until it has reason to believe that a specific crime has been or is being committed is thereby wholly aborted. Likewise the statute's failure to describe with particularity the conversations sought gives the officer a roving commission to seize any and all conversations. It is true that the statute requires the naming of "the person or persons whose communications, conversations or discussions are to be overheard or recorded . . . ." But this does no more than identify the person whose constitutionally protected area is to be invaded rather than "particularly describing" the communications, conversations, or discussions to be seized. As with general warrants this leaves too much to the discretion of the officer executing the order. Secondly, authorization of eavesdropping for a two-month period is the equivalent of a series of intrusions, searches, and seizures pursuant to a single showing of probable cause. Prompt execution is also avoided. During such a long and continuous (24 hours a day) period the conversations of any and all persons coming into the area covered by the device will be seized indiscriminately and without regard to their connection to the crime under investigation. Moreover, the statute permits, as was done here, extensions of the original two-month period—presumedly for two months each—on a mere showing that such extension is "in the public interest." Apparently the original grounds on which the eavesdrop order was initially issued also form the basis of the renewal. This we believe insufficient without a showing of present probable cause for the continuance of the eavesdrop. Third, the statute places no termination date on the eavesdrop once the conversation sought is seized. This is left entirely in the discretion of the officer. Finally, the statute's procedure, necessarily because its success depends on secrecy, has no requirement for notice as do conventional warrants, nor does it overcome this defect by requiring some showing of special facts. On the contrary, it permits uncontested entry without any showing of exigent circumstances. Such a showing of exigency, in order to avoid notice would appear more important in eavesdropping, with its inherent dangers, than that required when conventional procedures of search and seizure are utilized. Nor does the statute provide for a return on the warrant thereby leaving full discretion in the officer as to the use of seized conversations of innocent as well as guilty parties. In short, the statute's blanket grant of permission to eavesdrop is without adequate judicial supervision or protective procedures.

It is said with fervor that electronic eavesdropping is a most important technique of law enforcement and that outlawing it will severely cripple crime detection. The monumental report of the President's Crime Commission entitled "The Challenge of Crime in a Free Society" informs us that the majority of law enforcement officials say that this is especially true in the detection of organized crime. As the Commission reports, there can be no question about the serious proportions of professional criminal activity in this country. However, we have found no empirical statistics on the use of electronic devices (bugging) in the fight against organized crime. Indeed, there are even figures available in the wiretap category which indicate to the contrary. See, Dash, Schwartz, and Knowlton. The Eavesdroppers (1959), District Attorney Silver's poll, 105, 117–119. * * * Brooklyn's District Attorney Silver's poll of the State of New York indicates that during the 12-year period (1942–1954) duly authorized wiretaps in bribery and corruption cases constituted only a small percentage of the whole. It indicates that this category only involved 10% of the total wiretaps. The overwhelming majority were in the categories of larceny, extortion, coercion, and blackmail, accounting for almost 50%. Organized gambling was about 11%. Statistics are not available on subsequent years. Dash, supra, p. 40.

An often repeated statement of District Attorney Hogan of New York County was made at a hearing before the Senate Judiciary Committee at which he advocated the amendment of the Federal Communications Act of 1934, supra, so as to permit "telephonic interception" of conversations. As he testified, "Federal statutory law [the 1934 Act] has been interpreted in such a way as to bar us from divulging wiretap evidence, even in the courtroom in the course of criminal prosecution". Mr. Hogan then said that "without it [wiretaps] my own office could not have convicted . . . top figures in the underworld." He then named nine persons his office had convicted and one on whom he had furnished "leads" secured from wiretaps to the authorities of New Jersey. Evidence secured from wiretaps, as Mr. Hogan said, was not admissible in "criminal prosecutions." He was advocating that the Congress adopt a measure that would make it admissible; Hearings on S. 2813 and S. 1495, before the Committee on the Judiciary of the United States Senate, 87th Cong., 2d Sess., pp. 173, 174 (1962). The President's Crime Commission also emphasizes in its report the need for wiretapping in the investigation of organized crime because of the telephone's "relatively free use" by those engaged in the business and the difficulty of infiltrating their organizations. The Congress, though long importuned, has not amended the 1934 Act to permit it.

We are also advised by the Solicitor General of the United States that the Federal Government has abandoned the use of electronic eavesdropping for "prosecutorial purposes." Despite these actions of the Federal Government there has been no failure of law enforcement in that field.

In any event we cannot forgive the requirements of the Fourth Amendment in the name of law enforcement. This is no formality that we require today but a fundamental rule that has long been recognized as basic to the privacy of every home in America. While "[t]he requirements of the Fourth Amendment are not inflexible, or obtusely unyielding to the legitimate needs of law enforcement," Lopez v. United States, supra, at 464, 83 S.Ct. at 1404, dissenting opinion of Brennan, J., it is not asking too much that officers be required to comply with the basic command of the Fourth Amendment before the innermost secrets of one's home or office are invaded. Few threats to liberty exist which are greater than that posed by the use of eavesdropping devices. Some may claim that without the use of such devices crime detection in certain areas may suffer some delays since eavesdropping is quicker, easier, and more certain. However, techniques and practices may well be developed that will operate just as speedily and certain—and what is more important—without attending illegality.

It is said that neither a warrant nor a statute authorizing eavesdropping can be drawn so as to meet the Fourth Amendment's requirements. If that be true then the "fruits" of eavesdropping devices are barred under the Amendment. On the other hand this Court has in the past, under specific conditions and circumstances, sustained the use of eavesdropping devices. In the latter case the eavesdropping device was permitted where the "commission of a specific offense" was charged, its use was "under the most precise and discriminating circumstances" and the effective administration of justice in a federal court was at stake. The States are under no greater restrictions. The Fourth Amendment does not make the "precincts of the home or office . . . sanctuaries where the law can never reach." but it does prescribe a constitutional standard that must be met before official invasion is permissible. Our concern with the statute here is whether its language permits a trespassory invasion of the home, by general warrant, contrary to the command of the Fourth Amendment. As it is written, we believe that it does.

Reversed.

[MR. JUSTICE DOUGLAS' concurring opinion is omitted.]

MR. JUSTICE STEWART, concurring in the result.

I fully agree with MR. JUSTICE BLACK, MR. JUSTICE HARLAN, and MR. JUSTICE WHITE, that this New York law is entirely constitutional. In short, I think that "electronic eavesdropping, *as such* or as it is permitted by this statute, is not an unreasonable search and seizure." The statute contains many provisions more stringent than the Fourth Amendment generally requires, as MR. JUSTICE BLACK has so forcefully pointed out. * * *

The issue before us, as MR. JUSTICE WHITE says, is "whether *this* search complied with Fourth Amendment standards." For me that issue is an extremely close one in the circumstances of this case. It certainly cannot be resolved by incantation of ritual phrases like "general warrant." Its resolution involves "the unavoidable task in any search and seizure case: was the particular search and seizure reasonable or not?"

I would hold that the affidavits on which the judicial order issued in this case did not constitute a showing of probable cause adequate to justify the authorizing order. The need for particularity and evidence of reliability in the showing required when judicial authorization is sought for the kind of electronic eavesdropping involved in this case is especially great. The standard of reasonableness embodied in the Fourth Amendment demands that the showing of justification match the degree of intrusion. By its very nature electronic eavesdropping for a 60-day period, even of a specified office, involves a broad invasion of a constitutionally protected area. Only the most precise and rigorous standard of probable cause should justify an intrusion of this sort. I think the affidavits presented to the judge who authorized the electronic surveillance of the Steinman office failed to meet such a standard.

So far as the record shows, the only basis for the Steinman order consisted of two affidavits. One of them contained factual allegations supported only by bare, unexplained references to "evidence" in the district attorney's office and "evidence" obtained by the Neyer eavesdrop. No underlying facts were presented on the basis of which the judge could evaluate these general allegations. The second affidavit was no more than a statement of another assistant district attorney that he had read his associate's affidavit and was satisfied on that basis alone that proper grounds were presented for the issuance of an authorizing order.

This might be enough to satisfy the standards of the Fourth Amendment for a conventional search or arrest. But I think it was constitutionally insufficient to constitute probable cause to justify an intrusion of the scope and duration that was permitted in this case.

Accordingly, I would reverse the judgment.

MR. JUSTICE BLACK, dissenting. * * * Evidence obtained by electronic eavesdropping was used to convict the petitioner here of conspiracy to bribe the chairman of the State Liquor Authority which controls the issuance of liquor licenses in New York. It is stipulated that without this evidence a conviction could not have been obtained and it seems apparent that use of that evidence showed petitioner to be a briber beyond all reasonable doubt. Notwithstanding petitioner's obvious guilt, however, the Court now strikes down his conviction in a way that plainly makes it impossible ever to convict him again. This is true because the Court not only holds that the judicial orders which were the basis of the authority to eavesdrop were insufficient, but holds that the New York eavesdropping statute is *on its face* violative of the Fourth Amendment. And while the Court faintly intimates to the contrary, it seems obvious to me that its holding, by creating osbtacles that cannot be overcome, makes it completely impossible for the State or the Federal Government ever to have a valid eavesdropping statute. All of this is done, it seems to me, in part because of the Court's hostility to eavesdropping as "ignoble" and "dirty business" and in part because of fear that rapidly advancing science and technology is making eavesdropping more and more effective. Neither of these, nor any other grounds that I can think of, are sufficient in my judgment to justify a holding that the use of evidence secured by eavesdropping is barred by the Constitution.

I.

Perhaps as good a definition of eavesdropping as another is that it is listening secretly and sometimes "snoopily" to conversations and discussions believed to be private by those who engage in them. Needless to say, eavesdropping is not ranked as one of the most learned or most polite professions, nor perhaps would an eavesdropper be selected by many people as a most desirable and attractive associate. But the practice has undoubtedly gone on since the beginning of human society, and during that time it has developed a usefulness of its own, particularly in the detection and prosecution of crime.

Eavesdroppers have always been deemed competent witnesses in English and American courts. The main test of admissibility has been relevance and first-hand knowledge, not by whom or by what method proffered evidence was obtained. It is true that in England people who obtained evidence by unlawful means were held liable in damages as in Entick v. Carrington, 19 How.St.Tr. 1029. But even that famous civil liberties case made no departure from the traditional common-law rule that relevant evidence is admissible, even though obtained contrary to ethics, morals, or law. And, for reasons that follow, this evidentiary rule is well adapted to our Government, set up, as it was, to "insure domestic tranquility" under a system of laws.

Today this country is painfully realizing that evidence of crime is difficult for governments to secure. Criminals are shrewd and constantly seek, too often successfully, to conceal their tracks and their outlawry from law officers. But in carrying on their nefarious practices professional criminals usually talk considerably. Naturally, this talk is done, they hope, in a secret way that will keep it from being heard by law enforcement authorities or by others who might report to the authorities. In this situation "eavesdroppers," "informers," and "squealers," as they are variously called, are helpful, even though unpopular, agents of law enforcement. And it needs no empirical studies or statistics to establish that eavesdropping testimony plays an important role in exposing criminals and bands of criminals who but for such evidence would go along their criminal way with little possibility of exposure, prosecution, or punishment. Such of course is this particular case before us.

The eavesdrop evidence here shows this petitioner to be a briber, a corrupter of trusted public officials, a poisoner of the honest administration of government, upon which good people must depend to obtain the blessings of a decent orderly society. No man's privacy, property, liberty, or life is secure, if organized or even unorganized criminals can go their way unmolested, ever and ever further in their unabandoned lawlessness. However obnoxious eavesdroppers may be they are assuredly not engaged in a more "ignoble" or "dirty business" than are bribers, thieves, burglars, robbers, rapists, kidnapers, and murderers, not to speak of others. And it cannot be denied that to deal with such specimens of our society, eavesdroppers are not merely useful, they are frequently a necessity. I realize that some may say, "Well, let the prosecuting officers use more scientific measures than eavesdropping." It is always easy to hint at mysterious means available just around the corner to catch outlaws. But crimes, unspeakably horrid crimes, are with us in this country, and we cannot afford to dispense with any known method of detecting and correcting them unless it is forbidden by the Constitution or deemed inadvisable by legislative policy—neither of which I believe to be true about eavesdropping.

II.

Since eavesdrop evidence obtained by individuals is admissible and helpful I can perceive no permissible reason for courts to reject it, even when obtained surreptitiously by machines, electric or otherwise. Certainly evidence picked up and recorded on a machine is not less trustworthy. In both perception and retention a machine is more accurate than a human listener. The machine does not have to depend on a defective memory to repeat what was said in its presence for it repeats the very words uttered. I realize that there is complaint that sometimes the words are jumbled or indistinct. But machine evidence need not be done away with to correct such occasional defective recording. The trial judge has ample power to refuse to admit indistinct or garbled recordings.

The plain facts are, however, that there is no inherent danger to a defendant in using these electronic recordings except that which results from the use of testimony that is so unerringly accurate that it is practically bound to bring about a conviction. In other words, this kind of transcribed eavesdropping evidence is far more likely to lead a judge or jury to reach a correct judgment or verdict—the basic and always-present objective of a trial.

III.

The superior quality of evidence recorded and transcribed on an electronic device is, of course, no excuse for using it against a defendant, if, as the Court holds, its use violates the Fourth Amendment. If that is true, no amount of common-law tradition or anything else can justify admitting such evidence. But I do not believe the Fourth Amendment, or any other, bans the use of evidence obtained by eavesdropping.

There are constitutional amendments that speak in clear unambiguous prohibitions or commands. * * * [P]rovisions of the First and Fifth Amendments, as well as others I need not mention at this time, are clear unconditional commands that something shall not be done. Particularly of interest in comparison with the Fourth Amendment is the Fifth Amendment's prohibition against compelling a person to be a witness against himself. The Fifth Amendment's language forbids a court to hear evidence against a person that he has been compelled to give, without regard to reasonableness or anything else. Unlike all of these just named Fifth Amendment provisions, the Fourth Amendment relating to searches and seizures contains no such unequivocal commands. It provides:

> "The right of the people to be secure in their persons, houses, papers, and effects, against unreasonable searches and seizures, shall not be violated, and no Warrants shall issue, but upon probable cause, supported by Oath or affirmation, and particularly describing the place to be searched, and the persons or things to be seized."

Obviously, those who wrote this Fourth Amendment knew from experience that searches and seizures were too valuable to law enforcement to prohibit them entirely, but also knew at the same time that while searches or seizures must not be stopped, they should be slowed down, and warrants should be issued only after studied caution. This accounts for use of the imprecise and flexible term, "unreasonable," the key word permeating this whole Amendment. Also it is noticeable that this Amendment contains no appropriate language, as does the Fifth, to forbid the use and introduction of search and seizure evidence even though secured "unreasonably." Nor does this Fourth Amendment attempt to describe with precision what was meant by its words, "probable cause"; nor by whom the "oath or affirmation" should be taken; nor what it need contain. Although the Amendment does specifically say that the warrant should particularly describe "the place to be searched, and the persons or things to be seized," it does not impose any precise limits on the spatial or temporal extent of the search or the quantitative extent of the seizure. Thus this Amendment, aimed against only "unreasonable" searches and seizures, seeks to guard against them by providing, as the Court says, that a "neutral and detached authority be interposed between the police and the public, Johnson v. United States." And, as the Court admits, the Amendment itself provides no sanctions to enforce its standards of searches, seizures, and warrants. This was left for Congress to carry out if it chose to do so.

Had the framers of this Amendment desired to prohibit the use in court of evidence secured by an unreasonable search or seizure, they would have used plain appropriate language to do so, just as they did in prohibiting the use of enforced self-incriminatory evidence in the Fifth Amendment. Since the Fourth Amendment contains no language forbidding the use of such evidence, I think there is no such constitutional rule. So I continue to believe that the exclusionary rule formulated to bar such evidence in the *Weeks* case is not rooted in the Fourth Amendment but rests on the "supervisory power" of this Court over the other federal courts. For these reasons and others to be stated, I do not believe the Fourth Amendment standing alone, even if applicable to electronic eavesdropping, commands exclusion of the overheard evidence in this case.

In reaching my conclusion that the Fourth Amendment itself does not bar the use of eavesdropping evidence in courts, I do not overlook the fact that the Court at present is reading the Amendment as expressly and unqualifiedly barring invasions of "privacy" rather than merely forbidding "unreasonable searches and seizures." On this premise of the changed command of the Amendment, the Court's task in passing on the use of eavesdropping evidence becomes a simple one. Its syllogism is this:

> The Fourth Amendment forbids invasion of privacy and excludes evidence obtained by such invasion;
>
> To listen secretly to a man's conversations or to tap his telephone conversations invades his privacy;
>
> Therefore, the Fourth Amendment bars use of evidence obtained by eavesdropping or by tapping telephone wires.

The foregoing syllogism is faulty for at least two reasons: (1) the Fourth Amendment itself contains no provision from which can be implied a purpose to bar evidence or anything else secured by an "unreasonable search or seizure"; (2) the Fourth Amendment's language, fairly construed, refers specifically to "unreasonable searches and seizures" and not to a broad undefined right to "privacy" in general. To attempt to transform the meaning of the Amendment, as the Court does here, is to play sleight-of-hand tricks with it. . . .

IV.

While the electronic eavesdropping here bears some analogy to the problems with which the Fourth Amendment is concerned, I am by no means satisfied that the Amendment controls the constitutionality of such eavesdropping. As pointed out, the Amendment only bans searches and seizures of "persons, houses, papers, and effects." This literal language imports tangible things, and it would require an expansion of the language used by the framers, in the interest of "privacy" or some equally vague judge-made goal, to hold that it applies to the spoken word. It simply requires an imaginative transformation of the English language to say that conversations can be searched and words seized. . . .

. . . Since the framers in the first clause of the Amendment specified that only persons, houses, and things were to be protected, they obviously wrote the second clause, regulating search warrants, in reference only to such tangible things. To hold, as the Court does, that the first clause protects words, necessitates either a virtual rewriting of the particularity requirements of the Warrant Clause or a literal application of that clause's requirements and our cases construing them to situations they were never designed to cover. I am convinced that the framers of the Amendment never intended this Court to do either, and yet it seems to me clear that the Court here does a little of both.

V.

Assuming, as the Court holds, that the Fourth Amendment applies to eavesdropping and that the evidence obtained by an eavesdrop which violates the Fourth Amendment must be excluded in state courts, I disagree with the Court's holding that the New York statute on its face fails to comport with the Amendment. I also agree with my BROTHER WHITE that the statute as here applied did not violate any of petitioner's Fourth Amendment rights—assuming again that he has some—and that he is not entitled to a reversal of his conviction merely because the statute might have been applied in some way that would not have accorded with the Amendment.

This case deals only with a trespassory eavesdrop, an eavesdrop accomplished by placing a "bugging" device in petitioner's office. Significantly, the Court does not purport to disturb the *Olmstead-Silverman-Goldman* distinction between eavesdrops which are accompanied by a physical invasion and those that are not. Neither does the Court purport to overrule the holdings of On Lee v. United States, and Lopez v. United States, which exempt from the Amendment's requirements the use of an electronic device to record, and perhaps even transmit, a conversation to which the user is a party. It is thus clear that at least certain types of electronic eavesdropping, until today, were completely outside the scope of the Fourth Amendment. Nevertheless, New York has made it a crime to engage in almost any kind of electronic eavesdropping, N.Y.Penal Law § 738, and the only way eavesdropping, even the kind this Court has held constitutional, can be accomplished with immunity from criminal punishment is pursuant to § 813–a. The Court now strikes down § 813–a in its entirety, and that may well have the result of making it impossible for state law enforcement officers merely to listen through a closed door by means of an inverted cone or some other crude amplifying device, eavesdropping which this Court has to date refused to hold violative of the Fourth Amendment. Certainly there is no justification for striking down completely New York's statute, covering all kinds of eavesdropping, merely because it fails to contain the "strict precautions" which the Court derives—or more accurately fabricates—as conditions to eavesdrops covered by the Fourth Amendment. In failing to distinguish between types of eavesdropping and in failing to make clear that the New York statute is invalid only as applied to certain kinds of eavesdropping, the Court's opinion leaves the definite impression that all eavesdropping is governed by the Fourth Amendment. Such a step would require overruling of almost every opinion this Court has ever written on the subject. . . .

VI.

[A] constitution like ours is not designed to be a full code of laws like some of our States and some foreign countries have made theirs. And if constitutional provisions require new rules and sanctions to make them as fully effective as might be desired my belief is that calls for action, not by us, but by Congress or state legislatures, vested with powers to choose between conflicting policies. Here, for illustration, there are widely diverging views about eavesdropping. Some would make it a crime, barring it absolutely and in all events; others would bar it except in searching for evidence in the field of "national security," whatever that means; still others would pass no law either authorizing or forbidding it, leaving it to follow its natural course. This is plainly the type of question that can and should be decided by legislative bodies, unless some constitutional provision *expressly* governs the matter, just as the Fifth Amendment *expressly* forbids enforced self-incrimination. There is no such express prohibition in the Fourth Amendment nor can one be implied. The Fourth Amendment can only be made to prohibit or to regulate eavesdropping by taking away some of its words and by adding others.

MR. JUSTICE HARLAN, dissenting. . . .

I turn to what properly is the central issue in this case: the validity under the Warrants Clause of the Fourth Amendment of the eavesdropping order under which the recordings employed at petitioner's trial were obtained. It is essential first to set out certain of the pertinent facts.

The disputed recordings were made under the authority of a § 813–a order, dated June 12, 1962, permitting the installation of an eavesdropping device in the business office of one Harry Steinman; the order, in turn, was, so far as this record shows, issued solely upon the basis of information contained in affidavits submitted to the issuing judge by two assistant district attorneys. The first affidavit, signed by Assistant District Attorney Goldstein, indicated that the Rackets Bureau of the District Attorney's Office of New York County was then conducting an investigation of alleged corruption in the State Liquor Authority, and that the Bureau had received information that persons desiring to obtain or retain liquor licenses were obliged to pay large sums to officials of the Authority. It described the methods by which the bribe money was transmitted through certain attorneys to the officials. The affidavit asserted that one Harry Neyer, a former employee of the Authority, served as a "conduit." It indicated that evidence had been obtained "over a duly authorized eavesdropping device installed in the office of the aforesaid Harry Neyer," that conferences "relative to the payment of unlawful fees" occurred in Steinman's office. The number and street address of the office were provided. The affidavit specified that the "evidence indicates that the said Harry Steinman has agreed to pay, through the aforesaid Harry Neyer, $30,000" in order to secure a license for the Palladium Ballroom, an establishment within New York City. The Palladium, it was noted, had been the subject of hearings before the Authority "because of narcotic arrests therein." On the basis of this information, the affidavit sought an order to install a recording device in Steinman's business office.

The second affidavit, signed by Assistant District Attorney Scotti, averred that Scotti, as the Chief of the Bureau to which Goldstein was assigned, had read Goldstein's affidavit, and had concluded that the order might properly issue under § 813–a.

The order as issued permitted the recording of "any and all conversations, communications and discussions" in Steinman's business office for a period of 60 days.

The central objections mounted to this order by petitioner, and repeated as to the statute itself by the Court, are three: first, that it fails to specify with adequate particularity the conversations to be seized; second, that it permits a general and indiscriminate search and seizure; and third, that the order was issued without a showing of probable cause.

Each of the first two objections depends principally upon a problem of definition: the meaning in this context of the constitutional distinction between "search" and "seizure." If listening alone completes a "seizure," it would be virtually impossible for state authorities at a probable cause hearing to describe with particularity the seizures which would later be made during extended eavesdropping; correspondingly, seizures would unavoidably be made which lacked any sufficient nexus with the offenses for which the order was first issued. There is no need for present purposes to explore at length the question's subtleties; it suffices to indicate that, in my view, conversations are not "seized" either by eavesdropping alone, or by their recording so that they may later be heard at the eavesdropper's convenience. Just as some exercise of dominion, beyond mere perception, is necessary for the seizure of tangibles so some use of the conversation beyond the initial listening process is required for the seizure of the spoken word. With this premise, I turn to these three objections.

The "particularity" demanded by the Fourth Amendment has never been thought by this Court to be reducible "to formula"; it has instead been made plain that its measurement must take fully into account the character both of the materials to be seized and of the purposes of the seizures. Accordingly, where the materials "are books, and the basis for their seizure is the ideas which they contain," the most "scrupulous exactitude" is demanded in the warrant's description; but where the special problems associated with the First Amendment are not involved, as they are not here, a more "reasonable particularity," is permissible. The degree of particularity necessary is best measured by that requirement's purposes. The central purpose of the particularity requirement is to leave "nothing . . . to the discretion of the officer executing the warrant," by describing the materials to be seized with precision sufficient to prevent "the seizure of one thing under a warrant describing another." The state authorities are not compelled at the probable cause hearing to wager, upon penalty of a subsequent reversal, that they can successfully predict each of the characteristics of the materials which they will later seize, such a demand would, by discouraging the use of the judicial process, defeat the Amendment's central purpose.

The materials to be seized are instead described with sufficient particularity if the warrant readily permits their identification both by those entrusted with the warrant's execution and by the court in any subsequent judicial proceeding. "It is," the Court has said with reference to the particularity of the place to be searched, "enough if the description is such that the officer . . . can, with reasonable effort ascertain and identify" the warrant's objects.

These standards must be equally applicable to the seizure of words, and, under them, this order did not lack the requisite particularity. The order here permitted the interception, or search, of any and all conversations occurring within the order's time limitations at the specified location; but this direction must be read in light of the terms of the affidavits, which, under § 813, form part of the authority for the eavesdropping. The affidavits make plain that, among the intercepted conversations, the police were authorized to seize only those "relative to the payment of unlawful fees to obtain liquor licenses." These directions sufficed to provide a standard which left nothing in the choice of materials to be seized to the "whim," of the state authorities. There could be no difficulty, either in the course of the search or in any subsequent judicial proceeding, in determining whether specific conversations were among those authorized for seizure by the order. The Fourth and Fourteenth Amendments do not demand more.

Nor was the order invalid because it permitted the search of any and all conversations occurring at the specified location; if the requisite papers have identified the materials to be seized with sufficient particularity, as they did here, and if the search was confined to an appropriate area, the order is not invalidated by the examination of all within that area reasonably necessary for discovery of the materials to be seized. I do not doubt that searches by eavesdrop must be confined in time precisely as the search for tangibles is confined in space, but the actual duration of the intrusion here, or for that matter the total period authorized by the order, was not, given the character of the offenses involved, excessive. All the disputed evidence was obtained within 13 days, scarcely unreasonable in light of an alleged conspiracy involving many individuals and a lengthy series of transactions.

The question therefore remains only whether, as petitioner suggests, the order was issued without an adequate showing of probable cause. . . . it suffices now simply to emphasize that the information presented to the magistrate or commissioner must permit him to "judge for himself the persuasiveness of the facts relied on by a complaining officer." The magistrate must "assess independently the probability" that the facts are as the complainant has alleged; he may not "accept without question the complainant's mere conclusion."

As measured by the terms of the affidavits here, the issuing judge could properly have concluded that probable cause existed for the order. . . . the judge was provided the evidence which supported the affiants' conclusions; he was not compelled to rely merely on their "affirmation of suspicion and belief." In my opinion, taking the Steinman affidavits on their face, the constitutional requirements of probable cause were fully satisfied. * * *

MR. JUSTICE WHITE, dissenting. . . .

Petitioner primarily argues that eavesdropping is invalid, even pursuant to court order or search warrant, because it constitutes a "general search" barred by the Fourth Amendment. Petitioner suggests that the search is inherently overbroad because the eavesdropper will overhear conversations which do not relate to criminal activity. But the same is true of almost all searches of private property which the Fourth Amendment permits. In searching for seizable matters, the police must necessarily see or hear, and comprehend, items which do not relate to the purpose of the search. That this occurs, however, does not render the search invalid, so long as it is authorized by a suitable search warrant and so long as the police, in executing that warrant, limit themselves to searching for items which may constitutionally be seized. Thus, while I would agree with petitioner that individual searches of private property through surreptitious eavesdropping with a warrant must be carefully circumscribed to avoid excessive invasion of privacy and security, I cannot agree that all such intrusions are constitutionally impermissible general searches.

* * *

The Court, however, seems irresistably determined to strike down the New York statute. The majority criticizes the *ex parte* nature of § 813–a court orders, the lack of a requirement that "exigent circumstances" be shown, and the fact that one court order authorizes "a series or a continuous surveillance." But where are such search warrant requirements to be found in the Fourth Amendment or in any prior case construing it? The Court appears intent upon creating out of whole cloth new constitutionally mandated warrant procedures carefully tailored to make eavesdrop warrants unobtainable. That is not a judicial function. The question here is whether *this* search complied with Fourth Amendment standards. There is no indication in this record that the District Attorney's office seized and used conversations not described in the Goldstein affidavit, nor that officials continued the search after the time when they had gathered the evidence which they sought. Given the constitutional adequacy of the Goldstein affidavit in terms of Fourth Amendment requirements of probable cause and particularity, I conclude that both the search and seizure in Steinman's office satisfied Fourth Amendment mandates. Regardless of how the Court would like eavesdropping legislation to read, our function ends in a state case with the determination of these questions.

Unregulated use of electronic surveillance devices by law enforcement officials and by private parties poses a grave threat to the privacy and security of our citizens. As the majority recognizes, New York is one of a handful of States that have reacted to this threat by enacting legislation that limits official use of all such devices to situations where designated officers obtain judicial authorization to eavesdrop. Except in these States, there is a serious lack of comprehensive and sensible legislation in this field, a need that has been noted by many, including the President's prestigious Commission on Law Enforcement and Administration of Justice (the "Crime Commission") in its just-published reports. Bills have been introduced at this session of Congress to fill this legislative gap, and extensive hearings are in progress. . . .

At least three positions have been presented at these hearings. Opponents of eavesdropping and wiretapping argue that they are so "odius" an invasion of privacy that they should never be tolerated. The Justice Department, in advocating the Administration's current position, asserts a more limited view; its bill would prohibit all wiretapping and eavesdropping by state and federal authorities except in cases involving the "national security," and in addition would ban judicial use of evidence gathered even in national security cases. A third position, adopted by many New York law enforcement personnel and by others, agrees that official eavesdropping and wiretapping must be stringently controlled but argues that such devices are irreplaceable investigative tools which are needed for the enforcement of criminal laws and which can be adequately regulated through legislation such as New York's § 813–a.

The grant of certiorari in this case has been widely noted, and our decision can be expected to have a substantial impact on the current legislative consideration of these issues. Today's majority does not, in so many words, hold that all wiretapping and eavesdropping are constitutionally impermissible. But by transparent indirection it achieves practically the same result by striking down the New York statute and imposing a series of requirements for legalized electronic surveillance that will be almost impossible to satisfy.

In so doing, the Court ignores or discounts the need for wiretapping authority and incredibly suggests that there has been no breakdown of federal law enforcement despite the unavailability of a federal statute legalizing electronic surveillance. The Court thereby impliedly disagrees with the carefully documented reports of the Crime Commission which, contrary to the Court's intimations, underline the serious proportions of professional criminal activity in this country, the failure of current national and state efforts to eliminate it, and the need for a statute permitting carefully controlled official use of electronic surveillance, particularly in dealing with organized crime and official corruption. How the Court can feel itself so much better qualified than the Commission, which spent months on its study, to assess the needs of law enforcement is beyond my comprehension. We have only just decided that reasonableness of a search under the Fourth Amendment must be determined by weighing the invasions of Fourth Amendment interests which wiretapping and eavesdropping entail against the public need justifying such invasions. In these terms, it would seem imperative that the Court at least deal with facts of the real world. This the Court utterly fails to do. In my view, its opinion is wholly unresponsive to the test of reasonableness under the Fourth Amendment.

The Court also seeks support in the fact that the Federal Government does not now condone electronic eavesdropping. But here the Court is treading on treacherous ground. It is true that the Department of Justice has now disowned the relevant findings and recommendations of the Crime Commission, and that it has recommended to the Congress a bill which would impose broad prohibitions on wiretapping and eavesdropping. But although the Department's communication to the Congress speaks of "exercis[ing] the full reach of our constitutional powers to outlaw electronic eavesdropping on private conversations," the fact is, as I have already indicated, that the bill does nothing of the kind. Both H.R. 5386 and its counterpart in the Senate, S. 928, provide that the prohibitions in the bill shall not be deemed to apply to interceptions in national security cases. Apparently, under this legislation, the President without court order would be permitted to authorize wiretapping or eavesdropping "to protect the Nation against actual or potential attack or other hostile acts of a foreign power or any other serious threat to the security of the United States, or to protect national security information against foreign intelligence activities."

There are several interesting aspects to this proposed national security exemption in light of the Court's opinion. First, there is no limitation on the President's power to delegate his authority, and it seems likely that at least the Attorney General would exercise it. Second, the national security exception would reach cases like sabotage and investigations of organizations controlled by a foreign government. For example, wiretapping to prove an individual is a member of the Communist Party, it is said, would be permissible under the statute. Third, information from authorized surveillance in the national security area would not be admissible in evidence; to the contrary, the surveillance would apparently be for investigative and informational use only, not for use in a criminal prosecution and not authorized because of any belief or suspicion that a crime is being committed or is about to be committed. Fourth, the Department of Justice has recommended that the Congress not await this Court's decision in the case now before us because whether or not the Court upholds the New York statute the power of Congress to enact the proposed legislation would not be affected. But if electronic surveillance is a "general search," or if it must be circumscribed in the manner the Court now suggests, how can surreptitious electronic surveillance of a suspected Communist or a suspected saboteur escape the strictures of the Fourth Amendment? It seems obvious from the Department of Justice bill that the present Administration believes that there are some purposes and uses of electronic surveillance which do not involve violations of the Fourth Amendment by the Executive Branch. Such being the case, even if the views of the Executive were to be the final answer in this case, the requirements imposed by the Court to constitutionalize wiretapping and eavesdropping are a far cry from the practice anticipated under the federal legislation now before the Congress.

But I do not think the views of the Executive should be dispositive of the broader Fourth Amendment issues raised in this case. If the security of the National Government is a sufficient interest to render eavesdropping reasonable, on what tenable basis can a contrary conclusion be reached when a State asserts a purpose to prevent the corruption of its major officials, to protect the integrity of its fundamental processes, and to maintain itself as a viable institution? The serious threat which organized crime poses to our society has been frequently documented. The interrelation between organized crime and corruption of governmental officials is likewise well established, and the enormous difficulty of eradicating both forms of social cancer is proved by the persistence of the problems if by nothing else. The Crime Commission has concluded that "only in New York have law enforcement officials been able to mount a relatively continuous and relatively successful attack on an organized crime problem," that "electronic surveillance techniques . . . have been *the* tools" making possible such an attack, and that practice under New York's § 813–a has achieved a proper balance between the interests of "privacy and justice." And New York County District Attorney Frank S. Hogan, who has been on the job almost as long as any member of this Court, has said of the need for legislation similar to § 813–a:

> "The judicially supervised system under which we operate has worked. It has served efficiently to protect the rights, liberties, property, and general welfare of the law-abiding members of our community. It has permitted us to undertake major investigations of organized crime. Without it, and I confine myself to top figures in the underworld, my own office could not have convicted Charles 'Lucky' Luciano, Jimmy Hines, Louis 'Lepke' Buchalter, Jacob 'Gurrah' Shapiro, Joseph 'Socks' Lanza, George Scalise, Frank Erickson, John 'Dio' Dioguardi, and Frank Carbo. Joseph 'Adonis' Doto, who was tried in New Jersey, was convicted and deported on evidence supplied by our office and obtained by assiduously following leads secured through wiretapping."
>
> . . .

To rebut such evidence of the reasonableness of regulated use of official eavesdropping, the Court presents only outdated statistics on the use of § 813–a in the organized crime and corruption arenas, the failure of the Congress thus far to enact similar legislation for federal law enforcement officials, and the blind hope that other "techniques and practices may well be developed that will operate just as speedily and certain." None of this is even remotely responsive to the question whether the use of eavesdropping techniques to unveil the debilitating corruption involved in this case was reasonable under the Fourth Amendment. At best, the Court puts forth an apologetic and grossly inadequate justification for frustrating New York law enforcement by invalidating § 813–a.

In any event, I do not consider this case a proper vehicle for resolving all of these broad constitutional and legislative issues raised by the problem of official use of wiretapping and eavesdropping. I would hold only that electronic surveillance was a reasonable investigative tool to apply in uncovering corruption among high state officials, compare Osborn v. United States, 385 U.S. 323, 87 S.Ct. 429, 17 L.Ed.2d 394, that the § 813–a court procedure as used in this case satisfied the Fourth Amendment's search warrant requirements, and that New York officials limited themselves to a constitutionally permissible search and seizure of petitioner's private conversations in executing that court order. Therefore, I would affirm.

[The decision in *Berger* was held not to apply to evidence acquired under 813–a prior to the date of *Berger*. Kaiser v. New York, 394 U.S. 280, 89 S.Ct. 1044 (1969)].

KATZ v. UNITED STATES

Supreme Court of the United States, 1967.
389 U.S. 347, 88 S.Ct. 507.

MR. JUSTICE STEWART delivered the opinion of the Court.

The petitioner was convicted in the District Court for the Southern District of California under an eight-count indictment charging him with transmitting wagering information by telephone from Los Angeles to Miami and Boston in violation of a federal statute. At trial the Government was permitted, over the petitioner's objection, to introduce evidence of the petitioner's end of telephone conversations, overheard by FBI agents who had attached an electronic listening and recording device to the outside of the public telephone booth from which he had placed his calls. In affirming his conviction, the Court of Appeals rejected the contention that the recordings had been obtained in violation of the Fourth Amendment, because "[t]here was no physical entrance into the area occupied by, [the petitioner]." We granted certiorari in order to consider the constitutional questions thus presented.

The petitioner has phrased those questions as follows:

"A. Whether a public telephone booth is a constitutionally protected area so that evidence obtained by attaching an electronic listening recording device to the top of such a booth is obtained in violation of the right to privacy of the user of the booth.

"B. Whether physical penetration of a constitutionally protected area is necessary before a search and seizure can be said to be violative of the Fourth Amendment to the United States Constitution."

We decline to adopt this formulation of the issues. In the first place the correct solution of Fourth Amendment problems is not necessarily promoted by incantation of the phrase "constitutionally protected area." Secondly, the Fourth Amendment cannot be translated into a general constitutional "right to privacy." That Amendment protects individual privacy against certain kinds of governmental intrusion, but its protections go further, and often have nothing to do with privacy at all. Other provisions of the Constitution protect personal privacy from other forms of governmental invasion. But the protection of a person's *general* right to privacy—his right to be let alone by other people—is, like the protection of his property and of his very life, left largely to the law of the individual States.

Because of the misleading way the issues have been formulated, the parties have attached great significance to the characterization of the telephone booth from which the petitioner placed his calls. The petitioner has strenuously argued that the booth was a "constitutionally protected area." The Government has maintained with equal vigor that it was not. But this effort to decide whether or not a given "area," viewed in the abstract, is "constitutionally protected" deflects attention from the problem presented by this case. For the Fourth Amendment protects people, not places. What a person knowingly exposes to the public, even in his own home or office, is not a subject of Fourth Amendment protection. But what he seeks to preserve as private, even in an area accessible to the public may be constitutionally protected.

The Government stresses the fact that the telephone booth from which the petitioner made his calls was constructed partly of glass, so that he was as visible after he entered it as he would have been if he had remained outside. But what he sought to exclude when he entered the booth was not the intruding eye—it was the uninvited ear. He did not shed his right to do so simply because he made his calls from a place where he might be seen. No less than an individual in a business office, in a friend's apartment, or in a taxicab, a person in a telephone booth may rely upon the protection of the Fourth Amendment. One who occupies it, shuts the door behind him, and pays the toll that permits him to place a call, is surely entitled to assume that the words he utters into the mouthpiece will not be broadcast to the world. To read the Constitution more narrowly is to ignore the vital role that the public telephone has come to play in private communication.

The Government contends, however, that the activities of its agents in this case should not be tested by Fourth Amendment requirements, for the surveillance technique they employed involved no physical penetration of the telephone booth from which the petitioner placed his calls. It is true that the absence of such penetration was at one time thought to foreclose further Fourth Amendment inquiry, although a closely divided Court supposed in *Olmstead* that surveillance without any trespass and without the seizure of any material object fell outside the ambit of the Constitution, we have since departed from the narrow view on which that decision rested. Indeed, we have expressly held that the Fourth Amendment governs not only the seizure of tangible items, but extends as well to the recording of oral statements overheard without any "technical trespass under . . . local property law." Once this much is acknowledged, and once it is recognized that the Fourth Amendment protects people—and not simply "areas"—against unreasonable searches and seizures it becomes clear that the reach of that Amendment cannot turn upon the presence or absence of a physical intrusion into any given enclosure.

We conclude that the underpinnings of *Olmstead* and *Goldman* have been so eroded by our subsequent decisions that the "trespass" doctrine there enunciated can no longer be regarded as controlling. The Government's activities in electronically listening to and recording the petitioner's words violated the privacy upon which he justifiably relied while using the telephone booth and thus constituted a "search and seizure" within the meaning of the Fourth Amendment. The fact that the electronic device employed to achieve that end did not happen to penetrate the wall of the booth can have no constitutional significance.

The question remaining for decision, then, is whether the search and seizure conducted in this case complied with constitutional standards. In that regard, the Government's position is that its agents acted in an entirely defensible manner: They did not begin their electronic surveillance until investigation of the petitioner's activities had established a strong probability that he was using the telephone in question to transmit gambling information to persons in other States, in violation of federal law. Moreover, the surveillance was limited, both in scope and in duration, to the specific purpose of establishing the contents of the petitioner's unlawful telephonic communications. The agents confined their surveillance to the brief periods during which he used the telephone booth, and they took great care to overhear only the conversations of the petitioner himself.

Accepting this account of the Government's actions as accurate, it is clear that this surveillance was so narrowly circumscribed that a duly authorized magistrate, properly notified of the need for such investigation, specifically informed of the basis on which it was to proceed, and clearly apprised of the precise intrusion it would entail, could constitutionally have authorized, with appropriate safeguards, the very limited search and seizure that the Government asserts in fact took place. . . .

The Government urges that, because its agents relied upon the decisions in *Olmstead* and *Goldman*, and because they did no more here than they might properly have done with prior judicial sanction, we should retroactively validate their conduct. That we cannot do.

It is apparent that the agents in this case acted with restraint. Yet the inescapable fact is that this restraint was imposed by the agents themselves, not by a judicial officer. They were not required, before commencing the search, to present their estimate of probable cause for detached scrutiny by a neutral magistrate. They were not compelled, during the conduct of the search itself, to observe precise limits established in advance by a specific court order. Nor were they directed, after the search had been completed, to notify the authorizing magistrate in detail of all that had been seized. In the absence of such safeguards, this Court has never sustained a search upon the sole ground that officers reasonably expected to find evidence of a particular crime and voluntarily confined their activities to the least intrusive means consistent with that end. * * *

[The government argues that] that surveillance of a telephone booth should be exempted from the usual requirement of advance authorization by a magistrate upon a showing of probable cause. We cannot agree. Omission of such authorization

> "bypasses the safeguards provided by an objective predetermination of probable cause, and substitutes instead the far less reliable procedure of an after-the-event justification for the . . . search, too likely to be subtly influenced by the familiar shortcomings of hindsight judgment."

And bypassing a neutral predetermination of the *scope* of a search leaves individuals secure from Fourth Amendment violations "only in the discretion of the police."

These considerations do not vanish when the search in question is transferred from the setting of a home, an office, or a hotel room, to that of a telephone booth. Wherever a man may be, he is entitled to know that he will remain free from unreasonable searches and seizures. The government agents here ignored "the procedure of antecedent justification . . . that is central to the Fourth Amendment," a procedure that we hold to be a constitutional precondition of the kind of electronic surveillance involved in this case. Because the surveillance here failed to meet that condition, and because it led to the petitioner's conviction, the judgment must be reversed.

It is so ordered.

Judgment reversed.

MR. JUSTICE MARSHALL took no part in the consideration or decision of this case.

[The concurring opinion of JUSTICES DOUGLAS and BRENNAN is omitted.]

MR. JUSTICE HARLAN, concurring.

I join the opinion of the Court, which I read to hold only (a) that an enclosed telephone booth is an area where, like a home, a person has a constitutionally protected reasonable expectation of privacy; (b) that electronic as well as physical intrusion into a place that is in this sense private may constitute a violation of the Fourth Amendment; and (c) that the invasion of a constitutionally protected area by federal authorities is, as the Court has long held, presumptively unreasonable in the absence of a search warrant.

As the Court's opinion states, "The Fourth Amendment protects people, not places." The question, however, is what protection it affords to those people. Generally, as here, the answer to that question requires reference to a "place." My understanding of the rule that has emerged from prior decisions is that there is a twofold requirement, first that a person have exhibited an actual (subjective) expectation of privacy and, second, that the expectation be one that society is prepared to recognize as "reasonable." Thus a man's home is, for most purposes, a place where he expects privacy, but objects, activities, or statements that he exposes to the "plain view" of outsiders are not "protected" because no intention to keep them to himself has been exhibited. On the other hand, conversations in the open would not be protected against being overheard, for the expectation of privacy under the circumstances would be unreasonable.

The critical fact in this case is that "[o]ne who occupies it, [a telephone booth] shuts the door behind him, and pays the toll that permits him to place a call, is surely entitled to assume" that his conversation is not being intercepted. The point is not that the booth is "accessible to the public" at other times, but that it is a temporarily private place whose momentary occupants' expectations of freedom from intrusion are recognized as reasonable. * * *

Finally, I do not read the Court's opinion to declare that no interception of a conversation one-half of which occurs in a public telephone booth can be reasonable in the absence of a warrant. As elsewhere under the Fourth Amendment, warrants are the general rule, to which the legitimate needs of law enforcement may demand specific exceptions. It will be time enough to consider any such exceptions when an appropriate occasion presents itself, and I agree with the Court that this is not one.

[The concurring opinion of JUSTICE WHITE is omitted.]

MR. JUSTICE BLACK, dissenting.

If I could agree with the Court that eavesdropping carried on by electronic means (equivalent to wiretapping) constitutes a "search" or "seizure," I would be happy to join the Court's opinion. For on that premise my BROTHER STEWART sets out methods in accord with the Fourth Amendment to guide States in the enactment and enforcement of laws passed to regulate wiretapping by government. In this respect today's opinion differs sharply from Berger v. State of New York, decided last Term, which held void on its face a New York statute authorizing wiretapping on warrants issued by magistrates on showings of probable causes. The *Berger* case also set up what appeared to be insuperable obstacles to the valid passage of such wiretapping laws by States. The Court's opinion in this case, however, removes the doubts about state power in this field and abates to a large extent the confusion and near paralyzing effect of the *Berger* holding. Notwithstanding these good efforts of the Court, I am still unable to agree with its interpretation of the Fourth Amendment.

* * *

I do not deny that common sense requires and that this Court often has said that the Bill of Rights' safeguards should be given a liberal construction. This principle, however, does not justify construing the search and seizure amendment as applying to eavesdropping or the "seizure" of conversations. The Fourth Amendment was aimed directly at the abhorred practice of breaking in, ransacking and seaching homes and other buildings and seizing peoples' personal belongings without warrants issued by magistrates. The Amendment deserves, and this Court has given it, a liberal construction in order to protect against warrantless searches of buildings and seizures of tangible personal effects. But until today this Court has refused to say that eavesdropping comes within the ambit of Fourth Amendment restrictions. * * *

[A]lthough the Court attempts to convey the impression that for some reason today *Olmstead* and *Goldman* are no longer good law, it must face up to the fact that these cases have never been overruled or even "eroded." It is the Court's opinions in this case and *Berger* which for the first time since 1790, when the Fourth Amendment was adopted, have declared that eavesdropping is subject to Fourth Amendment restrictions and that conversation can be "seized." I must align myself with all those judges who up to this year have never been able to impute such a meaning to the words of the Amendment.

Since I see no way in which the words of the Fourth Amendment can be construed to apply to eavesdropping, that closes the matter for me. In interpreting the Bill of Rights, I willingly go as far as a liberal construction of the language takes me, but I simply cannot in good conscience give a meaning to words which they have never before been thought to have and which they certainly do not have in common ordinary usage. I will not distort the words of the Amendment in order to "keep the Constitution up to date" or "to bring it into harmony with the times." It was never meant for this Court to have such power, which in effect would make us a continuously functioning constitutional convention.

With this decision the Court has completed, I hope, its rewriting of the Fourth Amendment, which started only recently when the Court began referring incessantly to the Fourth Amendment not so much as a law against *unreasonable* searches and seizures as one to protect an individual's privacy. By clever word juggling the Court finds it plausible to argue that language aimed specifically at searches and seizures of things that can be searched and seized may, to protect privacy, be applied to eavesdropped evidence of conversations that can neither be searched nor seized. Few things happen to an individual that do not affect his privacy in one way or another. Thus, by arbitrarily substituting the Court's language, designed to protect privacy, for the Constitution's language, designed to protect against unreasonable searches and seizures, the Court has made the Fourth Amendment its vehicle for holding all laws violative of the Constitution which offend the Court's broadest concept of privacy. As I said in Griswold v. State of Connecticut, "The Court talks about a constitutional 'right of privacy' as though there is some constitutional provision or provisions forbidding any law ever to be passed which might abridge the 'privacy' of individuals. But there is not." I made clear in that dissent my fear of the dangers involved when this Court uses the "broad, abstract and ambiguous concept" of "privacy" as a "comprehensive substitute for the Fourth Amendment's guarantee against 'unreasonable searches and seizures.' "

The Fourth Amendment protects privacy only to the extent that it prohibits unreasonable searches and seizures of "persons, houses, papers and effects." No general right is created by the Amendment so as to give this Court the unlimited power to hold unconstitutional everything which affects privacy. Certainly the Framers, well acquainted as they were with the excesses of governmental power, did not intend to grant this Court such omnipotent lawmaking authority as that. The history of governments proves that it is dangerous to freedom to repose such powers in courts.

For these reasons I respectfully dissent.

[Katz was held to be inapplicable to overhearings occurring prior to the date it was decided. See Desist v. United States, 394 U.S. 244, 89 S.Ct. 1030 (1969)].

NOTES

1. The history and interpretation of 47 U.S.C.A. § 605, the federal statute forbidding wiretapping, have been omitted because far-reaching legislative changes were enacted by Congress in 1968 as Title III of the "Omnibus Crime Control and Safe Streets Act". A discussion of the major cases construing the former § 605 may be found in Lee v. Florida, 392 U.S. 378, 88 S.Ct. 2096 (1968).

2. In light of the *Berger* and *Katz* opinions, consider the constitutionality of the following provisions of Title III governing eavesdropping and wiretapping.

TITLE III—WIRETAPPING AND ELECTRONIC SURVEILLANCE

FINDINGS

SEC. 801. On the basis of its own investigations and of published studies, the Congress makes the following findings:

(a) Wire communications are normally conducted through the use of facilities which form part of an interstate network. The same facilities are used for interstate and intrastate communications. There has been extensive wiretapping carried on without legal sanctions, and without the consent of any of the parties to the conversation. Electronic, mechanical, and other intercepting devices are being used to overhear oral conversations made in private, without the consent of any of the parties to such communications. The contents of these communications and evidence derived therefrom are being used by public and private parties as evidence in court and administrative proceedings, and by persons whose activities affect interstate commerce. The possession, manufacture, distribution, advertising, and use of these devices are facilitated by interstate commerce.

(b) In order to protect effectively the privacy of wire and oral communications, to protect the integrity of court and administrative proceedings, and to prevent the obstruction of interstate commerce, it is necessary for Congress to define on a uniform basis the circumstances and conditions under which the interception of wire and oral communications may be authorized, to prohibit any unauthorized interception of such communications, and the use of the contents thereof in evidence in courts and administrative proceedings.

(c) Organized criminals make extensive use of wire and oral communications in their criminal activities. The interception of such communications to obtain evidence of the commission of crimes or to prevent their commission is an indispensable aid to law enforcement and the administration of justice.

(d) To safeguard the privacy of innocent persons, the interception of wire or oral communications where none of the parties to the communication has consented to the interception should be allowed only when authorized by a court of competent jurisdiction and should remain under the control and supervision of the authorizing court. Interception of wire and oral communications should further be limited to certain major types of offenses and specific categories of crime with assurances that the interception is justified and that the information obtained thereby will not be misused.

SEC. 802. Part I of title 18, United States Code is amended by adding at the end the following new chapter:

"Chapter 119. WIRE INTERCEPTION AND INTERCEPTION OF ORAL COMMUNICATIONS

"§ 2510. Definitions

"As used in this chapter—

"(1) 'wire communication' means any communication made in whole or in part through the use of facilities for the transmission of communications by the aid of wire, cable, or other like connection between the point of origin and the point of reception furnished or operated by any person engaged as a common carrier in providing or operating such facilities for the transmission of interstate or foreign communications;

"(2) 'oral communication' means any oral communication uttered by a person exhibiting an expectation that such communication is not subject to interception under circumstances justifying such expectation;

"(3) 'State' means any State of the United States, the District of Columbia, the Commonwealth of Puerto Rico, and any territory or possession of the United States;

"(4) 'intercept' means the aural acquisition of the contents of any wire or oral communication through the use of any electronic, mechanical, or other device.

"(5) 'electronic, mechanical, or other device' means any device or apparatus which can be used to intercept a wire or oral communication other than—

"(a) any telephone or telegraph instrument, equipment or facility, or any component thereof, (i) furnished to the subscriber or user by a communications common carrier in the ordinary course of its business and being used by the subscriber or user in the ordinary course of its business; or (ii) being used by a communications common carrier in the ordinary course of its business, or by an investigative or law enforcement officer in the ordinary course of his duties;

"(b) a hearing aid or similar device being used to correct subnormal hearing to not better than normal;

"(6) 'person' means any employee, or agent of the United States or any State or political subdivision thereof, and any individual, partnership, association, joint stock company, trust, or corporation;

"(7) 'Investigative or law enforcement officer' means any officer of the United States or of a State or political subdivision thereof, who is empowered by law to conduct investigations of or to make arrests for offenses enumerated in this chapter, and any attorney authorized by law to prosecute or participate in the prosecution of such offenses;

"(8) 'contents', when used with respect to any wire or oral communication, includes any information concerning the identity of the parties to such communication or the existence, substance, purport, or meaning of that communication;

"(9) 'Judge of competent jurisdiction' means—

"(a) a judge of a United States district court or a United States court of appeals; and

"(b) a judge of any court of general criminal jurisdiction of a State who is authorized by a statute of that State to enter orders authorizing interceptions of wire or oral communications;

"(10) 'communication common carrier' shall have the same meaning which is given the term 'common carrier' by section 153(h) of title 47 of the United States Code; and

"(11) 'aggrieved person' means a person who was a party to any intercepted wire or oral communication or a person against whom the interception was directed.

"§ 2511. Interception and disclosure of wire or oral communications prohibited

"(1) Except as otherwise specifically provided in this chapter any person who—

"(a) willfully intercepts, endeavors to intercept, or procures any other person to intercept or endeavor to intercept, any wire or oral communication;

"(b) willfully uses, endeavors to use, or procures any other person to use or endeavor to use any electronic, mechanical, or other device to intercept any oral communication when—

"(i) such device is affixed to, or otherwise transmits a signal through, a wire, cable, or other like connection used in wire communication; or

"(ii) such device transmits communications by radio, or interferes with the transmission of such communication; or

"(iii) such person knows, or has reason to know, that such device or any component thereof has been sent through the mail or transported in interstate or foreign commerce; or

"(iv) such use or endeavor to use (A) takes place on the premises of any business or other commercial establishment the operations of which affect interstate or foreign commerce; or (B) obtains or is for the purpose of obtaining information relating to the operations of any business or other commercial establishment the operations of which affect interstate or foreign commerce; or

"(v) such person acts in the District of Columbia, the Commonwealth of Puerto Rico, or any territory or possession of the United States;

"(c) willfully discloses, or endeavors to disclose, to any other person the contents of any wire or oral communication, knowing or having reason to know that the information was obtained through the interception of a wire or oral communication in violation of this subsection; or

"(d) willfully uses, or endeavors to use, the contents of any wire or oral communication, knowing or having reason to know that the information was obtained through the interception of a wire or oral communication in violation of this subsection;

shall be fined not more than $10,000 or imprisoned not more than five years, or both.

"(2)(a) It shall not be unlawful under this chapter for an operator of a switchboard, or an officer, employee, or agent of any communication common carrier, whose facilities are used in the transmission of a wire communication, to intercept, disclose, or use that communication in the normal course of his employment while engaged in any activity which is a necessary incident to the rendition of his service or to the protection of the rights or property of the carrier of such communication: *Provided,* That said communication common carriers shall not utilize service observing or random monitoring except for mechanical or service quality control checks.

"(b) It shall not be unlawful under this chapter for an officer, employee, or agent of the Federal Communications Commission, in the normal course of his employment and in discharge of the monitoring responsibilities exercised by the Commission in the enforcement of chapter 5 of title 47 of the United States Code, to intercept a wire communication, or oral communication transmitted by radio, or to disclose or use the information thereby obtained.

"(c) It shall not be unlawful under this chapter for a person acting under color of law to intercept a wire or oral communication, where such person is a party to the communication or one of the parties to the communication has given prior consent to such interception.

"(d) It shall not be unlawful under this chapter for a person not acting under color of law to intercept a wire or oral communication where such person is a party to the communication or where one of the parties to the communication has given prior consent to such interception unless such communication is intercepted for the purpose of committing any criminal or tortious act in violation of the Constitution or laws of the United States or of any State or for the purpose of committing any other injurious act.

"(3) Nothing contained in this chapter or in section 605 of the Communications Act of 1934 (48 Stat. 1143; 47 U.S.C. 605) shall limit the constitutional power of the President to take such measures as he deems necessary to protect the Nation against actual or potential attack or other hostile acts of a foreign power, to obtain foreign intelligence information deemed essential to the security of the United States, or to protect national security information against foreign intelligence activities. Nor shall anything contained in this chapter be deemed to limit the constitutional power of the President to take such measures as he deems necessary to protect the United States against the overthrow of the Government by force or other unlawful means, or against any other clear and present danger to the structure or existence of the Government. The contents of any wire or oral communication intercepted by authority of the President in the exercise of the foregoing powers may be received in evidence in any trial hearing, or other proceeding only where such interception was reasonable, and shall not be otherwise used or disclosed except as is necessary to implement that power.

* * *

"§ 2515. Prohibition of use as evidence of intercepted wire or oral communications

"Whenever any wire or oral communication has been intercepted, no part of the contents of such communication and no evidence derived therefrom may be received in evidence in any trial, hearing, or other proceeding in or before any court, grand jury, department, officer, agency, regulatory body, legislative committee, or other authority of the United States, a State, or a political subdivision thereof if the disclosure of that information would be in violation of this chapter.

"§ 2516. Authorization for interception of wire or oral communications

"(1) The Attorney General, or any Assistant Attorney General specially designated by the Attorney General, may authorize an application to a Federal judge of competent jurisdiction for, and such judge may grant in conformity with section 2518 of this chapter an order authorizing or approving the interception of wire or oral communications by the Federal Bureau of Investigation, or a Federal agency having responsibility for the investigation of the offense as to which the application is made, when such interception may provide or has provided evidence of—

"(a) any offense punishable by death or by imprisonment for more than one year under sections 2274 through 2277 of title 42 of the United States Codes (relating to the enforcement of the Atomic Energy Act of 1954), or under the following chapters of this title: chapter 37 (relating to espionage), chapter 105 (relating to sabotage), chapter 115 (relating to treason), or chapter 102 (relating to riots);

"(b) a violation of section 186 or section 501(c) of title 29, United States Code (dealing with restrictions on payments and loans to labor organizations), or any offense which involves murder, kidnapping, robbery, or extortion, and which is punishable under this title;

"(c) any offense which is punishable under the following sections of this title: section 201 (bribery of public officials and witnesses), section 224 (bribery in sporting contests), section 1084 (transmission of wagering information), section 1503 (influencing or injuring an officer, juror, or witness generally), section 1510 (obstruction of criminal investigations), section 1751 (Presidential assassinations, kidnapping, and assault), section 1951 (interference with commerce by threats or violence), section 1952 (interstate and foreign travel or transportation in aid of racketeering enterprises), section 1954 (offer, acceptance, or solicitation to influence operations of employee benefit plan), section 659 (theft from interstate shipment), section 664 (embezzlement from pension and welfare funds), or sections 2314 and 2315 (interstate transportation of stolen property);

"(d) any offense involving counterfeiting punishable under section 471, 472, or 473 of this title;

"(e) any offense involving bankruptcy fraud or the manufacture, importation, receiving, concealment, buying, selling or otherwise dealing in narcotic drugs, marihuana, or other dangerous drugs, punishable under any law of the United States;

"(f) any offense including extortionate credit transactions under sections 892, 893, or 894 of this title; or

"(g) any conspiracy to commit any of the foregoing offenses.

"(2) The principal prosecuting attorney of any State, or the principal prosecuting attorney of any political subdivision thereof, if such attorney is authorized by a statute of that State to make application to a State court judge of competent jurisdiction for an order authorizing or approving the interception of wire or oral communications, may apply to such judge for, and such judge may grant in conformity with section 2518 of this chapter and with the applicable State statute an order authorizing, or approving the interception of wire or oral communications by investigative or law enforcement officers having responsibility for the investigation of the offense as to which the application is made, when such interception may provide or has provided evidence of the commission of the offense of murder, kidnapping, gambling, robbery, bribery, extortion, or dealing in narcotic drugs, marihuana or other dangerous drugs, or other crime dangerous to life, limb, or property, and punishable by imprisonment for more than one year, designated in any applicable State statute authorizing such interception, or any conspiracy to commit any of the foregoing offenses.

"§ 2517. Authorization for disclosure and use of intercepted wire or oral communications

"(1) Any investigative or law enforcement officer who, by any means authorized by this chapter, has obtained knowledge of the contents of any wire or oral communication, or evidence derived therefrom, may disclose such contents to another investigative or law enforcement officer to the extent that such disclosure is appropriate to the proper performance of the official duties of the officer making or receiving the disclosure.

"(2) Any investigative or law enforcement officer who, by any means authorized by this chapter, has obtained knowledge of the contents of any wire or oral communication or evidence derived therefrom may use such contents to the extent such use is appropriate to the proper performance of his official duties.

"(3) Any person who has received, by any means authorized by this chapter, any information concerning a wire or oral communication, or evidence derived therefrom intercepted in accordance with the provisions of this chapter may disclose the contents of that communication or such derivative evidence while giving testimony under oath or affirmation in any criminal proceeding in any court of the United States or of any State or in any Federal or State grand jury proceeding.

"(4) No otherwise privileged wire or oral communication intercepted in accordance with, or in violation of, the provisions of this chapter shall lose its privileged character.

"(5) When an investigative or law enforcement officer, while engaged in intercepting wire or oral communications in the manner authorized herein, intercepts wire or oral communications relating to offenses other than those specified in the order of authorization or approval, the contents thereof, and evidence derived therefrom, may be disclosed or used as provided in subsections (1) and (2) of this section. Such contents and any evidence derived therefrom may be used under subsection (3) of this section when authorized or approved by a judge of competent jurisdiction where such judge finds on subsequent application that the contents were otherwise intercepted in accordance with the provisions of this chapter. Such application shall be made as soon as practicable.

"§ 2518. Procedure for interception of wire or oral communications

"(1) Each application for an order authorizing or approving the interception of a wire or oral communication shall be made in writing upon oath or affirmation to a judge of competent jurisdiction and shall state the applicant's authority to make such application. Each application shall include the following information:

"(a) the identity of the investigative or law enforcement officer making the application, and the officer authorizing the application;

"(b) a full and complete statement of the facts and circumstances relied upon by the applicant, to justify his belief that an order should be issued, including (i) details as to the particular offense that has been, is being, or is about to be committed, (ii) a particular description of the nature and location of the facilities from which or the place where the communication is to be intercepted, (iii) a particular description of the type of communications sought to be intercepted, (iv) the identity of the person, if known, committing the offense and whose communications are to be intercepted;

"(c) a full and complete statement as to whether or not other investigative procedures have been tried and failed or why they reasonably appear to be unlikely to succeed if tried or to be too dangerous;

"(d) a statement of the period of time for which the interception is required to be maintained. If the nature of the investigation is such that the authorization for interception should not automatically terminate when the described type of communication has been first obtained, a particular description of facts establishing probable cause to believe that additional communications of the same type will occur thereafter;

"(e) a full and complete statement of the facts concerning all previous applications known to the individual authorizing and making the application, made to any judge for authorization to intercept, or for approval of interceptions of, wire or oral communications involving any of the same persons, facilities or places specified in the application, and the action taken by the judge on each such application; and "(f) where the application is for the extension of an order, a statement setting forth the results thus far obtained from the interception, or a reasonable explanation of the failure to obtain such results.

"(2) The judge may require the applicant to furnish additional testimony or documentary evidence in support of the application.

"(3) Upon such application the judge may enter an ex parte order, as requested or as modified, authorizing or approving interception of wire or oral communications within the territorial jurisdiction of the court in which the judge is sitting, if the judge determines on the basis of the facts submitted by the applicant that—

"(a) there is probable cause for belief that an individual is committing, has committed, or is about to commit a particular offense enumerated in section 2516 of this chapter;

"(b) there is probable cause for belief that particular communications concerning that offense will be obtained through such interception;

"(c) normal investigative procedures have been tried and have failed or reasonably appear to be unlikely to succeed if tried or to be too dangerous;

"(d) there is probable cause for belief that the facilities from which, or the place where, the wire or oral communications are to be intercepted are being used, or are about to be used, in connection with the commission of such offense, or are leased to, listed in the name of, or commonly used by such person.

"(4) Each order authorizing or approving the interception of any wire or oral communication shall specify—

"(a) the identity of the person, if known, whose communications are to be intercepted;

"(b) the nature and location of the communications facilities as to which, or the place where, authority to intercept is granted;

"(c) a particular description of the type of communication sought to be intercepted, and a statement of the particular offense to which it relates;

"(d) the identity of the agency authorized to intercept the communications, and of the person authorizing the application; and

"(e) the period of time during which such interception is authorized, including a statement as to whether or not the interception shall automatically terminate when the described communication has been first obtained.

"(5) No order entered under this section may authorize or approve the interception of any wire or oral communication for any period longer than is necessary to achieve the objective of the authorization, nor in any event longer than thirty days. Extensions of an order may be granted, but only upon application for an extension made in accordance with subsection (1) of this section and the court making the findings required by subsection (3) of this section. The period of extension shall be no longer than the authorizing judge deems necessary to achieve the purposes for which it was granted and in no event for longer than thirty days. Every order and extension thereof shall contain a provision that the authorization to intercept shall be executed as soon as practicable, shall be conducted in such a way as to minimize the interception of communications not otherwise subject to interception under this chapter, and must terminate upon attainment of the authorized objective, or in any event in thirty days.

"(6) Whenever an order authorizing interception is entered pursuant to this chapter, the order may require reports to be made to the judge who issued the order showing what progress has been made toward achievement of the authorized objective and the need for continued interception. Such reports shall be made at such intervals as the judge may require.

"(7) Notwithstanding any other provision of this chapter, any investigative or law enforcement officer, specially designated by the Attorney General or by the principal prosecuting attorney of any State or subdivision thereof acting pursuant to a statute of that State, who reasonably determines that—

> "(a) an emergency situation exists with respect to conspiratorial activities threatening the national security interest or to conspiratorial activities characteristic of organized crime that requires a wire or oral communication to be intercepted before an order authorizing such interception can with due diligence be obtained, and
>
> "(b) there are grounds upon which an order could be entered under this chapter to authorize such interception,

may intercept such wire or oral communication if an application for an order approving the interception is made in accordance with this section within forty-eight hours after the interception has occurred, or begins to occur. In the absence of an order, such interception shall immediately terminate when the communication sought is obtained or when the application for the order is denied, whichever is earlier. In the event such application for approval is denied, or in any other case where the interception is terminated without an order having been issued, the contents of any wire or oral communication intercepted shall be treated as having been obtained in violation of this chapter, and an inventory shall be served as provided for in subsection (d) of this section on the person named in the application.

"(8)(a) The contents of any wire or oral communication intercepted by any means authorized by this chapter shall, if possible, be recorded on tape or wire or other comparable device. The recording of the contents of any wire or oral communication under this subsection shall be done in such way as will protect the recording from editing or other alterations. Immediately upon the expiration of the period of the order, or extensions thereof, such recordings shall be made available to the judge issuing such order and sealed under his directions. Custody of the recordings shall be wherever the judge orders. They shall not be destroyed except upon an order of the issuing or denying judge and in any event shall be kept for ten years. Duplicate recordings may be made for use or disclosure pursuant to the provisions of subsections (1) and (2) of section 2517 of this chapter for investigations. The presence of the seal provided for by this subsection, or a satisfactory explanation for the absence thereof, shall be a prerequisite for the use or disclosure of the contents of any wire or oral communication or evidence derived therefrom under subsection (3) of section 2517.

"(b) Applications made and orders granted under this chapter shall be sealed by the judge. Custody of the applications and orders shall be wherever the judge directs. Such applications and orders shall be disclosed only upon a showing of good cause before a judge of competent jurisdiction and shall not be destroyed except on order of the issuing or denying judge, and in any event shall be kept for ten years.

"(c) Any violation of the provisions of this subsection may be punished as contempt of the issuing or denying judge.

"(d) Within a reasonable time but not later than ninety days after the filing of an application for an order of approval under section 2518(7)(b) which is denied or the termination of the period of an order or extensions thereof, the issuing or denying judge shall cause to be served, on the persons named in the order or the application, and such other parties to intercepted communications as the judge may determine in his discretion that is in the interest of justice, an inventory which shall include notice of—

"(1) the fact of the entry of the order or the application;

"(2) the date of the entry and the period of authorized, approved or disapproved interception, or the denial of the application; and

"(3) the fact that during the period wire or oral communications were or were not intercepted.

The judge, upon the filing of a motion, may in his discretion make available to such person or his counsel for inspection such portions of the intercepted communications, applications and orders as the judge determines to be in the interest of justice. On an ex parte showing of good cause to a judge of competent jurisdiction the serving of the inventory required by this subsection may be postponed.

"(9) The contents of any intercepted wire or oral communication or evidence derived therefrom shall not be received in evidence or otherwise disclosed in any trial, hearing, or other proceeding in a Federal or State court unless each party, not less than ten days before the trial, hearing, or proceeding, has been furnished with a copy of the court order, and accompanying application, under which the interception was authorized or approved. This ten-day period may be waived by the judge if he finds that it was not possible to furnish the party with the above information ten days before the trial, hearing, or proceeding and that the party will not be prejudiced by the delay in receiving such information.

"(10)(a) Any aggrieved person in any trial, hearing, or proceeding in or before any court, department, officer, agency, regulatory body, or other authority of the United States, a State, or a political subdivision thereof, may move to suppress the contents of any intercepted wire or oral communication, or evidence derived therefrom, on the grounds that—

"(i) the communication was unlawfully intercepted;

"(ii) the order of authorization or approval under which it was intercepted is insufficient on its face; or

"(iii) the interception was not made in conformity with the order of authorization or approval.

Such motion shall be made before the trial, hearing, or proceeding unless there was no opportunity to make such motion or the person was not aware of the grounds of the motion. If the motion is granted, the contents of the intercepted wire or oral communication, or evidence derived therefrom, shall be treated as having been obtained in violation of this chapter. The judge, upon the filing of such motion by the aggrieved person, may in his discretion make available to the aggrieved person or his counsel for inspection such portions of the intercepted communication or evidence derived therefrom as the judge determines to be in the interests of justice.

"(b) In addition to any other right to appeal, the United States shall have the right to appeal from an order granting a motion to suppress made under paragraph (a) of this subsection, or the denial of an application for an order of approval, if the United States attorney shall certify to the judge or other official granting such motion or denying such application that the appeal is not taken for purposes of delay. Such appeal shall be taken within thirty days after the date the order was entered and shall be diligently prosecuted.

"§ 2519. Reports concerning intercepted wire or oral communications

"(1) Within thirty days after the expiration of an order (or each extension thereof) entered under section 2518, or the denial of an order approving an interception, the issuing or denying judge shall report to the Administrative Office of the United States Courts—

"(a) the fact that an order or extension was applied for;

"(b) the kind of order or extension applied for;

"(c) the fact that the order or extension was granted as applied for, was modified, or was denied;

"(d) the period of interceptions authorized by the order, and the number and duration of any extensions of the order;

"(e) the offense specified in the order or application, or extension of an order;

"(f) the identity of the applying investigative or law enforcement officer and agency making the application and the person authorizing the application; and

"(g) the nature of the facilities from which or the place where communications were to be intercepted.

"(2) In January of each year the Attorney General, an Assistant Attorney General specially designated by the Attorney General, or the principal prosecuting attorney of a State, or the principal prosecuting attorney for any political subdivision of a State, shall report to the Administrative Office of the United States Courts—

"(a) the information required by paragraphs (a) through (g) of subsection (1) of this section with respect to each application for an order or extension made during the preceding calendar year;

"(b) a general description of the interceptions made under such order or extension, including (i) the approximate nature and frequency of incriminating communications intercepted, (ii) the approximate nature and frequency of other communications intercepted, (iii) the approximate number of persons whose communications were intercepted, and (iv) the approximate nature, amount, and cost of the manpower and other resources used in the interceptions;

"(c) the number of arrests resulting from interceptions made under such order or extension, and the offenses for which arrests were made;

"(d) the number of trials resulting from such interceptions;

"(e) the number of motions to suppress made with respect to such interceptions, and the number granted or denied;

"(f) the number of convictions resulting from such interceptions and the offenses for which the convictions were obtained and a general assessment of the importance of the interceptions; and

"(g) the information required by paragraphs (b) through (f) of this subsection with respect to orders or extensions obtained in a preceding calendar year.

"(3) In April of each year the Director of the Administrative Office of the United States Courts shall transmit to the Congress a full and complete report concerning the number of applications for orders authorizing or approving the interception of wire or oral communications and the number of orders and extensions granted or denied during the preceding calendar year. Such report shall include a summary and analysis of the data required to be filed with the Administrative Office by subsections (1) and (2) of this section. The Director of the Administrative Office of the United States Courts is authorized to issue binding regulations dealing with the content and form of the reports required to be filed by subsections (1) and (2) of this section.

"§ 2520. Recovery of civil damages authorized

"Any person whose wire or oral communication is intercepted, disclosed, or used in violation of this chapter shall (1) have a civil cause of action against any person who intercepts, discloses, or uses, or procures any other person to intercept, disclose, or use such communications, and (2) be entitled to recover from any such person—

"(a) actual damages but not less than liquidated damages computed at the rate of $100 a day for each day of violation or $1,000, whichever is higher;

"(b) punitive damages; and

"(c) a reasonable attorney's fee and other litigation costs reasonably incurred.

A good faith reliance on a court order or on the provisions of section 2518 (7) of this chapter shall constitute a complete defense to any civil or criminal action brought under this chapter."

* * *

3. § 2511(3) infers that the President may, in the exercise of his "constitutional power" to "protect the Nation against actual or potential attack or other hostile acts of a foreign power, to obtain foreign intelligence information deemed essential to the security of the United States, or to protect national security information against foreign intelligence activities" or "to protect the United States against the overthrow of the Government by force or other unlawful means, or against any other clear and present danger to the structure or existence of the United States" authorize eavesdropping or wiretapping, presumably without court order. Does the President possess such power? Is it limited by the Fourth Amendment? In this regard, reconsider the concurring and dissenting opinions in *Katz*. The same section further provides that evidence obtained by "Presidential eavesdropping" shall be admissible in a criminal trial if it is "reasonable". What standards would be used to determine the reasonableness of such eavesdropping?

In United States v. United States District Court, 407 U.S. 297, 92 S.Ct. 2125 (1972), the government sought to justify warrantless eavesdropping on the grounds that domestic security was involved. The Court held that the provision in 18 U.S.C. § 2511(3) that nothing in the chapter was deemed to limit the constitutional power of the President to take such action as necessary to protect the United States against overthrow of the Government was only a congressional disclaimer and an expression of neutrality. It did not grant authority. "[T]he statute is not a measure of the executive authority exercised in this case." The constitutional powers of the President are not found to override the requirements of the Fourth Amendment.

The Court also rejected the argument that internal security matters are too subtle and complex for judicial evaluation.

The Court emphasized the scope of its decision by pointing out it has expressed no opinion with respect to activities of foreign powers or their agents. Further, it recognized that Title Three of the Omnibus Crime Control and Safe Streets Act of 1968 does not apply to presidential action to meet domestic threats to national security and that there may be some changes by Congress so as to provide a lesser standard in dealing with domestic security surveillance. "Different standards may be compatible with the Fourth Amendment if they are reasonable both in relation to the legitimate need of Government for intelligence information and the protected rights of our citizens."

4. § 2515 has been held to authorize a person accused of contempt to defend on the grounds that the questions he refused to answer in the grand jury were based upon information acquired by illegal interceptions of communications. Mr. Justice White, who made the majority with his concurrence, added a significant proviso to his opinion:

> "Where the Government produces a court order for the interception, however, and the witness nevertheless demands a full blown suppression hearing to determine the legality of the order, there may be room for striking a different accommodation between the due functioning of the grand jury system and the federal wiretap statute. . . . It is well, therefore, that the Court has left this issue open for consideration by the District Court on remand. . . . Of course, where the Government officially denies the fact

of electronic surveillance of the witness, the matter is at an end and the witness must answer."

Gelbard v. United States, 408 U.S. 41, 92 S.Ct. 2357 (1972).

5. Does § 2516(2) of the Act require that a state pass a statute specifically authorizing electronic eavesdropping under the terms of the Act before state law enforcement agents may utilize this device? Would a general search warrant statute be the equivalent of "a statute of that State [allowing] . . . application to a State court judge of competent jurisdiction for an order authorizing or approving the interception of wire or oral communications . . . "?

6. Not infrequently an informer equipped with electronic devices will record or transmit to a third party conversations between the informer and a suspect. May the recordings or the testimony of the third party who overheard the conversations through use of the electronic device be admitted into evidence consistent with *Katz*? The Court has so held. See United States v. White, 401 U.S. 745, 91 S.Ct. 1122 (1971).

7. For a comprehensive survey of the law in this area, see Standards Relating To Electronic Surveillance, published by the A. B. A. Project on Minimum Standards For Criminal Justice (Tent.Draft, 1968).

HOLMES v. BURR

United States Court of Appeals, 9th Circuit, 1973.
486 F.2d 55.

BARNES, CIRCUIT JUDGE:

W. Thomas Holmes, appellant, is a former Arizona attorney convicted of grand theft of money under false pretenses in an Arizona state court. The state court found that Holmes fraudulently obtained $1,000 from a client, Sanford Marburger, a Tucson liquor store proprietor. Marburger claimed that the $1,000 was given to Holmes for payment of a fine imposed for an alleged liquor license violation of which Holmes had informed him. Subsequent to Holmes' receipt of the money Marburger discovered that no fine had been levied, and no fee had been paid on his behalf.

In cooperation with the Arizona State Liquor Department, Marburger engaged petitioner in a telephone conversation from the Liquor Department office on August 23, 1968. The parties discussed the alleged license violation and fine. With Marburger's consent, but without a warrant, the conversation was overheard and recorded by the state officials. The tape recording was admitted into evidence at Holmes' trial over timely objection. * * *

Holmes alleges several errors. We find only one question to have merit: whether the eavesdropping and recording of the Marburger-Holmes conversation violated Holmes' right to privacy pursuant to the Fourth and Fourteenth Amendments; or more specifically, his right to be secure in his person from unreasonable searches and seizures.

For this reason, and for purposes of judicial economy, we limit our discussion to this issue.

Prior to the Supreme Court's ruling in Katz v. United States, government interception of oral communications was permissible where one party to the conversation gave prior consent. [On Lee v. United States (1952); Rathbun v. United States (1957); and Lopez v. United States (1963).] It is now argued by Holmes, and it is the position of the dissent, that *Katz* makes consensual eavesdropping by the Government unconstitutional. We hold that the principles enunciated in *On Lee, Rathbun,* and *Lopez* are not unconstitutional, and therefore remain binding on the federal courts. United States v. Puchi, 441 F.2d 697 (1971).

Each of these cases is in certain respects factually similar to the matter before us. On Lee v. United States, *supra,* involved a face to face conversation between an indicted, but unconvicted, criminal defendant, and an old friend and accomplice, turned government informant. The informant elicited incriminating statements from On Lee to which the government informant was permitted to testify at On Lee's trial. Holmes argues, and the dissent concludes, that *On Lee* has been so eroded by recent Supreme Court decisions, particularly Katz v. United States, *supra* that it is no longer a controlling precedent. While we do not find that *On Lee* is not controlling, we do note that it has been severely criticized. See the concurring opinion of Warren, C. J., in Lopez v. United States. The thrust of the criticism, however, has been directed to the prosecution's failure in *On Lee* to call the informant-accomplice to testify. Unlike the posture of the informant in *On Lee,* Marburger testified himself; and the conversation, which was recorded here, was only used to corroborate Marburger's testimony—it was not primary evidence.

The consenting party to the intercepted conversation in Rathbun v. United States was the victim of a crime perpetrated by the nonconsenting party, as Marburger was the victim of a crime perpetrated by Holmes. Similarly, the eavesdropping was accomplished through a regularly used telephone extension; and the evidence obtained was used for corroboration purposes. With respect to the parties' privacy rights, the Supreme Court stated:

> "Each party to a telephone conversation takes the risk that the other party may have an extension telephone and may allow another to overhear the conversation. When such takes place there has been no violation of any privacy of which the parties may complain."

The only real distinction between *Rathbun* and *Holmes* is that Holmes' conversation was recorded. However, since the constitutional question centers around the *interception* by a government third party, we do not find the distinction in the *means of disclosure* dispositive.

We also note that *Rathbun* was approved by the Supreme Court in a decision subsequent to *Katz.* Lee v. Florida (1968).

In Lopez v. United States, an Internal Revenue Agent was equipped with a pocket tape recorder for the purpose of obtaining corroborative evidence of a bribe. During the recorded conversation, Lopez made additional bribes; and he was convicted only for the bribes made during that conversation. In upholding the admission into evidence of the recording, the Supreme Court first noted that the agent had a clear right to be present at the conversation in Lopez's office, and to which the agent had been invited, and to testify as to the subject matter of the conversation at Lopez's trial. For this reason, there was

> "no 'eavesdropping' whatever in any proper sense of that term. The Government did not use an electronic device to listen in on conversations it could not otherwise have heard. Instead, the device was used only to obtain the most reliable evidence possible of a conversation in which the Government's own agent was a participant and which that agent was fully entitled to disclose."

With respect to an alleged invasion of Lopez's right to privacy, the court stated that "the risk that (Lopez) took in offering a bribe to (the Government agent) fairly included the risk that the offer would be accurately reproduced in court, whether by faultless memory or mechanical recording." Id.

Although the instant case is factually closer to *Rathbun* (because *Rathbun* was concerned with an eavesdropping, and there was no eavesdropping present in *Lopez*), the Court's concern in *Lopez* with the preservation of accurate evidence is relevant to the Marburger-Holmes conversation. In this connection, we find that the use of the recording at Holmes' trial insured that the jury would hear exactly what Marburger heard. In her dissent, Judge Hufstedler states that one of the dangers of the recorded conversation is that the recording does not record facial expressions or other bodily gestures inherent in normal conversation. Without discussing the validity of this concern, we merely note that it is not appropriate under the facts of this case: facial expressions and bodily gestures were not transmitted over the telephone to Marburger; and the jury obtained the precise communication that Marburger received.

Katz v. United States is said to make the holdings in *On Lee, Rathbun,* and *Lopez* nugatory, not because of the factual holding in *Katz,* but because of the principles enunciated therein. In *Katz* a listening and recording device was attached to a public telephone booth by Government officials. No warrant had been obtained, and neither party to the conversation granted permission to the government for the latter's action. The Supreme Court held that "the Fourth Amendment protects people, not places," and disallowed the evidence, overruling the "trespass" approach to the Fourth Amendment in Olmstead v. United States. The Court stated that the government's activities "violated the privacy upon which . . .

(Katz) . . . justifiably relied while using the telephone booth and thus constituted a search and seizure within the meaning of the Fourth Amendment."

We first turn to circuit decisions. My sister Hufstedler disposes of the conclusions of other circuits approving "consensual" electronic surveillance by a brief mention in footnote [12] of her dissent. She does not discuss them, but dismisses them by the conclusion: "None of them undertakes any independent analysis. . . ."

Eight other circuits have supported this majority opinion (in addition to the Ninth) and declined to follow the position urged by the dissent.

Each have considered the question of the effect of *Katz* on consensual interception of oral communications. Each one has held that *Katz* is not applicable. Dancy v. United States, 390 F.2d 370 (5th Cir. 1968), in which *Katz* was held not to control the admission of a government agent's testimony obtained via a transmitter on the person of an informant; Holt v. United States, 404 F.2d 914 (10th Cir. 1968), in which the recorded conversation between the defendant and an informant was admitted for corroboration purposes, notwithstanding *Katz*; United States v. Kaufer, 406 F.2d 550 (2d Cir. 1969), in which *Lopez* and *Rathbun* were held to permit the admission of a recorded conversation of a bribe directed to a government agent, notwithstanding *Katz*; United States v. Gardner, 416 F.2d 879 (6th Cir. 1969), where *On Lee* was held to control the admission of testimony by a government agent obtained via transmitter attached to the person of an informant; and in which the court held that *On Lee* would continue to apply until overruled by the Supreme Court, in which a recorded conversation between a government agent and the defendant was admitted into evidence for corroboration purposes on the basis of *Lopez* and *Hoffa, Katz* not controlling; United States v. Hickman, 426 F.2d 515 (7th Cir. 1970), where evidence was admitted at the defendant's trial which was obtained by government agents listening on a regularly used extension telephone at a police station; and *Rathbun* and Lee v. Florida, *supra,* were held to control the question of the defendant's right to privacy under the Fourth Amendment; United States v. Riccobene, 320 F.Supp. 196 (E.D.Pa.) (1970), aff'd 451 F.2d 587 (3d Cir. 1971), where *Rathbun* and *Lopez* were held to control the admission into evidence for corroboration purposes of a recorded telephone conversation between a government witness and the defendant, *Katz* not controlling; United States v. Skillman, 442 F.2d 542 (8th Cir. 1971), in which the recorded conversation of the defendant and a co-conspirator was admitted into evidence for the purpose of impeachment on the basis of *Lopez.*

The Government argues that on the facts of this case, *Katz* is not controlling; instead, they would have the court rely upon United States v. White, 401 U.S. 745, 91 S.Ct. 1122 (1971). In *White,* a radio transmitter was attached to the person of a government informant through which incriminating statements made by White were overheard by government agents. The informant was unavailable for White's trial and the government agents were permitted to testify as to the conversations they overheard. No warrant was obtained for the eavesdropping, but the agents did not have the consent of the informant. The Supreme Court found the evidence permissible notwithstanding the Fourth Amendment.

> "If the conduct and revelations of an agent operating without electronic equipment do not invade the defendant's constitutionally justifiable expectations of privacy, neither does a simultaneous recording of the same conversations made by the agent or by others from transmissions received from the agent to whom the defendant is talking and whose trustworthiness the defendant necessarily risks."

Holmes would have this Court disregard *White* on the ground that the electronic surveillance was pre-*Katz.* In Desist v. United States, 394 U.S. 244, 89 S.Ct. 1030 (1969), the Supreme Court held that *Katz* only applied prospectively. Hence, Holmes urges that *White* was decided on constitutional principles no longer applicable because of *Katz.* This position represents only a partial reading of *White.* The Supreme Court did find that *White* required application of pre-*Katz* doctrine; but the Court also reached the constitutional questions in view of *Katz.*

> "In our view, the Court of Appeals misinterpreted both the *Katz* case and the Fourth Amendment and in any event erred in applying the *Katz* case to events that occurred before that decision was rendered by this Court."

After distinguishing *Katz* on the grounds that there was no consensual interception, the Court disposed of the Fourth Amendment right to privacy claim.

> "Hoffa v. United States (1966), which was left undisturbed by *Katz,* held that however strongly a defendant may trust an apparent colleague, his expectations in this respect are not protected by the Fourth Amendment when it turns out that the colleague is a government agent regularly communicating with the authorities. In these circumstances, 'no interest legitimately protected by the Fourth Amendment is involved,' for that amendment affords no protection to 'a wrongdoer's misplaced belief that a person to whom he voluntarily confides his wrongdoing will not reveal it.' "

Holmes and my sister Hufstedler's dissent strongly urge this Court to disregard *White* on the grounds that *White* was only a plurality decision, and therefore not binding precedent on this Court. In United States v. Puchi, supra, however, three judges of this circuit have found that *White* was binding precedent for the admission of a recorded telephone conversation between one Mitchell, a consenting private citizen and a seller of untaxed liquor. United States v. Puchi, 441 F.2d at 700.

Notwithstanding United States v. Puchi, we find that for purposes of finding the principles of *Katz* controlling on the issue of consensual third party interception of oral communications, we note that Black, J., concurred in *White* on the grounds that *Katz* was improperly decided. United States v. White, 401 U.S. at 754, 91 S.Ct. 1122. For this reason, *White* is a majority opinion.

For still another reason, we believe *White* is controlling. This Court is without power to overrule *White*. * * *

In this opinion, we have not referred to the provisions of 18 U.S.C. § 2511(2)(c); for while it specifically authorizes the consensual interception, we need not rely on it here.

Holmes and the dissent correctly note that the government's conduct raises serious questions as to the nature and extent on one's right to privacy. We agree. We conclude, however, that the question of the constitutionality of such conduct is foreclosed by *White* and *Puchi*. For this reason, as well as by reason of similar holdings in other circuits, and the total lack of any judicial precedents in support of appellant's position, the decision of the district court denying the petition for Writ of Habeas Corpus is Affirmed.

HUFSTEDLER, CIRCUIT JUDGE (dissenting):

* * *

The narrowest constitutional issue is whether the state overcame the per se unreasonableness of the warrantless electronic surveillance of Holmes' conversation by proof alone that Marburger gave his consent to the surveillance of Holmes. In my view, the Fourth and Fourteenth Amendments, as interpreted by controlling Supreme Court authority, compel a negative answer. Electronic surveillance of Holmes would have been legal if the state had obtained a warrant, a simple procedure in this case. The state's failure to obtain a warrant rendered the search and seizure constitutionally impermissible.

I.

Marburger, who owned a liquor store retained Holmes for an agreed fee of $2000 to represent him in connection with charges against him pending before the Arizona Liquor Department. According to Marburger, Holmes told him in March 1968 that he had settled the charges upon the basis of Marburger's paying a $1000 fine to the Department and receiving a five-day suspension of his liquor license. The day after this conversation Marburger paid Holmes $1000. The Department, in fact, had not levied any fine. Marburger contended that Holmes did not give him a receipt for the $1000. Marburger went to the Arizona Liquor Department for conferences on several occasions, and he eventually agreed to help the Department obtain corroborating evidence of Holmes' duplicity. For about two weeks,

Marburger, under the direction of the Arizona authorities, tried unsuccessfully to record face-to-face and telephone conversations with Holmes. On August 23, 1968, more than five months after the alleged commission of the crime, Marburger made the telephone call in issue. Marburger placed the call from the Arizona Liquor Department's office to Holmes' residence. With Marburger's consent, the law enforcement officers listened to the conversation on an extension telephone and electronically recorded it. A transcript of the complete conversation as recorded is set forth below.[1]

1. Child: Hello.

Marburger: Good evening. Is Mr. Holmes at home?

Child: Uh, yes.

Marburger: May I speak to him please?

Child: O.K.

Marburger: Thank you.

Mrs. Holmes: Hello.

Marburger: Hi Mrs. Holmes, Sandy.

Mrs. Holmes: Just a minute Sandy.

Marburger: All right.

T. Holmes: Hello.

Marburger: How are you feeling?

T. Holmes: Oh, terrible Sandy, they're putting me in the hospital I guess.

Marburger: Oh, my gosh, I hear you been under the weather quite some time.

T. Holmes: Yeah.

Marburger: Well, I hate like heck to bother you on this except I, I don't know I guess I got a problem on it and I . . .

T. Holmes: Well, what is the problem Sandy?

Marburger: Well, now

T. Holmes: I gave you a receipt and you know, if you recall at the time, I deliberately gave you a receipt.

Marburger: No I got the receipt.

T. Holmes: As an attorney's fees and everything so that you could write it off. In other words you can take it as an expense item.

Marburger: Yeah, but, you see, Uh then I . . .

T. Holmes: Otherwise you can't.

Marburger: Yeah, Well I didn't understand that, see. Now I told, when it came up when I put it on the book I put down, you know, that was a fine paid to the Liquor Department, My accountant picked it up.

T. Holmes: Well you just tell him to un-pick it! And, put it down and just write it off as attorney's fees! He hasn't filed your income tax yet.

Marburger: No, that's the whole thing but he's filed for that month see, that was March.

T. Holmes: Well, he hasn't—you've —what do you mean filed for that month?

Marburger: Look, every month he makes out a profit and loss sheet.

T. Holmes: Oh, well that's all right, but he can change that. That's the reason I deliberately did it that way was so you could take it as a write off.

Marburger: So what shall I tell him? Just that . . .

T. Holmes: Tell him to contact me if he wants to and I'll tell him what to do. It's real simple like. You have the receipt. You have everything. All you do is turn in the receipt to him. Nancy told me you lost the receipt.

Marburger: Well, I couldn't find the first one but Nancy gave me another one so that part's no problem.

T. Holmes: Just hand it to him and say, put it on the books this way and this is the way we do it.

Marburger: Yeah, and then if he says to me what about the fine and all?

T. Holmes: Tell him I took care of that personally, which I did, and that's my business.

Marburger: Tell him you, or me? I mean tell him Sandy Marburger took care of it or what?

T. Holmes: Tell him Tommy Holmes took care of it, but I gave you a bill in that manner and that's the way that he files your tax.

Marburger: OK, OK and then if he's got any problems . . .

T. Holmes: I have my reasons for doing that also Sandy.

Marburger: If he's got any problems, I'll let him call you.

T. Holmes: Have him give me a call.

Marburger: OK.

Holmes' version of the facts differed sharply from Marburger's. He admitted that he received the $1000, denied that he told Marburger that the money was for a fine, insisted that he had given Marburger a receipt for it, and maintained that the payment was part of his legal fees and costs.

Holmes' conviction could not have been sustained without the admission of the recorded conversation because Arizona law requires that a grand theft by false pretenses charge be corroborated by the testimony of two witnesses or of one witness and corroborating circumstances. . . .

At no time during the months elapsing between the alleged commission of the offense and the interception of Holmes' conversation in August 1968 did the officers attempt to obtain prior court approval for monitoring and recording Holmes' telephone conversations.

II.

The fate of any one man enmeshed in the criminal process is never inconsequential. But this is one of those cases in which the issues involved far transcend the particular factual setting in which the constitutional battle is fought. The case presents some of the most vexing and pressing problems of our day: What are the constitutional limitations on governmental electronic intrusions into privacy? Do the Fourth and Fourteenth Amendments circumscribe warrantless electronic intrusions as effectively as they limit corporeal invasions of privacy? Are the protections of the Fourth and Fourteenth Amendments diluted if the person subjected to the warrantless electronic intrusion is suspected of a crime?

Fear of invisible eyes and ears is pervasive. Today's sophisticated electronic devices are capable of surreptitious probing of every aspect of our lives . . .

Public fear of omnipresent electronic surveillance has escalated with increasing revelations of widespread wire-tapping, bugging,

T. Holmes: Olive will be back in a couple of weeks, I understand, in a couple of weeks and we'll get that other seventy five buck deal straightened out.

Marburger: OK fine.

T. Holmes: As quick as she gets back.

Marburger: OK Well then, I'm sorry I had to bother you on this, Mr. Holmes, but you know me, I don't know anything about and I want to make sure I was doing the right thing.

T. Holmes: Well, you're doing the right thing and that's the reason I did it that way was so that you would have a write off and, wouldn't have to pay taxes on it.

Marburger: OK fine, OK that's all.

T. Holmes: OK fine.

Marburger: Thank you, listen feel better now, will you?

T. Holmes: All right, well, they're gonna put me in the hospital I guess and go through a bunch of tests. You lay there in bed and you never see anybody—for days, you know, when those doctors get you in there.

Marburger: Well, I sure hope everything works out alright.

T. Holmes: Fine, well I know it will.

Marburger: Thank you, You'll give me a call then when Mrs. Keihl gets back in town.

T. Holmes: I will as quick as she gets back Sandy.

Marburger: OK thank you.

T. Holmes: OK, bye bye.

Marburger: Bye bye.

monitoring, and recording. Reported statistics of court-ordered interceptions of wire and oral communications show that, since the enactment of Title III of the Omnibus Crime Control and Safe Streets Act of 1968 (18 U.S.C. §§ 2510–20), authorized interceptions increased 184 percent.[2] "National Security" installations of electronic surveillance devices reported by the Department of Justice during the period 1969–1970, made without court approval, were massive; one of these "national security" wiretaps monitored more than 900 conversations during a 14-month period.[3] Government agencies have installed

2. FEDERAL AND STATE WIRETAPPING AND ELECTRONIC SURVEILLANCE

Court Authorized Devices

Year	*Federal*	*State*	*Total No.*	*Total No. of Days In Actual Use*
1968*	0	174	174	(Unavailable)
1969	33	269	302	9,019
1970	183	414	597	11,200.5
1971	285	531	816	14,582.5
1972	206	649	855	15,562**

* The 1968 reporting period covered only June 20, 1968, to December 31, 1968.

** This figure is lower than the actual total since this information was not provided by all reporting jurisdictions.

Source: Administrative Office of the U. S. Courts, Report on Applications for Orders Authorizing or Approving the Interception of Wire Or Oral Communications for 1968, 1969, 1970, 1971, 1972.

3. During the two-year period 1969–1970, the Department of Justice installed, without court approval, 207 "national security" electronic devices. The duration of use of such devices far surpassed those authorized by court orders during the same period. *See id.* at 334, 92 S.Ct. 2125 (appendix to op'n of Douglas, J., concurring):

FEDERAL WIRETAPPING AND BUGGING 1969–1970

	Court Ordered Devices		*Executive Ordered Devices*		
				Days in Use	
Year	*Number*	*Days in Use*	*Number*	*Minimum (Rounded)*	*Maximum (Rounded)*
1969	30	462	94	8,100	20,800
1970	180	2,363	113	8,100	22,600

	Ratio of Days Used Executive Ordered: Court Ordered		*Average Days in Use Per Device*		
				Executive Ordered Devices	
Year	*Minimum*	*Maximum*	*Court Ordered Devices*	*Minimum*	*Maximum*
1969	17.5*	45.0*	15.4	86.2	221.3
1970	3.4	9.6	13.1	71.7	200.0

* Ratios for 1969 are less meaningful than those for 1970, since court-ordered surveillance program was in its initial stage in 1969.

Source:

(1) Letter from Assistant Attorney General Robert Mardian to Senator Edward M. Kennedy, March 1, 1971. Source figures withheld at request of Justice Department.

(2) 1969 and 1970 Reports of the Administrative Office of the U. S. Courts.

secret observation booths in offices and restrooms.[4] The Government's uninvited ears and eyes have conjoined its cybernetic memory to compile hundreds of thousands of dossiers on high political figures,[5] domestic policial organizations,[6] dissident groups,[7] Black studies programs,[8] and average citizens.[9]

The full measure of the governmental electronic surveillance problem by no means emerges from these reports, which almost entirely involve probing without the knowledge of anyone whose activities were watched, heard, or recorded. The far more pervasive spectre is presented by governmental interceptions and recordings accomplished with the cooperation of one party to a communication but without the knowledge of the other. Such "participant monitoring" and "participant electronic surveillance" are much more widespread; estimates of such participant activities run in the tens of thousands per year.

In a pluralistic society dedicated to liberal democratic traditions, confidential communication serves as a lubricant for the smooth functioning of social and political institutions. Without "uninhibited, robust, and wide-open" public and private expression on the great issues of our day, as well as private discussion about the mundane, the trivial, and the banal, a once free society will soon become a nation of "hagridden and furtive" people.

> "The dangers posed by wiretapping and electronic surveillance strike at the very heart of the democratic philos-

4. *See generally* Hearings on Invasion of Privacy Before the Subcomm. on Administrative Practice and Procedure of the Senate Comm. on the Judiciary, 89th Cong., 1st Sess. (1965).

5. United States Army domestic intelligence operations have reportedly focused upon United States Senators Sam Ervin, Fred Harris, Harold Hughes, Edward Kennedy, George McGovern, and Edmund Muskie, N. Y. Times, Feb. 29, 1972, at 1, col. 3.

6. Senator Sam Ervin, Jr., Chairman of the Senate Subcommittee on Constitutional Rights, has disclosed that organizations subjected to Army surveillance have included the NAACP, ACLU, Operation Breadbasket, the Urban League, and the States' Rights Party. Brief for Senator Sam Ervin, Jr., as Amicus Curiae at 10, Laird v. Tatum (1972) 408 U.S. 1, 92 S.Ct. 2318, 33 L.Ed.2d 154. Army operations also infiltrated Resurrection City, the Poor People's Campaign, the 1968 Democratic and Republican Party nominating conventions. Federal Data Banks, Computers and the Bill of Rights, Hearings Before the Subcomm. on Constitutional Rights of the Senate Comm. on the Judiciary, 92d Cong., 1st Sess., pt. 1, at 197–201 (1971).

7. *See* Federal Data Banks, Computers and the Bill of Rights, at 201–06. The FBI has also been charged with electronic surveillance of Dr. Martin Luther King (V. Navasky, Kennedy Justice 135–55 (1971)) and with wiretapping Mrs. Eleanor Roosevelt and John L. Lewis (Theoharis & Meyer, The "National Security" Justification For Electronic Eavesdropping: An Elusive Exception, 14 Wayne L.Rev. 749, 760–61 (1968)).

8. Federal Data Banks, Computers and the Bill of Rights, supra note 7, at 185.

9. *See generally* Federal Data Banks, Computers and the Bill of Rights, supra note 7; A. Westin & F. Baker, Databanks in a Free Society (1972) (Report of the Project on Computer Databanks of the Computer Science and Engineering Board, National Academy of Sciences).

ophy. A free society is based on the premise that there are large zones of privacy into which the government may not intrude except in unusual circumstances.

> "Such practices can only have a damaging effect on our society. . . . The time may come when no one can be sure whether his words are being recorded for use at some future time; when everyone will fear that his most secret thoughts are no longer his own, but belong to the Government; when the most confidential and intimate conversations are always open to eager, prying ears. When that time comes, privacy, and with it liberty, will be gone. If a man's privacy can be invaded at will, who can say he is free? . . ." Osborn v. United States (1966) 385 U.S. 323, 353–354, 87 S.Ct. 429, 446 (Douglas, J., dissenting).

The corrosive impact of warrantless participant monitoring on our sense of security and freedom of expression is every bit as insidious as electronic surveillance conducted without the consent of any of the parties involved. In terms of the individual's reluctance to speak freely no qualitative difference exists between the danger posed by third party interception and the risk that his auditor has sanctioned a secret recording of their conversation. Extensive police-instigated and clandestine participant recordings, coupled with their use as evidence of any self-incriminating remarks of the speaker, pose "a grave danger of chilling all private, free, and unconstrained communication. . . . In a free society, people ought not to have to watch their every word so carefully." Lopez v. United States (Brennan, J., dissenting).

III.

The constitutional issues that Holmes raises could be avoided and the opinion confined to the application of the federal statute outlawing all nonjudicially authorized interceptions of any wire or oral communications (Omnibus Crime Control and Safe Streets Act of 1968), if the Holmes' surveillance did not fall within one of the kinds of surveillance expressly excepted by the Act. That avenue is foreclosed, however, because governmental participant monitoring is expressly exempted by 18 U.S.C. § 2511(2)(c):

> "It shall not be unlawful under this chapter for a person acting under color of law to intercept a wire or oral communication, where such person is a party to the communication or one of the parties to the communication has given prior consent to such interception."

* * *

The constitutional problem must be faced whether we ignore the Act altogether and concentrate on Holmes' direct constitutional attack, or we begin with the Act and confront the same constitutional challenge to the quoted exception to the Act. The frontal assault is conceptually neater. I therefore undertake the constitutional analysis independent of the Act, although I am aware of the impact of the analysis on the exception.

For the purpose of this constitutional analysis, I adopt Professor Westin's concept that "privacy" is "the claim of individuals, groups, or institutions to determine for themselves when, how, and to what extent information about them is communicated to others." (A. Westin, Privacy and Freedom (1967) at 7.) This constitutionalized right to privacy protects the individual's interest in preserving his essential dignity as a human being.

The generic term "electronic surveillance" is used here to encompass all forms of electronic interception, overhearing, or recording of wire or oral communications. "Participant monitoring" includes three situations; in each, one participant to a communication at the instance of, or under the direction of, a governmental agent or agency, without the knowledge of the second party, (1) himself records the conversation with the second party, or (2) uses an electronic device to transmit the conversation to a government agent or his nominee, or (3) consents to a government agent's or informant's using an electronic device to overhear and to record the communication. Holmes was subjected to participant monitoring of the third type.

* * *

IV.

[In] Olmstead v. United States, Mr. Chief Justice Taft held that warrantless wiretapping offended neither the Fourth nor Fifth Amendments because there was no corporeal search, no tangible seizure, no trespass, and no coercive physical presence of a government officer.

* * *

The holding of *Olmstead* was finally overruled in Katz v. United States (1967) 389 U.S. 347, 88 S.Ct. 507. "[T]he Fourth Amendment protects people, not places."

* * *

Tucked into *Olmstead* was a passing reference to the theory that persons subjected to warrantless electronic interception volunteer their statements to the Government by their very act of talking to each other. This theory later emerged as the constructive consent and assumption of the risk fictions relied on in On Lee v. United States, and Lopez v. United States. In *Lopez,* the majority added the variation that a person talking face-to-face with a known government agent assumes the risk that the agent will be able to repeat the conversation either by total personal recall or by a corroborative recording which in its nature is more reliable than human recollection. The theme was replayed in a slightly different key by the plurality in United States v. White.[10]

Using familiar jurisprudential tools, *Holmes* can be successfully distinguished from every Supreme Court decision directly bearing on the case other than *Katz*. Thus, *On Lee* and *Lopez* not only are factually dissimilar but, more importantly, were based on trespassory concepts destroyed by *Katz*. Rathbun v. United States (1957) 355 U. S. 107, 78 S.Ct. 161, dealt with governmental eavesdropping by extension telephone without electronic recording, and the decision was confined to an interpretation of section 605 of the 1934 Federal Communications Act (47 U.S.C. § 605). . . . The facts in *White* were closer to those in *On Lee* than to *Olmstead* or *Holmes*. But of much greater significance, *White* necessarily applied pre-*Katz* law because the electronic surveillance of White occurred before *Katz* was decided, and *Katz* had been earlier held nonretroactive in Desist v. United States. United States v. White is nevertheless important because it reveals continuing reliance by some of the Justices on the assumption of the risk doctrine.[11]

B.

Katz does apply to *Holmes* because the interception occurred after *Katz* became effective. However, two factual dissimilarities exist: (1) the mechanics of interception were not the same in both cases, and (2) *Katz* did not involve participant monitoring. In *Katz*, without the knowledge of either party to the conversation, the Government placed an electronic listening and recording device outside the public booth in which Katz was telephoning and thereby obtained evidence used to convict him for illegally transmitting wagering information. *Katz* itself defeats any argument that governmental choice of electronic devices is constitutionally significant. Thus, the only remaining issue is whether the participant feature of *Holmes* can defeat the warrant requirement of *Katz*. The majority opinion argues that it does, relying

10. Acting without a warrant, government agents overheard incriminating conversations between White and a confidant-government informant who transmitted his conversations with White to the agents by means of a radio transmitter concealed on his person. The informant was not produced at trial. The electronically eavesdropping government agents testified to the intercepted conversations. Mr. Justice White, speaking for a plurality (he did not command a majority on the point), said that a person contemplating illegal activity "must realize and risk" that his confidant may be a police informer who is fully wired for sound.

11. *See* United States v. White. Although the holding in *White* was based upon the nonretroactivity of *Katz*, several of the Justices did express views on the effect of *Katz* on participant electronic surveillance. Mr. Justice White, writing for the Chief Justice and Justices Stewart and Blackmun, suggested that *On Lee* remained sound law. Justices Brennan, Douglas, Harlan, and Marshall each wrote separate opinions arguing that the result in *On Lee* could not survive *Katz*. Mr. Justice Black, concurring in the judgment of the Court, did not address this issue, merely reasserting the position taken in his *Katz* dissent that electronic surveillance was not within the ambit of the Fourth Amendment.

on the theories of consent and assumption of the risk. Neither theory is acceptable.

Holmes never consented to having his conversations overheard by third parties or recorded by Marburger or other government agents. As the Court observed in *Katz,* "the very nature of electronic surveillance precludes its use pursuant to the suspect's consent." (389 U.S. at 358, 88 S.Ct. at 515.) Moreover, Marburger cannot waive Holmes' Fourth Amendment rights. To say that Marburger's consent is Holmes' consent is a fiction that has been expressly rejected by the Supreme Court in the context of warrantless searches and seizures. Marburger can no more consent for Holmes than a hotel manager can consent to a search of a guest's room on behalf of the guest (Stoner v. California (1964) 376 U.S. 483, 84 S.Ct. 889), or a landlord can give permission attributable to his tenant to search his tenant's quarters (Chapman v. United States (1961) 365 U.S. 610, 81 S.Ct. 776.

Although a majority of the Supreme Court has never relied on the assumption of the risk doctrine to validate interception of private conversations, references to the doctrine have threaded through a number of opinions applying pre-*Katz* law. This doctrine, relied upon by the majority in the case at bench, is a hybrid of factual and fictitious elements and of individual and societal judgments. If Holmes knew that his conversation might be electronically intercepted by the government, or if warrantless electronic monitoring were so pervasive that he is chargeable with such knowledge, a factual foundation would exist for invoking the venerable assumption of the risk doctrine. However, if he did not know and if he had no reason to be aware of the risk, that doctrine is inapt. To say that a person "assumes the risk" of electronic surveillance, although he was rightfully oblivious to the risk, is to mislabel a newly created rule of law limiting the scope of the Fourth Amendment. Indeed, none of the opinions in which the doctrine has been invoked to defeat Fourth Amendment claims attempts to justify its application on factual grounds. Instead, the result is explained by resorting to two intertwined theories: First, one must realize that a person in whom he confides may repeat the conversation to another; and he must also realize that his confidant may be a government informer who will choose to repeat the conversation by electronically recording and transmitting it. Assignment of both risks to a person who may be totally ignorant of the opportunity for electronic surveillance is considered appropriate because no significant difference exists between talking to a person who is electronically unaided and to one who is "wired for sound." Second, a person contemplating illegal activity assumes some risks that others do not. Among these risks is subjection to warrantless electronic surveillance. Neither theory withstands analysis.

Repetition of conversations thought to be confidential is a known risk. However, the risk that one's trusted friend may be a gossip is of an entirely different order than a risk that the friend may be transmitting and recording every syllable. The latter risk is not yet rooted in common American experience, and it should not be thrust upon us: the differences between talking to a person enswathed in electronic equipment and one who is not are very real, and they cannot be reduced to insignificance by verbal legerdemain. All of us discuss topics and use expressions with one person that we would not undertake with another and that we would never broadcast to a crowd. Few of us would ever speak freely if we knew that all our words were being captured by machines for later release before an unknown and potentially hostile audience. No one talks to a recorder as he talks to a person.

Proponents of the assumption of the risk doctrine, apparently recognizing the significant intrusion upon an individual's privacy caused by participant monitoring, do not say that everyone must anticipate and risk warrantless surveillance; rather, they limit its application to those who contemplate illegal activity. But never do these proponents explain how, absent the Fourth Amendment requirement of antecedent justification before a neutral magistrate, the sinful can be separated from the saintly without probing everyone or leaving the selection to the unbridled discretion of government agents. What is left of anyone's justifiable reliance on privacy (*see* Katz v. United States, supra, 389 U.S. at 353, 88 S.Ct. 507) if everyone must realize that he will be free from warrantless electronic intrusion only so long as someone in the government does not suspect him of improper conduct or wrong thinking?

Adoption of the assumption of the risk theory ultimately rests on the cynical conclusion that a warrantless search is justified by what it reveals. The conclusion has been firmly rejected in the context of physical entries and tangible seizures and in nonparticipant electronic surveillance. It should not be given vitality in participant monitoring cases.

C.

After mistaken notions of consent are corrected and the rubble of fictions is removed from electronic surveillance, participant monitoring is revealed to be squarely within the rule of *Katz.* In terms of expectations of privacy, expressed either as a subjective state of mind of the monitored suspect or as a societal judgment, Holmes' situation cannot be distinguished from Katz's. Holmes was just as ignorant as Katz of the presence of hovering governmental ears; and society has not yet reached a judgment that a lawyer talking on his residential telephone to a client must have a lesser expectation of privacy than a bookmaker transmitting wagering information to a confederate from a public telephone booth. Holmes' expectation of privacy, which was surely no less reasonable than Katz's, did not become unreasonable simply because his client, without his knowledge, invited the government to overhear and to record the conversation. *Katz* refused to leave the choice of suspects to be electronically monitored to the unreviewed discretion of government agents. The Government cannot escape *Katz* by committing the responsibility for surveillance to a private citizen. The guardian of the individual's right of privacy is the neutral magistrate, not a government informant.

The burden was on the state to obtain a warrant prior to subjecting Holmes to electronic surveillance (*Katz,* supra), or to prove facts that would bring the search and seizure within one of the carefully delineated exceptions to the warrant requirement. (United States v. United States District Court, supra, 407 U.S. at 318, 92 S.Ct. 2125.) Neither burden was met, and the surveillance was constitutionally impermissible.[12]

D.

Even if *Katz* could be successfully distinguished from *Holmes,* leaving the question of the constitutionality of participant surveillance open, the denouement would be the same. The constitutional values restated and reinforced in *Katz* and United States v. United States District Court, supra, are equally threatened by participant and nonparticipant warrantless electronic surveillance. Nevertheless, this constitutional bedrock has been obscured by three arguments which have been wholly or partially articulated to support warrantless electronic surveillance: (1) electronic recording produces more reliable evidence than human recollection; (2) law enforcement officers need unhampered authority to engage in electronic surveillance to protect us from crime; and (3) the exclusion of evidence obtained by electronic surveillance frees the guilty to the detriment of society.

Are machines more reliable than human beings? Unlike human beings, a machine neither remembers nor forgets. If the concept of reliability rested solely on ability to reproduce a conversation word for word, we would say machines are more reliable. But the concept is not that shallow. Machines are capable of distortion without regard to tampering and despite the invisibility of their presence. A tape recording preserves the spoken words, but not the gestures, facial expressions, and other subtle details which are often far more eloquent media than the words used to convey thoughts and feelings. Focus on a single element in a total environment can produce deceptive results. For example, a snapshot captures a person as he appeared in a fraction of a second. Is the picture an accurate portrayal of the person? Anyone who has seen a newspaper photograph of himself taken at a singularly unattractive moment will say "no."

12. I am aware of the authorities from this circuit and others upholding the constitutionality of warrantless participant electronic surveillance. Some of the cases cited by the majority can be effectively distinguished from *Holmes.* Others cannot. In my view, however, none of the circuit decisions can be harmonized with controlling Supreme Court authority. None of them undertake any independent analysis that supplies a defensible rationale for depriving a person subjected to warrantless participant surveillance of the protection of the Fourth Amendment.

A machine's capacity for distortion is enhanced when one party to a conversation knows that a recording is being made and the other does not. The knowledgeable person says nothing that he does not want to have graven on tape. The third ear affects his behavior as surely as knowledge of a camera's eye affects the pose of a witting subject. The behavior of one participant influences the response of the other in a conversation. When we evaluate the reliability of the electronic harvest of participant monitoring, we must not overlook the fact that the invisible machine can produce a very different conversation from the one that would have occurred if neither person had a recorder.

The supervening difficulty with the reliability rationale, however, is that it is a response to an irrelevant question. Contraband discovered in the course of an illegal entry by police is inadmissible although it is the best evidence that contraband was present. We exclude the evidence, not because it is unreliable, but because the values preserved by the Fourth Amendment are of greater societal moment than the use of that evidence to obtain a criminal conviction.

The second reason, and the one most often forwarded, is that unfettered governmental electronic surveillance is necessary to protect us from crime. Of course, the government has a great and legitimate interest in detecting and preventing crime, but that interest must be balanced against the individual's right to be free from unjustified intrusions. The balance was struck by the draftsmen of the Fourth Amendment: the governmental interest in combating crime is fully accommodated by permitting all searches and seizures, subject only to advance authorization by a magistrate upon a showing of probable cause; and the individual's expectations of privacy are protected by the knowledge that warrantless intrusions into his life will not be tolerated.

The third reason is rarely articulated, but hostility to the exclusionary rule permeates opinion after opinion, commencing with *Olmstead.* Dissatisfaction with the exclusionary rule as the predominate remedy for conduct violating the Fourth Amendment is understandable and defensible. Attacks on the constitutional right of privacy as the means of expressing dissatisfaction with the remedy are intellectually indefensible and dangerous. A constitutional right continuously diluted becomes no right. Destroying a right protected by the Fourth Amendment because of distaste for the remedy makes little more sense than destroying a patient for failure to respond to chosen medication. If the remedy is wrong, it is time to reexamine the remedy, not to diminish the right.

The threat to fundamental constitutional values and to the quality of life in our country which is created by the ruling of the majority can be revealed by even brief reflection upon the directions in which an insensitive embrace of electronic hardware will carry us. The fact that the issues have arisen in the context of a criminal case should not obscure the reality that the basic right at stake is the right of all of us to be free from unjustified governmental encroachments upon our privacy. This is the right that Mr. Justice Brandeis accurately described as "the most comprehensive of rights and the right most valued by civilized men." * * *

Do we want to live in a society in which all of us must anticipate that we are always subject to electronic monitoring? Must we be ever watchful because our clients, friends, and acquaintances may be recording all we say for relay to a suspicious government? Do we want to convert our courtrooms into arenas in which we pit men against machines, or in which a person's liberty is decided in a contest fought by electronic surrogates because machines are more "reliable" than human beings?

The chilling atmosphere that these questions evoke is neither fanciful nor remote. In a nation wracked by fear of crime and engulfed by Orwellian devices, that dehumanized world can become our own unless we build constitutional walls that can be breached neither by the boldest leader nor by legions of the timorous. * * *

Express recognition that the same constitutional right to be free from unjustifiable governmental penetrations of personality inheres in all persons, whether or not suspected of crime, would be a major step in constructing an effective barrier against untoward governmental interference with privacy. Yet this substantial protection of the basic right of privacy can be accomplished without any significant impairment of legitimate governmental interests. No one challenges the right of the government to employ modern technology in criminal law enforcement. The only issue is whether to interpose the Fourth Amendment warrant procedure between law enforcement agencies and the ordinary citizen. The warrant requirement will not end electronic surveillance. It would reassure us that "this capability will not be used to intrude upon cherished privacy of law-abiding citizens."

I would overturn United States v. Puchi as contrary to *Katz,* and reverse the order denying Holmes' habeas petition.

Chapter 12

THE EXCLUSIONARY RULE AND ITS ALTERNATIVES

A. THE EXCLUSIONARY RULE

The court-established rule whereby various kinds of evidence of guilt are excluded ("suppressed") from consideration in the course of a judicial determination of the issue of guilt or innocence usually involves one or more of the following provisions of the Bill of Rights (the first eight Amendments) of the Constitution of the United States, all of which have their counterparts in almost every state constitution:

The Fourth Amendment—

The right of the people to be secure in their persons, houses, papers, and effects, against unreasonable searches and seizures, shall not be violated, and no warrants shall issue, but upon probable cause, supported by oath or affirmation, and particularly describing the place to be searched, and the persons or things to be seized.

The Fifth Amendment—

No person shall be . . . compelled in any criminal case to be a witness against himself. . . .

The Sixth Amendment—

In all criminal prosecutions, the accused shall enjoy the right . . . to have the assistance of counsel for his defense.

The Fourteenth Amendment—

No State shall . . . deprive any person of life, liberty, or property, without due process of law; . . .

A central thesis of the exclusionary rule is that police will be compelled to comply with the substantive commands of the law if the penalty for failure to comply is the exclusion, from a criminal trial, of evidence of guilt which is otherwise relevant and competent. The following cases and note materials present the concept and philosophy of the rule, supplemented by commentaries upon the question of whether its central thesis is actually served in practice and whether there are workable alternatives which may be employed in its stead.

MAPP v. OHIO

Supreme Court of the United States, 1961.
367 U.S. 643, 81 S.Ct. 1684.

MR. JUSTICE CLARK delivered the opinion of the Court.

Appellant stands convicted of knowingly having had in her possession and under her control certain lewd and lascivious books, pictures, and photographs in violation of § 2905.34 of Ohio's Revised Code. As officially stated in the syllabus to its opinion, the Supreme Court of Ohio found that her conviction was valid though "based primarily upon the introduction in evidence of lewd and lascivious books and pictures unlawfully seized during an unlawful search of defendant's home. . . ."

On May 23, 1957, three Cleveland police officers arrived at appellant's residence in that city pursuant to information that "a person [was] hiding out in the home, who was wanted for questioning in connection with a recent bombing, and that there was a large amount of policy paraphernalia being hidden in the home." Miss Mapp and her daughter by a former marriage lived on the top floor of the two-family dwelling. Upon their arrival at that house, the officers knocked on the door and demanded entrance but appellant, after telephoning her attorney, refused to admit them without a search warrant. They advised their headquarters of the situation and undertook a surveillance of the house.

The officers again sought entrance some three hours later when four or more additional officers arrived on the scene. When Miss Mapp did not come to the door immediately, at least one of the several doors to the house was forcibly opened and the policemen gained admittance. Meanwhile Miss Mapp's attorney arrived, but the officers, having secured their own entry, and continuing in their defiance of the law, would permit him neither to see Miss Mapp nor to enter the house. It appears that Miss Mapp was halfway down the stairs from the upper floor to the front door when the officers, in this high-handed manner, broke into the hall. She demanded to see the search warrant. A paper, claimed to be a warrant, was held up by one of the officers. She grabbed the "warrant" and placed it in her bosom. A struggle ensued in which the officers recovered the piece of paper and as a result of which they handcuffed appellant because she had been "belligerent" in resisting their official rescue of the "warrant" from her person. Running roughshod over appellant, a policeman "grabbed" her, "twisted [her] hand," and she "yelled [and] pleaded with him" because "it was hurting." Appellant, in handcuffs, was then forcibly taken upstairs to her bedroom where the officers searched a dresser, a chest of drawers, a closet and some suitcases. They also looked into a photo album and through personal papers belonging to the appellant. The search spread to the rest of the second floor including the child's bedroom, the living room, the kitchen and a dinette. The basement of the building and a trunk found therein were also searched. The obscene materials for possession of which she was ultimately convicted were discovered in the course of that widespread search.

At the trial no search warrant was produced by the prosecution, nor was the failure to produce one explained or accounted for. At best, "There is, in the record, considerable doubt as to whether there ever was any warrant for the search of defendant's home." The Ohio Supreme Court believed a "reasonable argument" could be made that the conviction should be reversed "because the 'methods' employed to obtain the [evidence] were such as to 'offend "a sense of justice,"'" but the court found determinative the fact that the evidence had not been taken" from defendant's person by the use of brutal or offensive physical force against defendant . . ."

The State says that even if the search were made without authority, or otherwise unreasonably, it is not prevented from using the unconstitutionally seized evidence at trial, citing Wolf v. People of State of Colorado, 1949, 338 U.S. 25, 69 S.Ct. 1359, in which this Court did indeed hold "that in a prosecution in a State court for a State crime the Fourteenth Amendment does not forbid the admission of evidence obtained by an unreasonable search and seizure." On this appeal, of which we have noted probable jurisdiction, it is urged once again that we review that holding.

I.

Seventy-five years ago, in Boyd v. United States, 1886, 116 U.S. 616, 630, 6 S.Ct. 524, 532, considering the Fourth and Fifth Amendments as running "almost into each other" on the facts before it, this Court held that the doctrines of those Amendments

> "apply to all invasions on the part of the government and its employes of the sanctity of a man's home and the privacies of life. It is not the breaking of his doors, and the rummaging of his drawers, that constitutes the essence of the offence; but it is the invasion of his indefeasible right of personal security, personal liberty and private property . . . . Breaking into a house and opening boxes and drawers are circumstances of aggravation; but any forcible and compulsory extortion of a man's own testimony or of his private papers to be used as evidence to convict him of crime or to forfeit his goods, is within the condemnation . . . [of those Amendments]."

The Court noted that

> "constitutional provisions for the security of person and property should be liberally construed. . . . It is the duty of courts to be watchful for the constitutional rights of the citizen, and against any stealthy encroachments thereon."

Less than 30 years after Boyd, this Court, in Weeks v. United States, 1914, 232 U.S. 383, 34 S.Ct. 341, . . . stated that

> "the 4th Amendment . . . put the courts of the United States and Federal officials, in the exercise of their power and authority, under limitations and restraints [and] . . . forever secure[d] the people, their persons, houses, papers, and effects, against all unreasonable searches and seizures under the guise of law . . . and the duty of giving to it force and effect is obligatory upon all entrusted under our Federal system with the enforcement of the laws."

Specifically dealing with the use of the evidence unconstitutionally seized, the Court concluded:

> "If letters and private documents can thus be seized and held and used in evidence against a citizen accused of an offense, the protection of the Fourth Amendment declaring his right to be secure against such searches and seizures is of no value, and, so far as those thus placed are concerned, might as well be stricken from the Constitution. The efforts of the courts and their officials to bring the guilty to punishment, praiseworthy as they are, are not to be aided by the sacrifice of those great principles established by years of endeavor and suffering which have resulted in their embodiment in the fundamental law of the land."

Finally, the Court in that case clearly stated that use of the seized evidence involved "a denial of the constitutional rights of the accused." Thus, in the year 1914, in the Weeks case, this Court "for the first time" held that "in a federal prosecution the Fourth Amendment barred the use of evidence secured through an illegal search and seizure." Wolf v. People of State of Colorado, supra. This Court has ever since required of federal law officers a strict adherence to that command which this Court has held to be a clear, specific, and constitutionally required—even if judicially implied—deterrent safeguard without insistence upon which the Fourth Amendment would have been reduced to "a form of words." Holmes, J., Silverthorne Lumber Co. v. United States, 1920, 251 U.S. 385, 392, 40 S.Ct. 182, 183. It meant, quite simply, that "conviction by means of unlawful seizures and enforced confessions . . . should find no sanction in the judgments of the courts . . . ," Weeks v. United States, supra, and that such evidence "shall not be used at all." Silverthorne Lumber Co. v. United States, supra.

There are in the cases of this Court some passing references to the Weeks rule as being one of evidence. But the plain and unequivocal language of Weeks—and its later paraphrase in Wolf—to the effect that the Weeks rule is of constitutional origin, remains entirely undisturbed. In Byars v. United States, 1927, a unanimous Court declared that "the doctrine [cannot] . . . be tolerated *under our constitutional system*, that evidences of crime discovered by a federal officer in making a search without lawful warrant may be used against the victim of the unlawful search where a timely challenge has been interposed." (Emphasis added.) The Court, in Olmstead v. United States, 1928, 277 U.S. 438, at page 462, 48 S.Ct. 564, 567, 72 L.Ed. 944, in unmistakable language restated the Weeks rule:

> "The striking outcome of the Weeks case and those which followed it was the sweeping declaration that the Fourth Amendment, although not referring to or limiting the use of evidence in court, really forbade its introduction if obtained by government officers through a violation of the amendment." . . .

II.

In 1949, 35 years after Weeks was announced, this Court, in Wolf v. People of State of Colorado, supra, again for the first time, discussed the effect of the Fourth Amendment upon the States through the operation of the Due Process Clause of the Fourteenth Amendment. It said:

> "[W]e have no hesitation in saying that were a State affirmatively to sanction such police incursion into privacy it would run counter to the guaranty of the Fourteenth Amendment."

Nevertheless, after declaring that the "security of one's privacy against arbitrary intrusion by the police" is "implicit in 'the concept of ordered liberty' and as such enforceable against the States through the Due Process Clause," and announcing that it "stoutly adhere[d]" to the Weeks decision, the Court decided that the Weeks exclusionary rule would not then be imposed upon the States as "an essential ingredient of the right." . . . The Court's reasons for not considering essential to the right to privacy, as a curb imposed upon the States by the Due Process Clause, that which decades before had been posited as part and parcel of the Fourth Amendment's limitation upon federal encroachment of individual privacy, were bottomed on factual considerations.

While they are not basically relevant to a decision that the exclusionary rule is an essential ingredient of the Fourth Amendment as the right it embodies is vouchsafed against the States by the Due Process Clause, we will consider the current validity of the factual grounds upon which Wolf was based.

The Court in Wolf first stated that "[t]he contrariety of views of the States" on the adoption of the exclusionary rule of Weeks was "particularly impressive" . . . ; and, in this connection, that it could not "brush aside the experience of States which deem the incidence of such conduct by the police too slight to call for a deterrent remedy . . . by overriding the [States'] relevant rules of evidence." . . . While in 1949, prior to the Wolf case, almost two-thirds of the States were opposed to the use of the exclusionary rule, now, despite the Wolf case, more than half of those since passing upon it, by their own legislative or judicial decision, have wholly or partly adopted or adhered to the Weeks rule. . . . Significantly, among those now following the rule is California, which, according to its highest court, was "compelled to reach that conclusion because other remedies have completely failed to secure compliance with the constitutional provisions. . . ." People v. Cahan, 1955, . . . In connection with this California case, we note that the second basis elaborated in Wolf in support of its failure to enforce the exclusionary doctrine against the States was that "other means of protection" have been afforded "the right to privacy." . . . The experience of California that such other remedies have been worthless and futile is buttressed by the experience of other States. The obvious futility of relegating the Fourth Amendment to the protection of other remedies has, moreover, been recognized by this Court since Wolf. See Irvine v. People of State of California, 1954, . . .

Likewise, time has set its face against what Wolf called the "weighty testimony" of People v. Defore, 1926, 242 N.Y. 13, 150 N.E. 585. There Justice (then Judge) Cardozo, rejecting adoption of the Weeks exclusionary rule in New York, had said that "[t]he Federal rule as it stands is either too strict or too lax." However, the force of that reasoning has been largely vitiated by later decisions of this Court. These include the recent discarding of the "silver platter" doctrine which allowed federal judicial use of evidence seized in violation of the Constitution by state agents, Elkins v. United States, [364 U.S. 206, 80 S.Ct. 1437]; the relaxation of the formerly strict requirements as to standing to challenge the use of evidence thus seized, so that now the procedure of exclusion, "ultimately referable to constitutional safeguards," is available to anyone even "legitimately on [the] premises" unlawfully searched, Jones v. United States, 1960; and finally, the formulation of a method to prevent state use of evidence unconstitutionally seized by federal agents, Rea v. United States, 1956. Because there can be no fixed formula, we are admittedly met with "recurring questions of the reasonableness of searches," but less is not to be expected when dealing with a Constitution, and, at any rate, "[r]easonableness is in the first instance for the [trial court] to determine." . . .

It, therefore, plainly appears that the factual considerations supporting the failure of the Wolf Court to include the Weeks exclusionary rule when it recognized the enforceability of the right to privacy against the States in 1949, while not basically relevant to the constitutional consideration, could not, in any analysis, now be deemed controlling.

III.

[Omitted]

IV.

Since the Fourth Amendment's right of privacy has been declared enforceable against the States through the Due Process Clause of the Fourteenth, it is enforceable against them by the same sanction of exclusion as is used against the Federal Government. Were it otherwise, then just as without the Weeks rule the assurance against unreasonable federal searches and seizures would be "a form of words", valueless and undeserving of mention in a perpetual charter of inestimable human liberties, so too, without that rule the freedom from state invasions of privacy would be so ephemeral and so neatly severed from its conceptual nexus with the freedom from all brutish means of coercing evidence as not to merit this Court's high regard as a freedom "implicit in 'the concept of ordered liberty.'" At the time that the Court held in Wolf that the Amendment was applicable to the States through the Due Process Clause, the cases of this Court, as we have seen, had steadfastly held that as to federal officers the Fourth Amendment included the exclusion of the evidence seized in violation of its provisions. Even Wolf "stoutly adhered" to that proposition. The right to privacy, when conceded operatively enforceable against the States, was not susceptible of destruction by avulsion of the sanction upon which its protection and enjoyment had always been deemed dependent under the Boyd, Weeks and Silverthorne cases. Therefore, in extending the substantive protections of due process to all constitutionally unreasonable searches—state or federal—it was logically and constitutionally necessary that the exclusion doctrine—an essential part of the right to privacy—be also insisted upon as an essential ingredient of the right newly recognized by the Wolf case. In short, the admission of the new constitutional right by Wolf could not consistently tolerate denial of its most important constitutional privilege, namely, the exclusion of the evidence which an accused had been forced to give by reason of the unlawful seizure. To hold otherwise is to grant the right but in reality to withhold its privilege and enjoyment. Only last year the Court itself recognized that the purpose of the exclusionary rule "is to deter—to compel respect for the constitutional guaranty in the only effectively available way—by removing the incentive to disregard it."

Indeed, we are aware of no restraint, similar to that rejected today, conditioning the enforcement of any other basic constitutional right. The right to privacy, no less important than any other right carefully and particularly reserved to the people, would stand in marked contrast to all other rights declared as "basic to a free society." Wolf v. People of State of Colorado, supra, . . . This Court has not hesitated to enforce as strictly against the States as it does against the Federal Government the rights of free speech and of a free press, the rights to notice and to a fair, public trial, including, as it does, the right not to be convicted by use of a coerced confession, however logically relevant it be, and without regard to its reliability. And nothing could be more certain than that when a coerced confession is involved, "the relevant rules of evidence" are overridden without regard to "the incidence of such conduct by the police," slight or frequent. Why should not the same rule apply to what is tantamount to coerced testimony by way of unconstitutional seizure of goods, papers, effects, documents, etc.? We find that, as to the Federal Government, the Fourth and Fifth Amendments and, as to the States, the freedom from unconscionable invasions of privacy and the freedom from convictions based upon coerced confessions do enjoy an "intimate relation" in their perpetuation of "principles of humanity and civil liberty [secured] . . . only after years of struggle." Bram v. United States, 1897. They express "supplementing phases of the same constitutional purpose—to maintain inviolate large areas of personal privacy." Feldman v. United States, 1944. The philosophy of each Amendment and of each freedom is complementary to, although not dependent upon, that of the other in its sphere of influence—the very least that together they assure in either sphere is that no man is to be convicted on unconstitutional evidence. . . .

V.

Moreover, our holding that the exclusionary rule is an essential part of both the Fourth and Fourteenth Amendments is not only the logical dictate of prior cases, but it also makes very good sense. There is no war between the Constitution and common sense. Presently, a federal prosecutor may make no use of evidence illegally seized, but a State's attorney across the street may, although he supposedly is operating under the enforceable prohibitions of the same Amendment. Thus the State, by admitting evidence unlawfully seized, serves to encourage disobedience to the Federal Constitution which it is bound to uphold. Moreover, as was said in Elkins, "[t]he very essence of a healthy federalism depends upon the avoidance of needless conflict between state and federal courts." Such a conflict, hereafter needless, arose this very Term, in Wilson v. Schnettler, 1961, in which, and in spite of the promise made by Rea, we gave full recognition to our practice in this regard by refusing to restrain a federal officer from testifying in a state court as to evidence unconstitutionally seized by him in the performance of his duties. Yet the double standard recognized until today hardly put such a thesis into practice. In nonexclusionary States, federal officers, being human, were by it invited to and did, as our cases indicate, step across the street to the State's attorney with their unconstitutionally seized evidence. Prosecution on the basis of that evidence was then had in a state court in utter disregard of the enforceable Fourth Amendment. If the fruits of an unconstitutional search had been inadmissible in both state and federal courts, this inducement to evasion would have been sooner eliminated. There would be no need to reconcile such cases as Rea and Schnettler, each pointing up the hazardous uncertainties of our heretofore ambivalent approach.

Federal-state cooperation in the solution of crime under constitutional standards will be promoted, if only by recognition of their now mutual obligation to respect the same fundamental criteria in their approaches. "However much in a particular case insistence upon such rules may appear as a technicality that inures to the benefit of a guilty person, the history of the criminal law proves that tolerance of shortcut methods in law enforcement impairs its enduring effectiveness." Denying shortcuts to only one of two cooperating law enforcement agencies tends naturally to breed legitimate suspicion of "working arrangements" whose results are equally tainted. . . .

There are those who say, as did Justice (then Judge) Cardozo, that under our constitutional exclusionary doctrine "[t]he criminal is to go free because the constable has blundered." People v. Defore [supra]. In some cases this will undoubtedly be the result. But, as was said in Elkins, "there is another consideration—the imperative of judicial integrity." . . . The criminal goes free, if he must, but it is the law that sets him free. Nothing can destroy a government more quickly than its failure to observe its own laws, or worse, its disregard of the charter of its own existence. As Mr. Justice Brandeis, dissenting, said in Olmstead v. United States, 1928, 277 U.S. 438, 485, 48 S.Ct. 564, 575: "Our government is the potent, the omnipresent teacher. For good or for ill, it teaches the whole people by its example. . . . If the government becomes a lawbreaker, it breeds contempt for law; it invites every man to become a law unto himself; it invites anarchy." Nor can it lightly be assumed that, as a practical matter, adoption of the exclusionary rule fetters law enforcement. Only last year this Court expressly considered that contention and found that "pragmatic evidence of a sort" to the contrary was not wanting. Elkins v. United States, supra. The Court noted that

> "The federal courts themselves have operated under the exclusionary rule of Weeks for almost half a century; yet it has not been suggested either that the Federal Bureau of Investigation has thereby been rendered ineffective, or that the administration of criminal justice in the federal courts has thereby been disrupted. Moreover, the experience of the states is impressive . . . . The movement towards the rule of exclusion has been halting but seemingly inexorable."

. . .

The ignoble shortcut to conviction left open to the State tends to destroy the entire system of constitutional restraints on which the liberties of the people rest. Having once recognized that the right to privacy embodied in the Fourth Amendment is enforceable against the States, and that the right to be secure against rude invasions of privacy by state officers is, therefore, constitutional in origin, we can no longer permit that right to remain an empty promise. Because it is enforceable in the same manner and to like effect as other basic rights secured by the Due Process Clause, we can no longer permit it to be revocable at the whim of any police officer who, in the name of law enforcement itself, chooses to suspend its enjoyment. Our decision, founded on reason and truth, gives to the individual no more than that which the Constitution guarantees him, to the police officer no less than that to which honest law enforcement is entitled, and, to the courts, that judicial integrity so necessary in the true administration of justice.

The judgment of the Supreme Court of Ohio is reversed and the cause remanded for further proceedings not inconsistent with this opinion.

Reversed and remanded.

MR. JUSTICE BLACK, concurring.

. . .

I am still not persuaded that the Fourth Amendment, standing alone, would be enough to bar the introduction into evidence against an accused of papers and effects seized from him in violation of its commands. For the Fourth Amendment does not itself contain any provision expressly precluding the use of such evidence, and I am extremely doubtful that such a provision could properly be inferred from nothing more than the basic command against unreasonable searches and seizures. Reflection of the problem, however, in the light of cases coming before the Court since Wolf, has led me to conclude that when the Fourth Amendment's ban against unreasonable searches and seizures is considered together with the Fifth Amendment's ban against compelled self-incrimination, a constitutional basis emerges which not only justifies but actually requires the exclusionary rule.

The close interrelationship between the Fourth and Fifth Amendments, as they apply to this problem, has long been recognized and, indeed, was expressly made the ground for this Court's holding in Boyd v. United States. There the Court fully discussed this relationship and declared itself "unable to perceive that the seizure of a man's private books and papers to be used in evidence against him is substantially different from compelling him to be a witness against himself." . . . In the final analysis, it seems to me that the Boyd doctrine, though perhaps not required by the express language of the Constitution strictly construed, is amply justified from an historical standpoint, soundly based in reason, and entirely consistent with what I regard to be the proper approach to interpretation of our Bill of Rights—an approach well set out by Mr. Justice Bradley in the Boyd case:

> "[C]onstitutional provisions for the security of person and property should be liberally construed. A close and literal construction deprives them of half their efficacy, and leads to gradual depreciation of the right, as if it existed more in sound than in substance. It is the duty of [the] courts to be watchful for the constitutional rights of the citizen, and against any stealthy encroachments thereon."

. . . . As I understand the Court's opinion in this case, we . . . set aside this state conviction in reliance upon the precise, intelligible and more predictable constitutional doctrine enunciated in the Boyd case. I fully agree with Mr. Justice Bradley's opinion that the two Amendments upon which the Boyd doctrine rests are of vital importance in our constitutional scheme of liberty and that both are entitled to a liberal rather than a niggardly interpretation. The courts of the country are entitled to know with as much certainty as possible what scope they cover. The Court's opinion, in my judgment, dissipates the doubt and uncertainty in this field of constitutional law and I am persuaded, for this and other reasons stated, to depart from my prior views, to accept the Boyd doctrine as controlling in this state case and to join the Court's judgment and opinion which are in accordance with that constitutional doctrine.

MR. JUSTICE DOUGLAS, concurring.

Though I have joined the opinion of the Court, I add a few words. This criminal proceeding started with a lawless search and seizure. The police entered a home forcefully, and seized documents that were later used to convict the occupant of a crime.

She lived alone with her fifteen-year-old daughter in the second-floor flat of a duplex in Cleveland. At about 1:30 in the afternoon of May 23, 1957, three policemen arrived at this house. They rang the bell, and the appellant, appearing at her window, asked them what they wanted. According to their later testimony, the policemen had come to the house on information from "a confidential source that there was a person hiding out in the home, who was wanted for questioning in connection with a recent bombing." To the appellant's question, however, they replied only that they wanted to question her and would not state the subject about which they wanted to talk.

The appellant, who had retained an attorney in connection with a pending civil matter, told the police she would call him to ask if she should let them in. On her attorney's advice, she told them she would let them in only when they produced a valid search warrant. For the next two and a half hours, the police laid siege to the house. At four o'clock, their number was increased to at least seven. Appellant's lawyer appeared on the scene; and one of the policemen told him that they now had a search warrant, but the officer refused to show it. Instead, going to the back door, the officer first tried to kick it in and, when that proved unsuccessful, he broke the glass in the door and opened it from the inside.

The appellant, who was on the steps going up to her flat, demanded to see the search warrant; but the officer refused to let her see it although he waved a paper in front of her face. She grabbed it and thrust it down the front of her dress. The policemen seized her, took the paper from her, and had her handcuffed to another officer. She was taken upstairs, thus bound, and into the larger of the two bedrooms in the apartment; there she was forced to sit on the bed. Meanwhile, the officers entered the house and made a complete search of the four rooms of her flat and of the basement of the house.

The testimony concerning the search is largely nonconflicting. The approach of the officers; their long wait outside the home, watching all its doors; the arrival of reinforcements armed with a paper; breaking into the house; putting their hands on appellant and handcuffing her; numerous officers ransacking through every room and piece of furniture, while the appellant sat, a prisoner in her own bedroom. . . . One must understand that this case is based on the knowing possession of four little pamphlets, a couple of photographs and a little pencil doodle—all of which are alleged to be pornographic.

* * *

We held in Wolf v. People of State of Colorado, [supra] that the Fourth Amendment was applicable to the States by reason of the Due Process Clause of the Fourteenth Amendment. But a majority held that the exclusionary rule of the Weeks case was not required of the States, that they could apply such sanctions as they chose. That position had the necessary votes to carry the day. But with all respect it was not the voice of reason or principle.

As stated in the Weeks case, if evidence seized in violation of the Fourth Amendment can be used against an accused, "his right to be secure against such searches and seizures, is of no value, and . . . might as well be stricken from the Constitution." . . .

When we allowed States to give constitutional sanction to the "shabby business" of unlawful entry into a home . . . we did indeed rob the Fourth Amendment of much meaningful force. There are, of course, other theoretical remedies. One is disciplinary action within the hierarchy of the police system, including prosecution of the police officer for a crime. Yet as Mr. Justice Murphy said in Wolf v. People of State of Colorado, . . . "Self-scrutiny is a lofty ideal, but its exaltation reaches new heights if we expect a District Attorney to prosecute himself or his associates for well-meaning violations of the search and seizure clause during a raid the District Attorney or his associates have ordered."

The only remaining remedy, if exclusion of the evidence is not required, is an action of trespass by the homeowner against the offending officer. Mr. Justice Murphy showed how onerous and difficult it would be for the citizen to maintain that action and how meagre the relief even if the citizen prevails. The truth is that trespass actions against officers who make unlawful searches and seizures are mainly illusory remedies.

Without judicial action making the exclusionary rule applicable to the States, Wolf v. People of State of Colorado in practical effect reduced the guarantee against unreasonable searches and seizures to "a dead letter," as Mr. Justice Rutledge said in his dissent.

Wolf v. People of State of Colorado, supra, was decided in 1949. The immediate result was a storm of constitutional controversy which only today finds its end. I believe that this is an appropriate case in which to put an end to the asymmetry which Wolf imported into the law. It is an appropriate case because the facts it presents show—as would few other cases—the casual arrogance of those who have the untrammelled power to invade one's home and to seize one's person.

. . .

Moreover, continuance of Wolf v. People of State of Colorado in its full vigor breeds the unseemly shopping around of the kind revealed in Wilson v. Schnettler, 365 U.S. 381, 81 S.Ct. 632. Once evidence, inadmissible in a federal court, is admissible in a state court a "double standard" exists which, as the Court points out, leads to "working arrangements" that undercut federal policy and reduce some aspects of law enforcement to shabby business. The rule that supports that practice does not have the force of reason behind it.

[The Memorandum of MR. JUSTICE STEWART is omitted.]

MR. JUSTICE HARLAN, whom MR. JUSTICE FRANKFURTER and MR. JUSTICE WHITTAKER join, dissenting.

In overruling the Wolf case the Court, in my opinion, has forgotten the sense of judicial restraint which, with due regard for *stare decisis*, is one element that should enter into deciding whether a past decision of this Court should be overruled. Apart from that I also believe that the Wolf rule represents sounder Constitutional doctrine than the new rule which now replaces it.

I.

From the Court's statement of the case one would gather that the central, if not controlling, issue on this appeal is whether illegally state-seized evidence is Constitutionally admissible in a state prosecution, an issue which would of course face us with the need for re-examining Wolf. However, such is not the situation. For, although that question was indeed raised here and below among appellant's subordinate points, the new and pivotal issue brought to the Court by this appeal is whether § 2905.34 of the Ohio Revised Code making criminal the *mere* knowing possession or control of obscene material, and under which appellant has been convicted, is consistent with the rights of fee thought and expression assured against state action by the Fourteenth Amendment. That was the principal issue which was decided by the Ohio Supreme Court, which was tendered by appellant's Jurisdictional Statement, and which was briefed and argued in this Court.

In this posture of things, I think it fair to say that five members of this Court have simply "reached out" to overrule Wolf. With all respect for the views of the majority, and recognizing that *stare decisis* carries different weight in Constitutional adjudication than it does in nonconstitutional decision, I can perceive no justification for regarding this case as an appropriate occasion for re-examining Wolf.

Since the demands of the case before us do not require us to reach the question of the validity of Wolf, I think this case furnishes a singularly inappropriate occasion for reconsideration of that decision, if reconsideration is indeed warranted. Even the most cursory examination will reveal that the doctrine of the Wolf case has been of continuing importance in the administration of state criminal law. Indeed, certainly as regards its "nonexclusionary" aspect, Wolf did no more than articulate the then existing assumption among the States that the federal cases enforcing the exclusionary rule "do not bind [the States], for they construe provisions of the federal Constitution, the Fourth and Fifth Amendments, not applicable to the states." Though, of course, not reflecting the full measure of this continuing reliance, I find that during the last three Terms, for instance, the issue of the inadmissibility of illegally state-obtained evidence appears on an average of about fifteen times per Term just in the *in forma pauperis* cases summarily disposed of by us. This would indicate both that the issue which is now being decided may well have untoward practical ramifications respecting state cases long since disposed of in reliance on Wolf, and that were we determined to re-examine that doctrine we would not lack future opportunity.

The occasion which the Court has taken here is in the context of a case where the question was briefed not at all and argued only extremely tangentially. The unwisdom of overruling Wolf without full-dress argument is aggravated by the circumstance that that decision is a comparatively recent one (1949) to which three members of the present majority have at one time or other expressly subscribed, one to be sure with explicit misgivings. I would think that our obligation to the States, on whom we impose this new rule, as well as the obligation of orderly adherence to our own processes would demand that we seek that aid which adequate briefing and argument lends to the determination of an important issue. It certainly has never been a postulate of judicial power that mere altered disposition, or subsequent membership on the Court, is sufficient warrant for overturning a deliberately decided rule of Constitutional law. * * *

I am bound to say that what has been done is not likely to promote respect either for the Court's adjudicatory process or for the stability of its decisions. Having been unable, however, to persuade any of the majority to a different procedural course, I now turn to the merits of the present decision.

II.

Essential to the majority's argument against Wolf is the proposition that the rule of Weeks v. United States, [supra] excluding in federal criminal trials the use of evidence obtained in violation of the Fourth Amendment, derives not from the "supervisory power" of this Court over the federal judicial system, but from Constitutional requirement. This is so because no one, I suppose, would suggest that this Court possesses any general supervisory power over the state courts. Although I entertain considerable doubt as to the soundness of this foundational proposition of the majority, . . . I shall assume, for present purposes, that the Weeks rule "is of constitutional origin."

At the heart of the majority's opinion in this case is the following syllogism: (1) the rule excluding in federal criminal trials evidence which is the product of an illegal search and seizure is a "part and parcel" of the Fourth Amendment; (2) Wolf held that the "privacy" assured against federal action by the Fourth Amendment is also protected against state action by the Fourteenth Amendment; and (3) it is therefore "logically and constitutionally necessary" that the Weeks exclusionary rule should also be enforced against the States.

This reasoning ultimately rests on the unsound premise that because Wolf carried into the States, as part of "the concept of ordered liberty" embodied in the Fourteenth Amendment, the principle of "privacy" underlying the Fourth Amendment . . ., it must follow that whatever configurations of the Fourth Amendment have been developed in the particularizing federal precedents are likewise to be deemed a part of "ordered liberty," and as such are enforceable against the States. For me, this does not follow at all.

It cannot be too much emphasized that what was recognized in Wolf was not that the Fourth Amendment *as such* is enforceable against the States as a facet of due process, a view of the Fourteenth Amendment which, as Wolf itself pointed out . . ., has long since been discredited, but the principle of privacy "which is at the core of the Fourth Amendment." . . . It would not be proper to expect or impose any precise equivalence, either as regards the scope of the right or the means of its implementation, between the requirements of the Fourth and Fourteenth Amendments. For the Fourth, unlike what was said in Wolf of the Fourteenth, does not state a general principle only; it is a particular command, having its setting in a pre-existing legal context on which both interpreting decisions and enabling statutes must at least build.

Thus, even in a case which presented simply the question of whether a particular search and seizure was constitutionally "unreasonable"—say in a tort action against state officers—we would not be true to the Fourteenth Amendment were we merely to stretch the general principle of individual privacy on a Procrustean bed of federal precedents under the Fourth Amendment. But in this instance more than that is involved, for here we are reviewing not a determination that what the state police did was Constitutionally permissible (since the state court quite evidently assumed that it was not), but a determination that appellant was properly found guilty of conduct which, for present purposes, it is to be assumed the State could Constitutionally punish. Since there is not the slightest suggestion that Ohio's policy is "affirmatively to sanction . . . police incursion into privacy," what the Court is now doing is to impose upon the States not only federal substantive standards of "search and seizure" but also the basic federal remedy for violation of those standards. For I think it entirely clear that the Weeks exclusionary rule is but a remedy which, by penalizing past official misconduct, is aimed at deterring such conduct in the future.

I would not impose upon the States this federal exclusionary remedy. The reasons given by the majority for now suddenly turning its back on Wolf seem to me notably unconvincing.

First, it is said that "the factual grounds upon which Wolf was based" have since changed, in that more States now follow the Weeks exclusionary rule than was so at the time Wolf was decided. While that is true, a recent survey indicates that at present one-half of the States still adhere to the common-law non-exclusionary rule, and one, Maryland, retains the rule as to felonies. Berman and Oberst, Admissibility of Evidence Obtained by an Unconstitutional Search and Seizure, 55 N.W.L.Rev. 525, 532–533. But in any case surely all this is beside the point, as the majority itself indeed seems to recognize. Our concern here, as it was in Wolf, is not with the desirability of that rule but only with the question whether the States are Constitutionally free to follow it or not as they may themselves determine, and the relevance of the disparity of views among the States on this point lies simply in the fact that the judgment involved is a debatable one. Moreover, the very fact on which the majority relies, instead of lending support to what is now being done, points away from the need of replacing voluntary state action with federal compulsion.

The preservation of a proper balance between state and federal responsibility in the administration of criminal justice demands patience on the part of those who might like to see things move faster among the States in this respect. Problems of criminal law enforcement vary widely from State to State. One State, in considering the totality of its legal picture, may conclude that the need for embracing the Weeks rule is pressing because other remedies are unavailable or inadequate to secure compliance with the substantive Constitutional principle involved. Another, though equally solicitous of Constitutional rights, may choose to pursue one purpose at a time, allowing all evidence relevant to guilt to be brought into a criminal trial, and dealing with Constitutional infractions by other means. Still another may consider the exclusionary rule too rough-and-ready a remedy, in that it reaches only unconstitutional intrusions which eventuate in criminal prosecution of the victims. Further, a State after experimenting with the Weeks rule for a time may, because of unsatisfactory experience with it, decide to revert to a non-exclusionary rule. And so on. From the standpoint of Constitutional permissibility in pointing a State in one direction or another, I do not see at all why "time has set its face against" the considerations which led Mr. Justice Cardozo, then chief judge of the New York Court of Appeals, to reject for New York in People v. Defore, [supra], the Weeks exclusionary rule. For us the question remains, as it has always been, one of state power, not one of passing judgment on the wisdom of one state course or another. In my view this Court should continue to forbear from fettering the States with an adamant rule which may embarrass them in coping with their own peculiar problems in criminal law enforcement.

Further, we are told that imposition of the Weeks rule on the States makes "very good sense," in that it will promote recognition by state and federal officials of their "mutual obligation to respect the same fundamental criteria" in their approach to law enforcement, and will avoid " 'needless conflict between state and federal courts.' " Indeed the majority now finds an incongruity in Wolf's discriminating perception between the demands of "ordered liberty" as respects the basic right of "privacy" and the means of securing it among the States. That perception, resting both on a sensitive regard for our federal system and a sound recognition of this Court's remoteness from particular state problems, is for me the strength of that decision.

An approach which regards the issue as one of achieving procedural symmetry or of serving administrative convenience surely disfigures the boundaries of this Court's functions in relation to the state and federal courts. Our role in promulgating the Weeks rule and its extensions in such cases as Rea, Elkins, and Rios was quite a different one than it is here. There, in implementing the Fourth Amendment, we occupied the position of a tribunal having the ultimate responsibility for developing the standards and procedures of judicial administration within the judicial system over which it presides. Here we review state procedures whose measure is to be taken not against the specific substantive commands of the Fourth Amendment but under the flexible contours of the Due Process Clause. I do not believe that the Fourteenth Amendment empowers this Court to mould state remedies effectuating the right to freedom from "arbitrary intrusion by the police" to suit its own notions of how things should be done, as, for instance, the California Supreme Court did in People v. Cahan, . . . with reference to procedures in the California courts or as this Court did in Weeks for the lower federal courts.

A state conviction comes to us as the complete product of a sovereign judicial system. Typically a case will have been tried in a trial court, tested in some final appellate court, and will go no further. In the comparatively rare instance when a conviction is reviewed by us on due process grounds we deal then with a finished product in the creation of which we are allowed no hand, and our task, far from being one of over-all supervision, is, speaking generally, restricted to a determination of whether the prosecution was Constitutionally fair. The specifics of trial procedure, which in every mature legal system will vary greatly in detail, are within the sole competence of the States. I do not see how it can be said that a trial becomes unfair simply because a State determines that evidence may be considered by the trier of fact, regardless of how it was obtained, if it is relevant to the one issue with which the trial is concerned, the guilt or innocence of the accused. Of course, a court may use its procedures as an incidental means of pursuing other ends than the correct resolution of the controversies before it. Such indeed is the Weeks rule, but if a State does not choose to use its courts in this way, I do not believe that this Court is empowered to impose this much-debated procedure on local courts, however efficacious we may consider the Weeks rule to be as a means of securing Constitutional rights.

Finally, it is said that the overruling of Wolf is supported by the established doctrine that the admission in evidence of an involuntary confession renders a state conviction Constitutionally invalid. Since such a confession may often be entirely reliable, and therefore of the greatest relevance to the issue of the trial, the argument continues, this doctrine is ample warrant in precedent that the way evidence was obtained, and not just its relevance, is Constitutionally significant to the fairness of a trial. I believe this analogy is not a true one. The "coerced confession" rule is certainly not a rule that any illegally obtained statements may not be used in evidence. I would suppose that a statement which is procured during a period of illegal detention is, as much as unlawfully seized evidence, illegally obtained, but this Court has consistently refused to reverse state convictions resting on the use of such statements. Indeed it would seem the Court laid at rest the very argument now made by the majority when in Lisenba v. People of State of California, a state-coerced confession case, it said:

> "It may be assumed [that the] treatment of the petitioner [by the police] . . . deprived him of his liberty without due process and that the petitioner would have been afforded preventive relief if he could have gained access to a court to seek it.
>
> "But illegal acts, as such, committed in the course of obtaining a confession . . . do not furnish an answer to the constitutional question we must decide. . . . The gravamen of his complaint is the unfairness of the *use* of his confessions, and what occurred in their procurement is relevant only as it bears on that issue." (Emphasis supplied.)

The point, then, must be that in requiring exclusion of an involuntary statement of an accused, we are concerned not with an appropriate remedy for what the police have done, but with something which is regarded as going to the heart of our concepts of fairness in judicial procedure. The operative assumption of our procedural system is that "Ours is the accusatorial as opposed to the inquisitorial system. Such has been the characteristic of Anglo-American criminal justice since it freed itself from practices borrowed by the Star Chamber from the Continent whereby an accused was interrogated in secret for hours on end." . . . The pressures brought to bear against an accused leading to a confession, unlike an unconstitutional violation of privacy, do not, apart from the use of the confession at trial, necessarily involve independent Constitutional violations. What is crucial is that the trial defense to which an accused is entitled should not be rendered an empty formality by reason of statements wrung from him, for then "a prisoner . . . [has been] made the deluded instrument of his own conviction." 2 Hawkins, Pleas of the Crown (8th ed., 1824), c. 46, § 34. That this is a *procedural right*, and that its violation occurs at the time his improperly obtained statement is admitted at trial, is manifest. For without this right all the careful safeguards erected around the giving of testimony, whether by an accused or any other witness, would become empty formalities in a procedure where the most compelling possible evidence of guilt, a confession, would have already been obtained at the unsupervised pleasure of the police.

This, and not the disciplining of the police, as with illegally seized evidence, is surely the true basis for excluding a statement of the accused which was unconstitutionally obtained. In sum, I think the coerced confession analogy works strongly *against* what the Court does today.

In conclusion, it should be noted that the majority opinion in this case is in fact an opinion only for the *judgment* overruling Wolf, and not for the basic rationale by which four members of the majority have reached that result. For my Brother Black is unwilling to subscribe to their view that the Weeks exclusionary rule derives from the Fourth Amendment itself, but joins the majority opinion on the premise that its end result can be achieved by bringing the Fifth Amendment to the aid of the Fourth. On that score I need only say that whatever the validity of the "Fourth-Fifth Amendment" correlation which the Boyd case [supra] found, we have only very recently again reiterated the long-established doctrine of this Court that the Fifth Amendment privilege against self-incrimination is not applicable to the States. . . .

I regret that I find so unwise in principle and so inexpedient in policy a decision motivated by the high purpose of increasing respect for Constitutional rights. But in the last analysis I think this Court can increase respect for the Constitution only if it rigidly respects the limitations which the Constitution places upon it, and respects as well the principles inherent in its own processes. In the present case I think we exceed both, and that our voice becomes only a voice of power, not of reason.

NOTES

1. The exclusionary rule has been under recent attack. In one recent decision, the Oregon Supreme Court refused to exclude evidence which had been seized in violation of a state statutory provision governing searches. See State v. Valentine, 504 P.2d 84 (Ore.1972). At the end of the 1970 Term at least four justices indicated their willingness to overrule Mapp v. Ohio. Chief Justice Burger indicated his views in a dissent in Bivens v. Six Unknown Named Agents, 403 U.S. 388, 91 S.Ct. 1999 (1971). This opinion is reprinted infra at p. 765. In Coolidge v. New Hampshire, 403 U.S. 443, 91 S.Ct. 2022 (1971), police officers secured a search warrant from the prosecuting attorney who under state law had authority to issue one. The Court held that the warrant was invalid because it was not issued by a "neutral and detached magistrate". The Court then considered various exceptions to the rule which require a warrant prior to search and found all of them inapplicable. There was no dispute that the police did have adequate probable cause to justify a search but the evidence was suppressed for failure to secure a *valid* warrant or to fit the case within the warrant exception categories. Applicable language from the opinions in *Coolidge* concerning the exclusionary rule follow:

"MR. JUSTICE BLACK, concurring and dissenting.

"After a jury trial in a New Hampshire state court, petitioner was convicted of murder and sentenced to life imprisonment. Holding that certain evidence introduced by the State was seized during an 'unreasonable' search and that the evidence was inadmissible under the judicially created exclusionary rule of the Fourth Amendment, the majority reverses that conviction. Believing that the search and seizure here was reasonable and that the Fourth Amendment properly construed contains no such exclusionary rule, I dissent. * * *

"The Fourth Amendment prohibits unreasonable searches and seizures. The Amendment says nothing about consequences. It certainly nowhere provides for the exclusion of evidence as the remedy for violation. The Amendment states: 'The right of the people to be secure in their persons, houses, papers and effects, against unreasonable searches and siezures, shall not be violated, and no Warrants shall issue, but upon probable cause, supported by Oath or affirmation, and particularly describing the place to be searched, and the persons or things to be seized.' No examination of that text can find an exclusionary rule by a mere process of construction.

"In striking contrast to the Fourth Amendment, the Fifth Amendment states in express, unambiguous terms that no person 'shall be compelled in any criminal case to be a witness against himself.' The Fifth Amendment in and of itself directly and explicitly commands its own exclusionary rule—a defendant cannot be compelled to give evidence against himself. Absent congressional action taken pursuant to the Fourth Amendment, if evidence is to be excluded, it must be under the Fifth Amendment, not the Fourth. . . . That was the thrust of my concurring opinion in Mapp v. Ohio, 367 U.S. 643, 661, 81 S.Ct. 1684, 1694 (1961).

"The evidence seized by breaking into Mrs. Mapp's house and the search of all her possessions, was excluded from evidence, not by the Fourth

Amendment which contains no exclusionary rule, but by the Fifth Amendment which does. * * *

"The majority treats the exclusionary rule as a judge-made rule of evidence designed and utilized to enforce the majority's own notions of proper police conduct. The Court today announces its new rules of police procedure in the name of the Fourth Amendment, then holds that evidence seized in violation of the new 'guidelines' is automatically inadmissible at trial. The majority does not purport to rely on the Fifth Amendment to exclude the evidence in this case. Indeed it could not. The majority prefers instead to rely on 'changing times' and the Court's role as it sees it, as the administrator in charge of regulating the contacts of officials with citizens. The majority states that in the absence of a better means of regulation, it applies a court-created rule of evidence. * * *

"It is difficult for me to believe the Framers of the Bill of Rights intended that the police be required to prove a defendant's guilt in a 'little trial' before the issuance of a search warrant. . . . No such proceeding was required before or after the adoption of the Fourth Amendment, until this Court decided *Aguilar* and *Spinelli*. Likewise, eavesdroppers were deemed to be competent witnesses in both English and American courts up until this Court in its Fourth Amendment 'rulemaking' capacity undertook to lay down rules for electronic surveillance. * * *

"Our Government is founded upon a written Constitution. The draftsmen expressed themselves in careful and measured terms corresponding with the immense importance of the powers delegated to them. The Framers of the Constitution, and the people who adopted it, must be understood to have used words in their natural meaning, and to have intended what they said. The Constitution itself contains the standards by which the seizure of evidence challenged in the present case and the admissibility of that evidence at trial is to be measured in the absence of congressional legislation. It is my conclusion that both the seizure of the rifle offered by petitioner's wife and the seizure of the automobile at the time of petitioner's arrest were consistent with the Fourth Amendment and that the evidence so obtained under the circumstances shown in the record in this case could not be excluded under the Fifth Amendment. * * *"

[MR. JUSTICE BLACKMUN joins MR. JUSTICE BLACK in that portion which is to the effect that the Fourth Amendment supports no exclusionary rule.]

MR. JUSTICE HARLAN, concurring.

"From the several opinions that have been filed in this case it is apparent that the law of search and seizure is due for an overhauling. State and federal law enforcement officers and prosecutorial authorities must find quite intolerable the present state of uncertainty, which extends even to such an everyday question as the circumstances under which police may enter a man's property to arrest him and seize a vehicle believed to have been used during the commission of a crime.

"I would begin this process of re-evaluation by overruling Mapp v. Ohio, 367 U.S. 643, 81 S.Ct. 1684 (1961), and Ker v. California, 374 U.S. 23, 83 S.Ct. 1623 (1963). The former of these cases made the federal 'exclusionary rule' applicable to the States. The latter forced the States to follow all the ins and outs of this Court's Fourth Amendment decisions, handed down in federal cases.

"In combination *Mapp* and *Ker* have been primarily responsible for bringing about serious distortions and incongruities in this field of constitutional law. . . . First, the States have been put in a federal mold with respect to this aspect of criminal law enforcement, thus depriving the country of the opportunity to observe the effects of different procedures in similar settings. See, e. g., Oaks, Studying the Exclusionary Rule in Search and Seizure, 37 U.Chi.L.Rev. 665 (1970), suggesting that the assumed "deterrent value" of the exclusionary rule has never been adequately demonstrated or disproved and pointing out that because of *Mapp* all comparative statistics are 10 years old and no new ones can be obtained. Second, in order to leave some room for the States to cope with their own diverse problems, there has been generated a tendency to relax federal requirements under the Fourth Amendment, which now govern state procedures as well. . . . Until we face up to the basic constitutional mistakes of *Mapp* and *Ker,* no solid progress in setting things straight in search and seizure law will, in my opinion, occur.

"But for *Mapp* and *Ker,* I would have little difficulty in voting to sustain this conviction, for I do not think that anything the State did in this case could be said to offend those values which are 'at the core of the Fourth Amendment'."

Despite the impossibility of conducting comparative statistical studies on the effectiveness of the exclusionary rule after *Mapp,* a study has been conducted comparing search and seizure practices in Toronto, Canada with those in Chicago. The study concluded that "the deterrent rationale for the rule does not seem to be justified [by the empirical study and] Canada's experience with the tort remedy suggests that viable alternatives to the . . . rule do exist". See Spiotto, "The Search and Seizure Problem—Two Approaches: The Canadian Tort Remedy And The U.S. Exclusionary Rule", 1 J.Pol.Sci. & Admin. 36 (1973). A detailed analysis of Chicago search and seizure statistics leading to the conclusion that the exclusionary rule does not deter illegal police conduct is found in Spiotto, "Search and Seizure: An Empirical Study Of The Exclusionary Rule And Its Alternatives", 2 J.Legal Studies 243 (1973).

Finally, in United States v. Calandra, 414 U.S. 338, 94 S.Ct. 613 (1974), the Supreme Court of the United States held that the exclusionary rule does not apply at grand jury proceedings. The Court, with six Justices concurring held clearly that the sole justification for the exclusionary rule was its supposed deterrent effect against unlawful police conduct. The Court held that application of the rule to grand jury proceedings would have only minimal, if any, deterrent effect and therefore would not be invoked. The majority noted the conflict over the efficacy of the rule at trial itself but did not consider the question of the rule's continued viability. Most significantly, however, the three dissenters based their argument, not on deterrent effect, but upon the impropriety of judicial participation in, and approval of, police lawlessness that they thought inherent whenever a court admitted illegally seized materials into evidence. Near the end of his dissent Mr. Justice Brennan stated:

"In *Mapp,* the Court thought it had "close[d] the only courtroom door remaining open to evidence secured by official lawlessness" in violation of Fourth Amendment rights, 367 U.S. at 654–655. The door is again ajar. As a consequence, I am left with the uneasy feeling that today's decision may signal that a majority of my colleagues have positioned themselves to reopen the door still further and abandon altogether the exclusionary rule in search and seizure cases; for surely they cannot believe that application of the exclusionary rule at trial furthers the goal of deterrence, but that its application in grand jury proceedings will not "significantly" do so. Unless we are to shut our eyes to the evidence that crosses our desks every day, we must concede that official lawlessness has not abated and that no empirical data distinguishes trials from grand jury proceedings. I thus fear that when next we confront a case of a conviction rested on illegally seized evidence, today's decision will be invoked to sustain the conclusion in that case also that "it is unrealistic to assume" that application of the rule at trial would "significantly further" the goal of deterrence—though, if the police are presently undeterred, it is difficult to see how removal of the sanction of exclusion will induce more lawful official conduct.

"The exclusionary rule gave life to Madison's prediction that "independent tribunals of justice . . . will be naturally led to resist every encroachment upon rights expressly stipulated for in the Constitution by the declaration of rights." We betray the trust upon which that prediction rested by today's long step toward abandonment of the exclusionary rule."

Quere: Is Mr. Justice Brennan abandoning all reliance on the deterrent rationale for the exclusionary rule?

2. During the 1972 Term the Court heard arguments in two cases seeking the modification of Mapp v. Ohio. In California v. Krivda, one question presented was whether the exclusionary rule should be modified in state trials. The Court did not decide the question but remanded for a determination of whether the state court had based its decision on federal or state grounds. 409 U.S. 33, 93 S.Ct. 32 (1972). In Schneckloth v. Bustamonte, 412 U.S. 218, 93 S.Ct. 2041 (1973), the Court was urged to hold that the legality of a search and seizure by state officers may not be relitigated in a federal habeas corpus proceeding. Although the case was disposed of by a holding that the search was a consensual one, three of the Justices (Burger, Powell, and Rehnquist) were of the opinion that the Court should have ruled that federal habeas corpus was unavailable in such cases. A fourth (Blackmun) expressed a concurrence in that viewpoint but thought the issue should be reserved for another case, and Justice Stewart, who wrote the majority opinion, merely stated that it was unnecessary to consider that issue in this particular case.

During the 1973 Term, the Court heard an attack upon the exclusionary rule in federal criminal trials, in United States v. Robinson, 471 F.2d 1082 (D.C.Cir.1972), cert. granted, 410 U.S. 982, 93 S.Ct. 1500. The Court decided the case on other grounds and its opinion appears supra at p. 542. The State of Illinois filed an amicus curiae brief in this case (as well as in California v. Krivda), which contains an excellent summary of the arguments against the rule. Following are excerpts from that brief:

"On ethical grounds, the rule in its direct application, seems unfair. It benefits only the guilty. The innocent man whose rights are violated must sue civilly to secure damages; he must pursue a remedy that this Court has found to be ineffective. Further, the application of the rule punishes society and not the offending officer.

"In terms of judicial administration, the rule requires diversion from the fundamental concerns of guilt or innocence. At the very least, the determination of the ultimate question is substantially delayed and witnesses for both sides become discouraged or unavailable. At the worst, counsel for defendants become so concerned with the question of suppression that they never seriously prepare for trial or explore defenses on the merits.

"The public perception of the delay, the procedural gamesmanship and the clear benefit to the guilty serves to diminish confidence in the courts.

"The exclusionary rule creates a haven for a corrupt policeman or prosecutor. The rule allows the officer to immunize an offender while appearing to do an aggressive job of law enforcement. An officer may conduct a massive gambling raid without securing adequate evidence of probable cause. The officer appears to be doing his job cracking down on gambling only to be frustrated by the courts. The officer may reap both the benefits of public approval and consideration from the gambler. One study found that 'an examination of the records and a period of observation of this practice in the court is fairly convincing that the raids are made to immunize the gamblers while at the same time satisfying the public that gamblers are being harassed by the police.' Dash, 'Cracks in the Foundation of Criminal Justice,' 46 Ill.L.Rev. 385, 392 (1951). See also, Peterson, 'Restrictions in the Law of Search and Seizure,' 52 Nw. L.Rev. 45, 57–58, 58–59 (1957). The courts are compromised by aiding this kind of corruption. And the courts, not the police, are the recipients of public disapproval when they suppress meaningful, or overwhelming evidence. The corrupt policeman blames the courts for his ineffectiveness and the Courts cannot respond.

"The exclusionary rule is thought to deter illegal police conduct. There is no evidence that proves this is so. See Oaks, 'Studying the Exclusionary Rule in Search and Seizure,' 37 U.Chi.L.Rev. 665 (1970). The fact that there is no proof of deterrence should cause the rule to be abandoned. If due process requires the exclusionary rule, it would seem clear that the proponent of the rule ought to sustain the burden. It seems clear to us that even without statistics a realistic analysis of the incentives and pressures upon the police would show that the exclusionary rule cannot deter.

"The primary pressure upon the police is to apprehend criminals and prevent crime. It is an unceasing public pressure which arises not from some irrational public prejudice but from the indisputable assessment that crime is both an ethical and social evil. Further, there is the internal standard of every ordinary man in law enforcement that murderers, robbers, etc., ought to be punished for their crimes. The effect of the exclusionary rule in search and seizure cases is not deterrence but perjury. The rule fosters false testimony by law officers who feel they must apprehend offenders and are fearful that minor technical errors will result in their escape. In short, police officers who would not alter their testimony in any respect to help the prosecution establish guilt may well be driven to such extremes when the question is not one of guilt but rather of the admissibility of reliable evidence.

"There are institutional pressures which work against deterrence. The police organizational structure asks the policeman why he didn't arrest rather than why he did.

"[One eminent judge has adopted a standard for search and seizure which reflects this concern: 'When a police officer could justifiably be disciplined for failure to act, his action can hardly be characterized as unreasonable.' People v. Moore, 35 Ill.2d 399, 403, 220 N.E.2d 443, 445 (1966) (Schaefer, J.).]

"The police encourage seizure of contraband and place a premium on police alertness. The desire to prevent crime often causes the police to engage in practices which are not permitted when the object is the prosecution of offenders. The police structure is responsive to public norms. The police do not feel morally blameworthy because the public does not condemn. See Skolnick, Justice Without Trial, 219–26 (1966). La Fave, 'Improving Police Performance Through the Exclusionary Rule,' 30 Mo.L. Rev. 391, 442–44 (1965).

"It is this abiding, powerful and rational pressure to suppress crime that leads police to prefer, in many cases, to engage in the forbidden practices and forego prosecution. The Court has recognized the inability of the rule to deter in certain contexts. See Terry v. Ohio, 392 U.S. 1, 12–15 (1968). Studies have shown that the police have an incentive to arrest without any thought of conviction. An arrest disrupts illegal business and clears the streets for a time. Narcotics and weapons are destroyed and the arrestee bears the costs of freeing himself through court action. See La Fave, 'Improving Police Performance Through the Exclusionary Rule,' 30 Mo.L.Rev. 391, 422–29, 447–55 (1965); Waite, 'Police Regulation by Rules of Evidence,' 42 Mich.L.Rev. 679, 685–87 (1944). It is important to reiterate that the police do not act out of malice, they act because the public demands that they act and that demand is more forceful than the demands made by judges.

"It is our view that the only effective control upon police conduct is the community in which the police function. Excesses and abuses of police power occur rarely because the citizens will not tolerate them, not because the police fear that months later a judge will suppress evidence they seize. In our experience, the only effective means of changing police procedures which aggrieve segments of the community is by community pressure. The exclusionary rule has been in effect in Illinois since 1923 and yet there is no evidence that complaints concerning police abuses have diminished. In one city in Illinois, it is claimed that one minority group is persistently harassed by police. Though many allegations have proven unfounded, there have apparently been enough incidents to cause several changes in police procedure and high ranking personnel. The incentive for change was not a new rule of court or a far-reaching opinion but rather the pressure of citizens groups. In light of several recent jury verdicts acquitting unpopular defendants, it seems absurd to argue that the community will tolerate police excesses against minority groups.

"In this connection, it is worth observing that an officer who acts in good faith is not going to be deterred by the exclusionary rule. See Horowitz, 'Excluding the Exclusionary Rule,' 47 L.A.Bar Bull. 91, 92

(1972). By definition, such an officer acts because he thinks, albeit mistakenly, that he is acting within the law. The officer who acts in bad faith will not be deterred either. 'The officer who takes bribes or shakes down prisoners or extorts money on threat of arrest, or brutally mistreats prisoners or otherwise consciously abuses his authority can be controlled only by the imposition of direct penalties . . . the exclusionary rule has no impact in such a situation.' Barrett, 'Exclusion of Evidence Obtained by Illegal Searches,' 43 Calif.L.Rev. 565, 592–93 (1955).

"The incentives and pressures which work against the exclusionary rule are not the only factors which account for its limited value as a tool of deterrence. The rule itself is applied in a context inimical to its purposes. There is, first, a distinct failure to communicate the rules of search and seizure laid down by courts to the police in a manner comprehensible to the police. La Fave and Remington, 'Controlling the Police: The Judge's Role in Making and Reviewing Law Enforcement Decisions,' 63 Mich.L.Rev. 987, 991–93, 1003–1008 (1965). There is also the admitted failure of courts to prescribe consistent and comprehensible rules governing search and seizure. See Coolidge v. New Hampshire, 403 U.S. 443, 483 (1971). It may be inherently impossible to devise coherent Fourth Amendment precepts. If that is the case then the exclusionary rule is clearly out of place. It is unreasonable to expect deterrence when the subject does not know what he is forbidden to do. The lack of clarity in the law contributes to both public and police disrespect for the rules of search and seizure. Nothing is more incomprehensible to the policeman who accepts judicial supervision of searches by securing a warrant than to have another court say that the first court was wrong in issuing the warrant. See La Fave, 'Improving Police Performance Through the Exclusionary Rule, ' 30 Mo.L.Rev. 391, 411–415 (1966).

"There is a particularly striking and inexplicable anomaly in our treatment of police officers vis a vis lawyers. We excuse a lawyer who mistakenly judges a law to be constitutional and advises his client to plead guilty. See Brady v. United States, 397 U.S. 742, 756–757 (1970). Yet by a divided court we condemn a police officer who decides to search upon his mistaken judgment that he has met the requirements of the law. It is unfair to tax an officer, usually a layman, with the endless permutations of search and seizure law. The appearance to the officer, is that the law is capricious and meaningless, an attitude which scarcely encourages eager compliance.

"Many who recognize the validity of objections to the rule will advocate that the rule not be abandoned until a reasonable alternative is provided. The most popular suggestion for an alternative is to provide a remedy reminiscent of Industrial Commission (Workmen's Compensation) procedures. See Horowitz, 'Excluding the Exclusionary Rule, Can There Be an Effective Alternative,' 47 Los Angeles Bar Bull. 91, 94 et seq. (1972); Barrett, Exclusion of Evidence Obtained By Illegal Searches, 43 Calif.L.Rev. 565, 594–95 (1955). Bivins v. Six Unknown Fed. Narcotics Agents, 403 U.S. 388, 422–23 (1971) (Burger C. J. dissenting).

"It seems to us that concern over a viable alternative should not prevent this Court from reconsidering the exclusionary rule. If the exclusionary rule were effective and meaningful as a deterrent, it might be proper to ponder the necessity for replacing it with something else. But it appears that the exclusionary rule cannot and does not serve the purpose of deterrence. If the exclusionary rule has no deterrent effects, its absence will not leave a void to be filled. It might be said that an outright abolition of the exclusionary rule may have a symbolic effect and encourage police abuse. We doubt that this would occur. The public resentment of arbitrary police conduct is now and will remain the primary restraint on the police. Further, the continuation of the exclusionary rule will encourage the other police abuses attendant upon the administration of the rule.

"This Court need not resolve the issues presented by a complete abandonment of the exclusionary rule. Instead, a more modest approach can and ought to be pursued.

"The exclusionary rule in federal cases was adopted in Weeks v. United States, 232 U.S. 383 (1914). The crime there was use of the mails to transport lottery tickets. The police action there was conducted without any authority. It consisted of a complete search of the room of the defendant in his absence and a seizure of his private letters and correspondence and other private papers. Under the rule in Boyd v. United States, 116 U.S. 616 (1886), the seizure may well have violated the Fifth Amendment.

"The exclusionary rule was imposed upon the States in Mapp v. Ohio, 367 U.S. 643 (1961). The conduct of the police in that case can properly be characterized as flagrant. The offense charged could not today be constitutionally classified as a crime. See Stanley v. Georgia, 394 U.S. 557 (1969). The Court held that it must exclude 'evidence secured by official lawlessness in flagrant abuse of that basic right [of privacy]' 367 U.S. at 654–55.

"The nature of police conduct in both *Weeks* and *Mapp* was exceptionally violative of the suspect's rights. Indeed, in neither case, did the officers attempt to defend their actions on the merits or as taken in good faith. No rationale appears in either case for applying the exclusionary rule to reasonable, good faith but erroneous action by the police.

"Judge Friendly has suggested that 'the object of deterrence would be sufficiently achieved if the police were denied the fruit of activity intentionally or flagrantly illegal—where there was no reasonable cause to believe there was reasonable cause.' Friendly, The Bill of Rights as a Code of Criminal Procedure, 53 Calif.L.Rev. 929, 952 (1965). See also A.L.I. Model Code of Pre-Arraignment Procedure, § 8.02(2) (Tent.Draft No. 4, 1971). It appears to us at least that this is what *Mapp* said. When Mr. Justice (then Chief Judge) Cardozo rejected the idea that the criminal should go free because the constable 'blundered' he meant exactly what he said. A blundering constable was not the subject of *Mapp,* rather there a deliberate, methodical violation of a suspect's rights was involved.

"The exclusionary rule ought to be applied also in light of the severity of the crime involved. Justice Cardozo's opinion in People v. Defore is often cited but there is significant language in the opinion of Justice Finch in the Appellate Division opinion:

> 'To be unable to find a murderer guilty, although competent evidence is before the court to warrant a conviction, for the reason that someone else is guilty of petty larceny in connection with obtaining such evidence seems a handicap rather than a help to the administration of justice.' People v. Defore, 213 App.Div. 643, 652; 211 N.Y.S. 134, 142 (1925).

"['. . . judicial exceptions . . . should depend somewhat upon the gravity of the offense. If we assume, for example, that a child is kidnapped and the officers throw a roadblock about the neighborhood and search every outgoing car, it would be a drastic and undiscriminating use of the search. The officers might be unable to show probable cause for searching any particular car. However, I should candidly strive hard to sustain such an action, executed fairly and in good faith, because it might be reasonable to subject travelers to that indignity if it was the only way to save a threatened life and detect a vicious crime. But I should not strain to sustain such a roadblock and universal search to salvage a few bottles of bourbon and catch a bootlegger.' Brinegar v. United States, 338 U.S. 160, 183 (Jackson J. dissenting).]"

"The ethical quandary posed by the application of the exclusionary rule without regard to the nature of the crime involved is a significant one. 'However much we may be revolted by the methods used by the police to obtain the evidence we cannot rationally say that the defendant whose crime may be at least equally revolting should have a personal right to go free as a result.' The exclusionary rule assumes 'that the policeman's action always involves a greater social evil than the defendant.' Barrett, Exclusion of Evidence Obtained By Illegal Searches, 43 Calif.L.Rev. 565, 581 (1955).

* * *

"The other factor that ought to be considered is the nature of the police conduct.

"It has never been adequately explained why a case like *Mapp* involving extremely flagrant police misconduct used for the prosecution of the most trivial offense leads to the suppression of evidence seized with probable cause in good faith reliance upon a statutorily authorized warrant used for the prosecution of murder as in Coolidge v. New Hampshire, 403 U.S. 443 (1971). Without that explanation the rule should never have been extended to its present breadth.

"We do not ask now for the overruling of *Mapp*; we ask that the exclusionary rule be limited to those cases like *Mapp* which caused the rule to be promulgated. The exclusionary rule has assumed a scope far beyond the justifications offered when it was put upon the States. There is no valid rationale for its automatic extension to all classes of cases regardless of the nature of the police conduct and the gravity of the crime. As a minimum measure, the reach of the rule should be reduced to conform with the reasons offered for the rule in *Mapp*."

3. A rather flexible compromise exclusionary rule has been developed in Scotland. There the particular facts and merits of each case situation will determine whether the illegally seized evidence is to be admitted. In this way the Scottish courts seek to strike a balance between "(a) the interest of the citizen to be protected from illegal or irregular invasions of his liberties by the authorities and (b) the interest of the state to secure that evidence bearing upon the commission of crime and necessary to enable justice to be done shall not be withheld from courts of law on any merely formal or technical ground." See Lawrie v. Muir [1950] Scots.L.T.R. 37, in which the court, after referring to (a) and (b) above, said: "Neither of these objects can be insisted upon to the uttermost. The protection of the citizen is primarily for the innocent citizen against unwarranted, wrongful and perhaps high-handed interference . . . . The protection is not

intended as a protection for the guilty citizen against the efforts of the public prosecutor to vindicate the law. On the other hand, the interest of the State cannot be magnified to the point of causing all the safeguards for the protection of the citizen to vanish, and of offering a positive inducement to the authorities to proceed by irregular methods."

For another Scottish case, in addition to the one above, which resulted in a rejection of illegally seized evidence by reason of the foregoing consideration, see H. M. Advocate v. Turnbull [1951] Scots.L.T.R. 409. But for a case which applied the same test and upheld the admissibility of illegally seized evidence, see Fairley v. Fishmongers of London [1951] Scots.L.T.R. 54.

In England and throughout the commonwealth generally, the illegality of a seizure does not bar the admissibility of evidence. See Kuruma v. R. [1955] 2 W.L.R. 223, [1955] 1 All Eng.R. 236; Cowen and Carter, Essays on the Law of Evidence (1956), ch. 3; and 74 Scottish L.Rev. 73 (1958). For a recent comparison between the English and American search and seizure practice, see Karlen, Sawer & Wise, Anglo-American Criminal Justice 107–33 (Oxford U.Press, 1967).

4. Conceding that questions of the admissibility of ordinary types of evidence (proof of corpus delicti, testimony of accomplices, hearsay, etc.) ought to be left up to the courts, should a distinction be made as regards a basic policy decision such as that involved in the issue of the admissibility of illegally seized evidence? The United States Supreme Court recognized this distinction in Fisher v. United States, 328 U.S. 463, 66 S.Ct. 1318 (1945), where it deferred to Congress on the issue of whether mental deficiency should be considered in determining the capacity of an accused person to harbor the intent required for a first degree murder prosecution.

Is not the legislative process a more democratic one for such a basic policy decision as a shift from the non-exclusionary rule to the exclusionary rule? In the judicial process, a change in the thinking of a single judge out of five, seven or nine members of an appellate court may produce a substantial policy change, whereas a larger number of changed minds is ordinarily required for a legislative shift of viewpoint. Moreover, before legislative changes occur there ordinarily would be committee hearings at which opposing viewpoints would be presented—not just by the attorneys for the prosecution and defense, but rather by persons and groups with a broader interest, an interest in the policy issue rather than the outcome of a particular case. Similarly, the legislative determination, either on the committee level or by the entire body itself, would be based on policy considerations and not upon the consideration of the shocking facts for or against the accused in a particular case. In other words, might there not be more objectivity behind a legislative change?

5. Finally, consider the following suggestion to the police voiced by one of the authors (Thompson) at a national conference on "The Supreme Court and the Police," and appearing in 57 J.Crim.L., C. & P.S. 419, 424–5 (1966).

"There exists, among police, a dogged and seemingly unshakeable notion that Supreme Court decisions restricting police practices in the enforcement of the criminal law are not only aimed 'personally' at them, but, supposedly undermining their effectiveness, make *them* 'responsible' to the citizenry for rising crime rates and the inability to capture, charge and convict all persons who have committed crimes.

"It is high time that the police of America rid themselves of this patellar-like reaction to decisions such as [*Mapp*] and the others. The Fourth, Fifth and Sixth amendments were put into our Constitution long ago. It is the duty of the Supreme Court to interpret these constitutional provisions and whether particular decisions be thought right or wrong they must be accepted or else the Constitution should be changed. The Supreme Court has adopted the device of the exclusionary rule because it has found no worthy alternative to enforce compliance with these fundamental restrictions upon the power of society to deal with those accused of crime. To the extent that credible evidence is excluded from the fact finding process supposedly designed to find 'truth' therefore, we must accept the fact that some persons whom we know to have committed offenses will go unpunished.

"The point is that *this is not the fault of the police* and *they* ought to quit blaming themselves for their inability—if no honest alternatives to practices condemned by exclusionary rules can be found—to prevent crimes and catch criminals. So long as the American people are willing to tolerate a system of constitutional regulation which in some instances restricts society's power to deal with criminals on a totally efficient basis, the police cannot be blamed for gaps in the war against crime. Too often, the police are on their own 'backs'; their frustrations, cynicism and bitterness at not being able to 'do their job' are too often self-imposed. If the police act within the rules that all the people—not just the Supreme Court—have sanctioned; if they are supplied with the money, manpower and training necessary to raise the profession—and it is a profession—to the level where it must be placed, then all that *can* be expected of *them* will have been done."

6. Michigan attempted a compromise solution to the exclusionary rule problem by amending its constitutional search and seizure provision to read as follows:

Art. 2, § 10: "The person, houses, papers and possessions of every person shall be secure from unreasonable searches and seizures. No warrant to search any place or to seize any person or things shall issue without describing them, nor without probable cause, supported by oath or affirmation. *Provided, however*, that the provisions of this section shall not be construed to bar from evidence in any court of criminal jurisdiction, or in any criminal proceeding held before any magistrate or justice of the peace, any narcotic drug or drugs, any firearm, rifle, pistol, revolver, automatic pistol, machine gun, bomb, bomb shell, explosive, blackjack, slingshot, billy, metallic knuckles, gas-ejecting device, or any other dangerous weapon or thing, seized by any peace officer outside the curtilage of any dwelling house in this state." [The phrase "any narcotic drug or drugs" was inserted by reason of a 1952 amendment to the Michigan constitution; the remainder of the proviso regarding firearms, etc., resulted from a 1936 amendment.]

At the 1962 Michigan constitutional convention—even though the convention delegates were fully aware of *Mapp*—the above quoted provision of the Michigan constitution was retained. Is it constitutional?

In Lucas v. Michigan, 420 F.2d 259 (6th Cir. 1970), the United States Court of Appeals held the Michigan rule unconstitutional in so far as it permitted to be used as evidence certain items unlawfully seized. After reviewing the Michigan case law, the Sixth Circuit panel held that because the Michigan reviewing courts had demonstrated an unwillingness to strike down the Michigan provision, prisoners convicted on evidence unlawfully seized but admitted into evidence under the Michigan rule could make immediate application for federal habeas corpus relief since resort to the state reviewing courts would undoubtedly prove futile. Subsequently the Michigan Supreme Court held the Michigan provision to be in violation of the United States Constitution. People v. Pennington, 383 Mich. 611, 178 N.W.2d 471 (1970).

B. TORT LIABILITY OF THE POLICE—THE FEDERAL CIVIL RIGHTS ALTERNATIVE

MONROE v. PAPE

Supreme Court of the United States, 1961.
365 U.S. 167, 81 S.Ct. 473.

MR. JUSTICE DOUGLAS delivered the opinion of the Court.

This case presents important questions concerning the construction of R.S. § 1979, 42 U.S.C.A. § 1983, which reads as follows:

> "Every person who, under color of any statute, ordinance, regulation, custom, or usage, of any State or Territory, subjects, or causes to be subjected, any citizen of the United States or other person within the jurisdiction thereof to the deprivation of any rights, privileges, or immunities secured by the Constitution and laws, shall be liable to the party injured in an action at law, suit in equity, or other proper proceeding for redress."

The complaint alleges that 13 Chicago police officers broke into petitioners' home in the early morning, routed them from bed, made them stand naked in the living room, and ransacked every room, emptying drawers and ripping mattress covers. It further alleges that Mr. Monroe was then taken to the police station and detained on "open" charges for 10 hours, while he was interrogated about a two-day-old murder, that he was not taken before a magistrate, though one was accessible, that he was not permitted to call his family or attorney, that he was subsequently released without criminal charges being preferred against him. It is alleged that the officers had no search warrant and no arrest warrant and that they acted "under color of the statutes, ordinances, regulations, customs and usages" of Illinois and of the City of Chicago. . . .

The City of Chicago moved to dismiss the complaint on the ground that it is not liable under the Civil Rights Acts nor for acts committed in performance of its governmental functions. All defendants moved to dismiss, alleging that the complaint alleged no cause of action under those Acts or under the Federal Constitution.

The District Court dismissed the complaint. The Court of Appeals affirmed. * * *

I.

Petitioners claim that the invasion of their home and the subsequent search without a warrant and the arrest and detention of Mr. Monroe without a warrant and without arraignment constituted a deprivation of their "rights, privileges, or immunities secured by the Constitution" within the meaning of R.S. § 1979. It has been said that when 18 U.S.C.A. § 241 made criminal a conspiracy "to injure, oppress, threaten, or intimidate any citizen in the free exercise or enjoyment of any right or privilege secured to him by the Constitution," it embraced only rights that an individual has by reason of his relation to the central government, not to state governments. United States v. Williams, 341 U.S. 70, 71 S.Ct. 581. But the history of the section of the Civil Rights Act presently involved does not permit such a narrow interpretation.

Section 1979 came onto the books as § 1 of the Ku Klux Act of April 20, 1871. It was one of the means whereby Congress exercised the power vested in it by § 5 of the Fourteenth Amendment to enforce the provisions of that Amendment. * * * Allegation of facts constituting a deprivation under color of state authority of a right guaranteed by the Fourteenth Amendment satisfies to that extent the requirement of R.S. § 1979. See Douglas v. Jeannette, 319 U.S. 157, 161–162, 63 S.Ct. 877, 880. So far petitioners are on solid ground. For the guarantee against unreasonable searches and seizures contained in the Fourth Amendment has been made applicable to the States by reason of the Due Process Clause of the Fourteenth Amendment. * * *

II.

There can be no doubt at least since Ex parte Virginia, 100 U.S. 339, 346–347, that Congress has the power to enforce provisions of the Fourteenth Amendment against those who carry a badge of authority of a State and represent it in some capacity, whether they act in accordance with their authority or misuse it. See Home Tel. & Tel. Co. v. Los Angeles, 227 U.S. 278, 287–296, 33 S.Ct. 312, 314, 318. The question with which we now deal is the narrower one of whether Congress, in enacting § 1979, meant to give a remedy to parties deprived of constitutional rights, privileges and immunities by an official's abuse of his position.

We conclude that it did so intend.

It is argued that "under color of" enumerated state authority excludes acts of an official or policeman who can show no authority under state law, state custom, or state usage to do what he did. In this case it is said that these policemen, in breaking into petitioners' apartment, violated the Constitution and laws of Illinois. It is pointed out that under Illinois law a simple remedy is offered for that violation and that, so far as it appears, the courts of Illinois are available to give petitioners that full redress which the common law affords for violence done to a person; and it is earnestly argued that no "statute, ordinance, regulation, custom or usage" of Illinois bars that redress.

The Ku Klux Act grew out of a message sent to Congress by President Grant on March 23, 1871, reading:

> "A condition of affairs now exists in some States of the Union rendering life and property insecure and the carrying of the mails and the collection of the revenue dangerous. The proof that such a condition of affairs exists in some localities is now before the Senate. That the power to correct these evils is beyond the control of State authorities I do not doubt; that the power of the Executive of the United States, acting within the limits of existing laws, is sufficient for present emergencies is not clear. Therefore, I urgently recommend such legislation as in the judgment of Congress shall effectually secure life, liberty, and property, and the enforcement of law in all parts of the United States. . . "

The legislation—in particular the section with which we are now concerned—had several purposes. There are threads of many thoughts running through the debates. One who reads them in their entirety sees that the present section had three main aims.

First, it might, of course, override certain kinds of state laws. * * *

Second, it provided a remedy where state law was inadequate. * * *

But the purposes were much broader. The *third* aim was to provide a federal remedy where the state remedy, though adequate in theory, was not available in practice. The opposition to the measure complained that "It overrides the reserved powers of the States," just as they argued that the second section of the bill "absorb[ed] the entire jurisdiction of the States over their local and domestic affairs."

This Act of April 20, 1871, sometimes called "the third 'force bill,'" was passed by a Congress that had the Klan "particularly in mind." The debates are replete with references to the lawless conditions existing in the South in 1871. . . . It was not the unavailability of state remedies but the failure of certain States to enforce the laws with an equal hand that furnished the powerful momentum behind this "force bill." * * *

While one main scourge of the evil—perhaps the leading one—was the Ku Klux Klan, the remedy created was not a remedy against it or its members but against those who representing a State in some capacity were *unable* or *unwilling* to enforce a state law. * * *

There was, it was said, no quarrel with the state laws on the books. It was their lack of enforcement that was the nub of the difficulty. * * *

It was precisely that breadth of the remedy which the opposition emphasized. * * *

The debates were long and extensive. It is abundantly clear that one reason the legislation was passed was to afford a federal right in federal courts because, by reason of prejudice, passion, neglect, intolerance or otherwise, state laws might not be enforced and the claims of citizens to the enjoyment of rights, privileges, and immunities guaranteed by the Fourteenth Amendment might be denied by the state agencies. . . .

Although the legislation was enacted because of the conditions that existed in the South at that time, it is cast in general language and is as applicable to Illinois as it is to the States whose names were mentioned over and again in the debates. It is no answer that the State has a law which if enforced would give relief. The federal remedy is supplementary to the state remedy, and the latter need not be first sought and refused before the federal one is invoked. Hence the fact that Illinois by its constitution and laws outlaws unreasonable searches and seizures is no barrier to the present suit in the federal court.

We had before us in United States v. Classic, supra, § 20 of the Criminal Code, 18 U.S.C.A. § 242, which provides a criminal punishment for anyone who "under color of any law, statute, ordinance, regulation, or custom" subjects any inhabitant of a State to the deprivation of "any rights, privileges, or immunities secured or protected by the Constitution or laws of the United States." * * * The right involved in the *Classic* case was the right of voters in a primary to have their votes counted. The laws of Louisiana required the defendants "to count the ballots, to record the result of the count, and to certify the result of the election." United States v. Classic, supra, 313 U.S. 325–326, 61 S.Ct. 1043. But according to the indictment they did not perform their duty. In an opinion written by Mr. Justice (later Chief Justice) Stone, in which Mr. Justice Roberts, Mr. Justice Reed, and Mr. Justice Frankfurter joined, the Court ruled, "Misuse of power, possessed by virtue of state law and made possible only because the wrongdoer is clothed with the authority of state law, is action taken 'under color of' state law." There was a dissenting opinion; but the ruling as to the meaning of "under color of" state law was not questioned.

That view of the meaning of the words "under color of" state law, 18 U.S.C.A. § 242, was reaffirmed in Screws v. United States. The acts there complained of were committed by state officers in performance of their duties, *viz.*, making an arrest effective. It was urged there, as it is here, that "under color of" state law should not be construed to duplicate in federal law what was an offense under state law (dissenting opinion). It was said there, as it is here, that the ruling in the *Classic* case as to the meaning of "under color of" state law was not in focus and was ill-advised (dissenting opinion). It was argued there, as it is here, that "under color of" state law included only action taken by officials pursuant to state law (dissenting opinion). We rejected that view. * * * it is beyond doubt that this phrase should be accorded the same construction in both statutes—in § 1979 and in 18 U.S.C.A. § 242.

Since the *Screws* and *Williams* decisions, Congress has had several pieces of civil rights legislation before it.

If the results of our construction of "under color of" law were as horrendous as now claimed, if they were as disruptive of our federal scheme as now urged, if they were such an unwarranted invasion of States' rights as pretended, surely the voice of the opposition would have been heard in Committee reports. Their silence and the new uses to which "under color of" law have recently been given reinforce our conclusion that our prior decisions were correct on this matter of construction.

We conclude that the meaning given "under color of" law in the *Classic* case and in the *Screws* and *Williams* cases was the correct one; and we adhere to it.

In the *Screws* case we dealt with a statute that imposed criminal penalties for acts "wilfully" done. We construed that word in its setting to mean the doing of an act with "a specific intent to deprive a person of a federal right." We do not think that gloss should be placed on § 1979 which we have here. The word "wilfully" does not appear in § 1979. Moreover, § 1979 provides a civil remedy, while in the *Screws* case we dealt with a criminal law challenged on the ground of vagueness. Section 1979 should be read against the background of tort liability that makes a man responsible for the natural consequences of his actions.

So far, then, the complaint states a cause of action. There remains to consider only a defense peculiar to the City of Chicago.

III.

The City of Chicago asserts that it is not liable under § 1979. We do not stop to explore the whole range of questions tendered us on this issue at oral argument and in the briefs. For we are of the opinion that Congress did not undertake to bring municipal corporations within the ambit of § 1979.

When the bill that became the Act of April 20, 1871, was being debated in the Senate, Senator Sherman of Ohio proposed an amendment which would have made "the inhabitants of the county, city, or parish" in which certain acts of violence occurred liable "to pay full compensation" to the person damaged or his widow or legal representative. The amendment was adopted by the Senate. The House, however, rejected it. . . . In a second conference the Sherman amendment was dropped. . . . Mr. Poland, speaking for the House Conferees about the Sherman proposal to make municipalities liable, said:

> "We informed the conferees on the part of the Senate that the House had taken a stand on that subject and would not recede from it; that that section imposing liability upon towns and counties must go out or we should fail to agree."

It is said that doubts should be resolved in favor of municipal liability because private remedies against officers for illegal searches and seizures are conspicuously ineffective, and because municipal liability will not only afford plaintiffs responsible defendants but cause those defendants to eradicate abuses that exist at the police level. We do not reach those policy considerations. Nor do we reach the constitutional question whether Congress has the power to make municipalities liable for acts of its officers that violate the civil rights of individuals.

The response of the Congress to the proposal to make municipalities liable . . . was so antagonistic that we cannot believe that the word "person" was used in this particular Act to include them. . . .

[The concurring opinion of MR. JUSTICE HARLAN is omitted.]

MR. JUSTICE FRANKFURTER, dissenting. . . .

[All] the evidence converges to the conclusion that Congress by § 1979 created a civil liability enforceable in the federal courts only in instances of injury for which redress was barred in the state courts because some "statute, ordinance, regulation, custom, or usage" sanctioned the grievance complained of. . . . The jurisdiction which Article III of the Constitution conferred on the national judiciary reflected the assumption that the state courts, not the federal courts, would remain the primary guardians of that fundamental security of person and property which the long evolution of the common law had secured to one individual as against other individuals. The Fourteenth Amendment did not alter this basic aspect of our federalism.

Its commands were addressed to the States. Only when the States, through their responsible organs for the formulation and administration of local policy, sought to deny or impede access by the individual to the central government in connection with those enumerated functions assigned to it, or to deprive the individual of a certain minimal fairness in the exercise of the coercive forces of the State, or without reasonable justification to treat him differently than other persons subject to their jurisdiction, was an overriding federal sanction imposed. * * * This conception begot the "State action" principle on which, from the time of the Civil Rights Cases, 109 U.S.

3, 3 S.Ct. 18, this Court has relied in its application of Fourteenth Amendment guarantees. As between individuals, that body of mutual rights and duties which constitute the civil personality of a man remains essentially the creature of the legal institutions of the States.

But, of course, in the present case petitioners argue that the wrongs done them were committed not by individuals but by the police as state officials. There are two senses in which this might be true. It might be true if petitioners alleged that the redress which state courts offer them against the respondents is different than that which those courts would offer against other individuals, guilty of the same conduct, who were not the police. This is not alleged. It might also be true merely because the respondents *are* the police—because they are clothed with an appearance of official authority which is in itself a factor of significance in dealings between individuals. Certainly the night-time intrusion of the man with a star and a police revolver is a different phenomenon than the night-time intrusion of a burglar. The aura of power which a show of authority carries with it has been created by state government. The pretense of authority alone might seem to Congress sufficient basis for creating an exception to the ordinary rule that it is to the state tribunals that individuals within a State must look for redress against other individuals within that State. The same pretense of authority might suffice to sustain congressional legislation creating the exception. See Ex parte Virginia, 100 U.S. 339. Congress has not in § 1979 manifested that intention.

[E]xtending federal civil jurisdiction into the traditional realm of state tort law presents problems of policy appropriately left to Congress. Suppose that a state legislature or the highest court of a State should determine that within its territorial limits no damages should be recovered in tort for pain and suffering, or for mental anguish, or that no punitive damages should be recoverable. Since the federal courts went out of the business of making "general law," Erie R. Co. v. Tompkins, 304 U.S. 64, 58 S.Ct. 817, such decisions of local policy have admittedly been the exclusive province of state lawmakers. Should the civil liability for police conduct which can claim no authority under local law, which is actionable as common-law assault or trespass in the local courts, comport different rules? Should an unlawful intrusion by a policeman in Chicago entail different consequences than an unlawful intrusion by a hoodlum? These are matters of policy in its strictly legislative sense, not for determination by this Court. . . . If § 1979 is made a vehicle of constitutional litigation in cases where state officers have acted lawlessly at state law, difficult questions of the federal constitutionality of certain official practices—lawful perhaps in some States, unlawful in others—may be litigated between private parties without the participation of responsible state authorities which is obviously desirable to protect legitimate state interests, but also to better guide adjudication by competent record-making and argument.

Of course, these last considerations would be irrelevant to our duty if Congress had demonstrably meant to reach by § 1979 activities like those of respondents in this case. But where it appears that Congress plainly did not have that understanding, respect for principles . . . of our federalism should avoid extension of a statute beyond its manifest area of operation into applications which invite conflict with the administration of local policies. Such an extension makes the extreme limits of federal constitutional power a law to regulate the quotidian business of every traffic policeman, every registrar of elections, every city inspector or investigator, every clerk in every municipal licensing bureau in this country. The text of the statute, reinforced by its history, precludes such a reading.

In concluding that police intrusion in violation of state law is not a wrong remediable under R.S. § 1979, the pressures which urge an opposite result are duly felt. The difficulties which confront private citizens who seek to vindicate in traditional common-law actions their state-created rights against lawless invasion of their privacy by local policemen are obvious, and obvious is the need for more effective modes of redress. The answer to these urgings must be regard for our federal system which presupposes a wide range of regional autonomy in the kinds of protection local residents receive. If various common-law concepts make it possible for a policeman—but no more possible for a policeman than for any individual hoodlum intruder—to escape without liability when he has vandalized a home, that is an evil. But, surely, its remedy devolves, in the first instance, on the States. Of course, if the States afford less protection against the police, as police, than against the hoodlum—if under authority of state "statute, ordinance, regulation, custom, or usage" the police are specially shielded—§ 1979 provides a remedy which dismissal of petitioners' complaint in the present case does not impair. . . . Federal intervention may in the long run do the individual a disservice by deflecting responsibility from the state lawmakers, who hold the power of providing a far more comprehensive scope of protection. Local society, also, may well be the loser, by relaxing its sense of responsibility and, indeed, perhaps resenting what may appear to it to be outside interference where local authority is ample and more appropriate to supply needed remedies.

This is not to say that there may not exist today, as in 1871, needs which call for congressional legislation to protect the civil rights of individuals in the States. Strong contemporary assertions of these needs have been expressed. Report of the President's Committee on Civil Rights, To Secure These Rights (1947); Chafee, Safeguarding Fundamental Human Rights: The Tasks of States and Nation, 27 Geo.Wash.L.Rev. 519 (1959). But both the insistence of the needs and the delicacy of the issues involved in finding appropriate means for their satisfaction demonstrate that their demand is for legislative, not judicial, response. We cannot expect to create an effective means of protection for human liberties by torturing an 1871 statute to meet the problems of 1960.

* * *

It is not a work for courts to melt and recast this statute. "Under color" of law meant by authority of law in the nineteenth century. No judicial sympathy, however strong, for needs now felt can give the phrase—a phrase which occurs in a statute, not in a constitution—any different meaning in the twentieth.

* * *

This meaning, no doubt, poses difficulties for the case-by-case application of § 1979. Manifestly the applicability of the section in an action for damages cannot be made to turn upon the actual availability or unavailability of a state-law remedy for each individual plaintiff's situation. Prosecution to adverse judgment of a state-court damage claim cannot be made prerequisite to § 1979 relief. In the first place, such a requirement would effectively nullify § 1979 as a vehicle for recovering damages. In the second place, the conclusion that police activity which violates state law is not "under color" of state law does not turn upon the existence of a state tort remedy. Rather, it recognizes the freedom of the States to fashion their own laws of torts in their own way under no threat of federal intervention save where state law makes determinative of a plaintiff's rights the particular circumstance that defendants are acting by state authority. Section 1979 was not designed to cure and level all the possible imperfections of local common-law doctrines, but to provide for the case of the defendant who can claim that some particular dispensation of state authority immunizes him from the ordinary processes of the law.

It follows that federal courts in actions at law under § 1979 would have to determine whether defendants' conduct is in violation of, or under color of, state law often with little guidance from earlier state decisions. Such a determination will sometimes be difficult, of course. But Federal District Courts sitting in diversity cases are often called upon to determine as intricate and uncertain questions of local law as whether official authority would cloak a given practice of the police from liability in a state-court suit. Certain fixed points of reference will be available. If a plaintiff can show that defendant is acting pursuant to the specific terms of a state statute or of a municipal ordinance, § 1979 will apply. See Lane v. Wilson, 307 U.S. 268, 59 S.Ct. 872. If he can show that defendant's conduct is within the range of executive discretion in the enforcement of a state statute, or municipal ordinance, § 1979 will apply. See Hague v. C. I. O., 307 U.S. 496, 59 S.Ct. 954. Beyond these cases will lie the admittedly more difficult ones in which he seeks to show some " 'custom or usage' which has become common law." . . .

The present case comes here from a judgment sustaining a motion to dismiss petitioners' complaint. That complaint, insofar as it describes the police intrusion, makes no allegation that that intrusion was authorized by state law other than the conclusory and unspecific claim that "During all times herein mentioned the individual defendants and each of them were acting under color of the statutes, ordinances, regulations, customs and usages of the State of Illinois, of the County of Cook and of the defendant City of Chicago." In the face of Illinois decisions holding such intrusions unlawful and in the absence of more precise factual averments to support its conclusion, such a complaint fails to state a claim under § 1979.

However, the complaint does allege, as to the ten-hour detention of Mr. Monroe, that "it was, and it is now, the custom or usage of the Police Department of the City of Chicago to arrest and confine individuals in the police stations and jail cells of the said department for long periods of time on 'open' charges." These confinements, it is alleged, are for the purpose of interrogating and investigating the individuals arrested, in the aim of inducing incriminating statements, permitting possible identification of suspects in lineups, holding suspects *incommunicado* while police conduct field investigations of their associates and background, and punishing the arrested persons without trial. Such averments do present facts which, admitted as true for purposes of a motion to dismiss, seem to sustain petitioners' claim that Mr. Monroe's detention—as contrasted with the night-time intrusion into the Monroe apartment—was "under color" of state authority. Under the few relevant Illinois decisions it is impossible to say with certainty that a detention *incommunicado* for ten hours is unlawful *per se,* or that the courts of that State would hold that the lawless circumstances surrounding Mr. Monroe's arrest made his subsequent confinement illegal. On this record, then, petitioners' complaint suffices to raise the narrow issue of whether the detention *incommunicado,* considered alone, violates due process.

Since the majority's disposition of the case causes the Court not to reach that constitutional issue, it is neither necessary nor appropriate to discuss it here.

NOTES

1. In Bivens v. Six Unknown Named Agents of Federal Bureau of Narcotics, 403 U.S. 388, 91 S.Ct. 1999 (1971), the petitioner claimed that federal agents had unconstitutionally forced their way into his house, arrested him, manacled him in front of his wife and children, threatened arrest of the entire family, searched his home exhaustively, and transported him to a courthouse where he was interrogated, booked and strip searched. Section 1983 applies only to persons acting under color of state law and not to federal officers, although the Court held that a civil remedy could be based upon a Fourth Amendment violation. A federal cause of action is inherent in the Amendment and does not require Congressional action. Three dissenters (Burger, C. J., Black and Blackmun, JJ.) all agreed that only Congress could create the remedy envisioned by the Court. The Court did not deal with the claim of immunity but on remand the immunity argument was rejected. See 456 F.2d 1339 (2nd Cir. 1972).

(The dissenting opinion of Chief Justice Burger appears infra, p. 765.)

2. Is tort liability—federal or state—on the part of a municipality or its officers effective as an alternative to the exclusionary rule, or even as a supplement to it? Consider the following criticisms from Mathes and Jones, Toward A "Scope Of Official Duty" Immunity For Police Officers In Damage Actions, 53 Geo.L.J. 889, 897–98, 907–08 (1965):

"A brief sketch of the liability scheme is in order. Police officers are normally held liable for de facto false arrests absent arrest warrants, unless the arrested person has committed an offense in the presence of the officer or there is 'reasonable cause' to believe the person arrested has committed a crime with the status of a felony. The burden, moreover, is upon the police officer to show he had 'reasonable cause' once the plaintiff has shown he was arrested without a warrant. 'Reasonable cause,' or 'probable cause' as it is sometimes called, means at least that "a man of ordinary care and prudence, knowing what the officer knows would be led to believe or conscientiously entertain a strong suspicion that the arrested person is guilty of a crime, even if there is room for doubt. Although actions for false arrest usually also involve damage claims for the ensuing false imprisonment, even in cases where the arrest was validly effected there remains the possibility that the officer may nevertheless be subject to an award of damages for false imprisonment if it be found that he failed in his statutory duty to take the arrested person before a magistrate without delay.

"Force, generally speaking, may be used to effect an arrest without a warrant only if the arrest is for a felony and the officer 'reasonably believes' the force necessary to accomplishment of his purpose. For any use of force beyond these limitations, whatever they mean, the officer qua individual must respond for all damages proximately resulting, both to the individual pursued and to the property of innocent bystanders. For example, in cases involving the right to arrest for a suspected misdemeanor, it is invariably held that an officer may be found negligent if he shoots a suspect to prevent his escape.

"It is ironic understatement to say that this situation puts the individual police officer on his mettle, perhaps on mettle he should not be expected to possess. In the split second or so in which he might have an opportunity to effect an arrest, he must at his peril go through a most problematic 'balancing' process to determine 'reasonable cause' for the arrest and the degree of force reasonably necessary. Confronted with such a delicate choice and personal responsibility for its correctness, it would not be surprising if police officers generally decided to err on the side of caution and think of home and family instead of the public interest in law enforcement. . . .

"From the viewpoint of public policy, it seems clear that there are at least seven defects in the present system of police officer liability:

"(1) The broad threat of personal financial liability hanging over police officers in the performance of official duty must serve—at least to men normally concerned with home and family—as a continual and substantial deterrent to vigorous law enforcement. Corollary to this consideration is the fact that law enforcement is necessarily impeded by having policemen devoting time and energy to the defense of actions in court rather than in carrying out their jobs. On this score the public, as well as the officer, suffers.

"(2) It is obviously unjust to penalize officers financially for the performance of the affirmative duties incumbent upon their jobs. This is particularly true where, as in the false imprisonment cases, their error is often simply one of 'reasonable judgment.' To be sure, there are cases where officers wilfully inflict injuries entirely without justification, but the individual-immunity theories have always expressly excepted wilful torts committed clearly beyond the limits of authority or 'jurisdiction.'

"(3) Except in the case where an officer acts outside the plain boundaries of official authority or in clear excess of lawful powers, he acts not for himself but for the state and the people. Accordingly, the real grievance of a victim of, say, false arrest is with the state and should be fought out on that ground. Individual-officer financial liability may be appropriate to an autonomous, decentralized constabulary, but as applied to large, highly centralized bureaucracies such as modern police departments, it may often work to fix the burden where the responsibility does not reside.

"(4) Competent studies, as well as experience, indicate that incentives to safety and proper execution of official duty are greatest where tort liability is imposed upon the large corporate defendant rather than upon the individual employee whose negligence or other misconduct causes injury to other persons. The reasons for this are rooted in characteristics of human nature. Certain persons are accident prone, careless or 'downright mean.' Despite imposition of individual financial liability upon them, such persons inevitably have more accidents or cause more injuries than people without these characteristics. By placing responsibility with the agency employing them, a greater incentive toward employing people less likely to cause the kind of harms with which we are concerned might be achieved.

"(5) Absent insurance factors, the financial remedy against the officer is probably illusory anyway. Since police officers are not often men of property, plaintiffs have little hope of substantial recovery in a suit against the officer unless a practice of indemnity prevails (as in Illinois). Indeed, the very existence of a right of recovery against the individual police officer often simply beclouds further the substantial question of whether governmental entities ought to assume responsibility for those really unjustifiable injuries which do occasionally occur.

"(6) Where a police officer's fault is the criterion of liability, actions to enforce individual liability often necessitate review by the courts of the propriety of police-executive action. This circumstance involves the courts in unseemly conflicts with a coordinate branch of government and in types of inquiry they are not well equipped to make. This is a fortiori true where activities of state police officers are at issue in federal courts and federal-state relations are involved.

"(7) There is reason to think that the threat of civil liability might discourage responsible people from entering public service. Immunity from individual liability for performance of official police duties should remove whatever deterrent here exists. . . .

"Perhaps the finest summary of the position of this article is this eloquent statement of Judge Learned Hand:

'It does indeed go without saying that an official, who is in fact guilty of using his powers to vent his spleen upon others, or for any other personal motive not connected with the public good, should not escape liability for the injuries he may so cause; and, if it were possible in practice to confine such complaints to the guilty, it would be monstrous to deny recovery. The justification for doing so is that it is impossible to know whether the claim is well founded until the case has been tried, and that to submit all officials, the innocent as well as the guilty, to the burden of a trial and to the inevitable danger of its outcome, would dampen the ardor of all but the most resolute, or the most irresponsible, in the unflinching discharge of their duties. Again and again the public interest calls for action which may turn out to be founded on a mistake, in the face of which an official may later find himself hard put to it to satisfy a jury of his good faith. There must indeed be means of punishing public officers who have been truant to their duties; but that is quite another matter from exposing such as have been honestly mistaken to suit by anyone who has suffered from their errors. As is so often the case, the answer must be found in a balance between the evils inevitable in either alternative. In this instance it has been thought in the end better to leave unredressed the wrongs done by dishonest officers than to subject those who try to do their duty to the constant dread of retaliation. Judged as res nova, we should not hesitate to follow the path laid down in the books.' *

"For the reasons stated, it is to be hoped that neither will the courts hesitate to apply this rationale to police officers. They could find no better 'golden text' than the words of Judge Hand.

"It cannot be gainsaid that hard cases do tend to make bad law; this is particularly true in cases of 'police brutality,' where the winds of passion on occasion blow out the candles of unbiased legal reason and sound public policy. Yet those who find the immunity doctrine harsh must remember that the alternatives are not 'punishment' or 'no punishment' of the individual police officer, for the criminal law will still stand to punish his excessive use or abuse of authority. Rather, the alternatives here are between imposing personal financial (tort) liability to the constant dread of the individual police officer, and shifting that financial responsibility to the public agency he serves. Law enforcement is bound to suffer more than we can afford when the never-overpaid police officer, assigned to risk his very life in the task of, say, ferreting out suspected criminals in a dark alley at three o'clock on a rainy winter morning, must stake the security of his family upon a snap determination as to whether some judge or jury, in the ivory-tower quiet of court or jury room, will find that he used more or greater force than was reasonably necessary under the circumstances. In this area of 'individual rights,' the past decade has afforded all too much proof of the validity of Mr. Justice Holmes' dictum that 'judges are apt to be naif, simple-minded men, and they need something of Mephistopheles.' "

PIERSON v. RAY

Supreme Court of the United States, 1967.
386 U.S. 547, 87 S.Ct. 1213.

MR. CHIEF JUSTICE WARREN delivered the opinion of the Court.

This case presents issues involving the liability of local police officers and judges under § 1 of the Civil Rights Act of 1871, 42 U.S.C. § 1983. Petitioners in Number 79 were members of a group of 15 white and Negro Episcopal clergymen who attempted to use segregat-

* Gregoire v. Biddle, 177 F.2d 579, 581 (2d Cir.1949).

ed facilities at an interstate bus terminal in Jackson, Mississippi, in 1961. They were arrested by respondents Ray, Griffith, and Nichols, policemen of the City of Jackson, and charged with violating § 2087.5 of the Mississippi Code, which makes guilty of a misdemeanor anyone who congregates with others in a public place under circumstances such that a breach of the peace may be occasioned thereby, and refuses to move on when ordered to do so by a police officer. Petitioners waived a jury trial and were convicted of the offense by respondent Spencer, a municipal police justice. They were each given the maximum sentence of four months in jail and a fine of $200. On appeal petitioner Jones was accorded a trial *de novo* in the County Court, and after the city produced its evidence the court granted his motion for a directed verdict. The cases against the other petitioners were then dropped.

Having been vindicated in the County Court, petitioners brought this action for damages in the United States District Court for the Southern District of Mississippi, Jackson Division, alleging that respondents had violated § 1983, supra, and that respondents were liable at common law for false arrest and imprisonment. A jury returned verdicts for respondents on both counts. On appeal, the Court of Appeals for the Fifth Circuit held that respondent Spencer was immune from liability under both § 1983 and the common law of Mississippi for acts committed within his judicial jurisdiction. As to the police officers, the court noted that § 2087.5 of the Mississippi Code was held unconstitutional as applied to similar facts in Thomas v. Mississippi, 380 U.S. 524, 85 S.Ct. 1327 (1965). Although *Thomas* was decided years after the arrest involved in this trial, the court held that the policeman would be liable in a suit under § 1983 for an unconstitutional arrest even if they acted in good faith and with probable cause in making an arrest under a state statute not yet held invalid. The court believed that this stern result was required by Monroe v. Pape, 365 U.S. 167, 81 S.Ct. 473 (1961). Under the count based on the common law of Mississippi, however, it held that the policemen would not be liable if they had probable cause to believe that the statute had been violated, because Mississippi law does not require police officers to predict at their peril which state laws are constitutional and which are not. Apparently dismissing the common-law claim, the Court of Appeals reversed and remanded for a new trial on the § 1983 claim against the police officers because defense counsel had been allowed to cross-examine the ministers on various irrelevant and prejudicial matters, particularly including an alleged convergence of their views on racial justice with those of the Communist Party. At the new trial, however, the court held that the ministers could not recover if it were proved that they went to Mississippi anticipating that they would be illegally arrested because such action would constitute consent to the arrest under the principle of *volenti non fit injuria*, he who consents to a wrong cannot be injured.

We granted certiorari to consider whether a local judge is liable for damages under § 1983 for an unconstitutional conviction and whether the ministers should be denied recovery against the police officers if they acted with the anticipation that they would be illegally arrested. We also granted the police officers' petition to determine if the Court of Appeals correctly held that they could not assert the defense of good faith and probable cause to an action under § 1983 for unconstitutional arrest.

The evidence at the federal trial showed that petitioners and other Negro and white Episcopal clergymen undertook a "prayer pilgrimmage" in 1961 from New Orleans to Detroit. The purpose of the pilgrimmage was to visit church institutions and other places in the North and South to promote racial equality and integration, and, finally, to report to a church convention in Detroit. Letters from the leader of the group to its members indicate that the clergymen intended from the beginning to go to Jackson and attempt to use segregated facilities at the bus terminal there, and that they fully expected to be arrested for doing so. The group made plans based on the assumption that they would be arrested if they attempted peacefully to exercise their right as interstate travelers to use the waiting rooms and other facilities at the bus terminal, and the letters discussed arrangements for bail and other matters relevant to arrests.

The ministers stayed one night in Jackson, and went to the bus terminal the next morning to depart for Chattanooga, Tennessee. They entered the waiting room, disobeying a sign at the entrance that announced "White Waiting Room Only—By Order of the Police Department." They then turned to enter the small terminal restaurant but were stopped by two Jackson police officers, respondents Griffith and Nichols, who had been awaiting their arrival and who ordered them to "move on." The ministers replied that they wanted to eat, and refused to move on. Respondent Ray, then a police captain and now the deputy chief of police, arrived a few minutes later. The ministers were placed under arrest and taken to the jail.

All witnesses including the police officers agreed that the ministers entered the waiting room peacefully and engaged in no boisterous or objectionable conduct while in the "White Only" area. There was conflicting testimony on the number of bystanders present and their behavior. Petitioners testified that there was no crowd at the station, that no one followed them into the waiting room, and that no one uttered threatening words or made threatening gestures. The police testified that some 25 to 30 persons followed the ministers into the terminal, that persons in the crowd were in a very dissatisfied and ugly mood, and that they were mumbling and making unspecified threatening gestures. The police did not describe any specific threatening incidents, and testified that they took no action against any persons in the crowd who were threatening violence because they "had determined that the ministers was the cause of the violence if any might occur," although the ministers were concededly orderly and polite and the police did not claim that it was beyond their power to control the allegedly disorderly crowd. The arrests and convictions were followed by this lawsuit.

We find no difficulty in agreeing with the Court of Appeals that Judge Spencer is immune from liability for damages for his role in these convictions. The record is barren of any proof or specific allegation that Judge Spencer played any role in these arrests and convictions other than to adjudge petitioners guilty when their cases came before his court. Few doctrines were more solidly established at common law than the immunity of judges from liability for damages for acts committed within their judicial jurisdiction, as this Court recognized when it adopted the doctrine, in Bradley v. Fisher, 13 Wall. (80 U.S.) 335, 20 L.Ed. 646 (1871). This immunity applies even when the judge is accused of acting maliciously and corruptly, and it "is not for the protection or benefit of a malicious or corrupt judge, but for the benefit of the public, whose interest it is that the judges should be at liberty to exercise their functions with independence, and without fear of consequences." It is a judge's duty to decide all cases within his jurisdiction that are brought before him, including controversial cases that arouse the most intense feelings in the litigants. His errors may be corrected on appeal, but he should not have to fear that unsatisfied litigants may hound him with litigation charging malice or corruption. Imposing such a burden on judges would contribute not to principled and fearless decision-making but to intimidation.

We do not believe that this settled principle of law was abolished by § 1983, which makes liable "any person" who under color of law deprives another person of his civil rights. The legislative record gives no clear indication that Congress meant to abolish wholesale all common-law immunities. Accordingly, this Court held in Tenney v. Brandhove, 341 U.S. 367, 71 S.Ct. 783 (1951), that the immunity of legislators for acts within the legislative role was not abolished. The immunity of judges for acts within the judicial role is equally well-established, and we presume that Congress would have specifically so provided had it wished to abolish the doctrine.

The common law has never granted police officers an absolute and unqualified immunity, and the officers in this case do not claim that they are entitled to one. Their claim is rather that they should not be liable if they acted in good faith and with probable cause in making an arrest under a statute that they believed to be valid. Under the prevailing view in this country a peace officer who arrests someone with probable cause is not liable for false arrest simply because the innocence of the suspect is later proved. Restatement (Second), Torts § 121 (1965). A policeman's lot is not so unhappy that he must choose between being charged with dereliction of duty if he does not arrest when he has probable cause, and being mulcted in damages if he does. Although the matter is not entirely free from doubt, the same consideration would seem to require excusing him from liability for acting under a statute that he reasonably believed to be valid but that was later held unconstitutional on its face or as applied.

The Court of Appeals held that the officers had such a limited privilege under the common law of Mississippi, and indicated that it would have recognized a similar privilege under § 1983 except that it felt compelled to hold otherwise by our decision in Monroe v. Pape (1961). Monroe v. Pape presented no question of immunity, however, and none was decided. The complaint in that case alleged that "13 Chicago police officers broke into petitioners' home in the early morning, routed them from bed, made them stand naked in the living room, and ransacked every room, emptying drawers and ripping mattress covers. It further allege[d] that Mr. Monroe was then taken to the police station and detained on 'open' charges for 10 hours, while he was interrogated about a two-day-old murder, that he was not taken before a magistrate, though one was accessible, that he was not permitted to call his family or attorney, that he was subsequently released without criminal charges being preferred against him." 365 U. S., at 169, 81 S.Ct., at 474. The police officers did not choose to go to trial and defend the case on the hope that they could convince a jury that they believed in good faith that it was their duty to assault Monroe and his family in this manner. Instead, they sought dismissal of the complaint, contending principally that their activities were so plainly illegal under state law that they did not act "under color of any statute, ordinance, regulation, custom or usage, of any State or Territory" as required by § 1983. In rejecting this argument we in no way intimated that the defense of good faith and probable cause was foreclosed by the statute. We also held that the complaint should not be dismissed for failure to state that the officers had "a specific intent to deprive a person of a federal right," but this holding, which related to requirements of pleading, carried no implications as to which defenses would be available to the police officers. As we went on to say in the same paragraph, § 1983 " 'should be read against the background of tort liability that makes a man responsible for the natural consequences of his actions.' " Part of the background of tort liability, in the case of police officers making an arrest, is the defense of good faith and probable cause.

We hold that the defense of good faith and probable cause, which the Court of Appeals found available to the officers in the common-law action for false arrest and imprisonment, is also available to them in the action under § 1983. This holding does not, however, mean that the complaint should be dismissed. The Court of Appeals ordered dismissal of the common-law count on the theory that the police officers were not required to predict our decision in Thomas v. Mississippi, supra. We agree that a police officer is not charged with predicting the future course of constitutional law. But the petitioners in this case did not simply argue that they were arrested under a statute later held unconstitutional. They claimed and attempted to prove that the police officers arrested them solely for attempting to use the "White Only" waiting room, that no crowd was present, and that no one threatened violence or seemed about to cause a disturbance. The officers did not defend on the theory that they believed in good faith that it was constitutional to arrest the ministers solely for using the waiting room. Rather, they claimed and attempted to prove that they did not arrest the ministers for the purpose of preserving the custom of segregation in Mississippi, but solely for the purpose of preventing violence. They testified, in contradiction to the ministers, that a crowd gathered and that imminent violence was likely. If the jury believed the testimony of the officers and disbelieved that of the ministers, and if the jury found that the officers reasonably believed in good faith that the arrest was constitutional, then a verdict for the officers would follow even though the arrest was in fact unconstitutional. The jury did resolve the factual issues in favor of the officers but, for reasons previously stated, its verdict was influenced by irrelevant and prejudicial evidence. Accordingly, the case must be remanded to the trial court for a new trial.

It is necessary to decide what importance should be given at the new trial to the substantially undisputed fact that the petitioners went to Jackson expecting to be illegally arrested. We do not agree with the Court of Appeals that they somehow consented to the arrest because of their anticipation that they would be illegally arrested, even assuming that they went to the Jackson bus terminal for the sole purpose of testing their rights to unsegregated public accommodations. The case contains no proof or allegation that they in any way tricked or goaded the officers into arresting them. The petitioners had the right to use the waiting room of the Jackson bus terminal, and their deliberate exercise of that right in a peaceful, orderly, and inoffensive manner does not disqualify them from seeking damages under § 1983.

The judgment of the Court of Appeals is affirmed in part and reversed in part, and the case is remanded for further proceedings consistent with this opinion.

It is so ordered.

Judgment of Court of Appeals affirmed in part and reversed in part and case remanded with directions.

MR. JUSTICE DOUGLAS, dissenting.

I do not think that all judges, under all circumstances, no matter how outrageous their conduct are immune from suit under R.S. § 1979, 42 U.S.C. § 1983. That ruling is not justified by the admitted need for a vigorous and independent judiciary, is not commanded by the common-law doctrine of judicial immunity, and does not follow inexorably from our prior decisions. * * *

The immunity which the Court today grants the judiciary is not necessary to preserve an independent judiciary. If the threat of civil action lies in the background of litigation, so the argument goes, judges will be reluctant to exercise the discretion and judgment inherent to their position and vital to the effective operation of the judiciary. We should, of course, not protect a member of the judiciary "who is in fact guilty of using his powers to vent his spleen upon others, or for any other personal motive not connected with the public good". Gregoire v. Biddle, 2 Cir., 177 F.2d 579, 581. To deny recovery to a person injured by the ruling of a judge acting for personal gain or out of personal motives would be "monstrous." Ibid. But, it is argued that absolute immunity is necessary to prevent the chilling effects of a judicial inquiry, or the threat of such inquiry, into whether, in fact, a judge has been unfaithful to his oath of office. Thus, it is necessary to protect the guilty as well as the innocent.[1]

The doctrine of separation of powers is, of course, applicable only to the relations of coordinate branches of the same government, not to the relations between the branches of the Federal Government and those of the States. See Baker v. Carr, 369 U.S. 186, 210, 82 S. Ct. 691, 706. Any argument that Congress could not impose liability on state judges for the deprivation of civil rights would thus have to be based upon the claim that doing so would violate the theory of division of powers between the Federal and State Governments. This claim has been foreclosed by the cases recognizing "that Congress has the power to enforce the provisions of the Fourteenth Amendment against those who carry a badge of authority of a State . . . ." Monroe v. Pape. In terms of the power of Congress, I can see no difference between imposing liability on a state police officer (Monroe v. Pape, supra) and on a state judge. The question presented is not of constitutional dimension; it is solely a question of statutory interpretation.

The argument that the actions of public officials must not be subjected to judicial scrutiny because to do so would have an inhibiting effect on their work, is but a more sophisticated manner of saying "The King can do no wrong." Chief Justice Cockburn long ago disposed of the argument that liability would deter judges:

> "I cannot believe judges . . . would fail to discharge their duty faithfully and fearlessly according to their oaths and consciences . . . from any fear of exposing themselves to actions at law. I am persuaded that the number of such actions would be infinitely small and would be easily disposed of. While, on the other hand, I can easily conceive cases in which judicial opportunity might be so perverted and abused for the purpose of injustice as that, on sound principles, the authors of such wrong ought to be responsible to the parties wronged." Dawkins v. Lord Paulet, L.R. 5 Q.B. 94, 110 (C. J. Cockburn, dissenting).

1. Other justifications for the doctrine of absolute immunity have been advanced: (1) preventing threat of suit from influencing decision; (2) protecting judges from liability for honest mistakes; (3) relieving judges of the time and expense of defending suits; (4) removing an impediment to responsible men entering the judiciary; (5) necessity of finality; (6) appellate review is satisfactory remedy; (7) the judge's duty is to the public and not to the individual; (8) judicial self-protection; (9) separation of powers. See generally, Jennings, Tort Liability of Administrative Officers, 21 Minn.L. Rev. 263, 271–272 (1937).

This is not to say that a judge who makes an honest mistake should be subjected to civil liability. It is necessary to exempt judges from liability for the consequences of their honest mistakes. The judicial function involves an informed exercise of judgment. It is often necessary to choose between differing versions of fact, to reconcile opposing interests, and to decide closely contested issues. Decisions must often be made in the heat of trial. A vigorous and independent mind is needed to perform such delicate tasks. It would be unfair to require a judge to exercise his independent judgment and then to punish him for having exercised it in a manner which, in retrospect, was erroneous. Imposing liability for mistaken, though honest judicial acts, would curb the independent mind and spirit needed to perform judicial functions. Thus, a judge who sustains a conviction on what he forthrightly considers adequate evidence should not be subjected to liability when an appellate court decides that the evidence was not adequate. Nor should a judge who allows a conviction under what is later held an unconstitutional statute.

But that is far different from saying that a judge shall be immune from the consequences of any of his judicial actions, and that he shall not be liable for the knowing and intentional deprivation of a person's civil rights. What about the judge who conspires with local law enforcement officers to "railroad" a dissenter? What about the judge who knowingly turns a trial into a "kangaroo" court? Or one who intentionally flouts the Constitution in order to obtain a conviction? Congress, I think, concluded that the evils of allowing intentional, knowing deprivations of civil rights to go unredressed far outweighed the speculative inhibiting effects which might attend an inquiry into a judicial deprivation of civil rights.[2]

The plight of the oppressed is indeed serious. Under City of Greenwood v. Peacock, 384 U.S. 808, 809, 86 S.Ct. 1800, 1803, the defendant cannot prevent a state court from depriving him of his civil rights by removing to a federal court. And under the rule announced today, the person cannot recover damages for the deprivation.

NOTE

In connection with the "good faith" defense under Pierson v. Ray, consider the following, pre-Pierson decision in Bowens v. Knazze, 237 F.Supp. 826 (N.D.Ill.1965):

WILL, DISTRICT JUDGE. Plaintiff brings this action under the Civil Rights Act, 42 U.S.C. § 1983, seeking the recovery of damages for an illegal search of his person.

2. A judge is liable for injury caused by a ministerial act; to have immunity the judge must be performing the judicial function. See, e. g., Ex parte Virginia, 100 U.S. 339, 25 L.Ed. 676, Harper & James, Law of Torts 1642, 1643 (1956). The presence of malice and the intention to deprive a person of his civil rights is wholly incompatible with the judicial function. When a judge acts intentionally and knowingly to deprive a person of his constitutional rights he exercises no discretion or individual judgment; he acts no longer as a judge, but as a "minister" of his own prejudices.

Defendant is an officer of the Chicago Police Department. Early on the morning of August 21, 1961, plaintiff, his wife and another couple were walking in the vicinity of 39th Street and Cottage Grove Avenue in the city of Chicago. Officer Knazze, and his partner, Officer Frawley, having been informed that plaintiff's wife was carrying a concealed weapon, stopped the two couples on the street. The weapon, concealed by newspapers, was in the possession of plaintiff's wife and was surrendered to Officer Knazze. Officer Frawley approached the plaintiff who attempted to run away, but later stopped. Frawley searched the plaintiff and found no weapon. As Frawley proceeded to search the second man in the group, Officer Knazze decided to make a more thorough search of the plaintiff. This second search yielded a package of heroin which had been concealed in the fly of plaintiff's trousers.

Plaintiff was then taken into custody and charged with the unlawful possession of narcotic drugs. . . .

Upon trial, Bowens moved to suppress the package of heroin found in his trousers. The trial judge, after a hearing on the motion, allowed the package to be admitted in evidence. On the basis of this evidence, plaintiff was convicted of the offense charged in the indictment.

Bowens appealed the judgment of conviction to the Supreme Court of Illinois, which reversed and vacated the conviction, holding that the heroin was obtained in an illegal search and that the trial judge erred in admitting it in evidence. People v. Bowen (sic), 29 Ill.2d 349, 194 N.E.2d 316 (1963). The court determined that the initial search by Officer Frawley was reasonable and lawful. However, since the officer had determined, to his satisfaction, that Bowens was unarmed, the subsequent and more thorough search by Officer Knazze was held to be unlawful. Inasmuch as the heroin was found in the second search, its use in evidence was proscribed. In reaching this conclusion, the court made no reference to prior decisions and it appears that the question of the lawfulness of a "double search" was before the Illinois court for the first time.

The defendant has filed a motion to dismiss the instant complaint, contending that it does not state a cause of action under § 1983. Responding to this motion, plaintiff urges only that each and every time a search is determined to be unlawful, the person searched has a cause of action under the Civil Rights Act. While § 1983 is written with broad strokes, we cannot conclude that it should be so automatically and comprehensively construed. . . . one essential requirement of an action under § 1983 is that the plaintiff show facts which indicate that the defendant, at the time he acted, knew or as a reasonable man should have known that his acts were ones which would deprive the plaintiff of his constitutional rights or might lead to that result.

. . .

The Civil Rights Act created a new type of tort: the invasion, under color of law, of a citizen's constitutional rights. The test of tortious conduct in an ordinary tort case is, as a general rule, whether at the time of the incident the defendant was negligent, whether he failed to act as a reasonably prudent man. In such cases the judgment of negligence is based on a standard of behavior left to the determination of the community. . . . These judgments pose no problem because they are merely the application of general standards which, by definition, the defendant should have been able to apply at the time the acts complained of occurred.

The tort created by the Civil Rights Act, however, is not amenable to such treatment in at least one respect. The measure of a citizen's constitutional rights is not left to the determination of the community-at-large. It is determined by the courts. If that standard has not yet been enunciated by a court in a manner which makes its applicability to the incident at hand clear, the potential defendant cannot be expected to conform his conduct to it. Unlike the requirements of a statute or the judgment of the community which can be applied retroactively, the retroactive application of the judgment of a court as to the requirements of the Constitution—based not on community standards but on legal reasoning—would place a defendant in an impossible position.

It would require law enforcement officers to respond in damages every time they miscalculated in regard to what a court of last resort would determine constituted an invasion of constitutional rights, even where, as here, a trial judge—more learned in the law than a police officer—held that no such violation occurred.

We would observe that, if plaintiff is correct and every act ultimately determined to be constitutionally improper gives rise to an action under § 1983, it would be reasonable to assume that we should hold the trial judge equally responsible as the police officer. Each has committed the identical error. Clearly, the Act does not purport to make such a judicial error actionable. It would be unreasonable to construe the Act in a manner which produces a different and more rigorous standard for the police officer.

So long as the defendant's conduct stemmed from his reasonable belief as to the requirements of the law and was not unreasonable in any other way, he cannot be held responsible. . . . "No one has a constitutional right to be free from a law officer's honest misunderstanding of the law or facts in making an arrest". Agnew v. City of Compton, 239 F.2d 226, 231 (9 Cir. 1956), cert. den. 353 U.S. 959, 77 S.Ct. 868. Thus, the action of a police officer cannot be tortious when the officer proceeds on the basis of his reasonable, good faith understanding of the law and does not act with unreasonable violence or subject the citizen to unusual indignity. The facts alleged in the complaint demonstrate conclusively that the defendant could not reasonably have foreseen that a deprivation of constitutional rights might have resulted from his conduct. Under such circumstances, the complaint must be dismissed.

. . .

Plaintiff suggests that the incident was one of "unusual indignity" inasmuch as the defendant unzipped his trousers to remove the package of heroin. It is clear that Officer Knazze, having determined that something was hidden in plaintiff's trousers, was entitled to remove the concealed object. That the plaintiff chose to hide the package in a particular place adds nothing to his complaint.

. . .

For the foregoing reasons, both the instant complaint and the related complaint subsequently filed will be dismissed for failure to state a cause of action under the Civil Rights Act, 42 U.S.C. § 1983.

C. CONTEMPT OF COURT

McNEAR v. RHAY

Supreme Court of Washington, 1965.
65 Wash.2d 530, 398 P.2d 732.

* * * FINLEY, JUDGE (concurring in the result). The decision of the United States Supreme Court in Mapp v. Ohio (1961), and the trend in subsequent state decisions clearly indicate that the exclusionary "fruit of the poison tree doctrine" of the Weeks case is now supported by the great weight of authority, in fact is the law of the land, unless and until revised by authoritative court decisions. Since our decision in State v. Rousseau, and my concurring opinion therein, I have been convinced of the soundness of the evaluation by the late John H. Wigmore that the Weeks case and its so-called exclusionary doctrine is a contagion of sentimentality—nothing more, nothing less. Furthermore, I think the policy considerations involved are unsound and unworkable and should not be perpetuated. In other words, if the courts are to "police the police," and I can agree that in some respects the courts probably should, other procedures or judicial mechanisms should be exercised, such as contempt of court,* to correct and control interference or obstruction of the administration of justice. This in my judgment would be much more effective in regulating questionable police methods and in establishing proper police practices than the present policy of the judiciary of relying upon the Weeks-Mapp doctrine. I question whether law enforcement officers read the advance sheets, or for that matter the opinions of appellate courts in the bound volumes. If they do, or if they hear of decisions of the Weeks and Mapp variety, I am very dubious about such decisions preventing a police officer from making an unlawful arrest, or search and seizure, when he is on the firing line, so to speak, attempting to apprehend a suspect, or trying to impound stolen goods or contraband. Suspension from duty, *and without pay,* compelled by contempt of court order under appropriate police disciplinary procedure and authority, has a much more convincing ring, and should be more reasonably effective in correcting over-reaching police tactics. The suggested alternative law enforcement supervisory procedure has a most important by-product: relevant, competent evidence, having effective and proper

* Blumrosen, Contempt of Court and Unlawful Police Action, 11 Rutgers L. Rev. 526, 532 (1957).

Unlawful arrest, search and seizure without warrant or probable cause could be prohibited and contempt proceedings could be authorized by promulgation of rules of court or by legislation, or both. Police officers violating the probation would be cited to show cause, or be held in contempt of court. Trial courts could impose sanctions, against offending officers, conditioned upon disciplinary action being taken against the officers by appropriate police authorities within a period of time specified by court order.

probative value (except for the Weeks-Mapp exclusionary policy) will be available and usable for the prosecution of criminal charges. It seems far-fetched, bordering on the grotesque, to expect to train police officers, and to better supervise questionable police tactics, by weakening the prosecution of criminal cases and actually in some cases turning criminals loose because, as Cardozo once said, "the constable has blundered." In addition, the Weeks-Mapp police administration policy is certainly not conducive to effective law enforcement respecting criminal offenders. The interests of the public in this and their protection from the predatory proclivities of the criminal element require some re-thinking in this area of the law apropos of a sounder solution of the problems of unlawful arrest, search and seizure, than I can find in Weeks and Mapp. I am convinced that a better solution can be found, and believe that the contempt of court procedure mentioned herein has rational and constructive possibilities. But only one or a few voices in dissent cannot hope to stem the present tide. And, for the time being at least, I am bound by Mapp v. Ohio, supra, so at the present time I reluctantly concur.

NOTES

The article cited by Judge Finley in his concurring opinion in the foregoing case contains the following criticisms of various alternatives which have been proposed for use in place of the exclusionary rule. See Blumrosen, Contempt of Court and Unlawful Police Action, 11 Rutgers L.Rev. 526, 529–32, 533–48 (1957):

"The second alternative, that of criminal prosecution of police officers who engage in unlawful investigative activity, poses other problems. The probability is low that such proceedings will be initiated by a prosecutor who has had the benefit of illegally procured evidence, either for purposes of prosecution or further investigation. Prosecutors themselves may feel that the rules relating to investigation are unduly restrictive. A feeling of ingratitude and inconsistency may restrain them from prosecuting the police officer who has furthered the performance of the prosecutor's duties. Evidence of non-prosecution is not lacking. The annotations following the federal criminal statutes dealing with illegal police activity reveal no decided cases.[1] Some prosecutions may be found under the Civil Rights Act, but there, the prosecuting agency is unrelated to the investigative officers. In some limited circumstances, prosecution may be brought for political reasons, but this seems a slim reed on which to rely for protection against arbitrary police activity. In short, the general objection to this alternative is that it has virtually no deterrent value, because prosecutors won't prosecute.

"Internal discipline within the police organization as an alternative method of control faces some of the same objections noted above, and one more. Police officers who are convinced of the guilt of their suspect tend to feel that the 'formalities' incident to arrest and prosecution are unfair in

1. 62 Stat. 803, 18 U.S.C. § 2236 (1948), 18 U.S.C.A. § 2236 (unlawful search and seizure); 62 Stat. 803. 18 U.S.C. § 2235 (1948), (malicious procurement of warrant); 62 Stat. 803, 18 U.S.C. § 2234 (1948) (exceeding authority under warrant).

that they hinder investigation and conviction.[2] Thus the likelihood of effective internal police supervision seems small. An increase in the knowledge by police of their duties has been noted where the exclusionary rules are in effect, but this improvement, when not coupled with effective sanctions against violators, is not likely to produce the maximum deterrent effect. An aggressive police commissioner can shape police behavior, but to do so, he must combat a highly developed body of resistence.

"The civil action against a police officer is apparently ineffective, particularly where plaintiff was convicted of a crime on the basis of evidence unlawfully obtained. The argument that he would not have been discovered in his illegal activities if the police officer had obeyed the rules, or that he would have been convicted three days sooner if he had been promptly arraigned is not calculated to stir the sensibilities of a jury, valid as it may be in the abstract.[3] In a number of civil actions where recovery has been allowed, plaintiffs were in fact innocent, and often had other virtues which commended themselves to the deciding body.[4]

"In such a civil action, the focus is on the two parties, and plaintiff who stands convicted or suspected of crime does not appear to be a good candidate for compensation, while the over-zealous marshall does not appear seriously at fault. Thus the civil action distorts the perspective of the prohibitions against unlawful police activity. The meaningful perspective is

2. An indication of the attitude of one police officer may be found in Noback v. Town of Montclair, 33 N.J.Super. 420, 110 A.2d 339 (Law Div.1954), an action for assault brought against a municipality and a police officer arising out of the shooting of a suspected disorderly person who fled when the officer approached him. When asked why he fired, the officer replied:

"A. Counsellor, my feeling at that time was when that man escaped me, I just couldn't understand why that man ran away and why would he run away from a policeman. He must have done something wrong. He must have been guilty of something. I didn't know whether it was just that particular incident. I didn't know whether it was something that he was afraid that he had done. I did not know that, but not knowing that man I had to get that man. I had never had anyone get away from me as long as I have been a policeman, and I just had to get that man and bring him in so if he had done something wrong or not, we would have found that out at headquarters." 33 N.J.Super. at 425, 110 A.2d at 342.

3. If plaintiff has been convicted of a crime on the basis of unlawfully seized evidence, may or will a jury award actual damages to compensate him for the time spent in prison?

4. See, for example, Bucher v. Krause, 200 F.2d 576 (7th Cir. 1952), cert. denied 345 U.S. 997 [73 S.Ct. 1141] (1953), a diversity case. Plaintiff, an innocent young man in Chicago to marry his fiance, was shot by police officers without justification and then detained in what might have been an effort to "cover up" the unjustifiable shooting. Damages: $100,000.

In Ware v. Dunn, 80 Cal.App.2d 936, 183 P.2d 128 (1947), plaintiffs were husband, in the navy, and his wife, who were accused and detained by vice squad men who doubted that they were married. Cf. Daniel v. McNeel, 217 Miss. 573, 64 So.2d 636 (1953), where elements of entrapment seemed to be present.

See Barrett, Exclusion of Evidence Obtained by Illegal Search, 43 Calif.L. Rev. 565 (1955). He refuses to discount the significance of the court action although he recognizes a need to streamline it. To the same effect, see Plumb, Illegal Enforcement of the Law, 24 Cornell L.Q. 337 (1939).

Obviously we are building on assumptions as to police behavior that could be evaluated better if empirical data were available. See Barrett, supra for an example of the use of some such data.

that we are here dealing with rules expressing some fundamental precepts concerning democratic government, based ultimately perhaps, on the fear that an executive armed with unlimited powers of arrest, detention, and search may be armed with a weapon inconsistent with our system of freedom. The enforcement of rules based on concepts such as these by a petty criminal in the civil courts narrows this perspective, and it is not surprising that the broader concept is lost because of the immediate context.

"The privilege of self-defense theoretically available at common law is so fraught with peril that it is not worth cataloguing as a separate remedy here.

"The alternative suggested here—contempt of court—would, if adopted, substantially overcome the objections to the other remedial devices. In jurisdictions which do not want to catch the cop and let the robber go, the contempt of court approach would enable a penal disposition of both wrongdoers. Since the initiation of contempt proceedings normally is by the court, which appoints prosecuting counsel, the objection to the criminal sanction—that prosecutors won't prosecute—would not apply.

"The issue in contempt proceedings would be different from that in a civil action. In contempt, the issue would be between the offending officer and the courts, as administrators of the judicial process, rather than, as in a civil action, between the officers and the suspect. Thus the problem of perspective mentioned earlier would be avoided. In contempt proceedings, the theory of prosecution would be that the officer has interfered with the administration of the judicial process, one function of which is to demarcate the limits of executive power.

"Thus far, contempt of court as a remedy for unlawful police activity commends itself. It avoids the weaknesses of the alternative remedies, and would seem to have far more effective deterrent potential than any of the alternative forms. It is one thing for an officer to risk losing his case against a suspect, a possible harsh word at headquarters, or a probably unsuccessful civil action, but quite another for him to risk the likelihood of a conviction for contempt with the attendant consequences of possible loss of position and imprisonment.

"A word of caution is in order. Arbitrary governmental action is no less arbitrary if it is court action. It will not do, in our desire to limit the police to lawful conduct, to subject them to unreasonable risks. While we do not want police officers to step over the line of permissible conduct where it is clearly drawn, we do want them to go up to that line in order to function effectively." . . .

D. ADMINISTRATIVE REVIEW

SECTION 1. DAMAGE CLAIMS

BIVENS v. SIX UNKNOWN NAMED AGENTS OF FEDERAL BUREAU OF NARCOTICS

Supreme Court of the United States, 1971.
403 U.S. 388, 91 S.Ct. 1999.

* * *.

MR. CHIEF JUSTICE BURGER, dissenting.

. . .

This case has significance far beyond its facts and its holding. For more than 55 years this Court has enforced a rule under which evidence of undoubted reliability and probative value has been suppressed and excluded from criminal cases whenever it was obtained in violation of the Fourth Amendment. The rule has rested on a theory that suppression of evidence in these circumstances was imperative to deter law enforcement authorities from using improper methods to obtain evidence.

The deterrence theory underlying the suppression doctrine, or exclusionary rule, has a certain appeal in spite of the high price society pays for such a drastic remedy. * * *

The plurality opinion in Irvine v. California, 347 U.S. 128, 136, 74 S.Ct. 381, 385 (1954), catalogued the doctrine's defects:

> "Rejection of the evidence does nothing to punish the wrong-doing official, while it may, and likely will, release the wrong-doing defendant. It deprives society of its remedy against one lawbreaker because he has been pursued by another. It protects one against whom incriminating evidence is discovered, but does nothing to protect innocent persons who are the victims of illegal but fruitless searches."

From time to time members of the Court, recognizing the validity of these protests, have articulated varying alternative justifications for the suppression of important evidence in a criminal trial. Under one of these alternative theories the rule's foundation is shifted to the "sporting contest" thesis that the government must "play the game fairly" and cannot be allowed to profit from its own illegal acts. But the exclusionary rule does not ineluctably flow from a desire to ensure that government plays the "game" according to the rules. If an effective alternative remedy is available, concern for official observance of the law does not require adherence to the exclusionary rule. Nor is it easy to understand how a court can be thought to endorse a violation of the Fourth Amendment by allowing illegally seized evidence to be introduced against a defendant if an effective remedy is provided against the government.

The exclusionary rule has also been justified on the theory that the relationship between the Self-Incrimination Clause of the Fifth Amendment and the Fourth Amendment requires the suppression of evidence seized in violation of the latter.

Even ignoring, however, the decisions of this Court that have held that the Fifth Amendment applies only to "testimonial" disclosures, it seems clear that the Self-Incrimination Clause does not protect a person from the seizure of evidence that is incriminating. It protects a person only from being the conduit by which the police acquire evidence. Mr. Justice Holmes once put it succinctly, "A party is privileged from producing the evidence, but not from its production." Johnson v. United States, 228 U.S. 457, 458, 33 S.Ct. 572 (1913).

It is clear, however, that neither of these theories undergirds the decided cases in this Court. Rather the exclusionary rule has rested on the deterrent rationale—the hope that law enforcement officials would be deterred from unlawful searches and seizures if the illegally seized, albeit trustworthy, evidence was suppressed often enough and the courts persistently enough deprived them of any benefits they might have gained from their illegal conduct.

This evidentiary rule is unique to American jurisprudence. Although the English and Canadian legal systems are highly regarded, neither has adopted our rule. See Martin, The Exclusionary Rule Under Foreign Law—Canada, 52 J.Crim.L.C. & P.S. 271, 272 (1961); Williams, The Exclusionary Rule Under Foreign Law—England, 52 J.Crim.L.C. & P.S. 272 (1961).

I do not question the need for some remedy to give meaning and teeth to the constitutional guarantees against unlawful conduct by government officials. Without some effective sanction, these protections would constitute little more than rhetoric. Beyond doubt the conduct of some officials requires sanctions. . . . But the hope that this objective could be accomplished by the exclusion of reliable evidence from criminal trials was hardly more than a wistful dream. Although I would hesitate to abandon it until some meaningful substitute is developed, the history of the suppression doctrine demonstrates that it is both conceptually sterile and practically ineffective in accomplishing its stated objective. . . .

Some clear demonstration of the benefits and effectiveness of the exclusionary rule is required to justify it in view of the high price it extracts from society—the release of countless guilty criminals. . . . But there is no empirical evidence to support the claim that the rule actually deters illegal conduct of law enforcement officials. . . .

There are several reasons for this failure. The rule does not apply any direct sanction to the individual official whose illegal conduct results in the exclusion of evidence in a criminal trial. With rare exceptions law enforcement agencies do not impose direct sanctions on the individual officer responsible for a particular judicial application of the suppression doctrine. Thus there is virtually nothing done to bring about a change in his practices. The immediate sanction triggered by the application of the rule is visited upon the prosecutor whose case against a criminal is either weakened or destroyed. The doctrine deprives the police in no real sense; except that apprehending wrongdoers is their business, police have no more stake in successful prosecutions than prosecutors or the public.

The suppression doctrine vaguely assumes that law enforcement is a monolithic governmental enterprise. For example, the dissenters in Wolf v. Colorado, *supra,* 338 U.S., at 44, 69 S.Ct., at 1370, argued that:

> "Only by exclusion can we impress upon the zealous *prosecutor* that violation of the Constitution will do him no good. And only when that point is driven home can the *prosecutor* be expected to emphasize the importance of observing the constitutional demands in *his instructions to the police.*" (Emphasis added.)

But the prosecutor who loses his case because of police misconduct is not an official in the police department; he can rarely set in motion any corrective action or administrative penalties. Moreover, he does not have control or direction over police procedures or police actions that lead to the exclusion of evidence. It is the rare exception when a prosecutor takes part in arrests, searches, or seizures so that he can guide police action.

Whatever educational effect the rule conceivably might have in theory is greatly diminished in fact by the realities of law enforcement work. Policemen do not have the time, inclination, or training to read and grasp the nuances of the appellate opinions that ultimately define the standards of conduct they are to follow. The issues that these decisions resolve often admit of neither easy nor obvious answers, as sharply divided courts on what is or is not "reasonable" amply demonstrate. Nor can judges, in all candor, forget that opinions sometimes lack helpful clarity.

The presumed educational effect of judicial opinions is also reduced by the long time lapse—often several years—between the original police action and its final judicial evaluation. Given a policeman's pressing responsibilities, it would be surprising if he ever becomes aware of the final result after such a delay. Finally, the exclusionary rule's deterrent impact is diluted by the fact that there are large areas of police activity that do not result in criminal prosecutions—hence the rule has virtually no applicability and no effect in such situations. . . .

Although unfortunately ineffective, the exclusionary rule has increasingly been characterized by a single, monolithic, and drastic judicial response to all official violations of legal norms. Inadvertent errors of judgment that do not work any grave injustice will inevitably occur under the pressure of police work. These honest mistakes have been treated in the same way as deliberate and flagrant *Irvine*-type violations of the Fourth Amendment.

. . .

Freeing either a tiger or a mouse in a schoolroom is an illegal act, but no rational person would suggest that these two acts should be punished in the same way. From time to time judges have occasion to pass on regulations governing police procedures. I wonder what would be the judicial response to a police order authorizing "shoot to kill" with respect to every fugitive. It is easy to predict our collective wrath and outrage. We, in common with all rational minds, would say that the police response must relate to the gravity and need; that a "shoot" order might conceivably be tolerable to prevent the escape of a convicted killer but surely not for a car thief, a pickpocket or a shoplifter.

I submit that society has at least as much right to expect rationally graded responses from judges in place of the universal "capital punishment" we inflict on all evidence when police error is shown in its acquisition. See ALI, Model Code of Pre-Arraignment Procedure § SS 8.02(2), p. 23 (Tent. Draft No. 4, 1971), reprinted in the Appendix to this opinion. Yet for over 55 years, and with increasing scope and intensity our legal system has treated vastly dissimilar cases as if they were the same.

Instead of continuing to enforce the suppression doctrine inflexibly, rigidly, and mechanically, we should view it as one of the experimental steps in the great tradition of the common law and acknowledge its shortcomings. But in the same spirit we should be prepared to discontinue what the experience of over half a century has shown neither deters errant officers nor affords a remedy to the totally innocent victims of official misconduct.

I do not propose, however, that we abandon the suppression doctrine until some meaningful alternative can be developed. In a sense our legal system has become the captive of its own creation. To overrule *Weeks* and *Mapp,* even assuming the Court was now prepared to take that step, could raise yet new problems. Obviously the public interest would be poorly served if law enforcement officials were suddenly to gain the impression, however erroneous, that all constitutional restraints on police had somehow been removed—that as open season on "criminals" had been declared. I am concerned lest some such mistaken impression might be fostered by a flat overruling of the suppression doctrine cases. For years we have relied upon it as the exclusive remedy for unlawful official conduct; in a sense we are in a situation akin to the narcotics addict whose dependence on drugs precludes any drastic or immediate withdrawal of the supposed prop, regardless of how futile its continued use may be.

Reasonable and effective substitutes can be formulated if Congress would take the lead, as it did for example in 1946 in the Federal Tort Claims Act. I see no insuperable obstacle to the elimination of the suppression doctrine if Congress would provide some meaningful and effective remedy against unlawful conduct by government officials.

The problems of both error and deliberate misconduct by law enforcement officials call for a workable remedy. Private damage actions against individual police officers concededly have not adequately met this requirement. . . . There is some validity to the claims that juries will not return verdicts against individual officers except in those unusual cases where the violation has been flagrant or where the error has been complete, as in the arrest of the wrong person or the search of the wrong house. There is surely serious doubt, for example, that a drug peddler caught packing his wares will be able to arouse much sympathy in a jury on the ground that the police officer did not announce his identity and purpose fully . . . Jurors may well refuse to penalize a police officer at the behest of a person they believe to be a "criminal" and probably will not punish an officer for honest errors of judgment. In any event an actual recovery depends on finding nonexempt assets of the police officer from which a judgment can be satisfied.

I conclude, therefore, that an entirely different remedy is necessary but it is one that in my view is as much beyond judicial power as the step the Court takes today. Congress should develop an administrative or quasi-judicial remedy against the government itself to afford compensation and restitution for persons whose Fourth Amendment rights have been violated. The venerable doctrine of *respondeat superior* in our tort law provides an entirely appropriate conceptual basis for this remedy. If, for example, a security guard privately employed by a department store commits an assault or other tort on a customer such as an improper search, the victim has a simple and obvious remedy—an action for money damages against the guard's employer, the department store. W. Prosser, The Law of Torts § 68, pp. 470–480 (3d ed., 1964). Such a statutory scheme would have the added advantage of providing some remedy to the completely innocent persons who are sometimes the victims of illegal police conduct—something that the suppression doctrine, of course, can never accomplish.

A simple structure would suffice. For example, Congress could enact a statute along the following lines:

(a) a waiver of sovereign immunity as to the illegal acts of law enforcement officials committed in the performance of assigned duties;

(b) the creation of a cause of action for damages sustained by any person aggrieved by conduct of governmental agents in violation of the Fourth Amendment or statutes regulating official conduct;

(c) the creation of a tribunal, quasi-judicial in nature or perhaps patterned after the United States Court of Claims to adjudicate all claims under the statute;

(d) a provision that this statutory remedy is in lieu of the exclusion of evidence secured for use in criminal cases in violation of the Fourth Amendment; and

(e) a provision directing that no evidence, otherwise admissible, shall be excluded from any criminal proceeding because of violation of the Fourth Amendment.

I doubt that lawyers serving on such a tribunal would be swayed either by undue sympathy for officers or by the prejudice against "criminals" that has sometimes moved lay jurors to deny claims. In addition to awarding damages, the record of the police conduct that is condemned would undoubtedly become a relevant part of an officer's personnel file so that the need for additional training or disciplinary action could be identified or his future usefulness as a public official evaluated. Finally, appellate judicial review could be made available on much the same basis that it is now provided as to district courts and regulatory agencies. This would leave to the courts the ultimate responsibility for determining and articulating standards.

Once the constitutional validity of such a statute is established, it can reasonably be assumed that the States would develop their own remedial systems on the federal model. Indeed there is nothing to prevent a State from enacting a comparable statutory scheme without waiting for the Congress. Steps along these lines would move our system toward more responsible law enforcement on the one hand and away from the irrational and drastic results of the suppression doctrine on the other. Independent of the alternative embraced in this dissenting opinion, I believe the time has come to re-examine the scope of the exclusionary rule and consider at least some narrowing of its thrust so as to eliminate the anomalies it has produced.

In a country that prides itself on innovation, inventive genius, and willingness to experiment, it is a paradox that we should cling for more than a half century to a legal mechanism that was poorly designed and never really worked. I can only hope now that the Congress will manifest a willingness to view realistically the hard evidence of the half-century history of the suppression doctrine revealing thousands of cases in which the criminal was set free because the constable blundered and virtually no evidence that innocent victims of police error—such as petitioner claims to be—have been afforded meaningful redress.

SECTION 2. DISCIPLINARY ACTION—CIVILIAN REVIEW BOARDS

WHO WILL WATCH THE WATCHMAN?

WARREN E. BURGER *

. . .

"I will anticipate the suggestion that what I am about to propose is theoretical, visionary or impractical, by pointing to procedures long used in industry to prevent industrial accidents. In every modern factory accidents cause injury to persons and damage to equipment or to products. More often than not the resulting losses are covered by insurance, but invariably the owner and the insurer working together conduct an inquiry into the causes of every accident. The purpose is to determine what happened, why it happened, to fix responsibility, to make monetary reparation in some cases and always to take preventive steps to avoid repetition of the accident.

"Industry does not like to have expensive machinery damaged; neither industry nor its workers want human beings injured. This combination of sound frugality and decent humanitarian considerations leads industry and its insurance companies to study and teach safety measures constantly. Chronic accident makers are removed from their jobs.

"Another example is found in the airline industry and the operation of aircraft generally. Every accident is made the subject of careful inquiry by a board of independent people who are qualified by training and experience to understand aircraft operations. When the cause of a failure or accident is determined, whether pilot error, mechanical failure, or other cause, a report is made and circulated in the industry. In order to prevent loss of life and property, all those who fly or maintain airplanes learn from the experience of others. The question at once suggests itself whether we can afford to be less concerned about protecting the functioning of the machinery of justice than the functioning of the machinery of industry. I think not.

"Training and education of police and the limitations which the law places upon them are not the central subject of discussion. Nevertheless, the years of judicial frustration at failure of police to observe the commands of the courts and the rising frequency of suppression of evidence cry out for better training of police officers and elevation of police standards. That improvements are possible, and that

* The quoted material is from an article by Chief Justice Burger under the title "Who Will Watch the Watchman?", in 14 Am.U.L.Rev. 1–2; 9–23 (1964). It was written when the author was a Judge of the United States Court of Appeals for the District of Columbia Circuit.

preventive measures are feasible, is suggested by the performance of some of the federal agencies, notably the Federal Bureau of Investigation, which has a remarkable record as to the incidence of suppression of evidence secured by its agents.

"Over the years most metropolitan police departments in the United States have developed some form of organization to receive and process complaints from civilians relating to alleged police misconduct. There is a wide variety of procedures and methods in use in one hundred or more cities and I would accept as true that these mechanisms have been established in a sincere desire to afford citizens the means by which a complaint may be registered with responsible administrators. I also believe that police administrators want this information in order to maintain fairness and improve police work. However, where these review bodies have been established they are almost invariably part of the police organization, often with a minority of civilian members. It is with no thought to disparage what has been done in this field that I suggest that none of the systems which are now in operation fully meets the need which exists.

"To accomplish the objective of maintaining lawful law enforcement calls for a commission or board which is predominantly *civilian* and external rather than an internal *police* agency. The civilian members should be persons well versed by experience in the legal subtleties of arrest, search, seizure, interrogations and related matters. Although such a review body would of necessity cooperate with a police department, it must be *independent* of police administration in the same sense—and for some of the same reasons—that courts must be independent of prosecutors.

"To provoke much-needed discussion, debate, and exploration, I will outline one suggested program to meet this need. I will be specific to some degree for the express purpose of engaging others to challenge and to offer alternatives. I believe debate among those who are interested in the improvement of the administration of justice may well develop a mechanism that would prevent a large proportion of the police errors causing the suppression of evidence. Over a period of time an independent Review Board would serve the much needed function of making clear to police officers generally, as well as to those called before the board, precisely where they had erred.

"There are certain features which seem to me fundamental and crucial in the structure of such a board as this. To make my points concrete I will direct them within the existing framework of the District of Columbia Government.

"(1) *Independence.* The Board should be independent of police administration and responsible directly to the Executive Branch of Government.

"(2) *Composition.* The Board should consist of five to seven members; two should be senior police officers of wide law enforcement experience, and the balance should be drawn from leaders of the legal profession, although one non-lawyer might well serve a useful purpose. The presence of a majority of lawyers on such a Board is indispensable, for they are trained in sorting out facts, getting at truth and then applying rules of law to known facts. To preserve continuity and allow for the accumulation of the special experience needed, members should have staggered terms so that not more than one-third of the membership would change each year.

"(3) *Subpoena Power.* Although the cooperation of most policemen and citizens can be assumed, the Board should be empowered to compel testimony and have access to police files. The matter of access to police files needs careful study in order to impose proper limits on using contents of such files; disclosure should not be permitted at any stage where it would prejudice or impede other pending criminal investigations.

"(4) *Pending Litigation.* Careful study would determine what provisions are needed to avoid conflict between Board review proceedings and other cases then pending in court or under study by the prosecution.

"(5) *Board Immunity.* Members of the Board acting in the performance of their duties and especially in making findings and recommendations should be covered by the same general immunity as that protecting members of a grand jury.

"(6) *Initiation of Complaints.* The mechanics and procedures for initiating complaints cannot be fully set forth without a joint study by police administrators and lawyers experienced in such matters. However, as a minimum, the Board's jurisdiction would include the following:

(a) The Board would consider complaints made directly to it by individuals.

(b) The Board would secure and review the transcript of every case in the District Court and the Court of General Sessions in which a motion to suppress evidence was granted.

(c) The Board would secure and review the appellate opinion and the basic transcript in every case in which an appellate court directs the suppression of evidence by the trial court.

"(7) *Nature of Hearing.* The Board should probably be empowered to conduct executive hearings within limits, provided that transcripts of hearings become public when findings are made public. Any officer appearing before the Board should be allowed counsel if desired. The details of how examination of witnesses should be conducted and to what extent rules of evidence would control require study in depth and to some extent would evolve from experience and practice.

"(8) *Counsel and Investigation.* A necessary incident of the independent status of the Board would be an independent investigator and counsel selected by the Board and responsible directly to the Board.

"(9) *Board Powers.* Careful study is needed to determine the scope of the Board's powers; the following areas of specific power should be considered:

(a) Power to direct or recommend suspension or dismissal of an officer; power to direct a hearing by a tribunal having disciplinary authority;

(b) Power to direct or recommend inquiry by the Police Department as to general police procedures;

(c) Power to direct or recommend reprimands short of dismissal or suspension;

(d) Power to direct or recommend specific in-job training for a particular officer;

(e) Power to direct or recommend that records be expunged, as for illegal arrest or illegal warrants.

I do not suggest this Review Board should have all these broad powers but only that these are some of the difficult problems which must be studied carefully before this machinery is set in motion. Our experience in other areas may indicate that direct action against an individual officer should not be within the jurisdiction of such a Review Board as this. The power to *recommend* such departmental action may be sufficient; when the officer's individual job rights or other related rights are in jeopardy, he is entitled to the protection of a separate proceeding with all the safeguards now afforded to an officer charged with a breach of duty.

"(10) *Board Action.* After hearing or inquiry the Review Board would render a report or make findings, depending upon the nature of the complaint and the facts disclosed. Its conclusions could take any one of several forms, for example:

(a) It might conclude that in all the circumstances the police action was justified or if not justified that it was due to an honest error of judgment.

Findings in this category could lead to recommendations that the officer be required to remedy defects in his basic training at a police training school.

(b) It might conclude that the officer had violated a statute or a constitutional provision without culpable intent and simply because he did not fully know the rules which limited his power to act or because he acted under the excitement of some emergency.

Findings in this second category might lead to recommendations for official reprimand, discipline, or limited suspension.

(c) It might conclude that the police acted in reckless or careless or conscious disregard of known rules, statutes or rights.

Such a flagrant case might well be one involving recommendation for departmental trial on charges leading to dismissal; this third category would, I hope, be the unusual case, but when found, firm action would be required.

"It is fair to anticipate that police administrators will look with skepticism on a Review Board which is independent and predominantly civilian in composition. Over the years judicial decisions have gradually taken from police many tools which were deeply imbedded in police practice and few substitute tools have been developed. Where the fault lies for failure to develop new tools, or whether new tools can be found, is beside the point at this stage. As I see it, the work of the Review Board would shed light on every aspect of the problem.

"One objection to a civilian Review Board is that non-experts are not competent to review the work of trained police. Certainly if the reviewers approach the problem in a spirit of hostility toward police or if the police respond in that spirit, progress would be difficult. But we must remember that suppression of evidence arises out of the application of provisions of the Constitution and statutes to concrete fact situations, and in this area it is the lawyer, not the policeman, who is the expert.

"It may be said that police administrators can put their own houses in order. I believe they can do so with the aid of such a Board, but the record up to this date is against the effectiveness of internal police controls. If police administrators find that they can establish effective internal controls, the need for external control would then have been eliminated.

"It may be said that the very existence of such an external Review Board would reflect on the integrity and competence of police administrators who are directly responsible, and would undermine police morale. This argument overlooks the fact that in a complex society virtually everyone at every level of government, and many outside government, is subject to external controls. Judges are in the forefront of those subject to this external influence. In Washington the Court of General Sessions is reviewed by the District of Columbia Court of Appeals; the United States Court of Appeals can in turn review the latter and the Supreme Court can review us. Even the Supreme Court is not fully immune, for in common with all judges they are at the mercy of the most cold-blooded external review ever devised by Man. I refer to the law professors who spend six months doing an autopsy on an appellate opinion often written under pressure in four or five days. Judges are indeed subject to deterrence by this unofficial 'external control' exercised by the academic community. When a law review article has laid bare the fact that a judge has written an opinion too broadly for the needs of a case, or that he has overlooked some important legislative history, or cited cases which do not support his thesis, there is no doubt the judge takes note. All rational human beings are subject to deterrence if there is prompt, direct, intelligent and affirmative purpose to the deterrence procedure. When the protest against external control is raised, we must also remember that law enforcement officers, like judges, congressmen, and presidents, work for the people and are accountable to them.

"It may be said that the very existence of such a Review Board will hamper police action, impede law enforcement by making officers timid and ineffective. Grave problems would arise if the members of such a Board approached their task in a spirit of hostility toward police or an attitude that they were the Commissars of the Police Force. No doubt there would be an interim period of adjustment during which some uncertainty would prevail, but I think a timid or immobilized police force can be avoided and is a spectre I have difficulty imagining. I point again to the example of the rigid control of every aircraft in this country, and particularly the regular airlines. I see no evidence that airlines have suffered. On the contrary they have benefited and the public has had the protection of safer and more efficient transportation because of the system of independent and external control. Moreover the surveillance of airlines is far more detailed and stringent on an hour-to-hour basis than anything needed for or appropriate to police operations.

"In this strong dissent in the *Olmstead* case, Justice Brandeis made a stirring plea for keeping law enforcement on a high plane:

> Decency, security and liberty alike demand that government officials shall be subjected to the same rules of conduct that are commands to the citizen. In a government of laws, existence of the government will be imperilled if it fails to observe the law scrupulously. Our Government is the potent, the omnipresent teacher. For good or for ill, it teaches the whole people by its example. Crime is contagious. If the Government becomes a lawbreaker, it breeds contempt for law; it invites every man to become a law unto himself; it invites anarchy. To declare that in the administration of the criminal law the end justifies the means—to declare that the Government may commit crimes in order to secure the conviction of a private criminal—would bring terrible retribution. Against that pernicious doctrine this Court should resolutely set its face.

No one can take issue with the Brandeis thesis, but there is another side to the coin.

"If a majority—or even a substantial minority—of the people in any given community, whether it be Washington, D.C., or Charlottesville, Virginia, come to believe that law enforcement is being frustrated by what laymen call 'technicalities,' there develops a sour and bitter feeling that is psychologically and sociologically unhealthy. Let me illustrate this. In recent years in Washington a series of cases involving the Suppression Doctrine has led to extended public debates, mass meetings, and bar association and congressional committees, all arousing bitter controversy. I refrain from naming the particular cases, for the very names have taken on the quality of slogans which tend to stifle thought and arouse emotions. National magazines have added to this unhealthy situation, describing Washington as a crime-ridden city; and genuinely thoughtful consideration has reached an impasse.

"I do not challenge these rules of law. But I do suggest that we may have come the full circle from the place where Brandeis stood, and that a vast number of people are losing respect for law and the administration of justice because they think that the Suppression Doctrine is *defeating* justice. That much of this reaction is due to lack of understanding does not mean we can ignore it. To a lesser degree this feeling can be found in many other cities in America. I suggest that this controversy, like both the rationale and the effect of the Suppression Doctrine itself, is sterile and futile. Apart from the imperative need to end this unwholesome controversy over some manifestations of the Suppression Doctrine and the need to improve law enforcement, we in the Nation's Capital have an added incentive to take some positive steps to change the unhappy image of Washington as a 'cesspool' of crime.

"The judges who shaped the Suppression Doctrine over the years may have been mistaken in particular cases, but we must remember that the rule was made to protect the integrity of law enforcement, not to cripple it. I suggest judges had a right to assume that other branches of government, and police in particular, would recognize that this mechanism of suppression was not an end in itself but a means, which needed implementation from the legislative and the executive branches. Those branches of government, not the courts, have the jurisdiction and power to make the doctrine a positive force. Courts cannot conduct post-mortem examinations of police action or conduct training courses for the police. That is the responsibility of others. Judges construe the Constitution and laws and define standards; beyond that all they can do is suggest, as I do tonight, the need for more.

"As you can readily observe the very statement, in barest outline, of the scope and function of such a Review Board demonstrates the complexity of the problems presented. The dimensions of these problems call for the most thoughtful study and consideration by leaders of the legal profession and police administrators. This is a study for which there are few guidelines and those who approach it must realize that they will be plowing in hard-packed soil filled with many rocks.

"It would be naive to suggest that Congress consider this problem at this stage, even though congressional action would ultimately be required. First, the entire subject should run the gauntlet of study and criticism by the legal profession and law enforcement agencies, and the results of such studies should be presented to Congress.

"The public has accepted—largely on faith in the Judiciary—the distasteful results of the Suppression Doctrine; but the wrath of public opinion may descend alike on police and judges if we persist in the view that suppression is a solution. At best it is a necessary evil and hardly more than a manifestation of sterile judicial indignation even in the view of well motivated and well informed laymen. We can well ponder whether any community is entitled to call itself an 'organized society' if it can find no way to solve this problem except by suppression of truth in the search for truth."

Chapter 13

SEARCHES PERMISSIBLE UPON LESS THAN PROBABLE CAUSE

A. STOP AND FRISK

TERRY v. OHIO

Supreme Court of the United States, 1968.
392 U.S. 1, 88 S.Ct. 1868.

MR. CHIEF JUSTICE WARREN delivered the opinion of the Court.

This case presents serious questions concerning the role of the Fourth Amendment in the confrontation on the street between the citizen and the policeman investigating suspicious circumstances.

Petitioner Terry was convicted of carrying a concealed weapon. Following the denial of a pretrial motion to suppress, the prosecution introduced in evidence two revolvers and a number of bullets seized from Terry and a codefendant, Richard Chilton, by Cleveland Police Detective Martin McFadden. At the hearing on the motion to suppress this evidence, Officer McFadden testified that while he was patrolling in plain clothes in downtown Cleveland at approximately 2:30 in the afternoon of October 31, 1963, his attention was attracted by two men, Chilton and Terry, standing on the corner of Huron Road and Euclid Avenue. He had never seen the two men before, and he was unable to say precisely what first drew his eye to them. However, he testified that he had been a policeman for 39 years and a detective for 35 and that he had been assigned to patrol this vicinity of downtown Cleveland for shoplifters and pickpockets for 30 years. He explained that he had developed routine habits of observation over the years and that he would "stand and watch people or walk and watch people at many intervals of the day." He added: "Now, in this case when I looked over they didn't look right to me at the time."

His interest aroused, Officer McFadden took up a post of observation in the entrance to a store 300 to 400 feet away from the two men. "I get more purpose to watch them when I seen their movements," he testified. He saw one of the men leave the other one and walk southwest on Huron Road, past some stores. The man paused for a moment and looked in a store window, then walked on a short distance, turned around and walked back toward the corner, pausing once again to look in the same store window. He rejoined his companion at the corner, and the two conferred briefly. Then the second man went through the same series of motions, strolling down Huron Road, looking in the same window, walking on a short distance, turning back, peering in the store window again, and returning to confer with the first man at the corner. The two men repeated this ritual alternately between five and six times apiece—in all, roughly a dozen trips. At one point, while the two were standing together on the corner, a third man approached them and engaged them briefly in conversation. This man then left the two others and walked west on Euclid Avenue. Chilton and Terry resumed their measured pacing, peering, and conferring. After this had gone on for 10 to 12 minutes, the two men walked off together, heading west on Euclid Avenue, following the path taken earlier by the third man.

By this time Officer McFadden had become thoroughly suspicious. He testified that after observing their elaborately casual and oft-repeated reconnaissance of the store window on Huron Road, he suspected the two men of "casing a job, a stick-up," and that he considered it his duty as a police officer to investigate further. He added that he feared "they may have a gun." Thus, Officer McFadden followed Chilton and Terry and saw them stop in front of Zucker's store to talk to the same man who had conferred with them earlier on the street corner. Deciding that the situation was ripe for direct action, Officer McFadden approached the three men, identified himself as a police officer and asked for their names. At this point his knowledge was confined to what he had observed. He was not acquainted with any of the three men by name or by sight, and he had received no information concerning them from any other source. When the men "mumbled something" in response to his inquiries, Officer McFadden grabbed petitioner Terry, spun him around so that they were facing the other two, with Terry between McFadden and the others, and patted down the outside of his clothing. In the left breast pocket of Terry's overcoat Officer McFadden felt a pistol. He reached inside the overcoat pocket, but was unable to remove the gun. At this point, keeping Terry between himself and the others, the officer ordered all three men to enter Zucker's store. As they went in, he removed Terry's overcoat completely, retrieved a .38 caliber revolver from the pocket and ordered all three men to face the wall with their hands raised. Officer McFadden proceeded to pat down the outer clothing of Chilton and the third man, Katz. He discovered another revolver in the outer pocket of Chilton's overcoat, but no weapons were found on Katz. The officer testified that he only patted the men down to see whether they had weapons, and that he did not put his hands beneath the outer garments of either Terry or Chilton until he felt their guns. So far as appears from the record, he never placed his hands beneath Katz's outer garments. Officer McFadden seized Chilton's gun, asked the proprietor of the store to call a police wagon, and took all three men to the station, where Chilton and Terry were formally charged with carrying concealed weapons.

On the motion to suppress the guns the prosecution took the position that they had been seized following a search incident to a lawful arrest. The trial court rejected this theory, stating that it "would be stretching the facts beyond reasonable comprehension" to find that Officer McFadden had had probable cause to arrest the men before he patted them down for weapons. However, the court denied the defendant's motion on the ground that Officer McFadden, on the basis of his experience, "had reasonable cause to believe . . . that the defendants were conducting themselves suspiciously, and some interrogation should be made of their action." Purely for his own protection, the court held, the officer had the right to pat down the outer clothing of these men, whom he had reasonable cause to believe might be armed. The court distinguished between an investigatory "stop" and an arrest, and between a "frisk" of the outer clothing for weapons and a full-blown search for evidence of crime. The frisk, it held, was essential to the proper performance of the officer's investigatory duties, for without it "the answer to the police officer may be a bullet, and a loaded pistol discovered during the frisk is admissible."

After the court denied their motion to suppress, Chilton and Terry waived jury trial and pleaded not guilty. The court adjudged them guilty . . .

I.

The Fourth Amendment provides that "the right of the people to be secure in their persons, houses, papers, and effects, against unreasonable searches and seizures, shall not be violated . . . ." This inestimable right of personal security belongs as much to the citizen on the streets of our great cities as to the homeowner closeted in his study to dispose of his secret affairs. * * *

Unquestionably petitioner was entitled to the protection of the Fourth Amendment as he walked down the street in Cleveland. The question is whether in all the circumstances of this on-the-street encounter, his right to personal security was violated by an unreasonable search and seizure.

We would be less than candid if we did not acknowledge that this question thrusts to the fore difficult and troublesome issues regarding a sensitive area of police activity—issues which have never before been squarely presented to this Court. Reflective of the tensions involved are the practical and constitutional arguments pressed with great vigor on both sides of the public debate over the power of the police to "stop and frisk"—as it is sometimes euphemistically termed—suspicious persons.

On the one hand, it is frequently argued that in dealing with the rapidly unfolding and often dangerous situations on city streets the police are in need of an escalating set of flexible responses, graduated in relation to the amount of information they possess. For this purpose it is urged that distinctions should be made between a "stop" and an "arrest" (or a "seizure" of a person), and between a "frisk" and a "search." Thus, it is argued, the police should be allowed to "stop" a person and detain him briefly for questioning upon suspicion that he may be connected with criminal activity. Upon suspicion that the person may be armed, the police should have the power to "frisk" him for weapons. If the "stop" and the "frisk" give rise to probable cause to believe that the suspect has committed a crime, then the police should be empowered to make a formal "arrest," and a full incident "search" of the person. This scheme is justified in part upon the notion that a "stop" and a "frisk" amount to a mere "minor inconvenience and petty indignity," which can properly be imposed upon the citizen in the interest of effective law enforcement on the basis of a police officer's suspicion.[1]

On the other side the argument is made that the authority of the police must be strictly circumscribed by the law of arrest and search as it has developed to date in the traditional jurisprudence of the Fourth Amendment. It is contended with some force that there is not—and cannot be—a variety of police activity which does not depend solely upon the voluntary cooperation of the citizen and yet which stops short of an arrest based upon probable cause to make such an arrest. The heart of the Fourth Amendment, the argument runs, is a severe requirement of specific justification for any intrusion upon protected personal security, coupled with a highly developed system of judicial controls to enforce upon the agents of the State the commands of the Constitution. Acquiescence by the courts in the compulsion inherent in the field interrogation practices at issue here, it is urged, would constitute an abdication of judicial control over, and indeed an encouragement of, substantial interference with liberty and personal security by police officers whose judgment is necessarily colored by their primary involvement in "the often competitive enterprise of ferreting out crime." Johnson v. United States, 333 U.S. 10, 14, 68 S.Ct. 367, 369 (1948). This, it is argued, can only serve to exacerbate police-community tensions in the crowded centers of our Nation's cities.

1. ". . . [T]he evidence needed to make the inquiry is not of the same degree or conclusiveness as that required for an arrest. The stopping of the individual to inquire is not an arrest and the ground upon which the police may make the inquiry may be less incriminating than the ground for an arrest for a crime known to have been committed. . . .

"And as the right to stop and inquire is to be justified for a cause less conclusive than that which would sustain an arrest, so the right to frisk may be justified as an incident to inquiry upon grounds of elemental safety and precaution which might not initially sustain a search. Ultimately the validity of the frisk narrows down to whether there is or is not a right by the police to touch the person questioned. The sense of exterior touch here involved is not very far different from the sense of sight or hearing—senses upon which police customarily act." People v. Rivera, 14 N.Y.2d 441, 445, 447, 201 N.E.2d 32, 34, 35, 252 N.Y.S.2d 458, 461, 463 (1964), cert. denied, 379 U.S. 978, 85 S.Ct. 679 (1965).

In this context we approach the issues in this case mindful of the limitations of the judicial function in controlling the myriad daily situations in which policemen and citizens confront each other on the street. The State has characterized the issue here as "the right of a police officer . . . to make an on-the-street stop, interrogate and pat down for weapons (known in the street vernacular as 'stop and frisk')." But this is only partly accurate. For the issue is not the abstract propriety of the police conduct, but the admissibility against petitioner of the evidence uncovered by the search and seizure. Ever since its inception, the rule excluding evidence seized in violation of the Fourth Amendment has been recognized as a principal mode of discouraging lawless police conduct. Thus its major thrust is a deterrent one, and experience has taught that it is the only effective deterrent to police misconduct in the criminal context, and that without it the constitutional guarantee against unreasonable searches and seizures would be a mere "form of words." The rule also serves another vital function—"the imperative of judicial integrity." Courts which sit under our Constitution cannot and will not be made party to lawless invasions of the constitutional rights of citizens by permitting unhindered governmental use of the fruits of such invasions. Thus in our system evidentiary rulings provide the context in which the judicial process of inclusion and exclusion approves some conduct as comporting with constitutional guarantees and disapproves other actions by state agents. A ruling admitting evidence in a criminal trial, we recognize, has the necessary effect of legitimizing the conduct which produced the evidence, while an application of the exclusionary rule withholds the constitutional imprimatur.

The exclusionary rule has its limitations, however, as a tool of judicial control. It cannot properly be invoked to exclude the products of legitimate police investigative techniques on the ground that much conduct which is closely similar involves unwarranted intrusions upon constitutional protections. Moreover, in some contexts the rule is ineffective as a deterrent. Street encounters between citizens and police officers are incredibly rich in diversity. They range from wholly friendly exchanges of pleasantries or mutually useful information to hostile confrontations of armed men involving arrests, or injuries, or loss of life. Moreover, hostile confrontations are not all of a piece. Some of them begin in a friendly enough manner, only to take a different turn upon the injection of some unexpected element into the conversation. Encounters are initiated by the police for a wide variety of purposes, some of which are wholly unrelated to a desire to prosecute for crime.[2] Doubtless some police "field interroga-

2. See Tiffany, McIntyre & Rotenberg, Detection of Crime: Stopping and Questioning, Search and Seizure, Encouragement and Entrapment 18–56 (1967). This sort of police conduct may, for example, be designed simply to help an intoxicated person find his way home, with no intention of arresting him unless he becomes obstreperous. Or the police may be seeking to mediate a domestic quarrel which threatens to erupt into violence. They may accost a woman in an area known for prostitution as part of a

tion" conduct violates the Fourth Amendment. But a stern refusal by this Court to condone such activity does not necessarily render it responsive to the exclusionary rule. Regardless of how effective the rule may be where obtaining convictions is an important objective of the police, it is powerless to deter invasions of constitutionally guaranteed rights where the police either have no interest in prosecuting or are willing to forego successful prosecution in the interest of serving some other goal.

Proper adjudication of cases in which the exclusionary rule is invoked demands a constant awareness of these limitations. The wholesale harassment by certain elements of the police community, of which minority groups, particularly Negroes, frequently complain,[3] will not be stopped by the exclusion of any evidence from any criminal trial. Yet a rigid and unthinking application of the exclusionary rule, in futile protest against practices which it can never be used effectively to control, may exact a high toll in human injury and frustration of efforts to prevent crime. No judicial opinion can comprehend the protean variety of the street encounter, and we can only judge the facts of the case before us. Nothing we say today is to be taken as indicating approval of police conduct outside the legitimate investigative sphere. Under our decision, courts still retain their traditional responsibility to guard against police conduct which is overbearing or harassing, or which trenches upon personal security without the objective evidentiary justification which the Constitution requires. When such conduct is identified, it must be condemned by the judiciary and its fruits must be excluded from evidence in criminal trials. And, of course, our approval of legitimate and restrained investigative conduct undertaken on the basis of ample factual justification

harassment campaign designed to drive prostitutes away without the considerable difficulty involved in prosecuting them. Or they may be conducting a dragnet search of all teenagers in a particular section of the city for weapons because they have heard rumors of an impending gang fight.

3. The President's Commission on Law Enforcement and Administration of Justice found that "in many communities, field interrogations are a major source of friction between the police and minority groups." President's Commission on Law Enforcement and Administration of Justice, Task Force Report: The Police 183 (1967). It was reported that the friction caused by "misuse of field interrogations" increases "as more police departments adopt 'aggressive patrol' in which officers are encouraged routinely to stop and question persons on the street who are unknown to them, who are suspicious, or whose purpose for being abroad is not readily evident." Id., at 184. While the frequency with which "frisking" forms a part of field interrogation practice varies tremendously with the locale, the objective of the interrogation, and the particular officer, see Tiffany, McIntyre & Rotenberg, supra, n. 9, at 47–48, it cannot help but be a severely exacerbating factor in police-community tensions. This is particularly true in situations where the "stop and frisk" of youths or minority group members is "motivated by the officers' perceived need to maintain the power image of the beat officer, an aim sometimes accomplished by humilating anyone who attempts to undermine police control of the streets." Id., at 47–48.

should in no way discourage the employment of other remedies than the exclusionary rule to curtail abuses for which that sanction may prove inappropriate.

Having thus roughly sketched the perimeters of the constitutional debate over the limits on police investigative conduct in general and the background against which this case presents itself, we turn our attention to the quite narrow question posed by the facts before us: whether it is always unreasonable for a policeman to seize a person and subject him to a limited search for weapons unless there is probable cause for an arrest. Given the narrowness of this question, we have no occasion to canvass in detail the constitutional limitations upon the scope of a policeman's power when he confronts a citizen without probable cause to arrest him.

II.

Our first task is to establish at what point in this encounter the Fourth Amendment becomes relevant. That is, we must decide whether and when Officer McFadden "seized" Terry and whether and when he conducted a "search." There is some suggestion in the use of such terms as "stop" and "frisk" that such police conduct is outside the purview of the Fourth Amendment because neither action rises to the level of a "search" or "seizure" within the meaning of the Constitution. We emphatically reject this notion. It is quite plain that the Fourth Amendment governs "seizures" of the person which do not eventuate in a trip to the station house and prosecution for crime—"arrests" in traditional terminology. It must be recognized that whenever a police officer accosts an individual and restrains his freedom to walk away, he has "seized" that person. And it is nothing less than sheer torture of the English language to suggest that a careful exploration of the outer surfaces of a person's clothing all over his or her body in an attempt to find weapons is not a "search." Moreover, it is simply fantastic to urge that such a procedure performed in public by a policeman while the citizen stands helpless, perhaps facing a wall with his hands raised, is a "petty indignity."[4] It is a serious intrusion upon the sanctity of the person, which may inflict great indignity and arouse strong resentment, and it is not to be undertaken lightly.[5]

4. Consider the following apt description:

"[T]he officer must feel with sensitive fingers every portion of the prisoner's body. A thorough search must be made of the prisoner's arms and armpits, waistline and back, the groin and area about the testicles, and entire surface of the legs down to the feet." Priar & Martin, Searching and Disarming Criminals, 45 J.Crim., L.C. & P.S. 481 (1954).

5. We have noted that the abusive practices which play a major, though by no means exclusive, role in creating this friction are not susceptible of control by means of the exclusionary rule, and cannot properly dictate our decision with respect to the powers of the police in genuine investigative and preventive situations. However, the degree of community resentment aroused by particular practices is clearly relevant to an assessment of the quality of the intrusion upon reasonable expectations of personal security caused by those practices.

The danger in the logic which proceeds upon distinctions between a "stop" and an "arrest," or "seizure" of the person, and between a "frisk" and a "search" is two-fold. It seeks to isolate from constitutional scrutiny the initial stages of the contact between the policeman and the citizen. And by suggesting a rigid all-or-nothing model of justification and regulation under the Amendment, it obscures the utility of limitations upon the scope, as well as the initiation, of police action as a means of constitutional regulation. This Court has held in the past that a search which is reasonable at its inception may violate the Fourth Amendment by virtue of its intolerable intensity and scope. The scope of the search must be "strictly tied to and justified by" the circumstances which rendered its initiation permissible. Warden v. Hayden, 387 U.S. 294, 310, 87 S.Ct. 1642, 1651, 1652 (1967) (Mr. Justice Fortas, concurring).

The distinctions of classical "stop-and-frisk" theory thus serve to divert attention from the central inquiry under the Fourth Amendment—the reasonableness in all the circumstances of the particular governmental invasion of a citizen's personal security. "Search" and "seizure" are not talismans. We therefore reject the notions that the Fourth Amendment does not come into play at all as a limitation upon police conduct if the officers stop short of something called a "technical arrest" or a "full-blown search."

In this case there can be no question, then, that Officer McFadden "seized" petitioner and subjected him to a "search" when he took hold of him and patted down the outer surfaces of his clothing. We must decide whether at that point it was reasonable for Officer McFadden to have interfered with petitioner's personal security as he did.[6] And in determining whether the seizure and search were "unreasonable" our inquiry is a dual one—whether the officer's action was justified at its inception, and whether it was reasonably related in scope to the circumstances which justified the interference in the first place.

III.

If this case involved police conduct subject to the Warrant Clause of the Fourth Amendment, we would have to ascertain whether "probable cause" existed to justify the search and seizure which took place. However, that is not the case. We do not retreat from our holdings that the police must, whenever practicable, obtain advance judicial

6. We thus decide nothing today concerning the constitutional propriety of an investigative "seizure" upon less than probable cause for purposes of "detention" and/or interrogation. Obviously, not all personal intercourse between policemen and citizens involves "seizures" of persons. Only when the officer, by means of physical force or show of authority, has in some way restrained the liberty of a citizen may we conclude that a "seizure" has occurred. We cannot tell with any certainty upon this record whether any such "seizure" took place here prior to Officer McFadden's initiation of physical contact for purposes of searching Terry for weapons, and we thus may assume that up to that point no intrusion upon constitutionally protected rights had occurred.

approval of searches and seizures through the warrant procedure . . . or that in most instances failure to comply with the warrant requirement can only be excused by exigent circumstances. But we deal here with an entire rubric of police conduct—necessarily swift action predicated upon the on-the-spot observations of the officer on the beat—which historically has not been, and as a practical matter could not be, subjected to the warrant procedure. Instead, the conduct involved in this case must be tested by the Fourth Amendment's general proscription against unreasonable searches and seizures.

Nonetheless, the notions which underlie both the warrant procedure and the requirement of probable cause remain fully relevant in this context. In order to assess the reasonableness of Officer McFadden's conduct as a general proposition, it is necessary "first to focus upon the governmental interest which allegedly justifies official intrusion upon the constitutionally protected interests of the private citizen," for there is "no ready test for determining reasonableness other than by balancing the need to search [or seize] against the invasion which the search [or seizure] entails." Camara v. Municipal Court, 387 U.S. 523, 534, 536–537, 87 S.Ct. 1727, 1733–1735 (1967). And in justifying the particular intrusion the police officer must be able to point to specific and articulable facts which, taken together with rational inferences from those facts, reasonably warrant that intrusion. The scheme of the Fourth Amendment becomes meaningful only when it is assured that at some point the conduct of those charged with enforcing the laws can be subjected to the more detached, neutral scrutiny of a judge who must evaluate the reasonableness of a particular search or seizure in light of the particular circumstances. And in making that assessment it is imperative that the facts be judged against an objective standard: would the facts available to the officer at the moment of the seizure or the search "warrant a man of reasonable caution in the belief" that the action taken was appropriate? Anything less would invite intrusions upon constitutionally guaranteed rights based on nothing more substantial than inarticulate hunches, a result this Court has consistently refused to sanction. And simple " 'good faith on the part of the arresting officer is not enough.' . . . If subjective good faith alone were the test, the protections of the Fourth Amendment would evaporate, and the people would be 'secure in their persons, houses, papers, and effects,' only in the discretion of the police."

Applying these principles to this case, we consider first the nature and extent of the governmental interests involved. One general interest is of course that of effective crime prevention and detection; it is this interest which underlies the recognition that a police officer may in appropriate circumstances and in an appropriate manner approach a person for purposes of investigating possibly criminal behavior even though there is no probable cause to make an arrest. It was this legitimate investigative function Officer McFadden was discharging when he decided to approach petitioner and his companions. He had observed Terry, Chilton, and Katz go through a series of acts, each of them perhaps innocent in itself, but which taken together warranted further investigation. There is nothing unusual in two men standing together on a street corner, perhaps waiting for someone. Nor is there anything suspicious about people in such circumstances strolling up and down the street, singly or in pairs. Store windows, moreover, are made to be looked in. But the story is quite different where, as here, two men hover about a street corner for an extended period of time, at the end of which it becomes apparent that they are not waiting for anyone or anything; where these men pace alternately along an identical route, pausing to stare in the same store window roughly 24 times; where each completion of this route is followed immediately by a conference between the two men on the corner; where they are joined in one of these conferences by a third man who leaves swiftly; and where the two men finally follow the third and rejoin him a couple of blocks away. It would have been poor police work indeed for an officer of 30 years' experience in the detection of thievery from stores in this same neighborhood to have failed to investigate this behavior further.

The crux of this case, however, is not the propriety of Officer McFadden's taking steps to investigate petitioner's suspicious behavior, but rather, whether there was justification for McFadden's invasion of Terry's personal security by searching him for weapons in the course of that investigation. We are now concerned with more than the governmental interest in investigating crime; in addition, there is the more immediate interest of the police officer in taking steps to assure himself that the person with whom he is dealing is not armed with a weapon that could unexpectedly and fatally be used against him. Certainly it would be unreasonable to require that police officers take unnecessary risks in the performance of their duties. American criminals have a long tradition of armed violence, and every year in this country many law enforcement officers are killed in the line of duty, and thousands more are wounded. Virtually all of these deaths and a substantial portion of the injuries are inflicted with guns and knives.

In view of these facts, we cannot blind ourselves to the need for law enforcement officers to protect themselves and other prospective victims of violence in situations where they may lack probable cause for an arrest. When an officer is justified in believing that the individual whose suspicious behavior he is investigating at close range is armed and presently dangerous to the officer or to others, it would appear to be clearly unreasonable to deny the officer the power to take necessary measures to determine whether the person is in fact carrying a weapon and to neutralize the threat of physical harm.

We must still consider, however, the nature and quality of the intrusion on individual rights which must be accepted if police officers are to be conceded the right to search for weapons in situations where probable cause to arrest for crime is lacking. Even a limited search of the outer clothing for weapons constitutes a severe, though brief, intrusion upon cherished personal security, and it must surely be an annoying, frightening, and perhaps humiliating experience. Petitioner contends that such an intrusion is permissible only incident to a lawful arrest, either for a crime involving the possession of weapons or for a crime the commission of which led the officer to investigate in the first place. However, this argument must be closely examined.

Petitioner does not argue that a police officer should refrain from making any investigation of suspicious circumstances until such time as he has probable cause to make an arrest; nor does he deny that police officers in properly discharging their investigative function may find themselves confronting persons who might well be armed and dangerous. Moreover, he does not say that an officer is always unjustified in searching a suspect to discover weapons. Rather, he says it is unreasonable for the policeman to take that step until such time as the situation evolves to a point where there is probable cause to make an arrest. When that point has been reached, petitioner would concede the officer's right to conduct a search of the suspect for weapons, fruits or instrumentalities of the crime, or "mere" evidence, incident to the arrest.

There are two weaknesses in this line of reasoning, however. First, it fails to take account of traditional limitations upon the scope of searches, and thus recognizes no distinction in purpose, character, and extent between a search incident to an arrest and a limited search for weapons. The former, although justified in part by the acknowledged necessity to protect the arresting officer from assault with a concealed weapon, Preston v. United States, 376 U.S. 364, 367, 84 S.Ct. 881, 883 (1964), is also justified on other grounds, *ibid.*, and can therefore involve a relatively extensive exploration of the person. A search for weapons in the absence of probable cause to arrest, however, must, like any other search, be strictly circumscribed by the exigencies which justify its initiation. Warden v. Hayden, 387 U.S. 294, 310, 87 S.Ct. 1642, 1651, 1652 (1967) (MR. JUSTICE FORTAS, concurring). Thus it must be limited to that which is necessary for the discovery of weapons which might be used to harm the officer or others nearby, and may realistically be characterized as something less than a "full" search, even though it remains a serious intrusion.

A second, and related, objection to petitioner's argument is that it assumes that the law of arrest has already worked out the balance between the particular interests involved here—the neutralization of danger to the policeman in the investigative circumstance and the sanctity of the individual. But this is not so. An arrest is a wholly different kind of intrusion upon individual freedom from a limited search for weapons, and the interests each is designed to serve are likewise quite different. An arrest is the initial stage of a criminal prosecution. It is intended to vindicate society's interest in having its laws obeyed, and it is inevitably accompanied by future interference with the individual's freedom of movement, whether or not trial or conviction ultimately follows. The protective search for weapons, on the other hand, constitutes a brief, though far from inconsiderable, intrusion upon the sanctity of the person. It does not follow that because an officer may lawfully arrest a person only when he is apprised of facts sufficient to warrant a belief that the person has committed or is committing a crime, the officer is equally unjustified, absent that kind of evidence, in making any intrusions short of an arrest. Moreover, a perfectly reasonable apprehension of danger may arise long before the officer is possessed of adequate information to justify taking a person into custody for the purpose of prosecuting him for a crime. Petitioner's reliance on cases which have worked out standards of reasonableness with regard to "seizures" constituting arrests and searches incident thereto is thus misplaced. It assumes that the interests sought to be vindicated and the invasions of personal security may be equated in the two cases, and thereby ignores a vital aspect of the analysis of the reasonableness of particular types of conduct under the Fourth Amendment. See Camara v. Municipal Court, supra.

Our evaluation of the proper balance that has to be struck in this type of case leads us to conclude that there must be a narrowly drawn authority to permit a reasonable search for weapons for the protection of the police officer, where he has reason to believe that he is dealing with an armed and dangerous individual, regardless of whether he has probable cause to arrest the individual for a crime. The officer need not be absolutely certain that the individual is armed; the issue is whether a reasonably prudent man in the circumstances would be warranted in the belief that his safety or that of others was in danger. And in determining whether the officer acted reasonably in such circumstances, due weight must be given, not to his inchoate and unparticularized suspicion or "hunch," but to the specific reasonable inferences which he is entitled to draw from the facts in light of his experience. Cf. Brinegar v. United States, supra.

IV.

We must now examine the conduct of Officer McFadden in this case to determine whether his search and seizure of petitioner were reasonable, both at their inception and as conducted. He had observed Terry, together with Chilton and another man, acting in a manner he took to be preface to a "stick-up." We think on the facts and circumstances Officer McFadden detailed before the trial judge a reasonably prudent man would have been warranted in believing petitioner was armed and thus presented a threat to the officer's safety while he was investigating his suspicious behavior. The actions of Terry and Chilton were consistent with McFadden's hypothesis that these men were contemplating a daylight robbery—which, it is reasonable to assume, would be likely to involve the use of weapons—and nothing in their conduct from the time he first noticed them until the time he confronted them and identified himself as a police officer gave him sufficient reason to negate that hypothesis. Although the trio had departed the original scene, there was nothing to indicate abandonment of an intent to commit a robbery at some point. Thus, when Officer McFadden approached the three men gathered before the display window at Zucker's store he had observed enough to make it quite reasonable to fear that they were armed; and nothing in their response to his hailing them, identifying himself as a police officer, and asking their names served to dispel that reasonable belief. We cannot say his decision at that point to seize Terry and pat his clothing for weapons was the product of a volatile or inventive imagination, or was undertaken simply as an act of harassment; the record evidences the tempered act of a policeman who in the course of an investigation had to make a quick decision as to how to protect himself and others from possible danger, and took limited steps to do so.

The manner in which the seizure and search were conducted is, of course, as vital a part of the inquiry as whether they were warranted at all. The Fourth Amendment proceeds as much by limitations upon the scope of governmental action as by imposing preconditions upon its initiation. The entire deterrent purpose of the rule excluding evidence seized in violation of the Fourth Amendment rests on the assumption that "limitations upon the fruit to be gathered tend to limit the quest itself." United States v. Poller, 43 F.2d 911, 914 (C.A.2d Cir. 1930). Thus, evidence may not be introduced if it was discovered by means of a seizure and search which were not reasonably related in scope to the justification for their initiation.

We need not develop at length in this case, however, the limitations which the Fourth Amendment places upon a protective seizure and search for weapons. These limitations will have to be developed in the concrete factual circumstances of individual cases. See Sibron v. New York, decided today. Suffice it to note that such a search, unlike a search without a warrant incident to a lawful arrest, is not justified by any need to prevent the disappearance or destruction of evidence of crime. The sole justification of the search in the present situation is the protection of the police officer and others nearby, and it must therefore be confined in scope to an intrusion reasonably designed to discover guns, knives, clubs, or other hidden instruments for the assault of the police officer.

The scope of the search in this case presents no serious problem in light of these standards. Officer McFadden patted down the outer clothing of petitioner and his two companions. He did not place his hands in their pockets or under the outer surface of their garments until he had felt weapons, and then he merely reached for and removed the guns. He never did invade Katz's person beyond the outer surfaces of his clothes, since he discovered nothing in his pat down which might have been a weapon. Officer McFadden confined his search strictly to what was minimally necessary to learn whether the men were armed and to disarm them once he discovered the weapons. He did not conduct a general exploratory search for whatever evidence of criminal activity he might find.

V.

We conclude that the revolver seized from Terry was properly admitted in evidence against him. At the time he seized petitioner and searched him for weapons, Officer McFadden had reasonable grounds to believe that petitioner was armed and dangerous, and it was necessary for the protection of himself and others to take swift measures to discover the true facts and neutralize the threat of harm if it materialized. The policeman carefully restricted his search to what was appropriate to the discovery of the particular items which he sought. Each case of this sort will, of course, have to be decided on its own facts. We merely hold today that where a police officer observes unusual conduct which leads him reasonably to conclude in light of his experience that criminal activity may be afoot and that the persons with whom he is dealing may be armed and presently dangerous; where in the course of investigating this behavior he identifies himself as a policeman and makes reasonable inquiries; and where nothing in the initial stages of the encounter serves to dispel his reasonable fear for his own or others' safety, he is entitled for the protection of himself and others in the area to conduct a carefully limited search of the outer clothing of such persons in an attempt to discover weapons which might be used to assault him. Such a search is a reasonable search under the Fourth Amendment, and any weapons seized may properly be introduced in evidence against the person from whom they were taken.

Affirmed.

* * *

MR. JUSTICE HARLAN, concurring.

While I unreservedly agree with the Court's ultimate holding in this case, I am constrained to fill in a few gaps, as I see them, in its opinion. I do this because what is said by this Court today will serve as initial guidelines for law enforcement authorities and courts throughout the land as this important new field of law develops. * * *

If the State of Ohio were to provide that police officers could, on articulable suspicion less than probable cause, forcibly frisk and disarm persons thought to be carrying concealed weapons, I would have little doubt that action taken pursuant to such authority could be constitutionally reasonable. Concealed weapons create an immediate and severe danger to the public, and though that danger might not warrant routine general weapons checks, it could well warrant action on less than a "probability." I mention this line of analysis because

I think it vital to point out that it cannot be applied in this case. On the record before us Ohio has not clothed its policemen with routine authority to frisk and disarm on suspicion; in the absence of state authority, policemen have no more right to "pat down" the outer clothing of passers-by, or of persons to whom they address casual questions, than does any other citizen. . . .

The state courts held, instead, that when an officer is lawfully confronting a possibly hostile person in the line of duty he has a right, springing only from the necessity of the situation and not from any broader right to disarm, to frisk for his own protection. This holding, with which I agree and with which I think the Court agrees, offers the only satisfactory basis I can think of for affirming this conviction. The holding has, however, two logical corollaries that I do not think the Court has fully expressed.

In the first place, if the frisk is justified in order to protect the officer during an encounter with a citizen, the officer must first have constitutional grounds to insist on an encounter, to make a *forcible* stop. Any person, including a policeman, is at liberty to avoid a person he considers dangerous. If and when a policeman has a right instead to disarm such a person for his own protection, he must first have a right not to avoid him but to be in his presence. That right must be more than the liberty (again, possessed by every citizen) to address questions to other persons, for ordinarily the person addressed has an equal right to ignore his interrogator and walk away; he certainly need not submit to a frisk for the questioner's protection. I would make it perfectly clear that the right to frisk in this case depends upon the reasonableness of a forcible stop to investigate a suspected crime.

Where such a stop is reasonable, however, the right to frisk must be immediate and automatic if the reason for the stop is, as here, an articulable suspicion of a crime of violence. Just as a full search incident to a lawful arrest requires no additional justification, a limited frisk incident to a lawful stop must often be rapid and routine. There is no reason why an officer, rightfully but forcibly confronting a person suspected of a serious crime, should have to ask one question and take the risk that the answer might be a bullet.

The facts of this case are illustrative of a proper stop and an incident frisk. Officer McFadden had no probable cause to arrest Terry for anything, but he had observed circumstances that would reasonably lead an experienced, prudent policeman to suspect that Terry was about to engage in burglary or robbery. His justifiable suspicion afforded a proper constitutional basis for accosting Terry, restraining his liberty of movement briefly, and addressing questions to him, and Officer McFadden did so. When he did, he had no reason whatever to suppose that Terry might be armed, apart from the fact that he suspected him of planning a violent crime. McFadden asked Terry his name, to which Terry "mumbled something." Whereupon McFadden, without asking Terry to speak louder and without giving him any chance to explain his presence or his actions, forcibly frisked him.

I would affirm this conviction for what I believe to be the same reasons the Court relies on. I would, however, make explicit what I think is implicit in affirmance on the present facts. Officer McFadden's right to interrupt Terry's freedom of movement and invade his privacy arose only because circumstances warranted forcing an encounter with Terry in an effort to prevent or investigate a crime. Once that forced encounter was justified, however, the officer's right to take suitable measures for his own safety followed automatically.

Upon the foregoing premises, I join the opinion of the Court.

MR. JUSTICE WHITE, concurring.

I join the opinion of the Court, reserving judgment, however, on some of the Court's general remarks about the scope and purpose of the exclusionary rule which the Court has fashioned in the process of enforcing the Fourth Amendment.

Also, although the Court puts the matter aside in the context of this case, I think an additional word is in order concerning the matter of interrogation during an investigative stop. There is nothing in the Constitution which prevents a policeman from addressing questions to anyone on the streets. Absent special circumstances, the person approached may not be detained or frisked but may refuse to cooperate and go on his way. However, given the proper circumstances, such as those in this case, it seems to me the person may be briefly detained against his will while pertinent questions are directed to him. Of course, the person stopped is not obliged to answer, answers may not be compelled, and refusal to answer furnishes no basis for an arrest, although it may alert the officer to the need for continued observation. In my view, it is temporary detention, warranted by the circumstances, which chiefly justifies the protective frisk for weapons. Perhaps the frisk itself, where proper, will have beneficial results whether questions are asked or not. If weapons are found, an arrest will follow. If none are found, the frisk may nevertheless serve preventive ends because of its unmistakable message that suspicion has been aroused. But if the investigative stop is sustainable at all, constitutional rights are not necessarily violated if pertinent questions are asked and the person is restrained briefly in the process.

MR. JUSTICE DOUGLAS, dissenting.

I agree that petitioner was "seized" within the meaning of the Fourth Amendment. I also agree that frisking petitioner and his companions for guns was a "search." But it is a mystery how that "search" and that "seizure" can be constitutional by Fourth Amendment standards, unless there was "probable cause" to believe that

(1) a crime had been committed or (2) a crime was in the process of being committed or (3) a crime was about to be committed.

The opinion of the Court disclaims the existence of "probable cause." If loitering were an issue and that was the offense charged, there would be "probable cause" shown. But the crime here is carrying concealed weapons; and there is no basis for concluding that the officer had "probable cause" for believing that crime was being committed. Had a warrant been sought, a magistrate would, therefore, have been unauthorized to issue one, for he can act only if there is a showing of "probable cause." We hold today that the police have greater authority to make a "seizure" and conduct a "search" than a judge has to authorize such action. We have said precisely the opposite over and over again.

In other words, police officers, up to today have been permitted to effect arrests or searches without warrants only when the facts within their personal knowledge would satisfy the constitutional standard of *probable cause.* At the time of their "seizure" without a warrant they must possess facts concerning the person arrested that would have satisfied a magistrate that "probable cause" was indeed present. The term "probable cause" rings a bell of certainty that is not sounded by phrases such as "reasonable suspicion." Moreover, the meaning of "probable cause" is deeply imbedded in our constitutional history. As we stated in Henry v. United States, 361 U.S. 98, 100–102, 80 S.Ct. 168, 171.

> "The requirement of probable cause has roots that are deep in our history. The general warrant, in which the name of the person to be arrested was left blank, and the writs of assistance, against which James Otis inveighed, both perpetuated the oppressive practice of allowing the police to arrest and search on suspicion. Police control took the place of judicial control, since no showing of 'probable cause' before a magistrate was required.
>
> . . . .
>
> "That philosophy [rebelling against these practices] later was reflected in the Fourth Amendment. And as the early American decisions both before and immediately after its adoption show, common rumor or report, suspicion, or even 'strong reason to suspect' was not adequate to support a warrant for arrest. And that principle has survived to this day.
>
> . . . .
>
> "It is important, we think, that this requirement [of probable cause] be strictly enforced, for the standard set by the Constitution protects both the officer and the citizen. If the officer acts with probable cause, he is protected even though it turns out that the citizen is innocent . . . And while a search without a warrant is, within limits, per-

missible if incident to a lawful arrest, if an arrest without a warrant is to support an incidental search, it must be made with probable cause . . . This immunity of officers cannot fairly be enlarged without jeopardizing the privacy or security of the citizen."

The infringement on personal liberty of any "seizure" of a person can only be "reasonable" under the Fourth Amendment if we require the police to possess "probable cause" before they seize him. Only that line draws a meaningful distinction between an officer's mere inkling and the presence of facts within the officer's personal knowledge which would convince a reasonable man that the person seized has committed, is committing, or is about to commit a particular crime. "In dealing with probable cause, . . . as the very name implies, we deal with probabilities. These are not technical; they are the factual and practical considerations of everyday life on which reasonable and prudent men, not legal technicians, act." Brinegar v. United States, 338 U.S. 160, 175, 69 S.Ct. 1302, 1310.

To give the police greater power than a magistrate is to take a long step down the totalitarian path. Perhaps such a step is desirable to cope with modern forms of lawlessness. But if it is taken, it should be the deliberate choice of the people through a constitutional amendment.

SIBRON v. NEW YORK

PETERS v. NEW YORK

Supreme Court of the United States, 1968.
392 U.S. 40, 88 S.Ct. 1889.

MR. CHIEF JUSTICE WARREN delivered the opinion of the Court.

These are companion cases to No. 67, Terry v. Ohio, decided today. They present related questions under the Fourth and Fourteenth Amendments, but the cases arise in the context of New York's "stop-and-frisk" law, N.Y.Code Crim.Proc. § 180–a. This statute provides:

> "1. A police officer may stop any person abroad in a public place whom he reasonably suspects is committing, has committed or is about to commit a felony or any of the crimes specified in section five hundred fifty-two of this chapter, and may demand of him his name, address and an explanation of his actions.
>
> "2. When a police officer has stopped a person for questioning pursuant to this section and reasonably suspects that he is in danger of life or limb, he may search such person

> for a dangerous weapon. If the police officer finds such a weapon or any other thing the possession of which may constitute a crime, he may take and keep it until the completion of the questioning, at which time he shall either return it, if lawfully possessed, or arrest such person."

The appellants, Sibron and Peters, were both convicted of crimes in New York state courts on the basis of evidence seized from their persons by police officers. The Court of Appeals of New York held that the evidence was properly admitted, on the ground that the searches which uncovered it were authorized by the statute. . . .

The facts in these cases may be stated briefly. Sibron, the appellant in No. 63, was convicted of the unlawful possession of heroin. . . . At the hearing on the motion to suppress, Officer Martin testified that while he was patrolling his beat in uniform on March 9, 1965, he observed Sibron "continually from the hours of 4:00 P.M. to 12:00, midnight . . . in the vicinity of 742 Broadway." He stated that during this period of time he saw Sibron in conversation with six or eight persons whom he (Patrolman Martin) knew from past experience to be narcotics addicts. The officer testified that he did not overhear any of these conversations, and that he did not see anything pass between Sibron and any of the others. Late in the evening Sibron entered a restaurant. Patrolman Martin saw Sibron speak with three more known addicts inside the restaurant. Once again, nothing was overheard and nothing was seen to pass between Sibron and the addicts. Sibron sat down and ordered pie and coffee, and as he was eating, Patrolman Martin approached him and told him to come outside. Once outside, the officer said to Sibron, "You know what I am after." According to the officer, Sibron "mumbled something and reached into his pocket." Simultaneously, Patrolman Martin thrust his hand into the same pocket, discovering several glassine envelopes, which, it turned out, contained heroin.

The State has had some difficulty in settling upon a theory for the admissibility of these envelopes of heroin. In his sworn complaint Patrolman Martin stated:

> "As the officer approached the defendant, the latter being in the direction of the officer and seeing him, he did put his hand in his left jacket pocket and pulled out a tinfoil envelope and did attempt to throw same to the ground. The officer never losing sight of the said envelope seized it from the def[endan]t's left hand, examined it and found it to contain ten glascine [*sic*] envelopes with a white substance alleged to be Heroin."

This version of the encounter, however, bears very little resemblance to Patrolman Martin's testimony at the hearing on the motion to suppress. In fact, he discarded the abandonment theory at the hearing.[1] Nor did the officer ever seriously suggest that he was in fear of bodily harm and that he searched Sibron in self-protection to find weapons.[2]

The prosecutor's theory at the hearing was that Patrolman Martin had probable cause to believe that Sibron was in possession of narcotics because he had seen him conversing with a number of known addicts over an eight-hour period. In the absence of any knowledge on Patrolman Martin's part concerning the nature of the intercourse between Sibron and the addicts, however, the trial court was inclined to grant the motion to suppress. As the judge stated, "All he knows about the unknown men: They are narcotics addicts. They might have been talking about the World Series. They might have been talking about prize fights." The prosecutor, however, reminded the judge that Sibron had admitted on the stand, in Patrolman Martin's absence, that he had been talking to the addicts about narcotics. Thereupon, the trial judge changed his mind and ruled that the officer had probable cause for an arrest.

Section 180–a, the "stop-and-frisk" statute, was not mentioned at any point in the trial court. The Appellate Term of the Supreme Court affirmed the conviction without opinion. In the Court of Appeals of New York, Sibron's case was consolidated with the *Peters* case, No. 74. The Court of Appeals held that the search in *Peters* was justified under the statute, but it wrote no opinion in Sibron's case. The dissents of Judges Fuld and Van Voorhis, however, indicate that the court rested its holding on § 180–a. At any rate, in its Brief in Opposition to the Jurisdictional Statement in this Court, the State sought to justify the search on the basis of the statute. After we noted probable jurisdiction, the District Attorney for Kings County confessed error.

1. Patrolman Martin stated several times that he put his hand into Sibron's pocket and seized the heroin before Sibron had any opportunity to remove his own hand from the pocket. The trial court questioned him on this point:

"Q. Would you say at that time that he reached into his pocket and handed the packets to you? Is that what he did or did he drop the packets?

"A. He did not drop them. *I do not know what his intentions were.* He pushed his hand into his pocket.

"Mr. Joseph [Prosecutor]: You intercepted it; didn't you, Officer?

"The Witness: Yes." (Emphasis added.)

It is of course highly unlikely that Sibron, facing the officer at such close quarters, would have tried to remove the heroin from his pocket and throw it to the ground in the hope that he could escape responsibility for it.

2. The possibility that Sibron, who never, so far as appears from the record, offered any resistance, might have posed a danger to Patrolman Martin's safety was never even discussed as a potential justification for the search. The only mention of weapons by the officer in his entire testimony came in response to a leading question by Sibron's counsel, when Martin stated that he "thought he [Sibron] might have been" reaching for a gun. Even so, Patrolman Martin did not accept this suggestion by the opposition regarding the reason for his action; the discussion continued upon the plain premise that he had been looking for narcotics all the time.

Peters, the appellant in No. 74, was convicted of possessing burglary tools under circumstances evincing an intent to employ them in the commission of a crime. Officer Samuel Lasky of the New York City Police Department testified at the hearing on the motion that he was at home in his apartment in Mount Vernon, New York, at about 1 p. m. on July 10, 1964. He had just finished taking a shower and was drying himself when he heard a noise at his door. His attempt to investigate was interrupted by a telephone call, but when he returned and looked through the peephole into the hall, Officer Lasky saw "two men tiptoeing out of the alcove toward the stairway." He immediately called the police, put on some civilian clothes and armed himself with his service revolver. Returning to the peephole, he saw "a tall man tiptoeing away from the alcove and followed by this shorter man, Mr. Peters, toward the stairway." Officer Lasky testified that he had lived in the 120-unit building for 12 years and that he did not recognize either of the men as tenants. Believing that he had happened upon the two men in the course of an attempted burglary,[3] Officer Lasky opened his door, entered the hallway and slammed the door loudly behind him. This precipitated a flight down the stairs on the part of the two men,[4] and Officer Lasky gave chase. His apartment was located on the sixth floor, and he apprehended Peters between the fourth and fifth floors. Grabbing Peters by the collar, he continued down another flight in unsuccessful pursuit of the other man. Peters explained his presence in the building to Officer Lasky by saying that he was visiting a girl friend. However, he declined to reveal the girl friend's name, on the ground that she was a married woman. Officer Lasky patted Peters down for weapons, and discovered a hard object in his pocket. He stated at the hearing that the object did not feel like a gun, but that it might have been a knife. He removed the object from Peters' pocket. It was an opaque plastic envelope, containing burglar's tools.

The trial court explicitly refused to credit Peters' testimony that he was merely in the building to visit his girl friend. It found that Officer Lasky had the requisite "reasonable suspicion" of Peters under § 180–a to stop him and question him. It also found that Peters'

3. Officer Lasky testified that when he called the police immediately before leaving his apartment, he "told the Sergeant at the desk that two burglars were on my floor."

4. Officer Lasky testified that when he emerged from his apartment, "I slammed the door, I had my gun and I ran down the stairs after them." A sworn affidavit of the Assistant District Aattorney, which was before the trial court when it ruled on the motion to suppress, stated that when apprehended Peters was "fleeing down the steps of the building." The trial court explicitly took note of the flight of Peters and his companion as a factor contributing to Officer Lasky's "reasonable suspicion" of them:

"We think the testimony at the hearing does not require further laboring of this aspect of the matter, unless one is to believe that it is legitimately normal for a man to tip-toe about in the public hall of an apartment house while on a visit to his unidentified girl-friend, and, when observed by another tenant, to rapidly descend by stairway in the presence of elevators."

response was "clearly unsatisfactory," and that "under the circumstances Lasky's action in frisking Peters for a dangerous weapon was reasonable, even though Lasky was himself armed." It held that the hallway of the apartment building was a "public place" within the meaning of the statute. The Appellate Division of the Supreme Court affirmed without opinion. The Court of Appeals also affirmed, essentially adopting the reasoning of the trial judge, with Judges Fuld and Van Voorhis dissenting separately. . . .

III.

The parties on both sides of these two cases have urged that the principal issue before us is the constitutionality of § 180–a "on its face." We decline, however, to be drawn into what we view as the abstract and unproductive exercise of laying the extraordinarily elastic categories of § 180–a next to the categories of the Fourth Amendment in an effort to determine whether the two are in some sense compatible. The constitutional validity of a warrantless search is pre-eminently the sort of question which can only be decided in the concrete factual context of the individual case. . . .

Section 180–a, deals with the substantive validity of certain types of seizures and searches without warrants. It purports to authorize police officers to "stop" people, "demand" explanations of them and "search [them] for dangerous weapon[s]" in certain circumstances upon "reasonable suspicion" that they are engaged in criminal activity and that they represent a danger to the policeman. The operative categories of § 180–a are not the categories of the Fourth Amendment, and they are susceptible of a wide variety of interpretations. New York is, of course, free to develop its own law of search and seizure to meet the needs of local law enforcement, see Ker v. California, 374 U.S. 23, 34, 83 S.Ct. 1623, 1630 (1963), and in the process it may call the standards it employs by any names it may choose. It may not, however, authorize police conduct which trenches upon Fourth Amendment rights, regardless of the labels which it attaches to such conduct. The question in this Court upon review of a state-approved search or seizure "is not whether the search [or seizure] was authorized by state law. The question is rather whether the search was reasonable under the Fourth Amendment. Just as a search authorized by state law may be an unreasonable one under that amendment, so may a search not expressly authorized by state law be justified as a constitutionally reasonable one." Cooper v. California, 386 U.S. 58, 61, 87 S.Ct. 788, 790 (1967).

Accordingly, we make no pronouncement on the facial constitutionality of § 180–a. The constitutional point with respect to a statute of this peculiar sort, as the Court of Appeals of New York recognized, is "not so much . . . the language employed as . . . the conduct it authorizes." People v. Peters, 18 N.Y.2d 238, 245, 219 N.E.2d 595, 599, 273 N.Y.S.2d 217, 222 (1966). We have held today in Terry v. Ohio, that police conduct of the sort with which § 180–a deals must be judged under the Reasonable Search and Seizure Clause of the Fourth Amendment. The inquiry under that clause may differ sharply from the inquiry set up by the categories of § 180–a. Our constitutional inquiry would not be furthered here by an attempt to pronounce judgment on the words of the statute. We must confine our review instead to the reasonableness of the searches and seizures which underlie these two convictions.

IV.

Turning to the facts of Sibron's case, it is clear that the heroin was inadmissible in evidence against him. The prosecution has quite properly abandoned the notion that there was probable cause to arrest Sibron for any crime at the time Patrolman Martin accosted him in the restaurant, took him outside and searched him. The officer was not acquainted with Sibron and had no information concerning him. He merely saw Sibron talking to a number of known narcotics addicts over a period of eight hours. It must be emphasized that Patrolman Martin was completely ignorant regarding the content of these conversations, and that he saw nothing pass between Sibron and the addicts. So far as he knew, they might indeed "have been talking about the World Series." The inference that persons who talk to narcotics addicts are engaged in the criminal traffic in narcotics is simply not the sort of reasonable inference required to support an intrusion by the police upon an individual's personal security. Nothing resembling probable cause existed until after the search had turned up the envelopes of heroin. It is axiomatic that an incident search may not precede an arrest and serve as part of its justification. Thus the search cannot be justified as incident to a lawful arrest.

If Patrolman Martin lacked probable cause for an arrest, however, his seizure and search of Sibron might still have been justified at the outset if he had reasonable grounds to believe that Sibron was armed and dangerous. Terry v. Ohio. We are not called upon to decide in this case whether there was a "seizure" of Sibron inside the restaurant antecedent to the physical seizure which accompanied the search. The record is unclear with respect to what transpired between Sibron and the officer inside the restaurant. It is totally barren of any indication whether Sibron accompanied Patrolman Martin outside in submission to a show of force or authority which left him no choice, or whether he went voluntarily in a spirit of apparent cooperation with the officer's investigation. In any event, this deficiency in the record is immaterial, since Patrolman Martin obtained no new information in the interval between his initiation of the encounter in the restaurant and his physical seizure and search of Sibron outside.

Although the Court of Appeals of New York wrote no opinion in this case, it seems to have viewed the search here as a self-protective search for weapons and to have affirmed on the basis of § 180–a, which authorizes such a search when the officer "reasonably suspects that he is in danger of life or limb." The Court of Appeals has, at any rate, justified searches during field interrogation on the ground that "the answer to the question propounded by the policeman may be a bullet; in any case the exposure to danger could be very great." People v. Rivera, 14 N.Y.2d 441, 446, 201 N.E.2d 32, 35, 252 N.Y.S. 2d 458, 463 (1964), cert. denied, 379 U.S. 978, 85 S.Ct. 679 (1965). But the application of this reasoning to the facts of this case proves too much. The police officer is not entitled to seize and search every person whom he sees on the street or of whom he makes inquiries. Before he places a hand on the person of a citizen in search of anything, he must have constitutionally adequate reasonable grounds for doing so. In the case of the self-protective search for weapons, he must be able to point to particular facts from which he reasonably inferred that the individual was armed and dangerous. Terry v. Ohio, supra. Patrolman Martin's testimony reveals no such facts. The suspect's mere act of talking with a number of known narcotics addicts over an eight-hour period no more gives rise to reasonable fear of life or limb on the part of the police officer than it justifies an arrest for committing a crime. Nor did Patrolman Martin urge that when Sibron put his hand in his pocket, he feared that he was going for a weapon and acted in self-defense. His opening statement to Sibron—"You know what I am after"—made it abundantly clear that he sought narcotics, and his testimony at the hearing left no doubt that he thought there were narcotics in Sibron's pocket.

Even assuming *arguendo* that there were adequate grounds to search Sibron for weapons, the nature and scope of the search conducted by Patrolman Martin were so clearly unrelated to that justification as to render the heroin inadmissible. The search for weapons approved in *Terry* consisted solely of a limited patting of the outer clothing of the suspect for concealed objects which might be used as instruments of assault. Only when he discovered such objects did the officer in *Terry* place his hands in the pockets of the men he searched. In this case, with no attempt at an initial limited exploration for arms, Patrolman Martin thrust his hand into Sibron's pocket and took from him envelopes of heroin. His testimony shows that he was looking for narcotics, and he found them. The search was not reasonably limited in scope to the accomplishment of the only goal which might conceivably have justified its inception—the protection of the officer by disarming a potentially dangerous man. Such a search violates the guarantee of the Fourth Amendment, which protects the sanctity of the person against unreasonable intrusions on the part of all government agents.

We think it is equally clear that the search in Peters' case was wholly reasonable under the Constitution. The Court of Appeals of New York held that the search was made legal by § 180–a, since Peters was "abroad in a public place," and since Officer Lasky was reasonably suspicious of his activities and, once he had stopped

Peters, reasonably suspected that he was in danger of life or limb, even though he held Peters at gun point. This may be the justification for the search under state law. We think, however, that for purposes of the Fourth Amendment the search was properly incident to a lawful arrest. By the time Officer Lasky caught up with Peters on the stairway between the fourth and fifth floors of the apartment building, he had probable cause to arrest him for attempted burglary. The officer heard strange noises at his door which apparently led him to believe that someone sought to force entry. When he investigated these noises he saw two men, whom he had never seen before in his 12 years in the building, tiptoeing furtively about the hallway. They were still engaged in these maneuvers after he called the police and dressed hurriedly. And when Officer Lasky entered the hallway, the men fled down the stairs. It is difficult to conceive of stronger grounds for an arrest, short of actual eyewitness observation of criminal activity. As the trial court explicitly recognized, deliberately furtive actions and flight at the approach of strangers or law officers are strong indicia of *mens rea*, and when coupled with specific knowledge on the part of the officer relating the suspect to the evidence of crime, they are proper factors to be considered in the decision to make an arrest.

As we noted in Sibron's case, a search incident to a lawful arrest, may not precede the arrest and serve as part of its justification. It is a question of fact precisely when, in each case, the arrest took place. Rios v. United States, 364 U.S. 253, 261–262, 80 S.Ct. 1431, 1436, 1437 (1960). And while there was some inconclusive discussion in the trial court concerning when Officer Lasky "arrested" Peters, it is clear that the arrest had for purposes of constitutional justification already taken place before the search commenced. When the policeman grabbed Peters by the collar, he abruptly "seized" him and curtailed his freedom of movement on the basis of probable cause to believe that he was engaged in criminal activity. At that point he had the authority to search Peters, and the incident search was obviously justified "by the need to seize weapons and other things which might be used to assault an officer or effect an escape, as well as by the need to prevent the destruction of evidence of the crime." Preston v. United States, 376 U.S. 364, 367, 84 S.Ct. 881, 883 (1964). Moreover, it was reasonably limited in scope by these purposes. Officer Lasky did not engage in an unrestrained and thorough-going examination of Peters and his personal effects. He seized him to cut short his flight, and he searched him primarily for weapons. While patting down his outer clothing, Officer Lasky discovered an object in his pocket which might have been used as a weapon. He seized it and discovered it to be a potential instrument of the crime of burglary.

We have concluded that Peters' conviction fully comports with the commands of the Fourth and Fourteenth Amendments, and must be affirmed. The conviction in No. 63, however, must be reversed, on the ground that the heroin was unconstitutionally admitted in evidence against the appellant.

It is so ordered.

MR. JUSTICE BLACK, concurring and dissenting.

I concur in the affirmance of the judgment against Peters but dissent from the reversal of No. 63, Sibron v. New York and would affirm this conviction. . . .

* * *

First. I think there was probable cause for the policeman to believe that when Sibron reached his hand to his coat pocket, Sibron had a dangerous weapon which he might use if it were not taken away from him. . . . It seems to me to be a reasonable inference that when Sibron, who had been approaching and talking to addicts for eight hours, reached his hand quickly to his left coat pocket, he might well be reaching for a gun. And as the Court has emphasized today in its opinions in the other stop and frisk cases, a policeman under such circumstances has to act in a split second; delay may mean death for him. No one can know when an addict may be moved to shoot or stab, and particularly when he moves his hand hurriedly to a pocket where weapons are known to be habitually carried, it behooves an officer who wants to live to act at once as this officer did. It is true that the officer might also have thought Sibron was about to get heroin instead of a weapon. But the law enforcement officers all over the Nation have gained little protection from the courts through opinions here if they are now left helpless to act in self defense when a man associating intimately and continuously with addicts, upon meeting an officer, shifts his hand immediately to a pocket where weapons are constantly carried.

* * *

Second, I think also that there was sufficient evidence here on which to base findings that after recovery of the heroin, in particular, an officer could reasonably believe there was probable cause to charge Sibron with violating New York's narcotics laws. As I have previously argued, there was, I think, ample evidence to give the officer probable cause to believe Sibron had a dangerous weapon and that he might use it. Under such circumstances the officer had a right to search him in the very limited fashion he did here. Since, therefore, this was a reasonable and justified search, the use of the heroin discovered by it was admissible in evidence.

I would affirm.

MR. JUSTICE HARLAN, concurring in the results.

I fully agree with the results the Court has reached in these cases. . . .

* * *

Turning to the individual cases, I agree that the conviction in No. 63, *Sibron,* should be reversed, and would do so upon the premises of *Terry* . . . .

The considerable confusion that has surrounded the "search" or "frisk" of Sibron that led to the actual recovery of the heroin seems to me irrelevant for our purposes. Officer Martin repudiated his first statement, which might conceivably have indicated a theory of "abandonment". No matter which of the other theories is adopted, it is clear that there was at least a forcible frisk, comparable to that which occurred in *Terry,* which requires constitutional justification.

Since carrying heroin is a crime in New York, probable cause to believe Sibron was carrying heroin would also have been probable cause to arrest him. As the Court says, Officer Martin clearly had neither. Although Sibron had had conversations with several known addicts, he had done nothing, during the several hours he was under surveillance, that made it "probable" that he was either carrying heroin himself or engaging in transactions with these acquaintances.

Nor were there here reasonable grounds for a *Terry*-type "stop" short of an arrest. . . .

The forcible encounter between Officer Martin and Sibron did not meet the *Terry* reasonableness standard. In the first place, although association with known criminals may, I think, properly be a factor contributing to the suspiciousness of circumstances, it does not, entirely by itself, create suspicion adequate to support a stop. There must be something at least in the activities of the person being observed or in his surroundings that affirmatively suggests particular criminal activity, completed, current, or intended. That was the case in *Terry,* but it palpably was not the case here. For eight continuous hours, up to the point when he interrupted Sibron eating a piece of pie, Officer Martin apparently observed not a single suspicious action and heard not a single suspicious word on the part of Sibron himself or any person with whom he associated. If anything, that period of surveillance pointed away from suspicion.

Furthermore, in *Terry,* the police officer judged that his suspect was about to commit a violent crime and that he had to assert himself in order to prevent it. Here there was no reason for Officer Martin to think that an incipient crime, or flight, or the destruction of evidence would occur if he stayed his hand; indeed, there was no more reason for him to intrude upon Sibron at the moment when he did than there had been four hours earlier, and no reason to think the situation would have changed four hours hence. While no hard-and-fast rule can be drawn, I would suggest that one important factor, missing here, that should be taken into account in determining whether there are reasonable grounds for a forcible intrusion is whether there is any need for immediate action.

For these reasons I would hold that Officer Martin lacked reasonable grounds to introduce forcibly upon Sibron. In consequence, the essential premise for the right to conduct a self-protective frisk was lacking. See my concurring opinion in *Terry.* I therefore find it unnecessary to reach two further troublesome questions. First, although I think that, as in *Terry,* the right to frisk is automatic when an officer lawfully stops a person suspected of a crime whose nature creates a substantial likelihood that he is armed, it is not clear that suspected possession of narcotics falls into this category. If the nature of the suspected offense creates no reasonable apprehension for the officer's safety, I would not permit him to frisk unless other circumstances did so. Second, I agree with the Court that even where a self-protective frisk is proper, its scope should be limited to what is adequate for its purposes. I see no need here to resolve the question whether this frisk exceeded those bounds.

Turning now to No. 74, *Peters,* I again agree that the conviction should be upheld, but here I would differ strongly and fundamentally with the Court's approach. The Court holds that the burglar's tools were recovered from Peters in a search incident to a lawful arrest. I do not think that Officer Lasky had anything close to probable cause to arrest Peters before he recovered the burglar's tools. Indeed, if probable cause existed here, I find it difficult to see why a different rationale was necessary to support the stop and frisk in *Terry* and why States such as New York have had to devote so much thought to the constitutional problems of field interrogation. This case will be the latest in an exceedingly small number of cases in this Court indicating what suffices for probable cause. While, as the Court noted in *Terry,* the influence of this Court on police tactics "in the field" is necessarily limited, the influence of a decision here on hundreds of courts and magistrates who have to decide whether there is probable cause for a real arrest or a full search will be large.

Officer Lasky testified that at 1 o'clock in the afternoon he heard a noise at the door to his apartment. He did not testify, nor did any state court conclude, that this "led him to believe that someone sought to force entry." He looked out into the public hallway and saw two men whom he did not recognize, surely not a strange occurrence in a large apartment building. One of them appeared to be tip-toeing. Lasky did not testify that the other man was tip-toeing or that either of them was behaving "furtively." Lasky left his apartment and ran to them, gun in hand. He did not testify that there was any "flight," though flight at the approach of gun-carrying strangers (Lasky was apparently not in uniform) is hardly indicative of *mens rea.*

Probable cause to arrest means evidence that would warrant a prudent and reasonable man (such as a magistrate, actual or hypothetical) in believing that a particular person has committed or is committing a crime. Officer Lasky had no extrinsic reason to think that a crime had been or was being committed, so whether it would have been proper to issue a warrant depends entirely on his statements of his observations of the men. Apart from his conclusory statement that he thought the men were burglars, he offered very little specific evidence. I find it hard to believe that if Peters had made good his escape and there were no report of a burglary in the neighborhood, this Court would hold it proper for a prudent neutral magistrate to issue a warrant for his arrest.

* * *

Although the articulable circumstances are somewhat less suspicious here than they were in *Terry,* I would affirm on the *Terry* ground that Officer Lasky had reasonable cause to make a forced stop. Unlike probable cause to arrest, reasonable grounds to stop do not depend on any degree of likelihood that a crime *has* been committed. An officer may forcibly intrude upon an incipient crime even where he could not make an arrest for the simple reason that there is nothing to arrest anyone for. Hence although Officer Lasky had small reason to believe that a crime had been committed, his right to stop Peters can be justified if he had a reasonable suspicion that he was about to attempt burglary.

It was clear that the officer had to act quickly if he was going to act at all, and, as stated above, it seems to me that where immediate action is obviously required, a police officer is justified in acting on rather less objectively articulable evidence than when there is more time for consideration of alternative courses of action. Perhaps more important, the Court's opinion in *Terry* emphasized the special qualifications of an experienced police officer. While "probable cause" to arrest or search has always depended on the existence of hard evidence that would persuade a "reasonable man," in judging on-the-street encounters it seems to me proper to take into account a police officer's trained instinctive judgment operating on a multitude of small gestures and actions impossible to reconstruct. Thus the statement by an officer that "he looked like a burglar to me" adds little to an affidavit filed with a magistrate in an effort to obtain a warrant. When the question is whether it was reasonable to take limited but forcible steps in a situation requiring immediate action, however, such a statement looms larger. A court is of course entitled to disbelieve the officer (who is subject to cross-examination), but when it believes him and when there are some articulable supporting facts, it is entitled to find action taken under fire to be reasonable.

Given Officer Lasky's statement of the circumstances, and crediting his experienced judgment as he watched the two men, the state courts were entitled to conclude, as they did, that Lasky forcibly stopped Peters on "reasonable suspicion." The frisk made incident to that stop was a limited one, which turned up burglar's tools. Although the frisk is constitutionally permitted only in order to protect the officer, if it is lawful the State is of course entitled to the use of any other contraband that appears.

For the foregoing reasons I concur in the results in these cases.

MR. JUSTICE WHITE, concurring.

. . . With respect to appellant Peters, I join the affirmance of his conviction, not because there was probable cause to arrest, a question I do not reach, but because there was probable cause to stop Peters for questioning and thus to frisk him for dangerous weapons. See my concurring opinion in Terry v. Ohio. While patting down Peters' clothing the officer "discovered an object in his pocket which might have been used as a weapon." That object turned out to be a package of burglar's tools. In my view those tools were properly admitted into evidence.

[The concurring opinions of JUSTICES DOUGLAS and FORTAS are omitted.]

NOTE

1. Following is an editorial which appeared in the Journal of Criminal Law, Criminology and Police Science (Vol. 59, No. 3, 1968), soon after the *Terry* case decision, under the imprint of the President and Vice-President of *Americans for Effective Law Enforcement, Inc.*:

STOP AND FRISK: THE POWER AND THE OBLIGATION OF THE POLICE

"On June 10, the Supreme Court of the United States, in the case of Terry v. Ohio, rendered a decision that will greatly aid the police in their efforts to prevent crime and apprehend criminals. That decision, however, must not be interpreted by the police as a green light for indiscriminate, arbitrary stopping and frisking, or for any other unworthy purpose.

"*Americans for Effective Law Enforcement, Inc.*, a non-partisan, non-political, not-for-profit educational corporation, which was founded last Summer for the purpose of advancing the cause of effective law enforcement, filed an 'amicus curiae' (friend of the Court) brief in the Terry case last November. It urged the Court to rule as it did.

"Upon the reasonable assumption that our brief had a persuasive effect upon the Supreme Court, we feel privileged to now admonish the police to assume the proper *responsibility* that must accompany this *privilege* so newly sanctioned by the Court.

"The Terry decision only authorizes action upon *reasonable* suspicion of criminality and a frisking *reasonably* necessary for the officer's protection. And all this must be performed in a *reasonable* manner.

"The Court's opinion sets up general guidelines for the police. The actual holding of the case, however, indicates that the Court intended to confine the power to 'stop' to situations which clearly call for investigation of criminally suspicious circumstances and the power of 'frisk' to situations where there is a probability that the person to be frisked or searched is armed and may be dangerous to the officer or other citizens. The Court said:

'. . . where a police officer observes unusual conduct which leads him reasonably to conclude in light of his experience that criminal activity may be afoot and that the persons with whom he is dealing may be armed and presently dangerous; where in the course of investigating this behavior he identifies himself as a policeman and makes reasonable inquiries;

and where nothing in the initial stages of the encounter serves to dispel his reasonable fear for his own or others' safety, he is entitled for the protection of himself and others in the area to conduct a carefully limited search of the outer clothing of such persons in an attempt to discover weapons which might be used to assault him. Such a search is a reasonable search under the Fourth Amendment, and any weapons seized may properly be introduced in evidence against the person from whom they were taken.'

"Of course, the decision is not limited to the kind of facts set out in the Terry case. It encompasses a variety of suspicious conduct which the police meet every day during the course of field investigation and interrogation. For this reason, police training schools and police legal advisors must relay the message of the Court in meaningful terms to the police officer, with the use of appropriate examples of what is and what is not reasonable action in stop and frisk situations. Reference to the Court's holding, however, makes it unmistakably clear that the Court will not tolerate 'dragnet' seizures and frisks which, though designed to achieve ostensibly worthy objectives, e. g., gun control or harassment of vice offenders and juvenile gangs, do not measure up to the Fourth Amendment requirement of reasonableness.

"By its decision in the Terry case, the Supreme Court delivered into the hands of the police a very powerful weapon for the prevention and detection of crime. This power, however, is readily subject to abuse by an ignorant, brutal, or corrupt police officer. And any abuse of the power may easily lead to deterioration of police-citizen relationship, especially in the tense and emotionally charged slum areas of our large cities. All measures necessary to prevent this abuse must be taken by those in command positions within the police force itself.

"AELE is proud of the effort it made in the Terry case to persuade the Supreme Court to uphold the right of the police to 'stop and frisk.' In our brief we pledged the Court that law enforcement agencies would not abuse the power we requested the Court to sanction. We now ask that the police of this country make good our word, and that they proceed to exercise their newly won legitimate power with tolerance, understanding, tact, and caution. What the Supreme Court has granted, the legislatures can take away upon evidence of police abuse of that power.

"How well the police use the power may play an important part in future cases coming before the courts in which they are asked to rule in favor of the needs of law enforcement. This factor may also shape the course of events in the halls of Congress and before other legislative bodies whenever proposals are under consideration for additional grants of police powers.

"We urge the police to use well and fairly the power they now clearly have, for the protection and preservation of the rights of all citizens."

2. The same organization, *Americans for Effective Law Enforcement, Inc.*, issued a "Position Paper" urging the enactment of legislation in conformity with the *Terry* decision, and AELE prepared and disseminated to the various legislatures and to other governmental leaders a Model "Stop-and-Frisk" bill. They are as follows:

AELE POSITION PAPER ON "STOP-AND-FRISK"

"An appreciation of the need for 'stop and frisk' legislation and a proper understanding of the nature of the practice requires answers to the following questions: What is a 'stop and frisk'? How does it differ from an arrest and search? When may it be employed by the police? What is the risk of police abuse?

The Meaning of 'Stop and Frisk'

"The following hypothetical case discloses the meaning of 'stop and frisk':

"Two police officers are on a routine beat patrol at 3:00 A.M. in a residential neighborhood. It is dark and the streets are deserted. As the police car proceeds down an alley, the figure of a man is seen. He steps to the side, behind a telephone pole. The police car speeds up, and when the officers arrive at the scene they find a man dressed in dark non-descript clothing, standing next to a garage. For all the police know at that moment, he might be a householder who owns the garage—or he may be a recently paroled burglar; he may live next door—or he may live miles away; he may be able to give a good explanation for being there—or he may be prepared to tell a demonstrably false story.

"In our hypothetical case three things are clear: (a) the actions of the man are suspicious; but (b) there is no probable cause to *arrest* him for the commission of a *crime*, and yet (c) the police ought to *do something*. The question is, what should they do? What can they do? Are they forced to choose between doing nothing, proceeding on their way, or falsely arresting the suspect for a 'crime'.

"If the officers do nothing, a burglar, robber or rapist might be left in the alley to proceed with his plan unhindered. If the officers make an arrest, the arrestee may turn out to be an innocent resident of the neighborhood, who will thereafter have a police record. Moreover, even if developments subsequent to an actual arrest establish that the suspect was in fact plotting a crime, or had committed one unknown at the time of his arrest, a gun or other evidence obtained from him may be excluded from usage in court because of an arrest made without the constitutional requirement of 'probable cause'.

"Because of these various difficulties, proper police investigative technique demands the employment of another procedure—a middle ground approach—one between police inaction and illegal action. What is needed is the employment of an authorized 'stop and frisk' procedure. In this hypothetical case, for instance, the police officers would stop their car, alight from the vehicle and ask the suspect such questions as 'Who are you?', 'What are you doing in the alley?', 'May we see some identification?'. The officers must also have the right to frisk the suspicious person if they reasonably think that he may be armed with a dangerous weapon.

"Necessarily, the right to ask the questions includes the power to temporarily detain the suspect, even against his will, for a brief time. Since a suspect could defeat the whole purpose of stop and frisk simply by walking away from the inquiring police, under 'stop and frisk' authorization he will not be privileged to do so.

"Since even a brief detention is a 'seizure' of the person within the meaning of the Fourth Amendment of the Constitution, it must be 'reasonable', that is, based upon some identifiable and objective standard of suspicion of criminal behavior. It cannot be based upon an officer's whim, caprice, prejudice or inarticulated 'hunch'.

"Suppose that the suspect in our hypothetical case refuses to answer questions asked by the police. He cannot, after all, be compelled to do so, and he may take advantage of his Fifth Amendment right to say nothing. What then? Does this destroy the value of the 'stop and frisk' power? The answer is a sure 'no', because a quick investigation of the surrounding area may provide enough evidence to give the police probable cause to arrest him for a criminal offense. For example, suppose that in shining their flashlights on the door of the garage next to which the suspect was found the police find fresh 'jimmy' marks. They would then have probable cause to arrest the suspect for attempted burglary. If, upon searching him after the arrest, they find a jimmy, or screwdriver that matches the marks on the door, another burglar may well be on his way to the penitentiary.

"Even when the police are forced to release the suspect because of his refusal to answer questions or because no evidence of an attempted crime is found at the scene, the very act of temporary detention and questioning may deter, at least for that night, a potential criminal act of violence. That, in itself, would be a worthwhile result, since the duty of the police is not only to apprehend persons who have already committed criminal acts, but also to prevent crimes from occurring in the first place.

"Moreover, in many instances a person stopped under circumstances such as the one involved in our hypothetical case will respond to the questions asked by the police; and his answers may supply the necessary information either to dispel the police suspicion or else escalate the suspicion into probable cause for an arrest.

" 'Stop and frisk' may be used in a number of fact situations: for instance, a teenage boy walking from car to car and apparently testing the windows or looking in for keys left in ignition locks; the person who furtively and repeatedly looks into the window of a business establishment about to close; the man who has been trailing two teenage girls for several blocks. The possibilities are numerous.

The Objections to 'Stop and Frisk'

"The charge has been made by some persons that 'stop and frisk' is a tactic for the repression of minority groups; that it is a racist practice designed to keep the ghetto resident 'in his place'; and that it is a tactic to show the teenage gang member, the addict, and the prostitute who 'rules the turf' on the officer's patrol beat.

"As with all other professions or occupations, there are some policemen who do not deserve the honor of a police badge and the privilege of carrying a gun—just as there are misfit doctors, unethical and incompetent lawyers, and corrupt public officials. On occasions some police, in all parts of the country, have used the power of their office to engage in various kinds of illegal and coercive practices. But that fact does not warrant the withholding of needed authorization to those police officers who do conform to proper standards, and who must have such authorization for the protection of the public and also for their own safety.

The Answer

"The basic answer to the concern over possible police abuse of the power of 'stop and frisk', as well as of all the other powers the police possess, is the development of better procedures for the selection of police applicants, so as to reject the psychological misfits, the ones whose past conduct evidences a lack of the required integrity, and those whose social values are incompatible with the role of protector of all members of our society.

"Adequate compensation must be provided in order to attract applicants with the required qualifications, and to retain in office those who are selected.

"Proper internal supervision will also be needed, along with meaningful sanctions for the police who misuse the powers of their office."

AELE's Model State Statute on "Stop-and-Frisk"

§ 1. Whenever any peace officer of this state encounters any person under circumstances which reasonably indicate that such person has committed, is committing, or is about to commit a criminal offense, he may detain such person.

§ 2. Such detention shall be for the purpose of ascertaining the identity of the person detained and the circumstances surrounding his presence abroad which led the officer to believe that he had committed, was committing, or was about to commit a criminal offense, but no person shall be compelled to answer any inquiry of any peace officer.

§ 3. No person shall be detained under the provisions of § 2 of this Act longer than is reasonably necessary to effect the purposes of that subsection, and in no event longer than 15 minutes. Such detention shall not extend beyond the place where it was first effected or the immediate vicinity thereof.

§ 4. If at any time after the onset of the detention authorized by § 1 of this Act, probable cause for arrest of the person shall appear, the person shall be arrested. If, after an inquiry into the circumstances which prompted the detention, no probable cause for the arrest of the person shall appear, he shall be released.

§ 5. Whenever any peace officer authorized to detain any person under the provisions of § 1 of this Act reasonably believes that any person whom he has detained, or is about to detain, is armed with a dangerous weapon and therefore offers a threat to the safety of the officer or another, he may search his person to the extent necessary to disclose, and for the purpose of disclosing the presence of such weapon. If such a search discloses a weapon or any evidence of a criminal offense it may be seized.

§ 6. Nothing seized by a peace officer in any such search shall be admissible against any person in any court of this state unless the search which disclosed its existence was authorized by, and conducted in compliance with, the provisions of this Act.

ADAMS v. WILLIAMS

Supreme Court of the United States, 1972.
407 U.S. 143, 92 S.Ct. 1921.

MR. JUSTICE REHNQUIST delivered the opinion of the Court.

Respondent Robert Williams was convicted in a Connecticut state court of illegal possession of a handgun found during a "stop and frisk," as well as possession of heroin that was found during a full search incident to his weapons arrest.

Police Sgt. John Connolly was alone early in the morning on car patrol duty in a high crime area of Bridgeport, Connecticut. At approximately 2:15 a. m. a person known to Sgt. Connolly approached his cruiser and informed him that an individual seated in a nearby vehicle was carrying narcotics and had a gun at his waist.

After calling for assistance on his car radio, Sgt. Connolly approached the vehicle to investigate the informant's report. Connolly tapped on the car window and asked the occupant, Robert Williams to open the door. When Williams rolled down the window instead, the sergeant reached into the car and removed a fully loaded revolver from Williams' waistband. The gun had not been visible to Connolly from outside the car, but it was in precisely the place indicated by the informant. Williams was then arrested by Connolly for unlawful possession of the pistol. A search incident to that arrest was conducted after other officers arrived. They found substantial quantities of heroin on Williams' person and in the car, and they found a machete and a second revolver hidden in the automobile.

Respondent contends that the initial seizure of his pistol, upon which rested the later search and seizure of other weapons and narcotics, was not justified by the informant's tip to Sgt. Connolly. He claims that absent a more reliable informant, or some corroboration of the tip, the policeman's actions were unreasonable under the standards set forth in Terry v. Ohio, supra.

After respondent's conviction was affirmed by the Supreme Court of Connecticut, State v. Williams, 157 Conn. 114, 249 A.2d 245 (1968), Williams' petition for federal habeas corpus relief was denied by the District Court and by a divided panel of the Second Circuit, 436 F.2d 30 (1970), but on rehearing *en banc* the Court of Appeals granted relief. 441 F.2d 394 (1971). That court held that evidence introduced at Williams' trial had been obtained by an unlawful search of his person and car, and thus the state court judgments of conviction should be set aside. Since we conclude that the policeman's actions here conformed to the standards this Court laid down in Terry v. Ohio, we reverse.

In *Terry* this Court recognized that "a police officer may in appropriate circumstances and in an appropriate manner approach a person for purposes of investigating possibly criminal behavior even though there is no probable cause to make an arrest." The Fourth Amendment does not require a policeman who lacks the precise level of information necessary for probable cause to arrest to simply shrug his shoulders and allow a crime to occur or a criminal to escape. On the contrary, *Terry* recognizes that it may be the essence of good police work to adopt an intermediate response. A brief stop of a suspicious individual, in order to determine his identity or to maintain the status quo momentarily while obtaining more information, may be most reasonable in light of the facts known to the officer at the time.

The Court recognized in *Terry* that the policeman making a reasonable investigatory stop should not be denied the opportunity to protect himself from attack by a hostile suspect. "When an officer is justified in believing that the individual whose suspicious behavior he is investigating at close range is armed and presently dangerous to the officer or to others," he may conduct a limited protective search for concealed weapons. The purpose of this limited search is not to discover evidence of crime, but to allow the officer to pursue his investigation without fear of violence, and thus the frisk for weapons might be equally necessary and reasonable whether or not carrying a concealed weapon violated any applicable state law. So long as the officer is entitled to make a forcible stop and has reason to believe that the suspect is armed and dangerous, he may conduct a weapons search limited in scope to this protective purpose.

Applying these principles to the present case we believe that Sgt. Connolly acted justifiably in responding to his informant's tip. The informant was known to him personally and had provided him with information in the past. This is a stronger case than obtains in the case of an anonymous telephone tip. The informant here came forward personally to give information that was immediately verifiable at the scene. Indeed, under Connecticut law, the informant herself might have been subject to immediate arrest for making a false complaint had Sgt. Connolly's investigation proven the tip incorrect [for false reporting of a crime]. Thus, while the Court's decisions indicate that this informant's unverified tip may have been insufficient for a narcotics arrest or search warrant, the information carried enough indicia of reliability to justify the officer's forcible stop of Williams.

In reaching this conclusion, we reject respondent's argument that reasonable cause for a stop and frisk can only be based on the officer's personal observation, rather than on information supplied by another person. Informants' tips, like all other clues and evidence coming to a policeman on the scene, may vary greatly in their value and reliability. One simple rule will not cover every situation. Some tips, completely lacking in indicia of reliability, would either warrant no police response or require further investigation before a forcible stop of a suspect would be authorized. But in some situations—for example, when the victim of a street crime seeks immediate police aid and gives a description of his assailant, or when a credible informant warns of a specific impending crime—the subtleties of the hearsay rule should not thwart an appropriate police response.

While properly investigating the activity of a person who was reported to be carrying narcotics and a concealed weapon and who was sitting alone in a car in a high crime area at 2:15 in the morning, Sgt. Connolly had ample reason to fear for his safety.[1] When Williams rolled down his window, rather than complying with the policeman's request to step out of the car so that his movements could more easily be seen, the revolver allegedly at Williams' waist became an even greater threat. Under these circumstances the policeman's action in reaching to the spot where the gun was thought to be hidden constituted a limited intrusion designed to insure his safety, and we conclude that it was reasonable. The loaded gun seized as a result of this intrusion was therefore admissible at Williams' trial. Terry v. Ohio.

Once Sgt. Connolly had found the gun precisely where the informant had predicted, probable cause existed to arrest Williams for unlawful possession of the weapon. Probable cause to arrest depends "upon whether, at the moment the arrest was made . . . the facts and circumstances within [the arresting officers'] knowledge and of which they had reasonably trustworthy information were sufficient to warrant a prudent man in believing that the [suspect] had committed or was committing an offense." Beck v. Ohio. In the present case the policeman found Williams in possession of a gun in precisely the place predicted by the informant. This tended to corroborate the reliability of the informant's further report of narcotics, and together with the surrounding circumstances certainly suggested no lawful explanation for possession of the gun. Probable cause does not require the same type of specific evidence of each element of the offense as would be needed to support a conviction. See Draper v. United States. Rather, the court will evaluate generally the circumstances at the time of the arrest to decide if the officer had probable cause for his action:

> "In dealing with probable cause, however, as the very name applies, we deal with probabilities. These are not technical; they are the factual and practical considerations of everyday life on which reasonable and prudent men, not legal technicians, act." Brinegar v. United States, 338 U.S. 160, 175, 69 S.Ct. 1302, 1310, 93 L.Ed. 1879 (1949).

1. Figures reported by the Federal Bureau of Investigation indicate that 125 policemen were murdered in 1971, with all but five of them having been killed by gunshot wounds. Federal Bureau of Investigation Law Enforcement Bulletin, February 1972, p. 33. According to one study, approximately 30% of police shootings occurred when a police officer approached a suspect seated in an automobile. Bristow, Police Officer Shootings—A Tactical Evaluation, 54 J.Crim.L.C. & P.S. 93 (1963).

See also id., at 177. Under the circumstances surrounding Williams' possession of the gun seized by Sgt. Connolly, the arrest on the weapons charge was supported by probable cause, and the search of his person and of the car incident to that arrest was lawful. The fruits of the search were therefore properly admitted at Williams' trial.

MR. JUSTICE DOUGLAS, with whom MR. JUSTICE MARSHALL concurs, dissenting.

My views have been stated in substance by Judge Friendly in the Court of Appeals. 436 F.2d 30, 35. Connecticut allows its citizens to carry weapons, concealed or otherwise, at will, provided they have a permit. Conn.Gen.Stat. §§ 29–35, 29–38. Connecticut law gives its police no authority to frisk a person for a permit. Yet the arrest was for illegal possession of a gun. The only basis for that arrest was the informer's tip on the narcotics. Can it be said that a man in possession of narcotics will not have a permit for his gun? Is that why the arrest for possession of a gun in the free-and-easy State of Connecticut becomes constitutional?

The police problem is an acute one not because of the Fourth Amendment, but because of the ease with which anyone can acquire a pistol. A powerful lobby dins into the ears of our citizenry that these gun purchases are constitutional rights protected by the Second Amendment which reads, "A well regulated Militia, being necessary to the security of a free State, the right of the people to keep and bear Arms, shall not be infringed."

There is under our decisions no reason why stiff state laws governing the purchase and possession of pistols may not be enacted. There is no reason why pistols may not be barred from anyone with a police record. There is no reason why a State may not require a purchaser of a pistol to pass a psychiatric test. There is no reason why all pistols should not be barred to everyone except the police.

Critics say that proposals like this water down the Second Amendment. Our decisions belie that argument, for the Second Amendment, as noted, was designed to keep alive the militia. But if watering-down is the mood of the day, I would prefer to water down the Second rather than the Fourth Amendment.

MR. JUSTICE BRENNAN, dissenting.

The crucial question on which this case turns, as the Court concedes, is whether, there being no contention that Williams acted voluntarily in rolling down the window of his car, the State had shown sufficient cause to justify Officer Connolly's "forcible" stop. I would affirm, believing, for the following reasons stated by Judge, now Chief Judge, Friendly, 436 F.2d at 38–39, that the State did not make that showing: I would not find the combination of Officer Connolly's almost meaningless observation and the tip in this case to be sufficient justification for the intrusion. The tip suffered from a threefold defect, with each fold compounding the others. The informer was unnamed, he was not shown to have been reliable with respect to guns or narcotics, and he gave no information which demonstrated personal knowledge or—what is worse—could not readily have been manufactured by the officer after the event. To my mind, it has not been sufficiently recognized that the difference between this sort of tip and the accurate prediction of an unusual event is as important on the latter score as on the former. [In Draper v. United States], Narcotics Agent Marsh would hardly have been at the Denver Station at the exact moment of the arrival of the train Draper had taken from Chicago unless *someone* had told him *something* important, although the agent might later have embroidered the details to fit the observed facts. . . . There is no such guarantee of a patrolling officer's veracity when he testifies to a 'tip' from an unnamed informer saying no more than that the officer will find a gun and narcotics on a man across the street, as he later does. If the state wishes to rely on a tip of that nature to validate a stop and frisk, revelation of the name of the informer or demonstration that his name is unknown and could not reasonably have been ascertained should be the price.

"Terry v. Ohio was intended to free a police officer from the rigidity of a rule that would prevent his doing anything to a man reasonably suspected of being about to commit or having just committed a crime of violence, no matter how grave the problem or impelling the need for swift action, unless the officer had what a court would later determine to be probable cause for arrest. It was meant for the serious cases of imminent danger or of harm recently perpetrated to persons or property, not the conventional ones of possessory offenses. If it is to be extended to the latter at all, this should be only where observation by the officer himself or well authenticated information shows 'that criminal activity may be afoot.' I greatly fear that if the [contrary view] should be followed, *Terry* will have opened the sluicegates for serious and unintended erosion of the protection of the Fourth Amendment."

MR. JUSTICE MARSHALL, with whom MR. JUSTICE DOUGLAS joins, dissenting.

Terry did not hold that whenever a policeman has a hunch that a citizen is engaging in criminal activity, he may engage in a stop and frisk. It held that if police officers want to stop and frisk, they must have specific facts from which they can reasonably infer that an individual is engaged in criminal activity and is armed and dangerous. It was central to our decision in *Terry* that the police officer acted on the basis of his own personal observations and that he carefully scrutinized the conduct of his suspects before interfering with them in any way. When we legitimated the conduct of the officer in *Terry* we did so because of the substantial *reliability* of the information on which the officer based his decision to act.

If the Court does not ignore the care with which we examined the knowledge possessed by the officer in *Terry* when he acted, then I cannot see how the actions of the officer in this case can be upheld. The Court explains what the officer knew about respondent before accosting him. But what is more significant is what he did not know. With respect to the scene generally, the officer had no idea how long respondent had been in the car, how long the car had been parked, or to whom the car belonged. With respect to the gun [1] the officer did not know if or when the informant had ever seen the gun, or whether the gun was carried legally, as Connecticut law permitted, or illegally. And with respect to the narcotics, the officer did not know what kind of narcotics respondent allegedly had, whether they were legally or illegally possessed, what the basis of the informant's knowledge was, or even whether the informant was capable of distinguishing narcotics from other substances.

Unable to answer any of these questions, the officer nevertheless determined that it was necessary to intrude on respondent's liberty. I believe that his determination was totally unreasonable. As I read *Terry*, an officer may act on the basis of *reliable* information short of probable cause to make a stop, and ultimately a frisk, if necessary; but, the officer may not use unreliable, unsubstantiated, conclusory hearsay to justify an invasion of liberty. *Terry* never meant to approve the kind of knee-jerk police reaction that we have before us in this case.

Even assuming that the officer had some legitimate reason for relying on the informant, *Terry* requires, before any stop and frisk is made, that the reliable information in the officer's possession demonstrate that the suspect is both armed and *dangerous*. The fact remains that Connecticut specifically authorizes persons to carry guns so long as they have a permit. Thus, there was no reason for the officer to infer from anything that the informant said that the respondent was dangerous. His frisk was, therefore, illegal under *Terry*.

Even if I could agree with the Court that the stop and frisk in this case was proper, I could not go further and sustain the arrest, and the subsequent searches. It takes probable cause to justify an arrest and search and seizure incident thereto. Probable cause means that the "facts and circumstances before the officer are such as to warrant a man of prudence and caution in believing that the offense has been committed . . ."

Once the officer seized the gun from respondent, it is uncontradicted that he did not ask whether respondent had a license to carry it, or whether respondent carried it for any other legal reason under

1. The fact that the respondent carried his gun in a high crime area is irrelevant. In such areas it is more probable than not that citizens would be more likely to carry weapons authorized by the State to protect themselves.

Connecticut law. Rather, the officer placed him under arrest immediately and hastened to search his person. Since Connecticut has not made it illegal for private citizens to carry guns, there is nothing in the facts of this case to warrant a man "of prudence and caution" to believe that any offense had been committed merely because respondent had a gun on his person. Any implication that respondent's silence was some sort of a tacit admission of guilt would be utterly absurd.

It is simply not reasonable to expect someone to protest that he is not acting illegally before he is told that he is suspected of criminal activity. It would have been a simple matter for the officer to ask whether respondent had a permit, but he chose not to do so. In making this choice, he clearly violated the Fourth Amendment.

NOTES

1. In order to stop and frisk, the officer must be able to establish that a reasonable officer would be able to entertain a reasonable suspicion that criminal activity may be afoot and that the person suspected is armed and dangerous. The officer does not have to establish that he personally feared the suspect. The validity of the stop and frisk is not based on the existence of actual fear but rather on whether a hypothetical reasonable officer could have reasonably been suspicious. See Brown v. State, 295 A.2d 575 (Del. 1972). But see United States v. Green, 465 F.2d 620 (D.C.Cir. 1972).

2. During a stop and frisk, prying into places which could not contain a weapon or exploration of soft bulges is not permitted. Tinney v. Wilson, 408 F.2d 912 (9th Cir. 1969); United States v. Gonzalez, 319 F.Supp. 563 (D.Conn.1970); State v. Washington, 82 N.M. 284, 480 P.2d 174 (1971); People v. McKelvy, 23 Cal.App.3d 1027, 100 Cal.Rptr. 661 (1972).

However, if an officer does no more than is necessary to accomplish a frisk and discovers seizable material that is not a weapon, he may seize it. Worthy v. United States, 409 F.2d 105 (D.C.Cir. 1968) ("The need to seize weapons and the potential instruments of crime, thus indicated as relevant to the scope of a search, does not limit its admissible fruit to weapons if conducted consistently with a proper search for weapons").

3. The properly conducted stop and frisk, as in Terry v. Ohio and Adams v. Williams, may escalate into situations allowing broader searches. One example of this is Dell v. Louisiana, 468 F.2d 324 (5th Cir. 1972):

"At 2:30 a. m. on December 16, 1969, the attendant of a gas station reported to the police that he had just been held up by an armed black man with a paper bag mask over his head. He reported that the robber has escaped with two rolls of wrapped nickels, an ESSO envelope containing loose change and bills, and a .25 caliber automatic belonging to the station manager. Shortly thereafter, a police officer responding to the call noticed a car driving very slowly past the gas station. In the car were two black men who were staring intently at the gas station. The police officer summoned the car to the curb and the driver, petitioner in this case, ignored the command until the officer lifted his shotgun, at which time petitioner pulled over. The police officer asked petitioner to step out of the car and display his identification. When the door opened, the officer could plainly see a .25

caliber automatic on the front floorboard and an ESSO envelope, identical to the one taken from the gas station, on the rear floorboard. When petitioner failed to produce his driver's license, he was placed under arrest for driving without a license. See La.Stat.Ann.-Rev.Stat. 32:427. The search of petitioner's person pursuant to this initial arrest produced a roll of wrapped nickels. When the other occupant of the car stepped out to show his identification, a second officer who had arrived on the scene noticed a revolver and two paper bags on the floor of the car. At that point petitioner was placed in the back seat of the police car and the envelope, paper bags and guns which had been observed in the automobile were removed by the officers.

"The general rule is that a police officer may stop a vehicle and request the production of a driver's license with somewhat less than probable cause as a requisite. E. g., United States v. Marlow, 5 Cir. 1970, 423 F.2d 1064. *See* La.Stat.Ann.-Rev.Stat. 32:411(D). Here the initial stopping took place at 2:30 a. m., under suspicious circumstances, and we are not prepared to say that merely requesting the production of a driver's license under such conditions was unreasonable.

. . .

"The initial arrest for driving without a license did not take place until after petitioner admitted he had no license; therefore, probable cause clearly existed for the initial arrest. The search of petitioner's person pursuant to this initial arrest was a valid search incident to the arrest, therefore, the discovery and seizure of the roll of nickels from his person was clearly lawful. At the point in time when the nickels were seized and prior to the seizure from the car, the officer was cognizant of the following: the stolen nickels found on petitioner's person, the guns, envelope, and masks lying in plain view in the car and petitioner's suspicious behavior, including the fact that he was driving without a license at 2:30 a. m. at the scene of the robbery moments after the robbery. In sum, it is indisputable that probable cause to arrest petitioner for the further crime of armed robbery existed prior to the time the items were seized from the car."

4. Recent efforts to detect potential airplane hijackers including the use of metal detection devices and the hijacker's profile (consisting of a list of twenty five or more characteristics in which hijackers differ from the ordinary air traveler) are generally approved. If these techniques and interviews by airline personnel and marshals indicate that further steps might be needed, the passenger is frisked for weapons. This practice is sometimes justified on the basis of "implied" consent to submit by virtue of purchasing a ticket and seeking to board the plane. United States v. Allen, 349 F.Supp. 749 (N.D.Cal.1972) (meeting profile, giving inadequate explanation of possession of another person's ticket and identification is not sufficient to justify frisk). Usually the Courts hold that the practice is justified as reasonable under the less than probable cause standards in Terry v. Ohio. See United States v. Epperson, 454 F.2d 796 (4th Cir. 1972); United States v. Bell, 464 F.2d 667 (2nd Cir. 1972); United States v. Slocum, 464 F.2d 1180 (3rd Cir. 1972); United States v. Lindsey, 451 F.2d 701 (3rd Cir. 1971) (man gave wrong name for reservation and appeared nervous).

5. On the question of sufficient suspicion to justify a stop, *compare* Commonwealth v. Mamon, 449 Pa. 249, 297 A.2d 471 (1972) (information given independently by two unproven informants is sufficient); Steph-

enson v. United States, 296 A.2d 606 (D.C.Ct.App.1972) (false statement to police justifies frisk); State v. Taras, 19 Ariz.App. 7, 504 P.2d 548 (1972) (flight from police justifies stop); State v. Brooks, 281 So.2d 55 (Fla.App. 1973) (frisk permitted where, in a high crime area, police heard a shot and the only two persons in the immediate area denied even hearing the gunshot); People v. Juarez, 35 Cal.App.3d 631, 110 Cal.Rptr. 865 (1973) (police may frisk a person found near the scene of a burglary who gives a dubious explanation for his presence); *with* United States v. Mallides, 473 F.2d 859 (9th Cir. 1973) (frisk not justified when Mexican occupants of an auto being driven in a Mexican neighborhood failed to turn their heads as a police car passed); United States v. Page, 298 A.2d 233 (D.C. Ct.App. 1972) (equivocal gesture while committing a traffic offense fails to sustain claims of a reasonable stop and frisk); In re State in interest D.S., 63 N.J. 541, 310 A.2d 460 (1973) (improper to frisk youths who split up their group as the police approached); State v. Jackson, 213 Kan. 219, 515 P.2d 1108 (1973) (improper to frisk an individual simply because he is walking on a highway late at night).

PEOPLE v. MORALES

Court of Appeals of New York, 1968.
22 N.Y.2d 55, 238 N.E.2d 307.

JASEN, JUDGE. This appeal squarely presents the issue of the authority of law enforcement officials to temporarily detain and question suspects upon less than probable cause for charges of crime after advising them of their Fifth and Sixth Amendment rights.

At about 3:00 A.M. on October 4, 1964, Addie Brown was brutally stabbed 31 times while in the elevator of the apartment building in which she lived in New York City. Two men, attracted by her screams, heard running footsteps and the slamming or closing of a door. Mrs. Brown was unable to respond to questioning and died at 3:30 A.M.

The police questioned a large number of persons and conducted an investigation which established that no one witnessed the murder or observed the killer leave the scene of the crime. They were unable to discover any direct evidence concerning the identity of the killer. During the course of this investigation, the police conducted a "canvass" of the apartment building during which they learned that defendant had been present in the building at the time of the crime. They also learned that defendant, a known narcotics addict, who constantly frequented the apartment house, had not been seen since the killing.[1] The police made several fruitless attempts to locate defendant through his mother who lived in the same apartment building. They interpreted Mrs. Morales' statements to them to mean that she did not know where defendant was. Finally,

1. Defendant testified that he returned to his mother's apartment in the building on several occasions after the murder. However, this fact was unknown to the apprehending detectives.

on the tenth day of defendant's continued "absence" from the area of the crime, October 13, Detectives Carroll and Daum staked out Mrs. Morales' beauty parlor.

Defendant appeared at his mother's business establishment on October 13 because he knew the police were attempting to locate him through his mother for questioning, and was apprehended by detectives upon his arrival at 8:00 P.M. He was told, "We [were] looking for you" and placed in Detective Daum's car. He was not informed that he was under arrest. In response to defendant's question concerning the reason for placing him in the car, Detective Carroll replied, "Well don't worry about it, I will ask you a few questions, that's all." Mrs. Morales was not allowed to speak to her son, nor did he ask to speak to her. However, the apprehending detectives informed her that defendant would be released in an hour or so after questioning. Defendant was then driven to the 42nd Precinct Station in the Bronx, where he was questioned.

The record does not indicate that physical force was used in taking defendant to the 42nd Precinct. In fact, defendant testified that he was so loosely guarded when taken from the car to the station that he could have safely escaped but did not because he had no reason to do so. However, he was not free to leave at the time he was apprehended and would have been restrained had he attempted to flee.

Upon arrival at the 42nd Precinct at about 8:30 P.M. and prior to being questioned, defendant was informed of the subject matter of the investigation, his right to remain silent, his right to have a lawyer at any time, and advised that any answers he gave could be used against him. Shortly thereafter, defendant confessed that he killed Addie Brown when she resisted his attempts to rob her for money to buy narcotics. The substance of this confession was reduced to writing and signed by defendant at 9:05 P.M.

Defendant was convicted after a jury trial of felony murder . .

On this appeal defendant contends that his confessions should have been suppressed because they were evidence obtained as a result of an unreasonable seizure proscribed by the Fourth Amendment. Specifically, he argues that these statements were illegally taken because they were obtained during a period of detention which was unlawful because it had not been predicated upon probable cause.

It may be conceded that the apprehending detectives did not have probable cause to justify an arrest of defendant at the time they took him into custody. Moreover, the record does not support a finding that defendant consented to his detention and questioning. However, it does not follow that defendant was *unreasonably* detained within the meaning of the Fourth Amendment. Considering the totality of the circumstances of this case, we conclude that defendant's temporary detention for questioning represented a reasonable exercise of the police power. * * *

Concluding then that defendant was technically not arrested within the meaning of our arrest statute, the question narrows to whether the police *unreasonably* seized defendant within the meaning of the Fourth Amendment by taking him to the 42nd Precinct Station for questioning. . . .

This court recognized the common-law authority of law enforcement officials to detain persons for investigation as a reasonable and necessary exercise of the police power for the prevention of crime and the preservation of public order in People v. Rivera, . . . Indeed, we recently upheld the constitutionality of section 180–a of the Code of Criminal Procedure, popularly known as the "Stop and Frisk" law. . . .

Of course, this statute is limited to the stopping, questioning and frisking of persons in public places upon reasonable suspicion. We have also held that probable cause can be obtained during a "stop" authorized by common law and by section 180–a, and this probable cause will support a formal arrest and a contemporaneous incidental search. . . .

Other courts have recognized the power to detain for investigation as extending to the police station. . . . The Court of Appeals, Second Circuit, upholds the power of the police to detain a person for a reasonable period of time for the purpose of interrogation. . . . Indeed, LUMBARD, Ch. J., in United States v. Vita, 294 F.2d 524, 529–534 [2d Cir., 1961], expressed the view that four or five hours of police detention for the purpose of questioning does not constitute an arrest. . . . However, we need not go so far in this case. It is enough that the police were justified in the record as developed in detaining and questioning defendant for a short and reasonable period of time.

This question is complicated by the fact that the Supreme Court has never settled the perimeters of constitutionally unreasonable seizures. . . .

* * *

We are thus squarely confronted with the perplexing question of the authority of law enforcement officials, though lacking sufficient cause to justify an arrest, to detain defendant for a reasonable period of time for questioning as a constitutional issue of first impression. The resolution of this issue requires striking a balance between the right of the individual to move freely without undue restraint or interference and society's need to prevent crime and bring criminals expeditiously to justice. . . .

* * *

Broadly viewed then, the issue can be stated as whether the police possessed sufficient cause to interfere with defendant's movement to the extent revealed by the facts of this case. This problem involves weighing the seriousness of the known crime (a brutal murder) and the degree of suspicion possessed by the police against the magnitude of the personal rights encroached upon.

. . . As [previously] recognized by this court it is the duty and function of police officers to enforce criminal laws and bring violators of these laws to justice. Interrogation of those who know something about the facts is the chief means of solution of crime. The public interest requires that such interrogation not be completely forbidden so long as it is conducted fairly, reasonably, within proper limits and with full regard to the rights of those being questioned. Indeed, the interest of the State in bringing a criminal to justice is so vital that one known to be innocent may be detained, in the absence of bail, as a material witness.

* * *

This prerogative of police officers to detain persons for questioning is not only essential to effective criminal investigation, but it also protects those who are able to exculpate themselves from being arrested and having formal charges made against them before their explanations are considered. The fact that detention is not recorded as an arrest and may not be considered by the individual as an arrest is also important.

The evil to be guarded against is the danger posed to constitutional rights by incommunicado questioning, without advice as to a suspect's rights. This evil can be controlled by fully advising a person of his rights and providing counsel upon request. Where, as here, the defendant is advised of his rights, . . . he is confronted with a clear choice. If he declines to talk, the police must release him unless they have probable cause to arrest on a charge of crime. The fact that defendant was questioned in a police station should not be controlling, although, of course, it is considered with all the other circumstances in determining the reasonableness of police conduct. Police station interrogation facilitates questioning because trained investigators and stenographic facilities are present. Its privacy eliminates the distractions caused by crowds which may form during questioning conducted on the street.

In conclusion, the police were justified in questioning defendant in the manner in which they did because of the exceptional circumstances of this case. There was a high degree of public interest involved resulting from the confluence of a brutal crime and a lack of practical alternative investigative techniques. The checkerboard square of the police investigation, although resting upon circumstantial evidence, pointed only to defendant. The public interest in questioning defendant was, therefore, great. In fact, defendant was the only person the police could have reasonably detained for questioning based upon the instant record. Finally, custodial interrogation, the investigative technique, was reasonably applied to the needs of the situation. The explanation of defendant's constitutional rights clearly exceeded the requirements of the law as it was understood at the time of his interrogation. The period of proposed detention was brief, approximately one hour. Defendant, experienced in police procedures, could not have regarded his temporary detention as tantamount to an arrest. Of course, when defendant confessed approximately 15 minutes after questioning began, detectives then had probable cause to arrest him on a charge of crime.

Nothing is more offensive to our deep concern for the dignity of the individual than unnecessary restraint by the police. Lengthy detention on mere suspicion breeds abuse of those safeguards which a civilized society must erect to protect even the most reprehensible of its members. However, the possibility that power given to law enforcement officers may be abused does not require that they be left powerless to make reasonable inquiry. The reasonableness of their behavior may be assured by close judicial supervision of the methods used.

It is recognized that detention for questioning has its manifest evils and dangers. This decision is, therefore, limited to the exceptional circumstances presented on this appeal involving a serious crime affecting the public safety. We hold merely that a suspect may be detained upon reasonable suspicion for a reasonable and brief period of time for questioning under carefully controlled conditions protecting his Fifth and Sixth Amendment rights. Mass detentions for questioning are never permissible. The scope of the authority to question is limited to those persons reasonably suspected of possessing knowledge of the crime under investigation in circumstances involving crimes presenting a high degree of public concern affecting the public safety.

Our review of the other questions raised on this appeal finds no error requiring reversal of this judgment of conviction.

Accordingly, the judgment of the Appellate Division should be affirmed.

BURKE, SCILEPPI, BERGAN, KEATING and BREITEL JJ., concur.

FULD, C. J., concurs in result but solely on the ground that the record established that defendant waived his constitutional rights and acquiesced in his being interrogated by the police at the police station.

Judgment affirmed.

MORALES v. NEW YORK

Supreme Court of the United States, 1969.
396 U.S. 102, 90 S.Ct. 291.

PER CURIAM. On October 4, 1964, a murder by stabbing took place in an elevator of an apartment building where petitioner Morales' mother lived and where Morales frequently visited. On October 13, his mother informed Morales by telephone that the police wished to talk with him; petitioner said that he would come that evening to his mother's place of business. This he did. He was apprehended by police officers and taken to the police station, arriving at 8:30 p. m. Within 15 minutes he had confessed to the crime and by 9:05 p. m. he had written and signed a statement. In response to subsequent questioning by police officers, Morales later repeated the substance of this confession. At the trial, the court held a separate hearing on the voluntariness of the confessions, found them voluntary, and admitted them over Morales' objection. . . . In the New York Court of Appeals, Morales for the first time raised a Fourth Amendment issue, claiming that there was no probable cause for his detention at the time of his confessions and that the confessions, even if voluntary, were inadmissible fruits of the illegal detention. The State asserted that the issue had not been decided below and that there had hence been no opportunity to make a record of the relevant facts; moreover, the State claimed that Morales had voluntarily surrendered himself for questioning and that in any event the voluntary confessions were the result of an independent choice by Morales such that the legality of the detention was irrelevant to the admissibility of the confessions.

The Court of Appeals affirmed, accepting without discussion the trial court's finding as to the voluntariness of Morales' confessions. . . . The court dealt with and rejected the Fourth Amendment claim not on the ground that there was probable cause to arrest but rather on the ground that the police conduct involved was reasonable under the circumstances of the case. Although Morales was not free to leave at the time he was apprehended and would have been restrained had he attempted to flee, the Court of Appeals stated that his detention was not a formal arrest under New York law and that had he refused to answer questions in the police station (where he was entitled to have a lawyer if he desired one) he would have been free to leave. The Court of Appeals held that the State had authority under the Fourth Amendment to conduct brief custodial interrogation of "those persons reasonably suspected of possessing knowledge of the crime under investigation in circumstances involving crimes presenting a high degree of public concern affecting the public safety." We granted certiorari. . . .

After considering the full record, we do not disturb the determination of the trial court, affirmed by the New York appellate courts, that Morales' confessions were voluntarily given. The trial occurred prior to Miranda v. Arizona, 384 U.S. 436, 86 S.Ct. 1602 (1966), and the totality of the circumstances surrounding the confessions shows that the confessions were voluntary, not coerced.

We should not, however, decide on the record before us whether Morales' conviction should otherwise be affirmed. The ruling below, that the State may detain for custodial questioning on less than probable cause for a traditional arrest, is manifestly important, goes beyond our decisions in Terry v. Ohio, and Sibron v. New York. But we have concluded after considering the parties' briefs and hearing oral argument that there is merit in the State's position that the record does not permit a satisfactory evaluation of the facts surrounding the apprehension and detention of Morales. A lengthy hearing was held on the question of the voluntariness of the confessions, but the basis for the apprehension of Morales does not appear to have been fully explored since no challenge to the lawfulness of the apprehension was raised until the case came to the Court of Appeals. Although that court stated that "[i]t may be conceded that the apprehending detectives did not have probable cause to justify an arrest of defendant at the time they took him into custody," . . . the court later said that "[t]he checkerboard square of the police investigation, although resting upon circumstantial evidence, pointed only to defendant. . . . In fact, defendant was the only person the police could have reasonably detained for questioning based upon the instant record." . . .

Given an opportunity to develop in an evidentiary hearing the circumstances leading to the detention of Morales and his confessions, the State may be able to show that there was probable cause for an arrest or that Morales' confrontation with the police was voluntarily undertaken by him or that the confessions were not the product of illegal detention. In any event, in the absence of a record which squarely and necessarily presents the issue and fully illuminates the factual context in which the question arises, we choose not to grapple with the question of the legality of custodial questioning on less than probable cause for a full-fledged arrest.

We accordingly vacate the judgment below and remand the case for further proceedings not inconsistent with this opinion.

It is so ordered.

MR. JUSTICE BLACK dissents.

NOTES

1. Subsequent to the Supreme Court decision in *Morales*, one New York court concluded that investigative detention for interrogation upon less than probable cause for arrest was permissible. The court held that:

"In our opinion the reasonableness of a detention for interrogation purposes is measured by standards less than those requiring probable cause for arrest. Accordingly, if any reasonable basis exists for suspecting a person of having committed or participated in the commission of a crime or for attributing to that person some questionable relationship with respect thereto, the police should not be frustrated in pursuing their investigation to the point of detention and interrogation either on the spot or at the police station as long as such detention and interrogation are not tantamount to an arrest within the purview of section 167 of the Code of Criminal Procedure. If such reasonable basis short of probable cause exists, a detention and interrogation which follows would, in our opinion, be lawful and proper. In such event, absent involuntariness, a confession obtained in the course thereof would be admissible and could not be considered the product of illegality, even under the rationale of Morales v. New York, 396 U.S. 102, 90 S.Ct. 291, or the result of indiscriminate invasions of privacy and wholesale roundups and harassment of innocent persons of which the court in Davis v. Mississippi, 394 U.S. 721, 726, 89 S.Ct. 1394, was apprehensive."

The court then remanded the case for further hearings to develop the facts of the case. People v. Pounds, 35 App.Div.2d 969, 317 N.Y.S.2d 884 (1970).

2. The use of investigative detention to secure physical evidence and the use of investigative detention to secure the presence of a suspect for a lineup identification are considered in Chapter 14.

3. In United States v. Van Leeuwen, 397 U.S. 249, 90 S.Ct. 1029 (1970) a unanimous Court approved an investigative detention of two pieces of first class mail. A postal clerk in Washington state advised a policeman of his suspicions about two recently mailed packages of coins. The officer examined the packages and perceived that the return addresses were fictitious. He noted that the individual who mailed the packages drove a car with Canadian license plates. The packages were then held while investigators discovered that the addresses in California and Tennessee were under investigation for trafficking in stolen coins. After this was learned, a search warrant was secured. The packages had been delayed for a little more than one day before the warrants were secured. The Court said that although "detention of mail could at some point become an unreasonable seizure of 'papers' or 'effects' within the meaning of the Fourth Amendment," Terry v. Ohio authorized this "detentions, without a warrant, while an investigation was made." The Court noted that the investigation was conducted promptly and that most of the delay was attributable to the fact that because of the time differential the Tennessee authorities could not be reached until the following day.

B. ADMINISTRATIVE SEARCHES

CAMARA v. MUNICIPAL COURT OF SAN FRANCISCO

Supreme Court of the United States, 1967.
387 U.S. 523, 87 S.Ct. 1727.

MR. JUSTICE WHITE delivered the opinion of the Court.

On November 6, 1963, an inspector of the Division of Housing Inspection of the San Francisco Department of Public Health entered an apartment building to make a routine annual inspection for possible violations of the city's Housing Code. The building's manager informed the inspector that appellant, lessee of the ground floor, was using the rear of his leasehold as a personal residence. Claiming that the building's occupancy permit did not allow residential use of the ground floor, the inspector confronted appellant and demanded that he permit an inspection of the premises. Appellant refused to allow the inspection because the inspector lacked a search warrant.

The inspector returned on November 8, again without a warrant, and appellant again refused to allow an inspection. A citation was then mailed ordering appellant to appear at the district attorney's office. When appellant failed to appear, two inspectors returned to his apartment on November 22. They informed appellant that he was required by law to permit an inspection under § 503 of the Housing Code:

> "Sec. 503. RIGHT TO ENTER BUILDING. Authorized employees of the City departments or City agencies, so far as may be necessary for the performance of their duties, shall, upon presentation of proper credentials, have the right to enter, at reasonable times, any building, structure, or premises in the City to perform any duty imposed upon them by the Municipal Code."

Appellant nevertheless refused the inspectors access to his apartment without a search warrant. Thereafter, a complaint was filed charging him with refusing to permit a lawful inspection in violation of § 507 of the Code.

In Frank v. State of Maryland, [359 U.S. 360, 79 S.Ct. 804] this Court upheld the conviction of one who refused to permit a warrantless inspection of private premises for the purposes of locating and abating a suspected public nuisance. . . . the *Frank* opinion has generally been interpreted as carving out an additional exception to the rule that warrantless searches are unreasonable under the Fourth Amendment.

To the *Frank* majority, municipal fire, health, and housing inspection programs "touch at most upon the periphery of the important interests safeguarded by the Fourteenth Amendment's protection against official intrusions," because the inspections are merely to determine whether physical conditions exist which do not comply with minimum standards prescribed in local regulatory ordinances.

We may agree that a routine inspection of the physical condition of private property is a less hostile intrusion than the typical policeman's search for the fruits and instrumentalities of crime. . . . But we cannot agree that the Fourth Amendment interests at stake in these inspection cases are merely "peripheral." It is surely anomalous to say that the individual and his private property are fully protected by the Fourth Amendment only when the individual is suspected of criminal behavior. For instance, even the most law-abiding citizen has a very tangible interest in limiting the circumstances under which the sanctity of his home may be broken by official authority, for the possibility of criminal entry under the guise of official sanction is a serious threat to personal and family security. And even accepting Frank's rather remarkable premise, inspections of the kind we are here considering do in fact jeopardize "self protection" interests of the property owner. Like most regulatory laws, fire, health, and housing codes are enforced by criminal processes. . . .

The *Frank* majority suggested, and appellee reasserts, two other justifications for permitting administrative health and safety inspections without a warrant. First, it is argued that these inspections are "designed to make the least possible demand on the individual occupant." The ordinances authorizing inspections are hedged with safeguards, and at any rate the inspector's particular decision to enter must comply with the constitutional standard of reasonableness even if he may enter without a warrant. In addition, the argument proceeds, the warrant process could not function effectively in this field. The decision to inspect an entire municipal area is based upon legislative or administrative assessment of broad factors such as the area's age and condition. Unless the magistrate is to review such policy matters, he must issue a "rubber stamp" warrant which provides no protection at all to the property owner.

In our opinion, these arguments unduly discount the purposes behind the warrant machinery contemplated by the Fourth Amendment. Under the present system, when the inspector demands entry, the occupant has no way of knowing whether enforcement of the municipal code involved requires inspection of his premises, no way of knowing the lawful limits of the inspector's power to search, and no way of knowing whether the inspector himself is acting under proper authorization. These are questions which may be reviewed by a neutral magistrate without any reassessment of the basic agency decision to canvass an area. Yet, only by refusing entry and risking a criminal conviction can the occupant at present challenge the inspector's decision to search. And even if the occupant possesses sufficient fortitude to take this risk, as appellant did here, he may never learn any more about the reason for the inspection than that the law generally allows housing inspectors to gain entry. The practical effect of this system is to leave the occupant subject to the discretion of the official in the field. This is precisely the discretion to invade private property which we have consistently circumscribed by a requirement that a disinterested party warrant the need to search.

The final justification suggested for warrantless administrative searches is that the public interest demands such a rule: it is vigorously argued that the health and safety of entire urban populations is dependent upon enforcement of minimum fire, housing, and sanitation standards, and that the only effective means of enforcing such codes is by routine systematized inspection of all physical structures. Of course, in applying any reasonableness standard, including one of constitutional dimension, an argument that the public interest demands a particular rule must receive careful consideration. But we think this argument misses the mark. The question is not, at this stage at least, whether these inspections may be made, but whether they may be made without a warrant. . . .

It has nowhere been urged that fire, health, and housing code inspection programs could not achieve their goals within the confines of a reasonable search warrant requirement. Thus, we do not find the public need argument dispositive.

In summary, we hold that administrative searches of the kind at issue here are significant intrusions upon the interests protected by the Fourth Amendment, that such searches when authorized and conducted without a warrant procedure lack the traditional safeguards which the Fourth Amendment guarantees to the individual . . . Because of the nature of the municipal programs under consideration, however, these conclusions must be the beginning, not the end of our inquiry. The *Frank* majority gave recognition to the unique character of these inspection programs by refusing to require search warrants; to reject that disposition does not justify ignoring the question whether some other accommodation between public need and individual rights is essential.

II.

The Fourth Amendment provides that, "no Warrants shall issue but upon probable cause." Borrowing from more typical Fourth Amendment cases, appellant argues not only that code enforcement inspection programs must be circumscribed by a warrant procedure, but also that warrants should issue only when the inspector possesses probable cause to believe that a particular dwelling contains violations of the minimum standards prescribed by the code being enforced. We disagree.

Unlike the search pursuant to a criminal investigation, the inspection programs at issue here are aimed at securing city-wide compliance with minimum physical standards for private property. The primary governmental interest at stake is to prevent even the unintentional development of conditions which are hazardous to public health and safety. Because fires and epidemics may ravage large urban areas, because unsightly conditions adversely affect the economic values of neighboring structures, numerous courts have upheld the police power of municipalities to impose and enforce such minimum standards even upon existing structures. In determining whether a particular inspection is reasonable—and thus in determining whether there is probable cause to issue a warrant for that inspection—the need for the inspection must be weighed in terms of these reasonable goals of code enforcement.

There is unanimous agreement among those most familiar with this field that the only effective way to seek universal compliance with the minimum standards required by municipal codes is through routine periodic inspections of all structures. It is here that the probable cause debate is focused, for the agency's decision to conduct an area inspection is unavoidably based on its appraisal of conditions in the area as a whole, not on its knowledge of conditions in each particular building. Appellee contends that, if the probable cause standard urged by appellant is adopted, the area inspection will be eliminated as a means of seeking compliance with code standards and the reasonable goals of code enforcement will be dealt a crushing blow.

In meeting this contention, appellant argues first, that his probable cause standard would not jeopardize area inspection programs because only a minute portion of the population will refuse to consent to such inspections, and second, that individual privacy in any event should be given preference to the public interest in conducting such inspections. The first argument, even if true, is irrelevant to the question whether the area inspection is reasonable within the meaning of the Fourth Amendment. The second argument is in effect an assertion that the area inspection is an unreasonable search. Unfortunately, there can be no ready test for determining reasonableness other than by balancing the need to search against the invasion which the search entails. But we think that a number of persuasive factors combine to support the reasonableness of code enforcement area inspections. First, such programs have a long history of judicial and public acceptance. Second, the public interest demands that all dangerous conditions be prevented or abated, yet it is doubtful that any other canvassing technique would achieve acceptable results. Many such conditions—faulty wiring is an obvious example—are not observable from outside the building and indeed may not be apparent to the inexpert occupant himself. Finally, because the inspections are neither personal in nature nor aimed at the discovery of evidence of crime, they involve a relatively limited invasion of the urban citizen's privacy. . . .

* * *

Having concluded that the area inspection is a "reasonable" search of private property within the meaning of the Fourth Amendment, it is obvious that "probable cause" to issue a warrant to inspect must exist if reasonable legislative or administrative standards for conducting an area inspection are satisfied with respect to a particular dwelling. Such standards, which will vary with the municipal program being enforced, may be based upon the passage of time, the nature of the building (e. g., a multi-family apartment house), or the condition of the entire area, but they will not necessarily depend upon specific knowledge of the condition of the particular dwelling. It has been suggested that so to vary the probable cause test from the standard applied in criminal cases would be to authorize a "synthetic search warrant" and thereby to lessen the overall protections of the Fourth Amendment. But we do not agree. The warrant procedure is designed to guarantee that a decision to search private property is justified by a reasonable governmental interest. But reasonableness is still the ultimate standard. If a valid public interest justifies the intrusion contemplated, then there is probable cause to issue a suitably restricted search warrant. . . . Such an approach neither endangers time-honored doctrines applicable to criminal investigations nor makes a nullity of the probable cause requirement in this area. It merely gives full recognition to the competing public and private interests here at stake and, in so doing, best fulfills the historic purpose behind the constitutional right to be free from unreasonable government invasions of privacy. . . .

III.

Since our holding emphasizes the controlling standard of reasonableness, nothing we say today is intended to foreclose prompt inspections, even without a warrant, that the law has traditionally upheld in emergency situations. See North American Cold Storage Co. v. City of Chicago, 211 U.S. 306, 29 S.Ct. 101 (seizure of unwholesome food); Jacobson v. Commonwealth of Massachusetts, 197 U.S. 11, 25 S.Ct. 358 (compulsory smallpox vaccination); Compagnie Francaise de Navigation à Vapeur v. Louisiana State Board of Health, 186 U.S. 380, 22 S.Ct. 811 (health quarantine); Kroplin v. Truax, 119 Ohio St. 610, 165 N.E. 498 (summary destruction of tubercular cattle). On the other hand, in the case of most routine area inspections, there is no compelling urgency to inspect at a particular time or on a particular day. Moreover, most citizens allow inspections of their property without a warrant. Thus, as a practical matter and in light of the Fourth Amendment's requirement that a warrant specify the property to be searched, it seems likely that warrants should normally be sought only after entry is refused unless there has been a citizen complaint or there is other satisfactory reason for securing immediate entry. . . .

SEE v. CITY OF SEATTLE

Supreme Court of the United States, 1967.
387 U.S. 541, 87 S.Ct. 1737.

MR. JUSTICE WHITE delivered the opinion of the Court.

Appellant seeks reversal of his conviction for refusing to permit a representative of the City of Seattle Fire Department to enter and inspect appellant's locked commercial warehouse without a warrant and without probable cause to believe that a violation of any municipal ordinance existed therein. The inspection was conducted as part of a routine, periodic city-wide canvass to obtain compliance with Seattle's Fire Code.

As governmental regulation of business enterprise has mushroomed in recent years, the need for effective investigative techniques to achieve the aims of such regulation has been the subject of substantial comment and legislation. Official entry upon commercial property is a technique commonly adopted by administrative agencies at all levels of government to enforce a variety of regulatory laws; thus, entry may permit inspection of the structure in which a business is housed, as in this case, or inspection of business products, or a perusal of financial books and records. This Court has not had occasion to consider the Fourth Amendment's relation to this broad range of investigations. However, we have dealt with the Fourth Amendment issues raised by another common investigative technique, the administrative subpoena of corporate books and records. We find strong support in these subpoena cases for our conclusion that warrants are a necessary and a tolerable limitation on the right to enter upon and inspect commercial premises.

It is now settled that, when an administrative agency subpoenas corporate books or records, the Fourth Amendment requires that the subpoena be sufficiently limited in scope, relevant in purpose, and specific in directive so that compliance will not be unreasonably burdensome. The agency has the right to conduct all reasonable inspections of such documents which are contemplated by statute, but it must delimit the confines of a search by designating the needed documents in a formal subpoena. In addition, while the demand to inspect may be issued by the agency, in the form of an administrative subpoena, it may not be made and enforced by the inspector in the field, and the subpoenaed party may obtain judicial review of the reasonableness of the demand prior to suffering penalties for refusing to comply.

It is these rather minimal limitations on administrative action which we think are constitutionally required in the case of investigative entry upon commercial establishments. The agency's particular demand for access will of course be measured, in terms of probable cause to issue a warrant, against a flexible standard of reasonableness that takes into account the public need for effective enforcement of the particular regulation involved. But the decision to enter and inspect will not be the product of the unreviewed discretion of the enforcement officer in the field. Given the analogous investigative functions performed by the administrative subpoena and the demand for entry, we find untenable the proposition that the subpoena, which has been termed a "constructive" search, . . . is subject to Fourth Amendment limitations which do not apply to actual searches and inspections of commercial premises.

We therefore conclude that administrative entry, without consent, upon the portions of commercial premises which are not open to the public may only be compelled through prosecution or physical force within the framework of a warrant procedure. We do not in any way imply that business premises may not reasonably be inspected in many more situations than private homes, nor do we question such accepted regulatory techniques as licensing programs which require inspections prior to operating a business or marketing a product. Any constitutional challenge to such programs can only be resolved, as many have been in the past, on a case-by-case basis under the general Fourth Amendment standard of reasonableness.

[Dissenting opinion in both *Camara* and *See*]

MR. JUSTICE CLARK with whom MR. JUSTICE HARLAN and MR. JUSTICE STEWART join, dissenting.

Eight years ago my Brother Frankfurter wisely wrote in Frank v. State of Maryland . . . :

> "Time and experience have forcefully taught that the power to inspect dwelling places, either as a matter of systematic area-by-area search or, as here, to treat a specific problem, is of indispensable importance to the maintenance of community health; a power that would be greatly hobbled by the blanket requirement of the safeguards necessary for a search of evidence of criminal acts. The need for preventive action is great, and city after city has seen this need and granted the power of inspection to its health officials; and these inspections are apparently welcomed by all but an insignificant few."

Today the Court renders this municipal experience, which dates back to Colonial days, for naught by overruling Frank v. State of Maryland and by striking down hundreds of city ordinances throughout the country and jeopardizing thereby the health, welfare, and safety of literally millions of people.

But this is not all. It prostitutes the command of the Fourth Amendment that "no Warrants shall issue, but upon probable cause" and sets up in the health and safety codes area inspection a newfangled "warrant" system that is entirely foreign to Fourth Amendment standards. It is regrettable that the Court wipes out such a long and widely accepted practice and creates in its place such enormous confusion in all of our towns and metropolitan cities in one fell swoop. I dissent.

The great need for health and safety inspection is emphasized by the experience of San Francisco, a metropolitan area known for its cleanliness and safety ever since it suffered earthquake and fire back in 1908. For the fiscal year ending June 30, 1965, over 16,000 dwelling structures were inspected, of which over 5,600 required some type of compliance action in order to meet code requirements. . . .

In the larger metropolitan cities such as Los Angeles, over 300,000 inspections (health and fire) revealed over 28,000 hazardous violations. In Chicago during the period November 1965 to December 1966, over 18,000 buildings were found to be rodent infested out of some 46,000 inspections. . . . And in New York City the problem is even more acute. A grand jury in Brooklyn conducted a housing survey of 15 square blocks in three different areas and found over 12,000 hazardous violations of code restrictions in those areas alone. Prior to this test there were only 567 violations reported in the entire area. The pressing need for inspection is shown by the fact that some 12,000 additional violations were actually present at that very time.

An even more disastrous effect will be suffered in plumbing violations. These are not only more frequent but also the more dangerous to the community. Defective plumbing causes back siphonage of sewage and other household wastes. Chicago's disastrous amoebic dysentery epidemic is an example. Over 100 deaths resulted. Fire code violations also often cause many conflagrations. Indeed, if the fire inspection attempted in District of Columbia v. Little, 339 U.S. 1, 70 S.Ct. 468 (1950), had been permitted a two-year-old child's death resulting from a fire that gutted the home involved there on August 6, 1964, might well have been prevented.

Inspections also play a vital role in urban redevelopment and slum clearance. Statistics indicate that slums constitute 20% of the residential area of the average American city, still they produce 35% of the fires, 45% of the major crimes, and 50% of the disease. Today's decision will play havoc with the many programs now designed to aid in the improvement of these areas. We should remember the admonition of Mr. Justice Douglas in Berman v. Parker:

> "Miserable and disreputable housing conditions may do more than spread disease and crime and immorality. They may also suffocate the spirit by reducing those who live there to the status of cattle. They may indeed make living an almost insufferable burden."

The majority propose two answers to this admittedly pressing problem of need for constant inspection of premises for fire, health, and safety infractions of municipal codes. First, they say that there will be few refusals of entry to inspect. Unlike the attitude of householders as to codes requiring entry for inspection, we have few empirical statistics on attitudes where consent must be obtained. It is true that in the required entry to inspect situations most occupants welcome the periodic visits of municipal inspectors. In my view this will not be true when consent is necessary. The City of Portland, Oregon, has a voluntary home inspection program. The 1966 record shows that out of 16,171 calls where the occupant was at home, entry was refused in 2,540 cases—approximately one out of six. This is a large percentage and would place an intolerable burden on the inspection service when required to secure warrants. What is more important is that out of the houses inspected 4,515 hazardous conditions were found! Hence, on the same percentage, there would be approximately 800 hazardous situations in the 2,540 in which inspection was refused in Portland. . . .

The majority seems to hold that warrants may be obtained after a refusal of initial entry; I can find no such constitutional distinction or command. This boxcar warrant will be identical as to every dwelling in the area, save the street number itself. I daresay they will be printed up in pads of a thousand or more—with space for the street number to be inserted—and issued by magistrates in broadcast fashion as a matter of course.

I ask: Why go through such an exercise, such a pretense? As the same essentials are being followed under the present procedures, I ask: Why the ceremony, the delay, the expense, the abuse of the search warrant? In my view this will not only destroy its integrity but will degrade the magistrate issuing them and soon bring disrepute not only upon the practice but upon the judicial process. It will be very costly to the city in paperwork incident to the issuance of the paper warrants, in loss of time of inspectors and waste of the time of magistrates and will result in more annoyance to the public. . . .

NOTES

1. Since *See* and *Camara*, the Court has dealt on three occasions with administrative searches:

a. In Colonnade Catering Corp. v. United States, 397 U.S. 72, 90 S.Ct. 774 (1970) the Court excluded evidence seized by federal agents who had, without a warrant, forcibly entered a locked storeroom on the premises of a federally licensed dealer in alcoholic beverages. The Court decided that the Act of Congress which authorized inspection of such premises did not authorize forcible entry. The statute took the alternative position of making it a criminal offense to refuse admission to the inspectors.

b. In Wyman v. James, 400 U.S. 309, 91 S.Ct. 381 (1971) the Court approved a state law which required welfare recipients to admit caseworkers into their homes or else face termination of benefits. The Court based its holding on several factors: the caseworkers are reasonably attempting to determine if aid is properly given to dependent children, the refusal to permit entry is not made a criminal offense, written notice of visits must be made several days in advance, forcible entry or entry under false pretenses is prohibited, visits must occur during normal working hours, the essential information secured by home visits is not available from other sources and the visit is not conducted by a law-enforcement officer looking for criminal violations.

c. In United States v. Biswell, 406 U.S. 311, 92 S.Ct. 1593 (1972) the Court approved a federal agent's inspection of a federally licensed gun dealer's storeroom. The gun dealer objected to the inspection but acquiesced upon being shown a copy of the federal statute specifically authorizing such inspections during business hours. The court distinguished *Colonnade* by asserting the absence of forcible entry and holding that submission by the dealer to *lawful* authority rather than risking a criminal charge by refusing entry is a valid basis for the inspector's entry into the storeroom. The Court also said:

"In See v. Seattle, supra, the mission of the inspection system was to discover and correct violations of the building code, conditions that were relatively difficult to conceal or to correct in a short time. Periodic inspection sufficed, and inspection warrants could be required and privacy given a measure of protection with little if any threat to the effectiveness of the inspection system there at issue. We expressly refrained in that case from questioning a warrantless regulatory search such as that authorized by § 923 of the Gun Control Act. Here, if inspection is to be effective and serve as a credible deterrent, unannounced, even frequent, inspections are essential. In this context, the prerequisite of a warrant could easily frustrate inspection; and if the necessary flexibility as to time, scope and frequency is to be preserved, the protections afforded by a warrant would be negligible."

2. There are many recognized forms of administrative searches or seizures which are permissible regardless of the absence of probable cause. Some common categories are these:

a. Border searches and customs inspections are exempt from the requirement of probable cause but must be reasonable. Border searches include searches well within the border or at checkpoints. Duprez v. United States, 435 F.2d 1276 (9th Cir. 1970), or searches where observation has been continuous since border was crossed. Thomas v. United States, 372 F.2d 252 (5th Cir. 1967); United States v. DeLeon, 462 F.2d 170 (5th Cir. 1972) (10 miles from border). Searches some distance from the border must be specially justified by circumstances known to the border officers although probable cause is not necessary. In striking down a search made sixty three miles from the border one Court required a special justification saying that "any other doctrine would render travelers who had recently entered this country subject to almost unlimited search and seizure without any cause save the simple request from a border official to one at an interior point." Marsh v. United States, 344 F.2d 317 (5th Cir. 1965). Ordinary border searches need not even be based on real suspicion but where the search extends to body cavities, a very real suspicion (although not necessarily amounting to probable cause) must be demonstrated. Henderson v. United States, 390 F.2d 805 (9th Cir. 1967). One court applied the real suspicion test to "mere" strip searches, United States v. Johnson, 425 F.2d

630 (9th Cir. 1970) (cert. granted but case later dismissed by stipulation of parties). Generally it is said that test should be different since search through underclothing that has been removed is less offensive than search through same clothing still being worn. People v. Eggleston, 15 Cal.App.3d 1026, 93 Cal.Rptr. 776 (1971). Border search theory has been extended to justify the search of a car believed to have been loaded with Mexican marijuana although car itself did not cross border. United States v. Markham, 440 F.2d 1119 (9th Cir. 1971).

b. In a related area, immigration authorities had been granted the right to make a random stop of automobiles within 100 miles of an international border and to look anywhere (in the trunk, under the seat) where an illegal alien might be hidden, but the Court overturned this practice in Almeida-Sanchez v. United States, 413 U.S. 266, 93 S.Ct. 2535 (1973). Almeida-Sanchez involved a Mexican alien, with a valid work permit, whose car was stopped and searched at a point 25 miles north of the Mexican border. A search of the trunk discovered marijuana for the possession of which the alien was convicted. Excerpts from the Court's opinion follow:

MR. JUSTICE STEWART delivered the opinion of the Court:

"The Border Patrol conducts three types of surveillance along inland roadways, all in the asserted interest of detecting the illegal importation of aliens. Permanent checkpoints are maintained at certain nodal intersections; temporary checkpoints are established from time to time at various places; and finally, there are roving patrols such as the one that stopped and searched the petitioner's car. In all of these operations, it is argued, the agents are acting within the Constitution when they stop and search automobiles without a warrant, without probable cause to believe the cars contain aliens, and even without probable cause to believe the cars have made a border crossing. The only asserted justification for this extravagant license to search is § 287(a) of the Immigration and Nationality Act, 8 U.S.C. § 1357(a), which simply provides for warrantless searches of automobiles and other conveyances 'within a reasonable distance from any external boundary of the United States,' as authorized by regulations to be promulgated by the Attorney General. The Attorney General's regulation, 8 CFR § 287.1, defines 'reasonable distance' as 'within 100 air miles from any external boundary of the United States.'

* * *

"In Camara v. Municipal Court, the Court held that administrative inspections to enforce community health and welfare regulations could be made on less than probable cause to believe that particular dwellings were the sites of particular violations. Yet the Court insisted that the inspector obtain either consent or a warrant supported by particular physical and demographic characteristics of the areas to be searched. The search in the present case was conducted in the unfettered discretion of the members of the Border Patrol, who did not have a warrant, probable cause, or consent. The search thus embodied precisely the evil the Court saw in *Camara* when it insisted that the 'discretion of the official in the field' be circumscribed by obtaining a warrant prior to the inspection.

Two other administrative inspection cases relied upon by the Government are equally inapposite. Colonnade Catering Corporation v. United

States and United States v. Biswell, both approved warrantless inspections of commercial enterprises engaged in businesses closely regulated and licensed by the Government. In *Colonnade,* the Court stressed the long history of federal regulation and taxation of the manufacture and sale of liquor. In *Biswell,* the Court noted the pervasive system of regulation and reporting imposed on licensed gun dealers.

* * *

"Moreover, in *Colonnade* and *Biswell,* the searching officers knew with certainty that the premises searched were in fact utilized for the sale of liquor or guns. In the present case, by contrast, there was no such assurance that the individual searched was within the proper scope of official scrutiny—that is, there was no reason whatever to believe that he or his automobile had even crossed the border, much less that he was guilty of the commission of an offense.

* * *

"[Here the statute merely] purports to authorize automobiles to be stopped and searched, without a warrant and 'within a reasonable distance from any external boundary of the United States.' It is clear, of course, that no Act of Congress can authorize a violation of the Constitution. But under familiar principles of constitutional adjudication, our duty is to construe the statute, if possible, in a manner consistent with the Fourth Amendment.

"It is undoubtedly within the power of the Federal Government to exclude aliens from the country. It is also without doubt that this power can be effectuated by routine inspections and searches of individuals or conveyances seeking to cross our borders. . . .

"Whatever the permissible scope of intrusiveness of a routine border search might be, searches of this kind may in certain circumstances take place not only at the border itself, but at its functional equivalents as well. For example, searches at an established station near the border, at a point marking the confluence of two or more roads that extend from the border, might be functional equivalents of border searches. For another example, a search of the passengers and cargo of an airplane arriving at a St. Louis airport after a nonstop flight from Mexico City would clearly be the functional equivalent of a border search.

"But the search of the petitioner's automobile by a roving patrol, on a California road that lies at all points at least 20 miles north of the Mexican border, was of a wholly different sort. In the absence of probable cause or consent, that search violated the petitioner's Fourth Amendment right to be free of 'unreasonable searches and seizures.'

MR. JUSTICE POWELL (concurring).

* * *

" . . . Nothing in the papers before us demonstrates that it would not be feasible for the Border Patrol to obtain advance judicial approval of the decision to conduct roving searches on a particular road or roads for a reasonable period of time. According to the Government, the incidence of illegal transportation of aliens on certain roads is predictable, and the roving searches are apparently planned in advance or carried out according to a predetermined schedule. The use of an area warrant procedure would surely not 'frustrate the governmental purpose behind the search.' Camara v. Municipal Court. It would of course entail some inconvenience, but inconvenience alone has never been thought to be an adequate reason for abrogating the warrant requirement.

"Although standards for probable cause in the context of this case are relatively unstructured (cf. United States v. United States District Court, supra, 407 U.S., at 322), there are a number of relevant factors which would merit consideration: they include (i) the frequency with which aliens illegally in the country are known or reasonably believed to be transported within a particular area; (ii) the proximity of the area in question to the border; (iii) the extensiveness and geographic characteristics of the area, including the roads therein and the extent of their use, and (iv) the probable degree of interference with the rights of innocent persons, taking into account the scope of the proposed search, its duration, and the concentration of illegal alien traffic in relation to the general traffic of the road or area.

* * *

"For the reasons stated above, I think a rational search warrant procedure is feasible in cases of this kind. As no warrant was obtained here, I agree that the judgment must be reversed. I express no opinion as to whether there was probable cause to issue a warrant on the facts of this particular case.

MR. JUSTICE WHITE with whom the CHIEF JUSTICE and JUSTICES BLACKMUN and REHNQUIST join, dissenting.

* * *

"Since 1875, Congress has given 'almost continuous attention . . . to the problems of immigration and of excludability of certain defined classes of aliens. The pattern generally has been one of increasing control . . . .' Kleindienst v. Mandel. It was only as the illegal entry of aliens multiplied that Congress addressed itself to enforcement mechanisms. In 1917, immigration authorities were authorized to board and search all conveyances by which aliens were being brought into the United States. Act of February 5, 1917, 39 Stat. 874, 886. This basic authority, substantially unchanged, is incorporated in 8 U.S.C. § 1225(a).

"In 1946, it was represented to Congress that '[i]n the enforcement of the immigration laws it is at times desirable to stop and search vehicles within a reasonable distance from the boundaries of the United States and legal right to do so should be conferred by law.' H.R.Rep.No.186, 79th Cong., 1st Sess. 2. The House Committee on Immigration and Naturalization was 'of the opinion that the legislation is highly desirable,' and its counterpart in the Senate, S.Rep.No.632, stated that '[t]here is no question but that this is a step in the right direction.' The result was express statutory authority, Act of August 7, 1946, 60 Stat. 865, to conduct searches of vehicles for aliens within a reasonable distance from the border without warrant or possible cause. Moreover, in the Immigration and Nationality Act of 1952, 66 Stat. 163, Congress permitted the entry of private lands, excluding dwellings, within a distance of 25 miles from any external boundaries of the country 'for the purpose of patrolling the borders to prevent the illegal entry of aliens into the United States . . . .'

"The judgment of Congress obviously was that there are circumstances in which it is reasonably necessary, in the enforcement of the immigration laws, to search vehicles and other private property for aliens, without warrant or probable cause, and at locations other than at the border. To disagree with this legislative judgment is to invalidate § 1357 in the face of the contrary opinion of Congress that its legislation comported with the standard of reasonableness of the Fourth Amendment. This I am quite unwilling to do.

"The external boundaries of the United States are extensive. The Canadian border is almost 4,000 miles in length; the Mexican, almost 2,000. Surveillance is maintained over the established channels and routes of communication. But not only is inspection at regular points of entry not infallible, but it is also physically impossible to maintain continuous patrol over vast stretches of our borders. The fact is that illegal crossings at other than the legal ports of entry are numerous and recurring. If there is to be any hope of intercepting illegal entrants and of maintaining any kind of credible deterrent, it is essential that permanent or temporary check points be maintained away from the borders, and roving patrols be conducted to discover and intercept illegal entrants as they filter to the established roads and highways and attempt to move away from the border area. It is for this purpose that the Border Patrol maintained the roving patrol involved in this case and conducted random, spot checks of automobiles and other vehicular traffic.

"The United States in this case reports that in fiscal year 1972, Border Patrol traffic checking operations located over 39,000 deportable aliens, of whom approximately 30,000 had entered the United States by illegally crossing the border at a place other than a port of entry. This was said to represent nearly 10% of the number of such aliens located by the Border Patrol by all means throughout the United States.

"Section 1357(a)(3) authorizes only searches for aliens and only searches of conveyances and other property. No searches of the person or for contraband are authorized by the section. The authority extended by the statute is limited to that reasonably necessary for the officer to assure himself that the vehicle or other conveyance is not carrying an alien who is illegally within this country; and more extensive searches of automobiles without probable cause are not permitted by the section. Guided by the principles of *Camara, Colonnade*, and *Biswell*, I cannot but uphold the judgment of Congress that for purposes of enforcing the immigration laws it is reasonable to treat the exterior boundaries of the country as a zone, not a line, and that there are recurring circumstances in which the search of vehicular traffic without warrant and without probable cause may be reasonable under the Fourth Amendment although not carried out at the border itself.

. . .

"I also think that § 1357(a) was validly applied in this case and that the search for aliens and the discovery of marihuana were not illegal under the Fourth Amendment. It was stipulated that the highway involved here was one of the few roads in California moving away from the Mexican border that did not have an established check station and that it is commonly used by alien smugglers to evade regular check points. The automobile, when stopped sometime after midnight, was 50 miles along the road from the border town of Calexico, proceeding toward Blythe, California; but as a matter of fact it appears that the point at which the car was stopped was approximately only 20 miles due north of the Mexican border. Given the large number of illegal entries across the Mexican border at other than established ports of entry, as well as the likelihood that many illegally entering aliens cross on foot and meet prearranged transportation in this country, I think that under all the circumstances the stop of petitioner's car was reasonable, as was the search for aliens under the rear seat of the car pursuant to an official bulletin suggesting search procedures based on experience. Given a valid search of the car for aliens, it is in no way contended that the discovery and seizure of the marihuana was contrary to law."

See also Abel v. United States, 362 U.S. 217, 80 S.Ct. 683 (1960) (immigration service administrative warrant approved).

c. Some cases hold that the Fourth Amendment is not violated when probationers or parolees are searched without probable cause. See People v. Chinnici, 51 Misc.2d 570, 273 N.Y.S.2d 538 (1966) (probationer's car by probation officer); People v. Adams, 36 App.Div.2d 784, 319 N.Y.S.2d 372 (1971) parolee's apartment by parole officer); United States ex rel. Santos v. New York State Board of Parole, 441 F.2d 1216 (2d Cir. 1971) (parolee's premises by parole officer); People v. Mason, 5 Cal.3d 759, 97 Cal.Rptr. 302, 488 P.2d 630 (1972) (warrantless search of probationer's apartment).

One possible limitation of searches of parolees and probationers may occur if the searches are conducted by parole or probation officers at the instance of the police or the prosecutor. If there is no legitimate relationship between the search and the parole or probation supervision of the subject, the search may be considered unjustifiably abusive. There have been warnings against the use of administrative searches solely for law enforcement purposes (Abel v. United States, 362 U.S. 217, 80 S.Ct. 683 (1960)), and one court has considered excluding parole search evidence from criminal cases. People v. Way, 65 Misc.2d 865, 319 N.Y.S.2d 16 (1971). In any event evidence seized during a parole or probation search would be admissible at a hearing to revoke parole or probation. See United States ex rel. Sperling v. Fitzpatrick, 426 F.2d 1161 (2nd Cir. 1970); United States ex rel. Lombardino v. Heyd, 318 F.Supp. 648 (E.D.La.1970).

d. Inspection of automobile identification numbers is valid on less than probable cause. United States v. Power, 439 F.2d 373 (4th Cir. 1971). Some courts do not consider such inspections to be searches. United States v. Ware, 457 F.2d 828 (7th Cir. 1972); United States v. Johnson, 431 F.2d 441 (5th Cir. 1970).

C. EMERGENCY SEARCHES

PATRICK v. STATE

Supreme Court of Delaware, 1967.
227 A.2d 486.

The defendant appeals from his conviction of murder in the second degree on the grounds . . . that evidence introduced at trial was illegally obtained.

The pertinent threshold facts are undisputed:

Ernest R. Patrick, the defendant, lived with Joseph Woods and Beverly Goodwyn. Beverly was Woods' mistress but she was also intimate with Patrick on occasion. On the night before the killing, Beverly and Woods had an altercation, over her leaving the house without him, during which Woods struck Beverly, drawing blood, and she attempted to cut him with a razor blade. Beverly and Patrick spent the next day and evening together. After some drinking, they returned to the Woods apartment about 11:00 P.M. En route, Beverly expressed fear of what Woods might do when they arrived. The door of the apartment was open; they entered the living room; and Beverly asked Patrick if Woods was in the bedroom. Patrick went to the bedroom and returned, saying that Woods was there.

Against this background, the jury heard Beverly, called by the State, testify as follows:

That after returning to the living room, Patrick stated that he was going to kill Woods; that Patrick picked up a brick supporting the sofa, entered the hallway, and turned toward the bedroom. Beverly testified that she heard noises which sounded like a brick hitting the bed and like Woods choking; that it did not sound like the brick was hitting Woods. Beverly testified that Patrick returned to the living room with blood on his hands, saying Woods was dead, and then went to the bathroom to wash his hands; that she went into the bedroom and saw Woods' bloody body on the bed; that, in response to her question, Patrick repeated that Woods was dead; that she and Patrick immediately left the apartment and returned to her sister's home where they spent the balance of the night.

Patrick, testifying in his own defense, stated that it was Beverly who took the brick from under the sofa, went to the bedroom, and killed Woods; that it was he in the living room, not Beverly, who heard the thuds of the blows.

Admitted in evidence was the shirt worn by Patrick on the night in question, bearing stains of Group A blood—Woods' blood type but not Patrick's. Also admitted were pieces of brick, stained with Group A blood, found on the bed and headboard, bloodstained bed clothing, and other items taken by the police from the room in which Woods' body was found. The State proved that the cause of Woods' death was depressed fracture of the skull. Patrick was indicted for murder in the second degree and was found guilty. He appeals. . . .

The defendant claims that articles introduced in evidence against him were obtained by the police by unlawful search and seizure. The facts pertinent to this issue are as follows:

Woods' body was discovered by his employer, W. A. Larrimore, on the morning after the killing. Larrimore found Woods in bed, a bloody "mess", with his head "beaten in with a brick." Larrimore, "panicked"; he could not tell whether Woods was dead or alive. He immediately called the police and, upon their arrival, stated that Woods had a head wound and might be dead. The police officers immediately entered the premises. They found Woods dead, with fragments of brick "five to six inches from his left ear"; and on the headboard of the bed they found half a brick bearing apparent blood stains. The police took photographs in the room, had the body removed, and took into custody the brick pieces, the bed clothing, Woods' clothing, and a wire cord. All items taken were open to view in the room in which the body was found. The police had no search warrant when they entered the premises.

The contention is now made that, absent a warrant, the articles were taken in violation of . . . the defendant's constitutional guaranties against unreasonable search and seizure; that the admission in evidence of such articles requires reversal of the conviction.

The basic question is whether the police were in the Woods apartment lawfully. That this question must be answered in the affirmative is obvious.

The general rules governing searches and seizures are subject to the exception of emergency situations, sometimes called the "exigency rule." The reasonableness of an entry by the police upon private property is measured by the circumstances then existing. The right of police to enter and investigate in an emergency, without an accompanying intent either to seize or arrest, is inherent in the very nature of their duties as peace officers, and derives from the common law. United States v. Barone (C.A.2) 330 F.2d 543 (1964). The preservation of human life is paramount to the right of privacy protected by search and seizure laws and constitutional guaranties; it is an overriding justification for what otherwise may be an illegal entry. It follows that a search warrant is not required to legalize an entry by police for the purpose of bringing emergency aid to an injured person. Frequently, the report of a death proves inaccurate and a spark of life remains, sufficient to respond to emergency police aid. As a general rule, we think, an emergency may be said to exist, within the meaning of the "exigency" rule, whenever the police have credible information that an unnatural death has, or may have, occurred. And the criterion is the reasonableness of the belief of the police as to the existence of an emergency, not the existence of an emergency in fact. Wayne v. United States, 115 U.S.App.D.C. 234, 318 F.2d 205 (1963); Davis v. State, 236 Md. 389, 204 A.2d 76 (1964); compare Miller v. United States, 357 U.S. 301, 78 S.Ct. 1190, 1200 (1958).

Applying these tenets to the instant case, we have no doubt that the entry of the police was reasonable under the circumstances. The officers were informed by Larrimore that Woods was dead or dying from a head wound. Clearly, the police had good reason to believe that a life was in balance and that emergency aid might be needed. Under the circumstances, it was the duty of the police to act forthwith upon the report of the emergency—not to speculate upon the accuracy of the report or upon legal technicalities regarding search warrants. It follows that the entry by the police was reasonable and lawful.

After the entry, there was no further search by the officers. All articles taken were in open view in the room in which the body was found. The seizure of evidence in open view upon a lawful entry violates no right of privacy. Wayne v. United States, supra. That which is in open view is not the product of a search. United States v. Barone, supra; Ker v. State of California, 374 U.S. 23, 36–37, 83 S.Ct. 1623, 1635 (1963).

Accordingly, we conclude that there was no violation of statute or constitutional guaranty as to the evidence here in question. . . .

NOTE

1. If the police enter a dwelling under emergency circumstances and discover a corpse or a seriously wounded person, may they inspect the premises (presumably after the dead or injured are removed)? One court has held that a further search may be made only after securing a warrant. See State v. Pires, 55 Wis.2d 597, 201 N.W.2d 153 (1972).

Compare State v. Davidson, 44 Wis.2d 177, 170 N.W.2d 755 (1969). Other courts have sustained such searches. United States v. Birrell, 470 F.2d 113, 116–17 (2nd Cir. 1972). Thomas v. State, 118 Ga.App. 359, 163 S.E.2d 850 (1968); Palmore v. State, 283 Ala. 501, 218 So.2d 830 (1969). The Supreme Judicial Court of Maine concurred:

"We are satisfied that if the police cannot after lawful entry make the sort of prompt, orderly and methodical investigation of the scene of a violent death . . . the protection of the legitimate interests of society will be seriously weakened." State v. Chapman, 250 A.2d 203, 207—12 (Me. 1969).

The rules governing emergency searches are reviewed in People v. Sirhan, 7 Cal.3d 369, 710, 497 P.2d 1121 (1972) (holding that the mere possibility that evidence of a conspiracy to assassinate prominent political leaders justifies entry and search of the home of the person accused of killing a presidential candidate).

2. In United States v. Dunavan, 485 F.2d 201 (6th Cir.1973) the Court affirmed an "emergency" search of substantial scope:

"At about 4 p. m. on Sunday, May 17, 1970, Dunavan was found by passers-by at a beach near Pensacola, Florida, in a disabled car which had set the grass on fire below it. He was foaming at the mouth and unable to talk. They removed him from the car, put out the fire, and went through the automobile seeking to identify him, thereby finding a Social Security card, $961 in cash, a motel key, and a car rental agreement for the automobile in appellant Mitchell's name. They also found two locked briefcases and called the police. All of these items were turned over to a Deputy Sheriff, who dispatched Dunavan to the hospital and then went to the motel, taking the briefcases with him. He testified that he and other officers who saw Dunavan at the scene 'thought he was going to die,' and that he and two other officers entered Dunavan's motel room with the key which had been turned over to him:

> So, we decided to go on in the room and see if we could find some identification or information or something to give the hospital about Mr. Dunavan.

"In the motel room the officers found two small keys which opened one of the briefcases. It was full of money, banded with Green Hills Branch Bank bands, marked with red dye and smelling of gas. Some of the money was "bait" money (identifiable) and the dye and gas resulted from a bank anti-robbery device.

"The officers had seen a woman emerge from an adjoining room as they arrived and had seen that the door was open between the two rooms. On questioning this woman they learned that one of two men occupying the rooms was a diabetic and kept his insulin in one of the briefcases. After an officer was sent to the hospital to get a key to it from Dunavan, this case was then opened. The insulin and a syringe were found, along with a lot more money marked like the money in the first case.

" . . .

"The District Judge made the following findings:

" . . . 'that the defendant was brought to the hospital on May 17, 1970, while unconscious, and was given an intravenous injection of Sodium Amytal at 4:43 p. m., was finally given an injection of Dextrose at approximately 6:25 p. m., and, as a result of the latter injection, regained consciousness sometime after 6:30 p. m. He definitely was not conscious before the 6:25 injection. The Court also finds that the police officers entered the motel room at approximately 5:15 p. m. on the same day and that the first briefcase was opened a few minutes thereafter, probably about 5:20 p. m. It is manifestly clear, therefore, that the police not only did not know the defendant had regained consciousness when they entered the room and when they opened the first briefcase, he in fact had not regained consciousness at those times.'

" . . . The District Judge . . . denied the motion to suppress evidence, holding that the officers' conduct was pursuant to a lawful life-saving mission. . . .

"Appellants, as we read their briefs, do not appear to dispute the proposition that a lawful entry on private premises may be made by law enforcement officers for emergency life-saving measures.

"No emergency life-saving exception to the Fourth Amendment's warrant requirement appears to have been spelled out in any Supreme Court case up to this point. But cases in both the Eighth Circuit and the Second Circuit do support it.

"In one of these, the Eighth Circuit said:

> For purposes of the instant case, the emergency or exigency doctrine may be stated as follows: police officers may enter a dwelling without a warrant to render emergency aid and assistance to a person whom they reasonably believe to be in distress and in need of that assistance.

. . .

"If anything, the Second Circuit's holding is more emphatic:

> The right of the police to enter and investigate in an emergency without the accompanying intent to either search or arrest is inherent in the very nature of their duties as peace officers, and derives from the common law. See generally Read v. Case, 4 Conn. 166 (1822). Indeed it is obvious that had the patrolmen been denied entry to the apartment they would have had the right, if not the duty, to gain entry forcibly. United States v. Barone, 330 F.2d 543, 545 (2d Cir.).

"We are aware that there may be cases where police assertions of Good Samaritan motives might (as charged here) be pretextual rather than real. On the other hand, particularly in big city life, the Good Samaritan of today is more likely to wear a blue coat than any other. While we believe the government would have the burden of proving the defense (as it clearly has done here), we agree with the holdings of the Eighth and Second Circuits quoted above, that a legitimate life-saving purpose may provide another example of the exigent circumstances which excuse failure to follow the warrant requirements of the Fourth Amendment."

Chapter 14

COURT COMPELLED EVIDENCE

A. NON-TESTIMONIAL EVIDENCE

SCHMERBER v. CALIFORNIA

Supreme Court of the United States, 1966.
384 U.S. 757, 86 S.Ct. 1826.

MR. JUSTICE BRENNAN delivered the opinion of the Court.

Petitioner was convicted in Los Angeles Municipal Court of the criminal offense of driving an automobile while under the influence of intoxicating liquor. He had been arrested at a hospital while receiving treatment for injuries suffered in an accident involving the automobile that he had apparently been driving. At the direction of a police officer, a blood sample was then withdrawn from petitioner's body by a physician at the hospital. The chemical analysis of this sample revealed a percent by weight of alcohol in his blood at the time of the offense which indicated intoxication, and the report of this analysis was admitted in evidence at the trial. Petitioner objected to receipt of this evidence of the analysis on the ground that the blood had been withdrawn despite his refusal, on the advice of his counsel, to consent to the test. He contended that in that circumstance the withdrawal of the blood and the admission of the analysis in evidence denied him due process of law under the Fourteenth Amendment, as well as specific guarantees of the Bill of Rights secured against the States by that Amendment; his privilege against self-incrimination under the Fifth Amendment; his right to counsel under the Sixth Amendment; and his right not to be subjected to unreasonable searches and seizures in violation of the Fourth Amendment. The Appellate Department of the California Superior Court rejected these contentions and affirmed the conviction. In view of constitutional decisions since we last considered these issues we granted certiorari. We affirm.

I.

THE DUE PROCESS CLAUSE CLAIM.

[Breithaupt v. Abram, 352 U.S. 432, 77 S.Ct. 408] was also a case in which police officers caused blood to be withdrawn from the driver of an automobile involved in an accident, and in which there was ample justification for the officer's conclusion that the driver was under the influence of alcohol. There, as here, the extraction was made by a physician in a simple, medically acceptable manner in a hospital environment.

There, however, the driver was unconscious at the time the blood was withdrawn and hence had no opportunity to object to the procedure. We affirmed the conviction there resulting from the use of the test in evidence, holding that under such circumstances the withdrawal did not offend "that 'sense of justice' of which we spoke in Rochin v. [People of] California, 1952, 342 U.S. 165, 72 S.Ct. 205." *Breithaupt* thus requires the rejection of petitioner's due process argument, and nothing in the circumstances of this case [1] or in supervening events persuades us that this aspect of *Breithaupt* should be overruled.

II.

THE PRIVILEGE AGAINST SELF-INCRIMINATION CLAIM.

Breithaupt summarily rejected an argument that the withdrawal of blood and the admission of the analysis report involved in that state case violated the Fifth Amendment privilege of any person not to "be compelled in any criminal case to be a witness against himself," citing Twining v. State of New Jersey, 211 U.S. 78, 29 S.Ct. 14. But that case, holding that the protections of the Fourteenth Amendment do not embrace this Fifth Amendment privilege, has been succeeded by Malloy v. Hogan, 378 U.S. 1, 8, 84 S.Ct. 1489, 1493. We there held that "[t]he Fourteenth Amendment secures against state invasion the same privilege that the Fifth Amendment guarantees against federal infringement—the right of a person to remain silent unless he chooses to speak in the unfettered exercise of his own will, and to suffer no penalty . . . for such silence." We therefore must now decide whether the withdrawal of the blood and admission in evidence of the analysis involved in this case violated petitioner's privilege. We hold that the privilege protects an accused only from being compelled to testify against himself, or otherwise provide the State with evidence of a testimonial or communicative nature,[2] and that the withdrawal

1. We "cannot see that it should make any difference whether one states unequivocally that he objects or resorts to physical violence in protest or is in such condition that he is unable to protest." Breithaupt v. Abram. It would be a different case if the police initiated the violence, refused to respect a reasonable request to undergo a different form of testing, or responded to resistance with inappropriate force.

2. A dissent suggests that the report of the blood test was "testimonial" or "communicative," because the test was performed in order to obtain the testimony of others, communicating to the jury facts about petitioner's condition. Of course, all evidence received in court is "testimonial" or "communicative" if these words are thus used. But the Fifth Amendment relates only to acts on the part of the person to whom the privilege applies, and we use these words subject to the same limitations. A nod or headshake is as much a "testimonial" or "communicative" act in this sense as are spoken words. But the terms as we use them do not apply to evidence of acts noncommunicative in nature as to the person asserting the privilege, even though, as here, such acts are compelled to obtain the testimony of others.

of blood and use of the analysis in question in this case did not involve compulsion to these ends.

It could not be denied that in requiring petitioner to submit to the withdrawal and chemical analysis of his blood the State compelled him to submit to an attempt to discover evidence that might be used to prosecute him for a criminal offense. He submitted only after the police officer rejected his objection and directed the physician to proceed. The officer's direction to the physician to administer the test over petitioner's objection constituted compulsion for the purposes of the privilege. The critical question, then, is whether petitioner was thus compelled "to be a witness against himself." [3]

If the scope of the privilege coincided with the complex of values it helps to protect, we might be obliged to conclude that the privilege was violated. In Miranda v. Arizona, 384 U.S. 436, at 460, 86 S.Ct. 1602, at 1620, the Court said of the interests protected by the privilege: "All these policies point to one overriding thought: the constitutional foundation underlying the privilege is the respect a government—state or federal—must accord to the dignity and integrity of its citizens. To maintain a 'fair state-individual balance,' to require the government 'to shoulder the entire load,' . . . to respect the inviolability of the human personality, our accusatory system of criminal justice demands that the government seeking to punish an individual produce the evidence against him by its own independent labors, rather than by the cruel, simple expedient of compelling it from his own mouth." The withdrawal of blood necessarily involves puncturing the skin for extraction, and the percent by weight of alcohol in that blood, as established by chemical analysis, is evidence of criminal guilt. Compelled submission fails on one view to respect the "inviolability of the human personality." Moreover, since it enables the State to rely on evidence forced from the accused, the compulsion violates at least one meaning of the requirement that the State procure the evidence against an accused "by its own independent labors."

As the passage in *Miranda* implicitly recognizes, however, the privilege has never been given the full scope which the values it helps to protect suggest. History and a long line of authorities in lower

3. Many state constitutions, including those of most of the original Colonies, phrase the privilege in terms of compelling a person to give "evidence" against himself. But our decision cannot turn on the Fifth Amendment's use of the word "witness." "[A]s the manifest purpose of the constitutional provisions, both of the states and of the United States, is to prohibit the compelling of testimony of a self-incriminating kind from a party or a witness, the liberal construction which must be placed upon constitutional provisions for the protection of personal rights would seem to require that the constitutional guaranties, however differently worded, should have as far as possible the same interpretation . . . ." Counselman v. Hitchcock, 142 U.S. 547, 584–585, 12 S.Ct. 195, 206. 8 Wigmore, Evidence § 2252 (McNaughton rev. 1961).

courts have consistently limited its protection to situations in which the State seeks to submerge those values by obtaining the evidence against an accused through "the cruel, simple expedient of compelling it from his own mouth. . . . In sum, the privilege is fulfilled only when the person is guaranteed the right 'to remain silent unless he chooses to speak in the unfettered exercise of his own will.'" The leading case in this Court is Holt v. United States, 218 U.S. 245, 31 S.Ct. 2. There the question was whether evidence was admissible that the accused, prior to trial and over his protest, put on a blouse that fitted him. It was contended that compelling the accused to submit to the demand that he model the blouse violated the privilege. Mr. Justice Holmes, speaking for the Court, rejected the argument as "based upon an extravagant extension of the 5th Amendment," and went on to say: "[T]he prohibition of compelling a man in a criminal court to be witness against himself is a prohibition of the use of physical or moral compulsion to extort communications from him, not an exclusion of his body as evidence when it may be material. The objection in principle would forbid a jury to look at a prisoner and compare his features with a photograph in proof." [4]

It is clear that the protection of the privilege reaches an accused's communications, whatever form they might take, and the compulsion of responses which are also communications, for example, compliance with a subpoena to produce one's papers. Boyd v. United States, 116 U.S. 616, 6 S.Ct. 524. On the other hand, both federal and state courts have usually held that it offers no protection against compulsion to submit to fingerprinting, photographing, or measurements, to write or speak for identification, to appear in court, to stand, to assume a stance, to walk, or to make a particular gesture. The distinction which has emerged, often expressed in different ways, is that the privilege is a bar against compelling "communications" or "testimony," but that compulsion which makes a suspect or accused the source of "real or physical evidence" does not violate it.

Although we agree that this distinction is a helpful framework for analysis, we are not to be understood to agree with past applications in all instances. There will be many cases in which such a distinction is not readily drawn. Some tests seemingly directed to obtain "physical evidence," for example, lie detector tests measuring changes in body function during interrogation, may actually be directed to eliciting responses which are essentially testimonial. To compel a person to submit to testing in which an effort will be made to determine his guilt or innocence on the basis of physiological responses, whether willed or not, is to evoke the spirit and history of the Fifth

4. Compare Wigmore's view, "that the privilege is limited to testimonial disclosures. It was directed at the employment of legal process to *extract from the person's own lips* an admission of guilt, which would thus take the place of other evidence." 8 Wigmore, Evidence § 2263 (McNaughton rev. 1961). California adopted the Wigmore formulation. Our holding today, however, is not to be understood as adopting the Wigmore formulation.

Amendment. Such situations call to mind the principle that the protection of the privilege "is as broad as the mischief against which it seeks to guard." Counselman v. Hitchcock, 142 U.S. 547, 562.

In the present case, however, no such problem of application is presented. Not even a shadow of testimonial compulsion upon or enforced communication by the accused was involved either in the extraction or in the chemical analysis. Petitioner's testimonial capacities were in no way implicated; indeed, his participation, except as a donor, was irrelevant to the results of the test, which depend on chemical analysis and on that alone.[5] Since the blood test evidence, although an incriminating product of compulsion, was neither petitioner's testimony nor evidence relating to some communicative act or writing by the petitioner, it was not inadmissible on privilege grounds.

III.

THE RIGHT TO COUNSEL CLAIM.

This conclusion also answers petitioner's claim that, in compelling him to submit to the test in face of the fact that his objection was made on the advice of counsel, he was denied his Sixth Amendment right to the assistance of counsel. Since petitioner was not entitled to assert the privilege, he has no greater right because counsel erroneously advised him that he could assert it. His claim is strictly limited to the failure of the police to respect his wish, reinforced by counsel's advice to be left inviolate. No issue of counsel's ability to assist petitioner in respect of any rights he did possess is presented. The limited claim thus made must be rejected.

5. This conclusion would not necessarily govern had the State tried to show that the accused had incriminated himself when told that he would have to be tested. Such incriminating evidence may be an unavoidable by-product of the compulsion to take the test, especially for an individual who fears the extraction or opposes it on religious grounds. If it wishes to compel persons to submit to such attempts to discover evidence, the State may have to forego the advantage of any *testimonial* products of administering the test—products which would fall within the privilege. Indeed, there may be circumstances in which the pain, danger, or severity of an operation would almost inevitably cause a person to prefer confession to undergoing the "search," and nothing we say today should be taken as establishing the permissibility of compulsion in that case. But no such situation is presented in this case. Petitioner has raised a similar issue in this case, in connection with a police request that he submit to a "breathalyzer" test of air expelled from his lungs for alcohol content. He refused the request, and evidence of his refusal was admitted in evidence without objection. He argues that the introduction of this evidence and a comment by the prosecutor in closing argument upon his refusal is ground for reversal under Griffin v. State of California, 380 U.S. 609, 85 S.Ct. 1229. We think general Fifth Amendment principles, rather than the particular holding of *Griffin*, would be applicable in these circumstances. Since trial here was conducted after our decision in Malloy v. Hogan, supra, making those principles applicable to the States, we think petitioner's contention is foreclosed by his failure to object on this ground to the prosecutor's question and statements.

IV.

The Search and Seizure Claim.

In *Breithaupt*, as here, it was also contended that the chemical analysis should be excluded from evidence as the product of an unlawful search and seizure in violation of the Fourth and Fourteenth Amendments. The Court did not decide whether the extraction of blood in that case was unlawful, but rejected the claim on the basis of Wolf v. People of State of Colorado, 338 U.S. 25, 69 S.Ct. 1359. That case had held that the Constitution did not require, in state prosecutions for state crimes, the exclusion of evidence obtained in violation of the Fourth Amendment's provisions. We have since overruled *Wolf* in that respect, holding in Mapp v. Ohio that the exclusionary rule adopted for federal prosecutions must also be applied in criminal prosecutions in state courts. The question is squarely presented therefore, whether the chemical analysis introduced in evidence in this case should have been excluded as the product of an unconstitutional search and seizure.

The overriding function of the Fourth Amendment is to protect personal privacy and dignity against unwarranted intrusion by the State . . .

The values protected by the Fourth Amendment thus substantially overlap those the Fifth Amendment helps to protect. History and precedent have required that we today reject the claim that the Self-Incrimination Clause of the Fifth Amendment requires the human body in all circumstances to be held inviolate against state expeditions seeking evidence of crime. But if compulsory administration of a blood test does not implicate the Fifth Amendment, it plainly involves the broadly conceived reach of a search and seizure under the Fourth Amendment. That Amendment expressly provides that "[t]he right of the people to be secure in their *persons*, houses, papers, and effects, against unreasonable searches and seizures, shall not be violated . . . ." (Emphasis added.) It could not reasonably be argued, and indeed respondent does not argue, that the administration of the blood test in this case was free of the constraints of the Fourth Amendment. Such testing procedures plainly constitute searches of "persons," and depend antecedently upon seizures of "persons," within the meaning of that Amendment.

Because we are dealing with intrusions into the human body rather than with state interferences with property relationships or private papers—"houses, papers, and effects"—we write on a clean slate. Limitations on the kinds of property which may be seized under warrant, as distinct from the procedures for search and the permissible scope of search, are not instructive in this context. We begin with the assumption that once the privilege against self-incrimination has been found not to bar compelled intrusions into the body for blood to be analyzed for alcohol content, the Fourth Amendment's proper function is to constrain, not against all intrusions as such, but against intrusions which are not justified in the circumstances, or which are made in an improper manner. In other words, the questions we must decide in this case are whether the police were justified in requiring petitioner to submit to the blood test, and whether the means and procedures employed in taking his blood respected relevant Fourth Amendment standards of reasonableness.

In this case, as will often be true when charges of driving under the influence of alcohol are pressed, these questions arise in the context of an arrest made by an officer without a warrant. Here, there was plainly probable cause for the officer to arrest petitioner and charge him with driving an automobile while under the influence of intoxicating liquor. The police officer who arrived at the scene shortly after the accident smelled liquor on petitioner's breath, and testified that petitioner's eyes were "bloodshot, watery, sort of a glassy appearance." The officers saw petitioner again at the hospital, within two hours of the accident. There he noticed similar symptoms of drunkenness. He thereupon informed petitioner "that he was under arrest and that he was entitled to the services of an attorney, and that he could remain silent, and that anything that he told me would be used against him in evidence."

While early cases suggest that there is an unrestricted "right on the part of the government always recognized under English and American law, to search the person of the accused when legally arrested, to discover and seize the fruits or evidences of crime," the mere fact of a lawful arrest does not end our inquiry. The suggestion of these cases apparently rests on two factors—first, there may be more immediate danger of concealed weapons or of destruction of evidence under the direct control of the accused; second, once a search of the arrested person for weapons is permitted, it would be both impractical and unnecessary to enforcement of the Fourth Amendment's purpose to attempt to confine the search to those objects alone. Whatever the validity of these considerations in general, they have little applicability with respect to searches involving intrusions beyond the body's surface. The interests in human dignity and privacy which the Fourth Amendment protects forbid any such intrusions on the mere chance that desired evidence might be obtained. In the absence of a clear indication that in fact such evidence will be found, these fundamental human interests require law officers to suffer the risk that such evidence may disappear unless there is an immediate search.

Although the facts which established probable cause to arrest in this case also suggested the required relevance and likely success of a test of petitioner's blood for alcohol, the question remains whether the arresting officer was permitted to draw these inferences himself, or was required instead to procure a warrant before proceeding with the test. Search warrants are ordinarily required for searches of dwellings, and absent an emergency, no less could be required where intrusions into the human body are concerned. The requirement that a warrant be obtained is a requirement that inferences to support the search "be drawn by a neutral and detached magistrate instead of being judged by the officer engaged in the often competitive enterprise of ferreting out crime." The importance of informed, detached and deliberate determinations of the issue whether or not to invade another's body in search of evidence of guilt is indisputable and great.

The officer in the present case, however, might reasonably have believed that he was confronted with an emergency, in which the delay necessary to obtain a warrant, under the circumstances, threatened "the destruction of evidence." We are told that the percentage of alcohol in the blood begins to diminish shortly after drinking stops, as the body functions to eliminate it from the system. Particularly in a case such as this, where time had to be taken to bring the accused to a hospital and to investigate the scene of the accident, there was no time to seek out a magistrate and secure a warrant. Given these special facts, we conclude that the attempt to secure evidence of blood-alcohol content in this case was an appropriate incident to petitioner's arrest.

Similarly, we are satisfied that the test chosen to measure petitioner's blood-alcohol level was a reasonable one. Extraction of blood samples for testing is a highly effective means of determining the degree to which a person is under the influence of alcohol. Such tests are a commonplace in these days of periodic physical examinations and experience with them teaches that the quantity of blood extracted is minimal, and that for most people the procedure involves virtually no risk, trauma, or pain. Petitioner is not one of the few who on grounds of fear, concern for health, or religious scruple might prefer some other means of testing, such as the "breathalyzer" test petitioner refused. We need not decide whether such wishes would have to be respected.

Finally, the record shows that the test was performed in a reasonable manner. Petitioner's blood was taken by a physician in a hospital environment according to accepted medical practices. We are thus not presented with the serious questions which would arise if a search involving use of a medical technique, even of the most rudimentary sort, were made by other than medical personnel or in other than a medical environment—for example, if it were administered by police in the privacy of the stationhouse. To tolerate searches under these conditions might be to invite an unjustified element of personal risk of infection and pain.

We thus conclude that the present record shows no violation of petitioner's right under the Fourth and Fourteenth Amendments to be free of unreasonable searches and seizures. It bears repeating, however, that we reach this judgment only on the facts of the present record. The integrity of an individual's person is a cherished value of our society. That we today hold that the Constitution does not forbid the State's minor intrusions into an individual's body under stringently limited conditions in no way indicates that it permits more substantial intrusions, or intrusions under other conditions.

Affirmed.

MR. JUSTICE HARLAN, whom MR. JUSTICE STEWART joins, concurring.

In joining the Court's opinion I desire to add the following comment. While agreeing with the Court that the taking of this blood test involved no testimonial compulsion, I would go further and hold that apart from this consideration the case in no way implicates the Fifth Amendment. Cf. my dissenting opinion and that of Mr. Justice White in Miranda v. Arizona, 384 U.S. 504, 526, 86 S.Ct. 1643, 1655.

MR. CHIEF JUSTICE WARREN, dissenting.

While there are other important constitutional issues in this case, I believe it is sufficient for me to reiterate my dissenting opinion in Breithaupt v. Abram, as the basis on which to reverse this conviction.

MR. JUSTICE BLACK with whom MR. JUSTICE DOUGLAS joins, dissenting.

I would reverse petitioner's conviction. I agree with the Court that the Fourteenth Amendment made applicable to the States the Fifth Amendment's provision that "No person . . . shall be compelled in any criminal case to be a witness against himself . . . ." But I disagree with the Court's holding that California did not violate petitioner's constitutional right against self-incrimination when it compelled him, against his will, to allow a doctor to puncture his blood vessels in order to extract a sample of blood and analyze it for alcoholic content, and then used that analysis as evidence to convict petitioner of a crime.

The Court admits that "the State compelled [petitioner] to submit to an attempt to discover evidence [in his blood] that might be [and was] used to prosecute him for a criminal offense." To reach the conclusion that compelling a person to give his blood to help the State convict him is not equivalent to compelling him to be a witness against himself strikes me as quite an extraordinary feat. The Court, however, overcomes what had seemed to me to be an insuperable obstacle to its conclusion by holding that

> ". . . the privilege protects an accused only from being compelled to testify against himself, or otherwise provide the State with evidence of a testimonial or communicative nature, and that the withdrawal of blood and use of the analysis in question in this case did not involve compulsion to these ends."

I cannot agree that this distinction and reasoning of the Court justify denying petitioner his Bill of Rights' guarantee that he must not be compelled to be a witness against himself.

In the first place it seems to me that the compulsory extraction of petitioner's blood for analysis so that the person who analyzed it could give evidence to convict him had both a "testimonial" and a "communicative nature." The sole purpose of this project which proved to be successful was to obtain "testimony" from some person to prove that petitioner had alcohol in his blood at the time he was arrested. And the purpose of the project was certainly "communicative" in that the analysis of the blood was to supply information to enable a witness to communicate to the court and jury that petitioner was more or less drunk.

I think it unfortunate that the Court rests so heavily for its very restrictive reading of the Fifth Amendment's privilege against self-incrimination on the words "testimonial" and "communicative." These words are not models of clarity and precision as the Court's rather labored explication shows. Nor can the Court, so far as I know, find precedent in the former opinions of this Court for using these particular words to limit the scope of the Fifth Amendment's protection. There is a scholarly precedent, however, in the late Professor Wigmore's learned treatise on evidence. He used "testimonial" which, according to the latest edition of his treatise revised by McNaughton, means "communicative" (8 Wigmore, Evidence § 2263 (McNaughton rev. 1961), p. 378), as a key word in his vigorous and extensive campaign designed to keep the privilege against self-incrimination "within limits the strictest possible." 8 Wigmore, Evidence § 2251 (3d ed. 1940), p. 318. Though my admiration for Professor Wigmore's scholarship is great, I regret to see the word he used to narrow the Fifth Amendment's protection play such a major part in any of this Court's opinions.

I am happy that the Court itself refuses to follow Professor Wigmore's implication that the Fifth Amendment goes no further than to bar the use of forced self-incriminating statements coming from a "person's own lips." It concedes, as it must so long as Boyd v. United States, stands, that the Fifth Amendment bars a State from compelling a person to produce papers he has that might tend to incriminate him. It is a strange hierarchy of values that allows the State to extract a human being's blood to convict him of a crime because of the blood's content but proscribes compelled production of his lifeless papers. Certainly there could be few papers that would have any more "testimonial" value to convict a man of drunken driving than would an analysis of the alcoholic content of a human being's blood introduced in evidence at a trial for driving while under the influence of alcohol. In such a situation blood, of course, is not oral testimony given by an accused but it can certainly "communicate" to a court and jury the fact of guilt.

The Court itself expresses its own doubts, if not fears, of its own shadowy distinction between compelling "physical evidence" like blood which it holds does not amount to compelled self-incrimination, and "eliciting responses which are essentially testimonial." And in explanation of its fears the Court goes on to warn that

> "To compel a person to submit to testing [by lie detectors for example] in which an effort will be made to determine his guilt or innocence on the basis of physiological responses, whether willed or not, is to evoke the spirit and history of the Fifth Amendment. Such situations call to mind the principle that the protection of the privilege 'is as broad as the mischief against which it seeks to guard.' Counselman v. Hitchcock."

A basic error in the Court's holding and opinion is its failure to give the Fifth Amendment's protection against compulsory self-incrimination the broad and liberal construction that *Counselman* and other opinions of this Court have declared it ought to have.

The liberal construction given the Bill of Rights' guarantee in Boyd v. United States, supra, which Professor Wigmore criticized severely, see 8 Wigmore, Evidence, § 2264 (3d ed. 1940), pp. 366–373, makes that one among the greatest constitutional decisions of this Court. In that case all the members of the Court decided that civil suits for penalties and forfeitures incurred for commission of offenses against the law,

> ". . . are within the reason of criminal proceedings for all the purposes of . . . that portion of the fifth amendment which declares that no person shall be compelled in any criminal case to be a witness against himself; . . . within the meaning of the fifth amendment to the constitution . . . ."

Obviously the Court's interpretation was not completely supported by the literal language of the Fifth Amendment. Recognizing this, the Court announced a rule of constitutional interpretation that has been generally followed ever since, particularly in judicial construction of Bill of Rights guarantees:

> "A close and literal construction [of constitutional provisions for the security of persons and property] deprives them of half their efficacy, and leads to gradual depreciation of the right, as if it consisted more in sound than in substance. It is the duty of courts to be watchful for the constitutional rights of the citizen, and against any stealthy encroachments thereon."

The Court went on to say, at 637, 6 S.Ct. at 536, that to require "an owner to produce his private books and papers, in order to prove his breach of the laws, and thus to establish the forfeiture of his property, is surely compelling him to furnish evidence against himself." The Court today departs from the teachings of *Boyd*. Petitioner Schmerber has undoubtedly been compelled to give his blood "to furnish evidence against himself," yet the Court holds that this is not forbidden by the Fifth Amendment. With all deference I must say that the Court here gives the Bill of Rights' safeguard against compulsory self-incrimination a construction that would generally be considered too narrow and technical even in the interpretation of an ordinary commercial contract.

The Court apparently, for a reason I cannot understand, finds some comfort for its narrow construction of the Fifth Amendment in this Court's decision in Miranda v. Arizona. I find nothing whatever in the majority opinion in that case which either directly or indirectly supports the holding in this case. In fact I think the interpretive constitutional philosophy used in *Miranda*, unlike that used in this case, gives the Fifth Amendment's prohibition against compelled self-incrimination a broad and liberal construction in line with the wholesome admonitions in the *Boyd* case. The closing sentence in the Fifth Amendment section of the Court's opinion in the present case is enough by itself, I think, to expose the unsoundness of what the Court here holds. That sentence reads:

> "Since the blood test evidence, although an incriminating product of compulsion, was neither petitioner's testimony nor evidence relating to some communicative act or writing by the petitioner, it was not inadmissible on privilege grounds."

How can it reasonably be doubted that the blood test evidence was not in all respects the actual equivalent of "testimony" taken from petitioner when the result of the test was offered as testimony, was considered by the jury as testimony, and the jury's verdict of guilt rests in part on that testimony? The refined, subtle reasoning and balancing process used here to narrow the scope of the Bill of Rights' safeguard against self-incrimination provides a handy instrument for further narrowing of that constitutional protection, as well as others, in the future. Believing with the Framers that these constitutional safeguards broadly construed by independent tribunals of justice provide our best hope for keeping our people free from governmental oppression, I deeply regret the Court's holding. . . .

MR. JUSTICE DOUGLAS, dissenting.

I adhere to the views of The Chief Justice in his dissent in Breithaupt v. Abram, and to the views I stated in my dissent in that case and add only a word.

We are dealing with the right of privacy which, since the *Breithaupt* case, we have held to be within the penumbra of some specific guarantees of the Bill of Rights. Thus, the Fifth Amendment marks "a zone of privacy" which the Government may not force a person to surrender. Likewise the Fourth Amendment recognizes that right when it guarantees the right of the people to be secure "in their persons." Ibid. No clearer invasion of this right of privacy can be imagined than forcible bloodletting of the kind involved here.

MR. JUSTICE FORTAS, dissenting.

I would reverse. In my view, petitioner's privilege against self-incrimination applies. I would add that, under the Due Process Clause, the State, in its role as prosecutor, has no right to extract blood from an accused or anyone else, over his protest. As prosecutor, the State has no right to commit any kind of violence upon the person, or to utilize the results of such a tort, and the extraction of blood, over protest, is an act of violence. . . .

NOTES

1. Consider the following alternative to the procedure utilized by the police in the *Schmerber* case. It is known as an "Implied Consent Law". This one appears in the McKinney's New York Vehicle and Traffic Law, § 1194:

"1. Any person who operates a motor vehicle or motorcycle in this state shall be deemed to have given his consent to a chemical test of his breath, blood, urine, or saliva for the purpose of determining the alcoholic or drug content of his blood provided that such test is administered at the direction of a police officer having reasonable grounds to believe such person to have been driving in an intoxicated condition, or while his ability to operate such motor vehicle or motorcycle was impaired by the consumption of alcohol or the use of a drug as defined in this chapter, and in accordance with the rules and regulations established by the police force of which he is a member. If such person having been placed under arrest and having thereafter been requested to submit to such chemical test refuses to submit to such chemical test, the test shall not be given, but the commissioner shall revoke his license or permit to drive and any non-resident operating privilege; provided, however, the commissioner shall grant such person an opportunity to be heard but a license, permit or non-resident operating privilege may, upon the basis of a sworn report of the police officer that he had reasonable grounds to believe such arrested person to have been driving in an intoxicated condition or, while his ability to operate such motor vehicle or motorcycle was impaired by the consumption of alcohol or the use of a drug as defined in this chapter, and that said person had refused to submit to such test, be temporarily suspended without notice pending the determination upon any such hearing . . . ."

2. For an excellent analysis of the cases involving "strip" searching, retrieving objects from body cavities, and obtaining body fluid or breath for analysis in drunk driving cases, consult McIntyre and Chabraja, The Intensive Search of a Suspect's Body and Clothing, 58 J.Crim.L., C. & P.S. 18 (1967).

DAVIS v. MISSISSIPPI

Supreme Court of the United States, 1969.
394 U.S. 721, 89 S.Ct. 1394.

MR. JUSTICE BRENNAN delivered the opinion of the Court.

Petitioner was convicted of rape and sentenced to life imprisonment by a jury in the Circuit Court of Lauderdale County, Mississippi.

The only issue before us is whether fingerprints obtained from petitioner should have been excluded from evidence as the product of a detention which was illegal under the Fourth and Fourteenth Amendments.

The rape occurred on the evening of December 2, 1965, at the victim's home in Meridian, Mississippi. The victim could give no better description of her assailant than that he was a Negro youth. Finger and palm prints found on the sill and borders of the window through which the assailant apparently entered the victim's home constituted the only other lead available at the outset of the police investigation. Beginning on December 3, and for a period of about 10 days, the Meridian police, without warrants, took at least 24 Negro youths to police headquarters where they were questioned briefly, fingerprinted, and then released without charge. The police also interrogated 40 or 50 other Negro youths either at police headquarters, at school, or on the street. Petitioner, a 14-year-old youth who had occasionally worked for the victim as a yardboy, was brought in on December 3 and released after being fingerprinted and routinely questioned. Between December 3 and December 7, he was interrogated by the police on several occasions—sometimes in his home or in a car, other times at police headquarters. This questioning apparently related primarily to investigation of other potential suspects. Several times during this same period petitioner was exhibited to the victim in her hospital room. A police officer testified that these confrontations were for the purpose of sharpening the victim's description of her assailant by providing a "a gauge to go by on size and color." The victim did not identify petitioner as her assailant at any of these confrontations.

On December 12, the police drove petitioner 90 miles to the city of Jackson and confined him overnight in the Jackson jail. The State conceded on oral argument in this Court that there was neither a warrant nor probable cause for this arrest. The next day, petitioner, who had not yet been afforded counsel, took a lie detector test and signed a statement [which was not used at the trial]. He was then returned to and confined in the Meridian jail. On December 14, while so confined, petitioner was fingerprinted a second time. That same day, these December 14 prints, together with the fingerprints of 23 other Negro youths apparently still under suspicion, were sent to the Federal Bureau of Investigation in Washington, D. C., for comparison with the latent prints taken from the window of the victim's house. The FBI reported that petitioner's prints matched those taken from the window. Petitioner was subsequently indicted and tried for the rape, and the fingerprint evidence was admitted in evidence at trial over petitioner's timely objections that the fingerprints should be excluded as the product of an unlawful detention. The Mississippi Supreme Court sustained the admission of the fingerprint evidence and affirmed the conviction. 204 So.2d 270 (1967). We granted certiorari. 393 U.S. 821, 89 S.Ct. 149 (1968). We reverse.

At the outset, we find no merit in the suggestion in the Mississippi Supreme Court's opinion that fingerprint evidence, because of its trustworthiness, is not subject to the proscriptions of the Fourth and Fourteenth Amendments.[1] Our decisions recognize no exception to the rule that illegally seized evidence is inadmissible at trial, however relevant and trustworthy the seized evidence may be as an item of proof. The exclusionary rule was fashioned as a sanction to redress and deter overreaching governmental conduct prohibited by the Fourth Amendment. To make an exception for illegally seized evidence which is trustworthy would fatally undermine these purposes. Thus, in Mapp v. Ohio, 367 U.S. 643, 655, 81 S.Ct. 1684 (1961), we held that "*all* evidence obtained by searches and seizures in violation of the Constitution is, by that same authority, inadmissible in a state court." (Italics supplied.) Fingerprint evidence is no exception to this comprehensive rule. We agree with and adopt the conclusion of the Court of Appeals for the District of Columbia Circuit in Bynum v. United States, 104 U.S.App.D.C. 368, 370, 262 F.2d 465, 467 (1958):

> "True, fingerprints can be distinguished from statements given during detention. They can also be distinguished from articles taken from a prisoner's possession. Both similarities and differences of each type of evidence to and from the others are apparent. But all three have the decisive common characteristic of being something of evidentiary value which the public authorities have caused an arrested person to yield to them during illegal detention. If one such product of illegal detention is proscribed, by the same token all should be proscribed."

We turn then to the question whether the detention of petitioner during which the fingerprints used at trial were taken constituted an unreasonable seizure of his person in violation of the Fourth Amendment. The opinion of the Mississippi Supreme Court proceeded on the mistaken premise that petitioner's prints introduced at trial were taken during his brief detention on December 3. In fact, as both parties before us agree, the fingerprint evidence used at trial was obtained on December 14, while petitioner was still in detention following his December 12 arrest. The legality of his arrest was not determined by the Mississippi Supreme Court. However, on oral argument here, the State conceded that the arrest on December 12 and the ensuing detention through December 14 were based on neither a warrant nor probable cause and were therefore constitutionally invalid. The State argues, nevertheless, that this invalidity should not prevent us from affirming petitioner's conviction. The December 3 prints were validly obtained, it is argued, and "it should make no difference

1. Fingerprint evidence would seem no more "trustworthy" than other types of evidence—such as guns, narcotics, gambling equipment—which are routinely excluded if illegally obtained.

in the practical or legal sense which [fingerprint] card was sent to the F.B.I. for comparison." It may be that it does make a difference in light of the objectives of the exclusionary rule, see Bynum v. United States, supra, at 371–372, 262 F.2d, at 468–469,[2] but we need not decide the question since we have concluded that the prints of December 3 were not validly obtained.

The State makes no claim that petitioner voluntarily accompanied the police officers to headquarters on December 3 and willingly submitted to fingerprinting. The State's brief also candidly admits that "[a]ll that the Meridian Police could possibly have known about petitioner at the time . . . would not amount to probable cause for his arrest. . . ." The State argues, however, that the December 3 detention was of a type which does not require probable cause. Two rationales for this position are suggested. First, it is argued that the detention occurred during the investigatory rather than accusatory stage and thus was not a seizure requiring probable cause. The second and related argument is that, at the least, detention for the sole purpose of obtaining fingerprints does not require probable cause.

It is true that at the time of the December 3 detention the police had no intention of charging petitioner with the crime and were far from making him the primary focus of their investigation. But to argue that the Fourth Amendment does not apply to the investigatory stage is fundamentally to misconceive the purposes of the Fourth Amendment. Investigatory seizures would subject unlimited numbers of innocent persons to the harassment and ignominy incident to involuntary detention. Nothing is more clear than that the Fourth Amendment was meant to prevent wholesale intrusions upon the personal security of our citizenry, whether these intrusions be termed "arrests" or "investigatory detentions."[3] We made this explicit only

2. The Government argued in *Bynum* that the controversy over the introduction in evidence of a particular set of fingerprints was "much ado over very little," because another set properly taken was available and might have been used. The Court of Appeals rejected this argument: "It bears repeating that the matter of primary judicial concern in all cases of this type is the imposition of effective sanctions implementing the Fourth Amendment guarantee against illegal arrest and detention. Neither the fact that the evidence obtained through such detention is itself trustworthy or the fact that equivalent evidence can conveniently be obtained in a wholly proper way militates against this overriding consideration. It is entirely irrelevant that it may be relatively easy for the government to prove guilt without using the product of illegal detention. The important thing is that those administering the criminal law understand that they must do it that way." 104 U.S.App. D.C., at 371–372, 262 F.2d at 468–469. On Bynum's retrial another set of fingerprints in no way connected with his unlawful arrest was used, and he was again convicted. The Court of Appeals affirmed this conviction. 107 U.S.App.D.C. 109, 274 F.2d 767 (1960).

3. The State relies on various statements in our cases which approve general questioning of citizens in the course of investigating a crime. See Miranda v. Arizona, 384 U.S. 436, 477–478, 86 S.Ct. 1602, 1629–1630 (1966); Culombe v. Connecticut, 367 U.S. 568, 635, 81 S.Ct. 1860, 1896 (concurring opinion) (1961). But these statements merely reiterated the settled principle

last Term in Terry v. Ohio, 392 U.S. 1, 19, 88 S.Ct. 1868, 1878 (1968), when we rejected "the notions that the Fourth Amendment does not come into play at all as a limitation upon police conduct if the officers stop short of something called a 'technical arrest' or a 'full-blown search.' "

Detentions for the sole purpose of obtaining fingerprints are no less subject to the constraints of the Fourth Amendment. It is arguable, however, that, because of the unique nature of the fingerprinting process, such detentions might, under narrowly defined circumstances, be found to comply with the Fourth Amendment even though there is no probable cause in the traditional sense. See Camara v. Municipal Court, 387 U.S. 523, 87 S.Ct. 1727 (1967). Detention for fingerprinting may constitute a much less serious intrusion upon personal security than other types of police searches and detentions. Fingerprinting involves none of the probing into an individual's private life and thoughts that marks an interrogation or search. Nor can fingerprint detention be employed repeatedly to harass any individual, since the police need only one set of each person's prints. Furthermore, fingerprinting is an inherently more reliable and effective crime-solving tool than eyewitness identifications or confessions and is not subject to such abuses as the improper line-up and the "third degree." Finally, because there is no danger of destruction of fingerprints, the limited detention need not come unexpectedly or at an inconvenient time. For this same reason, the general requirement that the authorization of a judicial officer be obtained in advance of detention would seem not to admit of any exception in the fingerprinting context.

We have no occasion in this case, however, to determine whether the requirements of the Fourth Amendment could be met by narrowly circumscribed procedures for obtaining, during the course of a criminal investigation, the fingerprints of individuals for whom there is no probable cause to arrest. For it is clear that no attempt was made here to employ procedures which might comply with the requirements of the Fourth Amendment: the detention at police headquarters of petitioner and the other young Negroes was not authorized by a judicial officer; petitioner was unnecessarily required to undergo two fingerprinting sessions; and petitioner was not merely fingerprinted during the December 3 detention but also subjected to interrogation. The judgment of the Mississippi Supreme Court is therefore

Reversed.

MR. JUSTICE FORTAS took no part in the consideration or decision of this case.

that while the police have the right to request citizens to answer voluntarily questions concerning unsolved crimes they have no right to compel them to answer.

MR. JUSTICE HARLAN, concurring.

I join the opinion of the Court, with one reservation. The Court states in dictum that, because fingerprinting may be scheduled for a time convenient to the citizen, "the general requirement that the authorization of a judicial officer be obtained in advance of detention would seem not to admit of any exception in the fingerprinting context." Ante, this page. I cannot concur in so sweeping a proposition. There may be circumstances, falling short of the "dragnet" procedures employed in this case, where compelled submission to fingerprinting would not amount to a violation of the Fourth Amendment even in the absence of a warrant, and I would leave that question open.

MR. JUSTICE BLACK, dissenting.

The petitioner here was convicted of a brutal rape of a woman, committed in her own home. Fingerprints of the petitioner, left on the window sill of her home, were the clinching evidence bringing about petitioner's conviction. The Court, by once more expanding the reach of the judicially declared exclusionary rule, obstensibly resting on the Fourth Amendment, holds the fingerprint evidence constitutionally inadmissible and thereby reverses petitioner's conviction. The rape occurred on December 2, 1965, and, as was their duty, the police authorities began to make a searching investigation the morning of December 3. The raped woman was originally able to describe the rapist only as a young Negro male. With this evidence the police proceeded to interrogate a number of young Negroes on the streets, at their homes, or at the police station, and then permitted them to go on their way. The petitioner was among those so interrogated on December 3, at which time his fingerprints were made. The fingerprints were again taken on December 14. The record does not show that petitioner or any other young man who was questioned and fingerprinted ever made the slightest objection. Apparently all of them cooperated with the police in efforts to find out who had committed the rape. This case is but one more in an ever-expanding list of cases in which this Court has been so widely blowing up the Fourth Amendment's scope that its original authors would be hard put to recognize their creation. For this most unnecessary expansion of the Amendment, the Court is compelled to put its chief reliance on a Court of Appeals decision, Bynum v. United States, 104 U.S.App.D.C. 368, 262 F.2d 465. I think it is high time this Court, in the interest of the administration of criminal justice, made a new appraisal of the language and history of the Fourth Amendment and cut it down to its intended size. Such a judicial action would, I believe, make our cities a safer place for men, women, and children to live.

I dissent from this reversal.

MR. JUSTICE STEWART, dissenting.

I do not disagree with the Court's conclusion that the petitioner was arrested and detained without probable cause. But it does not follow that his fingerprints were inadmissible at the trial.

Fingerprints are not "evidence" in the conventional sense that weapons or stolen goods might be. Like the color of a man's eyes, his height, or his very physiognomy, the tips of his fingers are an inherent and unchanging characteristic of the man. And physical impressions of his fingertips can be exactly and endlessly reproduced.

We do not deal here with a confession wrongfully obtained or with property wrongfully seized—so tainted as to be forever inadmissible as evidence against a defendant. We deal, instead, with "evidence" that can be identically reproduced and lawfully used at any subsequent trial.[1]

I cannot believe that the doctrine of Mapp v. Ohio, 367 U.S. 643, 81 S.Ct. 1684, requires so useless a gesture as the reversal of this conviction.

NOTES

1. Though Davis v. Mississippi left room for the development of techniques for securing physical evidence without requiring probable cause, some courts expressed a reluctance to take up the challenge. See e. g. United States v. Jennings, 468 F.2d 111 (9th Cir. 1972):

"Appellee points out that the Supreme Court in Davis v. Mississippi, 394 U.S. 721, 727–728, 89 S.Ct. 1394 (1969), intimated that a detention for fingerprinting, which lacked probable cause for arrest, might be found to comply with the Fourth Amendment under certain narrowly defined circumstances, presumably with judicial authorization. It is contended that appellant's detention at the Sheriff's office is constitutionally sufficient within *Davis*. The language in *Davis* was, however, dicta.

"This Court is not inclined to adopt on its own initiative, the suggestion that probable cause to arrest need not exist to impose burdens substantially like those of arrest-transportation to the police station, fingerprinting, photographing and completion of a lengthy arrest form."

In light of these comments, would it be wise for the police to adopt a practice of taking portable fingerprint and camera equipment to where the suspect lives or works and secure the needed physical evidence without taking the suspect to the police station and detaining him there?

2. On October 1, 1969, shortly after the decision in Davis v. Mississippi, the Colorado Supreme Court adopted Rule 41.1 which specifically empowers a court to issue an order for fingerprinting upon a showing that there is reason to believe that fingerprinting will aid in the apprehension of the unknown perpetrator of a known offense or that there is reason to suspect that the named individual is connected with perpetration of the crime.

A broader proposal has been made with respect to the Federal Rules of Criminal Procedure. The proposed Rule 41.1 (reported at 52 F.R.D. 462) reads as follows:

RULE 41.1. NONTESTIMONIAL IDENTIFICATION.

(a) AUTHORITY TO ISSUE ORDER. A nontestimonial identification order authorized by this rule may be issued by a federal magistrate

1. At the original trial the victim of the rape, under oath, positively identified the petitioner as her assailant. There now exists, therefore, ample probable cause to detain him and take his fingerprints.

upon request of a federal law enforcement officer or an attorney for the government.

(b) TIME OF APPLICATION. A request for a nontestimonial identification order may be made prior to the arrest of a suspect, after arrest and prior to trial or, when special circumstances of the case make it appropriate, during trial.

(c) BASIS FOR ORDER. An order shall issue only on an affidavit or affidavits sworn to before the federal magistrate and establishing the following grounds for the order:

(1) that there is probable cause to believe that an offense has been committed;

(2) that there are reasonable grounds, not amounting to probable cause to arrest, to suspect that the person named or described in the affidavit committed the offense; and

(3) that the results of specific nontestimonial identification procedures will be of material aid in determining whether the person named in the affidavit committed the offense.

(d) ISSUANCE. Upon a showing that the ground specified in subdivision (c) exist, the federal magistrate shall issue an order requiring the person named in the affidavit to appear at a designated time and place for nontestimonial identification. If it appears from the affidavit that a person named or described in the affidavit may, upon service of the order to appear, either flee or alter or destroy the nontestimonial evidence, the federal magistrate may direct a marshal or other federal law enforcement officer to bring the person before the federal magistrate. The federal magistrate shall then direct that the designated nontestimonial identification procedures be conducted expeditiously. After such identification procedures have been completed, the person shall be released or charged with an offense.

(e) MODIFICATION OF ORDER. At the request of the person named in the affidavit, the federal magistrate shall modify the order with respect to time and place of appearance whenever it appears reasonable under the circumstances to do so.

(f) FAILURE TO APPEAR. Any person who fails without adequate excuse to obey an order to appear served upon him pursuant to this section may be held in contempt of the court which issued the order or, in the event that the order was issued by a United States magistrate, may be held in contempt of the district court of the district in which the magistrate is sitting.

(g) SERVICE OF ORDER. An order to appear pursuant to this section may be served by a federal law enforcement officer. The order shall be served upon the person named or described in the affidavit by delivery of a copy to him personally. Service may be had at any place within the jurisdiction of the United States.

(h) CONTENTS OF ORDER. An order to appear shall be signed by the federal magistrate and shall state:

(1) that the presence of the person named in the affidavit is required for the purpose of permitting nontestimonial identification procedures in order to aid in the investigation of the offense specified therein;

(2) the time and place of the required appearance;

(3) the nontestimonial identification procedures to be conducted, the methods to be used, and the approximate length of time such procedures will require;

(4) the grounds to suspect that the person named in the affidavit committed the offense specified therein;

(5) that the person will be under no legal obligation to submit to any interrogation or to make any statement during the period of his appearance except for that required for voice identification;

(6) that the person may request the federal magistrate to make a reasonable modification of the order with respect to time and place of appearance, including a request to have any nontestimonial identification procedure other than a lineup conducted at his place of residence; and

(7) that the person, if he fails to appear, may be held in contempt of court.

(i) IMPLEMENTATION OF ORDER. Nontestimonial identification procedures may be conducted by any federal law enforcement officer or other person designated by the federal magistrate. Blood tests shall be conducted under medical supervision, and the federal magistrate may require medical supervision for any other test ordered pursuant to this section when he deems such supervision necessary. No person who appears under an order of appearance issued pursuant to this section shall be detained longer than is reasonably necessary to conduct the specified nontestimonial identification procedures unless he is arrested for an offense.

(j) RETURN. Within forty-five days after the nontestimonial identification procedure, a return shall be made to the federal magistrate who issued the order setting forth an inventory of the products of the nontestimonial identification procedures obtained from the person named in the affidavit. If, at the time of such return, probable cause does not exist to believe that such person has committed the offense named in the affidavit or any other offense, the person named in the affidavit shall be entitled to move that the federal magistrate issue an order directing that the products of the nontestimonial identification procedures, and all copies thereof, be destroyed. Such motion shall, except for good cause shown, be granted.

(k) NONTESTIMONIAL IDENTIFICATION ORDER AT REQUEST OF DEFENDANT. A person arrested for or charged with an offense may request the federal magistrate to order a nontestimonial identification procedure. If it appears that the results of specific nontestimonial identification procedures will be of material aid in determining whether the defendant committed the offense, the federal magistrate shall order the government to conduct such identification procedure involving the defendant under such terms and conditions as the federal magistrate shall prescribe.

(*l*) DEFINITION OF TERMS. As used in this rule, the following terms have the designated meaning:

(1) "Offense" means an offense defined by any Act of Congress or triable in any court established by Act of Congress and which is punishable by imprisonment for more than one year.

(2) "Federal law enforcement officer" means any government agent who is engaged in the enforcement of the criminal laws and who is autho-

rized by the Attorney General to apply for or execute a nontestimonial identification order.

(3) "Nontestimonial identification" includes identification by fingerprints, palm prints, footprints, measurements, blood specimens, urine specimens, saliva samples, hair samples, or other reasonable physical or medical examination, handwriting exemplars, voice samples, photographs, and lineups.

Congress has under consideration a proposal to enact 18 U.S.C. § 3507 (S. 2997, 91st Cong., 1st Sess.) which provides for issuance of a temporary detention subpoena for physical characteristics upon a showing that an offense (punishable by more than one year) has been committed and that procurement of the physical characteristics of a named individual may contribute to identification of the perpetrator and that the evidence cannot be obtained from another law enforcement agency.

Arizona has enacted Ariz.Rev.Stat. 13–1424 the terms of which are:

§ 13–1424. Detention for obtaining evidence of identifying physical characteristics.

A. A peace officer who is engaged, within the scope of his authority, in the investigation of an alleged criminal offense punishable by at least one year in the state prison, may make written application upon oath or affirmation to a magistrate for an order authorizing the temporary detention, for the purpose of obtaining evidence of identifying physical characteristics, of an identified or particularly described individual residing in or found in the jurisdiction over which the magistrate presides. The order shall require the presence of the identified or particularly described individual at such time and place as the court shall direct for obtaining the identifying physical characteristic evidence. Such order may be issued by the magistrate upon a showing of all of the following:

1. Reasonable cause for belief that a specifically described criminal offense punishable by at least one year in the state prison has been committed.

2. Procurement of evidence of identifying physical characteristics from an identified or particularly described individual may contribute to the identification of the individual who committed such offense.

3. Such evidence cannot otherwise be obtained by the investigating officer from either the law enforcement agency employing the affiant or the criminal identification division of the Arizona department of public safety.

B. Any order issued pursuant to the provisions of this section shall specify the following:

1. The alleged criminal offense which is the subject of the application.

2. The specific type of identifying physical characteristic evidence which is sought.

3. The relevance of such evidence to the particular investigation.

4. The identity or description of the individual who may be detained for obtaining such evidence.

5. The name and official status of the investigative officer authorized to effectuate such detention and obtain such evidence.

6. The place at which the obtaining of such evidence shall be effectuated.

7. The time that such evidence shall be taken except that no person may be detained for a period of more than three hours for the purpose of taking such evidence.

8. The period of time, not exceeding fifteen days, during which the order shall continue in force and effect. If the order is not executed within fifteen days, a new order may be issued, pursuant to the provisions of this section.

C. The order issued pursuant to this section shall be returned to the court not later than thirty days after its date of issuance and shall be accompanied by a sworn statement indicating the type of evidence taken. The court shall give to the person from whom such evidence was taken a copy of the order and a copy of the sworn statement indicating what type of evidence was taken, if any.

D. For the purposes of this section, "identifying physical characteristics" includes, but is not limited to, the fingerprints, palm prints, footprints, measurements, handwriting, handprinting, sound of voice, blood samples, urine samples, saliva samples, hair samples, comparative personal appearance, or photographs of an individual.

3. Securing temporary custody of a suspect for a line-up has always presented particularly difficult problems. The line-up is not a simple routine procedure like fingerprinting, photographing or taking samples of hair or even blood. One court has held that a trial judge has inherent power to order a suspect to appear in a lineup upon a showing that does not meet the requirements of probable cause. Consider these excerpts from Wise v. Murphy, 275 A.2d 205 (D.C.Ct.App.1971):

"Nebeker, J.:

. . .

"In [these] cases, the . . . judge . . . has issued a summons and an order requiring the subjects to appear before him, with counsel, or for the appointment of counsel, and to set a time and date for the lineup. The summonses also informed the subjects of the date and time of the offense. The affidavits submitted by the Government were furnished to the subjects and their counsel.

"Under the contemplated lineups, it is clear that if identified, the person will be arrested and dealt with according to law. If not identified, protective measures have been ordered insulating the event from future public and official notice. * * *

"Appointed counsel requested, and the Assistant United States Attorney agreed, that he be furnished with previous statements of description by the victims and any other witnesses to the offense, and that he be permitted to interview such persons before the lineups. All Statements made at the lineups will be recorded with a view to permitting verbal reconstruction and eliminating the possibility that counsel may also have to be a witness at any future proceedings. At oral argument before this court, the United States also agreed that, as usual in lineups in the District of Columbia, photographs of the lineups will be made, and the names and addresses of all participants will be kept for possible visual reconstruction of the lineups.

"In addition, the United States acknowledged that it could arrange a lineup without using convicted or suspected prisoners together with the necessary security safeguards and devices. It also agreed that nothing resulting from such lineup need be used officially in any other way. Thus, the lineup need not be photographed for use in connection with any other proceeding concerning others standing in it. The subjects need not be commingled with others accused or suspected of crime. The total time for assembly and viewing need hardly be more than a few minutes. In short, the process is to be as antiseptic as possible. * * *

"We recognize, however, that what is contemplated here is a seizure of the person. To be sure it is a more severe seizure than the monetary one of *Terry*, but obviously of lesser magnitude than a formal arrest. * * *

"Recognizing the seriousness of the intrusion, we take note of the governmental interest on the other end of the scales.

"The police are confronted with a woman who reports that she was forced into an alley in a high-crime area and raped at knife point at about 10:40 p. m. Surely, there exists a compelling interest for the state to apprehend the offender—not only to punish him but also to improve a desperate situation regarding urban safety and lawlessness. To this extent the Government has not only a right, but indeed a duty, to employ every reasonable law enforcement device to maintain the integrity of the state in its role of insuring an ordered and peaceful community.

"If the police are to know whether the right man has been singled out, or whether they must continue to look for him they will be forced to arrange some other confrontation. Such possibilities come to mind as arranging for the woman to go to the subject's home, place of employment, or other location that he frequents. * * *

"Aside from the obvious suggestibility inherent in such procedures, it is apparent that the subject and his counsel are deprived of meaningful cross-examination as to the verity of any courtroom identification.

"What thus becomes obvious is that the administration of criminal justice can and ought to devise a procedure which reasonably makes persons "available for line-up identification in respect of other crimes for which there is less than probable cause to [make a formal] arrest." Adams v. United States, 130 U.S.App.D.C. 203, 208, 399 F.2d 574, 579 (1968). * * *

"On balance, and realistically viewing the impact of a court-ordered line-up of the kind here contemplated on liberty, we conclude, under the test expressed in Camara v. Municipal Court, 387 U.S. 523, 87 S.Ct. 1727 (1967), that the public interest can validly require this intrusion.

"Grave reservations exist, however, as to whether this type of court-ordered lineup, not connected with a formal arrest, may be used constitutionally in other than serious felonies involving grave personal injuries or threats of the same. The governmental interest, though serious, is not of the same magnitude in commercial crimes involving property or money such as forgery or false pretenses or other less serious offenses. * * *

"In such cases it is highly likely that the governmental interests in law enforcement cannot outweigh the right of liberty, or freedom from being ordered into even the most antiseptic lineup, under circumstances short of traditional probable cause for formal arrest. * * *

"We turn then to the question whether on the facts as presented [have] the requisite specificity to permit meaningful evaluation of the reasonableness of the proposed order.

"The record reveals a complaint of rape at knife point and a statement by the victim that one subject's photograph among pictures of "possible suspects" reveals "facial features similar to those of the man who assaulted her." The victim also said that to be positive she would have to see the suspect in person.

"We are not unmindful that often this is all the police are told by a complainant and we do not wish to imply that more specific or dogmatic identification from the victim is expected or constitutionally required. Surely, the police should not be encouraged to demand more positive identification than the victim is honestly able to furnish. But such tentative and hesitant identification must be taken in complete context to know whether a lineup may reasonably be required. * * *

"We think it is necessary for the police to specify how they arrived at their conclusion that the individuals in the group of photographs were possible suspects. It may be that they were previous sex offenders with similar *modus operandi*, or that they had opportunity to commit the offense because of residence, employment, or known presence generally in the vicinity of the offense. It may be that those persons were previous acquaintances of the victim. In some cases, possible suspects may be singled out because of similar characteristics of description. These or a combination of these and other factors may have led the police to their conclusions regarding this group of suspects. There is every reason, with the exception of a case involving a reliable confidential informant, for the police to disclose all factors they possess shedding light on the likelihood that the tentative identification is the correct one. * * *

"With a sufficiently detailed recitation of articulable facts the judicial officer will be able to perform his all-important function of evaluating the reasonableness of the proposed intrusion against its impact, though limited to the extent possible, on personal liberty."

FICKLING, J. (dissenting):

"[The majority adopts] a completely flexible standard varying with all the circumstances of a case. This concept, variable probable cause, [is] unlike our present concept where we focus on only one issue—is there probable cause *to believe* the person is guilty of a crime—this test would call for the examination of a variety of factors such as: the gravity of the crime; whether the police are concerned mainly with detention rather than prevention; the seriousness of the intrusion necessitated by the type of detention employed. For instance, where a crime as serious as murder is involved and the police are only seeking a 10-minute detention for the purpose of taking fingerprints, a magistrate might be justified in issuing a warrant though the quantum of evidence was sufficient to show only probable cause *to suspect*, rather than probable cause to believe, guilt. Moreover, if the victim happened to be a police officer shot down in the course of duty, this same quantum of evidence might justify more lengthy detention or even the issuance of a search warrant. In essence, probable cause becomes one of a number of factors balanced in a test to determine the overriding standard of reasonableness. Search, frisk, arrest, or detention—variable probable cause applies to all.

I believe it is far too late in the day to argue that this theory applies to arrests or full criminal searches. Such a result would call for a reversal of our jurisprudence surrounding this area of the law. Courts have developed the standard of probable cause to believe and, until it is met, *any arrest* is legally unreasonable. If the type of detention employed, however, does not involve an arrest or a full criminal search, we are faced with a different question.

There is another possible conclusion, in the wake of *Terry*, in regard to the status of probable cause. With this alternative the existing standard calling for probable cause to believe is observed where an arrest or full criminal search is involved; when that standard is not met, the conduct is unreasonable per se. However, the existence of a detention involving something less than an arrest is recognized. Since a "seizure" is involved, the Fourth Amendment applies, however, the reasonableness standard and the warrant clause's requirement for probable cause may be satisfied and the seizure sanctioned, despite a failure to meet the traditional probable cause to believe test. It is only when these lesser detentions are involved that variable probable cause comes into play and suspicion becomes legitimate.

It appears that the majority adopts this latter alternative. Under this test the crucial question is whether there is an arrest. If there is, then we must look for traditional probable cause.

The majority holds that the intrusion upon liberty brought about by the proposed lineup order is less than a formal arrest. * * *

Despite the fact that detention and arrest may not be synonymous, to assert that the detention contemplated by the lineup order is not an arrest is to participate in semantic nonsense. It would appear that, at the least, two factors must be present before a distinction from an arrest could be justified:

(1) the time involved must be extremely brief, and (2) it must involve only a stop rather than an affirmative command to move somewhere else. Within these narrow confines, it is conceivable that the Fourth Amendment reasonableness standard *might* be satisfied.

The step from a brief stop to a trip to the station house and forced stint in a lineup is a giant step backward to the age of investigatory arrests. To contend that this is not a formal arrest renders the term "arrest" meaningless. To contend that a citizen can be ordered to a police station against his will and then further ordered to stand on a stage and be viewed, again against his will, and not be under arrest is beyond reason. What does it matter that the lineup is "antiseptic"? The fact that no official record will be kept and therefore the citizen will, hopefully, be spared some public humiliation is irrelevant. I recognize that this is less an "intrusion upon liberty" than placing a man in jail for a few days, yet, nonetheless, both are arrests. * * *

In conclusion I wish to stress that I share the majority's concern for "the desperate situation regarding urban safety and lawlessness." Yet, if this nation is to remain free, it is necessary for the judiciary to maintain a perspective and at all times to act in a constitutional manner."

4. In connection with detention for eyewitness identification, consider the following holding:

"The three defendants were . . . found guilty of sexual intercourse with a child 14 years of age [arising from an incident involving several victims]. At the time these young victims were rescued they were understandably distraught. The police were confronted with the problem of identifying the assailants from among fourteen members of a motorcycle gang. To that end, it was not only proper but essential that all of those present be taken into custody until the children regained their composure and were able to make an intelligent identification. There was no impropriety in this procedure. The record fully supports a determination that the victims had ample opportunity to view their assailants. By the very nature of the crimes, the proximity of the parties during the assault and the time which necessarily elapsed permitted the children to make a reliable identification."

State v. Gengler, 294 Minn. 503, 200 N.W.2d 187 (1972).

UNITED STATES v. DIONISIO

Supreme Court of the United States, 1973.
410 U.S. 1, 93 S.Ct. 764.

MR. JUSTICE STEWART delivered the opinion of the Court.

A special grand jury was convened in the Northern District of Illinois in February 1971, to investigate possible violations of federal criminal statutes relating to gambling. In the course of its investigation the grand jury received in evidence certain voice recordings that had been obtained pursuant to court orders.[1]

The grand jury subpoenaed approximately 20 persons, including the respondent Dionisio, seeking to obtain from them voice exemplars for comparison with the recorded conversations that had been received in evidence. Each witness was advised that he was a potential defendant in a criminal prosecution. Each was asked to examine a transcript of an intercepted conversation, and to go to a nearby office of the United States Attorney to read the transcript into a recording device. The witnesses were advised that they would be allowed to have their attorneys present when they read the transcripts. Dionisio

1. The court orders were issued pursuant to 18 U.S.C. § 2518, a statute authorizing the interception of wire communications upon a judicial determination that "(a) there is probable cause for belief that an individual is committing, has committed, or is about to commit a particular offense enumerated in section 2516 of this chapter [including the transmission of wagering information]; (b) there is probable cause for belief that particular communications concerning that offense will be obtained through such interception; (c) normal investigative procedures have been tried and have failed or reasonably appear to be unlikely to succeed if tried or to be too dangerous; (d) there is probable cause for belief that the facilities from which, or the place where, the wire or oral communications are to be intercepted are being used, or are about to be used, in connection with the commission of such offense, or are leased to, listed in the name of, or commonly used by such person."

and other witnesses refused to furnish the voice exemplars, asserting that these disclosures would violate their rights under the Fourth and Fifth Amendments.

The Government then filed separate petitions in the United States District Court to compel Dionisio and the other witnesses to furnish the voice exemplars to the grand jury. The petitions stated that the exemplars were "essential and necessary" to the grand jury investigation, and that they would "be used solely as a standard of comparison in order to determine whether or not the witness is the person whose voice was intercepted . . . ."

Following a hearing, the district judge rejected the witnesses' constitutional arguments and ordered them to comply with the grand jury's request.

* * *

When Dionisio persisted in his refusal to respond to the grand jury's directive, the District Court adjudged him in civil contempt and ordered him committed to custody until he obeyed the court order, or until the expiration of 18 months.[2]

The Court of Appeals for the Seventh Circuit reversed. 442 F.2d 276. It agreed with the District Court in rejecting the Fifth Amendment claims, but concluded that to compel the voice recordings would violate the Fourth Amendment. In the Court's view, the grand jury was "seeking to obtain the voice exemplars of the witnesses by the use of its subpoena powers because probable cause did not exist for their arrest or for some other, less unusual method of compelling the production of the exemplars." The Court found that the Fourth Amendment applied to grand jury process, and that "under the fourth amendment law enforcement officials may not compel the production of physical evidence absent a showing of the reasonableness of the seizure. Davis v. Mississippi, 394 U.S. 721, 89 S.Ct. 1394 . . . ."

In *Davis* this Court held that it was error to admit the petitioner's fingerprints into evidence at his trial for rape, because they had been obtained during a police detention following a lawless wholesale round-up of the petitioner and more than 20 other youths. Equating the procedures followed by the grand jury in the present case to the fingerprint detentions in *Davis*, the Court of Appeals reasoned that "[t]he dragnet effect here, where approximately twenty persons were subpoenaed for purposes of identification, has the same invidious effect on fourth amendment rights as the practice condemned in *Davis*."

* * *

I

The Court of Appeals correctly rejected the contention that the compelled production of the voice exemplars would violate the Fifth

2. The life of the special grand jury was 18 months, but could be extended for an additional 18 months. 18 U.S.C. § 3331.

Amendment. It has long been held that the compelled display of identifiable physical characteristics infringes no interest protected by the privilege against compulsory self-incrimination. In Holt v. United States, 218 U.S. 245, 252, 31 S.Ct. 2, 6, Mr. Justice Holmes, writing for the Court, dismissed as an "extravagant extension of the Fifth Amendment" the argument that it violated the privilege to require a defendant to put on a blouse for identification purposes. He explained that "the prohibition of compelling a man in a criminal court to be witness against himself is a prohibition of the use of physical or moral compulsion to extort communications from him, not an exclusion of his body as evidence when it may be material."

More recently, in Schmerber v. California, 384 U.S. 757, 86 S.Ct. 1826, we relied on *Holt*, and noted that "both federal and state courts have usually held that [the privilege] it offers no protection against compulsion to submit to fingerprinting, photographing, or measurements, to write or speak for identification, to appear in court, to stand, to assume a stance, to walk, or to make a particular gesture. The distinction which has emerged often expressed in different ways, is that the privilege is a bar against compelling 'communications' or 'testimony,' but that compulsion which makes a suspect or accused the source of 'real or physical evidence' does not violate it."

The Court held that the extraction and chemical analysis of a blood sample involved no "shadow of testimonial compulsion upon or enforced communication by the accused."

These cases led us to conclude in Gilbert v. California, 388 U.S. 263, 87 S.Ct. 1951, that handwriting exemplars were not protected by the privilege against compulsory self-incrimination. While "[o]ne's voice and handwriting are, of course, means of communication," we held that a "mere handwriting exemplar, in contrast to the content of what is written, like the voice or body itself, is an identifying physical characteristic outside its protection." And similarly in United States v. Wade, 388 U.S. 218, 87 S.Ct. 1926, we found no error in compelling a defendant accused of bank robbery to utter in a line-up words that had allegedly been spoken by the robber. The accused there was "required to use his voice as an identifying physical characteristic, not to speak his guilt."

Wade and *Gilbert* definitively refute any contention that the compelled production of the voice exemplars in this case would violate the Fifth Amendment. The voice recordings were to be used solely to measure the physical properties of the witnesses' voices, not for the testimonial or communicative content of what was to be said.

II

The Court of Appeals held that the Fourth Amendment required a preliminary showing of reasonableness before a grand jury witness could be compelled to furnish a voice exemplar, and that in this case the proposed "seizures" of the voice exemplars would be unreasonable because of the large number of witnesses summoned by the grand jury and directed to produce such exemplars. We disagree.

The Fourth Amendment guarantees that all people shall be "secure in their persons, houses, papers, and effects, against unreasonable searches and seizures . . . ." Any Fourth Amendment violation in the present setting must rest on a lawless governmental intrusion upon the privacy of "persons" rather than on interference with "property relationships or private papers." Schmerber v. California, 384 U.S. 757, 767, 86 S.Ct. 1826, 1833; see United States v. Doe (Schwartz), 2 Cir., 457 F.2d 895, 897. In Terry v. Ohio, 392 U.S. 1, 88 S.Ct. 1868, the Court explained the protection afforded to "persons" in terms of the statement in Katz v. United States, 389 U.S. 347, 88 S.Ct. 507, that "the Fourth Amendment protects people, not places," and concluded that "wherever an individual may harbor a reasonable 'expectation of privacy,' . . . he is entitled to be free from unreasonable governmental intrusion."

As the Court made clear in *Schmerber*, supra, the obtaining of physical evidence from a person involves a potential Fourth Amendment violation at two different levels—the "seizure" of the "person" necessary to bring him into contact with government agents, see Davis v. Mississippi, 394 U.S. 721, 89 S.Ct. 1394, and the subsequent search for and seizure of the evidence. In *Schmerber* we found the initial seizure of the accused justified as a lawful arrest, and the subsequent seizure of the blood sample from his body reasonable in light of the exigent circumstances. And in *Terry*, we concluded that neither the initial seizure of the person, an investigatory "stop" by a policeman, nor the subsequent search, a pat down of his outer clothing for weapons, constituted a violation of the Fourth and Fourteenth Amendments. The constitutionality of the compulsory production of exemplars from a grand jury witness necessarily turns on the same dual inquiry—whether either the initial compulsion of the person to appear before the grand jury, or the subsequent directive to make a voice recording is an unreasonable "seizure" within the meaning of the Fourth Amendment.

It is clear that a subpoena to appear before a grand jury is not a "seizure" in the Fourth Amendment sense, even though that summons may be inconvenient or burdensome. Last Term we again acknowledged what has long been recognized, that "[c]itizens generally are not constitutionally immune from grand jury subpoenas . . . ." Branzburg v. Hayes, 408 U.S. 665, 682, 92 S.Ct. 1646, 2656. We concluded that:

> "[a]lthough the powers of the grand jury are not unlimited and are subject to the supervision of a judge, the longstanding principle that 'the public . . . has a right to every man's evidence,' except for those persons protected by a constitutional, common-law, or statutory privilege, United States v. Bryan, 339 U.S. 323, 331, 70 S.Ct. 724, 730 (1950); Black-

mer v. United States, 284 U.S. 421, 438, 52 S.Ct. 252, 255 (1932); 8 J. Wigmore, Evidence § 2192 (McNaughton rev. 1961), is particularly applicable to grand jury proceedings."

These are recent reaffirmations of the historically grounded obligation of every person to appear and give his evidence before the grand jury. "The personal sacrifice involved is a part of the necessary contribution of the individual to the welfare of the public." Blair v. United States, 250 U.S. 273, 281, 39 S.Ct. 468, 471. And while the duty may be "onerous" at times, it is "necessary to the administration of justice." Blair v. United States.[3]

The compulsion exerted by a grand jury subpoena differs from the seizure effected by an arrest or even an investigative "stop" in more than civic obligation. For, as Judge Friendly wrote for the Court of Appeals for the Second Circuit:

> "The latter is abrupt, is effected with force or the threat of it and often in demeaning circumstances, and, in the case of arrest, results in a record involving social stigma. A subpoena is served in the same manner as other legal process; it involves no stigma whatever; if the time for appearance is inconvenient, this can generally be altered; and it remains at all times under the control and supervision of a court."

Thus the Court of Appeals for the Seventh Circuit correctly recognized in a case subsequent to the one now before us, that a "grand jury subpoena to testify is not that kind of governmental intrusion on privacy against which the Fourth Amendment affords protection once the Fifth Amendment is satisfied." Fraser v. United States, 452 F.2d 616, 620.

This case is thus quite different from Davis v. Mississippi, supra, on which the Court of Appeals primarily relied. For in *Davis* it was the initial seizure—the lawless dragnet detention—that violated the Fourth and Fourteenth Amendments—not the taking of the fingerprints. We noted that "[i]nvestigatory seizures would subject unlimited numbers of innocent persons to the harassment and ignominy incident to involuntary detention," and we left open the question whether, consistently with the Fourth and Fourteenth Amendments, narrowly circumscribed procedures might be developed for obtaining fingerprints from people when there was no probable cause to arrest them.[4] *Davis* is plainly inapposite to a case where the initial restraint does not itself infringe the Fourth Amendment.

3. The obligation to appear is no different for a person who may himself be the subject of the grand jury inquiry.

4. Judge Weinfeld correctly characterized *Davis* as "but another application of the principle that the Fourth Amendment applies to all searches and seizures of the person, no matter what the scope or duration. It held that in the circumstances there presented the detention for the sole purpose of fingerprinting was in violation of the Fourth Amendment ban against unreasonable search and seizure." Thom v. New York Stock Exchange, D.C., 306 F.Supp. 1002, 1007.

This is not to say that a grand jury subpoena is some talisman that dissolves all constitutional protections. The grand jury cannot require a witness to testify against himself. It cannot require the production by a person of private books and records that would incriminate him. The Fourth Amendment provides protection against a grand jury subpoena *duces tecum* too sweeping in its terms "to be regarded as reasonable." Hale v. Henkel, 201 U.S. 43, 76, 26 S.Ct. 370, 379. And last Term, in the context of a First Amendment claim, we indicated that the Constitution could not tolerate the transformation of the grand jury into an instrument of oppression: "Official harassment of the press undertaken not for purposes of law enforcement but to disrupt a reporter's relationship with his news sources would have no justification. Grand juries are subject to judicial control and subpoenas to motions to quash. We do not expect courts will forget that grand juries must operate within the limits of the First Amendment as well as the Fifth." Branzburg v. Hayes, 408 U.S. 665, 707–708, 92 S.Ct. 2646, 2669–2670.

But we are here faced with no such constitutional infirmities in the subpoena to appear before the grand jury or in the order to make the voice recordings. There is, as we have said, no valid Fifth Amendment claim. There was no order to produce private books and papers, and no sweeping subpoena *duces tecum*. And even if *Branzburg* be extended beyond its First Amendment moorings and tied to a more generalized due process concept, there is still no indication in this case of the kind of harassment that was of concern there.

The Court of Appeals found critical significance in the fact that the grand jury had summoned approximately 20 witnesses to furnish voice exemplars.[5] We think that fact is basically irrelevant to the constitutional issues here. The grand jury may have been attempting to identify a number of voices on the tapes in evidence, or it might have summoned the 20 witnesses in an effort to identify one voice. But whatever the case, "[a] grand jury's investigation is not fully carried out until every available clue has been run down and all witnesses examined in every proper way to find if a crime has been committed . . . ." United States v. Stone, 2 Cir., 429 F.2d 138, 140. As the Court recalled last Term, "Because its task is to inquire into the existence of possible criminal conduct and to return only well-founded indictments, its investigative powers are necessarily broad." Branzburg v. Hayes, 408 U.S., at 688,[6] 92 S.Ct., at 2659. The grand

5. As noted above, ante p. 879, there is no valid comparison between the detentions of the 24 youths in *Davis*, and the grand jury subpoenas to the witnesses here. While the dragnet detentions by the police did constitute substantial intrusions into the Fourth and Fourteenth Amendment rights of each of the youths in *Davis*, no person has a justifiable expectation of immunity from a grand jury subpoena.

6. "[The grand jury] is a grand inquest, a body with powers of investigation and inquisition, the scope of whose inquiries is not to be limited narrowly by questions of propriety or forecasts of the probable result of the investigation, or by doubts whether any particular individual will be found properly subject to an accusation of crime. As has been said before, the identity of the offender, and the precise nature of the offense, if

jury may well find it desirable to call numerous witnesses in the course of an investigation. It does not follow that each witness may resist a subpoena on the ground that too many witnesses have been called. Neither the order to Dionisio to appear, nor the order to make a voice recording was rendered unreasonable by the fact that many others were subjected to the same compulsion.

But the conclusion that Dionisio's compulsory appearance before the grand jury was not an unreasonable "seizure" is the answer to only the first part of the Fourth Amendment inquiry here. Dionisio argues that the grand jury's subsequent directive to make the voice recording was itself an infringement of his rights under the Fourth Amendment. We cannot accept that argument.

In Katz v. United States, supra, we said that the Fourth Amendment provides no protection for what "a person knowingly exposes to the public, even in his own home or office . . . . " The physical characteristics of a person's voice, its tone and manner, as opposed to the content of a specific conversation, are constantly exposed to the public. Like a man's facial characteristics, or handwriting, his voice is repeatedly produced for others to hear. No person can have a reasonable expectation that others will not know the sound of his voice, any more than he can reasonably expect that his face will be a mystery to the world. As the Court of Appeals for the Second Circuit stated:

> "Except for the rare recluse who chooses to live his life in complete solitude, in our daily lives we constantly speak and write, and while the content of a communication is entitled to Fourth Amendment protection, . . . the underlying identifying characteristics—the constant factor throughout both public and private communications—are open for all to see or hear. There is no basis for constructing a wall of privacy against the grand jury which does not exist in casual contacts with strangers. Hence no intrusion into an individual's privacy results from compelled execution of handwriting or voice exemplars; nothing is being exposed to the grand jury that has not previously been exposed to the public at large." United States v. Doe (Schwartz), 2 Cir., 457 F.2d 895, 898–899.

The required disclosure of a person's voice is thus immeasurably further removed from the Fourth Amendment protection than was the intrusion into the body effected by the blood extraction in *Schmerber*. "The interests in human dignity and privacy which the Fourth Amendment protects forbid any such intrusions on the mere chance that desired evidence might be obtained." Schmerber v. Cali-

there be one, normally are developed at the conclusion of the grand jury's labors, not at the beginning. Blair v. United States, 250 U.S. 273, 282, 39 S.Ct. 468, 471.

fornia, 384 U.S. 757, 769–770, 86 S.Ct. 1826, 1835. Similarly, a seizure of voice exemplars does not involve the "severe, though brief, intrusion upon cherished personal security," effected by the "pat down" in *Terry*—"surely . . . an annoying, frightening, and perhaps humiliating experience." Rather, this is like the fingerprinting in *Davis*, where, though the initial dragnet detentions were constitutionally impermissible, we noted that the fingerprinting itself, "involves none of the probing into an individual's private life and thoughts that marks an interrogation or search." Davis v. Mississippi, 394 U.S. 721, 727, 89 S.Ct. 1394, 1398, 22 L.Ed.2d 676.

Since neither the summons to appear before the grand jury, nor its directive to make a voice recording infringed upon any interest protected by the Fourth Amendment, there was no justification for requiring the grand jury to satisfy even the minimal requirement of "reasonableness" imposed by the Court of Appeals. A grand jury has broad investigative powers to determine whether a crime has been committed and who has committed it. The jurors may act on tips, rumors, evidence offered by the prosecutor, or their own personal knowledge. No grand jury witness is "entitled to set limits to the investigation that the grand jury may conduct." Blair v. United States, 250 U.S. 273, 282, 39 S.Ct. 468, 471. And a sufficient basis for an indictment may only emerge at the end of the investigation when all the evidence has been received.

> "It is impossible to conceive that . . . the examination of witnesses must be stopped until a basis is laid by an indictment formally preferred, when the very object of the examination is to ascertain who shall be indicted." Hale v. Henkel, 201 U.S. 43, 65, 26 S.Ct. 370, 375, 50 L.Ed. 652.

Since Dionisio raised no valid Fourth Amendment claim, there is no more reason to require a preliminary showing of reasonableness here than there would be in the case of any witness who, despite the lack of any constitutional or statutory privilege, declined to answer a question or comply with a grand jury request. Neither the Constitution nor our prior cases justify any such interference with grand jury proceedings.[7]

The Fifth Amendment guarantees that no civilian may be brought to trial for an infamous crime "unless on a presentment or indictment of a Grand Jury." This constitutional guarantee presupposes an in-

7. Mr. Justice MARSHALL in dissent suggests that a preliminary showing of "reasonableness" is required where the grand jury subpoenas a witness to appear and produce handwriting or voice exemplars, but not when it subpoenas him to appear and testify. Such a distinction finds no support in the Constitution. The dissent argues that there is a potential Fourth Amendment violation in the case of a subpoenaed grand jury witness because of the asserted intrusiveness of the initial subpoena to appear—the possible stigma from a grand jury appearance and the inconvenience of the official restraint. But the initial directive to appear is as intrusive if the witness is called simply to testify as it is if he is summoned to produce physical evidence.

vestigative body "acting independently of either prosecuting attorney or judge," Stirone v. United States, 361 U.S. 212, 218, 80 S.Ct. 270, 273, whose mission is to clear the innocent, no less than to bring to trial those who may be guilty.[8] Any holding that would saddle a grand jury with mini-trials and preliminary showings would assuredly impede its investigation and frustrate the public's interest in the fair and expeditious administration of the criminal laws.[9] The grand jury may not always serve its historic role as a protective bulwark standing solidly between the ordinary citizen and an overzealous prosecutor, but if it is even to approach the proper performance of its constitutional mission, it must be free to pursue its investigations unhindered by external influence or supervision so long as it does not trench upon the legitimate rights of any witness called before it.

Since the Court of Appeals found an unreasonable search and seizure where none existed, and imposed a preliminary showing of reasonableness where none was required, its judgment is reversed and this case is remanded to that Court for further proceedings consistent with this opinion.

It is so ordered.

Judgment reversed and case remanded.

UNITED STATES v. MARA

Supreme Court of the United States, 1973.
410 U.S. 19, 93 S.Ct. 774.

MR. JUSTICE STEWART delivered the opinion of the Court.

The respondent, Richard J. Mara, was subpoenaed to appear before the September 1971 Grand Jury in the Northern District of Illinois that was investigating thefts of interstate shipments. On two

8. "[T]he institution was adopted in this country, and is continued from considerations similar to those which give to it its chief value in England, and is designed as a means, not only of bringing to trial persons accused of public offences upon just grounds, but also as a means of protecting the citizen against unfounded accusation, whether it comes from government, or be prompted by partisan passion or private enmity. No person shall be required, according to the fundamental law of the country, except in the cases mentioned, to answer for any of the higher crimes unless this body, consisting of not less than sixteen nor more than twenty-three good and lawful men, selected from the body of the district, shall declare, upon careful deliberation, under the solemnity of an oath, that there is good reason for his accusation and trial." Ex parte Bain, 121 U.S. 1, 11, 7 S.Ct. 781, 786, 30 L.Ed. 849 (quoting grand jury charge of Justice Field).

9. The possibilities for delay caused by requiring initial showings of "reasonableness" are illustrated by the Court of Appeals' subsequent decision in In re September 1971 Grand Jury, 7 Cir., 454 F.2d 580, rev'd sub nom., United States v. Mara, 410 U.S. 19, 93 S.Ct. 774, 35 L.Ed.2d 99, where the Court held that the Government was required to show in an adversary hearing that its request for exemplars was reasonable, and "reasonableness" included proof that the exemplars could not be obtained from other sources.

separate occasions he was directed to produce handwriting and printing exemplars to the grand jury's designated agent. Each time he was advised that he was a potential defendant in the matter under investigation. On both occasions he refused to produce the exemplars.

The Government then petitioned the United States District Court to compel Mara to furnish the handwriting and printing exemplars to the grand jury. The petition indicated that the exemplars were "essential and necessary" to the grand jury investigation and would be used solely as a standard of comparison to determine whether Mara was the author of certain writings. The petition was accompanied by an affidavit of an FBI agent, submitted *in camera,* which set forth the basis for seeking the exemplars. The District Judge rejected the respondent's contention that the compelled production of such exemplars would constitute an unreasonable search and seizure, and he ordered the respondent to provide them. When the witness continued to refuse to do so, he was adjudged to be in civil contempt and was committed to custody until he obeyed the court order or until the expiration of the grand jury term.

The Court of Appeals for the Seventh Circuit reversed. Relying on its earlier decision in In re Dionisio, the Court found that the directive to furnish the exemplars would constitute an unreasonable search and seizure. "[I]t is plain that compelling [Mara] to furnish exemplars of his handwriting and printing is forbidden by the Fourth Amendment unless the Government has complied with its reasonableness requirement. . . ." 454 F.2d, at 582.

The court then turned to two issues necessarily generated by its decision in *Dionisio*—the procedure the Government must follow and the substantive showing it must make to establish the reasonableness of the grand jury's directive. It rejected the *in camera* procedure of the District Court, and held that the Government would have to present its affidavit in open court in order that Mara might contest its sufficiency. The Court ruled that to establish "reasonableness" the Government would have to make a substantive showing: "that the grand jury investigation was properly authorized, for a purpose Congress can order, that the information sought is relevant to the inquiry, and that . . . the grand jury process is not being abused. . . . [T]he Government's affidavit must also show why satisfactory handwriting and printing exemplars cannot be obtained from other sources without grand jury compulsion." 454 F.2d, at 584–585.

* * *

We have held today in *Dionisio,* that a grand jury subpoena is not a "seizure" within the meaning of the Fourth Amendment, and further, that that Amendment is not violated by a grand jury directive compelling production of "physical characteristics" which are "constantly exposed to the public." Handwriting, like speech, is repeatedly shown to the public, and there is no more expectation of privacy in the physical characteristics of a person's script than there is in the tone of his voice. Consequently the Government was under no obligation here, any more than in *Dionisio,* to make a preliminary showing of "reasonableness."

Indeed, this case lacks even the aspects of an expansive investigation that the Court of Appeals found significant in *Dionisio.* In that case 20 witnesses were summoned to give exemplars; here there was only one. The specific and narrowly drawn directive requiring the witness to furnish a specimen of his handwriting* violated no legitimate Fourth Amendment interest. The District Court was correct, therefore, in ordering the respondent to comply with the grand jury's request.

[Concurring and dissenting opinions in both United States v. Dionisio and United States v. Mara.]

MR. JUSTICE BRENNAN, concurring in part and dissenting in part.

I agree, for the reasons stated by the Court, that petitioners' Fifth Amendment claims are without merit. I dissent, however, from the Court's rejection of petitioners' Fourth Amendment claims as also without merit. I agree that no unreasonable seizure in violation of the Fourth Amendment is effected by a grand jury subpoena limited to requiring the appearance of a suspect to *testify.* But insofar as the subpoena requires a suspect's appearance in order to obtain his voice or handwriting exemplars from him, I conclude, substantially in agreement with Part II of my Brother MARSHALL's dissent, that the reasonableness under the Fourth Amendment of such a seizure cannot simply be presumed. I would therefore affirm the judgments of the Court of Appeals reversing the contempt convictions and remand with directions to the District Court to afford the Government the opportunity to prove reasonableness under the standard fashioned by the Court of Appeals.

MR. JUSTICE DOUGLAS, dissenting.

Judge William Campbell, who has been on the District Court in Chicago for over 32 years, recently made the following indictment against the grand jury:

> "This great institution of the past has long ceased to be the guardian of the people for which purpose it was created at Runnymede. Today it is but a convenient tool for the prosecutor—too often used solely for publicity. Any experienced prosecutor will admit that he can indict anybody at any time for almost anything before any grand jury."

It is indeed common knowledge that the grand jury, having been conceived as a bulwark between the citizen and the Government, is now a tool of the Executive. The concession by the Court that the grand jury is no longer in a realistic sense "a protective bulwark standing solidly between the ordinary citizen and over-zealous prosecutor" is reason enough to affirm these judgments.

It is not uncommon for witnesses summoned to appear before the grand jury at a designated room to discover that the room is the room of the prosecutor. The cases before us today are prime examples of this perversion.

Respondent Dionisio and approximately 19 others were subpoenaed by the Special February 1971 Grand Jury for the Northern District of Illinois in an investigation of illegal gambling operations. During the investigation the grand jury had received as exhibits voice recordings obtained under court orders, on warrants issued under 18 U.S.C.A. § 2518 authorizing wiretaps. The witnesses were instructed to go to the U. S. Attorney's office, with their own counsel if they desired, and in the company of an FBI agent who had been appointed as an agent of the grand jury by its foreman, and to read the transcript of the wire interception. The readings were recorded. The grand jury then compared the voices taken from the wiretap and the witnesses' record. Dionisio refused to make the voice exemplars on the grounds they were violating his rights under the Fourth and Fifth Amendments. . . .

The Special September 1971 Grand Jury, also in the Northern District of Illinois, was convened to investigate thefts of interstate shipments of goods that occurred in the State. Respondent Mara was subpoenaed and was requested to submit before the grand jury a sample of his handwriting. Mara refused. . . .

Under the Fourth Amendment law enforcement officers may not compel the production of evidence absent a showing of the reasonableness of the seizure. Davis v. Mississippi, 394 U.S. 721, 89 S.Ct. 1394. The test protects the person's expectation of privacy over the thing. We said in Katz v. United States, "the Fourth Amendment protects people, not places. What a person knowingly exposes to the public, even in his own home or office, is not a subject of Fourth Amendment protection. * * * But what he seeks to preserve as private, even in an area accessible to the public, may be constitutionally protected." The Government asserts that handwriting and voice exemplars do not invade the privacy of an individual when taken because they are physical characteristics that are exposed to the public. It argues that, unless the person involved is a recluse, these characteristics are not meant to be private to the individual and thus are not subject to the aid of the Fourth Amendment.

In *Davis* the sheriff in Mississippi rounded up 24 Blacks when a rape victim described her assailant only as a young Negro. Each was fingerprinted and then released.

. . . The dragnet effect in *Dionisio*, where approximately 20 people were subpoenaed for purposes of identification, was just the kind of invasion that the *Davis* case sought to prevent. Facial features can be presented to the public regardless of the cooperation or compulsion of the owner of the features. But to get the exemplars, the individual must be involved. So, although a person's handwriting is used in everyday life and speech is the vehicle of normal, social intercourse, when these personal characteristics are sought for purposes of identification, the government enters the zone of privacy and in my view must make a showing of reasonableness before seizures may be made.

The Government contends that since the production was before the grand jury, a different standard of constitutional law exists because the grand jury has broad investigatory powers. Blair v. United States, 250 U.S. 273, 39 S.Ct. 468, 63 L.Ed. 979. The Government concedes that the Fourth Amendment applies to the grand jury and prevents it from executing subpoenas *duces tecum* that are overly broad. Hale v. Henkel, 201 U.S. 43, 76, 26 S.Ct. 370, 379–380. It asserts, however, that that is the limit of its application. But the Fourth Amendment is not so limited, as this Court has held in *Davis*, supra, and reiterated in Terry v. Ohio, 392 U.S. 1, 88 S.Ct. 1868, where it held that the Amendment comes into effect whether or not there is a fullblown search. The essential purpose is to extend its protection "wherever an individual may harbor a reasonable 'expectation of privacy.' " 392 U.S. 1, 9, 88 S.Ct. 1868, 1873.

Just as the nature of the Amendment rebels against the limits that the Government seeks to impose on its coverage, so does the nature of the grand jury itself. It was secured at Runnymede from King John as a cornerstone of the liberty of the people. It was to serve as a buffer between the State and the offender. But here, as the Court of Appeals said, "It is evident that the grand jury is seeking to obtain the voice exemplars of the witnesses by the use of its subpoena powers because probable cause did not exist for their arrest or for some other, less unusual, method of compelling the production of the exemplars." Dionisio v. United States, 7 Cir., 442 F.2d 276, 280. Are we to stand still and watch the prosecution evade its own constitutional restrictions on its powers by turning the grand jury into its agents? Are we to allow the Government to usurp powers that were granted to the people by Magna Carta and codified in our Constitution? That will be the result of the majority opinion unless we continue to apply to the grand jury the protection of the Fourth Amendment.

The executive, acting through a prosecutor, could not have obtained these exemplars as he chose, for as stated by the Court of Appeals for the Eighth Circuit, "We conclude that the taking of the handwriting exemplars . . . . was a search and seizure under the Fourth Amendment." United States v. Harris, 453 F.2d 1317, 1319.

* * *

The showing required by the Court of Appeals in the *Mara* case was that the Government's showing of need for the exemplars be "reasonable," which "is not necessarily synonymous with probable cause." 7 Cir., 454 F.2d 580, 584. When we come to grand juries, probable cause in the strict Fourth Amendment meaning of the term does not have in it the same ingredients pointing toward guilt as it does in the arrest and trial of people. In terms of probable cause in the setting of the grand jury, the question is whether the exemplar sought is in some way connected with the suspected criminal activity under investigation. Certainly less than that showing would permit the Fourth Amendment to be robbed of all of its vitality.

* * *

It would be a travesty of justice to allow the prosecutor to do under the cloak of the grand jury what he could not do on his own.

In view of the disposition which I would make of these cases, I need not reach the Fifth Amendment question. But lest there be any doubt as to my position, I adhere to my dissents in United States v. Wade, and in Schmerber v. California, to the effect that the Fifth Amendment is not restricted to testimonial compulsion.

MR. JUSTICE MARSHALL, dissenting.

[In Part I of his dissent, Justice Marshall stated his reasons for disagreeing with the Court's limitation of the Fifth Amendment privilege to testimonial evidence and exclusion of voice and handwriting exemplars from the protection of the constitutional privilege.] . . .

II

* * *

The Court seems to reason that the exception to the Fourth Amendment for grand jury subpoenas directed at persons is justified by the relative unintrusiveness of the grand jury process on an individual's liberty. The Court, adopting Chief Judge Friendly's analysis in United States v. Doe (Schwartz), 457 F.2d 895, 898 (CA2 1972), suggests that arrests or even investigatory "stops" are inimical to personal liberty because they may involve the use of force; they may be carried out in demeaning circumstances; and at least an arrest may yield the social stigma of a record. By contrast, we are told, a grand jury subpoena is a simple legal process, which is served in an unoffensive manner; it results in no stigma; and a convenient time for appearance may always be arranged. The Court would have us believe, in short, that, unlike an arrest or an investigatory "stop," a grand jury subpoena entails little more inconvenience than a visit to an old friend. Common sense and practical experience indicate otherwise.

It may be that service of a grand jury subpoena does not involve the same potential for momentary embarrassment as does an arrest or investigatory "stop." But this difference seems inconsequential in comparison to the substantial stigma which—contrary to the Court's assertion—may result from a grand jury appearance as well as from an arrest or investigatory seizure. Public knowledge that a man has been summoned by a federal grand jury investigating, for instance, organized criminal activity can mean loss of friends, irreparable injury to business, and tremendous pressures on one's family life. Whatever nice legal distinctions may be drawn between police and prosecutor, on the one hand, and the grand jury, on the other, the public often treats an appearance before a grand jury as tantamount to a visit to the station house. Indeed, the former is frequently more damaging than the latter, for a grand jury appearance has an air of far greater gravity than a brief visit "downtown" for a "talk." The Fourth Amendment was placed in our Bill of Rights to protect the individual citizen from such potentially disruptive governmental intrusion into his private life unless conducted reasonably and with sufficient cause.

Nor do I believe that the constitutional problems inherent in such governmental interference with an individual's person are substantially alleviated because one may seek to appear at a "convenient time." In Davis v. Mississippi it was recognized that an investigatory detention effected by the police "need not come unexpectedly or at an inconvenient time." But this fact did not suggest to the Court that the Fourth Amendment was inapplicable; it was considered to affect, at most, the type of showing a State would have to make to justify constitutionally such a detention. No matter how considerate a grand jury may be in arranging for an individual's appearance, the basic fact remains that his liberty has been officially restrained for some period of time. In terms of its effect on the individual, this restraint does not differ meaningfully from the restraint imposed on a suspect compelled

* * *

The Court of Appeals in *Mara* did not impose a requirement that the Government establish probable cause to support a grand jury's request for exemplars. It correctly recognized that "examination of witnesses by a grand jury need not be preceded by a formal charge against a particular individual," since the very purpose of the grand jury process is to ascertain probable cause. Consistent with the Court's decision in Hale v. Henkel, it ruled only that the request for physical evidence such as exemplars should be subject to a showing of reasonableness. This "reasonableness" requirement has previously been explained by this Court, albeit in a somewhat different context, to require a showing by the Government that: (1) "the investigation is authorized by Congress"; (2) the investigation "is for a purpose Congress can order"; (3) the evidence sought is "relevant"; and (4) the request is "adequate, but not excessive, for the purposes of the relevant inquiry." This was the interpretation of the "reasonableness" requirement properly adopted by the Court of Appeals. And, in elaborating on the requirement that the request not be "excessive," it added that the Government would bear the burden of showing that it was not conducting "a general fishing expedition under grand jury sponsorship."

These are not burdensome limitations to impose on the grand jury when it seeks to secure physical evidence, such as exemplars, that has traditionally been gathered directly by law enforcement officials. The essence of the requirement would be nothing more than a showing that the evidence sought is relevant to the purpose of the investigation and that the particular grand jury is not the subject of prosecutorial abuse—a showing that the Government should have little difficulty making, unless it is in fact acting improperly. Nor would the requirement interfere with the power of the grand jury to call witnesses before it, to take their testimony, and to ascertain their knowledge concerning criminal activity. It would only discourage prosecutorial abuse of the grand jury process. The "reasonableness" requirement would do no more in the context of these cases than the Constitution compels—protect the citizen from unreasonable and arbitrary governmental interference, and ensure that the broad subpoena powers of the grand jury which the Court now recognizes are not turned into a tool of prosecutorial oppression.[1]

B. IMMUNIZED TESTIMONY

KASTIGAR v. UNITED STATES

Supreme Court of the United States, 1972.
406 U.S. 441, 92 S.Ct. 1653.

MR. JUSTICE POWELL delivered the opinion of the Court.

This case presents the question whether the United States Government may compel testimony from an unwilling witness, who invokes the Fifth Amendment privilege against compulsory self-incrimination, by conferring on the witness immunity from use of the compelled testimony in subsequent criminal proceedings, as well as immunity from use of evidence derived from the testimony.

Petitioners were subpoenaed to appear before a United States grand jury in the Central District of California on February 4, 1971.

1. It may be that my differences with the Court are not as great as may first appear, for despite the Court's rejection of the applicability of the Fourth Amendment to grand jury subpoenas directed at "persons," it clearly recognizes that abuse of the grand jury process is not outside a court's control. Beside the Fourth Amendment, the First Amendment and both the Due Process Clause and the privilege against compulsory self-incrimination contained in the Fifth Amendment erect substantial barriers to "the transformation of the grand jury into an instrument of oppression."

The Government believed that petitioners were likely to assert their Fifth Amendment privilege. Prior to the scheduled appearances, the Government applied to the District Court for an order directing petitioners to answer questions and produce evidence before the grand jury under a grant of immunity conferred pursuant to 18 U.S.C. §§ 6002, 6003. Petitioners opposed issuance of the order, contending primarily that the scope of the immunity provided by the statute was not coextensive with the scope of the privilege against self-incrimination, and therefore was not sufficient to supplant the privilege and compel their testimony. The District Court rejected this contention, and ordered petitioners to appear before the grand jury and answer its questions under the grant of immunity.

Petitioners appeared but refused to answer questions, asserting their privilege against compulsory self-incrimination. They were brought before the District Court, and each persisted in his refusal to answer the grand jury's questions, notwithstanding the grant of immunity. The court found both in contempt, and committed them to the custody of the Attorney General until either they answered the grand jury's questions or the term of the grand jury expired. The Court of Appeals for the Ninth Circuit affirmed. This Court granted certiorari to resolve the important question whether testimony may be compelled by granting immunity from the use of the compelled testimony and evidence derived therefrom ("use and derivative use" immunity), or whether it is necessary to grant immunity from prosecution for offenses to which compelled testimony relates ("transactional" immunity).

I

The power of government to compel persons to testify in court or before grand juries and other governmental agencies is firmly established in Anglo-American jurisprudence. The power with respect to courts was established by statute in England as early as 1562, and Lord Bacon observed in 1612 that all subjects owed the King their "knowledge and discovery." While it is not clear when grand juries first resorted to compulsory process to secure the attendance and testimony of witnesses, the general common law principle that "the public has a right to every man's evidence" was considered an "indubitable certainty" which "cannot be denied" by 1742. The power to compel testimony, and the corresponding duty to testify, are recognized in the Sixth Amendment requirements that an accused be confronted with the witnesses against him, and have compulsory process for obtaining witnesses in his favor. The first Congress recognized the testimonial duty in the Judiciary Act of 1789, which provided for compulsory attendance of witnesses in the federal courts.

But the power to compel testimony is not absolute. There are a number of exemptions from the testimonial duty, the most important of which is the Fifth Amendment privilege against compulsory self-incrimination. The privilege reflects a complex of our fundamental values and aspirations, and marks an important advance in the development of our liberty. It can be asserted in any proceeding, civil or criminal, administrative or judicial, investigatory or adjudicatory; and it protects against any disclosures which the witness reasonably believes could be used in a criminal prosecution or could lead to other evidence that might be so used. This Court has been zealous to safeguard the values which underlie the privilege.

Immunity statutes, which have historical roots deep in Anglo-American jurisprudence, are not incompatible with these values. Rather they seek a rational accommodation between the imperatives of the privilege and the legitimate demands of government to compel citizens to testify. The existence of these statutes reflects the importance of testimony, and the fact that many offenses are of such a character that the only persons capable of giving useful testimony are those implicated in the crime. Indeed, their origins were in the context of such offenses, and their primary use has been to investigate such offenses. Congress included immunity statutes in many of the regulatory measures adopted in the first half of this century. Indeed, prior to the enactment of the statute under consideration in this case, there were in force over 50 federal immunity statutes. In addition, every State in the Union, as well as the District of Columbia and Puerto Rico, has one or more such statutes. The commentators, and this Court on several occasions, have characterized immunity statutes as essential to the effective enforcement of various criminal statutes. As Mr. Justice Frankfurter observed, such statutes have "become part of our constitutional fabric."

II

Petitioners contend first that the Fifth Amendment's privilege against compulsory self-incrimination, which is that "no person . . . shall be compelled in any criminal case to be a witness against himself," deprives Congress of power to enact laws which compel self-incrimination, even if complete immunity from prosecution is granted prior to the compulsion of the incriminatory testimony. In other words, petitioners assert that no immunity statute, however drawn, can afford a lawful basis for compelling incriminatory testimony. They ask us to reconsider and overrule Brown v. Walker, 161 U.S. 591, 16 S.Ct. 644 (1896), and Ullmann v. United States, 350 U.S. 422, 76 S.Ct. 497 (1956), decisions which uphold the constitutionality of immunity statutes. We find no merit to this contention and reaffirm the decisions in *Brown* and *Ullmann*.

III

Petitioners' second contention is that the scope of immunity provided by the federal witness immunity statute, 18 U.S.C. § 6002, is not coextensive with the scope of the Fifth Amendment privilege against compulsory self-incrimination, and therefore is not sufficient to supplant the privilege and compel testimony over a claim of the privilege. The statute provides that when a witness is compelled by district court order to testify over a claim of the privilege:

> "the witness may not refuse to comply with the order on the basis of his privilege against self-incrimination; but no testimony or other information compelled under the order (or any information directly or indirectly derived from such testimony or other information) may be used against the witness in any criminal case, except a prosecution for perjury, giving a false statement, or otherwise failing to comply with the order."

The constitutional inquiry, rooted in logic and history, as well as in the decisions of this Court, is whether the immunity granted under this statute is coextensive with the scope of the privilege. If so, petitioners' refusals to answer based on the privilege were unjustified, and the judgments of contempt were proper, for the grant of immunity has removed the dangers against which the privilege protects. If, on the other hand, the immunity granted is not as comprehensive as the protection afforded by the privilege, petitioners were justified in refusing to answer, and the judgments of contempt must be vacated.

Petitioners draw a distinction between statutes which provide transactional immunity and those which provide, as does the statute before us, immunity from use and derivative use. They contend that a statute must at a minimum grant full transactional immunity in order to be coextensive with the scope of the privilege. [T]he Compulsory Testimony Act of 1893 removed the privilege against self-incrimination in hearings before the Interstate Commerce Commission and provided that:

> "no person shall be prosecuted or subjected to any penalty or forfeiture for or on account of any transaction, matter or thing, concerning which he may testify, or produce evidence, documentary or otherwise. . . ."

This transactional immunity statute became the basic form for the numerous federal immunity statutes until 1970, when, after re-examining applicable constitutional principles and the adequacy of existing law, Congress enacted the statute here under consideration. . . .

The statute's explicit proscription of the use in any criminal case of "testimony or other information compelled under the order (or any information directly or indirectly derived from such testimony or other information)" is consonant with Fifth Amendment standards. We hold that such immunity from use and derivative use is coextensive with the scope of the privilege against self-incrimination, and therefore is sufficient to compel testimony over a claim of the privilege. While a grant of immunity must afford protection commensurate with that afforded by the privilege, it need not be broader. Transactional immunity, which accords full immunity from prosecution for the offense to which the compelled testimony relates, affords the witness considerably broader protection than does the Fifth Amendment privilege. The privilege has never been construed to mean that one who invokes it cannot subsequently be prosecuted. Its sole concern is to afford protection against being "forced to give testimony leading to the infliction of 'penalties affixed to . . . criminal acts.'" Immunity from the use of compelled testimony and evidence derived directly and indirectly therefrom affords this protection. It prohibits the prosecutorial authorities from using the compelled testimony in *any* respect, and it therefore insures that the testimony cannot lead to the infliction of criminal penalties on the witness.

* * *

In Murphy v. Waterfront Comm'n, 378 U.S. 52, 84 S.Ct. 1594 (1964), the Court carefully considered immunity from use of compelled testimony and evidence derived therefrom. The *Murphy* petitioners were subpoenaed to testify at a hearing conducted by the Waterfront Commission of New York Harbor. After refusing to answer certain questions on the ground that the answers might tend to incriminate them, petitioners were granted immunity from prosecution under the laws of New Jersey and New York. They continued to refuse to testify, however, on the ground that their answers might tend to incriminate them under federal law, to which the immunity did not purport to extend. They were adjudged in civil contempt, and that judgment was affirmed by the New Jersey Supreme Court.

The issue before the Court in *Murphy* was whether New Jersey and New York could compel the witnesses, whom these States had immunized from prosecution under their laws, to give testimony which might then be used to convict them of a federal crime. Since New Jersey and New York had not purported to confer immunity from federal prosecution, the Court was faced with the question what limitations the Fifth Amendment privilege imposed on the prosecutorial powers of the Federal Government, a nonimmunizing sovereign. After undertaking an examination of the policies and purposes of the privilege, the Court overturned the rule that one jurisdiction within our federal structure may compel a witness to give testimony which could be used to convict him of a crime in another jurisdiction. The Court held that the privilege protects state witnesses against incrimination under federal as well as state law, and federal witnesses against incrimination under state as well as federal law. Applying this principle to the state immunity legislation before it, the Court held the constitutional rule to be that:

> "a state witness may not be compelled to give testimony which may be incriminating under federal law unless the compelled testimony and its fruits cannot be used in any manner

> by federal officials in connection with a criminal prosecution against him. We conclude, moreover, that in order to implement this constitutional rule and accommodate the interests of the State and Federal Government in investigating and prosecuting crime, the Federal Government must be prohibited from making any such use of compelled testimony and its fruits."

The Court emphasized that this rule left the state witness and the Federal Government, against which the witness had immunity only from the *use* of the compelled testimony and evidence derived therefrom, "in substantially the same position as if the witness had claimed his privilege in the absence of a state grant of immunity."

* * *

. . . [B]oth the reasoning of the Court in *Murphy* and the result reached compel the conclusion that use and derivative use immunity is constitutionally sufficient to compel testimony over a claim of the privilege. Since the privilege is fully applicable and its scope is the same whether invoked in a state or in a federal jurisdiction, the *Murphy* conclusion that a prohibition on use and derivative use secures a witness' Fifth Amendment privilege against infringement by the Federal Government demonstrates that immunity from use and derivative use is coextensive with the scope of the privilege. As the *Murphy* Court noted, immunity from use and derivative use "leaves the witness and the Federal Government in substantially the same position as if the witness had claimed his privilege" in the absence of a grant of immunity. The *Murphy* Court was concerned solely with the danger of incrimination under federal law, and held that immunity from use and derivative use was sufficient to displace the danger. This protection coextensive with the privilege is the degree of protection which the Constitution requires, and is all that the Constitution requires even against the jurisdiction compelling testimony by granting immunity.

IV

Although an analysis of prior decisions and the purpose of the Fifth Amendment privilege indicates that use and derivative use immunity is coextensive with the privilege, we must consider additional arguments advanced by petitioners against the sufficiency of such immunity. We start from the premise, repeatedly affirmed by this Court, that an appropriately broad immunity grant is compatible with the Constitution.

Petitioners argue that use and derivative use immunity will not adequately protect a witness from various possible incriminating uses of the compelled testimony: for example, the prosecutor or other law enforcement officials may obtain leads, names of witnesses, or other information not otherwise available which might result in a prosecution. It will be difficult and perhaps impossible, the argument goes, to identify, by testimony or cross-examination the subtle ways in which the compelled testimony may disadvantage a witness, especially in the jurisdiction granting the immunity.

This argument presupposes that the statute's prohibition will prove impossible to enforce. The statute provides a sweeping proscription of any use, direct or indirect, of the compelled testimony and any information derived therefrom:

> "no testimony or other information compelled under the order (or any information directly or indirectly derived from such testimony or other information) may be used against the witness in any criminal case. . . . " 18 U.S.C. § 6002.

This total prohibition on use provides a comprehensive safeguard, barring the use of compelled testimony as an "investigatory lead," and also barring the use of any evidence obtained by focusing investigation on a witness as a result of his compelled disclosures.

A person accorded this immunity under 18 U.S.C. § 6002, and subsequently prosecuted, is not dependent for the preservation of his rights upon the integrity and good faith of the prosecuting authorities. As stated in *Murphy:*

> "Once a defendant demonstrates that he has testified, under a state grant of immunity, to matters related to the federal prosecution, the federal authorities have the burden of showing that their evidence is not tainted by establishing that they had an independent, legitimate source for the disputed evidence."

This burden of proof, which we reaffirm as appropriate, is not limited to a negation of taint; rather, it imposes on the prosecution the affirmative duty to prove that the evidence it proposes to use is derived from a legitimate source wholly independent of the compelled testimony.

This is very substantial protection, commensurate with that resulting from invoking the privilege itself. The privilege assures that a citizen is not compelled to incriminate himself by his own testimony. It usually operates to allow a citizen to remain silent when asked a question requiring an incriminatory answer. This statute, which operates after a witness has given incriminatory testimony, affords the same protection by assuring that the compelled testimony can in no way lead to the infliction of criminal penalties. The statute, like the Fifth Amendment, grants neither pardon nor amnesty. Both the statute and the Fifth Amendment allow the government to prosecute using evidence from legitimate independent sources.

* * *

There can be no justification in reason or policy for holding that the Constitution requires an amnesty grant where, acting pursuant to statute and accompanying safeguards, testimony is compelled in exchange for immunity from use and derivative use when no such amnesty is required where the government, acting without colorable right, coerces a defendant into incriminating himself.

We conclude that the immunity provided by 18 U.S.C. § 6002 leaves the witness and the prosecutorial authorities in substantially the same position as if the witness had claimed the Fifth Amendment privilege. The immunity therefore is coextensive with the privilege and suffices to supplant it. . . .

Affirmed.

MR. JUSTICE BRENNAN and MR. JUSTICE REHNQUIST took no part in the consideration or decision of this case.

[The dissenting opinion of JUSTICE DOUGLAS is omitted.]

MR. JUSTICE MARSHALL, dissenting.

Today the Court holds that the United States may compel a witness to give incriminating testimony, and subsequently prosecute him for crimes to which that testimony relates. I cannot believe the Fifth Amendment permits that result.

The Fifth Amendment gives a witness an absolute right to resist interrogation, if the testimony sought would tend to incriminate him. A grant of immunity may strip the witness of the right to refuse to testify, but only if it is broad enough to eliminate all possibility that the testimony will in fact operate to incriminate him. It must put him in precisely the same position, *vis-à-vis* the government that has compelled his testimony, as he would have been in had he remained silent in reliance on the privilege. . . . I cannot agree that a ban on use will in practice be total, if it remains open for the Government to convict the witness on the basis of evidence derived from a legitimate independent source. The Court asserts that the witness is adequately protected by a rule imposing on the Government a heavy burden of proof if it would establish the independent character of evidence to be used against the witness. But in light of the inevitable uncertainties of the fact-finding process, a greater margin of protection is required in order to provide a reliable guarantee that the witness is in exactly the same position as if he had not testified. That margin can be provided only by immunity from prosecution for the offenses to which the testimony relates, *i. e.*, transactional immunity.

I do not see how it can suffice merely to put the burden of proof on the Government. First, contrary to the Court's assertion, the Court's rule does leave the witness "dependent for the preservation of his rights upon the integrity and good faith of the prosecuting authorities." For the information relevant to the question of taint is uniquely within the knowledge of the prosecuting authorities. They alone are in a position to trace the chains of information and investigation that lead to the evidence to be used in a criminal prosecution. A witness who suspects that his compelled testimony was used to develop a lead will be hard pressed indeed to ferret out the evidence necessary to prove it. And of course it is no answer to say he need not prove it, for though the Court puts the burden of proof on the Government, the Government will have no difficulty in meeting its burden by mere assertion if the witness produces no contrary evidence. The good faith of the prosecuting authorities is thus the sole safeguard of the witness' rights. Second, even their good faith is not a sufficient safeguard. For the paths of information through the investigative bureaucracy may well be long and winding, and even a prosecutor acting in the best of faith cannot be certain that somewhere in the depths of his investigative apparatus, often including hundreds of employees, there was not some prohibited use of the compelled testimony. The Court today sets out a loose net to trap tainted evidence and prevent its use against the witness, but it accepts an intolerably great risk that tainted evidence will in fact slip through that net.

* * *

NOTE

In the companion case of Zicarelli v. New Jersey State Commission of Investigation, 406 U.S. 472, 92 S.Ct. 1670 (1972), the Supreme Court upheld the validity of the New Jersey use immunity statute. The Court also held that the statutory condition of a "responsive answer" (inserted as a safeguard against a witness giving himself a complete "immunity bath" beyond the subject matter of the investigation) was not unconstitutionally vague since the phrase "responsive answer" has a clearly understood meaning, and, moreover, the person examined has the right to counsel before the Commission who could "secure clarification of vague and ambiguous questions in advance of a responsé by the witness".

GARRITY v. NEW JERSEY

Supreme Court of the United States, 1967.
385 U.S. 493, 87 S.Ct. 616.

MR. JUSTICE DOUGLAS delivered the opinion of the Court.

Appellants were police officers in certain New Jersey boroughs. The Supreme Court of New Jersey ordered that alleged irregularities in handling cases in the municipal courts of those boroughs be investigated by the Attorney General, invested him with broad powers of inquiry and investigation, and directed him to make a report to the court. The matters investigated concerned alleged fixing of traffic tickets.

Before being questioned each appellant was warned (1) that anything he said might be used against him in any state criminal proceeding; (2) that he had the privilege to refuse to answer if the disclosure would tend to incriminate him; but (3) that if he refused to answer he would be subject to removal from office.[1]

Appellants answered the questions. No immunity was granted, as there is no immunity statute applicable in these circumstances. Over their objections, some of the answers given were used in a subsequent prosecution for conspiracy to obstruct the administration of the traffic laws. Appellants were convicted and their conviction was sustained over their protests that their statements were coerced,[2] by reason of the fact that, if they refused to answer, they could lose their positions with the police department.

* * *

The choice imposed on appellants was one between self-incrimination or job forfeiture. Coercion that vitiates a confession can be "mental as well as physical"; "the blood of the accused is not the only hallmark of an unconstitutional inquisition." Subtle pressures may be as telling as coarse and vulgar ones. The question is whether the accused was deprived of his "free choice to admit, to deny, or to refuse to answer."

We adhere to Boyd v. United States, 116 U.S. 616, 6 S.Ct. 524, a civil forfeiture action against property. A statute offered the owner an election between producing a document or forfeiture of the goods at issue in the proceeding. This was held to be a form of compulsion in violation of both the Fifth Amendment and the Fourth Amendment.

1. "Any person holding or who has held any elective or appointive public office, position or employment (whether State, county, or municipal), who refuses to testify upon matters relating to the office, position or employment in any criminal proceeding wherein he is a defendant or is called as a witness on behalf of the prosecution, upon the ground that his answer may tend to incriminate him or compel him to be a witness against himself or refuses to waive immunity when called by a grand jury to testify thereon or who willfully refuses or fails to appear before any court, commission or body of this state which has the right to inquire under oath upon matters relating to the office, position or employment of such person or who, having been sworn, refuses to testify or to answer any material question upon the ground that his answer may tend to incriminate him or compel him to be a witness against himself, shall, if holding elective or public office, position or employment, be removed therefrom or shall thereby forfeit his office, position or employment and any vested or future right of tenure or pension granted to him by any law of this State provided the inquiry relates to a matter which occurred or arose within the preceding five years. Any person so forfeiting his office, position or employment shall not thereafter be eligible for election or appointment to any public office, position or employment in this State." N.J. Rev.Stat. § 2A:81–17.1 (Supp.1965), N.J.S.A.

2. At the trial the court excused the jury and conducted a hearing to determine whether, *inter alia*, the statements were voluntary. The State offered witnesses who testified as to the manner in which the statements were taken; the appellants did not testify at that hearing. The court held the statements to be voluntary.

The choice given appellants was either to forfeit their jobs or to incriminate themselves. The option to lose their means of livelihood or to pay the penalty of self-incrimination is the antithesis of free choice to speak out or to remain silent. That practice . . . is "likely to exert such pressure upon an individual as to disable him from making a free and rational choice." We think the confessions were infected by the coercion inherent in this scheme of questioning and cannot be sustained as voluntary under our prior decisions.

It is said that there was a "waiver." That, however, is a federal question for us to decide. . . .

Where the choice is "between the rock and the whirlpool," duress is inherent in deciding to "waive" one or the other. . . .

Mr. Justice Holmes, in McAuliffe v. New Bedford, 155 Mass. 216, 29 N.E. 517, stated a dictum on which New Jersey heavily relies:

> "The petitioner may have a constitutional right to talk politics, but he has no constitutional right to be a policeman. There are few employments for hire in which the servant does not agree to suspend his constitutional right of free speech as well as of idleness by the implied terms of his contract. The servant cannot complain, as he takes the employment on the terms which are offered him. On the same principle the city may impose any reasonable condition upon holding offices within its control."

The question in this case, however, is not cognizable in those terms. Our question is whether the Government, contrary to the requirement of the Fourteenth Amendment, can use the threat of discharge to secure incriminatory evidence against an employee.

We held in Slochower v. Board of Education, 350 U.S. 551, 76 S.Ct. 637, that a public school teacher could not be discharged merely because he had invoked the Fifth Amendment privilege against self-incrimination when questioned by a congressional committee:

> "The privilege against self-incrimination would be reduced to a hollow mockery if its exercise could be taken as equivalent either to a confession of guilt or a conclusive presumption of perjury. . . . The privilege serves to protect the innocent who otherwise might be ensnared by ambiguous circumstances."

We conclude that policemen, like teachers and lawyers, are not relegated to a watered-down version of constitutional rights.

There are rights of constitutional stature whose exercise a State may not condition by the exaction of a price. . . . We now hold the protection of the individual under the Fourteenth Amendment against coerced confessions prohibits use in subsequent criminal proceedings of confessions obtained under threat of removal from office, and that it extends to all, whether they are policemen or other members of our body politic.

Reversed.

MR. JUSTICE HARLAN, whom MR. JUSTICE CLARK and MR. JUSTICE STEWART join, dissenting.

* * *

The majority is apparently engaged in the delicate task of riding two unruly horses at once: it is presumably arguing simultaneously that the statements were involuntary as a matter of fact . . . , and that the statements were inadmissible as a matter of law, on the premise that they were products of an impermissible condition imposed on the constitutional privilege. These are very different contentions and require separate replies, but in my opinion both contentions are plainly mistaken, for reasons that follow.

I.

I turn first to the suggestion that these statements were involuntary in fact. An assessment of the voluntariness of the various statements in issue here requires a more comprehensive examination of the pertinent circumstances than the majority has undertaken.

The petitioners were at all material times policemen in the boroughs of Bellmawr and Barrington, New Jersey. Garrity was Bellmawr's chief of police and Virtue one of its police officers; Holroyd, Elwell, and Murray were police officers in Barrington. Another defendant below, Mrs. Naglee, the clerk of Bellmawr's municipal court, has since died. In June 1961 the New Jersey Supreme Court *sua sponte* directed the State's Attorney General to investigate reports of traffic ticket fixing in Bellmawr and Barrington. Subsequent investigations produced evidence that the petitioners, in separate conspiracies, had falsified municipal court records, altered traffic tickets, and diverted moneys produced from bail and fines to unauthorized purposes. In the course of these investigations the State obtained two sworn statements from each of the petitioners; portions of those statements were admitted at trial. The petitioners were convicted in two separate trials of conspiracy to obstruct the proper administration of the state motor traffic laws, the cases being now consolidated for purposes of our review. The Supreme Court of New Jersey affirmed all the convictions.

The first statements were taken from the petitioners by the State's Deputy Attorney General in August and November 1961. All of the usual indicia of duress are wholly absent. As the state court noted, there was "no physical coercion, no overbearing tactics of psychological persuasion, no lengthy incommunicado detention, or efforts to humiliate or ridicule the defendants." The state court found no evidence that any of the petitioners were reluctant to offer statements, and concluded that the interrogations were conducted with a "high degree of civility and restraint."

These conclusions are fully substantiated by the record. The statements of the Bellmawr petitioners were taken in a room in the local firehouse, for which Chief Garrity himself had made arrangements. None of the petitioners were in custody before or after the depositions were taken; each apparently continued to pursue his ordinary duties as a public official of the community. The statements were recorded by a court stenographer, who testified that he witnessed no indications of unwillingness or even significant hesitation on the part of any of the petitioners. The Bellmawr petitioners did not have counsel present, but the Deputy Attorney General testified without contradiction that Garrity had informed him as they strolled between Garrity's office and the firehouse that he had arranged for counsel, but thought that none would be required at that stage. The interrogations were not excessively lengthy, and reasonable efforts were made to assure the physical comfort of the witnesses. Mrs. Naglee, the clerk of the Bellmawr municipal court, who was known to suffer from a heart ailment, was assured that questioning would cease if she felt any discomfort.

The circumstances in which the depositions of the Barrington petitioners were taken are less certain . . . The defense did not contend that the statements were the result of physical or mental coercion, or that the wills of the Barrington petitioners were overborne. Accordingly, the State was never obliged to offer evidence of the voluntariness in fact of the statements. We are, however, informed that the three Barrington petitioners had counsel present as their depositions were taken. Insofar as the majority suggests that the Barrington statements are involuntary in fact . . . , it has introduced a factual contention never urged by the Barrington petitioners and never considered by the courts of New Jersey.

As interrogation commenced, each of the petitioners was sworn, carefully informed that he need not give any information, reminded that any information given might be used in a subsequent criminal prosecution, and warned that as a police officer he was subject to a proceeding to discharge him if he failed to provide information relevant to his public responsibilities. The cautionary statements varied slightly, but all, except that given to Mrs. Naglee, included each of the three warnings.* Mrs. Naglee was not told that she could be re-

* The warning given to Chief Garrity is typical. "I want to advise you that anything you say must be said of your own free will and accord without any threats or promises or coercion and anything you say may be, of course, used against you or any other person in any subsequent criminal proceedings in the courts of our state.

"You do have, under our law, as you probably know, a privilege to refuse to make any disclosure which may tend to incriminate you. If you make a disclosure with knowledge of this right or privilege, voluntarily, you thereby waive that right or privilege in relation to any other questions which I might put to you relevant to such disclosure in this investigation.

"This right or privilege which you have is somewhat limited to the extent that you as a police officer under the laws

moved from her position at the court if she failed to give information pertinent to the discharge of her duties. All of the petitioners consented to give statements, none displayed any significant hesitation, and none suggested that the decision to offer information was motivated by the possibility of discharge.

A second statement was obtained from each of the petitioners in September and December 1962. These statements were not materially different in content or circumstances from the first. The only significant distinction was that the interrogator did not advert even obliquely to any possibility of dismissal. All the petitioners were cautioned that they were entitled to remain silent, and there was no evidence whatever of physical or mental coercion.

All of the petitioners testified at trial, and gave evidence essentially consistent with the statements taken from them. At a preliminary hearing conducted at the Bellmawr trial to determine the voluntariness of the statements, the Bellmawr petitioners offered no evidence beyond proof of the warning given them.

The standards employed by the Court to assess the voluntariness of an accused's statements have reflected a number of values, and thus have emphasized a variety of factual criteria. The criteria employed have included threats of imminent danger, physical deprivations, repeated or extended interrogation, limits on access to counsel or friends, length and illegality of detention under state law, Haynes v. State of Washington, individual weakness or incapacities, Lynumn v. State of Illinois, and the adequacy of warnings of constitutional rights. Whatever the criteria employed, the duty of the Court has been "to examine the entire record," and thereby to determine whether the accused's will "was overborne by the sustained pressures upon him."

It would be difficult to imagine interrogations to which these criteria of duress were more completely inapplicable, or in which the requirements which have subsequently been imposed by this Court on police questioning were more thoroughly satisfied. Each of the petitioners received a complete and explicit reminder of his constitutional privilege. Three of the petitioners had counsel present; at least a fourth had consulted counsel but freely determined that his presence was unnecessary. These petitioners were not in any fashion "swept from familiar surroundings into police custody, surrounded by antagonistic forces, and subjected to the techniques of persuasion

of our state . . . may be subjected to a proceeding to have you removed from office if you refuse to answer a question put to you under oath pertaining to your office or your function within that office. It doesn't mean, however, you can't exercise that right. You do have the right."

A. "No, I will cooperate."

Q. "Understanding this, are you willing to proceed at this time and answer any questions?"

A. "Yes."

. . . ." I think it manifest that, under the standards developed by this Court to assess voluntariness, there is no basis for saying that any of these statements were made involuntarily.

The issue remaining is whether the statements were inadmissible because they were "involuntary as a matter of law," in that they were given after a warning that New Jersey policemen may be discharged for failure to provide information pertinent to their public responsibilities. What is really involved on this score, however, is not in truth a question of "voluntariness" at all, but rather whether the condition imposed by the State on the exercise of the privilege against self-incrimination, namely dismissal from office, in this instance serves in itself to render the statements inadmissible. Absent evidence of involuntariness in fact, the admissibility of these statements thus hinges on the validity of the consequence which the State acknowledged might have resulted if the statements had not been given. If the consequence is constitutionally permissible, there can surely be no objection if the State cautions the witness that it may follow if he remains silent. If both the consequence and the warning are constitutionally permissible, a witness is obliged, in order to prevent the use of his statements against him in a criminal prosecution, to prove under the standards established since Brown v. State of Mississippi that as a matter of fact the statements were involuntarily made. The central issues here are . . . whether consequences may properly be permitted to result to a claimant after his invocation of the constitutional privilege, and if so, whether the consequence in question is permissible. . . . [N]othing in the logic or purposes of the privilege demands that all consequences which may result from a witness' silence be forbidden merely because that silence is privileged. The validity of a consequence depends both upon the hazards, if any, it presents to the integrity of the privilege and upon the urgency of the public interests it is designed to protect.

It can hardly be denied that New Jersey is permitted by the Constitution to establish reasonable qualifications and standards of conduct for its public employees. Nor can it be said that it is arbitrary or unreasonable for New Jersey to insist that its employees furnish the appropriate authorities with information pertinent to their employment. Finally, it is surely plain that New Jersey may in particular require its employees to assist in the prevention and detection of unlawful activities by officers of the state government. The urgency of these requirements is the more obvious here, where the conduct in question is that of officials directly entrusted with the administration of justice. The importance for our systems of justice of the integrity of local police forces can scarcely be exaggerated. In evidence, it need only be recalled that this Court itself has often intervened in state criminal prosecutions precisely on the ground that this might encourage high standards of police behavior. It must be concluded, therefore, that the sanction at issue here is reasonably calculated to serve the most basic interests of the citizens of New Jersey.

The final question is the hazard, if any, which this sanction presents to the constitutional privilege. The purposes for which, and the circumstances in which, an officer's discharge might be ordered under New Jersey law plainly may vary. It is of course possible that discharge might in a given case be predicated on an imputation of guilt drawn from the use of the privilege, as was thought by this Court to have occurred in Slochower v. Board of Higher Ed., supra. But from our vantage point, it would be quite improper to assume that New Jersey will employ these procedures for purposes other than to assess in good faith an employee's continued fitness for public employment. This Court, when a state procedure for investigating the loyalty and fitness of public employees might result either in the *Slochower* situation or in an assessment in good faith of an employee, has until today consistently paused to examine the actual circumstances of each case. I am unable to see any justification for the majority's abandonment of that process; it is well calculated both to protect the essential purposes of the privilege and to guarantee the most generous opportunities for the pursuit of other public values. The majority's broad prohibition, on the other hand, extends the scope of the privilege beyond its essential purposes, and seriously hampers the protection of other important values. As the majority's prohibition is applied in this case, it seems implicit in it, despite the majority's disclaimer, that it would entirely forbid a sanction which presents, at least on its face, no hazard to the purposes of the constitutional privilege, and which may reasonably be expected to serve important public interests. We are not entitled to assume that discharges will be used either to vindicate impermissible inferences of guilt or to penalize privileged silence, but must instead presume that this procedure is only intended and will only be used to establish and enforce standards of conduct for public employees. As such, it does not minimize or endanger the petitioners' constitutional privilege against self-incrimination.

I would therefore conclude that the sanction provided by the State is constitutionally permissible. From this, it surely follows that the warning given of the possibility of discharge is constitutionally unobjectionable. Given the constitutionality both of the sanction and of the warning of its application, the petitioners would be constitutionally entitled to exclude the use of their statements as evidence in a criminal prosecution against them only if it is found that the statements were, when given, involuntary in fact. For the reasons stated above, I cannot agree that these statements were involuntary in fact.

I would affirm the judgments of the Supreme Court of New Jersey.

GARDNER v. BRODERICK

Supreme Court of the United States, 1968.
392 U.S. 273, 88 S.Ct. 1913.

MR. JUSTICE FORTAS delivered the opinion of the Court.

Appellant brought this action in the Supreme Court of the State of New York seeking reinstatement as a New York City patrolman and back pay. He claimed he was unlawfully dismissed because he refused to waive his privilege against self-incrimination. In August 1965, pursuant to subpoena, appellant appeared before a New York County grand jury which was investigating alleged bribery and corruption of police officers in connection with unlawful gambling operations. He was advised that the grand jury proposed to examine him concerning the performance of his official duties. He was advised of his privilege against self-incrimination [1] but he was asked to sign a "waiver of immunity" after being told that he would be fired if he did not sign.[2] Following his refusal, he was given an administrative hearing and was discharged solely for this refusal, pursuant to § 1123 of the New York City Charter.

Our decisions establish beyond dispute the breadth of the privilege to refuse to respond to questions when the result may be self-incriminatory and the need fully to implement its guaranty. . . . The privilege is applicable to state as well as federal proceedings. . . . The privilege may be waived in appropriate circumstances if the waiver is knowingly and voluntarily made. Answers may be compelled regardless of the privilege if there is immunity from federal and state use of the compelled testimony or its fruits in connection with a criminal prosecution against the person testifying. . . .

1. The Assistant District Attorney said to appellant:

"You understand * * * that under the Constitution of the United States, as well as the Constitution of New York, no one can be compelled to testify against himself, and that he has a right, the absolute right to refuse to answer any questions that would tend to incriminate him?"

2. Appellant was told:

"You understand * * * that under the Constitution of the United States, as the Charter of the City of New York, * * * a public officer, which includes a police officer, when called before a Grand Jury to answer questions concerning the conduct of his public office and the performance of his duties is required to sign a waiver of immunity if he wishes to retain that public office?"

The document appellant was asked to sign was phrased as follows:

"I * * * do hereby waive all benefits, privileges, rights and immunity which I would otherwise obtain from indictment, prosecution, and punishment for or on account of, regarding or relating to any matter, transaction or things, concerning the conduct of my office or the performance of my official duties, or the property, government or affairs of the State of New York or of any county included within its territorial limits, or the nomination, election, appointment or official conduct of any officer of the city or of any such county, concerning any of which matters, transactions or things I may testify or produce evidence documentary or otherwise, before the [blank] Grand Jury in the County of New York in the investigation being conducted by said Grand Jury."

The question presented in the present case is whether a policeman who refuses to waive the protections which the privilege gives him may be dismissed from office because of that refusal.

About a year and a half after New York City discharged petitioner for his refusal to waive this immunity, we decided Garrity v. State of New Jersey, 385 U.S. 493, 87 S.Ct. 616 (1967). * * *

The New York Court of Appeals considered that *Garrity* did not control the present case. It is true that *Garrity* related to the attempted use of compelled testimony. It did not involve the precise question which is presented here: namely, whether a State may discharge an officer for refusing to waive a right which the Constitution guarantees to him. The New York Court of Appeals also distinguished our post-*Garrity* decision in Spevack v. Klein, 385 U.S. 511, 87 S.Ct. 625. In *Spevack*, we ruled that a lawyer could not be disbarred solely because he refused to testify at a disciplinary proceeding on the ground that his testimony would tend to incriminate him. The Court of Appeals concluded that *Spevack* does not control the present case because different considerations apply in the case of a public official such as a policeman. A lawyer, it stated, although licensed by the state is not an employee. This distinction is now urged upon us. It is argued that although a lawyer could not constitutionally be confronted with Hobson's choice between self-incrimination and forfeiting his means of livelihood, the same principle should not protect a policeman. Unlike the lawyer, he is directly, immediately, and entirely responsible to the city or State which is his employer. He owes his entire loyalty to it. He has no other "client" or principal. He is a trustee of the public interest, bearing the burden of great and total responsibility to his public employer. Unlike the lawyer who is directly responsible to his client, the policeman is either responsible to the State or to no one.

We agree that these factors differentiate the situations. If appellant, a policeman, had refused to answer questions specifically, directly, and narrowly relating to the performance of his official duties, without being required to waive his immunity with respect to the use of his answers or the fruits thereof in a criminal prosecution of himself, . . . the privilege against self-incrimination would not have been a bar to his dismissal.

The facts of this case, however, do not present this issue. Here, petitioner was summoned to testify before a grand jury in an investigation of alleged criminal conduct. He was discharged from office, not for failure to answer relevant questions about his official duties, but for refusal to waive a constitutional right. He was dismissed for failure to relinquish the protections of the privilege against self-incrimination. The Constitution of New York State and the City Charter both expressly provided that his failure to do so, as well as his failure to testify, would result in dismissal from his job. He was dismissed solely for his refusal to waive the immunity to which he is entitled if he is required to testify despite his constitutional privilege.

We need not speculate whether, if appellant had executed the waiver of immunity in the circumstances, the effect of our subsequent decision in Garrity v. State of New Jersey, supra, would have been to nullify the effect of the waiver. New York City discharged him for refusal to execute a document purporting to waive his constitutional rights and to permit prosecution of himself on the basis of his compelled testimony. Petitioner could not have assumed—and certainly he was not required to assume—that he was being asked to do an idle act of no legal effect. In any event, the mandate of the great privilege against self-incrimination does not tolerate the attempt, regardless of its ultimate effectiveness, to coerce a waiver of the immunity it confers on penalty of the loss of employment. It is clear that petitioner's testimony was demanded before the grand jury in part so that it might be used to prosecute him, and not solely for the purpose of securing an accounting of his performance of his public trust. If the latter had been the only purpose, there would have been no reason to seek to compel petitioner to waive his immunity. Proper regard for the history and meaning of the privilege against self-incrimination, . . . dictate the conclusion that the provision of the New York City Charter pursuant to which petitioner was dismissed cannot stand. Accordingly, the judgment is reversed.

Reversed.

MR. JUSTICE BLACK concurs in the result.

NOTES

1. Does Gardner v. Broderick permit a police department to immunize its officers from criminal prosecution by requiring them to answer questions concerning their conduct while on duty—for instance, a case involving the questionable shooting of a citizen? Granted that after *Kastigar* the immunity provided in such a situation would probably be use immunity rather than transactional immunity, the burden would still be on the prosecution to show that none of its evidence is derived from the "compelled" testimony given by the officer under threat of loss of job if the self-incrimination privilege is invoked in an official police internal investigation. Would the prosecution do better to refuse to examine the internal investigation reports for fear of tainting a criminal prosecution? Is this solution practical?

2. The *Gardner* solution to a difficult Fifth Amendment problem, permitting the compulsion of testimony upon the promise that it may not be used, is one example of the "use exclusion" doctrine which had its origins in Murphy v. Waterfront Commissioner, 378 U.S. 52, 84 S.Ct. 1594 (1964). There a state investigative agency granted a witness immunity from state prosecution. The witness claimed that he still had a right to invoke the Fifth Amendment because his answers could subject him to prosecution under federal law. In upholding the statute, the Court prohibited the subsequent use by federal authorities of the testimony thus compelled. Although the California Supreme Court had adopted this sort of compromise to up-

hold its "stop and report" law applicable to motorists involved in auto accidents, the Supreme Court of the United States rejected it in California v. Byers, 402 U.S. 424, 91 S.Ct. 1535 (1971). (In *Byers* the Court held that such a statute did not violate Fifth Amendment principles and that evidence derived from compliance could be used in a criminal prosecution). The rejection and judicially created use-immunity doctrines under such circumstances can ordinarily be justified by reference to legislative intent. For instance, it seems clear that the California legislature did not intend to grant use immunity in enacting its stop-and-report law. Nothing suggests it was willing to make criminal prosecution more difficult when it enacted the law in question. See also Marchetti v. United States, 390 U.S. 39, 88 S.Ct. 697 (1968), where in striking down certain gambling registration requirements, the Court refused to "save" the federal statute by creating a use-immunity doctrine which would have made state gambling prosecutions more difficult where the purpose of the statute was to do quite the opposite.

Carried to its logical extreme, the use-exclusion doctrine would permit a judge to order a witness who has invoked the Fifth Amendment in any proceeding to testify on the theory that testimony given under such an order, and evidence derived from such testimony, could not be used against him in a federal prosecution. The *Murphy* Court said that state compulsion of testimony would be permissible in the future because under such circumstances, the Court would prohibit the use of such testimony in a federal prosecution. Thus *Murphy* appears to permit a state prosecutor to grant immunity (use, not transactional) in federal prosecutions.

One criticism of use-immunity doctrines arises out of reflection upon *Gardner* and *Murphy*. Historically, grants of immunity have been given only where (1) a statute specifically authorizing immunity exists and (2) the prosecutor of the jurisdiction in question has exercised his discretion to seek judicial approval of a grant of immunity. In *Gardner* and *Murphy* someone other than that prosecutor is making the decision to grant immunity.

Use-exclusion is often proposed as a method of upholding statutory schemes which arguably compel a person to give testimony against himself. In *Byers, supra,* under a statute which required a driver involved in an accident to stop and report his name and address, it was argued that the Fifth Amendment issue should be resolved by upholding the statute but prohibiting the use of any evidence derived from the driver's compliance with the statute not be used in a criminal prosecution. The fallacy is that the procedure would permit a grant of immunity without specific statutory authorization and, in many instances, without any prosecutorial participation in the decision to grant immunity.

Chapter 15

EYE–WITNESS IDENTIFICATION PROCEDURES

A. THE RIGHT TO PRESENCE OF COUNSEL

UNITED STATES v. WADE

Supreme Court of the United States, 1967.
388 U.S. 218, 87 S.Ct. 1926.

MR. JUSTICE BRENNAN delivered the opinion of the Court.

The question here is whether courtroom identifications of an accused at trial are to be excluded from evidence because the accused was exhibited to the witnesses before trial at a post-indictment lineup conducted for identification purposes without notice to and in the absence of the accused's appointed counsel.

The federally insured bank in Eustace, Texas, was robbed on September 21, 1964. A man with a small strip of tape on each side of his face entered the bank, pointed a pistol at the female cashier and the vice president, the only persons in the bank at the time, and forced them to fill a pillowcase with the bank's money. The man then drove away with an accomplice waiting in a stolen car outside the bank. On March 23, 1965, an indictment was returned against respondent Wade and two others for conspiring to rob the bank, and against Wade and the accomplice for the robbery itself. Wade was arrested on April 2, and counsel was appointed to represent him on April 26. Fifteen days later an FBI agent, without notice to Wade's lawyer, arranged to have the two bank employees observe a lineup made up of Wade and five or six other prisoners and conducted in a courtroom of the local county courthouse. Each person in the line wore strips of tape such as allegedly worn by the robber and upon direction each said something like "put the money in the bag," the words allegedly uttered by the robber. Both bank employees identified Wade in the lineup as the bank robber.

At trial the two employees, when asked on direct examination if the robber was in the courtroom, pointed to Wade. The prior lineup identification was then elicited from both employees on cross-examination. At the close of testimony, Wade's counsel moved for a judgment of acquittal or, alternatively, to strike the bank officials' courtroom identifications on the ground that conduct of the lineup, without notice to and in the absence of his appointed counsel, violated his Fifth Amendment privilege against self-incrimination and his Sixth Amendment right to the assistance of counsel. The motion was denied, and Wade was convicted. The Court of Appeals for the Fifth Circuit reversed the conviction and ordered a new trial at which the in-court identification evidence was to be excluded, holding that, though the lineup did not violate Wade's Fifth Amendment rights, "the lineup, held as it was, in the absence of counsel, already chosen to represent appellant, was a violation of his Sixth Amendment rights . . . ." We granted certiorari and set the case for oral argument with Gilbert v. State of California, and Stovall v. Denno, which present similar questions. We reverse the judgment of the Court of Appeals and remand to that court with direction to enter a new judgment vacating the conviction and remanding the case to the District Court for further proceedings consistent with this opinion.

I.

Neither the lineup itself nor anything shown by this record that Wade was required to do in the lineup violated his privilege against self-incrimination. We have only recently reaffirmed that the privilege "protects an accused only from being compelled to testify against himself, or otherwise provide the State with evidence of a testimonial or communicative nature . . . ." Schmerber v. California, 384 U.S. 757, 86 S.Ct. 1826. We there held that compelling a suspect to submit to a withdrawal of a sample of his blood for analysis for alcohol content and the admission in evidence of the analysis report was not compulsion to those ends. That holding was supported by the opinion in Holt v. United States . . . in which case a question arose as to whether a blouse belonged to the defendant. A witness testified at trial that the defendant put on the blouse and it had fit him. The defendant argued that the admission of the testimony was error because compelling him to put on the blouse was a violation of his privilege. The Court rejected the claim as "an extravagant extension of the Fifth Amendment," Mr. Justice Holmes saying for the Court:

> "[T]he prohibition of compelling a man in a criminal court to be witness against himself is a prohibition of the use of physical or moral compulsion to extort communications from him, not an exclusion of his body as evidence when it may be material."

* * *

We have no doubt that compelling the accused merely to exhibit his person for observation by a prosecution witness prior to trial involves no compulsion of the accused to give evidence having testimonial significance. It is compulsion of the accused to exhibit his physical characteristics, not compulsion to disclose any knowledge he might have. It is no different from compelling Schmerber to provide a blood sample or Holt to wear the blouse, and, as in those instances, is not within the cover of the privilege. Similarly, compelling Wade to speak within hearing distance of the witnesses, even to utter words purportedly uttered by the robber, was not compulsion to utter statements of a "testimonial" nature; he was required to use his voice as an identifying physical characteristic, not to speak his guilt. We held in *Schmerber*, supra, that the distinction to be drawn under the Fifth Amendment privilege against self-incrimination is one between an accused's "communications" in whatever form, vocal or physical, and "compulsion which makes a suspect or accused the source of 'real or physical evidence,' ". We recognized that "both federal and state courts have usually held that . . . [the privilege] offers no protection against compulsion to submit to fingerprinting, photography, or measurements, to write or speak for identification, to appear in court, to stand, to assume a stance, to walk, or to make a particular gesture." None of these activities becomes testimonial within the scope of the privilege because required of the accused in a pretrial lineup.

Moreover, it deserves emphasis, that this case presents no question of the admissibility in evidence of anything Wade said or did at the lineup which implicates his privilege. The Government offered no such evidence as part of its case, and what came out about the lineup proceedings on Wade's cross-examination of the bank employees involved no violation of Wade's privilege.

II.

The fact that the lineup involved no violation of Wade's privilege against self-incrimination does not, however, dispose of his contention that the court room identifications should have been excluded because the lineup was conducted without notice to and in the absence of his counsel. Our rejection of the right to counsel claim in *Schmerber* rested on our conclusion in that case that "no issue of counsel's ability to assist petitioner in respect of any rights he did possess is presented." In contrast, in this case it is urged that the assistance of counsel at the lineup was indispensable to protect Wade's most basic right as a criminal defendant—his right to a fair trial at which the witnesses against him might be meaningfully cross-examined.

* * * When the Bill of Rights was adopted, there were no organized police forces as we know them today. The accused confronted the prosecutor and the witnesses against him, and the evidence was marshalled, largely at the trial itself. In contrast, today's law enforcement machinery involves critical confrontations of the accused by the prosecution at pretrial proceedings where the results might well settle the accused's fate and reduce the trial itself to a mere formality. In recognition of these realities of modern criminal prosecution, our cases have construed the Sixth Amendment guarantee to apply to "critical" stages of the proceedings. * * *

* * * It is central to that principle that in addition to counsel's presence at trial, the accused is guaranteed that he need not stand alone against the State at any stage of the prosecution, formal or informal, in court or out, where counsel's absence might derogate the accused's right to a fair trial. . . . The presence of counsel at such critical confrontations, as at the trial itself, operates to assure that the accused's interests will be protected consistently with our adversary theory of criminal prosecution.

In sum, the principle of Powell v. Alabama and succeeding cases requires that we scrutinize *any* pretrial confrontation of the accused to determine whether the presence of his counsel is necessary to preserve the defendant's basic right to a fair trial as affected by his right meaningfully to cross-examine the witnesses against him and to have effective assistance of counsel at the trial itself. It calls upon us to analyze whether potential substantial prejudice to defendant's rights inheres in the particular confrontation and the ability of counsel to help avoid that prejudice.

III.

The Government characterizes the lineup as a mere preparatory step in the gathering of the prosecution's evidence, not different—for Sixth Amendment purposes—from various other preparatory steps, such as systematized or scientific analyses of the accused's fingerprints, blood sample, clothing, hair, and the like. We think there are differences which preclude such stages being characterized as critical stages at which the accused has the right to the presence of his counsel. Knowledge of the techniques of science and technology is sufficiently available, and the variables in techniques few enough, that the accused has the opportunity for a meaningful confrontation of the Government's case at trial through the ordinary processes of cross-examination of the Government's expert witnesses and the presentation of the evidence of his own experts. The denial of a right to have his counsel present at such analyses does not therefore violate the Sixth Amendment; they are not critical stages since there is minimal risk that his counsel's absence at such stages might derogate his right to a fair trial.

IV.

But the confrontation compelled by the State between the accused and the victim or witnesses to a crime to elicit identification evidence is peculiarly riddled with innumerable dangers and variable factors which might seriously, even crucially, derogate from a fair trial. The vagaries of eyewitness identification are well-known; the annals of criminal law are rife with instances of mistaken identification.[1] Mr. Justice Frankfurter once said: "What is the worth of identification testimony even when uncontradicted? The identification of strangers is proverbially untrustworthy. The hazards of such testimony are established by a formidable number of instances in the records of English and American trials. These instances are recent—not due to the brutalities of ancient criminal procedure." The Case of Sacco and Vanzetti 30 (1927). A major factor contributing to the high incidence of miscarriage of justice from mistaken

1. Borchard, Convicting the Innocent; Frank & Frank, Not Guilty; Wall, Eyewitness Identification in Criminal Cases, 3 Wigmore, Evidence § 786(a) (3d ed. 1940); Rolph, Personal Identity; Gross, Criminal Investigation 47–54 (Jackson ed. 1962); Williams, Proof of Guilt 83–98 (1952); Wills, Circumstantial Evidence 192–205 (7th ed. 1937); Wigmore, The Science of Judicial Proof §§ 250–253.

identification has been the degree of suggestion inherent in the manner in which the prosecution presents the suspect to witnesses for pretrial identification. A commentator has observed that "the influence of improper suggestion upon identifying witnesses probably accounts for more miscarriages of justice than any other single factor—perhaps it is responsible for more such errors than all other factors combined." Wall, Eyewitness Identification in Criminal Cases 26. Suggestion can be created intentionally or unintentionally in many subtle ways. And the dangers for the suspect are particularly grave when the witness' opportunity for observation was insubstantial, and thus his susceptibility to suggestion the greatest.

Moreover, "it is a matter of common experience that, once a witness has picked out the accused at the line-up, he is not likely to go back on his word later on, so that in practice the issue of identity may (in the absence of other relevant evidence) for all practical purposes be determined there and then, before the trial." [2]

The pretrial confrontation for purpose of identification may take the form of a lineup, also known as an "identification parade" or "showup," as in the present case, or presentation of the suspect alone to the witness, as in Stovall v. Denno, post. It is obvious that risks of suggestion attend either form of confrontation and increase the dangers inhering in eyewitness identification. But as is the case with secret interrogations, there is serious difficulty in depicting what transpires at lineups and other forms of identification confrontations. "Privacy results in secrecy and this in turn results in a gap in our knowledge as to what in fact goes on . . . ." Miranda v. State of Arizona, supra. For the same reasons, the defense can seldom reconstruct the manner and mode of lineup identification for judge or jury at trial. Those participating in a lineup with the accused may often be police officers; in any event, the participants' names are rarely recorded or divulged at trial.[3] The impediments to an objective observation are increased when the victim is the witness. Lineups are prevalent in rape and robbery prosecutions and present a particular hazard that a victim's understandable outrage may excite vengeful or spiteful motives. In any event, neither witnesses nor lineup participants are apt to be alert for conditions prejudicial to the suspect. And if they were, it would likely be of scant benefit to the suspect since neither witnesses nor lineup participants are likely to be schooled in the detection of suggestive influences.[4] Improper influences may go undetected by a suspect, guilty or not, who

2. Williams & Hammelmann, Identification Parades, Part I, [1963] Crim.L. Rev. 479, 482.

3. See Rolph, Personal Identity 50; "The bright burden of identity, at these parades, is lifted from the innocent participants to hover about the suspects, leaving the rest featureless and unknown and without interest."

4. An additional impediment to the detection of such influences by participants, including the suspect, is the physical conditions often surrounding the conduct of the lineup. In many, lights shine on the stage in such a way that the suspect cannot see the witness. In some a one-way mirror is used and what is said on the witness' side cannot be heard.

experiences the emotional tension which we might expect in one being confronted with potential accusers. Even when he does observe abuse, if he has a criminal record he may be reluctant to take the stand and open up the admission of prior convictions. Moreover any protestations by the suspect of the fairness of the lineup made at trial are likely to be in vain; [5] the jury's choice is between the accused's unsupported version and that of the police officers present.[6] In short, the accused's inability effectively to reconstruct at trial any unfairness that occurred at the lineup may deprive him of his only opportunity meaningfully to attack the credibility of the witness' courtroom identification.

What facts have been disclosed in specific cases about the conduct of pretrial confrontations for identification illustrate both the potential for substantial prejudice to the accused at that stage and the need for its revelation at trial. A commentator provides some striking examples:

> "In a Canadian case . . . the defendant had been picked out of a lineup of six men, of which he was the only Oriental. In other cases, a blackhaired suspect was placed upon a group of light-haired persons, tall suspects have been made to stand with short nonsuspects, and, in a case where the perpetrator of the crime was known to be a youth, a suspect under twenty was placed in a lineup with five other persons, all of whom were forty or over."

Similarly state reports, in the course of describing prior identifications admitted as evidence of guilt, reveal numerous instances of suggestive procedures, for example, that all in the lineup but the suspect

5. See In re Groban, 352 U.S. 330, 340, 77 S.Ct. 510, 516 (Black, J., dissenting). The difficult position of defendants in attempting to protest the manner of pretrial identification is illustrated by the many state court cases in which contentions of blatant abuse rested on their unsupportable allegations, usually controverted by the police officers present. . . . For a striking case in which hardly anyone agreed upon what occurred at the lineup, including who identified whom, see Johnson v. State, 237 Md. 283, 206 A.2d 138 (1965).

6. An instructive example of the defendant's predicament may be found in Proctor v. State, 223 Md. 394, 164 A.2d 708 (1960). A prior identification is admissible in Maryland only under the salutary rule that it cannot have been made "under conditions of unfairness or unreliability." Against the defendant's contention that these conditions had not been met, the Court stated:

"In the instant case, there are no such facts as, in our judgment, would call for a finding that the identification . . . was made under conditions of unfairness or unreliability. The relatively large number of persons put into the room together for [the victim] to look at is one circumstance indicating fairness, and the fact that the police officer was unable to remember the appearances of the others and could not recall if they had physical characteristics similar to [the defendant's] or not is at least suggestive that they were not of any one type or that they all differed markedly in looks from the defendant. There is no evidence that the Police Sergeant gave the complaining witness any indication as to which of the thirteen men was the defendant; the Sergeant's testimony is simply that he asked [the victim] if he could identify [the defendant] after having put the thirteen men in the courtroom."

were known to the identifying witness, that the other participants in a lineup were grossly dissimilar in appearance from the suspect, that only the suspect was required to wear distinctive clothing which the culprit allegedly wore, that the witness is told by the police that they have caught the culprit after which the defendant is brought before the witness alone or is viewed in jail, that the suspect is pointed out before or during a lineup, and that the participants in the lineup are asked to try on an article of clothing which fits only the suspect.[7]

The potential for improper influence is illustrated by the circumstances, insofar as they appear, surrounding the prior identifications in the three cases we decide today. In the present case, the testimony of the identifying witnesses elicited on cross-examination revealed that those witnesses were taken to the courthouse and seated in the courtroom to await assembly of the lineup. The courtroom faced on a hallway observable to the witnesses through an open door. The cashier testified that she saw Wade "standing in the hall" within sight of an FBI agent. Five or six other prisoners later appeared in the hall. The vice president testified that he saw a person in the hall in the custody of the agent who "resembled the person that we identified as the one that entered the bank." [8]

The lineup in *Gilbert* was conducted in an auditorium in which some 100 witnesses to several alleged state and federal robberies charged to Gilbert made wholesale identifications of Gilbert as the robber in each others' presence, a procedure said to run counter to the most elemental precepts of the psychology of suggestion. And the vice of suggestion created by the identification in *Stovall* was the presentation to the witness of the suspect alone handcuffed to police officers. It is hard to imagine a situation more clearly conveying the suggestion to the witness that the one presented is believed guilty by the police.

The few cases that have surfaced therefore reveal the existence of a process attended with hazards of serious unfairness to the criminal accused and strongly suggest the plight of the more numerous defendants who are unable to ferret out suggestive influences in the secrecy of the confrontation. We do not assume that these risks are the result of police procedures intentionally designed to prejudice an accused. Rather we assume they derive from the dangers inherent in eyewitness identification and the suggestibility inherent in the context of the pretrial identification. Glanville Williams, in one of the most comprehensive studies of such forms of identification, said "[T]he fact that the police themselves have, in a given case, little

7. [For case citations supporting the foregoing statements, consult original footnotes 18 through 21.]

8. See Wall, supra, n. 7, at 48; Napley, Problems of Effecting the Presentation of the Case for a Defendant, 66 Col.L.Rev. 94, 99 (1966): "[W]hile many identification parades are conducted by the police with scrupulous regard for fairness, it is not unknown for the identifying witness to be placed in a position where he can see the suspect before the parade forms . . . ."

or no doubt that the man put up for identification has committed the offense, and that their chief preoccupation is with the problem of getting sufficient proof, because he has not 'come clean,' involves a danger that this persuasion may communicate itself even in a doubtful case to the witness in some way . . . ." Williams & Hammelmann, Identification Parades, Part I, [1963] Crim.L.Rev. 479, 483.

Insofar as the accused's conviction may rest on a courtroom identification in fact the fruit of a suspect pretrial identification which the accused is helpless to subject to effective scrutiny at trial, the accused is deprived of that right of cross-examination which is an essential safeguard to his right to confront the witnesses against him. . . . And even though cross-examination is a precious safeguard to a fair trial, it cannot be viewed as an absolute assurance of accuracy and reliability. Thus in the present context, where so many variables and pitfalls exist, the first line of defense must be the prevention of unfairness and the lessening of the hazards of eyewitness identification at the lineup itself. The trial which might determine the accused's fate may well not be that in the courtroom but that at the pretrial confrontation, with the State aligned against the accused, the witness the sole jury, and the accused unprotected against the overreaching, intentional or unintentional, and with little or no effective appeal from the judgment there rendered by the witness—"that's the man."

Since it appears that there is grave potential for prejudice, intentional or not, in the pretrial lineup, which may not be capable of reconstruction at trial, and since presence of counsel itself can often avert prejudice and assure a meaningful confrontation at trial,[9]

9. One commentator proposes a model statute providing not only for counsel, but other safeguards as well:

"Most if not all, of the attacks on the lineup process could be averted by a uniform statute modeled upon the best features of the civilian codes. Any proposed statute should provide for the right to counsel during any lineup or during any confrontation. Provision should be made that any person, whether a victim or a witness, must give a description of the suspect before he views any arrested person. A written record of this description should be required, and the witness should be made to sign it. This written record would be available for inspection by defense counsel for copying before the trial and for use at the trial in testing the accuracy of the identification made during the lineup and during the trial.

This ideal statute would require at least six persons in addition to the accused in a lineup, and these persons would have to be of approximately the same height, weight, coloration of hair and skin, and bodily types as the suspect. In addition, all of these men should, as nearly as possible, be dressed alike. If distinctive garb was used during the crime, the suspect should not be forced to wear similar clothing in the lineup unless all of the other persons are similarly garbed. A complete written report of the names, addresses, descriptive details of the other persons in the lineup, and of everything which transpired during the identification would be mandatory. This report would include everything stated by the identifying witness during this step, including any reasons given by him as to what features, etc., have sparked his recognition.

This statute should permit voice identification tests by having each person in the lineup repeat identical innocuous phrases, and it would be imper-

there can be little doubt that for Wade the post-indictment lineup was a critical stage of the prosecution at which he was "as much entitled to such aid [of counsel] . . . as at the trial itself." . . . Thus both Wade and his counsel should have been notified of the impending lineup, and counsel's presence should have been a requisite to conduct of the lineup, absent an "intelligent waiver." . . . No substantial countervailing policy considerations have been advanced against the requirement of the presence of counsel. Concern is expressed that the requirement will forestall prompt identifications and result in obstruction of the confrontations. As for the first, we note that in the two cases in which the right to counsel is today held to apply, counsel had already been appointed and no argument is made in either case that notice to counsel would have prejudicially delayed the confrontations. Moreover, we leave open the question whether the presence of substitute counsel might not suffice where notification and presence of the suspect's own counsel would result in prejudicial delay.[10] And to refuse to recognize the right to counsel for fear that counsel will obstruct the course of justice is contrary to the basic assumptions upon which this Court has operated in Sixth Amendment cases. We rejected similar logic in Miranda v. State of Arizona, concerning presence of counsel during custodial interrogation:

> "[A]n attorney is merely exercising the good professional judgment he has been taught. This is not cause for considering the attorney a menace to law enforcement. He is merely carrying out what he is sworn to do under his oath—to protect to the extent of his ability the rights of his client. In fulfilling this responsibility the attorney plays a vital role in the administration of criminal justice under our Constitution."

In our view counsel can hardly impede legitimate law enforcement; on the contrary, for the reasons expressed, law enforcement may be assisted by preventing the infiltration of taint in the prosecution's identification evidence.[11] That result cannot help the guilty avoid

missible to force the use of words allegedly used during a criminal act.

The statute would enjoin the police from suggesting to any viewer that one or more persons in the lineup had been arrested as a suspect. If more than one witness is to make an identification, each witness should be required to do so separately and should be forbidden to speak to another witness until all of them have completed the process.

The statute could require the use of movie cameras and tape recorders to record the lineup process in those states which are financially able to afford these devices. Finally, the statute should provide that any evidence obtained as the result of a violation of this statute would be inadmissible." Murray, The Criminal Lineup at Home and Abroad, 1966 Utah L.Rev. 610, 627–628.

10. Although the right to counsel usually means a right to the suspect's own counsel, provision for substitute counsel may be justified on the ground that the substitute counsel's presence may eliminate the hazards which render the lineup a critical stage for the presence of the suspect's *own* counsel.

11. Concern is also expressed that the presence of counsel will force divul-

conviction but can only help assure that the right man has been brought to justice.[12]

Legislative or other regulations, such as those of local police departments, which eliminate the risks of abuse and unintentional suggestion at lineup proceedings and the impediments to meaningful confrontation at trial may also remove the basis for regarding the stage as "critical." [13] But neither Congress nor the federal authorities has seen fit to provide a solution. What we hold today "in no way creates a constitutional strait-jacket which will handicap sound efforts at reform, nor is it intended to have this effect." . . .

V.

We come now to the question whether the denial of Wade's motion to strike the courtroom identification by the bank witnesses at trial because of the absence of his counsel at the lineup required, as the Court of Appeals held, the grant of a new trial at which such evidence is to be excluded. We do not think this disposition can be justified without first giving the Government the opportunity to establish by clear and convincing evidence that the in-court identifications were based upon observations of the suspect other than the lineup identification. . . . Where, as here, the admissibility of evidence of the lineup identification itself is not involved, a per se rule of exclusion of courtroom identification would be unjustified. . . . A rule limited solely to the exclusion of testimony concerning identifi-

gence of the identity of government witnesses whose identity the Government may want to conceal. To the extent that this is a valid or significant state interest there are police practices commonly used to effect concealment, for example, masking the face.

12. Most other nations surround the lineup with safeguards against prejudice to the suspect. In England the suspect must be allowed the presence of his solicitor or a friend, Napley, supra, at 98–99; Germany requires the presence of retained counsel; France forbids the confrontation of the suspect in the absence of his counsel; Spain, Mexico, and Italy provide detailed procedures prescribing the conditions under which confrontation must occur under the supervision of a judicial officer who sees to it that the proceedings are officially recorded to assure adequate scrutiny at trial. Murray, The Criminal Lineup at Home and Abroad, 1966 Utah L. Rev. 610, 621–627.

13. Thirty years ago Wigmore suggested a "scientific method" of pretrial identification "to reduce the risk of error hitherto inherent in such proceedings." Wigmore, The Science of Judicial Proof 541 (3d ed. 1937). Under this approach, at least 100 talking films would be prepared of men from various occupations, races, etc. Each would be photographed in a number of stock movements, with and without hat and coat, and would read aloud a standard passage. The suspect would be filmed in the same manner. Some 25 of the films would be shown in succession in a special projection room in which each witness would be provided an electric button which would activate a board backstage when pressed to indicate that the witness had identified a given person. Provision would be made for the degree of hesitancy in the identification to be indicated by the number of presses. Of course, the more systematic and scientific a process or proceeding, including one for purposes of identification, the less the impediment to reconstruction of the conditions bearing upon the reliability of that process or proceeding at trial. . . .

cation at the lineup itself, without regard to admissibility of the courtroom identification, would render the right to counsel an empty one. The lineup is most often used, as in the present case, to crystallize the witnesses' identification of the defendant for future reference. We have already noted that the lineup identification will have that effect. The State may then rest upon the witnesses' unequivocal courtroom identification, and not mention the pretrial identification as part of the State's case at trial. Counsel is then in the predicament in which Wade's counsel found himself—realizing that possible unfairness at the lineup may be the sole means of attack upon the unequivocal courtroom identification, and having to probe in the dark in an attempt to discover and reveal unfairness, while bolstering the government witness' courtroom identification by bringing out and dwelling upon his prior identification. Since counsel's presence at the lineup would equip him to attack not only the lineup identification but the courtroom identification as well, limiting the impact of violation of the right to counsel to exclusion of evidence only of identification at the lineup itself disregards a critical element of that right.

We think it follows that the proper test to be applied in these situations is that quoted in Wong Sun v. United States, 371 U.S. 471, 488, 83 S.Ct. 407, 417, "Whether, granting establishment of the primary illegality, the evidence to which instant objection is made has been come at by exploitation of that illegality or instead by means sufficiently distinguishable to be purged of the primary taint." . . . Application of this test in the present context requires consideration of various factors; for example, the prior opportunity to observe the alleged criminal act, the existence of any discrepancy between any prelineup description and the defendant's actual description, any identification prior to lineup of another person, the identification by picture of the defendant prior to the lineup, failure to identify the defendant on a prior occasion, and the lapse of time between the alleged act and the lineup identification. It is also relevant to consider those facts which, despite the absence of counsel, are disclosed concerning the conduct of the lineup.

We doubt that the Court of Appeals applied the proper test for exclusion of the in-court identification of the two witnesses. The court stated that "it cannot be said with any certainty that they would have recognized appellant at the time of trial if this intervening lineup had not occurred," and that the testimony of the two witnesses "may well have been colored by the illegal procedure [and] was prejudicial." Moreover, the court was persuaded, in part, by the "compulsory verbal responses made by Wade at the instance of the Special Agent." This implies the erroneous holding that Wade's privilege against self-incrimination was violated so that the denial of counsel required exclusion.

On the record now before us we cannot make the determination whether the in-court identifications had an independent origin. This was not an issue at trial, although there is some evidence relevant to a determination. That inquiry is most properly made in the District Court. We therefore think the appropriate procedure to be followed is to vacate the conviction pending a hearing to determine whether the in-court identifications had an independent source, or whether, in any event, the introduction of the evidence was harmless error, and for the District Court to reinstate the conviction or order a new trial, as may be proper. See United States v. Shotwell Mfg. Co., 355 U.S. 233, 245–246, 78 S.Ct. 245, 253.

The judgment of the Court of Appeals is vacated and the case is remanded to that court with direction to enter a new judgment vacating the conviction and remanding the case to the District Court for further proceedings consistent with this opinion. It is so ordered.

Judgment of Court of Appeals vacated and case remanded with direction.

THE CHIEF JUSTICE joins the opinion of the Court except for Part I, from which he dissents for the reasons expressed in the opinion of MR. JUSTICE FORTAS.

MR. JUSTICE DOUGLAS joins the opinion of the Court except for Part I. On that phase of the case he adheres to the dissenting views in Schmerber v. State of California, that compulsory lineup violates the privilege against self-incrimination contained in the Fifth Amendment.

MR. JUSTICE CLARK, concurring.

With reference to the lineup point involved in this case I cannot, for the life of me, see why a lineup is not a critical stage of the prosecution. Identification of the suspect—a prerequisite to establishment of guilt—occurs at this stage, and with Miranda v. State of Arizona on the books, the requirement of the presence of counsel arises, unless waived by the suspect. I dissented in *Miranda* but I am bound by it now, as we all are. Schmerber v. State of California, precludes petitioner's claim of self-incrimination. I therefore join the opinion of the Court.

MR. JUSTICE BLACK, dissenting in part and concurring in part.

* * *

The Court in Part I of its opinion rejects Wade's Fifth Amendment contention. From that I dissent. In Parts II–IV of its opinion, the Court sustains Wade's claim of denial of right to counsel in the out-of-court lineup, and in that I concur. In Part V, the Court remands the case to the District Court to consider whether the courtroom identification of Wade was the fruit of the illegal lineup, and if it were, to grant him a new trial unless the court concludes that the courtroom identification was harmless error. I would reverse the Court of Appeals' reversal of Wade's conviction, but I would not remand for further proceedings since the prosecution not having used the out-of-court lineup identification against Wade at his trial, I believe the conviction should be affirmed.

I.

In rejecting Wade's claim that his privilege against self-incrimination was violated by compelling him to appear in the lineup wearing the tape and uttering the words given him by the police, the Court relies on the recent holding in Schmerber v. State of California. In that case the Court held that taking blood from a man's body against his will in order to convict him of a crime did not compel him to be a witness against himself. I dissented from that holding, and still dissent. The Court's reason for its holding was that the sample of Schmerber's blood taken in order to convict him of crime was neither "testimonial" nor "communicative" evidence. I think it was both. It seems quite plain to me that the Fifth Amendment's Self-incrimination Clause was designed to bar the Government from forcing any person to supply proof of his own crime, precisely what Schmerber was forced to do when he was forced to supply his blood. The Government simply took his blood against his will and over his counsel's protest for the purpose of convicting him of crime. So here, having Wade in its custody awaiting trial to see if he could or would be convicted of crime, the Government forced him to stand in a lineup, wear strips on his face, and speak certain words, in order to make it possible for government witnesses to identify him as a criminal. Had Wade been compelled to utter these or any other words in open court, it is plain that he would have been entitled to a new trial because of having been compelled to be a witness against himself. Being forced by Government to help convict himself and to supply evidence against himself by talking outside the courtroom is equally violative of his constitutional right not to be compelled to be a witness against himself. Consequently, because of this violation of the Fifth Amendment, and not because of my own personal view that the Government's conduct was "unfair," "prejudicial," or "improper," I would prohibit the prosecution's use of lineup identification at trial.

II.

I agree with the Court, in large part because of the reasons it gives, that failure to notify Wade's counsel that Wade was to be put in a lineup by government officers and to be forced to talk and wear tape on his face denied Wade the right to counsel in violation of the Sixth Amendment. Once again, my reason for this conclusion is solely the Sixth Amendment's guarantee that "the accused shall enjoy the right . . . to have the assistance of counsel for his defence." As this Court's opinion points out, "[t]he plain wording of this guarantee thus encompasses counsel's assistance whenever necessary to assure a meaningful 'defence.'" And I agree with the Court that a lineup is a "critical stage" of the criminal proceedings against an accused, because it is a stage at which the Government makes use of his custody to obtain crucial evidence against him. Besides counsel's presence at the lineup being necessary to protect the defendant's specific constitutional rights to confrontation and the assistance of counsel at the trial itself, the assistance of counsel at the lineup is also necessary to protect the defendant's in-custody assertion of his privilege against self-incrimination, for contrary to the Court, I believe that counsel may advise the defendant not to participate in the lineup or to participate only under certain conditions.

I agree with the Court that counsel's presence at the lineup is necessary to protect the accused's right to a "fair trial," only if by "fair trial" the Court means a trial in accordance with the "law of the land" as specifically set out in the Constitution. But there are implications in the Court's opinion that by a "fair trial" the Court means a trial which a majority of this Court deems to be "fair" and that a lineup is a "critical stage" only because the Court, now assessing the "innumerable dangers" which inhere in it, thinks it is such. That these implications are justified is evidenced by the Court's suggestion that "legislative or other regulations . . . which eliminate the abuse . . . at lineup proceedings . . . may also remove the basis for regarding the stage as 'critical.'" * * * I am wholly unwilling to make the specific constitutional right of counsel dependent on judges' vague and transitory notions of fairness and their equally transitory, though "practical," assessment of the "risk that . . . counsel's absence . . . might derogate from a fair trial." . . .

III.

I would reverse Wade's conviction without further ado had the prosecution at trial made use of his lineup identification either in place of courtroom identification or to bolster in a harmful manner crucial courtroom identification. But the prosecution here did neither of these things. After prosecution witnesses under oath identified Wade in the courtroom, it was the defense, and not the prosecution, which brought out the prior lineup identification. While stating that "a *per se* rule of exclusion of courtroom identification would be unjustified," the Court, nevertheless remands this case for "a hearing to determine whether the in-court identifications had an independent source," or were the tainted fruits of the invalidly conducted lineup. From this holding I dissent.

In the first place, even if this Court has power to establish such a rule of evidence I think the rule fashioned by the Court is unsound. The "taint"-"fruit" determination required by the Court involves more than considerable difficulty. I think it is practically impossible. How is a witness capable of probing the recesses of his mind to draw a sharp line between a courtroom identification due exclusively to an earlier lineup and a courtroom identification due to memory not based on the lineup? What kind of "clear and convincing evidence" can the prosecution offer to prove upon what particular events memories resulting in an in-court identification rest? How long will trials be delayed while judges turn psychologists to probe the subconscious minds of witnesses? All these questions are posed but not answered by the Court's opinion. In my view, the Fifth and Sixth Amendments are satisfied if the prosecution is precluded from using lineup identification as either an alternative to or corroboration of courtroom identification. If the prosecution does neither and its witnesses under oath identify the defendant in the courtroom, then I can find no justification for stopping the trial in midstream to hold a lengthy "taint"-"fruit" hearing. The fact of and circumstances surrounding a prior lineup identification might be used by the defense to impeach the credibility of the in-court identifications, but not to exclude them completely.

But more important, there is no constitutional provision upon which I can rely that directly or by implication gives this Court power to establish what amounts to a constitutional rule of evidence to govern, not only the Federal Government, but the States in their trial of state crimes under state laws in state courts. See Gilbert v. California, post. The Constitution deliberately reposed in States very broad power to create and to try crimes according to their own rules and policies. . . . Before being deprived of this power, the least that they can ask is that we should be able to point to a federal constitutional provision that either by express language or by necessary implication grants us the power to fashion this novel rule of evidence to govern their criminal trials. * * *

Perhaps the Court presumes to write this constitutional rule of evidence on the Fourteenth Amendment's Due Process Clause. This is not the time or place to consider that claim. Suffice it for me to say briefly that I find no such authority in the Due Process Clause. It undoubtedly provides that a person must be tried in accordance with the "Law of the Land." Consequently, it violates due process to try a person in a way prohibited by the Fourth, Fifth, or Sixth Amendments of our written Constitution. But I have never been able to subscribe to the dogma that the Due Process Clause empowers this Court to declare any law, including a rule of evidence, unconstitutional which it believes is contrary to tradition, decency, fundamental justice, or any of the other wide-meaning words used by judges to claim power under the Due Process Clause. . . . I have an abiding idea that if the Framers had wanted to let judges write the Constitution on any such day-to-day beliefs of theirs, they would have said so instead of so carefully defining their grants and prohibitions in a written constitution. With no more authority than the Due Process Clause I am wholly unwilling to tell the state or federal courts that the United States Constitution forbids them to allow courtroom identification without the prosecution first proving that the identification does not rest in whole or in part on an illegal lineup. Should I do so, I would feel that we are deciding what the Constitution is, not from what it says, but from what we think it would have been wise for the Framers to put in it. That to me would be "judicial activism" at its worst. I would leave the States and Federal Government free to decide their own rules of evidence. That, I believe, is their constitutional prerogative.

I would affirm Wade's conviction.

MR. JUSTICE WHITE, whom MR. JUSTICE HARLAN and MR. JUSTICE STEWART join, dissenting in part and concurring in part.

The Court has again propounded a broad constitutional rule barring the use of a wide spectrum of relevant and probative evidence, solely because a step in its ascertainment or discovery occurs outside the presence of defense counsel. This was the approach of the Court in Miranda v. State of Arizona. I objected then to what I thought was an uncritical and doctrinaire approach without satisfactory factual foundation. I have much the same view of the present ruling and therefore dissent from the judgment and from Parts II, IV, and V of the Court's opinion.

The Court's opinion is far reaching. It proceeds first by creating a new *per se* rule of constitutional law: a criminal suspect cannot be subjected to a pretrial identification process in the absence of his counsel without violating the Sixth Amendment. If he is, the State may not buttress a later courtroom identification of the witness by any reference to the previous identification. Furthermore, the courtroom identification is not admissible at all unless the State can establish by clear and convincing proof that the testimony is not the fruit of the earlier identification made in the absence of defendant's counsel—admittedly a heavy burden for the State and probably an impossible one. For all intents and purposes, courtroom identifications are barred if pretrial identifications have occurred without counsel being present.

The rule applies to any lineup, to any other techniques employed to produce an identification and *a fortiori* to a face-to-face encounter between the witness and the suspect alone, regardless of when the identification occurs, in time or place, and whether before or after indictment or information. It matters not how well the witness knows the suspect, whether the witness is the suspect's mother, brother, or long-time associate, and no matter how long or well the witness observed the perpetrator at the scene of the crime. The kidnap victim who has lived for days with his abductor is in the same category as the witness who had had only a fleeting glimpse of the criminal. Neither may identify the suspect without defendant's counsel being present. The same strictures apply regardless of the number of other witnesses who positively identify the defendant and regardless of the corroborative evidence showing that it was the defendant who has committed the crime.

The premise for the Court's rule is not the general unreliability of eyewitness identifications nor the difficulties inherent in observation, recall, and recognition. The Court assumes a narrower evil as the basis for its rule—improper police suggestion which contributes to erroneous identifications. The Court apparently believes that improper police procedures are so widespread that a broad prophylactic rule must be laid down, requiring the presence of counsel at all pretrial identifications, in order to detect recurring instances of police misconduct.[1] I do not share this pervasive distrust of all official investigations. None of the materials the Court relies upon supports it.[2] Certainly, I would bow to solid fact, but the Court quite obviously does not have before it any reliable, comprehensive survey of current police practices on which to base its new rule. Until it does, the Court should avoid excluding relevant evidence from state criminal trials.

The Court goes beyond assuming that a great majority of the country's police departments are following improper practices at pretrial identifications. To find the lineup a "critical" stage of the proceeding and to exclude identifications made in the absence of counsel, the Court must also assume that police "suggestion," if it occurs at all, leads to erroneous rather than accurate identifications and that reprehensible police conduct will have an unavoidable and largely undiscoverable impact on the trial. This in turn assumes that there is now no adequate source from which defense counsel can learn about the circumstances of the pretrial identification in order to place before the jury all of the considerations which should enter into an appraisal of courtroom identification evidence. But these are treacherous and unsupported assumptions resting as they do on the notion that the defendant will not be aware, that the police and the witnesses will forget or prevaricate, that defense counsel will be unable to bring out the truth and that neither jury, judge, nor appellate court is a sufficient safeguard against unacceptable police conduct occurring at a pretrial identification procedure. I am unable to share the Court's view of the willingness of the police and the ordinary citizen-witness to dissemble, either with respect to the identification of the defendant or with respect to the circumstances surrounding a pretrial identification.

1. Yet in Stovall v. Denno, 388 U.S. 293, 87 S.Ct. 1967, the Court recognizes that improper police conduct in the identification process has not been so widespread as to justify full retroactivity for its new rule.

2. In Miranda v. State of Arizona, the Court noted that O'Hara, Fundamentals of Criminal Investigation (1956) is a text that has enjoyed extensive use among law enforcement agencies and among students of police science. The quality of the work was said to rest on the author's long service as observer, lecturer in police science, and work as a federal crime investigator. O'Hara does not suggest that the police should or do use identification machinery improperly; instead he argues for techniques that would increase the reliability of eyewitness identifications, and there is no reason to suggest that O'Hara's views are not shared and practiced by the majority of police departments throughout the land.

There are several striking aspects to the Court's holding. First, the rule does not bar courtroom identifications where there have been no previous identifications in the presence of the police, although when identified in the courtroom, the defendant is known to be in custody and charged with the commission of a crime. Second, the Court seems to say that if suitable legislative standards were adopted for the conduct of pretrial identifications, thereby lessening the hazards in such confrontations, it would not insist on the presence of counsel. But if this is true, why does not the Court simply fashion what it deems to be constitutionally acceptable procedures for the authorities to follow? Certainly the Court is correct in suggesting that the new rule will be wholly inapplicable where police departments themselves have established suitable safeguards.

Third, courtroom identification may be barred, absent, counsel at a prior identification, regardless of the extent of counsel's information concerning the circumstances of the previous confrontation between witness and defendant—apparently even if there were recordings or sound-movies of the events as they occurred. But if the rule is premised on the defendant's right to have his counsel know, there seems little basis for not accepting other means to inform. A disinterested observer, recordings, photographs—any one of them would seem adequate to furnish the basis for a meaningful cross-examination of the eyewitness who identifies the defendant in the courtroom.

I share the Court's view that the criminal trial, at the very least, should aim at truthful factfinding, including accurate eyewitness identifications. I doubt, however, on the basis of our present information, that the tragic mistakes which have occurred in criminal trials are as much the product of improper police conduct as they are the consequence of the difficulties inherent in eyewitness testimony and in resolving evidentiary conflicts by court or jury. I doubt that the Court's new rule will obviate these difficulties, or that the situation will be measurably improved by inserting defense counsel into the investigative processes of police departments everywhere.

But, it may be asked, what possible state interest militates against requiring the presence of defense counsel at lineups? After all, the argument goes, he *may* do some good, he *may* upgrade the quality of identification evidence in state courts and he can scarcely do any harm. Even if true, this is a feeble foundation for fastening an ironclad constitutional rule upon state criminal procedures. Absent some reliably established constitutional violation, the processes by which the States enforce their criminal laws are their own prerogative. The States *do* have an interest in conducting their own affairs, an interest which cannot be displaced simply by saying that there are no valid arguments with respect to the merits of a federal rule emanating from this Court.

Beyond this, however, requiring counsel at pretrial identifications as an invariable rule trenches on other valid state interests. One of them is its concern with the prompt and efficient enforcement of its criminal laws. Identifications frequently take place after arrest but before indictment or information is filed. The police may have arrested a suspect on probable cause but may still have the wrong man. Both the suspect and the State have every interest in a prompt identification at that stage, the suspect in order to secure his immediate release and the State because prompt and early identification enhances *accurate* identification and because it must know whether it is on the right investigative track. Unavoidably, however, the absolute rule requiring the presence of counsel will cause significant delay and it may very well result in no pretrial identification at all. Counsel must be appointed and a time arranged convenient for him and the witnesses. Meanwhile, it may be necessary to file charges against the suspect who may then be released on bail, in the federal system very often on his own recognizance, with neither the State nor the defendant having the benefit of a properly conducted identification procedure.

Nor do I think the witnesses themselves can be ignored. They will now be required to be present at the convenience of counsel rather than their own. Many may be much less willing to participate if the identification stage is transformed into an adversary proceeding not under the control of a judge. Others may fear for their own safety if their identity is known at an early date, especially when there is no way of knowing until the lineup occurs whether or not the police really have the right man.[3]

Finally, I think the Court's new rule is vulnerable in terms of its own unimpeachable purpose of increasing the reliability of identification testimony.

Law enforcement officers have the obligation to convict the guilty and to make sure they do not convict the innocent. They must be dedicated to making the criminal trial a procedure for the ascertainment of the true facts surrounding the commission of the crime. To this extent, our so-called adversary system is not adversary at all; nor should it be. But defense counsel has no comparable obligation to ascertain or present the truth. Our system assigns him a different mission. He must be and is interested in not convicting the innocent, but, absent a voluntary plea of guilty, we also insist that he defend his client whether he is innocent or guilty. The State has the obligation to present the evidence. Defense counsel need present nothing, even if he knows what the truth is. He need furnish no witnesses to the police, reveal any confidences of his client, nor furnish any other information to help the prosecution's case. If he can confuse a witness, even a truthful one, or make him appear at a disadvantage, unsure or indecisive, that will be his normal course. Our interest in not

3. I would not have thought that the State's interest regarding its sources of identification is any less than its interest in protecting informants, especially those who may aid in identification but who will not be used as witnesses.

convicting the innocent permits counsel to put the State to its proof, to put the State's case in the worst possible light regardless of what he thinks or knows to be the truth. Undoubtedly there are some limits which defense counsel must observe but more often than not, defense counsel will cross-examine a prosecution witness, and impeach him if he can, even if he thinks the witness is telling the truth, just as he will attempt to destroy a witness who he thinks is lying. In this respect, as part of our modified adversary system and as part of the duty imposed on the most honorable defense counsel, we countenance or require conduct which in many instances has little, if any, relation to the search for truth.

I would not extend this system, at least as it presently operates, to police investigations and would not require counsel's presence at pretrial identification procedures. Counsel's interest is in not having his client placed at the scene of the crime, regardless of his whereabouts. Some counsel may advise their clients to refuse to make any movements or to speak any words in a lineup or even to appear in one. To that extent the impact on truthful factfinding is quite obvious. Others will not only observe what occurs and develop possibilities for later cross-examination but will hover over witnesses and begin their cross-examination then, menacing truthful factfinding as thoroughly as the Court fears the police now do. Certainly there is an implicit invitation to counsel to suggest rules for the lineup and to manage and produce it as best he can. I therefore doubt that the Court's new rule, at least absent some clearly defined limits on counsel's role, will measurably contribute to more reliable pretrial identifications. My fears are that it will have precisely the opposite result. It may well produce fewer convictions, but that is hardly a proper measure of its long-run acceptability. In my view, the State is entitled to investigate and develop its case outside the presence of defense counsel. This includes the right to have private conversations with identification witnesses, just as defense counsel may have his own consultations with these and other witnesses without having the prosecutor present.

Whether today's judgment would be an acceptable exercise of supervisory power over federal courts is another question. But as a constitutional matter, the judgment in this case is erroneous and although I concur in Parts I and III of the Court's opinion I respectfully register this dissent.

MR. JUSTICE FORTAS, with whom THE CHIEF JUSTICE and MR. JUSTICE DOUGLAS join, concurring in part and dissenting in part.

1. I agree with the Court that the exhibition of the person of the accused at a lineup is not itself a violation of the privilege against self-incrimination. In itself, it is no more subject to constitutional objection than the exhibition of the person of the accused in the courtroom for identification purposes. It is an incident of the State's power to arrest, and a reasonable and justifiable aspect of the State's custody resulting from arrest. It does not require that the accused take

affirmative, volitional action, but only that, having been duly arrested he may be seen for identification purposes. It is, however, a "critical stage" in the prosecution, and I agree with the Court that the opportunity to have counsel present must be made available.

2. In my view, however, the accused may not be compelled in a lineup to speak the words uttered by the person who committed the crime. I am confident that it could not be compelled in court. It cannot be compelled in a lineup. It is more than passive, mute assistance to the eyes of the victim or of witnesses. It is the kind of volitional act—the kind of forced cooperation by the accused—which is within the historical perimeter of the privilege against compelled self-incrimination.

Our history and tradition teach and command that an accused may stand mute. The privilege means just that; not less than that. According to the Court, an accused may be jailed—indefinitely—until he is willing to say, for an identifying audience, whatever was said in the course of the commission of the crime. Presumably this would include, "Your money or your life"—or perhaps, words of assault in a rape case. This is intolerable under our constitutional system.

I completely agree that the accused must be advised of and given the right to counsel before a lineup—and I join in that part of the Court's opinion; but this is an empty right unless we mean to insist upon the accused's fundamental constitutional immunities. One of these is that the accused may not be compelled to speak. To compel him to speak would violate the privilege against self-incrimination, which is incorporated in the Fifth Amendment.

* * *

An accused cannot be compelled to utter the words spoken by the criminal in the course of the crime. I thoroughly disagree with the Court's statement that such compulsion does not violate the Fifth Amendment. The Court relies upon Schmerber v. State of California to support this. . . . But *Schmerber* which authorized the forced extraction of blood from the veins of an unwilling human being, did not compel the person actively to cooperate—to accuse himself by a volitional act which differs only in degree from compelling him to act out the crime, which, I assume, would be rebuffed by the Court. . . .

To permit *Schmerber* to apply in any respect beyond its holding is, in my opinion, indefensible. To permit its insidious doctrine to extend beyond the invasion of the body, which it permits, to compulsion of the will of a man, is to deny and defy a precious part of our historical faith and to discard one of the most profoundly cherished instruments by which we have established the freedom and dignity of the individual. We should not so alter the balance between the rights of the individual and of the state, achieved over centuries of conflict.

3. While the Court holds that the accused must be advised of and given the right to counsel at the lineup, it makes the privilege

meaningless in this important respect. Unless counsel has been waived or, being present, has not objected to the accused's utterance of words used in the course of committing the crime, to compel such an utterance is constitutional error.*

Accordingly, while I join the Court in requiring vacating of the judgment below for a determination as to whether the identification of respondent was based upon factors independent of the lineup, I would do so not only because of the failure to offer counsel before the lineup but also because of the violation of respondent's Fifth Amendment rights.

NOTES

1. In Gilbert v. California, 388 U.S. 263, 87 S.Ct. 1951 (1967), the Court elaborated on its several holdings in *Wade.* The Court held that requiring a suspect to give handwriting exemplars in the absence of counsel violated neither Fifth nor Sixth Amendment rights. The Court further held that a lineup conducted without notice to Gilbert's counsel some sixteen days after indictment violated Gilbert's right to counsel. With respect to those witnesses who identified Gilbert at trial, the Court held that Gilbert was entitled to a hearing whether their courtroom identification was untainted by their observations of Gilbert at the illegal lineup. The Court finally held that testimony concerning the pre-trial confrontation introduced by the prosecution was erroneously admitted. Such testimony, according to the Court, was the direct product of illegal law-enforcement conduct and "only a per se exclusionary rule as to such testimony can be an effective sanction to assure that law enforcement authorities will respect the accused's constitutional right to the presence of his counsel at the critical lineup."

2. Can the right to counsel at lineups be waived? Every court that has considered the question has answered in the affirmative. See State v. Taylor, 456 S.W.2d 9 (Mo.1970); Hayes v. State, 46 Wis.2d 93, 175 N.W.2d 625 (1970); Compare State v. Bass, 280 N.C. 435, 186 S.E.2d 384 (1972) with State v. Mems, 281 N.C. 709, 190 S.E.2d 164 (1972). A waiver must be voluntary. Compare Redding v. State, 10 Md.App. 601, 272 A.2d 70 (1971) with Chambers v. State, 46 Ala.App. 247, 240 So.2d 370 (1970) (waiver voluntary when suspect was told he could go home if he was not identified). Warnings of the right to counsel *at the lineup* must be given. The mere giving of Miranda warnings is not sufficient (United States v. Ayers, 426 F.2d 524 (2nd Cir. 1970)) but such warnings may be considered as supplementing other warnings specifically concerning the lineup. See People v. Evans, 16 Cal.App.3d 510, 94 Cal.Rptr. 88 (1971).

* While it is conceivable that legislation might provide a meticulous lineup procedure which would *satisfy* constitutional requirements, I do not agree with the Court that this would "remove the basis for regarding the [lineup] stage as 'critical.' "

KIRBY v. ILLINOIS

Supreme Court of the United States, 1972.
406 U.S. 682, 92 S.Ct. 1877.

MR. JUSTICE STEWART announced the judgment of the Court in an opinion in which THE CHIEF JUSTICE, MR. JUSTICE BLACKMUN, and MR. JUSTICE REHNQUIST join.

* * * In the present case we are asked to extend the *Wade-Gilbert per se* exclusionary rule to identification testimony based upon a police station showup that took place *before* the defendant had been indicted or otherwise formally charged with any criminal offense.

On February 21, 1968, a man named Willie Shard reported to the Chicago police that the previous day two men had robbed him on a Chicago street of a wallet containing, among other things, travellers checks and a Social Security card. On February 22, two police officers stopped the petitioner and a companion, Ralph Bean, on West Madison Street in Chicago. When asked for identification, the petitioner produced a wallet that contained three travellers checks and a Social Security card, all bearing the name of Willie Shard. Papers with Shard's name on them were also found in Bean's possession. When asked to explain his possession of Shard's property, the petitioner first said that the travellers checks were "play money," and then told the officers that he had won them in a crap game. The officers then arrested the petitioner and Bean and took them to a police station.

Only after arriving at the police station, and checking the records there, did the arresting officers learn of the Shard robbery. A police car was then dispatched to Shard's place of employment, where it picked up Shard and brought him to the police station. Immediately upon entering the room in the police station where the petitioner and Bean were seated at a table, Shard positively identified them as the men who had robbed him two days earlier. No lawyer was present in the room, and neither the petitioner nor Bean had asked for legal assistance, or been advised of any right to the presence of counsel.

* * * A pretrial motion to suppress Shard's identification testimony was denied, and at the trial Shard testified as a witness for the prosecution. In his testimony he described his identification of the two men at the police station on February 22, and identified them again in the courtroom as the men who had robbed him on February 20. He was cross-examined at length regarding the circumstances of his identification of the two defendants. The jury found both defendants guilty, and the petitioner's conviction was affirmed on appeal. The Illinois appellate court held that the admission of Shard's testimony was not error, relying upon an earlier decision of the Illinois Supreme Court, People v. Palmer, 41 Ill.2d 571, 244 N.E.

2d 173, holding that the *Wade-Gilbert per se* exclusionary rule is not applicable to preindictment confrontations. We granted certiorari, limited to this question.

I

We note at the outset that the constitutional privilege against compulsory self-incrimination is in no way implicated here. * * *

It follows that the doctrine of Miranda v. Arizona has no applicability whatever to the issue before us. For the *Miranda* decision was based exclusively upon the Fifth and Fourteenth Amendment privilege against compulsory self-incrimination, upon the theory that custodial *interrogation* is inherently coercive.

The *Wade-Gilbert* exclusionary rule, by contrast, stems from a quite different constitutional guarantee—the guarantee of the right to counsel contained in the Sixth and Fourteenth Amendments. Unless all semblance of principled constitutional adjudication is to be abandoned, therefore, it is to the decisions construing that guarantee that we must look in determining the present controversy.

In a line of constitutional cases in this Court stemming back to the Court's landmark opinion in Powell v. Alabama, 287 U.S. 45, 53 S.Ct. 55, it has been firmly established that a person's Sixth and Fourteenth Amendment right to counsel attaches only at or after the time that adversary judicial proceedings have been initiated against him.

This is not to say that a defendant in a criminal case has a constitutional right to counsel only at the trial itself. The *Powell* case makes clear that the right attaches at the time of arraignment, and the Court has recently held that it exists also at the time of a preliminary hearing. But the point is that, while members of the Court have differed as to existence of the right to counsel in the contexts of some of the above cases, *all* of those cases have involved points of time at or after the initiation of adversary judicial criminal proceedings—whether by way of formal charge, preliminary hearing, indictment, information, or arraignment.

The only seeming deviation from this long line of constitutional decisions, was Escobedo v. Illinois, 378 U.S. 478, 84 S.Ct. 1758. But *Escobedo* is not apposite here for two distinct reasons. First, the Court in retrospect perceived that the "prime purpose" of *Escobedo* was not to vindicate the constitutional right to counsel as such, but, like *Miranda*, "to guarantee full effectuation of the privilege against self-incrimination. . . ." Secondly, and perhaps even more important for purely practical purposes, the Court has limited the holding of *Escobedo* to its own facts, and those facts are not remotely akin to the facts of the case before us.

The initiation of judicial criminal proceedings is far from a mere formalism. It is the starting point of our whole system of adversary criminal justice. For it is only then that the Government has committed itself to prosecute, and only then that the adverse positions of Government and defendant have solidified. It is then that a defendant finds himself faced with the prosecutorial forces of organized society, and immersed in the intricacies of substantive and procedural criminal law. It is this point, therefore, that marks the commencement of the "criminal prosecutions" to which alone the explicit guarantees of the Sixth Amendment are applicable.

In this case we are asked to import into a routine police investigation an absolute constitutional guarantee historically and rationally applicable only after the onset of formal prosecutorial proceedings. We decline to do so. Less than a year after *Wade* and *Gilbert* were decided, the Court explained the rule of those decisions as follows: "The rationale of those cases was that an accused is entitled to counsel at any 'critical stage of the *prosecution*,' and that a post-indictment lineup is such a 'critical stage.'" (Emphasis supplied.) Simmons v. United States, 390 U.S. 377, 382–383, 88 S.Ct. 967, 970. We decline to depart from that rationale today by imposing a *per se* exclusionary rule upon testimony concerning an identification that took place long before the commencement of any prosecution whatever.

II

What has been said is not to suggest that there may not be occasions during the course of a criminal investigation when the police do abuse identification procedures. Such abuses are not beyond the reach of the Constitution. As the Court pointed out in *Wade* itself, it is always necessary to "scrutinize *any* pretrial confrontation. . . ." The Due Process Clause of the Fifth and Fourteenth Amendments forbids a lineup that is unnecessarily suggestive and conducive to irreparable mistaken identification. When a person has not been formally charged with a criminal offense, *Stovall* strikes the appropriate constitutional balance between the right of a suspect to be protected from prejudicial procedures and the interest of society in the prompt and purposeful investigation of an unsolved crime.

The judgment is affirmed.

MR. CHIEF JUSTICE BURGER, concurring.

I agree that the right to counsel attaches as soon as criminal charges are formally made against an accused and he becomes the subject of a "criminal prosecution." Therefore, I join in the Court's opinion and holding.

MR. JUSTICE POWELL, concurring in the result.

As I would not extend the *Wade-Gilbert per se* exclusionary rule, I concur in the result reached by the Court.

MR. JUSTICE BRENNAN, with whom MR. JUSTICE DOUGLAS and MR. JUSTICE MARSHALL join, dissenting. * * *

While it should go without saying, it appears necessary, in view of the plurality opinion today, to re-emphasize that *Wade* did not require the presence of counsel at pretrial confrontations for identification purposes simply on the basis of an abstract consideration of the words "criminal prosecutions" in the Sixth Amendment. Counsel is required at those confrontations because "the dangers inherent in eyewitness identification and the suggestibility inherent in the context of the pretrial identification," mean that protection must be afforded to the "most basic right [of] a criminal defendant—his right to a fair trial at which the witnesses against him might be meaningfully cross-examined,". Indeed, the Court expressly stated that "[L]egislative or other regulations, such as those of local police departments, which eliminate the risks of abuse and unintentional suggestion at lineup proceedings and the impediments to meaningful confrontation at trial may also remove the basis for regarding the stage as 'critical.'" Hence, "the initiation of adversary judicial criminal proceedings," *ante,* at 1882, is completely irrelevant to whether counsel is necessary at a pretrial confrontation for identification in order to safeguard the accused's constitutional rights to confrontation and the effective assistance of counsel at his trial.

In view of *Wade,* it is plain, and the plurality today does not attempt to dispute it, that there inhere in a confrontation for identification conducted after arrest * the identical hazards to a fair trial that inhere in such a confrontation conducted "after the onset of formal prosecutorial proceedings." The plurality apparently considers an arrest, which for present purposes we must assume to be based upon probable cause to be nothing more than part of "a routine police investigation," ibid., and thus not "the starting point of our whole system of adversary criminal justice,". An arrest, according to the plurality, does not face the accused "with the prosecutorial forces of organized society," nor immerse him "in the intricacies of substantive and procedural criminal law." Those consequences ensue, says the plurality, only with "[t]he initiation of judicial criminal proceedings," "[f]or it is only then that the Government has committed itself to prosecute, and only then that the adverse positions of Government and defendant have solidified." If these propositions do not amount to "mere formalism," ibid., it is difficult to know how to characterize them. An arrest evidences the belief of the police that the perpetrator of a crime has been caught. A post-arrest confrontation for identification is not "a mere preparatory step in the gathering of the prosecution's evidence." A primary, and frequently sole, purpose of

* This case does not require me to consider confrontations that take place before custody, see e. g., Bratten v. Delaware, 307 F.Supp. 643 (Del.1969); nor accidental confrontations not arranged by the police, see, e. g., United States v. Pollack, 427 F.2d 1168 (CA5 1970); nor on-the-scene encounters shortly after the crime, see, e. g. Russell v. United States, 408 F.2d 1280 (D.C.Cir.1969).

the confrontation for identification at that stage is to accumulate proof to buttress the conclusion of the police that they have the offender in hand. The plurality offers no reason, and I can think of none, for concluding that a post-arrest confrontation for identification, unlike a post-charge confrontation, is not among those "critical confrontations of the accused by the prosecution at pretrial proceedings where the results might well settle the accused's fate and reduce the trial itself to a mere formality."

The highly suggestive form of confrontation employed in this case underscores the point. This showup was particularly fraught with the peril of mistaken identification. In the setting of a police station squad room where all present except petitioner and Bean were police officers, the danger was quite real that Shard's understandable resentment might lead him too readily to agree with the police that the pair under arrest, and the only persons exhibited to him, were indeed the robbers. * * * Shard's testimony itself demonstrates the necessity for such safeguards. On direct examination, Shard identified petitioner and Bean not as the alleged robbers on trial in the courtroom, but as the pair he saw at the police station. * * *

The plurality today "decline[s] to depart from [the] rationale" of *Wade* and *Gilbert*. The plurality discovers that "rationale" not by consulting those decisions themselves, which would seem to be the appropriate course, but by reading one sentence in Simmons v. United States, 390 U.S. 377, 382–383, 88 S.Ct. 967, 970 (1968), where no right to counsel claim was either asserted or considered. The "rationale" the plurality discovers is, apparently, that a post-indictment confrontation for identification is part of the prosecution. The plurality might have discovered a different "rationale" by reading one sentence in Foster v. California, 394 U.S. 440, 442, 89 S.Ct. 1127 (1969), a case decided after *Simmons*, where the Court explained that in *Wade* and *Gilbert* "this Court held that because of the possibility of unfairness to the accused in the way a lineup is conducted, a lineup is a 'critical stage' in the prosecution, at which the accused must be given the opportunity to be represented by counsel." In *Foster*, moreover, although the Court mentioned that the lineups took place after the accused's arrest, it did not say whether they were also after the information was filed against him. Instead, the Court simply pointed out that under Stovall v. Denno, *Wade* and *Gilbert* were "applicable only to lineups conducted after those cases were decided." Similarly, in Coleman v. Alabama, 399 U.S. 1, 90 S.Ct. 1999 (1970), another case involving a pre-*Wade* lineup, no member of the Court saw any significance in whether the accused had been formally charged with a crime before the lineup was held.

* * *

Wade and *Gilbert*, of course, happened to involve post-indictment confrontations. Yet even a cursory perusal of the opinions in those cases reveals that nothing at all turned upon that particular circumstance. In short, it is fair to conclude that rather than "declin[ing] to depart from [the] rationale" of *Wade* and *Gilbert*, the plurality today, albeit purporting to be engaged in "principled constitutional adjudication," refuses even to recognize that "rationale." For my part, I do not agree that we "extend" *Wade* and *Gilbert*, by holding that the principles of those cases apply to confrontations for identification conducted after arrest. Because Shard testified at trial about his identification of petitioner at the police station showup, the exclusionary rule of *Gilbert*, requires reversal.

MR. JUSTICE WHITE, dissenting.

United States v. Wade, and Gilbert v. California, govern this case and compel reversal of the judgment of the Illinois Supreme Court.

NOTES

1. Prior to the *Kirby* decision there were several lines of demarcation. It was held that the right to counsel did not apply to confrontations occurring shortly after the crimes, to accidental confrontations or to confrontations occurring when the suspect was not in custody. Some courts had restricted right to counsel to post-indictment lineups, People v. Palmer, 41 Ill. 2d 571, 244 N.E.2d 173 (1969), but most rejected this limitation, People v. Fowler, 1 Cal.3d 335, 82 Cal.Rptr. 363, 461 P.2d 643 (1969).

Those courts which applied right to counsel more broadly than required by *Kirby* may now reduce the scope of their rules to bring them into conformity with *Kirby*. The Supreme Court of California has done this in People v. Chojnacky, 8 Cal.3d 759, 106 Cal.Rptr. 106, 505 P.2d 530 (1973). See also Commonwealth v. Lopes, 287 N.E.2d 118 (Mass.1972). But see Chandler v. State, 501 P.2d 512 (Okl.Crim.App.1972).

Two serious questions arise with reference to the scope of *Kirby*. First, in some jurisdictions a suspect is brought to a "bond" court shortly after arrest. Does this court appearance, which is limited solely to the setting of bail, represent the onset of formal prosecutorial proceedings? Does it make a difference whether a prosecutor appears at the hearing or the police appear without a prosecutor? Second, if the police get an arrest warrant from a court does this signify the commencement of prosecution? Some courts have answered in the affirmative. United States ex rel. Robinson v. Zelker, 468 F.2d 159 (2d Cir. 1972), the court said:

> "The first question we have is whether 'adversary judicial proceedings' had been 'initiated' within Kirby v. Illinois. * * *
>
> . . .
>
> "Here the arrest warrant itself commanded that appellant be brought forthwith before the Criminal Court 'to answer the said charge, and to be dealt with according to law.' These were formal criminal proceedings, for the warrant had been signed by a judge based on an 'information upon oath' that appellant did commit the crimes of assault, robbery and possession of a dangerous weapon. This being true, *Wade* required counsel at the show-up, for we see no distinction based on the chance fact that the identifying witness was also a police officer. Time was not of the essence, a lineup could have been arranged and there appeared to be no 'substantial

countervailing policy considerations' against requiring the presence of counsel as suggested in *Wade*."

In dissent Judge Hayes said:

> "I cannot agree with the majority's conclusion that 'adversary judicial criminal proceedings,' within the meaning of Kirby v. Illinois, had been begun in this case at the time of the pre-trial show-up, entitling Robinson to counsel at that show-up. In *Kirby* the Court said:
>
> > 'The initiation of judicial criminal proceedings is far from a mere formalism. It is the starting point of our whole system of adversary criminal justice. *For it is only then that the Government has committed itself to prosecute, and only then that the adverse positions of Government and defendant have solidified.* It is this point, therefore, that marks the commencement of the "criminal prosecutions" to which alone the explicit guarantees of the Sixth Amendment are applicable.'
>
> "Here the only judicial action taken against Robinson was the issuance of a warrant of arrest. He was not even arraigned until the day after the show-up. . . . It seems clear that such a warrant is not a point at which 'the Government has committed itself to prosecute, and . . . the adverse positions of Government and defendant have solidified' ".

See Arnold v. State, 484 S.W.2d 248 (Mo.1972). See also State v. Earle, 60 N.J. 550, 292 A.2d 2 (1972) (rule does not apply when suspect is in custody on an unrelated charge). Does the answer to the question depend on whether, under local law, a complaint for an arrest warrant, which may only state the facts showing probable cause, is sufficient to meet the formal requirements for complaints charging a crime, i. e., affirmative allegations of each of the elements of the crime, citation to the statute violated, etc.? Would it make a difference if the prosecutor assisted the police in drafting the complaint or if a prosecutor approved the application for the warrant?

2. The question of right to counsel has also arisen in connection with identification from photographs. Without exception every court considering the question has held that there is no right to counsel when police show photographs of suspects who are not in custody. What is the basis for this holding? The same result has been reached by the majority of courts when the Sixth Amendment claim was made on behalf of a suspect in custody.

In United States v. Ash, 413 U.S. 300, 93 S.Ct. 2568 (1973), the Court resolved the question. Following are exerpts from the opinion:

MR. JUSTICE BLACKMUN delivered the opinion of the Court.

In this case the Court is called upon to decide whether the Sixth Amendment grants an accused the right to have counsel present whenever the Government conducts a post-indictment photographic display, containing a picture of the accused, for the purpose of allowing a witness to attempt an identification of the offender. The United States Court of Appeals for the District of Columbia Circuit, sitting *en banc*, held, by a 5-to-4 vote, that the accused possesses this right to counsel. The court's holding is inconsistent with decisions of the court of appeals of nine other circuits. . . .

I

On the morning of August 26, 1965, a man with a stocking mask entered a bank in Washington, D. C., and began waving a pistol. He ordered an employee to hang up the telephone and instructed all others present not to move. Seconds later a second man, also wearing a stocking mask, entered the bank, scooped up money from tellers' drawers into a bag, and left. The gunman followed, and both men escaped through an alley. The robbery lasted three or four minutes.

A Government informer, Clarence McFarland, told authorities that he had discussed the robbery with Charles J. Ash, Jr., the respondent here. Acting on this information, an FBI agent, in February 1966, showed five black-and-white mug shots, of Negro males of generally the same age, height, and weight, one of which was of Ash, to four witnesses. All four made uncertain identifications of Ash's picture. At this time Ash was not in custody and had not been charged. On April 1, 1966, an indictment was returned charging Ash and a codefendant, John L. Bailey, in five counts related to this bank robbery, in violation of D.C.Code § 22–2901 and 18 U.S.C. § 2113(a).

Trial was finally set for May 1968, almost three years after the crime. In preparing for trial, the prosecutor decided to use a photographic display to determine whether the witnesses he planned to call would be able to make in-court identifications. Shortly before the trial, an FBI agent and the prosecutor showed five color photographs to the four witnesses who previously had tentatively identified the black-and-white photograph of Ash. Three of the witnesses selected the picture of Ash, but one was unable to make any selection. None of the witnesses selected the picture of Bailey which was in the group. This post-indictment identification provides the basis for respondent Ash's claim that he was denied the right to counsel at a "critical stage" of the prosecution. . . .

At trial, the three witnesses who had been inside the bank identified Ash as the gunman, but they were unwilling to state that they were certain of their identifications. None of these made an in-court identification of Bailey. The fourth witness, who had been in a car outside the bank and who had seen the fleeing robbers after they had removed their masks, made positive in-court identifications of both Ash and Bailey. Bailey's counsel then sought to impeach this in-court identification by calling the FBI agent who had shown the color photographs to the witnesses immediately before trial. Bailey's counsel demonstrated that the witness who had identified Bailey in court had failed to identify a color photograph of Bailey. During the course of the examination, Bailey's counsel also, before the jury, brought out the fact that this witness had selected another man as one of the robbers. At this point the prosecutor became concerned that the jury might believe that the witness had selected a third person when, in fact, the witness had selected a photograph of Ash. After a conference at the bench, the trial judge ruled that all five color photographs would be admitted into evidence. The Court of Appeals held that this constituted the introduction of a post-indictment identification at the prosecutor's request and over the objection of defense counsel.

McFarland testified as a Government witness. He said he had discussed plans for the robbery with Ash before the event and, later, had discussed the results of the robbery with Ash in the presence of Bailey. McFarland was shown to possess an extensive criminal record and a history as an informer.

The jury convicted Ash on all counts. It was unable to reach a verdict on the charges against Bailey, and his motion for acquittal was granted. . . .

II

The Court of Appeals relied exclusively on that portion of the Sixth Amendment providing, "In all criminal prosecutions, the accused shall enjoy the right . . . to have the Assistance of Counsel for his defence." The right to counsel in Anglo-American law has a rich historical heritage, and this Court has regularly drawn on that history in construing the counsel guarantee of the Sixth Amendment. . . .

This historical background suggests that the core purpose of the counsel guarantee was to assure "Assistance" at trial, when the accused was confronted with both the intricacies of the law and the advocacy of the public prosecutor. Later developments have led this Court to recognize that "Assistance" would be less than meaningful if it were limited to the formal trial itself.

This extension of the right to counsel to events before trial has resulted from changing patterns of criminal procedure and investigation that have tended to generate pretrial events that might appropriately be considered to be parts of the trial itself. At these newly emerging and significant events, the accused was confronted, just as at trial, by the procedural system, or by his expert adversary, or by both. . . .

The Court consistently has applied an historical interpretation of the guarantee, and has expanded the constitutional right to counsel only when new contexts appear presenting the same dangers that gave birth initially to the right itself.

Recent cases demonstrate the historical method of this expansion. In Hamilton v. Alabama (1961), and in White v. Maryland (1963), the accused was confronted with the procedural system and was required, with definite consequences, to enter a plea. In Massiah v. United States (1964), the accused was confronted by prosecuting authorities who obtained, by ruse and in the absence of defense counsel, incriminating statements. In Coleman v. Alabama (1970), the accused was confronted by his adversary at a "critical stage" preliminary hearing at which the uncounseled accused could not hope to obtain so much benefit as could his skilled adversary.

The analogy between the unrepresented accused at the pretrial confrontation and the unrepresented defendant at trial, implicit in the cases mentioned above, was explicitly drawn in *Wade*:

> "The trial which might determine the accused's fate may well not be that in the courtroom but that at the pretrial confrontation, with the State aligned against the accused, the witness the sole jury, and the accused unprotected against the overreaching, intentional or unintentional, and with little or no effective appeal from the judgment there rendered by the witness—'that's the man.'"

Throughout this expansion of the counsel guarantee to trial-like confrontations, the function of the lawyer has remained essentially the same as his function at trial. In all cases considered by the Court, counsel has continued to act as a spokesman for, or advisor to, the accused. The accused's right to the "Assistance of Counsel" has meant just that, namely, the right of the accused to have counsel acting as his assistant. In *Hamilton* and *White,* for example, the Court envisioned the lawyer as advising the accused on available defenses in order to allow him to plead intelligently. In *Massiah* counsel could have advised his client on the benefits of the Fifth Amendment and could have sheltered him from the overreaching of the prosecution. In *Coleman* the skill of the lawyer in examining witnesses, probing for evidence, and making legal arguments was relied upon by the Court to demonstrate that, in the light of the purpose of the preliminary hearing under Alabama law, the accused required "Assistance" at that hearing.

The function of counsel in rendering "Assistance" continued at the lineup under consideration in *Wade* and its companion cases. Although the accused was not confronted there with legal questions, the lineup offered opportunities for prosecuting authorities to take advantage of the accused. Counsel was seen by the Court as being more sensitive to, and aware of, suggestive influences than the accused himself, and as better able to reconstruct the events at trial. Counsel present at lineup would be able to remove disabilities of the accused in precisely the same fashion that counsel compensated for the disabilities of the layman at trial. Thus the Court mentioned that the accused's memory might be dimmed by "emotional tension," that the accused's credibility at trial would be diminished by his status as defendant, and that the accused might be unable to present his version effectively without giving up his privilege against compulsory self-incrimination. 388 U.S., at 230–231, 87 S.Ct., at 1933, 1934. It was in order to compensate for these deficiencies that the Court found the need for the assistance of counsel.

This review of the history and expansion of the Sixth Amendment counsel guarantee demonstrates that the test utilized by the Court has called for examination of the event in order to determine whether the accused required aid in coping with legal problems or assistance in meeting his adversary. Against the background of this traditional test, we now consider the opinion of the Court of Appeals.

III

* * *

After the Court in *Wade* held that a lineup constituted a trial-like confrontation requiring counsel, a more difficult issue remained in the case for consideration. The same changes in law enforcement that led to lineups and pretrial hearings also generated other events at which the accused was confronted by the prosecution. The Government had argued in *Wade* that if counsel was required at a lineup, the same forceful considerations would mandate counsel at other preparatory steps in the "gathering of the prosecution's evidence," such as, for particular example, the taking of fingerprints or blood samples.

The Court concluded that there were differences. Rather than distinguishing these situations from the lineup in terms of the need for counsel to assure an equal confrontation at the time, the Court recognized that there were times when the subsequent trial would cure a one-sided confrontation between prosecuting authorities and the uncounseled defendant. In other words, such stages were not "critical." Referring to fingerprints, hair, clothing, and other blood samples, the Court explained:

> "Knowledge of the techniques of science and technology is sufficiently available, and the variables in techniques few enough, that the accused has the opportunity for a meaningful confrontation of the Government's case at trial through the ordinary processes of cross-examination of the Government's expert witnesses and the presentation of the evidence of his own experts."

The structure of *Wade*, viewed in light of the careful limitation of the Court's language to "confrontations," makes it clear that lack of scientific precision and inability to reconstruct an event are not the tests for requiring counsel in the first instance. These are, instead, the tests to determine whether confrontation with counsel at trial can serve as a substitute for counsel at the pretrial confrontation. If accurate reconstruction is possible, the risks inherent in any confrontation still remain, but the opportunity to cure defects at trial causes the confrontation to cease to be "critical." . . .

The Court of Appeals considered its analysis complete after it decided that a photographic display lacks scientific precision and ease of accurate reconstruction at trial. That analysis, under *Wade*, however, merely carries one to the point where one must establish that the trial itself can provide no substitute for counsel if a pretrial confrontation is conducted in the absence of counsel. Judge Friendly, writing for the Second Circuit in United States v. Bennett, 409 F.2d 888 (1969), recognized that the "criticality" test of *Wade*, if applied outside the confrontation context, would result in drastic expansion of the right to counsel:

> "None of the classical analyses of the assistance to be given by counsel, Justice Sutherland's in Powell v. Alabama . . . and Justice Black's in Johnson v. Zerbst . . . and Gideon v. Wainwright . . . suggests that counsel must be present when the prosecution is interrogating witnesses in the defendant's absence even when, as here, the defendant is under arrest; counsel is rather to be provided to prevent the defendant himself from falling into traps devised by a lawyer on the other side and to see to it that all available defenses are proffered. Many other aspects of the prosecution's interviews with a victim or a witness to a crime afford just as much opportunity for undue suggestion as the display of photographs; so, too, do the defense's interviews, notably with alibi witnesses."

We now undertake the threshold analysis that must be addressed.

IV

A substantial departure from the historical test would be necessary if the Sixth Amendment were interpreted to give Ash a right to counsel at the photographic identification in this case. Since the accused himself is not present at the time of the photographic display, and asserts no right to be present, Brief for the Respondent 40, no possibility arises that the accused might be misled by his lack of familiarity with the law or overpowered by his professional adversary. Similarly, the counsel guarantee would not be used to produce equality in a trial-like adversary confrontation. Rather, the guarantee was used by the Court of Appeals to produce confrontation at an event that previously was not analogous to an adversary trial.

Even if we were willing to view the counsel guarantee in broad terms as a generalized protection of the adversary process, we would be unwilling to go so far as to extend the right to a portion of the prosecutor's trial-preparation interviews with witnesses. Although photography is relatively new, the interviewing of witnesses before trial is a procedure that predates the Sixth Amendment. In England in the 16th and 17th centuries counsel regularly interviewed witnesses before trial. The traditional counterbalance in the American adversary system for these interviews arises from the equal ability of defense counsel to seek and interview witnesses himself.

That adversary mechanism remains as effective for a photographic display as for other parts of pretrial interviews. No greater limitations are placed on defense counsel in constructing displays, seeking witnesses, and conducting photographic identifications than those applicable to the prosecution. Selection of the picture of a person other than the accused, or the inability of a witness to make any selection, will be useful to the defense in precisely the same manner that the selection of a picture of the defendant would be useful to the prosecution. In this very case, for example, the initial tender of the photographic display was by Bailey's counsel, who sought to demonstrate that the witness had failed to make a photographic identification. Although we do not suggest that equality of access to photographs removes all potential for abuse, it does remove any inequality in the adversary process itself and thereby fully satisfies the historical spirit of the Sixth Amendment's counsel guarantee.

The argument has been advanced that requiring counsel might compel the police to observe more scientific procedures or might encourage them to utilize corporeal rather than photographic displays. This Court has recognized that improved procedures can minimize the dangers of suggestion. Simmons v. United States (1968). Commentators have also proposed more accurate techniques.

Pretrial photographic identifications, however, are hardly unique in offering possibilities for the actions of the prosecutor unfairly to prejudice the accused. Evidence favorable to the accused may be withheld; testimony of witnesses may be manipulated; the results of laboratory tests may be contrived. In many ways the prosecutor, by accident or by design, may improperly subvert the trial. The primary safeguard against abuses of this kind is the ethical responsibility of the prosecutor, who, as so often has been said, may "strike hard blows" but not "foul ones." If that safeguard fails, review remains available under due process standards. These same safeguards apply to misuse of photographs. See Simmons v. United States.

We are not persuaded that the risks inherent in the use of photographic displays are so pernicious that an extraordinary system of safeguards is required.

We hold, then, that the Sixth Amendment does not grant the right to counsel at photographic displays conducted by the Government for the purpose of allowing a witness to attempt an identification of the offender. . . .

Reversed and remanded.

MR. JUSTICE STEWART, concurring in the judgment.

* * *

A photographic identification is quite different from a lineup, for there are substantially fewer possibilities of impermissible suggestion when photographs are used, and those unfair influences can be readily reconstructed at trial. It is true that the defendant's photograph may be markedly different from the others displayed, but this unfairness can be demonstrated at trial from an actual comparison of the photographs used or from the witness' description of the display. Similarly, it is possible that the photographs could be arranged in a suggestive manner, or that by comment or gesture the prosecuting authorities might single out the defendant's picture. But these are the kinds of overt influence that a witness can easily recount and that would serve to impeach the identification testimony. In short, there are few possibilities for unfair suggestiveness—and those rather blatant and easily reconstructed. Accordingly, an accused would not be foreclosed from an effective cross-examination of an identification witness simply because his counsel was not present at the photographic display. For this reason, a photographic display cannot fairly be considered a "critical stage" of the prosecution. . . .

Preparing witnesses for trial by checking their identification testimony against a photographic display is little different, in my view, from the prosecutor's other interviews with the victim or other witnesses before trial. While these procedures can be improperly conducted, the possibility of irretrievable prejudice is remote, since any unfairness that does occur can usually be flushed out at trial through cross-examination of the prosecution witnesses. The presence of defense counsel at such pretrial preparatory sessions is neither appropriate nor necessary under our adversary system of justice "to preserve the defendant's basic right to a fair trial as affected by his right meaningfully to cross-examine the witnesses against him and to have effective assistance of counsel at the trial itself."

MR. JUSTICE BRENNAN, with whom MR. JUSTICE DOUGLAS and MR. JUSTICE MARSHALL join, dissenting.

* * *

In my view, today's decision is wholly unsupportable in terms of such considerations as logic, consistency and, indeed, fairness. As a result, I must reluctantly conclude that today's decision marks simply another step towards the complete evisceration of the fundamental constitutional principles established by this Court, only six years ago, in United States v. Wade. I dissent.

* * *

III

As the Court of Appeals recognized, "the dangers of mistaken identification . . . set forth in *Wade* are applicable in large measure to photographic as well as corporeal identifications." 461 F.2d, at 100. To the extent that misidentification may be attributable to a witness' faulty memory or perception, or inadequate opportunity for detailed observation during the crime, the risks are obviously as great at a photographic display as at a lineup. But "[b]ecause of the inherent limitations of photography, which presents its subject in two dimensions rather than the three dimensions of reality, . . . a photographic identification, even when properly obtained, is clearly inferior to a properly obtained corporeal identification." P. Wall, Eye-Witness Identification in Criminal Cases 70 (1965). Indeed, noting "the hazards of initial identification by photograph," we have expressly recognized that "a corporeal identification . . . is normally more accurate" than a photographic identification. Thus, in this sense at least, the dangers of misidentification are even greater at a photographic display than at a lineup.

Moreover, as in the lineup situation, the possibilities for impermissible suggestion in the context of a photographic display are manifold. Such suggestion, intentional or unintentional, may derive from three possible sources. First, the photographs themselves might tend to suggest which of the pictures is that of the suspect. For example, differences in age, pose, or other physical characteristics of the persons represented, and variations in the mounting, background, lighting or markings of the photographs all might have the effect of singling out the accused.

Second, impermissible suggestion may inhere in the manner in which the photographs are displayed to the witness. The danger of misidentification is, of course, "increased if the police display to the witness . . . the pictures of several persons among which the photograph of a single such individual recurs or is in some way emphasized." Simmons v. United States, supra, at 383, 88 S.Ct., at 971. And if the photographs are arranged in an asymetrical pattern, or if they are displayed in a time sequence that tends to emphasize a particular photograph, "any identification of the photograph which stands out from the rest is no more reliable than an identification of a single photograph, exhibited alone." P. Wall, supra, at 81.

Third, gestures or comments of the prosecutor at the time of the display may lead an otherwise uncertain witness to select the "correct" photograph. For example, the prosecutor might "indicate to the witness that [he has] other evidence that one of the persons pictured committed the crime," and might even point to a particular photograph and ask whether the person pictured "looks familiar." More subtly, the prosecutor's inflection, facial expressions, physical motions and myriad other almost imperceptible means of communication might tend, intentionally or unintentionally, to compromise the witness' objectivity. Thus, as is the case with lineups, "[i]mproper photographic identification procedures, . . . by exerting a suggestive influence upon the witnesses, can often lead to an erroneous identification . . . ." P. Wall, supra, at 89. And "[r]egardless of how the initial misidentification comes about, the witness thereafter is apt to retain in his memory the image of the photograph rather than of the person actually seen. . . ." Simmons v. United States, supra, 390 U.S., at 383–384, 88 S.Ct., at 971. As a result, " 'the issue of identity may (in the absence of other relevant evidence) for all practical purposes be determined there and then, before the trial.' " Wade v. United States, supra, 388 U.S., at 229, 87 S.Ct., at 1933, quoting Williams and Hammelmann, supra, at 482.

Moreover, as with lineups, the defense can "seldom reconstruct" at trial the mode and manner of photographic identification. It is true, of course, that the photographs used at the pretrial display might be preserved for examination at trial. But "it may also be said that a photograph can preserve the record of a lineup; yet this does not justify a lineup without counsel." 461 F.2d, at 100–101. Cf. United States v. Wade, supra, 388 U.S., at

239 and n. 30, 87 S.Ct., at 1938. Indeed, in reality, preservation of the photographs affords little protection to the unrepresented accused. For although retention of the photographs may mitigate the dangers of misidentification due to the suggestiveness of the photographs themselves, it cannot in any sense reveal to defense counsel the more subtle, and therefore more dangerous, suggestiveness that might derive from the manner in which the photographs were displayed or any accompanying comments or gestures. Moreover, the accused cannot rely upon the witnesses themselves to expose these latter sources of suggestion, for the witnesses are not "apt to be alert for conditions prejudicial to the suspect. And if they were, it would be of scant benefit to the suspect" since the witnesses are hardly "likely to be schooled in the detection of suggestive influences." United States v. Wade, supra, at 230, 87 S.Ct., at 1934.

Finally, and *unlike* the lineup situation, the accused himself is not even present at the photographic identification, thereby reducing the likelihood that irregularities in the procedures will ever come to light. . . .

* * *

IV

Ironically, the Court does not seriously challenge the proposition that presence of counsel at a pretrial photographic display is essential to preserve the accused's right to a fair trial on the issue of identification. Rather, in what I can only characterize a triumph of form over substance, the Court seeks to justify its result by engrafting a wholly unprecedented—and wholly unsupportable—limitation on the Sixth Amendment right of "the accused . . . to have the Assistance of Counsel for his defense." Although apparently conceding that the right to counsel attaches, not only at the trial itself, but at all "critical stages" of the prosecution, see ante, at 2573–2575, the Court holds today that, in order to be deemed "critical," the particular "stage of the prosecution" under consideration must, at the very least, involve the physical "presence of the accused," at a "trial-like confrontation" with the Government, at which the accused requires the "guiding hand of counsel." A pretrial photographic identification does not, of course, meet these criteria. . . .

The fundamental premise underlying *all* of this Court's decisions holding the right to counsel applicable at "critical" pretrial proceedings, is that a "stage" of the prosecution must be deemed "critical" for the purposes of the Sixth Amendment if it is one at which the presence of counsel is necessary to protect the fairness of *the trial itself*.

This established conception of the Sixth Amendment guarantee is, of course, in no sense dependent upon the physical "presence of the accused," at a "trial-like confrontation" with the Government, at which the accused requires the "guiding hand of counsel." On the contrary, in Powell v. Alabama (1932), the seminal decision in this area, we explicitly held the right to counsel applicable at a stage of the pretrial proceedings involving *none* of the three criteria set forth by the Court today. In *Powell,* the defendants in a State felony prosecution were not appointed counsel until the very eve of trial. This Court held, in no uncertain terms, that such an appointment could not satisfy the demands of the Sixth Amendment, for " '[i]t is vain . . . to guarantee [the accused] counsel without giving the latter any opportunity to acquaint himself with the facts or law of the case.' " In other words, *Powell* made clear that, in order to preserve the accused's right to a fair trial and to "effective and substantial" assistance of counsel at that trial, the Sixth Amendment guarantee necessarily encompasses a reasonable period of time before trial during which counsel might prepare the defense. Yet it can hardly be said that this preparatory period of research and investigation involves the physical "presence of the accused," at a "trial-like confrontation" with the Government, at which the accused requires the "guiding hand of counsel." . . .

Thus, contrary to the suggestion of the Court, the conclusion in *Wade* that a pretrial lineup is a "critical stage" of the prosecution did not in any sense turn on the fact that a lineup involves the physical "presence of the accused" at a "trial-like confrontation" with the Government. And that conclusion most certainly did not turn on the notion that presence of counsel was necessary so that counsel could offer legal advice or "guidance" to the accused at the lineup. On the contrary, *Wade* envisioned counsel's function at the lineup to be primarily that of a trained observer, able to detect the existence of any suggestive influences and capable of understanding the legal implications of the events that transpire. Having witnessed the proceedings, counsel would then be in a position effectively to reconstruct at trial any unfairness that occurred at the lineup, thereby preserving the accused's fundamental right to a fair trial on the issue of identification.

There is something ironic about the Court's conclusion today that a pretrial lineup identification is a "critical stage" of the prosecution because counsel's presence can help to compensate for the accused's deficiencies as an observer, but that a pretrial photographic identification is not a "critical stage" of the prosecution because the accused is not able to observe at all. In my view, there simply is no meaningful difference, in terms of the need for attendance of counsel, between corporeal and photographic identifications. And applying established and well-reasoned Sixth Amendment principles, I can only conclude that a pretrial photographic display, like a pretrial lineup, is a "critical stage" of the prosecution at which the accused is constitutionally entitled to the presence of counsel.

3. The cases decided after *Wade* and *Gilbert* have held the essential purpose served by counsel at the lineup is that of a witness or observer. See United States v. Gholston, 437 F.2d 260 (6th Cir. 1971); Wright v. State, 46 Wis.2d 75, 175 N.W.2d 646 (1971). See also Comment, Right To Counsel At Police Identification Proceedings, 29 U.Pitt.L.Rev. 65 (1967). Counsel cannot stop a lineup simply by walking away. See Vernen v. State, 12 Md.App. 430, 278 A.2d 609 (1971). There are some inherent problems for defense counsel who appears at a lineup for his client. Does he have a duty to make suggestions about how to make the lineup fairer? If he does make suggestions, should they be designed to produce a fair lineup or one weighted as heavily as possible in favor of his client? A searching criticism of the use of counsel to correct lineup abuses is found in Read, Lawyers at Lineups, Constitutional Necessity or Avoidable Extravagance?, 17 U.C.L.A.L.Rev. 339 (1969). Consider these excerpts:

"(a) *Those participating may be police officers.*

> How will a lawyer's presence change this and is this an evil in and of itself? It must be remembered that the purpose of a lineup is to aid the police in investigating a crime. Certainly it must be conceded that police should be able to participate in their own investigative techniques.

"(b) *The participants' names are rarely divulged.*

The obvious remedy is to require the names to be divulged. In the District of Columbia a 'sheet' is routinely kept, listing the names of those participating in the lineup and the names of the conducting officers. The sheet is available to the defense.

"(c) *The victim is not an effective witness as to what occurred.*

Neither is the defendant's lawyer. Audio and visual recording devices, photographs, and the like are much more effective. Even a lay observer, in the absence of such devices, would probably make a better witness than the defendant's lawyer. It is my view the jury would be much more likely to believe an independent observer than an accused's own attorney testifying on behalf of his client.

"(d) *The victim's outrage may excite 'vengeful or spiteful motives' and the victim will not be alert to conditions prejudicial to the suspect.*

A lawyer's presence will not change this. Only regularized lineup procedures that are faithfully followed can minimize suggestive procedures that may point the victim's outrage at the wrong person.

"(e) *Neither witnesses nor lineup participants are alert for conditions 'prejudicial' to the suspect or schooled in the detection of suggestive influence.*

A lawyer is not necessarily 'schooled' in detecting suggestive influences either. A psychologist might be better equipped for the task. Even assuming the lawyer spots such conditions, what can he do about them except prepare himself to be a witness at trial? Certainly any impartial observer, acquainted with the problem and given examples of what to look for, could do as well as any lawyer. Better yet, since the purpose of a lawyer's presence is to acquaint judge and jury with what occurred, photographs, videotapes, or recordings would do this much more vividly. And adoption of regularized procedures might avoid suggestive conditions in the first place.

"(f) *Jury will not believe a suspect's version of what occurred.*

Will it be much more likely to believe the suspect's lawyer's version of what occurred? Probably not. Therefore, objective reproduction by mechanical devices again will better counter this evil."

Professor Read studied one jurisdiction (District of Columbia) in which efforts were made to provide counsel at lineups. His finding:

"Legal Aid seems to concede that under present conditions there is no real reason for defense counsel to appear at the lineup. First, except for minor alterations, the police will not change their set procedures. Second, there is no one there to record any objection that might be made. Legal Aid personnel seem generally to be of the opinion that the presence of an attorney at a lineup is simply not necessary if the attorney is to take a limited role.

* * *

"Experienced police officers and prosecuting attorneys are convinced that any discovery of a witness' name by some defense attorneys is tantamount to disclosure of that name to that lawyer's client. These same police officers and prosecuting attorneys feel that many prospective witnesses are refusing to participate in lineup procedures because of real fear of retaliation from the accused or friends of the accused once a witness' identity is discovered. A particularly sensitive situation evidently exists in the District of Columbia. It was reported that fear of physical intimidation seems especially acute among many Negro witnesses and victims of crime who are asked to cooperate with the police. Police officers charged that the real problem with the lineups is not that witnesses are too susceptible to suggestion but, on the contrary, witnesses are too reluctant to participate freely in the process. Several defense attorneys conceded that a serious problem of witness intimidation does exist and that Wade's command that a lawyer be present at lineups may have exacerbated the situation.

"Another vigorously raised complaint of police and prosecution attorneys relates to the conduct of defense counsel in altering the appearance of their clients prior to their client's participation in a lineup. For example, a young defendant may be arrested while sporting a mustache, an 'Afro haircut' and very bright clothing. When he shows up for the lineup, his Afro haircut is removed, his mustache is shaved off, and he is wearing a suit and tie. An extreme example of this occurred when a female impersonator was arrested in his feminine disguise and then showed up for the lineup in typical male attire. The United States Attorney's Office thus feels that intimidation and disguise of suspects by defense lawyers is the 'other side of the coin' from the suggestive influence problem."

[Ed. Note. The incident of changed appearance cited by Professor Read is quite similar to that occurring in United States v. Jackson, 476 F.2d 249 (7th Cir. 1973)]:

"My observations and conversations with police, prosecuting attorneys and defense attorneys have convinced me that the lineup is a necessary tool in the arsenal of investigatory techniques available to the police. However, it is also my view that the presence of defense counsel at a lineup is simply not necessary to insure the fairness of the procedure. His passive role renders him basically impotent; he is unable to change the slightest detail in any way unless the police decide to cooperate; he is unable to make and have recorded any objections he may have; and he has no way of preserving what occurred except through his own notes and memory.

"Not only is the defense lawyer's presence only minimally effective in preventing unfairness and preserving a record of what occurred, his presence, in certain cases, can actually hinder the administration of criminal justice. Some lawyers have turned the lineup, a police investigatory technique, into a discovery proceeding. A serious danger of intimidation exists in many cases when the identity of witnesses is discovered and disclosed to defendants. Furthermore, by drastically altering the appearance of defendants, defense counsel can actually nullify the usefulness of the lineup process as an investigatory tool. Wade was intended to protect an accused from suggestive lineup procedures; however, in certain cases, the real effect of the Wade remedy is to destroy the utility of the lineup procedure and to make intimidation of witnesses easier."

4. In *Wade* it was suggested that "Legislative or other regulations, such as those of local police departments, which eliminate the risk of abuse and unintentional suggestion at lineup proceedings and the impediments to meaningful confrontation at trial may also remove the basis for regarding the stage as 'critical' ", United States v. Wade, 388 U.S. at 239. Yet, that language was explicitly disavowed by four of six Justices joining in the opinion. (Black, J. and Fortas, J. joined by Warren, C. J. and Douglas J.). A fifth Justice implicitly rejected the proposition. (Clark, J.).

The only attempt to rely on the suggestion that regulations might obviate the right to counsel has been rebuffed with the reasoning that such regulations would be adequate only if they succeeded in elevating eyewitness identification procedures to the level of reliability present in procedures for analyzing fingerprints, blood samples and hair. See People v. Fowler, 1 Cal.3d 355, 461 P.2d 643, 652 (1969). If this is the standard to be met by legislation or regulation, then is acceptable regulation possible? Is this the appropriate standard by which to judge lineup regulations?

5. In 1968 Congress enacted the following provision as part of the "Omnibus Crime Control And Safe Streets Act of 1968":

§ *3502. Admissibility in evidence of eye witness testimony*

The testimony of a witness that he saw the accused commit or participate in the commission of the crime for which the accused is being tried shall be admissible in evidence in a criminal prosecution in any trial court ordained and established under Article III of the Constitution of the United States.

Is this provision constitutional?

B. SUGGESTIVENESS IN IDENTIFICATION PROCEDURE

STOVALL v. DENNO

Supreme Court of the United States, 1967.
388 U.S. 293, 87 S.Ct. 1967.

MR. JUSTICE BRENNAN delivered the opinion of the Court. * * *

Dr. Paul Behrendt was stabbed to death in the kitchen of his home in Garden City, Long Island, about midnight August 23, 1961. Dr. Behrendt's wife, also a physician, had followed her husband to the kitchen and jumped at the assailant. He knocked her to the floor and stabbed her 11 times. The police found a shirt on the kitchen floor and keys in a pocket which they traced to petitioner. They arrested him on the afternoon of August 24. An arraignment was promptly held but was postponed until petitioner could retain counsel.

Mrs. Behrendt was hospitalized for major surgery to save her life. The police, without affording petitioner time to retain counsel, arranged with her surgeon to permit them to bring petitioner to her hospital room about noon of August 25, the day after the surgery. Petitioner was handcuffed to one of five police officers who, with two members of the staff of the District Attorney, brought him to the hospital room. Petitioner was the only Negro in the room. Mrs. Behrendt identified him from her hospital bed after being asked by an officer whether he "was the man" and after petitioner repeated at the direction of an officer a "few words for voice identification." None of the witnesses could recall the words that were used. Mrs. Behrendt and the officers testified at the trial to her identification of the petitioner in the hospital room, and she also made an in-court identification of petitioner in the courtroom. * * *

We hold that *Wade* and *Gilbert* affect only those cases and all future cases which involve confrontations for identification purposes conducted in the absence of counsel after this date. The rulings of *Wade* and *Gilbert* are therefore inapplicable in the present case. We think also that on the facts of this case petitioner was not deprived of due process of law in violation of the Fourteenth Amendment. The judgment of the Court of Appeals is, therefore, affirmed. * * *

We turn now to the question whether petitioner, although not entitled to the application of *Wade* and *Gilbert* to his case, is entitled to relief on his claim that in any event the confrontation conducted in this case was so unnecessarily suggestive and conducive to irreparable mistaken identification that he was denied due process of law. This is a recognized ground of attack upon a conviction independent of any right to counsel claim. Palmer v. Peyton, 359 F.2d 199 (C.A. 4th Cir. 1966). The practice of showing suspects singly to persons for the purpose of identification, and not as part of a lineup, has been widely condemned. However, a claimed violation of due process of law in the conduct of a confrontation depends on the totality of the circumstances surrounding it, and the record in the present case reveals that the showing of Stovall to Mrs. Behrendt in an immediate hospital confrontation was imperative. The Court of Appeals, *en banc,* stated, 355 F.2d at 735.

> "Here was the only person in the world who could possibly exonerate Stovall. Her words, and only her words, 'He is not the man' could have resulted in freedom for Stovall. The hospital was not far distant from the courthouse and jail. No one knew how long Mrs. Behrendt might live. Faced with the responsibility of identifying the attacker, with the need for immediate action and with the knowledge that Mrs. Behrendt could not visit the jail, the police followed the only feasible procedure and took Stovall to the hospital room. Under these circumstances, the usual police station line-up, which Stovall now argues he should have had, was out of the question."

The judgment of the Court of Appeals is affirmed. It is so ordered.

Affirmed.

NOTES

1. *Stovall* prohibits "unnecessarily suggestive" confrontations and held that the procedure involving Stovall himself was proper because it was *necessarily* suggestive. Are there any other forms of necessarily suggestive confrontations? Consider the 6′ 10″ or the 4′ 10″ suspect, or the suspect with prominent scars or tattoos. See State v. Mallette, 159 Conn. 143, 267 A.2d 438 (1970); People v. Faulkner, 28 Cal.App.3d 625, 104 Cal.Rptr. 625 (1972). Consider also the suspect who engages in conduct which attracts attention, i. e., protests his arrest, buries his head in his hands, etc. See United States v. Holsey, 437 F.2d 250 (10th Cir. 1970); People v. Nelson, 40 Ill.2d 146, 238 N.E.2d 378 (1968). What value has the notion that in difficult cases the police ought to use photographic identification procedures? Is the notion based on the assumption that eyewitness identification is based exclusively on facial characteristics? If so, is that a valid assumption? Is photographic identification as reliable as corporeal identification? In the last analysis does the presence of unusual physical characteristics make identification more or less reliable? If a suspect is so unusual that he cannot be placed in an adequate lineup, is it fairer to use a one to one "showup"?

2. The first test by which a line-up or a photographic display is judged is whether it is suggestive (the question of necessity need be reached only if there is suggestiveness).

Suggestiveness is tested by looking at what the witness sees and then asking which of the persons in the line-up stands out. A line-up must also be weighed in terms of the individual witnesses. For example, a line-up may include several fairly similar men all wearing eyeglasses only one of which has horn rim frames. If the witness described the criminal as wearing eyeglasses, the line-up may be perfectly valid. If the witness specifically described the criminal's glasses as hornrimmed, a different view of the line-up might be taken. Generally speaking, few objective standards for fair line-ups can be definitely established but the courts have not had great difficulty making the determination on a case by case basis. Sometimes, however, the judgment is difficult to make at the trial level. Both court and counsel are familiar with what the defendant looks like, and in a line-up photograph, the defendant will stand out. Whether the defendant would stand out to the eyes of a witness who had observed only the crime is another question and, of course, the only question that has to be answered.

3. Suggestiveness may also inhere in circumstances occurring outside the limited sphere of what the witness sees at a line-up. The police may indirectly tell a witness that a particular man is their candidate for prosecution, i. e., "Take a good look at the third man from the left." The fact that the police say that they have a suspect in custody does not constitute a suggestive practice so long as no particular suspect is pointed out by police. See People v. Wooley, 127 Ill.App.2d 249, 262 N.E.2d 237 (1967); State v. McClure, 107 Ariz. 351, 488 P.2d 971 (1971). The reasoning of these courts is that any witness who is asked to view a line-up will obviously conclude that the police have a suspect. See Coleman v. Alabama, 399 U.S. 1, 6, 90 S.Ct. 1999, 2001 (1970).

4. In *Stovall* the Supreme Court specifically noted that "The practice of showing suspects singly to persons for the purpose of identification, and not as part of a line-up has been widely condemned." Yet an exception to this rule has been found in cases involving confrontations occurring shortly after the crime. A discussion of one-man showups is contained in Bates v. United States, 405 F.2d 1104 (D.C.Cir. 1968), which involved a pre-*Wade* Confrontation. In affirming, the Court (Burger, C. J.) said:

"There is no prohibition against a view of a suspect alone in what is called a 'one-man show-up' when this occurs near the time of the alleged criminal act; such a course does not tend to bring about misidentification but rather tends under some circumstances to insure accuracy. The rationale underlying this is in some respects not unlike that which the law relies on to make an exception to the hearsay rule, allowing spontaneous utterances a standing which they would not be given if uttered at a later point in time. An early identification is not in error. Of course, proof of infirmities and subjective factors, such as hysteria of a witness, can be explored on cross-examination and in argument. Prudent police work would confine these on-the-spot identification to situations in which possible doubts as to identification needed to be resolved promptly; absent such need the conventional line-up viewing is the appropriate procedure.

". . . [T]he police action in returning the suspect to the vicinity of the crime for immediate identification fosters the desirable objective of fresh, accurate identification which in some instances may lead to the immediate release of an innocent suspect and at the same time enable the police to resume the search for the fleeing culprit while the trial is fresh".

How prompt must a confrontation be in order to come within this exception? The usual case involves an identification made no more than two or three hours after the offense. See Virgin Islands v. Callwood, 440 F.2d 1206 (3rd Cir. 1971); State v. Sears, 182 Neb. 384, 155 N.W.2d 332 (1967).

A similar doctrine has arisen when a witness accidentally encounters a suspect as in the case where both are injured and brought to the same emergency room. In such a case Stovall is not likely to affect admissibility. This conclusion rests on two factors: (a) there is no deliberate misconduct by the police, see Coleman v. Alabama, 399 U.S. 1, 90 S.Ct. 1999 (1970), and, (b) if the confrontation is truly accidental then there is likely to have been no suggestive aspect leading to an unreliable identification. See United States v. Johnson, 448 F.2d 963 (9th Cir. 1971); United States v. Pollack, 427 F.2d 1168 (5th Cir. 1970); (court building); State v. Dutton, 112 N.J.Super. 402, 271 A.2d 593 (1970) (at hospital—victim on a stretcher); Commonwealth v. Leaster, —— Mass. ——, 287 N.E.2d 122 (1972).

5. *Stovall* has not been thought to affect the validity of normal courtroom identification procedures. It is completely within the discretion of the trial court whether to grant a defense or prosecution request for a lineup in the courtroom to test witness identification. See People ex rel. Blassick v. Callahan, 50 Ill.2d 330, 279 N.E.2d 1 (1972) (thorough citation of cases on point). Consider the comments of the court in United States v. Hamilton, 469 F.2d 880 (9th Cir. 1972):

> "It might well be argued that the deeply-rooted practice of allowing witnesses to identify the defendant in open court is no less a suggestive show-up than those condemned by *Stovall* and *Foster*.* But we decline to take the giant step of holding in-court identifications inadmissible. It is sufficient safeguard that the accused be allowed to question the weight to be given the 'in-court' identification considering the length of time the witness saw the perpetrator of the crime, the elapsed time between the act and the trial, and the fact that the witness had made no other identification of the defendant."

NEIL v. BIGGERS

Supreme Court of the United States, 1972.
409 U.S. 188, 93 S.Ct. 375.

MR. JUSTICE POWELL delivered the opinion of the Court.

In 1965, after a jury trial in a Tennessee court, respondent was convicted of rape and was sentenced to 20 years' imprisonment. The State's evidence consisted in part of testimony concerning a station house identification of respondent by the victim. * * *

The District Court, after a hearing, held in an unreported opinion that the station house identification procedure was so suggestive

* "One of the things which is hardest for me to understand about this entire line of decisions is the faith in the Court that the fair and reliable and true evidence of identification is the witness's testimony from the stand that the defendant is the man. It seems to me that of all possible identifications that you could conceive of this identification, this in-court identification, although subject to cross-examination, is certainly the most unreliable.

* * * * * *

"This isn't an identification. Far from being a lineup, it is just a ritual. He knows exactly that it is the man sitting there with the three uniformed guards sitting behind him, with their arms crossed. That is the man he is supposed to pick out."

Panel Discussion, "The Role of the Defense Lawyer at a Line-Up in Light of the Wade, Gilbert, and Stovall Decisions," 4 Crim.L.Bull. 273, 283–84 (1968) (Remarks of H. Richard Uviller).

as to violate due process. The Court of Appeals affirmed. Biggers v. Neil, 448 F.2d 91 (1971). * * *

The victim testified at trial that on the evening of January 22, 1965, a youth with a butcher knife grabbed her in the doorway to her kitchen:

> "A. [H]e grabbed me from behind, and grappled—twisted me on the floor. Threw me down on the floor.
>
> "Q. And there was no light in that kitchen?
>
> "A. Not in the kitchen.
>
> "Q. So you couldn't have seen him then?
>
> "A. Yes, I could see him; when I looked up in his face.
>
> "Q. In the dark?
>
> "A. He was right in the doorway—it was enough light from the bedroom shining through. Yes, I could see who he was.
>
> "Q. You could see? No light? And you could see him and know him then?
>
> "A. Yes." Tr. of Rec., pp. 33–34.

When the victim screamed, her 12-year-old daughter came out of her bedroom and also began to scream. The assailant directed the victim to "tell her [the daughter] to shut up, or I'll kill you both." She did so, and was then walked at knifepoint about two blocks along a railroad track, taken into a woods, and raped there. She testified that "the moon was shining brightly, full moon." After the rape, the assailant ran off, and she returned home, the whole incident having taken between 15 minutes and half an hour.

She then gave the police what the Federal District Court characterized as "only a very general description," describing him as "being fat and flabby with smooth skin, bushy hair and a youthful voice." Additionally, though not mentioned by the District Court, she testified at the habeas corpus hearing that she had described her assailant as being between 16 and 18 years old and between five feet ten inches and six feet tall, as weighing between 180 and 200 pounds, and as having a dark brown complexion. This testimony was substantially corroborated by that of a police officer who was testifying from his notes.

On several occasions over the course of the next seven months, she viewed suspects in her home or at the police station, some in lineups and others in showups, and was shown between 30 and 40 photographs. She told the police that a man pictured in one of the photographs had features similar to those of her assailant, but identified none of the suspects. On August 17, the police called her to the station to view petitioner, who was being detained on another charge. In an effort to construct a suitable lineup, the police checked the city jail and the city juvenile home. Finding no one at either place fitting petitioner's unusual physical description, they conducted a showup instead.

The showup itself consisted of two detectives walking respondent past the victim. At the victim's request, the police directed petitioner to say "shut up or I'll kill you." The testimony at trial was not altogether clear as to whether the victim first identified him and then asked that he repeat the words or made her identification after he had spoken.[1] In any event, the victim testified that she had "no doubt" about her identification. At the habeas corpus hearing, she elaborated in response to questioning.

> "A. That I have no doubt, I mean that I am sure that when—see, when I first laid eyes on him, I knew that it was the individual, because his face—well, there was just something that I don't think I could ever forget. I believe—
>
> "Q. You say when you first laid eyes on him, which time are you referring to?
>
> "A. When I identified him in the courthouse when I was took up to view the suspect." Pet.App., p. 127.

We must decide whether, as the courts below held, this identification and the circumstances surrounding it failed to comport with due process requirements.

We have considered on four occasions the scope of due process protection against the admission of evidence deriving from suggestive identification procedures. In Stovall v. Denno, 388 U.S. 293 (1967), the Court held that the defendant could claim that "the confrontation conducted . . . was so unnecessarily suggestive and conducive to irreparable mistaken identification that he was denied due process of law." This, we held, must be determined "on the totality of the circumstances." We went on to find that on the facts of the case then before us, due process was not violated, emphasizing that the critical condition of the injured witness justified a showup in her hospital room. At trial, the witness, whose view of the suspect at the time of the crime was brief, testified to the out-of-court identification, as did several police officers present in her hospital room, and also made an in-court identification.

1. At trial, one of the police officers present at the identification testified explicitly that the words were spoken after the identification. The victim testified:

"Q. What physical characteristics, if any, caused you to be able to identify him?

"A. First of all,—uh—his size,—next I could remember his voice.

"Q. What about his voice? Describe his voice to the Jury.

"A. Well, he has the voice of an immature youth—I call it an immature youth. I have teen-age boys. And that was the first thing that made me think it was the boy."

The colloquy continued, with the victim describing the voice and other physical characteristics. At the habeas corpus hearing, the victim and all of the police witnesses testified that a visual identification preceded the voice identification.

Subsequently, in a case where the witnesses made in-court identifications arguably stemming from previous exposure to a suggestive photographic array, the Court restated the governing test:

> "[W]e hold that each case must be considered on its own facts, and that convictions based on eyewitness identification at trial following a pretrial identification by photograph will be set aside on that ground only if the photographic identification procedure was so impermissibly suggestive as to give rise to a very substantial likelihood of irreparable misidentification." Simmons v. United States, 390 U.S. 377, 384 (1968).

Again we found the identification procedure to be supportable, relying both on the need for prompt utilization of other investigative leads and on the likelihood that the photographic identifications were reliable, the witnesses having viewed the bank robbers for periods of up to five minutes under good lighting conditions at the time of the robbery.

The only case to date in which this Court has found identification procedures to be violative of due process is Foster v. California, 394 U.S. 440, 442 (1969). There, the witness failed to identify Foster the first time he confronted him, despite a suggestive lineup. The police then arranged a showup, at which the witness could make only a tentative identification. Ultimately, at yet another confrontation, this time a lineup, the witness was able to muster a definite identification. We held all of the identifications inadmissible, observing that the identifications were "all but inevitable" under the circumstances. 394 U.S., at 443.

In the most recent case of Coleman v. Alabama, 399 U.S. 1 (1970), we held admissible an in-court identification by a witness who had a fleeting but "real good look" at his assailant in the headlights of a passing car. The witness testified at a pretrial suppression hearing that he identified one of the petitioners among the participants in the lineup before the police placed the participants in a formal line. JUSTICE BRENNAN for four members of the Court stated that this evidence could support a finding that the in-court identification was "entirely based upon observations at the time of the assault and not at all induced by the conduct of the lineup." 399 U.S., at 5–6.[2]

2. [Ed. Note: The Facts in Coleman are these]:

At the trial Reynolds testified that at about 11:30 p. m. on July 24, 1966, he was engaged in changing a tire when three men approached from across the highway. One of them shot him from a short distance away. The three then ran up to within three or four feet. Reynolds arose from his stooped position and held on to his wife, who had left the car to watch him as he worked. One of the men put his hand on Mrs. Reynolds' shoulder. Reynolds testified that this was Coleman. Within a few seconds a car with its lights on approached, and the three men turned and "ran across the road * * *." As they turned to go, Reynolds was shot a second time. He identified petitioner Stephens as the gunman, stating that he saw him "in the car lights" while "looking straight at

Some general guidelines emerge from these cases as to the relationship between suggestiveness and misidentification. It is, first of all, apparent that the primary evil to be avoided is "a very substantial likelihood of irreparable misidentification." While the phrase was coined as a standard for determining whether an in-court identification would be admissible in the wake of a suggestive out-of-court identification, with the deletion of "irreparable" it serves equally well as a standard for the admissibility of testimony concerning the out-of-court identification itself. It is the likelihood of misidentification which violates a defendant's right to due process, and it is this which was the basis of the exclusion of evidence in *Foster*. Suggestive confrontations are disapproved because they increase the likelihood of misidentification, and unnecessarily suggestive ones are condemned for the further reason that the increased chance of misidentification is gratuitous. But as *Stovall* makes clear, the admission of evidence of a showup without more does not violate due process.

What is less clear from our cases is whether, as intimated by the District Court, unnecessary suggestiveness alone requires the exclusion of evidence. While we are inclined to agree with the courts below that the police did not exhaust all possibilities in seeking persons physically comparable to petitioner, we do not think that the evidence must therefore be excluded. The purpose of a strict rule barring evidence of unnecessarily suggestive confrontations would be to deter the police from using a less reliable procedure where

him." Reynolds repeated on cross-examination his testimony on direct; he said he saw Coleman "face to face"; "I looked into his face," "got a real good look at him."

At the pretrial hearing on petitioners' motion to suppress identification evidence, Detective Fordham testified that he had spoken briefly to Reynolds at the hospital two days after the assault and about two weeks later, and that on neither occasion was Reynolds able to provide much information about his assailants. At the hospital he gave a vague description—that the attackers were "young, black males, close to the same age and height." Petitioners are both Negro; but Stephens was 18 and 6′2″ and Coleman, 28 and 5′4½″. However, Detective Fordham also testified that at the time Reynolds gave this description he was in considerable pain, and that consequently the questioning was very brief. The detective further stated that Reynolds did not identify any of his assailants from mug shots, but it does not appear whether pictures of petitioners were among those shown him. Detective Hart testified that a lineup was held on October 1 at the request of the police. He stated that Reynolds identified petitioner Stephens spontaneously before the formal lineup even began. "[T]he six men were brought in by the warden, up on the stage, and as Otis Stephens—he didn't get to his position on the stage, which was number one, when Mr. Reynolds identified him as being one of his assailants." Reynolds gave similar testimony: "As soon as he stepped inside the door—I hadn't seen him previous to then until he stepped inside the door, and I recognized him * * *. Just as soon as he stepped up on the stage, I said, 'That man, there, is the one; he is the one that shot me.'" Reynolds also testified that he identified Coleman at the lineup before Coleman could act on a request Reynolds had made that the lineup participants speak certain words used by the attackers. Reynolds admitted that he did not tell Detective Hart of his identification until later during the lineup, and the detective stated he could not recall whether Reynolds told him of the identification before or after Coleman spoke the words.

a more reliable one may be available, not because in every instance the admission of evidence of such a confrontation offends due process. Such a rule would have no place in the present case, since both the confrontation and the trial preceded Stovall v. Denno, supra, when we first gave notice that the suggestiveness of confrontation procedures was anything other than a matter to be argued to the jury.

We turn, then, to the central question, whether under the "totality of the circumstances" the identification was reliable even though the confrontation procedure was suggestive. As indicated by our cases, the factors to be considered in evaluating the likelihood of misidentification include the opportunity of the witness to view the criminal at the time of the crime, the witness' degree of attention, the accuracy of the witness' prior description of the criminal, the level of certainty demonstrated by the witness at the confrontation, and the length of time between the crime and the confrontation. Applying these factors, we disagree with the District Court's conclusion.

In part, as discussed above, we think the District Court focused unduly on the relative reliability of a lineup as opposed to a showup, the issue on which expert testimony was taken at the evidentiary hearing. It must be kept in mind also that the trial was conducted before *Stovall* and that therefore the incentive was lacking for the parties to make a record at trial of facts corroborating or undermining the identification. The testimony was addressed to the jury, and the jury apparently found the identification reliable. Some of the State's testimony at the federal evidentiary hearing may well have been self-serving in that it too neatly fit the case law, but it surely does nothing to undermine the state record, which itself fully corroborated the identification.

We find that the District Court's conclusions on the critical facts are unsupported by the record and clearly erroneous. The victim spent a considerable period of time with her assailant, up to half an hour. She was with him under adequate artificial light in her house and under a full moon outdoors, and at least twice, once in the house and later in the woods, faced him directly and intimately. She was no casual observer, but rather the victim of one of the most personally humiliating of all crimes. Her description to the police, which included the assailant's approximate age, height, weight, complexion, skin texture, build, and voice, might not have satisfied Proust but was more than ordinarily thorough. She had "no doubt" that respondent was the person who raped her. In the nature of the crime, there are rarely witnesses to a rape other than the victim, who often has a limited opportunity of observation. The victim here, a practical nurse by profession, had an unusual opportunity to observe and identify her assailant. She testified at the habeas corpus hearing that there was something about his face "I don't think I could ever forget." Pet. App., p. 128.

There was, to be sure, a lapse of seven months between the rape and the confrontation. This would be a seriously negative factor in most cases. Here, however, the testimony is undisputed that the victim made no previous identification at any of the showups, lineups, or photographic showings. Her record for reliability was thus a good one, as she had previously resisted whatever suggestiveness inheres in a showup. Weighing all the factors, we find no substantial likelihood of misidentification. The evidence was properly allowed to go to the jury.

Reversed in part and remanded.

MR. JUSTICE MARSHALL took no part in the consideration or decision of this case.

MR. JUSTICE BRENNAN, with whom MR. JUSTICE DOUGLAS and MR. JUSTICE STEWART concur, concurring in part and dissenting in part. [Opinion omitted.]

NOTES

1. The testimony of an eyewitness is subject to a complex set of exclusionary rules. Evidence of pre-trial identification (testimony by the witness on direct examination that he attended a line-up and picked out the defendant as the offender) is subject to two per se rules of exclusion. If the pre-trial confrontation is conducted in violation of the right to counsel (Wade-Gilbert), evidence of the pre-trial confrontation is excluded. If the pre-trial confrontation is unnecessarily suggestive (Stovall) evidence of the pre-trial confrontation is similarly excluded. Evidence of in-court identification (i. e. testimony by the witness that the offender is the defendant sitting in the courtroom) is subject to derivative exclusionary rules. If, and only if, the Court has found that the pre-trial confrontation violates one (or both) of the per se exclusionary rules, will there be suppression of evidence of in-court identification. People v. Rodriguez, 10 Cal.App.3d 18, 88 Cal. Rptr. 789 (1970). However, if the prosecution can prove by clear and convincing evidence that the in-court identification has a source independent of the illegal pre-trial confrontation, then evidence of the in-court identification is admissible. An excellent analysis of these rules is found in Clemons v. United States, 408 F.2d 1230 (D.C.Cir.1968).

In determining whether there was an independent source of an in-court identification, several factors are considered. The most common of these are:

> (1) prior opportunity of witnesses to observe the criminal act, (2) existence of a discrepancy between any pre-lineup description and the actual appearance of the accused, (3) any identification of another person prior to the lineup, (4) failure to identify the accused on a prior occasion, (5) lapse of time between the criminal act and the lineup identification, (6) prior photographic identification from a large group of photographs, (7) the presence of distinctive physical characteristics in defendant, (8) prior acquaintance of witness with the suspect, (9) ability and training at identification, (10) the exercise of unusual care to make observations, (11) prompt identification at first confrontation.

See United States ex rel. Geralds v. Deegan, 292 F.Supp. 968 (S.D.N.Y. 1968) and 307 F.Supp. 56 (S.D.N.Y.1969).

If the trial court decides to suppress evidence of pre-trial confrontation but refuses to suppress evidence of in-court identification, the defense has the option to bring the pre-trial confrontation out at trial if it is thought helpful to a defense attack on the courtroom identification. Davis v. State, 467 P.2d 521 (Okl.Cr.App.1970). If the defense brings out some of the facts concerning the pre-trial confrontation, the state may bring out the rest of the circumstances. Commonwealth v. Redmond, 357 Mass. 475, 258 N.E.2d 287 (1970).

An error in the admission of identification evidence does not constitute automatic reversible error. Such errors may be harmless. See Gilbert v. California, 388 U.S. 263, 274, 87 S.Ct. 1951 (1967); United States v. Wade, 388 U.S. 218, 242, 87 S.Ct. 1926 (1967).

2. Can it be said from the point of view of the prosecutor that Stovall is far more significant a case than Wade because as a practical matter only the application of Stovall can cause the loss of the entire testimony of a witness, and that the worst consequence of a violation of Wade-Gilbert is the suppression of evidence of a pre-trial identification by a witness?

Assume a case arising this year where a defendant is placed in a post-indictment lineup without waiving counsel. Wade-Gilbert has been violated. But assume that the lineup is perfectly fair, consisting of seven men of the same height, hair color, race and general appearance, all similarly dressed. If the victim identifies the defendant, the victim will not be able to testify concerning the lineup. But the witness will be able to make a courtroom identification because it is clear that a perfectly fair lineup could not have tainted the courtroom identification. See Nielsen v. State, 456 S.W.2d 928 (Tex.1970). Indeed, the fairness of the lineup itself, coupled with a positive identification, is clear and convincing evidence that the witness had a strong basis for identification prior to the lineup. The ease with which a court can sustain an identification when the pre-trial procedures have been exemplary is found in Butler v. State, 226 Ga. 56, 172 S.E. 2d 399 (1970). . . . A Stovall violation is of far greater potential consequence than a Wade-Gilbert violation. The former tends to impugn the integrity of the witness' courtroom identification while the latter does not. In those jurisdictions where the prosecution is prohibited from showing that a witness made a prior identification the effect of Wade-Gilbert alone is negligible. See 4 Wigmore, Evidence, Sec. 1130 (3rd Ed.1940); 71 A.L. R.2d 449.

In those jurisdictions where evidence of pre-trial identification is admissible what value does this evidence have? See United States v. Williams, 421 F.2d 1166 (D.C.Cir. 1970). In an urban jurisdiction a jury may hear evidence of an in-court identification a year or more after the date of the crime. Could the absence of evidence of pre-trial identification affect their verdict?

3. Can it be said that Neil v. Biggers (and Coleman v. Alabama) evince a general attitude that the courts ought not be too ready to suppress in-court identification evidence?

Chapter 16

INTERROGATIONS AND CONFESSIONS

A. MIRANDA v. ARIZONA

It is quite possible that the next main case, Miranda v. Arizona, will be overruled. One strong indication is the fact that in 1968 two of the present members of the court, Justices Stewart and White, along with the late Justice Harlan, stated in Mathis v. United States, 391 U.S. 1, 88 S.Ct. 1503 (1968), that *Miranda* should be abandoned, "thus avoiding the reversal of this conviction because of the introduction at trial of statements by the defendants that were unquestionably voluntary". Since this statement was made, there has been a replacement on the court of three of the Justices (Warren, Black, and Goldberg) who were among the five constituting the majority in *Miranda*. Also, in Harris v. New York (reported infra, p. 1045), there was some erosion of *Miranda* when a majority of the court held that a confession obtained without the required warnings could nevertheless be used to impeach the confessor after he had taken the stand and denied the commission of the offense.

Another erosion occurred in a June 10, 1974 decision of the Supreme Court in Michigan v. Tucker, — U.S. —, 94 S.Ct. 2357. A majority of the Court held that the prosecution properly used as a witness an individual whose name was given to a police interrogator by the defendant (for false alibi purposes), even though he had not received the full Miranda warnings. (Also consider the implications of the 1969 case of Frazier v. Cupp, reported later in this casebook at page 1066.)

Then, too, there is the provision in the 1968 Omnibus Crime Bill whereby Congress declared that the test of confession admissibility (in federal cases) was to be the test of voluntariness, and that the absence of the warnings prescribed in *Miranda* were only factors to be considered in determining voluntariness; in other words, the absence of the warnings would no longer categorically outlaw a confession.

Despite these developments, however, we cannot safely assume that *Miranda* will necessarily be abandoned by the Supreme Court. Moreover, there is the possibility, of course, that some state courts or legislatures will retain the *Miranda* requirements, as would be their privilege. We have concluded, therefore, to include that case as a main one in this casebook, supplemented by notes explanatory of the meaning of its various requirements. Moreover, the case has value with respect to the history of confession admissibility rules, and as regards the practical aspects of law enforcement interrogation practices.

MIRANDA v. ARIZONA

VIGNERA v. NEW YORK

WESTOVER v. UNITED STATES

CALIFORNIA v. STEWART

Supreme Court of the United States, 1966.
384 U.S. 436, 86 S.Ct. 1602.

MR. CHIEF JUSTICE WARREN delivered the opinion of the Court.

The cases before us raise questions which go to the roots of our concepts of American criminal jurisprudence: the restraints society must observe consistent with the Federal Constitution in prosecuting individuals for crime. More specifically, we deal with the admissibility of statements obtained from an individual who is subjected to custodial police interrogation and the necessity for procedures which assure that the individual is accorded his privilege under the Fifth Amendment to the Constitution not to be compelled to incriminate himself.

We dealt with certain phases of this problem recently in Escobedo v. State of Illinois, 378 U.S. 478, 84 S.Ct. 1758 (1964).

There, as in the four cases before us, law enforcement officials took the defendant into custody and interrogated him in a police station for the purpose of obtaining a confession. The police did not effectively advise him of his right to remain silent or of his right to consult with his attorney. Rather, they confronted him with an alleged accomplice who accused him of having perpetrated a murder. When the defendant denied the accusation and said "I didn't shoot Manuel, you did it," they handcuffed him and took him to an interrogation room. There, while handcuffed and standing, he was questioned for four hours until he confessed. During this interrogation, the police denied his request to speak to his attorney, and they prevented his retained attorney, who had come to the police station, from consulting with him. At his trial, the State, over his objection, introduced the confession against him. We held that the statements thus made were constitutionally inadmissible.

This case has been the subject of judicial interpretation and spirited legal debate since it was decided two years ago. Both state and federal courts, in assessing its implications, have arrived at varying conclusions. A wealth of scholarly material has been written tracing its ramifications and underpinnings. Police and prosecutor have speculated on its range and desirability. We granted certiorari in these cases, . . . in order further to explore some facets of the problems, thus exposed, of applying the privilege against self-incrimination to in-custody interrogation, and to give concrete constitutional guidelines for law enforcement agencies and courts to follow.

We start here, as we did in *Escobedo,* with the premise that our holding is not an innovation in our jurisprudence, but is an application of principles long recognized and applied in other settings. We have undertaken a thorough re-examination of the *Escobedo* decision and the principles it announced, and we reaffirm it. That case was but an explication of basic rights that are enshrined in our Constitution—that "No person . . . shall be compelled in any criminal case to be a witness against himself," and that "the accused shall . . . have the Assistance of Counsel"—rights which were put in jeopardy in that case through official overbearing. These precious rights were fixed in our Constitution only after centuries of persecution and struggle. And in the words of Chief Justice Marshall, they were secured "for ages to come, and . . . designed to approach immortality as nearly as human institutions can approach it," . . .

It was necessary in *Escobedo,* as here, to insure that what was proclaimed in the Constitution had not become but a "form of words," . . . in the hands of government officials. And it is in this spirit, consistent with our role as judges, that we adhere to the principles of *Escobedo* today.

Our holding will be spelled out with some specificity in the pages which follow but briefly stated it is this: the prosecution may not use statements, whether exculpatory or inculpatory, stemming from custodial interrogation of the defendant unless it demonstrates the use of procedural safeguards effective to secure the privilege against self-incrimination. By custodial interrogation, we mean questioning initiated by law enforcement officers after a person has been taken into custody or otherwise deprived of his freedom of action in any significant way.[1] As for the procedural safeguards to be employed, unless other fully effective means are devised to inform accused persons of their right of silence and to assure a continuous opportunity to exercise it, the following measures are required. Prior to any questioning, the person must be warned that he has a right to remain silent, that any statement he does make may be used as evidence against him, and that he has a right to the presence of an attorney, either retained or appointed. The defendant may waive effectuation of these rights, provided the waiver is made voluntarily, knowingly and intelligently. If, however, he indicates in any manner and at any stage of the process that he wishes to consult with an attorney before speaking there can be no questioning. Likewise, if the individual is alone and indicates in any manner that he does not wish to be interrogated, the police may not question him. The mere fact that he may have answered some questions or volunteered some statements on his own does not deprive him of the right to refrain from answering any further inquiries until he has consulted with an attorney and thereafter consents to be questioned.

1. This is what we meant in *Escobedo* when we spoke of an investigation which had focused on an accused.

I.

The constitutional issue we decide in each of these cases is the admissibility of statements obtained from a defendant questioned while in custody or otherwise deprived of his freedom of action in any significant way. In each, the defendant was questioned by police officers, detectives, or a prosecuting attorney in a room in which he was cut off from the outside world. In none of these cases was the defendant given a full and effective warning of his rights at the outset of the interrogation process. In all the cases, the questioning elicited oral admissions, and in three of them, signed statements as well which were admitted at their trials. They all thus share salient features—incommunicado interrogation of individuals in a police-dominated atmosphere, resulting in self-incriminating statements without full warnings of constitutional rights.

An understanding of the nature and setting of this in-custody interrogation is essential to our decisions today. The difficulty in depicting what transpires at such interrogations stems from the fact that in this country they have largely taken place incommunicado. From extensive factual studies undertaken in the early 1930's, . . . it is clear that police violence and the "third degree" flourished at that time. In a series of cases decided by this Court long after these studies, the police resorted to physical brutality—beatings, hanging, whipping—and to sustained and protracted questioning incommunicado in order to extort confessions. The Commission on Civil Rights in 1961 found much evidence to indicate that "some policemen still resort to physical force to obtain confessions." The use of physical brutality and violence is not, unfortunately, relegated to the past or to any part of the country. Only recently in Kings County, New York, the police brutally beat, kicked and placed lighted cigarette butts on the back of a potential witness under interrogation for the purpose of securing a statement incriminating a third party.

The examples given above are undoubtedly the exception now, but they are sufficiently widespread to be the object of concern. Unless a proper limitation upon custodial interrogation is achieved—such as these decisions will advance—there can be no assurance that practices of this nature will be eradicated in the foreseeable future. . . .

* * *

Again we stress that the modern practice of in-custody interrogation is psychologically rather than physically oriented. As we have stated before, . . . "this Court has recognized that coercion can be mental as well as physical, and that the blood of the accused is not the only hallmark of an unconstitutional inquisition." Interrogation still takes place in privacy. Privacy results in secrecy and this in turn results in a gap in our knowledge as to what in fact goes on in the interrogation rooms. A valuable source of information about present police practices, however, may be found in various police manuals and texts which document procedures employed with success in the past, and which recommended various other effective tactics. These texts are used by law enforcement agencies themselves as guides.[2] It should be noted that these texts professedly present the most enlightened and effective means presently used to obtain statements through custodial interrogation. By considering these texts and other data, it is possible to describe procedures observed and noted around the country.

The officers are told by the manuals that the "principal psychological factor contributing to a successful interrogation is privacy—being alone with the person under interrogation." [Inbau and Reid] The efficacy of this tactic has been explained as follows:

> "If at all practicable, the interrogation should take place in the investigator's office or at least in a room of his own choice. The subject should be deprived of every psychological advantage. In his own home he may be confident, indignant, or recalcitrant. He is more keenly aware of his rights and more reluctant to tell of his indiscretions or criminal behavior within the walls of his home. Moreover his family and other friends are nearby, their presence lending moral support. In his office, the investigator possesses all the advantages. The atmosphere suggests the invincibility of the forces of the law." [O'Hara]

To highlight the isolation and unfamiliar surroundings, the manuals instruct the police to display an air of confidence in the suspect's guilt and from outward appearance to maintain only an interest in confirming certain details. The guilt of the subject is to be posited as a fact. The interrogator should direct his comments toward the reasons why the subject committed the act, rather than court failure by asking the subject whether he did it. Like other men, perhaps the subject has had a bad family life, had an unhappy childhood, had too much to drink, had an unrequited desire for women. The of-

2. The methods described in Inbau & Reid, Criminal Interrogation and Confessions (1962), are a revision and enlargement of material presented in three prior editions of a predecessor text, Lie Detection and Criminal Interrogation (3d ed. 1953). The authors and their associates are officers of the Chicago Police Scientific Crime Detection Laboratory and have had extensive experience in writing, lecturing and speaking to law enforcement authorities over a 20-year period.* They say that the techniques portrayed in their manuals reflect their experiences and are the most effective psychological stratagems to employ during interrogations. Similarly, the techniques described in O'Hara, Fundamentals of Criminal Investigation (1956), were gleaned from long service as observer, lecturer in police science, and work as a federal criminal investigator. All these texts have had rather extensive use among law enforcement agencies and among students of police science, with total sales and circulation of over 44,000.

[Editors' note: Inbau was Director of the Laboratory from 1938–1941; he has had no official connection with it since then. Reid was on the Laboratory staff from 1938 to 1947; he too has had no official connection with it since that time.]

ficers are instructed to minimize the moral seriousness of the offense, to cast blame on the victim or on society. These tactics are designed to put the subject in a psychological state where his story is but an elaboration of what the police purport to know already—that he is guilty. Explanations to the contrary are dismissed and discouraged.

The texts thus stress that the major qualities an interrogator should possess are patience and perseverance. One writer describes the efficacy of these characteristics in this manner:

> "In the preceding paragraphs emphasis has been placed on kindness and strategems. The investigator will, however, encounter many situations where the sheer weight of his personality will be the deciding factor. Where emotional appeals and tricks are employed to no avail, he must rely on an oppressive atmosphere of dogged persistence. He must interrogate steadily and without relent, leaving the subject no prospect of surcease. He must dominate his subject and overwhelm him with his inexorable will to obtain the truth. He should interrogate for a spell of several hours pausing only for the subject's necessities in acknowledgement of the need to avoid a charge of duress that can be technically substantiated. In a serious case, the interrogation may continue for days, with the required intervals for food and sleep, but with no respite from the atmosphere of domination. It is possible in this way to induce the subject to talk without resorting to duress or coercion. The method should be used only when the guilt of the subject appears highly probable." [O'Hara]

The manuals suggest that the suspect be offered legal excuses for his actions in order to obtain an initial admission of guilt. Where there is a suspected revenge-killing, for example, the interrogator may say:

> "Joe, you probably didn't go out looking for this fellow with the purpose of shooting him. My guess is, however, that you expected something from him and that's why you carried a gun—for your own protection. You knew him for what he was, no good. Then when you met him he probably started using foul, abusive language and he gave some indication that he was about to pull a gun on you, and that's when you had to act to save your own life. That's about it, isn't it, Joe?" [Inbau & Reid]

Having then obtained the admission of shooting, the interrogator is advised to refer to circumstantial evidence which negates the self-defense explanation. This should enable him to secure the entire story. One text notes that "Even if he fails to do so, the inconsistency between the subject's original denial of the shooting and his present admission of at least doing the shooting will serve to deprive him of a self-defense 'out' at the time of trial." [Inbau & Reid]

When the techniques described above prove unavailing, the texts recommend they be alternated with a show of some hostility. One ploy often used has been termed the "friendly-unfriendly" or the "Mutt and Jeff" act:

> ". . . In this technique, two agents are employed. Mutt, the relentless investigator, who knows the subject is guilty and is not going to waste any time. He's sent a dozen men away for this crime and he's going to send the subject away for the full term. Jeff, on the other hand, is obviously a kindhearted man. He has a family himself. He has a brother who was involved in a little scrape like this. He disapproves of Mutt and his tactics and will arrange to get him off the case if the subject will cooperate. He can't hold Mutt off for very long. The subject would be wise to make a quick decision. The technique is applied by having both investigators present while Mutt acts out his role. Jeff may stand by quietly and demur at some of Mutt's tactics. When Jeff makes his plea for cooperation, Mutt is not present in the room." [O'Hara]

The interrogators sometimes are instructed to induce a confession out of trickery. The technique here is quite effective in crimes which require identification or which run in series. In the identification situation, the interrogator may take a break in his questioning to place the subject among a group of men in a line-up. "The witness or complainant (previously coached, if necessary) studies the line-up and confidently points out the subject as the guilty party." [O'Hara] Then the questioning resumes "as though there were now no doubt about the guilt of the subject." A variation on this technique is called the "reverse line-up":

> "The accused is placed in a line-up, but this time he is identified by several fictitious witnesses or victims who associated him with different offenses. It is expected that the subject will become desperate and confess to the offense under investigation in order to escape from the false accusations." [O'Hara]

The manuals also contain instructions for police on how to handle the individual who refuses to discuss the matter entirely, or who asks for an attorney or relatives. The examiner is to concede him the right to remain silent. "This usually has a very undermining effect. First of all, he is disappointed in his expectation of an unfavorable reaction on the part of the interrogator. Secondly, a concession of this right to remain silent impresses the subject with the apparent fairness of his interrogator." [Inbau & Reid] After this psychological conditioning, however, the officer is told to point out the incriminating significance of the suspect's refusal to talk:

> "Joe, you have a right to remain silent. That's your privilege and I'm the last person in the world who'll try to take it away from you. If that's the way you want to leave this,

> O.K. But let me ask you this. Suppose you were in my shoes and I were in yours and you called me in to ask me about this and I told you, 'I don't want to answer any of your questions.' You'd think I had something to hide, and you'd probably be right in thinking that. That's exactly what I'll have to think about you, and so will everybody else. So let's sit here and talk this whole thing over." [Inbau & Reid]

Few will persist in their initial refusal to talk, it is said, if this monologue is employed correctly.

In the event that the subject wishes to speak to a relative or an attorney, the following advice is tendered:

> "[T]he interrogator should respond by suggesting that the subject first tell the truth to the interrogator himself rather than get anyone else involved in the matter. If the request is for an attorney, the interrogator may suggest that the subject save himself or his family the expense of any such professional service, particularly if he is innocent of the offense under investigation. The interrogator may also add, 'Joe, I'm only looking for the truth, and if you're telling the truth, that's it. You can handle this by yourself.' " [Inbau & Reid]

From these representative samples of interrogation techniques, the setting prescribed by the manuals and observed in practice becomes clear. In essence, it is this: To be alone with the subject is essential to prevent distraction and to deprive him of any outside support. The aura of confidence in his guilt undermines his will to resist. He merely confirms the preconceived story the police seek to have him describe. Patience and persistence, at times relentless questioning, are employed. To obtain a confession, the interrogator must "patiently maneuver himself or his quarry into a position from which the desired objective may be attained." When normal procedures fail to produce the needed result, the police may resort to deceptive stratagems such as giving false legal advice. It is important to keep the subject off balance, for example, by trading on his insecurity about himself or his surroundings. The police then persuade, trick, or cajole him out of exercising his constitutional rights.

Even without employing brutality, the "third degree" or the specific stratagems described above, the very fact of custodial interrogation exacts a heavy toll on individual liberty and trades on the weakness of individuals. This fact may be illustrated simply by referring to three confession cases decided by this Court in the Term immediately preceding our *Escobedo* decision. In Townsend v. Sain (1963), the defendant was a 19-year-old heroin addict, described as a "near mental defective." The defendant in Lynumn v. State of Illinois (1963), was a woman who confessed to the arresting officer after being importuned to "cooperate" in order to prevent her children from being taken by relief authorities. This Court as in those cases reversed the conviction of a defendant in Haynes v. State of Washington (1963), whose persistent request during his interrogation was to phone his wife or attorney. In other settings, these individuals might have exercised their constitutional rights. In the incommunicado police-dominated atmosphere, they succumbed.

In the cases before us today, given this background, we concern ourselves primarily with this interrogation atmosphere and the evils it can bring. In No. 759, Miranda v. Arizona, the police arrested the defendant and took him to a special interrogation room where they secured a confession. In No. 760, Vignera v. New York, the defendant made oral admissions to the police after interrogation in the afternoon, and then signed an inculpatory statement upon being questioned by an assistant district attorney later the same evening. In No. 761, Westover v. United States, the defendant was handed over to the Federal Bureau of Investigation by local authorities after they had detained and interrogated him for a lengthy period, both at night and the following morning. After some two hours of questioning, the federal officers had obtained signed statements from the defendant. Lastly, in No. 584, California v. Stewart, the local police held the defendant five days in the station and interrogated him on nine separate occasions before they secured his inculpatory statement.

In these cases, we might not find the defendants' statements to have been involuntary in traditional terms. Our concern for adequate safeguards to protect precious Fifth Amendment rights is, of course, not lessened in the slightest. In each of the cases, the defendant was thrust into an unfamiliar atmosphere and run through menacing police interrogation procedures. The potentiality for compulsion is forcefully apparent, for example, in *Miranda,* where the indigent Mexican defendant was a seriously disturbed individual with pronounced sexual fantasies, and in *Stewart,* in which the defendant was an indigent Los Angeles Negro who had dropped out of school in the sixth grade. To be sure, the records do not evince over physical coercion or patent psychological ploys. The fact remains that in none of these cases did the officers undertake to afford appropriate safeguards at the outset of the interrogation to insure that the statements were truly the product of free choice.

It is obvious that such an interrogation environment is created for no purpose other than to subjugate the individual to the will of his examiner. This atmosphere carries its own badge of intimidation. To be sure, this is not physical intimidation, but it is equally destructive of human dignity. The current practice of incommunicado interrogation is at odds with one of our Nation's most cherished principles—that the individual may not be compelled to incriminate himself. Unless adequate protective devices are employed to dispel the compulsion inherent in custodial surroundings, no statement obtained from the defendant can truly be the product of his free choice.

From the foregoing, we can readily perceive an intimate connection between the privilege against self-incrimination and police custodial questioning. It is fitting to turn to the Self-Incrimination Clause to determine its applicability in this situation.

II.

* * *

The question in these cases is whether the privilege is fully applicable during a period of custodial interrogation. In this Court, the privilege has consistently been accorded a liberal construction. . . . We are satisfied that all the principles embodied in the privilege apply to informal compulsion exerted by law-enforcement officers during in-custody questioning. An individual swept from familiar surroundings into police custody, surrounded by antagonistic forces, and subjected to the techniques of persuasion described above cannot be otherwise than under compulsion to speak. As a practical matter, the compulsion to speak in the isolated setting of the police station may well be greater than in courts or other official investigations, where there are often impartial observers to guard against intimidation or trickery.

* * *

Our decision in Malloy v. Hogan (1964) necessitates an examination of the scope of the privilege in state cases as well. In *Malloy,* we squarely held the privilege applicable to the States, and held that the substantive standards underlying the privilege applied with full force to state court proceedings. . . . the reasoning in *Malloy* made clear what had already become apparent—that the substantive and procedural safeguards surrounding admissibility of confessions in state cases had become exceedingly exacting, reflecting all the policies embedded in the privilege. The voluntariness doctrine in the state cases, as *Malloy* indicates, encompasses all interrogation practices which are likely to exert such pressure upon an individual as to disable him from making a free and rational choice. . . .

Our holding there stressed the fact that the police had not advised the defendant of his constitutional privilege to remain silent at the outset of the interrogation, and we drew attention to that fact at several points in the decision. This was no isolated factor, but an essential ingredient in our decision. The entire thrust of police interrogation there, as in all the cases today, was to put the defendant in such an emotional state as to impair his capacity for rational judgment. The abdication of the constitutional privilege—the choice on his part to speak to the police—was not made knowingly or competently because of the failure to apprise him of his rights; the compelling atmosphere of the in-custody interrogation, and not an independent decision on his part, caused the defendant to speak.

A different phase of the *Escobedo* decision was significant in its attention to the absence of counsel during the questioning. There, as in the cases today, we sought a protective device to dispel the compelling atmosphere of the interrogation. In *Escobedo,* however, the police did not relieve the defendant of the anxieties which they had created in the interrogation rooms. Rather, they denied his request for the assistance of counsel. This heightened his dilemma, and made his later statements the product of this compulsion. The denial of the defendant's request for his attorney thus undermined his ability to exercise the privilege—to remain silent if he chose or to speak without any intimidation, blatant or subtle. The presence of counsel, in all the cases before us today, would be the adequate protective device necessary to make the process of police interrogation conform to the dictates of the privilege. His presence would insure that statements made in the government-established atmosphere are not the product of compulsion.

It was in this manner that *Escobedo* explicated another facet of the pre-trial privilege, noted in many of the Court's prior decisions: the protection of rights at trial. That counsel is present when statements are taken from an individual during interrogation obviously enhances the integrity of the fact-finding processes in court. The presence of an attorney, and the warnings delivered to the individual, enable the defendant under otherwise compelling circumstances to tell his story without fear, effectively, and in a way that eliminates the evils in the interrogation process. Without the protections flowing from adequate warning and the rights of counsel, "all the careful safeguards erected around the giving of testimony, whether by an accused or any other witness, would become empty formalities in a procedure where the most compelling possible evidence of guilt, a confession, would have already been obtained at the unsupervised pleasure of the police." Mapp v. Ohio (1961).

III.

Today, then, there can be no doubt that the Fifth Amendment privilege is available outside of criminal court proceedings and serves to protect persons in all settings in which their freedom of action is curtailed in any significant way from being compelled to incriminate themselves. . . .

It is impossible for us to foresee the potential alternatives for protecting the privilege which might be devised by Congress or the States in the exercise of their creative rule-making capacities. Therefore we cannot say that the Constitution necessarily requires adherence to any particular solution for the inherent compulsions of the interrogation process as it is presently conducted. Our decision in no way creates a constitutional strait-jacket which will handicap sound efforts at reform, nor is it intended to have this effect. We encourage Congress and the States to continue their laudable search for increasingly effective ways of protecting the rights of the individual while promoting efficient enforcement of our criminal laws. However, unless we are shown other procedures which are at least as effective in apprising accused persons of their right of silence and in assuring a continuous opportunity to exercise it, the following safeguards must be observed.

At the outset, if a person in custody is to be subjected to interrogation, he must first be informed in clear and unequivocal terms that he has the right to remain silent. For those unaware of the privilege, the warning is needed simply to make them aware of it—the threshold requirement for an intelligent decision as to its exercise. More important, such a warning is an absolute prerequisite in overcoming the inherent pressures of the interrogation atmosphere. It is not just the subnormal or woefully ignorant who succumb to an interrogator's imprecations, whether implied or expressly stated, that the interrogation will continue until a confession is obtained or that silence in the face of accusation is itself damning and will bode ill when presented to a jury. Further, the warning will show the individual that his interrogators are prepared to recognize his privilege should he choose to exercise it.

The Fifth Amendment privilege is so fundamental to our system of constitutional rule and the expedient of giving an adequate warning as to the availability of the privilege so simple, we will not pause to inquire in individual cases whether the defendant was aware of his rights without a warning being given. Assessments of the knowledge the defendant possessed, based on information as to his age, education, intelligence, or prior contact with authorities, can never be more than speculation; a warning is a clearcut fact. More important, whatever the background of the person interrogated, a warning at the time of the interrogation is indispensable to overcome its pressures and to insure that the individual knows he is free to exercise the privilege at that point in time.

The warning of the right to remain silent must be accompanied by the explanation that anything said can and will be used against the individual in court. This warning is needed in order to make him aware not only of the privilege, but also of the consequences of foregoing it. It is only through an awareness of these consequences that there can be any assurance of real understanding and intelligent exercise of the privilege. Moreover, this warning may serve to make the individual more acutely aware that he is faced with a phase of the adversary system—that he is not in the presence of persons acting solely in his interest.

The circumstances surrounding in-custody interrogation can operate very quickly to overbear the will of one merely made aware of his privilege by his interrogators. Therefore, the right to have counsel present at the interrogation is indispensable to the protection of the Fifth Amendment privilege under the system we delineate today. Our aim is to assure that the individual's right to choose between silence and speech remains unfettered throughout the interrogation process. A once-stated warning, delivered by those who will conduct the interrogation, cannot itself suffice to that end among those who most require knowledge of their rights. A mere warning given by the interrogators is not alone sufficient to accomplish that end. Prosecutors themselves claim that the admonishment of the right to remain silent without more "will benefit only the recidivist and the professional." Brief for the National District Attorneys Association as *amicus curiae*, p. 14. Even preliminary advice given to the accused by his own attorney can be swiftly overcome by the secret interrogation process. Thus, the need for counsel to protect the Fifth Amendment privilege comprehends not merely a right to consult with counsel prior to questioning, but also to have counsel present during any questioning if the defendant so desires.

The presence of counsel at the interrogation may serve several significant subsidiary functions as well. If the accused decides to talk to his interrogators, the assistance of counsel can mitigate the dangers of untrustworthiness. With a lawyer present the likelihood that the police will practice coercion is reduced, and if coercion is nevertheless exercised the lawyer can testify to it in court. The presence of a lawyer can also help to guarantee that the accused gives a fully accurate statement to the police and that the statement is rightly reported by the prosecution at trial. . . .

An individual need not make a pre-interrogation request for a lawyer. While such request affirmatively secures his right to have one, his failure to ask for a lawyer does not constitute a waiver. No effective waiver of the right to counsel during interrogation can be recognized unless specifically made after the warnings we here delineate have been given. The accused who does not know his rights and therefore does not make a request may be the person who most needs counsel. . . .

* * *

Accordingly we hold that an individual held for interrogation must be clearly informed that he has the right to consult with a lawyer and to have the lawyer with him during interrogation under the system for protecting the privilege we delineate today. As with the warnings of the right to remain silent and that anything stated can be used in evidence against him, this warning is an absolute prerequisite to interrogation. No amount of circumstantial evidence that the person may have been aware of this right will suffice to stand in its stead. Only through such a warning is there ascertainable assurance that the accused was aware of this right.

If an individual indicates that he wishes the assistance of counsel before any interrogation occurs, the authorities cannot rationally ignore or deny his request on the basis that the individual does not have or cannot afford a retained attorney. The financial ability of the individual has no relationship to the scope of the rights involved here. . . .

In order fully to apprise a person interrogated of the extent of his rights under this system then, it is necessary to warn him not only that he has the right to consult with an attorney, but also that if he is indigent a lawyer will be appointed to represent him. . . .

Once warnings have been given, the subsequent procedure is clear. If the individual indicates in any manner, at any time prior to or during questioning, that he wishes to remain silent, the interrogation must cease. At this point he has shown that he intends to exercise his Fifth Amendment privilege; any statement taken after the person invokes his privilege cannot be other than the product of compulsion, subtle or otherwise. Without the right to cut off questioning, the setting of in-custody interrogation operates on the individual to overcome free choice in producing a statement after the privilege has been once invoked. If the individual states that he wants an attorney, the interrogation must cease until an attorney is present. At that time, the individual must have an opportunity to confer with the attorney and to have him present during any subsequent questioning. If the individual cannot obtain an attorney and he indicates that he wants one before speaking to police, they must respect his decision to remain silent.

This does not mean, as some have suggested, that each police station must have a "station house lawyer" present at all times to advise prisoners. It does mean, however, that if police propose to interrogate a person they must make known to him that he is entitled to a lawyer and that if he cannot afford one, a lawyer will be provided for him prior to any interrogation. If authorities conclude that they will not provide counsel during a reasonable period of time in which investigation in the field is carried out, they may refrain from doing so without violating the person's Fifth Amendment privilege so long as they do not question him during that time.

If the interrogation continues without the presence of an attorney and a statement is taken, a heavy burden rests on the government to demonstrate that the defendant knowingly and intelligently waived his privilege against self-incrimination and his right to retained or appointed counsel. . . . Since the State is responsible for establishing the isolated circumstances under which the interrogation takes place and has the only means of making available corroborated evidence of warnings given during incommunicado interrogation, the burden is rightly on its shoulders.

An express statement that the individual is willing to make a statement and does not want an attorney followed closely by a statement could constitute a waiver. But a valid waiver will not be presumed simply from the silence of the accused after warnings are given or simply from the fact that a confession was in fact eventually obtained. . . . Moreover, where in-custody interrogation is involved, there is no room for the contention that the privilege is waived if the individual answers some questions or gives some information on his own prior to invoking his right to remain silent when interrogated. . . .

Whatever the testimony of the authorities as to waiver of rights by an accused, the fact of lengthy interrogation or incommunicado incarceration before a statement is made is strong evidence that the accused did not validly waive his rights. In these circumstances the fact that the individual eventually made a statement is consistent with the conclusion that the compelling influence of the interrogation finally forced him to do so. It is inconsistent with any notion of a voluntary relinquishment of the privilege. Moreover, any evidence that the accused was threatened, tricked, or cajoled into a waiver will, of course, show that the defendant did not voluntarily waive his privilege. The requirement of warnings and waiver of rights is a fundamental with respect to the Fifth Amendment privilege and not simply a preliminary ritual to existing methods of interrogation.

The warnings required and the waiver necessary in accordance with our opinion today are, in the absence of a fully effective equivalent, prerequisites to the admissibility of any statement made by a defendant. No distinction can be drawn between statements which are direct confessions and statements which amount to "admissions" of part or all of an offense. . . . Similarly, for precisely the same reason, no distinction may be drawn between inculpatory statements and statements alleged to be merely "exculpatory." If a statement made were in fact truly exculpatory it would, of course, never be used by the prosecution. In fact, statements merely intended to be exculpatory by the defendant are often used to impeach his testimony at trial or to demonstrate untruths in the statement given under interrogation and thus to prove guilt by implication. These statements are incriminating in any meaningful sense of the word and may not be used without the full warnings and effective waiver required for any other statement. . . .

The principles announced today deal with the protection which must be given to the privilege against self-incrimination when the individual is first subjected to police interrogation while in custody at the station or otherwise deprived of his freedom of action in any significant way. It is at this point that our adversary system of criminal proceedings commences, distinguishing itself at the outset from the inquisitorial system recognized in some countries. Under the system of warnings we delineate today or under any other system which may be devised and found effective, the safeguards to be erected about the privilege must come into play at this point.

Our decision is not intended to hamper the traditional function of police officers in investigating crime. When an individual is in custody on probable cause, the police may, of course, seek out evidence in the field to be used at trial against him. Such investigation may include inquiry of persons not under restraint. General on-the-scene questioning as to facts surrounding a crime or other general questioning of citizens in the fact-finding process is not affected by our holding. It is an act of responsible citizenship for individuals to give whatever information they may have to aid in law enforcement. In such situations the compelling atmosphere inherent in the process of in-custody interrogation is not necessarily present.[3]

In dealing with statements obtained through interrogation, we do not purport to find all confessions inadmissible. Confessions remain a proper element in law enforcement. Any statement given freely and voluntarily without any compelling influences is, of course, admissible in evidence. The fundamental import of the privilege while an individual is in custody is not whether he is allowed to talk to the police without the benefit of warnings and counsel, but whether he can be interrogated. There is no requirement that police stop a person who enters a police station and states that he wishes to confess to a crime, or a person who calls the police to offer a confession or any other statement he desires to make. Volunteered statements of any kind are not barred by the Fifth Amendment and their admissibility is not affected by our holding today.

To summarize, we hold that when an individual is taken into custody or otherwise deprived of his freedom by the authorities in any significant way and is subjected to questioning, the privilege against self-incrimination is jeopardized. Procedural safeguards must be employed to protect the privilege and unless other fully effective means are adopted to notify the person of his right of silence and to assure that the exercise of the right will be scrupulously honored, the following measures are required. He must be warned prior to any questioning that he has the right to remain silent, that anything he says can be used against him in a court of law, that he has the right to the presence of an attorney, and that if he cannot afford an attorney one will be appointed for him prior to any questioning if he so desires. Opportunity to exercise these rights must be afforded to him throughout the interrogation. After such warnings have been given, and such opportunity afforded him, the individual may knowingly and intelligently waive these rights and agree to answer questions or make a statement. But unless and until such warnings and waiver are demonstrated by the prosecution at trial, no evidence obtained as a result of interrogation can be used against him.

IV.

A recurrent argument made in these cases is that society's need for interrogation outweighs the privilege. . . .

* * *

In announcing these principles, we are not unmindful of the burdens which law enforcement officials must bear, often under trying circumstances. We also fully recognize the obligation of all citi-

3. The distinction and its significance has been aptly described in the opinion of a Scottish court:

"In former times such questioning, if undertaken, would be conducted by police officers visiting the house or place of business of the suspect and there questioning him, probably in the presence of a relation or friend. However convenient the modern practice may be, it must normally create a situation very unfavourable to the suspect." Chalmers v. H. M. Advocate, [1954] Sess.Cas. 66, 78 (J.C.).

zens to aid in enforcing the criminal laws. This Court, while protecting individual rights, has always given ample latitude to law enforcement agencies in the legitimate exercise of their duties. The limits we have placed on the interrogation process should not constitute an undue interference with a proper system of law enforcement. As we have noted, our decision does not in any way preclude police from carrying out their traditional investigatory functions. Although confessions may play an important role in some convictions, the cases before us present graphic examples of the overstatement of the "need" for confessions. In each case authorities conducted interrogations ranging up to five days in duration despite the presence, through standard investigating practices, of considerable evidence against each defendant.[4] Further examples are chronicled in our prior cases. . . .

* * *

Over the years the Federal Bureau of Investigation has compiled an exemplary record of effective law enforcement while advising any suspect or arrested person at the outset of an interview, that he is not required to make a statement, that any statement may be used against him in court, that the individual may obtain the services of an attorney of his own choice and, more recently, that he has a right to free counsel if he is unable to pay. . . .

The practice of the FBI can readily be emulated by state and local enforcement agencies. The argument that the FBI deals with different crimes than are dealt with by state authorities does not mitigate the significance of the FBI experience.

The experience in some other countries also suggests that the danger to law enforcement in curbs on interrogation is overplayed. . . .

* * *

It is also urged upon us that we withhold decision on this issue until state legislative bodies and advisory groups have had an opportunity to deal with these problems by rule making. . . . We have already pointed out that the Constitution does not require any specific code of procedures for protecting the privilege against self-incrimination during custodial interrogation. Congress and the States are free to develop their own safeguards for the privilege, so long as they are fully as effective as those described above in informing accused persons of their right of silence and in affording a continuous opportunity to exercise it. In any event, however, the issues presented are of constitutional dimensions and must be determined by the courts. The admissibility of a statement in the face of a claim that it was obtained in violation of the defendant's constitutional rights is an issue the resolution of which has long since been undertaken by this

4. Miranda, Vignera, and Westover were identified by eyewitnesses. Marked bills from the bank robbed were found in Westover's car. Articles stolen from the victim as well as from several other robbery victims were found in Stewart's home at the outset of the investigation.

Court. . . . Where rights secured by the Constitution are involved, there can be no rule making or legislation which would abrogate them.

* * * * * * * * * *

[Miranda reversed; Vignera reversed; Westover reversed; Stewart (state appellate court reversal of conviction) affirmed.]

MR. JUSTICE CLARK, dissenting in Nos. 759, 760, and 761, and concurring in the result in No. 584.

It is with regret that I find it necessary to write in these cases. However, I am unable to join the majority because its opinion goes too far on too little, while my dissenting brethren do not go quite far enough. Nor can I join in the Court's criticism of the present practices of police and investigatory agencies as to custodial interrogation. The materials it refers to as "police manuals" are, as I read them, merely writings in this field by professors and some police officers. Not one is shown by the record here to be the official manual of any police department, much less in universal use in crime detection. Moreover the examples of police brutality mentioned by the Court are rare exceptions to the thousands of cases that appear every year in the law reports. The police agencies—all the way from municipal and state forces to the federal bureaus—are responsible for law enforcement and public safety in this country. I am proud of their efforts, which in my view are not fairly characterized by the Court's opinion.

I.

The *ipse dixit* of the majority has no support in our cases. Indeed, the Court admits that "we might not find the defendants' statements [here] to have been involuntary in traditional terms." In short, the Court has added more to the requirements that the accused is entitled to consult with his lawyer and that he must be given the traditional warning that he may remain silent and that anything that he says may be used against him. Now, the Court fashions a constitutional rule that the police may engage in no custodial interrogation without additionally advising the accused that he has a right under the Fifth Amendment to the presence of counsel during interrogation and that, if he is without funds, counsel will be furnished him. When at any point during an interrogation the accused seeks affirmatively or impliedly to invoke his rights to silence or counsel, interrogation must be forgone or postponed. The Court further holds that failure to follow the new procedures requires inexorably the exclusion of any statement by the accused, as well as the fruits thereof. Such a strict constitutional specific inserted at the nerve center of crime detection may well kill the patient.[5] Since there is at this time a

5. The Court points to England, Scotland, Ceylon and India as having equally rigid rules. As my Brother Harlan points out, post, . . . the Court is mistaken in this regard, for it overlooks counterbalancing prosecutorial advantages. Moreover, the requirements of the Federal Bureau of

paucity of information and an almost total lack of empirical knowledge on the practical operation of requirements truly comparable to those announced by the majority, I would be more restrained lest we go too far too fast.

II.

Custodial interrogation has long been recognized as "undoubtedly an essential tool in effective law enforcement." Recognition of this fact should put us on guard against the promulgation of doctrinaire rules. . . . To require all [the warnings and rights] at one gulp should cause the Court to choke over more cases than Crooker v. State of California, (1958), and Cicenia v. La Gay, (1958), which it expressly overrules today.

The rule prior to today . . . depended upon "a totality of circumstances evidencing an involuntary . . . admission of guilt." . . .

III.

I would continue to follow that rule. Under the "totality of circumstances" rule . . . I would consider in each case whether the police officer prior to custodial interrogation added the warning that the suspect might have counsel present at the interrogation and, further, that a court would appoint one at his request if he was too poor to employ counsel. In the absence of warnings, the burden would be on the State to prove that counsel was knowingly and intelligently waived or that in the totality of the circumstances, including the failure to give the necessary warnings, the confession was clearly voluntary.

Rather than employing the arbitrary Fifth Amendment rule which the Court lays down I would follow the more pliable dictates of the Due Process Clauses of the Fifth and Fourteenth Amendments which we are accustomed to administering and which we know from our cases are effective instruments in protecting persons in police custody. In this way we would not be acting in the dark nor in one full sweep changing the traditional rules of custodial interrogation which this Court has for so long recognized as a justifiable and proper tool in balancing individual rights against the rights of society. It will be soon enough to go further when we are able to appraise with somewhat better accuracy the effect of such a holding.

* * *

MR. JUSTICE HARLAN, whom MR. JUSTICE STEWART and MR. JUSTICE WHITE join, dissenting.

I believe the decision of the Court represents poor constitutional law and entails harmful consequences for the country at large. How

Investigation do not appear . . . to be as strict as those imposed today in at least two respects: (1) The offer of counsel is articulated only as "a right to counsel"; nothing is said about a right to have counsel present at the custodial interrogation . . . ; [and (2) the warning issued by the FBI does not indicate that the agent "will secure counsel"].

serious these consequences may prove to be only time can tell. But the basic flaws in the Court's justification seem to me readily apparent now once all sides of the problem are considered.

I. INTRODUCTION

* * *

. . . The new rules are not designed to guard against police brutality or other unmistakably banned forms of coercion. Those who use third-degree tactics and deny them in court are equally able and destined to lie as skillfully about warnings and waivers. Rather, the thrust of the new rules is to negate all pressures, to reinforce the nervous or ignorant suspect, and ultimately to discourage any confession at all. The aim in short is toward "voluntariness" in a utopian sense, or to view it from a different angle, voluntariness with a vengeance.

To incorporate this notion into the Constitution requires a strained reading of history and precedent and a disregard of the very pragmatic concerns that alone may on occasion justify such strains. . . .

II. CONSTITUTIONAL PREMISES

It is most fitting to begin an inquiry into the constitutional precedents by surveying the limits on confessions the Court has evolved under the Due Process Clause . . . because these cases show that there exists a workable and effective means of dealing with confessions in a judicial manner; because the cases are the baseline from which the Court now departs and so serve to measure the actual as opposed to the professed distance it travels; and because examination of them helps reveal how the Court has coasted into its present position.

The earliest confession cases in this Court emerged from federal prosecutions and were settled on a nonconstitutional basis, the Court adopting the common-law rule that the absence of inducements, promises, and threats made a confession voluntary and admissible. Hopt v. People of Territory of Utah [1884]; Pierce v. United States [1896]. While a later case said the Fifth Amendment privilege controlled admissibility, this proposition was not itself developed in subsequent decisions. The Court did, however, heighten the test of admissibility in federal trials to one of voluntariness "in fact," Ziang Sung Wan v. United States [1921], and then by and large left federal judges to apply the same standards the Court began to derive in a string of state court cases.

This new line of decisions, testing admissibility by the Due Process Clause, began in 1936 with Brown v. State of Mississippi, . . . While the voluntariness rubric was repeated . . ., the Court never pinned it down to a single meaning . . . To travel quickly over the main themes, there was an initial emphasis on reliability, e. g., Ward v. State of Texas [1942], supplemented by concern over the legality and fairness of the police practices, e. g., Ashcraft v. State of Tennessee [1944], in an "accusatorial" system of law enforcement, Watts v. State of Indiana [1949], and eventually by close attention to the individual's state of mind and capacity for effective choice, e. g., Gallegos v. State of Colorado [1962] . . . The outcome was a continuing re-evaluation on the facts of each case of *how much* pressure on the suspect was permissible.

Among the criteria often taken into account were threats or imminent danger, e. g., Payne v. State of Arkansas [1958], physical deprivations such as lack of sleep or food, e. g., Reck v. Pate [1961], repeated or extended interrogation, e. g., Chambers v. State of Florida [1940], limits on access to counsel or friends, Crooker v. State of California [1958]; Cicenia v. La Gay [1958], length and illegality of detention under state law, e. g., Haynes v. State of Washington [1963], an individual weakness or incapacities, Lynumn v. State of Illinois [1963]. Apart from direct physical coercion, however, no single default or fixed combination of defaults guaranteed exclusion, and synopses of the cases would serve little use because the overall gauge has been steadily changing, usually in the direction of restricting admissibility. But to mark just what point had been reached before the Court jumped the rails in Escobedo v. State of Illinois [1964], it is worth capsulizing the then-recent case of Haynes v. State of Washington [1963]. There, Haynes had been held some 16 or more hours in violation of state law before signing the disputed confession, had received no warnings of any kind, and despite requests had been refused access to his wife or to counsel, the police indicating that access would be allowed after a confession. Emphasizing especially this last inducement and rejecting some contrary indicia of voluntariness, the Court in a 5-to-4 decision held the confession inadmissible.

There are several relevant lessons to be drawn from this constitutional history. The first is that with over 25 years of precedent the Court has developed an elaborate, sophisticated, and sensitive approach to admissibility of confessions. It is "judicial" in its treatment of one case at a time, see Culombe v. Connecticut [1961], flexible in its ability to respond to the endless mutations of fact presented, and ever more familiar to the lower courts. Of course, strict certainty is not obtained in this developing process, but this is often so with constitutional principles, and disagreement is usually confined to that borderland of close cases where it matters least.

. . . In practice and from time to time in principle, the Court has given ample recognition to society's interest in suspect questioning as an instrument of law enforcement. Cases countenancing quite significant pressures can be cited without difficulty, and the lower courts may often have been yet more tolerant. Of course the limitations imposed today were rejected by necessary implication in case after case, the right to warnings having been explicitly rebuffed in this Court many years ago. . . .

Finally, the cases disclose that the language in many of the opinions overstates the actual course of decision. It has been said, for example, that an admissible confession must be made by the suspect "in the unfettered exercise of his own will," Malloy v. Hogan [1964], and that "a prisoner is not 'to be made the deluded instrument of his own conviction,'" Culombe v. Connecticut [1961]. Though often repeated, such principles are rarely observed in full measure. Even the word "voluntary" may be deemed somewhat misleading, especially when one considers many of the confessions that have been brought under its umbrella. The tendency to overstate may be laid in part to the flagrant facts often before the Court; but in any event one must recognize how it has tempered attitudes and lent some color of authority to the approach now taken by the Court.

I turn now to the Court's asserted reliance on the Fifth Amendment, an approach which I frankly regard as a *trompe l'oeil*. . . .

The Court's opening contention, that the Fifth Amendment governs police station confessions, is perhaps not an impermissible extension of the law but it has little to commend itself in the present circumstances. Historically, the privilege against self-incrimination did not bear at all on the use of extra-legal confessions, for which distinct standards evolved; indeed, "the *history* of the two principles is wide apart, differing by one hundred years in origin, and derived through separate lines of precedents. . . ." . . . Even those who would readily enlarge the privilege must concede some linguistic difficulties since the Fifth Amendment in terms proscribes only compelling any person "in any criminal case to be a witness against himself." . . .

. . . Certainly the privilege does represent a protective concern for the accused and an emphasis upon accusatorial rather than inquisitorial values in law enforcement, although this is similarly true of other limitations such as the grand jury requirement and the reasonable doubt standard. Accusatorial values, however, have openly been absorbed into the due process standard governing confessions; this indeed is why at present "the kinship of the two rules [governing confessions and self-incrimination] is too apparent for denial." . . . Since extension of the general principle has already occurred, to insist that the privilege applies as such serves only to carry over inapposite historical details and engaging rhetoric and to obscure the policy choices to be made in regulating confessions.

Having decided that the Fifth Amendment privilege does apply in the police station, the Court reveals that the privilege imposes more exacting restrictions than does the Fourteenth Amendment's voluntariness test. It then emerges . . . that the Fifth Amendment requires for an admissible confession that it be given by one distinctly aware of his right not to speak and shielded from "the compelling atmosphere" of interrogation. From these key premises, the Court finally develops the safeguards of warning, counsel, and so forth. I do not believe these premises are sustained by precedents under the Fifth Amendment.

The more important premise is that pressure on the suspect must be eliminated though it be only the subtle influence of the atmosphere and surroundings. The Fifth Amendment, however, has never been thought to forbid *all* pressure to incriminate one's self in the situations covered by it. On the contrary, it has been held that failure to incriminate one's self can result in denial of removal of one's case from state to federal court; in refusal of a military commission; in denial of a discharge in bankruptcy; and in numerous other adverse consequences. This is not to say that short of jail or torture any sanction is permissible in any case; policy and history alike may impose sharp limits. However, the Court's unspoken assumption that *any* pressure violates the privilege is not supported by the precedents and it has failed to show why the Fifth Amendment prohibits that relatively mild pressure the Due Process Clause permits.

The Court appears similarly wrong in thinking that precise knowledge of one's rights is a settled prerequisite under the Fifth Amendment to the loss of its protections. A number of lower federal court cases have held that grand jury witnesses need not always be warned of their privilege, . . . and Wigmore states this to be the better rule for trial witnesses. . . . No Fifth Amendment precedent is cited for the Court's contrary view. . . .

A closing word must be said about the Assistance of Counsel Clause of the Sixth Amendment, which is never expressly relied on by the Court but whose judicial precedents turn out to be linchpins of the confession rules announced today. To support its requirement of a knowing and intelligent waiver, the Court cites [a number of cases which] concerned counsel at trial or on appeal. While the Court finds no pertinent difference between judicial proceedings and police interrogation, I believe the differences are vast . . .

The only attempt in this Court to carry the right to counsel into the station house occurred in *Escobedo,* the Court repeating several times that that stage was no less "critical" than trial itself. This is hardly persuasive when we consider that a grand jury inquiry, the filing of a certiorari petition, and certainly the purchase of narcotics by an undercover agent from a prospective defendant may all be equally "critical" yet provision of counsel and advice on the score have never been thought compelled by the Constitution in such cases. The sound reason why this right is so freely extended for a criminal trial is the severe injustice risked by confronting an untrained defendant with a range of technical points of law, evidence, and tactics familiar to the prosecutor but not to himself. This danger shrinks markedly in the police station where indeed the lawyer in fulfilling his professional responsibilities of necessity may become an obstacle to truthfinding.

. . .

III. Policy Considerations

. . . Legal history has been stretched before to satisfy deep needs of society. In this instance, however, the Court has not and cannot make the powerful showing that its new rules are plainly desirable in the context of our society, something which is surely demanded before those rules are engrafted onto the Constitution and imposed on every State and county in the land.

Without at all subscribing to the generally black picture of police conduct painted by the Court, I think it must be frankly recognized at the outset that police questioning allowable under due process precedents may inherently entail some pressure on the suspect and may seek advantage in his ignorance or weaknesses. The atmosphere and questioning techniques, proper and fair though they be, can in themselves exert a tug on the suspect to confess, and in this light "[t]o speak of any confessions of crime made after arrest as being 'voluntary' or 'uncoerced' is somewhat inaccurate, although traditional. A confession is wholly and incontestably voluntary only if a guilty person gives himself up to the law and become his own accuser." . . . Until today, the role of the Constitution has been only to sift out *undue* pressure, not to assure spontaneous confessions. . . .

The Court's new rules aim to offset these minor pressures and disadvantages intrinsic to any kind of police interrogation. The rules do not serve due process interests in preventing blatant coercion since, as I noted earlier, they do nothing to contain the policeman who is prepared to lie from the start. The rules work for reliability in confessions almost only in the Pickwickian sense that they can prevent some from being given at all.[6] . . .

What the Court largely ignores is that its rules impair, if they will not eventually serve wholly to frustrate, an instrument of law enforcement that has long and quite reasonably been thought worth the price paid for it. There can be little doubt that the Court's new code would markedly decrease the number of confessions. To warn the suspect that he may remain silent and remind him that his confession may be used in court are minor obstructions. To require also an express waiver by the suspect and an end to questioning whenever he demurs must heavily handicap questioning. And to suggest or provide counsel for the suspect simply invites the end of the interrogation.

How much harm this decision will inflict on law enforcement cannot fairly be predicted with accuracy. Evidence on the role of confessions is notoriously incomplete, and little is added by the Court's reference to the FBI experience and the resources believed wasted in interrogation. We do know that some crimes cannot be solved without confessions, that ample expert testimony attests to their impor-

6. The Court's vision of a lawyer "mitigat[ing] the dangers of untrustworthiness" by witnessing coercion and assisting accuracy in the confession is largely a fancy; for if counsel arrives, there is rarely going to be a police station confession. Watts v. State of Indiana, [1949] (separate opinion of Jackson, J.): "[A]ny lawyer worth his salt will tell the suspect in no uncertain terms to make no statement to police under any circumstances." . . .

tance in crime control, and that the Court is taking a real risk with society's welfare in imposing its new regime on the country. The social costs of crime are too great to call the new rules anything but a hazardous experimentation.

While passing over the costs and risks of its experiment, the Court portrays the evils of normal police questioning in terms which I think are exaggerated. Albeit stringently confined by the due process standards interrogation is no doubt often inconvenient and unpleasant for the suspect. However, it is no less so for a man to be arrested and jailed, to have his house searched, or to stand trial in court, yet all this may properly happen to the most innocent given probable cause, a warrant, or an indictment. Society has always paid a stiff price for law and order, and peaceful interrogation is not one of the dark moments of the law.

. . . it may make the analysis more graphic to consider the actual facts of one of the four cases reversed by the Court. Miranda v. Arizona serves best, being neither the hardest nor easiest of the four under the Court's standards.

On March 3, 1963, an 18-year-old girl was kidnapped and forcibly raped near Phoenix, Arizona. Ten days later, on the morning of March 13, petitioner Miranda was arrested and taken to the police station. At this time Miranda was 23 years old, indigent, and educated to the extent of completing half the ninth grade. He had "an emotional illness" of the schizophrenic type, according to the doctor who eventually examined him; the doctor's report also stated that Miranda was "alert and oriented as to time, place, and person," intelligent within normal limits, competent to stand trial, and came within the legal definition. At the police station, the victim picked Miranda out of a lineup, and two officers then took him into a separate room to interrogate him, starting about 11:30 a. m. Though at first denying his guilt, within a short time Miranda gave a detailed oral confession and then wrote out in his own hand and signed a brief statement admitting and describing the crime. All this was accomplished in two hours or less without any force, threats or promises and—I will assume this though the record is uncertain, without any effective warnings at all.

Miranda's oral and written confessions are now held inadmissible under the Court's new rules. One is entitled to feel astonished that the Constitution can be read to produce this result. These confessions were obtained during brief, daytime questioning conducted by two officers and unmarked by any of the traditional indicia of coercion. They assured a conviction for a brutal and unsettling crime, for which the police had and quite possibly could obtain little evidence other than the victim's identifications, evidence which is frequently unreliable. There was, in sum, a legitimate purpose, no perceptible unfairness, and certainly little risk of injustice in the interrogation. Yet the resulting confessions, and the responsible course of police practice they represent, are to be sacrificed to the Court's own finespun conception of fairness which I seriously doubt is shared by many thinking citizens in this country.

* * *

The Court in closing its general discussion invokes the practice in federal and foreign jurisdictions as lending weight to its new curbs on confessions for all the States. A brief résumé will suffice to show that none of these jurisdictions has struck so one-sided a balance as the Court does today. Heaviest reliance is placed on the FBI practice. Differing circumstances may make this comparison quite untrustworthy, but in any event the FBI falls sensibly short of the Court's formalistic rules. For example, there is no indication that FBI agents must obtain an affirmative "waiver" before they pursue their questioning. Nor is it clear that one invoking his right to silence may not be prevailed upon to change his mind. And the warning as to appointed counsel apparently indicates only that one will be assigned by the judge when the suspect appears before him; the thrust of the Court's rules is to induce the suspect to obtain appointed counsel before continuing the interview. Apparently American military practice, briefly mentioned by the Court, has these same limits and is still less favorable to the suspect than the FBI warning, making no mention of appointed counsel.

The law of the foreign countries described by the Court also reflects a more moderate conception of the rights of the accused as against those of society when other data are considered. Concededly, the English experience is most relevant. In that country, a caution as to silence but not counsel has long been mandated by the "Judges' Rules," which also place other somewhat imprecise limits on police cross-examination of suspects. However, in the court's discretion confessions can be and apparently quite frequently are admitted in evidence despite disregard of the Judges' Rules, so long as they are found voluntary under the common-law test. Moreover, the check that exists on the use of pretrial statements is counterbalanced by the evident admissibility of fruits of an illegal confession and by the judge's often-used authority to comment adversely on the defendant's failure to testify. [Other examples are the absence of exclusionary rules for unlawfully seized evidence, and, in Scotland, guilt based on majority jury verdicts] . . .

* * *

. . . Despite the Court's disclaimer, the practical effect of the decision made today must inevitably be to handicap seriously sound efforts at reform, not least by removing options necessary to a just compromise of competing interests. Of course legislative reform is rarely speedy or unanimous, though this Court has been more patient in the past. But the legislative reforms when they come would have the vast advantage of empirical data and comprehensive study, they would allow experimentation and use of solutions not open to the courts, and they would restore the initiative in criminal law reform to those forums where it truly belongs.

* * *

In conclusion: Nothing in the letter or the spirit of the Constitution or in the precedents squares with the heavy-handed and one-sided action that is so precipitously taken by the Court in the name of fulfilling its constitutional responsibilities. The foray which the Court makes today brings to mind the wise and far-sighted words of Mr. Justice Jackson: "This Court is forever adding new stories to the temples of constitutional law, and the temples have a way of collapsing when one story too many is added."

MR. JUSTICE WHITE, with whom MR. JUSTICE HARLAN and MR. JUSTICE STEWART join, dissenting.

* * *

That the Court's holding today is neither compelled nor even strongly suggested by the language of the Fifth Amendment, is at odds with American and English legal history, and involves a departure from a long line of precedent does not prove either that the Court has exceeded its powers or that the Court is wrong or unwise in its present reinterpretation of the Fifth Amendment. It does, however, underscore the obvious—that the Court has not discovered or found the law in making today's decision, nor has it derived it from some irrefutable sources; what it has done is to make new law and new public policy in much the same way that it has in the course of interpreting other great clauses of the Constitution. This is what the Court historically has done. Indeed, it is what it must do and will continue to do until and unless there is some fundamental change in the constitutional distribution of governmental powers.

But if the Court is here and now to announce new and fundamental policy to govern certain aspects of our affairs, it is wholly legitimate to examine the mode of this or any other constitutional decision in this Court and to inquire into the advisability of its end product in terms of the long-range interest of the country. At the very least, the Court's text and reasoning should withstand analysis and be a fair exposition of the constitutional provision which its opinion interprets. Decisions like these cannot rest alone on syllogism, metaphysics or some ill-defined notions of natural justice, although each will perhaps play its part. In proceeding to such constructions as it now announces, the Court should also duly consider all the factors and interests bearing upon the cases, at least insofar as the relevant materials are available; and if the necessary considerations are not treated in the record or obtainable from some other reliable source, the Court should not proceed to formulate fundamental policies based on speculation alone.

First, we may inquire what are the textual and factual bases of this new fundamental rule. To reach the result announced on the grounds it does, the Court must stay within the confines of the Fifth

Amendment, which forbids self-incrimination only if *compelled*. Hence the core of the Court's opinion is that because of the "compulsion inherent in custodial surroundings, no statement obtained from [a] defendant [in custody] can truly be the product of his free choice," absent the use of adequate protective devices as described by the Court. However, the Court does not point to any sudden inrush of new knowledge requiring the rejection of 70 years' experience. Nor does it assert that its novel conclusion reflects a changing consensus among state courts, see Mapp v. Ohio or that a succession of cases had steadily eroded the old rule and proved it unworkable, . . . Rather than asserting new knowledge, the Court concedes that it cannot truly know what occurs during custodial questioning, because of the innate secrecy of such proceedings. It extrapolates a picture of what it conceives to be the norm from police investigatorial manuals, published in 1959 and 1962 or earlier, without any attempt to allow for adjustments in police practices that may have occurred in the wake of more recent decisions of state appellate tribunals or this Court. But even if the relentless application of the described procedures could lead to involuntary confessions, it most assuredly does not follow that each and every case will disclose this kind of interrogation or this kind of consequence.[7] Insofar as appears from the Court's opinion, it has not examined a single transcript of any police interrogation, let alone the interrogation that took place in any one of these cases which it decides today. Judged by any of the standards for empirical investigation utilized in the social sciences the factual basis for the Court's premise is patently inadequate.

Although in the Court's view in-custody interrogation is inherently coercive, the Court says that the spontaneous product of the coercion of arrest and detention is still to be deemed voluntary. An accused, arrested on probable cause, may blurt out a confession which will be admissible despite the fact that he is alone and in custody, without any showing that he had any notion of his right to remain silent or of the consequences of his admission. Yet, under the Court's rule, if the police ask him a single question such as "Do you have anything to say?" or "Did you kill your wife?" his response, if there is one, has somehow been compelled, even if the accused has been clearly warned of his right to remain silent. Common sense informs us to the contrary. While one may say that the response was "involuntary" in the sense the question provoked or was the occasion for the response and thus the defendant was induced to speak out

7. In fact, the type of sustained interrogation described by the Court appears to be the exception rather than the rule. A survey of 399 cases in one city found that in almost half of the cases the interrogation lasted less than 30 minutes. Barrett, Police Practices and the Law—From Arrest to Release or Charge, 50 Calif.L.Rev. 11, 41–45 (1962). Questioning tends to be confused and sporadic and is usually concentrated on confrontations with witnesses or new items of evidence, as these are obtained by officers conducting the investigation. See generally LaFave, Arrest: The Decision to Take a Suspect into Custody 386 (1965); ALI, A Model Code of Pre-Arraignment Procedure, Commentary § 5.01, at 170, n. 4 (Tent.Draft No. 1, 1966).

when he might have remained silent if not arrested and not questioned, it is patently unsound to say the response is compelled.

Today's result would not follow even if it were agreed that to some extent custodial interrogation is inherently coercive. The test has been whether the totality of circumstances deprived the defendant of a "free choice to admit, to deny, or to refuse to answer," and whether physical or psychological coercion was of such a degree that "the defendant's will was overborne at the time he confessed," . . . The duration and nature of incommunicado custody, the presence or absence of advice concerning the defendant's constitutional rights, and the granting or refusal of requests to communicate with lawyers, relatives or friends have all been rightly regarded as important data bearing on the basic inquiry. . . . [8]

But it has never been suggested, until today, that such questioning was so coercive and accused persons so lacking in hardihood that the very first response to the very first question following the commencement of custody must be conclusively presumed to be the product of an overborne will.

If the rule announced today were truly based on a conclusion that all confessions resulting from custodial interrogation are coerced, then it would simply have no rational foundation. . . . *A fortiori* that would be true of the extension of the rule to exculpatory statements, which the Court effects after a brief discussion of why, in the Court's view, they must be deemed incriminatory but without any discussion of why they must be deemed coerced. Even if one were to postulate that the Court's concern is not that all confessions induced by police interrogation are coerced but rather that some such confessions are coerced and present judicial procedures are believed to be inadequate to identify the confessions that are coerced and those that are not, it would still not be essential to impose the rule that the Court has now fashioned. Transcripts or observers could be required, specific time limits, tailored to fit the cause, could be imposed, or other devices could be utilized to reduce the chances that otherwise indiscernible coercion will produce an inadmissible confession.

On the other hand, even if one assumed that there was an adequate factual basis for the conclusion that all confessions obtained during in-custody interrogation are the product of compulsion, the rule propounded by the Court will still be irrational, for, apparently, it is only if the accused is also warned of his right to counsel and waives both that right and the right against self-incrimination that

8. By contrast, the Court indicates that in applying this new rule it "will not pause to inquire in individual cases whether the defendant was aware of his rights without a warning being given." The reason given is that assessment of the knowledge of the defendant based on information as to age, education, intelligence, or prior contact with authorities can never be more than speculation, while a warning is a clear-cut fact. But the officers' claim that they gave the requisite warnings may be disputed, and facts respecting the defendant's prior experience may be undisputed and be of such a nature as to virtually preclude any doubt that the defendant knew of his rights. . . .

the inherent compulsiveness of interrogation disappears. But if the defendant may not answer without a warning a question such as "Where were you last night?" without having his answer be a compelled one, how can the Court ever accept his negative answer to the question of whether he wants to consult his retained counsel or counsel whom the court will appoint? And why if counsel is present and the accused nevertheless confesses, or counsel tells the accused to tell the truth, and that is what the accused does, is the situation any less coercive insofar as the accused is concerned? The Court apparently realizes its dilemma of foreclosing questioning without the necessary warnings but at the same time permitting the accused, sitting in the same chair in front of the same policemen to waive his right to consult an attorney. It expects, however, that the accused will not often waive the right; and if it is claimed that he has, the State faces a severe, if not impossible burden of proof.

All of this makes very little sense in terms of the compulsion which the Fifth Amendment proscribes. That amendment deals with compelling the accused himself. It is his free will that is involved. Confessions and incriminating admissions, as such, are not forbidden evidence; only those which are compelled are banned. I doubt that the Court observes these distinctions today. By considering any answers to any interrogation to be compelled regardless of the content and course of examination and by escalating the requirements to prove waiver, the Court not only prevents the use of compelled confessions but for all practical purposes forbids interrogation except in the presence of counsel. That is, instead of confining itself to protection of the right against compelled self-incrimination the Court has created a limited Fifth Amendment right to counsel—or, as the Court expresses it, a "need for counsel to protect the Fifth Amendment privilege . . . ." The focus then is not on the will of the accused but on the will of counsel and how much influence he can have on the accused. Obviously there is no warrant in the Fifth Amendment for thus installing counsel as the arbiter of the privilege.

In sum, for all the Court's expounding on the menacing atmosphere of police interrogation procedures, it has failed to supply any foundation for the conclusions it draws or the measures it adopts.

Criticism of the Court's opinion, however, cannot stop with a demonstration that the factual and textual bases for the rule it propounds are, at best, less than compelling. Equally relevant is an assessment of the rule's consequences measured against community values. The Court's duty to assess the consequences of its action is not satisfied by the utterance of the truth that a value of our system of criminal justice is "to respect the inviolability of the human personality" and to require government to produce the evidence against the accused by its own independent labors. More than the human dignity of the accused is involved; the human personality of others in the society must also be preserved. Thus the values reflected by the privilege are not the sole desideratum; society's interest in the general security is of equal weight.

The obvious underpinning of the Court's decision is a deep-seated distrust of all confessions. As the Court declares that the accused may not be interrogated without counsel present, absent a waiver of the right to counsel, and as the Court all but admonishes the lawyer to advise the accused to remain silent, the result adds up to a judicial judgment that evidence from the accused should not be used against him in any way, whether compelled or not. This is the not so subtle overtone of the opinion—that it is inherently wrong for the police to gather evidence from the accused himself. And this is precisely the nub of this dissent. I see nothing wrong or immoral, and certainly nothing unconstitutional, in the police's asking a suspect whom they have reasonable cause to arrest whether or not he killed his wife or in confronting him with the evidence on which the arrest was based, at least where he has been plainly advised that he may remain completely silent. Until today, "the admissions or confessions of the prisoner, when voluntarily and freely made, have always ranked high in the scale of incriminating evidence." . . . Particularly when corroborated, as where the police have confirmed the accused's disclosure of the hiding place of implements or fruits of the crime, such confessions have the highest reliability and significantly contribute to the certitude with which we may believe the accused is guilty. Moreover, it is by no means certain that the process of confessing is injurious to the accused. To the contrary it may provide psychological relief and enhance the prospects for rehabilitation.

This is not to say that the value of respect for the inviolability of the accused's individual personality should be accorded no weight or that all confessions should be indiscriminately admitted. This Court has long read the Constitution to proscribe compelled confessions, a salutary rule from which there should be no retreat. But I see no sound basis, factual or otherwise, and the Court gives none, for concluding that the present rule against the receipt of coerced confessions is inadequate for the task of sorting out inadmissible evidence and must be replaced by the *per se* rule which is now imposed. Even if the new concept can be said to have advantages of some sort over the present law, they are far outweighed by its likely undesirable impact on other very relevant and important interests.

The most basic function of any government is to provide for the security of the individual and of his property. These ends of society are served by the criminal laws which for the most part are aimed at the prevention of crime. Without the reasonably effective performance of the task of preventing private violence and retaliation, it is idle to talk about human dignity and civilized values.

The modes by which the criminal laws serve the interest in general security are many. First the murderer who has taken the life of another is removed from the streets, deprived of his liberty and thereby prevented from repeating his offense. In view of the statistics on recidivism in this country and of the number of instances in which apprehension occurs only after repeated offenses, no one can sensibly claim that this aspect of the criminal law does not prevent crime or contribute significantly to the personal security of the ordinary citizen.

Secondly, the swift and sure apprehension of those who refuse to respect the personal security and dignity of their neighbor unquestionably has its impact on others who might be similarly tempted. That the criminal law is wholly or partly ineffective with a segment of the population or with many of those who have been apprehended and convicted is a very faulty basis for concluding that it is not effective with respect to the great bulk of our citizens or for thinking that without the criminal laws, or in the absence of their enforcement, there would be no increase in crime. Arguments of this nature are not borne out by any kind of reliable evidence that I have seen to this date.

Thirdly, the law concerns itself with those whom it has confined. The hope and aim of modern penology, fortunately, is as soon as possible to return the convict to society a better and more law-abiding man than when he left. Sometimes there is success, sometimes failure. But at least the effort is made, and it should be made to the very maximum extent of our present and future capabilities.

The rule announced today will measurably weaken the ability of the criminal law to perform these tasks. It is a deliberate calculus to prevent interrogations, to reduce the incidence of confessions and pleas of guilty and to increase the number of trials. Criminal trials, no matter how efficient the police are, are not sure bets for the prosecution, nor should they be if the evidence is not forthcoming. Under the present law, the prosecution fails to prove its case in about 30% of the criminal cases actually tried in the federal courts. But it is something else again to remove from the ordinary criminal case all those confessions which heretofore have been held to be free and voluntary acts of the accused and to thus establish a new constitutional barrier to the ascertainment of truth by the judicial process. There is, in my view, every reason to believe that a good many criminal defendants who otherwise would have been convicted on what this Court has previously thought to be the most satisfactory kind of evidence will now under this new version of the Fifth Amendment, either not be tried at all or will be acquitted if the State's evidence, minus the confession, is put to the test of litigation.

I have no desire whatsoever to share the responsibility for any such impact on the present criminal process.

In some unknown number of cases the Court's rule will return a killer, a rapist or other criminal to the streets and to the environment which produced him, to repeat his crime whenever it pleases him. As a consequence, there will not be a gain, but a loss, in human dignity. The real concern is not the unfortunate consequences of this new decision on the criminal law as an abstract, disembodied series of authoritative proscriptions, but the impact on those who rely on the public authority for protection and who without it can only engage in violent self-help with guns, knives and the help of their neighbors similarly inclined. There is, of course, a saving factor: the next victims are uncertain, unnamed and unrepresented in this case.

Nor can this decision do other than have a corrosive effect on the criminal laws as an effective device to prevent crime. A major component in its effectiveness in this regard is its swift and sure enforcement. The easier it is to get away with rape and murder, the less the deterrent effect on those who are inclined to attempt it. This is still good common sense. If it were not, we should posthaste liquidate the whole law enforcement establishment as a useless, misguided effort to control human conduct.

And what about the accused who has confessed or would confess in response to simple, noncoercive questioning and whose guilt could not otherwise be proved? Is it so clear that release is the best thing for him in every case? Has it so unquestionably been resolved that in each and every case it would be better for him not to confess and to return to his environment with no attempt whatsoever to help him? I think not. It may well be that in many cases it will be no less than a callous disregard for his own welfare as well as for the interests of his next victim.

There is another aspect to the effect of the Court's rule on the person whom the police have arrested on probable cause. The fact is that he may not be guilty at all and may be able to extricate himself quickly and simply if he were told the circumstances of his arrest and were asked to explain. This effort, and his release, must now await the hiring of a lawyer or his appointment by the court, consultation with counsel and then a session with the police or the prosecutor. Similarly, where probable cause exists to arrest several suspects, as where the body of the victim is discovered in a house having several residents, it will often be true that a suspect may be cleared only through the results of interrogation of other suspects. Here too the release of the innocent may be delayed by the Court's rule.

Much of the trouble with the Court's new rule is that it will operate indiscriminately in all criminal cases, regardless of the severity of the crime or the circumstances involved. It applies to every defendant, whether the professional criminal or one committing a crime of momentary passion who is not part and parcel of organized crime. It will slow down the investigation and the apprehension of confederates in those cases where time is of the essence, such as kidnapping, . . . those involving national security . . . and some of those involving organized crime. In the latter context the lawyer who arrives may also be the lawyer for the defendant's colleagues and can be relied upon to insure that no breach of the organization's security takes place even though the accused may feel that the best thing he can do is to cooperate.

At the same time, the Court's *per se* approach may not be justified on the ground that it provides a "bright line" permitting the authorities to judge in advance whether interrogation may safely be pursued without jeopardizing the admissibility of any information obtained as a consequence. Nor can it be claimed that judicial time and effort, assuming that is a relevant consideration, will be conserved because of the ease of application of the new rule. Today's decision leaves open such questions as whether the accused was in custody, whether his statements were spontaneous or the product of interrogation, whether the accused has effectively waived his rights, and whether nontestimonial evidence introduced at trial is the fruit of statements made during a prohibited interrogation, all of which are certain to prove productive of uncertainty during investigation and litigation during prosecution. For all these reasons, if further restrictions on police interrogation are desirable at this time, a more flexible approach makes much more sense than the Court's constitutional straitjacket which forecloses more discriminating treatment by legislative or rule-making pronouncements.

NOTES

1. Assuming the continued employment of the exclusionary rule as a device by which police conduct is conformed to the requirements of substantive law, the question remains, how far should a court—particularly the Supreme Court—go in laying down *specific* rules of police conduct? See Friendly, The Bill of Rights As A Code Of Criminal Procedure, 53 Cal.L. Rev. 929 (1965). What form should such "rules" take? Between the decision in *Escobedo* and that in *Miranda*, one writer suggested that the Supreme Court ought to promulgate rules outside the vehicle of an adjudicated case, and that the Congress, under its power to enforce the Fourteenth Amendment, ought to enact a code of criminal procedure to govern state law enforcement officers. Consider the following materials from Dowling, Escobedo And Beyond: The Need For A Fourteenth Amendment Code Of Criminal Procedure, 56 J.Crim.L., C. & P.S. 143, 153–57 (1965).

"The readily traceable reason for the inaction of Congress and the absence of court rules specially promulgated by the Supreme Court for the area of state-federal criminal procedure is the division of powers between the states and the federal government inherent in our history and emphasized in the ninth and tenth amendments. The reason rested on bedrock when that division existed and where it legitimately continues to exist. But when the reservation of powers of the states in the criminal area is brought into the penumbra of the federal system, it is inefficient, foolhardy and contrary to our form of government to permit the federal-fourteenth amendment part of state-federal criminal procedure to drift forward, backward, or stand still, exclusively on the pages of the *Supreme Court Reports*. Moreover, it is a disservice to make state law enforcement officials and state courts flounder in their duties upon a sea of doubt over which they have no navigable control. If the states are to operate the state-federal criminal system, they ought to be allowed to participate in the full panoply of governmental processes which control that system—which means legislative participation as well as judicial imposition. The resolution of the demands and challenges of the fourteenth amendment to afford fair criminal proceedings against the citizen and on behalf of the state should not be exclusively reposited in the Supreme Court.

"It is, of course, true that the states are left to their own devices in meeting the dictates of the Supreme Court. But obedience, even when it is willing and eager, can be misguided and—when it comes to operating a system of criminal justice within a state—grossly inefficient. . . . I do not suggest that we need to find a way to curb the Court. On the contrary, as to the Court, I suggest that to supplement its present role in making state-federal criminal law on a case-by-case basis, it be encouraged to perform the further function of promulgating rules which would be helpful to the states and lead to greater efficiency in the administration of the state-federal law. The scope of these rules would be within the range of power generally conceded to appellate courts administering laws over which they have jurisdiction.

"Professor Allen's point is sound that many of the problems of fair and decent criminal procedure are, apart from those of the limits of constitutional power, ones of policy and common sense. And legislative initiative on the local level should not preclude legislation *for* the local level by a conglomerate legislature representing thousands of localities and fifty states with *common* local problems under the fourteenth amendment. If the Congress is intelligently advised, perhaps through a Committee on State-Federal Criminal Law with local sub-groups, legislation meeting the demands of decency and efficiency to the citizens prosecuted and the state as law-enforcer could be passed and included in a title to the United States code recognizing and implementing the existing, growing body of state-federal case law under the fourteenth amendment.

"The relationship of the states to the federal government in this area has understandably, but needlessly, been a touchy subject. Fourteenth amendment doctrine has been developed by the Court under a tip-toe method which the states have found leaves the scuff-marks of the big boot. The Supreme Court, while reassuring the states of exclusive jurisdiction in procedural matters concerning the operation of state systems of criminal justice, at the same time dictates requirements under the fourteenth amendment which generally affect the most important aspects of criminal procedure followed within the states. Consider the then thought to be reassuring language of Mr. Justice Burton in Bute v. Illinois, a 1948 decision following the now discarded rule of Betts v. Brady:

" 'The Fourteenth Amendment . . . does not say that no state shall deprive any person of liberty without following the *federal* process of law as prescribed for the federal courts in comparable federal cases. . . . This *due* process is not an equivalent for the process of the federal courts or for the process of any particular state. It has reference rather to a standard of process that may cover many varieties of processes that are expressive of differing combinations of historical or modern, local or other judicial standards, provided they do not conflict with the 'fundamental principles of liberty and justice which lie at the base of all our civil and political institutions' . . . . This clause in the Fourteenth Amendment leaves room for much of the freedom which, under our Constitution of the United States and in accordance with its purposes, was originally reserved to the states for their exercise of their own police powers and for their control over the procedure to be followed in criminal trials in their respective courts. . . .

"Can it really be said that the problems confronting the California, Oregon, Rhode Island and Illinois Supreme Courts, the New York trial judge, the one from Tennessee and, no doubt, hundreds of other trial judges, are 'local' problems? Are there 'varieties of processes' open to the state courts to be divined out of their own local, historical or modern settings—the fifty separate precincts—to comport with 'this *due* process' which, it is said, is not an equivalent for federal process or the process of any given state? Is the question whether a man charged with misdemeanor is entitled to appointment of counsel, a question left over from *Gideon*, a 'local' question, assuming the man's indigency? Is whether a man suspected of, say, murder entitled to be provided with a free lawyer if he is poor and wants one during police interrogation, a 'local' question? Is whether *Escobedo* should be made to apply retrospectively subject to 'local' resolution? Or whether we should do away with the voluntary confession altogether? Or what rights a man ought to be told he has before we elicit a confession from him? Or just how to go about 'effectively' telling him about those rights? These questions could be posed for quite some time before one got down to the really 'local' issues: how to charge an offense, as long as one is intelligibly charged; how to provide counsel, as long as counsel is provided; how to provide appellate review of convictions, as long as it is open to all; how to conduct a post-conviction hearing, as long as there is a hearing; and how to conduct a criminal trial, as long as it is conducted fairly. The local and the national procedures can be sorted out for quite some time, and this is the hub of what I propose we do; not just by a majority, but by the fifty states through the Congress.

"Until the Supreme Court of the United States articulates answers to these questions, law enforcement officials will continue to perform their duties as they see them. There is no mysterious process at arriving at the answers that makes the Supreme Court more fit to articulate them than the Congress. There is nothing inherent in our system, other than Congressional lethargy, some lack of imagination, the force of legislative inertia at rest, and the willingness to pass the buck to judicial interpolation, that restricts Congress from legislating fourteenth amendment requirements for state criminal processes.

"We do not have to nationalize the criminal procedure of the several States. But we do have to 'fourteenth amendmentize' their procedure. And the code of fourteenth amendment criminal procedure that we have to start thinking about cannot be thought about in terms of traditional procedural codes. For the code that will have to be worked out with all of the originality that went into drafting the Constitution does not now exist. To be sure, the Congress will have to draw on the best talent in this nation to do the sorting-out and, indeed, the drafting. The statesmen will have to be assembled. For until the job is done, with the full participation of the states, we are going to keep hearing statements like the one of the trial judge from Tennessee, and someone is going to feel the pinches of those statements.

"We do not have to search very far for the answer to the question: does the Congress have authority to enact legislation for the federal part of the state-federal trial that the states are now administering? Section five of the fourteenth amendment states: 'The Congress shall have power to enforce, by appropriate legislation, the provisions of this article.' Mr. Justice Strong, construing this provision for the Supreme Court of the United States in Ex Parte Virginia, stated:

" 'It is the power of Congress which has been enlarged. Congress is authorized to *enforce* the prohibitions by appropriate legislation. Some legislation is contemplated to make the amendment fully effective. Whatever legislation is appropriate, that is, adapted to carry out the objects the amendments have in view . . . is brought within the domain of congressional power.

" 'Nor does it make any difference that such legislation is restrictive of what the State might have done before the constitutional amendment was adopted. The prohibitions of the Fourteenth Amendment are directed to the States, and they are to a degree restrictions of State power. It is these which Congress is empowered to enforce, and to enforce against State action, however put forth, whether that action be executive, legislative, or judicial. Such enforcement is no invasion of State sovereignty. No law can be, which the people of the States have, by the Constitution of the United States, empowered Congress to enact.'

That the concept of section five of the fourteenth amendment as stated in Ex Parte Virginia still has vitality is borne out by a 1961 decision of the Supreme Court, where Mr. Justice Douglas, speaking for the Court, said:

" 'There can be no doubt at least since Ex Parte Virginia . . . that Congress has the power to enforce provisions of the Fourteenth Amendment.' [Monroe v. Pape, 365 U.S. 167, 81 S.Ct. 473.]

"Assuming Congressional authority to enact a code of fourteenth amendment criminal procedure applicable to state criminal cases, and further assuming a desire on the part of Congress to legislate with a genuine sensitivity to concepts of fairness developed by the Supreme Court and those still being debated in chambers, such a code could contribute substantially to the efficient and sound administration of criminal justice in the United States. Congressional participation potentially offers a greater degree of certainty and predictability for state systems of criminal justice. It offers a wider forum for resolution of important problems confronting the administration of criminal justice, including the opportunity for Congress to solicit the reasoned judgment of members of the state judiciary on important constitutional problems confronting the nation—not just the judiciary.

"Justice Walter V. Schaefer of the Supreme Court of Illinois has said that '[s]uperimposed upon the recency of many of our procedural safeguards is the novelty of federal intervention in the field.' Since Justice Schaefer made that statement in 1956 the 'novelty' has begun to wear off. Nevertheless we remain lulled by the sense of transiency that goes with novelty. The Supreme Court, standing at the summit of our constitutional system, will continue to intervene on a case-by-case basis so long as we—through our Congress—continue to default in our responsibilities to provide uniform machinery to meet the ever-evolving demands and challenges of the fourteenth amendment. But if we use it, there is reason to believe the Court will heed our common sense."

2. The following provision was enacted by Congress as part of Title II of the "Omnibus Crime Control and Safe Streets Act of 1968". Although the statute on its face purports to set forth only a test of "voluntariness", in fact the point of the legislation was to "overrule" the *Miranda* decision. Does Congress have the power to do so? Would the act be constitutional if it reached *state* trials under the authority of Congress to "implement" the Fourteenth Amendment?

SEC. 701. (a) Chapter 223, title 18, United States Code (relating to witnesses and evidence), is amended by adding at the end thereof the following new sections:

"§ 3501. Admissibility of confessions

"(a) In any criminal prosecution brought by the United States or by the District of Columbia, a confession, as defined in subsection (e) hereof, shall be admissible in evidence if it is voluntarily given. Before such confession is received in evidence, the trial judge shall, out of the presence of the jury, determine any issue as to voluntariness. If the trial judge determines that the confession was voluntarily made it shall be admitted in evidence and the trial judge shall permit the jury to hear relevant evidence on the issue of voluntariness and shall instruct the jury to give such weight to the confession as the jury feels it deserves under all the circumstances.

"(b) The trial judge in determining the issue of voluntariness shall take into consideration all the circumstances surrounding the giving of the confession, including (1) the time elapsing between arrest and arraignment of the defendant making the confession, if it was made after arrest and before arraignment, (2) whether such defendant knew the nature of the offense with which he was charged or of which he was suspected at the time of making the confession, (3) whether or not such defendant was advised or knew that he was not required to make any statement and that any such statement could be used against him, (4) whether or not such defendant had been advised prior to questioning of his right to the assistance of counsel; and (5) whether or not such defendant was without the assistance of counsel when questioned and when giving such confession.

"The presence or absence of any of the above-mentioned factors to be taken into consideration by the judge need not be conclusive on the issue of voluntariness of the confession. . . .

"(d) Nothing contained in this section shall bar the admission in evidence of any confession made or given voluntarily by any person to any other person without interrogation by anyone, or at any time at which the person who made or gave such confession was not under arrest or other detention.

"(e) As used in this section, the term 'confession' means any confession of guilt of any criminal offense or any self-incriminating statement made or given orally or in writing."

3. One week after the decision in *Miranda*, the Court held that neither *Escobedo* nor *Miranda* were to apply to cases in which the *trials* were commenced prior to the dates of decision in those cases. Johnson v. New Jersey, 384 U.S. 719, 86 S.Ct. 1772 (1966). In 1969 the Court further limited the effect of *Miranda* by declaring it inapplicable on re-trial of any case where the original trial occurred before *Miranda*, Jenkins v. Delaware, 395 U.S. 213, 89 S.Ct. 1699 (1969).

B. INTERPRETATION OF THE MIRANDA REQUIREMENTS

SECTION 1. THE MEANING OF "CUSTODY"

UNITED STATES v. HALL

United States Court of Appeals, Second Circuit, 1969.
421 F.2d 540, certiorari denied 1970, 397 U.S. 990, 90 S.Ct. 1123.

FRIENDLY, CIRCUIT JUDGE. This appeal from a conviction for bank robbery, vindicates the observation by a penetrating scholar: "Probably the most difficult and frequently raised question in the wake of [Miranda v. Arizona] is what constitutes the 'in-custody interrogation' or 'custodial questioning' which must be preceded by the *Miranda* warnings."

. . . At approximately 7:55 A.M. on Thursday, December 12, 1968, Mrs. Richer, the head teller, parked her automobile at the rear of the bank. Approaching it, she sensed she was being followed. A man wearing a stocking mask over his face and carrying a rifle directed her into the bank. He herded Mrs. Richer, Mr. Corbett, the assistant manager, and two other tellers into a vault. There he instructed Mrs. Richer to put the cash, $37,872.44, into a bag and give him the keys to her car. He then made his exit. Later Mrs. Richer saw her car in the parking lot of a bowling alley some 100′ away from the back parking lot of the bank.

Unfortunately for the robber, an observant young lady, Barbara Costick, had driven onto the bowling alley parking lot around 7:45 A.M. She saw a maroon or red colored car backed up against the edge of the parking lot and facing the rear of the bank. . . . She noticed that the man in the car was wearing a gray hat and topcoat—a description of the robber's costume generally tallying with Mrs. Richer's. As Miss Costick drove by, the man put his left arm up to the window to shield his face. She was sufficiently struck by this conduct to look at the license plate and, after driving a hundred yards or so and coming to a stop, to write down on a card the number—OA 1587. About five minutes later, Stanley Costick noticed that the red car, which he identified as a Chevrolet, had moved to the other side of the parking lot closer to the bank. Later observation of footprints in the snow by a county sheriff made it evident that the robber had walked from this position up to the bank parking lot and had returned to the same position from Mrs. Richer's car.

The license number was speedily traced . . . a Chevrolet car bearing that number had been assigned to defendant Hall. . . .

At 4:22 P.M. Special Agent Schaller and two other F.B.I. agents arrived at Hall's apartment in North Tonawanda, N. Y. The apartment, in the rear of the first floor of a three family dwelling, was a small one, with a living room some 12′ × 14′ furnished with a couch and two chairs, a kitchen, a bedroom and bath. After identifying himself and his companions Schaller told Hall they would like to come in and speak to him. He said they were welcome. Schaller related that a bank near Syracuse had been robbed that morning, that a car tallying Hall's in description and license number had then been observed nearby, and that he would like to talk to Hall about the latter's activities during the week of December 9 to 12. [Hall then answered the agent's questions about his car].

. . . After some seventeen minutes Schaller sought permission to search the apartment and the car, and Hall signed waivers and consents. No money was found.

The interview was resumed shortly after 5 P.M. Schaller advised [Hall of his Miranda rights; Hall waived his rights].

The serious question concerns the initial seventeen minutes of questioning which elicited the false exculpatory statement that Hall's car was in front of his apartment at 9:00 A.M. The parties have devoted a large portion of their briefs and arguments to whether during this period Hall had become the "focus" of the investigation. As put the question is unanswerable. Certainly the agents had "focused" on Hall more than on all residents of Cicero or on other residents of North Tonawanda; on the other hand the focus was not so sharp that they had anything approaching certain, indeed even probable cause to believe he was the robber. Furthermore, the "focus" question, derived from Escobedo v. Illinois, is not the appropriate test. The phrase was there used in an effort to define the point when the Sixth Amendment forbids the deprivation of a suspect's access to his lawyer. Moreover, the coming of that point was defined not in terms of "focus" alone but of focus plus. It is well to attend to precisely what the Court said: "We hold, therefore, that where, as here, the investigation is no longer a general inquiry into an unsolved crime but has begun to focus on a particular suspect, the suspect has been taken into police custody, the police carry out a process of interrogations that lends itself to eliciting incriminating statements, the suspect has requested and been denied an opportunity to consult with his lawyer, and the police have not effectively warned him of his absolute constitutional right to remain silent, the accused has been denied 'the Assistance of Counsel' in violation of the Sixth Amendment to the Constitution * * *." "We hold only that when the process shifts from investigatory to accusatory—when its focus is on the accused *and* its purpose is to elicit a confession—our adversary system begins to operate, and, *under the circumstances here,* the accused must be permitted to consult with his lawyer." [Emphasis supplied.] No claim is or could reasonably be made here that the early questioning of Hall violated Sixth Amendment rights.

It is equally plain that "focus" alone does not trigger the need for *Miranda* warnings. As appears from the first *Escobedo* extract we have quoted custody as well as focus and other factors were essential to that decision. Under *Miranda* custody alone suffices. We fail to perceive how one can reason from these two propositions to a conclusion that "focus" alone is enough to bring *Miranda* into play. The only possible basis for such an argument would be that, after limiting *Miranda* to custodial interrogation and defining this as "questioning initiated by law enforcement officers after a person has been taken into custody or otherwise deprived of his freedom of action in any significant way," Chief Justice Warren dropped a footnote:

> This is what we meant in *Escobedo* when we spoke of an investigation which had focused on an accused.

While much dialectic skill has been expended on this footnote, the one thing that is undeniable is that the opinion said that focus means custody, not that custody means focus. As Professor Kamisar has put it, "*Miranda's* use of 'custodial interrogation' actually marks a *fresh start* in describing the point at which the Constitutional protections begin," *id.*—Fifth Amendment protections, that is.

This still leaves the courts with the far from easy task of determining whether questioning was initiated "after a person has been taken into custody or otherwise deprived of his freedom of action in any significant way." The only two relevant Supreme Court decisions since *Miranda* shed little light. In Mathis v. United States (1968), the person interrogated by a federal revenue agent was in custody under any standard; he was in a state prison serving a sentence for a wholly unrelated crime. If the decision has any significance here, which may be doubtful, it would be that the Court favors a rule-of-thumb approach, assumed to be easily applicable, rather than a detailed inquiry into the coerciveness of the "custody" in the particular case since, as pointed out in Mr. Justice White's dissent, Mathis was not coerced into answering the questions "any more than is the citizen interviewed at home by a revenue agent or interviewed in a Revenue Service office to which citizens are requested to come for interviews." Orozco v. Texas (1969) put beyond doubt that custodial interrogation may take place outside the station-house, as the *Miranda* opinion had rather clearly indicated although none of the four cases there decided had presented the point. But the officers conceded that "from the moment he [Orozco] gave his name * * * petitioner was not free to go where he pleased but was 'under arrest,'" and the decision rested upon that.

Schaller was not asked concerning his intentions about holding Hall during the first stage of the interview, and Hall did not say how he regarded his situation. Doubtless this was just as well. The Court could scarcely have intended the issue whether the person being interrogated had "been taken into custody or otherwise deprived of his liberty in any significant way" to be decided by swearing contests in which officers would regularly maintain their lack of intention to assert power over a suspect save when the circumstances would make such a claim absurd, and defendants would assert with equal regularity that they considered themselves to be significantly deprived of their liberty the minute officers began to inquire of them. Moreover, any formulation making the need for *Miranda* warnings depend upon how each individual being questioned perceived his situation would require a prescience neither the police nor anyone else possesses. On the other hand, a standard hinging on the inner intentions of the police would fail to recognize *Miranda's* concern with the coercive effect of the "atmosphere" from the point of view of the person being questioned.

The test must thus be an objective one. Clearly the Court meant that *something* more than official interrogation must be shown. It is hard to suppose that suspicion alone was thought to constitute that something; almost all official interrogation of persons who later become criminal defendants stems from that very source. While the Court's language in *Miranda* was imprecise, doubtless deliberately so, it conveys a flavor of some affirmative action by the authorities other than polite interrogation. This view is strengthened by the passage at 384 U.S. 478, 86 S.Ct. 1630, where the Chief Justice, after referring to "the compelling atmosphere inherent in the process of in-custody interrogation" and just before a second and slightly altered affirmation of the test, inserted a footnote reading:

> The distinction and its significance has been aptly described in the opinion of a Scottish court [in 1954];
> "In former times such questioning, if undertaken, would be conducted by police officers visiting the house or place of business of the suspect and there questioning him, probably in the presence of a relation or friend. However convenient the modern practice [of interrogation at the police station] may be, it must normally create a situation very unfavourable to the suspect."

Even without the light of *Orozco* we would not have thought this to mean that questioning in the home could never come within the mandate of *Miranda;* we do think it suggests that in the absence of actual arrest something must be said or done by the authorities, either in their manner of approach or in the tone or extent of their questioning, which indicates that they would not have heeded a request to depart or to allow the suspect to do so. This is not to say that the amount of information possessed by the police, and the consequent acuity of their "focus," is irrelevant. The more cause for believing the suspect committed the crime, the greater the tendency to bear down in interrogation and to create the kind of atmosphere of significant restraint that triggers *Miranda,* and *vice versa.* But this is simply one circumstance, to be weighed with all the others.

The *Gibson* case [392 F.2d 373 (4th Cir. 1968)] is closer to this one than any other we have found. There the West Virginia police had received information that Gibson was driving a stolen car with Indiana license plates bearing a designated number. They located the car outside a bar where Gibson was seated. An officer invited him outside and asked whether the car was his; after initial denial, he admitted it was and produced a registration which showed alteration.

The police then arrested him and gave the warnings. Writing for the court, Judge Sobeloff did "not read *Miranda* as requiring officers to preface with a warning all non-coercive questioning conducted in the course of a routine investigation as in the circumstances of this case. * * * In the complete absence of the element of coercion, actual or potential, or police dominance of the individual's will, the mild police activity shown here should not prevent the introduction of statements freely made." While the instant case is a bit stronger for the defendant in the restricted size of his quarters, the number of officers present, and the somewhat more extensive questioning, these factors must be weighed against the point that the only piece of information the agents then had was the presence of Hall's car near the scene and at the time of the robbery. Although this was suspicious, it could have been thought susceptible of innocent explanation, especially since Hall's work apparently often took him near Syracuse.

It is altogether too easy to fall into the error of allowing the first seventeen minutes of interrogation to be significantly colored by what developed later. The picture presented to us is one of F.B.I. agents conscientiously interviewing a man, engaged in a respectable occupation, who was under considerable suspicion but whom they knew they could not lawfully arrest, and sedulously abstaining from any threat that they would. We have no reason to believe the agents would not have departed on request or allowed Hall to do so—as indeed they did the next morning when he indicated a desire to see his lawyer—although they might well have kept him under surveillance. It is immaterial that if Hall had attempted to bolt, thereby furnishing added evidence of guilt, the agents would doubtless have restrained him.

NOTES

1. One of the central issues of *Miranda* is the scope of the phrase "custodial interrogation". It is and will always be a complex issue simply because the determination of whether interrogation is "custodial" depends upon a consideration of many circumstances. However, the frequency of cases in which the issue arises may diminish with the passage of time. The issue was of great significance initially because many interrogations conducted prior to *Miranda* were being judged against *Miranda* standards. Since adequate warnings were rarely given, the only issue for the court to consider was whether the interrogation was custodial. In time, as the police have established a practice of warning, the issues will shift to the adequacy of warning and waiver. The issue of custody will always be the subject of some opinions, for as often as the police may give warnings, they will not, nor can they be expected to, go through a warning and waiver process lasting from thirty seconds to a minute or more every time and every place they ask a citizen a question.

2. The foregoing *Hall* case deals with the intermesh of notions of focus and custody. The attention given to the problem has been substantial and the consequences of adopting one or another view has a significant effect on the outcome of cases.

In the leading case of Lowe v. United States, 407 F.2d 1391 (9th Cir. 1969), it was held that the "Court's decision in *Miranda* clearly abandoned 'focus of investigation' as a test to determine when rights attach in confession cases." In essence, the *Lowe* court held that it does not matter what the officer knew about the defendant's guilt or what the officer intended to do with defendant so long as the officer did nothing to make the defendant believe he was in custody.

In line with this reasoning the majority of courts have generally held that (1) the fact an officer knows the suspect committed the crime, or (2) intends to arrest the suspect at the end of the interview, or (3) would not allow the suspect to leave if he tried, does *not* require that *Miranda* warnings be given if the interview is not otherwise custodial. People v. Hazel, 252 Cal.App.2d 412, 60 Cal.Rptr. 437 (1967); People v. Rodney P., 21 N.Y. 2d 1, 286 N.Y.S.2d 225, 233 N.E.2d 255 (1967); State v. Sandoval, 92 Idaho 853, 452 P.2d 350 (1969). In essence, the courts have regarded the intent or knowledge of the officer as irrelevant so long as it is unvoiced, i. e., not stated to the suspect, Allen v. United States, 390 F.2d 476 (D.C.Cir. 1968); State v. Crossen, —— Or.App. ——, 499 P.2d 1357 (1972); United States v. Davis, 259 F.Supp. 496 (1st Cir. 1966) (defendant unaware of arrest warrant in possession of interrogator). In these cases the courts held that intent of the interrogating officer is unimportant. See United States v. Charpentier, 438 F.2d 721 (10th Cir. 1971); United States v. Jaskiewich, 433 F.2d 415 (3rd Cir. 1970); United States v. Squeri, 398 F.2d 785 (2nd Cir. 1968). The most striking example of this interpretation of *Miranda* is People v. Allen, 28 A.D.2d 724, 281 N.Y.S.2d 602 (1967). There an officer with probable cause to arrest and an intention to arrest went to the suspect's home and questioned him in the presence of his family without telling him he was under arrest. After the conversation the suspect was arrested. The court held that warnings were not required.

The courts which adhere generally to the view that the focus concept is to be discarded have formulated an "objective" test of custody, i. e., whether under the circumstances of the case, a reasonable man would believe himself to be in custody. The key phrase is a "reasonable" belief on the part of the "reasonable" suspect. The mere subjective assertion of a suspect that he considered himself under arrest is not enough. Freije v. United States, 408 F.2d 100 (1st Cir. 1969); People v. Morse, 70 Cal.2d 711, 76 Cal.Rptr. 391, 452 P.2d 607 (1969). Extraordinary frailties and sensitivities of the individual are not relevant. People v. Rodney P., 21 N.Y.2d 1, 286 N.Y.S.2d 225, 233 N.E.2d 255 (1969) holds that the issue is "not what the defendant thought but rather what a *reasonable man, innocent of any crime,* would have thought had he been in the defendant's position."

For two cases adopting the standard of what a reasonable man, innocent of any crime, would have thought had he been in defendant's position as a guide to resolving questions of custody, see Green v. United States, 275 A. 2d 555 (D.C.App.1971) and Hicks v. United States, 382 F.2d 158 (D.C.Cir. 1967).

Under the objective test, the court in People v. Arnold, 66 Cal.2d 438, 58 Cal.Rptr. 415, 426 P.2d 515 (1967) refused to accept the simple assertion of a suspect who said she thought she had no alternative but to appear for questioning. The court asked the trial court to consider "the precise language used by the deputy district attorney in summoning Mrs. Arnold to his office, . . . any statements of the deputy not transcribed, made before or after formal interrogation and . . . the physical surroundings . . . the extent to which the authorities confronted defendant with evidence of her guilt, the pressures exerted to detain defendant and any other circumstances which might have led defendant reasonably to believe that she could not leave freely."

At the other end of the spectrum are those courts which use focus as the definitive test. These courts reason that custody arises at the latest when the officer has probable cause to arrest. See Campbell v. Superior Court, 106 Ariz. 542, 479 P.2d 685 (1971) (when officer determines arrest is to be made); People v. Orf, 172 Colo. 253, 472 P.2d 123 (1970) (little doubt in the officer's mind that they had the offender); State v. Kinn, 288 Minn. 31, 178 N.W.2d 888 (1970) (when the officer determines to take the suspect into custody); Windsor v. United States, 389 F.2d 530 (5th Cir. 1968).

Most jurisdictions which initially decided some cases on focus tests have abandoned or modified them with the passage of time. See People v. Murphy, 105 Cal.Rptr. 138, 503 P.2d 594 (1972); People v. Algien, — Colo. —, 501 P.2d 468 (1972); State v. Bainch, 109 Ariz. 77, 505 P.2d 248 (1973); McMillian v. United States, 399 F.2d 458 (5th Cir. 1968). One jurisdiction has oscillated between the two tests. Compare Commonwealth v. Sites, 427 Pa. 486, 235 A.2d 387 (1967) with Commonwealth v. Marabel, 445 Pa. 435, 283 A.2d 1285 (1971), and with Commonwealth v. D'Nicuola, 488 Pa. 54, 292 A.2d 333 (1972).

There are decisions which apply the focus test to Internal Revenue Service investigations because of the peculiar mix of civil and criminal investigative functions performed by a single agency. See United States v. Dickerson, 413 F.2d 1111 (7th Cir. 1969). This rule has been limited to I.R.S. cases by the court that adopted it. (United States v. Sicilia, 475 F.2d 308 (7th Cir. 1973)), and most courts reject the rule even in I.R.S. cases. See Cohen v. United States, 405 F.2d 34 (8th Cir. 1968); United States v. Lockyer, 448 F.2d 417 (10th Cir. 1971).

The arguments against a pure focus test were stated in United States v. Hall. The focus cases have also been criticised for ignoring the implication in Hoffa v. United States, 385 U.S. 293, 309–10, 87 S.Ct. 408 (1966), that whether the police have probable cause has no relevance to when the right of a suspect to receive warnings attaches. In *Hoffa*, an informer in Hoffa's group recorded several conversations in which the informer participated and which constituted evidence of jury tampering. In answer to the contention that when the informer and the Government had probable cause to arrest Hoffa, they should have done so instead of continuing to participate in additional conversations, the Court said:

> "Law enforcement officers are under no constitutional duty to call a halt to a criminal investigation the moment they have the minimum evidence to establish probable cause, a quantum of evidence which may fall short of the amount necessary to support a criminal conviction."

Judge Friendly's opinion in the *Hall* case suggests at least one reason why the pure focus test is applied in some cases. He notes that in *Hall* both sides accepted implicitly the focus test and spent their argument on the issue of whether focus was present. The failure of counsel to apprehend the issues may account for a good number of the judicial opinions that become the subject of criticism with the passage of time.

Several courts, as in *Hall*, adopt a middle ground. Focus is not a determinative factor but it is a significant one. The degree of significance attached to focus varies from case to case. Agius v. United States, 413 F. 2d 915 (5th Cir. 1969) (existence of focus requires close scrutiny).

The court in *Hall* seems to view "focus" more as a factor for aiding judgment as to the relative credibility of interrogator and suspect as they each contend for a finding favorable to their position. There is much validity in this contention. However, experience has shown that the formula generally works in reverse. That is, the lack of focus is usually the operative fact in reported decisions. And the courts have reasoned, in effect, that since the police had no reason to take anyone into custody—the person interviewed was not, in fact, in custody. People v. Richards, 120 Ill.App.2d 313, 256 N.E.2d 475 (1970) (autopsy which uncovered homicide had not yet been performed); Coward v. State, 10 Md.App. 127, 268 A.2d 508 (1970) (defendant not a suspect); State v. Farmer, 3 Wash.App. 575, 476 P.2d 129 (1970) (defendant resembled suspect but he was cooperative, open and apparently of good demeanor and officer had doubts as to whether he was the man). Another facet of the use of focus is found in those cases where the person in custody is being held not as a suspect but as a witness. In short, the court relies on the purpose for the detention to establish that *Miranda* is inapplicable. See People v. Goedecke, 65 Cal.2d 850, 56 Cal.Rptr. 625, 423 P.2d 777 (1967); State v. Cole, 252 Or. 146, 448 P.2d 523 (1968). But see People v. Clayton, 28 App.Div.2d 543, 279 N.Y.S.2d 605 (1967).

Does the custody test (and a fair reading of *Miranda*) permit what has been termed a "tactical" interrogation? This is a "designed" non-custodial interview conducted with an individual who is known or suspected of having committed a crime. The purpose of the interview is to secure damaging evidence. In this connection it is worthwhile to consider the words of Chief Justice Weintraub in dealing with a *Miranda* problem, in State v. McKnight, 52 N.J. 35, 52–53, 243 A.2d 240 (1968):

> "There is no right to escape detection. There is no right to commit a perfect crime or to an equal opportunity to that end. The Constitution is not at all offended when a guilty man stubs his toe. On the contrary, it is decent to hope that he will. Nor is it dirty business to use evidence a defendant himself may furnish in the detectional stage . . . As to the culprit who reveals his guilt unwittingly with no intent to shed his inner burden, it is no more unfair to use the evidence he thereby reveals than it is to turn against him clues at the scene of the crime which a brighter, better informed or more gifted criminal would not have left. . . . It is consonant with good morals and the Constitution to exploit a criminal's ignorance or stupidity in the detectional process."

Are Chief Justice Weintraub's views consistent with those of Chief Justice Warren?

3. What facts and circumstances are weighed by the courts in determining custody? A summary of the rules follows:

(a) Place of Interrogation

The place of interrogation is a vital, but not conclusive factor. See 31 A.L.R.3d 656. Usually the cases evince a concern with the location of the interrogation but the physical circumstances of the room in which the interrogation takes place is significant. United States v. Lackey, 413 F.2d 655 (7th Cir. 1969) (small room); People v. Bryant, 87 Ill.App.2d 238, 231 N.

E.2d 4 (1967) (closed room); State v. Seefeldt, 51 N.J. 472, 242 A.2d 322 (1968) (law library in prosecutor's office).

In all four of the cases decided under the *Miranda* label, the suspect was questioned in a police station after arrest and usually police station interrogation is custodial. Nevertheless, it is clear that interrogation inside what one Court has called "buildings housing law enforcement personnel" (Evans v. United States, 377 F.2d 535 (5th Cir. 1967) is not necessarily custodial. In Hicks v. United States, 382 F.2d 158 (D.C.Cir.1967) it was held that statements given in response to interrogation at police headquarters were not custodial when defendant voluntarily went to headquarters upon request. Under proper circumstances, which do not arise often, courts have accepted the proposition that someone can legitimately be said to have been invited to a police station; Thompson v. United States, 382 F.2d 390 (9th Cir. 1967). See United States v. Freije, 408 F.2d 100 (1st Cir. 1969) (officer told defendant he would meet with him wherever defendant preferred). In addition to these kinds of cases the courts have held police station interrogation to be non-custodial when the person questioned is present as a witness. Clark v. United States, 400 F.2d 83 (9th Cir. 1968) (two drivers in an accident; both brought into station for report); People v. Pugliese, 26 N.Y.2d 478, 311 N.Y.S.2d 851, 260 N.E.2d 499 (1970) (defendant was a complainant of whom police were suspicious and who was asked to give an oath). There are cases in which the defendant walks into the station essentially on his own initiative. In People v. Hill, 70 Cal.2d 678, 76 Cal.Rptr. 225, 452 P.2d 329 (1969), the defendant called the police station and volunteered some information concerning a crime; he then offered to and did come to the police station and gave a statement. The questioning was held to be non-custodial. Questioning in police vehicles is also common and where the presence of the person interrogated is clearly a result of invitation the questioning has been held non-custodial. State v. Caha, 184 Neb. 70, 165 N.W.2d 362 (1969). Such questioning, however, has usually been characterized as custodial. State v. Saunders, 102 Ariz. 565, 435 P.2d 39 (1969); Myers v. State, 3 Md.App. 534, 240 A.2d 288 (1968).

In Mathis v. United States, 391 U.S. 1, 88 S.Ct. 1503 (1968) the Court, by a vote of 5–3, reversed the Fifth Circuit Court and held that one who was incarcerated in a penitentiary for one offense was in custody for purposes of interrogation conducted by I.R.S. agents with respect to another offense. Indeed the general rule is that if the suspect is in jail he is in custody for purposes of any interrogation.

In Commonwealth v. O'Toole, 351 Mass. 627, 223 N.E.2d 87 (1967), aff'd on habeas corpus sub nom. O'Toole v. Scafati, 386 F.2d 168 (1st Cir. 1968), cert. denied 390 U.S. 385, 88 S.Ct. 1109, the defendant was the City Manager of Revere, Massachusetts. He was the principal suspect in a rather large series of misappropriations of city funds. Defendant was aware of this fact. He was asked to come to the Office of the District Attorney. The Assistant District Attorney asked for an explanation of certain records and disbursements. The defendant's explanations were used against him at his trial. The court held that the failure of the prosecutor to warn O'Toole of his rights was irrelevant. O'Toole was not in custody in the prosecutor's office nor was he brought there under arrest. Under these circumstances the interrogation was held to be non-custodial under *Miranda*. The courts have regarded interrogations in prosecutor's office with a fair degree of willingness to find them non-custodial. State v. Seefeldt, 51 N.J. 472, 242 A.2d 322 (1968).

Ordinarily interrogation in a suspect's home is not custodial, but this principle is not absolute. In Orozco v. Texas, 394 U.S. 324, 89 S.Ct. 1095 (1969), a suspect was questioned at 4 a. m. in his bedroom by four officers, one of whom testified that the suspect was under arrest. The Court held that the suspect was the subject of custodial interrogation even though the questioning was brief and took place in his own bedroom. Of course, the key factors were the time of the interrogation (at 4 a. m., and after the officers were told defendant was asleep), the number of officers, and the evidence of formal arrest (though this is unclear).

Most cases of interrogation at homes involve less severe circumstances, and generally the holding is that questioning a suspect in his own home without arrest is not custodial interrogation. United States v. Agy, 374 F. 2d 94 (6th Cir. 1967); United States v. Kubik, 266 F.Supp. 501 (S.D.Iowa, 1967) (defendant questioned *several times* at his own home); People v. Allen, 28 App.Div.2d 724, 281 N.Y.S.2d 602 (1967), (defendant questioned at home in the presence of family by officers who intended to arrest him after the interview was over); People v. Rodney P., 21 N.Y.2d 1, 286 N.Y.S.2d 225, 233 N.E.2d 255 (1967) (defendant was questioned in his back yard); People v. Miller, 71 Cal.2d 459, 78 Cal.Rptr. 449, 455 P.2d 377 (1969) (the questioning of defendant in his front yard was non-custodial although the officer suspected the defendant to be involved in what turned out to be a homicide); Virgin Islands v. Berne, 412 F.2d 1055 (3rd Cir. 1969) (officers questioned a man who they strongly suspected committed rape—he was questioned at his home and surrendered some clothes from the trunk of his car—this was held non-custodial). Questioning of a person at his friend's or relative's home is also generally ruled non-custodial. Steigler v. Superior Court, 252 A.2d 300 (Del.1969) (neighbor's home); People v. Rogers, 14 Mich.App. 207, 165 N.W.2d 337 (1968) (grandmother's house). There have been a few, but very few cases in which custodial interrogation was held to have occurred in the suspect's home. These cases have arisen, however, from special circumstances; for instance, People v. Paulin, 61 Misc.2d 289, 305 N.Y.S.2d 607, aff'd. 25 N.Y.2d 445, 306 N.Y.S.2d 929, 255 N.E.2d 164 (1970) ("police dominated" atmosphere).

Interrogation of a suspect in his place of business is usually considered non-custodial. As in the case of homes, the place of business represents a familiar surrounding. United States v. Gallagher, 430 F.2d 1222 (7th Cir. 1970) (suspect's law office); Brown v. State, 278 A.2d 462 (D.C.App.1971) (postal employee questioned at place of employment).

The rationale of familiar surroundings applicable to questioning in homes and offices does not invariably apply when the interrogation occurs in a restaurant or bar. However, the usual view in such cases is that the interrogation is not custodial. This result is due to the fact that the suspect is, if not in a completely familiar place, at least in a place of his own choosing. Another significant factor is the lack of isolation from the outside world and the distinct absence of police station atmosphere. See Lucas v. United States, 408 F.2d 835 (9th Cir. 1969) (night club); United States v. Messina, 388 F.2d 393 (2nd Cir. 1968) (park bench and restaurant).

Questioning of a suspect who is confined in a hospital as a patient, but who is not under arrest, is often held not to be custodial interrogation. State v. District Court, 150 Mont. 128, 432 P.2d 93 (1967) (Sheriff questioned prime suspect in murder who was confined as a private patient in a hospital); People v. Gilbert, 8 Mich.App. 393, 154 N.W.2d 800 (1967) (Police in hospital questioned a defendant walking around the emergency room who was involved in an auto accident and whose breath smelled of liquor); State v. Zucconi, 50 N.J. 361, 235 A.2d 193 (1967) (defendant involved in a fatal auto accident and the principal evidence against him were his admissions on two separate occasions to an interrogating State Trooper that he was driving the car; the court said, "defendant never was in the custody of the police nor was he deprived of his freedom by authorities. The questioning here took place in defendant's hospital room and at his home, surroundings totally lacking in the compelling atmosphere inherent in the process of in-custody interrogation". On the other hand hospital interviews have often been held custodial in nature. See People v. Braun, 98 Ill.App.2d 5, 241 N.E.2d 25 (1968) (suspect informed that officers had a ticket for him); People v. Tanner, 31 App.Div.2d 148, 295 N.Y.S.2d 709 (1968) (relay questioning); Shedrick v. State, 10 Md.App. 579, 271 A.2d 773 (1970) (suspect at hospital is considered in custody when, aware of the victim's poor condition, he was questioned in a small room by two officers).

Although most cases in which a suspect is questioned in his automobile are usually resolved on the theory that a traffic stop does not constitute custody, there are some cases that emphasize the fact that a suspect in his own car is in familiar surroundings. Under either rationale these cases generally find a lack of custody. Williams v. United States, 381 F.2d 20 (9th Cir. 1967) (defendant stopped his car himself at a border station); Cornish v. State, 6 Md.App. 167, 251 A.2d 23 (1969) (suspect stopped car on his own volition); State v. Miller, 35 Wis.2d 454, 151 N.W.2d 157 (1967) (suspect was driving his car to the police station with a policeman as passenger). Contra: People v. McFall, 259 Cal.App.2d 172, 66 Cal.Rptr. 277 (1968); People v. Ceccone, 260 Cal.App.2d 886, 67 Cal.Rptr. 499 (1968).

In *Miranda* the Court said that its decision was "not intended to hamper the traditional function of police officers in investigating crime . . . General on-the-scene questioning as to facts surrounding a crime or other general questioning of citizens in the fact finding process is not affected by our holding. It is an act of responsible citizenship for individuals to give whatever information they may have to aid in law enforcement. In such situations the compelling atmosphere inherent in the process of in-custody interrogation is not necessarily present." Accordingly, questioning of a suspect prior to arrest near the scene of crime is not custodial interrogation: Laury v. State, 260 A.2d 907 (Del.1969) (accosting suspect at robbery scene); Nevels v. State, 216 So.2d 529 (Miss.1968) (at the end of chase and search); People v. Schwartz, 30 App.Div.2d 385, 292 N.Y.S.2d 518 (1968) (two questions of persons leaving scene of reported assault); State v. Largo, 24 Utah 2d 430, 473 P.2d 895 (1970) (interrogation at school of sixty boys concerning incident where some boys invaded a girl's dormitory and raped one girl). Several cases have reached the same conclusion with respect to questioning at the scene of an automobile accident. People v. Routt, 100 Ill.App.2d 388, 241 N.E.2d 206 (1968); State v. Desjardins, 110 N.H. 511, 272 A.2d 599 (1970) (inquiry as to who operated vehicle). The most commonly reported instance of on-the-scene questioning involves homicides: Tate v. State, 219 Tenn. 698, 413 S.W.2d 366 (1967) (the defendant shot his boss at the office and his defense at trial was self-defense. Officers testified that they arrived on the scene and asked who did the shooting. In the presence of others, defendant said that he did. The officers asked why and he said because the boss was firing him from his job. This questioning was held to be within the scope of general investigation). See also Bell v. State, 442 S.W.2d 716 (Tex.Crim.App.1969) ("what happened?"); Ison v. State, 281 Ala. 189, 200 So.2d 511 (1967) ("Did you shoot him?").

The crime scene situation as well as several others, i. e., street encounters, traffic stops, and stop and frisk often involve an officer who will testify that if the suspect had tried to leave, the officer would have stopped him. This does not usually create a custodial situation so long as such an intent to stop is unvoiced. Can it be argued that, even if the officer at the scene of a crime asks one or more persons to remain at the scene, this should not be thought to establish custody? The Court in *Miranda* referred to deprivation "of freedom of action in any significant way" and declared that its opinion did not apply to "general on-the-scene" interviews, and that "it is an act of responsible citizenship" for persons to give information to the police. Did the Court envision the brief retention of all potential witnesses at the scene of a crime and exclude this kind of interviewing from *Miranda*? Would an ordinary innocent person directed by an officer not to leave the scene of a crime consider himself in custody or under arrest? See People v. Garrison, 491 P.2d 971 (Colo.1971); Arnold v. United States, 382 F.2d 4 (9th Cir. 1967).

Another form of general on-the-scene questioning occurs when an officer makes inquiries of persons on the public ways under suspicious circumstances. See United States v. Thomas, 396 F.2d 310 (2nd Cir. 1968) (Suspect prowling in railroad yard); United States v. Diaz, 427 F.2d 636 (1st Cir. 1970) (request for identification from a hitchhiker); People v. Cartwright, 26 Mich.App. 687, 182 N.W.2d 811 (1970) (two persons stopped in the vicinity of a break-in); United States v. Owens, 431 F.2d 349 (5th Cir. 1970) (where an officer simply finds someone he is seeking on the street and there makes inquiries of him; the incident is non-custodial in nature). The basic premise underlying these decisions is that the officers were confronted with suspicious circumstances which could have been resolved with an explanation from the person questioned. The absence of a custodial atmosphere is significant but the investigative nature of the encounter is foremost. Of course, under certain circumstances street and scene encounters may be deemed custodial. See Allen v. United States, 404 F.2d 1335 (D.C.Cir.1968); State v. Shoffner, 31 Wis.2d 412, 143 N.W.2d 458 (1966).

(b) Time of Interrogation

The intrusion of police in the early morning hours to make inquiries would create serious doubts as to whether an ordinary man would consider himself in custody. (Consider Orozco v. Texas, 394 U.S. 324, 89 S.Ct. 1095 (1969).) Of course, on the scene questioning shortly after the commission of a crime may permissibly take place at odd hours, but seeking out someone some distance away from the scene, as was done in *Orozco*, may create a custodial situation.

(c) The Persons Present at the Interrogation

The language of *Miranda* evinces concern for a suspect "cut off from the outside world". It follows that the presence of friends or neutrals at an interview is a fact of some relevance. Accordingly, several courts have considered the presence of friends as indicative of non-custody. Archer v. United States, 393 F.2d 124 (5th Cir. 1968) (suspect's husband); United States v. Manni, 270 F.Supp. 103 (D.Mass.1967), aff'd 391 F.2d 922 (1st Cir. 1968) (suspect's wife); People v. Butterfield, 258 Cal.App.2d 586, 65 Cal. Rptr. 765 (1968) (suspect's mother); State v. Davis, 157 N.W.2d 907 (Iowa 1968) (doctor and nurses). By the same token the deliberate removal of a suspect from the presence of his family and friends tends to support a finding of custody. Commonwealth v. Sites, 427 Pa. 486, 235 A.2d 387 (1967). Cf. Pemberton v. Peyton, 288 F.Supp. 920 (E.D.Va.1968) (driving a suspect 65 miles to give him a Polygraph, and then interrogation without Polygraph). The "balance of power" may also be significant in cases where the sheer number of police is inferential of police dominated atmosphere. See People v. Paulin, 61 Misc.2d 289, 305 N.Y.S.2d 607 (1969), aff'd 308 N.Y.S. 2d 883, 33 App.Div.2d 105 (1969), aff'd 25 N.Y.2d 445, 306 N.Y.S.2d 929, 255 N.E.2d 164 (1969). Presumably the reverse is true and the officer who is significantly outnumbered by suspects or a suspect's friends may be found to have conducted a non-custodial interview. See People v. Robinson, 22 Mich.App. 124, 177 N.W.2d 234 (1970) (single officer). The fact that the interviewer is a uniformed policeman does not render the interview, per se, custodial. State v. Hall, 12 Ariz.App. 147, 468 P.2d 598 (1970); State v. Meunier, 126 Vt. 176, 224 A.2d 922 (1966). But the presence of a uniformed officer has been considered as one circumstance supporting a finding of custody. People v. Bliss, 53 Misc.2d 472, 278 N.Y.S.2d 732 (1967).

(d) Indicia of Arrest

The courts have generally recognized that the existence of physical restraint is a significant factor in determining questions of custody. The absence of physical restraint has led several courts to the conclusion that the defendant was not under arrest or in custody. United States v. Fiorillo, 376 F.2d 180 (2nd Cir. 1967) (telephone conversation with suspect); People v. Merchant, 260 Cal.App.2d 875, 67 Cal.Rptr. 459 (1968) (police asked questions from outside locked screen door). But the absence of physical restraint does not automatically require a finding of non-custody. United States v. Bekowies, 432 F.2d 9 (9th Cir. 1970). The existence of physical restraint has almost invariably led to a finding of custody. United States v. Averell, 296 F.Supp. 1004 (S.D.N.Y.1969) (handcuffing); State v. Saunders, 102 Ariz. 565, 435 P.2d 39 (1967) (officer placed his hand on suspect's arm and led him to patrol car). The courts also recognize that in certain cases restraint may be non-physical in nature, but the drawing of lines is not simple. In People v. Gilbert, 21 Mich.App. 442, 175 N.W.2d 547 (1970), a suspect was asked to come to a police car and there informed of an accusation of rape. The court found custody. In Priestly v. State, 446 P.2d 405 (Wyo.1968), custody was found where the officer told the suspect to get into his car. On the other hand, the mere request of an officer to a suspect to step aside does not create a custodial situation. United States v. Arnold, 382 F.2d 4 (9th Cir. 1967); People v. Rodney P., 233 N.E.2d 255 (N.Y. 1967). Nor does a request to step outside a cafe for routine questions create custody. United States v. Gibson, 392 F.2d 373 (4th Cir. 1968). See People v. Pantoja, 28 Mich.App. 681, 184 N.W.2d 762 (1970) (request to step into separate room at tavern did not establish custody). Holding a gun on a suspect clearly creates a custodial situation. State v. Intogna, 101 Ariz. 275, 419 P.2d 59 (1967). The fact that a suspect is himself armed should be weighed strongly against a finding of custody. Yates v. United States, 384 F.2d 586 (5th Cir. 1967); Ison v. State, 281 Ala. 189, 200 So.2d 511 (1967). This sort of situation is not rare; armed felons often make damaging admissions when holding off police. See People v. Tahl, 65 Cal. 2d 719, 56 Cal.Rptr. 318, 423 P.2d 246 (1967). And an officer who arrives at the scene of a shooting may also find that his suspect is armed.

It has been recognized in the earliest cases that the absence of fingerprinting, photographing, and other booking procedures are indicative of the non-custodial interview. Hicks v. United States, 382 F.2d 158 (D.C.Cir. 1967). The use of booking procedures, however, leads to the contrary conclusion. People v. Ellingsen, 258 Cal.App.2d 535, 65 Cal.Rptr. 744 (1968) (fingerprinting and removal of clothes). Similarly, the absence of frisk or search helps to show absence of custody. United States v. Thomas, 396 F. 2d 310 (2nd Cir. 1968). The reverse is true. United States v. Averell, 296 F.Supp. 1004 (S.D.N.Y.1969).

A related problem arises when a suspect is interviewed on premises where the officer is executing a search warrant. A single question to a suspect whose apartment was being searched was held permissible in People v. Cerrato, 24 N.Y.2d 1, 298 N.Y.S.2d 688, 246 N.E.2d 501 (1969), and People v. Fischetti, 47 Ill.2d 92, 264 N.E.2d 191 (1970). Contra: People v. Wilson, 268 Cal.App.2d 581, 74 Cal.Rptr. 131 (1968); United States v. Bekowies, 432 F.2d 8 (9th Cir. 1970). Where the search is illegal the statements may be suppressed as fruits of the poisoned tree. People v. Hendricks, 25 N.Y.2d 129, 303 N.Y.S.2d 33, 250 N.E.2d 323 (1969).

The officer who tells a suspect that he is not under arrest and is free to leave at any time has fairly definitely established that the interview is non-custodial. Lucas v. United States, 408 F.2d 835 (9th Cir. 1969). The only exception to this rule has occurred in a jurisdiction which, at the time of the decision, used a pure focus concept to determine custody. Windsor v. United States, 389 F.2d 530 (5th Cir. 1968).

If a suspect is told he is under arrest then, of course, there is custody for *Miranda* purposes. In all such cases a reasonable man would reasonably conclude that he is in custody. It is also clear that custody exists in all cases after formal arrest. There is a scattering of cases relying on what the officer did not say concerning arrest. In State v. Caha, 184 Neb. 70, 165 N.W.2d 362 (1969), the court relied partially on the fact that the suspect had never been told he was under arrest to negate custody. In People v. Ellingsen, 258 Cal.App.2d 535, 65 Cal.Rptr. 744 (1968), the fact that a defendant was never told he was free to go was one circumstance leading to a finding of custody.

Finally, the demeanor of the officer may be significant. The higher the level of courtesy and deference toward the suspect, the more likely a court is to find that the suspect did not reasonably believe he was in custody: State v. Bode, 108 N.J.Super. 363, 261 A.2d 396 (1970) (police chief questioning subordinate with the aim of protecting his fellow officer); Commonwealth v. Willman, 434 Pa. 489, 255 A.2d 534 (1969) (friendly attitude of officers). Where, however, the officer is accusatory and insistently confronts the suspect with evidence of his guilt, the argument that custody existed is strengthened. People v. Arnold, 66 Cal.2d 438, 58 Cal.Rptr. 115, 426 P.2d 515 (1967).

One rather incongruous problem is whether *the giving* of gratuitous warnings establishes the existence of custody. Gratuitous warnings may be given when an individual officer incorrectly believes that warnings are necessary under *Miranda.* One court has held that the fact that warnings are given does not establish the existence of custody. United States v. Owens, 431 F.2d 349 (5th Cir. 1970). It has been held that the giving of unnecessary warnings shows a courteous and respectful attitude on the part of the officer and supports a finding of non-custody. State v. McLam, 82 N.M. 242, 478 P.2d 570 (1970).

(e) The Length and Form of Questions

The length and nature of the interrogation is of considerable significance. Almost all of the cases approving crime scene and street interrogations conducted without warnings rely upon the additional fact that questioning was brief, consuming little time and involving a few, very general inquiries. Brief, routine police inquiries are indicative of a non-custodial interview designed to clarify a questionable situation. In Allen v. United States, 390 F.2d 476 (D.C.Cir.1968), modified in 404 F.2d 1335, an officer stopped a car driven by defendant. There was a passenger in the car who was bleeding and injured. The driver gave some suspicious answers to the officer's questions and the officer asked the passenger if he had been beaten or by whom he had been beaten. The passenger mumbled incoherently and pointed at the driver. The officer asked the driver if he had done it and the driver said "yes". The court held that the officer had to clarify the situation and that he did so properly by asking routine questions. The court found that such questioning was permissible under *Miranda* and pointed out that warnings demean routine police investigation and make cooperative citizens nervous. The courts have generally reached the same result where short, neutral (non-accusatory) inquiries were put, i. e., Who are you?; Where do you live?; What are you doing here?; Where do you come from?; Is this car (or other item) yours?; Where did you get it?; etc.

The existence of lengthy interrogations indicates custody. People v. Ryff, 28 App.Div.2d 1112, 284 N.Y.S.2d 953 (1967). The use of relay questioning or repeated interviews is highly damaging to a contention of no custody. People v. Tanner, 31 App.Div.2d 148, 295 N.Y.S.2d 709 (1968); Commonwealth v. Banks, 429 Pa. 53, 239 A.2d 416 (1968). The use of accusatory and leading questions, close and persistent questioning, confronting the suspect with evidence against him, and discounting the suspect's denials, are all indicative of custody. United States v. Phelps, 443 F.2d 246 (5th Cir. 1971); United States v. Bekowies, 432 F.2d 8 (9th Cir. 1970). The logic behind the latter cases is fairly sound; confrontation and accusation by the police in many situations would give rise to a reasonable belief of a suspect that he is in custody. Finally those courts that use the concept of focus may approve routine interrogation on the additional grounds that the routine nature of the inquiry tends to show lack of focus.

(f) Summoning the Police and Initiating the Interviews

The fact that a suspect summons the police and/or initiates the interview supports the premise that the interview was non-custodial. The rationale is similar to that underlying the admission of volunteered statements; the element of compulsion is lacking and the statements are not solely the result of police action. It may also be thought that where the suspect initiates contact with the police the police are likely not to assume, at least in the beginning, that he is a guilty party. People v. Lee, 33 App. Div.2d 397, 308 N.Y.S.2d 412 (1970) (defendant flagged down a police car and stated that he shot a would-be robber, who was the true victim). State v. Huson, 73 Wash.2d 660, 440 P.2d 192 (1968) (the defendant arranged for an officer to pick him up at an agreed place; the conversation at the agreed place was held not custodial).

(g) The Lack of Arrest After the Interview

The fact that a suspect was arrested immediately following an interview does not mean the interview was necessarily custodial. In nearly every case dealing with non-custodial interviews the suspect was, in fact, promptly arrested thereafter.

However, the case where a suspect is allowed to go free after the interview is almost certainly one in which the interrogation was non-custodial. United States v. Manglona, 414 F.2d 642 (9th Cir. 1969); United States v. Scully, 415 F.2d 680 (2nd Cir. 1969).

(h) Statements Constituting the Crime and Statements to Undercover Agents

Where a suspect in custody attempts to bribe an officer, his statement constitutes a crime in itself and should be admissible even though he may make the bribe offer during a period of custodial interrogation without having received warnings. People v. Ricketson, 129 Ill.App.2d 365, 264 N.E.2d 220 (1970) ("you take the stuff and let us go"—a bribe offer not within *Miranda*).

If a suspect does not know he is speaking to a policeman he can hardly be said to have a reasonable belief that he is in custody. Nevertheless, it has been argued that undercover police should give warnings when the investigation focuses on the particular suspect, but this argument clearly conflicts with Hoffa v. United States, 385 U.S. 293, 87 S.Ct. 408 (1966), and has been rejected by every court that has considered it. Garcia v. United States, 364 F.2d 306 (10th Cir. 1966); United States v. Baker, 373 F.2d 28 (6th Cir. 1967). The ordinary situation involving an undercover agent is clearly non-custodial in all respects. United States v. Viviano, 437 F.2d 295 (2nd Cir. 1971) (no "police compulsion" to meet with supposedly corrupt inspector). There are cases dealing with a jailed suspect who makes a statement to his cellmate who conveys the information to the police. This has twice been approved. Holston v. State, 208 So.2d 98 (Fla.1968); State v. Spence, 271 N.C. 23, 155 S.E.2d 802 (1967). There is an inherent, subsequently to be discussed, *Massiah* problem involved in such situations however.

(i) Statements After Traffic Stops

Questioning of the driver of a vehicle stopped for traffic violations is considered non-custodial. This result is justified by several elements present in traffic stop cases; (a) the traffic stop is a common everyday occurrence endured by most citizens, one or more times, and is not likely to create a belief that one is under arrest or in custody; (b) the questions are usually brief and non-accusatory; (c) the situation seems to fit within the rubric of "general on-the-scene" investigation; and (d) there is usually no definite "focus" on the person questioned with respect to a specific crime. United States v. Balperio, 452 F.2d 389 (9th Cir. 1971); Wilson v. Porter, 361 F.2d 412 (9th Cir. 1966).

(j) Statements During the Course of Stop-And-Frisk

In most jurisdictions having stop-and-frisk procedures, the officer is usually authorized to ask a few simple questions, i. e., name, address, and explanation of actions. People v. Rosemond, 26 N.Y.2d 101, 308 N.Y.S.2d 836, 257 N.E.2d 23 (1970); United States v. Brown, 436 F.2d 702 (9th Cir. 1970) ("There is nothing ipso facto unconstitutional in the brief detention of citizens for purposes of limited inquiry in the course of routine police investigation even when the circumstances are not such as to justify an arrest"). In People v. Manis, 268 Cal.App.2d 653, 74 Cal.Rptr. 423 (1969), the court held that a short period of on the street questioning in connection with a stop-and-frisk does not require *Miranda* warnings. The California Court reasoned that a stop-and-frisk, though a deprivation of freedom of action, was not a *significant* deprivation and thus *Miranda* was inapplicable. United States v. Thomas, 396 F.2d 310 (2nd Cir. 1968); Green v. United States, 234 A.2d 177 (D.C.1967); Utsler v. State, 84 S.D. 360, 171 N.W.2d 739 (1969); People v. Armstrong, 298 N.Y.S.2d 630 (N.Y.App.1969); State v. Lister, 2 Wash.App. 737, 469 P.2d 597 (1970). It must be emphasized that the courts sustaining stop-and-frisk inquiries rely heavily on the brevity and neutrality of the questions. This suggests that what underlies the opinions is not only the belief that the situation is not "custodial", but also the belief that what takes place does not constitute "interrogation" as the Court in *Miranda* used the word. See United States v. Ganter, 436 F.2d 369 (7th Cir. 1970).

In People v. Ramos, 17 Mich.App. 515, 170 N.W.2d 189 (1969), the suspect's wife told the officers he had a gun. They apprehended the suspect and asked him where the gun was. He denied having it and was told to quit kidding and tell where it was. He pointed to his belt. The court relied on the right of the officers to protect themselves as justifying the asking of the questions. Similarly, a court has upheld the actions of an officer who interrupted his fellow officer, while he was giving the warnings, to ask where the gun was. State v. Lane, 77 Wash.2d 860, 467 P.2d 304 (1970).

SECTION 2. THE MEANING OF "INTERROGATION"

HAIRE v. SARVER

United States Court of Appeals, Eighth Circuit, 1971.
437 F.2d 1262, certiorari denied 404 U.S. 910, 92 S.Ct. 235.

MEHAFFY, CIRCUIT JUDGE. L. V. Haire, defendant, was convicted of second degree murder . . .

The mother of the deceased reported his disappearance and stated to investigating officers that he was last seen leaving the mother's house in the company of defendant's wife who was subsequently identified and taken into custody. She apparently promptly admitted that the deceased had been murdered and that she and her husband committed the crime. While she was being questioned, defendant appeared voluntarily at the jail and was arrested. Defendant's wife told the officers that the body was in a wheat field on the right side of a county road. She was taken to the area where a search was conducted without success. Defendant was also taken to the scene and when his wife was asked whether she had not told the officers that the body was on the right hand side of the road, defendant, without waiting for her reply, stated, "no, Honey, on the left side." The wife was then asked where the gun was hidden and she replied that it was under the bed at her home. Again, defendant corrected her and stated that the gun was hidden in the fireplace. Defendant had not been given the *Miranda* warnings and was not interrogated. The body was found at the location defendant indicated. The two investigating officers accompanied by defendant's wife went to their house and found the gun where defendant said it was located. It was proven that the gun was the murder weapon from which six bullets had been fired into the body of the deceased. . . .

Defendant argues in brief that in permitting evidence of self-incriminating statements of a person in custody but not in response to a direct question the Arkansas Supreme Court as well as the federal district court engrafted an exception to the *Miranda* rule. It is asserted that such a ruling is not countenanced by the explicit language of the Supreme Court in *Miranda*. We do not agree. Such an interpretation of *Miranda* as suggested would require a broad extension of *Miranda*—one that was not contemplated by the majority of the Supreme Court as clearly reflected by its opinion.

Defendant's argument assumes without record justification that he was interrogated but he was not interrogated at the scene or at any other time. He was under arrest and in custody and was taken to the scene. His wife had previously told the officers the location of the body. They could not find the body so the officers obviously thought that Mrs. Haire might be mistaken as to its location. It was in this light that questions were asked her. No question was put to defendant and his wife jointly, but only to the wife. The answer by defendant was freely, spontaneously and voluntarily given without any semblance of compelling influence. There is no evidence that he was interrogated prior to that time, and indeed there was no need to interrogate him as his wife had apparently immediately admitted that she and her husband had murdered Freddie Jackson. Both the Supreme Court of Arkansas and the federal district court found that the statements by defendant were voluntary and spontaneous and not in response to any interrogation of defendant by the officers. Defendant at no time was asked a single question and at the time he made the voluntary statements both he and his wife apparently were cooperative with the officers. There is no background or atmosphere here in any wise comparable to the four cases in *Miranda*.

In the very first paragraph of Chief Justice Warren's majority opinion in *Miranda*, he stated:

> "More specifically, we deal with the admissibility of statements obtained from an individual who is *subjected to custodial police interrogation* . . ."

In fact we find that the word "interrogation" is used at least one hundred twenty-nine times in the course of his opinion.

The Chief Justice made quite plain that statements given freely and voluntarily without any compelling influence are admissible and that the fundamental import of the privilege while an individual is in custody is not whether he is allowed to talk to the police without the benefit of warnings and counsel but whether he can be interrogated.

". . . The fundamental import of the privilege while an individual is in custody is not whether he is allowed to talk to the police without the benefit of warnings and counsel, but whether he can be interrogated. There is no requirement that police stop a person who enters a police station and states that he wishes to confess to a crime, or a person who calls the police to offer a confession or any other statement he desires to make. Volunteered statements of any kind are not barred by the Fifth Amendment and their admissibility is not affected by our holding today. . . .

In the case at bar, despite the fact that defendant was in custody for several hours before the statements were made, there is no allegation that he was questioned at all during this period and no evidence of any semblance of pressure or coercion or lack of voluntariness of the statements. "If authorities conclude that they will not provide counsel during a reasonable period of time in which investigation in the field is carried out, they may refrain from doing so without violating the person's Fifth Amendment privilege so long as they do not question him during that time." 384 U.S. at 474, 86 S.Ct. at 1628. We hold that the district court was correct in finding that defendant's statements were spontaneous and voluntary and note that it is not controverted that defendant actually made the statements.

BRIGHT, CIRCUIT JUDGE (dissenting).

Relying upon the testimony of Deputy Sheriff Lewis, and upon his further conclusionary, and somewhat incredible, testimony that the appellant "automatically told us where the body was", the Arkansas courts and the federal district court concluded that appellant's statements were not produced as a result of police interrogation and thus fell outside the dimensions of *Miranda*. Lewis' testimony furnishes but a slender reed to support the conclusion that *Miranda* is inapplicable in this case. On the other hand, the record clearly discloses the following circumstances surrounding the obtaining of appellant's incriminating statements which, considered together, carry their own "badge of intimidation": (1) Sheriff's deputies initially separated Haire from his wife and took her into custody for interrogation; (2) Police arrested Haire and his two friends without a warrant immediately upon their arrival at the jailhouse; (3) Three deputies took Haire's wife to the rural "Bottoms" area to search for the victim's body; (4) Approximately four hours after his arrest, sheriff's deputies brought Haire, then handcuffed, to the "Bottoms" to help find the body; (5) The search took place at night with a search party consisting of five policemen and a friend of one of them; (6) Haire remained in handcuffs throughout this entire nighttime excursion; (7) The sheriff's officers interrogated Mrs. Haire in Haire's presence; and (8) Haire requested permission to join his wife in an automobile immediately after making the incriminating statements.

It is most significant upon the issue of whether Haire spoke voluntarily or under compulsion that the record discloses that upon being advised of his constitutional rights by the prosecuting attorney on the following morning, the accused immediately demanded and received counsel. I think it immaterial that Deputy Sheriff Lewis testified that Haire responded to questions directed at his wife, rather than himself. *Miranda* renders compelled disclosures inadmissible into evidence. . . . Here, questions directed at either one of the beleaguered pair would likely demand responses from either. The circumstances presented in the instant case are easily distinguishable from examples of spontaneous, voluntary statements or confessions to which *Miranda* is inapplicable. . . .

Upon reviewing this record, I believe that the Arkansas courts, as well as the federal district court and the majority, misinterpret the scope of *Miranda*. The issue is not solely whether an accused in custody speaks without responding to a specific question, but whether the inherent pressures of an interrogation atmosphere compelled that response. The circumstances in the instant case constituted the very evil which Chief Justice Warren decried in *Miranda*: "incommunicado interrogation of individuals in a police-dominated atmosphere, resulting in self-incriminating statements without full warnings of constitutional rights." . . . Responses elicited under such pressures are, absent appropriate *Miranda* warnings, excluded from evidence.

In Bosley v. United States, 426 F.2d 1257 (1970), the court enunciated what I believe to be the proper interpretation of *Miranda*:

> [A]t some point in time during the course of the arrest it could no longer be contended that the police were without opportunity to give the *Miranda* warning. We believe that *Miranda* does require the police to warn an arrested suspect of his rights as immediately as practicable after arresting him. A heavy burden rests on the Government to prove any contention that the arrested suspect volunteered a statement without any "interrogation," explicit or implicit, on the part of the police and before he could be warned of his rights.

I would apply that rule to this case. Sheriff's deputies had more than ample opportunity to advise the appellant of his constitutional rights as required by *Miranda*, but chose not to do so. Moreover, I am unconvinced that the prosecution has sustained its heavy burden of proving that appellant's incriminating statements were made without any interrogation, either express or implied.

NOTES

1. In *Miranda* the Court stated that "volunteered statements of any kind are not barred by the Fifth Amendment and their admissibility is not affected by our holding today." A volunteered statement is one that is *not* made in response to questioning by an officer. The relative simplicity of this concept makes the determination of whether a statement is volunteered a much easier issue than the question of custody.

Volunteered statements occur when a man simply walks into a police station or talked to a policeman and makes a damaging admission. These sorts of volunteered statements are probably also admissible as non-custodial in nature.

Volunteered statements most frequently occur after a suspect has been taken into custody. Such statements may occur before, during or after actual interrogation so long as they are clearly volunteered. See Anderson v. United States, 399 F.2d 753 (10th Cir. 1968) (suspect told police that his companion had nothing to do with it); United States v. Maret, 433 F.2d 1064 (8th Cir. 1970) (volunteered during warnings); United States v. McNeil, 433 F.2d 1109 (D.C.Cir. 1969) (volunteered after warnings).

Volunteered statements also occur during interrogation when the suspect makes a damaging admission that is not responsive to the officer's question. For example, an officer may ask "What is your name?" and the response may be "I'm sorry I killed her". See Parson v. United States, 387 F.2d 944 (10th Cir. 1968). DeHart v. State, 468 S.W.2d 435 (Tex.1971) ("Do you know your father is dead? I know, I only wish it had been my mother.")

On occasion conversations among co-defendants are overheard as are conversations of defendants with relatives, victims and friends. Admissions made during these conversations are not the product of *Miranda* interrogation. Caton v. United States, 407 F.2d 367 (8th Cir. 1969); (Co-defendant); Soolook v. State, 447 P.2d 555 (Alaska, 1968) (parents); Edington v. State, 243 Ark. 10, 418 S.W.2d 637 (1967) (girl friend); Chancellor v. Commonwealth, 438 S.W.2d 783 (Ky.1969) (offer of restitution to victim).

The police have no duty to interrupt a volunteered statement in order to warn a suspect of his rights. Taylor v. Page, 381 F.2d 717 (10th Cir. 1967); Ballay v. People, 160 Colo. 309, 419 P.2d 446 (1966).

Finally, a volunteered statement is admissible regardless of when it was made, i. e., while in custody, after indictment, after counsel is retained, etc., People v. Sunday, 275 Cal.App.2d 473, 79 Cal.Rptr. 752 (1969).

2. Apart from the purely volunteered statement the courts have recognized a category which, for want of a better term, may be called non-interrogation questioning. There are four basic types of such questions.

(a) Threshold And Clarifying Questions

The problem of threshold questioning arises because most volunteered admissions are not very detailed. In People v. Savage, 102 Ill.App.2d 477, 242 N.E.2d 446 (1968) a man walked into a police station and said "I done it. I done it. Arrest me. Arrest me." Naturally the officer asked him what he did and when the man said he killed his wife the officer asked him how and he replied, "With an axe, that's all I had." The Court held that this was "threshold questioning" and was permitted by *Miranda*.

The rule is stated in People v. Sunday, 76 Cal.Rptr. 668 and 275 Cal.App.2d 473, 79 Cal.Rptr. 752 (Cal.App.1969) where the defendant, who was in custody, initiated an interview with the police. His statement was largely a monologue but some routine questions were asked. The Court held that a statement is volunteered even if some questions are asked, as long as the questions are neutral, intended to clarify and are not designed to expand the scope of the statement the witness wants to make. See also People v. Superior Court, 3 Cal.App.3d 476, 83 Cal.Rptr. 777 (1970) ("I did it, I am sorry" "What happened?" "Where is the knife?"); Campbell v. State, 4 Md.App. 448, 243 A.2d 642 (1968) ("How much time can I get for this" "For what?" "For robbing that old lady"); But see, People v. Mathews, 264 Cal.App.2d 557, 70 Cal.Rptr. 756 (1968) (exceeded permissible scope of clarification); People v. Connor, 270 Cal.App.2d 630, 75 Cal.Rptr. 905 (1969) (same—32 page transcript of "clarifying" questions.).

(b) Routine Questions And Booking Procedures

The questions asked during booking of suspects by the booking officer are usually held to be non-interrogative. See Toohey v. United States, 404 F.2d 907 (9th Cir. 1968) (information secured in normal booking process is admissible); United States v. Schipani, 414 F.2d 1262 (2nd Cir. 1969) (routine personal history survey in prison is admissible); People v. Hernandez, 263 Cal.App.2d 242, 69 Cal.Rptr. 448 (1968) (age); Clarke v. State, 3 Md.App. 447, 240 A.2d 291 (1968) (name, address, employment); Contra, Proctor v. United States, 404 F.2d 819 (D.C.Cir. 1968) (routine question about employment inadmissible under *Miranda*).

The rationale that brief, routine questions are not interrogation extends to cases beyond the booking procedure. The courts seem to read *Miranda* as directed toward the combination of custody coupled with a series of authoritative demands for answers. See State v. Travis, 250 Or. 213, 441 P.2d 597 (1968). And from this it is concluded that the simple run-of-the-mill question does not constitute interrogation. Further, courts rely heavily in such situations on the lack of focus or intent to incriminate on the part of the officer asking the question. See People v. Ashford, 265 Cal.App.2d 673, 71 Cal.Rptr. 619 (1968) (question from bailiff "How's it going, Ashford?"); Rubey v. City of Fairbanks, 456 P.2d 470 (Alaska 1969) (request for marked money made after arrest).

A most interesting example of non-interrogative questioning is found in State v. Barnes, 54 N.J. 1, 252 A.2d 398 (1969). In that case the defendant was arrested as an escapee pursuant to a warrant. She and her companions were arrested and searched. During a cursory search of their car an officer spotted some checks on the floor of the car. He asked defendant, "Whose stuff is this?" She replied that they were hers. She was in custody. She had not been warned. The officers did not know that the checks were stolen checks nor were they aware that any checks had been recently stolen. After defendant answered the one question, no further questions were asked, and only later did the officers learn the checks were stolen. The Supreme Court of New Jersey affirmed on the grounds that the question was not calculated but was a spontaneous reaction of the officer. Finally, the Court distinguished the prolonged interrogations found in *Miranda* and pointed out that defendant in their case was not suspected of any connection with stolen checks. For a similar case see People v. Stout, 66 Cal.2d 184, 57 Cal.Rptr. 152, 424 P.2d 704 (1967).

(c) Spontaneous Questions

In People v. Morse, 70 Cal.2d 711, 76 Cal.Rptr. 391, 452 P.2d 607 (1969) a jailer and a guard were called to a cell area where they found one prisoner garroted near death. While tending to this prisoner they asked the defendant, who was also a prisoner, questions about what happened and received incriminating replies. The Court upheld this questioning as not a deliberate effort to elicit damaging evidence but rather general on-the-scene questioning by an "astonished" jailer.

The spontaneity or impulsive nature of questioning depends upon the circumstances in which the question is asked. Though very few courts, of the courts which rely upon the brevity of questions in sustaining the admissibility of the answers explicitly mention the spontaneous nature of the questions, it can be persuasively argued that spontaneity is at least a subliminal factor supporting those judgments. In State v. Barnes, 54 N.J. 1, 252 A.2d 398 (1969) the Court did consider spontaneity. See also United States v. Ganter, 436 F.2d 364 (7th Cir. 1970) (officers made "natural" inquiry concerning the location of the suspect's gun); Dennis v. Commonwealth, 464 S.W.2d 253 (Ky.1971) (after arrest for intoxication defendant who had blood on his arm was asked "What happened?").

(d) Emergency Questions

In the case of search and seizure the police may act in an emergency to protect human life without first securing a warrant. United States v. Barone, 330 F.2d 543 (2nd Cir. 1964). Similarly, where the interest of the police is justifiable self-protection they may ask if the suspect is armed or where his weapon is. See People v. Ramos, 17 Mich.App. 515, 170 N.W.2d 189 (1970); State v. Lane, 77 Wash.2d 860, 467 P.2d 304 (1970); Contra: United States v. Pelensky, 300 F.Supp. 976 (Vt.1969).

Where the officer asks the defendant a question about what happened in order to aid the medical treatment of the victim, this has been considered non-interrogative. People v. Paton, 255 Cal.App.2d 347, 62 Cal.Rptr. 865 (1968).

3. Another category of non-interrogation techniques involves situations in which admissions are made in response not to direct interrogation, but to other forms of police conduct.

(a) Confronting the Suspect with the Evidence Against Him

Generally speaking, it is proper to confront a suspect with the evidence against him, or with other facts of the case. This has been approved even when the police misstate or falsely represent the state of the evidence, i. e., that an accomplice has confessed. Frazier v. Cupp, 394 U.S. 731, 89 S.Ct. 1420 (1969). The issue under *Miranda* is whether confrontation is a form of interrogation. The Courts have divided over the issue. In Howell v. State, 5 Md.App. 337, 247 A.2d 291 (1968) a suspect was told his cohort had confessed after he had refused to talk—the volunteered response of the suspect was held admissible. In State v. Burnett, 429 S.W.2d 239 (Mo. 1968) it was held that confronting a person with stolen money was not silent interrogation.

In People v. Sunday, 275 Cal.App.2d 473, 79 Cal.Rptr. 752 (1969) the Court argued that informing the defendant of the evidence against him may be viewed as helpful to him in deciding intelligently whether to waive his rights. In Commonwealth v. Franklin, 438 Pa. 411, 265 A.2d 361 (1970) the suspect volunteered a statement after being told by the officer that his statement was not needed because there were witnesses. The Court found the statements admissible because there was no subterfuge.

In People v. Doss, 44 Ill.2d 541, 256 N.E.2d 753 (1970) it was held that confrontation with an accomplice is not a continuation of interrogation; and in Combs v. Commonwealth, 438 S.W.2d 82 (Ky.1969) the Court ruled that confronting a suspect with an adverse ballistics report was not interrogation—over a dissent saying, "the purpose of a question is to get an answer. Anything else that has the same purpose falls in the same category and is susceptible of the same abuses *Miranda* seeks to prevent." Neither the ruling in *Doss* nor that in *Combs* survived federal review on habeas corpus. See United States ex rel. Doss v. Bensinger, 463 F.2d 576 (7th Cir. 1972); Combs v. Wingo, 465 F.2d 96 (6th Cir. 1972). See also United States v. Barnes, 432 F.2d 89 (5th Cir. 1970) holding that a confrontation with an accomplice after the defendant had asserted his right to silence was in violation of *Miranda*.

All of the cases disapproving confrontation techniques involved suspects who had first asserted their rights and only then were confronted with evidence. Should the result be any different if the suspect is arrested, brought to a police station, never warned of his rights or asked any questions, but is shown, without comment, his accomplice's confession after which he volunteers some admission?

Statements volunteered after a line-up identification are usually held admissible. Camacho v. United States, 407 F.2d 39 (9th Cir. 1969); State v. Gallicchio, 51 N.J. 313, 240 A.2d 166 (1968). So too, where a victim accused the defendant at the scene of the crime, the defendant volunteered incriminating statements which were held admissible. Gregg v. State, 446 S.W.2d 630 (Mo.1969).

When the suspect is present at the discovery of some piece of evidence —his volunteered statements are admissible. Brown v. State, 226 Ga. 114, 172 S.E.2d 666 (1970) (One officer tells his partner to look at blood on suspect's hand). Similarly, where the suspect learns that the police are undertaking an investigation which he knows will result in the discovery of evidence against him, he may volunteer a statement which will be admissible. United States v. Godfrey, 409 F.2d 1338 (10th Cir. 1969) (suspect was told a check was being run to learn if the car was stolen).

(b) Statements in Response to Statements by Others

Closely related to statements volunteered after confrontation with evidence are statements volunteered in response to comments (not questions) by police officers. A slightly stronger case for admissibility is present in this situation because, usually, there is no intent to elicit anything from the suspect. And in this respect these cases usually differ from confrontation cases. See People v. Jenkins, 131 Ill.App.2d 49, 268 N.E.2d 198 (1971) ("You just killed a woman"—"the bitch needed killing"—volunteered); State v. Williams, 182 N.W.2d 396 (Iowa 1971) (comments by officers on ride back to jurisdiction where crime occurred).

On the other hand in People v. Paulin, 61 Misc.2d 289, 305 N.Y.S.2d 607 (1969) aff'd 33 App.Div.2d 105, 308 N.Y.S.2d 883 (1969) aff'd 25 N.Y.2d 445, 306 N.Y.S.2d 929, 255 N.E.2d 164 (1969) the Court held that remarks concerning the death of the decedent, i. e., "this is a terrible tragedy," "what about funeral arrangements", etc., were a form of subtle interrogation designed to elicit damaging admissions, and were especially impermissible since the suspect had said she wanted to talk to a lawyer and had previously undergone interrogation in a police dominated atmosphere.

SECTION 3. THE REQUIRED WARNINGS

UNITED STATES ex rel. WILLIAMS v. TWOMEY

United States Court of Appeals, Seventh Circuit, 1972.
467 F.2d 1248.

DILLIN, DISTRICT JUDGE (by designation).

Appellant . . . appealed, primarily on the grounds that five statements, four oral and one written, were taken in violation of Miranda . . .

His state remedies exhausted, appellant petitioned the district court for a writ of habeas corpus, submitting the petition for consideration upon the state court record. That court denied the petition, ruling that the record established that appellant had been adequately warned of his rights under *Miranda* and had voluntarily and knowingly waived them. We likewise rely upon the state court record.

I

The record reveals that Fleming was killed sometime during the early morning hours of October 15, 1967, in his Chicago apartment. Appellant was first arrested and taken into custody, also in the early morning hours of October 15, 1967, following an automobile accident he had on the Indiana Toll Road while driving Fleming's car. At the accident scene appellant presented Fleming's registration and credit cards to an Indiana State Trooper when asked for identification. The trooper took appellant to a police station to administer a Breathalizer test. Prior to the test the trooper read to appellant the legend printed on a standard form used by the Indiana State Police.[1]

* * *

Appellant challenges the adequacy of the advice of his right to an attorney, in light of the qualifying language, "We have no way of furnishing you with an attorney, but one will be appointed for you, if you wish, if and when you go to court."

Miranda requires a clear and unequivocal warning to an accused of his constitutional rights, prior to the taking of any statement, whether exculpatory or inculpatory, during interrogation occurring after an accused is taken into custody. One of those rights is, of course, the right to the presence of counsel, hired or appointed. . . .

We hold that the warning given here was not an "effective and express explanation;" to the contrary, it was equivocal and ambiguous. In one breath appellant was informed that he had the right to appointed counsel during questioning. In the next breath, he was told that counsel could not be provided until later. In other words, the statement that no lawyer can be provided at the moment and can only be obtained if and when the accused reaches court substantially restricts the absolute right to counsel previously stated; it conveys the contradictory alternative message that an indigent is first entitled to counsel upon an appearance in court at some unknown, future time. The entire warning is therefore, at best, misleading and confusing and, at worst, constitutes a subtle temptation to the un-

1. The form reads: "Warning as to Rights

"Before we ask you any questions, it is our duty as police officers to advise you of your rights and to warn you of the consequences of waiving your rights.

"You have the absolute right to remain silent.

"Anything you say to us can be used against you in court.

"You have the right to talk to an attorney before answering any questions and to have an attorney present with you during questioning.

"You have this same right to the advice and presence of an attorney whether you can afford to hire one or not. We have no way of furnishing you with an attorney, but one will be appointed for you, if you wish, if and when you go to court.

"If you decide to answer questions now without an attorney present, you will still have the right to stop answering at any time. You also have the right to stop answering any time until you talk to an attorney.

"Waiver

"I have read the above statement of my rights, and it has been read to me. I understand what my rights are. I wish to make a voluntary statement, and I do not want an attorney. No force, threats, or promises of any kind or nature have been used by anyone in any way to influence me to waive my rights. I am signing this statement after having been advised of my rights before any questions have been asked of me by the police."

sophisticated, indigent accused to forego the right to counsel at this critical moment.

The practice of police interrogation of an accused, after informing him that counsel cannot be provided at the present time, is a practice anticipated and expressly prohibited by the *Miranda* decision.

> ". . . if police propose to interrogate a person they must make known to him that he is entitled to a lawyer and that if he cannot afford one, a lawyer will be provided for him prior to any interrogation. If authorities conclude that they will not provide counsel during a reasonable period of time in which investigation in the field is carried out, they may refrain from doing so without violating the person's Fifth Amendment privilege so long as they do not question him during that time." . . .

Consistent with the above, many courts encountering similarly qualified warnings have recognized them as deficient.

We are not unmindful of the fact that a warning identical to that here used by the Indiana trooper has been approved by a divided Supreme Court of Indiana in related cases of Jones v. State, 252 N.E.2d 572 (1969), and Rouse v. State, 266 N.E.2d 209 (1971). As above noted, it was likewise approved by the Appellate Court of Illinois in the appeal of the Illinois conviction here involved. Further, a warning including the phrase that a lawyer would be appointed for the defendant "if and when you go to court," has been given approval by this Court, although the opinion does not set out the entire warning.

In view of the foregoing, we have considered our holding in accordance with the criteria set forth in Stovall v. Denno (1967), and have determined that this decision should be given a prospective application. Our holding, therefore, will apply only to interrogations taking place after the date of this decision.

We reverse the district court order denying the petition for the writ and remand with direction to grant the relief prayed for in the petition unless the Illinois authorities grant Williams a new trial within a reasonable period to be fixed by the district court.

PELL, CIRCUIT JUDGE (dissenting).

While I agree with the majority that its decision should be only prospective, I must respectfully dissent from the holding of the opinion. We have before us a case in which there is little doubt that the defendant committed the homicide with which he was charged, a case in which the conviction was substantially based on his own admissions which were not extracted from him by physical duress and arguably not by psychological stress, but a case in which there is a real possibility that, lacking other independent proof, the defendant may be freed because of noncompliance with an overly technical application of the *Miranda* rule.

My principal point of disagreement with the majority opinion stems from the holding which finds the Indiana State Police warning of October 15, 1967, to be constitutionally deficient. There seems to be no claim that the warning given would not have passed muster if it had not included the words, "[w]e have no way of furnishing you with an attorney, but one will be appointed for you, if you wish, if and when you go to court."

The majority opinion does not purport to overrule United States v. Johnson, yet the issue seems to have been squarely before this court and Judge Kiley stated the following at 1115:

> "Harry Johnson was told that a lawyer would be appointed 'if and when you go to court' and claims this did not fully advise him of his right to have an attorney present during the custodial interrogation. However, he signed a statement which, read as a whole, complied with the *Miranda* requirements. Having signed the written waiver form, without evidence to the contrary, he cannot now contend that he did not understand his rights."

While the *Johnson* case does not set out the entire warning given there, the fair inference seems to be that the remainder of the statement complies with the *Miranda* requirements. Likewise here, as pointed out above, there seems to be no faulting of the balance of the warning statement.

As pointed out in the majority opinion, the inclusion of the "not until court" language in an otherwise proper *Miranda* warning has been held not to be a fatal constitutional defect by the state courts of both Indiana and Illinois.

* * *

While we are not bound by the state court decision, I do not think we should ignore the realistic analysis of the very warning before us given by Judge Burman of the Illinois Appellate Court in *Williams*:

> "The warnings which were read to the defendant informed him (1) that he had a right to remain silent, (2) that anything he said could be used against him in court, (3) that he had a right to talk to a lawyer before and during questioning, (4) that he had a right to a lawyer's advice and pressence even if he could not afford to hire one, (5) that a lawyer would be appointed for him, if and when he went to court, and (6) that he had a right to stop answering questions at any time until he talked to a lawyer. The defendant by signing the waiver acknowledged that he had read the warning and that he understood his rights. The above warnings when read in combination, clearly and understandably informed the defendant that he was entitled to appointed counsel prior to questioning."

It seems to me considering the *Miranda* statement here given as a whole that Williams was definitely informed that he did not have to talk without an attorney. He was informed that there were no facilities for getting him an attorney at the time in the jail but it seems nevertheless to me that it was made clear to him that he did not have to talk unless he voluntarily desired to do so. Certainly, the state police had and have no facilities for appointing attorneys and the impact of the majority decision virtually is that the police have to bring in an attorney before they can ever interrogate, irrespective of the warning. Whether this language is in the standard *Miranda* warnings which have been approved or not, it is implicitly there because there is no way of which I am aware by which the police in the initial interrogation of a suspect are able to provide him with counsel at that point. They do have to advise him, however, of his right not to speak without counsel and it seems to me that was adequately done here.

I cannot agree with the correctness of the statement of Lathers v. United States (5th Cir. 1968), that the "*Miranda* warning must effectively convey to the accused that he is entitled to a government-furnished counsel here and now." If "here and now" means the police station, this is just not a realistic statement because police stations do not furnish government counsel. It seems to me that the most that can be said is that, as the *Lathers* court itself said, "[t]he words must asseverate with conviction that any accused can have a lawyer before speaking." With that I cannot disagree. However, if the accused, after being warned, states that he wants a lawyer, either now or later, then while no necessary obligation exists to provide him one "here and now," there is a *Miranda* impediment against further interrogation. If it is contended that the accused, notwithstanding a request for counsel at a time of unavailability of the same, did nevertheless proceed to talk or answer questions on a voluntary basis, there would be indeed a heavy burden upon the state to demonstrate voluntariness. I would not hold, however, that it was an impossible burden.

NOTES

1. The warnings required under *Miranda* are these: (1) Right to silence: "At the outset, if a person in custody is to be subjected to interrogation, he must first be informed in clear and unequivocal terms that he has the right to remain silent." The Court's reasoning is that this warning is needed (a) to assist the uninformed to exercise intelligently this right, (b) to overcome the "inherent pressures of the interrogation atmosphere", and (c) to assure the accused that his interrogators will recognize this right; (2) Courtroom use of the statement: The accused must be given to understand "that anything said can and will be used against the individual in court." In this way the Court states, (a) the accused is made aware of the right that he has to refuse to talk and he is alerted to the consequences that he faces in waiving this right, and (b) he is made to realize "that he is not in the presence of persons acting solely in his interest"; (3) Right to assistance of counsel during interrogation: "An individual held for interroga-

tion must be clearly informed that he has the right to consult with a lawyer and to have the lawyer with him during interrogation under the system for protecting the privilege we delineate today"; The accused must be warned "not only that he has the right to consult with an attorney, but also that if he is indigent a lawyer will be appointed to represent him". The Court specifically holds the interrogator to this measure: "If an individual indicates that he wishes the assistance of counsel before any interrogation occurs, the authorities cannot rationally ignore or deny his request on the basis that the individual does not have or cannot afford a retained attorney".

There has been almost no dispute concerning the substance of the *Miranda* warnings. The only contention made with any frequency at all is that the suspect must be warned that anything he says "can and will" be used against him. However, the courts have uniformly rejected the argument holding that it is enough to warn the suspect that what he says "might", "can", or "could" be used against him. United States v. Grady, 423 F.2d 1091 (5th Cir. 1970); United States v. Sanchez, 422 F.2d 1198 (2nd Cir. 1970); Davis v. United States, 425 F.2d 673 (9th Cir. 1970). One court has held that the warning that a statement could be used "for or against you" is misleading. See Commonwealth v. Singleton, 439 Pa. 185, 266 A.2d 753 (1970). There has been some dispute as to whether additional warnings other than those mentioned should be given. Although suspects are often warned of their right to stop answering questions at any time, Sanchez v. State, 454 S.W.2d 210 (Tex.1970), it has been held that such a warning is not necessary. Flannagin v. State, 289 Ala. 177, 266 So.2d 643 (1972); Katzensky v. State, 228 Ga. 6, 183 S.E.2d 749 (1971); People v. Tubbs, 22 Mich.App. 549, 177 N.W.2d 622 (1970) (an admonition advising the defendant that he had the right to stop answering questions at any time was not required by *Miranda*); State v. Harper, 467 S.W.2d 547 (Mo.1971). It is also held that a suspect need not be warned that his refusal to answer questions cannot be used against him nor need he be informed of certain applicable legal rules, i. e., felony murder. State v. McRae, 276 N.C. 308, 172 S.E.2d 37 (1970). The suspect need not be told that he needs or could use the help of a lawyer in deciding to waive his rights. United States v. Hall, 396 F.2d 841 (4th Cir. 1968). The suspect need not specifically be told that oral statements are admissible where the suspect is willing to give an oral statement but not a written one. United States v. Ruth, 394 F.2d 134 (3rd Cir. 1968). But see Frazier v. United States, 419 F.2d 1161 (D.C. Cir. 1969).

Some courts require additional admonishment concerning the nature of the charge or subject of investigation. See Commonwealth v. Boykin, 450 Pa. 25, 298 A.2d 258 (1972). Some courts do not. United States v. Campbell, 431 F.2d 97 (9th Cir. 1970) (suspect need not be warned that he was being investigated for Dyer Act violations). In any event the issue will not arise often because a suspect generally knows the nature of the charge and because local statutes and police procedures usually require such admonishments. Are the cases that do insist that the suspect be fully informed of the charge in conflict with the precedents approving interrogation in homicide cases where the police do not inform the suspect that the victim has died? See Satterfield v. Boles, 297 F.Supp. 609, aff'd 408 F.2d 1029 (4th Cir. 1969); Sanchez v. State, 454 S.W.2d 210 (Tex.1970).

2. Williams v. Twomey is an example of the most common challenge to the propriety of any given warning. Either the officer merely says the

suspect has a right to counsel, or he says counsel will be appointed by the Court, or he informs the suspect that the police have no way of getting counsel for him immediately. To say either of the latter two is to mandate reversal in most cases. See Gilpin v. United States, 415 F.2d 638 (5th Cir. 1969) (no way to give you a lawyer now); Square v. State, 283 Ala. 548, 219 So.2d 377 (1968); People v. Ansley, 18 Mich.App. 659, 171 N.W.2d 649 (1969) (Court will appoint a lawyer); People v. Watts, 35 App.Div.2d 802, 315 N.Y.S.2d 669 (1970) (could not provide counsel on Saturday afternoon). Contra, Steel v. State, 246 Ark. 75, 436 S.W.2d 800 (1969); Bohachef v. State, 50 Wis.2d 694, 185 N.W.2d 339 (1971).

It is understandable that police officers would make these statements —in nearly all cases there is no way they can provide a lawyer immediately. But it is clear from *Miranda* that they must offer the services of a lawyer before interrogation. They need not tender counsel immediately but they must make it clear that, if the suspect wants a lawyer, they will not question him until he has the opportunity to consult with one. Mayzak v. United States, 402 F.2d 152 (5th Cir. 1968).

The rationale for this view was expressed in Mayzak v. United States, 402 F.2d 152, 155 (5th Cir. 1968):

> "The fact that the FBI agent truthfully informed Mayzak that the F. B. I. could not furnish a lawyer until federal charges were preferred against him does not vitiate the sufficiency of an otherwise adequate warning. Mayzak knew he could remain silent. He knew he could refuse the interview or terminate it at any point by a simple request. Yet he neither exercised his right of silence nor requested legal counsel.
>
> "We are asked to find that the sufficiency of a Miranda warning is diluted or destroyed because the promise of an attorney is not accompanied by a concurrent tender of one. To so hold would be to allow a defendant to use his right to an attorney as a weapon against his custodians. He would simply argue if you will not furnish me an attorney now, even though I am told I can remain silent, I will talk and after talking object to my words going into evidence. This argument is both hollow and specious. The Miranda warnings given to Mayzak were constitutionally adequate. That he chose of his own free will to speak without the assistance of counsel should give him no cause for complaint."

See also United States v. Lacy, 446 F.2d 511 (5th Cir. 1971); State v. Blanchey, 75 Wash.2d 926, 454 P.2d 841 (1969). Is *Mayzak* consistent with Williams v. Twomey? Would the result in Williams v. Twomey have been different if immediately after making the statement about "an attorney . . . will be appointed for you . . . when you go to court" the officer had added "and you do not have to say anything until you go to court and talk to your appointed attorney"? Can it be said that Williams v. Twomey requires the police officer to simply say "an attorney will be appointed for you anytime you wish including now". That statement would, of course, be untrue. If the suspect took up the offer of counsel, the consequence would not be the appointment of counsel but rather the cessation of interrogation. Is there anything wrong with this practice? It is clear that the issue with respect to provision of counsel is not whether the police can make good on their offer of counsel but whether the defendant declined the offer and waived his right. See People v. Cooper, 10 Cal.App.3d 96, 88 Cal.Rptr. 919 (1970). On the other hand, if the suspect asks for counsel and it is not provided, may not the suspect become uncertain about the willingness of the police to respect his other rights?

The right to counsel extends to the period prior to questioning and continues during questioning. Failure to make this clear is error. See United States v. Oliver, 421 F.2d 1034 (10th Cir. 1970); United States v. Garcia, 431 F.2d 134 (9th Cir. 1970). But see Klingler v. United States, 409 F. 2d 299 (8th Cir. 1969); People v. Gilleylem, 34 Mich.App. 393, 191 N.W.2d 96 (1971) ("before questioning" is sufficient).

One court has sanctioned a less rigorous form of warning for "field interrogation" in two tandem decisions. In both cases the defendants were arrested on the street and given warnings with respect to counsel that were inadequate. In one case defendant was told he had a "right to an attorney"; in the other, that he had a "right to an attorney while making a statement". The court held that both warnings were proper in context and held that they were adequate for on the street interrogation. The court indicated that a more careful warning procedure would be required for a stationhouse interrogation. The dichotomy between street warning and stationhouse warnings was based on the practical differences between the two situations both in terms of police security and custodial atmosphere. See United States v. Lamia, 429 F.2d 373 (2nd Cir. 1970); United States v. Cusomano, 429 F.2d 378 (2nd Cir. 1970).

3. *Miranda* warnings must be given in a clear, unhurried manner—in such a way that the individual would feel free to claim his rights without fear. The warnings should not be given in a perfunctory fashion. United States v. Vanterpool, 394 F.2d 697 (2nd Cir. 1968); Lathers v. United States, 396 F.2d 524 (5th Cir. 1968). But, "*Miranda* does not require law enforcement officials to insist upon or to suggest the refusal of cooperation. As long as the suspect is clearly told and clearly understands that he need not talk, that he may consult a lawyer before deciding whether or not to talk, and that he may have one present when he talks, if he decides to talk, all of the requirements of *Miranda* are met". United States v. Duke, 409 F.2d 669 (4th Cir. 1969).

When warnings are given to an illiterate or subnormal person, "Miranda requires meaningful advice . . . in language which he can comprehend and on which he can knowingly act. The crucial test is whether the words used by the officers, in view of the age, intelligence and demeanor of the individual being interrogated (conveyed) a clear understanding of all his rights." Jenkins v. State, 214 So.2d 470 (Miss.1968). (For an example of great care in warning one of subnormal intelligence, see Anderson v. State, 6 Md.App. 688, 253 A.2d 387 (1969).

In dealing with suspects who do not speak English, the warnings, of course, must be given in a language they understand. De La Fe v. United States, 413 F.2d 543 (5th Cir. 1969). Warnings may be read from a card (Hammond v. State, 244 Ark. 1113, 428 S.W.2d 639 (1968)) and written warnings are sufficient where the suspect is literate. United States v. Lucarz, 430 F.2d 1051 (9th Cir. 1970).

It seems clear that claims arising from an improper manner of admonishment will be settled in trial courts. If the required warnings are fully stated it is impossible for anyone but a trier of fact to determine whether admittedly proper warnings were given in an improper manner. It is doubtful that a court of review can effectively deal with such claims. See State v. Lay, 427 S.W.2d 394 (Mo.1968) (hollow recitation); People v. McCottrell, 117 Ill.App.2d 1, 254 N.E.2d 284 (1969) (hurried recitation); State v. Ortega, 95 Idaho 239, 506 P.2d 466 (1973) (15–20 second warning is not per se improper).

4. The warnings must be given at the very beginning of the interrogation, State v. Johnson, 106 N.J.Super. 295, 255 A.2d 777 (1969), but need not be repeated as the questioning moves from one crime to another, Heard v. State, 244 Ark. 44, 424 S.W.2d 179 (1968); State v. Jennings, 448 P.2d 62 (1968); State v. Davidson, 252 Or. 617, 451 P.2d 481 (1969), or after a short break, United States v. Osterburg, 423 F.2d 704 (9th Cir. 1970); United States v. Hopkins, 433 F.2d 1041 (7th Cir. 1970) (no need to rewarn where there was no significant interval between state and federal interrogations); Mitchell v. State, 458 S.W.2d 630 (Tenn.Cr.App.1970) (where warnings with respect to first interrogation concerning one crime are clearly adequate, interrogation with respect to another crime the next day need not begin with warnings). When the questioning is taken over by a new officer, he does not have to rewarn. Commonwealth v. Bradley, 449 Pa. 19, 295 A.2d 842 (1972). It has been held that the warnings must precede only the incriminating question and answer; it need not precede all questions. Commonwealth v. Bartlett, 446 Pa. 392, 288 A.2d 796 (1972).

5. The testimony of an officer that he gave the warnings is sufficient. It need not be corroborated even if contradicted by defendant. Neitz v. People, 170 Colo. 428, 462 P.2d 498 (1969); State v. Bower, 73 Wash.2d 634, 440 P.2d 167 (1968); Bridges v. State, 255 Ind. 201, 263 N.E.2d 368 (1970). But see Williams v. State, 220 So.2d 325 (Miss.1969) (fact of warnings contradicted, prosecution failed to prove warnings when it did not call second interrogating officer).

The precise nature of the warnings given must be clearly shown in the record. Conclusory testimony that defendant "was given his rights and agreed to talk" is insufficient. (State v. Graham, 240 So.2d 486 (Fla.App. 1970); State v. Seefeldt, 51 N.J. 472, 242 A.2d 322 (1968)). However, it is not necessary to tape record warnings, or to have them stenographically reported. People v. Baxter, 7 Cal.App.3d 579, 86 Cal.Rptr. 812 (1970).

Often, officers read warnings from a card to be certain they omit nothing. If so, it is essential to either introduce the card into evidence or have it read into evidence. Moll v. United States, 413 F.2d 1233 (5th Cir. 1969); Contra: Tudela v. State, 212 So.2d 387 (Fla.App.1968) (court took judicial notice of the text of the warning card).

Where written or oral warnings are given and one is defective and the other not, the courts have considered the correct warning as reparative of the inadequate one. Brooks v. State, 229 A.2d 833 (Del.1967) (inadequate written warnings); State v. Taggert, 443 S.W.2d 168 (Mo.1969) (inadequate written warnings); People v. Swift, 32 App.Div.2d 183, 300 N.Y.S.2d 639 (1969) (inadequate oral warning). But see United States v. Garcia, 431 F.2d 134 (9th Cir. 1970) (conflict between two different warnings serves only to confuse.)

SECTION 4. THE ADEQUACY OF WAIVER

STATE v. DAVIS

Supreme Court of Washington, 1971.
73 Wash.2d 271, 438 P.2d 185.

NEILL, JUDGE. Defendant Belknap, along with three co-defendants, was convicted of attempted escape. . . .

A pretrial confession hearing established the following undisputed facts: (1) after discovery of the attempted escape, a sheriff's captain had a conversation with Belknap; (2) an undersheriff was present at, but did not participate in, this conversation; (3) the captain informed Belknap of his constitutional rights as required by Miranda; (4) Belknap understood his rights; and (5) Belknap was requested to give a written statement which he refused to do.

Other material factual details surrounding this conversation are in dispute. The sheriff's captain testified that: (1) after being informed of his rights, Belknap stated that he understood them, that he would waive his rights, would answer questions he felt it was wise to answer and would refuse to answer questions he felt it was unwise to answer, unless his attorney would be present; (2) defendant was told that the authorities knew he had not sawed on the floor but that he had sawed on a table brace; (3) Belknap replied that four men were involved in the attempt and that he had played his part by sawing on the table brace and acting as a lookout; (4) Belknap was requested to give a written statement; (5) he requested time to consider whether he would do so or whether he would consult his attorney first; (6) Belknap later informed the captain that he would not do so; (7) the captain did not know Belknap had an attorney; (8) Belknap did not request an attorney at any time prior to making the oral admissions; (9) Belknap was not told that charges might not be brought if he cooperated. Conversely, Belknap testified that: (1) after being warned of his rights, he told the captain that he would not say anything until he talked with his attorney; (2) he was informed that the captain had learned, from other inmates, of Belknap's part in the escape; (3) the state might not prosecute if Belknap cooperated; (4) the captain asked if it was true that defendant had sawed on a table brace and acted as a lookout; (5) Belknap replied that he would not answer until after consulting his attorney; (6) Belknap informed the captain of the name of his attorney; (7) Belknap informed the captain that he had no statement to give, written or otherwise. The trial court believed the captain's version of the disputed facts and ruled that Belknap's alleged admissions were voluntary and admissible. . . .

[Succinctly stated, the real issued in the instant case is whether, in light of *Miranda's* placing a heavy burden of proof on the prosecution, we must now require a greater quantum and quality of proof than we did in pre-*Miranda* cases]. . . . [*Miranda* is emphatic that no presumptions are available to aid the prosecution in its attempt to prove a valid waiver of the rights to counsel and to remain silent.]

. . . *Miranda* specifically points out certain factual criteria which should be considered in determining the validity of a waiver, including the existence of tricks, cajolery, lengthy interrogation, or incommunicado incarceration prior to the waiver, as well as the time interval between the alleged waiver and the giving of a statement. But these factual criteria are of little value in determining whether the police in a particular case have followed the mandate of *Miranda,* if the only proof relative to such criteria is the testimony of one interrogating officer—the very person who allegedly violated the accused's constitutional rights. If in fact an accused's waiver is not valid, often his only means of proving the invalidity is his own testimony to that effect. But a review of cases, in which the issue of the admissibility of a confession had to be resolved on the basis of a "swearing contest," indicates that almost invariably the police officer was held by the trial court to be more credible than the accused. In contrast to the accused's inadequate means of establishing evidence, the police, when interrogating the accused within the confines of a station house, have readily available numerous methods and techniques of establishing corroborating testimony and independent supporting evidence, e. g., (1) the officers, in addition to the interrogating officer, who may witness the accused's waiver; (2) stenographers; (3) tape recordings; (4) motion pictures; and (5) video tape recordings.

With respect to certain of the factual criteria mentioned in the preceding paragraph, the court in *Miranda* stated:

> *Whatever the testimony of the authorities* as to waiver of rights by an accused, the fact of lengthy interrogation or incommunicado incarceration before a statement is made is strong evidence that the accused did not validly waive his rights. * * * Moreover, *any evidence* that the accused was threatened, tricked, or cajoled into a waiver will, of course, show that the defendant did not voluntarily waive his privilege. (Italics ours.)

The language quoted above, particularly as emphasized, has been interpreted by some authorities to mean:

> [T]hat confessions achieved by custodian interrogation are regarded with so much distrust by the *Miranda* justices that something resembling a presumption against their admissibility is taking shape. Though calling this a presumption of police misconduct and perjury might not be accurate, and would doubtless be resented, it should be recognized that the evidentiary problem of proving a valid waiver of *Miranda* rights is not much different from what it would be if such a presumption existed. 19 Am.Jur. Proof of Facts 72.

See also Justice White's dissenting opinion, *Miranda*. While we do not particularly subscribe to this interpretation, we do believe that the Supreme Court intended a mandate to require the adoption of more credible and sophisticated techniques of proof than was formerly the case. So long as interrogation takes place in isolated circumstances, with no one present who is either favorable to the accused or suited for the role of a neutral and impartial observer, some firmer guaranty that constitutional rights have been observed will normally be necessary than can be provided by a mere "swearing contest" between the accused and one interrogating police officer.

Considering the facts as presented in the case at bar, we cannot hold that the prosecution has met the burden of proving the validity of Belknap's alleged waiver as required by the holding in *Miranda*: (1) the admission was made while the defendant was in police custody within the confines of the police station; (2) presumably the police had both the opportunity and the means readily available to establish substantial corroborating evidence; (3) the only evidence presented by the prosecution consisted of the testimony of one interrogating officer; (4) the officer's testimony was neither corroborated by other testimony nor supported by other independent evidence; (5) the officer's testimony was completely contradicted by the defendant; and (6) a second officer, who was the only other person present during the interrogation, was not called as a corroborating witness by the prosecution nor was his absence explained, and in the instant case this last element may be deemed determinative.

NOTES

1. The issue of waiver under *Miranda* will, in time, become the most dominant issue. And the resolution of waiver issues, as is the case with custody issues, will be complex. Where once there were claims of coerced confession there may now arise claims of coerced waiver. See Miranda v. Arizona, 384 U.S. at 476, 86 S.Ct. at 1628, 1629; Coyote v. United States, 380 F.2d 305 (10th Cir. 1967); State v. LaFernier, 37 Wis.2d 365, 155 N.W. 2d 93 (1967). Indeed, debates over the existence of waiver will parallel the old debates over voluntariness because voluntariness of waiver must be determined by the same "totality of the circumstances" that once determined voluntariness of confession. See People v. Hill, 39 Ill.2d 125, 233 N.E.2d 367 (1968).

In State v. Davis the Court discussed the problems of administering the "heavy burden" test of *Miranda*. The use of the term "heavy burden" may not be particularly helpful. It is often said that no one really understands how heavy is the burden of proof beyond a reasonable doubt or by preponderance of the evidence. These are vague abstractions. Perhaps the Court meant that the prosecution should show unequivocally that there was a waiver. At least the prosecution's case should show waiver clearly if the defendant denies waiver; then the trier of fact decides, but initially the prosecution must be clear in its proof. See United States v. Springer, 460 F.2d 1344 (7th Cir. 1972) (if prosecution shows waiver, then accused has burden of going forward with evidence of involuntariness). And if there is any doubt it must be resolved against the finding of waiver; for example, a case where a suspect is warned, acknowledges his understanding of rights and does not assert his rights, he may say something that muddies the water such as "I should see my lawyer now" but never asks for a lawyer. In such a case, there should be an express waiver of counsel before interrogation continues. Craig v. State, 216 So.2d 19 (Fla.App.1968). For a case in which clarification was carefully made see People v. Smith, 270 Cal.App.2d 715, 76 Cal.Rptr. 53 (1969). On the necessary clarity of the State's proof see Thomas v. State, 458 S.W.2d 817 (Tex.1970) (warnings given by a judge; confession witnessed by disinterested citizen); Madkins v. State, 50 Wis.2d 347, 184 N.W.2d 144 (1971) (slight variation between testimony of two officers is not fatal to proof of waiver). The court in State v. Davis suggested the use of mechanical devices to record waiver but did not require them. See also People v. Baxter, 7 Cal.App.3d 579, 86 Cal.Rptr. 812 (1970) (tape recording not required).

The courts have singled out certain facts which particularly support findings of waiver. The selective exercise of certain rights, i. e., refusal to answer some questions, tends to show the existence of a deliberate waiver with respect to the questions answered. United States v. Lovell, 378 F.2d 799 (3rd Cir. 1967); United States v. Barnhill, 429 F.2d 340 (8th Cir. 1970); Mitchess v. United States, 434 F.2d 483 (D.C. Cir. 1970) (request for counsel immediately after statement); The existence of a motive to make a statement is supportive of a conscious waiver. State v. Collins, 74 Wash.2d 729, 446 P.2d 325 (1968) (attempt to secure deal for providing evidence); State v. LaFernier, 37 Wis.2d 365, 155 N.W.2d 93 (1967) (desire to avoid publicity). A suspect's extensive criminal experience will also serve to substantiate existence of a knowing waiver. Mingo v. People, 171 Colo. 474, 468 P.2d 849 (1970).

Finally, the "heavy burden" language of *Miranda* is now subject to some question. Under the decision in Lego v. Twomey, 404 U.S. 477, 92 S. Ct. 619 (1972), the prosecution may introduce a confession upon proof of its voluntariness by a preponderance of the evidence. It can be argued that coercion of a confession is a far more serious matter than violation of *Miranda*. If this is the case, and it obviously is, it may be argued that the prosecution should not bear a greater burden of proof in showing compliance with *Miranda* than it does in establishing voluntariness. Therefore, it can be argued that the language in *Miranda* concerning "heavy burden" is either dictum or has been rendered void in light of *Lego*.

2. Even if there are adequate warnings the question may arise as to whether the suspect was mentally competent to waive his rights. A leading case sustaining waiver is People v. Lara, 67 Cal.2d 365, 62 Cal.Rptr. 586, 432 P.2d 202 (1967). In Dover v. State, 227 So.2d 296 (Miss.1969) a suspect with an I.Q. of 60 with lowered ability in stress situations was held incompetent to waive his right. The question of competency to waive will normally deal with the effect of youth, mental capacity, insanity, drug, alcohol and injury upon the ability to comprehend the rights involved and the gravity of the decision to waive. The decisions on these questions are voluminous.

On the subject of youth, consider: Commonwealth v. Darden, 441 Pa. 41, 271 A.2d 257 (1970) (waiver by 15 year old, mild retarded juvenile upheld); State v. Smith, 192 S.E.2d 870 (S.C.1972) (waiver by 13 year old upheld); In re P., 7 Cal.3d 801, 103 Cal.Rptr. 425, 500 P.2d 1 (1972) (waiver by 14 year old retarded shortly after he was wakened is invalid); Thomas v. North Carolina, 447 F.2d 1320 (4th Cir. 1971) (waiver by 15 year old with I.Q. of 72 invalid after 14 hours in custody).

Insanity or Retardation: Compare United States v. Bush, 466 F.2d 236 (5th Cir. 1972) (waiver by suspect with I.Q. of 68 and mental age of 6 upheld); People v. Stanis, 41 Mich.App. 565, 200 N.W.2d 473 (1972) (waiver by suspect with six year old mind is invalid). Low intelligence does not by itself invalidate a waiver. Commonwealth v. White, 285 N.E.2d 110 (Mass. 1972); State v. Smith, 492 P.2d 317 (Ore.App.1971) (waiver upheld where psychiatrist testified that *Miranda* warnings were simply and easily understood); See also Criswell v. State, 86 Nev. 573, 472 P.2d 342 (1970) (waiver by paranoid schizophrenic).

Intoxication: People v. Duke, 63 Misc.2d 407, 311 N.Y.S.2d 312 (1970) (accused cannot challenge waiver on grounds of self-inflicted intoxication); State v. Pease, 129 Vt. 70, 271 A.2d 835 (1970) (intoxication does not invalidate a waiver per se); People v. Moore, 20 Cal.App.3d 444, 97 Cal.Rptr. 601 (1971) (blood alcohol reading of .21 is not sufficient to invalidate waiver); People v. Roy, 49 Ill.2d 113, 273 N.E.2d 363 (1971) (intoxication voids waiver); People v. Gurley, 23 Cal.App.3d 536, 100 Cal.Rptr. 407 (1972) (influence of heroin voids waiver); State v. Hoskins, 292 Minn. 111, 193 N.W. 2d 802 (1972) (suspect using tranquilizing medication may validly waive his rights).

Injury: See State v. Pressel, 2 Or.App. 477, 468 P.2d 915 (1970) (wounded suspect may make a valid waiver); State v. Parker, 55 Wis.2d 131, 197 N.W.2d 742 (1972) (suspect with a minor wound may validly waive rights even though wound was thought to be major).

The decision as to competency is usually based on the totality of the circumstances (State v. Smith, 4 Or.App. 130, 476 P.2d 802 (1970)) and the trial court's ruling is usually determinative. United States v. Cowley, 452 F.2d 243 (10th Cir. 1971). There has been debate over one suggested per se rule, that is, that to secure a waiver from a juvenile, the juvenile's parents must be present or be notified or that the juvenile must be told of his right to have his parents present. The courts have been severely divided on the issue. Decisions holding that parents need not be involved in the waiver process are O'Neil v. State, 2 Tenn.Cr.App. 518, 455 S.W.2d 597 (1970); State v. Dawson, 278 N.C. 351, 180 S.E.2d 140 (1971); Commonwealth v. Porter, 449 Pa. 153, 295 A.2d 311 (1972); Mullen v. State, 505 P.2d 305 (Wyo.1973). To the contrary are In re B. D., 110 N.J.Super. 585, 266 A.2d 326 (1969); Lewis v. State, 288 N.E.2d 138 (Ind.1972); Ezell v. State, 489 P.2d 781 (Okl.1971).

The *Miranda* opinion says two things about waiver. First, it says that waiver cannot be inferred from silence. Second, *Miranda* noted that an express statement of the suspect that he is willing to make a statement and does not want an attorney followed closely by a statement *might* constitute a waiver. The Supreme Court has yet to take a waiver case and resolve unanswered questions. And there is really only one thing that is clear from the *Miranda* opinion; that a warning followed by complete silence does not constitute a waiver. But what if the suspect is asked if he understands the rights and says yes and then gives a statement? When the Court specified a certain clear form of waiver and said that a subject *might* waive *Miranda* rights, did the Court mean *might* in the sense that the example given is one of many possible forms of waiver that *might* occur? Or, did they mean that even this degree of waiver *might* not pass muster?

The difficult issue is whether waiver may be implied when there is no specific verbal waiver. In State v. Kremens, 52 N.J. 303, 245 A.2d 313 (1968) the court held: "Any clear manifestation of a desire to waive is sufficient. The test is the showing of a knowing intent, not the utterance of a shibboleth. The criterion is not solely the language employed but a combination of that articulation and the surrounding facts and circumstances."

In United States v. Hayes, 385 F.2d 375 (4th Cir. 1967) waiver was implied when after warnings defendant made no acknowledgement but asked to use a phone. He was allowed to do so. After the call he returned to the room and answered questions for a half an hour. He then stopped, asked for a lawyer, and no further questions were put.

In Brown v. State, 3 Md.App. 313, 239 A.2d 761 (1968) a suspect turned himself in and volunteered information. He was warned and made no explicit waiver but promptly answered questions. The Court construed his actions prior to warning as supporting a conclusion of implied waiver.

The principle that waiver may be implied is generally recognized. See e. g., Commonwealth v. Fisher, 354 Mass. 549, 238 N.E.2d 525 (1968) (Suspect declines use of phone, says he wants to talk, agrees to Polygraph test); People v. Matthews, 22 Mich.App. 619, 178 N.W.2d 94 (1970) (waiver is implied from defendant's initiating conversation).

By the same token a claim of privilege need not be formal in nature, i. e., "Don't bother me" is an assertion of the right to remain silent. State v. Klimczak, 159 Conn. 608, 268 A.2d 372 (1970).

4. The courts have rarely dealt with a model *Miranda* waiver, i. e., State v. Ranson, 182 Neb. 243, 153 N.W.2d 916 (1967). The area of waiver is one where "problems do exist". United States v. Corbins, 397 F.2d 790 (7th Cir. 1968). Not the least problem is the indecisive suspect who seems never to quite get to the point of waiving or claiming his rights. See especially People v. Hiles, 172 Colo. 463, 474 P.2d 153 (1970) (upholding waiver of suspect who refused to acknowledge understanding his rights and refused to waive them but insisted for half an hour that he wanted to talk).

The courts have coped with the problems in the following ways:

When it is clear that a defendant has been fully informed of his rights any reasonable verbal acknowledgement of understanding or willingness to speak is acceptable. United States v. Boykin, 398 F.2d 483 (3rd Cir. 1968) (after warnings, suspect said "I might as well tell you about it"); Miller v. United States, 396 F.2d 492 (8th Cir. 1968) (acknowledged understanding, stated "I waive" and signed written waiver); People v. Samaniego, 263 Cal.App.2d 804, 69 Cal.Rptr. 904 (1968) (Will you waive? "Yes"); Patrick v. State, 203 So.2d 62 (Fla.App.1967) (after warnings suspect said "I don't need a lawyer"); State v. Brown, 250 La. 1125, 202 So.2d 274 (1967) (after warning, suspect said "I know all that"); State v. Kremens, 52 N.J. 303, 245 A.2d 313 (1968) (after warnings, suspect said "I'll tell you"); State v. Montoya, 78 N.M. 294, 430 P.2d 865 (1967) ("I don't need an attorney. I want to straighten it out"); State v. Lightsey, 6 N.C.App. 745, 171 S.E.2d 27 (1969) (after warnings, suspect said, "I've been in trouble enough to know my rights"),

The most commonly encountered form of waiver is the acknowledgement that the suspect understands, followed by a statement. It is usually held that once the defendant has been informed of his rights and indicates that he understands those rights, it would seem that his choosing to speak and not requesting a lawyer is sufficient evidence that he knows of his rights and chooses not to exercise them. People v. Johnson, 70 Cal.2d 541, 75 Cal.Rptr. 401, 450 P.2d 865 (1969). This rule is probably valid only if the statement of the defendant follows immediately after he says he understands the warnings. Billings v. People, 171 Colo. 236, 466 P.2d 474 (1970). The cases upholding this rule are a legion; e. g., United States v. Osterburg, 423 F.2d 704 (9th Cir. 1970); United States v. Daniel, 441 F.2d 374 (5th Cir. 1971). Some earlier opinions required specific waiver of the right to counsel; e. g., Sullins v. United States, 389 F.2d 985 (10th Cir. 1968), but this is a distinct minority view. United States ex rel. Falconer v. Pate, 319 F.Supp. 206 (N.D.Ill.1970). Nor must a suspect acknowledge understanding after each specific warning. United States v. Mix, 446 F.2d 615 (5th Cir. 1971).

In addition, the courts have also approved non-verbal waivers such as nods and shrugs. State v. Flores, 9 Ariz.App. 502, 454 P.2d 172 (1969) (nodding head); State v. Brammeier, 1 Or.App. 612, 464 P.2d 717 (1970) (shrug); People v. Hurlic, 14 Cal.App.3d 122, 92 Cal.Rptr. 55 (1971) (head shake).

The signing of a written waiver is usually sufficient if the suspect is literate; e. g. Brooks v. United States, 416 F.2d 1044 (5th Cir. 1969); United States v. Chapman, 448 F.2d 1381 (3rd Cir. 1971). The fact that the written acknowledgment of waiver was not made until confession was completed after oral warning and waiver is not crucial. State v. Jones, 257 La. 966, 244 So.2d 849 (1971). Written waivers are not legally necessary. United States v. Crisp, 435 F.2d 354 (7th Cir. 1970); United States v. Jenkins, 440 F.2d 574 (7th Cir. 1970); United States v. McNeil, 433 F.2d 1109 (D.C.Cir. 1969). A written waiver may not always be sufficient. United States v. Hall, 396 F.2d 841 (4th Cir. 1968).

5. A suspect who says that he would talk to an attorney later but presently would answer questions without counsel has waived his right to counsel. State v. Green, 457 P.2d 505 (Hawaii, 1969) (would retain counsel upon release); State v. Capitan, 2 Or.App. 338, 468 P.2d 533 (1970) (wanted no lawyer "at this time"); but see State v. Prossen, 235 So.2d 740 (Fla.App.1970) (sustaining trial court's finding that such language was a request for counsel). A request for counsel made by a suspect to a friend or relative does not have the effect of a request made upon the police even if the police are aware that such a request was made. People v. Smith, 108 Ill.App.2d 172, 246 N.E.2d 689 (1969).

For cases dealing with the effect of an unsuccessful attempt to reach an attorney, see Rouse v. State, 255 Ind. 670, 266 N.E.2d 209 (1971) (valid waiver after failure to reach an attorney); State v. Slobodian, 57 N. J. 18, 268 A.2d 849 (1970) (no right to question after unsuccessful attempt to secure a lawyer); United States v. Coleman, 322 F.Supp. 550 (E.D.Pa. 1971) (the fact that after waiver suspect asked to and was allowed to call a lawyer did not operate to retract the waiver); Grimsley v. State, 251 So.2d 671 (Fla.App.1971) (answer to question concerning counsel—"I don't know" —does not vitiate written waiver).

A suspect who requests to see someone other than a lawyer has not asserted his rights under *Miranda*. State v. Franklin, 103 R.I. 715, 241 A.2d 219 (1968); State v. Deardurff, 186 Neb. 92, 180 N.W.2d 890 (1970) (not an assertion of a *Miranda* right). Note, The Right to Non-Legal Counsel During Police Interrogation, 70 Colum.L.Rev. 757 (1970). However, a denial of such a request may lead to a valid challenge on the issue of voluntariness. See Haynes v. Washington, 373 U.S. 503, 83 S.Ct. 1336 (1963).

6. In Frazier v. United States, 419 F.2d 1161 (D.C.Cir. 1969), the suspect objected to the taking of notes. The court held that this inveighed against a finding of waiver because it implied that the suspect thought oral statements could not be used against him. This ruling was made despite the existence of a written waiver. See also United States v. Ramos, 448 F. 2d 398 (5th Cir. 1971) (refusal to sign a written confession militates against waiver finding); United States v. Van Dusen, 431 F.2d 1278 (1st Cir. 1970) (suggests suspect should be told that refusal to sign the written waiver does not mean he can speak with impunity).

The *Frazier* decision has run contrary to the majority rule. No state court has adopted it and most federal courts reject it. Indeed, after remand for additional findings, the court in the *Frazier* case itself upheld *en banc* the waiver, 476 F.2d 891 (D.C.Cir. 1973). The general rule is that refusal to sign a written statement does not impeach the validity of the suspect's waiver with respect to oral statements. Pettyjohn v. United States, 419 F.2d 651 (D.C.Cir. 1969) (refusal to sign acknowledgment of warnings does not constitute non-comprehension of the warnings and such a written acknowledgment is not legally required); United States v. Jenkins, 440 F.2d 574 (7th Cir. 1971) (must be a clear oral waiver after a refusal to sign a written waiver); United States v. Ellis, 457 F.2d 1204 (8th Cir. 1972) (willing to give oral statements but not to sign without lawyer).

The same general rule applies to the refusal to sign a written waiver of rights while persisting in an oral waiver. See Cummings v. United States, 398 F.2d 377 (8th Cir. 1968) (suspect would not sign waiver because his attorney told him to sign nothing; however, he waived his rights and specifically stated he did not want his attorney present); Parks v. United States, 387 F.2d 944 (10th Cir. 1968); United States v. Thompson, 417 F.2d 196 (4th Cir. 1969); Klingler v. United States, 409 F.2d 299 (8th Cir. 1969); United States v. Devall, 462 F.2d 137 (5th Cir. 1972). But see Frazier v. United States, 419 F.2d 1161 (D.C.Cir. 1969); Pettyjohn v. United States, 419 F.2d 651 (D.C.Cir. 1969).

The refusal to answer some particular questions is the right of the suspect; however, a suspect who generally answers some questions, but refuses to answer others and does not indicate that all questioning cease, has not asserted his right to remain silent in the sense that the police must stop all questioning. State v. Adams, 76 Wash.2d 650, 458 P.2d 558 (1969); United States v. Brown, 459 F.2d 319 (5th Cir. 1972). Indeed, such events are thought to show clearly a deliberate waiver of rights as to the questions answered. See Note 1, supra.

SECTION 5. PERMISSIBILITY OF MULTIPLE INTERROGATIONS

JENNINGS v. UNITED STATES

United States Court of Appeals, Fifth Circuit, 1968.
391 F.2d 512, certiorari denied 393 U.S. 868, 89 S.Ct. 154.

COLEMAN, CIRCUIT JUDGE. Jacob Jennings . . . was convicted of unlawfully transporting a motor vehicle in interstate commerce.

. . .

James Blakely, a police officer in Fort Pierce, . . . arrested Jennings but told him he would not question him any further until he got to the police station. Upon arrival at the station, the officer advised Jennings of his rights. After Jennings had answered a few questions too rapidly for the officer to write down the answers, he announced that he would not answer further and the interrogation immediately stopped.

In the meantime, an agent of the Federal Bureau of Investigation had been notified. Within about an hour he arrived at the police station. He did not know, and neither the Fort Pierce police nor the defendant told him, that defendant had announced an unwillingness to answer any further questions. Proceeding as if there had been no prior interrogation, the F. B. I. agent again gave full and complete warnings. Subsequent to these warnings, the appellant signed a waiver and did not hesitate to discuss the matter with the agent. After they had talked awhile, appellant's statement was reduced to writing and he signed it.

The warnings given by the Fort Pierce police were clearly adequate. Appellant admits in his brief that the F. B. I. warning was adequate but further contends that since appellant had already refused to answer any more questions it was improper, under *Miranda*, for the F. B. I. agent to question him. In support of this contention appellant quotes from *Miranda*,

> "If however, he indicates in any manner and at any stage of the process that he wishes to consult with an attorney before speaking there can be no questioning. Likewise, if the individual is alone and indicates in any manner that he does not wish to be interrogated, the police may not question him. The mere fact that he may have answered some questions or volunteered some statements on his own does not deprive him of the right to refrain from answering any further inquiries until he has consulted with an attorney and thereafter consents to be questioned".

> "Once warnings have been given, the subsequent procedure is clear. If the individual indicates in any manner, at any time prior to or during questioning, that he wishes to remain silent, the interrogation must cease. At this point he has shown that he intends to exercise his Fifth Amendment privilege; any statement taken after the person invokes his privilege cannot be other than the product of compulsion, subtle or otherwise. Without the right to cut off questioning, the setting of in-custody interrogation operates on the individual to overcome free choice in producing a statement after the privilege has been once invoked".

Appellant then argues that the present case is similar to Westover v. United States, a case included in the *Miranda* decision.

We do not agree with these contentions. It seems clear to us that what the Court sought to interdict in *Miranda* were those situations in which a person has indicated his desire to exercise his constitutional right of silence but the police refuse to take "no" for an answer. Disregarding his constitutional claim, they continue to ask questions. These techniques were not used in this case. It is admitted that the local police ceased interrogation immediately upon appellant's expression of an unwillingness to proceed further.

In *Westover*, the defendant was arrested by local police. With no preliminary warning of his rights, they kept him in custody for over fourteen hours and interrogated him at length during that period. They obtained no statement. The F. B. I. interrogation began immediately and was conducted in the same police headquarters. The Supreme Court said, "Despite the fact that F. B. I. agents gave warnings at the outset of the interview, from Westover's point of view the warning came at the end of the interrogation process. In these circumstances an intelligent waiver of constitutional rights cannot be assumed". On the other hand, Jennings was first thoroughly warned by the Fort Pierce police. He found out that immediately upon expressing an unwillingness to proceed the interrogation would promptly stop. He had been in custody only about an hour, and the questioning had been brief. When the F. B. I. agent repeated the warnings, appellant for some reason satisfactory to himself, failed to express the same unwillingness theretofore exercised against the local police. The situation lacks a long way of coming within the *Westover* rule. There was no error in the admission of the statement obtained by the F. B. I.

NOTES

The language of *Miranda* suggests a three part division of the problem of multiple interrogation. First, the accused may indicate a desire to see an attorney. The language in *Miranda* indicates the questioning must cease until he has seen an attorney.

Several courts, however, have allowed a second interrogation prior to the time a suspect actually seeks counsel if a very clear waiver of counsel is given prior to the second interrogation. In some of these cases the courts rely upon the fact that the accused had an opportunity to consult with counsel even if he did not do so. See United States v. Brady, 421 F.2d 681 (2nd Cir. 1970); United States v. Grady, 423 F.2d 1091 (5th Cir. 1970) (F.B.I. was unaware of prior request for counsel directed to state agents 12 hours previously); People v. Williams, 131 Ill.App.2d 149, 264 N.E.2d 901 (1970) (during a third interrogation defendant demands a lawyer and interrogation ceases—later defendant says he does not want a lawyer—he is rewarned and waives and his statement is admissible); Rouse v. State, 255 Ind. 670, 266 N.E.2d 209 (1971) (proper to secure waiver after the suspect tried and failed to reach his attorney); State v. Welch, 4 Or.App. 225, 476 P.2d 822 (1970) (proper to attempt second interrogation with waiver where defendant first refused to make a written statement without his attorney and was then confronted by his co-defendant). State v. Turner, 281 N.C. 118, 187 S.E.2d 750 (1972) (suspect requests attorney and speaks to one who is unable to take the case, suspect may then be questioned after new warnings and explicit waiver of counsel)

The interpretation of *Miranda* which allows interrogation after a suspect requests counsel but before he sees one is defensible, but, it can be argued persuasively, incorrect. See United States v. Nielson, 392 F.2d 849 (7th Cir. 1968); Mims v. State, 255 Ind. 37, 262 N.E.2d 638 (1970) (improper to attempt fourth interrogation after three prior assertions of rights); State v. Slobodian, 57 N.J. 18, 268 A.2d 849 (1970) (improper to attempt second interrogation after defendant unsuccessfully sought to contact his lawyer); People v. Watts, 35 App.Div.2d 802, 315 N.Y.S.2d 669 (1970) (improper to attempt interrogation after indicating on three occasions that counsel could not be provided because of the late hour). Commonwealth v. Nathan, 445 Pa. 470, 285 A.2d 175 (1971) (ignorance of second officer concerning first interrogation is no excuse).

Jurisdictions which prohibit interrogation after a request for counsel probably would not prohibit such interrogation when it is initiated by the suspect. People v. Randall, 1 Cal.3d 948, 83 Cal.Rptr. 658, 464 P.2d 114 (1970); and it is clear, from the *Miranda* opinion, that after requesting and consulting with counsel an accused may thereafter consent to be questioned. De La Fe v. United States, 413 F.2d 543 (5th Cir. 1969); Coughlan v. United States, 391 F.2d 371 (9th Cir. 1968).

In a second class of cases, the defendant may say nothing about seeing or wanting an attorney but will assert his right to silence. The *Miranda* opinion is somewhat ambiguous as to the existence of limitations upon a second attempt to interrogate.

Several courts have simply approved second attempts to question but sometimes with a caveat that successive attempts to interview after an initial refusal will be viewed with caution. United States v. Collins, 462 F.2d 792 (2nd Cir. 1972) (suspect must be rewarned); State v. Godfrey, 182 Neb. 451, 155 N.W.2d 438 (1968) (warning repeated before second interrogation); Franklin v. State, 6 Md.App. 572, 252 A.2d 487 (1969) (usually should give warning at second interrogation); United States v. Crisp, 435 F.2d 354 (7th Cir. 1970) (proper to interrogate where defendant summoned agents and gave statements after new warnings; improper to ask defendant whether he is willing to talk about what occurred before and after the robbery when he declares that he is unwilling to talk about the robbery); McIntyre v. New York, 329 F.Supp. 9 (E.D.N.Y.1971) (permissible where new inquiry occurred after eye witness identification); Gardner v. State, 10 Md.App. 691, 272 A.2d 410 (1970) (an initial refusal to speak is a heavy factor to be overcome when it is claimed that there was a subsequent waiver); State v. Deardurff, 186 Neb. 92, 180 N.W.2d 890 (1970) (a valid waiver is found where defendant was arrested and warned, after which he asked to see his wife and was told he could not because she was in custody; he then said he did not want to talk and also that he neither knew, could afford, or wished to see a lawyer; on the next day, after being rewarned, defendant made a statement); People v. Lyons, 18 Cal.App.3d 760, 96 Cal.Rptr. 76 (1971) (permissible where interrogation concerned second crime newly discovered); Bronson v. State, 270 N.E.2d 751 (Ind. 1971) (heavy burden upon state to show valid waiver).

The opposite conclusion was reached in People v. Fioritto, 68 Cal.2d 714, 68 Cal.Rptr. 817, 411 P.2d 625 (1968) (interrogation must cease after the suspect invokes his right to silence). See also People v. Milton, 270 Cal.2d 408, 75 Cal.Rptr. 803 (1969) (prohibitive rule applies even where the second interrogator is unaware of the initial refusal); People v. McIntyre, 31 App.Div.2d 964, 299 N.Y.S.2d 88 (1969) (refusal to be interviewed does not evaporate because the police change the subject of discussion to another offense). United States v. Brown, 466 F.2d 493 (10th Cir. 1972) (repeated attempts are improper).

As in the case with interrogation after request for counsel, all courts tend to approve interrogation after refusal to talk when some of the initiative comes from the defendant. People v. Brockman, 2 Cal.App.3d 1002, 83 Cal.Rptr. 70 (1969) (defendant refused to talk but said he might like to talk about in a couple of days and police questioned him two days later); State v. Lucia, 74 Wash.2d 819, 447 P.2d 606 (1968) (defendant initiated the second interview); Conway v. State, 7 Md.App. 400, 256 A.2d 178 (1969) (conditional refusal and request for time to think about it does not bar second interrogation where warnings were given); United States v. Jackson, 436 F.2d 39 (9th Cir. 1970) (defendant refused to see a lawyer and said he had something to say later; four days later he was asked about what he had to say and he waived his rights after being rewarned); People v. Atkins, 10 Cal.App.3d 1042, 89 Cal.Rptr. 588 (1970) (request to speak to a particular officer).

In the third class of cases, the suspect may waive his rights and submit to interrogation, and after an interval of time he may, of course, be interrogated a second time. Tucker v. United States, 375 F.2d 363 (8th Cir. 1967). The issue is whether warnings must be given before the second interrogation. A few cases require the repetition of warnings. Davis v. State, 44 Ala.App. 145, 204 So.2d 490 (1967); Brown v. State, 6 Md.App. 564, 252 A.2d 272 (1969). It is probably the better practice to re-warn. United States v. Thomas, 296 F.2d 310 (2nd Cir. 1968); United States v. Brady, 421 F.2d 681 (2nd Cir. 1970). But it is the general rule that the warnings need not be repeated. Maguire v. United States, 396 F.2d 327 (9th Cir. 1968); Miller v. United States, 396 F.2d 492 (8th Cir. 1968); United States v. Mansfield, 381 F.2d 961 (7th Cir. 1967); People v. Hill, 66 Cal.2d 536, 426 P.2d 908 (1967); People v. Hill, 39 Ill.2d 125, 233 N.E.2d 367 (1968); State v. Rowe, 77 Wash.2d 955, 468 P.2d 1000 (1970); United States v. Canseco, 465 F.2d 383 (5th Cir. 1972); Commonwealth v. Abrams, 443 Pa. 295, 278 A.2d 902 (1971) (unnecessary).

SECTION 6. RELATED ISSUES

(a) USE OF THE INADMISSIBLE STATEMENT AGAINST THE DEFENDANT WHO TESTIFIES AT TRIAL

HARRIS v. NEW YORK

Supreme Court of the United States, 1971.
401 U.S. 222, 91 S.Ct. 643.

MR. CHIEF JUSTICE BURGER delivered the opinion of the Court.

We granted the writ in this case to consider petitioner's claim that a statement made by him to police under circumstances rendering it inadmissible to establish the prosecution's case in chief under Miranda v. Arizona (1966), may not be used to impeach his credibility.

The State of New York charged petitioner in a two-count indictment with twice selling heroin to an undercover police officer. At a subsequent jury trial the officer was the State's chief witness, and he testified as to details of the two sales. A second officer verified collateral details of the sales, and a third offered testimony about the chemical analysis of the heroin.

Petitioner took the stand in his own defense. He admitted knowing the undercover police officer but denied a sale on January 4, 1966. He admitted making a sale of contents of a glassine bag to the officer on January 6 but claimed it was baking powder and part of a scheme to defraud the purchaser.

On cross-examination petitioner was asked seriatim whether he had made specified statements to the police immediately following his arrest on January 7—statements that partially contradicted petitioner's direct testimony at trial. In response to the cross-examination, petitioner testified that he could not remember virtually any of the questions or answers recited by the prosecutor. At the request of petitioner's counsel the written statement from which the prosecutor had read questions and answers in his impeaching process was placed in the record for possible use on appeal; the statement was not shown to the jury.

The trial judge instructed the jury that the statements attributed to petitioner by the prosecution could be considered only in passing on petitioner's credibility and not as evidence of guilt. In closing summations both counsel argued the substance of the impeaching statements. The jury then found petitioner guilty on the second count of the indictment.

At trial the prosecution made no effort in its case in chief to use the statements allegedly made by petitioner, conceding that they were inadmissible under Miranda v. Arizona. The transcript of the interrogation used in the impeachment, but not given to the jury, shows that no warning of a right to appointed counsel was given before questions were put to petitioner when he was taken into custody. Petitioner makes no claim that the statements made to the police were coerced or involuntary.

Some comments in the *Miranda* opinion can indeed be read as indicating a bar to use of an uncounseled statement for any purpose, but discussion of that issue was not at all necessary to the Court's holding and cannot be regarded as controlling. *Miranda* barred the prosecution from making its case with statements of an accused made while in custody prior to having or effectively waiving counsel. It does not follow from *Miranda* that evidence inadmissible against an accused in the prosecution's case in chief is barred for all purposes, provided of course that the trustworthiness of the evidence satisfies legal standards.

In Walder v. United States (1954), the Court permitted physical evidence, inadmissible in the case in chief, to be used for impeachment purposes.

> "It is one thing to say that the Government cannot make an affirmative use of evidence unlawfully obtained. It is quite another to say that the defendant can turn the illegal method by which evidence in the Government's possession was obtained to his own advantage, and provide himself with a shield against contradiction of his untruths. Such an extension of the *Weeks* doctrine would be a perversion of the Fourth Amendment.
>
> "[T]here is hardly justification for letting the defendant affirmatively resort to perjurious testimony in reliance on the Government's disability to challenge his credibility."

It is true that Walder was impeached as to collateral matters included in his direct examination, whereas petitioner here was impeached as to testimony bearing more directly on the crimes charged. We are not persuaded that there is a difference in principle that warrants a result different from that reached by the Court in *Walder*. Petitioner's testimony in his own behalf concerning the events of January 7 contrasted sharply with what he told the police shortly after his arrest. The impeachment process here undoubtedly provided valuable aid to the jury in assessing petitioner's credibility, and the benefits of this process should not be lost, in our view, because of the speculative possibility that impermissible police conduct will be encouraged thereby. Assuming that the exclusionary rule has a deterrent effect on proscribed police conduct, sufficient deterrence flows when the evidence in question is made unavailable to the prosecution in its case in chief.

Every criminal defendant is privilged to testify in his own defense, or to refuse to do so. But that privilege cannot be construed to include the right to commit perjury. Having voluntarily taken the stand, petitioner was under an obligation to speak truthfully and accurately, and the prosecution here did no more than utilize the traditional truth-testing devices of the adversary process.[1] Had inconsistent statements been made by the accused to some third person, it could hardly be contended that the conflict could not be laid before the jury by way of cross-examination and impeachment.

The shield provided by *Miranda* cannot be perverted into a license to use perjury by way of a defense, free from the risk of confrontation with prior inconsistent utterances. We hold, therefore, that petitioner's credibility was appropriately impeached by use of his earlier conflicting statements.

Affirmed.

MR. JUSTICE BLACK dissents.

MR. JUSTICE BRENNAN, with whom MR. JUSTICE DOUGLAS and MR. JUSTICE MARSHALL, join, dissenting.

* * *

The State's case against Harris depended upon the jury's belief of the testimony of the undercover agent that petitioner "sold" the officer heroin on January 4 and again on January 6. Petitioner took the stand and flatly denied having sold anything to the officer on January 4. He countered the officer's testimony as to the January 6 sale with testimony that he had sold the officer two glassine bags containing what appeared to be heroin, but that actually the bags contained only baking powder intended to deceive the officer in order to obtain $12. The statement contradicted petitioner's direct testimony as to the events of both days. The statement's version of the events on January 4 was that the officer had used petitioner as a middleman to buy some heroin from a third person with money furnished by the officer. The version of the events on January 6 was that petitioner had again acted for the officer in buying two bags of heroin from a third person for which petitioner received $12 and a part of the heroin. Thus, it is clear that the statement was used to impeach petitioner's direct testimony not on collateral matters but on matters directly related to the crimes for which he was on trial.

Walder v. United States was not a case where tainted evidence was used to impeach an accused's direct testimony on matters directly related to the case against him. In *Walder* the evidence was used to

1. If, for example, an accused confessed fully to a homicide and led the police to the body of the victim under circumstances making his confession inadmissible, the petitioner would have us allow that accused to take the stand and blandly deny every fact disclosed to the police or discovered as a "fruit" of his confession, free from confrontation with his prior statements and acts. The voluntariness of the confession would, on this thesis, be totally irrelevant. We reject such an extravagant extension of the Constitution.

impeach the accused's testimony on matters *collateral* to the crime charged. Walder had been indicted in 1950 for purchasing and possessing heroin. When his motion to suppress use of the narcotics as illegally seized was granted, the Government dismissed the prosecution. Two years later Walder was indicted for another narcotics violation completely unrelated to the 1950 one. Testifying in his own defense, he said on direct examination that he had never in his life possessed narcotics. On cross-examination he denied that law enforcement officers had seized narcotics from his home two years earlier. The Government was then permitted to introduce the testimony of one of the officers involved in the 1950 seizure, that when he had raided Walder's home at that time he had seized narcotics there. The Court held that on facts where "the defendant went beyond a mere denial of complicity in the crimes of which he was charged and made the sweeping claim that he had never dealt in or possessed any narcotics," the exclusionary rule of Weeks v. United States (1914), would not extend to bar the Government from rebutting this testimony with evidence, although tainted, that petitioner had in fact possessed narcotics two years before. The Court was careful, however, to distinguish the situation of an accused whose testimony, as in the instant case, was a "denial of complicity in the crimes of which he was charged," that is, where illegally obtained evidence was used to impeach the accused's direct testimony on matters directly related to the case against him. As to that situation, the Court said:

> "Of course, the Constitution guarantees a defendant the fullest opportunity to meet the accusation against him. He must be free to deny all the elements of the case against him without thereby giving leave to the Government to introduce by way of rebuttal evidence illegally secured by it, and therefore not available for its case in chief."

From this recital of facts it is clear that the evidence used for impeachment in *Walder* was related to the earlier 1950 prosecution and had no direct bearing on "the elements of the case" being tried in 1952. The evidence tended solely to impeach the credibility of the defendant's direct testimony that he had never in his life possessed heroin. But that evidence was completely unrelated to the indictment on trial and did not in any way interfere with his freedom to deny all elements of that case against him. In contrast, here, the evidence used for impeachment, a statement concerning the details of the very sales alleged in the indictment, was directly related to the case against petitioner.

While *Walder* did not identify the constitutional specifics that guarantee "a defendant the fullest opportunity to meet the accusation against him * * * [and permit him to] be free to deny all the elements of the case against him," in my view Miranda v. Arizona identified the Fifth Amendment's privilege against self-incrimination as one of those specifics. It is fulfilled only when an accused is guaranteed the right "to remain silent unless he chooses to speak in the *unfettered* exercise of his own will," (emphasis added). The choice of whether to testify in one's own defense must therefore be "unfettered," since that choice is an exercise of the constitutional privilege, Griffin v. California. *Griffin* held that comment by the prosecution upon the accused's failure to take the stand or a court instruction that such silence is evidence of guilt is impermissible because it "fetters" that choice—"[i]t cuts down on the privilege by making its assertion costly." For precisely the same reason the constitutional guarantee forbids the prosecution to use a tainted statement to impeach the accused who takes the stand: The prosecution's use of the tainted statement "cuts down on the privilege by making its assertion costly."

Ibid. Thus, the accused is denied an "unfettered" choice when the decision whether to take the stand is burdened by the risk that an illegally obtained prior statement may be introduced to impeach his direct testimony denying complicity in the crime charged against him.

* * *

The objective of deterring improper police conduct is only part of the larger objective of safeguarding the integrity of our adversary system. The "essential mainstay" of that system, Miranda v. Arizona, 384 U.S., at 460, 86 S.Ct. 1602, is the privilege against self-incrimination, which for that reason has occupied a central place in our jurisprudence since before the Nation's birth. Moreover, "we may view the historical development of the privilege as one which groped for the proper scope of governmental power over the citizen. * * * All these policies point to one overriding thought: the constitutional foundation underlying the privilege is the respect a government * * * must accord to the dignity and integrity of its citizens." Ibid. These values are plainly jeopardized if an exception against admission of tainted statements is made for those used for impeachment purposes. Moreover, it is monstrous that courts should aid or abet the law-breaking police officer. It is abiding truth that "[n]othing can destroy a government more quickly than its failure to observe its own laws, or worse, its disregard of the charter of its own existence." Mapp v. Ohio. Thus even to the extent that *Miranda* was aimed at deterring police practices in disregard of the Constitution, I fear that today's holding will seriously undermine the achievement of that objective. The Court today tells the police that they may freely interrogate an accused incommunicado and without counsel and know that although any statement they obtain in violation of *Miranda* cannot be used on the State's direct case, it may be introduced if the defendant has the temerity to testify in his own defense. This goes far toward undoing much of the progress made in conforming police methods to the Constitution. I dissent.

NOTES

1. Consider *Harris* in relation to the dispute over whether a defendant may be cross-examined regarding his prior failure to tell the police the story he has related from the stand. In this regard *Harris* was distinguished

in United States ex rel. Burt v. Yeager, 342 F.Supp. 188 (D.C.N.J.1972), and held not to disrupt the *Miranda* rationale, the court stating (at 195):

> "The instant case does not involve prior inconsistent statements. To include the case at bar within the *Harris* rationale would be to expressly contradict that portion of *Miranda* not faced by the *Harris* Court."

But in United States v. Ramirez, 441 F.2d 950 (5th Cir. 1971), the court held that the "analogy to *Harris* was inescapable," and allowed the impeachment.

2. One state court has rejected the *Harris* rule, in exercise of its option to adopt a stricter standard than the federal one. State v. Santiago, 53 Hawaii 254, 492 P.2d 657 (1971).

3. The dissent in *Harris* implicitly assumes that the decision is an invitation to the police to violate Miranda? Is it? Would a police officer ordinarily know at the time he first questions a suspect whether he has a legally sufficient case against the suspect and will only need the suspect's admissions for possible impeachment? Would a police officer ordinarily know that his other evidence, i. e. physical evidence and eyewitness identification will not be subject to exclusion? In short, is it likely an officer will know at the interrogation that he doesn't need the statements for the state's case in chief?

(b) MIRANDA AND MASSIAH

In Massiah v. United States, 377 U.S. 201, 84 S.Ct. 1199 (1964) an informer sought out a defendant who was under indictment and was represented by counsel. The Supreme Court reversed because "there was used against him at trial evidence of his own incriminating words, which federal agents had deliberately elicited from him after he had been indicted and in the absence of counsel."

Massiah and *Miranda* doctrines become intertwined when, prior to indictment, a suspect, who is represented by counsel, is questioned.

Technically, *Massiah* is not violated because there has been no indictment, but it can be argued that the Sixth Amendment rights have been violated. On the other hand, the fact that defendant has retained counsel should make his waiver under *Miranda* of his right to counsel much more persuasive, since he could secure the assistance of counsel with one phone call. Further, if he had the advice of counsel, his decision to waive his rights may be said to be more fully informed. People v. Smith, 42 Ill.2d 479, 248 N.E.2d 68 (1969); People v. McKie, 25 N.Y.2d 19, 302 N.Y.S.2d 534, 250 N.E.2d 36 (1969); State v. Adams, 76 Wash.2d 650, 458 P.2d 558 (1969); Commonwealth ex rel. Craig v. Maroney, 348 F.2d 22 (3rd Cir. 1965), rehearing denied 352 F.2d 30 (3rd Cir.) (en banc).

The majority rule in both pre and post *Miranda* cases is that a voluntary statement made by one who has retained counsel is admissible if he voluntarily elects to speak in the absence of that counsel or waives the right to have counsel present. These holdings are scattered with dissents. In a few cases the courts have alluded to canons of ethics to conclude that such practices are not favored. See Coughlan v. United States, 391 F.2d 371 (9th Cir. 1969); United States v. Fellabaum, 408 F.2d 220 (7th Cir. 1969) (post-*Miranda*); Reinke v. United States, 405 F.2d 228 (9th Cir. 1969) (defendant initiated conversation); Wilson v. United States, 398 F.2d 331 (5th Cir. 1968); United States v. Springer, 460 F.2d 1344 (7th Cir. 1972) (limited to certain circumstances); Taylor v. State, 282 Ala. 567, 213 So.2d 566 (1968); State v. Sample, 107 Ariz. 407, 489 P.2d 44 (1971); Jordan v. People, 161 Colo. 54, 419 P.2d 656 (1966); Commonwealth v. Kleciak, 350 Mass. 679, 216 N.E.2d 417 (1966); State v. Renfrew, 280 Minn. 276, 159 N.W.2d 111 (1968); State v. Graham, 59 N.J. 366, 283 A.2d 321 (1972); State v. Lopez, 80 N.M. 130, 452 P.2d 199 (1969); State v. Temple, 269 N.C. 57, 152 S.E.2d 206 (1967); State v. Fields, 184 Neb. 565, 169 N.W.2d 437 (1969); State v. Morris, 248 Or. 480, 435 P.2d 1018 (1967) (defendant expressed desire not to have counsel); Commonwealth v. Dickerson, 428 Pa. 564, 237 A.2d 229 (1968); Callands v. Commonwealth, 208 Va. 340, 157 S.E.2d 198 (1967); Sabatini v. State, 14 Md.App. 431, 287 A.2d 511 (1972); State v. Moore, 189 Neb. 354, 202 N.W.2d 740 (1972); State v. Adams, 76 Wash.2d 650, 458 P.2d 558 (1969) (en banc).

Other jurisdictions have banned such interrogation outright, or, at least, when it is initiated by police. People v. Vella, 21 N.Y.2d 249, 287 N.Y.S.2d 369, 234 N.E.2d 422 (1967); People v. Arthur, 22 N.Y.2d 325, 292 N.Y.S.2d 663, 239 N.E.2d 537 (1968); United States v. Thomas, 475 F.2d 115 (10th Cir. 1973) (must notify counsel); State v. Witt, 422 S.W.2d 304 (Mo.1967) (relying on *Massiah*); People v. Randall, 1 Cal.3d 948, 83 Cal. Rptr. 658, 464 P.2d 114 (1970); Hart v. State, 484 P.2d 1334 (Okla.1971); Constantine v. People, 495 P.2d 208 (Colo.1972) (one ground for exclusion).

The language of the *Miranda* opinion implies that the majority rule is the correct one; it refers to a defendant who "has consulted with an attorney and thereafter consents to be questioned" 384 U.S. at 474. But this is an implication, not a holding.

The minority of jurisdictions recognize several exceptions to their rule.

In People v. McKie, 25 N.Y.2d 19, 302 N.Y.S.2d 534, 250 N.E.2d 36 (1969), a defendant, represented by counsel, was followed by police. The defendant then approached the police and initiated an argument during which he made a damaging admission. The court held there was no custody, that the defendant was aware of his rights and initiated the conversation. The conversation is interesting: After the initial foray the defendant said, "You can be killed, too." The officers replied, "You're not dealing with any little old lady now; you weren't so brave when you killed that little old lady". The defendant said, "Sure I did, but you guys can't prove it".

Where defense counsel has instructed the police not to question his client or asks to be present during interrogation or instructs the police to notify him if they want to question his client, it is doubtful that any Court could allow in evidence statements taken when these instructions of defense counsel were ignored. See United States v. Wiedra, 343 F.Supp. 1183 (S.D.N.Y.1972); People v. Baker, 23 N.Y.2d 307, 296 N.Y.S.2d 745, 244 N.E.2d 232 (1968); Commonwealth v. McKenna, 355 Mass. 313, 244 N.E.2d 560 (1969); Holt v. State, 202 Kan. 759, 451 P.2d 221 (1969). But see United States v. Moriarity, 375 F.2d 901 (7th Cir. 1967).

(c) MIRANDA AND THE DERIVATIVE EVIDENCE RULE

When a statement taken in violation of *Miranda* leads to other incriminating evidence does the fruit of the poisoned tree doctrine operate to exclude this derivative evidence?

As previously noted (at p. 962), the Supreme Court of the United States, in the June 10, 1974 decision of Michigan v. Tucker, held that the prosecution properly used as a witness an individual whose name had been given to the police by the defendant (for false alibi purposes), even though he had not received the full Miranda warnings. The omitted warning was with reference to the right of appointed counsel if he could not afford one.

In the *Tucker* case the trial court had excluded the use of the defendant's confession; all that was allowed was the derivative use of the witness' identity and his testimony. Consequently, the Supreme Court's decision is not subject to the interpretation that *Miranda* has been abandoned. The Court has yet to face that broader issue.

The derivative use problem is somewhat different than in *Tucker* when the case situation involves a second statement taken in adherence to *Miranda* but taken after the suspect gave a first statement without warnings. The Court in *Miranda* recognized that the taint of the first statement in one of the cases (Westover) might be deemed removed if the second statement were given at a time and place remote from the time and place of original statement. Ultimately, the issue will be resolved on the facts of each individual case.

Compare United States ex rel. B. v. Shelly, 430 F.2d 215 (2nd Cir. 1970) (also relying on youth and inexperience of the suspect), and State v. Dickson, 82 N.M. 408, 482 P.2d 916 (1971) (illegality of second confession presumed unless clearly rebutted), with People v. Young, 131 Ill.App.2d 113, 266 N.E.2d 160 (1970) (removed in time and place, warned twice and questioned by an officer who did not know of the first confession); Klamant v. Cupp, 437 F.2d 1153 (9th Cir. 1970) (Second statement volunteered); Williams v. Commonwealth, 211 Va. 609, 179 S.E.2d 512 (1971) (Second statement made in response to stepmother's question). In United States v. Trabucco, 424 F.2d 1311 (5th Cir. 1970) it was held that when an initial inadmissible statement is exculpatory the "cat has not been let out of the bag" and there is little compulsion to give a second statement admitting the crime. The court also held that being caught in a lie in the first statement is not a sufficient cause to believe the second statement flowed from the first inadmissible one.

The final question arising when *Miranda* is considered in relation to the fruit of the poisoned tree doctrine is whether the giving of *Miranda* warnings operates to dissipate the taint of some earlier illegality. Most opinions have dealt with confessions secured after illegal arrest. See Note, 61 J.Crim.L.C. & P.S. 207 (1970). One court has held that such a confession is inadmissible and the giving of warnings does not break the taint. See People v. Young, 35 App.Div.2d 1061, 316 N.Y.S.2d 379 (1970). However, most courts will not rule that an illegal arrest destroys the admissibility of a statement that is taken in compliance with *Miranda*. See Mulligan v. State, 10 Md.App. 429, 271 A.2d 385 (1971); State v. Newell, 462 S.W.2d 794 (Mo.1971) (illegal arrest-three day interval and warnings eliminate taint); People v. Zakrzewski, 36 App.Div.2d 646, 318 N.Y.S.2d 94 (1971) (illegal arrest-warnings help to eliminate taint); State v. Hooper, 25 Ohio St.2d 59, 267 N.E.2d 285 (1971) (*Miranda* warnings eliminate taint of unlawful arrest).

(d) MIRANDA AND PRIVATE CITIZEN INTERROGATIONS

It is invariably held that a suspect who makes damaging admissions in response to interrogation by private citizens need not have been warned of his rights. The cases are United States v. Thomas, 396 F.2d 310 (2nd Cir. 1968) (railroad detectives); Yates v. United States, 384 F.2d 586 (5th Cir. 1967) (hotel clerks); Truex v. State, 282 Ala. 191, 210 So.2d 424 (1968) (neighbor); Soolook v. State, 447 P.2d (Alaska 1968) (parents); State v. Lombardo, 104 Ariz. 598, 457 P.2d 275 (1969); State v. Fisk, 92 Idaho 675, 448 P.2d 768 (1968) (wife and daughter of victim); Edington v. State, 243 Ark. 10, 418 S.W.2d 637 (1967) (paramour); Edwards v. State, 244 Ark. 1145, 429 S.W.2d 92 (1968) (doctor); People v. Petker, 254 Cal.App.2d 652, 62 Cal.Rptr. 215 (1967) (parents); People v. Cheatham, 263 Cal.App.2d 458, 69 Cal.Rptr. 679 (1968) (tenant in burglarized house); People v. Amata, 270 Cal.App.2d 575, 75 Cal.Rptr. 860 (1969) (private investigator); Holston v. State, 208 So.2d 100 (Fla.1968) (cellmate); Franklin v. State, 114 Ga.App. 304, 151 S.E.2d 191 (1967) (private investigator); People v. Morehead, 45 Ill.2d 326, 259 N.E.2d 8 (1970); People v. Shipp, 96 Ill.App.2d 364, 239 N.E.2d 296 (1968) (school principal); Lipps v. State, 254 Ind. 141, 258 N.E.2d 622 (1970) (newspaper reporter that suspect asked to see); State v. Master, 154 N.W.2d 133 (Iowa 1967) (storemanager); State v. Little, 201 Kan. 94, 439 P.2d 387 (1968) (store proprietor); Peek v. Commonwealth, 415 S.W.2d 854 (Ky.1967) (bail bondsman); State v. Kemp, 251 La. 592, 205 So.2d 411 (1967) (armed group of citizens); Hubbard v. State, 2 Md.App. 364, 234 A.2d 775 (1967) (pharmacists); State v. Watson, 28 Ohio St.2d 15, 275 N.E.2d 153 (1971) (reporter); United States v. Wilkerson, 460 F.2d 725 (5th Cir. 1972) (persons without power to arrest); McElroy v. State, 204 So.2d 463 (Miss.1967) (victim); Schaumberg v. State, 83 Nev. 372, 432 P.2d 500 (1967) (security officers); Skinner v. State, 83 Nev. 380, 432 P.2d 675 (1967) (suspect's friends); Gallegos v. State, 84 Nev. 608, 446 P.2d 656 (1968) (suspect's niece coming to the station at his request); People v. Lee, 33 App.Div.2d 397, 308 N.Y.S.2d 412 (1970) (victim); State v. Valpredo, 75 Wash.2d 368, 450 P.2d 979 (1969) (victim); United States v. Antonel, 434 F.2d 335 (2nd Cir. 1970) (gateman employed by private detective agency); Mulligan v. State, 10 Md.App. 429, 271 A.2d 385 (1970) (defendant's wife—in presence of law officers); People v. Morgan, 24 Mich.App. 660, 180 N.W.2d 842 (1970) (store security officer); State v. Archuleta, 82 N.M. 378, 482 P.2d 242 (1970) (insurance company investigators).

In dealing with private citizen cases, the courts have kept to a precise technical definition of the interrogator's status. In Pratt v. State, 9 Md. App. 220, 263 A.2d 247 (1970) it was held that a private security guard who had been commissioned as a special officer by the Governor was required to give *Miranda* warnings. The same result was reached in a state where parole officers have statutory police powers, State v. Lekas, 201 Kan. 579, 442 P.2d 11 (1968). The mere fact that the private citizen is employed by the state does not require him to give *Miranda* warnings. People v. Wright, 249 Cal.App.2d 692, 57 Cal.Rptr. 781 (1967). The reliance upon the technical status of the interrogator also requires the holding that *Miranda* is inapplicable even if a private citizen falsely represents himself to be a law officer when he questions a suspect. See People v. Vlcek, 114 Ill. App.2d 74, 252 N.E.2d 377 (1969).

These generally recognized rules are subject to one universally recognized qualification. That is, the police are forbidden to use private citizens or foreign officers as their agents in order to escape the *Miranda* rule. Nearly every case cited for the proposition that private citizens are not governed by *Miranda* also states that the police may not use the private citizen as an agent. There are cases illustrative of the agency concept.

In State v. Kelly, 439 S.W.2d 487 (Mo.1969) the Court found that while *Miranda* generally was inapplicable to private witnesses it did apply in a case where the defendant was in police custody and has indicated his desire to remain silent. The defendant was in a room with the interrogating officer and the victim. The officer did not question him further but the victim did and soon after the officer joined in the interrogation. The court held that the victim's interrogation was merely a continuation of the police interrogation. In Commonwealth v. Bordner, 432 Pa. 405, 247 A.2d 612 (1968) it was held that the police used the suspect's parents as their agents. Where the suspect asked to speak to the victim and the victim agreed if the suspect were behind bars and the conversation taped, the victim was not a police agent where no questions were suggested by police. People v. Holzer, 25 Cal.App.3d 456, 102 Cal.Rptr. 11 (1972).

(e) MIRANDA AND THE SUSPECT WHO DOES NOT NEED THE WARNINGS

In one apparent pre-*Miranda* case a defendant complained about lack of warnings at his interrogation. The court brushed his complaint aside because the defendant was a judge. Commonwealth v. Schwartz, 210 Pa.Super. 360, 233 A.2d 904 (1967). What of the defendant who is a lawyer or a policeman? The *Miranda* opinion was very clear on this point:

> "We will not pause to inquire in individual cases whether the defendant was aware of his rights without a warning" (on the basis of his education, intelligence and experience); "a warning is a clearcut fact" . . . "More important, whatever the background of the person interrogated, a warning at the time of interrogation is indispensible to overcome its pressures and to insure that the individual knows he is free to exercise his privilege at that point in time".

In Dupont v. United States, 259 A.2d 355 (D.C.1969) a defendant was about to be warned when he said, "I know my rights". The court held that his statement was taken in violation of *Miranda*. When the suspect states that he knows his rights the officer should insist on continuing the warn-by the state does not require him to give *Miranda* warnings. People v. Wright, 249 Cal.App.2d 692, 57 Cal.Rptr. 781 (1967). The reliance upon the technical status of the interrogator also requires the holding that *Miranda* is inapplicable even if a private citizen falsely represents himself to be a law officer when he questions a suspect. See People v. Vlcek, 114 Ill. App.2d 74, 252 N.E.2d 377 (1969).

These generally recognized rules are subject to one universally recognized qualification. That is, the police are forbidden to use private citizens or foreign officers as their agents in order to escape the *Miranda* rule. Nearly every case cited for the proposition that private citizens are not governed by *Miranda* also states that the police may not use the private citizen as an agent. There are cases illustrative of the agency concept.

In State v. Kelly, 439 S.W.2d 487 (Mo.1969) the Court found that while *Miranda* generally was inapplicable to private witnesses it did apply in a case where the defendant was in police custody and has indicated his desire to remain silent. The defendant was in a room with the interrogating officer and the victim. The officer did not question him further but the victim did and soon after the officer joined in the interrogation. The court held that the victim's interrogation was merely a continuation of the police interrogation. In Commonwealth v. Bordner, 432 Pa. 405, 247 A.2d 612 (1968) it was held that the police used the suspect's parents as their agents. Where the suspect asked to speak to the victim and the victim agreed if the suspect were behind bars and the conversation taped, the victim was not a police agent where no questions were suggested by police. People v. Holzer, 25 Cal.App.3d 456, 102 Cal.Rptr. 11 (1972).

(e) MIRANDA AND THE SUSPECT WHO DOES NOT NEED THE WARNINGS

In one apparent pre-*Miranda* case a defendant complained about lack of warnings at his interrogation. The court brushed his complaint aside because the defendant was a judge. Commonwealth v. Schwartz, 210 Pa.Super. 360, 233 A.2d 904 (1967). What of the defendant who is a lawyer or a policeman? The *Miranda* opinion was very clear on this point:

> "We will not pause to inquire in individual cases whether the defendant was aware of his rights without a warning" (on the basis of his education, intelligence and experience); "a warning is a clearcut fact" . . . "More important, whatever the background of the person interrogated, a warning at the time of interrogation is indispensible to overcome its pressures and to insure that the individual knows he is free to exercise his privilege at that point in time".

In Dupont v. United States, 259 A.2d 355 (D.C.1969) a defendant was about to be warned when he said, "I know my rights". The court held that his statement was taken in violation of *Miranda*. When the suspect states that he knows his rights the officer should insist on continuing the warnings. Brown v. Heyd, 277 F.Supp. 899 (D.La.1967); State v. Pressel, 2 Or.App. 477, 468 P.2d 915 (1970) (en banc). Contra, State v. Perez, 182 Neb. 680, 157 N.W.2d 162 (1968) (suspect refused to listen further). One reasonable deviation from the absolute rule is found in Kear v. United States, 369 F.2d 78 (9th Cir. 1966) where it was held unnecessary to warn a defendant of his right to remain silent when he said "I know I don't have to make a statement". In this case it is clear on the face of the record that the defendant knew specifically of his right to remain silent.

The prior criminal experience of the defendant can be used to help establish that the warnings given in the interrogation were understood because they had been given before in other cases. Jordan v. United States, 421 F.2d 493 (9th Cir. 1970); Thessen v. State, 454 P.2d 341 (Alaska 1969); State v. Collins, 74 Wash.2d 729, 446 P.2d 325 (1968). And prior experience may serve to support the validity of a waiver of rights, Heard v. State, 244 Ark. 44, 424 S.W.2d 179 (1968); State v. Miller, 35 Wis.2d 454, 151 N.W.2d 157 (1967).

A different problem is presented by the wealthy defendant. To warn him of his right to the services of a lawyer seems to be enough; the right is made no more meaningful to him if he is told that a lawyer will be appointed if he cannot afford one. For purposes of making a decision to waive his rights, it is enough for him to know he can see a lawyer before interrogation. In essence, the warning concerning appointed counsel is not itself a basic *Miranda* right; rather, it is a safety device designed to protect what is a basic *Miranda* right, the right to counsel. This conclusion is supported by implication in *Miranda*, 384 U.S. at 473 n. 43, 86 S.Ct. at 1627 (n. 43).

There have been various holdings to the effect that a non-indigent need not be warned of his right to appointed counsel. Some of these Courts have required the State to show non-indigency or require that it be apparent to the interrogators that the suspect is not indigent. Some Courts simply hold that if there is no claim of indigency then they will not presume that failure to warn of the right to appointed counsel is prejudicial. See United States v. Lubitsch, 266 F.Supp. 294 (S.D.N.Y.1967) (must be clear that suspect is not indigent); United States v. Messina, 388 F.2d 393 (2nd Cir. 1968) (same); State v. Bliss, 238 A.2d 848 (Del.1968) (there must be evidence of indigency); James v. State, 233 So.2d 52 (Fla.App.1969) (State must show it was aware of non-indigency at time of statement); Griffith v. State, 223 Ga. 543, 156 S.E.2d 903 (1967) (Defendant must contend he is indigent); Brown v. Commonwealth, 445 S.W.2d 845 (Ky.1969) (apparent to officers that defendant was not indigent); People v. Braun, 98 Ill.App. 2d 5, 241 N.E.2d 25 (1968) (where shown that suspect was not indigent); Commonwealth v. Wilbur, 353 Mass. 376, 231 N.E.2d 919 (1967) (apparent non-indigency); People v. Post, 23 N.Y.2d 157, 295 N.Y.S.2d 665, 242 N.E. 2d 830 (1968) (evidence must show indigency); State v. Gray, 268 N.C. 69, 150 S.E.2d 1 (1966) (apparent non-indigency); Commonwealth v. Yount, 435 Pa. 276, 256 A.2d 464 (1969) (police must know of suspect's non-indigency); State v. Gendreau, 106 R.I. 332, 259 A.2d 855 (1969) (State must prove non-indigency); Floyd v. State, 1 Tenn.Cr.App. 106, 430 S.W.2d 888 (1968) (indigency must be shown); McCandless v. State, 425 S.W.2d 636 (Tex.1968) (evidence must show indigency); Dickey v. State, 444 P.2d 373 (Wyo.1968) (officers knew of non-indigency); Stallings v. State, 255 Ind.

365, 264 N.E.2d 618 (1970) (no claim of indigency); State v. Crump, 277 N.C. 573, 178 S.E.2d 336 (1971) (record showed non-indigency); Mora v. People, 173 Colo. 552, 481 P.2d 729 (1971) (where record showed defendant told officers he had counsel).

* * *

"The presence of counsel . . . would be the adequate protective device necessary to make the process of police interrogation conform to the dictates of the privilege. . . . His presence would insure that statements made in the government-established atmosphere are not the product of compulsion." Miranda v. Arizona, 384 U.S. at 466, 86 S.Ct. at 1624.

The rule that statements made in the presence of counsel are admissible is also found in United States v. Jackson, 390 F.2d 317 (2nd Cir. 1968); United States v. Stribling, 437 F.2d 765 (6th Cir. 1971); United States v. Turzynski, 268 F.Supp. 847 (N.D.Ill.1967) (unless counsel is incompetent).

It is still the better practice to warn such suspects to avoid later disputes about the lawyer's competence or the fact of retention. See Commonwealth v. Leaming, 432 Pa. 326, 247 A.2d 590 (1968).

In analogous cases, it has been held that no warnings need be given where the attorney for the defendant contacted the police and said his client wished to make a statement. The court assumed that counsel knew of the interview and did not wish to be present. Dempsey v. State, 225 Ga. 208, 166 S.E.2d 884 (1969); Jones v. State, 47 Wis.2d 642, 178 N.W.2d 42 (1970). But see Commonwealth v. Goldsmith, 438 Pa. 83, 263 A.2d 322 (1970) (cannot assume suspect knew of his rights because he came to the station with a lawyer).

C. THE TEST OF INHERENT COERCION AND INVOLUNTARINESS

DAVIS v. NORTH CAROLINA

Supreme Court of the United States, 1966.
384 U.S. 737, 86 S.Ct. 1761.

Opinion of the Court by MR. CHIEF JUSTICE WARREN, announced by MR. JUSTICE BRENNAN.

Petitioner, Elmer Davis, Jr., was tried before a jury in the Superior Court of Mecklenburg County, North Carolina, on a charge of rape-murder. At trial, a written confession and testimony as to an oral confession were offered in evidence. Defense counsel objected on the ground that the confessions were involuntarily given. The trial judge heard testimony on this issue, ruled that the confessions were made voluntarily, and permitted them to be introduced in evidence. The jury returned a verdict of guilty without a recommendation for life imprisonment, and Davis was sentenced to death.

We are not called upon in this proceeding to pass on the guilt or innocence of the petitioner of the atrocious crime that was committed. Nor are we called upon to determine whether the confessions obtained are true or false. Rogers v. Richmond, 365 U.S. 534, 81 S.Ct. 735 (1961). The sole issue presented for review is whether the confessions were voluntarily given or were the result of overbearing by police authorities. Upon thorough review of the record, we have concluded that the confessions were not made freely and voluntarily but rather that Davis' will was overborne by the sustained pressures upon him. Therefore, the confessions are constitutionally inadmissible and the judgment of the court below must be reversed.

Had the trial in this case before us come after our decision in Miranda v. Arizona, we would reverse summarily. Davis was taken into custody by Charlotte police and interrogated repeatedly over a period of 16 days. There is no indication in the record that police advised him of any of his rights until after he had confessed orally on the 16th day.[1] This would be clearly improper under *Miranda.* Similarly, no waiver of rights could be inferred from this record since it shows only that Davis was repeatedly interrogated and that he denied the alleged offense prior to the time he finally confessed.

We have also held today, in Johnson v. New Jersey, 384 U.S. 719, 86 S.Ct. 1772, that our decision in *Miranda,* delineating procedures to safeguard the Fifth Amendment privilege against self-incrimination during in-custody interrogation is to be applied prospectively only. Thus the present case may not be reversed solely on the ground that warnings were not given and waiver not shown. As we pointed out in *Johnson,* however, the nonretroactivity of the decision in *Miranda* does not affect the duty of courts to consider claims that a statement was taken under circumstances which violate the standards of voluntariness which had begun to evolve long prior to our decision in *Miranda.*

The review of voluntariness in cases in which the trial was held prior to our decisions in *Escobedo* and *Miranda* is not limited in any manner by these decisions. On the contrary, that a defendant was not advised of his right to remain silent or of his right respecting counsel at the outset of interrogation, as is now required by *Miranda,* is a significant factor in considering the voluntariness of statements later made. Thus, the fact that Davis was never effectively advised of his rights gives added weight to the other circumstances described below which made his confessions involuntary.

As is almost invariably so in cases involving confessions obtained through unobserved police interrogation, there is a conflict in the testimony as to the events surrounding the interrogations. Davis alleged

1. The written confession which Davis subsequently signed contained a notation that he was advised he did not have to make a statement and that any statement made could be used for or against him in court. A police officer testified at trial that he told Davis if the statement was not the truth he did not have to sign it.

that he was beaten, threatened, and cursed by police and that he was told he would get a hot bath and something to eat as soon as he signed a statement. This was flatly denied by each officer who testified. Davis further stated that he had repeatedly asked for a lawyer and that police refused to allow him to obtain one. This was also denied. Davis' sister testified at the habeas corpus hearing that she twice came to the police station and asked to see him, but that each time police officers told her Davis was not having visitors. Police officers testified that, on the contrary, upon learning of Davis' desire to see his sister, they went to her home to tell her Davis wanted to see her, but she informed them she was busy with her children. These factual allegations were resolved against Davis by the District Court and we need not review these specific findings here.

. . . Wholly apart from the disputed facts, a statement of the case from facts established in the record, in our view, leads plainly to the conclusion that the confessions were the product of a will overborne.

Elmer Davis is an impoverished Negro with a third or fourth grade education. His level of intelligence is such that it prompted the comment by the court below, even while deciding against him on his claim of involuntariness, that there is a moral question whether a person of Davis' mentality should be executed. Police first came in contact with Davis while he was a child when his mother murdered his father, and thereafter knew him through his long criminal record, beginning with a prison term he served at the age of 15 or 16.

In September 1959, Davis escaped from a state prison camp near Asheville, North Carolina, where he was serving sentences of 17 to 25 years. On September 20, 1959, Mrs. Foy Belle Cooper was raped and murdered in the Elmwood Cemetery in the City of Charlotte, North Carolina. On September 21, police in a neighboring county arrested Davis in Belmont, 12 miles from Charlotte. He was wearing civilian clothes and had in his possession women's undergarments and a billfold with identification papers of one Bishel Buren Hayes. Hayes testified at trial that his billfold and shoes had been taken from him while he lay in a drunken sleep near the Elmwood Cemetery on September 20.

Charlotte police learned of Davis' arrest and contacted the warden of the state prison to get permission to take Davis into their custody in connection with the Cooper murder and other felonies. Having obtained permission, they took Davis from Belmont authorities and brought him to the detective headquarters in Charlotte. From the testimony of the officers, it is beyond dispute that the reason for securing Davis was their suspicion that he had committed the murder.

The second and third floors of the detective headquarters building contain lockup cells used for detention overnight and occasionally for slightly longer periods. It has no kitchen facilities for preparing meals. The cell in which Davis was placed measures 6 by 10 feet and contains a solid steel bunk with mattress, a drinking fountain, and a commode. It is located on the inside of the building with no view of daylight. It is ventilated by two exhaust fans located in the ceiling of the top floor of the building. Despite the fact that a county jail equipped and used for lengthy detention is located directly across the street from detective headquarters, Davis was incarcerated in this cell on an upper floor of the building for the entire period until he confessed. Police Chief Jesse James testified: "I don't know anybody who has stayed in the city jail as long as this boy."

When Davis arrived at the detective headquarters, an arrest sheet was prepared giving various statistics concerning him. On this arrest sheet was typed the following illuminating directive: *Hold for Hucks & Fesperman re-Mrs. Cooper. Escapee from Haywood County still has 15 years to pull. Do not allow anyone to see Davis. Or allow him to use telephone.*" Both at trial and at the habeas corpus hearing the testimony of police officers on this notation was nearly uniform. Each officer testified that he did not put that directive on the arrest sheet, that he did not know who did, and that he never knew of it. The police captain first testified at trial that there had never been an order issued in the police department that Davis was not to see or talk to anybody. He cited as an example the fact that Davis' sister came to see him (after Davis had confessed). He testified later in the trial, however:

> "I don't know, it is possible I could have ordered this boy to be held without privilege of communicating with his friends, relatives and held without the privilege of using the telephone or without the privilege of talking to anybody. . . . No, I did not want him to talk to anybody. For the simple reason he was an escaped convict and it is the rules and regulations of the penal system that if he is a C grade prisoner he is not permitted to see anyone alone or write anyone letters and I was trying to conform to the state regulations." [2]

The District Court found as a fact that from September 21 until after he confessed on October 6, neither friend nor relative saw Davis. It concluded, however, that Davis was not held incommunicado because he would have been permitted visitors had anyone requested to see

2. Transcript of Evidence on Appeal. His testimony at the habeas corpus hearing was very similar. He first stated somewhat confusingly:

"Inasmuch as he was an escaped convict, I would have asked them what was the purpose of placing this do not allow anyone to see Davis or allow him to use the telephone. To be perfectly honest with you, why put it in writing when you can do the same thing verbally. I mean there is no question about it. The question is that each individual is allowed due process of law. And if they had been asked in any way or if I had been asked for anyone to see Elmer, they would have been given permission. Nobody asked to my knowledge."

He later testified:

"I didn't want anybody to talk to him without me knowing it as he was a prisoner of the State of North Carolina, and he was a C grade prisoner and not entitled to visitors without the permission of the warden."

him. In so finding, the District Court noted specifically the testimony that police officers contacted Davis' sister for him. But the court made no mention whatever of the notation on the arrest sheet or the testimony of the police captain.

The stark wording of the arrest sheet directive remains, as does Captain McCall's testimony. The denials and evasive testimony of the other officers cannot wipe this evidence from the record. Even accepting that police would have allowed a person to see Davis had anyone actually come, the directive stands unassailably as an indicium of the purpose of the police in holding Davis. As the dissenting judges below stated: "The instruction not to permit anyone access to Davis and not to allow him to communicate with the outside world can mean only that it was the determination of his custodians to keep him under absolute control where they could subject him to questioning at will in the manner and to the extent they saw fit, until he would confess." 339 F.2d, at 780. Moreover, the uncontested fact that *no one* other than the police spoke to Davis during the 16 days of detention and interrogation that preceded his confessions is significant in the determination of voluntariness.

During the time Davis was held by Charlotte police, he was fed two sandwiches, described by one officer as "thin" and "dry," twice a day. This fare was occasionally supplemented with peanuts and other "stuff" such as cigarettes brought to him by a police officer.[3] The District Court found that the food was the same served prisoners held overnight in the detention jail and that there was no attempt by police to weaken Davis by inadequate feeding. The State contends that "two sandwiches twice a day supplemented by peanuts 'and other stuff' was not such a poor diet, for an idle person doing no work, as to constitute a violation of due process of law."

We may readily agree that the record does not show any deliberate attempt to starve Davis, and that his diet was not below a minimum necessary to sustain him. Nonetheless, the diet was extremely limited and may well have had a significant effect on Davis' physical strength and therefore his ability to resist. There is evidence in the record, not rebutted by the State, that Davis lost 15 pounds during the period of detention.

From the time Davis was first brought to the overnight lockup in Charlotte on September 21, 1959, until he confessed on the 16th day of detention, police officers conducted daily interrogation sessions with him in a special interrogation room in the building.[4] These sessions each lasted "forty-five minutes or an hour or maybe a little more," according to one of the interrogating officers. Captain McCall testified that he had assigned his entire force of 26 to 29 men to investigate the case. From this group, Detectives Hucks and Fesperman

3. During the 16-day period, this diet varied only for two meals on the day he was taken to Asheville and on one other occasion when an officer brought him two hamburgers.

4. As the Police Chief explained: "An interrogation room should be void of all materials so that you can talk to a man in complete quiet and keep his attention."

had primary responsibility for interrogating Davis. These officers testified to interrogating him once or twice each day throughout the 16 days. Three other officers testified that they conducted several interrogation sessions at the request of Hucks and Fesperman. Although the officers denied that Davis was interrogated at night, one testified that the interrogation periods he directed were held some time prior to 11 p. m. Captain McCall also interrogated Davis once.

According to each of the officers, no mention of the Cooper murder was made in any of the interrogations between September 21 and October 3. Between these dates they interrogated Davis extensively with respect to the stolen goods in his possession. It is clear from the record, however, that these interrogations were directly related to the murder and were not simply questioning as to unrelated felonies. The express purpose of this line of questioning was to break down Davis' alibis as to where he had obtained the articles. By destroying Davis' contention that he had taken the items from homes some distance from Charlotte, Davis could be placed at the scene of the crime.

In order to put pressure on Davis with respect to these alibis, police took him from the lockup on October 1 to have him point out where he had stolen the goods. Davis had told the officers that he took the items from houses along the railroad line between Canton and Asheville. To disprove this story, Davis was aroused at 5 a. m. and driven to Canton. There his leg shackles were removed and he walked on the railroad tracks, handcuffed to an officer, 14 miles to Asheville. When Davis was unable to recognize any landmark along the way or any house that he had burglarized, an officer confronted him with the accusation that his story was a lie. The State points out that Davis was well fed on this day, that he agreed to make the hike, and contends that it was not so physically exhausting as to be coercive. The coercive influence was not, however, simply the physical exertion of the march, but also the avowed purpose of that trek—to break down his alibis to the crime of murder.

On the afternoon of October 3, two officers planned and carried out a ruse to attempt to get Davis to incriminate himself in some manner. They engaged Davis in idle conversation for 10 to 20 minutes and then inquired whether he would like to go out for "some fresh air." They then took Davis from the jail and drove him into the cemetery to the scene of the crime in order to observe his reaction.

The purpose of these excursions and of all of the interrogation sessions was known to Davis. On the day of the drive to the cemetery, the interrogators shifted tactics and began questioning Davis specifically about the matter. They asked him if he knew why he was being held. He stated that he believed it was with respect to the Cooper murder. Police then pressed him, asking, "Well, did you do it?" He denied it. The interrogation sessions continued through the next two days. Davis consistently denied any knowledge of the crime.

On October 6, Detectives Hucks and Fesperman interrogated Davis for the final time. Lieutenant Sykes, who had known Davis' family, but who had not taken part in any of the prior interrogation sessions because he had been away on vacation, asked to sit in. During this interrogation, after repeated earlier denials of guilt, Davis refused to answer questions concerning the crime. At about 12:45 p. m., Lieutenant Sykes inquired of Davis if he would like to talk to any of the officers alone about Mrs. Cooper. Davis said he would like to talk to Sykes. The others left the room. Lieutenant Sykes then asked Davis if he had been reading a testament which he was holding. Davis replied that he had. Sykes asked Davis if he had been praying. Davis replied that he did not know how to pray and agreed he would like Sykes to pray for him. The lieutenant offered a short prayer. At that point, as the dissent below aptly put it, the prayers of the police officer were answered—Davis confessed. He was driven to the cemetery and asked to re-enact the crime. Police then brought him back to the station where he repeated the confession to several of the officers. In the presence of six officers, a two-page statement of the confession Davis had made was transcribed. Although based on the information Davis had given earlier, Captain McCall dictated this statement employing his own choice of format, wording, and content. He paused periodically to ask Davis if he agreed with the statement so far. Each time Davis acquiesced. Davis signed the statement.[5] Captain McCall then contacted the press and stated, "He finally broke down today."

The concluding paragraphs of this confession, dictated by the police, contain, along with the standard disclaimer that the confession was free and voluntary, a statement that unwittingly summarizes the coercive effect on Davis of the prolonged period of detention and interrogation. They read:

> "In closing, I want to say this. I have known in my own mind that [*sic*] you people were holding me for, and all the time I have been lying in jail, it has been worrying me, and I knew that sooner or later, I would have to tell you about it.
>
> "I have made this statement freely and voluntarily. Captain McCall has dictated this statement in the presence of Detectives W. F. Hucks, E. F. Fesperman, H. C. Gardner, C. E. Davis, and Detective Lieutenant C. L. Sykes. I am glad it is over, because I have been going thru a big strain."

The facts established on the record demonstrate that Davis went through a prolonged period in which substantial coercive influences

5. After Davis signed the written confession, Police Chief Jesse James appeared to question Davis about his treatment. In response to this questioning, Davis stated that he had been treated all right. The following morning, a minister who knew Davis' family and had read of his arrest 16 days earlier in the newspaper, appeared to talk to Davis. He testified that Davis told him his treatment had been very fine and that everyone had been courteous and kind to him. The minister indicated further that he often cooperated with police in such matters.

were brought to bear upon him to extort the confessions that marked the culmination of police efforts. Evidence of extended interrogation in such a coercive atmosphere has often resulted in a finding of involuntariness by this Court. We have never sustained the use of a confession obtained after such a lengthy period of detention and interrogation as was involved in this case.

The fact that each individual interrogation session was of relatively short duration does not mitigate the substantial coercive effect created by repeated interrogation in these surroundings over 16 days. So far as Davis could have known, the interrogation in the overnight lockup might still be going on today had he not confessed. Moreover, as we have noted above, the fact that police did not directly accuse him of the crime until after a substantial period of eroding his will to resist by a tangential line of interrogation did not reduce the coercive influence brought to bear upon him. Similarly, it is irrelevant to the consideration of voluntariness that Davis was an escapee from a prison camp. Of course Davis was not entitled to be released. But this does not alleviate the coercive effect of his extended detention and repeated interrogation while isolated from everyone but the police in the police jail.

In light of all of the factors discussed above, the conclusion is inevitable—Davis' confessions were the involuntary end product of coercive influences and are thus constitutionally inadmissible in evidence. Accordingly, the judgment of the Court of Appeals for the Fourth Circuit must be reversed and the case remanded to the District Court. On remand, the District Court should enter such orders as are appropriate and consistent with this opinion, allowing the State a reasonable time in which to retry petitioner.

Reversed and remanded.

MR. JUSTICE BLACK concurs in the result.

MR. JUSTICE CLARK, with whom MR. JUSTICE HARLAN joins, dissenting.

The rationale of the Court's opinion is that Davis, "an impoverished Negro with a third or fourth grade education," was overborne when he gave his confession to the rape-murder.

Davis, a 39-year-old man, admits that he has "been in a lot of jails." The record indicates that his intelligence was far above that of a fourth grader. His own testimony at his trial reveals a highly retentive memory. He described in detail his numerous arrests, convictions, prison sentences, and escapes over a 15-year span. Furthermore, during the federal habeas corpus hearing Davis showed his awareness of legal technicalities. At one point the prosecutor sought to cross-examine Davis as to whether he had "been tried and convicted of various offenses." Despite the fact that there was no objection to the question by his lawyer, Davis turned to the judge and said: "Your Honor, do I have to answer that question? This is in the past."

After some argument about the admissibility of the evidence, the judge recessed the hearing for 10 minutes to give counsel an opportunity to present legal authority. Davis' objection was thereafter sustained.

This case goes against the grain of our prior decisions. The Court first confesses that the rule adopted under the Fifth Amendment in Miranda v. Arizona, that an accused must be effectively advised of his right to counsel before custodial interrogation, is not retroactive and therefore does not apply to this case. However, it obtains the same result by reading the Due Process Clause as requiring that heavy weight must be given the failure of the State to afford counsel during interrogation as "a significant factor in considering the voluntariness of statements." Through this change of pace Davis' guilty handwriting is stamped a forgery and his conviction is reversed.

I have found no case dealing with lengthy detention by state officers which supports reversal here. The Court cites three: all of which were treated in terms of due process. But these cases are clearly distinguishable on their facts with respect to the character of the accused and the circumstances under which interrogation took place. [In one (*Culombe*), the defendant] was a "mental defective of the moron class" who had twice been in state mental institutions. He had no previous criminal record. [In another (*Fikes*), the defendant] was "a schizophrenic and highly suggestible." He had only one prior conviction—for burglary. The interrogation of both these men was more concentrated than that of Davis. [In the third, (*Turner*), the defendant] was subjected to continual interrogation by a relay of officers, falsely told that others had implicated him, and not permitted to see his family or friends. The prosecutor admitted that his arraignment was delayed, in violation of a state statute, until the police could secure a confession. Turner had no prior criminal record.

On the other hand, Davis had a long criminal record. At the time of his arrest he was an escapee from state prison, and so could be properly held in custody. It is therefore wrong to compare police conduct here to the detention of an ordinary suspect until he confesses. Moreover, the sporadic interrogation of Davis can hardly be denominated as sustained or overbearing pressure. From the record it appears that he was simply questioned for about an hour each day by a couple of detectives. There was no protracted grilling. Nor did the police officers operate in relays.

The Court makes much of an "arrest sheet" which informed the jailer that Davis was being held in connection with the murder of Mrs. Cooper and that he was an escaped convict. This sheet further directed: "Do not allow anyone to see Davis. Or allow him to use telephone." No witness was able to identify the author of this notation. It is true Captain McCall said that he "might" have done it. But he said that, even so, it was merely a notice to the jailer that Davis was an escapee and, therefore, not permitted to see or talk to anyone.

On the contrary, however, the record shows that Davis was not held incommunicado. Upon his request, the police located his sister the second day after his arrest, informed her that Davis was in custody, and on two separate occasions invited her to visit him. The officers first called on his sister for the sole purpose of telling her that Davis wished to see her. A few days later they also asked whether she was missing any of the clothes which were found on Davis. He made no request to see anyone else. Moreover, it is undenied that visitors from churches and schools entered the jail with scripture pamphlets. And Davis had one of these booklets in his hands the day of his confession.

Witnesses testified that Davis had told them that his treatment was "very fine and that everybody was courteous and kind to him." As for the hike of some 14 miles along the railroad tracks, Davis described the purpose of it clearly:

> "Well, we had some clothes and things, what I took up there, and we wanted to go up there and get it straightened out; but the place where I took the stuff I couldn't locate the place because it was at night, you understand, when I took the clothes and things off the line."

As to the "prayer" of Lieutenant Sykes, there is no testimony whatever that it was in any way "coercive." Indeed, one witness, Davis' preacher, quoted him as saying "that he had nothing but praise for Lieutenant Sykes, especially in the way in which he dealt with him." At another point the parson testified: "Elmer told me that he appreciated the prayer of Lieutenant Sykes." The Court disregards the fact that Davis had a copy of the scriptures in his hands when Sykes came into the room and continued to hold them as they talked. After Sykes—a lay preacher—noticed the testament, it was only natural that the conversation would turn to the scriptures and prayer. Sykes asked if Davis wished him to give a prayer. Davis said that he did, and Sykes prayed with him. The prayer was entirely unsuggestive.

It is said also that the food was not sufficient. But the uncontradicted evidence is that Davis never complained about the meals he received while in custody.* Davis testified that he lost 15 pounds in jail. But this does not warrant a finding that he was improperly fed. No one could contradict or substantiate this contention because the record does not show that his weight was taken upon arrest. And Davis was found to be untruthful in most of his testimony. Indeed, Davis did not paint his treatment with a black brush until his habeas corpus hearing, although he testified at length at his trial in the state court.

Under these circumstances, it appears to me that the trial judge's findings cannot be found to be clearly erroneous. To the contrary, they are fully supported by the entire record. I would affirm.

* On the morning that Davis left the jail to walk along the railroad tracks, a police officer asked him "if he was hungry," and his natural reply at that time of day was "yes." The officer then gave Davis breakfast.

NOTE

In connection with the standards of Voluntariness, consider the decision in Garrity v. New Jersey in Chapter 14.

D. PERMISSIBLE INTERROGATION TACTICS AND TECHNIQUES

FRAZIER v. CUPP

Supreme Court of the United States, 1969.
394 U.S. 731, 89 S.Ct. 1420.

MR. JUSTICE MARSHALL delivered the opinion of the Court.

* * *

I.

Petitioner's first argument centers on certain allegedly prejudicial remarks made during the prosecutor's opening statement. [The Court held that there was no error with regard to this issue.]

II.

Petitioner's second argument concerns the admission into evidence of his own confession. The circumstances under which the confession was obtained can be summarized briefly. Petitioner was arrested about 4:15 p. m. on September 24, 1964. He was taken to headquarters where questioning began at about 5 p. m. The interrogation, which was tape-recorded, ended slightly more than an hour later, and by 6:45 p. m. petitioner had signed a written version of his confession.

After the questioning had begun and after a few routine facts were ascertained, petitioner was questioned briefly about the location of his Marine uniform. He was next asked where he was on the night in question. Although he admitted that he was with his cousin Rawls, he denied being with any third person. Then petitioner was given a somewhat abbreviated description of his constitutional rights. He was told that he could have an attorney if he wanted one and that anything he said could be used against him at trial. Questioning thereafter became somewhat more vigorous, but petitioner continued to deny being with anyone but Rawls. At this point, the officer questioning petitioner told him, falsely, that Rawls had been brought in and that he had confessed. Petitioner still was reluctant to talk, but after the officer sympathetically suggested that the victim had started a fight by making homosexual advances, petitioner began to spill out his story. Shortly after he began he again showed signs of reluctance and said, "I think I had better get a lawyer before I talk any more. I am going to get into trouble more than I am in now." The officer replied simply, "You can't be in any more trouble than you are in now," and the questioning session proceeded. A full confession was obtained and, after further warnings, a written version was signed.

Since petitioner was tried after this Court's decision in Escobedo v. Illinois (1964), but before the decision in Miranda v. Arizona (1966), only the rule of the former case is directly applicable. Johnson v. New Jersey (1966). Petitioner argues that his statement about getting a lawyer was sufficient to bring *Escobedo* into play and that the police should immediately have stopped the questioning and obtained counsel for him. We might agree were *Miranda* applicable to this case, for in *Miranda* this Court held that "[i]f . . . [a suspect] indicates in any manner and at any stage of the process that he wishes to consult with an attorney before speaking there can be no questioning." But *Miranda* does not apply to this case. This Court in Johnson v. New Jersey pointedly rejected the contention that the specific commands of *Miranda* should apply to all post-*Escobedo* cases. The Court recognized "[t]he disagreements among other courts concerning the implications of *Escobedo*," and concluded that the States, although free to apply *Miranda* to post-*Escobedo* cases were not required to do so. The Oregon Supreme Court, in affirming petitioner's conviction, concluded that the confession was properly introduced into evidence. Under *Johnson*, we would be free to disagree with this conclusion only if we felt compelled to do so by the specific holding of *Escobedo*.

We do not believe that *Escobedo* covers this case. Petitioner's statement about seeing an attorney was neither as clear nor as unambiguous as the request Escobedo made. The police in *Escobedo* were unmistakably informed of their suspect's wishes; in fact Escobedo's attorney was present and repeatedly requested permission to see his client. Here, on the other hand, it is possible that the questioning officer took petitioner's remark not as a request that the interrogation cease but merely as a passing comment. Petitioner did not pursue the matter, but continued answering questions. In this context, we cannot find the denial of the right to counsel which was found so crucial in *Escobedo*.

Petitioner also presses the alternative argument that his confession was involuntary and that it should have been excluded for that reason. The trial judge, after an evidentiary hearing during which the tape recording was played, could not agree with this contention, and our reading of the record does not lead us to a contrary conclusion. Before petitioner made any incriminating statements, he received partial warnings of his constitutional rights; this is, of course, a circumstance quite relevant to a finding of voluntariness. Davis v. North Carolina, 384 U.S. 737, 740, 741 (1966). The questioning was of short duration, and petitioner was a mature individual of normal intelligence. The fact that the police misrepresented the statements that Rawls had made is, while relevant, insufficient in our view to make this otherwise voluntary confession inadmissible. These cases must be decided by viewing the "totality of the circumstances," see, e. g., Clewis v. Texas, 386 U.S. 707, 708 (1967), and on the facts of this case we can find no error in the admission of petitioner's confession.

* * *

III.

Petitioner's final contention can be dismissed rather quickly. He argues that the trial judge erred in permitting some clothing seized from petitioner's duffel bag to be introduced into evidence. This duffel bag was being used jointly by petitioner and his cousin Rawls and it had been left in Rawls' home. The police, while arresting Rawls, asked him if they could have his clothing. They were directed to the duffel bag and both Rawls and his mother consented to its search. During this search, the officers came upon petitioner's clothing and it was seized as well. Since Rawls was a joint user of the bag, he clearly had authority to consent to its search. The officers therefore found evidence against petitioner while in the course of an otherwise lawful search. . . .

Because we find none of petitioner's contentions meritorious, we affirm the judgment of the Court of Appeals.

Affirmed.

MR. CHIEF JUSTICE WARREN and MR. JUSTICE DOUGLAS concur in the result.

MR. JUSTICE FORTAS took no part in the consideration or decision of this case.

In view of the foregoing opinion and decision in Frazier v. Cupp, consider the following Table of Contents from the 1967 edition (published after *Miranda*) of Criminal Interrogation and Confessions, by Inbau and Reid, two of the authors referred to in the *Miranda* opinion:

A.

Tactics and Techniques for the Interrogation of Suspects Whose Guilt is Definite or Reasonably Certain

A. Display an Air of Confidence in the Subject's Guilt

B. Point out Some, but by No Means All, of the Circumstantial Evidence Indicative of a Subject's Guilt

C. Call Attention to the Subject's Physiological and Psychological Symptoms of Guilt

D. Sympathize with the Subject by Telling Him That Anyone Else under Similar Conditions or Circumstances Might Have Done the Same Thing

E. Reduce the Subject's Guilt Feelings by Minimizing the Moral Seriousness of the Offense

F. Suggest a Less Revolting and More Morally Acceptable Motivation or Reason for the Offense Than That Which Is Known or Presumed

G. Sympathize with the Subject by (1) Condemning His Victim, (2) Condemning His Accomplice, or (3) Condemning Anyone Else Upon Whom Some Degree of Moral Responsibility Might Conceivably Be Placed for the Commission of the Crime in Question

H. Utilize Displays of Understanding and Sympathy in Urging the Subject to Tell the Truth

I. Point Out the Possibility of Exaggeration on the Part of the Accuser or Victim or Exaggerate the Nature and Seriousness of the Offense Itself

J. Have the Subject Place Himself at the Scene of the Crime or in Some Sort of Contact with the Victim or the Occurrence

K. Seek an Admission of Lying about Some Incidental Aspect of the Occurrence

L. Appeal to the Subject's Pride by Well-Selected Flattery or by a Challenge to His Honor

M. Point out the Futility of Resistance to Telling the Truth

N. Point out to the Subject the Grave Consequences and Futility of a Continuation of His Criminal Behavior

O. Rather Than Seek a General Admission of Guilt, First Ask the Subject a Question as to Some Detail of the Offense, or Inquire as to the Reason for its Commission

P. When Co-Offenders Are Being Interrogated and the Previously Described Techniques Have Been Ineffective, "Play One Against the Other"

B.

Tactics and Techniques for the Interrogation of Suspects Whose Guilt is Uncertain

Q. Ask the Subject if He Knows Why He is Being Questioned

R. Ask the Subject to Relate All He Knows about the Occurrence, the Victim, and Possible Suspects

S. Obtain from the Subject Detailed Information about His Activities before, at the Time of, and after the Occurrence in Question

T. Where Certain Facts Suggestive of the Subject's Guilt are Known, Ask Him about Them Rather Casually and as Though the Real Facts Were Not Already Known

U. At Various Intervals Ask the Subject Certain Pertinent Questions in a Manner which Implies that the Correct Answers Are Already Known

V. Refer to Some Non-Existing Incriminating Evidence to Determine whether the Subject Will Attempt to Explain It Away; if He Does, That Fact is Suggestive of His Guilt

W. Ask the Subject whether He Ever "Thought" about Committing the Offense in Question or One Similar To It

X. In Theft Cases, if a Suspect Offers to Make Restitution, That Fact Is Indicative of Guilt

Y. Ask the Subject whether He Is Willing to Take a Lie-Detector Test. The Innocent Person Will Almost Always Steadfastly Agree to Take Practically Any Test to Prove His Innocence, whereas the Guilty Person Is More Prone to Refuse to Take the Test or to Find Excuses for not Taking It, or for Backing Out of His Commitment To Take It

Z. A Subject Who Tells the Interrogator, "All Right, I'll Tell You What You Want, but I Didn't Do It", Is, in all Probability, Guilty.

The employment of any of the foregoing techniques, or, indeed of any interrogation whatsoever, of an arrested person, or of one who has been "deprived of his freedom in any significant way" presupposes, of course, the issuance of the *Miranda* warnings, followed by a waiver of those rights.

The authors of the foregoing text, Criminal Interrogation and Confessions (1967), expressed the following views (at pp. 213–219) with regard to the practical necessity for the interrogation of criminal suspects and witnesses:

"One completely false assumption accounts for most of the legal restrictions on police interrogations. It is this, and the fallacy is certainly perpetuated to a very considerable extent by mystery writers, the movies, and TV: whenever a crime is committed, if the police will only look carefully at the crime scene they will almost always find some clue that will lead them to the offender and at the same time establish his guilt; and once the offender is located, he will readily confess or disclose his guilt by trying to shoot his way out of the trap. But this is pure fiction; in actuality the situation is quite different. As a matter of fact, the art of criminal investigation has not developed to a point where the search for and the examination of physical evidence will always, or even in most cases, reveal a clue to the identity of the perpetrator or provide the necessary proof of his guilt. In criminal investigations, even of the most efficient type, there are many, many instances where physical clues are entirely absent, and the only approach to a possible solution of the crime is the interrogation of the criminal suspect himself, as well as others who may possess significant information. Moreover, in most instances these interrogations, particularly of the suspect himself, must be conducted under conditions of privacy and for a reasonable period of time; and they frequently require the use of psychological tactics and techniques that could well be classified as 'unethical,' if we are to evaluate them in terms of ordinary, everyday social behavior.

"To protect ourselves from being misunderstood, we want to make it unmistakably clear that we are not advocates of the so-called 'third degree'. We are unalterably opposed to the use of any interrogation tactic or technique that is apt to make an innocent person confess. We are opposed, therefore, to the use of force, threats, or promises of leniency—all of which might well induce an innocent person to confess; but we do approve of such psychological tactics and techniques as trickery and deceit that are not only helpful but frequently necessary in order to secure incriminating information from the guilty, or investigative leads from otherwise uncooperative witnesses or informants.

"Our position, then, is this, and it may be presented in the form of three separate points, each accompanied by case illustrations:

1. *Many Criminal Cases, Even When Investigated by the Best Qualified Police Departments, Are Capable of Solution Only by Means of an Admission or Confession from the Guilty Individual or upon the Basis of Information Obtained from the Questioning of Other Criminal Suspects.*

"As to the validity of this statement, we suggest that consideration be given to the situation presented by cases such as these. A man is hit on the head while walking home late at night. He does not see his assailant, nor does anyone else. A careful and thorough search of the crime scene reveals no physical clues. Then take the case of a woman who is grabbed on the street at night and dragged into an alley and raped. Here, too, the assailant was unaccommodating enough to avoid leaving his hat or other means of identification at the crime scene, and there are no other physical clues. All the police have to work on is the description of the assailant given by the victim herself. She describes him as about six feet tall, white, and wearing a dark suit. Or consider this case, an actual one in Illinois. Three women are vacationing in a wooded resort area. Their bodies are found dead, the result of physical violence, alongside a foot trail, and no physical clues are present.

"In cases of this kind—and they all typify the difficult investigation problem that the police frequently encounter—how else can they be solved, if at all, except by means of the interrogation of suspects or of others who may possess significant information?

"There are times, too, when a police interrogation may result not only in the apprehension and conviction of the guilty, but also in the release of the innocent from well-warranted suspicion. Here is one such actual case within our own professional experience.

"The dead body of a woman was found in her home. Her skull had been crushed, apparently with some blunt instrument. A careful police investigation of the premises did not reveal any clues to the identity of the killer. No fingerprints or other significant evidence was located; not even the lethal instrument itself could be found. None of the neighbors could give any helpful information. Although there was some evidence of a slight struggle in the room where the body lay, there were no indications of a forcible entry into the home. The deceased's young daughter was the only other resident of the home, and she had been away in school at the time of the crime. The daughter could not give the police any idea of what, if any, money or property had disappeared from the home.

"For several reasons the police considered the victim's husband a likely suspect. He was being sued for divorce; he knew his wife had planned on leaving the state and taking their daughter with her; and the neighbors reported that the couple had been having heated arguments, and that the husband was of a violent temper. He also lived conveniently near—in a garage adjoining the home. The police interrogated him and although his alibi was not conclusive his general behavior and the manner in which he answered the interrogator's questions satisfied the police of his innocence. Further investigation then revealed that the deceased's brother-in-law had been financially indebted to the deceased; that he was a frequent gambler; that at a number of social gatherings which he had attended money disappeared from some of the women's purses; that at his place of employment there had been a series of purse thefts; and that on the day of the killing he was absent from work. The police apprehended and questioned him. As the result of a few hours of competent interrogation—unattended by any abusive methods, but yet conducted during a period of delay in presenting the suspect before a committing magistrate as required by state statute—the suspect confessed to the murder. He told of going to the victim's home for the purpose of selling her a radio which she accused him of stealing. An argument ensued and he hit her over the head with a mechanic's wrench he was carrying in his coat pocket. He thereupon located and took some money he found in the home and also a diamond ring. After fleeing from the scene he threw the wrench into a river, changed his clothes, and disposed of the ones he had worn at the time of the killing by throwing them away in various parts of the city. He had hidden the ring in the attic of his mother's home, where it was found by the police after his confession had disclosed its presence there. Much of the stolen money was also recovered or else accounted for by the payment of an overdue loan.

"Without an opportunity for interrogation the police could not have solved this case. The perpetrator of the offense would have remained at liberty, perhaps to repeat his criminal conduct.

2. *Criminal Offenders, Except, of Course, Those Caught in the Commission of Their Crimes, Ordinarily Will Not Admit Their Guilt unless Questioned under Conditions of Privacy, and for a Period of Perhaps Several Hours.*

"This point is one which should be readily apparent not only to any person with the least amount of criminal investigative experience, but also to anyone who will reflect momentarily upon the behavior of ordinary law-abiding persons when suspected or accused of nothing more than simple social indiscretions. Self-condemnation and self-destruction not being normal behavior characteristics, human beings ordinarily do not utter unsolicited, spontaneous confessions. They must first be questioned regarding the offense. In some instances, a little bit of information inadvertently given to a competent interrogator by the suspect may suffice to start a line of investigation which might ultimately establish guilt. On other occasions, a full confession, with a revelation of details regarding a body, the loot, or the instruments used in the crime, may be required to prove the case; but whatever the possible consequences may be, it is impractical to expect any but a very few confessions to result from a guilty conscience unprovoked by an interrogation. It is also impractical to expect admissions or confessions to be obtained under circumstances other than privacy. Here again recourse to our everyday experience will support the basic validity of this requirement. For instance, in asking a personal friend to divulge a secret, or embarrassing information, we carefully avoid making the request in the presence of other persons, and seek a time and place when the matter can be discussed in private. The very same psychological factors are involved in a criminal interrogation, and even to a greater extent. For related psychological considerations, if an interrogation is to be had at all, it must be one based upon an unhurried interview, the necessary length of which will in many instances extend to several hours, depending upon various factors, such as the nature of the case situation and the personality of the suspect.

3. *In Dealing with Criminal Offenders, and Consequently Also with Criminal Suspects Who May Actually Be Innocent, the Interrogator Must of Necessity Employ Less Refined Methods Than Are Considered Appropriate for the Transaction of Ordinary, Everyday Affairs by and between Law-Abiding Citizens.*

"To illustrate this point, let us revert to the previously discussed case of the woman who was murdered by her brother-in-law.

His confession was obtained largely by the interrogator's adoption of a friendly attitude in questioning the suspect, when concededly no such genuine feeling existed; by his pretense of sympathizing with the suspect because of his difficult financial situation; by his suggestion that perhaps the victim had done or said something which aroused the suspect's anger and which would have aroused the anger of anyone else similarly situated to such an extent as to provoke a violent reaction; and by his resort to other similar expressions, or even overtures of friendliness and sympathy such as a pat on the suspect's shoulder. In all of this, of course, the interrogation was 'unethical' according to the standards usually set for professional, business, and social conduct, but the pertinent issue in this case was no ordinary, lawful, professional, business, or social matter. It involved the taking of a human life by one who abided by no code of fair play toward his fellow human beings. The killer would not have been moved one bit toward a confession by subjecting him to a reading or lecture regarding the morality of his conduct. It would have been futile merely to give him a pencil and paper and trust that his conscience would impel him to confess. Something more was required—something which was in its essence an 'unethical' practice on the part of the interrogator; but, under the circumstances involved in this case, how else would the murderer's guilt have been established? Moreover, let us bear this thought in mind. From the criminal's point of view, *any* interrogation of him is objectionable. To *him* it may be a 'dirty trick' to be talked into a confession, for surely it was not done for his benefit. Consequently, any interrogation of him might be labeled as deceitful or unethical.

"Of necessity, criminal interrogators must deal with criminal offenders [or suspects] on a somewhat lower moral plane than that upon which ethical, law-abiding citizens are expected to conduct their everyday affairs. That plane, in the interest of innocent suspects, need only be subject to the following restriction: Although both 'fair' and 'unfair' interrogation practices are permissible, nothing shall be done or said to the subject that will be apt to make an innocent person confess.

"If we view this whole problem realistically, we must come to the conclusion that an interrogation opportunity is necessary and that legislative provision ought to be made for a privately conducted police interrogation, covering a reasonable period of time, of suspects who are not unwilling to be interviewed; and that the only tactics or techniques that are to be forbidden are those which are apt to make an innocent person confess.

"There are other ways to guard against abuses in police interrogation short of taking the privilege away from them. Moreover, we could no more afford to do that than we could stand the effect of a law requiring automobile manufacturers to place governors on all cars so that, in order to make the highways safe, no one could go faster than twenty miles an hour.

"The only real, practically attainable protection we can set up for ourselves against police interrogation abuses (just as with respect to arrest and detention abuses) is to see to it that our police are selected and promoted on a merit basis, that they are properly trained and adequately compensated, and that they are permitted to remain substantially free from politically inspired interference. In the hands of men of this competence there will be a minimum degree of abusive practices. Once again we suggest that the real interest that should be exhibited by the legislatures and the courts is with reference to the protection of the innocent from the hazards of tactics and techniques that are apt to produce confessions of guilt or other false information. Individual civil liberties can survive in such an atmosphere, alongside the protective security of the public."

The authors of the foregoing text, in addressing themselves to their criminal interrogator readership, state the following (at p. 157):

"The sharp differences of viewpoint that prevail among the members of the United States Supreme Court and the uncertainty that exists in the various opinions of the Court itself leave the inquiring criminal interrogator in a quandary as to what is or is not permissible. In an effort to offer some guidance, about all we can suggest—until such time as the Supreme Court settles upon a clear-cut test of its own—is this, and we put it in the form of a question which the interrogator may ask of himself:

Is what I am about to do, or say, apt to make an innocent person confess?

"If the answer to the above question is 'No', the interrogator should go ahead and do or say whatever was contemplated; on the other hand, if the answer is 'Yes', the interrogator should refrain from doing or saying what he had in mind.

"In our judgment this is the only understandable test of confession admissibility. It is also the only one of any practical value and utility. Moreover, it is also the only test that is fair both to the public and to the accused or suspected individual."

E. REMEDIES FOR ABUSIVE INTERROGATIONS

The previous discussion makes it unmistakably clear that an improperly obtained confession is inadmissible as substantive evidence. As with the exclusion of illegally seized tangible evidence, however, this provides little consolation for the innocent person who is never brought to trial (and hence does not benefit by a suppressed confession) but whose rights and personal dignity were nevertheless violated. Discussion is warranted, therefore, of the remedies to which this person can turn, as well as supplemental remedies available to the individual who has already benefited by suppression.

SECTION 1. CIVIL REMEDIES

Under recent case law, a federal civil rights action may lie for a person who has been the victim of a coerced confession or even an abusive interrogation. The pertinent federal statute (Tit. 42 U.S.C. § 1983) reads:

> Every person who, under color of any statute, ordinance, regulation, custom, or usage, of any State or Territory, subjects, or causes to be subjected, any citizen of the United States or other person within the jurisdiction thereof to the deprivation of any rights, privileges, or immunities secured by the Constitution and laws, shall be liable to the party injured in an action at law, suit in equity, or other proper proceeding for redress.

While there is authority which holds that all *Miranda* violations are not actionable per se under this provision, that an illegally obtained confession must be introduced at trial in order to give rise to an action, Ambek v. Clark, 287 F.Supp. 208 (E.D.Penn.1968), and Ransom v. City of Philadelphia, 311 F.Supp. 973 (E.D.Penn.1970), recent decisions have broadened the scope of a § 1983 action in this regard. In Kerr v. City of Chicago, 424 F.2d 1134 (7th Cir. 1970), cert. denied, 400 U.S. 833, 91 S.Ct. 66 (1970) (see casenote, 20 De Paul L.Rev. 984 (1971)), a complaint alleged that he was illegally detained for 18 hours and a confession was coerced from him through force, threats, and deprivation of food and other necessities of life. The reviewing court reversed the lower court's refusal to admit evidence of the circumstances surrounding the interrogation. The court wrote:

> . . . the jury was entitled to hear the testimony surrounding all the events from the moment Kerr was taken from his home until his indictment by the Grand Jury. All of the acts of commission and omission—the totality of all the circumstances—are of great importance in determining whether plaintiff's confession was coerced in violation of his civil rights and thereby cognizable under 42 U.S.C. § 1983 . . .

The court further stated:

> . . . in a civil rights action alleging the extraction of an involuntary confession, the issue of guilt or innocence is irrelevant . . .

Since this is an emerging body of law, there are as yet no concrete guidelines to define the kind and quality of constitutional infringement that must be alleged in order to state a cause of action. Consider the court's opinion in Duncan v. Nelson, 466 F.2d 939 (7th Cir. 1972), cert. denied 409 U.S. 894, 93 S.Ct. 116 (1972):

> There is no indication from . . . any other case that physical violence need be present to produce the coercion necessary to constitute an involuntary confession cognizable under § 1983 [citation omitted]. In fact, Mr. Justice Harlan in his concurrence in Monroe v. Pape . . . recognized the possibility that psychological coercion leading to a confession would constitute damages under § 1983 . . .

SECTION 2. CRIMINAL SANCTIONS

A civil rights violation which gives rise to a civil suit under 42 U.S.C. § 1983, may also precipitate a criminal indictment against the offending officer(s) under 18 U.S.C. § 242. That provision reads as follows:

> Whoever, under color of any law, statute, ordinance, regulation, or custom, willfully subjects any inhabitant of any State, Territory, or District to the deprivation of any rights, privileges, or immunities secured or protected by the Constitution or laws of the United States, or to different punishments, pains, or penalties, on account of such inhabitant being an alien, or by reason of his color, or race, than are prescribed for the punishment of citizens, shall be fined not more than $1,000 or imprisoned not more than one year, or both; and if death results shall be subject to imprisonment for any term of years or for life.

If two or more persons are involved, the civil rights conspiracy statute may be invoked (18 USC § 242). That statute provides for a 10 year penalty and a $10,000 fine.

A criminal sanction specifically drafted to encompass the problems under discussion here is the Illinois provision, Ch. 38 § 12–7:

> **Compelling Confession or Information by Force or Threat**
>
> (a) A person who, with intent to obtain a confession, statement or information regarding any offense, inflicts or

threatens to inflict physical harm upon the person threatened or upon any other person commits the offense of compelling a confession or information by force or threat.

(b) Sentence.

Compelling a confession or information is a Class 4 felony.

While criminal prosecutions alleging improper interrogation are not requiring prosecutors to work overtime, the recent expansion of the civil side of this question may well lead to an accompanying increase in criminal indictments.

Chapter 17

PROSECUTORIAL DISCRETION

Any discussion of the prosecutor, and the discretion that he employs in the selection of cases to prosecute or decline, must begin with a recognition that he is the single most powerful officer in the criminal justice system. This quality of his office stems from two factors: (a) the influence he exercises upon the actions of other agencies within the system and (b) his freedom from review—except in the most extraordinary circumstances—of the decisions he makes as to whether to prosecute or not to prosecute.

More than any other agency, the influence of a prosecutor's office is felt at every stage of the proceedings within the system. He is usually an advisor to, and sometimes a supervisor of, the police or other investigative agencies. His views, therefore, may influence the course of investigations directly, or, even if unsupervised in a particular area, the police may tailor their actions to accommodate the known preferences or prejudices of their local prosecutor. After verdict, the prosecutor's relationship to the judge, or the influence of his standing in the community, may influence the decision of the judge in the imposition of sentence. On appeal, the prosecutor, by virtue of his power to concede issues or, in some jurisdictions, to press a cross-appeal, may continue to shape the case even after it has been decided by the trial court.

After the defendant has been incarcerated, the influence of the prosecutor is still felt. Prison authorities may accept his view of the kind of custodial care which is required in individual cases. In many jurisdictions it is commonplace for the prosecutor to send a letter to the prison authorities giving his views of the nature of the charge, the evidence presented, and the character of the defendant. When parole authorities are considering parole or executive clemency, the view of the prosecutor, especially if vigorously and publicly pressed, may well be the controlling factor in determining whether the prisoner wins release or is continued in custody.

In short, not only does the prosecutor occupy the most powerful position in the system by virtue of his control over who is prosecuted and who is not, but the influence of his office is felt at every stage from arrest to parole and pardon.

The second factor contributing to the power of the prosecutor is his almost unbridled right, both formal and informal, to make the decision either to prosecute or not to prosecute a particular defendant.

This right is largely a product of tradition rather than a studied determination by legislatures; nevertheless, generations of acceptance by legislatures as well as the courts have endowed it with an almost unquestioned character which prosecutors are anxious to see unchanged.

This immense prosecutorial power becomes even more apparent when contrasted with that possessed by other agencies of government involved in the law enforcement process and the administration of criminal justice—the legislatures, the police, and the courts.

In contrast to the prosecutor's almost complete freedom from review by other persons or agencies, even the power of the legislature to define offenses and set punishments is subject to some controls by the executive branch of government, whose police may not arrest offenders and whose prosecutors may not initiate prosecutions. Moreover, the validity of legislative enactments is subject to judicial scrutiny.

Although the actions of the police are subject to the control of the executive branch which governs them, their power to make arrests, searches and seizures, and conduct other investigative procedures may come to naught if the prosecutor declines to process their cases through the prosecution stage. Moreover, trial judges, and later on, appellate judges may nullify as evidence the results of police investigative efforts. Then, too, there are always legislative initiatives to confine the investigative and apprehension powers and practices of the police.

Trial judges in the federal system are subject to review by federal courts of appeal as well as by the Supreme Court. The decisions of state trial judges must withstand the scrutiny, not only of the appellate courts within the state system, but, where federal constitutional rights are involved, federal trial and appellate courts are increasingly quick to review the conclusions of state trial and appellate judges.

Even prison and parole authorities, historically insulated by the concept of "discretion", now find themselves checked by the recent willingness of judges, especially federal judges, to set minimum standards of prison housekeeping and disciplinary procedures within the context of civil rights or damage actions. Moreover, parole and pardon authorities, long undisputed guardians of their own procedures for determining eligibility for parole or the exercise of executive clemency, have now been told that there are minimum due process rights with which their procedures must comply.

From these comparisons the reader will all the more recognize the unique position occupied by the prosecutor with regard to his broad discretionary power. There exists one fairly remote control, of course, and that, rejection by the electorate when he runs for reelection; or, if he holds the office by virtue of an appointment he could be removed for misfeasance, but this would rarely apply with respect to a matter of prosecutorial discretion.

Control of a prosecutor's budget by the legislative authority may conceivably act as a brake in curbing prosecutorial zeal in pursuing particular cases, but the ability of the prosecutor to shift his resources may neutralize such a control attempt; moreover, power over the budget cannot compel the prosecutor to act affirmatively with regard to particular case situations.

Finally, judicial control over the prosecutor is felt only with regard to those matters which the prosecutor chooses to place within the system by initiating a prosecution. Even this control is largely negative, in the sense that it operates only to curb prosecutorial misbehavior in the gathering of evidence or during the trial of a case.

From this perspective, then, we turn to a discussion of the factors which may influence the decision of the prosecutor to proceed with, or decline to bring, criminal prosecutions.

1. The Prosecutor and His Office

Who and what the prosecutor is must be taken into account in assessing how and why he makes his decisions. A federal prosecutor, for example, is normally subject to the control only of the President and the Attorney General. He may however, be a powerful political figure in his own right, or he may be politically weak and thus dependent upon the favor of the senior Senator of the President's party, who traditionally recommends both prosecutorial and judicial nominees within the federal system. On the other hand, a state prosecutor, the attorney general of a state, may be elected, or appointed by the governor. A county prosecutor may be elected, or appointed by the Governor or the Attorney General.

The area in which the prosecutor operates may also influence his decisions to some degree. Thus the problems faced by the rural prosecutor are much different than those faced by the urban or suburban prosecutor. Since his priorities of law enforcement are bound to be different, so too are his decisions to prosecute or not to prosecute. For example, prosecutors in rural or suburban areas tend to regard commercial offenses, i. e., embezzlement, forgery, check "kiting", and petty theft, with more seriousness than their urban counterparts who cope with a much larger number of such offenses and who may not have such close personal relationships with community merchants.

Discretion is also affected by the quality of assistant prosecutors and the method of their selection and retention. If the office is regarded as a political stepping-stone, and if appointments are made as part of a political patronage system, political factors or favors may weigh in the balance. Sensitivity to community opinion (more precisely, the prosecutor's conception of community opinion) may be more influential. If the prosecutor, even an elected one, has served for a long time, and his assistants are chosen from outside the political system, or are civil service employees, less concern may be shown in this regard.

The stage of the principal prosecutor's career may also be important. If the prosecutor is young and at the beginning of a legal or political career, he may tend to caution in investigations and prosecutions to lessen the chances of mistakes which will adversely affect that career. Or, if the political balance is such, he may assume the role of the "white knight" who charges forth in an aggressive manner to joust with the established order or political hierarchy. A career prosecutor will tend to steer a more even, balanced course. And an older prosecutor, perhaps one to whom a small community has turned because of the shortage of lawyers, may be less concerned with community opinion.

The size of the office is also important. In one, two or three-man offices discretion will remain largely with the principal prosecutor since control of the assistants and their decisions is more easily attained. In larger offices, with 50 or 100 assistants, or more, control is more structured, with fewer decisions flowing to the top. The result is that initial, and often controlling discretion rests largely with assistants who may be new, inexperienced or who do not share, to the same degree, the philosophy of enforcement of the principal prosecutor. His discretion is thus supervisory, rather than original, and his control of their decisions depends heavily upon the ability of his supervisory staff and the formal structure of office authority. Thus, discretion in a large prosecutor's office may be that of many persons, rather than one, with review often hurried or haphazard. As a result discretion may be exercised in an internally inconsistent manner.

2. General Factors Influencing Discretion

Before examining those considerations which may influence the discretion to prosecute or decline in a particular case, some mention of *general* factors which shape a prosecutor's discretion should be made.

The first decision to be made is whether a criminal statute should be enforced at all. Though the statutory duty of prosecutors is often cast in mandatory terms, in practice selective enforcement or non-enforcement of particular statutes is not uncommon. Whether due to the personal predilections of the prosecutor, the tolerance of the local community, or the antiquity or irrationality of the statute, some laws are enforced only *pro forma* or sporadically in response to media pressure, and some laws are not enforced at all.

The second problem faced is how many criminal offenders are to be prosecuted if all cannot be. For example, if a federal prosecutor in a large urban area decided to prosecute all thefts from the mail, or all forgeries of government instruments, or all false statements on government employment applications, or all Dyer Act offenses, he would be able to prosecute nothing else.

Third, if a particular offender has committed more than one offense, should he be prosecuted for all? Or only for the most serious? Should the decision on other offenses be reserved until the disposition of the first offense charged? If one serious offense may be charged, should the prosecutor consider filing a less serious one—an "included" or "reduced" offense?

A prosecutor must also consider the views of the police agencies with which he works. Some police agencies, whose abilities to win appropriations depends upon the statistics they are able to present to a budget director or a legislative body, exert pressures upon a prosecutor to maintain a high level of prosecutions in selected areas within their jurisdiction. Under other circumstances, the desires of the investigative agencies may have little effect upon the decision to prosecute, except within the framework of a prosecutor's desire to maintain "good relations". Some prosecutors, when dealing with agencies which are especially cooperative on a regular basis, may, in return, prosecute more of that agencies' cases, or go on borderline cases where the agency has a particular interest in proceeding.

The decision may also turn upon what alternative remedies are open to the prosecutor and the administrative or investigative agency. For example, if a federal prosecutor declines to prosecute a theft from interstate shipment, no alternative (other than state prosecution) is available to satisfy the FBI. But if he declines to prosecute a case of fraud on the Social Security Administration, the agency may recoup lost monies from future payments. The failure to prosecute food stamp violations ferreted out by agents from the Department of Agriculture does not preclude the imposition of administrative sanctions by the agency. On occasion there may be pressure from a police agency to at least initiate prosecution to protect agents from the threat of civil litigation in cases where the arrest or search techniques were questionable. And, in a related area, there may be occasional industry pressures to proceed with a weak case against an employee, e. g., a theft case against a truck driver, to forestall union demands for reinstatement in the face of management's desire to discharge the errant employee.

The kind of offense under consideration may also affect the decision to prosecute or decline. A county prosecutor, for example, would rarely decline to prosecute a crime of violence or a narcotics charge, except for insufficiency of evidence or unlawful police practices which would result in suppression and consequent acquittal. Discretion in these instances is limited to legal assessments of these two potential problems. On the other hand, when considering whether to prosecute low level visibility offenses not involving threats to life or safety, and not particularly outrageous from society's standpoint, guilt is not, ordinarily, in issue—indeed a confession may be commonplace—and the decision to prosecute turns upon other factors. It is, of course, a truism that the lower the visibility of the offense and the lower the visibility of the prosecution, the easier it is to exercise discretion in deciding whether to prosecute.

The particular deterrence rationale involved may also be a factor. Is the offense one which is likely to produce a fairly effective deterrent to the commission of crimes by *others* if prosecuted vigorously and notoriously, e. g., tax evasion, embezzlement, and other crimes involving substantial periods of contemplation and planning to carry out a scheme? Or is the offense one which is likely to be the product of momentary aberration, perhaps not to be repeated, in which the deterrence of others is of little moment and the primary question is one of safeguarding society from a repetition of the acts by the *same* offender, e. g., marital assaults or reckless homicide. Or is the offense one which simply does not respond well to the criminal process, e. g., drunken and disorderly conduct, gambling, prostitution and other "victimless" offenses?

A prosecutor must also consider what kind of office he wants to run, for almost every prosecutor's office reflects the personal philosophies and priorities of the principal prosecutor. Does he strive for a statistical result, i. e., a high "conviction rate"? If so, he will be inclined to be cautious and will refuse to proceed with cases which are doubtful or risky. What kind of community credibility does he seek to attain? If the office is used as a political lance, then he will probably seek to be aggressive, though hopefully not reckless. If he deliberately seeks community recognition in certain high visibility areas of prosecution, e. g., public corruption, narcotics, financial frauds, civil rights, or pollution, then he will probably be keenly aware of the difference between merely "winning" and "not losing".

Finally, the stage of the prosecution at which the decision is being made is a factor to consider in the exercise of prosecutorial discretion. Is the prosecutor being called upon to decide whether to proceed before arrest? Or after the decision to arrest has been made by the police without his concurrence, but before a complaint has been filed? Should a case in which a complaint has been filed be taken through the grand jury process? Should the case be reassessed after indictment but before trial? Is there any reason, after conviction, to acquiesce in a motion for new trial? If a case is reversed on appeal some period of time after commission of the offense, the decision to reprosecute is often made after consideration of totally different factors than those which made up the initial decision to proceed, e. g., the current state of the evidence, the current climate of community opinion, a possible change in prosecutors, the expense of a retrial, a sentence mostly served awaiting appeal, and similar considerations.

3. The Specific Factors of Discretion

We turn then to a consideration of some of the *specific* factors which may enter into a prosecutor's decision of whether to proceed with a charge of a criminal offense. We assume, for these purposes, the sufficiency of the evidence.

Not all of these factors may enter into the decision in every case. And a prosecutor may not consciously be aware that he is even considering some of those that do enter into the case, for, depending upon his experience, his ability to analyze summaries of evidence and the time devoted to such analysis, he may conclude very quickly that a case is worth prosecuting or it is not.

The first question to be considered is whether the case fits within the prosecution priorities of the office. Especially in large offices, many cases in which the guilt of the accused is clear are not prosecuted simply because the office resources are not sufficient to proceed in every instance. For example, in a large United States Attorney's office, small cases of theft, embezzlement, marijuana possession and the like may be declined in order to allow the prosecutor to proceed with more serious offenses. Sometimes the potential defendants are placed in a status of "probation without conviction", which, if successfully completed, results in eventual dismissal of the charge. The federal prosecutor may decline in favor of local prosecution. If the offender is a member of the armed forces, he may be returned to the processes of military justice. A juvenile may be turned over to local juvenile authorities. Or the case may simply be declined, especially where restitution (in theft or fraud cases) has been made before the prosecutor must exercise his discretion.

In some cases, a prosecutor will decide that the arrest and temporary incarceration before release on bail was a sufficient sanction to promote deterrence. For example, the drunken business man who makes threatening remarks aboard an aircraft, and who spends the night in jail before release, is unlikely to need the additional sanction of actual prosecution to carry home the gravity of the offense. Care must be exercised in these cases, however, to prevent the concept of "trial" or "punishment" by arrest or incarceration from becoming a stated concept of law enforcement, especially one to be engaged in by investigative agencies in their discretion.

The defendant's background is also important. Prosecuting authorities tend to be more lenient with youthful and elderly offenders, with women, with persons who have led disadvantaged lives, with people who have wretched family situations which may have been contributing factors in the commission of the offense, with defendants who have many children or whose earnings are near the poverty level, with defendants who have creditable military service records, with people who have no prior arrest or conviction records, and with defendants who have been ill or who have mental problems not amounting to insanity. Sometimes these factors may have little or nothing to do with the commission of the offense, but, since prosecutors may feel a natural sympathy for the disadvantaged, they weigh in the balance when the decision to prosecute or decline is made. If a prosecutor receives 100 small embezzlement cases a year and has the resources to prosecute only twenty, it is likely that he will look for extenuating factors as an excuse to rationalize his dismissal of the eighty on grounds other than lack of resources.

The defendant's record of embroilment with the law on collateral charges is also important. If a defendant has just been convicted of another offense in the same or a sister jurisdiction, the likelihood is that a presently pending charge will not go forward, especially if the prosecutor suspects that conviction of a second offense will simply result in the imposition of a concurrent sentence. On the other hand, if the defendant has just been acquitted of another charge, particularly in a sister jurisdiction, and there is reason to believe that the acquittal was not based upon the merits, e. g., if crucial evidence was suppressed, or, assuming conviction, if the sentence for the other offense is thought to be too lenient, the decision may well be to proceed with the pending offense.

Even though guilt of the offense is clear, the quality of the prosecution's case must be constantly scrutinized. This is especially true when the prosecutor deals with a witness to a succession of offenses, e. g., an accomplice in a number of prosecutions against different hijackers or "fences." While the state of the evidence in earlier prosecutions may have been convincing and convictions may have been obtained, witnesses who testify repeatedly for the government sometimes "wear out", their testimony may become less credible because either they or the prosecutor become careless by reason of earlier successes, or continued trials furnish additional impeaching material. If the string of victories ends, and the prosecutor suffers several setbacks, he may well reconsider prosecuting the balance of the cases which looked promising a year earlier, and were therefore indicted. On the other hand, a prior loss with the same key government witness does not necessarily foreclose prosecution of a case in a new jurisdiction. The new prosecutors, jurors, community opinion, and differences in corroborating evidence may justify proceeding with an indictment in one jurisdiction even though the case is based substantially upon the testimony of a witness who has previously testified in a losing prosecution in another jurisdiction.

The age of a case may also persuade a prosecutor not to proceed. The case may be old when the offense is discovered, or the case may have lain dormant too long within the police agency or the lower courts and the evidence may now be stale. This factor is particularly important when, following reversal for reasons other than the sufficiency of the evidence, a decision whether a case should be retried must be made. Here, the factors of cost and manpower, which may not have been considered when the initial decision to prosecute was made, may outweigh the advantages of finally achieving a verdict of guilty. This is often true when the controversial nature of a case may have stretched a trial for a lesser offense beyond the limits which ordinarily would be reached in a trial for a misdemeanor.

Even though legal guilt is clear, a prosecutor who has set prosecution goals or wishes to maintain a community posture of invincibility in priority areas, e. g., public corruption or narcotics cases, may closely weigh the "winability" of a case. If there are factors upon which a jury might rest a verdict of acquittal despite the evidence of guilt, a prosecutor may fear the harmful effect of that acquittal upon the deterrence which a previous string of victories has presumably generated among potential offenders and decide that the prosecution is not worth the risk. In an analogous area, a prosecutor may also decide to delay the institution of a prosecution, even though the offense is complete at that point and there is sufficient evidence of guilt, because the case may have more "jury appeal" if subsequent conditions change. For example, if a defendant has obtained a large number of loans by means of false financial statements submitted to various lending institutions, he may be guilty of several offenses and the evidence may be sufficient to indict. But if all the loans are current and there are no losses to the banks, the case may not have the "jury appeal" necessary to obtain a conviction. Delay in the institution of prosecution until the loans go bad may appear to be a more discrete course of action of the part of the cautious prosecutor.

Prosecutors may also exercise their discretion to punish or reward defendants and, sometimes, their lawyers. Prosecution may be foregone as part of an agreement to obtain the defendant's co-operation against others. Or a case that, by application of routine standards might be declined, is pressed when a defendant refuses to co-operate with investigating or prosecuting authorities.

Occasionally, the fortuitous choice of a lawyer may work to the advantage of a defendant in his invocation of the prosecutor's discretion. If a lawyer has established a close relationship with a prosecutor, and if he has been of material assistance in other cases, e. g., persuading guilty clients not only to plead, but to testify against others, the prosecutor may be more inclined to deal leniently with a current client. Conversely, if a lawyer is employed who has an antagonistic relationship with the principal prosecutor or his assistants, the current client may find that his borderline case is decided in favor of prosecution.

The decision to make "new law" by instituting a criminal prosecution for the first time under a statute not previously utilized is one of the most difficult for a prosecutor. Many criminal statutes—particularly in the regulatory area—are broadly drawn and when their breadth is teamed with a prosecutor's ingenuity, practices close to the line—particularly in the business community—may be swept within the net of criminal prosecution.

How may a prosecutor proceed fairly in this area? Where the application of the statute is clear enough, and only a new or more vigorous program of enforcement is in issue, the question is relatively easy. For example, upon the imposition of wage and price controls, the government, in order to achieve national uniformity and maximum compliance, will prosecute, with maximum public exposure, all cases brought by the investigative agency, whether large or small. When the enforcement program is well under way and a sufficient compliance has been obtained, the prosecutor will invoke his discretion only in those cases which will clear doubtful areas of the law or which because of the visibility of the offense or the offender will presumably serve special deterrent purposes.

When the statute has been in force for some time and the question whether certain conduct is violative of the act is without precedent, how does the prosecutor proceed? If the conduct in question is asserted to have some claim to legitimacy—either by widespread or long time acceptance in the business community or by the assertion of industry leaders—it may well be the fairer course to publicly announce a prosecutorial conclusion that the conduct in question is viewed as unlawful. If the conduct ceases, the objectives of criminal prosecution have been accomplished. If offenders persist, then at least they have had fair warning. For example, assume that a federal prosecutor believes that reciprocal loans to each other by officers of two banks violates Title 18, § 215, which forbids the receipt of a thing of value in return for making a loan. Should a prosecution be brought without warning to the banking community? Or should the prosecutor correspond with officials of the offender banks, or perhaps with officials of banking associations, to convey his views to them?

Finally, a prosecutor always takes account of how a prosecution will be perceived by the defendant and his associates, by the press and public, by the court, by the investigative agency and by fellow lawyers. A case which is otherwise perfectly ripe for prosecution may be declined if, for example, a United States Attorney believes it is not "worthy" of being brought in a federal court, or, at least, suspects that a federal judge would think so. Or a case may be declined if the press or public would consider a prosecutor's priorities out of kilter if he brought it, e. g., the theft of a pair of shoes from a veterans' hospital supply room by a patient. And if cases too close to the borderline are prosecuted with sudden regularity, the investigative agencies might legitimately conclude that the prosecutor's standards have undergone unspoken adjustment and readjust their investigative priorities without consultation with the prosecutor.

NOTES

1. Compare the following from the ABA Standards Relating to the Prosecution Function:

3.9 Discretion in the charging decision

(a) In addressing himself to the decision whether to charge, the prosecutor should first determine whether there is evidence which would support a conviction.

(b) The prosecutor is not obliged to present all charges which the evidence might support. The prosecutor may in some circumstances and for good cause consistent with the public interest decline to prosecute, notwithstanding that evidence exists which would support a conviction. Illustrative of the factors which the prosecutor may properly consider in exercising his discretion are:

(i) the prosecutor's reasonable doubt that the accused is in fact guilty;

(ii) the extent of the harm caused by the offense;

(iii) the disproportion of the authorized punishment in relation to the particular offense or the offender;

(iv) possible improper motives of a complainant;

(v) prolonged non-enforcement of a statute, with community acquiescence;

(vi) reluctance of the victim to testify;

(vii) cooperation of the accused in the apprehension or conviction of others;

(viii) availability and likelihood of prosecution by another jurisdiction.

(c) In making the decision to prosecute, the prosecutor should give no weight to the personal or political advantages or disadvantages which might be involved or to a desire to enhance his record of convictions.

(d) In cases which involve a serious threat to the community, the prosecutor should not be deterred from prosecution by the fact that in his jurisdiction juries have tended to acquit persons accused of the particular kind of criminal act in question.

(e) The prosecutor should not bring or seek charges greater in number or degree than he can reasonably support with evidence at trial.

Commentary

a. Basic criteria

The charging decision is the heart of the prosecution function. The broad discretion given to a prosecutor in deciding whether to bring charges and in choosing the particular charges to be made requires that the greatest effort be made to see that this power is used fairly and uniformly. By its very nature the exercise of discretion cannot be reduced to a formula. Nevertheless, certain guidelines for the exercise of discretion can be established. See §§ 1.1, 2.5, supra. The standards contained in this section are not intended to be a substitute for working out appropriate prosecution policies on a local level. At most they are illustrative of certain basic factors which should be included or excluded in the exercise of discretion.

The prosecutor ordinarily should prosecute if after full investigation he finds that a crime has been committed, he can identify the perpetrator, and he has evidence which will support a verdict of guilty. See ABA Code DR 7–103(A). Although this proposition may seem to be laboring the obvious, it is stated in order to place in proper perspective factors which may be validly persuasive reasons for not bringing all or any charges; subsequent comments undertake to illustrate factors which may be relevant to the decision.

b. Factors which may properly be considered

The breadth of criminal legislation necessarily means that much conduct which falls within its literal terms should not always lead to criminal prosecution. It is axiomatic that all crimes cannot be prosecuted even if this were desirable. Realistically, there are not enough enforcement agencies to investigate and prosecute every criminal act which occurs. Some violations occur in circumstances in which there is no significant impact on the community or on any of its members. See Breitel, Controls in Criminal Law Enforcement, 27 U.Chi.L.Rev. 427, 431 (1960). A prosecutor must adopt a first-things-first policy, giving his greatest concern to those areas of criminal activity that pose a threat to the security and order of the community.

Nor is it desirable that he prosecute all crimes at the highest degree available. Necessarily crimes are defined in broad terms that encompass situations of greatly differing gravity. Differences in the circumstances under which the crime took place, the motives or pressures activating the offender, mitigating factors of the situation or the offender's age, prior record, general background, his role in the offense, and a host of other particular factors require that the prosecutor view the whole range of possible charges as a set of tools from which he must carefully select the proper instrument to bring the charges warranted by the evidence. In exercising discretion in this way, the prosecutor is not neglecting his public duty or discriminating among offenders. The public interest is best served and even-handed justice best dispensed not by a mechanical application of the "letter of the law" but by a flexible and individualized application of its norms through the exercise of the trained discretion of the prosecutor as an administrator of justice.

The standards provide a series of guidelines for the exercise of the prosecutor's discretion. In addition to the obvious factor of reasonable doubt of guilt of the accused, the extent of harm caused by the offense is an important factor to be considered in deciding whether to charge and what charges to bring. ABA Standards, Pleas of Guilty § 1.8(a)(iii) (Approved Draft, 1968).

If the prosecution is sought by a private party out of malice or to exert coercion on the defendant, as is sometimes the case in matters involving sexual offenses or debt collection, for example, the prosecutor may properly decline to prosecute.

Use of so-called "obsolete" criminal laws not generally enforced in order to discriminate against particular persons or groups is not warranted. Another related problem in the so-called "obsolescence" of laws arises when there has been a prolonged practice of non-enforcement of a particular law with the result that the community is lulled into an impression that the particular conduct is not prohibited. Strictly speaking, no "law" is obsolete, of course, but some laws are spoken of in these terms. Usually the attitude cannot develop with respect to conduct which significantly endangers the community or the safety of any individual. An example is found in wagering statutes which may, literally construed, prohibit "Bingo." If for any reason a prosecutorial decision is made to enforce the statute strictly so as to make playing "Bingo" a criminal act, a prosecutor probably has some duty to make this known by appropriate public announcement.

Another relevant consideration is the refusal of the victim to testify. A prosecutor may have difficulty making out a case if an indispensable witness declines to testify—for example, if the case involves evidence which, if made public, will cause great pain or harm to the victim of the crime. In serious cases, however, the interests of the community require that the prosecutor try to obtain the victim's cooperation and in some instances it may be his duty to use the subpoena power to compel his attendance as a witness. Prosecution of less serious offenses may be foregone because of lack of witness cooperation. See LaFave, Arrest 142 n. 66 (1965). A common instance of such an exercise of discretion occurs in family conflicts where minor violence occurs. Often the injured party who calls the police is later reluctant about prosecution, either because the dispute has been resolved or because of the harmful consequences of prosecution to the family. See Wright, Duties of a Prosecutor, 33 Conn.B.J. 293 (1959).

Prosecutors frequently and properly choose a lenient course with one participant in criminal activity in order to bring other more serious offenders to justice. See Baker, The Prosecutor—Initiation of Prosecution, 23 J. Crim.L.C. & P.S. 770, 788–90 (1933). The underlying policy is represented in statutes, found in many jurisdictions, permitting the grant of immunity from prosecution in exchange for testimony. See, e. g., Murphy v. Waterfront Comm'n, 378 U.S. 52 (1964). The decision to prosecute one defendant at the cost of letting another go free is often difficult. This Committee Report is consistent with the position of the Advisory Committee on the Criminal Trial of this ABA Project, which proposed a standard that charge and sentence concessions are appropriate to a defendant whose "cooperation has resulted or may result in the successful prosecution of one or more other offenders engaged in equally serious or more serious criminal conduct." ABA Standards, Pleas of Guilty § 1.8(a)(v) (Approved Draft, 1968).

The present broad span of federal criminal statutes presents many cases of overlapping federal and state jurisdiction. Particularly where federal laws are largely auxiliary to state laws, the federal prosecutor is faced with the problem that his power to prosecute may result in a defendant's being punished in two tribunals for the same conduct. In situations where there may be such overlapping federal and state jurisdiction,

> in general it can be said that federal action is justified in the presence of one or more of the following circumstances: (1) When the states are unable or unwilling to act; (2) when the jurisdictional feature, e. g., use of the mails, is not merely incidental or accidental to the offense, but an important ingredient of its success; (3) when, although the particular jurisdictional feature is incidental, another substantial federal interest is protected by the assertion of federal power; (4) when the criminal operation extends into a number of states, transcending the local interests of any one; (5) when it would be inefficient administration to refer to state authorities a complicated case investigated and developed on the theory of federal prosecution.

Schwartz, Federal Criminal Jurisdiction and Prosecutors' Discretion, 13 Law & Contemp.Probs. 64, 73 (1948).

When the possibility of double prosecution arises because the crime is punishable in more than one state, similar considerations should be taken into account in deciding whether to defer to the other jurisdiction's right to prosecute. Where the issues have already been tried in another state, the prosecutor should not seek to relitigate the case by bringing a new prosecution. See, e. g., Ill.Ann.Stat. ch. 38, § 3–4(c) (1964); Minn.Stat.Ann. § 609.045 (1964); N.Y.Code Crim.Proc. § 139 (1967).

c. Personal advantage not to be considered

The prosecutor should avoid measuring his record by the "conviction rate" of his office. He should never allow the decision to proceed in a particular case to be influenced by a desire to inflate his record of success in obtaining convictions. Nor should he hesitate to reduce a charge or decline a prosecution because of such considerations.

d. Community indifference to serious crime

There are cases where even in the face of probability or even certainty of acquittal, perhaps because of hostile community attitudes toward minority groups, a prosecutor should proceed if he is satisfied a serious crime has been committed, can identify the offender, and has the necessary evidence. Another example is found in a situation where there has been widespread corruption in government in circumstances where conviction is difficult. A prosecutor may have a duty in such situations to take a case to the grand jury and, if successful in obtaining an indictment, then proceed with trial even in the face of knowledge that a conviction will be difficult to obtain. These situations represent more than a gesture, for, hopefully, the prosecution would by this process alert the entire community to the existing conditions and in time arouse the community conscience.

e. Discretion in selecting the number and degree of charges

The structure of the substantive law of crimes is such that often a single criminal event will give rise to potential criminal liability for a number of different crimes. Constitutional double jeopardy provisions only narrowly limit the potential of multiple punishment in these situations. To some extent courts have found limitations inherent in the statutes defining the offenses. See, e. g., Heflin v. United States, 358 U.S. 415 (1959); Prince v. United States, 352 U.S. 322 (1957). Sometimes this has been accomplished by a statutory or judicial doctrine restricting punishment for several crimes embraced in a single episode to the maximum of the crime which was the "primary objective." See Neal v. State, 55 Cal.2d 11, 357 P.2d 839 (1961); Note, 50 Minn.L.Rev. 1102 (1966). But a broad area of prosecution discretion still remains. See Remington & Joseph, Charging, Convicting and Sentencing the Multiple Criminal Offender, 1961 Wis.L.Rev. 528, 530–31.

The chief criticism voiced by defense counsel with respect to the exercise of prosecution discretion in this area is that prosecutors "overcharge" in order to obtain leverage for plea negotiations. Although it is difficult to give a definition of "overcharging" in verbal form, it is clear that the heart of this criticism is a belief that prosecutors bring charges not in the good faith belief that they are appropriate under the circumstances and with an intention of prosecuting them to a conclusion, but merely as a harassing and coercive device, in the expectation that a guilty plea will result and that it will not be necessary to proceed to trial, verdict and sentence on all of the charges or at the degree of crime originally stated.

From the prosecutor's point of view, the charging decision is one which must be made at an early stage when all the evidence is not necessarily before him in the form it will take at trial. He must make a preliminary evaluation in order to proceed, knowing that at several later stages he may dismiss some charges or may be compelled to elect. He should not be forced to make these crucial decisions in the pre-indictment stage; hence he may charge in accordance with what he then believes he can establish as a prima facie case. If the facts warrant multiple charges growing out of a single episode, the prosecutor is entitled to charge broadly. A defendant accused of housebreaking, robbery, rape and murder committed in a single course of conduct involving one victim can hardly complain of "overcharging" if there is evidence of his conduct which supports each charge. At some stage, of course, a prosecutor might well voluntarily dismiss one or more of the lesser charges, but he cannot fairly be criticized for charging on all counts initially. The boundary line which separates so-called "overcharging" from the sound exercise of prosecutorial discretion is too vague and subjective to make this a matter for more definitive treatment than as stated in section

3.9(e). Obviously, a prosecutor must have a broad discretion at the charging stage; the trial court in turn has ultimate power to deal with abuse of the prosecutor's discretion.

2. Recently one Court of Appeals dealt with the power of a court to control discretion. The problem has two aspects: (a) the power of a court to dismiss a charge that it thinks was improperly filed, and (b) the power of a court to compel the prosecutor to bring a charge when the prosecutor has refused to do so.

(a) In United States v. Falk, 479 F.2d 616 (7th Cir. 1973) (en banc), held that a court could dismiss a charge if it were shown that the prosecutor exercised his discretion in an improperly discriminatory manner. Falk, for example, claimed that he was prosecuted for violating a seldom invoked provision of the Selective Service Act solely because he claimed to be a conscientious objector. Similar judicial sentiments have been voiced in a case involving alleged prosecution under the census act solely because the accused was a leader of a census resistance movement (United States v. Steele, 461 F.2d 1148 (9th Cir. 1972), and in a case in which an ordinance was allegedly enforced only against members of one race (Yick Wo. v. Hopkins, 118 U.S. 356 (1886). The rule that discriminatory enforcement of the law will result in dismissal of charges has long been recognized, yet such discrimination is nearly impossible to prove and the opinion in *Falk* (decided with three dissents) is one of the very rare instances of the application of the rule.

(b) In Littleton v. Berbling, 468 F.2d 389 (7th Cir. 1972) vacated and remanded *sub nom.* Spomer v. Littleton, 414 U.S. 514, 94 S.Ct. 685 (1974), it was held that a federal court could require a state prosecutor to bring charges if it could be shown that his refusal to prosecute was based upon considerations of race. This decision was the first of its kind and was contrary to the unanimous views of other courts to the effect that a judge has no power to compel a prosecutor to charge a crime: United States v. Cox, 342 F.2d 167 (5th Cir. 1965); Powell v. Katzenbach, 123 U.S.App.D.C. 250, 359 F.2d 234 (1965); Moses v. Kennedy, 219 F.Supp. 762 (D.D.C. 1963); Pugach v. Klein, 193 F.Supp. 630 (S.D.N.Y.1961). The continued validity of the holding in Littleton v. Berbling, even in the court that decided it, is subject to some doubt in light of the decision of the Supreme Court in O'Shea v. Littleton, 414 U.S. 488, 94 S.Ct. 669 (1974).

*

APPENDIX

Provisions of the Constitution of the United States, and certain Amendments thereto, of particular significance in the administration of criminal justice:

Preamble

We the People of the United States, in Order to form a more perfect Union, establish Justice, insure domestic Tranquility, provide for the common defense, promote the general Welfare, and secure the Blessings of Liberty to ourselves and our Posterity, do ordain and establish this Constitution for the United States of America.

Article I.

. . .

Section 8. The Congress shall have Power To lay and collect Taxes, Duties, Imposts and Excises, to pay the Debts and provide for the common Defence and general Welfare of the United States; but all Duties, Imposts and Excises shall be uniform throughout the United States; . . .

To regulate Commerce with foreign Nations, and among the several States and with the Indian Tribes; . . .

To provide for the Punishment of counterfeiting the Securities and current Coin of the United States; . . .

To constitute Tribunals inferior to the supreme Court;

To define and punish Piracies and Felonies committed on the high Seas, and Offences against the Law of Nations;

To declare War, grant Letters of Marque and Reprisal, and make Rules concerning Captures on Land and Water; . . .

To make Rules for the Government and Regulation of the land and naval forces;

To provide for calling forth the Militia to execute the Laws of the Union, suppress Insurrections and repel Invasions;

To provide for organizing, arming, and disciplining, the Militia, and for governing such Part of them as may be employed in the Service of the United States, reserving to the States respectively, the Appointment of the Officers, and the Authority of training the Militia according to the discipline prescribed by Congress;

To exercise exclusive Legislation in all Cases whatsoever, over such District (not exceeding ten Miles square) as may, by Cession of particular States, and the Acceptance of Congress, become the

Seat of the Government of the United States, and to exercise like Authority over all Places purchased by the Consent of the Legislature of the State in which the Same shall be, for the Erection of Forts, Magazines, Arsenals, dock-Yards, and other needful Buildings;—And

To make all Laws which shall be necessary and proper for carrying into Execution the foregoing Powers, and all other Powers vested by this Constitution in the Government of the United States, or in any Department or Officer thereof.

Section 9.

. . .

No Bill of Attainder or ex post facto Law shall be passed.

Article III.

Section 1. The judicial Power of the United States, shall be vested in one supreme Court, and in such inferior Courts as the Congress may from time to time ordain and establish. The Judges, both of the supreme and inferior Courts, shall hold their Offices during good Behaviour, and shall, at stated Times, receive for their Services, a Compensation, which shall not be diminished during their Continuance in Office.

Section 2.

. . . the supreme Court shall have appellate Jurisdiction, both as to Law and Fact, with such Exceptions, and under such Regulations as the Congress shall make.

The Trial of all Crimes, except in Cases of Impeachment, shall be by Jury; and such Trial shall be held in the State where the said Crimes shall have been committed; but when not committed within any State, the Trial shall be at such Place or Places as the Congress may by Law have directed.

Section 3. Treason against the United States, shall consist only in levying War against them, or in adhering to their Enemies, giving them Aid and Comfort. No Person shall be convicted of Treason unless on the Testimony of two Witnesses to the same overt Act, or on Confession in open Court.

The Congress shall have Power to declare the Punishment of Treason, but no Attainder of Treason shall work Corruption of Blood, or Forfeiture except during the Life of the Person attainted.

Article VI.

. . .

This Constitution, and the Laws of the United States which shall be made in Pursuance thereof; and all Treaties made, or which shall be made, under the Authority of the United States, shall be the supreme Law of the Land; and the Judges in every State shall be bound thereby, any Thing in the Constitution or Laws of any State to the Contrary notwithstanding.

. . .

AMENDMENTS

Amendment I.

Congress shall make no law respecting an establishment of religion, or prohibiting the free exercise thereof; or abridging the freedom of speech, or of the press; or the right of the people peaceably to assemble, and to petition the Government for a redress of grievances.

Amendment II.

A well regulated militia, being necessary to the security of a free State, the right of the people to keep and bear arms, shall not be infringed.

Amendment III.

No Soldier shall, in time of peace be quartered in any house, without the consent of the owner, nor in time of war, but in a manner to be prescribed by law.

Amendment IV.

The right of the people to be secure in their persons, houses, papers, and effects, against unreasonable searches and seizures, shall not be violated, and no warrants shall issue, but upon probable cause, supported by oath or affirmation, and particularly describing the place to be searched, and the persons or things to be seized.

Amendment V.

No person shall be held to answer for a capital, or otherwise infamous crime, unless on a presentment or indictment of a Grand Jury, except in cases arising in the land or naval forces, or in the militia, when in actual service in time of war or public danger; nor shall any person be subject for the same offence to be twice put in jeopardy of life or limb; nor shall be compelled in any criminal case to be a witness against himself, nor be deprived of life, liberty, or property, without due process of law; nor shall private property be taken for public use, without just compensation.

Amendment VI.

In all criminal prosecutions, the accused shall enjoy the right to a speedy and public trial, by an impartial jury of the State and district wherein the crime shall have been committed, which district shall have been previously ascertained by law, and to be informed of the nature and cause of the accusation; to be confronted with the witnesses against him; to have compulsory process for obtaining witnesses in his favor, and to have the assistance of Counsel for his defence.

Amendment VII.

In Suits at common law, where the value in controversy shall exceed twenty dollars, the right of trial by jury shall be preserved, and no fact tried by a jury, shall be otherwise re-examined in any Court of the United States, than according to the rules of the common law.

Amendment VIII.

Excessive bail shall not be required, nor excessive fines imposed, nor cruel and unusual punishments inflicted.

Amendment IX.

The enumeration in the Constitution, of certain rights, shall not be construed to deny or disparage others retained by the people.

Amendment X.

The powers not delegated to the United States by the Constitution, nor prohibited by it to the States, are reserved to the States respectively, or to the people.

. . .

Amendment XIII.

SECTION 1. Neither slavery nor involuntary servitude, except as a punishment for crime whereof the party shall have been duly convicted, shall exist within the United States, or any place subject to their jurisdiction.

SECTION 2. Congress shall have power to enforce this article by appropriate legislation.

Amendment XIV.

SECTION 1. All persons born or naturalized in the United States, and subject to the jurisdiction thereof, are citizens of the United States and of the State wherein they reside. No State shall make or enforce any law which shall abridge the privileges or immunities of citizens of the United States; nor shall any State deprive any person of life, liberty, or property, without due process of law; nor deny to any person within its jurisdiction the equal protection of laws.

. . .

SECTION 5. The Congress shall have power to enforce, by appropriate legislation, the provisions of this article.

Amendment XV.

SECTION 1. The right of citizens of the United States to vote shall not be denied or abridged by the United States or by any State on account of race, color, or previous condition of servitude.

SECTION 2. The Congress shall have power to enforce this article by appropriate legislation.

Amendment XVI.

The Congress shall have power to lay and collect taxes on incomes, from whatever source derived, without apportionment among the several States, and without regard to any census or enumeration.
. . .

*

INDEX

References are to Pages

References are to Pages

END OF VOLUME